乌尔第三王朝王后
贡牲机构档案重建与研究

王俊娜◎著

中国社会科学出版社

图书在版编目(CIP)数据

乌尔第三王朝王后贡牲机构档案重建与研究 / 王俊娜著 . —北京：中国社会科学出版社，2017. 3

ISBN 978-7-5161-9955-8

Ⅰ. ①乌… Ⅱ. ①王… Ⅲ. ①两河流域-畜禽-饲养管理-组织机构-档案-研究-前 2110-前 2003 Ⅳ. ①F337. 063

中国版本图书馆 CIP 数据核字(2017)第 042203 号

出 版 人 赵剑英
责任编辑 任 明
责任校对 韩天炜
责任印制 李寡寡

出 版 中国社会科学出版社
社 址 北京鼓楼西大街甲 158 号
邮 编 100720
网 址 http：//www. csspw. cn
发 行 部 010-84083685
门 市 部 010-84029450
经 销 新华书店及其他书店

印刷装订 北京市兴怀印刷厂
版 次 2017 年 3 月第 1 版
印 次 2017 年 3 月第 1 次印刷

开 本 710×1000 1/16
印 张 24. 5
插 页 2
字 数 408 千字
定 价 98. 00 元

目　　录

下卷 档案重建

引　言

古代两河流域地区在希腊语中被称为 Mesopotamia，意为“两河之间的土地”。它是以幼发拉底河和底格里斯河流域为中心，包括现今伊拉克的全境以及叙利亚东北部、土耳其东南部及伊朗西南部的古文明区。人类最早的文明就产生在这块土地上①。古代两河流域可以分为南北两部分，以今之希特（Hīt）—萨马腊（Sūmarrā）为界，北部称为亚述（Assyria），南部称为巴比伦尼亚（Babylonia）。巴比伦尼亚又分为南、北两部分，尼普尔城（今努法尔 Nuffar）以北称为阿卡德（Akkad），以南称为苏美尔（Sumer）。

古代两河流域文明最早产生在南部苏美尔地区，历经了哈拉夫文化时期（Halaf 约公元前 5500—4500 年）、埃瑞都-欧贝德文化时期（Eridu-Ubeid Period 约公元前 4500—前 3500 年）、乌鲁克文化时期（Uruk Period 约公元前 3500—前 3100 年）、乌鲁克 IV-III 层（Uruk IV-III）和捷姆迭特-那色原始文字时期（Jemdet Nasr Period 约公元前 3100—前 2950 年）、古苏美尔城邦争霸时期（约公元前 2800 年—前 2370 年）②。阿卡德王朝兴起后，苏美尔城邦一度衰落，至库提人霸权时期（约公元前 2230 年—前 2110 年）得到恢复。在乌图赫旮勒（Utu-hegal）驱逐蛮族之后，乌尔王乌尔那穆（Ur-Nammu）统一南部两河流域地区，建立了苏美尔人的乌尔第三王朝（Ur III Dynasty 约公元前 2110—前 2003 年），这一时期也称新苏美尔时期。乌尔第三王朝共经历五王：乌尔那穆（约公元前 2110—2093 年）、舒勒吉（Šulgi 约公元前 2092—2045 年）、阿马尔辛（Amar-

① 古代两河流域文明的产生参见刘文鹏、吴宇虹、李铁匠《古代西亚北非文明》，中国社会科学出版社 1999 年版，第 203—208 页。

② Alberto R.W.Green, *The Storm-God in The Ancient Near East*, Winona Lake, Indiana: Eisenbrauns, 2003, Chronological Chart.

Sîn 约公元前 2044—2036 年)、舒辛 (Šu-Sîn 约公元前 2035—2027 年)和伊比辛 (Ibbi-Sîn 约公元前 2026—2003 年),共统治 108 年,最终被埃兰 (Elam) 所灭。这一时期苏美尔文明和两河流域地区在政治、经济、军事、外交和文化方面都有了很大的发展,也是苏美尔文明最后和最辉煌的时期。

经过乌尔那穆的励精图治以及舒勒吉的南征北战,到舒勒吉统治中后期,两河流域南部呈现出军事强大和经济稳定发展的繁荣局面。大概在舒勒吉 21 年或更早[①],舒勒吉开始称自己是神,将自己神化,王权与神权紧密结合,国王的权力和地位空前强大。根据国王舒勒吉 39 年的年名"普兹瑞什达干司被建立之年"(苏美尔人的记年方法通常是把国家前一年的某些重大事件作为下一年的年名内容),舒勒吉于其统治的第 38 年在供奉神王恩里勒的尼普尔圣城附近建立了一个专门管理王朝贡牲的机构(牲畜存栏和记账中心)——普兹瑞什达干司(É-Puzriš-Dagan)。普兹瑞什达干司的遗址在现今伊拉克的德莱海姆村(Drehem)。在尼普尔城附近设立贡牲中心的主要目的是有效地管理王室、贵族和其他人及机构向苏美尔的宗教中心尼普尔城的神王恩里勒、图马勒庙区的宁里勒和其他有关神明献祭的大量牲畜和其他的动物牺牲。普兹瑞什达干贡牲中心规模很大,每天有来自各种官吏和机构的大量牲畜被送到这里,由中心官员发放到需要它们的地方,被诸神明、王室、外国使节、高级官吏和士兵消费。所有收入和支出的牲畜都由贡牲中心的书吏官员们加以登记并进行账目管理。贡牲中心由一位中心总管统一管理牲畜的收入和支出,下设各类官员管理具体事务。中心总管和各级官员都有各自的收支凭证和账簿,我们统称为"经济档案"。这些经济档案由日结、多日结、月结、年结甚至多年结的账目组成。贡牲中心每月经手的动物数以千计,每天的文件也可多达几十份。根据国际亚述学研究网站 CDLI(《楔形文字数字图书馆工程》加利福尼亚大学洛杉矶分校 http://www.cdli.ucla.edu/index_ html)和 BDTNS(《新苏美尔原文数据库》马德里,高等科学研究院语言研究所 http://bdtns.filol.csic.es/)所提供的原始文献统计,目前贡牲中心出土的泥板数量多达 12215 件[②]。

---

① P.Steinkeller, "More on the Ur III Royal Wives", *ASJ* 3 (1981), p.78.

② 非常感谢 CDLI 和 BDTNS 提供的文献原文给我的工作提供了极大的帮助。

由于现存的乌尔第三王朝各城邦的经济文献多是盗挖出土，因此文献分散到世界各个博物馆和私人手中，原来的档案秩序已全部被破坏。数量众多的德莱海姆泥板文书是在20世纪初由当地人盗挖出土，并在文物市场出卖后，引起学术界的注意。对这些散乱发表的档案文件加以重建一定对研究乌尔第三王朝的政治、经济、军事和宗教等社会状况以及王朝的政治结构和官员分工等具体情况具有非常重大的意义。东北师范大学的"Drehem Project"（Archives of Animal Center of Ur III Dynasty in Drehem《乌尔第三王朝贡牲中心档案重建工程》）的目标就是按时间重建贡牲中心散失各个官员的档案并给予基础性的研究，为国际学术界研究这一时期的政治和经济等提供必不可少的、经过系统建立而恢复了原貌和全貌的文献原文和翻译。对历经约38年的上万块泥板文书进行编年、排序、原文拉丁化和翻译是一项十分复杂和艰苦的工作。目前国际上尚无人做这类档案重建工作。本文是这一宏大工程的一部分。

舒勒吉新提王后贡牲机构的档案是贡牲中心档案中比较特殊的一个。同贡牲中心其他官员的档案一样，舒勒吉新提王后贡牲机构的档案也被分散在数以百计的出版物中。但是在西方学者对德莱海姆出土的文献进行了整理、发表和研究之后，发现一批文件均与乌尔第三王朝的第二王舒勒吉的王后舒勒吉新提有关，并且这一档案开始的时间是在贡牲中心建立即舒勒吉38年之前，因此学术界将这一类档案称为"早期档案"。贡牲中心的另一个早期档案是那冉伊里（*Na-ra-am-ì-lí*）的档案。目前学术界尚无人对舒勒吉新提王后贡牲机构的档案进行全面的、按日期排列的整理重建。因此，本文试图重建王后贡牲机构的经济档案，为分析贡牲中心建立前期及初期的经济情况提供较完整的参考。重建方法是对每件泥板文书的拉丁化的苏美尔原文按时间顺序进行排列，同时对苏美尔原文作出英文和中文翻译。

舒勒吉新提王后贡牲机构的档案覆盖时间是从舒勒吉28年1月到舒勒吉48年10月。舒勒吉新提王后贡牲机构的主要作用是为了舒勒吉新提王后祭祀自己负责的贝拉特苏赫尼尔（*Belat-Suhnir*）和贝拉特达腊班（*Belat-Darra-ban*）两位女神及其他诸神的节日，以及为祭祀朔月、上弦月和望月等活动提供动物牺牲并进行账目管理。王后贡牲机构档案的一个常用术语是"舒勒吉新提的送入项"（mu-túm *Šulgi-simti*），其意思是"为舒勒吉新提送入的（动物牲畜）"。王后贡牲机构的负责官员除了阿希马（*Ahima* 舒勒吉 28 年 1 月到舒勒吉 36 年 5 月）和卡兰希那吉（Kalam-henagi 舒勒吉 45 年 2 月 15 日到舒勒吉 48 年 2 月 10 日）这两位“配合负责官员”外，其他负责官员的任期基本衔接。根据任期排序，他们依次是舒库布姆（*Šukubum* 舒勒吉 28 年 3 月到舒勒吉 32 年 10 月）、贝里沓卜（*Beli-ṭab* 舒勒吉 33 年 5 月到舒勒吉 37 年 6 月）、阿皮里亚（*Apiliya* 舒勒吉 37 年 9 月到舒勒吉 41 年 10 月 11 日）、阿皮拉吞（*Apilatum* 舒勒吉 41 年 11 月 26 日到舒勒吉 45 年 6 月 15 日）、卢旮勒埃邓卡（Lugal-eden-ka 舒勒吉 45 年 7 月 12 日到舒勒吉 47 年 4 月 28 日）和舒勒吉伊里（*Šulgi-ili* 从舒勒吉 47 年 4 月 30 日到舒勒吉 48 年 10 月）

舒勒吉 48 年 10 月，国王舒勒吉去世。其王后舒勒吉新提贡牲机构的档案也随之结束。阿马尔辛 1 年 11 月，阿比新提（*Abī-simtī*）——与舒勒吉新提王后重要性相同的王后出现在贡牲机构的档案中。通过作者和吴宇虹教授的研究发现，舒勒吉新提与阿比新提是同一个人。在舒勒吉统治时期，舒勒吉新提（*Šulgi-simtī*）的名字的意思是“舒勒吉是我的骄傲”。在舒勒吉之子阿马尔辛和舒辛统治时期，新王因忌讳其父舒勒吉的名字而把母亲即王太后名字中的“舒勒吉”（Šulgi）改为“阿比”（中译“我的父亲”），王太后的新名阿比新提意为“我的父亲是我的骄傲”。这是舒勒吉之子阿马尔辛王和舒辛王朝廷上下对王太后的尊称。

有关阿比新提王太后的文件覆盖时间是从阿马尔辛 1 年 11 月 2 日到舒辛 9 年 12 月 17 日。其档案由贡牲中心官员之间的接管文件、记录阿比新提消费的月供应文件和记录贡牲中心官员把贡入的牲畜分配给阿比新提的文件组成。在文件中，阿比新提规律性地接收贡牲中心向其支付的牲畜。在贡牲中心官员为祭祀女神支出牲畜的文件中，阿比新提王太后常以“经由人”身份参加祭祀女神的活动。同时，阿比新提王太后主持王朝的祭祀“晦日”（ud-nú-a，意为“他（月神）躺下的那天”）的活动。目前发现最早的一个向阿比新提王太后的“饮水地”（ki-a-naĝ，古代苏美尔人祭祀祖先的地方）献祭的文件（ASJ 03 092 3）写于舒辛 9 年 12 月 17 日。这说明阿比新提王太后在舒辛 9 年 12 月 17 日之前去世。从此，阿比新提王太后从中心的档案中消失了。

为了更好地研究舒勒吉新提王后贡牲机构这一早期的档案，本文重建了与这一早期档案同时期的早期负责图马勒（Tummal）庙区的羊、猪和家禽官员阿什尼乌的档案（Š 40 iv–Š 44 i/12）以及死牲负责官员贝里阿瑞克的档案（Š 42 xi–Š 43 vi/24）。对贡牲中心这两位早期官员的档案的重建，为我们研究舒勒吉新提王后贡牲机构的档案提供了借鉴。

上卷　档案研究

第一部分　舒勒吉新提王后贡牲机构档案分析(Š 28 i–Š 48 x)

第一章　舒勒吉新提王后的贡牲机构及其生平

第一节　普兹瑞什达干贡牲中心简介

舒勒吉统治时期为了更好地管理各地向国王和众神进贡的日益增多的动物牲畜，国王舒勒吉在圣城尼普尔附近建立了一个大型贡牲中心——普兹瑞什达干司（é-Puzriš-Dagan）。贡牲中心建于尼普尔城附近的原因是为了更好地管理王室、贵族和其他人及机构向苏美尔的宗教中心尼普尔城的神王恩里勒、王配偶和其他有关大神献祭的牲畜。

由于苏美尔人的纪年方法通常是把国家前一年的某些重大事件作为下一年的年名内容，根据舒勒吉 39 年的年名“普兹瑞什达干司被建立之年”，普兹瑞什达干贡牲中心建立于舒勒吉统治的第 38 年，即公元前 2056 年。舒勒吉 40 年和 41 年的年名同样沿用了普兹瑞什达干司被建的内容，其年名分别为：普兹瑞什达干司被建年之次年；普兹瑞什达干司被建年之次年：之次年。同一年名内容多次被使用在不同年名中的原因可能是，国王由于某种特殊的原因，在新的一年开始时并没有马上公布新年名，所以书吏使用“……之后”（ús-sa）和之前的年名连用作为临时年名，其意思是“某年的下一年”，这类年名一直使用到国王颁布新的正式年名时。临时年名一般只用在年初的几个月，但是，也有全年都使用临时年名的情况，如：舒勒吉 33 年的年名“席穆润第三次被毁年之次年”，其苏美尔语为：mu ús-sa a-rá-3-kam Si-mu-ru-um^{ki} ba-hul。

贡牲中心建立的早期还不具规模，目前仅知道舒勒吉新提王后贡牲机构档案（Š 28 i–Š 48 x）和早期库房管理员那冉伊里的档案（Š 26 viii–AS 3 iv）。舒勒吉 39 年普兹瑞什达干司被建成后，它发展成为大型的牲畜管理机构。其规律性的基本账目从舒勒吉 40 年开始。乌尔第三王朝的末王伊比辛三年（公元前 2024 年）时，乌尔第三王朝开始衰落，王权逐渐失去对各行省的控制，贡牲中心因无贡可收而关闭。

根据美国学者施奈德在《乌尔第三王朝的苏美尔经济文献》（Sumerian Economic Texts from the Third Ur Dynasty）中的论述，普兹瑞什达干贡牲中心的档案可以分为早期档案和晚期档案两种类型①。早期档案的覆盖时间约从舒勒吉 28 年到舒勒吉 48 年，晚期档案的覆盖时间约从阿马尔辛 1 年到伊比辛 3 年。早期档案文献在内容与措辞方面与后期的档案文献不同。在早期文献中，负责收支动物的官员与后期贡牲中心负责相同工作的官员有所不同。早期贡牲中心的官员比较少，管理的物品种类比较繁多，不仅包括牛、羊、鸟、禽及野生动物等，还常包括羊毛、皮革等制成品和大麦等饲料的管理。

从舒勒吉 39 年开始，普兹瑞什达干贡牲中心设有一个中心主管部门，由中心总管负责记账和调拨贡牲中心接收和支出的牲畜和物品。其下设有养狗场、养驴场、牛、羊圈以及王室厨房（消费）和仓库等不同的部门，尼普尔圣城神庙的牺牲及其他用途的消费由中心总管直接支出。乌鲁克、乌尔或其他祭祀中心的牺牲由管理官员安排从普兹瑞什达干贡牲中心运往目的地。贡牲中心先后共有三名官员担任中心总管，分别是：（1）匿名的那萨（Nasa）②：工作时间从舒勒吉 42 年 10 月至舒勒吉 47 年 1 月；署名的那萨：工作时间从舒勒吉 46 年至阿马尔辛 1 年；（2）阿巴萨旮（Abba-saĝa）：工作时间从阿马尔辛 1 年至阿马尔辛 9 年；（3）尹塔埃阿（Intae-a）：工作时间从阿马尔辛 9 年至伊比辛 2 年。中心总管统一管理各种牲畜或物品的收入和支出，下设各类官员管理具体事物，例如：中心总管下设各种管理官员，他们主要负责管理不同地点和种类的动物牺牲。

① Tom B.Jones and John W.Snyder, *Sumerian Economic Texts from the Third Ur Dynasty*, University of Minnesota Press, 1961, pp.203–211.

② Wu Yuhong, The Anonymous Nasa and nasa of the Animal Center during Š44–48 and the Camel (gú-Gur$_5$), hunchbacked ox (Gur$_8$-Gur$_8$), UBI, HABUM and the confusion of the deer (lulim) with Donkey (anše) or šeg$_9$, *JAC*, 2010 (25), pp.1–19.

贡牲中心设有育肥师，他们的职责是将分配来的动物用大麦进行育肥，育肥之后献祭给主神明或在庆典上使用。贡牲中心的总管和各种官员都有各自记录的收支凭证和账簿。贡牲中心的档案由日结、多日结、月结、多月结、年结甚至多年结的账目文件组成。

贡牲中心账目文件的主要术语有以下几种：一是收入动物的文件，包括："接管"（ì-dab$_5$）文件、"收到"（šu~ ba-ti）文件和"新出生……接管"（ù-tud-da...ì-dab$_5$）文件。"接管"（ì-dab$_5$）文件是记录官员接收活牲的文件；"收到"（šu~ ba-ti）文件是记录官员收到死牲或物品的文件；"新出生……接管"（ù-tud-da...ì-dab$_5$）文件是记录新增加的牲畜幼崽的文件；与收入文件对应的账目文件是支出（zi-ga 或 ba-zi）文件。早期的档案文件中支出牲畜或物品时一般使用分词 zi-ga（"支出"）。从舒勒吉 46 年 7 月那萨署名中心总管开始，文件中的支出术语改为谓语动词 ba-zi（"被支出"）。

普兹瑞什达干贡牲中心建立于乌尔第三王朝的稳定、繁荣时期。根据 CDLI 和 BDTNS 网的数据统计，伊比辛 3 年贡牲中心的文件仅有 12 块，这表明这一时期乌尔第三王朝已经衰落，贡牲中心不得不关闭了。舒勒吉和阿马尔辛统治时期，普兹瑞什达干贡牲中心日结的动物牲畜有时会达到成百上千只，舒辛时期，贡牲中心的文件开始减少，到伊比辛 3 年，贡牲中心总的文件仅有 12 块。因此，普兹瑞什达干贡牲中心的建立、发展、完善到其衰落并最终被关闭的历史，从经济领域具象地反映了乌尔第三王朝从繁荣、鼎盛到其逐渐衰落的历史。可以说，普兹瑞什达干贡牲中见证了乌尔第三王朝的兴亡。

第二节　舒勒吉新提王后

一　舒勒吉新提王后的出身和生平

舒勒吉新提是乌尔第三王朝和第二王舒勒吉统治时期的王后。舒勒吉新提的阿卡德语名字是 *Šulgi-simtī*，意思是"舒勒吉是我的骄傲"。有时其名字也写成舒勒吉新吞（*Šulgi-simtum*），意思是"舒勒吉是骄傲"。舒勒吉新提王后的阿卡德语名字表明舒勒吉新提来自阿卡德地区。国王舒勒吉可能是为了团结当地的阿卡德人、与阿卡德人和平共处，娶了一位当地的公主作为妻子。

最早的一个祭祀国王舒勒吉“饮水地”（ki-a-naĝ 苏美尔人祭祀祖先的地方）的文件是写于舒勒吉48年11月2日①，这说明国王舒勒吉是在其统治的48年11月2日的前几天去世。而舒勒吉新提王后贡牲机构的档案结束于舒勒吉48年10月（Princeton 1 037）。此外，我们还发现了一个阿马尔辛1年3月28日同时向国王舒勒吉、舒勒吉新提王后以及舒勒吉的另一位妻子吉美宁里勒的“饮水地”献祭的文件ZVO 25 134 2②，该文件表明舒勒吉新提死于阿马尔辛1年3月28日之前。根据以上三个文件我们推测舒勒吉新提死于舒勒吉48年10月到阿马尔辛1年3月28日之间的某一天。由于国王和王后同时消失于舒勒吉48年10月中或底，以此推测：在国王舒勒吉去世时，消失的王后舒勒吉新提可能随之自杀陪葬，吉美宁里勒和国王的其他配偶也许同时殉葬。但是，通过对阿马尔辛和舒辛时期的阿比新提的文献材料的研究，我们认为舒勒吉新提没有随舒勒吉陪葬，而是改名为阿比新提，以王太后的身份继续辅助其两个儿子执政。

二 舒勒吉新提王后的头衔

在舒勒吉新提王后贡牲机构的档案文件中，舒勒吉新提被王后贡牲机构的官员们称为nin。苏美尔语nin的意思是“王后或女主人”，它常被用于对女神、王后或其他贵族女子的称谓，其相对应的阿卡德语是*šarratum*或*bēltum*。目前收集到的王后贡牲机构的档案中，仅有一个文件（MVN 08 097）同时提到舒勒吉新提和其“王后（nin）”的头衔，文件内容是：3只育肥公绵羊到厨房，**乌尔杜穆孜（厨师）督办（maškim）**；1只育肥公绵羊为宫殿，**阿皮里亚督办**；3只育肥公绵羊为厨房：当国王离开尼普

---

① 该文件的内容是：+10只公绵羊和+10只公山羊为舒勒吉的饮水地（ki-a-naĝ）……从那萨处支出了（zi-ga）（OrNS 46 225）。

② 文件内容是：1只育肥公绵羊、1只育肥雄绵羊羔、2只育肥肥尾公绵羊、5只肥尾公绵羊和1吃奶雄山羊崽到厨房，以上为舒勒吉的饮水地（ki-a-naĝ ᵈŠul-gi--ra）；1只育肥公绵羊和1只肥尾公绵羊为吉美宁里勒的饮水地（ki-a-naĝ Gemé-ᵈNin-líl-lá）；1只肥尾公绵羊为舒勒吉新提的饮水地（ki-a-naĝ ᵈ *Šul-gi-sí-im-ti*）；那冉伊里督办，从那鲁处，被支出（ba-zi）于乌尔城。文件中吉美宁里勒排在舒勒吉新提之前，并且祭祀吉美宁里勒的“饮水地”是2只羊，而对舒勒吉新提“饮水地”的祭祀仅用1只羊，可以看出，舒勒吉新提的地位应该低于吉美宁里勒。

尔前往乌鲁克时，**乌尔杜穆孜为督办**，以上支出**经由王后舒勒吉新提（gìr nin ᵈ *Šul–gi–sí–im–ti*）**，于乌尔，从阿希马（*Ahima*，王后贡牲机构的负责官员）处支出了（舒勒吉 32 年 5 月）。

在王后贡牲机构的档案文件中，舒勒吉新提一般被称为苏美尔和古巴比伦时期特有的特殊的妻子头衔"神妻"。"神妻"的苏美尔语是 lukur，意为"女祭司"，被认为是男神在人间的"妻子"，其对应的阿卡德语是 *nadītum* 或 *qadištum*。乌尔第三王朝和古巴比伦时期，"神妻（lukur）"拥有和男子相同的较高的社会地位，其中不少是王室或贵族的女儿①。一些贵族的妻子也称为 lukur"神妻"，她们也是神庙中神的妻子。古巴比伦时期一些女祭司因为神职身份不能生育，没有证据表明苏美尔时期的 lukur"神妻"也不能生育。可能在舒勒吉 21 年或之前，舒勒吉开始自称为神，在此时的文件中，舒勒吉的名字前加有神名的定义符（diĝir）。因此，从此时期开始，舒勒吉的妻子（dam）也成为了名副其实的舒勒吉的"神妻（lukur）"。

根据目前出土的文献记载，国王舒勒吉至少拥有六位"神妻（lukur）"，分别是：埃阿尼沙（*Ea–niša*）、吉美宁里拉（Geme–Ninlila）、宁卡拉（Nin–kala）、席马特埃阿（*Simat–Ea*）、舒勒吉新提（*Šulgi–simti*）和舒库尔吞（*Šūqurtum*?）②。在一个记录国王舒勒吉、王后舒勒吉新提以及其陪同下属们在参加一次重要活动中使用和获得的金银饰品、器皿等礼品的大文件 history.smsu.edu Phillips 13 中，接受礼品的 42 个人物被分为 7 个阶层：（1）国王舒勒吉；（2）王后舒勒吉新提；（3）3个王妃；（4）5 个贵妇人，分为 4 个等级；（5）7 个女大祭司和 1 个王子；（6）舒勒吉新提王后的 19 个女官，分 3 个等级；（7）舒勒吉新提王后的 5 个使节。在礼品单中，舒勒吉新提王后收到的礼品数量仅次于国王舒勒吉，种类比国王略为减少；而排在舒勒吉新提之后的舒勒吉王的 3 个妃子：宁卡拉、席马特埃阿和埃阿尼沙，她们收到的礼品远远少于舒勒吉新

---

① Wu Yuhong, "*Naram–ili*, Šu–Kabta and *Nawir–ilum* in the Archives of Ĝaršana, Puzriš–Dagan and Umma", *JAC* 23（2008）, p.8, p.12, Garšana 档案中提到公主 Me–Ištaran 和高官的夫人 A–na–a的印章都自称为 lukur。

② 见 D.Frayne, *Ur III Period*, RIME 3/2, Toronto: University of Toronto Press, 1997, Table 2: List of Members of the Ur III Royal Family, 由于舒库尔吞（*Šūqurtum*）的名字是恢复的，所以我们不确定舒勒吉的"神妻"中是否有舒库尔吞。

提，表明她们的地位低于王后舒勒吉新提①。并且在目前出土的文献中仅发现了舒勒吉新提王后贡牲机构的档案，这表明舒勒吉新提在舒勒吉的“神妻（lukur）”中拥有较高的地位。提到舒勒吉新提是舒勒吉的“神妻（lukur）”的印文见下表：

提到舒勒吉新提“神妻”（lukur）头衔的印文一览表

时间②	文件内容	官员	印文内容	出处
Š 32 vi	【1+】只公山羊崽和【1+】只羊羔为采鲁什达干之妹，由舒勒吉新吞送入	从埃阿巴尼处支出	舒勒吉是强大男子、乌尔之王和四方之王，**舒勒吉新吞是在旅途中陪伴他的lukur神妻**，马什古拉使官是你的仆人。	RT 37 130
Š 35 viii	1只鲶鱼（gú ~ su_6）、2只带壳鱼（peš - murgú）和4只zina鱼，自巴尔巴尔亚，为庙总管	哈里里接收	**舒勒吉新提是国王喜爱的lukur神妻**，舒伊里之子哈里里书吏是你的仆人。	OIP115 460
Š 46 viii	1头苇塘猪崽、19只幼鸭、22只家鸽和4只野鸽	乌尔卢旮勒埃邓卡补交	**舒勒吉新提，国王喜爱的lukur神妻**，库达-X之子乌尔卢旮勒埃邓卡书吏是你的仆人。	PDT 1 530

三 舒勒吉新提王后贡牲机构中的“我的王后”

在舒勒吉新提王后贡牲机构的档案中，一个被称为“我的王后（nin-ĝá）”的人物常被提到，她作为经由官员主要出现在女神祭祀和神庙祭祀的支出文件中。根据“我的王后”出现的文件中的负责官员，我们确定舒勒吉新提王后贡牲机构档案中的“我的王后”就是舒勒吉新提王后。例如文件PDT 2 1314：1+只优等育肥公绵羊为贝拉特苏赫尼尔和贝拉特达腊班庙，经由我的王后（gìr nin-ĝá），从舒库布姆（王后的贡牲官员）处支出了（舒勒吉29年10月）。此类文件的统计表如下：

① 参见李学彦、吴宇虹《从一件大礼品单看乌尔第三王朝国王和王后的豪华生活》，《历史教学》2011年4月下半期。

② 时间中Š加数字表示国王舒勒吉统治的年份，i-xii为月份。

经由"我的王后"向诸女神和男神献祭支出（zi-ga）一览表

（两女神 = 贝拉特苏赫尼尔和贝拉特达腊埃班，公羊 = 公绵羊）

时间	文件内容	支出官员	地点	文献出处
Š 29 x	1+只优等肥公羊为两女神庙	舒库布姆		PDT 2 1314
Š 31 viii	1 公崽为恩基；1 公山羊为古腊；1 公羊为宁基什凯什达	舒库布姆	乌鲁克	PDT 2 1363
Š 33 v	1 头肥公牛为安奴尼吞女神	贝里沓卜	乌尔	PDT 2 1017
Š 33 ix	1 只育肥公绵羊为大门楼	阿希马		MVN 2 336
Š 33 ix	2 肥公羊为阿奴尼吞，1 肥公羊为乌勒马席吞，阿拉吞、伊什哈腊同上，1 为伊南那于城墙的吉腊努姆仪式	阿希马		AnOr 7 053
Š 35 xi	1 头育肥公牛为圣殿，1 只 zag-ga!-lá 食草公绵羊为卧室	贝里沓卜	乌鲁克	MVN 3 145
Š 36 v	2 只肥公羊为两女神庙，1 只肥公绵羊为那那亚神	贝里沓卜	乌尔	Torino 1 178
Š 36 x	1 肥公羊和 1 羔为阿拉古拉庙，1 肥公羊和 1 羔为宁里勒庙，1 肥公羊和 1 羔为恩里勒，1 公羊为宁旮吉阿庙，为满月牺牲	贝里沓卜	尼普尔	SAT 2 0153
Š 37 i	1 肥公羊为伊南那庙，2 肥公羊、2 羊为阿拉古拉庙，2 肥公牛、2 肥公羊和 1 羊为宁里勒神庙，2 肥公羊和 1 羊为恩里勒神庙，1 羊为神王像，1 肥公羊和 2 羊为宁旮吉亚神庙，以上为"牛田节"	贝里沓卜	尼普尔	OIP 115 032
Š 37 v	2 肥公羊和 1 羔为圣殿门，1 羔为那那亚消失处牺牲，1 公崽为围绕城市哭泣的仪式，1 公崽为举起围攻城市的武器之时，1 肥公羊为祭司寝宫，1 肥公羊和 1 羔为那那亚庙	贝里沓卜	乌鲁克	CTNMC 09
Š 37 v	2 肥公羊、2 羊、2 公崽为贝拉特苏赫尼尔庙	贝里沓卜	乌尔	SET 042
Š 37 v	2 肥公羊为月供，1 肥羔为丹尼亚之妻，1 肥公羊为阿拉吞女神祭祀，1 肥公羊和 1 崽为阿拉古拉女神，1 肥公羊和 1 羔为宁里勒神庙，1 肥公羊和 1 崽为恩里勒神庙，1 肥公羊为宁埃吉亚，以上为初七上玄月	贝里沓卜	尼普尔	
Š 40 xi	1 公羊和 2 羔为宁里勒，1 肥公羊和 2 羔为恩里勒，1 母绵羊为宁旮吉亚，1 公羊为阿拉古拉；1 肥公羊和 1 羔为宁里勒，1 崽为恩里勒，1 肥公羊为伊南那，1 肥公羊为宁乌尔塔，1 肥公羊为努斯库，以上为哀悼祭	阿皮里亚	尼普尔	SumRecDreh.05
Š 41 ii	2 肥羊和 1 公羊为阿巴恩里勒艮之女的倒啤酒宴会，1 肥公羊为阿拉吞祭，阿拉古拉同上，1 肥公羊和 1 羔为宁里勒，恩里勒同上，1 公羊为宁旮吉阿，以上为初七上玄月	阿皮里亚	尼普尔	AnOr 07 068
Š 41 iv	1 幼鸭和 5 只野鸽为神庙的初七上玄月祭	阿皮里亚	尼普尔	SACT 1 133
Š 41 vii	1 肥公羊为修道院门，1 肥公羊为那那亚，2 肥公羊和 1 只羔为圣殿门，	阿皮里亚		AnOr 07 069

续表

时间	文件内容	支出官员	地点	文献出处
Š 45 viii	2公羊为两女神的涂油祭司，2雌崽为伊南那吉腊努姆仪式	乌尔卢旮勒埃丁卡		MVN 13 715
Š 45 ix	2公羊为阿卜朱，1公羊为阿拉穆什，宁旮勒、宁埃伊旮腊同上，1崽为伊尔汉沙，尼敏腊巴、安之子舒勒吉同上，1肥公牛、4肥公羊和1羔为大门楼，1公山羊为女观院的阿拉女神，1肥公羊为供奉，1公羊和1羔为宁荪，1公羊为供奉，2羊为伊什塔尔	乌尔卢旮勒埃丁卡	乌尔	AnOr 07 073
Š 45 xi	1肥公羊和【1羔】为宁里勒，恩里勒、宁舒布尔埃吉尔同上，1羔为宁廷乌格，1崽为舒马赫，1肥公牛、3肥公羊和1羔为宁廷乌格，2公羊为宁尼旮尔	卡兰希那吉		CDLJ 2007：109
Š 45xi	1肥崽为国王食物，1肥公牛、5肥公羊和2羔为那那亚，1肥公羊为舒勒吉，1崽为比勒旮美斯的牺牲，1公羊为舒勒吉，1雌崽为吉比勒牺牲，1羔为黑夜的食物，2肥公羊和1羔为那那亚的啤酒节	卡兰希那吉		PDT 1 582,
Š 45 xii	1肥公羊为月供，1羔为伊南那，1崽为宁乌尔塔，1崽为努斯库，1肥公羊和2羔为恩里勒，2肥公羊为宁里勒，1公羊为宁胡尔萨旮	乌尔卢旮勒埃丁卡		OIP 115 099
Š 46 v	2肥公羊、1公羊、1公山羊、1羔和1崽为两女神，1只公崽为神判河神	乌尔卢旮勒埃丁卡	乌尔	JCS 35 183 1
Š 46 x	1肥公羊为南那的月供，1肥公牛和2肥公羊为圣殿月供，1只肥公羊为月供，［x］［…］，为初七上弦月	乌尔卢旮勒埃丁卡	乌鲁克/尼普尔	OIP 115 105
Š 46 xi	1肥公羊为月供，1公羊为两女神，1公羊为阿达德的牺牲，1肥公羊和1羔为宁里勒，1肥公羊为月供，1崽为恩里勒	乌尔卢旮勒埃丁卡	尼普尔	AnOr 07 077
Š 47 xi	【1+】公羊为阿达德，【1+】公羊为古拉，1羔为那那亚消失处供奉，1肥公羊为月供，1羔为祭司寝宫，1肥公羊和1羔为那那亚，1肥公牛、2肥公羊和1羔为e-zar-zar的圣殿门	舒勒吉伊里	乌鲁克	AnOr 07 087

“我的王后”在舒勒吉新体贡牲机构的档案中更常见的是出现在“为我的王后的食物”（níĝ-gu$_7$ ~ nin-ĝá--šè）支出羊或禽类的文件中。例如：

1）3只育肥鸭、4只育肥家鸽、10只育肥野鸭为我的王后的食物……从阿皮里亚（贡牲机构的负责官员）支出了（舒勒吉38年8月，OIP 115 048）；

2）1只野鸽为我的王后的食物……从乌尔卢旮勒埃丁卡（贡牲机构的负责官员）支出了（舒勒吉46年6月22日，TRU 280）。

第三节　舒勒吉新提王后贡牲机构简介

舒勒吉新提王后贡牲机构是一个特殊的牲畜管理机构①。其设立主要是为了满足舒勒吉新提王后祭祀自己特殊崇拜的两位女神——贝拉特苏赫尼尔（*Belat- Suhnir*）和贝拉特达腊班（*Belat-Darraban*）及与她有关的其他女神和男神的节日，以及对每月三个重要的月相（朔月、上弦月和望月）奉献牺牲。

舒勒吉新提王后贡牲机构建立的年代不能确定。根据王后贡牲机构档案中出现的最早的文件（Princeton 2 134，舒勒吉28年1月），我们推测王后贡牲机构可能建立于舒勒吉28年或之前。舒勒吉新提王后于舒勒吉48年10月中或底随国王舒勒吉的去世而消失，而最后一个王后贡牲机构的档案文件出现在舒勒吉48年10月（Princeton 1 037），可以说舒勒吉新提王后贡牲机构随着舒勒吉统治的结束而结束了。

一　舒勒吉新提王后贡牲机构账目文件类型

目前收集到的舒勒吉新提王后贡牲机构的档案文件共有563件。其档案都是由收据类账目文件组成，主要记录动物牲畜的收支情况②。与普兹瑞什达干贡牲中心的账目文件一样，舒勒吉新提王后贡牲机构的账目文件也分为收入文件和支出文件两类。其中收入文件包括："接管"（ì-dab$_5$）文件、"收到"（šu~ ba-ti）文件和"新出生"（ù-tud-da）文件。由于王后贡牲机构的档案属于"早期档案"，其档案中的支出文件总是使用分词 zi-ga（"支出"）。

（一）舒勒吉新提王后贡牲机构账目文件中的送入和接管文件

王后贡牲机构档案文件属于收入类型的共有两种：（1）为"舒勒吉

① Marcel Sigrist, *Neo-Sumerian Texts From The Royal Ontario Museum*, Bethesda Maryland: CDL Press, 1995, pp.21-27.

② Walther Sallaberger, *Der kultische Kalender der Ur III-Zeit*, Berlin, New York: Walter de Gruyter, 1993, pp.18-25.

新提的送入项”送入的活牲和禽类（包括少数没提名字的送入项）；（2）新生幼畜的登记。

王后贡牲机构档案文件中常用的一个术语是“舒勒吉新提的送入项”（mu- túm *Šulgi-simtī*），其意思是“为舒勒吉新提送入项”，这一短语只出现在贡牲机构收入活牲的文件中。“舒勒吉新提的送入项”（mu-túm ᵈ*Šul-gi-sí-im-ti*）文件共有 169 个，未提及舒勒吉新提王后名字的送入项共计 33 个。“舒勒吉新提的送入项”文件的表述形式是：贡牲数量和种类，来自某人（有时带有其职业或头衔），为舒勒吉新提的送入项（mu-túm ᵈ*Šul-gi-sí-im-ti*），负责官员接管（ì-dab_5），月名，年名。在王后贡牲机构的档案中“舒勒吉新提的送入项”最早出现在舒勒吉 32 年 4 月：1 只公绵羊和 1 只公山羊崽来自扎拉亚（*Za-la-a*），为舒勒吉新提的送入项（MVN 2 308），在该文件中，没有提到贡入牲的接管官员，可能是早期的文件形式并不规范，但根据年代我们推测，此时接管贡入牲的官员可能是阿希马。“舒勒吉新提的送入项”文件最后一次在贡牲机构的档案中出现是在舒勒吉 47 年 11 月 5 日：2 只鸭来自卢旮勒美兰国使（Lugal-me-lám sukkal），于 5 日过去时，为舒勒吉新提的送入项，舒勒吉伊里接管了（OIP 115 115）。

王后贡牲机构中共有 33 个没有提及王后名字的“送入项——接管”（mu- túm……ì-dab_5）文件，可能是书吏省略了王后的名字。最早的没有提及王后名字的“送入项——接管”文件写于舒勒吉 28 年 3 月（MVN 03 117），最晚的没有提及王后名字的“送入项——接管”文件写于舒勒吉 47 年 2 月 26 日（MVN 13 677）。

舒库布姆接管的“舒勒吉新提的送入项”文件一览表

（带星号的是没有提及王后名字的送入项文件）

时间	舒勒吉新提的送入项	接管官员	文献出处
* Š 28iii	2 公羊和 1 公山羊自**伊坡胡尔之女**	舒库布姆	MVN 03 117
* Š 29 x	1+优等肥公羊自【X 之妻】，【1+优等肥公羊】自**达基基之妻**	舒库布姆	PDT 2 1039
* Š 29 xi	18 公羊和 2 崽自**台岑妈妈（阿马尔辛之女）**，7 公羊和 3 崽自**我的国王**，2 公羊和 1 公崽自**席马特埃阿（舒勒吉的 lukur 神妻）**，1 羔自**乌尔舒勒帕埃**（拉旮什的国务卿），1 崽自**埃台勒普达干**（王子）	舒库布姆	OIP 115016
* Š 31 iv	2 公羊和 1 崽自马干的人，3 公羊和 1 公崽自**王座之母**，1 羔自**庙总管库里姆**，1 羔自**卡扎鲁总督**	舒库布姆	OIP 115017

续表

时间	舒勒吉新提的送入项	接管官员	文献出处
＊Š 31 vi	2 公羊和 1 公崽自宁乌马，1 公羊和 1 公崽自**基尼阿沙朱之女**，1 公崽来自**埃阿巴尼**（埃瑞什的总督）	舒库布姆	BIN 3 360
Š 32 iv	1 公羊和 1 公崽自**扎拉亚**（监工）	无	MVN 2 308
Š 32 v	2 公羊来自**吉尔尼萨**（古拉神的庙总管）	无	Torino 1001

贝里沓卜接管的“舒勒吉新提的送入项”文件一览表

（带星号的是没有提及王后名字的送入项文件）

时间	舒勒吉新提的送入项	接管官员	文献出处
Š 33 v	1 公牛，10 羊自胡巴将军，1 公崽自**阿拉之妻**，1 公崽自**乌尔尼旮尔（舒如帕克的总督）之妻**	贝里沓卜	CST042
Š 33 vii	3 公羊和 1 公崽自杜杜，4 公羊和 1 公崽自伊瑞	贝里沓卜	MVN 15 309
Š 34 ii	6 公羊来自**塔巴达腊赫**（席穆润城之人），1 羔自**乌尔尼艮旮尔（舒如帕克的总督）之妻**，1 只羊羔来自马干城之人	贝里沓卜	OIP 115021
Š 34 v	1 头牛、10 羊来自**塔巴达腊赫**（席穆润城之人），1 羔自**阿达卜的总督卡斯卡勒之妻**	贝里沓卜	TLB 3 015
Š 34 x	6 头育肥公牛、38 只公羊、22 只公山羊来自阿姆扎坤	贝里沓卜	OIP 115022
＊Š 35 iv	1 公崽自**神庙总管伊隆巴尼**	贝里沓卜	OIP 115023
＊Š 35 vi	1 肥公牛、3 肥公羊、4 公羊、3 公羔自**乌尔舒勒帕埃**（拉旮什的国务卿）	贝里沓卜	Torino 1 049
＊Š 35 vi	10 肥公羊自温马的总督任职期间的月供	贝里沓卜	MVN 13 873
Š 35 viii	5 头肥公牛和 2 公羊自**普朱尔乌图将军**，2 只公崽自**伊隆巴尼庙总管**	贝里沓卜	MVN 03 143
Š 35 ix	2 只羔自**台岑妈妈**（阿马尔辛之女）	贝里沓卜	RT 37 129 ab.1
＊Š 35 x	5 肥公羊自吉尔苏总督任职期间的供奉	阿希马	Ontario 1059
Š 35 xi	1 头公牛和 10 只公羊自**尼尔伊达旮勒**（ÚR×A.HA^{ki}城的将军）	贝里沓卜	Aegyptus 29 106 34
Š 35 xii	1 羔来自**台岑妈妈（阿马尔辛女）**，2 公羊和 1 公崽自**庙总管伊隆巴尼**	贝里沓卜	Princeton 1 055
Š 36 i	2 只羔自**阿巴恩里勒艮（骑使）之女**，1 只羔自**埃台勒普达干（王子）**	贝里沓卜	BIN 3 347
Š 36 i	1 只羔自**国务卿之妻**	贝里沓卜	Hirose 013
Š 36 viii	1 肥牛和 7【肥】羊自**塔班达腊赫（席穆如王）之妻**，1 肥牛、10 羊自**舒卡卜塔之妻（Me-Iš-taran 公主）**，6 羊自**达基基之妻**，5 羊自伊米辛国使	贝里沓卜	OIP 115024
＊Š 36 x	2 肥公羊和 1 羔来自王座之母	贝里沓卜	Hirose 014

续表

时间	舒勒吉新提的送入项	接管官员	文献出处
Š 36 ix	1 牛、10 羊自国王，1 牛、9 公羊和 1 公崽自**美埃阿**（舒勒吉的 lukur 神妻），**乌尔舒勒帕埃国务卿**同上，4 肥公羊和 1 公崽自**尼尔伊达旮勒**（ÚR×A.HA^{ki} 城的将军），4 肥公羊和 1 羔自**执青铜官**，1 肥公牛、9 公羊和 1 公崽自**伊吉安那凯朱**（南那神的庙总管），**乌尔尼旮尔（王子）之妻，帕尼隆之妻**、**宁卡拉（舒勒吉的 lukur 神妻）**同上	贝里沓卜	AnOr 07 002
Š 37 i	2 只羔来自**埃台勒普达干**（王子）	贝里沓卜	JCS 40 237 8
Š 37 ii	1 雌崽自**塔伊吉伊恩里勒**，5 羊自**巴尼隆之妻**，1 羔自**伊兹阿瑞克**，1 羔来自伊南那的祭司	贝里沓卜	BIN 3 409
Š 37 ii	1 只羊羔自**庙总管伊鲁姆巴尼**，1 只羊羔自**台岑妈妈（阿马尔辛之女）**	贝里沓卜	Torino 1 028
Š 37 v	1 肥公牛、1 公牛、6 肥公羊和 10 只公羊和 4 只公崽自**丹尼亚之妹**	贝里沓卜	OIP 115025
* Š 37 vi	1 公崽来自卡扎鲁总督	贝里沓卜	MCS 7 16 Liv 51 63 27

阿皮里亚接管的“舒勒吉新提的送入项”文件一览表

（带星号的是没有提及王后名字的送入项文件）

时间	舒勒吉新提的送入项	接管官员	文献出处
* Š 37 ix	10 肥公羊自**舒勒吉新吞的月供**	阿皮里亚	Princeton 1 009
* Š 38 ii	2 肥公羊自**庙总管伊鲁姆巴尼**，1 羔自**埃台勒普达干**（王子）	阿皮里亚	Torino 1 050
* Š 38 iv	4 公羊和 1 羔自伊米辛	阿皮里亚	AnOr 01 024
* Š 38 iv	3 鸽来自巴尔巴尔尼亚	阿皮里亚	OIP 115035
Š 38 iv	8 公羊、1 公山羊和 1 公崽自**帕尼吞之妻**	阿皮里亚	PDT 2 0994
Š 38 iv	15 鸭由**乌尔尼旮尔（王子）之女**运送，30 只野鸽由 A-x-na 运送	阿皮里亚	TCS 358
Š 38 v	11 鸭和 3 白鸭来自**乌尔尼旮尔之子**，3 只家鸽来**自巴尔巴尔里亚**	阿皮里亚	NYPL 105
Š 38 v	2 肥尾公羊、2 公崽和 1 雌山羊崽自**乌尔库农那**	阿皮里亚	SACT 1 055
Š 38 v	2 羔自**宁里勒图米姆提**	阿皮里亚	Torino 1044
Š 38 vi	1 羔自**普朱尔伊什塔尔**（马瑞城的将军），于基苏腊	阿皮里亚	OIP 115036
Š 38 vi	31 只【家鸽】……15 只野鸽自捕鸟人阿达那赫	阿皮里亚	AnOr 01 001
Š 38 vii	10 公羊自帕尼吞，2 公羊和 1 公崽自埃阿巴尼，巴尔巴尔里亚和恩里勒伊沙格同上，2 只羊羔自**台岑妈妈（阿马尔辛之女）**	阿皮里亚	NYPL 235

续表

时间	舒勒吉新提的送入项	接管官员	文献出处
Š 38 viii	1 肥公牛、4 公牛、6 肥公羊、12 羊来自**舒沙马什妻**，1 公羊、1 羔来自牧羊人拉腊布姆，牧羊人伊米德伊里姆同上，监工为舒库布姆牲畜长	阿皮里亚	AnOr 7042
Š 38 viii	4 只肥公羊和 1 只羔自**乌图埃拉提将军**	阿皮里亚	Torino 1 030
Š 38 viii	2 公羊和 1 只公崽来自**库尔如卜埃尔腊**	阿皮里亚	Torino 1 029
Š 38ix	10 只鸭来自瓦特腊特	阿皮里亚	BIN 3 001
Š 38 x	6 羊自**舒伊邓之母**，5 羊来自**伊米辛妻**，1 公羊和 2 公崽自旮腊亚	阿皮里亚	AnOr 07 153
Š 38 x	2 公羊和 1 公崽自阿达图尔，1 公崽自舒勒巴拉亚，于乌鲁克，2 公羊和 1 公崽自**尼尔伊达旮勒**（ÚR×A.HA^{ki}城的将军），于大椰枣园中，2 公羊和 1 公山羊自鲁杜格旮拉，于卡伊德伊辛	阿皮里亚	MVN02 167
Š 38 xi	2 公牛、7 公羊、3 公崽自塔巴达腊赫（席穆润城之人），2 公羊、1 公崽自朱扎亚之子，3 公羊、2 公崽自庙总管之兄，1 羊羔自**台岑妈妈**	阿皮里亚	AnOr 07 040
Š 38 xii	2 只公羊和 1 只公崽自**伊什杜姆金**	阿皮里亚	Torino 1 031
Š 39 i	1 猪崽为女儿的奶妈自**埃台阿勒普达干（王子）**，2 只野鸽来自瑞喀穆沙	阿皮里亚	Torino 1 032
* Š 39 ii	1 雌崽自**台岑妈妈**，2 肥公羊自国王	阿皮里亚	Torino 1 051
Š 39 iii	6 只家鸽自巴尔巴尔里亚	阿皮里亚	MVN 03 161
Š 39 iii	3 羔和 1 公崽自**台岑妈妈**	阿皮里亚	MVN 03 162
Š 39 iii	1 鸭来自**女乐师恩尼亚**，10 家鸽，15 只鸟来自乌尔宁穆格，3 只野鸽、1+只 tu 鸟来自【舒】沙马什	阿皮里亚	OIP 115037
Š 39 iv/6	1 鸟自乌如卜城的人，58 野鸽来自**台岑妈妈**，2 只家鸽来自巴尔巴尔里亚	阿皮里亚	AUCT 1 952
Š 39 iv	3 只公羊和 1 只羊羔来自伊米新，2 只公羊和 1 只公崽来自旮腊亚，1 只雌羊羔崽来自乌如卜城的人，1 只羊羔来自马达提，1 只公崽来自 **x 之妻**	阿皮里亚	CST046
Š 39 iv	1 羔和 1 公崽自**瓦特腊特（王太后）监工**	阿皮里亚	SACT 1 056
Š 39 iv/28–30	4 只野鸽来自伊米新，6 只家鸽来自巴尔巴尔尼亚，2 只家鸽来自拉埃阿	阿皮里亚	OIP 115 038
Š 39 v	1 羔自**普朱尔伊什塔尔**（马瑞城的将军），1 崽自乌如卜城的人，1 羊自牧羊人**阿德穆**，1 羊自牧羊人尼达旮，1 崽自牧羊人乌尔美斯，1 羔自**卢旮勒埃载姆舒什**	阿皮里亚	AnOr 07 003
* Š 39 vi/15	130 肥公羊和 30 公山羊的账目平衡，来自恩迪弥尔	阿皮里亚	MVN 08 004
Š 39 vi	5 公羊和 1 羊羔自**伊什杜金（乌尔尼旮尔之子）**	阿皮里亚	Torino 1 033
Š 39 vii	1 只公牛、6 只公羊和 4 只公山羊来自**阿巴恩里勒艮（骑使）**	阿皮里亚	NYPL 253

续表

时间	舒勒吉新提的送入项	接管官员	文献出处
Š39viii/16	9只鸭子自**宁里勒吞伊姆提**	阿皮里亚	PDT 2 1006
Š 39viii/25	6只鸭子自**乌尔舒勒吉腊（将军）**	阿皮里亚	CST048
Š 39 viii	2只公羊和1只公崽自**丹尼亚之妻**，1只公崽自伊朱亚瑞克总督	阿皮里亚	CST049
Š 39 ix/22	12只鸭自乌图伊拉特（将军）	阿皮里亚	SumTemDocs.04
Š 39 ix/29	4只鸟	阿皮里亚	OIP 115039
Š 39 ix	1头公牛、1只公羊和3只公崽自**达基基之妻**	阿皮里亚	OIP 115 040
Š 39 x	1只羔和1只公崽自**台岑妈妈（阿马尔辛之女）**	阿皮里亚	Princeton 2 018
Š 39 xi	2公羊和1公崽自**卡里亚妻**，1羔自**库勒耐基阿格之妻**，1羔自埃乌埃（总督）	阿皮里亚	Princeton 1 007
Š 39 xi/25	2只育肥公牛和20只公羊自**努尼达（庙总管）之妻如巴吞**	阿皮里亚	OIP 115 042
Š 39 xii	4只公羊和1只瞪羚自**王座之母**	阿皮里亚	Princeton 1 010
Š 39	74只肥公羊、30只公羊和8只肥公山羊来自巴穆	阿皮里亚	Torino 1 034
Š 40 i	2只羔自扎克伊里，1只羔自乌尔尼旮尔（王子）之子伊什杜金	阿皮里亚	AUCT 1 089
Š 40 ii/19	1+肥羊、1+公崽自**伊吉安那凯朱（南那神的庙总管）**，5羊自阿皮里之妻，5肥羊、1公羊自**普朱尔伊什塔尔（马瑞城的将军）**	阿皮里亚	SACT 1 057
Š 40 ii	1只雌山羊崽来自埃乌埃（总督）	阿皮里亚	OIP 115043
*Š 40 iv/7，21	1+x鸽自伊尼姆沙腊之子沙腊卡姆，4鸭自**监工瓦特腊特王太后**	阿皮里亚	PDT 2 0993
Š 40 v	1羔自埃乌埃（总督），6只公羊自**努尼达（庙总管）之妻如巴吞**	阿皮里亚	OIP 115045
Š 40 v/9	1只肥公牛、9只肥公羊和1只公崽自**巴尼伊隆妻**	阿皮里亚	Ontario 1 011
Š 40 v/24	2只家鸽自**宁里勒吞伊姆提**	阿皮里亚	OIP 115044
Š 40 v/29	1只家鸽自埃乌埃（总督），2只家鸽自贝里巴尼（伊南那的庙总管）	阿皮里亚	RT 37 129 ml 2
Š 40 vi	1只雄羊羔和1只雌羔自**宁里勒吞伊姆提**	阿皮里亚	Torino 1 035
Š 40 vi/5	9只家鸽和2只野鸽自**宁里勒希姆提**	阿皮里亚	BIN 3 363
*Š40viii/29，30	3鸭自**伊尼姆沙腊（书吏）的新娘**，2+鸭自**宁里勒吞伊姆提**	阿皮里亚	CST051
Š 40ix10，19	1鸭自捕鸟人，2鸭自**台岑妈妈（阿马尔辛之女）**，1白鸭自辛那达	阿皮里亚	BIN 3 486
Š 40 ix/22	1只肥公羊和1只公羊来自**尼尔伊达旮勒（ÚR×A.HAki城的将军）**	阿皮里亚	RT 37 129 mr 3
Š 40 xi	1只羊羔自埃乌埃总督	阿皮里亚	Nisaba 08 169

续表

时间	舒勒吉新提的送入项	接管官员	文献出处
[Š 41] i	[⋯]，1 只鸭、10 只公山羊和 1 只羔自**采鲁什达干（席穆润总督）之妹**	阿皮里亚	TRU 076
Š 41 ii/22	3 只幼鸭自伊什杜姆金（马尔哈席城之人）	阿皮里亚	Torino 1 036
Š 41 vi/8，10	12 鸽自**席马特伊什塔尔（王子）**，2 鸭自瓦特腊特（王太后），【1+】鸽自马什马什里亚	阿皮里亚	BCT 2 246
Š 41 viii/17	9 只雏鸟自捕鸟人巴鲧	阿皮里亚	SAT 2 0294
Š 41 viii/23	3 只鸭自**采鲁什达干（席穆润总督）之妹**	阿皮里亚	YOS 18 005
Š41ix/10，14	【1+x】只鸭自**乐师阿旮农之女**，2 只鸭自捕猎网	阿皮里亚	MVN 03 179
*Š 41 ix	4 只羊羔和 2 只【母绵羊】	阿皮里亚	PDT 1 330

阿皮拉吞接管的“舒勒吉新提的送入项”文件一览表

（带星号的是没有提及王后名字的送入项文件）

时间	舒勒吉新提的送入项	接管官员	文献出处
*Š 41 xi/26	1 肥公牛和 10 公羊自伊尼姆沙腊（书吏）之子卡拉穆	阿皮拉吞	Torino 1 052
*Š 41 xii/2	2 只鸭自乌尔伊什塔蓝（阿马尔辛之子）	阿皮拉吞	Hirose 016
*Š41xii/[8]	2 肥羊和 1 崽自**王子那比乌姆**，4 肥公羊和 1 羔自国王之子【X】	阿皮拉吞	SET 005
Š 42 i/22	1 羔自伊南那的祭司，1 崽自塔林恩里勒，5 肥公羊和 3 羔自伊什杜金	阿皮拉吞	SET 006
Š 42 i/26	3 只幼鸭自宫殿	阿皮拉吞	Torino 1 037
Š 42 i/26	2 只肥公羊和 1 只羔来自庙总管伊米德伊隆	阿皮拉吞	OIP 115 069
Š 42 ii	1 只羊羔自布米扎之子	阿皮拉吞	OIP 115070
Š 42 ii/21，22，23，24	2 家鸽从宫殿带来，【⋯⋯】，13 家鸽自伊比辛交付的欠款，3 家鸽自巴尔巴尔里亚	阿皮拉吞	SET 007
Š 42 v/23	1 只肥公羊、1 只公羊和 1 只羔自旮拉亚	阿皮拉吞	CST 469
Š 42 v/28	3 只家鸽自**席马特伊什塔尔（王子）**	阿皮拉吞	Torino 1 039
Š 42 vi	4 只公羊和 1 只公崽自舒库布姆	阿皮拉吞	PDT 2 983
Š 42 vi/8	1+只家鸽自瓦特腊特（王太后）监工	阿皮拉吞	SA 045(Pl.003)
Š 42 vii/24	2 只鸭自国使沙闰伊里	阿皮拉吞	Torino 1038
Š 42 viii/5	8 只鸭自捕鸟人巴衮	阿皮拉吞	MVN 13 275
*Š 42 viii/22	1 鸭自沙闰伊里国使	阿皮拉吞	Princeton 1 059
Š 42 viii	1 只公羊和 1 只胸羊羔自**席亚亚**	阿皮拉吞	Torino 1040

续表

时间	舒勒吉新提的送入项	接管官员	文献出处
Š 42 viii	2 只公羊和 1 只公崽自库如卜埃腊	阿皮拉吞	Torino 1041
Š42 x/23，24	1 只鸭自阿亚马，3 只鸭自阿皮里	阿皮拉吞	OIP 115 071
* Š 42 xii	2 公羊和 1 公崽自吞腊亚，1 羔自**台岑妈妈（阿马尔辛之女）**	阿皮拉吞	Hirose 019
Š43 ii/1，4，9	2 鸽自看守阿拉穆，4 鸭自宁里勒吞伊姆提，2 鸭、12 鸽自尼尔伊达吞勒（ÚR×A.HA[ki]城的将军）	阿皮拉吞	OIP 115 072
Š 43 ii/30	2 羊自牧羊人塔巴伊里，3 肥羊自瓦特腊特（王太后）监工，2 羊自**席马特伊什塔尔（王子）**	阿皮拉吞	OLP 08 07 02
Š43 ix/17-22	3 只鸭自**沙腊坎之妻**，2 只鸭自**采鲁什达干之妹**，2 只鸭自载腊腊	阿皮拉吞	OIP 115074
* Š 43 xi/30	1 公羊和 1 羔自伊丁埃腊，3 公羊和 1 羊自执青铜官，2 崽自**普朱尔伊什塔尔（马瑞城的将军）**，1 公牛、7 公羊、1 母羊、1 公崽和 1 羔自妇女，1 公羊和 1 崽自阿尔西阿赫，1 崽自伊米德辛，1 羔来自马达提，2 公崽自**台岑妈妈（阿马尔辛之女）**，1 羔自王子舒伊什塔尔，2 肥公羊、1 公山羊和 1 公崽自采鲁什达干（席穆润的总督）	阿皮拉吞	RO 11 96 01
Š 43 xii/8	1 只幼鸭来自**沙腊刊（吉尔苏的总督）之妻**	阿皮拉吞	Hirose 022
Š 44 i/27，28，29，30	7 只野鸽自采鲁什达干（席穆润总督），32 只野鸽自达干古达干，9 只野鸽自伊尼姆库吞，4 只野鸽自达亚提	阿皮拉吞	MVN 03 200
Š 44 ii	1 只公崽自**瓦特腊特（王太后）**	阿皮拉吞	MVN 03 201
Š 44 ii	5 只家鸽自**乌尔尼之妻**，5 只家鸽和 14 只野鸽来自 X-基	阿皮拉吞	YOS 18 006
Š 44 ii/15	4 只幼鸭和 2 只家鸽自**席马特伊什塔尔（王子）**	阿皮拉吞	OIP 115075
Š 44 iii/7，11	120 家鸽自园丁们和 77 鸟自**沙腊闰伊里（国使）之妻**，120 只家鸽自乌尔达吞	阿皮拉吞	Torino 1 042
Š44iii/20，28	5 鸽自园丁们的生产产量，5 鸽自王子舒伊什塔尔，9 鸽自**乌尔尼妻**	阿皮拉吞	RA 19 192 07
Š 44 iv/15，17，19	5 鸽自瓦塔腊特（王太后），5 鸽自园丁们的生产定限，19 鸽自伊米德伊隆（牧羊人），4 鸽自园丁们的生产定限	阿皮拉吞	OIP 115076
Š 44 v/9	2 肥雌崽自普朱尔伊什塔尔将军，2 公羊和 1 公崽自**舒伊迪姆之母**，2 公羊和 1 公崽自库达提，1 只公崽自**瓦特腊特（王太后）**	阿皮拉吞	StOr 09-1 22 (pl.6)
Š 44 vi/15	1 绵羊和 1 雌崽从宫殿带来	阿皮拉吞	RT 37129 mi.4
* Š 44 vi/22	2 肥公羊自国王	阿皮拉吞	Torino 1 053
Š 44 vi/25	3 只公羊和 1 只公崽自采鲁什达干（席穆润总督）	阿皮拉吞	MVN 15 324
Š 44 vi	1 只羔自那姆兹塔腊（古杜阿的总督）	阿皮拉吞	SAT 2 0364

续表

时间	舒勒吉新提的送入项	接管官员	文献出处
* Š 44 vii/3, 6	1 羔自西伊什塔尔，1 肥羔自**监工（王太后）瓦特腊特**，7 肥公羊和 3 公羊自乌如卜城的人的使官，5 羔自 X，1 雌羔和 1 雌崽自宫殿	阿皮拉吞	Hirose 029
Š 44 vii/17–20	3 肥羊和 2 公羊自**努伊达之妻**，6 公羊和 1 公崽自努伊达，2 肥羊自国王，2 肥羊、2 公羊和 1 公山羊自尼普尔总督乌尔尼萨巴，3 肥羊和 2 公山羊自监工**（王太后）瓦特腊特**，2 雌崽自普朱尔伊什塔尔（马瑞城的将军）	阿皮拉吞	OrSP 18 pl.02 06
Š 44 ix	4 羊和 1 羔自伊提埃腊，1+只公羊、1 羔和 1 公崽自伊米德伊隆	阿皮拉吞	RT 37 130 ab.6
Š 44 ix/6	1 只鸭自**席马特伊什塔尔（王子）**	阿皮拉吞	Torino 1 043
Š 44x/13, 14	1 鸭自西巴特埃库尔，1 只鸭自【……】	阿皮拉吞	TRU 077
Š 44 xi	1 只雌崽自伊米德伊隆，2 只公羊和 1 只公崽自贝里巴尼	阿皮拉吞	UCP 9-2-2 070
Š 44 xi/2	5 只鸭自**沙润伊里（国使）之妻**	阿皮拉吞	BIN 3 007
Š 44 xi/21	2 公羊和 1 公崽自西马特埃库尔，2 肥羊和 1 只羔自**沙腊刊之妻**	阿皮拉吞	Orient 16 041 6
Š 44 xii/4	4 只家鸽自**瓦特腊特（王太后）监工**	阿皮拉吞	OIP 115077
Š 44 xii/15	2 只白母山羊来自伊尼姆库旮	阿皮拉吞	SACT 1 058
Š 44 xii	2 只白鸟自卡库旮	阿皮拉吞	SETDA 58
Š 44 xii	30 羊自**宁里勒希姆提**，1 羔自**扎腊腊之妻**，1 公崽自乌尔尼旮尔官员	阿皮拉吞	SET 008
* Š 45 i	2 公羊自采鲁什达干（席穆润总督），2 羔自**台岑妈妈（阿马尔辛之女）**，1 新生羊自育肥房，2 羊自**普朱尔伊什塔尔（马瑞城的将军）**，1 羔自乌尔尼旮尔（王子），1 羔自**宁里勒吞伊姆提**	阿皮拉吞	BIN 3 335
Š 45 i/7, 10	1 羔和 1 公崽自普朱尔伊什塔尔（**马瑞城的将军**），1 幼鸭自**席马特伊什塔尔（王子）**，1 公崽自马干国的人，1 肥公牛自伊库农，10 公羊来自埃台阿勒普达干（王子），1 羔来自**宁里勒吞伊姆提**	阿皮拉吞	Babyl.8 Pupil 17
Š 45 i/20, 23	2 鸭和 3 鸽自**宁里勒吞伊姆提**，40 鸽自捕鸟人巴穌，1 肥公羊自普朱尔伊什塔尔（**马瑞城的将军**），1 羔自伊米德伊隆	阿皮拉吞	Durand RA 73, no 1
Š 45 iii/23	9 只 LAGAB 鸟来自鲁乌如卡尔	阿皮拉吞	RT 37 129 be.5
Š 45 v/22	4 只公羊和 1 只公崽自沙润伊里总督，1 只羔自恩里勒伊萨，2 只育肥公羊和 1 只育肥羔自伊库隆，2 只家鸽自**哈拉亚之妻**	阿皮拉吞	PDT 1 475
Š45 vi	4 只公羊和 1 只公崽自伊尼姆库旮	阿皮拉吞	PDT 2 982
Š45 vi/15	1 母绵羊和 1 雌崽从宫殿带来，1 新生羔自育肥房，29 野鸽自捕鸟人巴衮	阿皮拉吞	NABU 1997: 099

乌尔卢旮勒埃丁卡接管的“舒勒吉新提的送入项”文件一览表

（带星号的是没有提及王后名字的送入项文件）

时间	舒勒吉新提的送入项	接管官员	文献出处
Š 45viii	2 母牛、10 只公羊和 10 只公山羊自**将军舒勒吉伊里妻**	乌尔卢旮勒埃丁卡	RT 37130 mi.7
* Š45viii/27	2 鸭和 1 鸟自**监工（王太后）瓦特腊特**	乌尔卢旮勒埃丁卡	MVN 04 105
Š 45 ix/29	7 只鸭自**席马特伊什塔尔（王子）**，1 羔自卢旮勒图尔塞，10 鸭自阿皮拉吞补交的欠款	乌尔卢旮勒埃丁卡	RA 49 86 04
Š 45 xi	2 只羔自**席马特伊什塔尔（王子）**	乌尔卢旮勒埃丁卡	OIP 115 085
Š 45 xi	1 只公羊和 1 只羔自**阿皮里之妻**	乌尔卢旮勒埃丁卡	SACT 1 059
Š 46 i/8，15	1 鸭和 5 鸽自沙林，20 鸽自采鲁什达干（席穆润总督）之子，3 鸽自鲁基瑞扎勒，8 鸽自**沙腊坎（吉尔苏总督）之妻**，2 猪自**席马特伊什塔尔（王子）**	乌尔卢旮勒埃丁卡	JCS 29 117 1
Š 46 ii/1	1 羔和 1 雄豚，【x】自乌如卜城的人，1 羔自【...的人】，【1+】野鸽自 X-达干丹，【1】羔从宫殿带来，1 羔自伊米德伊隆，	乌尔卢旮勒埃丁卡	OIP 115086
Š 46 iii/3	6 鸽自埃台勒普达干（王子），5 羊自**努尼达之妻巴巴吞**	乌尔卢旮勒埃丁卡	PDT 2 1035
Š 46 iv/24：	2 羔、3 鸽自**宁里勒希姆提**，1 羔自育肥房	乌尔卢旮勒埃丁卡	MVN 13 664
Š 46 viii	5 羊自如巴吞，49 公羊和 1 羔自采鲁什达干（席穆润总督），20 公绵来自 X，腊皮皮勒之子	乌尔卢旮勒埃丁卡	PDT 2 1013
Š 46 ix/6	2 肥公山羊自尼尔伊达旮勒，3 肥公羊、4 公羊和 3 公崽自**席马特伊什塔尔**，1 公羊自西巴特埃库尔，2 肥公羊和 1 雌崽自伊米德沙卜腊	乌尔卢旮勒埃丁卡	TRU 282
Š 46 x	1 羔自**席马特伊什塔尔（王子）**，1 公崽来自阿皮里，1 只羔来自库如卜埃腊	乌尔卢旮勒埃丁卡	Aegyptus 29 108 37
Š 46 x	1 肥公猪、1 肥公猪自乌尔卢旮勒埃丁卡，10 猪崽为军团的月供	乌尔卢旮勒埃丁卡	OIP 115 087
Š 46 x/28	5 鸭自采鲁什达干（席穆润总督），8 鸭自阿吉什旮尔捕鸟人，1 鸭来自卡库旮	乌尔卢旮勒埃丁卡	OIP 115 106
Š 46 xi	1 羔自扎克伊里	乌尔卢旮勒埃丁卡	MVN 13 675
Š 46 xii	1 羔自伊什杜姆金（马尔哈席尔城之人），1 羔自阿穆尔乌图，1 公崽自伊米德伊隆，1 羔自普朱尔伊什塔尔（马瑞城的将军）	乌尔卢旮勒埃丁卡	AnOr 07 011
* Š 46xii/15,18,22	3 肥公猪自沙如姆使官，3 鸭和 3 家鸽自**席马特伊什塔尔（王子）**，20 鸭自伊什塔尔阿勒舒（王子），1 鸭自乌尔美斯	乌尔卢旮勒埃丁卡	OIP 115 89

续表

时间	舒勒吉新提的送入项	接管官员	文献出处
Š 46 xii/22	【3+】羔，10 肥公羊，1 肥公牛、10 羊和 1 瞪羚自王子伊什塔尔阿勒舒，5 羔，10 公羊，3 肥公羊，自乌尔美斯书吏，【1+】头公牛、6+公羊、3 公山羊和 1 羔来自布达干，1 公崽来自阿穆尔乌图，2 羔自伊米德伊隆官员，总计 1+公牛，总计 30+公羊和公崽	乌尔卢旮勒埃丁卡	MVN 13 794
Š 47 i/11	1 只鸭和 2 只家鸽自尼尔伊达旮勒（ÚR×A.HA^{ki} 城的将军）	乌尔卢旮勒埃丁卡	TRU 078
Š 47 i/20	13 只野鸽自采鲁什达干（席穆润总督）	乌尔卢旮勒埃丁卡	SA 041
Š 47 i/23	2 只幼鸭自舒伊什塔尔（王子）	乌尔卢旮勒埃丁卡	PDT 2 1022
Š 47 i/29	2 育肥公羊和 1 羔自乌尔伊什塔蓝（阿马尔辛之子）	乌尔卢旮勒埃丁卡	SACT 1 060
Š 47 i	2 只羔自**瓦特腊特（王太后）监工**	乌尔卢旮勒埃丁卡	AnOr 07 016
Š 47 i	1 只羔自库如卜埃腊，1 只羔自伊米辛	乌尔卢旮勒埃丁卡	PDT 1 113
Š 47 i	2 只公羊和 1 只公山羊自塔巴伊里牧羊人，7 只公崽自 X–乌图	乌尔卢旮勒埃丁卡	TCS 335
* Š 47ii/26	2 家鸽自西拉马斯	乌尔卢旮勒埃丁卡	MVN 13 677
Š 47 ii	1 公崽自伊米德伊隆官员	乌尔卢旮勒埃丁卡	Torino 1 046
Š 47 ii	1 只羔自沙润伊里使官	乌尔卢旮勒埃丁卡	OIP 115 091
Š 47 ii/2	1 牛和 5 公羊自卡腊，1 肥牛、7 肥羊和 3 公山羊自沙腊刊，1 羔自伊南那的祭司，2 肥羊和 1 公崽自尼尔伊达旮勒（ÚR×A.HA^{ki} 城的将军），1 公崽自采鲁什达干（席穆润总督）	乌尔卢旮勒埃丁卡	OIP 115090
Š 47 iii	2 只公羊和 1 只羔自库如卜埃腊	乌尔卢旮勒埃丁卡	PDT 2 1003
Š 47 iii/21	4 只幼鸭自阿皮勒金	乌尔卢旮勒埃丁卡	OIP 115 092
Š 47 iv/3	1 肥公羊自月供，1 肥公羊、2 公羊和 1 公崽自西巴特埃库尔	乌尔卢旮勒埃丁卡	PDT 1 157

舒勒吉伊里接管的“舒勒吉新提的送入项”文件一览表

（带星号的是没有提及王后名字的送入项文件）

时间	舒勒吉新提的送入项	接管官员	文献出处
* Š 45 viii	1 头 kunga 母驴送入为国王，从那萨处	舒勒吉伊里	Torino 1 092

续表

时间	舒勒吉新提的送入项	接管官员	文献出处
Š 47 iv	2 羊自苏如什金，1 母山羊自**台岑妈妈（阿马尔辛之女）**，【1+】羔自舒埃什塔尔（王子）	舒勒吉伊里	Torino 1 024
Š 47 v	1 雌崽自普朱尔伊什塔尔（马瑞城的将军）	舒勒吉伊里	AnOr 07 014
Š 47 vi	1 只公崽自扎克里里	舒勒吉伊里	OIP 115 109
Š 47 vii	1 只公崽自舒伊什塔尔（王子），1 只公崽自旮腊亚	舒勒吉伊里	Princeton 1 036
Š 47 vii	3 只公羊和 1 只公崽自舒库布姆	舒勒吉伊里	Princeton 1 041
Š 47 vii/22	1 只鸭和 4 只野鸽自**采鲁什达干（（席穆润总督））的妹妹**	舒勒吉伊里	OIP 115 110
Š 47 vii	【1+】只羔自**舒伊什塔尔（王子）**，1 只公崽自马达提	舒勒吉伊里	Torino 1 047
Š 47 ix/2	2 只鸭自卡库旮	舒勒吉伊里	SACT 1 061
Š 47 ix/2	1 崽自王座之母，2 肥羊自乌如卜城人的月供，2 羊和 1 羔自库如卜埃腊	舒勒吉伊里	AnOr 07 015
Š 47 ix/11	3 只鸭自**沙如姆伊里军尉之妻**	舒勒吉伊里	OIP 115 111
Š 47 ix/13	2 公崽自**席马特伊什塔尔**（王子），3 肥羊自伊库农，1 公崽自沙润伊里，1 公羊和 1 公崽自尼尔伊达旮勒，1 羔自伊南那的祭司，1 羔自阿达图尔	舒勒吉伊里	Orient 16 044 16，
Š 47 ix/15	1 肥牛、3 肥羊、5 公羊、1 肥羊和 1 肥崽自尼尔伊达旮勒（ÚR×A.HA^{ki}城将军）	舒勒吉伊里	BIN 3 021
Š 47 ix/18	2 只鸭自**卡腊之妻**	舒勒吉伊里	Torino 1 048
Š 47 ix/20	2 肥公羊和 1 肥公山羊崽自阿皮【拉提】，1 肥公羊自舒库布姆	舒勒吉伊里	OIP 115 112
Š 47 ix/23	10 只鸭自**阿皮里之妻**	舒勒吉伊里	CST 184
Š 47 ix	2 公牛、16 公羊和 4 公山羊自舒勒吉伊里将军，1 羔自扎克伊里	舒勒吉伊里	OIP 115 113
Š 47 x	2 只羔自**宁里勒吞伊姆提**	舒勒吉伊里	OIP 115 114
Š 47 x/28	6 只鸭自捕鸟人巴鲧	舒勒吉伊里	PDT 1 139
Š 47 xi/5	2 只鸭自卢旮勒美兰国使	舒勒吉伊里	OIP 115 115

“新出生”（ù-tu-da）文件是记录王后贡牲机构收到的来自育肥房的猪或羊的新生幼崽数量以及其接管官员的文件。王后贡牲机构档案中的“新出生”文件共计 9 个。“新出生”文件的表述形式通常是：新出生动物牲畜的数量和种类，为舒勒吉新提的送入项，贡牲机构的负责官员接管。王后贡牲机构收到的新生猪共计 35 头（雌豚 20 头，雄豚 15 头）、新生公绵羊羔 9 只和新生公山羊崽 2 只。

贡牲机构的“新出生”牲畜登记简表

日期	文件内容	接管官员	文献出处
Š 41 xii/1	4 头雌豚和 1 头雄豚，为新生	阿皮拉吞	Torino 1 73
Š 44 vi/15	1 只新生公绵羊羔自育肥房，为舒勒吉新吞的送入项	阿皮拉吞	RT 37 129
Š 45 i	1 只新生公山羊崽来自育肥房	阿皮拉吞	BIN 3 335
Š 45 i	1 只新生公山羊崽自育肥房	阿皮拉吞	BIN 3 335
Š 45 vi/15	1 只新生公绵羊羔自育肥房，为舒勒吉新吞的送入项	阿皮拉吞	NABU 1997：099
Š 46 iv/24	1 只新生公绵羊羔自育肥房，为舒勒吉新吞的送入项	乌尔卢旮勒埃丁卡	MVN 13 664
Š 46 x	16 雌豚和 14 雄豚由 5 母猪生于育肥房，为舒勒吉新提送入项	乌尔卢旮勒埃丁卡	OIP 115 087
Š 46 xi	2 只新生公绵羊羔于育肥房，为送入项	乌尔卢旮勒埃丁卡	OIP 115 088
Š 46 xi	4 只新生公绵羊羔	舒勒吉伊里	OIP 115 492

（二）舒勒吉新提王后贡牲机构账目文件中的支出文件①

王后贡牲机构的支出（zi–ga）文件可以分为两类：一类是支出活牲的文件。王后贡牲机构支出活牲主要是为祭祀神明提供牺牲和为王后提供食物（偶尔有国王或贵族等来访，也会为他们提供食物）；另一类是支出死牲的文件。王后贡牲机构支出的死牲通常被送入宫殿，作为宫殿女工或士兵的食物。有时这两类支出写在同一个文件中。其支出的记账形式为：动物牺牲的数量和种类和目的，某人督办（maškim）和（或）经由（gìr）某人，日期，从负责官员处支出（zi–ga），有时还会提到支出的地点，最后是月名、年名。

二　舒勒吉新提王后贡牲机构的特点

舒勒吉新提王后贡牲机构与普兹瑞什达干贡牲中心相比，呈现出诸多不同的特点。首先王后贡牲机构的规模较小，它只是负责管理舒勒吉新提王后所有的牲畜，而普兹瑞什达干贡牲中心则统管整个王朝的牲畜或物品的收支。其次，二者档案中记录的文件内容和使用的文件术语等也有所不同。王后贡牲机构的负责官员管理的动物牲畜种类较多，负责官员可同时

① 舒勒吉新提王后贡牲机构的支出活动分析见第三章。

收支羊、牛、猪以及各种家禽，而贡牲中心的官员则集中负责一种牲畜；表达日期的术语方面，王后贡牲机构的档案文件采用 iti--ta ud-x ba-ra-zal（有时用 iti--ta ud-x ba-ta- zal），在普兹瑞什达干贡牲中心的档案文件中，接收死牲的文件采用 ud-x-kam①，而在接管活牲的文件中，以羊牲育肥官员那鲁的档案为例②，舒勒吉 47 年之前其接管活牲文件的日期表达是 iti-ud-x ba-zal，在舒勒吉 47 年之后，接管活牲文件的日期表达和接收死牲时一样，都采用 ud-x-kam；在“支出”一词的术语表达方面，王后贡牲机构的档案文件中，总是使用 zi-ga；而普兹瑞什达干贡牲中心，在那萨署名中心总管之后（舒勒吉 47 年 7 月 13 日），其档案文件开始使用 ba-zi（“被支出”）代替 zi-ga。此外，舒勒吉新提王后贡牲机构中送入动物牲畜或物品的人员多数是女性。这表明乌尔第三王朝时期，女性可以积极地参与社会的经济或宗教事务。

① 付世强：《乌尔第三王朝贡牲中心厨房死牲官员舒勒吉乌如穆的档案重建》，东北师范大学，硕士学位论文，2009 年。

② 王颖杰：《乌尔第三王朝贡牲中心羊牲育肥官员那鲁的档案重建》，东北师范大学，博士学位论文，2009 年。

第二章　舒勒吉新提王后贡牲机构的负责官员们

舒勒吉新提王后贡牲机构中共有八位负责收支动物牲畜的官员①，他们是育肥师阿希马（*Ahima*）、骑使舒库布姆（*Šukubum*）、育肥师贝里沓卜（*Beli-ṭab*）、阿皮里亚（*Apiliya*）、育肥师阿皮拉吞（*Apilatum*）、育肥师和书吏乌尔卢旮勒埃邓卡（Ur-Lugal-edenka）、骑使舒勒吉伊里（*Šulgi-ili*）和卡兰希那吉（Kalam-henagi）。其中前五位负责官员和骑使舒勒吉伊里的名字都是阿卡德语（只有两位负责官员的名字是苏美尔语），这反映出舒勒吉新提王后的阿卡德背景。除第一位负责官员阿希马和最后一位负责官员卡兰希那吉外，其余六位负责官员的任期依次接替。

舒勒吉新提王后贡牲机构负责官员头衔及任期一览表

官员	头衔	工作时间	历　时
阿希马	育肥师	Š 28 i– Š 36 v	8年4个月
舒库布姆	骑使	Š28 iii–Š 32 x	4年7个月
贝里沓卜	育肥师	Š33 v–Š 37 vi	4年1个月
阿皮里亚		Š37 ix–Š 41 x/11	4年1个月
阿皮拉吞	育肥师	Š41 xi/26–Š 45 vi/15	3年7个月
乌尔卢旮勒埃邓卡	育肥师、书吏	Š45 vii/12–Š 47 iv/28	1年9个月
舒勒吉伊里	骑使	Š47 iv/30–Š 48 x	1年6个月
卡兰希那吉		Š44 xi–Š 48 ii/10	3年3个月

王后贡牲机构收入和支出的动物牲畜的种类主要有以下几种：

（1）育肥牛和普通牛：育肥公牛（gud-niga）、2岁育肥母牛（áb-

---

① Marcel Sigrist, *Drehem*, Bethesda, MD: CDL Press, 1992, pp.222-246.

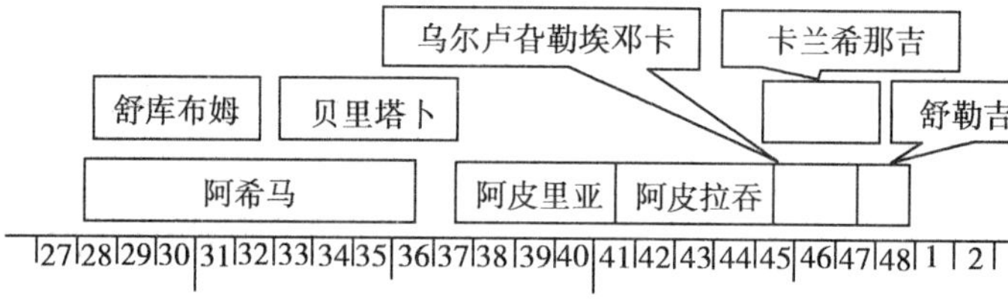

舒勒吉新提王后贡牲机构负责官员任期图

mu-2-niga)、食草公牛（gud-ú)、公牛（gud)、食草母牛（áb-ú)、母牛（áb）和一种不确定的牛羊类（amar-UDU.KU_6-tenu)。

（2）育肥羊和普通羊：育肥公绵羊（udu-niga)、育肥母绵羊（u_8-niga)、牛后级育肥公绵羊（udu-niga~gud-e-ús-sa)、育肥雄羔（$sila_4$-niga)、育肥公山羊（máš-gal-niga)、育肥母山羊（ud_5-niga)、育肥公山羊崽（máš-niga)、育肥雌山羊崽（^{f}ašgar-niga)、公绵羊（udu)、母绵羊（u_8)、大尾巴公绵羊（gukkan)、雄羔（$sila_4$)、雌羔（kir_{11})、公山羊（máš-gal)、母山羊（ud_5)、无崽母山羊（ud_5-máš-nú-a)、公山羊崽（máš)、雌崽（^{f}ašgar)、食草公绵羊（udu-ú)、食草公山羊（máš-gal-ú）和吃奶公山羊（máš~ga-gu_7)、剪毛羔（kir_{11}-ur_4)。

（3）家禽和鸟类：育肥鸭（uz-tur-niga)、鸭（uz-tur)、幼鸭（amar-sag~uz-tur)、野鸽（ir_7/kaskal)、家鸽（tu-$gur_4^{mušen}$)、白鸟（uz-babbar)、舵燕鸦（u_5-$sim^{mušen}$)。

（4）猪：猪崽（$šáh^{zah}$-tur)、苇塘雄豚（$šáh^{zah}$-tur-giš-gi)、苇塘雌豚（šáh-tur-munus-giš-gi）和驯养雌豚（šáh-izi-tur-munus-uru)。

第一节　王后贡牲机构的八位负责官员

一　牛、羊育肥师阿希马（Š 28 i– Š 36 v）

负责官员阿希马（*Ahima*）是王后贡牲机构档案中出现的第一位负责官员。其任期时间是从舒勒吉 28 年 1 月到舒勒吉 36 年 5 月，共 8 年 4 个月①。

① 阿希马的任期时间是从舒勒吉 28 年 1 月到舒勒吉 36 年 5 月，但是我们还发现了一个阿希马在舒勒吉 44 年 3 月 27 日支出羊牲的文件（MVN 2 333），据此我们推测王后贡牲机构的负责官员可能在卸任贡牲机构的职务后，偶尔还有负责贡牲机构的收支工作。

从档案文件分析，他的工作相对独立，任期时间较长，与舒勒吉新提王后贡牲机构的负责官员舒库布姆和贝里沓卜的收支工作重叠，可能是配合舒库布姆和贝里沓卜支出肥牛、肥羊及禽。目前，在王后贡牲机构出土的档案文献中尚未发现阿希马的印章。但根据他在一个文件中的称呼，我们知道阿希马的身份是育肥师。该文件内容是：1 只育肥公绵羊为乌勒马席吞女神、3 只育肥公绵羊为安努尼吞女神的祭祀，于埃如巴吞（食）神牛时（ud～ *E-ru-ba-tum* diĝir gud-gud-ka），从**育肥师阿希马**处支出了，经由阿皮里亚（舒勒吉 36 年 5 月，CST 41）。阿希马在王后贡牲机构中的头衔是 kurušda/gurušda，意思为"育肥师"。"育肥师"是对贡牲机构专门负责育肥牲畜官员的称呼。乌尔第三王朝时期，神明祭祀以及宗教庆典都需要优等育肥的活牲祭品，育肥师就是专门提供"育肥牲"的官员。育肥师阿希马管理的动物都是牛、羊和禽（1 个文件），没有猪。在阿希马工作的 8 年多中，他主要负责王后贡牲机构的支出工作，他支出的动物种类主要有：肥羊（76 只）、肥牛（3 头）、羊（123 只）、宰杀羊（82 只）、宰杀牛（1 头）、宰杀鸭（5 只）、宰杀鸽（2 只），鸽和鸭第一次出现。注意在他的文件中，只有 1 个接管文件。王后贡牲机构的负责官员们支出的育肥羊是给神明和王室成员食用；羔、崽和禽都是高级肉食，羔有时给神，禽一般来说是王后喜爱的食物；宰杀牲通常给下级人员食用并收获牛筋和皮毛等原材料。

育肥师阿希马收支动物的数量和种类一览表

时间	牲畜数量和种类	文件类型	时间	牲畜数量和种类	文件类型
Š 28 i	4 肥羊	支出	Š 33	98 羊、20 崽	支出
Š 30 vi，ix	4 肥羊	支出	Š 34 iii	14 肥羊、2 肥牛	支出
Š 31 i	14 **宰杀羊**	支出	Š 35 iv	4 肥羊	支出
Š 32 iv	1 肥牛	支出	Š 35 v	3 崽、1 羔	支出
Š 32 v	7 肥羊	支出	Š 35 v	1+羊	支出
Š 33 i	63 羊、5 肥羊、1 牛为**宰杀牲**	支出	Š 35 vi	2 肥羊	支出
Š 33 iii/29	5 鸭和 2 鸽为**宰杀牲**	支出	Š 35 vi–viii	9 肥羊	支出
Š 33 ix	1 肥羊	支出	Š 35 x	5 肥羊	**接管**
Š 33 ix	15 肥羊	支出	Š 36 v	4 肥羊	支出

二 骑使舒库布姆（Š 28 iii- Š 32 x）

舒库布姆（*Šukubum*）是王后贡牲机构的第一任正式的负责官员。他的任期时间是从舒勒吉 28 年 3 月到舒勒吉 32 年 10 月，共 4 年 7 个月，与阿希马同时。舒勒吉新提王后贡牲机构档案文献中发现了两个舒库布姆的印文，见下表：

日期	文献内容	官员	地点	印章内容	出处
Š 28 xii	1 只死雌野山羊尸体，它的角和皮毛都完整无缺	自那鲁处，舒库布姆收到了	乌尔	乌尔王舒勒吉之妻（dam）吉美辛，**舒库布姆骑使（rá-gaba）**是你的仆人。	JCS 31 133 01
Š 32 x	1 头死 UDU.Ku_6-tenu 牛犊	舒库布姆接收	乌尔	乌尔王舒勒吉之妻吉美辛：**舒库布姆骑使（rá-gaba）**是你的仆人。	JCS 28 169

rá-gaba 的意思是“骑使”，其对应的阿卡德语是 *rakbum*。在乌尔第三王朝时期，“骑使”是专为贵夫人服务的官员。舒库布姆的两个印文表明在舒勒吉 28 年到舒勒吉 32 年之间他是舒勒吉的一个妻子吉美辛的“骑使”。由于舒库布姆是舒勒吉新提王后贡牲机构的负责官员，我们推测吉美辛可能是舒勒吉新提的旧名。王后的名字是 *Šulgi-simtī*“舒勒吉是我的骄傲”，很明显这是她成为王后之后的新名。在舒库布姆卸任贡牲机构职务后，贡牲机构的官员阿皮里亚的一个文件（AnOr 7 042）中提到一个职务为牲畜长（šùš）的舒库布姆是牧羊人们的统领（ugula）①。该文件中的舒库布姆可能不是舒勒吉新提王后贡牲机构中担任负责官员的那个舒库布姆。

骑使舒库布姆收支牲畜的数量和种类一览表

文件时间	牲畜数量和种类	文件类型	文件时间	牲畜数量和种类	文件类型
Š28 iii	2 羊、1 崽	**接管**	Š 30 viii	【2 肥羊】	支出

① 该文件写于舒勒吉 38 年 8 月，内容是：1 头育肥公牛、1 头食草公牛、6 只育肥公绵羊、6 只公绵羊、3 头公牛、1 只公绵羊羔、3 只雌山羊崽和 2 公山羊崽来自舒沙马什之妻，1 只公绵羊和 1 只公绵羊羔来自牧羊人（na-gada）拉腊布姆，1 只公绵羊和 1 只公绵羊羔来自牧羊人（na-gada）伊米德伊里姆，监工为舒库布姆驯牲师（ugula *Šu-ku*$_8$*-bu-um* šùš），为舒勒吉新提的送入项，阿皮里亚接管了。

续表

文件时间	牲畜数量和种类	文件类型	文件时间	牲畜数量和种类	文件类型
Š 28 xii	1 宰杀的野山羊尸体	**收到**	Š 30 x/4	13 肥羊	支出
Š 29 vi	1+【肥】羊，2 肥羊	支出	Š 31 i	12 宰杀羊、2 宰杀崽	支出
Š 29 vi	1 肥牛、6 肥羊	支出	Š31 iii	3 羊	**接管**
Š 29 x	2+肥羊	**接管**	Š 31 iv	5 羊、2 崽、2 羔	**接管**
Š 29 x	2 肥羊	支出	Š 31 vi	3 羊、3 崽	**接管**
Š 29 x:	1+肥羊	支出	Š 31 viii	1 崽、2 羊	支出
Š 29 xi	27 羊、7 崽、1 羔	**接管**	Š 32 i	1 肥羊	支出
Š 29 xi	4+肥羊	支出	Š 32 iv	2 羊	支出
Š 30 v	5 羊、1 宰杀羊	支出	Š 32 x	1 宰杀牛	**接收**
Š 30 vii	2【肥】羊	支出			

骑使舒库布姆**支出**的牲畜主要有：肥羊（32+只）、肥牛（1 头）、羊（9 只）、崽（1 只）、宰杀羊（15 只）和宰杀牛（1 头）。

他**接管**的牲畜有：肥羊（2+只）、羊（40 只）、崽（13 只）、羔（3 只）、宰杀牛（1 头）和宰杀野山羊（1 头）。

三　牛、羊育肥师贝里沓卜（Š 33 v–Š 37 vi）

贝里沓卜（*Beli-ṭab*）是王后贡牲机构的第二任负责官员。他的任期时间是从舒勒吉 33 年 5 月到舒勒吉 37 年 6 月，共 4 年 1 个月。贝里沓卜和舒库布姆的接替日期有 7 个月的空白，可能是这一时期他们的文件没有被发现。在王后贡牲机构的档案文件中仅有一个表明贝里沓卜是育肥师的印文。1 头公牛和 48 只公绵羊羊为育肥师贝里沓卜补交的欠账。（印章：）贝里沓卜是舒勒吉新吞的**育肥师**（舒勒吉 43 年，AnOr 07 144）。

同时，舒勒吉新提王后贡牲机构的档案中，有 19 个文件的内容中提到贝里沓卜是“育肥师”。例如文件：

（1）1 只公山羊崽为古塔尔拉之妻，从**育肥师**贝里沓卜处支出（舒勒吉 34 年 6 月，SAT 2 0107）。

（2）5 头育肥公牛和 2 只食草公绵羊来自普朱尔乌图将军，2 只公山羊崽来自伊隆巴尼庙总管，为舒勒吉新吞的送入项，**育肥师**贝里沓卜接管（舒勒吉 35 年 8 月，MVN 03 143）。

（3）1 头公牛和 10 只食草公绵羊来自尼尔伊达旮勒（将军），为舒勒吉新吞的送入项，**育肥师**贝里沓卜接管（舒勒吉 35 年 11 月，Aegyptus 29 106 34）。

（4）1 头公牛为伊提卜西那特，2 只公绵羊为埃什塔闰米，从**育肥师**贝里沓卜支出（舒勒吉 35 年 11 月，Torino 1 177）。

育肥师贝里沓卜**支出**的牲畜包括：肥羊（102 只）、肥崽（2 只）、肥牛（22 头）、羊（170 只）、崽（35 只）、羔（11 只）、宰杀牛（3 头）和宰杀羊（65 只）。他**接管**的牲畜有：肥羊（29 只）、肥牛（16 头）、羊（207 只）、崽（13 只）和羔（18 只）。详见下表：

育肥师贝里沓卜收支牲畜的数量和种类一览表（Š 33 v–Š 37 vi）

文件时间	牲畜数量和种类	文件类型	文件时间	牲畜数量和种类	文件类型
Š 33 v	1 牛、9 羊、3 崽	**接管**	Š 35 xi	1 牛、5 羊、2 肥崽	支出
Š 33 v	1 肥牛、6 肥羊、4 羊、1 崽	支出	Š 35 xi	1 肥牛、1 羊	支出
Š 33 v	3+肥牛、7+肥羊	支出	Š 35 xii	1 羔、2 羊、1 崽	**接管**
Š 33 vi	1 肥羊、1 羊	支出	Š 36 i	7 肥羊	支出
Š 33 vi	1 肥羊	支出	Š 36 i	3 羔	**接管**
Š 33 vi	3 肥羊、4 羊、2 崽	支出	Š 36 i	1 羔	**接管**
Š 33 vii	7 羊、2 崽	**接管**	Š 36 ii	2 肥牛	支出
Š 33 vii	1 肥牛	支出	Š 36 ii	1 肥牛	支出
Š 33 ix	1 羊	支出	Š 36 v	4 肥羊	支出
Š 34 ii	6 羊、2 羔	**接管**	Š 36 vi	2 崽	支出
Š 34 ii	3 肥羊	支出	Š 36 viii	2 肥牛和 7【肥】羊、21 羊	**接管**
Š 34 iv	2 羊	支出	Š 36 ix	1 肥牛、5 牛、8 肥羊、57 羊	**接管**
Š 34 v	1 崽	支出	Š 36 x	1 肥牛、3 肥羊、5 羊	支出
Š 34 v	1 牛、8 羊、2 崽、1 羔	**接管**	Š 36 x	2 肥羊、1 羔	**接管**
Š 34 vi	2 羊	支出	Š 36 x	3 肥羊、3 羔、1 羊	支出
Š 34 vi	1 肥牛	支出	Š 37 i	2 羔	**接管**
Š 34 vi	1 崽	支出	Š 37 i	1 肥羊	支出
Š 34 ix	5 肥牛、7 肥羊、1 牛、6 羊	支出	Š 37 i	8 肥羊、7 羊、2 肥牛	支出
Š 34 x	1 肥牛、17 羊、1 崽	支出	Š 37 ii	1 崽、4 羊、3 羔	**接管**

续表

文件时间	牲畜数量和种类	文件类型	文件时间	牲畜数量和种类	文件类型
Š 34 x	6 肥牛、60 羊	接管	Š 37 ii	2 羔	接管
Š 35 ii	3 牛尸、58 羊尸、7 崽尸	支出	Š 37 ii	5 肥羊、2 崽	支出
Š 35 iv	1 崽	接管	Š 37 v	8 肥羊、6 羊、6 崽、1 肥牛	支出
Š 35 v	3 崽、1 羔	支出	Š 37 v	10 肥羊、1 羊、3 羔、2 崽	支出
Š 35 vi	2 崽	支出	Š 37 v	5 肥羊、1 肥牛、14 羊	支出
Š 35 vi	1 肥牛、3 肥羊、7 羊	接管	Š 37 v	1 肥牛、6 肥羊、1 牛、14 羊	接管
Š 35 vi	2 崽	支出	Š 37 v/7	8 肥羊、2 崽、1 羔	支出
Š 35 vi	10 肥羊	接管	Š 37 vi	1 肥牛、9 肥羊、7 羊	支出
Š 35 viii	5 肥牛、2 羊、2 崽	接管	Š 37 vi	3 崽、1 肥羊	支出
Š 35 ix	2 羔	接管	Š 37 vi	2 肥羊、1 崽	支出
Š 35 ix	4 羊、1 羔、2 崽	支出	Š 37 vi	1 崽	接管
Š 35 xi	1 牛、10 羊	接管	Š? vii	2 羔、2 崽、2 羊	支出
Š 35 xi	1 牛、2 羊	支出			

四　阿皮里亚（Š 37 ix- Š 41 x/11）

阿皮里亚（*Apiliya*）是王后贡牲机构的第三任负责官员。其任期时间是从舒勒吉 37 年 9 月到舒勒吉 41 年 10 月 11 日，共 4 年 1 个月。目前没有明确的证据给出他的头衔。但在阿皮里亚担任王后贡牲机构的负责官员前，他曾以“督办（maškim）”官员的身份出现在贡牲机构的档案中。督办官的职能是：向贡牲机构中的育肥师、牧羊人或保管员传达国王或王后为某种目的支出牲畜的命令，并把领取到的牲畜带到目的地。例如文件：

（1）3 只育肥公绵羊到厨房，乌尔杜穆孜（厨师）督办；1 只育肥公绵羊到宫殿，**阿皮里亚督办**……经由王后舒勒吉新提，于乌尔，从阿希马处支出了（舒勒吉 32 年 5 月，MVN 08 097）。

（2）2 只无崽母山羊为贝拉特苏赫尼尔和贝拉特达腊班的吉腊努姆仪式，于吉什廷安那之门，3 只无崽母山羊为宫殿的祭祀，**阿皮里亚督办**，以上为支出（舒勒吉32年9月，SAT 2 0047）。

阿皮里亚支出和接管的动物数量和种类情况如下：

（1）舒勒吉37年9月到舒勒吉38年12月，阿皮里亚**支出**的畜禽有：肥羊（8只）、肥崽（1只）、羊（9只）、羔（2只）、宰杀羊（1只）和宰杀禽（8只）；他**接管**的畜禽有：肥羊（26只）、肥牛（1头）、牛（6头）、羊（78只）、崽（20只）、羔（9只）和禽（家鸽、野鸽和鸭121只）。以上统计牲畜的种类和数量表明：从舒勒吉38年贡牲中心的建立开始，王后贡牲机构动物的数量和种类增多，禽类开始大量出现，猪的数量较少。

Š 37 ix–Š 39 i 阿皮里亚收支动物数量和种类一览表

时间	牲畜数量和种类	类型	时间	牲畜数量和种类	类型
Š 37 ix	10 肥羊	接管	Š 38viii	1 肥牛、4 牛、6 肥羊、16 羊	接管
Š 38 ii	2 肥羊、1 羔	接管	Š 38 viii	4 肥羊、1 羔	接管
Š 38 iv	4 羊、1 羔	接管	Š 38 viii	2 肥羊、1 崽	接管
Š 38 iv	9 羊、1 崽	接管	Š 38 viii	2 宰杀的野鸽	支出
Š 38 iv	15 鸭、30 野鸽	接管	Š 38 viii	1 肥崽	支出
Š 38 iv	3 家鸽	接管	Š 38 viii	13 肥鸭、4 肥鸽、1 死鸭、4 死鸽	支出
Š 38 iv	3 宰杀野鸽	支出	Š 38 ix	10 鸭	接管
Š 38 v	14 鸭、3 家鸽	接管	Š 38 x	10 羊、2 羔、2 崽	接管
Š 38 v	2 肥羊、3 崽	接管	Š 38 x	7 羊、3 崽	接管
Š 38 v	2 羔	接管	Š 38 xi	2 公牛、12 羊、6 崽、1 羔	接管
Š 38 v	2 宰杀野鸽	支出	Š 38 xi	1 肥羊	支出
Š 38 v	1 宰杀家鸽	支出	Š 38 xi	1 肥羊、2 羔、1 宰杀羔	支出
Š 38 vi	1 羔	接管	Š 38 xii	2 羊、1 崽	接管
Š 38vi	31【家鸽】、15 野鸽	接管	Š 38 xii	2 羊	支出
Š 38vii	16 羊、3 崽、2 羊	接管	Š38 xii–Š 39 i	7 羊、6 肥羊	支出

（2）舒勒吉39年阿皮里亚**支出**的畜禽有：肥羊（7只）、肥羔（1只）、崽（6只）、羊（26只）、羔（3只）、宰杀羊（1只）和宰杀禽（25只）。

他**接管**的畜禽种类有：肥羊（221只）、肥牛（2头）、牛（2头）、猪崽（1头）、羊（111只）、禽（142只）、崽（14只）、羔（14只）和瞪羚（1头）。

这一时期，王后贡牲机构的动物种类和数量都明显增多，猪和瞪羚第一次出现。详见下表：

Š 39 i –Š 39 xii/26，27 阿皮里亚收支动物数量和种类一览表

时间	牲畜数量和种类	类型	时间	牲畜数量和种类	类型
Š 39 i	1猪崽、2野鸽	接管	Š 39 vi/30	2肥羊和1羊	支出
Š 39 i	6鸽、1肥鸭为死牲、1肥鸭、3肥鸽	支出	Š 39 vi	5羊、1羔	接管
Š 39 ii	1崽、2肥羊	接管	Š 39 vii	1牛、10羊	接管
Š 39 iii	6家鸽	接管	Š 39 vii–viii	6崽、10羊	支出
Š 39 iii	3羔、1崽	接管	Š 39 vii–viii	20羊	接管
Š 39 iii	1鸭、13鸽、15鸟、1+tu鸟	接管	Š 39 viii/16	9鸭	接管
Š 39 iii	1鸭和2野鸽为宰杀牲	支出	Š 39 viii/25	6鸭	接管
Š 39 iii	1肥鸽	支出	Š 39 viiir	2羊、2崽	接管
Š 39 iii	1羔尸体、1肥羔尸体、1肥羔	支出	Š 39 ix/3	1+x家鸽和2野鸽宰杀牲	支出
Š 39 iv/6	1鸟、58野鸽、2家鸽	接管	Š 39 ix/22	12鸭	接管
Š 39 iv	5羊和3羔、2崽	接管	Š 39 ix/29	4鸟	接管
Š 39 iv	1羔和1公崽	接管	Š 39 ix	1牛、1羊和3崽	接管
Š39 iv	4死鸽、1死鸭和1死鸟、1鸭	支出	Š 39 x	1羔和1崽	接管
Š 39 iv/17，19	2宰杀鸽、1宰杀鸭	支出	Š 39 x/3	7肥羊、1羔	接管
Š 39 iv/28–30	4野鸽、8家鸽	接管	Š 39 x/27，29	5肥羊、1羊	支出
Š 39 v	2羔、2崽、2羊	接管	Š 39 xi	2羊、1崽、2羔	接管
Š 39 v/5	1肥鸭	支出	Š 39 xi/25	2肥牛、20羊	接管
Š 39 v/17，18	2肥鸭、2宰杀家鸽，5肥野鸽、	支出	Š 39 xi–xii	4鸭、3宰杀鸭	支出
39 v，vi	14羊、3羔	支出	Š 39 xi/?	3宰杀鸭	支出
Š 39 vi/2	1鸭、6野鸽	支出	Š 39 xii	4羊和1瞪羚	接管
Š 39 vi/14	1家鸽和3野鸽	支出	Š39xii/26，27	1宰杀鸭、1鸭、5野鸽	支出
Š 39 vi/15	130肥羊、30羊	接管	Š 39	82肥羊、30羊	接管

（3）舒勒吉40年阿皮里亚**支出**的畜禽有：肥羊（66只）、肥牛（5头）、牛（1头）、羊（110只）、羔（9只）、崽（8只）、宰杀羊（5只）、宰杀禽（43只）和宰杀猪崽（1头）；他**接管**的畜禽有：肥羊（18只）、羊（13只）、禽（35只）、崽（2只）、羔（7只）和肥牛（1头）。详见下表：

Š 40 i –Š 40 xii 阿皮里亚收支动物数量和种类一览表

时间	牲畜数量和种类	类型	时间	牲畜数量和种类	类型
Š 40 i	3 羔	**接管**	Š 40 vii/5–7	15 羊、9+肥羊、2+肥牛	支出
Š 40 i/6	2 肥羊	**接管**	Š 40 vii	1 肥羊、9 羊、1 崽为宰杀牲	支出
Š 40 i/20，22	1 宰杀鸭、1 鸭和 5 野鸽	支出	Š 40 vii	2+只宰杀鸽、2 鸽	支出
Š 40 i–ii	10 羊、4 崽、2 羔	支出	Š 40 viii/4，5	2 肥牛、10 肥羊、6 羊	支出
Š 40 ii/19	6+肥羊、1+崽、6 只羊	**接管**	Š 40viii/29，30	5+鸭	**接管**
Š 40 ii/22	1 宰杀的猪崽	支出	Š 40 iv–vii	40 羊	支出
Š 40 ii	1 崽	**接管**	Š 40 ix/5	3 羊、5 肥羊	支出
Š 40 iii/1	3 羊、6 肥羊、1 肥牛	支出	Š 40 ix/10，19	4 鸭	**接管**
Š 40 iii/8	1 鸭、5 野鸽	支出	Š 40 ix/12	1 鸭、2 鸽为宰杀牲	支出
Š 40 iii/	3 宰杀鸭、2 鸭和 8 野鸽	支出	Š 40 ix/16	1 肥羊	支出
Š 40 iv	2 鸽、2 鸭为宰杀牲、1 鸭	支出	Š 40 ix/19，20	4 鸭和 15 野鸽、1 鸟为宰杀牲	支出
Š 40 iv/7，21	1+x 鸽、4 鸭	**接管**	Š 40 ix/22	1 肥羊、1 羊	**接管**
Š 40 v	1 羔、6 羊	**接管**	Š 40 ix/30	6 肥羊、2 羊、1 羔	支出
Š 40 v/9	1 肥牛、9 肥羊和 1 崽	**接管**	Š 40 x/18	3 肥羊、4 羊	支出
Š 40 v/9	5 肥羊	支出	Š 40 x/28	4 肥羊、5 羊、2 宰杀羊	支出
Š 40 v/19，20	1 宰杀鸭和 1 宰杀鸽、2 鸭	支出	Š 40 xi/6，8	3 鸭、2 鸟、2 鸽为宰杀牲	支出
Š 40 v/24	2 鸽	**接管**	Š 40 xi/18	6 肥羊、5 羔、2 羊、1 崽	支出
Š 40 v/29	3 鸽	**接管**	Š 40 xi/25，30	1 牛、9 肥羊、4 羊	支出
Š 40 vi	2 羔	**接管**	Š 40 xi	1 羔	**接管**

续表

时间	牲畜数量和种类	类型	时间	牲畜数量和种类	类型
Š 40 vi/1，5	14 鸭、11 鸽	**接管**	Š 40 xii/25	3 宰杀羊、1 肥羊、	支出
Š 40 vi/13	1 鸭、5 野鸽、1 宰杀的野鸽	支出	Š 40 ix–xii	16 羊、5 崽和 1 羔	支出

（4）舒勒吉 41 年 1 月 4 日到舒勒吉 41 年 10 月 11 日阿皮里亚支出的畜禽有：肥羊（47 只）、肥牛（2 头）、崽（11 只）、羊（47 只）、羔（8 只）、牛（6 头）、禽（36 只）、宰杀羊（62 只）、宰杀牛（2 头）和宰杀禽（7 只）。他**接管**的畜禽种类有：羊（13 只）、禽（34 只）、羔（4 只）。详见下表：

Š 41 i /4–Š 41 x/11 阿皮里亚收支动物数量和种类一览表

时间	牲畜数量和种类	类型	时间	牲畜数量和种类	类型
Š 41 i/4	1 肥羊	支出	Š 41 v	9 羊、1 崽	支出
Š 41 i	1 鸭、1 死鸽、1 死“舵燕鸦”	支出	Š 41 vi/8，10	12 野鸽、2 鸭、【1+】家鸽	**接管**
Š 41 i/15	2 宰杀羊、4 肥和 3 羊	支出	Š 41 vi	3 肥羊	支出
Š 41 i/30	6 羊和 3 牛、3 肥羊	支出	Š 41 vii/2	4 肥羊、1 羔	支出
Š 41/30	4 羊、4 肥羊、1 牛	支出	Š 41 vii/26	10+只肥羊、4 羊	支出
Š 41 i	6 羊、1 宰杀羔	支出	Š 41 vii	4 羊、2 崽	支出
[Š 41] i	1 鸭、11 羊	**接管**	Š 41 viii/17	9 鸟	**接管**
Š 41 ii/4	6 肥羊、4 羊	支出	Š 41 viii/23	3 鸭	**接管**
Š 41 ii/ [5]	1 宰杀鸽、【1+羊】	支出	Š 41viii/26，30	12 鸽	支出
Š 41 ii/20	2 肥羊、3 羊、1 宰杀羔	支出	Š 41 ix	4 羔和 2【羊】	**接管**
Š 41 ii/22	3 鸭	**接管**	Š 41 ix/3	1 肥羊	支出
Š 41 ii	12 宰杀羊、1 宰杀羔	支出	Š 41 ix/6，10	2 死鸭、1 死鸽、2 鸽、15 鸭	支出
Š 41 i–ii	4 羊、2 羔、4 崽	支出	Š 41 ix/10，14	3+鸭	**接管**
Š 41 iii	1 宰杀公崽、1 宰杀羔	**接管**	Š 41 ix/28	2 肥羊	支出
Š 41 iii/1，4	1 宰杀崽、2 肥羊	支出	Š 41 ix	2 宰杀羔、1 宰杀羊	支出
Š 41 iv/2，5	1 宰杀鸭、1 鸭和 5 鸽	支出	Š 41 x	2 牛、37 羊、2 羔为宰杀牲	支出

续表

时间	牲畜数量和种类	类型	时间	牲畜数量和种类	类型
Š 41 iv	2羊、2羔和2崽	支出	Š 41 x	2崽、1羊、3羔	支出
Š 41 v/8	2宰杀羊、1肥羊	支出	Š 41 x/11	2肥牛、8肥羊、7羊、2肥崽	支出

五 牛、羊育肥师阿皮拉吞（Š 41 xi/26–Š 45 vi/15）

阿皮拉吞（*Apilatum*）是王后贡牲机构的第四任负责官员。其任期时间从舒勒吉41年11月26日到舒勒吉45年6月15日，共3年7个多月。王后贡牲机构的档案中没有发现阿皮拉吞的印章，但从两个文件的内容可以确定他的身份育肥师：

1）档案箱：**育肥师**阿皮拉吞的账目平衡，（总计）14个月，17天（舒勒吉43年10月到舒勒吉44年12月，ASJ 04 065 05）。

2）欠1头牛、欠41只家鸽和欠53只野鸽，以上从**育肥师**阿皮拉吞的收据中摘要（tur-ra）出（舒勒吉46年，CST 129）。

育肥师阿皮拉吞支出和接管的动物种类和数量情况如下：

1）舒勒吉41年11月26日到舒勒吉41年12月25日阿皮拉吞**支出**的畜禽有：肥猪（1头）、羊（7只）、猪（10头）、禽（7只）、宰杀羊（2只）、宰杀猪（3头）和宰杀禽（2只）。

他**接管**的畜禽有：肥羊（6只）、肥牛（1头）、羊（12只）和禽（2只）。详见下表：

值得注意的是这一时期，猪的数量开始增多。

Š 41 xi/26– Š 41 xii/25 育肥师阿皮拉吞收支牲畜数量和种类一览表

时间	牲畜数量和种类	类型	时间	牲畜数量和种类	类型
Š 41 xi/26	1肥牛、10羊	**接管**	Š 41 xii	2豚、5鸽、2**死**鸽和1**死**豚	支出
Š 41 xii/1	4雌豚、1雄豚	**接管**	Š 41 xii	6羊	支出
Š 41 xii/2	2鸭	**接管**	Š 41 xii	1肥猪	支出
Š 41 xii/5	3母猪、1鸭、1鸽	支出	Š 41 xii	1羊和1羔为**宰杀**牲	支出
Š 41 xii/［8］，9	6肥羊、2羊	**接管**	Š 41 xii/25	1肥崽	支出
Š 41 xii/15	2病**死**豚、1猪崽	支出			

2）**舒勒吉 42 年**阿皮拉吞**支出**的畜禽有：肥羊（46 只）、肥牛（3 头）、肥崽（1 只）、牛（4 头）、羊（32 只）、猪（6 头）、禽（25 只）、宰杀羊（9 只）和宰杀禽（3 只）。

这一时期，他**接管**的畜禽有：肥羊（12 只）、崽（4 只）、羔（12 只）、羊（12 只）和禽（40 只）。详见下表：

Š 42 i/22–Š 42 xii 育肥师阿皮拉吞收支牲畜数量和种类一览表

时间	牲畜数量和种类	类型	时间	牲畜数量和种类	类型
Š 42 i/22	4 羔、1 崽、5 肥羊	**接管**	Š 42 vii/15	4 肥羊和 4 羔、2 羊	**接管**
Š 42 i/26	3 鸭	**接管**	Š 42 vii/24	2 鸭	**接管**
Š 42 i/26	2 肥羊、1 羔	**接管**	Š 42 viii/5	8 鸭	**接管**
Š 42 ii	1 羔	**接管**	Š 42 viii/20	1 肥牛、2 + 肥羊、1 羊	支出
Š 42 ii/21–24	18 鸽	**接管**	Š 42 viii/22	1 鸭	**接管**
Š 42 ii/30	4 肥羊、4 羊	支出	Š 42 viii	1 宰杀鸭、1 雌豚	支出
Š 42 iii/［?］	【1+x 宰杀羊	支出	Š 42 viii	3 死羊、6 肥羊、1 牛，3 羊	支出
Š42 iii/13，14	9 肥羊、8 羊	支出	Š 42 viii	1 羊、1 羔	**接管**
Š 42 iv/1，3	2 宰杀鸽	支出	Š 42 viii	2 羊、1 崽	**接管**
Š 42 iv/3	1 宰杀肥羊	支出	Š 42 viii	1 宰杀羊	支出
Š 42 v/21	1 鸭、5 鸽	支出	Š 42 x/13，14	7 肥羊、4 羊、4 宰杀羊	支出
Š 42 v/23	1 肥羊、1 羊和 1 羔	**接管**	Š 42 x/23，24	4 鸭	**接管**
Š 42 v/24	1 牛、1 肥牛和 1 肥羊崽	支出	Š 42 xi/29	1 豚	支出
Š 42 v/28	3 家鸽	**接管**	Š 42 xi	6 羊	支出
Š 42 vi	4 羊和 1 崽	**接管**	Š 42 xi	2 宰杀崽	支出
Š 42 vi/8	1+鸽	**接管**	Š 42 xi/23	2 雌豚、1 雄豚	支出
Š 42 vi/24	1 雄豚、2 鸭、17 鸽	支出	Š 42 xii	2 羊、1 崽、1 羔来	**接管**
Š 42 vii/5–9	2 牛、15 肥羊、1 肥牛、5 羊	支出	Š 42 xii	4 肥羊	支出

3）**舒勒吉 43 年**阿皮拉吞**支出**的畜禽有：肥羊（19 只）、肥牛（1 头）、猪（6 头）、羊（11 只）、羔（4 只）、禽（40 只）、宰杀羊（7 只）

和宰杀禽（12 只）。

这一时期，他**接管**的畜禽有：肥羊（5 只）、牛（1 头）、羊（31 只）和禽（30 只）。

Š 43 i–Š 43 xii/8 育肥师阿皮拉吞收支牲畜数量和种类一览表

时间	牲畜数量和种类	类型	时间	牲畜数量和种类	类型
Š43 i	2 豚、2 鸭、5 鸽、4 **死**鸭和 1 **死**燕	支出	Š 43 v	4 崽、2 羊为**宰**杀牲	支出
Š 43 i	1 **宰杀**羊、8 肥羊、1 羊	支出	Š 43 vii	1 羊、1 羔	支出
Š 43 ii/1，4，9	14 鸽、6 鸭	**接管**	Š 43 ix	9 鸭	**接管**
Š 43 ii	9 鸟、3 豚、1 鸭为**宰杀**、2 鸭	支出	Š 43 ix	5 羊、1 肥羊	支出
Š 43 ii/21	1 肥牛和 5 肥羊	支出	Š 43 x/4，5	5 肥羊、3 羔	支出
Š 43 ii	1 **死**鸭、1 豚、1 鸭、15 鸟、1 **死**鸽	支出	Š 43 xi/30	27 羊、1 牛、2 肥羊	**接管**
Š 43 ii/30	4 羊、3 肥羊	**接管**	Š 43 xii/8	1 鸭	**接管**
Š 43 iii	3 **死**鸭、1 **死**鸽、1 鸭和 5 鸽	支出			

4）舒勒吉 44 年 1 月到舒勒吉 45 年 6 月 15 日阿皮拉吞的**支出**文件仅有 1 个，其支出的畜禽主要是：肥羊（1 只）、羊（1 只）、猪（1 头）、禽（4 只）和宰杀禽（1 只）。

这一时期，他**接管**的畜禽主要有：禽（包括鸭、家鸽和野鸽共：578 只）、崽（9 只）、肥崽（2 只）、肥牛（1 头）、牛（1 头）、羊（115 只）和肥羊（29 只）。

以上数据说明，这一时期育肥师阿皮拉吞的工作以接管为主，他接管的动物以禽类数量最多。

Š 44 i–Š 45 vi/15 育肥师阿皮拉吞收支牲畜数量和种类一览表

时间	牲畜数量和种类	类型	时间	牲畜数量和种类	类型
Š 44 i	52 鸽	接管	Š 44 ix/6	1 鸭	接管
Š 44 ii	1 崽	接管	Š 44 x/13，14	2 鸭	接管
Š 44 ii	10 家鸽、14 野鸽	接管	Š 44 xi	2 崽、2 羊	接管
Š 44 ii/15	4 鸭、2 家鸽	接管	Š 44 xi/2	5 鸭	接管

续表

时间	牲畜数量和种类	类型	时间	牲畜数量和种类	类型
Š 44 ii/15	1 牛和 12 羊、2 肥羊	接管	Š 44 xi/21	2 羊和 1 崽、2 肥羊、1 羔	接管
Š 44 iii/7，11	240 家鸽、77 鸟	接管	Š 44 xii/4	4 家鸽	接管
Š 44 iii/20，28	11 家鸽和 8 野鸽	接管	Š 44 xii/15	2 羊	接管
Š 44 iv	10 家鸽和 23 野鸽	接管	Š 44 xii	30 羊和、1 羔、1 崽	接管
Š 44 v/9	2 肥崽、7 羊	接管	Š 45 i	7 羊、2 羔	接管
Š 44 vi/15	1 羊和 1 崽、1 羔、29 鸽	接管	Š 45 i/7，10	14 羊、1 鸭、1 肥牛	接管
Š 44 vi/22	2 肥羊	接管	Š 45 i	2 鸭、43 鸽、1 肥羊、1 羔	接管
Š 44 vi/25	3 羊和 1 崽	接管	Š 45 iii	1 豚、4 鸽、1 鸭宰杀、1 肥羊、1 羊、	支出
Š 44 vi	1 羔	接管	Š 45 iii/23	9 鸟	接管
Š 44 vii/3，6	11 羊、8 肥羊	接管	Š 45 v/22	6 羊、3 肥羊，2 鸽	接管
Š 44 vii/17–20	10 肥羊、16 羊	接管	Š 45 vi	4 羊和 1 崽	接管
Š 44 ix	8+羊	接管	Š45 vi/15	1 羊、1 崽、1 羔、29 野鸽	接管

六　牛、羊育肥师乌尔卢旮勒埃邓卡（Š 45 vii/12–Š 47 iv/28）

乌尔卢旮勒埃邓卡（Ur–Lugal–edenka）是王后贡牲机构的第五任负责官员。他的任期时间是从舒勒吉 45 年 7 月 12 日到舒勒吉 47 年 4 月 28 日，共 1 年 9 个多月。虽然在一个文件的内容中他被称为是育肥师，而在该文件的印文中他也是一名书吏，这表明乌尔卢旮勒埃邓卡身兼育肥师和书吏的双重头衔。该文件内容是：1 头苇塘雄豚、19 只幼鸭、22 只家鸽和 4 只野鸽，乌尔卢旮勒埃邓卡**育肥师**（gurušda）补交了。（印章）：舒勒吉新提，国王喜爱的 lukur 神妻，库达–X 之子——乌尔卢旮勒埃邓卡**书吏**是你的仆人（舒勒吉 46 年 8 月，PDT 1 530）。

育肥师乌尔卢旮勒埃邓卡支出和接管的动物数量和种类情况如下：

（1）舒勒吉 45 年 7 月 12 日到舒勒吉 45 年 12 月乌尔卢旮勒埃邓卡**支出**的畜禽主要有：肥羊（28 只）、肥牛（1 头）、禽（16 只）、牛（3 头）、羊（54 只）、崽（3 只）、羔（1 只）、豚（5+头）、宰杀禽（35+只）、宰杀羊（16 只）、宰杀牛（2 头）和宰杀豚（2 头）。他**接管**的畜禽有：母牛（2头）、羊（21只）、禽（20只）和羔（2只）。

Š 45 vii/12– Š 45 xii 育肥师乌尔卢旮勒埃邓卡收支牲畜数量和种类一览表

时间	牲畜数量和种类	类型	时间	牲畜数量和种类	类型
Š 45 vii/12	1 鸽、10 宰杀鸽、1 羊	支出	Š 45 ix /30	2+x 猪崽	支出
Š 45 vii	2 宰杀羊、4 羊、3 肥羊、4 鸽	支出	Š 45 x/10，12，15	2 鸭和 2 鸽为宰杀牲、7 肥羊、2 豚、1 鸭、7 鸽、5 羊	支出
Š 45 vii	1 肥羊、4 羊、1 鸭和 7 鸽为宰杀牲、1 豚	支出	Š 45 x/30 t	2+羊、1+鸭、1+鸽和 1 豚为宰杀	支出
Š 45 vii/25	1 崽	支出	Š 45 xi	2 羔	接管
Š 45 viii	2 母牛、20 羊	接管	Š 45 xi	1 羊和 1 羔	接管
Š 45 viii	1 牛、10 羊、1 鸽和 8 鸭为宰杀牲、3 肥羊、2 崽	支出	Š 45 xi/4	1 牛、1 羊、1 鸭和 1 鸽为宰杀	支出
Š45 viii/25	1 牛、3 肥羊、3 羊	支出	Š 45 xi/20	1 羊和 1 豚为死牲、2（肥）羊、2（肥）豚	支出
Š 45 iii/27	2 鸭和 1 鸟	接管	Š 45 xi/24	1 羊和 1 鸭为宰杀牲	支出
Š 45 ix/13	17+羊，1 肥牛、5 肥羊	支出	Š 45 xii	1 羊和 1 鸭为死牲、3 肥羊、1 羊	支出
Š 45 ix/29	17 鸭、1 羔	接管	Š 45 xii	4 肥羊、6 羊	支出

（2）舒勒吉 46 年育肥师乌尔卢旮勒埃邓卡**支出**的畜禽有：肥羊（52 只）、肥牛（2 头）、肥羔（2 只）、牛（4 头）、羊（126 只）、崽（32 只）、羔（11 只）、豚（8 头）、禽（93 只）、宰杀禽（79 只）、宰杀羊（107 只）和宰杀豚（8 头）。他**接管**的畜禽有：肥羊（18 只）、肥牛（1 头）、羊（85 只）、禽（88 只）、猪（48 头）、羔（59 只）、崽（6 只）和瞪羚（1 头）。这一时期，育肥师乌尔卢旮勒埃邓卡支出的宰杀牲数量最多，这些宰杀牲通常被送入宫殿，作为士兵或下级仆人的食物，而它们的皮毛则被加工成制成品。

Š 46 i/8，15–Š 46 xii/30 育肥师乌尔卢旮勒埃邓卡收支牲畜数量和种类一览表

时间	牲畜数量和种类	类型	时间	牲畜数量和种类	类型
Š46 i/8，15	1 鸭、36 鸽、2 公猪	接管	Š 46 ix/27	1 鸭	支出
Š 46 i/18	1 肥羊和 1 羊、1 鸭、1 宰杀鸭	支出	Š 46 x	2 羔、1 崽	接管

续表

时间	牲畜数量和种类	类型	时间	牲畜数量和种类	类型
Š 46 ii/1	4 羔和 1 豚、【1+】鸽	接管	Š 46 x	30 雌豚	接管
Š 46 ii/4，6	4 羊、3 肥羊、1 宰杀羊、1 鸭	支出	Š 46 x	2 公猪、10 猪崽	接管
Š 46 iii/3	6 家鸽、5 羊	接管	Š 46 x	1 牛、40 羊、33 崽为死牲	支出
Š 46 iii/6	1 羔、3 鸽为宰杀牲	支出	Š 46 x/7	4 肥羊、1 肥牛、1 崽	支出
Š 46 iii/26–29	4 鸭、1 鸽和 1 羊为死牲、3 肥羊、14 羊、2 豚和 5 鸽	支出	Š 46 x/20	1 牛和 7 羊为宰杀、1 羊、1 肥羔	支出
Š 46 iv/24	3 羔、3 家鸽	接管	Š 46 x/28	1 豚、2 鸭、2 宰杀鸭	支出
Š 46 v/20	1 羔、3 宰杀鸽、1 崽、2 野鸽	支出	Š 46 x/28	14 鸭	接管
Š 46 v/21	2 肥羊、8 羊	支出	Š 46 x	5 肥羊、3 羊、13 崽、6 宰杀羊	支出
Š 46 v	2 羔	接管	Š 46 xi	1 羔	接管
Š 46 vi/22	1 鸭、5 鸽为宰杀牲、1 野鸽	支出	Š 46 xi/7	4 肥羊、1 羊、1 羔、1 宰杀崽	支出
Š 46 vi/25	1 肥牛、3 肥羊、2 羊	支出	Š 46 xi /8，9	2 羊、5 崽和 1 羔为宰杀牲、3 肥羊、2 羔、3 崽	支出
Š 46 vi	1 羊	接管	Š 46 xi /15	3 肥羊、5 羊、1 羔、2 崽为病死	支出
Š 46 vi	4 羊、3 肥羊、1 鸭、7 鸽和 1 豚	支出	Š 46 xi/29	1 肥羊、1 羊和 3 崽为病死	支出
Š 46 viii	4 肥羊	支出	Š 46 xi	2 羔	接管
Š 46 viii /5，6	2 羊、7 鸭、30 鸽为死牲、1 肥羊、1 羊、2 鸭、20 野鸽和 1 豚	支出	Š 46 xi/20	4 肥羊和 1 羊	支出
Š 46 viii	1 牛和 2 肥羊、2 羊	支出	Š 46 xi/29	1 肥羊、1 羊和 3 崽为病死	支出
Š 46 viii	1 肥羔、1 猪崽和 1 鸭	支出	Š 46 xii	53 羊和 28 崽为宰杀牲	支出
Š 46 viii	1 猪崽、19 鸭、26 鸽	补交	Š 46 xii	3 羔、1 崽	接管
Š 46 viii	74 羊、1 羔	接管	Š 46 xii	2 猪崽、7 鸭和 3 鸽为宰杀牲	支出
Š 46viii/18	2 宰杀鸭	支出	Š 46 xii	3 肥猪、3 鸽、24 鸭	接管

续表

时间	牲畜数量和种类	类型	时间	牲畜数量和种类	类型
Š 46 viii27	3 肥羊、6 崽、2 羊	支出	Š 46 xii/22	41 + 羔、13 肥羊、1 肥牛、1 瞪羚	**接管**
Š 46viii/30	2 豚、1 鸭和 13 鸽为**死牲**、1 豚、1 鸭和 5 鸽	支出	Š 46 xi/28	1 羊、1 **宰杀**的舵燕	支出
Š 46 ix/6	4 羊、2 牛、5 肥羊、4 崽、2 羔	支出	Š 46 xii/30	5 羔、1 肥羊、1 羊、4 崽	支出
Š 46 ix /6	7 肥羊、5 羊和 4 崽	**接管**			

（3）舒勒吉 47 年 1 月 1–2 到舒勒吉 47 年 4 月 28 日，乌尔卢旮勒埃邓卡**支出**的畜禽有：肥羊（23 只）、肥羔（2 只）、禽（8 只）、羊（8 只）、崽（9 只）、羔（16 只）、宰杀禽（25 只）、宰杀牛（2 头）、宰杀羊（24 只）和宰杀猪（6 头）。他**接管**的畜禽有：肥羊（4 只）、牛（2 头）、羊（20 只）、禽（24 只）、羔（9 只）和崽（9 只）。

Š 47 i /1，2–Š 47 iv/28 育肥师乌尔卢旮勒埃邓卡收支牲畜数量和种类一览表

时间	牲畜数量和种类	类型	时间	牲畜数量和种类	类型
Š 47 i /1，2	5 羔、2 肥羊	支出	Š 47 ii /2：	2 牛、11 羊、9 肥羊、	**接管**
Š 47 i /7	1 羔、1 肥羊、1 崽	支出	Š 47 ii /14	1 肥羊	支出
Š 47 i /8	1 羔、1 肥羊	支出	Š 47 ii /16	2 牛、4 肥羊、19 羊和 1 瞪羚**病死**	支出
Š 47 i /11	1 鸭、2 家鸽	**接管**	Š 47 ii/26	2 家鸽	**接管**
Š 47 i /13	3 肥羊、1 崽	支出	Š 47 ii /26	1 肥羊	支出
Š 47 i /19	2 野鸽、2 **宰杀**鸽	支出	Š 47 iii	2 羊、1 羔	**接管**
Š 47 i /20	13 野鸽	**接管**	Š 47 iii/7	2+肥羊、2 羔	支出
Š 47 i /23	2 幼鸭	**接管**	Š 47 iii/15	6 豚、6 鸭、11 鸽为**宰杀牲**	支出
Š 47 i /28	1 肥羔、3 崽、1 羔	支出	Š 47 iii/16	1 肥羊、4 羊和 4 羔	支出
Š 47 i /29	2 肥羊、1 羔	**接管**	Š 47 iii/21	4 幼鸭	**接管**
Š 47 i /30	4 崽、2 肥羊、1 羊	支出	Š 47 iv	2 羊和 2+羔	**接管**
Š 47 i	2 羔	**接管**	Š 47 iv/3	2 肥羊、2 羊和 1 崽	**接管**
Š 47 i	2 羔	**接管**	Š 47 iv/7	1 鸭、5 野鸽、1 **宰杀**鸭	支出
Š 47 i	3 羊、7 崽	**接管**	Š 47 iv/10	1 幼鸭、5 野鸽	支出

续表

时间	牲畜数量和种类	类型	时间	牲畜数量和种类	类型
Š 47 i	1 羔	支出	Š 47 iv/14	4 肥羊、1 羔、1 宰杀肥羊	支出
Š 47 ii	1 崽	**接管**	Š 47 iv/18	1 肥羊、1 肥羔	支出
Š 47 ii	1 羔	**接管**	Š 47 iv/28	5 宰杀鸭	支出

七　骑使舒勒吉伊里（Š 47 iv/30–Š 48 x）

舒勒吉伊里（*Šulgi-ili*）是王后贡牲机构的第六任负责官员。他正式上任时间是舒勒吉 47 年 4 月 30 日①，其工作到舒勒吉 48 年 10 月结束，共 1 年近 6 个月。王后贡牲机构档案中尚未发现其印章，但一个文件内容中舒勒吉伊里的身份和舒库布姆一样是“骑使”，即专为贵夫人服务的官员：70 只公绵羊和 10 只公山羊为国王的送入项，从那冉伊里处，骑使舒勒吉伊里接管了，舒勒吉新提的收据（kišib ^{d}*Šul-gi-sí -im-tum*）（舒勒吉 48 年 10 月，Princeton 1 037）。此外，在其前任乌尔卢旮勒埃邓卡工作期间，出现了三个舒勒吉伊里收支羊毛和衣料的文件②，这三个文件中的舒勒吉伊里是否是王后贡牲机构的负责官员舒勒吉伊里，有待考证。

从舒勒吉 45 年 8 月到舒勒吉 48 年 10 月，骑使舒勒吉伊里**支出**的畜禽有：肥羊（55 只）、肥牛（2 头）、牛（1 头）、羊（29 只）、崽（7 只）、羔（5 只）、禽（91 只）、猪（7 头）、宰杀禽（61 只）、宰杀羊（9 只）和宰杀猪（2 头）。

他**接管**的畜禽有：肥羊（14 只）、肥牛（1 头）、羊（117 只）、牛（2 头）、羔（9 只）、崽（6 只）、母驴（1 头）、猪（3 头）和禽（30 只）。

---

① 在舒勒吉伊里正式上任之前，我们发现了两个他接管牲畜的文件分别是：Torino 1 092（Š 45 viii）、OIP 115 492（Š 46 xi）。

② 这三个文件分别是：（1）2 件 4 等级 niĝlam 衣料和 7 件 4 等级的 guzza 衣料，这些完成的衣料为送入项，自**舒勒吉伊里**处（支出）（舒勒吉 46 年 9 月，NYPL 104）；（2）55 斤次羊毛来自**舒勒吉伊里**处，被送入宫殿（舒勒吉 46 年 10 月，TCS 350）；（3）1 件 4 等级的 guzza 衣料，其重量是 4 斤，这件被称过的衣料，为送入项，从**舒勒吉伊里**处（支出）（舒勒吉 46 年 10 月，OIP 115 470）。

Š 45 viii– Š 48 x 骑使舒勒吉伊里收支牲畜数量和种类一览表

文件时间	牲畜数量和种类	类型	文件时间	牲畜数量和种类	类型
Š 45 viii	1 母驴	接管	Š47 viii/8	1 猪、2 鸭和 21 鸽为宰杀、1 猪、1 鸭、21 鸽	支出
Š 46 xi	4 羔	接管	Š 47 ix	2 羊、1 崽为宰杀牲	支出
Š 47 iv/30	1 雌豚、2 雄豚	接管	Š 47 ix/2	2 鸭	接管
Š 47 iv	2 羊、2 羔	支出	Š 47 ix/2	1 崽、2 肥羊、2 羊、1 羔	接管
Š 47 v/14	1 只宰杀鸭、1 雄豚、2 野鸽	支出	Š 47 ix/11	3 鸭	接管
Š 47 v/20	1 肥猪、2 猪、1 鸭、1 宰杀鸭	支出	Š 47 ix/13	7 羊、3 肥羊	接管
Š 47 v/30	10+肥羊、2+羊	支出	Š 47 ix/15	1 肥牛、5 肥羊、5 羊	接管
Š 47 v	1 雌崽	接管	Š 47 ix/18	2 鸭	接管
Š 47 v	2 羊、2 公崽	支出	Š 47 ix/20	1 肥羊、1 崽	支出
Š 47 v/30	20 宰杀野鸽	支出	Š 47 ix/20	4 肥羊	接管
Š47 vi/7	7 宰杀野鸽、2 野鸽	支出	Š 47 ix/20	1 牛、4 宰杀羊、6 肥羊、3 羊	支出
Š47 vi/10	2 野鸽	支出	Š 47 ix/23	10 鸭	接管
Š47 vi/15	2 鸭	支出	Š 47 ix	3 羊	支出
Š47 vi/16	1 肥羊、2 羊	支出	Š 47 ix	2 牛、20 羊、1 羔	接管
Š47 vi/19	11 肥羊、5 公崽、4 羊、1 肥牛	支出	Š 47 x	2 羔	接管
Š47 vi/22	2 羊、3 肥羊	支出	Š 47 x/15	2 肥羊、1 羊	支出
Š47 vi	1 公崽	接管	Š 47 x/19	2 肥羊、2 羊	支出
Š 47vii	2 公崽	接管	Š 47 x/28	6 鸭	接管
Š 47vii	3 羊和 1 崽	接管	Š 47 x/30	2 鸭、1 母猪为死牲	支出
Š 47vii/15	15 肥羊、18 羊为病死、3 羊	支出	Š 47 xi/5	2 鸭	接管
Š 47 vii/22	1 鸭和 4 鸽	接管	Š 47 xi/7	3 鸭和 1 家鸽为宰杀牲	支出
Š 47 vii/22	10 鸭、2 鸟、5 宰杀鸭	支出	Š 47 xi/7	3+羊、4 肥羊、3 羔、1 肥牛	支出
Š 47 vii	48 鸽、2 猪、2 鸭	支出	Š 47 xi/19	7 鸭和 1 鸽病死牲、1 母猪	支出
Š 47 vii	2 宰杀崽	支出	Š 48 x	80 羊	接管
Š 47vii	【1+】羔、1 崽	接管			

八　卡兰希那吉（Š 44 xi–Š 48 ii/10）

卡兰希那吉（Kalam-henagi）在舒勒吉新提王后贡牲机构中的任期时间较长，从舒勒吉 44 年 11 月到舒勒吉 48 年 2 月 10 日，历时 3 年 3 个月，与贡牲机构的负责官员阿皮拉吞、乌尔卢旮勒埃邓卡和舒勒吉伊里的任期时间重叠。由于目前仅发现 15 个卡兰希那吉的文件，且这 15 个文件全部为卡兰希那吉支出的文件，因此，我们推测：在舒勒吉 44 年 11 月到舒勒吉 48 年 2 月 10 日这一时期内，卡兰希那吉是一位配合阿皮拉吞、乌尔卢旮勒埃邓卡和舒勒吉伊里工作的支出官员。在王后贡牲机构档案中，我们没有发现他印章，也无表明其身份的文件。

在卡兰希那吉工作的 3 年多时间里，他支出的牲畜主要有：肥羊（43 只）、肥牛（8 头）、羊（50 只）、猪（219 头）、崽（2 崽）和宰杀羊（9 只）。

Š 44 xi– Š 48 ii/10 卡兰希那吉支出牲畜的数量和种类一览表

文件时间	牲畜数量和种类	文件时间	牲畜数量和种类
Š 44 xi	2 肥羊、1 羊	Š 47 ix	4 羊、1 崽
Š44 xii/7	1 羊	Š 47 x	2+肥羊、1 羊
Š 45 i/22	7 肥羊、1 肥牛、4 羊	Š 47 xi	2 肥牛、4 羊为宰杀牲
Š 45 ii	2 羊	Š 47 xi/25	4 羊、1 肥牛和 4 肥羊
Š 45 v/12–14	7 肥羊、2 羊为宰杀牲、1 肥牛、8 羊	Š 48 i	1 崽、3 肥羊
Š 45 xi/11–14	2 宰杀肥羊、16 羊、6 肥羊、1 肥牛	Š 48 ii/10	2 羊、1 宰杀羔
Š 45 xi/17	9 肥羊、1 肥牛、7 羊	Š ? ix	3+肥羊
Š 46 iii	96 母猪、123 公猪		

第二节　舒勒吉新提王后贡牲机构负责官员的任职特点

通过对八位王后贡牲机构负责官员的任期时间和其文件类型的分析：（1）阿希马的任期时间与舒库布姆和贝里沓卜的任期时间交叠（阿希马的任期与舒库布姆有 4 年 7 个月的重合、与贝里沓卜的任期有 3 年的重合）；（2）卡兰希那吉的任期时间与阿皮拉吞、乌尔卢旮勒埃邓卡及舒勒吉伊里的任期时间交叠（卡兰希那吉与阿皮拉吞的任期有4个月的重合、与乌尔卢旮勒埃邓卡的任期有5个月的重合、与舒勒吉伊里的任期有5个月的重合）；（3）在目前发现的阿希马担任贡牲机构的负责官员的18个文件中，有17个都是支出文件；（4）目前发现的卡兰希那吉担任贡牲机构负责官员的15个文件都是支出文件，以上四点表明：阿希马与卡兰希那吉都是舒勒吉新提王后贡牲机构中的“配合”支出官员，他们主要辅助其他的负责官员进行动物牲畜的支出工作。

其次，从贡牲机构八位负责官员的身份来看：担任育肥师职务的有：阿希马、贝里沓卜、阿皮拉吞和乌尔卢旮勒埃邓卡；担任骑使职务的有：舒库布姆和舒勒吉伊里；只有阿皮里亚担任“督办”的职务、乌尔卢旮勒埃邓卡身兼书吏和育肥师的双重职务，而卡兰希那吉在目前发现的档案中无头衔。王后贡牲机构八位负责官员中，有四位担任贡牲机构育肥师的职务，直接体现出舒勒吉新提王后贡牲机构的建立主要是为了祭祀的目的。这是因为王后贡牲机构祭祀诸位神明、节日庆典及月相活动等需要大量的育肥牲，它们必须经由专门的育肥师使用大麦等高级饲料喂养牲畜而得来，所以贡牲机构中一半的负责官员担任育肥师的职务直接体现出其目的性。

此外，在舒勒吉新提王后贡牲机构的档案中，还发现了三件舒勒吉新提王后自己担任负责官员的文件，简表如下：

时间	文献内容	负责官员	文献出处
Š 35 vi	1头公牛为祭品台，1肥公牛为安努尼吞，于宫殿中	舒勒吉新提支出	TCS 337
Š 46 vii	118绵羊和2只公山羊，王送牲，从那冉伊里处	舒勒吉提接管	Torino 1 023
Š 48 ix	40只绵羊为王送牲，从那冉伊里处	舒勒吉新吞接管	OIP 115，13

第三章　舒勒吉新提王后贡牲机构中的支出项目研究

舒勒吉新提王后贡牲机构支出的动物牲畜主要有以下几个用途：(1) 为诸神明、月相以及节日庆典等祭祀活动提供牺牲；(2) 为国王、王后等王室成员及高级官员提供食物；(3) 死牲被送到厨房，作为士兵、女工等工人的食物。

第一节　舒勒吉新提王后贡牲机构的祭祀活动分析

古代两河流域的居民由于不能对诸多的自然现象进行科学的解释，因此对自然界的一切都充满了恐惧和敬重。他们发现风雨雷电、日月盈缺和季节更替等都具有规律性，并认为这些现象是由天上的和人形状一样的诸神所掌控。同时，他们认为人类的生老病死和自然界的变化一样也都是由神明主宰。因此，两河流域的居民借助于宗教和想象去解释自然，解释人类与自然的关系。他们把人世间的许多人类不能控制的事情都归诸神明的力量，把灾难视为神对人的惩罚。于是，两河流域的居民对天体和自然既畏惧又崇拜。他们通过向神明献祭祈求、保佑，并希望得到帮助。

古代两河流域的宗教思想是多神崇拜，即自然崇拜。最初，两河流域的居民是对日神、月神、天空（安）、金星（伊南那）、风神、淡水神等自然现象的崇拜，这主要是因为它们直接影响着原始时代居民的农业和畜牧业等经济活动。希望各种食物得到丰收是古代两河流域居民崇拜大自然的主要目的。随着社会的发展，古代两河流域的居民逐渐形成了一套完整的以七大主神为首的诸神体系。

七大主神

神明	祭祀地	神的描述	与众神关系	附注
安（An）	乌鲁克	众神之父、伊南那之父	安图的丈夫；宁胡尔萨格、恩里勒和马尔图之父；大地神基和那穆之子	安曾是苏美尔众神首领。随着人们对他崇拜减退，其权力转移给了恩里勒
恩基（Enki）	埃瑞都	水、智慧、巫医神；创造了书写和人类	那穆之子；杜穆兹、宁萨尔、乌图、宁杜腊和阿萨尔卢比之父；宁图的丈夫	恩基神的标志是手握两条蛇缠绕的权杖
恩里勒（Enlil）	尼普尔	众神之王，天地之间主宰	宁里勒的丈夫；宁胡尔萨格之兄；阿什楠、耐尔旮勒、宁阿朱、宁乌尔塔和南那之父；基和天神安之子	其妻是宁里勒神后
伊南那（Inanna）	乌鲁克	爱、战争、美及金星女神	南那和宁旮勒之女；杜穆兹之妻；乌图、南筛、尼萨巴和宁穆格之妹	伊南那女神的标志是8或16角星
南那（Nanna）	乌尔	月神、夜空之主	太阳神乌图和伊南那女神之父；宁里勒和恩里勒之子；宁旮勒之丈夫	南那神的标志是新月符号
宁胡尔萨格（Nin - hur-sag）	凯什	大母神、生育女神	安和那穆之女；宁乌尔塔、马尔图和宁卡斯之母	
乌图（Utu）	西帕尔拉尔萨	太阳神、正义之神	南那神和宁旮勒之子；伊南那女神之兄	乌图神的标志是太阳圆盘

一 舒勒吉新提王后所祭祀的“两女神”及有关女神和其他神明

除了上述七大诸神外，两河流域的居民还崇拜其他自然神和各种各样的地方神。从王后贡牲机构献祭的档案中，我们发现舒勒吉新提王后所崇拜的最重要的神明是两个阿卡德地区的姐妹女神——贝拉特苏赫尼尔（*Belat-Suhnir*，意为“苏赫尼尔地区之女主人”）和贝拉特达腊班（*Belat-Darraban*，“意为达腊班地区之女主人”），本文简称“两女神”。目前，我们已发现两个写有“两女神”名字的印文。一个是迪亚拉河地区的高官巴巴提的印文①。该印文一次是盖在埃什嫩那城的总督（ensí Áš-nun^{ki}）为尼尼微城的来访者（lú *Ni-nu-a*^{ki}）和其随从（lú ús-sa-ni）支出面粉（zì）的文件（舒辛3年10月，JCS 28 179）中。另一个印文是

① 巴巴提的印文中提到舒辛的母亲阿比新提就是我们的王后舒勒吉新提，关于阿比新提和舒勒吉新提身份同一的研究见本文第二部分第一章。

盖在从乌尔第三王朝独立出来的埃什嫩那城的第一位总督舒伊里亚（*Šu-ì-lí-a*）的一个铭文（OIP 043 143 6 630）上。根据下列舒伊里亚的印文，她们可能是埃什嫩那的主神提什帕克（^{d}*Tišpak*）的妻子。

乌尔第三王朝时期的两个有关“两女神”的印文

时间	文件内容	印文内容	文献出处
ŠS 3 x	10 斗 zì-gu 面粉和 13 斗 zì 面粉为提什阿塔勒，尼尼微城的人，100+【x】人是他的卫队，每人 x 斗面粉……从埃什嫩那的总督处支出了，巴巴提的印章	舒辛——强大之人、乌尔之王、四方之王赠予了（in-na-ba）他的奴仆巴巴提——账目总管（g̃á-dub-ba）、王室管理员（šà-tam lugal）、马什干沙润的将军（šakkan$_6$）、阿巴勒的总督（ensí），贝拉特苏赫尼尔和贝拉特台腊班（贝拉特达腊班）女神的【喜爱者】，他（舒辛）亲爱的母亲阿比新提的兄弟（该印章）	JCS 28 179；盖有巴巴提印文的文件还有：BRM 3 037（ŠS 6 v）、BRM 3 038（ŠS 6 xi）
Ibbi-Sîn	无	提什帕克——强大之王，瓦润国（*Warim*）的国王，四方之王，神舒伊里亚（^{d}*Šu-ì-lí-a*），他的儿子，贝拉特塔腊班、贝拉特【苏赫尼尔】、阿达德和贝拉特伊里喜爱之人，是【他的】虔诚的 *išippum* 祭司（*muštemiqum*）。	OIP 043 143 6 630

根据上述印文我们知道这一时期“两女神”是以阿卡德为主的迪亚拉河地区最重要的女神。因此，负责祭祀“两女神”的舒勒吉新提王后很可能来自该地区，具有阿卡德人的背景。舒勒吉新提王后的名字不使用苏美尔语，而使用阿卡德语 *Šulgi-simtī*，意为“舒勒吉是我的骄傲”，可以为这一推测提供佐证。舒勒吉新提王后贡牲机构的档案中多次记录了舒勒吉新提王后对“两女神”进行献祭，表明她们是王后心中最重要的女神，很可能王后把她故乡的女神作为她崇拜的主神。

舒勒吉新提王后贡牲机构为两女神祭祀提供牺牲的数量和种类情况见下表：

Š 33 ix–Š 47 ix 王后贡牲机构为祭祀两女神的提供牺牲的数量和种类一览表

时间	文件内容	时间	文件内容
Š 33 ix	4 肥羊为两女神的祭祀	Š 43 i/29	2 肥羊为两女神
Š 34 iii	2 肥牛和 8 肥羊为两女神	Š 45viii/ 15	2 肥羊为两女神
Š 34 ix	4 牛后级公绵羊为**贝拉特苏赫尼尔**	Š 46 i/18	1 肥羊和 1 羊为宫殿祭祀，为两女神
Š 35 v	2 公崽为两女神的祭祀	Š 46 v/21	2 肥羊、2 羊、1 羔和 3 崽为两女神

续表

时间	文件内容	时间	文件内容
Š 35 v	1+【公绵羊?】为两女神	Š 46 x/30	2 崽、1 肥雌崽和 1 肥羊为两女神
Š 35 vi	2 肥羊为两女神	Š 46 xi/15	1 公绵羊为两女神
Š 35 vii	2 肥羊分别为两女神	Š 46 xii/30	4 雌崽为两女神
Š 37 v	1 肥羊和 1 肥公山羊为两女神祭祀	Š 47 iv/14	1 肥公山羊为两女神
Š 39x/29	1 肥羊和 1 肥公山羊为两女神祭祀	Š 47 v	2 食草公绵羊为两女神
Š 40 ix/ 30	1 肥羊和 1 公山羊为两女神祭祀	Š 47 v/30	【1+】公山羊为两女神
Š 40 x/28	1 肥羊和 1 母绵羊为两女神祭祀	Š 47 vi/16	2 公绵羊为两女神
Š 40 xi/25	1 肥羊和 1 肥公山羊为两女神祭祀	Š47 vi/19，21	4 羊、2 公崽为两女神
Š 41 i/30	1 肥羊和 1 食草公绵羊为两女神的祭祀	Š 47 vi/22	2 食草公绵羊为两女神
Š 42x/13，14	1 肥羊和 1 母绵羊为**贝拉特苏赫尼尔**	Š 47 ix/20	1 肥羊和 1 公崽为两女神
Š 42 xii/30	2 肥羊为两女神	Š 47 ix	2 食草公绵羊为两女神

在贡牲机构的祭祀活动中，常与“两女神”同时出现的另两位女神分别是：安努尼吞（^{d}*An-nu-ni-tum*）女神和乌勒马席吞（^{d}*Ul-ma-ši-tum*）女神。安努尼吞女神在古巴比伦时期的阿卡德王那腊姆辛的王铭中多次以 Inanna-*Annunītum* 的形式被提及①。由于 *Annunītum* 的词源解释为“战斗、战争”之意，因此我们推测安努尼吞是苏美尔女神伊南那的战争神性的化身。乌勒马席吞女神是阿卡德帝国首都阿卡德城的乌勒马什庙区（Ulmaš）掌管爱与战的金星女神，她也是伊南那的一个化身。安努尼吞女神和乌勒马席吞女神与“两女神”的关系并不明确，但她们常作为“两女神”的陪祭女神出现。舒勒吉新提王后对这四位阿卡德的女神的崇拜清楚地表明她本人是阿卡德和迪亚拉地区的出身和历史。

王后贡牲机构的档案中对安努尼吞女神和乌勒马席吞女神献祭的文件共 8 件，其中安努尼吞女神 4 次被单独献祭，共有 2 次献祭牺牲是 1 头育肥公牛、1 次为 1 头育肥公牛和 2+育肥公绵羊、1 次为公绵羊羔。乌勒马席吞被献祭的牺牲通常只有 1 只育肥公绵羊，其献祭牺牲的数量和质量明

① D.Frayne，*The Royal Inscriptionof Mesopotamia*，Toronto：University of Toronto Press，1993，RIME 2，E 2.1.4.2；E 2.1.4.3；E 2.1.4.5.

显少于安努尼吞女神。以上统计数字表明在王后贡牲机构中安努尼吞女神比乌勒马席吞女神重要。

Š 33 v–Š 46 ix/6 王后贡牲机构为祭祀安努尼吞女神和乌勒马席吞女神提供牺牲的数量和种类一览表

时间	文件内容	时间	文件内容
Š 33 v	1 头肥牛为安努尼吞女神	Š 36 vi	2 雌崽为安努尼吞和乌勒马席吞祭祀
Š 33 ix	2 肥羊为安努尼吞，1 肥羊乌勒马席吞	Š 42 viii	1 头肥牛和 2+肥羊为安努尼吞
Š 35 vi	1 头肥牛为安努尼吞女神	Š45viii/25	1 公牛和 3 肥羊安努尼吞，1 羊乌勒马席吞
Š 36 v	1 肥羊为乌勒马席吞，3 肥羊安努尼吞	Š 46 ix/6	1 羔为安努尼吞

除了“两女神”、安努尼吞女神和乌勒马席吞女神外，苏美尔最重要的伊南那女神和那那亚女神也是舒勒吉新提王后贡牲机构献祭的主要对象。伊南那女神（^{d}Inanna）的阿卡德语对应女神是^{d}*Ištar*。她是古代两河流域最重要的女神。伊南那女神是乌鲁克城的保护神，其神庙名为“天房”（é-anna）。伊南那女神有三种性格特质：爱、战斗和金星。那那亚女神（^{d}Nanaya）是伊南那女神的姐妹。

王后贡牲机构的档案中，那那亚女神被单独献祭 14 次，其牺牲通常为 1 只育肥公羊，但在舒勒吉 45 年 11 月 15 日至 17 日三天的祭祀中，其牺牲多达 1 头育肥公牛、5 只育肥公绵羊和 2 只公绵羊羔。伊南那女神被单独献祭 11 次，其牺牲一般为 1 只育肥羊羔。舒勒吉 45 年 5 月 14 日的节日祭祀中，其牺牲则多达 1 头育肥公牛、3 只育肥公绵羊和 1 只公绵羊羔。这些统计数字表明在单独祭祀中那那亚女神比伊南那女神得到更多的重视，但是王后贡牲机构对伊南那的祭祀主要体现在其吉腊努姆仪式中。

Š 32 i–Š 48 ii/10 王后贡牲机构为祭祀伊南那女神和那那亚女神提供牺牲的数量和种类一览

时间	文件内容	时间	文件内容
Š 32 i	1 肥羊为伊南那	Š 46 vi/25	1 公崽为那那亚
Š 34 x	1 崽为伊南那	Š 46 ix/6	1 公崽为那那亚
Š 36 v	1 肥羊为那那亚	Š 46 x/30	1 肥羊为伊南那的牺牲

续表

时间	文件内容	时间	文件内容
Š 37 v	1 肥羊为那那亚	Š 46 xii/30	1 肥羊、2 羔为伊南那
Š 40 xi/25	1 公绵羊为那那亚	Š 47 i/1	1 羔为那那亚
Š 41 vii/2	1 肥羊为那那亚	Š 47 i/13	1 肥牛后级公绵羊为那那亚
Š 42 x/13, 14	1 肥羊为伊南那	Š 47 iii/7	1 羔为那那亚
Š 43 i/29	1 肥羊为伊南那	Š 47 v/30	【1+】肥雌崽为伊南那
Š 45 v/(12-) 14	1 肥牛、3 肥羊和 1 羔为伊南那	Š 47 ix/9, 10	3 公绵羊为伊南那，1 崽为那那亚
Š 45 vii/10, 15	1 牛后级公绵羊为伊南那	Š 47x/15	1 公绵羊为那那亚
Š 45 xi/17	1 肥牛、5 肥羊和 2 羔为那那亚	Š 47 x	1 公绵羊为那那亚
Š 45 xii/20-22	1 羔为伊南那	Š 47 xi/7	1 肥羊和 1 羔为那那亚
Š 46 ii/4, 6	1 肥羔、1 羔为伊南那	Š 48 ii/10	1 公绵羊为那那亚

此外，王后贡牲机构祭祀的神明还包括：

（1）阿拉吞女神（^{d}*Al-la-tum*）——统治冥界的女神，其苏美尔语名字是 Ereškigal（共献祭 12 次）；（2）阿达德（^{d}*Adad*）——雷雨神，其苏美尔语名字是^{d}Iškur（共献祭 12 次）；（3）宁荪（^{d}Nin-sún）——“母野牛之女主”，她是乌尔第三王朝的祭祀祖先和乌鲁克第一王朝第三位神王卢旮勒班达的妻子（共献祭 10 次）；（4）神王恩里勒（共献祭 8 次）；（5）神后宁里勒（共献祭 8 次）；（6）宁廷乌格（^{d}Nin-tin-ug_5）——治愈女神，相当于乌鲁克城和乌尔城的古拉神和伊辛城的宁伊辛（共献祭 3 次）。（7）爱之女神伊什哈腊（^{d}*Iš-ha-ra*）叙利亚地区的农神达干（Dagan）之妻（共献祭 3 次）；（8）努斯库（^{d}Nusku）——苏美尔的光神和火神，公正之神，文明之神（共献祭 1 次）；（9）宁乌尔塔（^{d}Nin-urta）——战神、农神，恩里勒之子和赞美诗中的英雄（共献祭 1 次）。

Š 29 vi-Š 47xi/7 王后贡牲机构为祭祀阿拉吞女神和阿达德女神提供牺牲的数量和种类一览表

时间	文件内容	时间	文件内容
Š 29 vi	1 肥牛、2 肥羊为阿拉吞女神	Š 45 x/10, 12, 15	1 羔为阿达德的牺牲
Š 30 x/4	1 肥羊为阿拉吞女神	Š 45 xii/16, x	1 肥牛后级公绵羊为阿达德

续表

时间	文件内容	时间	文件内容
Š 33 ix	1 肥羊为阿拉吞	Š 46 ii/4，6	1 肥羊为阿拉吞的供奉
Š 36 iv	1 公崽为阿拉吞祭祀	Š 46 v/21	1 公崽为阿达德
Š 36 v	1 肥羊为阿达德	Š 46 viii/5，6	1 肥牛后级公绵羊为阿拉吞
Š 40 ix/5	1 肥羊为阿拉吞的祭祀	Š 46 ix/6	1 肥羊和 1 羔为阿拉吞
Š 40 xi/25	1 公羊崽为阿达德祭祀	Š 46 x/20	1 食草公绵羊为阿达德的牺牲
Š 41 i/4	1 肥羊为阿拉吞的祭祀	Š 46 xi/7	1 牛后级肥羊为阿拉吞
Š 41 i	1 公绵羊为阿拉吞祭祀	Š 46 xi/15	1 食草公绵羊为阿达德的牺牲
Š 41 iii/4	1 肥羊为阿拉吞祭祀	Š 47 v	1 公崽为阿达德
Š 41 ix/3	1 肥羊为阿达德的祭祀	Š 47 ix	1 食草公绵羊为阿达德
Š 45 viii/15	1 牛后级公绵羊为阿达德	Š 47 xi/7	【1+】食草公绵羊为阿达德

Š 42 iii/14–Š 48 i/10 王后贡牲机构为祭祀神王恩里勒和神后宁里勒提供牺牲的数量和种类一览表

时间	文件内容	时间	文件内容
Š 42 iii/14	2 肥羊和 1 羔为宁里勒，恩里勒相同	Š 45 xii/20–22	1 羔为恩里勒
Š 45 v/12–14	1 羊为恩里勒，1 羊为宁里勒	Š 46 xi/15	1 肥羊和 1 羔宁里勒，1 崽恩里勒
Š 45 x/10，12，15	2 肥羊和 1 羔为宁里勒，1 羊和 1 羔恩里勒	Š 46 xii/30	2 羔为宁里勒，1 羔为恩里勒
Š 45 xi/11–14	1 肥羊和【1 羔】为宁里勒，恩里勒相同	Š 48 i/10	1 肥羊为宁里勒
Š 45 xii/20–22	1 肥羊和 1 羔为恩里勒，1 肥羊为宁里勒		

Š 31 viii–Š 48 i/10 王后贡牲机构为祭祀其他神明提供牺牲的数量和种类一览表

时间	文件内容	时间	文件内容
Š 31 viii	1 崽为恩基，1 羊为古腊	Š 32 iv	1 肥牛为萨格旮
Š 33 ix	1 肥羊为伊什哈腊	Š 34 iii	1 肥羊为安神
Š 35 v	1 公崽为宁胡尔萨格	Š 35 vii	1 肥羊为伊什哈腊，1 肥羊贝拉特那旮尔
Š 35 ix	1 公山羊为美斯兰塔埃阿	Š 36 iv	1 吃奶公山羊为美斯兰塔埃阿

续表

时间	文件内容	时间	文件内容
Š 40 viii/5	1 肥牛、2 肥羊和 1 崽为阿拉古拉，1 肥羊为宁廷乌格		
Š 40 ix/ 30	1 肥羊为南那神，1 肥雌山羊崽为宁荪		
Š 40 x/28	1 肥羊为南那，1 崽为宁荪	Š 40 xi/25	1 肥羊为南那，1 雌崽为宁荪
Š 41 i/30	1 肥羊为南那，1 崽为宁荪	Š 42 iii/14	1 肥羊为阿拉古拉
Š 42 viii	1 公山羊为宁廷乌格	Š 42 viii/28，30	1 肥羊为南那，1 公崽为宁荪
Š 45 v/12-14	1 肥羊为南那，宁旮勒相同，宁尼旮尔 1 羊，达达 1，神判河神 1，宁舒布尔 1		
Š 45 ix/13	2 羊为阿卜朱，1 羊为宁旮勒，2 羊为宁荪，2+羊为伊什塔尔		
Š 45 x/10，12	1 羊为宁旮吉阿		
Š 45 xi/11-14	1 崽为宁胡尔萨格，1 肥牛、3 肥羊和 4 羊为宁廷乌格		
Š 45 xii/16，x	1 肥羊为南那		
Š 45 xii/20-22	1 崽为宁乌尔塔，1 崽为努斯库，1 羊为宁胡尔萨旮		
Š 46 ii/4，6	1 崽为宁埃旮勒，1 羔为宁荪，1 肥公山羊，1 羊为神判河神		
Š 46 v/21	1 崽为神判河神	Š 46 viii/5，6	1 羊为神判河神
Š 46 viii/27	1 崽为宁荪		
Š 46 ix/6	1 羊为安，1 羊和 1 崽为伊什哈腊和贝拉特那古		
Š 46 x/30	11 公崽为宁荪	Š 46 xi/7	1 羊为神判河神，1 羔为南那
Š 47 i/7	1 崽为神判河神	Š 47 v/30	【1 肥羊】为宁荪
Š 47 vi/19，21	1 崽为神判河神，1 崽为安神		
Š 47 xi/7	【1+】羊为古拉	Š 48 i/10	1 崽为底格里西斯河神

舒勒吉新提王后贡牲机构除了对诸神直接进行献祭外，早期术语还用神庙代替女神的名字，对女神进行献祭。在舒勒吉 41 年以后这种以庙代替神的术语被放弃。王后贡牲机构献祭的神庙有："两女神"庙、贝拉特苏赫尼尔庙、阿拉吞神庙、伊什哈腊和贝拉特那旮尔神庙、沙特伊勒廷神庙、宁荪庙、阿达德庙、乌勒马席吞庙、阿达德图格庙、宁里勒庙、那那亚庙。对诸神庙献祭的牺牲通常是育肥公绵羊，但偶尔也有育肥公牛、公山羊崽和公绵羊羔，以及普通公绵羊。献祭牺牲的数量通常是 2 只育肥羊，但有时其数量也会多达 6 只（贝拉特苏赫尼尔庙和宁里勒庙）。

王后贡牲机构为祭祀神庙提供牺牲的数量和种类一览表（Š 29 vi–Š 41 vii/26）

时间	文件内容	时间	文件内容
Š 29 vi	2 肥羊为两女神庙	Š 29 x	2 肥羊为两女神庙
Š 29 x	1+优等肥羊为两女神庙	Š 29 xi	1+肥羊为贝拉特苏赫尼尔庙
Š 30 vi，ix	4 肥羊为两女神庙（共 2 次）	Š 30 vii	2 肥羊为两女神庙
Š 30 viii	2 肥羊为两女神庙	Š 34 ii	3 肥羊为尼萨巴庙
Š 34 ix	1 肥牛和 1 公牛为贝拉特苏赫尼尔庙		
Š 36 i	1 肥羊为阿拉吞神庙，2 肥羊为伊什哈腊和贝拉特那旮尔神庙，1 肥羊为沙特伊勒廷神庙		
Š 36 v	2 肥羊为两女神庙	Š 36 x	1 公羊和 1 公崽为那那亚庙
Š 37 v	1 肥羊、1 公羊和 1 羔为宁荪庙，1 肥羊、1 公羊和 1 羔为阿达德庙，1 公羊为乌勒马席吞庙		
Š 37 v	1 公山羊崽为宁伊吉兹巴腊庙，2 肥羊、2 牛后级公绵羊、2 公崽为贝拉特苏赫尼尔庙		
Š 37 vi	1 肥羊为那那亚庙	Š 38 xi	1 肥羊为阿拉古拉庙的毁坏祭
Š 40 vii/5–7	2 肥羊为两女神庙祭祀，【1+】为宁荪庙，1 肥羊和 1 羊为阿达德图格庙，1 肥羊为阿拉吞庙		
Š 40 viii	1 肥牛、4 肥羊和 1 公崽为宁里勒庙		
Š 40 x/18	1 肥羊和 1 公羊为宁荪庙，1 肥羊和 1 公羊为阿达德神庙		
Š 41 vii/26	【1+】肥羊为那那亚庙		

二　王后贡牲机构中女神的节日庆典

王后贡牲机构除了主要祭祀神明和特殊月相之外，还对与神明有关的节日庆典进行祭祀，主要有：吉腊努姆仪式（*gi–ra–núm*）、埃鲁努姆节（*è–lu–núm*）、那卜润节（*nabrûm*）、倒啤酒仪式（kaš–dé–a）、塞尔塞闰仪式（*šeršerum*）和神明进入庆典（ezem–DINĜIR–ku_4– ku_4）等。

（一）吉腊努姆仪式

吉腊努姆仪式是王后贡牲机构的一个主要祭祀节日。*gi–ra–núm* 的阿卡德语词源是 *girrānu*，其对应的苏美尔语是 ér，意为“哭泣、哀悼”。从贡牲机构的档案中，我们发现吉腊努姆仪式与伊南那女神、那那亚女神、“两女神”、安努尼吞女神和乌勒马席吞女神紧密联系，并且祭祀的地点主要是在乌鲁克和乌尔。伊南那女神的吉腊努姆仪式祭祀是在 1 月、3—

12月举行，也就是几乎全年每月都可以举行；那那亚女神的吉腊努姆仪式祭祀是在6月举行；“两女神”的吉腊努姆仪式祭祀通常是在3月、5—7月和10月举行；安努尼吞和乌勒马席吞女神的祭祀是在5—7月举行。在贡牲机构的档案中，伊南那的吉腊努姆仪式的祭祀文件总计27个、“两女神”的吉腊努姆祭祀共有6个文件；那那亚女神的吉腊努姆仪式祭祀共计2个文件；安努尼吞和乌勒马席吞女神的祭祀共3个文件。

从贡牲机构档案记录祭祀各女神的文件统计数字来看，贡牲机构主要祭祀的是伊南那女神的吉腊努姆仪式，这可能是为了祭祀金星伊南那的伏地阶段。由于两女神经常与金星女神伊南那和那那亚女神以及伊南那女神在阿卡德地区的两个化身安努尼吞和乌勒马席吞女神一起祭祀，我们推测两女神也可能是伊南那在迪亚拉河地区的化身，她们可能分别代表黄昏出现的金星和凌晨出现的金星（即中国的长庚星和启明星）。安努尼吞女神和乌勒马席吞女神同样代表晚、早分别出现的金星。这四位女神经常同时出现在王后舒勒吉新提王后的供奉表中，因此，我们统称为“四女神”。苏美尔女神伊南那和那那亚也可能表示黄昏和早晨的金星。王后贡牲机构中的“四女神”的吉腊努姆仪式可能是金星在东西方天空转换期间的一种祭祀活动。

王后贡牲机构为祭祀吉腊努姆仪式提供牺牲数量和种类一览表

时间	文件内容	时间	文件内容
Š 30 x/4	两女神的吉腊努姆仪式2肥羊	Š 40 vii/6	安努尼吞和乌勒马席吞吉腊努姆仪式2羊
Š 32 iv	安努尼吞和乌勒马席吞吉腊努姆仪式2羊	Š 40 viii/4	伊南那的吉腊努姆仪式1肥羊
Š 32 ix	两女神的吉腊努姆仪式2母山羊	Š 40 ix/30	伊南那的吉腊努姆仪式1肥羊
Š 33 v	【2+】肥羊为两女神的吉腊努姆仪式，于乌尔	Š 40 x/28	伊南那吉腊努姆仪式1肥羊
Š 33 v	伊南那吉腊努姆仪式1肥羊	Š 40 xi/30	伊南那的吉腊努姆仪式1肥羊
Š 33 vi	安努尼吞和乌勒马席吞吉腊努姆仪式2羊	Š 40 xii/25	伊南那的吉腊努姆仪式1肥羊
Š 35i	贝拉特苏赫尼尔庙的吉腊努姆仪式2崽，于乌尔	Š 41 i/15	伊南那吉腊努姆仪式1肥羊
Š 35 vi	伊南那吉腊努姆仪式1羊，那那亚吉腊努姆仪式	Š 41 i/30	伊南那吉腊努姆仪式1肥羊

续表

时间	文件内容	时间	文件内容
	1羊，两女神吉腊努姆仪式2羊	Š 41 vii/26	伊南那吉腊努姆仪式1肥羊、1羊（2次）
Š 35 vi	那那亚的吉腊努姆仪式1崽	Š 41 ix/28	伊南那吉腊努姆仪式1肥羊
Š 35 x	两女神的吉腊努姆仪式2羊，于乌尔	Š 42 iii/13	伊南那的吉腊努姆仪式1肥羊，两女神吉
Š 36 i	伊南那吉腊努姆仪式的月供1肥羊，于乌尔		腊努姆仪式1肥羊和1羊
Š 36 ix	伊南那吉腊努姆仪式1肥羊，于乌尔	Š 42 viii/30	伊南那的吉腊努姆仪式1肥羊，两女神吉
Š 37 i	伊南那神的吉腊努姆仪式1肥羊		腊努姆仪式1肥羊和1牛
Š 37 v	伊南那吉腊努姆仪式1肥羊	Š 42 xii/30	伊南那吉腊努姆仪式1肥羊
Š 37 v	安努尼吞和吉腊努姆仪式1崽，乌勒马席吞庙的	Š 45 v/13	伊南那的吉腊努姆仪式1肥羊
	吉腊努姆仪式1崽，于乌尔	Š 45 vii/13	伊南那的吉腊努姆仪式1羊
Š 37 v	贝拉特苏赫尼尔庙的吉腊努姆仪式2公崽	Š 45 vii/25	伊南那吉腊努姆仪式1羊
Š 37 vi	伊南那的吉腊努姆仪式的月供1肥羊	Š 45 viii 15	伊南那吉腊努姆仪式1肥羊、2羊（2次）
Š 37 vi	伊南那的吉腊努姆仪式1公崽，于图马勒	Š47 vi/21	安努尼吞和乌勒马席吞吉腊努姆仪式2羊
Š 39 x/27	伊南那吉腊努姆仪式1肥羊		

（二）支出牛羊为那那亚、四女神等女神的“倒啤酒”宴会和支出牛羊禽为王室的“倒啤酒”宴会

王后贡牲机构的档案中有三个文件记录了安努尼吞女神和乌勒马席吞女神的吉腊努姆仪式和“倒啤酒”宴会（kaš-dé-a）同时举行①，我们猜测在吉腊努姆仪式的祭祀中包含一个“倒啤酒”宴会。倒啤酒宴会可能是为了庆祝伊南那女神从冥界的回归而举办的宴会。王后的贡牲档案中，“两女神”于10月举行的“倒啤酒”宴会有1个文件、贝拉特苏赫尼尔女神于9月单独举行的“倒啤酒”宴会有1个文件、安努尼吞女神和乌勒马席吞女神于5—7月举行的“倒啤酒”宴会有3个文件、那那亚女神5月和9月举行的“倒啤酒”宴会有3个文件、阿拉吞女神和宁埃旮勒于

① 这三个文件分别是：AnOr 7 61（Š 37 v）、TRU 273（Š 40 vii/5，6，7）、AnOr 7 83（Š 47 vi/19，21）。

9月举行的“倒啤酒”宴会各1个文件。

Š 33 v–Š 41 x/11 王后贡牲机构为倒啤酒宴会提供牺牲的数量和种类

时间	文件内容	时间	文件内容
Š 33 v	那那亚的倒啤酒宴会【1+】肥牛	Š 33 ix	宁埃旮勒的倒啤酒宴会1肥羊
Š 34 ix	贝拉特苏赫尼尔的倒啤酒宴会2肥牛，那那亚的倒啤酒宴会1肥牛和5肥羊，阿拉吞的倒啤酒宴会1肥牛和2肥羊		
Š 36 ix	那那亚的倒啤酒宴会1肥羊和1崽		
Š 37 v	安努尼吞的啤酒宴会1公崽，于安努尼吞的啤酒宴会时		
Š 47 vi/19，21	1羊为乌勒马席吞和安努尼吞的啤酒宴会		
Š 40 vii/5-7	安努尼吞的倒啤酒宴会1羊	Š 41 x/11	两女神的倒啤酒宴会1肥羊、1羊

舒勒吉新提王后贡牲机构的档案中不仅提到为诸神明的倒啤酒宴会提供牺牲，同时还记录了为国王、王室成员埃阿尼沙（舒勒吉的lukur神妻）、塔丁伊什塔尔（阿马尔辛之女）和高官贵族阿巴恩里勒良（骑使）之女的倒啤酒仪式提供禽类（鸭、鸽）、育肥牲（羊和牛）和猪。

Š 40 i/22– Š 43 ii/21 王后贡牲机构为王室成员的倒啤酒宴会提供牛羊禽一览表

时间	文件内容	时间	文件内容
Š 40 i/22	国王的倒啤酒宴会1鸭和5野鸽	Š 42 x/13	国王的倒啤酒宴会2肥羊
Š 40 iii	埃阿尼沙的倒啤酒宴会1鸭和5野鸽	Š 43 ii/21	塔丁伊什塔尔的倒啤酒宴会1肥牛和5肥羊
Š 41 ii/4	阿巴恩里勒良之女倒啤酒宴会2肥羊、1羊	Š 43 ii/21	塔丁伊什塔尔倒啤酒宴会1豚、1鸭、11鸽

（三）女神们的埃鲁努姆节、那卜润节、塞尔塞润节和神明进入庆典

埃鲁努姆节（*è/é-lu-núm*）在贡牲机构的档案中主要与“两女神”有关，其具体意义不详。“两女神”的埃鲁努姆节的祭祀通常是在1—3月。目前，贡牲档案中记录“两女神”埃鲁努姆节的祭祀文件共2个（Š 41 ii/20，AnOr 07 067和Š 41/30，SET 044），贝拉特苏赫尼尔埃鲁努姆节的祭祀文件2个（Š 28 i，Princeton 2 134和Š 41 iii/1，JCS 52，127），其祭祀举行的地点是在乌尔。

王后贡牲机构为埃鲁努姆节提供牺牲的数量和种类一览表

时间	文件内容	文献出处	时间	文件内容	文献出处
Š 28 i	贝拉特苏赫尼尔庙的埃鲁努姆仪式 4 肥羊	Princeton 2 134	Š 41 ii/20	两女神的埃鲁努姆仪式 2 只羊	AnOr 07 067
Š 41/30	两女神的埃鲁努姆仪式 3 只羊和 1 只肥羊	SET 044	Š 41 iii/1	贝拉特苏赫尼尔的埃鲁努姆仪式 4 肥羊	JCS 52，127

那卜润节的阿卡德语是 *nabrûm*，其词根是 *barû*，意思是“占卜、预测”。那卜润节是为了预测来年命运的一种占卜祭祀。贡牲机构档案记载“两女神”的那卜润节祭祀是于 9 月在乌鲁克举行，安努尼吞女神和乌勒马席吞女神的那卜润节的祭祀是于 8 月在乌尔举行。贡牲档案中，“两女神”的那卜润节祭祀的文件共计 1 个（TRU 282）、贝拉特苏赫尼尔的那卜润节祭祀文件 1 个（TRU 272）、安努尼吞女神的那卜润节祭祀文件 2 个（PDT 2 0973、PDT 1 162）①。

Š34 ix–Š 46 ix/6 王后为乌尔的那卜润节提供牺牲的数量和种类一览表

时间	文件内容	文献出处
Š 34 ix	贝拉特苏赫尼尔庙的那卜润节 1 肥牛和 1 牛	TRU 272
Š 42 viii/20	安努尼吞 1 肥牛和 2+肥羊，宁廷【乌旮】1 羊，为安努尼吞于乌尔的那卜润节	PDT 2 0973
Š 45 viii/25	安努尼吞 1 牛和 3 肥羊，乌勒马席吞 1 羊，于那卜润节时	PDT 1 162
Š 46 ix/6	两女神那卜润节 2 牛、2 肥羊、2 肥羊和 2 崽	TRU 282

塞尔塞闰节（ezem-*še-er-še-er-ru-um*）意为“锁链节”②。由于两女神可能是伊南那金星的化身，而神话中的金星女神一度来到地府，她可能被锁链锁在冥界，塞尔塞闰节，即“锁链节”由此而来。贡牲机构档案中记录了舒勒吉 37 年 2 月和舒勒吉 40 年 3 月举行了“两女神”的塞尔塞闰节。

① 在舒勒吉新提王后贡牲机构的档案中，总是为安努尼吞女神和乌勒马席吞女神一起提供祭祀牲，或是为安努尼吞女神单独提供祭祀牲，从来没有文件记载单独为乌勒马席吞女神提供祭祀牲，这可能表明在乌尔安努尼吞女神是姐妹女神中较重要的一位。

② Mark E. Cohen, *The Cultic Calendars of the Ancient Near East*. CDL Press, Bethesda, Maryland, 1993, p.475.

王后贡牲机构为塞尔塞闰节提供牺牲的数量和种类一览表

时间	文件内容	文献出处
Š 37 ii	祭祀的月供 5 肥羊，消失处供奉 2 崽，以上为两女神庙的塞尔塞闰节	OIP 115033
Š 40 iii/1	两女神的塞尔塞闰节 2 肥羊和 2 羊	AnOr 07 063

神明进入庆典（ezem-diĝir-ku$_4$-ku$_4$）在乌尔城举行是为了使安努尼吞女神和乌勒马席吞女神在短时间内（通常是一天或几天）出现并重返她的神庙。除了神明进入庆典，两位女神在乌尔的膜拜还有神明进入日（*ud~ è-ru-ba-tum*）。神明进入庆典一般都是在 2 月到 5 月举行。贡牲机构档案中记录安努尼吞女神的进入庆典有 2 个文件（Š 40 vii/7，TRU 273 和 Š 40 iii/1，AnOr 07 063）、安努尼吞和乌勒马席吞女神的进入庆典有 1 个文件（Š 41/30，SET 044）。

王后贡牲机构为神明进入庆典提供牺牲的数量和种类一览表

时间	文件内容	地点	文献出处
Š 40 vii/7	2 羔 1 肥牛、4 肥羊、1 羊为安努尼吞神的进入庆典	乌尔	TRU 273
Š 40 iii/1	1 肥牛和 3 肥羊为安努尼吞的进入庆典	乌尔	AnOr 07 063
Š 41/30	1 公牛、3 肥羊和 1 羊为安努尼吞和乌勒马席吞的进入庆典	乌尔	SET 044

三 王后贡牲机构祭祀月相的活动

古代苏美尔人将一年分为夏季和冬季两个季节。夏季从 2 月至 3 月份开始，冬季从 9 月至 10 月份开始。其月份是严格的太阴月，从新月出现的那晚开始，每 29 天或 30 天为一月。古苏美尔人通常以农业活动或祭祀神名的节日为每月命名，各城市间每月的名字并不相同。由于月份对古代苏美尔人的日常生活的重要影响，所以他们非常重视对月相的祭祀活动。对于月相的祭祀也成为王后贡牲机构的重要献祭对象之一。月相是指由于月亮的盈缺变化而呈现出的不同现象。它包括四种月相：朔月（ud-sakar）或是新月初（sag~ ud-sakar）、初七上弦月（é-ud-7）、望月（é-ud-15）和下弦月（é-ud-23）。目前，在王后贡牲机构的档案中尚未发现祭祀下弦月的文件。

王后贡牲机构中，对朔月的祭祀一般是在一个月的 27 日到 30 日中的一天举行，档案中关于朔月的祭祀活动的文件共有 14 个；对初七上弦月的祭祀是在 4 日到 7 日间的任意一天举行，王后档案中共有 5 个记录祭祀上弦月的文件；对望月的祭祀是在一个月的 14 日或 15 日举行，王后档案中共有 8 个祭祀望月的文件。

舒勒吉新提王后贡牲机构中，为祭祀月相提供的牲畜种类有：育肥牲、普通牲和禽类。育肥牲包括：育肥公绵羊、“牛后级”育肥公绵羊、育肥公牛；普通牲包括：公绵羊、母绵羊、绵羊羔、公山羊崽、雌山羊崽；禽类主要有幼鸭和野鸽。

（一）在乌鲁克举行的朔月祭

朔月俗称新月，是月亮周期变化的一个现象。古代苏美尔人经过长期的对天空的细致观察，掌握了月亮周期的变化规律：每 7 天月亮的形状会出现一次规律性的变化。古苏美尔人把日落后初现新月时作为一个月的开始。王后贡牲机构中共有 14 个祭祀新月的文件，包括 4 个对新月初（saĝ~ud-sakar）祭祀的文件。新月的祭祀通常是在一个月的 27 日到 30 日中的一天举行，祭祀的地点是在乌鲁克。贡牲档案中，为新月初祭提供的牺牲为 2 只育肥公绵羊和 1 只公绵羊；为新月祭提供牺牲的数量从 1 只公绵羊到 3 只育肥公绵羊和 3 头公牛不等。

王后贡牲机构为祭祀新月支出牺牲一览表

时间	文献内容	支出官员	督办/经由	地点	文献出处
Š 35 ix	1 公羊为新月初祭，1 公绵羊为满月祭 1 公羊为新月祭（第 2 次）	贝里沓卜	伊皮克埃腊	乌鲁克	SET 041
Š 36 i	2 肥公绵羊为新月祭	贝里沓卜		乌鲁克	AnOr 7 57
Š 36 iv	1 公绵羊为新月祭	庙总管	伊皮克埃腊	乌鲁克	AnOr 7 59
Š 36 x	1 公绵羊为新月祭	贝里沓卜	贝里巴尼	乌鲁克	OIP115 30
Š 37 vi	2 公绵羊和 1 公崽为新月祭	贝里沓卜	阿皮拉提	乌鲁克	AnOr 07 062
Š 39 vi/30	2 肥公绵羊和 1 公绵羊为新月的祭祀	阿皮里亚	舒勒吉乌图伊吉穆	乌鲁克	CST047
Š 39 x/27	2 肥公绵羊和 1 公绵羊为新月初祭	阿皮里亚		乌鲁克	MVN 05 093
Š 40 ix/30	2 肥公绵羊和 1 公绵羊为新月初祭	阿皮里亚	马顺	乌鲁克	AnOr 07 065

续表

时间	文献内容	支出官员	督办/经由	地点	文献出处
Š 40 x/28	1 肥公绵羊、2 公山羊为新月祭	阿皮里亚	埃阿巴尼	乌鲁克	AnOr 07 066
Š 41 i/30	3 公绵羊和 3 公牛为新月祭	阿皮里亚	阿皮里亚	乌鲁克	TRU 274
Š 43 i/29	2 肥公绵羊和 1 母绵羊为新月初祭	阿皮拉吞		乌鲁克	OIP 115082
Š 46 x/30	2 只公绵羊为新月祭	乌尔卢旮勒埃丁卡		乌鲁克	PDT 1 414
Š 46 xii/30	1 母绵羊和 1 雌崽为新月祭	乌尔卢旮勒埃丁卡		乌鲁克	SumRecDreh.10
Š 47 v/30	1 肥公绵羊和 1 只羔为新月祭	舒勒吉伊里	伊皮辛	乌鲁克	OrAnt 11273 2

（二）在尼普尔举行的初七上弦月的祭祀

苏美尔太阴历中，初七时，月亮从月牙变为半圆（上弦），所以苏美尔人此时也要对月相进行祭祀。贡牲机构为初七上弦月祭祀支出牺牲是在 4 日、5 日或 7 日举行，地点通常是在尼普尔。在 4 日或 5 日是在上弦月出现之前为其祭祀支出牺牲，而 7 日是在上弦月出现当天为其祭祀支出牺牲。

贡牲机构为初七上弦月祭祀支出牺牲的文件共有 8 个。其中 4 个文件的祭祀项目较多，属于多项大型祭祀。舒勒吉 37 年 5 月、舒勒吉 41 年 2 月 4 日和舒勒吉 43 年 10 月 4 日和 5 日祭祀初七上弦月的文件中，同时祭祀的神明或神庙有：阿拉吞、阿拉古拉、宁里勒（神庙）、恩里勒（神庙）、宁旮吉亚神。文件中为阿拉吞和阿拉古拉支出的牺牲分别为 1 只育肥公绵羊；为宁里勒（神庙）、恩里勒（神庙）支出的牺牲为 1 只育肥公绵羊和 1 只公山羊崽/1 只公绵羊羔；为宁旮吉亚支出的牺牲为 1 只（育肥）公绵羊。舒勒吉 46 年 10 月 7 日的文件中，祭祀初七上弦月的文件中，还同时祭祀了南那神和圣殿：为南那神支出的牺牲为 1 只育肥公绵羊；为圣殿支出的牺牲为 1 头育肥公牛和 2 只育肥公绵羊。

王后贡牲机构为祭祀初七上弦月支出牺牲一览表

时间	文献内容	支出官员	督办/经由	地点	文献出处
Š36 iii	1 公崽为阿拉古拉庙，1 羔为宁埃旮勒庙，1 崽为恩里勒庙，为初七上弦月祭	庙总管	我的王后	尼普尔	ASJ 09 316 06

续表

时间	文献内容	支出官员	督办/经由	地点	文献出处
Š 37 v	1肥羊为阿拉吞女神祭祀，1肥羊和1崽为阿拉古拉女神，1肥羊和1羔为宁里勒神庙，1肥羊和1崽为恩里勒神庙，1肥公羊为宁旮吉亚，为**初七上弦月**	贝里沓卜	无	**尼普尔**	CST044
Š 41 ii/4	1肥羊为阿拉吞祭，阿拉古拉同，1肥羊和1羔为宁里勒，恩里勒同，1羊为宁旮吉亚，为**初七上弦月**	阿皮里亚	我的王后	**尼普尔**	AnOr 07 068
Š 41 ii/［5］	【1+公绵羊】为**初七上弦月祭**	阿皮里亚		**尼普尔**	DoCu EPHE 293
Š 41 iv/5	1幼鸭和5野鸽为神庙的**初七上弦月祭**	阿皮里亚	我的王后	**尼普尔**	SACT 1 133
Š 43 x/4，5	1肥羊为阿拉吞；2肥羊和1羔为宁里勒，1肥羊和1崽为恩里勒，1肥羊为阿拉古拉，1羊为宁旮吉亚，为**初七上弦月祭**	阿皮拉吞		**尼普尔**	AnOr 07 071
Š 46 x/7	1肥羊为南那的月供，1肥牛和2肥羊为圣殿月供，1肥羊为月供，为【初七上弦月?】	乌尔卢旮勒埃丁卡	我的王后	【尼普尔】?	OIP 115 105
Š46 xi/7	1肥羊为宁里勒，宁胡尔萨格同上，为**初七上弦月**	舒卢旮勒埃丁		**尼普尔**	（Babyl 7 pl 19 04

（三）在乌鲁克举行的望月祭

望月，俗称满月，它是月亮运行到第15天时呈现在天空的现象。贡牲机构为满月祭祀支出牺牲的时间是在24日（提前一天）或25日（祭祀当天），祭祀地点通常是在乌鲁克，但有2个文件（SAT 2 0153，OrSP 18 pl.06 21）记录了对满月的祭祀是在尼普尔，王后档案中共有12个为满月祭祀支出牺牲的文件。其中舒勒吉35年9月和舒勒吉36年4月的两个文件中为新月和满月祭同时支出牺牲，分别为1只公绵羊。在舒勒吉42年3月14日和舒勒吉45年2月的文件中，贡牲机构祭祀满月的同时，还祭祀的神明有阿拉古拉、宁里勒和恩里勒。为阿拉古拉祭祀提供牺牲为

1只育肥公绵羊、为宁里勒和恩里勒提供牺牲一次是2只育肥公绵羊和1只公绵羊羔，另一次是1只育肥公绵羊。

王后贡牲机构为祭祀满月支出牺牲一览表

时间	文献内容	支出官员	督办/经由	地点	文献出处
Š 35 ix	1公绵羊为新月初祭，1公绵羊为满月祭，1公绵羊为新月祭（第2次）	贝里沓卜	伊皮克埃腊	乌鲁克	SET 041
Š 36 iv	1公绵羊为新月祭 1公绵羊为满月祭	庙总管	伊皮克埃腊 阿皮里亚	乌鲁克	AnOr 7 59
Š 36 x	1肥公羊和1羔为阿拉古拉庙，1肥公羊和1羔为宁里勒庙，恩里勒同上，1公羊为宁旮吉亚庙，为满月牺牲	贝里沓卜	我的王后	尼普尔	SAT 2 0153
Š 42 iii/14	1肥羊为阿拉古拉，2肥和1羔为宁里勒，恩里勒同上，1公羊和3公山羊为满月祭	阿皮拉吞	无	尼普尔	OrSP 18 pl.06 21
Š 42 x/14	1肥羊、1肥公山羊和1母绵羊为满月祭	阿皮拉吞		乌鲁克	TRU 284
Š 44 xi	1肥公绵羊为那那亚，为满月祭	卡兰希那吉	舒哈马提	乌鲁克	Rochester 013
Š 45 ii	1肥羊为宁里勒，恩里勒同为满月祭	卡兰希那吉	阿亚南那阿尔卡拉		PDT 1 370
Š 45 vii/15	2只肥公绵羊为满月祭	乌尔卢旮勒埃丁卡	伊皮克埃腊	乌鲁克	AnOr 07 072
Š 45 viii/15	2肥公羊和1羊为满月祭	乌尔卢旮勒埃丁卡	伊皮克埃腊	乌鲁克	MVN 13 715
Š 47 iv/14	1羔为满月祭	乌尔卢旮勒埃丁卡	阿腊德朱尼		CST 170
Š 47 vii/15	1公崽为满月祭	舒勒吉伊里	努尔辛	乌鲁克	OIP 115 122

四　消失处供奉（níĝ~ ki-zàh）

消失处供奉可能是王后贡牲机构对在冥界消失的女神的供奉。贡牲机构档案中，“两女神”于7月、9月和10月的消失处供奉有6个文件、贝拉特苏赫尼尔于10月的消失处供奉有1个文件、那那亚女神于1月和5月的消失处供奉有5个文件、阿达德神1月、7月和9月的消失处供奉有3个文件。

王后贡牲机构为消失处供奉提供牺牲的数量和种类一览表

时间	文献内容	时间	文献内容
Š 34 iii	2肥公羊为两女神的消失处供奉	Š 42 x	2羔为贝拉特苏赫尼尔庙消失处
Š 34 ix	1公羊为阿达德庙的消失处供奉	Š 45 vii/10，15	1公羊为阿达德消失处供奉，1肥公
Š 35 iv	2只肥公羊为两女神庙的消失处		羊和1母羊为两女神消失处供奉
Š 35 vi	2只公崽为两女神的消失处牺牲	Š 45 viii/25	1公羊和1羔为两女神消失处供奉
Š 37 v	1只羔为那那亚消失处牺牲	Š 46 v/20	1只羔为那那亚的消失处供奉
Š 37 v	1只羔为那那亚消失处牺牲	Š 47 x/19	2公羊为两女神的消失处供奉
Š 37 vi	1羔为那那亚庙消失处牺牲	Š 47 xi/7	1只羔为那那亚消失处的供奉
Š 41 i	1只【食草】公羊为阿达德消失处供奉		

五　晨牲（siskúr～Á～gú-zi-ga）和黄昏牲（siskúr～Á-<ud>-ten-na）

贡牲机构档案中还记录了一些特殊的祭祀文件，即一天中进行两次祭祀的文件。一天中先进行的是黄昏祭，然后是晨祭。黄昏祭的对象有：宁里勒、恩里勒、宁旮吉亚、阿拉古拉、那那亚及祭祀寝宫；晨祭的神明有：宁里勒、恩里勒、伊南那、宁乌尔塔、努斯库、那那亚、圣殿门和祭祀寝宫。

时间	文献内容	文献出处
Š 29 xi	2肥公羊为贝拉特苏赫尼尔庙的晨牺牲	DoCu EPHE 306
Š 30 x/4	1只肥公羊为黄昏牺牲，1只肥公羊为晨牺牲	OIP 115020
Š 40 xi/18	1肥公羊和2羔为宁里勒，恩里勒同上，1母绵羊为宁旮吉亚，1公羊为阿拉古拉，以上于黄昏时；1肥公羊和1羊为宁里勒，1公崽为恩里勒，1肥公羊为伊南那，1肥公羊为宁乌尔塔，1肥公羊为努斯库，为晨时	SumRecDreh.05
Š 47 i/7	1只羔于黄昏时，1只育肥公绵羊为月供，于晨时，为祭司寝宫	Torino 1 191
Š 47 i/8	1只羔于黄昏时，1只育肥公绵羊于晨时，为祭司寝宫	Orient 16 042 11
Š 47 vi/21	1羔为黄昏	AnOr 07 083
Š 47 vii/24	8野鸽为晨牺牲（月供），1母猪、1鸭、9鸽为黄昏牺牲（月供）	OIP 115 124

六　王后贡牲机构对天神之船和大门楼的祭祀

贡牲机构中祭祀的其他对象还有：（1）对大门楼（dub-lá-mah）的祭祀，贡牲机构档案中共计有3个文件（RA 19 192 04、AnOr 07 073、MVN 2，336）；（2）对天神安之船（má-An-na）的祭祀。对天神安之船的祭祀主要是于月末在乌鲁克城举行。

王后贡牲机构为祭祀天神安之船提供牺牲的数量和种类一览表

时间	文献内容	地点	文献出处
Š 33 vii	1头育肥公牛为天神安之船的祭祀	乌鲁克	Torino 1 204
Š 34 vi	1肥公牛为天神安之船	乌鲁克	Hirose 012
Š 34 x	1肥公牛和2只公山羊为天神安之船	乌鲁克	PDT 1 459
Š 35 xi	2肥雌山羊崽为天神安之船		CST043
Š 36 x	1头育肥公牛和2只食草公绵羊为天神安之船	乌鲁克	OIP 115030
Š 37 vi	1肥牛、3肥公羊和1公羊为安神之船	乌鲁克	AnOr 07 062
Š 40 xi/25	1公牛和3肥公羊为天神安之船	乌鲁克	OIP 115062
Š 41 vii/26	【1+】肥【公羊】和【1+】肥【羔】为【安神之船】，3肥公羊和3肥羔为安神之船	乌鲁克	TRU 275
Š 42 vi/24	1雄豚、2鸭、3家鸽和14野鸽为安神之船		ArOr 25 562 23
Š 46 vi/25	1肥公牛和3肥公羊为安神之船	乌鲁克	Torino 1 189

七　王后贡牲机构举行祭祀活动的地点分析

王后贡牲机构举行祭祀活动的地点一般是在宗教中心尼普尔、首都乌尔、乌鲁克以及图马勒庙区。祭祀时，通常是先由督办官员/经由官员向贡牲机构的负责官员传达王后的命令，负责官员据此支出牺牲，再由督办官员/经由官员将牺牲带到祭祀地点。督办官员一般由御膳房或厨房的厨师、负责外交事务的使官或国务卿、负责祭祀活动的司仪或祭司担任。有时，在同一个文件中可能会同时出现几个督办官员，这是因为文件中除了为祭祀活动提供牺牲外，还包括为王室成员、地方总督或御膳房提供牲畜。支出动物牲畜的目的不同，所以督办官员也相应的不同。

（一）王后在尼普尔城为阿拉吞女神夫妇和恩里勒家族支出牺牲

王后贡牲机构档案中记录于尼普尔举行祭祀活动的文件共计17件。

其中有 9 个文件记录了于尼普尔举行的由王后主持的初七上弦月和满月的祭祀活动、2 个文件是关于毁坏祭（a-igi-nigín-na）和哀悼祭（ér-sù-a）的内容和 6 个文件是关于直接对神明或神庙进行祭祀的内容。

9 个记录月相祭祀活动的文件中，7 个文件是初七月相节，2 个文件是满月节。在王后主持的特殊月相祭祀活动中，牺牲献给阿拉古拉庙或阿拉吞夫妇、宁里勒庙和恩里勒庙或神王夫妇和其女宁旮吉阿。贡牲机构为这些神庙或神明提供牺牲的情况通常是：（1）为恩里勒和宁里勒的祭祀提供牺牲为 1 只肥羊牲加 1 只公山羊崽或 1 只公绵羊羔；（2）阿拉古拉神或其神庙祭祀提供的牺牲为 1 只公山羊崽，但有时也会是 1 只肥羊牲加 1 只公绵羊羔；（3）为阿拉吞女神提供 1 只肥牲；（4）为宁埃旮勒祭祀提供牺牲为 1 只公绵羊羔；（5）为宁旮吉亚或其庙提供 1 只公山羊；（6）为宁胡尔萨格祭祀提供 1 只肥牲。

贡牲机构在尼普尔举行的哀悼祭（ér-sù-a）为两次。一次是于舒勒吉 40 年 xi/18 日举行（SumRecDreh.05）；另一次哀悼祭是在舒勒吉 45 年 xii/20-22 日举行（OIP 115 099）。

除了以上两项在尼普尔举行的祭祀活动外，贡牲档案中，还记录有在尼普尔直接对神明或神庙祭祀的文件。直接祭祀的神明有：宁里勒、恩里勒、伊南那、阿达德、两女神、宁胡尔萨格、宁旮吉亚、阿拉吞、阿拉古拉、宁乌尔塔和努斯库。贡牲机构为其提供牺牲的情况是：通常为宁里勒和恩里勒提供 1 只育肥牲加 1 只公山羊崽或 1 只公绵羊羔，偶尔也会只有 1 只公山羊崽或 1 只公绵羊羔的情况；为其他神提供 1 只育肥牲或 1 只公山羊崽或 1 只公绵羊羔。

值得注意的是，在尼普尔举行的祭祀活动中，宁里勒女神通常被写于恩里勒神之前，可能是因为王后贡牲机构重视对女神的祭祀。

王后贡牲机构档案中的尼普尔城的祭祀活动一览表

时间	文件内容	经由官员	地点
Š 36 iii	1 崽为阿拉古拉庙，1 羔为宁埃旮勒庙，1 崽恩里勒庙，为**初七上弦月祭**	我的王后	尼普尔
Š 36 x	1 肥公羊和 1 羔为阿拉古拉庙，1 肥公羊和 1 羔为宁里勒庙，恩里勒同上，1 公羊为宁旮吉亚庙，为**满月牺牲**	我的王后	尼普尔

续表

时间	文件内容	经由官员	地点
Š 37 i	1 肥公羊为伊南那神庙，2 肥公羊、1 公羊和 1 羔为阿拉古拉神庙，2 肥公牛、2 肥公羊和 1 羔为宁里勒神庙，2 肥公羊和 1 羔为恩里勒神庙，1 公羊为神王像，1 肥公羊和 2 公崽为宁旮吉亚神庙	我的王后	尼普尔
Š 37 v	1 肥羊为阿拉吞女神祭祀，1 肥羊和 1 崽为阿拉古拉女神，1 肥羊和 1 羔宁里勒神庙，1 肥羊和 1 崽恩里勒神庙，1 肥羊宁旮吉亚，为**初七上弦月**		尼普尔
Š 38 xi	1 肥公羊为阿拉古拉庙		尼普尔
Š 40 xi/18	1 肥公羊和 2 羔为宁里勒，恩里勒同上，1 母绵羊为宁旮吉亚，1 公羊为阿拉古拉，于**黄昏时** 1 肥公羊和 1 羔为宁里勒，1 公崽为恩里勒，1 肥公羊为南那，1 肥绵羊为伊南那，1 肥公羊为宁乌尔塔，1 肥公羊为努斯库，于**黎明时**，以上为**哀悼祭**	我的王后	尼普尔
Š 41 ii/4	1 肥羊为阿拉吞祭，阿拉古拉同，1 肥公羊和 1 羔为宁里勒，1 和 1 公崽为恩里勒，1 羊为宁旮吉阿，为**初七上弦月**	我的王后	尼普尔
Š 41 ii/［5?］	【1+公羊】为**初七上弦月祭**		尼普尔
Š 41 iv/5	1 幼鸭和 5 野鸽为神庙的**初七上弦月祭**	我的王后	尼普尔
Š 42 iii/14	1 肥公羊为阿拉古拉，2 肥和 1 羔为宁里勒，恩里勒同上，1 公羊和 3 公山羊为**满月祭**		尼普尔
Š 43 x/4，5	1 肥公羊为阿拉吞；2 肥公羊和 1 羔为宁里勒，1 肥公羊和 1 公崽为恩里勒，1 肥公羊为阿拉古拉，1 公羊为宁旮吉阿，为**初七上弦月祭**		尼普尔
Š 45 xii /20-22	1 羔为伊南那，1 公崽为宁乌尔塔，1 公崽为努斯库，1 肥公羊和 1 羊羔为恩里勒，1 肥公羊为宁里勒；1 羔为恩里勒，1【肥公羊】为宁里勒月供，1 公羊为宁胡尔萨格，为**哀悼祭祀**		尼普尔
Š 46 xi/7	1 肥公羊为恩里勒月供，1 肥公羊为宁里勒，1 肥公羊为宁胡尔萨格，为**初七上弦月祭**		尼普尔
Š 46 xi/8-9	1 肥公羊为月供，1 羔为伊南那，1 公羊和 1 公崽为宁乌尔塔，1 公崽为努斯库，1 肥公羊和 1 羔为恩里勒，1 肥公羊为月供，1 只公崽为宁里勒	我的王后	尼普尔
Š 46 xi/15	1 公羊为两女神，1 公羊为阿达德的牺牲，1 肥公羊和 1 羔为宁里勒，1 公崽为恩里勒	我的王后	尼普尔
Š 46 xii/30	1 羔为伊南那，宁里勒、恩里勒同上（第 1 次）；1 羔为伊南那，宁里勒同（第 2 次）；1 肥公羊为伊南那的牺牲（第 3 次）		尼普尔
Š 47 ix/10	1 公山羊为伊南那		尼普尔

（二）王后贡牲机构档案中的乌鲁克城的祭祀活动

乌鲁克城是乌尔第三王朝的第三大城市，同时也是伊南那女神保护的城市。王后贡牲机构中记录在乌鲁克举行祭祀的文件共计 54 个。其具体情况为：

（1）对于乌鲁克月相的祭祀共计 21 个文件；

（2）对于乌鲁克的天神安之船的祭祀共计 8 个文件；

（3）直接为乌鲁克提供牺牲的文件共计 6 个。贡牲机构为乌鲁克提供牺牲，应该是为乌鲁克的保护神伊南那的祭祀提供牺牲，贡牲档案中可能是省略了伊南那的名字。贡牲机构为乌鲁克直接提供的牺牲通常是 2 只育肥公绵羊，或 1 只育肥公绵羊和 1 只育肥公山羊，或 1 只育肥公绵羊和 1 只公山羊崽。

（4）直接为神明（庙）或其他提供牺牲的文件共计 19 个。贡牲机构在乌鲁克直接祭祀的神明有：伊南那、那那亚、阿拉吞、伊什哈腊、贝拉特那喀尔和两女神，此外，还对乌鲁克的圣殿（门）、祭司寝宫等进行祭祀。贡牲机构为伊南那提供牺牲的情况一般是 1 只育肥公绵羊，但偶尔是 1 头公牛或 1 只普通的公绵羊；为那那亚女神提供牺牲通常是 1 只公绵羊羔，少数情况是 1 只育肥公绵羊或 1 只公山羊崽；为阿拉吞提供牺牲为 1 只育肥公绵羊；为伊什哈腊和贝拉特那喀尔神庙提供牺牲共计 2 只育肥公绵羊；为两女神提供牺牲是 2 只育肥公绵羊；为圣殿（门）提供牺牲通常是 1 只育肥公绵羊，但也有提供 1 头育肥公牛，1 只公绵羊羔，2 只育肥公绵羊和 1 只公绵羊羔的情况；为祭司寝宫提供牺牲为 1 只育肥公绵羊，但也有 1 只公山羊崽，或 1 只公绵羊羔，或 1 头育肥公牛的情况。

在乌鲁克的祭祀活动中，对于圣殿、那那亚女神和祭司寝宫的祭祀总是三者一起进行或是其中的两者一起进行（详情见下表加黑部分）。

王后贡牲机构档案中的乌鲁克城的祭祀活动一览表

时间	文献内容	支出官员	督办/经由	地点
Š 32 xii/20	1 公牛为伊南那	伊提伊什塔尔	阿皮里亚	乌鲁克
Š 33 vii	1 头肥公牛为天神安之船的祭祀	贝里沓卜	乌尔杜穆兹	乌鲁克
Š 33 ix	2 肥公羊为乌鲁克	阿席马	乌尔杜穆孜达	乌鲁克
Š 34 vi	1 头肥公牛为天神安之船	贝里沓卜	巴尔巴尔瑞	乌鲁克
Š 34 x	1 头肥公牛和 2 公山羊为天神安之船	贝里沓卜		乌鲁克
Š 35 iv	2 只肥公羊为乌鲁克	阿希马	马顺	乌鲁克

续表

时间	文献内容	支出官员	督办/经由	地点
Š 35 viii	2 肥公羊到乌鲁克	阿希马	乌尔杜穆孜达	乌鲁克
Š 35 ix	1 公羊为新月初祭，1 公羊为满月祭	贝里沓卜	伊皮克埃腊	乌鲁克
Š 35 x	1 羔为圣殿，1 公崽为那那亚，祭司寝宫同上	（贝里沓卜）	我的王后	乌鲁克
Š 35 xi	1 肥公牛为圣殿，1 公羊为祭司寝宫	贝里沓卜	我的王后	乌鲁克
Š 36 i	1 肥羊为伊南那于城墙的吉腊努姆仪式的月供；阿拉吞神庙同上，2 肥公羊为伊什哈腊和贝拉特那喀尔的神庙，新月牺牲同上	贝里沓卜		乌鲁克
Š 36 ii	1 肥公牛为祭司寝宫口月供，圣殿口月供同上	贝里沓卜		乌鲁克
Š 36 iv	1 公羊为新月祭 1 公羊为满月祭	庙总管	伊皮克埃腊 阿皮里亚	乌鲁克
Š 36 x	1 肥牛和 2 羊为天船，1 肥羊为黑夜圣殿月供应，1 公羊和 1 只公崽为那那亚庙，1 公羊为新月祭	贝里沓卜	贝里巴尼	乌鲁克
Š 37 v	1 肥羊为月供，伊南那的吉腊努姆仪式同上，2 肥羊为两女神牺牲，2 肥羊和 1 羊为满月牺牲 2 肥羊和 1 羔为圣殿门，1 羔为那那亚消失处，1 崽为围绕城市哭泣仪式，1 崽为举起围攻城市的武器时，1 肥羊为祭司寝宫，1 肥羊和 1 羔为那那亚	贝里沓卜	贝里巴尼 我的王后	乌鲁克
Š 37 v	1 公崽为宁伊吉兹巴腊庙	贝里沓卜	乌尔杜穆兹达	乌鲁克
Š 37 vi	1 肥牛、3 肥公羊和 1 公羊为安神的船，1 肥公羊为那那亚庙，1 肥公羊为黑夜圣殿，1 羔为那那亚庙消失处牺牲，2 公羊和 1 公崽为新月祭	贝里沓卜	阿皮拉提	乌鲁克
Š 39 vi/30	2 肥公羊和 1 公羊为新月的祭祀	阿皮里亚	舒勒吉乌图伊吉穆	乌鲁克
Š 39 x/27	2 肥公羊和 1 公羊为新月初祭	阿皮里亚		乌鲁克
Š 40 ix/30	2 肥公羊和 1 公羊为新月祭月初	阿皮里亚	马顺	乌鲁克
Š 40 x/28	1 肥公羊、2 公山羊为新月祭	阿皮里亚	埃阿巴尼	乌鲁克
Š 40 xi/25	1 牛和 3 肥羊为安神之船，1 肥羊为黑夜圣殿，1 羊为那那亚	阿皮里亚	伊皮克埃腊	乌鲁克
Š 41 i/15	2 只肥公羊和 1 只食草【公羊】为满月牺牲	阿皮里亚	伊皮克埃腊	乌鲁克
Š 41 i/30	3 公羊和 3 公牛为新月祭	阿皮里亚	阿皮里亚	乌鲁克
Š 41 vii/26	【1+】肥【羊】和【1+】肥【羔】为【安神船】，【1+】肥公羊为那那亚庙，1 公羊为黑夜圣殿	阿皮里亚	阿皮里亚	乌鲁克

续表

时间	文献内容	支出官员	督办/经由	地点
Š 42 ii/30	1 肥公羊和 1 公崽为乌鲁克的祭祀		马顺	乌鲁克
Š 42 iii/14	2 肥公羊和 1 公山羊为于乌鲁克的祭祀	阿皮拉吞	阿皮里亚	乌鲁克
Š 42 viii/30	1 肥公羊和 1 只肥公山羊为乌鲁克	阿皮拉吞		乌鲁克
Š 42 x/14	1 肥公羊、1 肥公山羊和 1 只母绵羊为满月祭	阿皮拉吞		乌鲁克
Š 43 i/29	2 肥公羊和 1 母绵羊为新月初祭	阿皮拉吞		乌鲁克
Š 44 xi	1 肥羊为圣殿，1 肥羊为祭司寝宫门，1 羊为那那亚	卡兰希那吉	舒哈马提	乌鲁克
Š 45 vii/15	2 只肥公羊为满月祭	乌尔卢旮勒埃丁卡	伊皮克埃腊	乌鲁克
Š 45 viii/15	2 肥公羊和 1 公羊为满月祭	乌尔卢旮勒埃丁卡	伊皮克埃腊	乌鲁克
Š 46 iii /26–29	1 肥羊为【……】吉腊努姆仪式，1 肥羊为宫殿中的伊南那，1 肥公羊为月供，2 羊为新月牲	乌尔卢旮勒埃邓卡	乌尔杜穆兹达	乌鲁克
Š 46 v/20	1 羔为那那亚的消失处供奉	乌尔卢旮勒埃丁卡		乌鲁克
Š 46 vi/25	1 肥牛和 3 肥羊为安神船，1 羊为黑夜圣殿，那那亚同上	乌尔卢旮勒埃丁卡	努尔辛	乌鲁克
Š 46 x/7	1 肥羊为南那的月供，1 肥牛和 2 肥羊为圣殿月供，1 肥公羊为月供，以上为【初七上弦月】	乌尔卢旮勒埃丁卡	我的王后	乌鲁克
Š 46 x/30	2 只公羊为新月祭	乌尔卢旮勒埃丁卡		乌鲁克
Š 46 xii/30	1 母绵羊和 1 雌崽为新月祭	乌尔卢旮勒埃丁卡		乌鲁克
Š 47 i/1	1 羔为圣殿门，那那亚同，月供 2 肥羊，3 羔为祭司寝宫	乌尔卢旮勒埃丁卡		乌鲁克
Š 47 i/28	1 肥羔、1 雌崽和 1 雌羔为祭司寝宫，1 公崽为竖琴，1 公崽为舒如帕克	乌尔卢旮勒埃丁卡		乌鲁克
Š 47 i/30	1 崽为牺牲，祭司寝宫的消失处牺牲同上，1 崽为那那亚消失处，于黄昏时，1 肥羊和 1 崽为圣殿门，1 肥羊为祭司寝宫，1 羊为那那亚，于晨时	乌尔卢旮勒埃丁卡		乌鲁克
Š 47 i	1 只羔为祭司寝宫	乌尔卢旮勒埃丁卡		乌鲁克
Š 47 ii/14	1 只肥公羊为祭司寝宫的月供	乌尔卢旮勒埃丁卡		乌鲁克

续表

时间	文献内容	支出官员	督办/经由	地点
Š 47 iii/7	1+肥公羊为月供，1 羔为圣殿门，1 只肥公羊为祭司寝宫的月供，1 只羔为那那亚	乌尔卢旮勒埃丁卡		乌鲁克
Š 47 v	1 公崽为祭司寝宫	舒勒吉伊里	马顺	乌鲁克
Š 47 v/30	1 肥羊为月供，1 肥羊和 1 羔为新月牺牲	舒勒吉伊里	伊比辛	乌鲁克
Š 47 vii/15	1 公崽为满月祭	舒勒吉伊里	努尔辛	乌鲁克
Š 47ix/9，10	1 公羊为伊南那	卡兰希那吉	阿亚南那尔拉	乌鲁克
Š 47 x/15	1 肥羊为圣殿门，1 肥羊为祭司寝宫月供，1 羊为那那亚	勒吉伊里		乌鲁克
Š 47 x	【1+】肥公羊为圣殿，祭司寝宫同上，1 公羊为那那亚	卡兰希那吉	阿胡瓦喀尔	乌鲁克
Š 47 xi/7	【1+】羊为阿达德，宫殿中的圣桌同上，1 肥羊为月供，1 羔为祭司寝宫，1 肥羊和 2 羔为那那亚，1 肥牛、2 肥羊和 1 羔为圣殿门	舒勒吉伊里	我的王后	乌鲁克

（三）王后贡牲机构档案中的乌尔城的祭祀活动

与在尼普尔和乌鲁克举行的祭祀活动不同的是，乌尔城的祭祀活动的对象主要以两女神、安努尼吞女神和乌勒马席吞女神为主，但偶尔也会祭祀伊南那女神、那那亚女神、阿拉吞女神和阿达德神等。贡牲档案中，为两女神在乌尔城的祭祀提供牺牲的文件共计 19 个、为安努尼吞和乌勒马席吞女神提供牺牲的文件共 9 个，有时对于两女神和安努尼吞、乌勒马席吞女神的祭祀会记录在同一文件中（该类文件共有 6 个）；为伊南那女神、那那亚女神、阿拉吞女神、阿达德和南那神的祭祀提供牺牲的文件共计 10 个。

王后贡牲机构档案中的乌尔城的祭祀活动一览表（共 38 个文件）

时间	祭祀内容	支出官员	经由/督办官	地点
Š 33 v	【1+】肥公羊为贝拉特苏赫尼尔，【1+】肥公羊为贝拉特达腊班，【1+】肥公牛为那那亚于宫殿的倒啤酒宴会	贝里沓卜		乌尔
Š 33 vi	1 肥公羊为南那的牺牲	贝里沓卜		乌尔
Š 33 vi	1 肥公羊为大门楼	贝里沓卜		乌尔
Š 35i	2 公崽为贝拉特苏赫尼尔庙的吉腊努姆仪式	庙总管	乌尔杜姆兹达	乌尔

续表

时间	祭祀内容	支出官员	经由/督办官	地点
Š 35 v	1+【公羊?】为两女神	阿希马	乌尔杜穆孜达	乌尔
Š 35 vi	2 公崽为两女神消失处牺牲	贝里沓卜		乌尔
Š 35 x	2 公羊为两女神庙的吉腊努姆仪式		马顺督办	乌尔
Š 36 i	1 肥公羊为沙特伊勒廷的神庙	贝里沓卜		乌尔
Š 36 ix	1 肥羊为伊南那于城墙的吉腊努姆仪式月供，1 肥羊为阿拉吞，2 公羊为伊什哈腊和贝拉特那旮尔庙，1 公羊为乌勒马席吞庙，1 肥羊为安努尼吞，1 肥羊为阿达德庙的消失处月供 2 肥公羊为月供，1 羔为乌勒马席吞庙，2 肥羊和 1 羔为安努尼吞，1 公羊为伊什哈腊，1 公羊和 1 羔为阿拉吞，1 肥母牛、1 肥公羊、2 公羊和 1 羔为晨祭，1 公崽为众神的牺牲，1 羔为消失处、1 肥羊和 1 公崽为那那亚的倒啤酒宴会		卢乌如卜	乌尔
Š 37 ii	5 肥羊为祭祀的月供，2 公崽为消失处，以上为两女神庙之塞尔塞闰节	贝里沓卜	贝里巴尼	乌尔
Š 37 v	1 崽为那那亚，1 公羊为乌勒马什庙	贝里沓卜		乌尔
Š 37 v	2 公崽为贝拉特苏赫尼尔庙的吉腊努姆仪式 2 肥公羊、2 公羊、2 公崽为贝拉特苏赫尼尔庙 1 肥公牛、3 肥公羊、6 只公羊和 1 只公崽为美埃阿的供奉	贝里沓卜	阿皮里亚 我的王后	乌尔
Š 37 vi	2 只公崽为两女神庙的消失处	贝里沓卜	贝里巴尼	乌尔
Š 40 iii/1	1 羊为安神的食物，2 肥羊和 2 羊为两女神的塞尔塞闰节，1 肥羊为乌勒马席吞，1 肥牛和 3 肥羊为安努尼吞的进入节	阿皮里亚	贝里巴尼	乌尔
Š 41/30	3 羊和 1 公山羊为两女神庙的埃鲁努姆节，1 牛、3 肥羊和 1 公羊为安努尼吞和乌勒马席吞进入她们的庙的庆典	阿皮里亚	伊皮克埃腊	乌尔
Š 41 i	1 公羊为阿达德消失处 1 只食草公羊为阿拉吞的祭祀	阿皮里亚	马顺 阿皮里亚	乌尔
Š 41 ii/20	2 肥公羊为安努尼吞，1 羊为乌勒马西吞，2 羊为两女神的埃鲁努姆节	阿皮里亚	马顺	乌尔
Š 41 vi	2 肥公羊为安努尼吞，1 公羊为乌勒马席吞		卢乌如卜	乌尔
Š 42 viii/20	1 肥公牛和 2+肥公羊为安努尼吞，1 公山羊为宁廷【乌旮】	阿皮拉吞	舒勒吉伊里	乌尔

续表

时间	祭祀内容	支出官员	经由/督办官	地点
Š 45 viii/25	1公牛和3肥公羊为安努尼吞，1公羊为乌勒马西吞于那卜润节时，1公羊和1羔为两女神消失处祭	乌尔卢旮勒埃丁卡	伊皮克埃腊	乌尔
Š 45 x/13	1肥牛、4肥羊和1羔为大门楼，1羊为女官院的阿拉女神，1公羊和1羔为宁荪，1公羊为供奉，2羊为伊什塔尔 2羔为两女神的耐耐旮尔节	乌尔卢旮勒埃丁卡	我的王后 马顺	乌尔
Š 46 v/21	1公崽为阿达德 2公崽为两女神 2肥羊、2羊、1羔和1崽为两女神，1崽为神判河神		舒勒吉伊里 努尔辛 我的王后	乌尔
Š 46 viii	1牛和2肥羊为月供，2羊为安努尼吞那卜润节		乌尔杜穆兹达	乌尔
Š 46 ix/5	1羊为安，2羊为消失处供奉，2牛、4肥羊和2崽为两女神的那卜润节，1肥羊和1羔为阿拉吞，2为伊什哈腊和贝拉特那古，1羔为安努尼吞，1崽为那那亚	乌尔卢旮勒埃丁卡		乌尔
Š 46 x/30	2公崽为两女神	乌尔卢旮勒埃丁卡	乌尔杜穆孜达	乌尔
Š 46 xii/30	4雌崽为两女神	乌尔卢旮勒埃丁卡	伊皮克埃腊	乌尔
Š 47 v	2食草公羊为两女神，1公崽为阿达德	舒勒吉伊里	贝里巴尼	乌尔
Š 47 vi/19，21	1肥羊为南那的月供，4肥羊、2崽为两女神，1崽为神判河神；2羊为安努尼吞和乌勒马西吞的吉腊努姆仪式，1崽为供奉中的神，1肥牛、4肥羊为月供，1羔为黄昏祭祀，1肥崽为蔬菜食物，1崽为乌勒马席吞走向他的庙宇，1羊为乌勒马西吞和安努尼吞的啤酒节	舒勒吉伊里		乌尔
Š 47 vi/22	2公羊为两女神	舒勒吉伊里	马顺	乌尔
Š 47 ix	2公羊为两女神，1只食草公羊为阿达德	舒勒吉伊里	马顺	乌尔
Š 47 x/19	1肥羊为祭司寝宫，阿达德月供同，2羊两女神的消失处	舒勒吉伊里		乌尔

（四）王后贡牲机构档案中的图马勒庙区的祭祀活动

王后贡牲机构的档案中，在图马勒庙区举行祭祀活动的支出文件共计6个。为祭祀提供牺牲的神明有宁里勒、阿拉古拉、宁穆、宁马赫、两女神、安努尼吞女神、乌勒马席吞女神、那那亚、南亚、河神、伊南那、宁吉尔拉和阿达德。

王后档案中的图马勒庙区的祭祀活动

时间	文件内容	支出官员	经由/督办	地点
Š 35 vi	1 崽为宁里勒，1 羔为阿拉古拉，1 羊为宁穆，1 羊为宁马赫 2 雌崽为两女神		我的王后 贝里巴尼	图马勒
Š 36 vi	2 雌崽为安努尼吞和乌勒马西吞祭祀	贝里沓卜	马顺	图马勒
Š 37 vi	1 公崽为那那亚祭祀，1 肥公羊为南那祭祀供奉	贝里沓卜	马顺	图马勒
Š 37 vi	1 肥公羊为神判河神的月供，1 公崽为伊南那的吉腊努姆仪式，1 肥公羊为宁吉尔拉牺牲的月供	贝里沓卜	马顺	图马勒
Š 45vii/15	1 羊为阿达德消失处供奉，1 肥公羊和 1 母绵羊为两女神消失处供奉	乌尔卢旮勒埃丁卡		图马勒

第二节　王后贡牲机构为王后及高官支出畜禽的活动分析

舒勒吉新提王后贡牲机构除了主要为各种祭祀活动支出动物牺牲外，其另一项较大的支出是为王后、国王等王室成员及高官提供畜禽。为其提供畜禽的王室成员有：我的国王（舒勒吉）、王后（舒勒吉新提）、瓦特腊特（王太后）、台岑妈妈（舒勒吉或阿马尔辛之女）、埃阿尼沙（舒勒吉的 lukur 神妻）、吉美伊吉萨萨旮（舒勒吉之女）、席马特伊什塔尔（舒勒吉之女）和普朱尔伊什塔尔（舒勒吉之子）。王后贡牲机构为其支出动物牲畜的高官有：贝拉特苏赫尼尔女神的祭司、“两女神”的涂油祭祀、席穆润的总督采鲁什达干及其儿子和妹妹、骑使舒勒吉伊里、国务卿之妻等。

王后贡牲机构为王后等王室成员和高官贵族等支出的食物主要有羊、禽和猪。羊的种类和祭神的牺牲一样，但多用羊羔；鸟和禽的种类有：野鸽（ir_7/kaskal）、家鸽（tu-$gur_4^{mušen}$）、舵燕（u_5-$sim^{mušen}$）、白鸟（uz-babbar）、鸭（uz-tur）和育肥鸭（uz-tur-niga）；猪的种类有：驯养雌豚（小猪，$šáh^{zah}$-tur-munus-uru）、苇塘雌豚（$šáh^{zah}$-tur-munus-giš-gi）和苇塘雄豚（$šáh^{zah}$-tur-níta-giš-gi）。王后贡牲机构的档案中共计为王后提供食物 246 只动物，其中禽和鸟共 180 只。统计数字表明禽和豚是王后的特殊喜好。

王后贡牲机构为王后（少数王室成员）及高官贵族
支出食物的数量和种类一览表

时间	文件内容	时间	文件内容
Š 29 vi	伊皮乌尔席那德 1+肥羊，基尼阿 2 羊	Š 41 xii/25	我的王后的食物 1 只肥雌山羊崽
Š 30 v	米那塔勒医生 5 羊	Š 42 v/21	我的王后的食物 1 只鸭和 5 只野鸽
Š 33 v	**台岑妈妈** 1 肥牛、5 肥羊、5 羊	Š 42 viii/28	我的王后的食物 1 只雌豚
Š 33 ix	贝里巴尼 1 羊	Š 42 x/14	**国王**（舒勒吉）的食物 1 只肥公绵羊
Š 34 iv	布扎 2 羊	Š 42 xi/23	**席马特伊什塔尔**（舒勒吉之女）3 只豚
Š 34 iv	布扎 1 崽	Š 42 xi/29	我的王后的食物 1 只苇塘雄豚
Š 34 vi	古塔尔拉之妻 1 崽	Š 43 ii/22	我的王后的食物 4 只鸟
Š 34 x	**瓦特腊特**（舒勒吉之母）10 羊	Š 43 iii/26	我的王后的食物 1 只鸭和 5 只野鸽
Š 34 x	埃台勒普朱尔达干 5 羊	Š 43 vii	乌阿巴 1 羔
Š 35 ix	我的王后的食物 1 只羔	Š 45 vii/12	我的王后的食物 1 只野鸽
Š 35 xi	伊皮乌尔席那德 1 牛，埃什塔闰米 2 羊	Š 45 vii/18	我的王后的食物 1 只苇塘雌豚
Š 35 xi	国务卿之妻的供奉 1 牛和 5 羊	Š 45 viii/15	两女神的涂油祭司 2 羊
Š 38 viii	**埃阿尼沙**食物 1 肥崽	Š 45 ix/30	我的王后的食物 2+x 只苇塘雄豚
Š 38 viii	我的王后食物 3 肥鸭、14 肥鸽	Š 45 x/10	**国王**食物 1 肥羊、1 肥羔、1 豚、1 鸭、
Š 38 xi	我的王后的食物 1 肥公绵羊，2 羔	Š 45 x/12，15	**国王食物** 7 鸽，王后食物 1 只雌豚
Š 38 xii	贝拉特苏赫尼尔女神的祭司 2 羊	Š 45 xi/17	**国王**的食物 1 育肥雌崽
Š 39 i	我的王后的食物 1 只肥鸭和 3 肥野鸽	Š 46 ii/ 6	我的王后的食物 1 只幼鸭
Š 39 iii	我的王后的食物 1 只肥家鸽	Š 46 v/20	我的王后的食物 2 只野鸽
Š 39 iii	我的王后的食物 1 只肥羊羔	Š 46 vi/22	我的王后的食物 1 只野鸽
Š 39 iv	我的王后的食物 1 只白鸭	Š 46 viii/5	我的王后食物 2 鸭、20 野鸽和 1 雌豚
Š 39 v	我的王后的食物 2 只肥鸭和 5 肥野鸽	Š 46viii/27	采鲁什达干之妹 2 肥羊
Š 39 v/5	采鲁什达干 1 肥鸭	Š 46 viii/30	我的王后的食物 1 雌豚、1 鸭、5 鸽

续表

时间	文件内容	时间	文件内容
Š 39 vi/2	我的王后的食物 1 只鸭和 6 只野鸽	Š 46 ix/27	我的王后的食物 1 只鸭
Š 39 vi/14	我的王后的食物 1 只家鸽和 3 只野鸽	Š 46 x/28	我的王后的食物 1 只苇塘雌豚和 2 只鸭
Š 39 xi/26	我的王后的食物 2 只鸭	Š 46 xi/20	采鲁什达干之子的供奉 4 肥羊和 1 羊
Š 39 xii 27	我的王后的食物 1 只鸭和 5 只野鸽	Š 47 i/19	我的王后的食物 2 只野鸽
Š 40 iii/8	我的王后的食物 1 只鸭和 5 只野鸽	Š 47 iii/16	阿布姆 4 羊和 4 羔
Š 40 iii/27	我的王后的食物 1 只幼鸭和 3 只野鸽	Š 47 iv/7	我的王后的食物 1 只鸭和 5 只野鸽
Š 40 iv/14	我的王后的食物 1 只鸭	Š 47 iv/30	我的王后的食物 1 雌豚和 1 苇塘雄豚
Š 40 v/9	巴尼隆妻 2 肥羊	Š 47 iv/30	席马特伊什塔尔的供奉 1 雄豚
Š 40 ix/5	国王的食物 2 肥羔	Š 47 v/14	我的王后的食物 1 只雄豚和 2 只野鸽
Š 40 ix/5	伊皮克埃腊 1 羊，舒勒吉伊里 1 羊	Š 47 v/20	我的国王的食物 1 只育肥苇塘雄豚
Š 40 x/18	普朱尔伊什塔尔 1 肥羊，吉美伊吉萨萨	Š 47 v/20	台岑妈妈 1 崽和 1 鸭，沙润伊里之妻 1
	旮 2 羊		猪
Š 41 i/8	我的王后的食物 1 只鸭	Š 47 vi/7	我的王后的食物 2 只野鸽
Š 41 v/8	努伊达之妻 1 肥羊	Š 47 vi/10	我的王后的食物 2 只野鸽
Š 41 v	阿布姆 9 羊、1 崽	Š 47 vi/15	我的王后的食物 2 只鸭
Š 41 vii/26	里布尔新提 1 羊，伊什塔尔乌米 1 羊	Š 47 vi/22	国王 1 只肥羊、1 只肥羔和 1 只肥雌崽
Š 41 viii/26	我的王后的食物 1 只家鸽和 5 只野鸽	Š 47 vii/22	我的王后的食物 10 只鸭和 2 只鸟
Š 41 xii/5	我的王后的食物 1 只雌豚和 1 只鸭	Š 47 viii/8	我的王后食物 1 只雌豚、1 鸭、21 鸽
Š 41 xii/15	我的王后的食物 1 只苇塘雄豚	Š 48 i/10	国王的食物 1 只肥公绵羊和 1 只肥羔
Š 41 xii/24	我的王后的食物 2 只雄豚和 5 只野鸽	Š 48 ii/10	国王的食物 1 只吃奶羔

第三节 支出宰杀的畜、禽到厨房

王后贡牲机构中的被宰杀的畜、禽通常被支出到宫殿（ba-úš...é-gal-la ba-an- ku_4），但是一般不提具体用途。这些动物也可以译为“死牲”，它们一般是不能供奉神明和贵族们食用的质量较差的畜和禽，很可能包括因生病或老弱而被宰杀的畜禽。在贡牲机构负责官员阿皮里亚的5个支出文件中提到了宰杀牲给士兵、编织女工和漂染工，据此我们推测这些宰杀牲被送入宫殿可能主要是为宫殿的工人提供食物。

提到王后贡牲机构支出宰杀牲为士兵、女工提供食物的文件一览表

时间	文件内容	文献出处
Š 38 xi	1只羊羔肉条（ad_6）为国王的士兵，于旅途中	Ontario 1 014
Š 39 iii	1羔肉条为编织女工，1肥羔肉条为编织女工，于基什，监管者是古孜戴	CST045
Š 40 ii/22	1只宰杀的苇塘雄豚，编织女工接收了	CST050
Š 41 ii	12只宰杀的食草公绵羊和1只宰杀的羊羔为乌尔的漂洗工，苦达顺监管	OIP 115064
Š 41 x	2公牛、34绵羊、2公羔、1母山羊、1公山羊和1公崽，以上宰杀牲为编织女工的食物	OIP 115066

王后贡牲机构送入宫殿的宰杀畜禽的数量和种类一览表

时间	死牲数量和种类	时间	死牲数量和种类
Š 38 viii	2只野鸽、1只鸭、4只家鸽	Š 43 i	1只牛后级公绵羊
Š 39 iii	1只白鸭和2只野鸽	Š 43 ii	1只白鸭，1只家鸽
Š 39 iv	2只家鸽和4只野鸽，2白鸭和1只鸟	Š 43 iii	2只幼鸭、1只野鸽，1只鸭
Š 39 v	2只家鸽	Š 43 v	4只公崽、【x】和2只母绵羊
Š 39 ix	1+x只家鸽和2只野鸽	Š 45 v	1只羔和1只公崽
Š 39 xi，xii	1只白鸭，2只鸭	Š 45 vii	1只肥公羊、6只羊、1只鸭和7只野鸽
Š 39 xii	1只鸭	Š 45 viii	1头牛、3只羊、5只鸭和1只野鸽
Š 40 i	1只幼鸭	Š 45 x	2只鸭和1只家鸽，1只野鸽
Š 40 iii	2只鸭，1只幼鸭	Š 45 xi	1牛、1肥羊、3羊、2鸭、1鸽和1豚

续表

时间	死牲数量和种类	时间	死牲数量和种类
Š 40 iv	1 只家鸽，1 只白鸭 1 只野鸽	Š 45 xii	1 只公绵羊和 1 只鸭
Š 40 vi	1 只野鸽	Š 46 i	1 只鸭
Š 40 vii	1 只肥羊、10 只羊、【2+x】鸽	Š 46 v	3 只野鸽
Š 40 ix	5 只鸭、17 只家鸽和 1 只白鸟	Š 46 vi	1 只鸭、3 只家鸽和 2 只野鸽
Š 40 x	1 只食草公绵羊，1 只母绵羊	Š 46 viii	10 只鸭、43 只鸽、2 只鸭、9 只羊、2 只豚
Š 40 xi	2 只鸭、2 只鸟和 2 只家鸽	Š 46 x	1 头公牛、86 只羊、1 头肥公牛、2 只鸭
Š 40 xii	1 只公绵羊、1 只母绵羊和 1 只羔	Š 46 xi	1 只雌崽、1 只肥羊、4 只羊
Š 41 i	1 只野鸽、1 只舵燕	Š 46 xii	81 羊、2 只豚、4 只鸭、3 家鸽和 1 燕
Š 41 ii	1 只羊羔	Š 47 i	2 只野鸽
Š 41 iii	2 只公山羊崽、1 只雌羔	Š 47 ii	2 头牛、2 只肥羊、21 只羊和 1 只瞪羚
Š 41 iv	1 只幼鸭	Š 47 iv	6 只鸭、1 只肥羊
Š 41 v	2 只食草公绵羊	Š 47 v	2 只鸭、20 只野鸽
Š 41 ix	2 只鸭和 1 只家鸽、3 只羊	Š 47 vi	7 只野鸽
Š 41 x	2 头公牛、39 只羊	Š 47 vii	13 只肥公羊、20 只羊、5 只鸭
Š 41 xii	4 只雌豚、3 只鸽和 1 只雄豚	Š 47 viii	1 只公猪、2 只鸭和 21 只野鸽
Š 42 iv	2 只家鸽、1 只肥公绵羊	Š 47 ix	2 只羊、1 只雌山羊崽
Š 42 viii	1 只鸭、1 只肥公羊、3 只羊	Š 47 x	2 只鸭和 1 只驯养的母猪
Š 42 x	4 只食草公绵羊	Š 47 xi	2 肥牛、4 羊、10 鸭、2 鸽、1 猪

第四章　结语

舒勒吉新提王后贡牲机构的档案文件共计 563 件。其档案覆盖时间是从舒勒吉 28 年 1 月到舒勒吉 48 年 10 月，共 20 年 9 个月。舒勒吉新提王后贡牲机构的档案由“舒勒吉新提的送入项——接管”（mu-túm～ [d]*Šul-gi-sí-im-ti*,…，ì-dab_5）文件、“新出生——接管”（ù-tud-da,…，ì-dab_5）文件以及支出（zi-ga）文件组成。

舒勒吉新提是舒勒吉的“神妻”（lukur），也是他统治时期的王后（nin）。在贡牲机构的档案中，舒勒吉新提常被负责官员们称作“我的王后”，并作为经由官员频繁地出现在祭祀女神和神庙的支出文件中。舒勒吉新提（*Šulgi-simtī*）名字的意思是“舒勒吉是我的骄傲”。她的名字表明她来自阿卡德地区，这可能是国王舒勒吉为了团结当地的阿卡德人娶了一位当地的公主作为妻子。由于王后贡牲机构的档案结束于舒勒吉 48 年 10 月，且我们目前发现的最早祭祀舒勒吉新提王后“饮水地”（ki-a-naĝ，苏美尔祭祀祖先的地方）的文件写于阿马尔辛 1 年 3 月 28 日，而最早的祭祀国王舒勒吉的“饮水地”的文件写于舒勒吉 48 年 11 月 2 日，因此，我们推测舒勒吉新提于舒勒吉 48 年 10 月中或底消失可能是为了给舒勒吉国王陪葬。但是，通过对阿马尔辛和舒辛时期有关阿比新提的文献研究，我们认为舒勒吉新提没有给舒勒吉陪葬，而是改名为阿比新提。

舒勒吉新提王后贡牲机构的设立主要是为了方便舒勒吉新提祭祀自己负责的贝拉特苏赫尼尔和贝拉特达腊班两位女神以及与之有关的诸神明及朔月、上弦月和望月的月相祭祀活动。

在王后贡牲机构建立的 20 年的时间里，共有八人担任贡牲机构的收支官员，他们分别是：育肥师阿希马（*Ahima*，Š 28 i-Š 36 v，历时 8 年 4 个月）、骑使舒库布姆（*Šukubum*，Š 28 iii-Š 32 x，历时 4 年 7 个月）、育肥师贝里沓卜（*Beli-ṭab*，Š 33 v-Š 37 vi，历时 4 年 1 个月）、阿皮里亚

（*Apiliya*，Š 37 ix–Š 41 x/11，历时 4 年 1 个月）、育肥师阿皮拉吞（*Apilatum*，Š 41 xi/26–Š 45 vi/15，历时 3 年 7 个月）、育肥师和书吏乌尔卢旮勒埃邓卡（Ur–Lugal–edenka，Š 45 vii/12–Š 47 iv/28，历时 1 年 9 个月）、骑使舒勒吉伊里（*Šulgi–ili*，Š 47 iv/30–Š 48 x，历时 1 年 6 个月）和卡兰希那吉（Kalam–henagi，Š 44 xi–Š 48 ii/10，历时 3 年 3 个月）。由于阿希马的工作时间与舒库布姆和贝里沓卜的工作时间重叠，卡兰希那吉的工作时间与阿皮拉吞、乌尔卢旮勒埃邓卡和舒勒吉伊里的工作时间重叠，而且阿希马和卡兰希那吉的文件基本全是支出文件，因此，他们二人是辅助与他们同时期的负责官员的工作。除此二人外，贡牲机构的其他六位负责官员们依次接替。

舒勒吉新提王后贡牲机构收入和支出的动物牲畜的种类主要有：育肥牛、普通牛、育肥羊、普通羊、绵羊羔、山羊崽、禽类（鸭、鸽、鸟）以及猪。育肥牲通常是给神明和王室成员食用；羔、崽和禽都是高级肉食，羔有时也献祭给神；禽类在舒勒吉 33 年 3 月 29 日第一次出现，在舒勒吉 38 年贡牲中心建立后，禽类开始大量出现。一般来说，禽类是王后喜爱的食物；宰杀牲被送到宫殿作为士兵及下级人员食用并可收获牛筋和皮毛等原材料。

舒勒吉新提王后贡牲机构的牲畜来源主要有两种：一是来自王室成员，包括：台岑妈妈（阿马尔辛之女）、我的国王（舒勒吉）、埃台勒普达干（王子）、美伊什塔兰（公主）等。二是来自高官或高官之妻的送入，包括：埃阿巴尼（埃瑞什的总督）、乌尔尼旮尔（舒如帕克的总督）之妻、阿达卜的总督卡斯卡勒之妻、尼尔伊达旮勒（ÚrxA.HA^{ki}城的将军）及庙总管伊隆巴尼等。

以上送入的牲畜其用途主要有三种：一是用于祭祀贝拉特苏赫尼尔和贝拉特达腊班两位女神及与之相关的诸神明、神庙、节日庆典、月相祭祀等；二是为王后等王室成员和高官贵族提供食物；三是把死牲支出到宫殿，作为士兵等人的食物。

舒勒吉新提王后贡牲机构祭祀的神明主要有：贝拉特苏赫尼尔、贝拉特达腊班两位女神、乌勒马席吞女神、安努尼吞女神、伊南那女神、那那亚女神、宁里勒女神、恩里勒、阿拉古拉和阿拉吞女神等；王后贡牲机构祭祀的节日庆典主要有：吉腊努姆节、“倒啤酒”宴会和那卜润节等。其祭祀的特殊月相是：在乌鲁克举行的朔月祭、在尼普尔举行的初七上弦月的祭祀和在乌鲁克举行的满月祭祀。

此外，舒勒吉新提王后贡牲机构的档案相较于贡牲中心的档案呈现出以下特点：第一，王后贡牲机构负责官员管理的动物牲畜的种类较多，不仅有牛、羊牲，还包括禽类、猪以及瞪羚羊等；第二，王后贡牲机构档案文件中表达日期时，通常使用 iti--ta ud-x ba-ta/ra-zal；第三，王后贡牲机构的档案中“支出”一词使用的是 zi-ga；第四，王后贡牲机构档案中送入动物牲畜的人员女性占有相当大的比重，这表明一些贵族女性在当时拥有一定的地位和权利，她们可以参与社会的经济和宗教事务。

舒勒吉新提王后贡牲机构的档案于舒勒吉 48 年 10 月结束。两个月之后，阿马尔辛 1 年 11 月阿比新提第一次出现在档案中。通过我们对有关阿比新提的档案文件的研究，最终得出阿比新提是阿马尔辛和舒辛王的母亲，是舒勒吉王的妻子，她与舒勒吉新提是同一个人。在舒勒吉统治时期，她的名字是舒勒吉新提，意为“舒勒吉是我的骄傲”。舒勒吉死后，其子阿马尔辛和舒辛因忌讳父名舒勒吉而给其母重新取名为阿比新提，意为“我的父亲是我的骄傲”。

第二部分　阿马尔辛和舒辛时期阿比新提王太后的有关文献分析（AS 1 xi–ŠS 9 xii）

第一章　阿比新提王太后的身份介绍[①]

舒勒吉 48 年 10 月，乌尔第三王朝的第二王舒勒吉去世。其王后舒勒吉新提的贡牲机构的档案也同时结束[②]。文件 ZVO 25 134 2 记录了贡牲中心在阿马尔辛 1 年 3 月 28 日同时向舒勒吉及其王后舒勒吉新提以及舒勒吉的另一位妻子吉美宁里勒的“饮水地”进行了祭祀。阿马尔辛 1 年 11 月，一个新的王后阿比新提（*Abī-simtī*）出现在贡牲机构的档案中。阿比新提在普兹瑞什达干中心的档案文献中出现的时间是从阿马尔辛 1 年 11 月到舒辛 9 年 12 月，其在文献中出现的时间约 18 年（阿马尔辛王和舒辛王统治的时间分别为 9 年）。根据埃什嫩那城的王朝高官巴巴提的印章，阿比新提是舒辛王的母亲。关于阿比新提究竟是舒勒吉的妻子还是阿马尔辛的妻子这一问题，学术界尚无定论。一种传统观点认为阿比新提是阿马尔辛的妻子以及舒辛的母亲。但最近的研究表明阿比新提可能是舒勒吉的妻子。我们通过对阿比新提的各种文献材料的研究，提出一个新的建议：阿比新提王后是舒勒吉的妻子，她是阿马尔辛和舒辛这一对兄弟的母亲。

---

① 本章内容已以论文的形式发表在《东北师大学报》2011 年第 2 期。

② 该文件为 OIP 115 014，关于舒勒吉新提王后贡牲机构档案的研究见王俊娜、吴宇虹：《乌尔第三王朝贡牲中心出土舒勒吉新提王后贡牲机构苏美尔语档案文献研究》，《古代文明》2010 年第 2 期，第 17—30 页。

第一节 阿比新提的身份和头衔

目前我们没有发现阿比新提的印章。但是迪亚拉河中心地区埃什嫩那城的王朝高官巴巴提的印章提到阿比新提是舒辛王的母亲、巴巴提的姊妹[①]：舒辛是强大之【王】、乌尔之王和四方之王，（他）赠予了（in-na-ba）他的奴仆巴巴提：账目总管（ĝá-dub-ba）、王室经济执行官（šà-tam lugal）、马什干沙润的将军（šakkana *Maš-gán-šar-ru-um*^{ki}）、阿巴勒的总督（ensí A-ba-al^{ki}），贝拉特苏赫尼尔和贝拉特达腊班女神的【喜爱者】，他（舒辛）亲爱的母亲阿比新提的兄弟（该印章）（JCS 28 179，舒辛 3 年 10 月；BRM 3 037，舒辛 6 年 5 月和 BRM 3 038，舒辛 6 年 11 月）。

阿比新提在阿马尔辛统治时期的档案文献中被称为“nin”。苏美尔语“nin”的意思是“王后（王太后）”或“女主人”。在阿马尔辛 8 年 9 月 9 日和阿马尔辛 8 年 9 月 18 日的两个文件中，乌尔伊格阿林被称为“王后的育肥师”（gurušda nin），根据上下文可确定此处的王后是阿比新提：

（1）10 头育肥公牛、16 只育肥公绵羊、4 只牛后级育肥公绵羊、10 只育肥公山羊、70 只公绵羊和 20 只公山羊为啤酒节，经由恩里勒孜沙旮勒（^{d}En-líl-zi-šà-gál），以上送入为阿比新提，自王后的育肥师乌尔伊格阿林处（ki～ Ur-^{d}Ig-alim gurušda nin--ta），于 9 日，以上送入阿巴萨旮（Ab-ba-sa$_6$-ga）接管了（SumRecDreh.19）。

（2）3 头公牛、1 只公绵羊和 2 只公山羊自乌如阿城之人（URUxA^{ki}），监工：舒勒吉孜穆（ugula *^{d}Šul-gi-zi-mu*），10 头育肥公牛、69 只公绵羊、1 只羔和 30 只公山羊自伊冉达干，为阿比新提的送入，自王后的育肥师乌尔伊格阿林处，于 18 日，以上送入阿巴萨旮接管了（TRU 126）。

在阿比新提的儿子舒辛统治时期，阿比新提仍然拥有“王（太）后”

① 我们还发现一个称作是王后的姊妹（nin$_9$-nin）的女人——比朱阿（*Bí-zu-a*，“我的眼泪”）的文件（OIP 121 164），文件写于阿马尔辛 4 年 9 月 8 日。

（nin）的头衔，地位依旧显赫。此时“nin”应是指“国王的母亲，即王太后”。文件 Studies Pettinato 160，167 09，171 提到了阿比新提的身份是“王太后”。该文件写于舒辛 3 年 4 月，其内容是：1 头次优育肥公牛为安努尼吞女神，经由阿比新提王太后（gìr *A-bí-sí-*<*im*>*-ti* nin-a），辛阿比（^{d}*Sîn-a-bí*）司酒（sagi）督办，自马【顺】处被支出，于乌尔。

写于舒辛 7 年 10 月 6 日的文件 PDT 1 431 记录了为阿比新提王太后和舒辛王的“神妻”库巴吞（*Kubatum*）一起支出牲畜的内容。该文件内容是：16 只食草公绵羊为阿比新提，10 只食草公绵羊为库巴吞，为祭司寝宫的供奉（igi-kár ki-pàr--šè），卢库朱督办（Lú-kù-zu maškim），于乌尔，6 日，自乌尔库依那处被支出（ki~ Ur-kù-nun-na--ta ba-zi），经由卢沙林书吏（gìr *Lú-ša-lim* dub-sar）。月名，年名，（总计）20 只羊。文件中为阿比新提王太后支出的牲畜是 16 只羊，为库巴吞王后支出的牲畜是 10 只羊，这说明阿比新提王太后的地位高于库巴吞王后。

在温马出土的档案文献中，我们还发现一个舒辛时期称阿比新提为“退休王后”（nin-ĝar）的文件（SET 288）①。该文件内容是：17 个占卜用的篮子，装有皮羊（17 ^{gi}hal kin-gi$_4$-a kuš si-ga），其用皮为 8 张，（发）给阿比新提“退休王后”（*A-bí-sí-im-ti* nin-ĝar），当她走向扎巴兰城时（ud~ Zabalàm^{ki}--šè ĝen-na），经由恩温米伊里骑使（gìr *En-um-mi-ì-lí* rá-gaba），自阿卡拉处（ki~ *A-kal-la*-ta），卢卡拉的印章（kišib Lú-kal-la），月名、年名。（印章）：卢卡拉书吏是乌尔埃驯牲师（kuš$_7$）之子②。

目前只发现一件向阿比新提的“饮水地”献祭的文件（ASJ 03 092 3）。该文件写于舒辛 9 年 12 月 17 日，内容是：3 只育肥四等公绵羊为阿拉吞的 níĝ-dab$_5$供奉，3 只育肥四等公绵羊到 EN.DÍM.GIG，以上为阿比新提的“饮水地”，经由南那刊理发师（šu-i），于乌尔，17 日，自舒勒吉伊里处被支出（ba-zi），经由卢南那行政官（šár-ra-ab-du）。文件表明阿比新提王后可能在舒辛 9 年 12 月 17 日之前去世。

---

① 苏美尔词“ĝar”，有时指退休高官，乌尔里斯（Ur-Lisi）退休后被称为“ensí-ĝar”，见 Jacob L. Dahl, *The Ruling Family of Ur III Umma: A Prosopographical Analysis of an Elite Family in Southern Iraq 4000 Years Ago*, Leiden: Nederlands Instituut voor het Nabije Oosten, 2007, pp.55–62。

② Frauke Weiershäuser. *Die königlichen Frauen der III. Dynastie von Ur* [M], Göttingen: Universitätsverlag Göttingen, 2008.pp.138–142.

第二节 阿比新提与阿马尔辛王和舒辛王的关系

一 阿比新提与阿马尔辛的关系

根据古巴比伦时期出现的苏美尔王表，乌尔第三王朝历经了乌尔那穆、舒勒吉、阿马尔辛、舒辛和伊比辛这五位国王的统治。其中舒勒吉是乌尔那穆之子、阿马尔辛是舒勒吉之子、舒辛是阿马尔辛之子及伊比辛是舒辛之子。晚期写成的苏美尔王表并不能确定王朝的继承关系，因此，学术界有人认为舒辛是舒勒吉之子，舒辛与阿马尔辛是兄弟①。

阿马尔辛王成为王之前的信息我们一无所知。其父舒勒吉统治时期，既无他的名字，也无他的印章，因此，我们怀疑此人的王名“阿马尔辛”是他继位后新改的名字。两河流域历史中经常有新王改用新名字的例子，如萨尔贡（*Šarrum-kin*），意为“真正的王”。因此，我们认为阿马尔辛是由王太子的名字改成的王名。美国亚述学者 P.Steinkeller 在 2010 年 7 月 22—24 日于马德里举办的乌尔第三王朝专题会议上提出：阿马尔辛可能就是曾担任过乌鲁克城将军的王子乌尔辛。他在继位后，将自己的名字“乌尔辛”（Ur-Sîn）改为“阿马尔辛”（Amar-Sîn）。“乌尔辛”意为“辛神的仆人”，“阿马尔辛”意为“辛神的牛犊”，有“辛神之子”之意。“辛神之子”比“辛神的仆人”更符合国王的身份。

至今发现的舒勒吉时期乌尔辛以“王子”（dumu-lugal）的身份活动的文件共计 18 个，其时间是从舒勒吉 34 年 8 月（MVN 10 149）到舒勒吉 47 年 2 月 7 日（MVN 05 105）。但在阿马尔辛统治时期，我们没发现任何记录乌尔辛是王子的文件。如果乌尔辛王子不是恰好在新王继位后死去，这一现象则支持着王太子改名的推断。因此，我们认为正是舒勒吉时期最重要的王子乌尔辛继承了父亲的王位并改名为阿马尔辛。

有三个舒勒吉时期的文件上的印章提到乌尔辛曾担任过乌鲁克城和

① Jacob L.Dahl, *The Ruling Family of Ur III Umma: A Prosopographical Analysis of an Elite Family in Southern Iraq 4000 Years Ago*, Leiden: Nederlands Instituut voor het Nabije Oosten, 2007, p. 19.

"天神城堡"（BÀD.An[ki]，可能是在乌鲁克城内或附近的城堡）的将军①。三枚印章分别属于：乌尔恩基、瑞施伊隆和马顺。

有关乌尔辛的3个印章和舒辛的2个印章

时间	文件内容	印文内容	文献出处
无	对乌尔萨旮说："让人给予达达8钟（240斗）大麦！"	**乌尔辛**是乌鲁克和"天神城堡"的将军，乌尔恩基（Ur–Enki）：城市长老（ab–ba uru），是你的仆人	BIN 5 316
Š 48	无文件内容	**乌尔辛**是乌鲁克和"天神城堡"的将军，瑞施伊隆（Ri ṣ ṣ–ilum）是他的骑使	RA 13 020 7
AS 1 i	1只公绵羊羔从阿巴萨旮处，马顺接管。	**乌尔辛**是乌鲁克和"天神城堡"的将军，马【顺】（Mašum）是【你的】仆人	Trouvaille 74
无	【1+】头死牛和4+头死公绵羊	舒勒吉是强大之人、乌尔之王和四方之王：**乌鲁克的将军舒辛**（Šu –[d] EN.［ZU］）是他的儿子②	BRM 3 052
AS 9 iii	3公绵羊为送入项，从阿巴萨旮处，舒勒吉伊里军尉接管了，（总计：）3只	**舒辛是戴尔城的将军**，舒勒吉伊里书吏：【某人之子】是你的仆人	Mesopotamia 1293 A

瑞施伊隆的印文表明他是乌尔辛（即阿马尔辛）的骑使。根据我们对瑞施伊隆骑使的文献材料的搜集和研究，他的职责主要是督办为阿比新提以及王室公主们提供食用牲畜的供应。一个文件（阿马尔辛8年4月，MVN 11 183）中称瑞施伊隆是王（太）后的骑使（rá–gaba nin），目前所知的阿马尔辛时期拥有"王（太）后"（nin）头衔的人只有阿比新提。由于瑞施伊隆既是王太子乌尔辛的骑使，也是王（太）后阿比新提的骑使，我们推测阿马尔辛（原名乌尔辛）与阿比新提之间存在亲密的关系：他们是母子。

① D.Frayne, *The Royal Inscription of Mesopotamia*, Toronto: University of Toronto Press, 1993, RIME 3/2 1.2.95, 96, 97.

② 由于此印文中舒辛的名字 Šu–[d]En.［Zu］的破损，有学者将它恢复成 Šu–[d]En［–líl］，参见：D.Frayne, *The Royal Inscription of Mesopotamia*, Toronto: University of Toronto Press, 1993, RIME 3/2 1.2.94。

王（太）后骑使瑞施伊隆督办王（太）后事物一览表

时间	文献内容	支出官员	文献出处
AS 4 vii	1 肥羊和 1 羊为舒勒吉的王座，沙塔库朱督办；1 肥牛、3 肥羊和 7 羊为塔丁伊什塔尔，1 肥牛、2 肥羊和 3 羊各为宁里勒图库勒提，吉美南那、帕基那那、沙特马米、宁希杜、吉美埃安那、台岑妈妈、卢旮勒马古瑞的妻子、美伊什塔蓝、沙润巴尼的妻子、卢南那的妻子，以上是（12 个）公主，2 肥羊和 3 羊各为基那特努努和库巴吞，（2 个）国王的奶妈，**瑞施伊隆骑使督办**……	阿巴萨旮	CTMMA 1 17
AS 4 vii/27	【1 羊】到御膳房……送入，乌尔巴巴督办；7+肥羊由采鲁什达干等人送入为**【阿比】新提**，【1+】为美伊什塔蓝（公主），由舒库卜塔送入，**瑞施伊隆骑使督办**	阿巴萨旮	BIN 3 081
AS 4 ix/26	9 羔和 2 肥羊由乌尔恩旮勒杜杜等人送入，为**阿比新提，瑞施伊隆骑使督办**；2 羔由……送入到御膳房，乌尔巴巴督办	阿巴萨旮	Princeton 1 081
AS 5 viii/16	14 肥羊、17+羊为**阿比新提，瑞施伊隆骑使督办**；1 肥崽到御膳房，阿亚卡拉督办	阿巴萨旮	Orient 16 046 28
AS 6 iii	2 环银，每环重 8 “锱”，自努希伊隆国使处为**阿比新提，瑞施伊隆督办**；2 环银，每环重 8 舍克勒，1 把 dalla 环银自……为苏萨的统治者沙润伊里军尉的妻子，西台拉尼督办，于晦日祭时，1 个青铜杯赠予阿哈斯布弓射手，<马顺>督办，于普兹瑞什达干	卢迪弥腊	JCS 10 31 11
AS 8 ii/9	2 幼瞪羚为**王（太）后，瑞施伊隆督办**	卢旮勒阿马尔库	AUCT 2 238
AS 8 iv	2 环银子，每环 9 舍克勒为那维尔伊隆医生的神妻阿那亚，埃尔贝里督办；1 环银子，每环 8 舍克勒为阿图马马，1 为他的哥哥乌尔南筛，以上是水手，**王（太）后的骑使瑞施伊隆督办**	卢迪弥尔腊	MVN 11 183

二　阿比新提与舒辛王的关系

在乌尔辛（即阿马尔辛）卸任乌鲁克和“天神城堡”的将军职位而继承王位后，舒辛成为了乌尔王朝王太子所担任的乌鲁克城和“天神城堡”的将军。一个文件中的印章表明王子舒辛在阿马尔辛统治时期担任过“天神城堡”的将军（印文内容见表一）[①]。虽然舒辛是舒勒吉之子，并且经常出现在文件中，但是舒勒吉时期的文件从不提他的头衔是“王

① 乌尔那马在乌鲁克第五王朝的基础上建立了乌尔第三王朝，因此，乌鲁克城作为仅次于乌尔城的双首都之一具有非常重要的地位，故而乌尔第三王朝常把乌鲁克城作为王储的封地。

子”，而舒勒吉其他的儿子在当时的文件中经常被称为王子。这说明舒辛在舒勒吉时期拥有极其特殊的地位，似乎每个人都知道舒辛是最重要的王子之一，故而省略了他的王子头衔。一件极可能是舒辛的印章的文件（BRM 3 052，无日期）可以证明舒辛是舒勒吉之子（见表一）。如果该印文的破损处不读成舒勒吉的另一个儿子舒恩里勒（Šu-^{d}En-［líl］），那么印文则表明舒辛是舒勒吉之子，他也曾担任乌鲁克城的将军。

一个舒辛时期的文件（Nesbit 66）中记录了一个官员的新改的名字是^{d}*Šu-Suen-walid-* ^{d}*Šulgi*，意为“神舒辛是神舒勒吉所生”，该人的名字也直接证实了舒辛是舒勒吉之子①。

在古巴比伦抄本的《舒辛赞美诗》（SRT 23）的第7、8行以及第17、18行中，明确指出：舒辛王是舒勒吉和阿比新提的儿子②。有关叙述如下：

（舒勒吉的爱人对王唱到）

1—3行：圣人生了（你，舒辛），圣人生了你。王（太）后（nin）生了（你），阿比新提生了（你）。

4—5行：我的（过去的）华服的织机衡木是我的（母亲）阿比新提。我的现在的美服的织机木梭是我的王后（nin）库巴吞。

7—8行：我的完美伟人，我的主神舒辛。我的命令……是我舒勒吉之子。

17—18行：让你的城市像……啊，主人，我的舒辛，让它像狮崽陷在你的脚下，是我的舒勒吉之子。

一件记录国王舒勒吉、王后舒勒吉新提以及其他王妃和贵族获得的金银饰品、器皿、镶金和银的家具和衣料、酥油等内容的一个大文件（HANE/S 6，pp.30-31，无日期）提到的唯一一位王子是舒辛，这也证明了国王舒勒吉和王后舒勒吉新提对舒辛的喜爱以及他在诸王子中仅次于

① 见 David I.Owen，“On the Patronymy of Šu-Suen”，*N.A.B.U.Nouvelles Assyriologiques Brevs et Utilitaires*，2001，No.17。

② Yitschak Sefati，*Love Songs in Sumerian Literature*，Ramat Gan：Bar-Ilan University Press，1998，pp.344-352.

王储的重要地位[1]。

“饮水地”是古代苏美尔人祭祀祖先的地方。最早的一件向阿马尔辛的“饮水地”（ki-a-nag）祭祀的文件写于阿马尔辛9年11月30日。文件（PDT 1 384）内容是：1头育肥公牛为舒勒吉的“饮水地”，1头育肥公牛为阿马尔辛的“饮水地”，自乌尔舒旮兰马处被支出，经由调味师（lú-ùr--ra）乌尔舒勒帕埃。此文件表明阿马尔辛于其统治的最后一年的11月30日之前去世。在阿马尔辛去世后，接替其王位的是阿马尔辛的弟弟、舒勒吉的另一个儿子舒辛。

在阿马尔辛统治时期，舒辛王弟的地位十分显赫。贡牲中心出土的文献中有5个文件表明舒辛是王子的身份[2]。这5个文件都属于阿马尔辛时期（1个文件的日期缺损）。但是没有证据表明阿马尔辛有一个儿子和其弟舒辛同名。这一舒辛应是王弟“（先）王之子舒辛”。

舒辛和阿马尔辛兄弟关系中的一个特殊的现象是：在阿马尔辛王的最后三年或四年中，二人可能曾经共同执政过。我们发现37个写于阿马尔辛6年到阿马尔辛9年9月的文件，但是却盖有称舒辛是王的印章[3]。其中温马出土的文件共34个，德莱海姆出土的文件共3个。在温马出土的文件中，以下官员的印章中称舒辛为王：温马的总督乌尔里席（Ur-Lisi）和阿（亚）卡拉（A（ya）kalla）以及书吏古杜杜（Gududu）[4]；在德莱海姆出土的文件中，其印章中称舒辛为王的官员有：司酒努尔舒勒吉（Nur-Šulgi，AUCT 1 048，阿马尔辛7年10月）、书吏卢旮勒乌尔腊尼（Lugal-úr-ra-ni，CBCY 3 NBC 10124，阿马尔辛7年7月）以及一个官

① 见李学彦、吴宇虹《从一件大礼品单看乌尔第三王朝国王和王后的豪华生活》，《历史教学》2011年4月下半期，第3—12页。

② 五个文件分别是：RA 62 08 11（阿马尔辛1年1月）、PDT 1 171（阿马尔辛2年3月30日）、HUCA 29 073 02（阿马尔辛5年3月21日）、MVN 15 015（阿马尔辛2年3月）和PDT 2 0959（日期缺损）。

③ 由于我们发现的最早向阿马尔辛的“饮水地”献祭的文件是写于阿马尔辛9年11月30日，而阿马尔辛去世的时间应是在这之前的1—2个月，因此，我们把该类印章的时间的下限定位在阿马尔辛9年9月。

④ 阿马尔辛时期，乌尔里席称舒辛是王的印章在阿马尔辛7年的2个文件中：Torino 2 534和Hirose 365；阿亚卡拉称舒辛是王的印章是从阿马尔辛6年（2个文件）、阿马尔辛7年（BPOA 6 0948和CBCY 3 NBC 04274）、阿马尔辛8年（12个文件）到阿马尔辛9年9月（15个文件）；古杜杜称舒辛为王的印章仅有1个（SACT 2 046，阿马尔辛7年5月）。

员名缺损的印章（AUCT 3 414，阿马尔辛 9 年 4 月）。最早一件盖有记录舒辛是王的印章的温马文件（UTI 3 1845 和 CBCY 3 NBC 05190）是写于阿马尔辛 6 年。印章内容是：舒辛是强大之王、乌尔之王、四方之王，温马的总督阿亚卡拉是你的仆人。

这些印章也许表明从阿马尔辛 6 年开始，在温马（也可能少数德莱海姆）的官员们就已承认阿马尔辛和其兄弟舒辛共同执政。虽然阿亚卡拉在阿马尔辛 8 年 11 月（MVN 16 627）才成为温马的总督，这与阿马尔辛 6 年阿亚卡拉印章的内容不符，但是温马的总督阿亚卡拉与舒辛王一样提前与其前任共同执政的解释似乎不太可能。因为共同执政在两河流域历史中是非常少见的现象，而且舒辛的印章出现在阿马尔辛的 6 年到 9 年其死前的文件中的现象只出现在温马（贡牲中心仅有 3 件），所以我们对此解释的另一可能性是，在温马一些官员有倒填文件日期的做法，即为了追补过去的账目，把舒辛 1 年以后写的文件的日期倒填为账目发生时的日期（阿马尔辛时期），但却使用当时的印章。

综上所述，阿马尔辛与他的继承者舒辛应该是兄弟，他们都是舒勒吉之子。由于阿比新提是舒辛之母，而阿比新提与阿马尔辛的关系也应该是母子，因此，阿比新提应是舒勒吉时期的王后以及阿马尔辛和舒辛时期的王太后。

第三节　舒勒吉王和舒勒吉新提王后即阿比新提王太后的关系

一个文件（ZVO 25 134 2）记录了在阿马尔辛 1 年 3 月 28 日，贡牲中心同时向舒勒吉及其两位妻子吉美宁里勒和舒勒吉新提各自的“饮水地”的献祭[①]。一般来说，向舒勒吉和其两位妻子的“饮水地”的献祭标志着他们已去世。但是在阿马尔辛 1 年 3 月 28 日之后，我们发现了一个舒勒吉新提在 4 月 4 日仍然活动的文件：25 只育肥公绵羊、3 只育肥母山羊、39 只公绵羊、1 只母绵羊、1 只吃奶羔、1 只公山羊和 1 只吃奶公山羊崽，以上羊为舒勒吉新提，自舒勒吉伊里育肥师处送入，那萨接管，月

① 王俊娜、吴宇虹：《乌尔第三王朝贡牲中心出土舒勒吉新提王后贡牲机构苏美尔语档案文献研究》，《古代文明》2010 年第 2 期。

名，年名，（总计：）71 只羊（阿马尔辛 1 年 4 月 4 日，PDT 2 1215）。

因此，舒勒吉新提可能在舒勒吉死后，没有为丈夫殉葬。这一时期也没有活人殉葬的考古记录。虽然在阿马尔辛 1 年 3 月 28 日，舒勒吉、吉美宁里勒和舒勒吉新提三个人都出现在“饮水地”，但是真正去世的只有舒勒吉国王，同年 4 月 4 日的文件（PDT 2 1215）证明舒勒吉新提很可能仍然活着[①]。向舒勒吉新提和吉美宁里勒的“饮水地”献祭可能仅仅表明她们作为舒勒吉妻子的身份已经死亡。但是作为新王的母亲舒勒吉新提并没有死。同样的在“饮水地”被祭祀后仍然活着的贵族的例子是国务卿（sukkal-mah）阿腊德南那（Arád-Nanna）。旮尔沙那（Ĝaršana）档案中的一个文件（CUSAS 3 no.971）记录了舒辛 7 年 8 月向阿腊德南那和阿拉吞女神的“饮水地”的献祭，但是之后直到伊比辛 3 年阿腊德南那仍在积极活动[②]。对于阿马尔辛 1 年 4 月 4 日之后舒勒吉新提的名字既没有作为先妣名被祭祀，也没有作为活人名出现过的现象比较合理的解释是，在国王舒勒吉去世后，由王后变为王太后的舒勒吉新提采用了新的名字——阿比新提。

由于阿比新提是新王阿马尔辛和继王舒辛兄弟之母，故而阿比新提是舒勒吉最重要且地位很高的一位妻子。舒勒吉的妻子中没有一个人叫阿比新提，与这个名字最相似的名字就是舒勒吉新提。阿马尔辛 4 年 11 月 1 日贡牲中心的文件（Torino）并列记录了先王舒勒吉和太后阿比新提的月供应[③]，这证明先王舒勒吉和阿比新提之间是国王和王后的关系。在国王舒勒吉去世后，王后放弃了她原来为赞美舒勒吉而新起的王后名字“舒勒吉新提”或者“舒勒吉新吞”，意为“舒勒吉是我的骄傲”（*Šulgi-simtī*）或者“舒勒吉是骄傲（的人）”（*Šulgi-simtum*），而采用新王因忌

① 日本学者尾崎亨也认为舒勒吉新提在阿马尔辛时期仍然活着。他根据的是文件 TCS 186=Torino 1 363，我们知道该文件是贡牲中心死牲官员舒勒吉乌如穆，而并非舒勒吉新提接收死牲的文件，所以其根据是错误的。另一个他提到的文件（UET 3 1211，日期破损）中的舒勒吉新提应是伊比辛时期的舒勒吉新提，见 Tohru Gomi，“Shulgi-simti and her Libation Place（ki-a-nag）”，*Orient*（12），1976，p.9。

② Wu Yuhong，“Naram-ili，Šu-Kabta and Nawir-ilum in the Archives of Ĝaršana，Puzriš-Dagan and Umma”，*JAC*（23），2008，pp.3，6-8。

③ 该文件的内容是：29 只育肥公绵羊为 29 天的日供应，1 只育肥公绵羊为满月，1 只育肥公绵羊为新月，以上增加的为舒勒吉的月供，30 只育肥公绵羊为阿比新提的月供，于 1 日，努希伊隆国使督办，自舒勒吉阿亚姆处被支出，月名，年名。

讳其父舒勒吉的名字给母亲重新起的王太后名字“阿比新提”，意为“我的父亲是我的骄傲”。对王太后本人来说，其名字的意义并没有变化，只是在她的国王丈夫活着时，她的名字中第一部分是舒勒吉的名字，在其国王丈夫死后，她的儿子新王为忌讳父名“舒勒吉”（Šulgi），而不直呼舒勒吉的名字，故将母后名字中第一部分的舒勒吉改称为“我的父亲”（*abī*）。王太后的新名“阿比新提”在阿马尔辛 1 年 11 月第一次出现在文献中。王太后在文献中缺席 7 个月（从阿马尔辛 1 年 4 月到 11 月）的原因可能是她还处于服丧期，所以没有参加新王朝的经济及宗教等活动。

通过对贡牲中心出土的舒勒吉新提王后贡牲机构档案的研究，我们知道舒勒吉新提王后负责祭祀的主要神明是阿卡德人聚居的迪亚拉河流域的两个重要女神——贝拉特苏赫尼尔和贝拉特达腊班女神（我们简称“两夫人”女神）。巴巴提的印章表明阿比新提的弟弟——这一地区的将军巴巴提是“两夫人”女神的喜爱者，即“两夫人”女神是巴巴提的主神，很可能巴巴提（阿卡德人名）来自于阿卡德人中心区迪亚拉河地区。如果是这样，他的姐姐阿比新提王太后则与舒勒吉新提王后一样来自阿卡德人中心区的迪亚拉河地区。苏美尔王与阿卡德人的联姻，可能是基于稳固王国边界以及和谐两河流域两大民族关系的政治需要。同时，阿比新提和舒勒吉新提两位王后都非常重视对伊南那女神以及安努尼吞女神和阿拉吞女神等阿卡德地区的女神的祭祀，这表明两个人的相同的特殊宗教信仰也支持二人身份的同一。

文件 ASJ 03 092 3 中记录了向阿比新提王太后的“饮水地”的献祭，表明阿比新提王太后可能在舒辛 9 年 12 月 17 日之前已去世。阿比新提（即舒勒吉新提）历经舒勒吉统治的 20 年（舒勒吉 28 年到舒勒吉 48）和其两个儿子阿马尔辛和舒辛统治的 18 年。如果她 18 岁嫁给舒勒吉，到她去世时，她活了 56 年，这也是古人正常的生存年龄。值得注意的是在伊比辛统治时期，我们发现了三个为舒勒吉新提提供大麦粗面粉（dabin–zì）及羊牲的文件①。有学者认为该时期的舒勒吉新提为

---

① 三个文件分别是：CDLI P105646（……6 斗大麦粗面粉（dabin–zì）为舒勒吉新提……伊比辛 1 年 6 月）、Ontario 1 164（1 只次优育肥公绵羊和 1 只 3 等育肥母绵羊为舒勒吉新提……伊比辛 1 年 7 月 20 日）、UET 3 0116（4 只育肥公绵羊和 3 只育肥公山羊为舒勒吉新提的月供，自努尔伊里处（支出），伊比辛 5 年 12 月）。

伊比辛国王的女儿①，但也有可能是在阿比新提王太后和其子舒辛去世后，乌尔第三王朝的第五王伊比辛将其祖母（或母亲）的名字“阿比新提”又恢复成其旧名“舒勒吉新提”。

---

① Jacob L.Dahl, *The Ruling Family of Ur III Umma: A Prosopographical Analysis of an Elite Family in Southern Iraq 4000 Years Ago*, Leiden: Nederlands Instituut voor het Nabije Oosten, 2007, p. 31.

第二章　阿比新提王太后享用各种来源的牲畜的文件

在有关阿比新提王太后的文献中，我们发现阿比新提规律性地接收贡牲中心向她支付的牲畜。同时，在贡牲中心官员为祭祀诸神明支出牲畜的文件中，阿比新提王太后常以“经由人”身份参加祭祀活动。

第一节　分配给阿比新提王太后的牲畜的三种文件类型

分配给阿比新提的牲畜的文件可以分为三种：一是贡牲中心官员间的接管文件。即“为阿比新提的送入项，从王太后的育肥师乌尔伊格阿林处，阿巴萨旮（贡牲中心总管）接管了”（mu-túm *Abī-simtī*，ki~ Ur-^{d}Ig-alim gurušda nin--ta，… Ab-ba-sa$_6$-ga ì-dab$_5$）；该类文件共有3件，其中的阿比新提的送入项都是来自她的育肥师乌尔伊格阿林处，最终由中心总管阿巴萨旮接管记账。贡牲中心提供给阿比新提的牲畜有育肥公牛、育肥公绵羊和普通羊牲。育肥公牛的数量为1头或10头，育肥公绵羊的数量为30只到376只不等，普通羊牲的数量从58只到100只不等，数量都比较大，具体用处没有表明。

中心总管接管的为阿比新提送入牲畜一览表

时间	为阿比新提的送入项的牲畜的数量和种类	接管官及文献号
AS 8 viii/18	1肥牛、376肥羊和58羊自伊拉隆（乌如萨格瑞格的总督，ensí Uru-sag-rig$_7$^{ki}），以上为**阿比新提的送入项**，自乌尔伊格阿林（王太后）育肥师处	阿巴萨旮 Nik.2 488
AS 8 ix/9	10肥牛、30肥羊和90羊为“啤酒宴会”（kaš-dé-a），经由恩里勒孜沙旮勒（A.Ha^{ki}城的总督），以上为**阿比新提的送入项**，自乌尔伊格阿林王太后育肥师处	阿巴萨旮 SumRecDreh.19
AS 8 ix/18	……10肥牛、100羊从伊冉达干，为**阿比新提的送入项**，从乌尔伊格阿林王太后育肥师处	阿巴萨旮 TRU 126

第二类文件是记录阿比新提日常消费的月供应。阿比新提的月供应（sá-dug$_4$）文件共8件。阿比新提的每月的供应是30只育肥绵羊，一天一只。其中有3个文件在登记阿比新提的月供应的同时，提到了为舒勒吉的月供、阿马尔辛的月供及库巴吞王后（舒辛的神妻）等的月供应。

关于阿比新提王太后的月供应的支出文件一览表

日期	为阿比新提的月供提供牲畜的数量	督办/经由官	支出官员	文献出处
AS 2 v	30肥羊为**阿比新提**一个月的月供应	努希伊隆国使	舒勒吉阿亚穆	SumRecDreh. 15
AS 3 ii	30肥羊为**阿比新提**的月供应	努希伊隆国使	卢迪弥腊	OIP 121 011
AS 4 xi/1	29【肥】羊为29天的日供，2肥羊为满月和新月的附加供应：**舒勒吉的月供**，30肥羊为**阿比新提的月供**	努希伊隆国使	舒勒吉阿亚穆	**Torino 1 259**
AS 5 xi	29肥羊为29天的日供；2肥羊为满月和新月（附加供应，为舒勒吉），30肥羊为**阿比新提**的一个月的月供	经由努希伊隆	舒勒吉阿亚穆	**Nisaba 08 373**
AS 6ix	180钟大麦为**阿比新提**灌溉村庄的月供应和大麦口粮		卢旮勒希旮勒	PDT 2 1174
AS 8ix	30肥羊为**阿比新提**一个月的月供应		朱巴旮	OIP 121 556
AS 9ix	30肥羊为**阿比新提**一个月的月供应	经由埃腊巴尼	朱巴旮	JCS 52 10 35
ŠS 2 x	29肥羊为29天的日供，2肥羊为满月和新月的附加供应：**舒勒吉的月供应**，29肥羊为29天的日供应，2肥羊为满月和新月的附加供应：**阿马尔辛的月供应**，【1+】肥羊为**阿比新提**的月供应，9+肥羊为哈尔西吞的月供应，……，【1+】肥【羊】为**库巴吞王后（舒辛的神妻）的【月供应】**，【1+】肥羊为阿巴巴什提的月供，2+肥羊为乌那巴瑞的月供，3羊为比那胡庙祭祀，6肥羊为采里里的月供，17肥羊为17天的月供	经由乌尔乌什吉达书吏和苦腊德伊里行政官	阿胡维尔	**BIN 3 558**

第三类是由贡牲中心官员把王朝和各地的高官贡入的牲畜分配给阿比新提的记录。很可能这些牲畜是送牲官员直接献给阿比新提王太后的。此类文件共41件。这些文件有时同时还记载为国王和其他王室人员①、外

① 国王、舒勒吉王座、塞莱布吞公主、阿腊德穆国务卿的儿媳吉美埃安那、美伊什塔蓝公主和舒辛王的妻子库巴吞王后。

国王公或使节①、御膳房、厨房、库房等的支出。常给阿比新提王太后贡献牲畜礼品的官员有：采鲁什达干（席穆润的总督）、阿达吞（马瑞城的将军）、混舒勒吉（温马城的将军）、乌尔萨萨旮（伊莘舒勒吉城的总督）、伊拉隆和乌尔美斯（乌如萨格瑞格的总督），以及舒马马（卡勒扎鲁城的总督）等。根据为阿比新提贡献礼物的这些高官和外国王公的名字，我们可以看到：阿比新提王太后在阿马尔辛和舒辛两朝的外交事务中扮演着重要的角色。

高官送给阿比新提王太后的牲畜一览表

日期	为阿比新提送入牲畜的数量和种类以及其督办/经由官	支出官员及文献出处
AS 1 xi/2	2 羊为**舒勒吉王座**，61 羊是图普图普（新郎）的聘礼，为塞莱布吞公主，2 牛、20 羊为**阿比新提**，1 牛和 5 羊为兹达农城人腊席，4 羊为席马农城人 X-那，2 羊为哈尔席城人提-x-提，31 羊到厨房，阿腊德穆督办	阿巴萨旮，AUCT 1 110
AS2xii/10	1 肥牛为信使，3 肥羊为**阿比新提**，3 肥羊为阿腊德穆国务卿的儿媳吉美埃安那，1 肥羊为孜达农城人腊西，经由卢旮勒卡吉那使官，阿腊德穆督办	卢迪弥腊，OIP 121 009
AS 3 i/1	1 瞪羚为**阿比新提**，普朱尔伊什塔尔送入，里尼辛督办	阿巴萨旮，AUCT2 152
AS 3 ix	132 羊为国王的送入，10 羊为**阿比新提**的送入	欠款，SAT 2 0759
AS3xi²/25	2 肥羊采鲁什达干（席穆润的总督）送入，3 公牛、31 羊伊瑞布送入，5 羊伊吉润送入，1 羔马尔达的总督送入，以上为**阿比新提**，阿腊德穆督办	阿巴萨旮，AUCT 2 099
AS3xi²/26	1 羊那冉埃阿送入，2 羔埃什塔尔伊里舒送入，1 只羔舒勒吉伊里送入，1 只羔库宁旮勒送入，以上为**阿比新提**，阿腊德穆督办	阿巴萨旮，TAD 55
	1 肥崽到御膳房，尼尔伊达旮勒送入，乌尔巴巴督办	
AS 4 ii/2，11	2 瞪羚到御膳房分别由阿亚卡拉和乌尔巴巴督办，4 瞪羚到库房由阿达吞等送入，2 羔分别由【普斯】总督阿胡【马】等人送入，为**阿比新提**，努尔阿达德骑使督办	阿巴萨旮，PDT 2 1293
AS 4 iii/2	10 牛自孜穆达尔城圣殿的涂油祭司，**阿比新提**被给予，经由埃腊巴尼	ZA68 37 NCBT1628

① 外国使节或王公有：席马农城人 X-那、哈尔席城人提-x-提、孜达农城之人腊西、阿摩利人那坡拉农、LÚ.SU 城的亚卜腊特、杜杜里城的人胡里巴尔、马尔哈席城之人马尔胡尼、耐吉耐混城之人旮达比、安山城之人达亚孜台、席穆润城之人基尔卜乌勒美、沙什如城之人阿瑞杜布克、吉吉卜尼城之人塞特帕塔勒和马瑞城之人舒达干、马尔哈席的总督里巴努格沙巴什、哈尔席的总督阿达吉那、乌如萨格瑞格城的总督伊拉隆和温马的将军混舒勒吉等。

续表

日期	为阿比新提送入牲畜的数量和种类以及其督办/经由官	支出官员及文献出处
AS4ix/26	8羔分别由乌尔恩旮勒杜杜（庙总管）、阿达吞（马瑞城的将军）、混舒勒吉（温马城的将军）、乌尔萨萨旮（伊莘舒勒吉城的总督）、舒勒吉兰马穆高官、沙腊神的祭司、阿达亚（庙总管）和伊提卜席那特（埃任伊舒尔城的监工）送入，2肥羊和1羔阿布尼（将军）送入，为**阿比新提**，瑞施伊隆骑使督办	阿巴萨旮，Princeton 1 081
	1羔扎孜送入，1羔卢库朱送入，以上到御膳房，乌尔巴巴督办	
AS5 i	5肥牛、10肥羊和20绵羊为**阿比新提**，图冉达干督办	阿巴萨旮，PDT 2，p.20
	4肥牲和7羊为马尔哈席的总督里巴努格沙巴什，2羊为舒勒吉阿比，1羊为混舒勒吉（温马城的将军），4肥羊和10羔为阿摩利人那坡拉农，乌尔沙如良督办	
AS 5 i/25	1羔和1瞪羚为**阿比新提**，乌尔达姆送入，卢旮勒库朱督办	阿巴萨旮，BAOM 6 141 179
AS 5 i/26	8肥羊分别由阿布尼（将军）、尼尔伊达旮勒（ÚRxA.HA^{ki}城的将军）、伊拉隆（乌尔萨格萨格城的总督）、贝里阿瑞克（苏萨城的总督）送入，4羔分别由马萨萨、舒马马（卡扎鲁城的总督）、舒勒吉伊里和乌尔美斯总督（乌尔萨格萨格城的总督）送入，1瞪羚伊比伊斯塔蓝（王子）送入，3肥羊和1羔乌尔恩旮勒杜杜（庙总管）送入，为**阿比新提**，努尔阿达德骑使督办	阿巴萨旮，MVN 13 849
AS 5 ii	1个盆、1个kundu容器、16个杯子、6个zahum盆、4个šušala容器、1个gigid工具和1个šendili kundu容器为**阿比新提**	卢迪弥腊，MVN 20，031
AS 5 viii/16	14肥羊、16 x x和1崽为**阿比新提**，瑞施伊隆骑使督办	阿巴萨旮，Orient 16 046 28
	1育崽到御膳房，阿亚卡拉督办	
AS 5 ix/11	10牛和120羊为**阿比新提**，60羊为**美伊什塔蓝**，贝里伊里督办	阿巴萨旮，OIP 121 271
	2羊为**舒勒吉的王座**，乌图杜督办	
	1牛和10羊为歌手达达，5羊为舒达干，20羊为采伊什库尔，20牛为士兵阿马那亚，10羊为伊拉隆，阿腊德穆督办	
AS5ix/23	1崽为**阿比新提**，由沙腊神的祭司送入，努尔阿达德骑使督办	阿巴萨旮 OIP 121 283
AS 6 ii/16	1肥羊由朱布什信使给LÚ.SU城的亚卜腊特于尼普尔，经由乌尔哈亚使官	阿胡维尔，阿腊穆督办，Ontario 1 048
	2肥羊为水煮肉，1肥牛和10肥羊为信使，5羊为士兵们，到厨房，2羊为**阿比新提**，到宫殿，经由舒勒吉乌如穆	
	1肥羊由里班什古比信使给马尔哈席的总督里巴努格沙巴什，经由舒舒勒吉国使	
	1肥羊由丹那里信使给杜杜里城的人胡里巴尔，经由拉拉穆使官	

续表

日期	为阿比新提送入牲畜的数量和种类以及其督办/经由官	支出官员及文献出处
AS 6 ii/3，5，11，17，20，23，25，26	2 羔、2 羊、2 瞪羚到御膳房，于 3、11、20 日，哈巴巴吞厨师督办	阿巴萨旮，Nisaba 08 026
	1 牛和 3 羊为伊拉隆，2 羊为达达，2 羊为乌尔宁古巴拉格，阿腊德穆督办，17 日	
	2 死瞪羚到仓库，于 21、25 日	
	1 母绵羊为乌鲁克的伊南那神的祭司，努尔伊什库尔骑使督办	
	7 肥羊、7 羔和 1 只公崽为**阿比新提**，那姆哈里国使督办	
AS6ix/13	3 牛、180 羊为**阿比新提**，阿腊德穆督办	阿巴萨旮，SAT 2 0914
AS 6 xi/1，3，4，5，7，11，13，15，20，21，24，25，27	20 羊、5 羊、1 肥羊为伊拉隆，于 3、5 日，阿腊德穆和舒舒勒吉骑使督办	阿巴萨旮，Nisaba 08 036
	7 羔、2 羊到御膳房，由乌尔巴巴和阿亚卡拉督办，3、5、11、15、24 日	
	10 公山羊为瑞巴旮达骑使，于 3 日，贝里伊里督办	
	6 羊、1 羔和 1 崽为歌手达达，于 4、7、21 日，分别由乌拉伊尼什和阿腊德穆督办	
	3 肥羊、15 羊为美伊什塔蓝，于 7、11 日，南那刊国使和宁哈姆提督办	
	6 淘汰级瞪羚到厨房，舒勒吉乌如穆督办	
	10 羊、1 公崽为乐师乌尔宁古巴拉格，于 13 日，阿腊德穆和伊拉隆督办	
	4 肥羊和 9 只羔为**阿比新提**，于 24 日，舒宁舒布尔骑使督办	
AS 8 i/18	【……】为**阿比新提**，经由舒马马	MVN 13 636
	1 肥羊为哈尔席的总督阿达吉那，马尔哈席城之人马尔胡尼同	
	【1+】肥羊自达布杜克信使为 LÚ.SU^{ki} 城的亚卜腊特，经由拉拉姆国使	
	1 羊为耐吉耐混城之人旮达比，经由杜阿国使	
	5 肥羊为那坡拉农处	
AS 9 iii	2 环银，每环 8 锱，**自沙塔库朱国使为阿比新提的问安礼，**2 环银子，每环 8 锱，为宫殿，拉伊里什【督办】	普朱尔埃腊，JCS 10 30 10
AS 9 xi/18	3 肥羊为哈马兹的总督乌尔伊什库尔的新娘的供应，舒宁舒布尔骑使督办	朱巴旮，经由阿达卡拉，Ontario 1 160
	1 肥羊为哈布瑞吞神，达干、伊什哈腊同上，为**阿比新提**，阿图司酒督办	
ŠS 1 ii/10	4 育羊、4 羔和 1 瞪羚为**阿比新提**，贝里伊里督办	尹塔埃阿，经由南那马巴，BCT 1 094

续表

日期	为阿比新提送入牲畜的数量和种类以及其督办/经由官	支出官员及文献出处
ŠS 1 viii/5	140 羊为**阿比新提**，4+羊，5 死牛为士兵们，阿腊德穆督办	杜旮，经由努尔阿达德书吏，PDT 2 1036
ŠS 2	1 肥牛为**阿比新提**，经由南那库朱	阿胡维尔，TAD 28
ŠS2 ix/23	2 公牛到厨房，为信使们，南那刊国使督办	阿胡维尔，经由乌尔卢旮勒班达和乌尔比尔旮美斯行政官，BIN 3 559
	35 肥羊、30 羊和 14 牛为**阿比新提**	
ŠS 2 xi/24	1 肥羊和 1 羊为 LÚ.SU 城的亚卜腊特，1 肥羊各为安山城之人达亚孜台、席穆润城之人基尔卜乌勒美、沙什如城之人阿瑞杜布克和吉吉卜尼城之人塞特帕塔勒，分别经由巴扎扎国使,、舒库布姆国使、拉齐普姆国使和拉拉穆国使，阿腊德穆督办	从阿胡维尔支出，经由乌尔卢旮勒班达和阿哈尼舒行政官，Babyl. 8 Pupil 30
	1 吃奶羔为**阿比新提**，库卜扎吉穆督办	
ŠS 4 iii	1 把青铜和金刀，埃拉拉铜匠送入，赠予**阿比新提**，于尼普尔	卢迪弥腊，SET 296
ŠS 4 ix/14	9 牛为**阿比新提**的送入项，9 牛为库巴吞的送入项	尹塔埃阿，AUCT 1 032
ŠS 6 xi/14	3 肥羊为伊南那于宫殿的祭祀，南那伊吉杜司酒午夜督办，……10 肥羊为**阿比新提**，于尼普尔，图冉达干督办	阿巴恩里勒艮，经由卢宁舒布尔，Amorites 21 (pl. 10)
ŠS 7 v/1	3+羊为**阿比新提**，经由南那马巴书吏	尹塔埃阿，UCP 9-2-2 085
ŠS 7 vi/8	1 瞪羚为**阿比新提**，舒辛那冉恩里勒骑使督办	乌尔库依那，经由卢沙林书吏，BIN 3 342
	4 羊为乌阿马尔巴舒乐师，南那刊国使督办	
ŠS7vii/14	1 瞪羚为**阿比新提**，宁里勒阿马穆督办	尹塔埃阿，经由南那马巴，PDT 1 610
ŠS 7 x/6	16 羊为**阿比新提**，10 羊为库巴吞，于乌尔，卢库朱督办	乌尔库依那，经由卢沙林，PDT 1 431
?	1 肥羊为**阿比新提**……	AR RIM 01 23 H36c
? xi/16	4+瞪羚为**阿比新提**，5 瞪羚为库巴吞，阿穆尔伊隆骑使督办	乌尔库依那，经由努尔辛，AUCT 1 399
	32 羊到厨房，为士兵们，阿腊德穆督办	

第二节　负责分配牲畜给阿比新提王太后的官员们

负责分配牲畜给阿比新提王太后的官员主要有：阿巴萨旮、阿胡维尔、卢迪弥尔腊、尹塔埃阿、杜旮及朱巴旮、乌尔库依那、舒勒吉阿亚穆和普朱尔恩里勒等。

为阿比新提王太后服务的负责官员及其支出文件数统计表①

阿巴萨旮	阿胡维尔	卢迪弥腊	尹塔埃阿	杜旮	普朱尔恩里勒	朱巴旮	舒勒吉阿亚穆	乌尔库依那	乌尔南那	阿巴恩里勒艮	恩里拉	舒勒吉伊里	舒马马	伊吉恩里勒篩	普朱尔埃腊	那鲁	库尔比拉克	伊尼姆南那
27	9	7	7	6	5	5	4	4	2	2	2	2	1	1	1	1	1	1

阿巴萨旮（Abba-saga）是阿马尔辛时期的普兹瑞什达干贡牲中心的总管②。他的身份是书吏，他是其前任中心总管那萨之子③。阿巴萨旮为阿比新提贡牲机构支出牛、羊牲的文件总数为 27 件。其支出文件的时间是从阿马尔辛 1 年 11 月 2 日到阿马尔辛 9 年 5 月 26 日。

舒勒吉阿亚穆（Šulgi-ayamu）是贡牲中心家畜官员。他为阿比新提贡牲机构支出动物的文件数为 4 件，文件支出时间是从阿马尔辛 2 年 5 月到阿马尔辛 5 年 9 月。

卢迪弥腊（Lu-diĝirra）为阿比新提贡牲机构支出的文件总数为 7 件，其中 6 件是支出动物牲畜的文件，另一个是关于埃拉拉铜匠（*E-la-la* tibira）赠予阿比新提青铜和金刀的支出文件（SET 296）。卢迪弥腊支出文件的时间是从阿马尔辛 2 年 12 月 10 日到舒辛 4 年 3 月。

阿胡维尔（*Ahu-wer*）育肥师是家畜管理运输官员，他在贡牲中心的工作时间是从阿马尔辛 3 年 12 月 3 日到舒辛 6 年 5 月④。阿胡维尔为阿比新提贡牲机构支出动物牲畜的文件总数为 9 件，其中三个文件中，阿胡维尔既是支出官员也是“经由官员”。阿胡维尔支出文件的时间是从阿马尔

① 统计表中共有 88 个有支出官员名的文件，阿比新提的档案中还有 6 个没提支出官员名的文件。

② 贡牲中心的四任总管分别是：舒勒吉时期的匿名官员和那萨、阿马尔辛时期的阿巴萨旮和舒辛时期的尹塔埃阿，见 Tom B.Jones & John W.Snyder，*Sumerian Economic Texts from the Third Ur Dynasty*，Minneapolis：University of Minnesota Press，1961，p.213。

③ 见王颖杰《乌尔第三王朝贡牲中心羊牲育肥官员那鲁的档案重建》，博士学位论文，东北师范大学古典文明史研究所，2009 年。

④ 见付世强《乌尔第三王朝厨房死牲官员舒勒吉乌如穆的档案重建》，硕士学位论文，东北师范大学古典文明史研究所，2009 年。

辛6年2月16日到舒辛3年3月。

杜旮（Duga）为王家兽苑（Na-gáb-tum）官员。他为阿比新提贡牲机构支出动物牲畜的文件总数为6件，支出文件时间是从阿马尔辛8年2月26日到舒辛1年8月5日。

朱巴旮（Zubaga）是贡牲中心家畜管理运输官员。他为阿比新提贡牲机构支出动物牲畜的文件总数为5件，其中1个文件中（SET 066）朱巴旮既是支出官员，也是“经由”官员，其支出文件的时间是从阿马尔辛8年9月到舒辛1年12月12日。

尹塔埃阿（Inta-ea）书吏为舒辛时期的贡牲中心总管。他为阿比新提贡牲机构支出动物牲畜的文件总数为7件，文件覆盖时间是从舒辛1年2月10日到舒辛7年5月1日。

乌尔库侬那（Ur-kununna）书吏是贡牲中心的羊圈官吏①。乌尔库侬那为阿比新提贡牲机构支出动物的文件数为4件，文件支出时间是从舒辛7年6月8日到舒辛9年10月。

普朱尔恩里勒（Puzur-Enlil）为阿比新提贡牲机构支出动物的文件数为5件，文件的时间是从舒辛7年7月18日到舒辛9年5月3日。

此外，贡牲中心官员乌尔南那（Ur-Nanna）、阿巴恩里勒良（Aba-Enlilgin）、恩里拉（Enlilla）和舒勒吉伊里（*Šulgi-ili*）分别为阿比新提贡牲机构支出动物的文件为2件；舒马马（Šu- Mama）、伊吉恩里勒筛（Igi-Enlilše）、普朱尔埃腊（*Puzur-Erra*）、那鲁（Nalu）、库尔比拉克（Kurbilak）和伊尼姆南那（Inim-Nanna）各为阿比新提贡牲机构支出动物的文件为1件。

① 见齐霄《乌尔第三王朝贡牲中心羊圈管理官员乌尔库侬那的档案重建》，硕士学位论文，东北师范大学古典文明史研究所，2008年。

第三章　阿比新提王太后在祭祀活动中的作用

第一节　阿比新提王太后在诸神祭祀活动中作用

阿比新提王太后以“经由人”（gìr）身份参加宗教祭祀活动的文件共计 19 个。伊南那女神可能是阿比新提王太后最重视的女神，7 个文件记录了她对伊南那女神的祭祀；叙利亚地区塞姆人的神王达干神（6 个文件）和其妻子伊什哈腊女神（3 个文件）、苏美尔的神王恩里勒（2 个文件）和其妻子宁里勒（2 个文件）也是阿比新提王太后关注的祭祀对象。此外，阿比新提王太后参加祭祀的神明还有：南那神（6 个文件）、宁库依那女神、安努尼吞女神、阿拉吞女神、那那亚女神、哈布瑞吞女神、宁库依那女神、大门楼和宁旮勒女神（各有 2 个文件记录了对他们的祭祀）、为宁廷乌旮女神、杜穆兹神、宁荪女神和古拉神（各有 1 个文件记录了对其的祭祀）。

“经由”阿比新提王太后的祭祀活动一览表

时间	为祭祀神明提供的牺牲数量和种类	“经由”和“督办”
AS 2 i/1	1 羔为安努尼吞女神，1 羔为那那亚女神	经由阿比新提，SAT 2 0693
AS8 vii/27	1 肥公牛为宁廷乌旮女神	经由阿比新提 NYPL 244 8
AS 9 iii/15	4 肥公羊为伊南那，3 肥羊为最高女祭司寝宫，2 肥羊为那那亚	经由阿比新提 NYPL 357
ŠS 1 iv/29	2 羊为杜穆兹，2 羊为伊南那女神，1 羊为神伊沙尔（^{d}I-šar），2 羊为正义神米沙尔（^{d}Mi-šar）和宁舒布尔女神，于巴德提比拉	经由阿比新提 BIN 3 215
ŠS 1 xii/12	2 肥羊为阿拉吞女神，为于宫殿的祭祀	经由阿比新提，达达司酒督办 Trouvaille 16

续表

时间	为祭祀神明提供的牺牲数量和种类	“经由”和“督办”
ŠS 2 x/2	6公牛为伊南那门【……】，为国王节日的祭祀	经由阿比新提 MVN 10 142
ŠS 3 iii	【1肥牛】各为【恩里勒】、宁里勒和伊南那女神于尼普尔	经由阿比新提 Ebla 1975-1985 287 B
ŠS 3 iv	1肥公牛为安努尼吞女神	经由阿比新提，辛阿比司酒督办 Studies Pettinato 160，167 09，171
ŠS 3 vi/7	【3】肥羊为恩里勒，宁里勒女神同	经阿比新提，恩里勒孜沙旮勒督办 PDT 2 1219
ŠS 3 xii/10	2肥羊和2羔为达干，2肥羊和2羔为伊什哈腊女神，1肥羊和1羔为伊南那女神	经由阿比新提和南那伊吉杜司酒 PDT 1 269
ŠS 4 iii/4	【2+】肥羊为达干，【2+】肥羊为伊什哈腊，1肥羊为伊南那，1肥羊为宁尼旮尔（^{d}Nin-nigar$_{x}$），1肥公羊为果园祭，2肥羊和1羔为哈布瑞吞女神（^{d}*Ha-bu-rí-tum*）	经由阿比新提，辛阿布书司酒督办
ŠS 7 vi/14	2肥羊为神阿妈腊朱（^{d}Ama-ra-zu）	经由阿比新提，辛阿布舒司酒督办 AUCT 1 479
ŠS 7 vii/4	1肥公绵羊为宁库侬那女神（^{d}Nin-kù-nun-na）	经由阿比新提，辛阿布舒督办 PDT 1 610
ŠS 7 vii/18	1羔为达干，1肥公绵羊为哈布瑞吞女神	经由阿比新提，辛阿布舒司酒督办 CST 440
ŠS 9 v/3	3肥羊为辛神，【……】，为辛祭地的牺牲；1肥羊为旦旮勒侬那（^{d}Dam-gal-nun-na），由国王送入宫廷，于尼普尔，2肥羊为宁廷乌【旮】女神（^{d}Nin-tin-ug$_{5}$-ga）和宁埃旮勒女神，2肥羊为南那，于普兹瑞什达干	经由阿比新提，辛阿布舒司酒督办 MVN 13 098
ŠS 9 vi/15	1肥牛为达干，1肥牛为伊什哈腊，于普兹瑞什达干	经由阿比新提，辛阿布尼司酒 SAT 3 1871
ŠS 9 x	10只公绵羊、5只食草公绵羊为伊南那女神	经由阿比新提，辛阿布舒司酒督办 AnOr 07 108
［?］vi/13	……1只吃奶羔为祭祀地的南那神	经由阿比新提 ASJ 04 140 01
［ŠS+］/23，29	【1】肥牛、【1】肥羊、【1+】为南那，2肥羊为“大门楼”，1肥羊为宁旮勒女神，2肥羊和2羔为宁苏女神，2+肥羊为宁古卜拉旮女神，以上于23日（下弦月祭）；2肥羊为南那的 níg-dab$_{5}$的猪供奉，2肥羊为阿卜朱，1肥牛、2肥羊为南那，1肥羊为“大门楼”，1肥羊为宁旮勒女神，1肥羊为依旮勒，2肥羊为宁库依那女神，1肥羊为乌尔那穆的王座祭地，2肥羊、3羊为古拉，1肥羊为阿拉吞，【……】以上为新月祭	经由阿比新提，努尔乌图骑使督办 MVN 13 550

第二节　阿比新提王太后在晦日祭中的重要作用（阿马尔辛和舒辛时期）

涉及王太后阿比新提晦日祭（ud-nú-a，直译为“他（月神）躺下的那天”）的文件共计26件。该类文件分为两类，一类是“……为她的晦日祭被送入宫殿或被供奉在现场”，另一类是“……为她的晦日祭的níĝ-dab_5供奉”。文件的日期是在各月的25—27日之间，以26日为主，其中26日有16件、25日有6件、27日有4件、24日有1件。乌尔第三王朝祭祀晦日的活动与乌尔城的保护神月神南那有关。古代苏美尔人认为在农历最后一天的晦日（29或30日月相消失），月神南那进入了冥界。对晦日进行祭祀可能是为了迎接月神再次回到人间，新的一月即将开始。也许是要提前为29日的晦日祭作准备，王太后一般在两三天前（26日或27日）就收到了祭祀所用的牺牲。

在现存的阿比新提王太后的文件中，对晦日的祭祀活动主要出现在阿马尔辛4年10月26日到阿马尔辛9年2月26日。阿马尔辛4年10月之前尚未发现其晦日祭的文件，而舒辛时期仅发现一个记录晦日祭的文件（AUCT 2 170）。阿马尔辛时期的晦日祭的主要形式是：1只（偶尔多只）肥羊或羔为阿比新提的晦日祭被送入宫殿（ud-nú-a-ka é-gal ba-an-ku_4，共计7件）。特殊的晦日祭形式出现在阿马尔辛8年（5件）：1（2）只羔为阿比新提，为其晦日祭的贡入项，奉献在现场（mu-túm ud~nú-a-ka-ni ki-ba ba-na-a-gar），经由乌尔巴巴厨师和阿亚卡拉厨师（宰杀）。此外，阿比新提王太后的晦日祭的最后一个文件是AUCT 2 170（舒辛9年3月25日），文件中没有特指牲畜被送入宫殿。

被送入宫殿的晦日祭用牲一览表

时间	为晦日祭提供的牺牲的数量、种类及其“经由”或督办	支出官员及文献出处
AS 4 x/26	1肥羊为晦日祭被送入宫殿，为**阿比新提**，经由舒勒吉阿亚穆	舒勒吉阿亚穆，OIP 121 048
AS 6 iii/25	1肥崽为晦日祭被送入宫殿，为**阿比新提**，经由阿胡维尔	阿胡维尔，NYPL 133

续表

时间	为晦日祭提供的牺牲的数量、种类及其“经由”或督办	支出官员及文献出处
AS 6 iv/26	1肥羊为晦日祭被送入宫殿，为**阿比新提**，经由阿胡维尔 1肥羊分别为马尔哈席总督里巴努格沙巴什、埃卜拉城人伊里达干、马瑞城之人舒伊什哈腊，分别经由卢达穆、那比辛和席台里国使，阿腊德穆督办	阿胡维尔支出，MVN 11 146
AS 6 v/26	1雌崽为晦日祭被送入宫殿，为**阿比新提**	卢迪弥腊，Torino1 249
AS 6 xii/25	1羔为晦日祭被送入宫殿，为**阿比新提**	卢迪弥腊，Prima dell´alfabeto no.17
AS 7 iii/26	1肥崽为晦日祭被送入宫殿，为**阿比新提**，经由阿胡维尔	阿胡维尔，OIP 121 027
AS 9 ii/26	2羊为阿马尔辛的王座，1肥牛、6羊和4肥羊为问安礼，1肥羊为阿摩利人那坡鲁农，到厨房，经由乌尔巴巴厨师 1羊为晦日祭被送入宫殿，为**阿比新提**，经由朱巴旮	朱巴旮，经由阿达卡拉书吏，SET 066
ŠS 9 iii/25	1肥羊为宁廷乌旮，为**国王**的洁净仪式的 níĝ-dab$_5$ 供奉，……，3肥羊为**阿比新提**，为她的晦日祭支出	AUCT 2 170

供奉在现场的晦日祭用牲一览表

时间	为晦日祭提供的牺牲的数量、种类及其“经由”或督办	支出官员及文献出处
AS 8 ii/26	1羔为**阿比新提**，为其晦日贡入项奉献在现场，经由舒马马，伊隆丹国使督办	舒马马，BIN 3 165
AS 8 ii/26	1羔为**阿比新提**，为其晦日贡入项奉献在现场，经由乌尔巴巴厨师	杜旮，BIN 3 403
AS 8 iv/26	1+为乌尔美斯乐师，经由舒勒吉里提什国使，伊隆丹国使督办 2羔为**阿比新提**，为她的晦日的贡入项，奉献在现场，乌尔巴巴督办	杜旮，PDT 2 1145
AS 8 v/25	1羔为**阿比新提**，为其晦日的贡入项，奉献在现场，乌尔巴巴督办	杜旮，ASJ 07 123 19
AS 8 vi/27	1羔为**阿比新提**，为其晦日的贡入项，奉献在现场，阿亚卡拉督办	杜旮，CTNMC 05

记录阿比新提的晦日祭的 níĝ-dab$_5$ 供奉文件（níĝ-dab$_5$ ud-nú-a-a-ka-ni）的时间是从阿马尔辛6年10月25日到舒辛8年2月26日（共计12件）。它与一般的晦日祭的不同之处在于其祭祀用牲的数量比较多，通常是20—23只牲畜，最少为12只，最多达126只。其用牲的种类也比较多，包括：猪、肥牛或羊、羊和瞪羚等。

阿比新提的晦日祭的 níĝ-dab$_5$ 供奉一览表

时间	为阿比新提的晦日祭 níĝ-dab$_5$ 供奉 提供牺牲数量和种类及经由和督办	支出官员和文献出处
AS 6 x/25	6 肥羊、14 羊和 1 瞪羚为**阿比新提**，舒宁舒布尔骑使督办，1 肥羊为卢旮勒马古瑞，阿腊德穆督办，从送入项中，为晦日祭	阿巴萨旮，TRU 315
AS 7 v/2，7， 8，11，13， 18，22，24， 29，30 **v/26**	10、2、5、1、10（共 28 只）羊分别于 2、8、22、30 日为**卢旮勒马古瑞（驸马）**，分别由乌尔巴巴、乌拉伊尼什、乌塔米沙蓝和里尼审督办	阿巴萨旮， Nisaba 08 070 （月结） 文件 Ontario 1 075 为单独记载的日结
	5 羊为**乌尔比隆城的那尼帕塔勒的新娘**，经由舒勒吉哈席斯，300 羊为**卢南那的妻子**，阿腊德姆督办，于 7 日	
	3 猪、1 驴、8 肥羊、8 羊为**美伊什塔蓝（公主）**，为满月的 níĝ-dab$_5$ 供奉，于 11 日，宁哈马提骑使督办	
	1 肥羊为圣桌，为**阿马尔辛的 níĝ-dab$_5$ 供奉**，于 13 日，阿图司酒督办	
	2 肥羊、5 羊分别于 18、22 日为**伊拉隆**，达亚提书吏和乌塔米沙蓝督办	
	6 羊为**舒辛**，于 24 日，乌塔米沙蓝督办	
	1 猪、10 肥羊、10 羔和 1 瞪羚为**阿比新提**，为晦日祭的 níĝ-dab$_5$ 供奉，于 26 日	
	10 羊为**美伊什塔蓝（公主）**，于 29 日，乌塔米沙蓝督办	
AS8vi/27	……13 肥羊和 9 羊为**阿比新提**，从送入项中为她的晦日祭的 níĝ-dab$_5$ 供奉	阿巴萨旮，SAT 2 1089
AS8vii/26	8 肥羊和 10 羊为**阿比新提**，从送入项中为她的晦日祭的 níĝ-dab$_5$ 供奉	阿巴萨旮，UDT 129
AS 8ix/26	2 羊到御膳房，乌尔巴巴厨师督办	阿巴萨旮，经由达亚提书吏，UDT 095
	2 肥牛、1 牛、2 肥羊、121 羊为**阿比新提**，为晦日祭的 níĝ-dab$_5$ 供奉	
AS 9 ii/26	2 肥羊为阿摩利人那坡拉农，经由卢旮勒卡吉那国使，21 肥羊、39 羊和 3 瞪羚为**阿比新提**，为她晦日祭的 níĝ-dab$_5$ 供奉，经乌拉里什骑使，阿腊德穆督办	阿巴萨旮，经由努尔辛书吏，PDT 1 579
AS 9 iv/25	6 肥羊、14 羊为她的晦日祭的 níĝ-dab$_5$ 供奉，宁里勒阿马穆骑使督办	阿巴萨旮，经由南那马巴，DoCu EPHE 259
	1 瞪羚为乌尔宁古卜拉格乐师，【x】督办	
AS 9 v/26	1 羊到御膳房，阿腊德穆厨师督办，9 肥羊和 17 羊为**阿比新提**，从贡入项中为晦日祭的 níĝ-dab$_5$ 供奉，经由努尔辛书吏	阿巴萨旮，PDT 2，p.19
ŠS 1 ii/24	6 肥羊、5 羔和 1 瞪羚崽为**阿比新提**，从贡入项中为的她的晦日祭的 níĝ-dab$_5$ 供奉，经由南那马巴书吏	尹塔埃阿，PDT 1 470
ŠS 2 iii/27	3 肥羊、8 羔和 3 瞪羚崽为**阿比新提**，从贡入项中为的她的晦日祭的 níĝ dab$_5$ 供奉，经由南那马巴书吏	尹塔埃阿， JEOL 34，28，2，

续表

时间	为阿比新提的晦日祭 níĝ-dab_5供奉提供牺牲数量和种类及经由和督办	支出官员和文献出处
ŠS 4 xii/27	9 肥羊、1 肥羔和 10 羊为**阿比新提**，从贡入项中为的她的晦日祭的 níĝ-dab_5供奉，经由南那马巴书吏	尹塔埃阿，BCT 1 100
ŠS 8 ii/26	7 肥羊、12 羔和 1 瞪羚公崽为**阿比新提**，为她的晦日祭的 níĝ-dab_5供奉，经由宁里勒阿马穆骑使	尹塔埃阿，经南那马巴书吏，YOS 18 020

此外，还有一个文件（JCS 10 31 11）是关于晦日祭时为阿比新提的使节提供的银环，同时接收银环的还有一个苏萨的军尉的苏美尔妻子。文件内容是：2 环银，每环重 8 锱，给阿比新提的使节努希伊隆国使，瑞施伊隆督办，2 环银，每环重 8 锱，1 个 dalla 环银为卢旮勒安那卜杜的女儿，即苏萨的统治者沙润伊里的军尉的妻子，西台拉尼督办，于**晦日祭**时（ud~ ba-nú-ša-a），<阿腊德穆>督办，从卢迪弥腊处支出了（阿马尔辛 6 年 3 月（26）日）。

第三节　阿比新提王太后与扎巴兰城伊南那女神的关系

温马出土的文献中有 9 件提到阿马尔辛 9 年、舒辛 1 年、3 年和 4 年，特别是舒辛 3 年（4 个文件），阿比新提王太后和扎巴兰城（Zabalàm^{ki}）有特殊的关系。扎巴兰城是古代两河流域祭祀金星女神——伊南那女神的一个中心。阿比新提王太后前往扎巴兰城是为了祭祀伊南那女神。温马是扎巴兰城所在地区的中心。为阿比新提王太后前往扎巴兰城时提供布料（gada-du）、芝麻油（ì-giš）、啤酒（kaš）、面包（ninda）、牛羊的文件共计 7 件；提到为扎巴兰城的伊南那女神奉献财物的文件共 2 件。这类文件绝大多数只有年名，没有月、日。仅有 3 个文件有年名和月名，但没有日号。在阿马尔辛 9 年、舒辛 3 年和 4 年，温马城负责布匹的官员伊卡拉分别为阿比新提王太后提供 1 件、9 件和 10 件布料。在舒辛 3 年，牛羊官吏乌什穆在扎巴兰城一次为阿比新提王太后提供 1 头牛和 10 只羊，一次经由阿比新提王太后向伊南那女神奉献 2 头肥牛、10 只肥羊、13 只绵羊羔和山羊崽。舒辛 4 年 7 月，经由阿比新提王太后向扎巴兰城的伊南那女神提供 415 斗各种啤酒和 325 斗 15 升各种面粉作为“谷仓中”（šà-ge-guru$_7$-a）奉献。阿马尔辛 9 年和舒辛 1 年 4 月，阿比新提王太后的随从王家骑使是恩温伊里。

阿比新提王太后和扎巴兰城关系一览表

时间	文件内容	文献出处
AS 9	1 件亚麻布支出为**阿比新提王太后**，于扎巴兰城，从伊卡拉（布料吏）处，恩温伊里骑使的收据	UTI 3 2003
ŠS 1 iv	17 个占卜用的篮子，镶有皮革，其用皮为 8 张，给**阿比新提“退休王后”**，当她前往扎巴兰城时，经由恩温伊里骑使，从阿卡拉处，卢卡拉的收据	SET 288
ŠS 1	$5^2/_3$升油支出为**阿比新提王太后**，当她前往扎巴兰城时，乌尔舒勒帕埃的收据	MVN 18 463
ŠS 3/ii	22 个壮丁工作 2 天把啤酒和面包运送并放在扎巴兰城，于**阿比新提**王太后前往那里时，【……】，卢卡拉的收据	AnOr 7 235
ŠS 3	7 件布料为**库巴吞王后的供应**，当她生产时；1 件布料为**国王**；9 件布料为**阿比新提的（igi-kár）供应**，当她前往扎巴兰城时……从伊卡拉处，总督的收据	MVN 16 960
ŠS 3	1 公牛、9 羊和 1 羔，以上支出为**阿比新提王太后**，于扎巴兰城，从乌什穆处，总督的收据	MVN 16 916
ŠS 3	1 优公牛、1 次优肥公牛、5 优等肥公羊、5 次优肥公羊、2 公羊、9 羔、3 肥公崽和 1 公崽为**扎巴兰城的伊南那女神，经由阿比新提王太后**，从乌什穆处，司酒阿比阿皮赫的收据	BIN 5 31
ŠS 4	10 件布料是**王太后阿比新提的供应，当她前往扎巴兰城**，从伊卡拉（布料吏）处，总督的收据	MVN 16 713
ŠS 4/vii	415 斗各种啤酒和 129、68 斗 6 升、【1+】斗、65 斗和 8 升、62 斗和【1+】升【……】各种面粉，**为扎巴兰城的伊南那女神的 šà-ge-guru$_7$-a 供奉，经由阿比新提王太后**，辛阿比舒的收据	AnOr 7 241

第四章　吉尔苏城的阿比新提王太后的纺织作坊及其他文件

除了在贡牲中心和温马出土的有关阿比新提王太后的文件外，我们还发现了一些阿比新提王太后在吉尔苏（Girsu）、乌尔（Ur）、旮尔沙那（Ĝaršana）以及不清楚出土地的文件。

目前发现的在吉尔苏出土的有关阿比新提王太后的文件共8件。文件日期仅有年名，无月、日。其中3个文件（仅有年名）是记录阿比新提王太后的牧羊人为她提供一年的各类羊毛登记表（见下页表）①。阿马尔辛6年的文件提到为阿比新提王太后提供115篮（gurdub），约重3122公斤的羊毛（siki-udu）。阿马尔辛8年的文件提到以阿比新提王太后为首的三个羊毛接收机构：（1）阿比新提王太后，其监工为SI.A-A牲畜官（$kuš_7$）；（2）宫殿，其监工为乌尔宁朱牲畜官；（3）塔丁伊什塔尔公主和乌尔伊什塔蓝王子，其监工为乌尔巴巴牲畜官。其中王太后机构拥有的羊毛最多，约重3365公斤，公主和王子拥有的羊毛合计为5228.5公斤，宫殿拥有的羊毛最少，为1478公斤。王太后机构原有19个牧羊人（na-gada，libir-àm），又加有5个，共计24个牧羊人。宫殿有6个牧羊人。公主有4个牧羊人、王子有7个牧羊人，二人共有11个牧羊人。日期破损的第三个羊毛文件仅记录了王太后机构的21个原有的牧羊人和后加的5个共26个牧羊人各自上交的各类羊毛，其上交羊毛为3273公斤②。

---

① 文件中的羊毛分为七个等级，分别是：御用级羊毛（siki-túg-lugal）、次御用级羊毛（siki-túg-ús-lugal）、三级羊毛（siki-túg-3-kam-ús）、四级羊毛（siki-túg-4-kam-ús）、五级guzza羊毛（siki-túg-guz-za-ĝen）、第六级普通羊毛（siki-túg-ĝen）和第七级黑羊毛（siki-ge_6），偶尔也有死羊的羊毛（siki-udu-ba-úš）。

② 注意在新的羊毛表中，阿马尔辛8年原有的19个旧牧羊人中有3个人变换了，新表中又加入了3个新的牧羊人。

两个文件中阿比新提王太后机构的牧羊人对比表

DAS 051	ITT 2，00873	DAS 051	ITT 2，00873
Lú-diĝir-ra	Lugal-ú-šim-e	Lugal-sa_{12}-du_5	Ur-^{d}Nanše
Lugal-sa_6-ga	Ha-an-du	Ba-zi	Ur-^{d}Nun-gal
Ha-an-du	Ab-ba-kal-la	Éb-gu-ul	Lú-$lagaš^{ki}$
Nam-ha-ni	Lugal-sa_6-ga	Sag-lugal-e-zu	É-hi-li
Ur-éš-dam	^{d}Utu-ik-ṣúr	É-hi-li	[···]
Lú-$nigin_9$-bar-ra	Lú-me-lám	Ur-sukkal	A-kal-la
Du-du	Lu-$nigin_9$-bar-ra	Ad-da-kal-la（新的）	Du-du
A-kal-la	Girì-né-ì-sa_6	^{d}Utu-sa_6-ga	Lugal-iri-mu
Ur-^{d}Nan-še	Ur-^{d}Lamma	^{d}Ba-ba_6-da	Ad-da-kal-la（新的）
Ur-^{d}Nun-gal	Lugal-engar	Ur-^{d}Ba-ba_6	^{d}Utu-sa_6-ga
Girì-né-ì-sa_6	Lugal-sa_{12}-du_5	Ur-mes	^{d}Ba-ba_6-da
Ur-^{d}Lamma	Ba-zi		Ur-^{d}Ba-ba_6
Lugal-engar	Éb-gu-ul		

综上所述，阿比新提机构拥有大量的羊毛，我们推测阿比新提王太后在吉尔苏可能拥有一间羊毛作坊。它是王朝最大的羊毛作坊之一，每年大量的纺织品在纺织作坊中被生产出来。

为阿比新提王太后提供羊毛的文件一览表①

时间	为阿比新提提供羊毛的总量及其监工	文献出处
AS 6	……总计：115 篮羊毛，其重 104 钧 4 斤 15 锱，以上羊毛为**阿比新提**，监工：沙腊刊总督	HLC 2 082
AS 8	……总计：112 钧 10 斤 5 锱重的羊毛为**阿比新提**，监工：席阿亚牲畜官；49 钧 16 斤 10 锱重的羊毛为宫殿，监工：乌尔宁朱牲畜官；174 钧 17 $^1/_3$斤 8 锱重的羊毛为塔丁伊什塔尔公主和乌尔伊什塔蓝王子，监工：乌尔巴巴牲畜官	DAS 051
【?】	……总计：109 钧 6 $^2/_3$斤 x 锱羊毛为**阿比新提**，【监工：席阿亚牲畜官】	TCTI 1 00873

① 羊毛的重量单位有：钧（gú）约等于 30 公斤、ma-na 约等于 1 斤、锱（gín）约等于 1 钱即 8.3 克。

吉尔苏的文件还包括舒辛5—6年关于阿比新提王太后、库巴吞王后及宫殿（é-gal）的档案箱（pisan-dub-ba）标签（无日期）①、1个记录从阿比新提处支出布料（túĝ）和油（ì）的文件（SEL 02 37，日期破损）以及1个记录了为阿比新提王太后提供面粉（zì）、啤酒（kaš）、鱼（ku_6）、葱（sum-sikil）、蒜（sum-gaz）、鸟蛋（nunuz-mušen）、芦苇（sa-gi）及面包（ninda）等供应品的文件（ITT 2 3802，日期破损）。

乌尔城出土的有关阿比新提王太后的文件仅2件。一个（UET 3，1757，无日期）记录了为阿比新提王太后提供的布料；另一个（UET 9，4，舒辛1年4月）是关于阿比新提的送入项的文件（内容破损）。

旮尔沙那有2个涉及阿比新提王太后的文件。一个（CUSAS 3，351，舒辛时期）记录了为阿比新提等人提供砖（sig_4）；另一个（CUSAS 3，1485，舒辛9年12月13日）是为阿比新提王太后等人发放酥油（ì-nun）和奶制品（ga-àr）的发放名单。

此外，我们还发现了3个不清楚文献出处地且无日期的文件。一个（TCS 1，041）是在信件中提到为阿比新提的祭祀提供各种面粉的文件；一个（JCS 54，07，52）是为阿比新提王太后及库巴吞王后等人提供各种宝石或金银的文件；第三个是为阿比新提提供绿松石鞋（^{kuš}e-sír du_8-ši-a）的文件（Christie's 199307 72 170）。

① 三个文件分别是：MVN 09，165（舒辛5年）、MTBM 257（舒辛6年）、ITT 5，9193（舒辛时期）。

第五章　结语

阿比新提王太后的有关文献开始于阿马尔辛 1 年 11 月，结束于舒辛 9 年 12 月，共近 18 年。有关阿比新提王太后的文献主要由贡牲中心官员间的接管文件、记录阿比新提日常消费的月供应文件和记录贡牲中心官员把王朝和各地高官贡入的牲畜分配给阿比新提文件三类收入文件组成。

根据迪亚拉河地区埃什嫩那城的高官巴巴提的印章，阿比新提是舒辛王的母亲。阿比新提在阿马尔辛统治时期的档案文献中被称为 nin，即“王后（王太后）”或“女主人”。在她的儿子舒辛统治时期，阿比新提仍然拥有“王（太）后”的头衔。此时，阿比新提的身份是舒辛王的母亲，即“王太后”。在舒辛时期温马出土的一个文件中，阿比新提也被称为“退休王后”（nin-ĝar）。

由于阿马尔辛在成为国王之前的信息我们一无所知，因此，我们怀疑“阿马尔辛”是他继位后新改的名字。阿马尔辛很可能就是曾担任过乌鲁克城将军的王子乌尔辛。“乌尔辛”意为“辛神的仆人”，“阿马尔辛”意为“辛神的牛犊”，有“辛神之子”之意，“辛神之子”比“辛神的仆人”更符合国王的身份。同时，乌尔辛王子只在舒勒吉 34 年 8 月到舒勒吉 47 年 2 月 7 日活动，阿马尔辛时期没有发现他活动的任何记录，这也支持着乌尔辛改名的论断。因此，我们认为舒勒吉时期的王子乌尔辛继承了王位并改名为阿马尔辛。此外，《舒辛赞美诗》、^{d}Šu-Suen-*walid*-^{d}Šulgi 的名字以及 HANE/S 6，pp.30-31 的文件证明舒辛是舒勒吉和舒勒吉新提的儿子，舒辛与阿马尔辛是兄弟。由于阿比新提是舒辛之母，而阿比新提也应是阿马尔辛之母，因此，阿比新提应是舒勒吉时期的王后以及阿马尔辛和舒辛时期的王太后。再加上阿比新提与舒勒吉新提名字的相似性，我们得出阿比新提就是舒勒吉新提。新王因忌讳其父舒勒吉的名字将母亲的名字舒勒吉新提（“舒勒吉是我的骄傲”*Šulgi-simtī*）改为阿比新提

(*abi-simtī*)，意为“我的父亲是我的骄傲”。

通过对阿比新提王太后的有关文献的分析，我们知道阿比新提王太后常以“经由人”身份参加祭祀诸神的活动。同时，阿比新提王太后与晦日祭（ud-nú-a）和扎巴兰城伊南那女神的祭祀密切相关。此外，我们在吉尔苏还发现了一些关于阿比新提拥有大量羊毛的文件，据此我们推测阿比新提王太后在吉尔苏可能拥有一间羊毛作坊。

阿比新提王太后（即舒勒吉新提王后）经历了舒勒吉王、阿马尔辛王和舒辛王共38年的统治。她亲历了普兹瑞什达干贡牲中心乃至整个乌尔第三王朝的兴盛和衰落。舒勒吉新提王后贡牲机构档案记录了贡牲中心建立前期、中期以及早中期的乌尔第三王朝的政治、经济、宗教等社会情况。舒勒吉新提王后贡牲机构的设置反映了舒勒吉统治时期王国政治上的强大、经济上的繁荣以及宗教祭祀活动的频繁。到舒勒吉的儿子阿马尔辛和舒辛统治时期，阿比新提王太后主要接收各地高官给她的供奉，并积极参与各类宗教祭祀活动，这说明阿比新提王太后此时在王朝的外交事务及宗教祭祀中扮演着重要的角色。在吉尔苏阿比新提王太后的羊毛作坊的存在反映了阿比新提王太后在经济生产活动中的重要作用。总之，对舒勒吉新提王后（阿比新提王太后）的贡牲文件的研究表明：乌尔第三王朝时期，王室及一些贵族女性在王朝的政治、经济、宗教、外交等事务积极活动，她们拥有较多的权利，在王朝的社会生活中具有举足轻重的地位。

同时，对舒勒吉新提和阿比新提王太后同一身份的研究，不仅让我们明确了乌尔第三王朝时期舒勒吉、舒勒吉新提、阿比新提、阿马尔辛和舒辛之间的婚姻和血缘关系，而且有益于我们了解乌尔第三王朝王室的丧葬习俗以及王位兄弟继承制度①。更为我们全面地了解和研究阿比新提王太后在政治、经济、宗教和外交事务中的活动以及整个乌尔第三王朝的政治、经济、军事、外交及宗教等社会情况提供了丰富的材料。

---

①　两河流域兄弟之间的王位继承的例子还有乌尔第三王朝的首王乌尔那穆（Ur-Nammu）和其兄乌鲁克第五王朝的乌图赫旮勒（Utu-hegal），参见D.Frayne，*The Royal Inscription of Mesopotamia*，Toronto：University of Toronto Press，1993，E 3/2.1.1，p.9。

第三部分　早期图马勒庙区羊、猪和家禽官员阿什尼乌以及死牲官员贝里阿瑞克司仪和苏萨总督贝里阿瑞克的档案分析

第一章　早期图马勒庙区羊、猪和家禽官员阿什尼乌的档案分析（Š 40 iv–Š 44 i/12）

阿什尼乌是贡牲中心早期管理图马勒庙区的牲畜和牲畜饲料的官员①。目前，尚未发现阿什尼乌的印章或表明其身份的文件。贡牲中心出土的阿什尼乌的文件共计32个，覆盖时间从舒勒吉40年4月到舒勒吉44年1月12日，共3年9个月。其中阿什尼乌的支出文件25个、接管文件4个、统领文件2个（PDT 2，1049和JCS 24，162 64）、档案箱文件1个（OIP 115 141）。阿什尼乌的档案文件表明他是专门负责图马勒庙区羊、猪和家禽的管理官员。根据阿什尼乌档案中文件的内容不同，其文件可以分为一下几类：（1）监管和向育肥师发放的育肥饲料；（2）从那冉伊里处接管国王送入项羊牲（Š 41 i–vii，仅2个文件）；（3）转交自己宰杀处理的羊牲给（厨师）巴穆（Š 40和Š 41）以及死牲管理官员贝里阿瑞克（Š 43 ii–vi/24）；（4）支出羊牲给图马勒庙区女神宁里勒、神王恩里勒和祖先祭祀地（Š 42 vi–viii），以及为上弦月的辛祭地、宫中的伊南那和御膳房（é-uz-ga）提供肥公羊和羊羔。

---

① 在图马勒管理羊圈的官员还有羊牲育肥官员那鲁以及恩丁吉尔牟，见王颖杰《乌尔第三王朝贡牲中心羊牲育肥官员那鲁的档案重建》，博士学位论文，东北师范大学世界古典文明史研究所，2009年。

第一节 阿什尼乌监管和向育肥师发放的育肥饲料

阿什尼乌档案中的前 2 个文件（Š 40 iv-v）记载了他管理的全部动物所用的大麦饲料。根据食用饲料的不同，动物可以分为五等：第一等级的动物每只食用 1.5 升大麦、第二等级的动物每只食用 1 升大麦、第三等级的动物每只食用 2/3 升大麦、第四等级的动物每只食用 1/2 升和第五等级的动物每只食物 1/3 升。我们从这两个文件可以看出，阿什尼乌在图马勒庙区的牲畜种类比较多，数量中等，第一个文件中（PDT 2，1049）共有 632 只羊、80 头猪和食用 120 斗大麦的鸟。第二个文件中（AUCT 1 733）共有 467 只羊、50 头猪和食用 120 斗大麦的鸟。值得注意的是文件中猪的种类繁多，主要有：苇塘公猪（šah-ĝiš-gi-nitá-gal）、母猪（šah-ama-gan）、成年公猪（šah-nitá-sa-gi_4-a）、成年母猪（šah-munus-gur_4）、公猪豚（šah-zé-da-nitá）、母猪豚（šah-zé-da-munus）、生育母猪（šáh-ama-gan）、性成熟公猪（šáh-nitá-ĝiš）、年轻猪（šáh-mú）。

此外，舒勒吉 41 年 1 月到 10 月的 3 个文件也记录了阿什尼乌接收和转交的动物大麦饲料。第一个文件（Princeton 1 123）记录到阿什尼乌接管了 9716 斗大麦为羊、猪和鸟的饲料；后两个文件（Š 41 ix ASJ 7 124 22 和 Š 41 x，AUCT 1 733）则提到阿什尼乌分别将作为公绵羊饲料的 1145 斗大麦、1560 斗国王的大麦转交给了乌尔宁图和阿亚卡拉。其中第一个文件还同时提到了为天神安之城（乌鲁克）的女人、“宫殿的圣桌”、国王以及女奴等分发口粮的情况。舒勒吉 43 年 6 月的一个文件（AUCT 1 746）也同时提到阿什尼乌接管了为国王提供的 60 斗大麦。

阿什尼乌监管和向育肥师发放的育肥饲料表

时间/文献	（优等）每只1.5升）	（次优等）每只1升	肥羔每只2/3升）	（普通）每只1/2升	（第五等）每只1/3升	30天的大麦合计/接管官员
	104只优等育肥公绵羊	158肥公羊、38肥羔、20母山羊		136公羊、8公山羊		1332斗，阿亚卡拉育肥师接管
	90肥公绵羊	78肥公绵羊				639斗，那鲁育肥师接管
Š 40 iv / 1–30	1苇塘公猪、23母猪	10成年公猪、17成年母猪			14公猪豚、15母猪豚	218斗，舒萨穆接管
(PDT 2, 1049)						120斗大麦为鸟，布朱亚接管
	（总计:）194肥绵羊、1苇塘公猪、23母猪	（总计:）236肥公绵羊、38肥羔、20雌山羊、27成年猪		（总计:）136公绵羊、8雄山羊崽	（总计:）14公猪豚、15母猪豚	120斗大麦为鸟、2309斗大麦为肥羊、猪和鸟，于图马勒，监管（ugula）：阿什尼乌
共计：632只羊、80头猪和120斗大麦饲料的鸟，2429斗大麦						
	111优等肥公羊、1+羊羔? 10山羊崽	196肥公羊、33肥羔、1+x母绵羊、8崽、[20]母山羊	61肥羊羔	90只公绵羊		1725.5斗大麦为肥公绵，阿卡拉羊牲育肥师接管
	[60]+20（+10）肥公绵羊	1+公绵羊		1+公绵羊		801斗大麦，那鲁羊牲育肥师接管
Š 40 v	1苇塘公猪、23生育母猪	10成年公猪、3性成熟公猪、13成年母猪		26年轻猪		222斗大麦为苇塘猪，舒萨穆接管
(JCS 24, 162 64)						
						120斗大麦为鸟，布朱亚接管
	（总计:）201?优等肥公羊、1+羔、10崽、24猪	（总计:）196肥公羊、33肥羔、8崽、20母山羊、1+母绵羊、26猪	61肥羔	（总计:）91+公绵羊、4羔、26猪、10公山羊		4猪大麦没有接管，120斗大麦为鸟、2871.5斗大麦为猪和鸟，于图马勒，监管（ugula）：阿什尼乌
共计：575+只羊、76头猪和食用120斗大麦的鸟，2991.5斗大麦						

续表

时间/文献	（优等）每只 1.5 升）	（次优等）每只 1 升	肥羔每只 2/3 升）	（普通）每只 1/2 升	（第五等）每只 1/3 升	30 天的大麦合计/接管官员
Š 41 i-iv Princeton 1 123	9716 王斗大麦为**羊、猪和鸟的饲料**，2496 斗为住在“天神安”之城（uru-an-na）的女人们的啤酒和面包月供应，48 斗大麦和 48 斗红小麦为“天神安”之城的宫殿的圣桌（zà-gú-lá），1216 斗大麦为女奴和孩子们				转交官员（ki...--ta）从基图什鲁处	接管官员（ì-dab$_5$）阿什尼乌
Š 41 ix（ASJ 7 124 22）	1145 斗大麦为**公绵羊的饲料**				从阿什尼乌处	乌尔宁图
Š 41 x（AUCT 1 733）	1560 王斗大麦为**公绵羊的饲料**				从阿什尼乌处	阿亚卡拉
Š 43 vi（AUCT 1 746）	60 王斗大麦，返还到愿地（图马勒）				从乌尔萨旮牛牧处	阿什尼乌

第二节 阿什尼乌从那冉伊里处接管国王送入项羊牲（Š 41 i-vii）

阿什尼乌的档案中共有 2 个文件记录了阿什尼乌从早期官员那冉伊里处接管了国王送入的牲畜。这些牲畜的种类主要有：瞪羚羊、公绵羊、羔和崽，其数量不等，舒勒吉 41 年 1 月的文件中（BIN 3 365）仅记录了有 1 只瞪羚羊为国王的送入项，而同年 7 月的文件（Torino 1 02）记录的国王送入项的羊牲多达 431 只。

阿什尼乌从那冉伊里处接管“国王送入项”羊牲的数量和种类一览表

时间	文件内容	转交官员（ki ~ *Na-ra-am-ì-lí* --ta）	文献出处
Š 41 i	1 只瞪羚羊为国王的送入（mu-túm）	那冉伊里	BIN 3 365
Š 41 vii	73 肥公绵羊、4 肥羊羔、6 肥山羊崽，1 雌崽，264 公羊，83 羔，为国王的送入	那冉伊里	Torino 1 020

第三节　阿什尼乌转交自己宰杀处理的羊牲给（厨师）巴穆（Š 40 和 Š 41）以及死牲管理官员贝里阿瑞克（Š 43 ii-vi/24）

阿什尼乌的档案中共有 9 个文件记录了阿什尼乌将宰杀牲转交给死牲管理官员贝里阿瑞克。舒勒吉 40 年 7 月 5—7 日的文件（OIP 115 138）提到阿什尼乌将宰杀牲转交给了（厨师）巴穆。舒勒吉 41 年 7 月 30 日的文件中没有提到接管宰杀牲的官员，由于该文件与舒勒吉 40 年 7 月 5—7 日的文件日期相近，我们推测该文件中的宰杀牲的接管官员也是厨师巴穆。此外，一个没有年名只有月、日的文件（v/7，Hirose 005）也没有提到宰杀牲的接管官员。阿什尼乌转交的宰杀牲的种类有：育肥羔、普通羔、公绵羊、母绵羊和山羊崽，其数量通常是 1 天 1 只，但有时也可 1 天 2 只。阿什尼乌将这些宰杀牲交给厨师或死牲管理官员可能主要是为士兵或女奴提供食物。

阿什尼乌转交的宰杀牲的数量和种类一览表

时间	文件内容	被宰杀地	转交官员（ki...--ta）	接收官员（šu~ba-ti）	文献出处
Š 40 vii/5-[8]	1 宰杀的肥羊羔，于 5 日于图马勒庙区	被宰杀于图马勒	阿什尼乌	巴穆（厨师）	OIP 115 138
	1 公绵羊，于 6 日				
	1 + x 宰杀公山羊，于【7】日				
Š 41 vii/30	1 只公羔，于 30 日	图马勒	阿什尼乌	巴穆?（厨师）	Torino 1 405
Š 43 ii/17，22	1 只公绵羊，于 17 日	图马勒	阿什尼乌	贝里阿瑞克	Torino 1 268
	1 只宰杀公绵羊，于 22 日				
Š 43 ii/25-28	1 公绵羊，于 25 日	被宰杀于图马勒	阿什尼乌	贝里阿瑞克	MVN 13 861
	1 公绵羊和 1 只母绵羊，于 26 日				
	1 只育肥羊羔，于 27 日				
	1 只母绵羊，于 28 日				
Š 43 ii/30	1 只宰杀公绵羊	图马勒	阿什尼乌	贝里阿瑞克	RT 37136 1
Š 43 iii/8	1 只宰杀公绵羊	图马勒	阿什尼乌	贝里阿瑞克	RA 9 40 SA 1

续表

时间	文件内容	被宰杀地	转交官员（ki...--ta）	接收官员（šu~ba-ti）	文献出处
Š 43 iii /10，13，14	1 只公绵羊【……】，于10日	被宰杀于图马勒	阿什尼乌	贝里阿瑞克	AnOr 01 005
	2 只公绵羊，于 13 日				
	1 只公羊，于 14 日				
Š 43 iv/1，2	1 只公绵羊，于 1 日	图马勒	阿什尼乌	贝里阿瑞克	Sumer 24，72 8
	1 只宰杀公绵羊，于 2 日				
Š 43 v/9，10	1 只公绵羊，于 9 日	图马勒	阿什尼乌	贝里阿瑞克	Nisaba 08 190
	1 只宰杀公绵羊，于 10 日				
Š 43 v/28	2 只宰杀公绵羊	图马勒	阿什尼乌	贝里阿瑞克	BIN 3 005
Š 43 vi/24	1 只肥山羊崽和 1 只公羊为宰杀牲	图马勒	阿什尼乌	贝里阿瑞克	RA 9 40 SA 2
v/7	1 只宰杀的母绵羊	图马勒	阿什尼乌		Hirose 005

第四节　阿什尼乌在图马勒庙区支出活动的分析

阿什尼乌在图马勒庙区支出羊牲的目的主要是为女神宁里勒、神王恩里勒和祖先祭祀地（Š 42 vi–viii），以及为上弦月的辛祭地、宫中的伊南那和御膳房（é-uz-ga）提供育肥公绵羊和羊羔。阿什尼乌为宁里勒的祭祀支出牲畜的文件共有 2 个（Š 42 vi，OIP 115 140 和 Š 42 viii/22，AUCT 1 686），其中第二个是为神王恩里勒和神后宁里勒的祭祀同时支出牲畜的文件，但在文件中恩里勒比宁里勒的祭祀用牲多 1 只育肥公绵羊。舒勒吉 42 年 6 月 1 日的文件（Torino 1 196）还记录了阿什尼乌为宁里勒的月供应支出了 30 只育肥公绵羊（每天天 1 只）。舒勒吉 43 年 6 月 4 日和 5 日的两个文件中（JCS 52 07 02 和 JCS 24，159 51）阿什尼乌为宫中的伊南那女神的牺牲提供了 1 到 2 只育肥公绵羊的同时，他还为御膳房支出了 1 只羊。阿什尼乌的档案中提到为国王、乌尔那穆的饮水地、农旮勒提供月供应各 1 次。

从图马勒庙区阿什尼乌（处）支出羊牲的数量和用途一览表（Š 42 vi–Š 43 vi/5）

时间	文件内容	支出地点 zi-gašà ~ Tummal	转交官员（ki ~ Aš-ni-u_{18}）	文献出处
Š 42 vi	1+x【肥】公羊为……宁里勒之口	于图马勒	阿什尼乌	OIP 115 140
Š 42 vi/12	2肥公羊为【……】月供，6肥公羊和2公羊为国王的月供，2肥公羊和1公羊为（先王）乌尔那穆的饮水地的月供，1肥公羊为农旮勒神的月供	于图马勒	阿什尼乌	OIP 115 139
Š 42 vi/1	30肥公羊为宁里勒的月供	于图马勒	阿什尼乌	Torino 1 196
Š 42 viii/22	3肥公羊和1羔为恩里勒，2肥公羊和1羔为宁里勒，南篩乌勒旮勒督办	于图马勒	阿什尼乌	AUCT 1 686
Š 43 vi/4	2肥公羊为宫中的伊南那的牺牲，埃腊那达督办，1公羊羔为水煮肉，到御膳房，**乌尔舒勒吉【督办】**	于图马勒	阿什尼乌	JCS 52 07 02
Š 43 vi/5	5肥公羊为辛之地，1肥公羊为宫中伊南那的牺牲，埃腊那达督办，1母羊为御膳房，**乌尔舒勒吉督办**	于图马勒	阿什尼乌	JCS 24，159 51

此外，阿什尼乌的档案中还有3个文件记录了他将芦苇转交给乌尔伊格阿林和鲁旮勒沙拉。在阿比新提王太后的文件中，共有2个文件提到乌尔伊格阿林是“王（太）后的育肥师”（AS 8 ix/9，SumRecDreh.19和AS 8 ix/18，TRU 126），我们推测：阿什尼乌在图马勒庙区的经济活动与阿比新提王太后（舒勒吉新提）密切相关。

阿什尼乌转交的芦苇情况一览表

时间	文件内容	转交官员（ki...--ta）	**接收官员**（…，šu ~ ba-ti）	**文献出处**
Š 41 vii	58堆giruš芦苇	阿什尼乌	乌尔伊格阿林	ASJ 19 201 3
Š 41 vii/4	1堆giruš芦苇	阿什尼乌	乌尔伊格阿林	PDT 1 257
Š 42	334堆芦苇捆，93堆芦苇捆来自图马勒	阿什尼乌	鲁旮勒沙拉	SAT 2 0999

阿什尼乌在图马勒庙区一系列的经济活动：先是接收饲养羊、猪和鸟的大麦饲料，再用这些大麦饲料育肥羊牲，并将育肥的羊牲用于祭祀或为

王室人员或神明提供月供，最后把宰杀的羊牲转交给死牲管理官员，这表明：阿什尼乌在图马勒庙区拥有一套完整的牲畜管理体系。对阿什尼乌的档案进行分析，有助于我们更好地了解贡牲中心早期的运作模式和规模，为我们理解舒勒吉新提王后贡牲机构这一早期档案提供了借鉴。

第二章 贝里阿瑞克的档案分析

舒勒吉新提王后贡牲机构的档案和那冉伊里的档案是在王朝贡牲中心成立之前开始的两个早期档案。为了更好地理解王后贡牲机构的设置以及管理等情况，本书又重建了贡牲中心早期接收宰杀或死亡牲畜的官员贝里阿瑞克的档案。通过对贝里阿瑞克档案的重建，我们知道贝里阿瑞克接收死牲开始于舒勒吉 42 年 11 月，结束于舒勒吉 43 年 6 月 24 日，共工作了 8 个月。在中期和晚期的阿马尔辛和舒辛时期，有一个高级官员的名字也叫贝里阿瑞克，在贡牲中心总管那萨、阿巴萨旮和尹塔埃阿的接管官员们为贡牲中心送入牲畜，特别是羔、崽给恩里勒夫妇的送入项——接管文件中，他已经是苏萨的总督了（ŠS 8 xii，TÉL 046）。他在文献中出现的时间是从舒勒吉 44 年 6 月到舒辛 9 年 11 月，共 22 年。

第一节 早期死牲官员贝里阿瑞克的身份及其工作（Š 42 xi–Š 43 vi/24）

贝里阿瑞克的 13 个档案文件表明，他是一位专门接收死牲的官员。其工作的时间是从舒勒吉 42 年 11 月（BIN 3，611）到舒勒吉 43 年 6 月 24 日（RA 09 040 SA 02）。目前我们只发现一个贝里阿瑞克的印章。该印章与贡牲中心死牲官员厨师乌尔尼旮尔（Ur–niĝar）的印章一起盖在一件记录舒勒吉 42 年 12 月那冉伊里送入 215 头牛肉体和 1401 头羊肉体的文件中，死牲的收到者（šu ~ ba – ti）是贝里阿瑞克和乌尔尼旮尔两人（NYPL 278）。该收据文件的数目较大，又是在 12 月，属于年结文件。贝里阿瑞克的印章提到他的身份是司酒（sagi）：舒勒吉强大之人，乌尔之王，四方之王：**司酒贝里阿瑞克是你的仆人**①。我们不清楚为什么这一官职的人还管理死牲。

贝里阿瑞克的职责是专门接收贡牲中心宰杀的牛、羊牲。贝里阿瑞克从早期官员那然伊里和中心账目主管那萨处接收了可能是在运输和存栏过程中死亡和因老弱病残而被处理掉的牛、羊，它们基本上是没有经过育肥的牲畜，质量较差。贡牲中心主管并不把这些死亡的牲畜写入其每天收支活牲的总账目中，因为这些非宰杀而死亡的动物不能用于祭祀诸神或王室和官员们食用。

在贝里阿瑞克和乌尔尼旮尔共同接收死牲期间，我们猜测乌尔尼旮尔是贝里阿瑞克的副手。从舒勒吉 43 年 9 月（BIN 3 006）开始，乌尔尼旮尔正式接替贝里阿瑞克的工作，成为专门接收死牲的官员，一直持续到阿马尔辛 3 年 4 月 6 日。从阿马尔辛 3 年 4 月 10 日开始，舒勒吉乌如穆接替了乌尔尼旮尔的工作②，一直到伊比辛 2 年。

贡牲中心接收死牲官员任期表

官员名	工作时间
乌尔尼旮尔	Š 40 v 没有明确的死牲
贝里阿瑞克	Š 42 xi-Š 43 v 与乌尔尼旮尔共同接收死牲
乌尔尼旮尔	Š 43 ix-AS 3 iv/6 单独接收死牲
舒勒吉乌如穆	AS 3 iv/8-IS 2 xii/23

目前收集到的贝里阿瑞克的档案文件共 13 个，在最早的舒勒吉 42 年 11 月和 12 月的 3 个贝里阿瑞克和乌尔尼旮尔从那冉伊里处收到死牲的文件中，用牛羊的肉体（ad_6）来表达死牲，③ 然而从 42 年开始，那冉伊里的早期档案的术语不同于后来的中心官员。那冉伊里作为库房管理员，他考虑到库存形式的肉、皮、筋，所以强调的是牛羊肉体，而不是牛羊。其后的其他官员转交死牲时所用的术语是被宰杀或死亡（ba-úš）的牛羊。那冉伊

① 苏美尔语 sagi 的直译是“执酒杯者”。

② 付世强：《乌尔第三王朝厨房死牲官员舒勒吉乌如穆的档案重建》，东北师范大学古典文明史研究所，2009。

③ 在贡牲机构的档案文件中对动物尸体的表述是用 ad_6（尸体），而表达死的或宰杀的动物牲畜时用 ba-úš。可能 ba-úš 表示运送中刚死亡的动物，而 ad_6 是加工过的动物尸体。

里之所以把牛羊肉体交给贝里阿瑞克，可能是他把牛羊皮、筋和羊毛存入自己的仓库中，只把牛羊肉交给贝里阿瑞克分发或交给低级人员食用。

贝里阿瑞克和乌尔尼旮尔共同接收死牲的第4个文件是二人从中心总管那萨处接管宰杀的牛羊。在贝里阿瑞克和乌尔尼旮尔4次共同接收死牲后，乌尔尼旮尔开始自己接收死亡的各种动物（包括野生动物）[①]。

Š 42 xi–Š 43 v 贝里阿瑞克和阿什尼乌共同接收的死牲文件一览表

（从早期官员那冉伊里和中心总管那萨处）

时间	文件内容	文献出处
Š 42 xi	78头牛尸、11头吃奶牛犊尸和312只羊尸是宰杀的牛羊，从**那冉伊里**处送入	BIN 3，611
Š 42 xi	42头公牛尸、39头牛犊尸，13头吃奶牛犊尸和1063羊尸，从**那冉伊里**处送入	TIM 6，27
Š 42 xii	159头牛尸、25头牛犊尸和31头吃奶牛犊尸，1385只羊尸和16只羔和山羊崽尸，从**那冉伊里**处送入	NYPL 278
Š 43 v	1头1岁母牛、4只母绵羊、1只公绵羊和1只山羊，为宰杀牲，从**那萨处**	OIP 115 296

贝里阿瑞克从贡牲中心的牛牲育肥师恩里拉处收到10只宰杀的牛牲。恩里拉的上司是贡牲中心总管那萨，其活动时间是从舒勒吉41年至舒辛2年9月，共19年。[②]

贝里阿瑞克8个月的死牲管理工作的另一个工作联系人是神后宁里勒的庙区图马勒的死牲官员阿什尼乌，其文件共计8个，覆盖时间从舒勒吉43年2月17日到6月24日，共4个月另7天。每次收到宰杀的羊数量较少，从1只到5只不等，反映了图马勒庙区的规模远小于尼普尔的诸神庙。

贝里阿瑞克从图马勒庙区的羊牲官员阿什尼乌处接收死牲一览表

时间	文件内容	转交官员	文献出处
Š 43 ii/17，22	1只公绵羊，1只宰杀公绵羊，以上为宰杀牲，于**图马勒**	阿什尼乌	Torino 1 268

---

① 乌尔尼旮尔的印章是：舒勒吉强大之人，乌尔之王，提如之子——乌尔尼旮尔厨师是你的仆人。

② 谢胜杰：《乌尔第三王朝贡牲中心牛圈管理官员恩里拉的档案重建》，硕士学位论文，东北师范大学古典文明史研究所，2006年。

续表

时间	文件内容	转交官员	文献出处
Š 43 ii/25-28	1 只公绵羊，1 只公绵羊和 1 只母绵羊，1 只育肥羊羔，1 只母绵羊，以上为宰杀牲，于**图马勒**	阿什尼乌	MVN 13 861
Š 43 ii/30	1 只宰杀公绵羊，于**图马勒**	阿什尼乌	RT 37136 1
Š 43 iii/8	1 只宰杀公绵羊，于**图马勒**	阿什尼乌	RA 09 040 SA 01
Š 43 iii/ 10，13，14	1 只公绵羊【……】，2 只公绵羊，1 只公羊，以上为宰杀牲，于**图马勒**	阿什尼乌	AnOr 01 005
Š 43 iv/1-2	1 只公绵羊，1 只宰杀公绵羊，于**图马勒**	阿什尼乌	Sumer 24，72 08
Š 43 v/9-10	1 只公绵羊，1 只宰杀公绵羊，于**图马勒**	阿什尼乌	Nisaba 08 190
Š 43 vi/24	1 只育肥山羊崽和 1 只公绵羊为宰杀牲，于**图马勒**	阿什尼乌	RA 09 040 SA 02

第二节　苏萨的总督贝里阿瑞克（Š 43 v/12-ŠS 9 xi）

在阿马尔辛和舒辛时期，有一个名叫贝里阿瑞克的高官出现在贡牲中心总管那萨、阿巴萨旮和尹塔埃阿的接管官员们为贡牲中心送入牲畜，特别是羔、崽给恩里勒夫妇的送入项——接管文件中。在苏萨的总督扎瑞克（*Za-rí-iq*）卸任后（其在任时间是从舒勒吉 41 年 7 月到阿马尔辛 5 年），阿马尔辛 6 年 3 月 9 日贝里阿瑞克荣升为苏萨的总督（Nik.2 479）。

表明贝里阿瑞克是苏萨的总督的文件一览表

时间	文件内容	文献出处
AS 6 iii/9	3586 公羊和 14 公山羊为育肥房，于苏萨……贝里阿瑞克接管……	Nik.2 479
ŠS 8 xii	45 升啤酒和 45 升面包为苏萨的总督贝里阿瑞克……	TÉL 046
?	……40 育肥公牛、5 四等育肥公绵羊、628 育肥牛后级公绵羊、41 育肥牛后级公山羊和 1 羔来自苏萨的总督贝里阿瑞克……	SACT 1 189
?	45 升普通啤酒和 45 升粗麦面粉为苏萨的总督贝里阿瑞克，当他离开苏萨时……	ITT 5 06779
?	……12 升啤酒、16 升面包和 1 升芝麻油为苏萨的总督贝里阿瑞克……	ITT 3 05241
? i	45 升啤酒和 45 升面包为苏萨的总督贝里阿瑞克，当他走向苏萨时……	RT 22 153 3

有关苏萨的总督贝里阿瑞克的文献中共有34个文件记录了贝里阿瑞克从舒勒吉44年6月到舒辛9年11月为祭祀等各种目的送入牲畜的情况。其中“送入项—接管”（mu-túm...ì-dab_5）文件共计21件，其接管官员分别是：匿名的那萨（3件）、署名的那萨（1件）、阿巴萨旮（10件）、尹塔埃阿（7件）。在阿巴萨旮的接管文件中，共有3个文件记录了为贝里阿瑞克的“倒啤酒”宴会提供牛羊牲的情况，阿马尔辛4年9月21日的2个文件（PDT 1 190，AUCT 1 603）提到为贝里阿瑞克的“倒啤酒”宴会提供3头牛、30只羊，而舒辛6年11月29日的文件（PDT 1 564）则提到为贝里阿瑞克的“倒啤酒”宴会提供7头肥牛、1头肥驴、1只肥高山公山羊、30只肥公绵羊、85只食草羊。这两个文件中，牛羊牲数量上的变化说明舒辛6年11月29日时，贝里阿瑞克已经从一名高官升任为苏萨的总督。而舒辛1年12月的1个支出文件（TLB 3 095）记录了为贝里阿瑞克的“倒啤酒”宴会支出24只公绵羊。

此外，阿马尔辛6年3月9日（Nik.2 479）和阿马尔辛6年4月（TAD 16）的2个文件还提到贝里阿瑞克在苏萨分别接管了3600只羊和150只羊为育肥房。

有关苏萨的总督贝里阿瑞克的支出文件共计9件，其中舒勒吉43年5月12日的文件（OIP 115 222）提到贝里阿瑞克督办了2个宰杀牲到仓库，70只羊到厨房；分别有3个文件记录了贝里阿瑞克为瓦工（Š 47 ix/13，MVN 02 309）、南那神（Š 48 xi/16，MVN 20，078）、美伊斯塔兰（AS 4x/27，AUCT 1 585）送入羊牲的情况。而阿马尔辛9年11月16日的1个文件（BAOM 6，138 297）提到朱巴旮为贝里阿瑞克的妻子支出1只牛后级育肥公绵羊到厨房的情况。

贝里阿瑞克的文件中，有10个文件没提到收支的类型。其中4个文件明确记录了为苏萨的总督贝里阿瑞克提供了啤酒、面包、面粉和芝麻油（ŠS 8 xii，TÉL 046，另3个文件分别ITT 5 06779，ITT 3 05241，RT 22 153 3，日期缺损）。还有1个日期缺损的文件（SACT 1 189）提到为苏萨的总督贝里阿瑞克提供了714只育肥羊和1只羔。此外，阿马尔辛8年的1个文件（Rochester 178）记录了8个工人工作三天为贝里阿瑞克的庄园的大坝。

有关苏萨的总督贝里阿瑞克的文件一览表（Š 43 v/12-ŠS 9 xi）

时间	文件内容	文件类型及官员	文献出处
Š 43 v/12	……2 绵羊为宰杀牲到仓库，29 绵羊、41 山羊到厨房为士兵们，贝里阿瑞克督办	以上为支出	OIP 115 222
Š 44 vi	……1 高山母绵羊来自贝里阿瑞克，……以上为送入项	匿名的那萨	OIP 115 174
Š 46 x	……1 高山母绵羊来自贝里阿瑞克，……以上为送入项	匿名的那萨	Torino 1 015
Š 46 v/21	……1 羔、1 雌山羊崽和 1 公绵羊来自贝里阿瑞克……以上为送入项	匿名的那萨	Nik.2 465
Š 47 ix/13	……【1+公绵羊】、6 公山羊和 1 雌山羊崽为瓦工埃什塔贝，贝里阿瑞克送入……	那萨支出	MVN 02 309
Š 48 xi/16	……1 羔为南那神，【……】贝里阿瑞克送入……	那萨支出	MVN 20，078
AS 1 iii/11	……1 羔、1 崽和 11 牛来自贝里阿瑞克……以上为送入项	那萨接管	PDT 1 422
AS 2 xi	……6 公绵羊、4 公山羊和 1 公崽来自贝里阿瑞克……为国王的送入项	阿巴萨旮接管	Studies Levine 115-119
AS 4 ix/19	……来自贝里阿瑞克的送入项……	阿巴萨旮支出	UDT 097
AS 4 ix/21	2 公牛、1 母牛、20 公绵羊和 10 公山羊为贝里阿瑞克的倒啤酒宴会……自阿巴萨旮处	舒勒吉阿亚穆接管	PDT 1 190
AS 4 ix/ 21	2 公牛、1 母牛、20 公绵羊和 10 公山羊为贝里阿瑞克的倒啤酒宴会……自阿巴萨旮处	阿胡维尔接管	AUCT 1 603
AS 4 x	……2 育肥公绵羊来自贝里阿瑞克的送入项……	国王支出	MVN 11 182
AS 4 x/27	1 羔为美伊斯塔兰，来自贝里阿瑞克的送入项……	阿巴萨旮支出	AUCT 1 585
AS 4 xii/13	……来自【贝】里阿瑞【克】……	阿巴萨旮接管	Nisaba 08 037
AS 5 i/10	……1 羔来自贝里阿瑞克……以上为送入项	阿巴萨旮接管	MVN 13 662
AS 5 i/26	……2 育肥公绵羊来自贝里阿瑞克的送入项……	阿巴萨旮支出	MVN 13 849
AS 5 iii/26	……2 育肥公绵羊和 1 羔自贝里阿瑞克……以上为送入项	阿巴萨旮接管	OIP 121 083
AS 5 iv/24	……2 肥公羊、1 肥 aslum 公羊、1 肥公山羊、2 种肥尾公绵羊和 1 羔来自贝里阿瑞克……以上为送入项	阿巴萨旮接管	PDT 1 167
AS 5 iv/26	……【1】高山公绵羊和 1 羔来自贝里阿瑞克……以上为送入项	阿巴萨旮接管	OIP 121 086

续表

时间	文件内容	文件类型及官员	文献出处
AS 5 viii/22	14 高山公山羊和 27 高山母山羊来自贝里阿瑞克……以上为送入项	阿巴萨旮接管	OIP 121 096
AS 5 viii/ 23	4 斑点公山羊和 3 野公山羊来自贝里阿瑞克……以上为送入项	阿巴萨旮接管	NYPL 272NYPL 272
AS 5 x/9	……1 羔来自贝里阿瑞克……以上为送入项	阿巴萨旮接管	JCS 17 008 2
AS 6 iii/9	3586 公羊和 14 公山羊为育肥房，于苏萨……	**贝里阿瑞克**接管	Nik.2 479
AS 6 iv	150 公山羊为育肥房，来自阿巴萨旮	**贝里阿瑞克**接管	TAD 16
AS 6 xi/2	1 羔来自贝里阿瑞克……	尹塔埃阿接管	OrSP 47-49 098
AS 7 vi	27 公羊和 2 公山羊为淘汰级，为贝里阿瑞克的羊……自尹塔埃阿处	舒马马接管	OrSP 47-49 106
AS 8	8 个工人工作三天为贝里阿瑞克的庄园的大坝，……		Rochester 178
AS 9 x/7	……3 育肥公绵羊和 1 羔来自贝里阿瑞克……以上为送入项	尹塔埃阿接管	BIN 3 546
AS 9? xi/16	1 牛后级育肥公绵羊到厨房，为贝里阿瑞克的妻子……	朱巴旮支出	BAOM 6，138 297
ŠS 1 vi/1	……2 育肥公绵羊和 1 羔来自贝里阿瑞克……以上为送入项	尹塔埃阿接管	BPOA 7 2650
ŠS 1 xii	……24 公绵羊为贝里阿瑞克的倒啤酒宴会……	以上为支出	TLB 3 095
ŠS 4 iv/5	4 三等育肥 aslum 公绵羊、8 四等育肥公绵羊和 1 羔来自贝里阿瑞克……为国王的送入项	尹塔埃阿接管	Akkadica 21 48
ŠS 4 viii	……为贝里阿瑞克王子，当他走向尼普尔时，经由 NI.URU 舒勒吉		MVN 16 0933
ŠS 5 xi/16	……120 食草公绵羊为贝里阿瑞克……从国王支出	自尹塔埃阿的倒啤酒宴会	SET 091
ŠS 5 xi/18	1 食草母山羊、2 公山羊和 2 雌崽来自贝里阿瑞克……	尹塔埃阿放于那处	BPOA 7 2824
ŠS 6 xi/29	7 肥公牛、1 肥驴、1 肥高山公山羊、30 肥公绵羊、60 食草公绵羊和 25 食草公山羊为贝里阿瑞克的倒啤酒宴会……以上为送入项	尹塔埃阿接管	PDT 1 564
ŠS 7 xii/25	2 次优育肥公绵羊和 1 羔来自贝里阿瑞克……以上为国王的送入项	尹塔埃阿接管	TRU 181
ŠS 8 xii	45 升啤酒和 45 升面包为苏萨的总督贝里阿瑞克……		TÉL 046
ŠS 9 xi	1 食草公牛来自贝里阿瑞克的牛送牲……来自普朱尔恩里勒处	乌尔库农那接管	BIN 3 588

续表

时间	文件内容	文件类型及官员	文献出处
?	……2 只野公山羊来自贝里阿瑞克……监工：贝里阿瑞克……1+育肥公绵羊和 1+羔来自贝里阿瑞克……		PDT 2 0959
?	……2 育肥 aslum 公绵羊和 1 羔来自贝里阿瑞克……		Ash m.1911-241
?	……4 育肥公绵羊和 1 羔来自贝里阿瑞克……以上送入	阿巴萨旮接管	PDT 2 0915
?	……45 公绵羊来自贝里阿瑞克的育肥公绵羊送入……120 公绵羊来自贝里阿瑞克处……		AUCT 1 973
?	……40 育肥公牛、5 四等育肥公绵羊、628 育肥牛后级公绵羊、41 育肥牛后级公山羊和 1 羔为苏萨的总督贝里阿瑞克……		SACT 1 189
?	45 升普通啤酒和 45 升粗麦面粉为苏萨的总督贝里阿瑞克，当他离开苏萨时……		ITT 5 06779
?	……12 升啤酒、16 升面包和 1 升芝麻油为苏萨的总督贝里阿瑞克……		ITT 3 05241
? i	45 升啤酒和 45 升面包为苏萨的总督贝里阿瑞克，当他走向苏萨时……		RT 22 153 3

根据上表我们可以知道，在有关贝里阿瑞克的文件中，记录的贝里阿瑞克送入牲畜的种类主要有：公绵羊、绵羊羔、山羊崽、高山母绵羊（u_8-hur-sag）、种羔（sila$_4$-giš-dù）、公牛（gud）、食草公牛（gud-ú）、母牛（áb）、牛后级育肥公绵羊、三等育肥 aslum 公绵羊、野公山羊（dara$_4$-nita）、斑点公山羊（máš-gal-gùn-a）等。

第三章　结语

舒勒吉新提王后贡牲机构的档案是王朝贡牲中心建立之前的一个早期档案，王朝贡牲中心的另一个早期档案是那冉伊里的档案。为了更好的理解王后贡牲机构的设置及管理等情况，本文又重建了贡牲中心早期管理图马勒庙区的牲畜和饲料的官员阿什尼乌的档案，以及接收宰杀或死亡牲畜的官员贝里阿瑞克的档案。

目前，发现的贡牲中心出土的阿什尼乌的文件共计 32 个，档案覆盖时间是从舒勒吉 40 年 4 月到舒勒吉 44 年 1 月 12 日，共 3 年 9 个月。

通过对阿什尼乌档案的重建和分析，我们可以得出：阿什尼乌是专门负责图马勒庙区羊、猪和禽的管理官员。根据他的档案文件内容的不同，其文件可以分为：阿什尼乌监管和向育肥师发放育肥饲料的文件、阿什尼乌从那冉伊里处接管国王送入项羊牲的文件、阿什尼乌转交自己宰杀处理的羊牲给巴穆和死牲管理官员贝里阿瑞克的文件、阿什尼乌支出羊牲给图马勒庙区女神宁里勒、神王恩里勒和祖先祭祀地等的文件。

阿什尼乌在图马勒庙区一系列的经济活动：先是接收饲养羊、猪和鸟的大麦饲料，再用这些大麦饲料育肥羊牲，并将育肥的羊牲用于祭祀或为王室人员或神明提供月供，最后把宰杀的羊牲转交给死牲管理官员，这表明：阿什尼乌在图马勒庙区拥有一套完整的牲畜管理体系。

我们仅发现了 13 个贡牲中心早期接收宰杀或死亡牲畜的官员贝里阿瑞克的档案文件。其档案覆盖时间是从舒勒吉 42 年 11 月到舒勒吉 43 年 6 月 24 日，共 8 个月。目前，我们只发现了一个贝里阿瑞克的印章，印章中提到他是一名司酒。在贝里阿瑞克的档案中，共有 4 个文件是他与乌尔尼旮尔共同从早期官员那冉伊里和中心总管那萨处接收死牲。从舒勒吉 43 年 9 月开始，乌尔尼旮尔单独接收死牲，因此，我们认为在他们二人共同接收死牲的时间里，乌尔尼旮尔是贝里阿瑞克的副手，他辅助贝里阿瑞克工作。贝里阿瑞克的工作联系人除了恩里拉外，其另一个重要的工作联系人是图马勒庙区的死牲官员阿什尼乌，他们之间工作联系的文件共8个，时间是从舒勒吉43年2月17日到4月24日，贡4个月又7天。

在阿马尔辛和舒辛时期，一个名为贝里阿瑞克的高官常出现在中心总管那萨、阿巴萨旮和尹塔埃阿接管从官员们送入牲畜的文件中，有关他的文件共48件。在苏萨的总督扎瑞克卸任后，阿马尔辛6年3月9日贝里阿瑞克荣升为苏萨的总督。共有6个文件表明贝里阿瑞克是苏萨的总督。

在有关苏萨的总督贝里阿瑞克的21个"送入项—接管"文件中，记录了为他的"倒啤酒"宴会等提供牲畜的情况。在其9个支出文件中，则提到贝里阿瑞克为瓦工、南那神、美伊斯塔兰等送入羊牲的情况。

总之，对阿什尼乌和贝里阿瑞克的档案重建和分析，有助于我们更好地了解贡牲中心建立早期的运作模式和规模，这为我们理解舒勒吉新提王后贡牲机构这一早期档案提供了借鉴。

下卷　档案重建

档案一　舒勒吉新提王后贡牲机构档案重建

时间和摘要	文献内容	英文翻译	中文翻译
Š 28 i： zi-ga 4 fat rams for**elunum festival of temple of Belat-Suhnir**，via **Barbarria**，withdr.fr.**Ahima**	4 udu-niga，***è-lu-núm* é-^{d}*Be-la-at-Suh-nir***，gìr***Bar-bar-ri-a***，*zi-ga* ***A-hi-ma.*** *iti-maš-dà ~ gu$_{7}$*，*mu en-Eridu^{ki} ba-huĝ-ĝá.* （*Princeton* 2 134，*P*201132）	4 *fattened rams for***elunum festival of the temple of Belat-Suhnir**，via **Barbarria**，were withdrawn from Ahima. Month of mašda-gu$_{7}$，Year of the en priestess（of Enki）of Eridu was installed.	4只育肥公绵羊为**贝拉特苏赫尼尔庙的埃鲁努姆节**，**经由巴尔巴瑞阿**，从阿希马支出了。食瞪羚月，埃瑞都的（恩基神的）女祭司被任命之年。
Š28 iii： **mu-túm，ì-dab$_{5}$** 2 grass rams and 1 kidwere deliveried by daughter of Iphur，**Šukubum** took over	2 udu-ú，1 máš **dumu-munus-*Ip-hur* mu-túm**，***Šu-ku$_{8}$*-［*bu*］*-um*** *ì-dab$_{5}$. iti-*［*u$_{5}$*］*-bí-gu$_{7}$*，*mu a-rá*［2］*-kam Ha-r*［*a-š*］*um^{ki} mu-hul.* （*MVN* 03 117，*P*113677）	2 *grass rams and* 1*kid were deliveried by the daughter of Iphur*，*Šukubum took over.Month of ubi-gu$_{7}$*，*Year after that of Harašum was destroyed.*	2只食草公绵羊和1只公山羊崽由伊坡胡尔之女送人，舒库布姆接管了。食乌比鸟月，哈尔西被毁年之次年。
Š 28 *xii*： **ba-úš，šu~ ba-ti** 1butchered female wild goat corpse，which horn and skin were intact，from Nalu，Šukubum received them in Ur	1 ad$_{6}$-darà-munus ~ ba-úš，á-bi kuš-bi，ì-silim，ki ~ **Na-lu$_{5}$**--ta，［***Šu***］***-ku-bu -um-e***［*šu*］~ *ba-ti*，［*šà*］~ **Urim^{ki}**-ma.［iti-še］-kin-kud，［mu］En-nam-šita-^{d}］Šul-gi-［ke$_{4}$-gub-ba ba-huĝ］. （Env.）1 ad$_{6}$-darà-munus ~ ba-úš，á-bi kuš-bi，ì-silim，ki~Na-lu$_{5}$--ta，［***Šu***］***-ku-bu-um-e***［*šu*］~*ba-ti*，［*šà*］~*Urim^{ki}-ma*，［*iti-še*］*-kin-kud*，［*mu*］*En-nam-šita-*［^{d}］*Šul-gi-*［*ke$_{4}$-gub-baba-huĝ*］. （*seal*）［*Gemé*］-^{d}*Sin*，［*dam*］*-Šul-gi*，*lugal Urim^{ki}-ma*，***Šu-ku-bu-***［***um***］*rá-gabaarád-*［*zu*］. （*JCS* 31 133 01，*P*112095）	1*butchered female wild goat corpse*，*which horn and skin were intact*，*from* **Nalu**，**Šukubum** received them in **Ur**. Month of še-kin-kud，Year of En-namšita-Šulgirake-guba（of Eridu）was installed. （Env.）1butchered female lú-bu（= habum）animal，which horn and skin were intact，from Nalu，Šukubum received them in Ur. Month of še-kin-kud，Year of En-namšita-Šulgirake-guba（of Eridu）was installed. （seal）Geme-Sin，the wife of Šulgi，king of Ur，Šukubum，the courier，is your servant.	1只宰杀的雌野山羊尸体，它的角和皮毛都完整无缺，从**那鲁**处，**舒库布姆收到了**，在**乌尔城**。大麦收割月，恩楠西塔舒勒吉腊凯古巴（女祭司）被任命之年。 （信封：）1只宰杀的雌野山羊尸体，它的角和皮毛都完整无缺，从那鲁处，舒库布姆收到了，在乌尔城。大麦收割月，恩楠西塔舒勒吉腊凯古巴（女祭司）被任命之年。 （印文：）吉美辛是乌尔之王舒勒吉的妻子，舒库布姆骑使是你的仆人。

续表

时间和摘要	文献内容	英文翻译	中文翻译
Š 29 vi: **zi-ga** 1+［fat］rams for**Itib-sinat**, 2 fat-tailed sheep for **Ki-ni-a**, were withdrawn from the place of **Šukubum**	［1+］udu-［niga］***I-ti*****! *-ib-si-na-at***, 2 *gukkal**Ki-ni-a***, *zi-ga ki~* ***Šu-ku$_8$-bu-um**--<ta>.* *iti-á-ki-ti*, *mu ús-sa en-Eridu^{ki}-ga ba-huĝ-ĝá.* (*TLB* 3 012, *P*134153)	1+［*fattened*］*rams for* **Itib-sinat**, 2 fat-tailed sheep for **Ki-ni-a**, were withdrawn from the place of Šukubum.Month of akiti, Year after that of the en-priestess (of Enki) of Eridu was installed.	1+只【育肥】公绵羊为**伊提卜席那特**，2只肥尾绵羊为**基尼阿**，从舒库布姆处支出了。阿基提月，埃瑞都（恩基神的）女祭司被任命年之次年。
Š 29 vi: **zi-ga** 1 fat bull, 2 fine fat rams for**Allatum**, 2 fat rams for **temple of Belat-Suhnir and Belat-Darraban**, **Apili**as deputy; 2 fat rams, **Maš**as royal deputy, for **temple of Belat-Suhnir and Belat-Darraban**, were withdrawn from **Šukubum**	1 gud-niga, 2 udu-niga-sig$_5$, ^{d}***Al-la-tum***, 2 *udu-niga*, (*é-*^{d}***Be-la-at-Suh-nir*** *ù* ^{d}***Be-la-at-Dar-ra-é-ba-an*****--*šè***), ***Á-pi$_5$-lí****maškim*; 2 *udu-niga*, **Maš** maškim, **é-^{d}*Be-la-at-Suh-nir*** *ù* ^{d}***Be-la-at-Dar-ra-é-ba-an**--šè*, *zi-ga* ***Šu-ku$_8$-bu-um****-ma. iti-á-ki ~ ti*, *mu ús-sa en-Eridu^{ki}-ga ba-huĝ-ĝá.* (*OIP* 115018, *P*123233)	1 *fattened bull*, 2 *fine fattened rams for***Allatum**, 2 fattened rams (**for temple of Belat-Suhnir and Belat-Darraban**), **Apili as royal deputy**; 2 fattened rams, **Maš as royal deputy**, for the **temple of Belat-Suhnir and Belat-Darra -eban**, were withdrawn from Šukubum.Month of Akiti, Year after that of the en priestess of Eridu was installed.	1头育肥公牛和2只优等育肥公绵羊为**女神阿拉吞**，2只育肥公绵羊（**为贝拉特苏赫尼尔和贝拉特达腊班庙**），**阿皮里督办**；2只育肥公绵羊，**马什督办**，为**贝拉特苏赫尼尔和贝拉特达腊埃班庙**，从舒库布姆支出了。阿基提月，埃瑞都的女祭司被任命之年之次年。
Š 29 x: **mu-túm, ì-dab$_5$** 1+ fat ram fr.［wife of x］,［1+ fine fat ram］delivered by the wife of Dakiki, **Šukubum** took over	［1+ udu-niga-s］ig$_5$,［**dam**....］,［1+ udu-niga-si］g$_5$, ***dam-Da-ki-ki***, *mu-túm*,［***Šu-k***］***u$_8$-bu-um*** *ì-dab$_5$.iti-ezem-An-na*, *mu ús-sa en Eridu^{ki}-ga ba-huĝ-ĝá.* (*PDT* 2 1039, *P*126379)	1+ *fine fattened ram from*［**the wife of x**］,［1+ fine fattened ram］, **the wife of Dakiki** delivered, Šukubum took over.Month of Ezem-Anna, Year after that of the priestess of Eridu was installed.	1+只优等肥公绵羊自【**X之妻**】,【1+只优等育肥公绵羊】由**达基基之妻**送入，舒库布姆接管了。天神庆典月，埃瑞都的女祭司被任命之年之次年。
Š 29 x: **zi-ga** 2 fat rams for**the temple of Belat-Suhnir and Belat-Darraeban**, Ur-Dumuzida as deputy, were withdrawn from **Šukubum**	2 udu-niga é-^{d}***Be-la-at-Suh-nir*** *ù*［^{d}］***Be-<la->-at-Dar-ra-é-ba-an***, **Ur-^{d}Dumu-zi-da**maškim, zi-ga ki~ ***Šu-ku-bu-um***. *iti-ezem-An-na mu ús-sa en Eridu^{ki}-ga ba-huĝ-ĝá.* (*ASJ* 04 064 01, *P*102133)	2 *fattened rams for* **the temple of Belat-Suhnir and Belat-Darraeban**, **Ur-Dumuzida as royal deputy**, were withdrawn from Šukubum.Month of Ezem-Anna, Year after that of the priestess of Eridu was installed.	2只育肥公绵羊为**贝拉特苏赫尼尔和贝拉特达腊埃班庙**，**乌尔杜穆孜达督办**，从舒库布姆处支出了。天神庆典月，埃瑞都的女祭司被任命之年之次年。
Š 29 x: **zi-ga** 1+x fat rams for［the tmeple］of **Belat-Suhnir and Belat-Darraeban**, via**my queen**, were **withdrawn from** Šukubum	［1+］udu-niga-sag$_5$,［é］-^{d}***Be-la-at-suh-nir*** *ù* ^{d}***Be-la-at-Dar-ra-é-ba-an***, gìr**nin-ĝá**, zi-ga ki ~ ***Šu-ku$_8$-bu-um***.*iti-ezem-An-na*, *mu ús-sa*［*en*］*-Eridu^{ki}-ga*［*ba*］*-huĝ-ĝá.* (*PDT* 2 1314, *P*126632)	1+*x fine fattened rams*, **for**［**the temple**］**of Belat-Suhnir and Belat-Darraeban**, via **my queen**, were withdrawn from Šukubum.Month of ezem-Ana, Year after that of the en priestess of Eridu was installed.	1+只优等育肥公绵羊为**贝拉特苏赫尼尔和贝拉特达腊埃班【庙】**，**经由我的王后**，从舒库布姆支出了。天神庆典月，埃瑞都的女祭司被任命之年之次年。

续表

时间和摘要	文献内容	英文翻译	中文翻译
Š 29 xi: **mu-túm, ì-dab$_5$** 18 grass rams, 2 kids from**Te ṣin-Mama**, 7 grass rams, 3 kids from **my king**; 2 grass rams, 1 kid from **Simat-Ea**; 1 lamb from **Ur-Šulpae**; 1 kid from **Etel-pu-Dagan**, which were deliveried, Šukubum **took over**	18 udu-ú, 2 máš, ***Te-ṣi-in-Ma-*** [***ma***], 7 *udu-ú*, 3 *máš*, **lugal-ĝu**, 2 udu-ú, 1 máš, ***Simat-É-a***, 1 *sila$_4$* **Ur-^{d}Šul-pa-è**, 1 máš, ***E-te-*** [***el***] ***-pù-^{d} Da-*** [***gan***], *mu-túm*, ***Šu-ku$_8$-bu-um*** *ì-dab$_5$*. *iti-Me-ki-ĝál*, *mu ús-sa en-Eridu^{ki}-ga ba-* [*huĝ*] *-* [*ĝá*]. (*OIP* 115016, *P*123365)	18 *grass rams*, 2 *kids from***Te ṣin-Mama**, 7 grass rams, 3 kids from **my king**; 2 grass rams, 1 kid from **Simat-Ea**; 1 lamb from **Ur-Šulpae**; 1 kid from **Etel-pu-Dagan**, which were deliveried, Šukubum took over.Month of Mekigal, Year after that of the en priestess of Eridu was installed.	18食草公绵羊和2公崽自**台岑妈妈**，7食草公绵羊和3公崽自**我的国王**，2食草公绵羊和1公崽自**席马特埃阿**，1公羔自**乌尔舒勒帕埃**，1公崽自**埃台勒普-达干**，以上是送入，**舒库布姆接管**了。神美基旮勒庆典月，埃瑞都的女祭司被任命之年之次年。
Š 29 xi: **zi-ga** 2 fat rams for **giranum festival**, 2 fat rams for the **Sacrifice of Dawn of the temple of Belat-Suhnir**, **via Šukubum**; 1+ fatrams for **the temple of Belat-Suhnir**, **via Barbarlia**, **withdr.fr.**Šukubum	2 udu-niga, ***gi-ra-núm***, 2 *udu-niga*, **siskúr~ á~gú-zi-ga**, *é-^{d} **Be-la-at-Suh$_6$-ni-ir**gìr* ***Šu-ku$_8$-bu-um***; [1+] *udu-niga*, *é-^{d}**Be-la-at-Suh$_6$-ni-ir*** gìr ***Bar-bar-lí-a***, *zi-ga ki~* ***Šu-ku$_8$-bu-um-ma***. *iti-ezem-Me-ki-ĝál*, *mu ús-sa en Eridu^{ki}-ga ba-huĝ-ĝá*. (DoCu EPHE 306, P109262)	2 fattened rams for**giranum festival**, 2 fattened rams for the **Sacrifice of Dawn of the temple of Belat-Suhnir**, **via Šukubum**; 1+ fattened rams for **the temple of Belat-Suhnir**, **via Barbarlia**, were withdrawn from Šukubum. Month of ezem-Mekigal, Year after that of the en priestess of Eridu was installed.	2只育肥公绵羊为**吉腊努姆仪式**，2只育肥公绵羊为**贝拉特苏赫尼尔庙的晨祭**，经由**舒库布姆**；1+育肥公绵羊为**贝拉特苏赫尼尔庙**，经由**巴尔巴瑞阿**，从舒库布姆处支出了。神美基旮勒庆典月，埃瑞都女祭司被任命之年之次年。
Š 30 v: **zi-ga** 5 grassrams for **Ahu-atal doctor**, 1 **butchered** grass ram, were withdrawn from Šukubum	5 udu-ú, ***A-<hu>-a-tal*** *a-zu*, 1 *udu-ú ba-úš*, *zi-ga ki~* ***Šu-ku$_8$-bu-um***. *iti-ezem-^{d} Nin-a-zu*, *mu dumu-munus-lugal-la énsi-An-ša-an^{ki} ba-an-tuku-a*. (*TLB* 3 092, P134233)	5 *grassrams for* **Ahu-atal doctor**, 1 butchered grass ram, were withdrawn from Šukubum.Month of ezem-Ninazu, Year of the daughter of king was married by the governor of Anšan.	5只食草公绵羊为**阿胡阿塔勒医生**，1只宰杀的食草公绵羊，（以上）从**舒库布姆处支出**了。神宁阿朱庆典月，王之女被安山的总督娶走之年。
Š 30 vi, ix: **zi-ga** 2 fatrams for **temple of Belat-Suhnir and Belat-Darraban** for 1st time, **month of akiti**; 2 fat rams for **temple of Belat-Suhnir and Belat-Darraban**, **month of ezem-mah**, withdr. from Ahima, **via Šukubum**	2 udu-niga, **é-^{d}*Be-la-at-Suh-nir*** *ù* ***^{d}Be-la-at-Dar-ra-ba-an*****--*šè***, *a-rá 1-kam*, **iti-á-ki~ti**; 2 udu-niga, **é-*^{d}Be-la-at-Suh-nir-ra*--*šè*** *ù* ***^{d}Be-la-at-Dar-ra-ba-an***. *iti-ezem mah*, *zi-ga ki~* ***A-hi-ma--ta***, *gìr* ***Šu-ku$_8$-bu-um***. *mu du-mu-munus-lugal énsi-An-ša-an^{ki}--ke$_4$ ba-an-tuku*. (*MVN* 15 057, *P*118337)	2 *fattenedrams for* **the temple of Belat-Suhnir and Belat-Darraban** for the 1st time, **month of akiti**; 2 fattened rams for **the temple of Belat-Suhnir and Belat-Darraban**, **month of ezem-mah**, were withdrawn from Ahima, **via Šukubum**. Year of the daughter of king was married by the governor of Anšan.	2只肥公绵羊为**贝拉特苏赫尼尔和贝拉特达腊班之庙**第一次，**阿基提月**；2只育肥公绵羊为**贝拉特苏赫尼尔和贝拉特达腊班之庙**（第二次），**大庆典月**，以上从阿希马处支出了，**经由舒库布姆**。王之女被安山的总督娶走之年。

续表

时间和摘要	文献内容	英文翻译	中文翻译
Š 30 vii： **zi-ga** 2［fattened］rams for **the temple of Belat-Suhnir and Belat-Darraban**，**via Barbarria**，were withdawn from Šukubum	2 udu-［niga］，*é-^{d} **Be-la-at-Suh-nir** ù ^{d}**Be-la-at-Dar-ra-ba-an**，**gìr Bar-bar-ri-a**，zi-ga ki ~* ***Šu-ku$_{8}$-bu-um-**ma--ta. iti-ezem-^{d} Šul-gi，mu dumu-mí-lugal énsi-An-ša-an^{ki}--ke$_{4}$ ba-an-tuku.*（*OIP* 115 019，*P*123333）	2［*fattened*］*rams for* **the temple of Belat-Suhnir and Belat-Darraban**，**via Barbarria**，were withdawn from Šukubum. Month of ezem-Šulgi，Year of the daughter of king was married by the governor of Anšan.	2只【育肥】公绵羊为**贝拉特苏赫尼尔和贝拉特达腊班之庙**，**经由巴尔巴瑞阿**，从舒库布姆处支出了。神舒勒吉庆典月，王之女被安山的总督娶走之年。
Š 30 viii： **zi-ga** ［2 fattened rams for **the temple of Belat-Suhnir and Belat-Darraban**］，were withdrawn from Šukubum	［2 udu-niga，*é-^{d} **Be-la-at-Suh-nir** ù* ^{d}**Be-la-at-Dar-ra-ba-an**］*x-a*，［*zi-g*］*a ki~* ***Šu-ku$_{8}$-bu-um-**ma--ta. iti-šu-eš-ša*， *mu dumu-munus-lugal énsi-An-ša-an^{ki}--ke$_{4}$ ba-an-tuku. gaba-ri*（*TLB* 3 093，*P*134234）	［2 *fattened rams for* **the temple of Belat-Suhnir and Belat-Darraban**］，were withdrawn from Šukubum. Month of šu-ešša，· Year of the daughter of king was married by the governor of Anšan. copy of the tablet	【2只育肥公绵羊为**贝拉特苏赫尼尔和贝拉特达腊班之庙**】，从舒库布姆处支出了。三只手月，王之女被安山的总督娶走之年。 原文抄件
Š 30 x/4： **zi-ga** 2 fattened rams for**giranum festival of Belat-Suhnir and Belat-Dareban**，1 fat ram for **Allatum**，1 fattened ram for the **Sacrifice of Dusk**，1 for **disappear place**，1 for **Sacrifice of Dawn**，on 1st day；1 fat bull，2 fat rams on 2nd day；2 fat rams on 3rd day；2 fat rams on 4th day，for **Ordeal Divine River**，**［cup-bearer］as deputy**，withdr. fr.Šukubum	2 udu-niga，***gi-ra-núm-**^{d} **Be-la-at-Suh-nir** ù* ^{d}**Be-la-at-Dar-é-ba-an**，1 *udu-niga*，*^{d}**Al-la-tum**，1 udu-niga*，**siskúr~ á-< ud >-ten-na**，1 udu-niga，**níĝ-< ki >-zàh**--šè，1 udu-niga，**siskúr ~ á-gú-zi-ga**，udu-1-kam；1 gud-niga，2 udu-niga，ud-2-kam；2 udu-niga，ud-3-kam；2 udu-niga ud-4-kam，［**mu..í**］**d lú-ru-gú--ta［…sa］gi maškim**，［zi-ga ***Šu-k***］***u$_{8}$-bu-um-**ma.*［*iti-ezem-An*］*-na*，［*mu dumu-mí-lu*］*gal énsi-*［*An-ša-an^{ki}--k*］*e$_{4}$ ba-an-tuku.*（*OIP* 115 020，*P*123290）	2 *fattened rams for the***giranum festival of Belat-Suhnir and Belat-Dareban**，1 fattened ram for **Allatum**，1 fattened ram for the **Sacrifice of Dusk**，1 fattened ram for **disappear place**，1 fattened ram for the **Sacrifice of Dawn**，on 1st day；1 fattened bull，2 fattened rams on 2nd day；2 fattened rams on the 3rd day；2 fattened rams on the 4th day，for **Ordeal Divine River**，**the［cup-bearer］as royal deputy**，were withdrawn from Šukubum. Month of ezem-Anna，Year of the daughter of king was married by the governor of Anšan.	2育肥公绵羊为**贝拉特苏赫尼尔和贝拉特达雷班的吉腊努姆仪式**，1育肥公绵羊为**阿拉吞女神**，1育肥公绵羊为**"黄昏"祭**，1育肥公绵羊为**消失处祭**，1育肥公绵羊为**晨祭**第一天；1头育肥公牛，2只育肥公绵羊为第二天；2只公绵羊为第三天；2只育肥公绵羊为第四天；【为了】**神判**，**【某某】司仪为督办**，从舒库布姆处支出了。天神庆典月，安山的总督娶国王之女之年。
Š 31 i： **zi-ga** 9**butchered** rams from place of **Lugal-Hamati**，3 butchered rams，2 butchered kids：these were butchered：from Ahima，**Ur-Ninmug fuller**，received：withdr.from Šukubum	10-lá-1 udu~ba-úš，ki~**Lugal-ha-ma-ti**，3 udu~ba-úš，2 máš~ba-úš，ug$_{7}$-ug$_{7}$-ga-àm，ki~ ***A-hi-ma**--ta*，**Ur-^{d}Nin-mug**，lú-túg，šu~ ba-ti， zi-ga ki~***Šu-ku$_{8}$-bu-um**-ma.* *iti-maš-dà~gu$_{7}$*， *mu a-rá-2-kam Kára-har^{ki} ba-hul.*（*NYPL* 163，*P*122701）	9*butchered rams of* **Lugal-Hamati**，3 butchered rams，2 butchered kids：these were butchered：from the place of Ahima，**Ur-Ninmug fuller**，received：were withdrawn from place of Šukubum. Month of mašda-gu$_{7}$，Year of Karahar was destroyed for second time.	9只宰杀的公绵羊在**卢旮勒哈马提处**，3只宰杀的公绵羊、2只宰杀的公山羊崽，以上宰杀牲**从阿希马处**，洗染工**乌尔尼穆格接收了**；从舒库布姆处支出了。食瞪羚月，卡腊哈尔第二次被毁灭之年。

续表

时间和摘要	文献内容	英文翻译	中文翻译
Š31 iii： **mu-túm，ì-dab$_5$** 2 grass rams and 1 he-goat deliveried by the **daughter of Iphur**，Šukubum took over	2 udu-ú，1 máš **dumu-munus-*Ip-hur*** *mu-túm*，***Šu-ku$_8$*-[*bu*] *-um*** [ì-da] b$_5$. iti-[u$_5$] -bí-gu$_7$，mu a-rá [2] -kam Ha-r [a-har]^{ki} (Kára-har^{ki}) ba-hul.（MVN 03 117，P113677）	2 grass rams and 1 he-goat deliveried by the **daughter of Iphur**，Šukubum took over. Month of ubi-gu$_7$，Year after that of Harahar（Karahar）was destroyed.	2只食草公绵羊和1只公山羊由**伊坡胡尔之女**送入，舒库布姆接管了。食乌比乌月，哈尔西被毁之年次年。
Š 31 iv： **mu-túm，ì-dab$_5$** 2 rams and 1 kid fr. **Lu-Magan**，3 rams and 1 kid from **Ama-barú**，1 lamb from **Kuligu majordomo**，1 lamb from **governor of Kazallu**，were deliveried，Šukubum took over	2 udu-ú，1 máš，**Lú-Má-gan^{ki}**， 3 udu-ú，1 máš，**Ama-barú**， 1 sila$_4$，**Ku-li-gu$_{10}$** šabra， 1 sila$_4$，**énsi-Ka-zal-lu^{ki}** mu-túm，***Šu-ku$_8$-bu-um*** *ì-dab$_5$*. *iti-ki-siki-^{d}Nin-a-zu*， *mu a-rá-2-kam* *Ha-ra-har^{ki}ba-hul.* （*OIP* 115017，*P*123237）	2 *grass rams and* 1 *kid from* **Lu-Magan**，3 grass rams and 1 kid from **Ama-barú**，1 lamb from **Kuligu majordomo**，1 lamb from **governor of Kazallu**，were deliveried，**Šukubum took over**.Month of ki-siki-Ninazu，Year of Harahar was destroyed for the second time.	2只食草公绵羊和1只公崽来自**鲁马干**，3只公绵羊和1只公崽来自**王座之母**，1只羊羔来自**庙总管库里古**，1只羊羔来自**卡扎鲁的总督**，以上送入，**舒库布姆接管**。神宁阿朱羊毛作坊月，哈腊哈尔第二次被毁灭之年。
Š 31 vi： **mu-túm，ì-dab$_5$** 2 grass rams and 1 kid from**Nin-uma**，1 grass ram and 1 kid from **daughter of Kini-ašazu**，1 kid from **Eabani**，**Šukubum took over**	2 udu-ú，1 máš **Nin-ù-ma**，1 udu-ú，1 máš **dumu-mu-nus-Ki-ni-a-šà-zu**，1 máš **É-a-ba-ni**，mu-túm，***Šu-ku$_8$-bu-um*** *ì-dab$_5$.iti-á-ki-ti*， *mu a-rá-2-kam Kará-har^{ki} ba-hul.* （*BIN* 3 360，*P*106166）	2 *grass rams and* 1 *kid from***Nin-uma**，1 grass ram and 1 kid from **daughter of Kini-ašazu**，1 kid from **Eabani**，these were deliveries，**Šukubum took over**.Month of akiti，Year of Karahar was destroyed for the second time.	2食草公绵羊和1公崽自**宁乌马**，1食草公绵羊和1公崽自**基尼阿沙朱之女**，1公崽来自**埃阿巴尼**，以上送入，**舒库布姆接管**了。阿基提月，卡腊哈尔第二次被毁灭之年。
Š 31 viii： **zi-ga** 1 kid for**Enki**，1 he-goat for **Gula**，1 grass ram for **Nin-giš-kešda**，**via my queen**，were withdrawn from Šukubum in **Uruk**	1 máš，**^{d}En-ki**，1 máš-x **^{d}Gu-la**，1 udu-ú，**^{d}Nin-giš-kešda-a**， gìr**nin-ĝá**，zi-ga ki～ ***Šu-ku$_8$-bu-um****-ma*，*šà*～ **Unug^{ki}**-ga.iti-šu-eš-ša，mu a-rá-2-kam Kára-har^{ki}ba-hul-a. （PDT 2 1363，P126672）	1 kid for**Enki**，1 he-goat for **Gula**，1 grass ram for **Nin-giš-kešda**，**via my queen**，were withdrawn from Šukubum in **Uruk**.Month of šu-ešša，Year of Karahar was destroyed for the second time.	1公崽为**恩基**，1公山羊为**古腊**，1食草公绵羊为**宁基什凯什达**，**经由我的王后**，以上从**乌鲁克**的舒库布姆处支出了。三只手月，卡腊哈尔第二次被毁灭之年。

续表

时间和摘要	文献内容	英文翻译	中文翻译
Š 32: **mu-túm** 1 kid fr. **wife of Balaya**, in **Uruk**, 2 rams and 2 fat-tailed sheep fr.prince **Urnigar**, 2 rams and 1 kid fr.**Allamu**, in temple of sagdana were deliveries for Šulgi-simtum	1 máš **dam-*Ba-la-a***, *šà~ Unug^{ki}-ga*, 2 *udu*, 2 *gukkal*, **Ur-ni$_9$-gar** dumu-lugal, 2 udu, 1 máš ***Al-la-mu***, *šà~* **é-sag-da-na**$^!$, mu-túm~ ***^{d}Šul-gi-sí-im-tum***. *mu a-rá-3-kam-aš Si-mu-ru-um^{ki} ba-hul.* (*BIN* 5 011, *P*106445)	1 *kid from* **the wife of Balaya**, in **Uruk**, 2 rams and 2 fat-tailed sheep from **Urnigar**, **the son of king**, 2 rams and 1 kid from **Allamu**, in the temple of sagdana were deliveries for Šulgi-simtum. Year of Simurum was destroyed for the third time	1 只公山羊崽来自**巴拉亚之妻**，于**乌鲁克**，2 只公绵羊和 2 只肥尾羊来自**王子乌尔尼旮尔**，2 只公绵羊和 1 只公崽来自**阿拉穆**，**于萨格达那庙**，为**舒勒吉新提的送入项**。席穆润第三次被毁灭之年。
Š 32 i: **zi-ga** 1 fattened ram for [x] **-Inanna**, [⋯] withdrawn from **Šukubum**	1 udu-niga, zi- [x] ^{d}Inanna- [x] ma-x [...], zi-[ga] ki~ ***Šu-ku$_8$-*** [***bu-um--ta***]. *iti-maš-dà~* [*gu$_7$*], *mu* [*a-rá 2-kam*] *Kará-har^{ki} ba-hul mu ús-sa-bi.* (*TLB* 3 094, *P*134235)	1 *fattened ram for* [*x*] **-Inanna**, [⋯] withdrawn from Šukubum.Month of mašda-gu$_7$, Year after that of Karahar was destroyed for the second time.	1 只育肥公绵羊为**伊南那**，从舒库布姆处支出了。食瞪羚月，卡腊哈尔第二次被毁灭之年次年。
Š 32 iv: 2 he-goats for **giranum festival of Annunitum and Ulmašitum**, **in the gate of Geštin-Anna**	2 máš-gal, ***gi-ra-núm-An-nu-ni-tum*** *ù* **^{d}Ul-ma-ši-tum**, *ká* **^{d}Geštin-an-na**.iti-ezem-^{d}Nin-a-zu, mu a-rá 3-kam-aš Si-mu-ru-um^{ki}ba-hul. ba-zi (OIP 115 128, P123552)	2 he-goats for **giranum festival of Annunitum and Ulmašitum**, **in the gate of Geštin-Anna**.Month of ezem-Ninazu, Year of Simurum was destroyed for the third time.were withdrawn (from Šukubum?)	2 只公山羊为**安努尼吞和乌勒马席吞的吉腊努姆仪式**，**于吉什廷安那之门**。神宁阿朱的庆典月，席穆润第三次被毁灭年。（从舒库布姆处?）支出
Š 32 iv: **mu-túm** 2 rams and 1 kid from **Zalaya**, were deliveries for Šulgi-simtum	2 udu, 1 máš, ***Za-la-a***, *mu-túm-*^{d}***Šul-gi-sí-im-tum***. *iti-ki-siki-^{d}Nin-a-zu*, *mu a-rá 3-kam-aš Si-mu-ru-um^{ki} ba-hul.* (*MVN* 2 308, *P*113607)	2 *rams and* 1 *kid from* **Zalaya**, were deliveries for Šulgi-simtum. Month of ki-siki-Ninazu, Year of Simurum was destroyed for the third time.	1 只公绵羊和 1 只公崽自**扎拉亚**，为舒勒吉新提的送入项。神宁阿朱羊毛作坊月，席穆润第三次被毁灭之年。
vi: **letter** is asking Ahima give 1 bull, 6 flocks for the festival of that year	*A-hi-ma*--ra ù-na-a-du$_{11}$ 1 gud, 5 udu, 1 máš, máš-da-ri-a á-ki-ti~mu, hé-ab-sá-e. (TCS 1 020, P108046)	Speak to Ahima, 1 bull, 5 rams, 1 kid for akiti festival of the year be prepared!	对阿希马说：1 只公牛、5 只公绵羊和 1 只公崽为这年的阿基提节准备好了。
Š 32 iv: **zi-ga** 1 fattened bull for**niĝ-provisions** [⋯] **of Sagga**, **via Apilatum**, was withdrawn from **Ahima**	1 gud- [niga], **níĝ-sì-ga** [...], **^{d}Sag$_9$-ga-x**, gìr ***Á-pi$_5$-la-tum***, *iti-ki-siki-^{d}Nin-a-zu*, *zi-ga* ***A-hi-ma***. *mu Si-mu-ru-um^{ki}a-rá-3-kam-ma-aš ba-hul.* (*PDT* 2 1373, *P*126681)	1 *fattened bull for***niĝ-provisions** [⋯] **of Sagga**, **via Apilatum**, month of ki-siki-Ninazu, was **withdrawn from Ahima**. Year of Simurum was destroyed for the third time.	1 只育肥公牛为**萨格旮的供品**，**经由阿皮拉吞**，神宁阿朱羊毛作坊月，从**阿希马**处支出了。席穆润第三次被毁灭之年。

续表

时间和摘要	文献内容	英文翻译	中文翻译
Š 32 v： **mu-túm** 2 rams from **Gir-nisa**, were deliveries for Šulgi-simtum	2 udu **Gìr-ni-ì-sa$_6$** mu-túm~ ^{d}***Šul-gi-sí-im-tum***. *iti-ezem-^{d}Nin-a-zu, mu a-rá-3-kam-aš Si-mu-ru-um ba-hul.* (*Torino* 1 001, *P*133833)	2 *rams from* **Gir-nisa**, were deliveries for Šulgi-simtum. Month of ezem-Ninazu, Year of Simurum was destroyed for the third time.	2只公绵羊来自**吉尔尼萨**，为舒勒吉新吞的送人项。神宁阿朱庆典月，席穆润第三次被毁灭之年。
Š 32 v： **ba-zi** 3 fattened rams to**the kitchen**, **Ur-Dumuzi as royal deputy**; 1 fattened ram to **the center of palace**, **Apilia as deputy**; 3 fattened rams to **the kitchen**, in **Uruk**, **Ur-Dumuzi as deputy**; **via the queen Šulgi-simti**, in **Ur**, were withdrawn from Ahima	3 udu-niga, **é! -muhaldim**--šè, **Ur-^{d}Dumu-zi**maškim; 1 udu-niga, šà~ **é-gal**--šè, ***Á-pi$_5$-lí-a***maškim; 3 *udu-ni-ga*, **é! -muhaldim**--šè Unug^{ki}--šè, ud-lugal ^{d}Nibru^{ki}--<ta> íb-ta-è-a, **Ur-^{d}Dumu-zi** maškim; gìr **nin** ^{d}***Šul-gi-sí-im-ti***, šà~ **Urim^{ki}**-ma, ki~ ***A-hi-ma--ta***, (*left*) *ba-zi* (*rev.*6). *iti-ezem-^{d}Nin-a-zu, mu a-rá-3-kam-aš Si-mu-ru-um^{ki}ba-hul.* (*MVN* 08 097, *P*115488)	3 *fattened rams to***the kitchen**, **Ur-Dumuzi as royal deputy**; 1 fattened ram to **the center of palace**, **Apilia as royal deputy**; 3 fattened rams to **the kitchen**, in **Uruk**, When the king left Nippur, **Ur-Dumuzi as royal deputy**; **via the queen Šulgi-simti**, in **Ur**, were withdrawn from Ahima. Month of ezem-Ninazu, Year of Simurum was destroyed for the third time.	3只育肥公绵羊**到厨房**，**乌尔杜穆孜（厨师）为督办**；1只育肥公绵羊为**内宫**，**阿皮里亚为督办**；3只育肥公绵羊为**厨房**：当国王离开尼普尔前往乌鲁克时，**乌尔杜穆孜为督办**，**经由王后舒勒吉新提**，于**乌尔**，从阿希马处支出了。神宁阿朱庆典月，席穆润第三次被毁灭之年。
Š 32 v： **mu-túm** 1 grass bull, 5 grass rams and 1 kid from**Kuli**, **the majordomo**, 1 lamb from **their shepherd**, were deliveries for **Šulgi-simtum**	1 gud-ú, 5 udu-ú, 1 máš, ***Ku-li*** *šabra*, 1 *sila$_4$* **sipa-e-ne**, mu-túm~ ^{d}***Šul-gi-sí-im-tum***. *iti-ezem-^{d}Nin-a-zu, mu a-rá-3-kam-aš Si-mu-ru-um^{ki} ba-hul.* (*DoCu Strasbourg* 53, *P*109138)	1 *grass bull*, 5 *grass rams and* 1 *kid from***Kuli**, **the majordomo**, 1 lamb from**their shepherd**, were deliveries for**Šulgi-simtum**. Month of ezem-Ninazu, Year of Simurum was destroyed for the third time.	1头食草公牛、5只食草公绵羊和1只公山羊崽**来自库里庙总管**，1只羊羔来自**他们的牧羊人**，为舒勒吉新吞的送人项。神宁阿朱庆典月，席穆润第三次被毁灭之年。
Š 32 vi： **zi-ga** [1+] kid and [1+] lamb for **the sister of Ṣiluš-Dagan**, were delivered of Šulgi-simtum, X in **Uruk**, **withdrawn from Ea-bani**	[1+] máš, [1+] sila$_4$, **nin$_9$**-***Ṣi-lu-uš-^{d}Da-gan*** mu-túm ^{d}***Šul-gi-sí-im-tum***, [*x x*] 8 *x`AN* [*x*] *Unug^{ki}-ga*, *zi-ga ki*~ ***É-a-ba-ni***. *iti-á-ki-ti*~ *še-numun, mu a-rá-3-kam-aš Si-mu-ru-um^{ki} ba-hul.* (*seal*)：^{d}*Šul-gi nita-kal-ga*, *lugal Urim^{ki}-ma*, *lugalan-ub-da limmú-ba*, ^{d}***Šul-gi-sí-im-tum*****lukur**！**kaskal-la-ka-ni**Maš-gu-la sukkal árad-zu.	[1+] kid and [1+] lamb for **the sister of Ṣiluš-Dagan**, were delivered of Šulgi-simtum, X in **Uruk**, **withdrawn from Ea-bani.** Month of akiti of barley seed, Year of Simurum was destroyed for the third time. (seal)：Šulgi is the strong man, the king of Ur, king of four-quarters, Šulgi-simtum is the lukur priestess wife on his journey, the envoy Mašgula is your servant.	【1+】公崽和【1+】只羊羔为**采鲁什达干之妹**，舒勒吉新吞的送人项，X **于乌鲁克**，**从埃阿巴尼**处支出了。大麦种子的阿基提月，席穆润第三次被毁灭之年。（印章）：舒勒吉是强大男子，乌尔的国王、四方之王，**舒勒吉新吞是在旅途中陪伴他的 lukur 神妻**，马什古拉国使，是你的仆人。

续表

时间和摘要	文献内容	英文翻译	中文翻译
Š 32 ix: **mu-túm** 2 rams and 1 [+ k] id from **Atalal**, 1 bull, 8 rams and 3 kids from **Ur-Šulpae**, 4 rams and 1 kid from **Nir-idagal**, 3 rams and 1 kid from **Ama-bara**, 1 kid from **Ea-bani**, the governor, were deliveries for **Šulgi-simti**	2 udu, 1 [+ m] áš *A-ta-làl*?, 1 *gud*, 8 *udu*, 3 *máš* **Ur-dŠul-pa-è**, 4 udu, 1 máš ***Nir-i-da-ĝál***, 3 *udu*, 1 *máš* **Ama-bára**, 1 máš **É-a-ba-ni** ensí, mu-túm~ ***dŠul-gi-sí-im-ti***. *iti-ezem-mah*, *mu a-rá-3-kam-aš Si-mu-ru-um*ki [*ba-hul*]. (*YOS* 4 079, *P*142143)	*2 rams and* 1 [+ *k*] *id from* **Atalal**, 1 bull, 8 rams and 3 kids from **Ur-Šulpae**, 4 rams and 1 kid from **Nir-idagal**, 3 rams and 1 kid from **Ama-bara**, 1 kid from **Ea-bani**, the governor, were deliveries for**Šulgi-simti**. Month of ezem-mah, Year of Simurrum was [destroyed] for the third time.	2公绵羊和1【+】公山羊自**阿塔拉勒**，1公牛、8公绵羊和3公崽自**乌尔舒勒帕埃**，4公绵羊和1公崽自**尼尔伊达旮勒**，3公绵羊和1公崽自**王座之母**，1公崽自**埃阿巴尼总督**，为舒勒吉新提的送入项。大庆典月，席穆润第三次被毁灭之年。
Š 32 ix: **zi-ga** 2 goats whose kid were dead for **giranum of Belat-Suhnir and Belat-Darraban**, **on gate of Geštin-Anna**, 3 goats whose kid were dead for **sacrifice of palace**, **Apiliya as deputy**, these were withdrawn	2 ud5-máš-nú-a, ***gi-ra-núm-dBe-la-at-Suh-nir*** ù ***dBe-la-at-Dar-ra-ba-an***, *ká~ dGeštin-an-na*, 3 *ud5-máš-nú-a siskúr šà~* **é-gal**, ***Á-pi5-lí-a***maškim *zi-ga*. *iti-ezem-mah*, *mu a-rá 3-kam-aš Si-mu-ru-um*ki*ba-hul*. (*SAT* 2 0047, P143246)	2*she-goats whose kid is dead for* **giranum festival of Belat-Suhnir and Belat-Darraban**, **on the gate of Geštin-Anna**, 3 she-goats whose kid is dead for **the sacrifice of center of palace**, **Apiliya as royal deputy**, these were withdrawn. Month of ezem-mah, Year of Simurrum was destroyed for the third time.	2只无山羊崽的母山羊为**贝拉特苏赫尼尔和贝拉特达腊班的吉腊努姆仪式，于吉什廷安那之门**，3只无山羊崽的母山羊为**宫殿中心的祭祀**，**阿皮里亚督办**，以上为支出。大庆典月，席穆润第三次被毁灭之年。
Š 32 x: **ba-úš, šu~ ba-ti** 1**butchered** calf of LU. HA-tenu in **Ur**, **Šukubum** reveived (**seal**): Geme-Sin, wife of Šulgi, king of Ur: **Šukubum** is your knight.	1 amarLu. HA-tenu ba-úš, šà~ **Urim**ki-ma, ***Šu-ku8-bu-um*** *šu~ ba-ti*, *iti-ezem-An-na*, **mu a-rá 3**!**-kam-aš Si-mu-ru-um**ki **ba-hul**. (env.): [1 amar LU]. HA-tenu ba-úš, Urimki-ma, [***Šu-ku8***] ***-bu-um-e*** [*šu*] *~ba-ti*, [*iti*] *-ezem-An-na*, [*mu*] *a-rá3-kam-aš Si-mu-*[*ru*] *-um*ki*ba-hul*. (**seal**): Gemé-dSuen, dam-Šul-gi lugal Urimki-ma, ***Šu-ku-bu-*** [***um***] *rá-gaba* **árad-zu**. (JCS 28 169, P112022)	1butchered calf of LU. HA-tenu **in Ur**, **Šukubum** reveived, Month of ezem-Anna, Year of Simurum was destroyed for the second time. (env.): 1butcheredcalf of LU. HA-tenu in Ur, Šukubum reveived, Month of ezem-Anna, Year of Simurum was destroyed for the third time. (**seal**): Geme-Sin, the wife of Šulgi, king of Ur: Šukubum is your knight.	1头宰杀的LU.HA-tenu牛犊于**乌尔**，**舒库布姆**接收了，天神安庆典月，席穆润被毁年之次年。 (文件:)1头宰杀的LU.HA-tenu牛犊于乌尔，舒库布姆接收了，天神安庆典月，席穆润第三次被毁灭之年。 (**印章**):乌尔王舒勒吉之妻——吉美辛：舒库布姆骑使是你的仆人。
Š 32 xii/20: **mu-túm** 44**corpses** of rams, 6 **corpses** of kids and 1 ram for É-NAR, 1 bull for **Inanna in Uruk**, **Apilliya as royal deputy**, were deliveries for **Šulgi-simtum**, fr. **Iti-Ištar**	44àd- [udu], 6 àd-máš, 1 udu, É-NAR?, 1 gud **d Inanna-Unug**ki, ***Á-pil-lí-a*** *maškim*, *mu-túm~* ***dŠul-gi-sí-im-tum***, *ki ~* ***I-ti-iš4-tár***-*ta*. *iti-še-kin-kud*, *ud-20-kam*, *mu a-rá-3-kam-aš Si-mu-ru-um*ki *ba-hul*. (*M.Sigrist*, *TPTS* 76)	44 *corpses of rams*, 6 *corpses of kids and* 1 *ram for* **É-NAR**, 1 bull for **Inanna in Uruk**, **Apilliya as royal deputy**, were deliveries for **Šulgi-simtum**, from **Iti-Ištar**. Month of še-kin-kud, on the 20th day, Year of Simurrum was destroyed for the third time.	44只公绵羊死尸、6只公崽死尸和1只公绵羊为É-NAR，1头公牛为**伊南那，于乌鲁克**，**阿皮里亚督办**，**为舒勒吉新吞的送入项**，**自伊提伊什塔尔处**。大麦收割月，于20日，席穆润第三次被毁灭之年。

续表

时间和摘要	文献内容	英文翻译	中文翻译
Š 33 i: ki～⋯-ta 50**corpses** of grass ram, 5 **corpses** of fattened ram, 13 **corpses** of kid and 1 butchered bull, were broken, fr.**Ahima**	50 ad_6-udu-ú, 5 ad_6-udu-niga, 13 ad_6-máš, 1 gud-úš, ki～ ***A-hi-ma***-*-ta. iti-maš-dà-*gu_7, *mu a-rá-3-kam Si-mu-ru-um*^{ki}*ba-hul mu-us-sa-bi.* zi-re-àm (OIP 115 129, P123534)	50 corpses of grass ram, 5 corpses of fattened ram, 13 corpses of kid and 1 butchered bull, were broken, from **Ahima**. Month of mašda-gu_7, Year after that of Simurum was destroyed for the third time	50食草公绵羊死尸、5肥公绵羊死尸、13只公崽死尸和1只宰杀的公牛，被分解了，自**阿希马**处。食瞪羚月，席穆润第三次被毁灭之年次年。
Š 33 iii/29: ki～⋯-ta 5 ducklets, 1dove and 1 pigeon, butchered ones were **withdrawn from Ahima**, (were sent to the palace)	5 uz-tur, $1ir_7$^{mušen}, 1 tu-gur_4^{mušen}, ud-30-lá-［1-k］am, ba-úš, ki～ ***A-hi-ma***? (*HA.A.UD*) -- ［*ta*］.*iti-*u_5-*bí-*gu_7, *mu a-rá-3-kam-aš Si-mu-ru-um*^{ki}*ba-hul-a mu-ús-sa-bi.* (*PDT* 2 1251, *P*126579)	5 *ducklets*, 1*dove and* 1 *pigeon*, *on the* 29th *day*, **butchered ones**, were **withdrawn from Ahima**, (were sent to the palace). Month of ubi-gu_7, Year after that of Simurum was destroyed for the third time.	5只幼鸭、1只野鸽和1只家鸽，于第29天，为宰杀牲，从**阿希马处（被送入宫殿）**。食乌比鸟月，席穆润第三次被毁灭之年次年。
Š 33 iv: **mu-túm** 5 rams and 1 kid**from majordomo Ilum-bani**, 2 rams and 1 kid from **captain Ur-Zababa**, 1 female kid from **governor Ea-bani**, 1 lamb for the 1st time, 1 lamb for the 2nd time, from **governor Kalum**, were deliveries for Šulgi-simtum	5 udu, 1 máš, **Ilum-ba-ni** šabra, 2 udu, 1 máš nu-bandà **Ur-**^{d}**Za-**ba_4**-**ba_4, 1^{f}ašgar **É-a-ba-ni** ensí, 1 $sila_4$ a-rá-1-kam, 1 $sila_4$a-rá-2-kam, ensí ***Ka-lu-um***, *mu-túm*～ ^{d}***Šul-gi-sí-im-tum***.*iti-ki-siki-*^{d}*Nin-a-zu*, *mu ús-sa a-rá-3-kam-aš Si-mu-ru-um*^{ki} *ba-hul.* (*MVN* 03 136, *P*113696)	5 *rams and* 1 *kid***from majordomo Ilum-bani**, 2 rams and 1 kid from **captain Ur-Zababa**, 1 female kid from **governor Ea-bani**, 1 lamb for the 1st time, 1 lamb for the 2nd time, from **governor Kalum**, were deliveries for Šulgi-simtum. Month of ki-siki-Ninazu, Year after that of Simurum was destroyed for the third time.	5只公绵羊和1只公崽来自**伊隆巴尼庙总管**，2只公绵羊和1只公崽来自**军尉乌尔扎巴巴**，1只雌崽来自**埃阿巴尼总督**，1只羔第1次，1只羔第2次，来自**总督卡隆**，以上为舒勒吉新吞的送入项。神宁阿朱羊毛作坊月，席穆润第三次被毁灭之年次年。
Š 33 v: **mu-túm**, **ì-**dab_5 1 bull, 9 grass rams, 1 kid fr.**Hubaya**, **the general**, 1 kid from **the wife of Alla**, 1 kid from the **wife of Ur-niĝar**, deliveries for Šulgi-simtum, **Beli-ṭab took over**	1 gud, 9 udu-ú, 1 máš, ***Hu-ba-a*** *šagina*, 1 *máš*, **dam-*Al-la***, 1 *máš*, **dam-Ur-**ni_9**-ĝar**, mu-túm-^{d}***Šul-gi-sí-im-tum***, **Be-lí-ṭàb** *ì-*dab_5*.iti-ezem-*^{d}*Nin-a-zu*, *mu ús-sa a-rá-3-kam Si-mu-ru-um*^{ki}*ba-hul* (*CST*042, *P*107554)	1 *bull*, 9 *grass rams*, 1 *kid from***Hubaya**, **the general**, 1 kid from **the wife of Alla**, 1 kid from the **wife of Ur-niĝar**, deliveries for Šulgi-simtum, **Beli-ṭab took over**. Month of ezem-Ninazu, Year after that of Simurum was destroyed for the third time.	1头公牛，9只食草公绵羊，1只公崽自**胡巴将军**，1只公崽自**阿拉之妻**，1只公崽来自**乌尔尼旮尔之妻**，以上为舒勒吉新吞送入项，**贝里沓卜接管了**。神宁阿朱庆典月，席穆润第三次被毁灭之年次年。

续表

时间和摘要	文献内容	英文翻译	中文翻译。
Š 33 v: **zi-ga** 1 fattened bull for **Annunitum**, **via my queen**; 1 fattened bull, 5 fat rams, 4 grass rams, 1 kid for **Te ṣin-Mama**, **via Apilati**; 1 fattened ram for **giranum festival of Inanna by the wall**, **Mašum as royaldeputy**, were withdrawn from **Beli-ṭab** in **Ur**	1 gud-niga, ***An-nu-ni-tum***, **gìr nin-ĝá**; 1 gud-niga, 5 udu-niga, 4 udu-ú, 1 máš, ***Te-ṣi-in-^{d}Ma-ma***, **gìr*Á-pi$_5$-la-ti***, 1 *udu-niga*, ***gi-ra-núm-***^{d}**Inanna**--da bàd-da, **Ma-šum maškim**; zi-ga šà~ **Urim^{ki}**--ma, ki~ ***Be-lí-ṭàb***--*ta. iti-ezem-^{d}* [*Nin-a-z*] *u*, *mu-ús-s* [*a a-rá-3-kam*] *Si-mu-r* [*u-um^{ki}ba-hul*]. (*PDT* 2 1017, P126359)	1 *fattened bull for* **Annunitum**, **via my queen**; 1 fattened bull, 5 fattened rams, 4 grass rams, 1 kid for**Te ṣin-Mama**, **via Apilati**; 1 fattened ram for**the giranum festival of Inanna by the wall**, **Mašum as the royal deputy**, were withdrawn from **Beli-ṭab** in **Ur**. Month of ezem-Ninazu, Year after that of Simurum was destroyed for the third time.	1 头育肥公牛为**安努尼吞女神**，**经由我的王后**； 1 头育肥公牛、5 只育肥公绵羊、4 只食草公绵羊和 1 只公崽为**台岑妈妈**，**经由阿皮拉提**；1 只育肥公绵羊为**伊南那的吉腊努姆仪式于城墙边**，**马顺督办**，从乌尔、贝里沓卜处支出了。神宁阿朱庆典月，席穆润第三次被毁灭之年次年。
Š 33 v: **zi-ga** 2 fat bullen and 2 fat rams for **animal manager**?, 2 fat rams for e**n-priestess of Nanna**, [1+] fat ram for **the belem of Nanna**,...the food, [1+] fattened ram for **Belat-Suhnir**, [1+] fattened ram for **Belat-Darraban**, **for the giranum festival**, [1+] fat ram for the **mother of queen**, [1+] fat bull for **"pouring-beer" festival of Nanaya in palace**, **withdr.fr.Beli-ṭab**, **in Ur**	2 gud-niga, 2 udu-niga šùš? (ÉxU) --šè, 2 udu-niga **en-^{d}Nanna**, [1+] udu-niga **šu-nir-^{d}Nanna**, [x] -e **níĝ-gu$_7$-a**, [1+] udu-niga ***^{d}Be-la-at-Suh-nir***, [1+] *udu-niga* ***^{d}Be-la-at-Dar-ra-ba-an gi-ra-núm***--*šè*, [1+] *udu-niga* **ama-nin-ĝá**, [1+] gud-niga **kaš-dé-a-*^{d}Na-na-a*** *šà~ é-gal--šè*, *zi-ga ki~* ***Be-lí-ṭab***-*ta*, *šà~* **Urim$_5$^{ki}**-ma. iti-ezem-^{d}Nin-a-zu, mu ús-sa a-rá-3-kam Si-mu-ru-um^{ki} ba-hul. (unp. Sigrist, Newark Public Library 11, R09)	2 fattened bullen and 2 fattened rams for**the animal manager**?, 2 fattened rams for e**n-priestess of Nanna**, [1+] fattened ram for **the emblem of Nanna**,...the food, [1+] fattened ram for **Belat-Suhnir**, [1+] fattened ram for **Belat-Darraban**, **for the giranum festival**, [1+] fattened ram for the **mother of queen**, [1+] fattened bull for **"pouring-beer" festival of Nanaya in palace**, were **withdrawn from Beli-ṭab**, in **Ur**. Month of ezem-Ninazu, Year after that of Simurum was destroyed for the third time.	2 只育肥公牛和 2 只育肥公绵羊为**牲畜长**，2 只育肥公绵羊为**南那神的祭司**，【1+】育肥公绵羊为**南那神的象征**，为……**食物**，【1+】肥公绵羊为**贝拉特苏赫尼尔**，【1+】育肥公绵羊为**贝拉特达腊班**，**为吉腊努姆仪式**，【1+】育肥公绵羊为**我的王后之母**，【1+】育肥公牛为**那那亚于宫殿的倒啤酒宴会**，从贝里沓卜支出了，于乌尔。 神宁阿朱庆典月，席穆润第三次被毁之年次年。
Š 33 vi: **zi-ga** 1 fat ram for**the sacrifice of Nanna**, 1 grass ram for **Ištar-ummi**, were withdrawn from **Beli-ṭab**, in **Ur**	1 udu-niga, **siskúr-^{d}Nanna**, 1 udu-ú, **mu~ *Iš$_8$-tár-um-mi*--*šè***, *zi-ga ki~* ***Be-lí-ṭàb***--*ta*, *šà~* **Urim^{ki}**-ma. iti-á-ki~ti, mu ús-sa a-rá-3-kam Si-mu-ru-um^{ki}ba-hul. (Torino 1 195, P131977)	1 fattened ram for**the sacrifice of Nanna**, 1 grass ram for **Ištar-ummi**, were withdrawn from **Beli-ṭab**, in **Ur**. Month of akiti, Year after that of Simurum was destroyed for the third time.	1 只育肥公绵羊为**南那的牺牲**，1 只食草公绵羊为**伊什塔尔温米**，从贝里沓卜于**乌尔**处支出了。阿基提月，席穆润第三次被毁灭之年次年。
Š 33 vi: **zi-ga** 1 fattened ram **for Dub-la-mah**, when my queen left it, withdrawn from the palce of Beli-ṭab, in **Ur**	1 udu-niga **Dub-lá-mah**, nin!-mu è-da-ni, zi-ga ki~ ***Be-lí-ṭàb***--*ta*, *šà~* **Urim^{ki}**-ma. iti-á-ki~ti, mu ús-sa a-rá-3-kam Si-mu-ru-um^{ki} ba-hul. (UCP 9-2-2 037, P136041)	1 fattened ram**for Dub-la-mah**, when my queen left it, withdrawn from the palce of Beli-ṭab, in **Ur**. Month of akiti, Year after that of Simurum was destroyed for the third time.	1 只育肥公绵羊为**大门楼**，于我的王后离开时，从**贝里沓卜**处支出了，于**乌尔**。阿基提月，席穆润第三次被毁灭之年次年。

续表

时间和摘要	文献内容	英文翻译	中文翻译
Š 33 vi: **zi-ga** 2 fat rams for**giranum on** 2 rams for **giranum**, 2 kid for **disppearing place of temple of Belat-Suhnir and Belat-Darraban** on, 1 fat ram for **giranum of Inanna by the side of wall**, **<u>via my queen</u>**, 2 rams for **giranum festival of Annunitum and Ulmasitum**, **<u>via Apilati</u>**, withdr.fr.**Beli-ṭab**	2 udu-niga***gi-ra-núm*****-**-*šè*, *a-rá-1-kam*, 2 *udu-ú* ***gi-ra-núm***-*šè*, 2 *máš* **níĝ-ki-zah** ***é-^{d}Be-la-at-Suh$^{!}$-nir*** *ù* ***^{d}Be-la-at-D*** [*ar*] ***-ra-ba-a*** [*n*], *a-rá-2-kam*, 1 *udu-niga*, ***gi-ra-núm*** **^{d}Inanna** da-bàd--da, **<u>gìr nin-ĝá!</u>**, 2 udu-ú ***gi-ra-núm An-nu-ni-tum*** ù ***^{d}Ul-ma-si-tum***, *gìr* ***<u>Á-pi$_5$-la! -ti</u>***, *zi-ga* ***Be-lí-ṭab$_6$***. *iti-á-ki-ti*, *mu ús-sa a-rá-3-kam Si$^{!}$-mu-ru-um^{ki} ba-hul.* (*F.N.H.al-Rowi*, *Iraq* 62, p28, *No*.59)	2 *fattened rams for***giranum on 1st time**, 2 grass rams for **giranum**, 2 kid for the **disppearing place of temple of Belat-Suhnir and Belat-Darraban** on 2nd time, 1 fattened ram for **giranum of Inanna by the side of wall**, **<u>via my queen</u>**, 2 grass rams for **giranum festival <u>of Annunitum</u> and Ulmasitum**, **<u>via Apilati</u>**, were withdrawn from **Beli-ṭab**. Month of akiti, Year after that of Simurum was destroyed for the third time.	2肥公绵羊为**吉腊努姆仪式**第1次，2食草公绵羊为**吉腊努姆仪式**，2公崽为**贝拉特苏赫尼尔和贝拉特达腊班庙的消失处**第2次，1肥公绵羊为**伊南那吉腊努姆仪式于城墙**，**经由我的王后**，2食草公绵羊为**安努尼吞和乌勒马席吞的吉腊努姆仪式**，**经由阿皮拉提**，从**贝里沓卜**支出。阿基提月，席穆润第三次被毁灭之年次年。
Š 33 vi: **mu-túm** 2 fattened rams and 1 kid from**Namutum**, were deliveries for **Šulgi-simtum**	2 udu-niga, 1 máš ***Na-mu-tum***, *mu-túm* ~ ***^{d}Šul-gi-sí-im-tum***. *iti-á-ki-ti-šu-numun*, *mu ús-sa a-rá-3-kam Si-mu-ru-um^{ki}ba-hul.* (*MVN* 03 137, *P*113697)	2 *fattened rams and* 1 *kid from***Namutum**, were deliveries for **Šulgi-simtum**. Month of akiti-šu-numun, Year after that of Simurum was destroyed for the third time.	2只育肥公绵羊和1只公崽来自**那穆吞**，为**舒勒吉新吞的送入项**。 阿基提种子月， 席穆润第三次被毁灭之年次年。
Š 33 vii: **mu-túm, ì-dab$_5$** 3 rams and 1 kid from**Dudu**, 4 rams and 1 kid from **Inmeri**, were deliveries for Šulgi-simti, **Beli-ṭab** took over	3 udu, 1 máš, **Du-du**?, 4 udu, 1 máš ***In-<me>-ri***, *mu-túm* ~ ***^{d}Šul-gi-sí-im-ti$^{!}$***, ***Be-lí-ṭàb*** *ì-dab$_5$*. *iti-ezem-^{d}Šul-gi*, *mu ús-sa a-rá-3-kam-aš Si-mu-ru-um^{ki} ba-hul.* (*MVN* 15 309, *P*118574)	3 *rams and* 1 *kid from***Dudu**, 4 rams and 1 kid from **Inmeri**, were deliveries for Šulgi-simti, **Beli-ṭab** took over. Month of ezem-Šulgi, Year after that of Simurum was destroyed for third time.	3公绵羊和1公崽自**杜杜**，4公绵羊和1公崽自**伊美瑞**，为舒勒吉新提的送入项，**贝里沓卜接管**了。舒勒吉庆典月，席穆润第三次被毁灭之年次年。
Š 33 vii: **zi-ga** 1 fat bull for **the sacrifice of boat of An, in Uruk**, **<u>Ur-Dumuzi as royal deputy</u>**, was withdrawn (fr. Beli-ṭab)	1 gud-niga **siskúr-má-An-na**, šà ~ **Unug^{ki}**-ga, **<u>Ur-^{d}Dumu-zi maškim</u>**, zi-ga.iti-ezem-^{d}Šul-gi, mu ús-sa a-rá-3-kam-aš Si-mu-ru-um^{ki} ba-hul. (Torino 1 204, P132036)	1 fattened bull for**the sacrifice of boat of An, in Uruk**, **<u>Ur-Dumuzi as royal deputy</u>**, was withdrawn.Month of ezem-Šulgi, Year after that of Simurum was destroyed for third time.	1头育肥公牛为**天神安之船的祭祀**，于**乌鲁克**，**乌尔杜穆兹督办**，从（贝里沓卜）支出了。舒勒吉庆典月，席穆润第三次被毁灭之年次年。
Š 33 viii: **ba-úš, šu~ba-ti** 1**butchered** calf of HA-tenu in **Ur**, **Šukubum** reveived	1 amar HA-tenu ~ ba-úš, šà ~ **Urim^{ki}**-ma, ***Šu-ku-bu-um*** *šu~ba-ti*. *iti-šu-eš-ša*, *mu ús-sa a-rá-3-kam-áš Si-mu-ru-um^{ki} ba-hul.* (*Syracuse* 330, *P*130881)	1**butchered** calf of HA-tenu in **Ur**, **Šukubum** reveived. Month ofšu-ešša, Year after that of Simurum was destroyed for third time.	1头宰杀的HA-tenu牛犊，于**乌尔**，**舒库布姆**接收了。三只手月， 席穆润第三次被毁灭之年次年。

续表

时间和摘要	文献内容	英文翻译	中文翻译
Š 33 ix: zi-ga 1 fattened ram forDublamah, via my queen, when (the king) left Nippur, were withdrawn from Ahima	1 udu-niga, ^{d}**Dub-lá-mah** gìr **nin-ĝá**, ud ~ **Nibru**^{ki} ba-ta-è, zi-ga *A-hi-ma*. *iti-ezem-mah*, *mu a-rá-3-kam Si-mu-ru-um*^{ki} *ba-hul mu-ús-sa-bi*. (*MVN* 2, 336, P113635)	1 *fattened ram for*Dublamah, via my queen, when (the king) left Nippur, were withdrawn from Ahima.Month of ezem-mah, Year after that of Simurum was destroyed for the third time.	1只育肥公绵羊为大门楼，经由我的王后，当（国王）离开尼普尔时，从阿希马处支出了。大庆典月，席穆润第三次被毁灭之年次年。
Š 33 ix: zi-ga 2 fat rams for Sacrifice of Belat-Suhnir and Belat-Darraban, Ur- [bi] as deputy; 2 fat rams for Annunitum, 1 for Ulmasitum, 1 for Allatum, 1 for Išhara, via my queen; 2 fat rams for Nenegar festival of temple of Belat-Suhnir and Belat-Darraban, via Apilatum; 2 for Belat-Suhnir and Belat-Darraban, viadaughter of Tabba-Darah, Urbias deputy; 1 for Giranum festival of Inanna by the wall, via my queen; 1 fat ram for "beer-pouring" of Nin-egalka, 2 fat rams for Uruk, via Ur-Dumuzida, withdr.fr.Ahima	2 udu-niga, **siskúr** ^{d}***Be-la-at-Suh***$_{6}$***-nir*** ù ***Be-la-*** [***at-Tár-ra***] ***-ba-an*** *Ur-* [*bi*] *maškim*; 2 *udu-niga*, ***An-nu-ni-tum***; 1 *udu-niga*, ^{d}***Ul-ma-si-tum***; 1 *udu-niga*, ^{d} ***Al-la-tum***; 1 *udu-niga*, ^{d} ***Iš-ha-ra***, gìr**nin-ĝá**; 2 udu-niga, ne-ne-gar é-^{d}***Be-la-at-Suh-nir*** ù ^{d}**Be-la-at-Suh-nir** (!), gìr ***Á-pi***$_{5}$***-la-tum***; 2 *udu-niga*, ^{d} ***Be-la-at-Suh***$_{6}$***-nir*** ù ^{d}***Be-la-at-Dar-ra-ba-an*** *gìrdumu-munus* ***Tab-ba-Da-ra-ah***, *Ur-bi maškim*; 1 *udu-niga*, ***gi-ra-núm*** ^{d}*Inanna--da bàd*, gìr**nin-ĝá**; 1 udu-niga, kaš-dé-a^{d} Nin-é-gal-ka, 2 udu-niga, Unug^{ki}--šè, gìr**Ur-**^{d}**Dumu-zi-da**, zi-ga***A-hi-ma***.*iti-ezem-mah*, *mu ús-sa a-rá 3-kam-aš Si-mu-ru-um*^{ki}*ba-hul*. (AnOr 7 053, P101348)	2 fattened rams for the Sacrifice of Belat-Suhnir and Belat-Darraban, Ur- [bi] as royal deputy; 2 fattened rams for Annunitum, 1 fattened ram for Ulmasitum, 1 fattened ram for Allatum, 1 fattened ram for Išhara, via my queen; 2 fattened rams for Nenegar festival of the temple of Belat-Suhnir and Belat-Darraban, via Apilatum; 2 fattened rams for Belat-Suhnir and Belat-Darraban, via the daughter of Tabba-Darah, Urbias royal deputy; 1 fattened ram for the Giranum festival of Inanna by the wall, via my queen; 1 fattened ram for "beer-pouring" of Nin-egalka, 2 fattened rams forUruk, via Ur-Dumuzida, were withdrawn from Ahima. Month of ezem-mah, Year after that of Simurum was destroyed for the third time.	2育肥公绵羊为贝拉特苏赫尼尔和贝拉特达腊班的祭祀，乌尔【比】督办；2育肥公绵羊为安努尼吞，1育肥公绵羊为乌勒马席吞，1育肥公绵羊为阿拉吞，1育肥公绵羊为伊什哈腊，经由我的王后；2育肥公绵羊为贝拉特苏赫尼尔和贝拉特达腊班庙之耐耐旮尔节，经由阿皮拉吞；2育肥公绵羊为贝拉特苏赫尼尔和贝拉特达腊班，经由塔巴达腊赫之女，乌尔比督办；1育肥公绵羊为伊南那于城墙的吉腊努姆仪式，经由我的王后；1育肥公绵羊为宁埃旮勒的倒啤酒宴会，2育肥公绵羊为乌鲁克，经由乌尔杜穆孜达，以上从阿希马支出了。大庆典月，席穆润第三次被毁灭之年次年。
Š 33 ix: zi-ga 1 grass ram forBeli-bani, was withdrawn from Beli-ṭab	1 udu-ú ***Be-lí-ba-ni***, *zi-ga* ***Be-lí-ṭàb***.*iti-ezem-mah*, *mu ús-sa a-rá-3-kam Si-mu-ru-um*^{ki} *ba-hul*. (*Torino* 1 176, P133895)	1 *grass ram for*Beli-bani, was withdrawn from Beli-ṭab. Month of ezem-mah, Year after that of Simurum was destroyed for the third time.	1只食草公绵羊为贝里巴尼，从贝里沓卜支出了。大庆典月，席穆润第三次被毁之年次年。
Š 33: zi-ga 98 grass rams, 20 kids for the monthly allowance of Belat-Suhnir, Belat-Darraban, Annunitum and Ulmašitum, the receipt of my queen's mother, withdr.from Ahima	98 udu-ú, 20 máš, sá-dug$_{4}$ ~ ^{d}***Be-la-at-Suh-nir***, ^{d}**Be-la-at-Dar-ra-ba-an**, **An-nu-ni-tum** ù ^{d}***Ul-ma-*** [***ši-tum***] *kišib* **ama nin-ĝá**--ka, zi-ga ki ~ ***A-hi-ma***--*ta. mu a-rá 3-kam-aš Si-mu-ru-um*^{ki}*ba-hul-a mu ús-sa-bi*. (*SA*001*a* (*Pl*.026), P128609)	98 *grass rams*, 20 *kids for* the monthly allowance of Belat-Suhnir, Belat-Darraban, Annunitum and Ulmašitum, thereceipt of my queen's mother, were withdrawn from Ahima. Year after that of Simurum was destroyed for the third time.	98只食草公绵羊、20只公崽为贝拉特苏赫尼尔、贝拉特达腊班，安努尼吞和乌勒马席吞的月供，（经由）我的王后之母的收据，从阿希马处支出了。席穆润第三次被毁灭之年次年。

续表

时间和摘要	文献内容	英文翻译	中文翻译
Š 34i/3: **mu-túm** 1 female kid was **delivery of Šulgisimtum**	1^{f}asgar, mu-túm~ <^{d} ***Šul-gi-sí-im-tum*** >, *ud-3-kam. iti-maš-kù-gu$_{7}$*, *mu An-ša-an^{ki} ba-hul.* (*T.Gomi*, *HCT* 11)	1 *female kid was* **delivery of Šulgisimtum**, on the 3rd day. Month of mašku-gu, Year of Anšan was destroyed.	1只雌崽为**舒勒吉新提的送入项**，于第3天。 食豚月， 安山被毁灭之年。
Š 34 ii: **mu-túm, ì-dab$_{5}$** 6 rams fr. **Taba-Darah**, 1 lamb from the **wife of Urnigar**, 1 lamb from **the man of Magan**, were delivery of Šulgisimtum, **Beli-ṭab** took	6 udu-ú, ***Ṫa-ba-Da-ra-ah***, 1 *sila$_{4}$*, **dam-Ur-ni$_{9}$-gar**, 1 sila$_{4}$, **lú-Má-gan^{ki}**, mu-túm *^{d}Šul-gi-sí-im-tum-ma*, ***Be-lí-ṭàb*** *ì-dab$_{5}$.iti-ze$_{x}$-da~gu$_{7}$*, *mu An-ša-an^{ki} ba-hul.* (*OIP* 115021, P123722)	6 *grass rams from* **Taba-Darah**, 1 lamb from the **wife of Urnigar**, 1 lamb from **the man of Magan**, were delivery of Šulgisimtum, **Beli-ṭab** took over. Month of zeda~gu$_{7}$, Year of Anšan was destroyed.	6只食草公绵羊来自**塔巴达腊赫**，1只羊羔来自**乌尔尼旮尔之妻**，1只羊羔来自**马干城之人**，（以上）**为舒勒吉新的送入项，贝里沓卜接管**了。食豚月，安山被毁灭之年。
Š 34 ii: **zi-ga** 3 fat rams for **the temple of Nisaba, via Barbarria**, were **withdrawn from Beli-ṭab**	3 udu-niga, é-^{d}**Nisaba**--šè, gìr ***Bar-bar-ri-a***, *zi-ga* ***Be-lí-ṭàb***.*iti-ze$_{x}$-da~gu$_{7}$*, *mu An-ša-an^{ki}ba-hul.* (*OIP* 115026, P123472)	3 *fattened rams for* **the temple of Nisaba, via Barbarria**, were **withdrawn from Beli-ṭab**. Month of zeda~gu$_{7}$, Year of Anšan was destroyed.	3只育肥公绵羊为**尼萨巴庙，经由巴尔巴瑞阿，从贝里沓卜处支出了**。 食豚月， 安山被毁灭之年。
Š 34 iii: **zi-g** 1 fat ram for **An**, 2 fat bulls, 6 fat rams for **Belat-Suhnir and Belat-Drraban**, 1 fat ram for **Sacrifice of Nanna**, 1 fat ram for **festival of gods entered**, 2 fat ram for **offering of Belat-Suhnir and Belat-Erraban**, 1 fat ram for **big tower**, 2 for **Belat-S.and Belat-E.**, withdr.fr.**Ahima**	1 udu-niga, **An-na**, 2 gud-niga, 6 udu-niga, ***^{d}Be-la-at-Suh$_{6}$-nir*** ù ***^{d}Be-la-at-Dar-ra-ba-an***, 1 *udu-niga*, *siskúr* ~ ^{d}**Nanna**, 1 gud-niga, ezem-diĝir-ku$_{4}$-ku$_{4}$, 2 udu-niga, níĝ-ki-zàh ***^{d}Be-la-at-Suh$_{6}$-nir*** ù ***^{d}Be-la-at-Èr-ra-ba-an***, 1 *udu-niga*, *Dub-lá-mah*, 2 *udu-niga*, ***^{d}Be-la-at-Suh$_{6}$-nir*** ù ***^{d}Be-la-at-Èr-ra-ba-an***, *zi-ga* ***A-hi-ma***.*iti-u$_{5}$-bí~gu$_{7}$*, *mu An-ša-an^{ki}ba-hul.* (*OrSP* 18 *pl.*01 01, P124847)	1 *fattened ram for* **An**, 2 fattened bulls, 6 fattened rams for **Belat-Suhnir and Belat-Drraban**, 1 fattened ram for **the Sacrifice of Nanna**, 1 fattened ram for **the festival of the gods entered**, 2 fattened ram for **the offering of Belat-Suhnir and Belat-Erraban**, 1 fattened ram for **the big tower**, 2 fattened rams for **Belat-Suhnir and Belat-Erraban**, were withdrawn from **Ahima**. Month of ubi~gu$_{7}$, Year of Anšan was destroyed.	1育肥公绵羊为**天神安**，2育肥公牛、6育肥公绵羊为**贝拉特苏赫尼尔和贝拉特埃腊班**，1育肥公绵羊为**南那神的祭祀**，1育肥公绵羊为**神明进入节**，2育肥公绵羊为**贝拉特苏赫尼尔和贝拉特埃腊班的消失处供奉**，1育肥公绵羊为**大门楼**，2育肥公绵羊为**贝拉特苏赫尼尔和贝拉特埃腊班，从阿希马处支出了**。食乌比乌月，安山被毁之年。
Š 34 iv: **zi-ga** 2 grass rams for **Buza**, were **withdrawn from Beli-ṭab**	2 udu-ú, **Bù-ú-za**, zi-ga ***Be-lí-ṭàb***. *iti-ki-siki-^{d} Nin-a-zu*, *mu An-ša-an^{ki}ba-hul.* (*OIP* 115027, P123517)	2 *grass rams for* **Buza**, were **withdrawn from Beli-ṭab**. Month of ki-siki-Ninazu, Year of Anšan was destroyed.	2只食草公绵羊为**布扎，从贝里沓卜处支出**。神宁阿朱羊毛作坊月，安山被毁灭之年。
Š 34 v: **zi-ga** 1 kid for **Buza**, was **withdrawn from Beli-ṭab**	1 máš, ***Bù-ú-za***, *zi-ga* ***Be-lí-ṭàb***.*iti-ezem-^{d}Nin-a-zu*, *mu An-ša-an^{ki}ba-hul.* (*PDT* 2 1148, P126483)	1 *kid for* **Buza**, was **withdrawn from Beli-ṭab**. Month of ezem-Ninazu, Year of Anšan was destroyed.	1只公崽为**布扎，从贝里沓卜处支出了**。神宁阿朱庆典月，安山被毁灭之年。

续表

时间和摘要	文献内容	英文翻译	中文翻译
Š 34 v: **ì-dab$_5$** 1 bull, 8 rams and 2 kids from**Tabba-Darah**, 1 lamb fr. wife in journey of **the governor of Adab**, for Šulgi-simtum, **Beli-ṭab took** over	1 gud, 8 udu, 2 máš ***Tab-ba-Da-ra-ah***, 1 *sila$_4$* **dam-kaskal**? ensí Adab^{ki}, ^{d}***Šul-gi-sí-im-tum***, ***Be-lí-ṭàb*** *ì-dab$_5$.iti-ezem-^{d}Nin-a-zu*, *mu An-ša-an^{ki} ba-hul.* (*TLB* 3 015, *P*134156)	1 *bull*, 8 *rams and* 2 *kids from***Tabba-Darah**, 1 lamb from the wife in the journey of **the governor of Adab**, for Šulgi-simtum, **Beli-ṭab took** over. Month of ezem-Ninazu, Year of Anšan was destroyed.	1头牛、8只公绵羊和2只公崽来自**塔巴达腊赫**，1只羔自**阿达卜的总督的旅行中的妻子**，为舒勒吉新吞的送入项，**贝里沓卜接管**了。神宁阿朱庆典月，安山被毁灭之年。
Š 34 v: **mu-túm** 1 bull, 9 rams and 1 kid fr. **Halhalla**; 1 fat bull, 6 rams and 4 kids fr. **Namutum**; 1 bull, 4 rams and 1 kid fr. **mother of Zalaya**; 4 fat rams and 1 kid fr. **Idrak-ili**; 2 fat rams and 1 lamb fr. **daughter of Kurgirneše**; 2 fat rams and 1 kid fr. **wife of Alla**; 1 fat bull, 9 rams and 1 kid fr. **Igi-annakezu**; 1 bull, 3 rams of after-ox-class, 6 rams and 1 kid from **Innuri**, were deliveries Šulgi-simtum	1 gud, 9 udu-ú, 1 máš ***Hal-hal-la***; 1 *gud-niga*, 6 *udu*, 4 *máš* ***Na-mu-tum***; 1 *gud*, 4 *udu*, 1 *máš*, **ama-*Za-la-a***; 4 *udu-niga*, 1 *máš*, ***Id-ra-ak-ì-lí***; 2 *udu-niga*, 1 *sila$_4$*, **dumu-munus-Kur-gìr-né-šè**; 2 udu-niga, 1 máš, **dam-*Al-la***; 1 *gud-niga*, 3 *udu-gud-e-ús*, 6 *udu-ú*, 1 *máš*, **Igi-an-na-ke$_4$-zu**; 1 gud, 3 udu-gud-e-ús, 6 udu-ú, 1 máš, ***In-nu-ri***; *mu-túm*~ ^{d}***Šul-gi-sí-im-tum***, *udu á-ki-ti.* *iti-ezem-^{d}Nin-a-zu*, *mu An-ša-an^{ki} ba-hul.* (*AnOr* 07 147, *P*101442)	1 *bull*, 9 *grass rams and* 1 *kid from***Halhalla**; 1 fattened bull, 6 rams and 4 kids from **Namutum**; 1 bull, 4 rams and 1 kid from **the mother of Zalaya**; 4 fattened rams and 1 kid from **Idrak-ili**; 2 fattened rams and 1 lamb from **the daughter of Kurgirneše**; 2 fattened rams and 1 kid from **the wife of Alla**; 1 fattened bull, 3 rams of after-ox-class, 6 grass rams and 1 kid from **Igi-annakezu**; 1 bull, 3 rams of after-ox-class, 6 grass rams and 1 kid from **Innuri**, were deliveries for Šulgi-simtum, for rams of akiti. Month of ezem-Ninazu, Year of Anšan was destroyed.	1牛、9食草公绵羊和1公崽自**哈勒哈拉**；1育肥公牛、6公绵羊和4公崽自**那穆吞**；1公牛、4公绵羊和1公崽自**扎拉亚之母**；4育肥公绵羊和1公崽来自**伊德腊克伊里**；2育肥公绵羊和1羔自**库尔吉尔耐筛的女儿**；2肥公绵羊和1公崽自**阿拉之妻**；1肥公牛、3牛后级公绵羊、6食草公绵羊和1公崽自**伊吉安那凯朱**；1公牛、3牛后级育肥公绵羊、6食草公绵羊和1公崽自**尹努瑞**，为舒勒吉新吞送入项，为阿基提的公绵羊。神宁阿朱庆典月，安山被毁灭之年。
Š 34 vi: **zi-ga** 2 grass rams from **Iṭib-šinat**, were withdrawn from **Beli-ṭab**	2 udu-ú ***I-ṭì-ib-ši-na-at***, *zi-ga ki*~ ***Be-lí-ṭàb***--*ta.iti-á-ki-ti*, *mu An-ša-an^{ki} ba-hul.* (*MVN* 13 415, *P*117188)	2 *grass rams from* **Iṭib-šinat**, were withdrawn from **Beli-ṭab**. Month of akiti, Year of Anšan was destroyed.	2只食草公绵羊来自**伊提卜西那特**，从**贝里沓卜**支出了。阿基提月，安山被毁灭之年。
Š 34 vi: **zi-ga** 1 fattened bull for the boat of**An**, in **Uruk**, **via Barbarre**, was withdrawn from **Beli-ṭàb**	1 gud-niga **má-An-na**, šà~ **Unug^{ki}**-ga, gìr ***Bar-bar-re***, *zi-ga* ***Be-lí-ṭàb***.*iti-á-ki-ti*, *mu An-ša-an^{ki} ba-hul.* (*Hirose* 012, *P*109483)	1 *fattened bull for the boat of***An**, in **Uruk**, **via Barbarre**, was withdrawn from **Beli-ṭàb**. Month of akiti, Year of Anšan was destroyed.	1头育肥公牛为**天神安之船**，于**乌鲁克**，经由**巴尔巴尔瑞**，从**贝里沓卜支出**了。阿基提月，安山被毁灭之年。
Š 34 vi: **zi-ga** 1 kid forwife of Gutarla, withdr. fr. **Beli-ṭàb** fattener	1 máš **dam-*Gú-tar-lá***, *zi-ga-****Be-lí-ṭàb*** *gurušda. iti-á-ki-ti*, *mu An-ša-an^{ki} ba-hul.* (*SAT* 2 0107, *P*143306)	1 *kid for***wife of Gutarla**, was withdrawn from **Beli-ṭàb**, the fattener. Month of akiti, Year of Anšan was destroyed.	1只公崽为**古塔尔拉之妻**，从育肥师**贝里沓卜支**出了。阿基提月，安山被毁灭之年。

续表

时间和摘要	文献内容	英文翻译	中文翻译
Š 34 vii, v, iii: (zi-ga) 1 fat ram for **Belat-Suhnir**, 1 for **Belat-D.**, **month of ezem-Šulgi**; 1 for **Nin-sun**, 1 for **Geštin-anna**, **month of ezem-Ninazu**; **via Tab-har-šum**, 4 for **elunum festival of Belat-S.**, **month of ubi~gu$_7$**; **via Apilanum and Iku--šum**, 2 for**Belat-S.**, 1 for **Allatum**, **month of ezem-Šulgi**; 1 for **the big tower**, 2 for **Belat-S.**, **month of ubi-gu$_7$**; **via Apilanum**	1 udu-niga^d***Be-la-at-Suh$_6$-nir^{ir}***, 1 *udu-niga* ^{d}***Be-la-at-<Dar>-ra-ba-an***, *iti-ezem-^{d}Šul-gi*; 1 *udu-niga* ^{d}**Nin-sún**, 1 udu-niga ^{d}**Geštin-an-na**, iti-ezem-^{d} Nin-a-zu; gìr ***Tab? -Har? -šum***, 4 *udu-niga* ***é-lu-núm-^{d} Be-la-at-Suh$_6$-nir^{ir}***, *iti-u$_5$-bí^{mušen}-gu$_7$ gìr* ***Á-pi$_5$-la-núm***ù ***I-ku-šum***; 2 *udu-niga* ^{d}***Be-la-at-suh$_6$-nir^{ir}***, 1 *udu-niga* ^{d}***Al-la-tum***, *iti-ezem-^{d}Šul-gi*; 1 *udu-niga* **dub-lá-mah--šè**, 2 udu-niga ^{d}***Be-la-at-suh$_6$-nir^{ir}***, *iti-u$_5$-bí^{mušen}-gu$_7$*; *gìr* ***Á-pi$_5$-la-núm.*** *mu An-ša-an^{ki} ba-hul.* (*RA* 19 192 04, P127734)	1 *fattened ram for***Belat-Suhnir**, 1 fattened ram for **Belat-Darraban**, **month of ezem-Šulgi**; 1 fattened ram for**Nin-sun**, 1 fattened ram for**Geštin-anna**, **month of ezem-Ninazu**; **via Tab-har-šum**, 4 fattened rams for**elunum festival of Belat-Suhnir**, **month of ubi~gu$_7$**; **via Apilanum and Iku-šum**, 2 fattened rams for**Belat-Suhnir**, 1 fattened ram for **Allatum**, **month of ezem-Šulgi**; 1 fattened ram for **the big tower**, 2 fattened rams for **Belat-Suhnir**, **month of ubi-gu$_7$**; **via Apilanum**. Year of Anšan was destroyed.	1肥公绵羊为贝拉特苏赫尼尔和1肥公绵羊为贝拉特达腊班，舒勒吉庆典月；1肥公绵羊为宁苏和1肥公绵羊为吉什廷安那，宁阿朱庆典月；经由塔卜哈尔顺，4肥公绵羊为贝拉特苏赫尼尔的埃鲁努姆，食乌比鸟月；经由阿皮拉农和伊苦顺，2肥公绵羊为贝拉特苏赫尼尔，1肥公绵羊为阿拉吞，舒勒吉庆典月；1肥公绵羊为大门楼，2只肥公绵羊为贝拉特苏和尼尔，食乌比鸟月，经由阿皮拉农。安山被毁灭之年。
Š 34 ix: **zi-ga** 1 fat bull, 1 bull for **Nabirum festival of temple of Belat-Suhnir**, 2 fat bulls for **"pouring beer" sacrifice of Belat-Suhnir in palace**, 1 ram for **offering of food of An of temple of Belat-Suhnir**, 1 ram for **offering of "disappearing place" of temple of Adad**, **Apili**as deputy; 1 fat bull, 5 fat rams for **"pouring beer" sacrifice of X**, 2 rams for offering of [⋯], 2 rams for [⋯] of **Belat-Suhnir**, 2 rams for **Belat-Suhnir**, **Ipiq-Erra** as deputy, 1 fat bull, 2 fat rams for **"pouring beer" sacrifice of Allatum**, **in palace**, withdr.fr.**Beli-ṭab**	1 gud-niga, 1 gud-ú, ***Na-bí-rí-um***, *é-^{d}* ***Be-la-at-Suh-nir***, 2 *gud-niga*, *kaš-dé-a-*^{d}***Be-la-at-Suh-nir*** *šà~ é-gal*, 1 *udu sá-dug$_4$* **nìĝ-gu$_7$-An-na**, *é-^{d}* ***Be-la-at-Suh-nir***, 1 *udu sá-dug$_4$ níĝ-ki-zàh~ é-*^{d}**Iškur**, ***Á-pi$_5$-lí****maškim*; 1 *gud-niga*, 2 *udu-niga a-rá-1-kam*, 2 *udu-niga a-rá-2-kam*, 1 *udu-niga a-rá-3-* [*kam*], **kaš-dé-a^d** [**...**], 2 udu sá-dug$_4$ [...], 2 udu gud-e-ús-sa [...], ^{d}***Be-la-at-Suh-*** [***nir***], 2 *udu gud-e-ús-sa* ^{d} ***Be-la-at-Suh-nir***, ***I-pi$_5$-iq-ìr-ra****maškim*, 1 *gud-niga*, 2 *udu-niga*, **kaš-dé-a** ^{d}***Al-la-tum***, **šà é-gal--šè**, zi-ga-***Be-lí- ṭàb***. *iti-ezem-mah*, *muAn-ša-an^{ki}ba-hul.* (*TRU* 272, P135036)	1 *fattened bull*, 1 *grass bull for***the Nabirum festival of temple of Belat-Suhnir**, 2 fattened bulls for **"pouring beer" sacrifice of Belat-Suhnir in palace**, 1 ram for **offering of food of Anna of temple of Belat-Suhnir**, 1 ram for **offering of "disappearing place" of temple of Adad**, **Apili**as royal deputy; 1 fattened bull, 2 fattened rams on 1st, 2 fattened rams on 2nd, 1 fattened ram on 3rd, **for "pouring beer" sacrifice of X**, 2 rams for offering of [⋯], 2 rams of after-ox-class for [⋯] of **Belat-Suhnir**, 2 rams of after-ox-class for **Belat-Suhnir**, **Ipiq-Erra** as deputy, 1 fattened bull, 2 fattened rams for **"pouring beer" sacrifice of Allatum**, **in palace**, were withdrawn from **Beli-ṭab**. Month of ezem-mah, Year of Anšan was destroyed.	1只育肥公牛和1只食草公牛为贝拉特苏赫尼尔庙的那卜润节，2只育肥公牛为贝拉特苏赫尼尔倒啤酒祭于宫殿，1只公绵羊为贝拉特苏赫尼尔庙的安神的食物的供奉，1只公绵羊为阿达德庙的消失处供奉，阿皮里督办；1只育肥公牛和2只育肥公绵羊第1次，2只育肥公绵羊第2次，1只育肥公绵羊第3次为X倒啤酒祭，2只牛后级公绵羊为贝拉特苏赫尼尔的【……】，2只牛后级公绵羊为贝拉特苏赫尼尔，伊皮克埃腊督办，1只育肥公牛和2只育肥公绵羊为阿拉吞的倒啤酒祭于宫殿， 从贝里杳卜支出了。 大庆典月， 安山被毁灭之年。

续表

时间和摘要	文献内容	英文翻译	中文翻译
Š 34 x: **zi-ga** 1 fat bull and 2 goats for **boat of An**, **in Uruk**, 5 rams and 5 goats for **Watar-tum**, 1 kid for **sacrifice of Inanna**, **in the orchard**, 5 he-goats, the big he-goats for **Etel-Puzur-Dagan**, **withdr. fr. Beli-ṭab**	1 gud-niga, 2 máš-gal, **má-An-na Unug^{ki}**-ga--šè, 5 udu, 5 máš-gal, **Watar-*tum***, 1 *máš* **siskúr-^{d}Inanna**, **šà~ ^{giš}kiri$_6$**, 5 máš-gal, maš-gu-la, **E-te<-el>-Pù-zur-^{d}Da-gan**, zi-ga ***Be-lí-ṭàb***.*iti-ezem-An-na*, *mu An-ša-an^{ki}ba-hul.* (*PDT* 1 459, *P*125875)	1 *fattened bull and* 2 *he-goats for***the boat of An**, **in Uruk**, 5 rams and 5 he-goats for **Watar-tum**, 1 kid for **sacrifice of Inanna**, **in the orchard**, 5he-goats, the big he-goats for **Etel-Puzur-Dagan**, were **withdrawn from Beli-ṭab**. Month of ezem-Anna, Year of Anšan was destroyed.	1头育肥公牛和2只公山羊为**天神安之船**，于**乌鲁克**，5只公绵羊和5只公山羊为**瓦塔尔吞**（舒勒吉之母），1只公崽为**伊南那的牺牲**，于**椰枣园**，5只公山羊为大山羊为**埃台勒普朱尔达干**，从贝里沓卜支出了。天神庆典月，安山被毁灭年。
Š 34 x: **mu-túm**, **ì-dab$_5$** 6 fat bulls, 38 rams, 22 goats from **Amzakum**, were **deliveries for Šulgi-simtum**, **Beli-ṭab took** over	6 gud-niga, 38 udu-ú, 22 máš-gal, ***Am-za-ku-um***, *mu-túm* ***^{d}Šul-gi-sí-im-tum***, ***Be-lí-ṭàb*** *ì-dab$_5$. iti-ezem-An-na*, *mu An-ša-an^{ki}ba-hul.* (*OIP* 115022, *P*123662)	6 *fattened bulls*, 38 *grass rams*, 22 *he-goats from* **Amzakum**, were **deliveries for Šulgi-simtum**, **Beli-ṭab took** over. Month of ezem-Ana, Year of Anšan was destroyed.	6头育肥公牛、38只食草公绵羊、22只公山羊来自**阿姆扎坤**，**为舒勒吉新吞的送入项**，**贝里沓卜接管了**。天神庆典月，安山被毁灭年。
Š 35i: **zi-ga** 2 kids for **giranum festival of temple of Belat-Suhnir**, **via Ur-Dumuzida**, **withdr. fr. mojorado**, **in Ur**	2 máš ***gi-ra-núm é-^{d}Be-la-at-Suh-nir***, *gìr* **Ur-^{d}Dumu-zi-da**, **zi-ga šabra**, šà~ **Urim$_5$^{ki}**-ma. iti-maš-dà~gu$_7$, mu ús-sa An-ša-an^{ki} ba-hul. (M.Sigrist, TPTS 95)	2 kids for **giranum festival of the temple of Belat-Suhnir**, **via Ur-Dumuzida**, were **withdrawn from the mojorado**, **in Ur**. Month of mašda~gu$_7$, Year after that of Anšan was destroyed.	2只公崽为**贝拉特苏赫尼尔庙的吉腊努姆仪式**，**经由乌尔杜姆兹达**，**从庙总管支出了**，**于乌尔**。食瞪羚月，安山国被毁之年次年。
Š 35 ii: **zi-ga** 3 **corpses** of bulls, 58 **corpses** of rams, 7 **corpses** of kids, were **withdr.from Beli-ṭab**	3 ad$_6$-gud, 58 ad$_6$-udu-ú, 7 ad$_6$-máš, zi-ga ki~ ***Be-lí-ṭàb***--*ta.iti-ze$_x$-da~gu$_7$*, *mu ús-sa An-ša-an^{ki} ba-hul.* (*OIP* 115028, *P*123525)	3 *corpses of bulls*, 58 *corpses of grass rams*, 7 *corpses of kids*, *were***withdrawn from Beli-ṭab**. Month of zeda~gu$_7$, Year after that of Anšan was destroyed.	3只公牛死尸、58只食草公绵羊死尸、7只公崽死尸，**从贝里沓卜处支出了**。食豚月，安山国被毁之年次年。
Š 35 iv: **mu-túm**, **ì-dab$_5$** 1 kid was**brought-in by Ilum-bani**, **majordomo**, **Beli-ṭab** took over	1 máš, ***Ilum-ba-ni*** *šabra mu-túm*, ***Be-lí-ṭàb*** *ì-dab$_5$.* *iti-ki-siki-^{d}Nin-a-zu*, *mu ús-sa An-ša-an^{ki} ba-hul.* (*OIP* 115023, *P*123656)	1 *kid was***brought-in by Ilum-bani**, **majordomo**, **Beli-ṭab** took over. Month of ki-siki-Ninazu, Year after that of Anšan was destroyed.	1只公山羊崽由**神庙总管伊隆巴尼带来**，**贝里沓卜接管了**。神宁阿朱羊毛作坊月，安山国被毁之年次年。

续表

时间和摘要	文献内容	英文翻译	中文翻译
Š 35 iv: **zi-ga** 2 fat rams for **disappearings place of temple of Be-lat-Suhnir and Belat-Darraban**, 2 fattened rams for **Uruk**, **via Mašum**, were withdrawn from **Ahima**	2 udu-niga**níĝ-ki-zàh é-^{d}** ***Be-la-at-Suh-nir*** *ù* ^{d}***Be-la-at-Dar-ra-ba-an***, 2 *udu-niga* **Unug^{ki}**-šè, gìr ***Ma-šum***, *zi-ga* ***A-hi-ma.*** *iti-ki-siki-^{d}Nin-a-zu, mu ús-sa An-ša-an^{ki} ba-hul.* (*Nisaba* 08 377, *P321028*)	2 *fattened rams for* **"everything disappearings" = (night?) of temple of Belat-Suhnir and Belat-Darraban**, 2 fattened rams for **Uruk**, **via Mašum**, were withdrawn from **Ahima**. Month of ki-siki-Ninazu, Year after that of Anšan was destroyed.	2只育肥公绵羊为**贝拉特苏赫尼尔和贝拉特达腊班庙的消失处祭**，2只育肥公绵羊为**乌鲁克**，经**由马顺**，从**阿希马**处支出了。神宁阿朱羊毛作坊月，安山国被毁之年次年。
Š 35 v: **zi-ga** 1 kid for**Ninhursag**, 2 kids for **sacrifice of Belat-Suhnir and Belat-Darraban**, **in the orchard**, 1 lamb for the palace of Kinia, **withdr. fr. Ahima**, from **Beli-ṭab**	1 máš, ^{d}**Nin-hur-sag**, 2 máš, siskúr ^{d}***Be-la-at-Suh-nir*** *ù* ^{d}**Be-la-at-Dar-ra-ba-an**, *šà* ~ *kiri$_{6}$*, 1 *sila$_{4}$*, **é-Ki-ni-a**-šè, zi-ga ***A-hi-ma***, *ki* ~ ***Be-lí-ṭàb***-ta. *iti-ezem-^{d}Nin-a-zu, mu ús-sa An-ša-an^{ki}ba-hul.* (*PDT* 20980, *P126327*)	1 *kid for***Ninhursag**, 2 kids for the **sacrifice of Belat-Suhnir and Belat-Darraban**, **in the orchard**, 1 lamb for the palace of ki-ni-a, were **withdrawn from Ahima**, from the place of **Beli-ṭab**. Month of ezem-Ninazu, Year after that of Anšan was destroyed.	1只公崽为**宁胡尔萨格**，2只公崽为**贝拉特苏赫尼尔和贝拉特达尔腊班的祭祀**，**于椰枣园中**，1只羊羔为**基尼阿的宫殿**，**从阿希马处**，**贝里沓卜**支出了。神宁阿朱庆典月，安山国被毁之年次年。
Š 35 v: **zi-ga** 1+［rams?］for**Belat-Suhnir and Belat-Darraban**, withdr.fr.Ahima, in **Ur**, **via Ur-Dumuzida**.è-x	[...] -x [...^{d}***Be-la-at***] ***-Suh-nir*** [*ù* ^{d}] ***Be-la-at-Dar-< ra>-ba-< an >***-šè, *zi-ga* ***A-hi-ma***, *šà* ~ **Urim$_{5}$^{ki}**-ma, gìr**Ur-^{d}Dumu-zi-da**, è-x. iti-ezem -^{d}Nin-a-zu mu ús-sa An-ša-an^{ki}ba-hul. (PDT 2 1027, P126369)	1+［rams?］for**Belat-Suhnir and Belat-Darraban**, were withdrawn from Ahima, in **Ur**, **via Ur-Dumu-zida**.è-x? Month of ezem-Ninazu, Year after that of Anšan was destroyed.	1+只【公绵羊?】为**贝拉特苏赫尼尔和贝拉特达腊班**，**从阿希马处**支出了**于乌尔**，**经由乌尔杜穆孜达**。神宁阿朱庆典月，安山国被毁之年次年。
Š 35 vi: **zi-ga** 2 kids for the**sacrifice of disappearing place of Be-lat-Suhnir and Belat-Darraban**, **withdrawn from Beli-ṭab**, **in Ur**	2 máš **níĝ-ki-zàh é-^{d}*Be-la-at-Suh-nir*** *ù* ^{d}***Be-la-at-Dar-ra-ba-an***, *zi-ga* **Be-lí-ṭàb**, šà~ **Urim$_{5}$^{ki}**-ma. iti-á-ki ~ ti, mu ús-sa An-ša-an^{ki} ba-hul. (ASJ 19 200 01, P102692)	2 kids for the**sacrifice of disappearing place of Be-lat-Suhnir and Belat-Darraban**, **were withdrawn from Beli-ṭab**, **in Ur**. Month of akiti, Year after that of Anšan was destroyed.	2只公崽为**贝拉特苏赫尼尔和贝拉特达腊班的消失处牺牲**， **从贝里沓卜支出了**， **于乌尔**。 阿基提月， 安山国被毁之年次年。
Š 35 vi: **zi-ga** 2 fat rams for **Belat-Suhnir and Belat-Darraban**, were **withdrawn from Ahima**, **via Apilatum**	2 udu-niga, ^{d} ***Be-la-at-Suh-ni-ir*** *ù* ^{d}***Be-la-at-Dar-ra-ba-an***, *ud~ má-è-a*, *zi-ga* ***A-hi-ma***, *gìr* ***Á-pi$_{5}$-la-tum***. *iti-á-ki~ti, mu ús-sa An-ša-an^{ki}ba-hul.* (*OIP* 115 130, *P123238*)	2 *fattened rams for***Belat-Suhnir and Belat-Darraban**, when the ship departed, were **withdrawn from Ahima**, **via Apilatum**. Month of akiti, Year after that of Anšan was destroyed.	2只育肥公绵羊为**贝拉特苏赫尼尔和贝拉特达腊班**，于船离开时，**从阿希马处支出了**，**经由阿皮拉吞**。阿基提月，安山国被毁之年次年。

续表

时间和摘要	文献内容	英文翻译	中文翻译
Š 35 vi: **zi-ga** 1 grass bull for**dais of food**, 1 fattened bull for **Annunitum**, **in the center of palace**, were withdrawn from Šulgi-simti	1 gud-ú, **barú-nîĝ-gu$_7$-a**, 1 gud-niga, ***An-nu-ni-tum***, *šà~é-gal*, *zi-ga* ***^{d}Šul-gi-sí-im-ti.*** iti-á-ki~ti, mu ús-sa An-ša-an^{ki}ba-hul. (TCS 337, P132122)	1 grass bull for**dais of food**, 1 fattened bull for **Annunitum**, **in the center of palace**, were withdrawn from Šulgi-simti. Month of akiti, Year after that of Anšan was destroyed.	1头食草公牛为**祭品台**，1头育肥公牛为**安努尼吞**，**于宫殿中**，从**舒勒吉新提处支出了**。 阿基提月， 安山国被毁之年次年。
Š 35 vi: **mu-túm, ì-dab$_5$** 1 fat bull, 3 fat rams, 4 rams, 3 kids from **Ur-Šulpae envoy**, these were deliveries, **in Ur**, **Beli-ṭab took over**	1 gud-niga, 3 udu-niga, 4 udu-ú, 3 máš, **Ur-^{d}Šul-pa-è** sukkal-mah$^{!}$, mu-túm, šà~ **Urim^{ki}**-ma, ***Be-lí-ṭàb***, *ì-dab$_5$.iti-á-ki~ti*, *mu ús-sa An-ša-an^{ki}ba-hul.* (*Torino* 1 049, P132000)	1 *fattened bull*, 3 *fattened rams*, 4 *grass rams*, 3 *kids from* **Ur-Šulpae**, the envoy, **these were deliveries**, **in Ur**, **Beli-ṭab took over.** Month of akiti, Year after that of Anšan was destroyed.	1头育肥公牛、3只育肥公绵羊、4只食草公绵羊、3只公羔自**乌尔舒勒帕埃国使**，（以上）送人，于乌尔，**贝里沓卜接管了**。阿基提月，安山国被毁之年次年。
Š 35 vi: **zi-ga** 1 kid for **giranum of Inanna**, **Ur-Dumuzida asdeputy**, 1 kid for **giranum of Nanaya**, **Ur-Dumuzida asdeputy**, 2 kids for **giranum of Belat-S.and Belat-D.**, **Ur-Dumuzida as deputy**, 2 lambs for **Belat-S.and Belat-D.**, **via my queen**, **withdr.**	1^{f}ašgar ***gi-ra-núm*** **^{d}Inanna**, **Ur-^{d}Dumu-zi-da maškim**, 1 ^{f}ašgar ***gi-ra-núm*** ***^{d}Na-na-a***, **Ur-^{d}Dumu-zi-da maškim**, 2 ^{f}ašgar ***gi-ra-núm*** ***^{d}Be-la-at -Suh-nir*** *ù* ***^{d}Be-la-at-Dar-ra-ba-an***, **Ur-^{d}Dumu-zi-da maškim**, 2 sila$_4$ ***^{d} Be-la-at-Suh-nir*** *ù* ***^{d}Be-la-at-Dar-ra-ba-an***, **gìrnin-ĝá**, zi-ga. iti-á-ki ~ ti, mu ús-sa An-ša-an^{ki} ba-hul. (AnOr 07 055, P101350)	1 female kid for **giranum festival of Inanna**, **Ur-Dumuzida as royal deputy**, 1 female kid for **giranum festival of Nanaya**, **Ur-Dumuzida as royal deputy**, 2 female kids for **giranum festival of Belat-Suhnir and Belat-Darraban**, **Ur-Dumuzida as royal deputy**, 2 lambs for **Belat-Suhnir and Belat-Darraban**, **via my queen**, were withdrawn. Month of akiti, Year after that of Anšan was destroyed.	1雌崽为**伊南那的吉腊努姆仪式**，**乌尔杜穆兹达督办**，1雌崽为**那那亚的吉腊努姆仪式**，**乌尔杜穆兹达督办**，2只雌崽为**贝拉特苏赫尼尔和贝拉特达腊班的吉腊努姆仪式**，**乌尔杜穆兹达督办**，2只羔为**贝拉特苏赫尼尔和贝拉特达腊班**，**经由我的王后**，以上支出了。阿基提月，安山国被毁之年次年。
Š 35 vi: **zi-ga** 1 kid for **giranum of Nanaya**, 1 kid for **center of temple**, **Mašum as royal deputy**, were withdrawn from **Beli-ṭab**	1^{f}ašgar, ***gi-ra-núm*** ***^{d}Na-na-a***, 1 *^{f}ašgar*, *šà~ é-gal--šè*, ***Ma-šum*****maškim**, zi-ga ***Be-lí-ṭàb.*** *iti-á-ki~ti*, *muús-sa An-ša-an^{ki}ba-hul.* (*PDT* 2 998, P126343)	1 *female kid for* **giranum festival of Nanaya**, 1 female kid for **center of temple**, **Mašum as royal deputy**, were withdrawn from **Beli-ṭab**. Month of akiti, Year after that of Anšan was destroyed.	1只雌山羊崽为**那那亚的吉腊努姆仪式**，1只雌山羊崽为**内殿**，**马顺为督办**，**从贝里沓卜处支出了**。阿基提月，安山国被毁之年次年。
Š 35 vi: **mu-túm, ì-dab** 10 fat rams fr. **allowance in duty period of governor of Umma**, these were deliveries, **Beli-ṭab took**	10 udu-niga**sá-dug$_4$** bala **ensí** Umma^{ki}, mu-túm, ***Be-lí-ṭàb*** *ì-dab$_5$.iti-á-ki~ti*, *mu ús-sa An-ša-an^{ki} ba-hul.* (*MVN* 13 873, P117645)	10 *fattened rams from***monthly allowance in duty period of governor of Umma**, these were deliveries, **Beli-ṭab took** over. Month of akiti, Year after that of Anšan was destroyed.	10只育肥公绵羊来自**温马的总督任职期间的月供**，以上送入，**贝里沓卜接管了**。阿基提月，安山国被毁之年次年。

续表

时间和摘要	文献内容	英文翻译	中文翻译
Š 35 viii，vi，vii： **zi-ga** 2 fat rams for **Uruk**，month of šu-ešša；3 fat rams for **throne of Šat-iltin**，month of akiti；1 fat ram for **Belat-Suhnir**，1 for **Belat-Darraban**，1 fat ram for **Išhara**，1 fat ram for **Belat-Naqar**，month of ezem-Šulgi，via **Ur-Dumuzida**，**withdr.fr.Ahima**	2 udu-niga，**Unug^{ki}**--šè，iti-šu-eš$_5$-ša； 3 udu-niga，**ki-^{geš}gu-za**，***Ša-at-il-ti-in***--*šè*，*iti-á-ki~ti*；1 *udu-niga*，^{d}***Be-la-at-Suh$_6$-nir***，1 *udu-niga*，^{d}***Be-la-at-Dar-ra-ba-an***，1 *udu-niga*，^{d}***Iš-ha-ra***，1 *udu-niga*，^{d}***Be-la-at-Na-qar***，*iti-ezem-*^{d}*Šul-gi*，*gìr* **Ur-^{d}Dumu-zi-da**，zi-ga ki~ ***A-hi-ma***. *mu ús-sa An-ša-*［*an^{ki}*］*ba-hul.* （*AnOr* 7 114，*P*101409）	2 *fattened rams for* **Uruk**，month of šu-ešša； 3 fattened rams for **the throne of Šat-iltīn**，month of akiti； 1 fattened ram for **Belat-Suhnir**，1 fattened ram for **Belat-Darraban**，1 fattened ram for **Išhara**，1 fattened ram for **Belat-Naqar**，month of ezem-Šulgi，via **Ur-Dumuzida**，were **withdrawn from Ahima**. Year after that of Anšan was destroyed.	2 育肥公绵羊到**乌鲁克**，三只手月；3 育肥公绵羊为**"两女神的女仆"的王座**，阿基提月；1 育肥公绵羊为**贝拉特苏赫尼尔**，1 育肥公绵羊为**贝拉特达腊班**，1 育肥公绵羊为**伊什哈腊**，1 育肥公绵羊为**贝拉特那喀尔**，舒勒吉庆典月，**经由乌尔杜穆孜达**，**从阿希马处支出**。安山国被毁之年次年。
Š 35 vii： **mu-túm** 2 rams of after-ox-class，2 rams and 1 kid **fr. governor of Nippur**，4 he-goats and 1 kid **fr. sister of Adalal**，1 ram and 1 lamb fr. **Zalaya**，were deliveries for Šulgi-simtum，**in Tummal**	2 udu-gud-e-úš-sa，2 udu-ú，1 máš，**énsi-Nibur^{ki}**，4 máš-gal，1 ^{f}ašgar，**nin$_9$-*A-da-làl*** *ugula-uš-bar*，1 *udu*，1 *sila$_4$*，***Za-la-a***， *mu-túm~* ^{d}***Šul-gi-sí-im-tum***， *šà~* **Tum-ma-al**.iti-ezem-^{d}Šul-gi， mu ús-sa An-ša-an^{ki} ba-hul. （Royal Ontario Museum 1，10）	2 rams of after-ox-class，2 grass rams and 1 kid **from the governor of Nippur**，4 he-goats and 1 female kid **from the sister of Adalal**，the overseer of weaver，1 ram and 1 lamb from **Zalaya**，were deliveries for Šulgi-simtum，**in Tummal**.Month of ezem of Šulgi，Year after that of Anšan was destroyed.	2 牛后级公绵羊、2 只食草公绵羊和 1 只公崽**自尼普尔的总督**，4 只公山羊和 1 只雌崽**自洗染工的监工阿达拉勒的妹妹**，1 只公绵羊和 1 只羔**自扎拉亚**，**为舒勒吉新吞的送入项**，**于图马勒**。舒勒吉庆典月，安山国被毁之年次年。
Š 35 viii： **mu-túm，ì-dab** 5 fat bulls and 2 rams fr. **Puzur-Utu general**，2 kids from **Ilum-bani** majordomo，deliveries for Šulgi-simtum，**Beli-ṭab fattener took over**	5 gud-niga，2 udu-ú，**Puzur$_4$-^{d}Utu** šakkan$_6$，2 máš ***Ilum-ba-ni*** *šabra*，*mu-túm~* ^{d}***Šul-gi-sí-im-tum***，***Be-lí-ṭàb*** *gurušda ì-dab$_5$. iti-šu-eš-ša*，*mu ús-sa An-ša-an^{ki} ba-hul.* （*MVN* 03 143，*P*113703）	5 *fattened bulls and* 2 *grass rams from* **Puzur-Utu**，the **general**，2 kids from **Ilum-bani**，the **majordomo**，were deliveries for Šulgi-simtum，**Beli-ṭab fattener took over**. Month of šu-ešša，Year after that of Anšan was destroyed.	5 头育肥公牛和 2 只食草公绵羊**来自普朱尔乌图将军**，2 只公崽**来自伊隆巴尼庙总管**，**为舒勒吉新吞的送入项**，**贝里沓卜育肥师接管了**。三只手月，安山国被毁之年次年。
Š 35 viii **šu~ ba-ti** 1 catfish，2 fishes with shell，4 zina fishes，**were from Barbaria**，**these were for the majordomo**，**Halili took**	1 gú~ su$_6$，2 peš-murgú，4 zí-na，ki *Bar-bar-ì-a*--ta，mu~ šabra--šè，*Ha-lí-lí* šu~ ba-ti. （OIP 115 460） （seal：）^{d}***Šul-gi-sí-im-***［*ti*］**lukur ki-áĝlugal**，*Ha-lí-lí*dub-sar dumu［*Šu*?］-*ì-lí*arad-zu. （OIP 115 460）	1 catfish，2 fishes with shell，4 zina fishes，**were from Barbaria**，**these were for the majordomo**，**Halili took** over. seal：Šulgi-simti，the beloved priestess of the king，the scribe Halili：the son of Šulgi-ili was your servant.	1 条鲶鱼、2 条带壳鱼和 4 条 zina 鱼，**来自巴尔巴尔亚**，**为庙总管**，**哈里里接收了**。 （印章）：**舒勒吉新提**，**国王喜爱的 lukur 神妻**，舒伊里之子哈里里书吏，是你的仆人。
Š 35 ix： **mu-túm，ì-dab** 2 lambs from **Te ṣ in-Mama**，deliveries for Šulgi-simtum，**Beli-ṭab took** voer	2 sila$_4$ ***Te-ṣ í-in-Ma-ma***，*mu-túm~* ^{d}***Šul-gi-sí-im-tum***，***Be-lí-ṭàb*** *ì-dab$_5$. iti-ezem-mah*，*mu ús-sa An-ša-an^{ki} ba-hul.* （*RT* 37 129 *ab*.1，*P*128392）	2 *lambs from* **Te ṣ in-Mama**，were deliveries for Šulgi-simtum，**Beli-ṭab took** voer. Month of ezem-mah，Year after that of Anšan was destroyed.	2 只羔来**自台岑妈妈**，为舒勒吉新吞的送入项，**贝里沓卜接管了**。大庆典月，安山国被毁之年次年。

续表

时间和摘要	文献内容	英文翻译	中文翻译
Š 35 ix: **zi-ga** 1 goat for**Meslam-taea**, **in the harbor of Gudua**; 1 ram for **sacrifice of the beginning of New Moon**, 1 ram for sacrifice of Full Moon, **in Uruk**, [...] Ur-^{d} [...], 1 lamb for **food of my queen**, **in Ka-sahar**, 2 kids for **the palace**, 1 ram for **sacrifice of New Moon**, **in Uruk**, **via Ipiq-Erra**, were withdrawn from **Beli-ṭab**	1 máš-gal ^{d}**Mes-lam-ta-è-a**, šà~ **kar Gú-du$_8$-a^{ki}**; 1 udu-ú**siskúr sag~ ud-sakar**, 1 udu **siskúr~ ud-15** šà ~ **Unug^{ki}**-ga; [...] Ur-^{d} [...], 1 sila$_4$ **níĝ-gu$_7$-nin-ĝá**--šè, šà~ **Ka-sahar-ra^{ki}**; 2^{f}ašgar šà~ **é-gal-la**--šè su-su-dam, 1 udu **siskúr~ ud-sakar** šà ~ **Unug^{ki}**-ga, gìr ***I-pi$_5$-iq-Èr-ra***, *zi-ga* ***Be-lí-ṭàb***. *iti-ezem-mah*, *mu ús-sa An-ša-an^{ki} ba-hul*. (*SET* 041, P129451)	1 *he-goat for***Meslam-taea**, **in the harbor of Gud-ua**; 1 grass ram for**sacrifice of the beginning of New Moon**, 1 ram for sacrifice of Full Moon, **in Uruk**, [...] Ur-^{d} [...], 1 lamb for **the food of my queen**, **in Ka-sahar**, 2 female kids for **the palace**, these are to be repaid, 1 ram for **sacrifice of New Moon**, **in Uruk**, **via Ipiq-Erra**, were withdrawn from **Beli-ṭab**.Month of ezem-mah, Year after that of Anšan was destroyed.	1只公山羊为**美斯兰塔埃阿**，于**古达阿港口**；1只食草公绵羊为**新月初牺牲**，1只公绵羊为**满月牺牲**，**于乌鲁克**；[...] Ur-^{d} [...]，1只羔为**我的王后的食物**，于**卡萨哈尔**；2雌崽为**内殿**，这些是补交的，1公绵羊为**新月牺牲**，**于乌鲁克**， **经由伊皮克埃腊**， **从贝里查卜支出**了。 大庆典月， 安山国被毁之年次年。
Š 35 x: **ì-dab** 5 fat ramsfrom **monthly allowance in the duty period of governor of Girsu**, **Ahima took**, **in Ur**	5 udu-niga, **sá-dug$_4$**, **bala**, **ensí Gír-su^{ki}**--ka, ***A-hi-ma*** *ì-dab$_5$*, *šà*~ **Urim^{ki}**-ma. iti-ezem-An-na, mu ús-sa An-ša-an-^{ki}ba-hul. (Ontario 1 059, P124472)	5 fattened ramsfrom **monthly allowance in the duty period of governor of Girsu**, **Ahima took** over, **in Ur**.Month of ezem-Ana, Year after that of Anšan was destroyed.	5只育肥公绵羊来自**吉尔苏总督任职期间的供奉**，**阿希马接管**了，**于乌尔**。天神庆典月，安山国被毁之年次年。
Š 35 x: **zi-ga** 1 lamb for **shrine**, 1 kid for **gate of cloister**, 1 kid for **Nanaya**, **in Uruk**, **via my queen**, 2 rams for **giranum of temple of Belat-Suhnir and Belat-Darraban**, **Mašum as deputy**, withdr.**in Ur**	1 sila$_4$ **èš**--šè, 1 máš **ka (ká) ~ gi$_6$-par$_4$-ra**, 1 máš ^{d}***Na-na-a***, *šà* ~ **Unug^{ki}**-ga, gìr-**nin-ĝá**, 2 udu ***gi-ra-núm*** *é*-^{d} ***Be-la-at-Suh-nir*** *ù* ^{d}***Be-la-at-Dar-ra-ba-an***, ***Ma-šum*** *maškim*, *zi-ga šà* ~ **Urim$_5$^{ki}**-ma. iti-ezem-An-na, mu ús-sa An-ša-an^{ki} ba-hul. (AnOr 07 056, P101351)	1 lamb for**the shrine**, 1 kid for the **gate of cloister**, 1 kid for **Nanaya**, **in Uruk**, **via my queen**, 2 rams for **giranum of temple of Belat-Suhnir and Belat-Darraban**, **Mašum as royal deputy**, were withdrawn **in Ur**. Month of ezem-Anna, Year after that of Anšan was destroyed.	1只羔为**圣殿**，1只公崽为**祭司寝宫门**，1只公崽为**那那亚**，**于乌鲁克**，**经由我的王后**，2只公绵羊为**贝拉特苏赫尼尔和贝拉特达腊班庙的吉腊努姆仪式**，**马顺督办**，以上支出**于乌尔**。天神庆典月，安山国被毁之年次年。
Š 35 xi: **mu-túm**, **ì-dab** 1 bull, 10 rams fr. **Nir-Idagal**, **deliveries for Šulgi-simtum**, **Beli-ṭab**, **the laborer took over**	1 gud, 10 udu-ú, **Nir-ì-da-ĝál**, *mu-túm*-^{d}***Šul-gi-sí-im-tum***, ***Be-lí-ṭàb*** *gurušda*, *ì-dab$_5$*.*iti-ezem-Me-ki-gál*, *mu ús-sa An-ša-an^{ki}ba-hul*. (*Aegyptus* 29 106 34, P100267)	1 *bull*, 10 *grass rams from***Nir-Idagal**, **deliveries for Šulgi-simtum**, **Beli-ṭab**, **the laborer took over**. Month of ezem-Mekiĝal, Year after that of Anšan was destroyed.	1头公牛和10只食草公绵羊自**尼尔伊达旮勒**，为舒勒吉新吞的送入项，**育肥师贝里沓卜接管了**。神美基旮勒庆典月，安山国被毁之年次年。

续表

时间和摘要	文献内容	英文翻译	中文翻译
Š 35 xi: **zi-ga** 1 bull for **Itib-šinat**, 2 rams for **Ištar-ummi**, withdrawn from **Beli-ṭab**, **fattener**	1 gud, ***I-ṭì-ib-ši-na-at***, 2 *udu*, ***Iš-tár-um-mi***, *zi-ga* ***Be-lí-ṭàb***, *gurušda. iti-ezem-Me-ki-ĝál*, *mu ús-sa An-ša-an^ki^ ba-hul.* (*Torino* 1 177, *P*133896)	1 *bull for* **Itib-šinat**, 2 rams for **Ištar-ummi**, were withdrawn from **Beli-ṭab**, **fattener**. Month of ezem-Mekiĝal, Year after that of Anšan was destroyed.	1头公牛为**伊提卜西那特**，2公绵羊为**埃什塔闰米**，从**育肥师贝里沓卜支出了**。神美基旮勒庆典月，安山国被毁之年次年。
Š 35 xi: **zi-ga** 1 bull and 5 rams for **provision of wife of ambassador**, 2 fat kids for **boat of heavens**, were withdrawn from Beli-ṭab	1 gud, 5 udu-ú, **igi-kár dam-sukkal-mah**, 2 ^f^ašgar-niga, **Má-an-na**--šè, zi-ga***Be-lí-ṭàb***. *iti-ezem-Me-ki-ĝál*, *mu ús-sa An-ša-an^ki^ ba-hul.* (*CST*043, *P*107555)	1 *bull and* 5 *grass rams for the* **provision of the wife of ambassador**, 2 fattened female kids for **boat of heavens**, were withdrawn from Beli-ṭab. Month of ezem-Mekiĝal, Year after that of Anšan was destroyed.	1头公牛和5只食草公绵羊为**国务卿之妻的供奉**，2只育肥雌山羊崽为**"天船"，从贝里沓卜支出**。神美基旮勒庆典月，安山国被毁之年次年。
Š 35 xi: **zi-ga** 1 fat bull for shrine, 1 zag-ga!-lá ram for **the bedroom**, in **Uruk**, <u>**via my queen**</u>, **withdr. from Beli-ṭab**	1 gud-niga **èš**--šè, 1 udu-ú ~ zag-ga!-lá **é-ki-nú**--šè, e-gi-LAGAB$_x$, šà ~ **Unug^ki^**-ga, gìr**nin-ĝá**, zi-ga ***Be-lí-ṭàb***. *iti-ezem-Me-ki-ĝál*, *mu ús-sa An-ša-an^ki^ ba-hul.* (*MVN* 03 145, *P*113705)	1 *fattened bull for the shrine*, 1 *zag-ga!-lá grass ram for* **the bedroom**, in **Uruk**, <u>**via my queen**</u>, **were withdrawn from Beli-ṭab**. Month of ezem-Mekiĝal, Year after that of Anšan was destroyed.	1头育肥公牛为**圣殿**，1只 zag-ga!-lá 食草公绵羊**为卧室**，于**乌鲁克**，<u>**经由我的王后**</u>，从贝里沓卜支出了。神美基旮勒庆典月，安山国被毁之年次年。
Š 35 xii: **mu-túm**, **ì-dab** 1 lamb fr. **Te ṣin-Mama**, 2 rams and 1 kid fr. **Ilum-bani**, deliveries for Šulgi-simtum, **Beli-ṭab took over**	1 sila$_4$ ***Te-ṣ í-in-Ma-ma***, 2 *udu*, 1 *máš* ***Ilum-ba-ni*** *šabra*, *mu-túm* ~ ***^d^Šul-gi-sí-im-tum***, ***Be-lí-ṭàb*** *ì-dab*$_5$. *iti-še-kin-kud*, *mu ús-sa An-ša-an^ki^ ba-hul.* (*Princeton* 1 055, *P*126744)	1 *lamb from* **Te ṣin-Mama**, 2 rams and 1 kid from **Ilum-bani**, the majordomo, were deliveries for Šulgi-simtum, **Beli-ṭab took over**. Month of še-kin-kud, Year after that of Anšan was destroyed.	1羔来自**台岑妈妈**，2公绵羊和1公崽自**庙总管伊隆巴尼**，为舒勒吉新吞的送入项，**贝里沓卜接管**了。大麦收割月，安山国被毁之年次年。

续表

时间和摘要	文献内容	英文翻译	中文翻译
Š 36 i: **zi-ga** 1 fat ram for **allowance of giranum of Inanna**, **by the wall**, 1 fat ram for **temple of Allatum**, 2 fat rams for **temple of Išhara and Belat-Nagar**, 2 fat rams for **sacrifice of New Moon**, in **Uruk**, 1 for **temple of Šat-iltin**, **withdrawn fr. Beli-ṭab**, the fattener, in **Ur**	1 udu-niga**sá-dug$_4$** ***gi-ra-núm-*** **^{d}Inanna**-da-bàd--da, 1 udu-niga é-^{d}***Al-la-tum***, 2 *udu-niga é-*^{d}***Iš-ha-ra*** *ù* ^{d}***Be-la-at-Na-gàr***, 2 *udu-niga* **siskúr-ud-sakar** šà ~ Unug^{ki}-ga, 1 udu-nigaé-***Ša-at-il-ti-in***--*šè*, *zi-ga**Be-lí-ṭàb*** *gurušda*, *šà ~ Urim^{ki}-ma.* *iti-maš-dà ~ gu$_7$*, *mu ús-sa An-ša-an^{ki} ba-hul mu ús-sa-bi.* (*AnOr* 07 057, *P*101352)	1 *fattened ram for***monthly allowance of giranum festival of Inanna**, **by the wall**, 1 fattened ram for **temple of Allatum**, 2 fattened rams for **temple of Išhara and Belat-Nagar**, 2 fattened rams for **sacrifice of New Moon**, in **Uruk**, 1 fattened ram for **temple of Šat-iltīn**, were **withdrawn from Beli-ṭab**, the fattener, in **Ur**. Month of mašda ~ gu$_7$, Year after that of Anšan was destroyed: after that.	1肥公绵羊为**伊南那的吉腊努姆仪式的月供**，于**城墙**；1肥公绵羊为**阿腊吞神庙**，2肥公绵羊为**伊什哈腊和贝拉特那旮尔的神庙**，2育肥公绵羊为**新月牺牲**，于**乌鲁克**，1只育肥公绵羊为**"两女神的女仆"的神庙**，从育肥师**贝里沓卜处支出**了，于**乌尔**。食瞪羚月，安山国被毁之年次年。
Š 36 i: **mu-túm**, **ì-dab** 2 lambs fr. **the daughter of Aba-Enlil-gin**, 1 lamb from **Etelpu-Daga**n, were deliveries for Šulgi-simtum, **Beli-ṭab took**	2 sila$_4$ **dumu-munus-A-ba-^{d}En-líl-gin$_7$**, 1 sila$_4$ ***E-te-<él>-pù-^{d}Da-gan***, *mu-túm ~* ^{d}***Šul-gi-sí-im-tum***, ***Be-lí-ṭàb*** *ì-dab$_5$*.*iti-maš-dà ~ gu$_7$*, *mu ús-sa An-ša-an^{ki} ba-hul mu ús-sa-bi.* (*BIN* 3 347, *P*106153)	2 *lambs from***the daughter of Aba-Enlil-gin**, 1 lamb from **Etelpu-Daga**n, were deliveries for Šulgi-simtum, **Beli-ṭab too**k over. Month of mašda ~ gu$_7$, Year after that of Anšan was destroyed: after that.	2只羔来自**阿巴恩里勒艮之女**，1只羔来自**埃台勒普达干**，为舒勒吉新吞的送入项，**贝里沓卜接管**了。食瞪羚月，安山国被毁之年次年。
Š 36 i: **mu-túm**, **ì-dab** 1 lamb from **the wife of the ambassador**, was delivery for Šulgi-simtum, **Beli-ṭab took**	1 sila$_4$ **dam-sukkal-mah**, mu-túm ~ ^{d}***Šul-gi-sí-im-tum***, [***Be-lí***] **-*ṭàb*** *ì-dab$_5$*. [*iti*] *-maš-dà ~ gu$_7$*, *mu ús-sa An-ša-an^{ki} ba-hul mu ús-sa-bi.* (*Hirose* 013, *P*109484)	1 *lamb from* **wife of ambassador**, was delivery for Šulgi-simtum, **Beli-ṭab took over**. Month of mašda ~ gu$_7$, Year after that of Anšan was destroyed: after that.	1只羔来自**国务卿之妻**，为舒勒吉新吞的送入项，**贝里沓卜接管**了。食瞪羚月，安山国被毁之年次年。

续表

时间和摘要	文献内容	英文翻译	中文翻译
Š 36 ii: **zi-ga** 1 fattened bull for**monthly allowance of the mouth of priestess residense**, 1 fattened bull for **monthly allowance of the mouth of shrine**, were withdrawn from **Šakultum of Inanna**, **in Uruk**, from **Beli-ṭab**	1 gud-niga, **<sú-dug$_4$>-ka~ĝi$_6$-pàr-ra**, 1 gud-niga, **<sú-dug$_4$>-ka~èš**, zi-ga***Ša-ku$_8$-ul-tum***-^{d}*Inanna*, šà~ **Unug^{ki}**-ga, ki~***Be-lí-ṭàb***--*ta*. *iti-ze$_x$-da~gu$_7$*, *mu a-rá-2-kam-aš^{d}Nanna-Kar-zi-da é-a-na ba-an-ku$_4$* (*SACT* 1 132, *P128887*)	1 *fattened bull for***monthly allowance of the mouth of priestess residense**, 1 fattened bull for **monthly allowance of the mouth of shrine**, were withdrawn from **Šakultum of Inanna**, **in Uruk**, from **Beli-ṭab**.Month of zeda~gu$_7$, Year of Nanna of Karzida was for the second time brought into his temple.	1头育肥公牛为**最高女祭司寝宫口的月供**, 1头育肥公牛为**圣殿口的月供**,从**伊南那的沙库勒吞那**,**于乌鲁克**, **贝里沓卜处支出了**。 食豚月, 卡尔孜达的神南那第二次被送入他的庙宇之年。
Š 36 ii: **zi-ga** 1 fat bull for **shrine**, was **withdrawn from Šulgi-simti**, the place of **Beli-ṭab**	1 gud-niga **šà~ èš**--šè, zi-ga ***^{d}Šul-gi-sí-im-ti***, *ki~* ***Be-lí-ṭàb***--*ta*. *iti-ze$_x$-da~gu$_7$*, *mu ús-sa An-ša-an^{ki} ba-hul mu ús-sa-bi*. (*Princeton* 1 096, *P126785*)	1 *fattened bullfor* **the center of shrine**, was **withdrawn from Šulgi-simti**, the place of **Beli-ṭab**. Month of zeda~gu$_7$, Year after that of Anšan was destroyed: after that.	1头育肥公牛为**圣殿**,从**舒勒吉新提**, **贝里沓卜处支出了**。 食豚月,安山国被毁之次年:之次年。
Š 36 iii: **zi-ga** 1 kid for **temple of Allagula**, 1 lamb for **temple of Ninegal**, 1 kid for **temple of Enlil**, **for sacrifice of the 7th day of Moon**, **in Nippur**, <u>**via my queen**</u>, were **withdrawn from the majordomo**	1 máš **é-*^{d}Al-la-gu-la***, 1 *sila$_4$* **é-^{d}Nin-é-gal**, 1 máš **é-^{d}En-líl**, **siskúr é-ud-7** šà~ **Nibru^{ki}**, gìr<u>**nin-ĝá**</u>, zi-ga šabra. iti-u$_5$-bí^{mušen}-gu$_7$, mu a-rá 2-kam-aš ^{d}Nanna kar-zi-da. (ASJ 09 316 06, P102370)	1 kid for **temple of Allagula**, 1 lamb for **temple of Ninegal**, 1 kid for **temple of Enlil**, **for sacrifice of the 7th day of Moon**, **in Nippur**, <u>**via my queen**</u>, were **withdrawn from the majordomo**. Month of ubi-gu$_7$, Year of Nanna of Karzida was for the second time brought into his temple.	1只公崽为**阿拉古拉庙**,1只羔为**宁埃旮勒庙**,1只公崽为**恩里勒庙**,**为初七上弦月祭**,**于尼普尔**,<u>**经由我的王后**</u>,**从庙总管支出了**。食乌比鸟月,卡尔孜达的神南那第二次被送入他的庙宇年。
Š 36 iv: **zi-ga** 1 ram for **the sacrifice of New Moon**, **via Ipiq-Erra**; 1 for **sacrifice of Full Moon in Uruk**, **via Apiliya**; 1 sucking goat for **Meslamta-Ea**, 1 kid for sacrifice of **Allatum**, <u>**Mašum as deputy**</u>, were withdrawn from the **majordomo**	1 udu **siskúr-ud-sakar**, gìr ***I-pi$_5$-iq-Èr-ra***, 1 *udu* **siskúr é-ud-15**, šà **Unug^{ki}**-ga, gìr ***Á-pi$_5$-lí-a***, 1 *máš~ga-gu$_7$* **^{d} Mes-lam-ta-è-a**, 1 máš siskúr-***^{d} Al-la-tum***, <u>***Ma-šum**maškim*</u>, *zi-ga*-**šabra**.iti-ki-siki-^{d}Nin-a-zu, mu a-rá 2-kam-aš^{d}Nanna Kar-zi-da. (AnOr 07 059, P101354)	1 ram for **the sacrifice of New Moon**, **via Ipiq-Erra**; 1 ram for **the sacrifice of Full Moon in Uruk**, **via Apiliya**; 1 sucking he-goat for **Meslamta-Ea**, 1 kid for the sacrifice of **Allatum**, <u>**Mašum as royal deputy**</u>, were withdrawn from the majordomo.Month of ki-siki-Ninazu, Year of Nanna of Karzida was for second time brought into his temple.	1只公绵羊为**新月祭**,**经由伊皮喀埃腊**;1只公绵羊为**满月祭于乌鲁克**,**经由阿皮里亚**;1只吃奶公山羊为**美斯兰塔埃阿**,1只公崽为**阿拉吞祭祀**,<u>**马顺督办**</u>,以上从庙总管处支出了。神宁阿朱羊毛作坊月,卡尔孜达的神南那第二次被送入他的庙宇年。

续表

时间和摘要	文献内容	英文翻译	中文翻译
Š 36 v: **zi-ga** 1 fat ram for **Ulma-šitum**, 3 fattened rams for the sacrifice of **Annunitum**, on the day of Erubatum (eating) of divine bulls, were **withdrawn from** Ahima, **the fattener**, **via Apilia**	1 udu-niga, ***dUl-ma-ši-tum***, 3 *udu-niga*, *siskúr-**dAn-nu-ni-tum***, *ud~ **E-ru-ba-tum** diĝir gud-gud-ka*, *zi-ga **A-hi-ma***, *gurušda*, *ĝìr<u>Á-pi₅-lí-a</u>.iti-ezem-dNin-a-zu*, *mudNanna-Kar-zi-da é-a-na ba-an-ku₄*. (CST 41, P107553)	1 fattened ram for**Ulma-šitum**, 3 fattened rams for the sacrifice of **Annunitum**, on the day of Erubatum (eating) of divine bulls, were **withdrawn from Ahima**, **the fattener**, <u>**via Apilia**</u>.Month of ezem-Ninazu, Year of Nanna of Karzida was brought into his temple.	1只育肥公绵羊为**乌勒马席吞**、3只育肥公绵羊为**安努尼吞的祭祀**，于埃如巴吞（食）神牛时，从**育肥师阿希马处支出了**，<u>**经由阿皮里亚**</u>。神宁阿朱的庆典月，卡尔孜达的神楠那被送入他的庙宇之年。
Š 36 v: **zi-ga** 2 fattened rams for**temple of Belat-Suhnir and Belat-Darraban**, 1 fattened ram for **Nanaya**, <u>**via my queen**</u>, 1 fattened ram for **Adad**, <u>**Mašum as royal deputy**</u>, were withdrawn from **Beli-ṭab**, in **Ur**	2 udu-niga, *é-d **Be-la-at-Suh₆-nir*** ù **dBe-la-at-Dar-ra-ba-an**, 1 *udu-niga*, ***dNa-na-a***, *ĝìr* <u>**nin-ĝá**</u>, 1 udu-niga, **dIškur**, <u>***Ma-šum*maškim**</u>, zi-ga-***Be-lí-ṭàb***, *šà*~ **Urim₅ki**-ma.iti-ezem-dNin-a-zu, mu dNanna-Kar-zi-da é-a-na ba-ku₄. (Torino 1 178, P132009)	2 fattened rams for**temple of Belat-Suhnir and Belat-Darraban**, 1 fattened ram for **Nanaya**, <u>**via my queen**</u>, 1 fattened ram for **Adad**, <u>**Mašum as royal deputy**</u>, were withdrawn from **Beli-ṭab**, in **Ur**. Month of ezem-Ninazu, Year of Nanna of Karzida was brought into his temple.	2只育肥公绵羊为**贝拉特苏赫尼尔和贝拉特达腊班庙**，1只育肥公绵羊为**那那亚神**，<u>**经由我的王后**</u>，1只育肥公绵羊为**阿达德**，<u>**马顺督办**</u>，（以上）从**贝里沓卜处被支出于乌尔**。神宁阿朱的庆典月，卡尔孜达的神楠那被送入他的庙宇之年。
Š 36 v: **mu-túm** 1 breast lamb fr.**governor of Kazallu**, 1 breast kid from **Bayalaya**, **in Nippur**, 1 breast kid fr. **wife of Bayalaya**, **were deliveries for Šulgi-simti**	1 sila₄-gaba **ensí** Ka-zal-luki-ka, 1 máš-gaba ***Ba-a-la-a***, *šà~ Nibruki*, 1 *máš-gaba* **dam-*Ba-a-la-a***, *mu-túm~* ***dŠul-gi-sí-im-ti***.*iti-ezem-dNin-a-zu*, *mu dNanna Kar-zi-da a-rá-2-kam-aš é ku₄-ra*. (*Orient* 16 040 3, P112841)	1 *breast lamb from* **the governor of Kazallu**, 1 breast kid from **Bayalaya**, **in Nippur**, 1 breast kid from **the wife of Bayalaya**, **were deliveries for Šulgi-simti**.Month of ezem-Ninazu, Year of Nanna of Karzida brought into his temple.	1雄公羔自**卡扎鲁的总督**，1雄公崽自**巴亚拉亚**，于**尼普尔**，1雄公崽来自**巴亚拉亚之妻**，为舒勒吉新吞的送入项。宁阿朱的庆典月，卡尔孜达的神南那被送入他的庙宇之年。
Š 36 vi: **zi-ga** 2 female kids for **the sacrifice of Annunitum and Ulmašitum**, <u>**Mašum as royal deputy**</u>, were **withdrawn from Beli-ṭab**, in **Tummal**.	2fašgar, **siskúr-*An-nu-ni-tum*** ù **dUl-ma-ši-tum**, <u>**Ma-šum***maškim*</u>, *zi-ga **Be-lí-ṭàb***, *šà*~ **Tum-ma-al**.iti-á-ki~ti, mu a-rá-2-kam-ašdNanna-Kar-zi-da é-a-na ba-ku₄ (OIP 115 029, P123645)	2 female kids for **the sacrifice of Annunitum and Ulmašitum**, <u>**Mašum as royal deputy**</u>, were **withdrawn from Beli-ṭab**, in **Tummal**.Month of akiti, Year of Nanna of Karzida was for the 2nd time brought into his temple.	2只雌山羊崽为**安努尼吞和乌勒马席吞祭祀**，<u>**马顺督办**</u>，（以上）从**贝里沓卜于图马勒庙区**支出了。阿基提月，卡尔孜达的神南那第二次被送入他的庙宇之年。

续表

时间和摘要	文献内容	英文翻译	中文翻译
Š 36 viii: **mu-túm, ì-dab** 1 fat bull, 7 [fat] goats from **the wife of Ṫabban-Darah**, 1 fattened cow of two years, 9 rams, 1 kid from **the wife of Šu-Kabta**, 5 rams, 1 lamb from **the wife of Dakiki**, 4 rams, 1 kid from **Imi-Sin**, were deliveries for Šulgi-simtum, Beli-ṭab **fattener took** over	1 gud-niga, 7 máš-[gal-niga], **dam *Ṫab-ba-Da-[ra-ah]***, 1 *áb-mu-2-niga*, 9 *udu*, 1 *máš*, **dam-Šu-^{d}Kabta (IDIM)**, 5 udu, 1 sila$_4$, **dam-*Da-ki-ki***, 4 *udu*, 1 *máš*, ***I-mi-^{d}Sîn***, *mu-túm-^{d}**Šul-gi-sí-im-tum***, ***Be-lí-ṭàb*** *gurušda ì-dab$_5$*. *iti-šu-eš-ša, mu a-rá-2-kam^{d} Nanna-Ka [r-zi-da] é-a-n [a ba-ku$_4$]*. (*OIP* 115024, *P*123716)	1 *fattened bull*, 7 [*fattened*] *he-goats from* **the wife of Ṫabban-Darah**, 1 fattened cow of two years, 9 rams, 1 kid from **the wife of Šu-Kabta**, 5 rams, 1 lamb from **the wife of Dakiki**, 4 rams, 1 kid from **Imi-Sin**, were deliveries for Šulgi-simtum, Beli-ṭab **fattener took** over. Month of šu-ešša, Year of Nanna of Karzida was for the second time brought into his temple.	1肥公牛和7【肥】公山羊自**沓班达腊赫（席穆如王）之妻**，1两岁育肥母牛、9公绵羊和1公崽自**舒卡卜塔之妻（Me-Ištaran公主）**，5公绵羊和1羊羔自**达基基之妻**，4公绵羊和1公崽自**伊米辛**，为舒勒吉新吞的送入项，**育肥师贝里沓卜**接管了。三只手月，卡尔孜达的神南那第二次被送入他的庙宇年。
Š 36 ix: **mu-túm, ì-dab** 1 bull, 8 rams and 2 kids, from the**place of king**, 1 bull, 3 rams of after-ox-class, 6 grass rams and 1 kid from **Me-Ea**, 1 bull, 9 rams and 1 kid fr. **Ur-Šulpae**, 4 fattened rams and 1 kid fr.**Nir-idagal**, 4 fat rams and 1 lamb fr. **zabar-dab**, 1 fat bull, 3 rams of after-ox-class, 6 rams and 1 kid fr.**Igi-anna-kezu**, 1 bull, 9 rams and 1 kid fr. **wife of Ur-niĝar**, 1 kid fr.**wife of Panilum**, 1 bull, 3 rams of after-ox-class, 6 rams and 1 kid fr.**Ninkalla**, deliveries for Šulgi-simti, **Beli-ṭab** **took over**	1 gud, 8 udu, 2 máš, ki~ **lugal**--ta, 1 gud, 3 udu-gud-e-ús-sa, 6 udu-ú, 1 máš, **Me-É-a**, 1 gud, 3 udu-gud-e ús-sa, 6 udu-ú, 1 máš, **Ur-^{d}Šul-pa-è** sukkal-mah, 4 udu-niga, 1 máš, ***Nir-ì-da-ĝál***, 4 *udu-niga*, 1 *sila$_4$*, **zabar-dab$_5$**, 1 gud-niga, 3 udu-gud-e-ús-sa, 6 udu-ú, 1 máš, **Igi-an-na-ke$_4$-zu**, 1 gud, 3 udu-gud-e-ús-sa, 6 udu-ú, 1 máš, **dam-Ur-ni$_9$-ĝar**, 1 máš **dam-*Pa-ni-lum***, 1 *gud*, 3 *udu-gud-e-ús-sa*, 6 *udu-ú*, 1 *máš* **Nin-kal-la**, mu-túm~ ***^{d}Šul-gi-<sí>-im-ti***, ***Be-lí-ṭàb*** *ì-dab$_5$*. *iti-ezem-mah, mu ^{d}Nanna Kar-zi-da a-rá-2$^{!}$-k [am] -aš é-na ba-an-ku$_4$*. (*AnOr* 07 002, *P*101297)	1 *bull*, 8 *rams and* 2 *kids*, *from the***place of king**, 1 bull, 3 rams of after-ox-class, 6 grass rams and 1 kid from **Me-Ea**, 1 bull, 3 rams of after-ox-class, 6 grass rams and 1 kid from **Ur-Šulpae**, the ambassador, 4 fattened rams and 1 kid from **Nir-idagal**, 4 fattened rams and 1 lamb from **zabar-dab**, 1 fattened bull, 3 rams of after-ox-class, 6 grass rams and 1 kid from **Igi-anna-kezu**, 1 bull, 3 rams of after-ox-class, 6 grass rams and 1 kid from **the wife of Ur-niĝar**, 1 kid from **wife of Panilum**, 1 bull, 3 rams of after-ox -class, 6 grass rams and 1 kid from **Ninkalla**, were deliveries for Šulgi-simti, **Beli-ṭab took over**. Month of ezem-mah, Year of Nanna of Karzida was for the 2nd time brought into his temple.	1牛、8公绵羊和2公崽自**国王处**，1牛、3牛后级公绵羊、6食草公绵羊和1公崽自**美埃阿**，1牛、3牛后级公绵羊、6食草公绵羊和1公崽自**乌尔舒勒帕埃国务卿**，4育肥公绵羊和1公崽自**尼尔伊达旮勒**，4育肥公绵羊和1羔自**执青铜官**，1育肥公牛、3牛后级公绵羊、6食草公绵羊和1公崽自**伊吉安那凯朱**，1牛、3牛后级公绵羊、6食草公绵羊和1公崽自**乌尔尼旮尔之妻**，1公崽自**帕尼隆之妻**，1牛、3牛后级公绵羊、6食草公绵羊和1公崽自**宁卡拉**，为舒勒吉新提送人，**贝里沓卜接管**。大庆典月，卡尔孜达的神南那第二次被送入他的庙宇年。

续表

时间和摘要	文献内容	英文翻译	中文翻译
Š 36 ix: **zi-ga** 2 fat rams for**allowance of Ili-išmani**, **in palace**, 1 fat ram for **allowance of giranum of Inanna** by side of wall, 1 fat ram for **Allatum**, 2 rams for **temple of Išhara and Belat-Nagar**, 1 ram for **temple of Ulmašitum**, 1 fat ram for **Annunitum**, 1 fat ram for **allowance of disappearing place of temple of Adad**, **viathe man of Urub**, 1 fat ram for **allowance**, 1 lamb for **temple of Ulmašitum**, 2 fat rams and 1 lamb for **Annunitum**, 1 fat ram for **allowance**, 1 ram for **temple of Išhara**, 1 ram and 1 lamb for **Allatum**, 1 fat cow, 1 fat ram, 2 rams and 1 lamb for **Dawn**, 1 kid for **sacrifice of deities**, 1 lamb for **disappearing place** on 1st time, 1 fat ram and 1 kid on 2nd time, for **pouring-beer of Nanaya**, were withdr., **in Ur**	2 udu-niga **sá-dug$_4$** ***Ì-lí-iš-ma-ni***, **šà~ é-gal**, 1 udu-niga**sá-dug$_4$** ***gi-ra-núm*** ^{d}**Inanna**--da-bàd--da, 1 udu-niga~ gud-e-ús ^{d}***Al-la-tum***, 2 *udu é-^{d}**Iš-ha-ra** ù ^{d}* ***Be-la-at-Na-gàr***--*šè*, 1 *udu-gud-e-ús-sa é-^{d}**Ul-ma-ši-tum***, 1 *udu-niga**An-nu-ni-tum***, 1 *udu-niga***sá-dug$_4$** **níĝ-ki-zàh** é-^{d} **Iškur**, **ĝìr** **lú-Urub** (**URUxKÁR^{ki}**) **sukkal**, 1 udu-niga sá-dug$_4$, 1 sila$_4$ é ^{d}***Ul-ma-ši-tum***, 2 *udu-niga*, 1 *sila$_4$* ***An-nu-ni-tum***, 1 *udu-niga* **sá-dug$_4$**, 1 udu-ú**é-^{d}*Iš-ha-ra*--*šè***, 1 *udu-gud-e-ús*, 1 *sila$_4$*, ^{d}***Al-la-tum***, 1*áb-niga*, 1 *udu-niga*, 2 *udu-ú*, 1 *sila$_4$* **á-gú-zi-ga**, 1 máš, **siskúr-diĝir-ne**, 1 sila$_4$ **níĝ-ki-zàh**--šè, ud-1-kam, 1 udu-niga, 1 máš ud-2-kam **kaš-dé-a-^{d}*Na-na-a***, *zi-ga* **šà~ Urim$_5$^{ki}-ma**. iti-ezem-mah, mu ^{d}Nanna Kar-zi-da a-rá-2-kam-aš é-na ba-an-ku$_4$. (AnOr 07 060, P101355)	2 fattened rams for**monthly allowance of Ili-išmani**, **in palace**, 1 fattened ram for **monthly allowance of giranum of Inanna** by side of wall, 1 fattened ram of after-ox-class for **Allatum**, 2 rams for **temple of Išhara and Belat-Nagar**, 1 ram of after-ox-class for **temple of Ulmašitum**, 1 fattened ram for **Annunitum**, 1 fattened ram for **monthly allowance of disappearing place of temple of Adad**, **via the envoy the man of Urub**, 1 fattened ram for **monthly allowance**, 1 lamb for **temple of Ulmašitum**, 2 fattened rams and 1 lamb for **Annunitum**, 1 fattened ram for **monthly allowance**, 1 grass ram for **temple of Išhara**, 1 ram of after-ox-class and 1 lamb for **Allatum**, 1 fattened cow, 1 fattened ram, 2 grass rams and 1 lamb for **Dawn**, 1 kid for **sacrifice of deities**, 1 lamb for **disappearing place** on 1st time, 1 fattened ram and 1 kid on 2nd time, for **pouring-beer of Nanaya**, were withdrawn, **in Ur**. Month of ezem-mah, Year of Nanna of Karzida was for the 2nd time brought into his temple.	2只育肥公绵羊为**伊里伊什马尼的月供于宫殿**，1只育肥公绵羊为**伊南那于城墙的吉腊努姆仪式月供**，1只育肥牛后级公绵羊为**阿拉吞**，2只公绵羊为**伊什哈腊和贝拉特那旮尔庙**，1只牛后级公绵羊为**乌勒马席吞庙**，1只育肥公绵羊为**安努尼吞**，1只育肥公绵羊为**阿达德庙的消失处月供**，**经由国使乌如卜城之人**，1只育肥公绵羊为**月供**，1只羔为**乌勒马席吞庙**，2只育肥公绵羊和1只羔为**安努尼吞**，1只育肥公绵羊为**月供**，1只食草公绵羊为**伊什哈腊**，1只牛后级公绵羊和1只羔为**阿拉吞**，1只育肥母牛、1只育肥公绵羊、2只食草公绵羊和1羔为**晨祭**，1公崽为**众神的牺牲**，1只羔为**消失处**第1次，1只育肥公绵羊和1只公崽第2次，为**那那亚的倒啤酒宴会**，以上支出于**乌尔**。大庆典月，卡尔孜达的神南那第二次被送入他的庙宇年。
Š 36 ix: **zi-ga** 1 bull, 3 rams of after-ox-class, 6 grass rams and 1 kid for **Nin-kalla**, when she ate them in é-GAR were **withdrawn**, **in Ur**	1 gud, 3 udu~ gud-e-ús-sa, 6 udu-ú, 1 máš, ***Nin$_9$-kal-la***, *ud-é$^!$-GAR bí-gu$_7$-a*, *zi-ga šà~ Urim$_5$^{ki}-ma. iti-ezem-mah*, *mu a-rá-2-kam-aš ^{d}Nanna Kar-zi-da é-a-na ba-an-ku$_4$*. (*TLB* 3 020, *P*134161)	1 *bull*, 3 *rams of after-ox-class*, 6 *grass rams and* 1 *kid for* **Nin-kalla**, when she ate them in é-GAR were **withdrawn**, **in Ur**. Month of ezem-mah, Year of Nanna of Karzida was for the second time brought into his temple.	1头公牛、3只牛后级公绵羊、6只食草公绵羊和1只公崽为**宁卡拉**，当她在é-GAR吃它们时，**支出于乌尔**。大庆典月，卡尔孜达的神南那第二次被送入他的庙宇年。

续表

时间和摘要	文献内容	英文翻译	中文翻译
Š 36 x: **zi-ga** 1 fattened bull, 2 grass rams for**boat of An**, 1 fattened ram for **monthly allowance of " night staying" shrine**, 1 grass ram, 1 kid for **the temple of Nanaya**, on the day of boat of heaven, 2 fat rams for **monthly allowance**, 1 grass ram for **sacrifice of New Moon**, in **Uruk**, **via Beli-bani**, withdr.fr.**Beli-ṭab fattener**	1 gud-niga, 2 udu-ú, **má-an-na**--šè, 1 udu-niga, **sá-dug$_4$-èš-gi$_6$-zal**--šè, 1 udu-ú, 1 máš, é-^{d} *Na-na-a*--šè, *ud* ~ **má-an-na**--ka, 2 udu-niga, **sá-dug$_4$**, 1 udu-ú, **siskúr-sag-ud-sakar**, šà~ **Unug^{ki}**-ga, gìr***Be-lí-ba-ni***, zi-ga-***Be-lí-ṭàb***, **gurušda**. iti-ezem-An-na, mu a-rá-2-kam-aš^{d}Nanna-Kar-zi-da é-a-na ba-an-ku$_4$. (OIP 115030, P123432)	1 fattened bull, 2 grass rams for**boat of An**, 1 fattened ram for **monthly allowance of " night staying" shrine**, 1 grass ram, 1 kid for **the temple of Nanaya**, on the day of the boat of heaven, 2 fattened rams for **monthly allowance**, 1 grass ram for **the sacrifice of New Moon**, in **Uruk**, **via Beli-bani**, were withdrawn from **Beli-ṭab fattener**. Month of ezem-An, Year of Nanna of Karzida was brought into his temple for the second time.	1头育肥公牛和2只食草公绵羊为**"天船"**，1只育肥公绵羊为**黑夜圣殿月供应**，1只食草公绵羊和1只公崽为**那那亚庙**，于天船时，2只育肥公绵羊为（**舒勒吉新提王后）月供应**，1只食草公绵羊为**新月于乌鲁克**，**经由贝里巴尼**，从**育肥师贝里沓卜支出了**。天神庆典月，卡尔孜达的神南那第二次被送入他的庙宇之年。
Š 36 x: **mu-túm, ì-dab** 2 fattened rams and 1 lamb from**Ama-bará**, these were deliveries, **Beli-ṭab took** over	2 udu-niga, 1 sila$_4$ **Ama-bará**, mu-túm, ***Be-lí-ṭab*** *ì-dab$_5$*. *iti-ezem-An-na*, *mu* ^{d}*Nanna Kar-zi-da a-rá-2-kam-aš é-a-na ba-an-ku$_4$*. (*Hirose* 014, *P*109485)	2 *fattened rams and* 1 *lamb from***Ama-bará**, these were deliveries, **Beli-ṭab took** over. Month of ezem-Anna, Year of Nanna of Karzida was for the second time brought into his temple.	2只育肥公绵羊和1只羔来自**王座之母**，以上送入，**贝里沓卜接管**了。天神安庆典月，卡尔孜达的神南那第二次被送入他的庙宇之年。
Š 36 x: **zi-ga** 1 fat ram and 1 lamb for**temple of Alla-gula**, 1 fat ram and 1 lamb for **temple of Ninlil**, 1 fattened ram and 1 lamb for **Enlil**, 1 ram of after-ox-class for **temple of Ningagia**, for the **sacrifice of Full Moon**, in **Nippur**, **via my queen**, were withdrawn from **Beli-ṭab**	1 udu-niga, 1 sila$_4$, é-^{d}***Al-la-gu-la***, [1 *udu-niga*], 1 *sila$_4$ é-*^{d}**Nin-líl-lá**, 1 udu-niga, 1 sila$_4$ ^{d}**En-líl**, 1 udu-gud-e-ús-sa é-^{d}**Nin-gá-gi$_4$-a**, **siskúr é-ud-15 šà~ Nibru^{ki}**, gìr-**nin-ĝá**, zi-ga***Be-lí-ṭàb***. *iti-ezem-An-na*, *mu a-rá 2-kam-aš* ^{d}*Nanna Kar-zi-da é-an-na ba-an-ku$_4$*. (*SAT* 2 0153, *P*143354)	1 *fattened ram and* 1 *lamb for***temple of Alla-gula**, 1 fattened ram and 1 lamb for **temple of Ninlil**, 1 fattened ram and 1 lamb for **Enlil**, 1 ram of after-ox-class for **temple of Ningagia**, for the **sacrifice of Full Moon**, in **Nippur**, **via my queen**, were withdrawn from **Beli-ṭab**. Month of ezem-Anna, Year of Nanna of Karzida was for the second time brought into his temple.	1只育肥公绵羊和1只羔为**阿拉古拉庙**， 1只育肥公绵羊和1只羔为**宁里勒庙**，1只育肥公绵羊和1只羔为**恩里勒**，1只牛后级公绵羊为**宁旮吉阿庙**，为**满月牺牲**，于**尼普尔**，**经由我的王后**，从**贝里沓卜支出**了。天神庆典月，卡尔孜达的神南那第二次被送入他的庙宇之年。

续表

时间和摘要	文献内容	英文翻译	中文翻译
Š 37 i: **mu-túm, ì-dab** 2 lamb from **Etel-pu-Dagan**, were deliveries for Šulgi-simtum, **Beli- ṭab took over**	1 sila$_4$ a-rá-1-kam, 1 sila$_4$a-rá-2-kam, **E-te-<él>-pù-^{d}Da-gan**, mu-túm~ ^{d}***Šul-gi-sí-im-tum***, ***Be-lí- ṭàb***--*ta* ì-*dab$_5$*.*iti-maš-dà~gu$_7$*, *mu ús-sa ^{d}Nanna Kar-zi-da.* (*JCS* 40 237 8, *P*112262)	1 *lamb for* 1st *time*, 1 *lamb for* 2nd *time*, *from* **Etel-pu-Dagan**, were deliveries for Šulgi-simtum, **Beli- ṭab took over**. Month of mašda~gu$_7$, Year after that of Nanna of Karzida. (was for the 2nd time brought into his temple)	1 只羔第 1 次，1 只羔第 2 次，来自**埃台勒普达干**，为舒勒吉新吞的送入项，**贝里沓卜接管**了。食瞪羚月，卡尔孜达的神南那（第二次被送入他的庙宇）之次年。
Š 37 i: **zi-ga** 1 fat ram for **offering of giranum of Inanna**, the gate of leaning, **Ipiq-Erra as royal deputy**, was **withdrawn from Beli- ṭab**, fattener	1 udu-niga, **sá-dug$_4$-*gi-ra-núm*-^{d}Inanna**, ká ú-ús, ***I-pi$_5$-iq-Èr-ra***maškim, zi-ga-***Be-lí- ṭàb*** *gurušda. iti-maš-dà~gu$_7$*, *mu ^{d}Šul-gi bàd ma-da ba-dù-a.* (*OIP* 115031, *P*123553)	1 *fattened ram for***the offering of giranum fesival of Inanna**, the gate of leaning, **Ipiq-Erra as royal deputy**, was **withdrawn from Beli- ṭab**, fattener. Month of mašdà~gu$_7$, Year of Šulgi built the wall of the land.	1 只育肥公绵羊为**伊南那神的吉腊努姆仪式供奉**，于"支臂"门，**伊皮喀埃腊为督办**，从育肥师**贝里沓卜**处支出了。食瞪羚月，舒勒吉建立国家的城墙之年。
Š 37 i: **zi-ga** 1 fat ram for **temple of Inanna**, 2 fat rams, 1 ram and 1 lamb for **temple of Alla-gula**, 2 fat bulls, 2 fat rams and 1 lamb for **temple of Nin-lil**, 2 fat rams and 1 lamb for **temple of Enlil**, 1 ram for **the statue of king**, 1 fattened ram and 2 kids for the **temple of Nin-gagiya**, for **festival of field of bull in Nippur**, **via my queen**, were **withdrawn from Beli- ṭab**, **fattener**,	1 udu-niga, **é-^{d}Inanna**--šè, 2 udu-niga, 1 udu-ú, 1 sila$_4$, é-^{d}**Al-la-gu-la**, 2 gud-niga, 2 udu-niga, 1 sila$_4$, é-^{d}**Nin-líl-lá**, 2 udu-niga, 1 sila$_4$, <é>-^{d}**En-líl-lá**, 1 udu-ú, ^{d}**Alan-lugal**, 1 udu-niga, 2 máš, é-^{d} **Nin-ĝá-gi$_4$-a**, **ezem-gud-gán**--šè, šà~ **Nibru^{ki}**, gìr-**nin-ĝá**, zi-ga***Be-lí- ṭàb***, *gurušda.iti-maš-dà~gu$_7$*, *mu ús-sa^{d}Nanna-Kar-zi-da é-a-na ba-an-ku$_4$.* (*OIP* 115032, *P*123625)	1 *fattened ram for* **temple of Inanna**, 2 fattened rams, 1 grass ram and 1 lamb for **the temple of Alla-gula**, 2 fattened bulls, 2 fattened rams and 1 lamb for **the temple of Nin-lil**, 2 fattened rams and 1 lamb for **the temple of Enlil**, 1 grass ram for **the statue of king**, 1 fattened ram and 2 kids for the **temple of Nin-gagiya**, for **festival of field of bull in Nippur**, **via my queen**, were **withdrawn from Beli- ṭab**, **fattener**. Month of mašda-gu$_7$, Year after that of Nanna of Karzida was for the 2nd time delivered of his temple.	1 育肥公绵羊为**伊南那神庙**，2 育肥公绵羊、1 食草公绵羊和 1 羊羔为**阿拉古拉神庙**， 2 育肥公牛、2 育肥公绵羊和 1 羊羔为**宁里勒神庙**，2 育肥公绵羊和 1 羊羔为**恩里勒神庙**， 1 只食草公绵羊为**神王像**，1 只育肥公绵羊和 2 只公崽为**宁旮吉亚神庙**，以上为**"牛田节"**，于尼普尔，**经由我的王后**，从**育肥师贝里沓卜支出**。食瞪羚月，卡尔孜达的神南那被送入他庙宇次年。
Š 37 ii: **mu-túm, ì-dab** 1 kid fr. **Talim-Enlil**, 4 rams and 1 lamb fr. **wife of Banilum**, 1 lamb fr. **Izi-arik**, 1 lamb fr. **priest of Inanna**, were deliveries for Šulig-simti, **Beli- ṭab took over**	1^{f}ašgar ***Tá-lim-*^{d}En-líl**, 4 udu-ú, 1 sila$_4$, **dam-*Ba-ni-lum***, 1 *sila$_4$* ***I-zi-a-ri-ik***, 1 *sila$_4$* **en-^{d}Inanna**, mu-túm~ ^{d}***Šul-gi-sí-im-ti***, ***Be-lí- ṭàb*** ì-*dab$_5$*.*iti-ze$_x$-da~gu$_7$*, *mu bàd ma-da ba-dù-a.* (*BIN* 3 409, *P*106216)	1 *female kid from***Talim-Enlil**, 4 grass rams and 1 lamb from **wife of Banilum**, 1 lamb from **Izi-arik**, 1 lamb from **the priest of Inanna**, were deliveries for Šulig-simti, **Beli- ṭab took over**. Month of zeda ~gu$_7$, Year of the wall of land was built.	1 只雌崽自**塔林恩里勒**，4 只食草公绵羊和 1 只羔自**巴尼隆之妻**，1 只羔自**伊兹阿瑞克**，1 只羔来自**伊南那的祭司**，为舒勒吉新提的送入项，**贝里沓卜接管**了。食豚月，国家的城墙被建立年。

续表

时间和摘要	文献内容	英文翻译	中文翻译
Š 37 ii: **mu-túm, ì-dab** 1 lamb fr.**Ilum-bani majordomo**, 1 lamb fr. **Te ṣ in-Mama**, celiveries for Šulgi-simti, **Beli-ṭab took**	1 sila$_4$, ***Ilum-ba-ni*** *šabra*, 1 *sila$_4$*, ***Te-ṣ i-in-^{d}Ma-ma***, *mu-túm* ~ ***^{d}Šul-gi-sí-im-ti***, **Be-lí-ṭab** *ì-dab$_5$*. *iti-zex-da* ~ *gu$_7$*, *mu bàd ma-da ba-dù-a*. (*Torino* 1 028, *P*131956)	1 *lamb from***Ilum-bani majordomo**, 1 lamb from **Te ṣ in-Mama**, were deliveries for Šulgi-simti, **Beli-ṭab took over**. Month of zeda-gu$_7$, Year that of wall of the land was built.	1只羊羔自**庙总管伊鲁姆巴尼**，1只羊羔自**台岑妈妈（阿马尔辛之女）**，为舒勒吉新提的送入项，**贝里沓卜接管**了。食豚月，国家城墙被建立年
Š 37 ii: **zi-ga** 5 fat rams for **allowance of sacrifice**, 2 kids for **offering of disappear place**, for **šeršerum festival of temple of Belat-S. and Belat-D.**, withdr. (fr. Beli-ṭab) **in Ur**, <u>**via Beli-bani**</u>	5 udu-niga, **sá-dug$_4$ siskúr--šè**, 2 máš, **níĝ~ ki-zàh--šè**, ***ezem-še-er -še-ru-um*** *é-^{d}****Be-la-at-Suh-nir*** *ù* ***^{d}Be-la-at-Dar-ra-ba-an***, *zi-ga šà~* **Urim^{ki}**-ma, <u>gìr-***Be-lí-ba-ni***</u>. *iti-šeš-da-kú*, *mu bàd <ma-da> ba-dù*. (*OIP* 115033, *P*123419)	5 *fattened rams for* **the monthly allowance of sacrifice**, 2 kids for **offering of disappear place**, for **šeršerum festival at the temple of Belat-Suhnir and Belat-Darraban**, were withdrawn (from Beli-ṭab) **in Ur**, <u>**via Beli-bani**</u>. Month of zeda ~ gu$_7$, Year that of wall of the land was built.	5只育肥公绵羊为**祭祀的月供**，2只公崽为"**消失处"供奉**，以上为**贝拉特苏赫尼尔和贝拉特达腊班神庙之 šeršerum 节**，从（贝里沓卜）于乌尔处支出了，<u>经由贝里巴尼</u>。食豚月，国家城墙被建立年。
Š 37 v: **zi-ga** 1 fat ram, 1 ram and 1 lamb for **temple of Nin-sun**, 1 fat ram, 1 ram and 1 lamb for **temple of Adad**, 1 fat ram for **Nanaya**, **in palace**, 1 kid for **giranum of Annunitum**, 1 kid for **giranum of temple of Ulmašitum**. 1 kid **in the courtyard**, **for the offering**, 1 fat bull, 4 fat rams, 1 ram for **statue of king**, 1 fat female kid, 1 kid for **food of fish and greenery**, 1 kid for**pouring beer festival of Annunitum**, **in palace**, 1 kid for **Nanaya**, 1 ram for **temple of Ulmaš**, withdr.**fr. Beli-ṭab** fattener, in**Ur**	1 udu-niga, 1 udu-ú, 1 sila$_4$ **é-^{d}Nin-sún**, 1 udu-niga, 1 udu-ú, 1 sila$_4$ **é-^{d}Iškur**, 1 udu-niga**^{d}Na-na-a** šà~ **é-gal**, 1 máš ***gi-ra-núm-An-nu-ni-tum***, 1 *máš* ***gi-ra-núm*** **é-*^{d}Ul-ma-ši-tum*** *-ma*, 1 *máš šà~* **kisal** gaba-ri-a, 1 gud-niga, 4 udu-niga, 1 udu, **alan lugal**, 1^{f}ašgar-niga, 1 máš níĝ-ku$_6$-nisig, 1 máš é-a-ni-šè du-a-ni, kaš-dé-a ***An-nu-ni-tum*** *šà~ é-gal*, 1 *máš* **^{d}Na-na-a** ud~ kaš-dé-a ***An-nu-ni-tum***, 1 *udu-ú***é-^{d}Ul-ma-áš**, zi-ga***Be-lí-ṭàb*** *gurušda*, *šà~ Uri$_5$^{ki}-ma*. *iti-ezem-^{d}Nin-a-zu*, *mu bàd ma-da ba-dù-a*. (*AnOr* 07 061, *P*101356)	1 *fattened ram*, 1 *grass ram and* 1 *lamb for* **temple of Nin-sun**, 1 fattened ram, 1 grass ram and 1 lamb for **temple of Adad**, 1 fattened ram for **Nanaya**, **in the palace**, 1 kid for **giranum festival of Annunitum**, 1 kid for **giranum festival of temple of Ulmašitum**, 1 kid **in the courtyard**, **for the offering**, 1 fattened bull, 4 fattened rams, 1 ram for **the statue of king**, 1 fattened female kid, 1 kid for **the food of fish and greenery**, 1 kid from his temple when he went, for **pouring beer festival of Annunitum**, **in the palace**, 1 kid for **Nanaya**, when pouring beer festival of Annunitum, 1 grass ram for **temple of Ulmaš**, were withdrawn **from Beli-ṭab** fattener, in **Ur**. Month of ezem-Ninazu, Year that of wall of land was built.	1育肥公绵羊、1食草公绵羊和1羔为**宁荪庙**， 1育肥公绵羊、1食草公绵羊和1羔为**阿达德庙**， 1育肥公绵羊为**那那亚**，于**宫殿**， 1公崽为**安努尼吞的吉腊努姆仪式**，1公崽为**乌勒马席吞庙的吉腊努姆仪式**，1公崽于**庭院**，为供奉，1育肥公牛、4育肥公绵羊和1公绵羊为**王像**，1育肥雌崽和1公崽为**鱼食和蔬菜**，1公崽来自她的庙当她离开时，**为安努尼吞啤酒节**，于**宫殿**，1公崽为**那那亚**，于安努尼吞的啤酒节时，1食草公绵羊为**乌勒马什庙**，从**育肥师贝里沓卜支出了**，于**乌尔**。神宁阿朱庆典月，国家城墙被建立年。

续表

时间和摘要	文献内容	英文翻译	中文翻译
Š 37 v: **zi-ga** 1 fat ram for **allowance of sacrifice of granary**, 1 for **giranum of Inanna**, 2 fat flocks for **sacrifice of Belat-S.and Belat-D.**, 2 fat rams, 1 ram for **sacrifice of Full Moon**, **in Uruk**, **via Beli-bani**, **in the storehouse**, 2 fat rams and 1 lamb for **gate of shrine**, 1 lamb for **sacrifice of disappearing place of Nanaya**, 1 kid for **weeping and going around city**, 1 kid for **day when raising up zí-na siege weapon**, 1 fat ram for **gate of bedroom of high priestess**, 1 fat ram and 1 lamb for **temple of Nanaya**, **via my queen**, **in Uruk**, **withdr.fr.Beli-ṭab**	1 udu-niga**sá-dug$_4$ siskúr šag$_4$-ge gu-ru-a**, 1 udu-niga***gi-ra-núm-***^{d}**Inanna**, 1 udu-niga, 1 máš-gal-niga **siskúr-**^{d}***Be-la-at-Suh$_6$-nir*** *ù* ^{d}***Be-la-at-Dar-ra-ba-an***, 2 *udu-niga*, 1 *udu-ú* **siskúr-é-ud-15** šà~ **Unug^{ki}**, gìr ***Be-lí-ba-ni***, šà~ *é-Sag-da-na*, 2 *udu-niga*, 1 *sila$_4$*, **ka~ èš**, 1 sila$_4$ **níg-ki-zàh-**^{d}**Na-na-a**, 1 máš **ér-uru-nigín-na**, 1 máš **ud~ zi-ga-zí-na**, 1 udu-niga **ka-gi$_6$-par$_4$-ra**, 1 udu-niga, 1 sila$_4$, **é-**^{d}**Na-na-a**, gìr **nin-ĝá**, šà~ **Unug^{ki}**-ga, zi-ga***Be-lí- ṭàb*** *gurušda.iti-ezem-*^{d}*Nin-a-zu*, *mu bàd ma-da ba-dù-a.* (*CTNMC* 09, *P*108740)	1 *fattened ram for***monthly allowance of sacrifice of granary**, 1 fattened ram for **giranum festival of Inanna**, 1 fattened ram, 1 fattened he-goat for **sacrifice of Belat-Suhnir and Belat-Darraban**, 2 fattened rams, 1 grass ram for **sacrifice of Full Moon**, **in Uruk**, **via Beli-bani**, **in the storehouse**, 2 fattened rams and 1 lamb for **gate of shrine**, 1 lamb for **sacrifice of disappearing place of Nanaya**, 1 kid for **weeping and going around city**, 1 kid for **the day when raising up the zí-na siege weapon**, 1 fattened ram for **gate of bedroom of high priestess**, 1 fattened ram and 1 lamb for **temple of Nanaya**, **via my queen**, **in Uruk**, **withdrawn from Beli-ṭab fattener**.Month of ezem-Ninazu, Year that of wall of land was built.	1只育肥公绵羊为**粮仓的牺牲的月供**, 1只育肥公绵羊为**伊南那的吉腊努姆仪式**,1只育肥公绵羊和1只育肥公山羊为**贝拉特苏赫尼尔和贝拉特达腊班的牺牲**,2只育肥公绵羊和1只食草公绵羊为**满月牺牲**,于**乌鲁克**,**经由贝里巴尼**,**于仓库**,2只育肥公绵羊和1只羔为**神殿门**,1只羔为**那那亚消失处牺牲**,1只公崽为**围绕城市哭泣的仪式**,1只公崽为**举起围攻城市的武器之时**,1只育肥公绵羊为**祭司寝宫**,1只育肥公绵羊和1只羔为**那那亚庙**,**经由我的王后**,**于乌鲁克**,从**育肥师贝里沓卜支出了**。神宁阿朱庆典月,国家城墙被建立年。
Š 37 v: **zi-ga** 1 kid for **temple of Nin-igi-zibarra**, **via Ur-Dumuzida**, in **Uruk**, 2 kids for **giranum of temple of Belat-Suhnir**, **via Apiliya**, 2 fat rams, 2 rams, 2 kids for **temple of Belat-Suhnir**, **via my queen**, 1 fat bull, 3 fat rams, 6 rams, 1 kid **for the provisions of Simat-Ea**, when she feed the dinner house in **Ur**, were **withdrawn from Beḷitab**	1 máš, é-^{d}**Nin-igi-zi-bar-ra**, gìr**Ur-**^{d}**Dumu-zi-da**, šà **Unug^{ki}**-ga, 2 máš, ***gi-ra-núm*** *é-*^{d}***Be-la-at-Suh$_6$-nir***, *gìr* ***Á-pi$_5$-lí-a***, 2 *udu-niga*, 2 *udu gud-e-ús-sa*, 2 *máš*, *é-*^{d} ***Be-la-at-Suh$_6$-nir***, *gìr* **nin-ĝá**, 1 gud-niga, 3 udu-niga, 6 udu-ú, 1 máš, **igi-kár *Simat-É-a***, **ud~ é-níĝ bí-gu$_7$-a**, **šà~ Urim^{ki}**-ma, zi-ga-***Be-lí- ṭab***. *iti-ezem* ^{d}*Nin -a-zu*, *mu bàd ma-da ba-dù-a.* (*SET* 042, *P*129452)	1 *kid for***the temple of Nin-igi-zibarra**, **via Ur-Dumuzida**, in **Uruk**, 2 kids for **the giranum festival of the temple of Belat-Suhnir**, **via Apiliya**, 2 fattened rams, 2 rams of the after ox class, 2 kids for **the temple of Belat-Suhnir**, **via my queen**, 1 fattened bull, 3 fattened rams, 6 grass rams, 1 kid **for the provisions of Simat-Ea**, when she feed the dinner house in **Ur**, were **withdrawn from Beḷitab**. Month of ezem-Ninazu, Year that of wall of the land was built.	1公崽为**宁伊吉兹巴腊庙**,**经由乌尔杜穆兹达**于**乌鲁克**,2公崽为**贝拉特苏赫尼尔庙的吉腊努姆仪式**,**经由阿皮里亚**,2育肥公绵羊、2牛后级公绵羊、2公崽为**贝拉特苏赫尼尔庙**,**经由我的王后**,1头肥公牛、3只育肥公绵羊、6只食草公绵羊和1只公崽为**美埃阿的供奉**,当她在供应饭厅时,**于乌尔**,以上**从贝里沓卜支出了**。神宁阿朱庆典月,国家城墙被建立年。

续表

时间和摘要	文献内容	英文翻译	中文翻译
Š 37 v: **mu-túm，ì-dab** 1 fat bull，1 bull，6 fattened rams，2 rams of after ox class，8 grass rams and 4 kids from **the sister of Danniya**，were deliveries for Šulgi-simtum，**Beli-ṭab fattener took over**	1 gud-niga，1 gud-ú，6 udu-niga， 2 udu，gud-e-ús-sa，8 udu-ú， 4 máš-gal，**nin$_9$-*Dan-ni-a***， *mu-túm-^{d}* ***Šul-gi-sí-im-tum-ma***，***Be-lí-ṭàb*** gurušda ì-dab$_5$.iti-ezem-^{d}Nin-a-zu，mu bàd ma-da ba-dù-a. （OIP 115025，P123319）	1 fattened bull，1 grass bull，6 fattened rams，2 rams of after ox class，8 grass rams and 4 kids from **the sister of Danniya**，were deliveries for Šulgi-simtum，**Beli-ṭab fattener took over**. Month of ezem-Ninazu，Year that of wall of the land was built.	1头育肥公牛、1头食草公牛、6只育肥公绵羊和2只牛后级公绵羊，8只食草公绵羊和4只公崽来自**丹尼亚之妹**，为舒勒吉新吞的送入项，**育肥师贝里杳卜接管**了。神宁阿朱庆典月，国家城墙被建立年。
Š 37 v/7: **zi-ga** 2 fat rams for **monthly allowance**，1 fat lamb for **wife of Danniya**，1 fat ram for **sacrifice of Allatum**，1 fat ram，1 kid for **temple of Alla-gula**，2 fat rams，1 lamb for **temple of Ninlil**，1 fat ram，1 kid for **temple of Enlil**，1［fat］ram of after-ox-class for **temple of Nin-egiya**，，**in Nippur**，<u>**via my queen**</u>，were **withdrawn from Beli-ṭab fattener**	2 udu-niga，**sá-dug$_4$**， 1 sila$_4$-niga mu～**dam-*Dan-ni-a*--šè**，1 *udu-niga*， **siskúr-^{d}*Al-la-tum***， 1 *udu-niga*，1 *máš*，*é*-**^{d}Al-la-gu-la**， 2 udu-niga，1 sila$_4$，é-**^{d}Nin-líl-lá**， 1 udu-niga，1 máš，**é-^{d}En-líl-lá**， 1 udu-<niga>-gud-e-ús-sa，é-**^{d}Nin-é-gi$_4$-a**， **ès-ès-é-ud-7**，šà～**Nibru^{ki}**， <u>**gìr～ nin-ĝá**</u>， zi-ga***Be-lí-ṭàb*** *gurušda.* *iti-ezem-^{d}Nin-a-zu*， *mu bàd-ma-da ba-dù-a.* （*CST*044，*P*107556）	2 *fattened rams for***monthly allowance**，1 fattened lamb for **wife of Danniya**，1 fattened ram for **sacrifice of Allatum**，1 fattened ram，1 kid for **the temple of Alla-gula**，2 fattened rams，1 lamb for **the temple of Ninlil**，1 fattened ram，1 kid for **the temple of Enlil**，1［fat］ram of after-ox-class for **the temple of Nin-egiya**，when festival of the 7th day of Moon，**in Nippur**，<u>**via my queen**</u>，were **withdrawn from Beli-ṭab fattener**.Month of ezem-Ninazu，Year that of wall of the land was built.	2只育肥公绵羊为**月供**，1只育肥羊羔为**丹尼亚之妻**，1只育肥公绵羊为**阿拉吞女神祭祀**，1只育肥公绵羊和1只公崽为**阿拉古拉女神**，1只育肥公绵羊和1只羊羔为**宁里勒神庙**，1只育肥公绵羊和1只公崽为**恩里勒神庙**，1只牛后级育肥公绵羊为**宁埃吉亚**，**初七上弦月**，于**尼普尔**，<u>**经由我的王后**</u>，从**育肥师贝里杳卜支出**。神宁阿朱庆典月，国家城墙被建立年。

续表

时间和摘要	文献内容	英文翻译	中文翻译
Š 37 vi: zi-ga 4 fat flocks, 1 ram for boat of An, 1 fat ram for temple of Nanaya, 1 fat ram for "night staying shrine", 1 lamb for sacrifice of disappearing place of Nanaya, 2 rams and 1 kid for sacrifice of New Moon, in Uruk, via Apillati, 1 fat ram for giranum festival of Inanna, 2 fat rams for allowance of sacrifice of Belat-S. and Belat-D., 1 lamb for the offering of disappearing place of palace, 1 for [...], 1 fat ram for sacrifice of Nanna, Ur-Dumuzi as deputy, withdr.fr. Beli-ṭab fattener, in storehouse	1 gud-niga, 3 udu-niga, 1 udu-ú, má-an-na-šè, 1 udu-niga é-^{d}Na-na-a, 1 udu-nigaèš~ĝi$_6$-zal-šè, 1 sila$_4$ níĝ-ki-zàh é-^{d}Na-na-a, 2 udu-gud-e-ús-sa, 1 máš, [sis] kúr-ud-sakar, šà~ Unug^{ki}-ga, gìr *Á-pil-la-ti*, 1 *udu-niga*sá-dug$_4$ *gi-ra-núm*-^{d}Inanna, 2 udu-nigasá-dug$_4$ siskúr-^{d}*Be-la-at-Suh-nir* ù ^{d}*Be-la-at-Dar-ra-ba-an*, 1 *sila$_4$* níĝ-ki-zàh, šà~ é-gal-la, 1 sila$_4$^{d} [...] -x, 1 udu-niga siskúr-^{d} Nanna, Ur-^{d}Dumu-zi maš [ki] m, zi-ga *Be-lí-ṭàb gurušda*, *šà é-sag-da-na.iti-á-ki-ti*, *mu bàd ma-da ba-dù*. (*AnOr* 07 062, *P*101357)	1 *fattened bull*, 3 *fattened rams*, 1 *grass ram for*boat of An, 1 fattened ram for temple of Nanaya, 1 fattened ram for "night staying shrine", 1 lamb for sacrifice of disappearing place of temple of Nanaya, 2 rams of after-ox-class and 1 kid for sacrifice of New Moon, in Uruk, via Apillati, 1 fattened ram for allowance of giranum festival of Inanna, 2 fattened rams for allowance of sacrifice of Belat-Suhnir and Belat-Darraban, 1 lamb for the offering of disappearing place of palace, 1 lamb for [...], 1 fattened ram for sacrifice of Nanna, Ur-Dumuzi as royal deputy, withdrawn from Beli-ṭab fattener, in the storehouse. Month of akiti, Year that of wall of land was built.	1育肥牛、3育肥公绵羊和1食草公绵羊为安神的船，1育肥公绵羊为那那亚庙，1育肥公绵羊为黑夜圣殿， 1羔为那那亚庙消失处牺牲，2牛后级公绵羊和1公崽为新月牺牲，于乌鲁克，经由阿皮拉提， 1育肥公绵羊为伊南那的吉腊努姆仪式的月供， 2育肥公绵羊为贝拉特苏赫尼尔和贝拉特达腊班牺牲的月供， 1羔为宫殿的消失处供奉，1羔为【……】，1育肥公绵羊为南那牺牲，乌尔杜姆兹督办， 从贝里耷卜育肥师支出了，于仓库。阿基提月，国家城墙被建立年。
Š 37 vi: zi-ga 1 kid for sacrifice of Nanaya, 1 fat ram for offering of sacrifice of Nanna, Mašum asdeputy, in Tummal, 2 kids for offering of disappearing place of Belat-S. and Belat-D., in Ur, via Beli-bani, withdr.fr. Beli-ṭab fattener	1 máš, siskúr-^{d}Na-na-a, 1 udu-niga, sá-dug$_4$-siskúr-^{d}Nanna, *Ma-šummaškim*, *šà*~ Tum-ma-al, 2 máš, níĝ~ ki-zàh-é-^{d}*Be-la-at-Suh-nir* ù ^{d}Be-la-at-Dar-ra-ba-an, *šà*~ Urim^{ki}-ma, gìr-*Be-lí-ba-ni*, *zi-ga-Be-lí-ṭàb gurušda.iti-á-ki-ti*, *mu bàd ma-da ba-dù*. (*OIP* 115034, *P*123504)	1 *kid for the* sacrifice of Nanaya, 1 fattened ram for the offering of sacrifice of Nanna, Mašum as royal deputy, in Tummal, 2 kids for offering of disappearing place of temple of Belat-Suhnir and Belat-Darraban, in Ur, via Beli-bani, were withdrawn from Beli-ṭab fattener. Month of akiti, Year that of wall of the land was built.	1只公崽为那那亚祭祀， 1只育肥公绵羊为南那祭祀的供奉，马顺督办，于图马勒（尼普尔）， 2只公崽为贝拉特苏赫尼尔和贝拉特达腊班神庙的消失处供奉，于乌尔，经由贝里巴尼， 从育肥师贝里耷卜支出了。阿基提月，国家城墙被建立年。

续表

时间和摘要	文献内容	英文翻译	中文翻译
Š 37 vi: **zi-ga** 1 fat ram for **allowance of sacrifice of Ordeal Divine River**, 1 kid for **giranum festival of Inanna**, 1 fat ram for **allowance of sacrifice of Nin-girla**, **Mašum as deputy**, were **withdrawn from Beli-ṭab**, **the fattener**, **in Tummal**	1 udu-niga**sá-dug$_4$ siskúr-I$_7$-lú-ru-gú**, 1 máš ***gi-ra-núm-*^{d}Inanna** a-rá-1-kam, 1 udu-niga **sá-dug$_4$** siskúr-^{d}Nin-gìr-lá, ***Ma*$^?$*-šum**maškim*, *zi-ga**Be-lí-ṭàb** gurušda*, *šà~ Tum-ma-al^{ki}.iti-á-ki-ti*, *mu bàd ma-da ba-dù*. (*MVN* 03 153, *P*113713)	1 *fattened ram for* **monthly allowance of sacrifice of Ordeal Divine River**, 1 kid for **giranum festival of Inanna** for 1st time, 1 fattened ram for **monthly allowance of sacrifice of Nin-girla**, **Mašum as royal deputy**, were **withdrawn from Beli-ṭab**, **the fattener**, **in Tummal**.Month of akiti, Year that of wall of the land was built.	1只育肥公绵羊为**神判河神牺牲的月供**, 1只公崽为**伊南那的吉腊努姆仪式**第1次, 1只育肥公绵羊为**宁吉尔拉牺牲的月供**, **马顺督办**, 从**育肥师贝里沓卜支出了**，于图马勒。 阿基提月, 国家城墙被建立年。
Š 37 vi: **ì-dab** 1 kid from **the governer of Kazallu**, **Beli-ṭab fattener took over**, in **Tummal**	1 máš **ensí-Ka-zal-lu^{ki}**, ***Be-lí-ṭàb*** *gurušda ì-dab$_5$*, *šà~ Tum-ma-al.iti-á-ki-ti*, *mu bàd ma-da ba-dù*. (*MCS* 7 16 *Liv* 51 63 27, *P*112840)	1 *kid from* **the governer of Kazallu**, **Beli-ṭab fattener took over**, in **Tummal**.Month of akiti, Year of the wall of the land was built.	1只公崽来自**卡扎鲁总督**，**育肥师贝里沓卜接管**了，于**图马勒**。 阿基提月, 国家城墙被建立年。
Š 37? vii: **zi-ga** 1 lamb for **shrine**, 1 kid for **high priestess**, 2 flocks for **Nanaya**, 1 lamb for **Nin-igi-zibar**, **Apillati as deputy**, 1 ram for **Full Moon**, in **Uruk**, **Beli-bani as deputy**, **withdr.fr.Beli-ṭab**	1 sila$_4$, **ká~èš**, 1 máš **ká~ĝi$_6$-par$_4$**, 1 udu, 1 máš, ^{d}**Na-na-a**, 1 sila$_4$^{d} **Nin-igi-zi-bar-ra**, ***Á-pil-la-ti**maškim*, 1 *udu* **siskúr-ud-15**$^!$ šà~ **Unug^{ki}**-ga, ***Be-lí-ba-ni**maškim*, *zi-ga **Be-lí-ṭàb**.iti-ezem-^{d}Šul-gi*. (*AnOr* 07 090, *P*101385)	1 *lamb for***gate of shrine**, 1 kid for **gate of bedroom of high priestess**, 1 ram and 1 kid for **Nanaya**, 1 lamb for **Nin-igi-zibar**, **Apillati as royal deputy**, 1 ram for **sacrifice of Full Moon**, in **Uruk**, **Beli-bani as royal deputy**, were **withdrawn from Beli-ṭab**. Month of ezem-Šulgi.	1只羔为**圣殿门**，1只公崽为**祭司寝宫**，1只公绵羊和1只公崽为**那那亚**，1只羔为**宁伊吉伊兹巴尔**，**阿皮拉提督办**，1只公绵羊为**满月牺牲**，于**乌鲁克**，**贝里巴尼督办**，从贝里沓卜支出了。 舒勒吉庆典月。
Š 37 ix: **ì-dab** 10 fat rams from **monthly allowance of Šulgi-simtum**, **Apliliya took over**	10 udu-niga, **sá-dug$_4$~ ^{d}*Šul-gi-sí-im-tum***, *bala* ^{d}**Ba-[x] -maš**, ***Á-pi$_5$-li-a*** *ì-dab$_5$.iti-ezem-mah*, *mu bàd ma-da ba-dù*. (*Princeton* 1 009, *P*126698)	10 *fattened rams from***monthly allowance of Šulgi-simtum**, in reign of Ba-x-maš, **Apliliya took over**. Month of ezem-mah, Year that of wall of the land was built.	10育肥公绵羊来自**舒勒吉新吞的月供**，于巴-X-马什任职期间，**阿皮里亚接管了**。大庆典月，国家城墙被建立年。

续表

时间和摘要	文献内容	英文翻译	中文翻译
Š 38 ii: **mu-túm, ì-dab** 2 fat rams from **Ilum-bani majordomo**, 1 lamb from **Etel-pu-Dagan**, these were deliveries, **Apiliya took over**	2 udu-niga, ***Ilum-ba-ni*** *šabra*, 1 *sila$_4$*, ***E-te-el-pù-^{d} Da-gan***, *mu-túm* ***Á-pi$_5$-lí-a***, *ì-dab$_5$.iti-ze$_x$-da~gu$_7$*, *mu ús-sa bàd-ma-da ba-dù*. (*Torino* 1 050, *P*132028)	2 *fattened rams from* **Ilum-bani majordomo**, 1 lamb from **Etel-pu-Dagan**, these were deliveries, **Apiliya took** over. Month of zeda~gu$_7$, Year after that of wall of land was bulit.	2只育肥公绵羊来自**庙总管伊隆巴尼**，1只羊羔来**自埃台勒普达干**，这些送入**阿皮里亚接管**了。食豚月，国家城墙被建立年之次年。
Š 38 iv: **mu-túm, ì-dab** 4 grass rams and 1 lamb from**Imi-Sin**, these were delivered, **Apiliya took over**	4 udu-ú, 1 sila$_4$ ***I-mi-^{d}Suen***, *mu-túm* ***Á-pi$_5$-lí-a*** *ì-dab$_5$.iti-ki-siki-^{d}Nin-a-zu*, *mu ús-sa bàd ma-da ba-dù*. (*AnOr* 01 024, P101015)	4 *grass rams and* 1 *lamb from***Imi-Sin**, these were delivered, **Apiliya took over**.Month of ki-siki-Ninazu, Year after that of wall of the land was bulit.	4只食草公绵羊和1只羊羔自**伊米辛**，以上送入**阿皮里亚接管**。宁阿朱羊毛作坊月，国家城墙被建立年之次年。
Š 38 iv: **mu-túm, ì-dab** 8 grass rams, 1 he-goat, 1 kid from**the wife of Pa-nitum**, were deliveries for Šulgi-simtum, **Apilia took**	8 udu-ú, 1 máš-gal, 1 máš, **dam-*Pa-ni-tum***, *mu-túm-**^{d}Šul-gi-sí-im-tum**-ma*, ***Á-pi$_5$-lí-a*** *ì-dab$_5$.iti-ki-siki-^{d}Nin-a-zu*, *mu ús-sa bàd-ma-da ba-dù*. (*PDT* 2 0994, *P*126340)	8 *grass rams*, 1 *he-goat*, 1 *kid from***the wife of Pa-nitum**, were deliveries for Šulgi-simtum, **Apilia took over**.Month of ki-siki-Ninazu, Year after that of wall of the land was bulit.	8食草公绵羊、1公山羊和1公崽来自**帕尼吞之妻**，为舒勒吉新吞送入项，**阿皮里亚接管**。神宁阿朱羊毛作坊月，国家城墙被建立年之次年。
Š 38 iv: **mu-túm, ì-dab** 15 ducksfrom the **daughter of Ur-niĝar**, 30 doves were delivered by **A-x-na**, these were deliveries for Šulgi-simti, **Apiliya took over**	15 uz-tur, mu-túm-**dumu-munus-Ur-ni$_9$-ĝar**, 30 tu-gur$_4$-<mušen>, mu-túm-**A-x-na**, mu-túm-***^{d}Šul-gi-sí-im-ti***, ***Á-pi$_5$-lá-a*** *ì-dab$_5$.iti-ki-siki-^{d}Nin-a-zu*, *mu ús-sa bàd-ma-da ba-dù*. (*TCS* 358, *P*132143)	15 *ducks were delivered by the***daughter of Ur-niĝar**, 30 doves were delivered by **A-x-na**, these were deliveries for Šulgi-simti, **Apiliya took over**.Month of ki-siki-Ninazu, Year after that of wall of the land was bulit.	15只鸭子由**乌尔尼旮尔之女**运送，30只野鸽子由**A-x-na**运送，以上送入给舒勒吉新提，**阿皮里亚接管**了。神宁阿朱羊毛作坊月，国家城墙被建立年之次年。
Š 38 iv: **mu-túm, ì-dab** 3 pigeons from**Barbarniya**, these were brought in, **Apiliya took over**	3 ir$_7$^{mušen}, ki~ ***Bar-bar-ni-a--ta***, *mu-túm* ***Á-pi$_5$-lí-a*** *ì-dab$_5$.iti-ki-siki-^{d}Nin-a-zu*, *mu ús-sa bàd-ma-da ba-dù-a*. (*OIP* 115035, *P*123706)	3 *pigeons from***Barbarniya**, these were brought in, **Apiliya took over**. Month of ki-siki-Ninazu, Year after that of wall of the land was bulit.	3只家鸽来自**巴尔巴尔尼亚**，这些送入**阿皮里亚接管**了。神宁阿朱羊毛作坊月，国家城墙被建立年之次年。

续表

时间和摘要	文献内容	英文翻译	中文翻译
Š 38 iv: **zi-ga，butchered** 3 **butcherd** doves were sent to the palace，were **withdrawn from Apiliya**	3 tu-gur$_4$^{mušen} ~ ba-úš，**é-gal-la** ba-an-ku$_4$，zi-ga ***Á-pi$_5$-lí-a***.*iti-ki-siki-^{d}Nin-a-zu*，*mu ús-sa bàd-ma-da ba-dù.* （*Torino* 1 179，*P*133897）	3**butchered** doves were sent to palace，withdrawn **from Apiliya**. Month of ki-siki-Ninazu，Year after that of wall of the land was bulit.	3只宰杀的野鸽被送入到宫殿，从**阿皮里亚支出**了。神宁阿朱羊毛作坊月，国家城墙被建立年之次年。
Š 38 v: **mu-túm，ì-dab** 11 ducks and 3 white ducks fr.**son of Ur-niĝar**，3 pigeons fr.**arbarliya**，were deliveries for Šulgi-simtum，**Apiliya took over**	11 uz-tur，3 uz-babbár，**dumu-Ur-niĝar**，3 ir$_7$（KASKAL）^{mušen} ***Bar-bar-lí-a***，*mu-túm*~ ***^{d}Šul-gi-sí-im-tum***，***Á-pi$_5$-lí-a*** *ì-dab$_5$.iti-ezem ^{d}Nin-a-zu*，*mu ús-sa bàd ma-da ba-dù.*（*NYPL* 105，*P*122641）	11 *ducks and* 3 *white ducks from***the son of Ur-niĝar**，3 pigeons from **Barbarliya**，were deliveries for Šulgi-simtum，**Apiliya took over**.Month of ezem-Ninazu，Year after that of wall of the land was bulit.	11只鸭和3只白鸭来自**乌尔尼旮尔之子**，3只家鸽来自**巴尔巴尔里亚**，为舒勒吉新吞的送入项，**阿皮里亚接管**了。神宁阿朱庆典月，国家城墙被建立年之次年。
Š 38 v: **mu-túm，ì-dab** 2 fat-tailed rams，2 kids，1 kid from **Ur-kununna**，were deliveries for Šulgi-simtum，**Apiliya took over**	2 gukkal，2 máš，1 ^{f}ašgar，**Ur-kug-nun-na**，mu-túm-^{d} ***Šul-gi-sí-im-tum***，***Á-pi$_5$-lí-a*** ì-dab$_5$. iti-ezem-^{d}Nin-a-zu，mu ús-sa bàd-ma-da ba-dù （SACT 1 055，P128810）	2 fat-tailed rams，2 kids，1 female kid from **Ur-kununna**，were deliveries for Šulgi-simtum，**Apiliya took over**.Month of ezem-Ninazu，Year after that of wall of the land was bulit.	2肥尾公绵羊、2公崽和1雌山羊崽来自**乌尔库农那**，为舒勒吉新提的送入项，**阿皮里亚接管**了。神宁阿朱庆典月，国家城墙被建立年次年。
Š 38 v: **mu-túm，ì-dab** 2 lamb from**Ninlil-tum-imti**，were deliveries for Šulgi-simti，**Apiliya took ove**	2 sila$_4$^{d} ***Nin-líl-tu*** ［*m*］***-im-ti***，*mu-túm-^{d}* ***Šul-gi-sí-im-ti***，***Á-pi$_5$-lí-a*** *ì-dab$_5$.iti-ezem-^{d}Ni*［*n-a-zu*］，*mu ú*［*s-sa bàd-ma*］*-d*［*a ba-dù*］. （*Torino* 1 044，*P*133852）	2 *lamb from***Ninlil-tum-imti**，were deliveries for Šulgi-simti，**Apiliya took over**.Month of ezem-Ninazu，Year after that of wall of the land was bulit.	2只羊羔来自**宁里勒图米姆提**，为舒勒吉新提的送入项，**阿皮里亚接管**了。神宁阿朱庆典月，国家城墙被建立年之次年。
Š 38 v: **zi-ga，butchered** 2**butchered** doves sent to the palace，were **withdrawn from Apiliya**	2 tu-gur$_8$^{mušen} ~ **ba-úš，é-gal-la ba-an-ku$_4$**，zi-ga-***Á-pi$_5$-lí-a***.*iti-ezem ^{d}Nin-a-zu*，*mu ús-sa bàd ma-da ba-dù.* （*OIP* 115 046，*P*123414）	2**butchered** doves sent to the palace，were **withdrawn from Apiliya**.Month of ezem-Ninazu， Year after that of wall of the land was bulit.	2只宰杀的野鸽被送入宫殿，从**阿皮里亚处支出**了。神宁阿朱庆典月， 国家城墙被建立年之次年。
Š 38 v: **zi-ga，butchered** 1**butchered** pigeon sent to the palace，was **withdrawn from Apiliya**	1 ir$_7$^{mušen}~ **ba-úš，é-gal-la ba-an-ku$_4$**，zi-ga-***Á-pi$_5$-lí-a***.*iti-ezem-^{d}Nin-a-zu*，*mu ús-sa-bàd-ma-da ba-dù.* （*Torino* 1 180，*P*133898）	1**butchered** pigeon sent to the palace，was **withdrawn from Apiliya**.Month of ezem-Ninazu， Year after that of wall of the land was bulit.	1只宰杀的家鸽被送入宫殿，从**阿皮里亚支出**了。 神宁阿朱庆典月， 国家城墙被建立年之次年。

续表

时间和摘要	文献内容	英文翻译	中文翻译
Š 38 vi： **mu-túm，ì-dab** 1 lamb from**Puzur-Ištar，in Kisurra，** was deliveries for Šulgi-simti，**Apiliya took over**	[1] sila$_4$，Puzur-Iš$_8$-tár，šà ~ Ki-sur-ra^{ki}-ka，mu-túm-^{d} ***Šul-gi-sí-im-ti***，***Á-pi$_5$-lí-a*** ì-dab$_5$. *iti-á-ki-ti*，*mu ús-sa bàd-ma-da ba-dù*.（*OIP* 115 036，*P*123514）	1 *lamb from***Puzur-Ištar，in Kisurra，** was deliveries for Šulgi-simti，**Apiliya took over**. Month of akiti，Year after that of wall of the land was bulit.	1只羊羔来**自普朱尔伊什塔尔于基苏腊**，为舒勒吉新提的送入项，**阿皮里亚接管**了。阿基提月，国家城墙被建立年之次年。
Š 38 vi： **mu-túm，ì-dab** 31 [pigeons]，…，15 doves from **Adanah，the bird-catcher**，were deliveries for Šulgi-simti，**Apiliya took**	31 [ir$_7$]^{mušen}，SAG? x x x，15 tu-gur$_4$^{mušen}，***A-da-na-ah*** *mušen-dù*，*mu-túm* ~ ^{d}***Šul-gi-sí-im-ti***，***Á-pi$_5$-lí-a*** *ì-dab$_5$.iti á-ki-ti*，*mu ús-sa bàd ma-da ba-dù*.（*AnOr* 01 001，*P*100992）	31 [*pigeons*]，…，15 *doves from* **Adanah，the bird-catcher**，were deliveries for Šulgi-simti，**Apiliya took over.** Month of akiti， Year after that of wall of the land was bulit.	31只【家鸽】……15只野鸽自**捕鸟人阿达那赫**，以上为舒勒吉新提的送入项，**阿皮里亚接管**了。阿基提月，国家城墙被建立年之次年。
Š 38 vii： **mu-túm，ì-dab** 10 grass rams from**Panitum**，2 rams and 1 kid from **Eani**，2 rams and 1 kid from **Barbarliya**，2 rams and 1kid from **Enlil-Išag**，2 lambs from **Te ṣ in-Mama**，were brought for Šulgi-simti，**Apiliya took over**	10 udu-ú ***Pa-ni-tum***，2 *udu*，1 *máš* **É-a-a-ni**，2 udu，[1] máš，***Bar-bar-lí-a***，2 *udu*，1 *máš*，^{d}**En-líl-ì-šag$_5$**，2 sila$_4$ ***Te-ṣ i-en$_6$-ma-ma***，*mu-túm-*^{d} ***Šul-gi-sí-im-tum-ma***，*šà Tum-ma-al^{ki}*，***Á-pi$_5$-lí-a*** *ì-dab$_5$.iti-ezem-^{d}Šul-gi*，*mu ús-sa bàd ma-da ba-dù*. （*NYPL* 235，*P*122773）	10 *grass rams from***Panitum**， 2 rams and 1 kid from **Eani**， 2 rams and 1 kid from **Barbarliya**，2 rams and 1kid from **Enlil-Išag**， 2 lambs from**Te ṣin-Mama**， were brought forŠulgi-simti，**Apiliya took over**. Month of ezem-Šulgi， Year after that of wall of the land was bulit.	10只食草公绵羊自**帕尼吞**，2只公绵羊和1只公崽自**埃阿尼**，2只公绵羊和1只公崽自**巴尔巴尔里亚**，2只公绵羊和1只公崽自**恩里勒伊沙格**，2只羊羔自**台岑妈妈**，**为舒勒吉新提的送入项**，**阿皮里亚接管**了。舒勒吉庆典月，国家城墙被建立年之次年。
Š 38 viii： **mu-túm，ì-dab** 1 fat bull，1 bull，6 fat rams，6 rams，3 bulls，1 lamb，5 kids，fr. **wife of Šu-Šamaš**，1 ram，1 lamb fr. **Larabum herdsman**，1 ram，1 lamb fr. **Imid-ilim herdsman，the overseer：Šukubum animal officer**， were deliveries for Šulgi-simti， **Apiliya took over**	1 gud-niga，1 gud-ú，6 udu-niga，6 udu，3 gud，1 sila$_4$，3 ^{f}áš-gàr，2 máš，**dam-Šu-^{d}Šamš**， 1 udu，1 sila$_4$，***La-ra-bu-um*** **na-gada**， 1 udu，1 sila$_4$，***I-mi-id-ilim***，*na-gada*， *ugula****Šu-ku$_8$-bu-um***，*šùš*（*kuš$_7$*）*mu-túm* ~ ^{d}***Šul-gi-sí-im-ti***，***Á-pi$_5$-lí-a*** *ì-dab$_5$.iti-šu-eš$_5$-ša*，*mu ús-sa bàd ma-da ba-dù*. （AnOr 7 042，P101337）	1 fattened bull，1 grass bull，6 fattened rams，6 rams，3 bulls，1 lamb，3 female kids，2 kids from**the wife of Šu-Šamaš**，1 ram，1 lamb from **Larabum herdsman**，1 ram，1 lamb from **Imid-ilim herdsman，the overseer：Šukubum animal officer**， were deliveries for Šulgi-simti，**Apiliya took over**. Month of šu-eššа，Year after that of wall of the land was bulit.	1育肥公牛、1食草公牛、6育肥公绵羊、6公绵羊、3公牛、1羊羔、3雌崽和2公崽来自**舒沙马什妻**，1公绵羊、1羊羔来自**牧羊人拉腊布姆**，1公绵羊、1羊羔来自**牧羊人伊米德伊里姆**，**监工为舒库布姆牲畜官员**，为舒勒吉新提的送入项，**阿皮里亚接管**。三只手月，国家城墙被建立年之次年。

续表

时间和摘要	文献内容	英文翻译	中文翻译
Š 38 viii： **mu-túm，ì-dab** 4 fat rams，1 lamb fr.**Utu-ellat**i general，deliveries for Šulgi-simti，**Apiliya took**	4 udu-niga，1 sila$_4$，^{d}**Utu-ellati** šagina，mu-túm-^{d}***Šul-gi-sí-im-ti***，***Á-pi$_5$-lí-a***，*ì-dab$_5$*. *iti-šu-eš$_5$-ša*，*mu ús-sa bàd ma-da ba-dù*. （*Torino* 1 030，*P*131843）	4 *fattened rams*，1 *lamb from***Utu-ellat**i，general，were deliveries for Šulgi-simti，**Apiliya took over**. Month of šu-eššа，Year after that of wall of the land was bulit.	4 肥公绵羊和 1 羊羔自**乌图埃拉提将**军，为舒勒吉新提的送入项，**阿皮里亚接管**了。三只手月，国家城墙被建立年之次年。
Š 38 viii： **mu-túm，ì-dab** 2 big-tailed rams，1 kid from **Kurrub-Err**a，was deliveries for Šulgi-simti，**Apiliya took**	2 gukkal，1 máš，***Kur-ru-ub-Èr-ra***，*mu-túm-*^{d}***Šul-gi-sí-im-ti***，***Á-pi$_5$-lí-a***，*ì-dab$_5$*. *iti-šu-eš$_5$-ša*，*mu-ús-sa bàd ma-da ba-dù*. （*Torino* 1 029，*P*132042）	2 *big-tailed rams*，1 *kid from* **Kurrub-Err**a，was deliveries for Šulgi-simti，**Apiliya took over**. Month of šu-eššа，Year after that of wall of the land was bulit.	2 肥尾公羊和 1 公崽来自**库尔如卜埃尔腊**，为舒勒吉新提的送入项，**阿皮里亚接管**了。三只手月，国家城墙被建立年之次年。
Š 38 viii： **zi-ga，butcherd** 2 doves were sent to the palace，**withdr.fr.Apiliya**	2 tu-gur$_4$^{mušen} **ba-úš，é-gal-la，ba-an-ku$_4$**，zi-ga-***Á-pi$_5$-lí-a***. *iti-šu-eš-ša*，*mu ús-sa bàd-ma-da ba-dù*.（*OIP* 115 046，*P*123414）	2**butchered** doves were sent to the palace，**with-drawn from Apiliya**. Month of šu-eššа，Year after that of wall of the land was bulit.	2 只宰杀的野鸽被送入宫殿，从**阿皮里亚支出**了。三只手月，国家城墙被建立年之次年。
Š 38 viii： **zi-ga** 1 fattened kid for**food of Ea-niša（priestess of Šulgi）**，was **withdrawn from Apiliya**	1 máš-niga，**níĝ-gu$_7$-*É-a-ni-ša*--šè**，*zi-ga* ***Á-pi$_5$-lí-a***. *iti-šu-eš-ša*， *mu ús-sa bàd-ma-da ba-dù*. （*OIP* 115047，*P*123667）	1 *fattened kid for***food of Ea-niša（priestess of Šulgi）**，was **withdrawn from Apiliya**. Month of šu-eššа，Year after that of wall of land was bulit.	1 育肥公崽为**埃阿尼沙（舒勒吉祭司妻子）的食物**，从**阿皮里亚支出**了。三只手月，国家城墙被建立年之次年。
Š 38 viii： **zi-ga，butchered** 3 fat ducks，4 fat pigeons，10 fat doves for **food of my queen，**1 **butchered** duck，4 **butchered** pigions were **sent to the palace**，were **withdrawn from Apiliya**	3 uz-tur-niga，4 ir$_7$（kaskal）^{mušen}-niga，10 tu-gur$_4$^{mušen}-niga，**níĝ-gu$_7$-nin-ĝá**--šè，1 uz-tur-ba-úš，4 ir$_7$^{mušen}-ba-úš，é-gal-la ba-an-ku$_4$，zi-ga ***Á-pi$_5$-lí-a***. *iti-šu-eš-ša*，*mu ús-sa bàd-ma-da ba-dù*. （*OIP* 115048，*P*123680）	3 *fattened ducks*，4 *fattened pigeons*，10 *fattened doves for***the food of my queen，**1 butchered duck，4 butchered pigions were **sent to the palace**，were **withdrawn from Apiliya**. Month of šu-eššа，Year after that of wall of the land was bulit.	3 只育肥鸭子、4 只育肥家鸽、10 只育肥野鸭**为我的王后的食物**， 1 只宰杀的鸭子、4 只宰杀的家鸽**被送入宫殿**，以上从**阿皮里亚支出**了。三只手月，国家城墙被建立年之次年。
Š 38ix： **mu-túm，ì-dab** 10 ducks from **Watrat**，were deliveries for Šulgi-simti，in the center of **Ur**，**Apiliya took**	10 uz-tur ***Wa-at-ra-at***，*mu-túm-*^{d} ***Šul-gi-sí-im-ti***，*šà* **Urim^{ki}**-ma，***Á-pi$_5$-lí-a*** *ì-dab$_5$*. *iti-ezem-mah*，*mu ús-sa bàd ma-da ba-dù*. （*BIN* 3 001，*P*105808）	10 *ducks from* **Watrat**，were deliveries for Šulgi-simti，in the center of **Ur**，**Apiliya took over**. Month of ezem-mah，Year after that of wall of the land was bulit.	10 只鸭子来自**瓦特腊特**，为舒勒吉新提的送入项，于**乌尔**中，**阿皮里亚接管**了。大庆典月，国家城墙被建立年之次年。

续表

时间和摘要	文献内容	英文翻译	中文翻译
Š 38 x: **mu-túm, ì-dab** 5 rams, 1 lamb fr. **mother of Šu-Idim**, 4 rams, 1 lamb fr. **wife of Imi-Sin**, 1 ram, 2 kids fr. **Garaya**, were deliveries for Šulgi-simti, **in journey**, **Apiliya took over**	5 udu, 1 sila$_4$, **ama-Šu-^{d}Idim**, 4 udu, 1 sila$_4$, ***dam-I-mi-^{d}Suen***, 1 *udu*, 2 *máš*, ***Ga-ra-a***, *mu-túm-*^{d}***Šul-gi-sí-im-ti***, *šà kaskal-la*, ***Á-pil-lí-a*** *ì-dab$_5$*. *iti-ezem-an-na*, *muús-sa bàd ma-da ba-dù*. (*AnOr* 07 153, *P*101448)	5 *rams*, 1 *lamb from***the mother of Šu-Idim**, 4 rams, 1 lamb from the **wife of Imi-Sin**, 1 ram, 2 kids from **Garaya**, were deliveries for Šulgi-simti, **in the journey**, **Apiliya took over**. Month of ezem-Anna, Year after that of wall of the land was bulit.	5公绵羊和1羔来自**舒伊邓之母**，4公绵羊和1羊羔来自**伊米辛妻**，1公绵羊和2公崽自**旮腊亚**，为舒勒吉新提的送入项，**于旅途中**，**阿皮里亚接管**了。天神安庆典月，国家城墙被建立年之次年。
Š 38 x: **mu-túm, ì-dab** 2 rams, 1 kid from **Addatur**, 1 kid from **Šulbalaya**, **in Uruk**, 2 rams, 1 kid from **Niridagal**, **in the big orchard**, 2 rams, 1 kid from **Luduggala**, in **Ka-id of Isin**, were deliveries for Šulgi-simtum, **Apiliya took over**	2 udu, 1 máš, **Ad-da-tur**, 1 máš, ***Šul-ba-la-a***, *šà* ~ **Unug**^{ki}-ga, 2 udu, 1 máš, **Nir-ì-da-gál**, šà ~ giš-kiri$_6$-mah, 2 udu, 1 máš, **Lú-dùg-ga-la**, **Ka-íd-Ì-si-[i] n^{ki}**, mu-túm ~ ^{d}***Šul-gi-sí-im-tum****-ma*, ***Á-pi$_5$-lí-a*** ì-dab$_5$. iti-ezem-an-na, mu ús-sa bàd ma-da ba-dù. (MVN02 167, P113466)	2 rams, 1 kid from **Addatur**, 1 kid from**Šulbalaya**, **in Uruk**, 2 rams, 1 kid from**Niridagal**, **in the big orchard**, 2 rams, 1 kid from**Luduggala**, in **Ka-id of Isin**, were deliveries forŠulgi-simtum, **Apiliya took over**. Month of ezem-Anna, Year after that of wall of the land was bulit.	2只公绵羊和1只公崽来自**阿达图尔**，1只公崽来自**舒勒巴拉亚于乌鲁克**，2只公绵羊和1只公崽来自**尼瑞达旮勒**，于**大椰枣园**中，2只公绵羊和1只公山羊来自**鲁杜格旮拉**，于**卡伊德伊辛**，为舒勒吉新提的送入项，**阿皮里亚接管**了。天神庆典月，国家城墙被建立年之次年。
Š 38 xi: **mu-túm, ì-dab** 2 bulls, 7 rams, 3 kids fr. **wife of Tabbadarah**, 2 rams, 1 kid fr. **son of Zuzaya**, 3 rams, 2 kids fr. **brother of majordomo**, 1 lamb from **Tezin-Mama**, were deliveries for Šulgi-simtum, **Apiliya took over**	2 gud-ú, 7 udu-ú, 3 máš, dam-***Tab-ba-da-ra-ah***, 2 *udu*, 1 *máš*, *dumu*-***Zu-za-a***, 3 *udu*, 2 *máš*, **šeš šabra**, 1 sila$_4$ ***Te-zí-in-Ma-ma***, *mu-túm-*^{d}***Šul-gi-sí-im-ti***, ***Á-pi$_5$-lí-a*** *ì-dab$_5$*. *iti-ezem-me-ki-ĝál*, *muús-sa bàd ma-da ba-dù*. (*AnOr* 07 040, *P*101335)	2 *grass bulls*, 7 *grass rams*, 3 *kids from* **the wife of Tabbadarah**, 2 rams, 1 kid from **the son of Zuzaya**, 3 rams, 2 kids from **the brother of ma-jordomo**, 1 lamb from **Tezin-Mama**, were deliveries for Šulgi-simtum, **Apiliya took over**. Month of ezem-Mekiĝal, Year after that of wall of the land was bulit.	2只食草公牛、7只食草公绵羊、3只公崽自**塔巴达腊赫**，2只公绵羊、1只公崽自**朱扎亚之子**，3只公绵羊、2只公崽来自**庙总管之兄**，1只羊羔来自**台岑妈妈**，为舒勒吉新提的送入项，**阿皮里亚接管**了。神美基旮勒庆典月，国家城墙被建立年之次年。

续表

时间和摘要	文献内容	英文翻译	中文翻译
Š 38 xi： **zi-ga** 1 fat ram for **the devastation sacrifice of temple of Allagula，withdrawn from Apiliya，in Nippur**	1 udu-niga，**a-igi-nigín-na**，*é-^{d}Al-la-gu-la*， *zi-ga* ***Á-pi$_5$-lí-a***，*šà~* **Nib-ru^{ki}**.iti-ezem-Me-ki-ĝál， muús-sa bàd ma-da ba-dù. （JEOL 26 51 13，P112276）	1 fattened ram for**the devastation sacrifice of temple of Allagula，withdrawn from Apiliya，in Nippur**.Month of ezem -Mekiĝal，Year after that of wall of the land was bulit.	1只育肥公绵羊为**阿拉古拉庙的毁坏祭**， 从**阿皮里亚支出了**， **于尼普尔**。 神美基旮勒庆典月， 国家城墙被建立年次年。
Š 38 xi： **zi-ga** 1 fat ram，2 lambs for **food of my queen**，**Ur-Dumuzida as royal deputy**，1 corpse of lamb for **the soldier of king**，**withdrawn from Apiliya**，**in the journey**	1 udu-niga，a-rá-1-a-kam，1 sila$_4$，a-rá-2-a-kam，1 sila$_4$，a-rá-3-a-kam，**níg-gu$_7$-nin-ĝá**--šè，**Ur-^{d}Dumu-zi-da** maškim，1 ad$_6$-sila$_4$，mu agà-ús **lugal**--ka--šè，zi-ga ***Á-pi$_5$-lí-a***，**šà~ kaskal-la**.iti-ezem-me-ki-ĝál，mu ús-sa bàd ma-da ba-dù. （Ontario 1 014，P124427）	1 fattened ram on the 1st time，1 lamb on the 2nd time，1 lamb on the 3rd time for the **food of my queen**，**Ur-Dumuzida as royal deputy**，1 corpse of lamb for **the soldier of king**，were **withdrawn from Apiliya**，**in the journey**. Month of ezem-Mekiĝal，Year after that of wall of the land was bulit.	1只育肥公绵羊第1次，1只羊羔第2次，1只羊羔第3次为**我的王后的食物**，**乌尔杜穆兹达督办**，1只羊羔死尸为**国王的士兵**，以上从**阿皮里亚支出了**，**于旅途中**。 神美基旮勒庆典月， 国家城墙被建立年次年。
Š 38 xii： **mu-túm，ì-dab** 2 grass rams，1 kid from**Išdum-kin**， were deliveries forŠulgi-simtum，**Apiliya took**	2 udu-ú，1 máš，***Išdum-ki-in***，*mu-túm-^{d}* ***Šul-gi-sí-im-ti***， ***Á-pi$_5$-lí-a*** *ì-dab$_5$*. *iti-še-kin-kud*，*mu ús-sa bàd-ma-da ba-dù.* （*Torino* 1 031，*P*132002）	2 *grass rams*，1 *kid from***Išdum-kin**， were deliveries forŠulgi-simtum，**Apiliya took over**. Month of še-kin-kud，Year after that of wall of the land was bulit.	2只食草公绵羊和1只公崽来自**伊什杜姆金**，为舒勒吉新提的送人项，**阿皮里亚接管**了。大麦收割月，国家城墙被建立年次年。
Š 38 xii： **zi-ga** 2 grass rams for**the priest of Belat-Suhnir**，were withdrawn from **Apiliya**	2 udu-ú，gúda（gudug）***^{d}Be-la-at-Suh-nir***，zi-ga ***Á-pi$_5$-lí-a***.*iti-še-kin-kud*，*mu ús-sa bàd-ma-da ba-dù.* （*OIP* 115049，*P*123239）	2 *grass rams for***the priest of Belat-Suhnir**，were withdrawn from **Apiliya**.Month of še-kin-kud，Year after that of wall of the land was bulit.	2只食草公绵羊为**贝拉特苏赫尼尔女神的祭司**，从**阿皮里亚支出**。大麦收割月，国家城墙被建立年次年。

续表

时间和摘要	文献内容	英文翻译	中文翻译
Š 38 xii -Š 39 i: (**zi-ga**) 3 sheep, 2 fat rams, 3 goats for offering of **Belat-Suhnir and Annunitum**, **month of še-kin-kud**; 3 fat rams, 1 sheep, 1 fat kid for **offering of month of Belat-Suhnir and Annunitum**	3 udu-u$_8$, 2 udu-niga, 3 ud$_5$, **sá-dug$_4$-^{d}*Be-la-at-Suh-ni-ir* ù *An-nu-ni-tum***, *iti-še-kin-kud*; 3 *udu-niga*, 1 *udu-u$_8$*, 1 *máš-niga*, **sá-dug$_4$-iti-^{d}*Be-la-at-Suh-ni-ir* ù An-nu-ni-tum**. *iti-maš-dà ~ gu$_7$*, *mu É-Puzr$_4$-iš-^{d}Da-gan ba-dù.* (*OIP* 115050, *P*123307)	3 *sheep*, 2 *fattened rams*, 3 *she-goats for the offering of* **Belat-Suhnir and Annunitum**, **month of še-kin-kud**; 3 fattened rams, 1 sheep, 1 fattened kid for **offering of month of Belat-Suhnir and Annunitum**.**month of maš-dà ~ gu$_7$**, Year that of the office of Puzriš-Dagan was built.	3只绵羊、2只育肥公绵羊和3只母山羊为**贝拉特苏赫尼尔和安努尼吞**于大麦收割月; 3只育肥公绵羊、1只羊和1只育肥山羊崽为**贝拉特苏赫尼尔和安努尼吞之月的供奉**。食瞪羚月,普兹瑞什达干司被建之年。
Š 39 i: **mu-túm, ì-dab** 1 piglet for**daughter's nursemaid from Eteal-pu-Dagan**, 2 doves from**Riqmu-ša**, were deliveries for Šulgi-simtum/ti, **Apiliya took**	1 šáh^{zah}-tur, eme-da (**um -me-da**) **-dumu-mí**, ***E-te-al-pù-^{d} Da-gan***, 2 *tu-gur$_4$^{mušen}*, ***Ri-iq-mu-ša***, *mu-*[*túm*] ~ **^{d}Šu** [***l-gi-sí***] ***-im-t*** [***um/ti***], ***Á-pi$_5$-lí-a***, *ì-dab$_5$.iti-maš-dà ~ gu$_7$*, *mu ús-sa bàd-ma-da ba-dù mu-ús-sa-bi.* (*Torino* 1 032, *P*133844)	1 *piglet for***daughter's nursemaid from Eteal-pu-Dagan**, 2 doves from**Riqmu-ša**, were deliveries for Šulgi-simtum/ti, **Apiliya took over**.Month of mašda ~ gu$_7$, Year after that of the wall of the land was built.	1头猪崽为**女儿的奶妈(或保姆)**来自**埃台阿勒普达干**,2只野鸽来自**瑞喀穆沙**,为舒勒吉新提的送入项,**阿皮里亚接管**了。食瞪羚月,国家城墙被建立年之次年:之次年。
Š 39 i: **zi-ga, butchered** 4 doves for 1st time, 1 fattened duck, 1 dove for 2nd time, 1 dove for 3rd time, **butchered ones, were sent to the palace**, 1 fattened duck, 3 fattened doves for **the food of my queen**, were **withdrawn from Apiliya**	4 tu-gur$_4$-mušen, a-rá-1-kam, 1 uz-tur-niga, 1 tu-gur$_4$-mušen, a-rá-2-kam, 1 tu-gur$_4$-mušen, a-rá-3-kam, **ba-úš é-gal-la ba-an-ku$_4$**, 1 uz-tur-niga, 3 tu-gur$_4$-mušen-niga, **ud~ dab$_5$-ba**, níĝ-kú-**nin-ĝá**--šè, zi-ga-***Á-pi$_5$-lí-a***.*iti-maš-dà ~ gu$_7$*, *mu ús-sa bàd-ma-da ba-dù mu-ús-sa-bi.* (*OIP* 115051, *P*123314)	4 *doves for 1st time*, 1 *fattened duck*, 1 *dove for 2nd time*, 1 *dove for 3rd time*, **butchered ones, were sent to the palace**, 1 fattened duck, 3 fattened doves, when were took over, for **the food of my queen**, were **withdrawn from Apiliya**. Month of mašda ~ gu$_7$, Year after that of the wall of the land was built.	4只野鸽第一次,1只育肥鸭子和1只野鸽第二次,1只野鸽第三次,**这些宰杀牲被送入宫殿**,1只育肥鸭子和3只育肥野鸽于接管之时为**我的王后的食物**,以上从**阿皮里亚支出**了。食瞪羚月,国家城墙被建立年之次年:之次年。
Š 39 ii: **mu-túm, ì-dab** 1 kid fr. 1 female kid from **Te ṣ in-Mama**, 2 fattened rams from the **king**, **Apiliya took**	1^{f}ašgar, ***Te-ṣ i-in-^{d} Ma-ma***, 2 *udu-niga*, *ki ~ lugal--ta*, ***Á-pi$_5$-lí-a***, *ì-dab$_5$.iti-ze$_x$-da ~ gu$_7$*, *mu é-Puzri$_4$-iš-^{d} Da-gan ba-dù.* (*Torino* 1 051, *P*132004)	1 *female kid from* **Te ṣ in-Mama**, 2 fattened rams from the **king**, **Apiliya took over**.Month of zeda ~ gu$_7$, Year that of the office of Puzriš-Dagan was built.	1只雌羊羔崽来自**台岑妈妈**,2只育肥公绵羊来自**国王**,**阿皮里亚接管**了。食豚月,普兹瑞什达干司被建之年。

续表

时间和摘要	文献内容	英文翻译	中文翻译
Š 39 iii: **mu-túm, ì-dab** 6 pigeons from**Barbarliya**, were deliveries for Šulgi-simti, **Apiliya took over**	6ir$_{7}^{mušen}$ **Bar-bar-lí-a**, *mu-túm-^{d}* ***Šul-gi-sí-im-ti***, ***Á-pi$_{5}$-lí-a*** *ì-dab$_{5}$. iti-u$_{5}$-bí-gu$_{7}$, mu é-Puzr$_{4}$-iš-^{d} Da-gan ba-dù.* (*MVN* 03 161, *P*113721)	6 *pigeons from***Barbarliya**, were deliveries for Šulgi-simti, **Apiliya took over**.Month of ubi-gu$_{7}$, Year that of the office of Puzriš-Dagan was built.	6只家鸽来自**巴尔巴尔里亚**，为舒勒吉新提的送入项，**阿皮里亚接管**了。食乌比乌月，普兹瑞什达干司被建之年。
Š 39 iii: **mu-túm, ì-dab** 3 lambs, 1 kid from**Te ṣin-Mama**, were deliveries for Šulgi-simti, **Apiliya took**	3 sila$_{4}$, 1 máš, ***Te-ṣi-en$_{6}$-ma-ma***, *mu-túm-^{d}****Šul-gi-sí-im-ti***, ***Á-pi$_{5}$-lí-a*** *ì-dab$_{5}$. iti-u$_{5}$-bí-gu$_{7}$, mu é-Puzr$_{4}$-iš-^{d} Da-gan ba-dù.* (*MVN* 03 162, *P*113722)	3 *lambs*, 1 *kid from***Te ṣin-Mama**, were deliveries for Šulgi-simti, **Apiliya took over**. Month of ubi-gu$_{7}$, Year that of the office of Puzriš-Dagan was built.	3只羊羔和1只公崽来自**台岑妈妈**，为舒勒吉新提的送入项，**阿皮里亚接管**了。食乌比乌月，普兹瑞什达干司被建之年。
Š 39 iii: **mu-túm, ì-dab** 1 ducklet fr. female musician **Enni-ya**, 10 pigeons for 1st time, 15 birds for 2nd time, fr.**Ur-Ninmug**, 3 doves, 1+ tu-birds fr. [**Šu**] -^{d}**Šamaš**, were deliveries for Šulgi-simti, **Apiliya took over**	1 amar-sag~ uz-tur, **En-ni-a**, nar-mí, 10 ir$_{7}^{mušen}$, a-rá-1-kam, 15 tu-mušen, a-rá-2-kam, **Ur-^{d}Nin-mug**, 3 tu-gur$_{4}$-mušen, 1+ tu^{mušen}, [Šu] -^{d}**Šamaš**, mu-túm-^{d}***Šul-gi-sí-im-ti***, ***Á-pi$_{5}$-lí-a*** *ì-dab$_{5}$. iti-u$_{5}$-bí-gu$_{7}$, mu É-Puzr$_{4}$-iš-^{d} Da-gan ba-dù.* (*OIP* 115037, *P*123578)	1 *ducklet from***Enni-ya**, the female musician, 10 pigeons for 1st time, 15 birds for 2nd time, from **Ur-Ninmug**, 3 doves, 1+ tu-birds from [**Šu**] -^{d}**Šamaš**, were deliveries forŠulgi-simti, **Apiliya took over**. Month of ubi-gu$_{7}$, Year that of the office of Puzriš-Dagan was built.	1只幼鸡来自**女乐师恩尼亚**， 10只家鸽第一次，15只鸟第二次，来自**乌尔宁穆格**，3只野鸽、1+只tu鸟来自【**舒**】**沙马什**， 以上为舒勒吉新提的送入项，**阿皮里亚接管**了。食乌比乌月，普兹瑞什达干司被建之年。
Š 39 iii: **zi-ga, butchered** 1 white duck and 2 doves, **butchered ones were sent to palace**, **withdr.fr.Apiliya**	1 uz-bar$_{6}$-bar$_{6}$, 2 tu-gur$_{4}$-mušen, ba-úš, é-gal-la ba-an-ku$_{4}$, zi-ga-***Á-pi$_{5}$-lí-a***. *iti-u$_{5}$-bí-gu$_{7}$, mu É-Puzr$_{4}$-iš-^{d} Da-gan ba-dù.* (*OIP* 115052, *P*123465)	1 *white duck and 2 doves*, **butchered ones were sent to the palace**, **withdrawn from Apiliya**. Month of ubi-gu$_{7}$, Year that of office of Puzriš-Dagan was built.	1只白鸭和2只野鸽，为**宰杀牲被送入宫殿**，从**阿皮里亚支出**了。食乌比乌月，普兹瑞什达干司被建之年。
Š 39 iii: **zi-ga** 1 fat pigeon for **food of my queen**, was sent to the palace, **withdrawn from Apiliya**	1 ir$_{7}^{mušen}$-niga, **níĝ-gu$_{7}$-nin-ĝá**--šè, é-gal-la, ba-an-ku$_{4}$, zi-ga-***Á-pi$_{5}$-lí-a***.*iti-u$_{5}$-bí-gu$_{7}$,* *mu É-Puzr$_{4}$-iš-^{d}Da-gan ba-dù.* (*OIP* 115053, *P*123560)	1 *fattened pigeon for***food of my queen**, was sent to the palace, **withdrawn from Apiliya**.Month of ubi-gu$_{7}$, Year that of the office of Puzriš-Dagan was built.	1只育肥家鸽为**我的王后的食物**，被送入宫殿，从**阿皮里亚支出**了。食乌比乌月，普兹瑞什达干司被建之年。

续表

时间和摘要	文献内容	英文翻译	中文翻译
Š 39 iii: **zi-ga, corpse** 1 corpse of lamb for**weaver women**, 1corpse of fat lamb for **weaver women**, in **Kiš**, **overseer: Guzide**, 1 fat lamb for **food of my queen**, **withdr. from Apiliya**	1 ad$_6$-sila$_4$, mu ~ **gemé-úš-bar-e-ne**--šè, 1 ad$_6$-sila$_4$-niga, mu ~ **gemé-úš-bar-e-ne**--šè, Kiš^{ki}--šè, ugula Gù-zi-dé, 1 sila$_4$-niga, **níĝ-gu$_7$-nin-ĝá**--šè, zi-ga-***Á-pi$_5$-lí-a***. *iti-u$_5$-bí-gu$_7$*, *mu É Puzr$_4$-iš-^{d}Da-gan ba-dù.* (*CST*045, P107557)	1 *corpse of lamb for***weaver women**, 1corpse of fattened lamb for **weaver women**, in **Kiš**, **the overseer: Guzide**, 1 fattened lamb for **the food of my queen**, were **withdrawn from Apiliya**. Month of ubi-gu$_7$, Year that of the office of Puzriš-Dagan was built.	1 只羊羔尸体为**编织女工**，1 只育肥羊羔尸体为**编织女工**，于**基什**，**监管者是古孜戴**，1 只育肥羊羔**为我的王后的食物**，以上从**阿皮里亚支出**。食乌比乌月，普兹瑞什达干司被建之年。
Š 39 iv/6: **mu-túm, ì-dab** 1 bird from **the man of Urub**, 58 doves from **Tezen-Mama**, 2 pigeons from **Barbarliya**, when the 6th day passed, were deliveries for Šulgi-simti, **Apiliya took over**	1 tu^{mušen}, lú-Urub (URUxKÁR)^{ki}, 60 lá 2 tu-gur$_4$^{mušen}, ***Te-ṣ í-en$_6$-Ma-ma***, 2 *ir$_7$^{mušen}* ***Bar-bar-lí-a***, *iti--ta ud-6-ba-ra-zal*, *mu-túm-*^{d} ***Šul-gi-sí-im-ti***, ***Á-pi$_5$-lí-a*** *ì-dab$_5$*. *iti-ki-siki-^{d}Nin-a-zu*, *mu é-Puzur$_4$-iš-^{d}Da-gan ba-dù.* (*AUCT* 1 952, P103797)	1 *bird from* **the man of Urub**, 58 doves from **Tezen-Mama**, 2 pigeons from **Barbarliya**, when the 6th day passed, were deliveries for Šulgi-simti, **Apiliya took over**. Month of ki-siki-Ninazu, Year that of the office of Puzriš-Dagan was built.	1 只鸟来自**乌如卜城的人**，58 只野鸽来自**台岑妈妈**，2 只家鸽来自**巴尔巴尔里亚**，于第 6 天过去时，为舒勒吉新提的送入项，**阿皮里亚接管**了。神宁阿朱羊毛作坊月，普兹瑞什达干司被建之年。
Š 39 iv: **mu-túm, ì-dab** 3 grass rams and 1 lamb from**Imi-Sin**, 2 grass rams and 1 kid from **Garaya**, 1.female kid from **the man of Urub**, 1 lamb fr.**Madati**, 1 kid fr.**wife of x**, were deliveries for Šulgi-simtum, **Apiliya took**	3 udu-ú, 1 sila$_4$, ***I-mi-^{d}Sîn***, 2 *udu-ú*, 1 *máš*, ***Ga-ra-a***, *^{1}ašgar*, *lú-Urub* (*URUxKÁR*)^{ki}, 1 *sila$_4$*, ***Ma-da-ti***, 1 *máš*, *dam-* [..] *-da*, [⋯], *mu-túm-*^{d}***Šul-gi-sí-im-tum***, ***Á-pi$_5$-lí-a*** *ì-dab$_5$*. *iti-ki-siki-^{d}Nin-a-zu*, *mu É-Puzr$_4$-iš-^{d}Da-gan ba-dù.* (*CST*046, P107558)	3 *grass rams and* 1 *lamb from***Imi-Sin**, 2 grass rams and 1 kid from **Garaya**, 1 female kid from**the man of Urub**, 1 lamb from **Madati**, 1 kid from the **wife of x**, were deliveries for Šulgi-simtum, **Apiliya took over**. Month of ki-siki-Ninazu, Year that of the office of Puzriš-Dagan was built.	3 食草公绵羊和 1 羔来自**伊米辛**，2 食草公绵羊和 1 公崽来自**旮腊亚**，1 只雌羊羔崽来自**乌如卜城的人**，1 只羊羔来自**马达提**，1 只公崽来自 x **之妻**，以上为舒勒吉新提的送入项，**阿皮里亚接管**了。神宁阿朱羊毛作坊月，普兹瑞什达干司被建之年。
Š 39 iv: **mu-túm, ì-dab** 1 lamb and 1 kid from**Watrat empress overseer**, were deliveries for Šulgi-simtum, **Apiliya took over**	1 sila$_4$, 1 máš, ***Wa-at-ra-at*** *ugula*, *mu-túm-*^{d}***Šul-gi-sí-im-ti***, **Á-pi$_5$-lí-a** *ì-dab$_5$*. *iti-ki-siki-^{d}Nin-a-zu*, *mu É-Puzr$_4$-iš-^{d}Da-gan ba-dù.* (*SACT* 1 056, P128811)	1 *lamb and* 1 *kid from***Watrat empress overseer**, were deliveries for Šulgi-simtum, **Apiliya took over**.Month of ki-siki-Ninazu, Year that of the office of Puzriš-Dagan was built.	1 羔和 1 公崽自**瓦特腊特（王太后）监工**，为舒勒吉新提送入项， **阿皮里亚接管**。 宁阿朱羊毛作坊月，普兹瑞什达干司被建之年。

续表

时间和摘要	文献内容	英文翻译	中文翻译
Š 39 iv/12，14，15： **zi-ga，butchered** 1 **butchered** pigeon，3 **butchered** doves，**were sent to palace**，1 white duck **for the food of my queen**，1 **butchered** white duck，1 **butchered** tu-bird were **sent to the palace**，were **withdrawn from Apiliya**	1 ir$_7$^{mušen}-ba-úš，3 tu-gur$_4$^{mušen}-ba-úš，iti--ta **ud-12** ba-ra-zal，**é-gal-la，ba-an-ku$_4$**，1 uz-bar$_6$-bar$_6$，iti--ta **ud-14** ba-ra-zal，**níĝ-gu$_7$-nin-ĝá**--šè，1 uz-bar$_6$-bar$_6$-ba-úš，1 tu^{mušen}-ba-úš，iti--ta **ud-15** ba-ra-zal，**é-gal-la ba-an-ku$_4$**，zi-ga-***Á-pi$_5$-lí-a***. *iti-ki-siki-^{d}Nin-a-zu*，*mu É-Puzr$_4$-iš-^{d}Da-gan ba-dù*. （*OIP* 115 054，*P*123356）	1 **butchered** pigeon，3 **butchered** doves，when **12th** day passed，**were sent to palace**，1 white duck，when **14th** day passed，**for food of my queen**，1 **butchered** white duck，1 **butchered** tu-bird，when **15th** day passed，were **sent to palace**，**withdrawn from Apiliya**. Month of ki-siki-Ninazu，Year that of the office of Puzriš-Dagan was built.	1只宰杀的家鸽和3只宰杀的野鸽于**13日**过去时**被送入宫殿**，1只白鸭子于14日过去时为**我的王后的食物**，1只**宰杀的**白鸭子和1只**宰杀的**tu鸟于**15日**过去时**被送入宫殿**，以上从**阿皮里亚支出**了。神宁阿朱羊毛作坊月，普兹瑞什达干司被建之年。
Š 39 iv/17，19： **zi-ga，butchered** 1**butchered** pigeon，1 **butchered** dove，1 **butchered** duck，were **sent to the palace**，were **withdrawn from Apiliya**	1 ir$_7$^{mušen}～ ba-úš，1 tu-gur$_4$^{mušen}～ ba-úš，iti--ta **ud-17** ba-ra-zal，1 uz-tur-ba-úš，iti--ta **ud-19** ba-ra-zal，**é-gal-la** ba-an-ku$_4$，zi-ga-***Á-pi$_5$-lí-a***. *iti-ki-siki-^{d}Nin-a-zu*，*mu É-Puzr$_4$-iš-^{d}Da-gan ba-dù*. （*Torino* 1 181，*P*133899）	1**butchered** pigeon，1 **butchered** dove，when **17th** day passed，1 **butchered** duck when **19th** day passed，were **sent to the palace**，**withdrawn from Apiliya**. Month of ki-siki-Ninazu，Year that of the office of Puzriš-Dagan was built.	1只**宰杀的**家鸽和1只**宰杀的**野鸽于第**17天**过去时，1只**宰杀**鸭于第**19天**过去时，以上**被送入宫殿**，从**阿皮里亚支出**了。神宁阿朱羊毛作坊月，普兹瑞什达干司被建之年。
Š 39 iv/28-30： **mu-túm，ì-dab** 4 doves when**from Imi-Sin**，6 pigeons from **Barbarniya**，2 pigeons when 30th day passed from **La-Ea**，were deliveries for Šulgi-simtum，**Apiliya took over**	4 tu-gur$_4$^{mušen}，iti--ta **ud-28** ba-ra-zal，***I-mi-^{d}Sîn***，6 *ir$_7$^{mušen}*，*iti--ta* **ud-29** ba-ra-zal，***Bar-bar-ni-a***，2 *ir$_7$^{mušen}*，*iti--ta* **ud-30** ba-ra-zal，**La-^{d}É-a**，mu-túm-^{d}***Šul-gi-sí-im-tum**-ma*，***Á-pi$_5$-lí-a*** *ì-dab$_5$*. *iti-ki-siki-^{d}Nin-a-zu*，*mu É-Puzr$_4$-iš-^{d}Da-gan ba-dù*.（*OIP* 115 038，*P*123701）	4 *doves when* 28th *day passed* **from Imi-Sin**，6 pigeons when 29th day passed from **Barbarniya**，2 pigeons when 30th day passed from **La-Ea**，were deliveries for Šulgi-simtum，**Apiliya took over**. Month of ki-siki-Ninazu，Year that of the office of Puzriš-Dagan was built.	4只野鸽于第**28天**过去时来自**伊米辛**，6只家鸽于第**29天**过去时来自**巴尔巴尔尼亚**，2只家鸽于第**30天**过去时来自**拉埃阿**，以上为舒勒吉新提的送入项，**阿皮里亚接管**了。神宁阿朱羊毛作坊月，普兹瑞什达干司被建之年。

续表

时间和摘要	文献内容	英文翻译	中文翻译
Š 39 v: **mu-túm, ì-dab** 1 lamb from**Puzur-Ištar**, 1 female kid from **the man of Urub**, 1 ram from **Admu hersman**, 1 ram from **Nidaga hersman**, 1 kid from **Ur-mes hersman**, 1 lamb from **Lugal-ezem-šuš**, deliveries forŠulgi-simti, **Apiliya took over**	1 sila$_4$ ***Puzur$_4$-Iš$_4$-tár***, 1^f*ašgar lú-Urub* (*URUxKÁR*)^{ki}, 1 *udu***Ad$_6$-mu** na-gada, 1 udu***Ni-da-ga*** *na-gada*, 1 *máš***Ur-mes** na-gada, 1 sila$_4$, **Lugal-ezem-šuš**, mu-túm-***^{d}Šul-gi-sí-im-ti***, ***Á-pi$_5$-lí-a*** *ì-dab$_5$.iti-ezem-^{d}Nin-a-zu*, *mu É-Puzr$_4$-iš-^{d}Da-gan ba-dù.* (*AnOr* 07 003, *P*101298)	1 *lamb from***Puzur-Ištar**, 1 female kid from **the man of Urub**, 1 ram from **Admu hersman**, 1 ram from **Nidaga hersman**, 1 kid from **Ur-mes hersman**, 1 lamb from **Lugal-ezem-šuš**, deliveries forŠulgi-simti, **Apiliya took over**. Month of ezem-Ninazu, Year that of the office of Puzriš-Dagan was built.	1只羔自**普朱尔伊什塔尔**，1雌崽自**乌如卜城的人**，1只公绵羊自**牧羊人阿德穆**，1只公绵羊自**牧羊人尼达旮**，1只公崽自**牧羊人乌尔美斯**，1只羊羔自**卢旮勒埃载姆舒什**，为舒勒吉新提送人项，**阿皮里亚接管**。神宁阿朱庆典月，普兹瑞什达干司被建之年。
Š 39 v/5: **zi-ga** 1 fattened duck**the supplies of Ṣiluš-Dagan** (gov.of Simurrum), **withdr.fr.Apiliya**	1 uz-tur-niga, iti--ta ud-5 ba-ra-zal, **igi-kár-*Ṣi-lu-uš-^{d}Da-gan***, *zi-ga-**Á-pi$_5$-lí_a.*** *iti-ezem-^{d}Nin-a-zu, mu é-Puzr$_4$-iš-^{d}Da-gan ba-dù.* (*OIP* 115055, *P*123475)	1 *fattened duck when* 5th *day passed for* **the supplies of Ṣ iluš-Dagan** (gov. of Simurrum), **withdrawn from Apiliya**. Month of ezem-Ninazu, Year that of the office of Puzriš-Dagan was built.	1只育肥鸭子于第5天过去时为**采鲁什达干（席穆润的总督）**，**从阿皮里亚支出了**。神宁阿朱庆典月，普兹瑞什达干司被建之年。
Š 39 v/17, 18: **zi-ga, butchered** […] for **food of my queen**, **withdr.fr.Apiliya**, 1 fattened duck, for the **food of my queen**, 1 **butchered** pigeon was **sent to the palace**, 5 fattened doves for the **food of my queen**, 1 **butchered** pigeon was **sent to the palace**, 1 fattened duck for the **food of my queen**	[…] **níĝ-gu$_7$-nin-** [**ĝá**--šè], zi-ga- ***Á-pi$_5$-lí-a***, *iti-ezem-^{d}Nin-a-zu* 1 *uz-tur-niga*, *iti--ta* **ud-17**-ba-ra-zal, **níĝ-gu$_7$-nin-ĝá**--šè, 1 ir$_7$^{mušen} ba-úš, iti--ta ud-17-ba-ra-zal, **é-gal -la ba-an-ku$_4$**, 5 tu-gur$_8$^{mušen}-niga, **níĝ-gu$_7$-nin -ĝá**--šè, 1 ir$_7$^{mušen}ba-úš, iti--ta **ud-18**-ba-ra-zal, **é-gal-la ba-an-ku$_4$**, 1 uz-tur-niga, **níĝ-gu$_7$-nin-ĝá**--šè.mu é-Puzr$_4$-iš-^{d}Da-gan ba-dù. (Babyl.8 HG 08, P104805)	[…] for the **food of my queen**, **withdrawn from Apiliya**, month of ezem-Ninazu, 1 fattened duck, when **17th** day passed, for the **food of my queen**, 1 **butchered** pigeon when **17th** day passed was **sent to the palace**, 5 fattened doves for the **food of my queen**, 1 **butchered** pigeon when **18th** day passed was **sent to the palace**, 1 fattened duck for **food of my queen**. Year that of office of Puzriš-Dagan was built.	**【……】**为**我的王后的食物**，**从阿皮里亚支出了**。神宁阿朱庆典月，1只育肥鸭于第**17天**过去时为**我的王后的食物**，1只**宰杀的家鸽**于第17天过去时**被送入宫殿**，5只育肥野鸽为**我的王后的食物**，1**宰杀的家鸽**于第**18天**过去时**被送入宫殿**，1育肥鸭为**我的王后的食物**。普兹瑞什达干司被建之年。

续表

时间和摘要	文献内容	英文翻译	中文翻译
39 v，vi： （**zi-ga**） 4 rams，3 ewes，1 sheared lamb；1 goats，1 sheared lamb，2 rams，4 goats **for allowance of Belat-Suhnir，Belat-Darraban，Annunitum and Ulmašitum**	4 udu-nitá，3 u$_{8}$，1 kir$_{11}$-ur$_{4}$，iti-ezem-^{d}Nin-a-zu； 1 ud$_{5}$，1 kir$_{11}$-ur$_{4}$，2 udu-nitá，4 máš-gal，iti-á-ki-ti，**sá-dug$_{4}$-^{d} *Be-la-at-Suh-nir*，^{d}Be-la-at-Dar-ra-ba-an，*An-nu-ni-tum* ù ^{d}*Ul-ma-ši-tum*.** *mu É-Puzr$_{4}$-iš-* ［^{d}］ *Da-*［*gan*］ *ba-dù.*（*Aegyptus* 19 236 04，*P100226*）	*4 rams*，*3 ewes*，*1 sheared lamb*，**month of ezem-Ninazu；** 1 she-goats，1 sheared lamb，2 rams，4 he-goats，**month of akiti，for the monthly allowance of Be-lat-Suhnir，Belat-Darraban，Annunitum and Ulmašitum.** Year that of the office of Puzriš-Dagan was built.	4只公绵羊、3只母绵羊和1只剪毛羔，**神宁阿朱庆典月**；1只母山羊、1只剪毛羔、2只公绵羊和4只公山羊，**阿基提月，为贝拉特苏赫尼尔、贝拉特达腊班、安努尼吞和乌勒马席吞的月供**。普兹瑞什达干司被建之年。
Š 39 vi/2： **zi-ga** 1 duck，6 dovesfor **the food of my queen**，were **withdrawn from Apiliy**	1 uz-tur，6 tu-gur$_{4}$^{mušen}，iti--ta ud-2 ba-ra-zal，［**níĝ**］-**gu$_{7}$-nin-ĝá**--šè，zi-ga-***Á-pi$_{5}$-lí-a***.*iti-á-ki-ti*，*mu É-Puzr$_{4}$-iš-^{d}Da-gan ba-dù.* （*Hirose* 015，*P109486*）	*1 duck*，*6 doves*，*when the 2nd day passed*，*for* **the food of my queen**，were **withdrawn from Apiliya.** Month of akiti，Year that of the office of Puzriš-Dagan was built.	1只鸭和6只野鸽于第2天过去时为**我的王后的食物**，从**阿皮里亚支出**了。阿基提月，普兹瑞什达干司被建之年。
Š 39 vi/14： **zi-ga** 1 pigeon and 3 doves when the 14th day passed for **the food of my queen**，were **withdrawn from Ap-iliya**	1ir$_{7}$^{mušen}，3 tu-gur$_{5}$^{mušen}， iti--ta ud-14 ba-ra-zal，**níĝ-gu$_{7}$-nin-ĝá**--šè zi-ga-***Á-pi$_{5}$-lí-a***.*iti-á-ki-ti*，*mu é-Puzr$_{4}$-iš-^{d}Da-gan ba-dù.* （*Ontario* 1 015，*P124428*）	*1 pigeon and 3 doves when the 14th day passed for* **the food of my queen**，were **withdrawn from Apiliya.** Month of akiti， Year that of the office of Puzriš-Dagan was built.	1只家鸽和3只野鸽于第14天过去时为**我的王后的食物**，从**阿皮里亚支**出了。阿基提月，普兹瑞什达干司被建之年。
Š 39 vi/15： **ì-dab$_{5}$** 130 fat rams and 30 goats of balance of account，from place of **En-diĝir-mu**， **Apiliya took**	130 udu-niga，30 máš-gal，si-ì-tum níg-ka$_{9}$-ak，ki～ **En-Diĝir-mu**--ta，iti--ta ud-15 ba-ra-zal，***Á-pi$_{5}$-lí-a*** *ì-dab$_{5}$.iti-á-ki-ti*，*mu é-Puzr$_{4}$-iš-^{d}Da-gan ba-dù.* （*MVN* 08 004，*P115395*）	130 *fattened rams and* 30 *he-goats of balance of ac-count*，*from place of***En-diĝir-mu**，when 15th day passed，**Apiliya took over.** Month of akiti，Year that of the office of Puzriš-Dagan was built.	130只育肥公绵羊和30只公山羊的账目平衡，来**自恩迪弥尔处**，于本月第15日过去时，**阿皮里亚接管**了。阿基提月，普兹瑞什达干司被建之年。

续表

时间和摘要	文献内容	英文翻译	中文翻译
Š 39 vi/30: **zi-ga** 2 fattened rams, 1 grass ram for**sacrifice of New Moon in Uruk, via Šulgi-Utu-igim**u, when 30th day passed, **were withdrawn from Apiliya**	2 udu-niga, 1 udu-ú, **siskúr sag-ud-sakar** šà ~ **Unug**^{ki}-ga, gìr-^{d}**Šul-gi-**^{d}**Utu-igi-mu**, iti--ta ud-30 ba-ra-zal, zi-ga-***Á-pi₅-lí-a***. *iti-á-ki-ti*, *mué-Puzr₄-iš-*^{d}*Da-gan ba-dù.* (*CST*047, *P*107559)	2 *fattened rams*, 1 *grass ram for***sacrifice of New Moon in Uruk, via Šulgi-Utu-igim**u, when 30th day passed, **were withdrawn from Apiliya**. Month of akiti, Year that of the office of Puzriš-Dagan was built.	2只育肥公绵羊和1只食草公绵羊为**新月的祭祀于乌鲁克，经由舒勒吉乌图伊吉穆**，于第30日过去时，从**阿皮里亚支出了**。阿基提月，普兹瑞什达干司被建之年。
Š 39 vi: **mu-túm, ì-dab₅** 5 grass rams, 1 lamb from**Išdum-kin**, were deliveries for Šulgi-simti, **Apiliya took**	5 udu-ú, 1 sila₄, ***Išdum-ki-in***, *mu-túm-*^{d}***Šul-gi-sím-ti***, ***Á-pi₅-lí-a*** *ì-dab₅. iti-á-ki-ti*, *mu é-Puzr₄-iš-*^{d}*Da-gan ba-dù.* (*Torino* 1 033, *P*133845)	5 *grass rams*, 1 *lamb from***Išdum-kin**, were deliveries for Šulgi-simti, **Apiliya took over**. Month of akiti, Year that of the office of Puzriš-Dagan was built.	5食草公绵羊和1羊羔自**伊什杜姆金**，为舒勒吉新提送入，**阿皮里亚接管**。阿基提月，普兹瑞什达干司被建之年。
Š 39 vii: **mu-túm, ì-dab₅** 5 grass rams, 1 lamb from**Išdum-kin**, were deliveries for Šulgi-simti, **Apiliya took over**	1 gud-ú, 6 udu-ú, 4 máš-gal, **A-ba-**^{d}**En-líl-gin₇**, mu-túm-^{d}***Šul-gi-sí-im-ti***, *šà* ~ **Tum-ma-al-la**^{ki}, ***Á-pi₅-lí-a*** *ì-dab₅. iti-ezem-*^{d}*Šul-gi*, *mu é-Pù-zur₈-iš-*^{d}*Da-gan ba-dù.* (*NYPL* 253, *P*122791)	1 *grass bull*, 6 *grass rams*, 4 *he-goats from Aba-Enlilgin*, *were deliveries for Šulgi-simti*, *in Tummal*, **Apiliya took over**. Month of ezem-Šulgi, Year that of the office of Puzriš-Dagan was built.	1食草公牛、6食草公羊和4公山羊自**阿巴恩里勒艮**，为舒勒吉新提的送入项，于**图马勒**，**阿皮里亚接管**了。舒勒吉庆典月，普兹瑞什达干司被建之年。
Š 39 vii-viii: (**zi-ga**) 6 kids, 6 ewe, 4 rams for **allowance of Belat-Suhnir, Belat-Darraban, Annunitum and Ulmaštum**	2 máš-nita, 2 ^{f}ašgar, 2 u₈, 2 udu-nita, **iti-ezem-**^{d}**Šul-gi**; 4 u₈, 2 udu-nita, 2 ^{f}ašgar, **iti-šu-eš-ša**; sá-dug₄ ^{d}***Be-la-at-Suh-nir***, ^{d} ***Be-la-at-Dar-ra-ba-an***, ***An-nu-ni-tum*** *ù* ^{d}***Ul-ma-ši-tum***, *mu é-Puzur₄-iš-*^{d}*Da-gan ba-dù.* (*TRU* 287, *P*135051)	2 *kids*, 2 *female kids*, 2 *ewe*, 2 *rams*, *month of ezem-Šulgi*; 4 *ewes*, 2 *rams*, 2 *female kids*, *month of šu-ešša*; *for* **the monthly allowance of Belat-Suhnir, Belat-Darraban, Annunitum and Ulmaštum**. Year that of the office of Puzriš-Dagan was built.	2公山羊崽、2母山羊崽、2母山羊和2公山羊舒勒吉庆典月；4母山羊、2公山羊、2母羊崽三只手月；为**贝拉特苏赫尼尔、贝拉特达腊班、安努尼吞和乌勒马席吞月供**。普兹瑞什达干司被建之年。
Š39 vii-viii: **ì-dab₅** 20 rams for**monthly allowance for 2 months, from Imid-Ilum, Apilli took over**	20 udu sá-dug₄, iti-2-kam, ki ~ ***I-mi-id-Ilum***--*ta*, ***Á-pil-lí*** *ì-dab₅. iti-ezem-*^{d}*Šul-gi--ta*, *iti-šu-eš-ša--šè*, *mu é-Puzur₄-iš-*^{d}*Da-gan ba-dù.* (*MVN* 20, 186 *P*143119)	20 *rams for***monthly allowance for 2 months, from Imid-Ilum, Apilli took over**. from month of ezem-Šulgi to month of šu-ešša, Year of the office of Puzriš-Dagan was built.	20只公绵羊为**两个月的月供**，从**伊米德伊隆**处，**阿皮里接管**了。从舒勒吉庆典月到三只手月，普兹瑞什达干司被建之年。

续表

时间和摘要	文献内容	英文翻译	中文翻译
Š 39 viii/16: **mu-túm, ì-dab$_5$** 9 ducks from **Ninlil-tumimti**, were deliveries for Šulgi-simtum, **Apiliya took over**	9 uz-tur, ^{d} ***Nin-líl-tum-im-ti***, *iti--ta-ud-16 ba-ra-zal*, *mu-túm-*^{d}***Šul-gi-sí-im-tum****-ma*, ***Á-pi$_5$-lí-a*** *ì-dab$_5$. iti-šu-eš$_5$-ša*, *mu é-Pù-zur$_8$-iš-^{d}Da-gan ba-dù.* (*PDT* 2 1006, *P*126351)	9 *ducks from* **Ninlil-tumimti**, when 16th day passed, were deliveries for Šulgi-simtum, **Apiliya took over**. Month of šu-ešša, Year that of the office of Puzriš-Dagan was built.	9只鸭子来自宁**里勒吞伊姆提**于第16日过去时，为舒勒吉新提的送入项，**阿皮里亚接管**了。三只手月，普兹瑞什达干司被建之年。
Š 39 viii/25: **mu-túm, ì-dab$_5$** 6 ducks from **Ur-Šulgira**, when 24th day passed, were deliveries for Šulgi-simtum, **Apiliya took over**	6 uz-tur, **Ur-^{d} Šul-gi**-ra, iti--ta ud-25 ba-ra-zal, mu-túm-^{d} ***Šul-gi-sí-im-tum-ma***, ***Á-pi$_5$-lí-a*** *ì-dab$_5$. iti-šu-eš-ša*, *mu é-Puzr$_4$-iš-^{d}Da-gan ba-dù.* (*CST*048, *P*107560)	6 *ducks from* **Ur-Šulgira**, when 24th day passed, were deliveries for Šulgi-simtum, **Apiliya took over**. Month of šu-ešša, Year that of the office of Puzriš-Dagan was built.	6只鸭子来自**乌尔舒勒吉腊**于第24日过去时，为舒勒吉新提的送入项，**阿皮里亚接管**了。 三只手月，普兹瑞什达干司被建之年。
Š 39 viii: **mu-túm, ì-dab$_5$** 2 rams, 1 kid fr. **wife of Danniya**, 1 kid fr. **Izuyarik governer**, deliveries for Šulgi-simtum, **Apiliya took over**	2 udu, 1 máš, **dam-*Dan-ni-a***, 1 *máš*, ***I-zu-a-ri-ik*** *énsi*, *mu-túm-*^{d} ***Šul-gi-sí-im-tum****-ma*, ***Á-pi$_5$-lí-a*** *ì-dab$_5$. iti-šu-eš-ša*, *mu é-Puzr$_4$-iš-^{d}Da-gan ba-dù.* (*CST*049, *P*107561)	2 *rams*, 1 *kid from* **the wife of Danniya**, 1 kid from **Izuyarik governer**, were deliveries for Šulgi-simtum, **Apiliya took over**. Month of šu-ešša, Year that of the office of Puzriš-Dagan was built.	2公绵羊和1公崽自**丹尼亚之妻**，1只公崽来自**伊朱亚瑞克总督**，为舒勒吉新提的送入项，**阿皮里亚接管**了。三只手月，普兹瑞什达干司被建之年。
Š 39 ix/3: **zi-ga** [1+x] pigecns, 2 doves, **butchered ones were sent to the palace**, **withdrawn from Apiliya**	[1+x] ir$_7$^{mušen}, 2 tu-gur$_4$^{mušen}, **ba-úš-úš**, **é-gal-la ba-an-ku$_4$**, iti--ta ud-3 ba-ra-zal, zi-ga-***Á-pi$_5$-lí-a***. *iti-ezem-mah*, *mu é-Puzr$_4$-iš-^{d}Da-gan ba-dù.* (*Princeton* 1 101, *P*126790)	[1+x] *pigeons*, 2 *doves*, **butchered ones were sent to the palace**, when the 3rd day passed, **withdrawn from Apiliya**. Month of ezem-mah, Year that of the office of Puzriš-Dagan was built.	1+x只家鸽和2只野鸽，**这些宰杀牲被送入宫殿**。于第3日过去时，从**阿皮里亚支出**了。 大庆典月，普兹瑞什达干司被建之年。
Š 39 ix/22: **mu-túm, ì-dab$_5$** 12 ducks from **Utu-illat**, when the 22nd day passed, were deliveries for Šulgi-simtum, **Apiliya took over**	12 uz-tur! (GAG), ^{d}**Utu-illat**, iti--ta ud-22 ba-ra! -zal, mu-túm-^{d} ***Šul-gi-sí-im-tum***, ***Á-pi$_5$-lí-a*** *ì-dab$_5$. iti-ezem-mah*, *mu é-Puzr$_4$-iš-^{d} Da-gan ba-dù.* (*SumTemDocs*.04, *P*130531)	12 *ducks from* **Utu-illat**, when the 22nd day passed, were deliveries for Šulgi-simtum, **Apiliya took over**. Month of ezem-mah, Year that of the office of Puzriš-Dagan was built.	12只鸭来自**乌图伊拉特**，于第22日过去时，为舒勒吉新提的送入项，**阿皮里亚接管**了。大庆典月，普兹瑞什达干司被建之年。
Š 39 ix/29: **mu-túm, ì-dab$_5$** 4 birds were deliveries for Šulgi-simtum, **Apiliya took over**	4 uz-tur^{mušen}-dù-ne, iti--ta ud-29 ba-ra-zal, mu-túm-^{d} ***Šul-gi-sí -im-tum****-ma*, ***Á-pi$_5$-lí-a*** *ì-dab$_5$. iti-ezem-mah*, *mu é-Puzr$_4$-iš-^{d} Da-gan ba-dù.* (*OIP* 115 039, P123513)	4 *birds when* 29th *day passed*, *were deliveries for Šulgi-simtum*, **Apiliya took over**. Month of ezem-mah, Year that of the office of Puzriš-Dagan was built.	4只鸟于第29天过去时为舒勒吉新提的送入项，**阿皮里亚接管**了。大庆典月，普兹瑞什达干司被建之年。

续表

时间和摘要	文献内容	英文翻译	中文翻译
Š 39 ix： **mu-túm，ì-dab$_5$** 1 grass bull，1 grass rams and 3 kids from**the wife of Dakiki**，were deliveries for Šulgi-simtum，**Apiliya took**	1 gud-ú，7 udu-ú，3 máš，**dam-*Da-ki-ki***，*mu-túm-^{d}* ***Šul-gi-sí-im-ti***，***Á-pi$_5$-lí-a*** *ì-dab$_5$. iti-ezem-mah*，*mu É-Puzr$_4$-iš-^{d}Da-gan ba-dù.* （*OIP* 115 040，*P*123644）	1 *grass bull*，1 *grass rams and* 3 *kids from***the wife of Dakiki**，were deliveries for Šulgi-simtum，**Apiliya took over.**Month of ezem-mah，Year that of the office of Puzriš-Dagan was built.	1 头食草公牛、1 只食草公绵羊和 3 只公崽来自**达基基之妻**，为舒勒吉新提的送入项，**阿皮里亚接管**了。大庆典月，普兹瑞什达干司被建之年。
Š 39 x： **mu-túm，ì-dab$_5$** 1 lamb and 1 kid from**Te ṣ in-Mama**，were delivered for Šulgi-simti，**Apiliya took**	1 sila$_4$，1 máš，***Te-ṣí-in-Ma-ma***，*mu-túm~* ***^{d}Šul-gi-sí-im-ti***，***Á-pi$_5$-lí-a*** *ì-dab$_5$. iti-ezem-An-na*，*mu é-Puzur$_4$-iš-^{d} Da-gan ba-dù.* （*Princeton* 2 018，*P*201016）	1 *lamb and* 1 *kid from***Te ṣ in-Mama**，were delivered for Šulgi-simti，**Apiliya took over.** Month of ezem-Anna，Year that of office of Puzriš-Dagan was built.	1 只羔和 1 只公崽来自**台岑妈妈**，为舒勒吉新提送入项，**阿皮里亚接管**。天神庆典月，普兹瑞什达干司被建之年。
Š 39 x/3： **mu-túm，ì-dab$_5$** 2 fattened rams，1 lamb from**zabar-idab official**，5 fattened rams from **Nir-idagal（general of Kuara）**，were deliveries for Šulgi-simtum，**Apiliya took over**	2 udu-niga，1 sila$_4$，**Zabar-｛ì｝-dab$_5$**，5 udu-niga，**Nir-ì-da-ĝál**，*mu-túm-***^{d}*Šul-gi-sí-im-ti***， ［***Á-p***］***i$_5$-lí-a*** *ì-dab$_5$.* *iti--ta ud-3 ba-ra-zal*，*iti-*［*ezem-An*］*-na*，*mu*［*é-P*］*uzr$_4$-iš-^{d}Da-gan ba-dù.* （*OIP* 115 041，*P*123545）	2 *fattened rams*，1 *lamb from***zabar-idab official（papanšen）**，5 fattened rams from **Nir-idagal**，were deliveries for Šulgi-simtum，**Apiliya took over**，when 3rd day passed. Month of ezem-Anna，Year that of office of Puzriš-Dagan was built.	2 育肥公绵羊和 1 羊羔自**“执青铜”官**，5 只育肥公绵羊来自**尼尔伊达旮勒（库阿腊将军）**，为舒勒吉新提的送入项，**阿皮里亚接管了**，于第 3 日过去时。天神庆典月，普兹瑞什达干司被建之年。
Š 39 x/27，29： **zi-ga** 2 fat rams and 1 ram for the **sacrifice of the beginning of New Moon in Uruk**，1 fattened ram for **giranum festival of Inanna**，when the **27th** day passed，1 fattened ram，1 fattened he-goat for the **sacrifice of Belat-Suhnir and Belat-Darraban**，**withdrawn from Apiliya**	2 udu-niga，1 udu-ú，**siskúr sag-ud-sakar** šà~ **Unu^{ki}**-ga，1 udu-niga，*gi-ra-núm-*^{d} **Inanna**，iti--ta **ud-27** ba-ra-zal，1 udu-niga，1 máš-gal-niga，**siskúr-^{d}** ***Be-la-at-Suh-nir*** *ù* ***^{d}Be-la-at-Dar-ra-ba-an***，*iti--ta* **ud-30 lá-1** ba-ra-zal， zi-ga-***Á-pi$_5$-lí-a.*** *iti-ezem-an-na*，*mu é-Puzr$_4$-iš-^{d}Da-gan ba-dù.* （*MVN* 05 093，*P*114313）	2 *fattened rams and* 1 *grass ram for the***sacrifice of the beginning of New Moon in Uruk**，1 fattened ram for **giranum festival of Inanna**，when the **27th** day passed，1 fattened ram，1 fattened he-goat for the **sacrifice of Belat-Suhnir and Belat-Darraban**，when the **29th** day passed，were **withdrawn from Apiliya**.Month of ezem-Anna，Year that of the office of Puzriš-Dagan was built.	2 只育肥公绵羊和 1 只食草公绵羊为**新月初祭，于乌鲁克**，1 只育肥公绵羊为**伊南那的吉腊努姆仪式**于第 **27** 日过去时，1 只育肥公绵羊和 1 只育肥公山羊为**贝拉特苏赫尼尔和贝拉特达腊班的祭祀**于第 **29** 日过去时，从**阿皮里亚支出了**。天神庆典月，普兹瑞什达干司被建之年。
Š 39 xi： **mu-túm，ì-dab$_5$** 2 rams and 1 kid from**the wife of Kalliya**，1 lamb from the **wife of Kulnekiag**，1 lamb from **E-u-e**，were deliveries for Šulgi-simti，**Apiliya took**	2 udu，1 máš，**dam-Kal-lí-a**，1 sila$_4$，**nin-^{ú} Kul-né-ki-áĝ**，1 sila$_4$，É-u$_6$-e，mu-túm-^{d} ***Šul-gi-sí-im-ti***，***Á-pi$_5$-lí-a*** *ì-dab$_5$. iti-ezem-Me-ki-ĝál*，*mu é-Puzr$_4$-iš-^{d} Da-gan ba-dù.* （*Princeton* 1 007，*P*126696）	2 *rams and* 1 *kid from***the wife of Kalliya**，1 lamb from the **wife of Kulnekiag**，1 lamb from **E-u-e**，were deliveries for Šulgi-simti，**Apiliya took over.** Month of ezem-Mekigal，Year that of the office of Puzriš-Dagan was built.	2 公绵羊和 1 公崽自**卡里亚之妻**，1 羔自**库勒耐基阿格之妻**，1 羔来自**埃乌埃**，为舒勒吉新提的送入项，**阿皮里亚接管了**。神美基旮勒庆典月，普兹瑞什达干司被建之年。

续表

时间和摘要	文献内容	英文翻译	中文翻译
Š 39 xi/25: **mu-túm, ì-dab$_5$** 2 fattened bulls, 20 grass rams from**Rubatum, the wife of Nunida**, were deliveries for Šulgi-simtum, **Apiliya took over**	2 gud-niga, 20 udu-ú, ***Ru-ba-tum*** *dam*-**Nu-ni-da**, iti--ta ud-25 ba-ra-zal, mu-túm~ ***^{d}Šul-gi-sí-im-tum****-ma*, ***Á-pi$_5$-lí-a*** *ì-dab$_5$. iti-ezem-Me-ki-gál, mu é-Puzr$_4$-iš-^{d}Da-gan ba-dù.* (*OIP* 115 042, *P*123575)	2 *fattened bulls*, 20 *grass rams from***Rubatum, the wife of Nunida**, when 25th day passed, were deliveries for Šulgi-simtum, **Apiliya took over.** Month of ezem-Mekigal, Year that of the office of Puzriš-Dagan was built.	2只育肥公牛和20只食草公绵羊自**努尼达之妻如巴吞**，于25日过去时，为舒勒吉新提的送入项，**阿皮里亚接管了**。神美基旮勒庆典月，普兹瑞什达干司被建之年。
Š 39 xi/26, 28, 30-xii/8, 10: **zi-ga, butchered** 26th: 1 duck when was took over for the **food of my queen**, 1 duck for the **food of my queen**, 28th: 1 **butchered** white duck, 30th: 1 **butchered** duck, **Month of ezem-Mekigal**; 8th: 2 ducks for the **beer sacrifice of Tadin-Ištar**, 10th: 1 **butchered** duck, **Šu-Sin as deputy, sent to palace,** were **withdrawn from Apiliya**	1 uz-tur, ud-dab$_5$-ba, **níĝ-gu$_7$-nin-ĝá**--šè, 1 uz-tur, **níĝ-gu$_7$-nin-ĝá**--šè, iti--ta **ud-26** ba-ra-zal, 1 uz-bar$_6$-bar$_6$ ba-úš, iti--ta **ud-28** ba-ra-zal, 1 uz-tur-ba-úš, iti--ta **ud-30** ba-ra-zal, **iti-ezem-Me-ki-gál**; 2 uz-tur, **kaš-dé-a**, ***Tá-din$^{!}$-Ištar***, *iti--ta* **ud-8** ba-ra-zal, 1 uz-tur-ba-úš, iti--ta **ud-10** ba-ra-zal, ***Šu-^{d} Sîn*** *maškim*, **é-gal-la ba-an-ku$_4$**, zi-ga-***Á-pi$_5$-lí a***. **iti-še-kin-kud**, mu é-Puzr$_4$-iš-^{d}Da-gan ba-dù. (OIP 115056, P123315)	1 duck when was took over for the**food of my queen**, 1 duck for the **food of my queen**, when 26th day passed, 1 **butchered** white duck when 28th day passed, 1 **butchered** duck when 30th day passed, **Month of ezem-Mekigal**; 2 ducks for the **beer sacrifice of Tadin-Ištar**, when 8th day passed, 1 **butchered** duck when 10th day passed, **Šu-Sin as royal deputy, sent to palace,** were **withdrawn from Apiliya**. Month of še-kin-kud, Year that of office of Puzriš-Dagan was built.	1鸭于被接管时为**我的王后的食物**和1鸭为**我的王后的食物**于**26**日过去时，1只**宰杀的**白鸭于**28**日过去时，1只**宰杀的**鸭于**30**日过去时，神美基旮勒庆典月；2只鸭为**塔丁伊什塔尔**（**阿马尔女**）**的啤酒节**于8日过去时，1只**宰杀的**鸭于10日过去时，**舒辛**（**王子**）**督办**，以上**被送入宫殿**，从**阿皮里亚支出**了。大麦收割月，普兹瑞什达干司被建之年。
Š 39 xi/?: **zi-ga, butchered** 3**butchered** duck was **sent to the palace**, when x day passed, **withdrawn from Apilliya**	3 uz-tur ba-ug$_7$, é-gal-la ba-an-ku$_4$, iti--ta ud-[...], zi-[ga] ***Á-pil-*** [***lí-a***]*.iti-ezem-Me-ki-*[*ĝál*], *mu é-Puzur$_4$-iš-^{d}Dagan ba-dù.* (*H.de Genouillac, Fouilles Francaises d'El-' Akhymer, tome* 2, *D.*49)	3**butchered** duck was **sent to the palace**, when x day passed, **withdrawn from Apilliya.** Month of ezem-Mekiĝal, Year that of the office of Puzriš-Dagan was built.	3只**宰杀鸭被送入宫殿**，于x天过去时， 从**阿皮里亚支出**了。 神美基旮勒庆典月， 普兹瑞什达干司被建之年。
Š 39 xii: **mu-túm, ì-dab$_5$** 4 rams and 1 gazelle fr.**Ama-bará**, were deliveries for Šulgi-simti, **Apiliya took over**	4 udu-ú, 1 maš-dà, **Ama-bará**, mu-túm-***^{d}Šul-gi-sí-im-ti***, ***Á-pi$_5$-lí-a*** *ì-dab$_5$.iti-še-kin-kud, mu é Puzur$_4$*-iš-^{d}Dagan ba-dù. (Princeton 1 010, P126699)	4 grass rams and 1 gazelle from**Ama-bará**, were deliveries for Šulgi-simti, **Apiliya took over.** Month of še-kin-kud, Year of the office of Puzuriš-Dagan was built.	4食草公绵羊和1只瞪羚来自**王座之母**，为舒勒吉新提的送入项，**阿皮里亚接管**了。大麦收割月，普兹瑞什达干司被建之年。
Š 39 xii/26, 27: **zi-ga, butchered** 26th: 1 **butchered** duck was sent to the palace, 27th: 1 duck and 5 doves when was took over for the **food of my queen**, were **withdrawn from Apiliya**	1 uz-tur ba-úš, iti--ta **ud-26**-ba-zal, **é-gal-la ba-an-ku$_4$**, 1 uz-tur, 5 tu-gur$_4$^{mušen}, ud-dab$_5$-ba **níĝ-gu$_7$-nin-ĝá**--šè, iti--ta **ud-27**-ba-ra-zal, zi-ga-***Á-pi$_5$-lí-a***. *iti-še-kin-kud, mu é Puzur$_4$*-iš-^{d} Da-gan ba-dù. (SAT 2 0226, P143427)	1 **butchered** duck when the **26th** day passed sent to the palace, 1 duck and 5 doves when was took over for the **food of my queen**, when the **27th** day passed, were **withdrawn from Apiliya**. Month of še-kin-kud, Year of the office of Puzuriš-Dagan was built.	1只**宰杀鸭**于**26**日过去时**被送入宫殿**， 1只鸭和5只野鸽于接管时为**我的王后的食物**， 于本月**27**日过去时， 以上从**阿皮里亚支出**了。大麦收割月，普兹瑞什达干司被建之年。

续表

时间和摘要	文献内容	英文翻译	中文翻译
Š 39: **ì-dab$_5$** 74 fat rams, 30 rams, 8 fat goats for monthly allowance of Šulgi-simti **from Ba-mu (cook), Apiliya took over**	74 udu-niga, 30 udu-ú, 8 máš-gal niga, **sá-dug$_4$-^{d}*Šul-gi-sí-im-ti***, *ki~ **Ba-mu**--ta*, ***Á-pi$_5$-lí-a** ì-dab$_5$*, *mu É-Puzr$_4$-iš-^{d}Da-gan ba-dù-a.* (*Torino* 1 034, *P*131860)	*74 fattened rams*, *30 grass rams*, *8 fattened he-goats for monthly allowance of Šulgi-simti* **from Ba-mu (cook), Apiliya took over**. Year that of the office of Puzriš-Dagan was built.	74只育肥公绵羊、30只食草公绵羊和8只育肥公山羊送给舒勒吉新提的月供，来自**巴穆**，**阿皮里亚接管了**。普兹瑞什达干司被建之年。
Š 40 i: **mu-túm, ì-dab$_5$** 2 lambs from**Zak-ili**, 1 lamb from **Išdum-kin**, twere deliveries for Šulgi-simtum, **Apiliya took over**	2 sila$_4$, ***Za-ak-ì-lí***, 1 *sila$_4$*, ***Išdum*** (**SUHUŠ**) ***-kí-in*** *dumu* **Ur-nîĝar^{gar}**, mu-túm ~ ***^{d}Šul-gi-sí-im-tum**-ma*, ***Á-pi$_5$-lí-a** ì-dab$_5$.iti-maš-dà~gu$_7$*, *mu ús-sa é-Puzr$_4$-iš-^{d} Da-gan ba-dù.* (*AUCT* 1 089, *P*102935)	*2 lambs from***Zak-ili**, 1 lamb from **Išdum-kin**, the son of Ur-nîĝar, were deliveries for Šulgi-simtum, **Apiliya took over**.Month of mašda~gu$_7$, Year after that of the office of Puzriš-Dagan was built.	2只羊羔自**扎克伊里**，1只羊羔自**乌尔尼旮尔之子伊什杜金**，以上为舒勒吉新吞的送入项，**阿皮里亚接管了**。食瞪羚月，普兹瑞什达干司被建年之次年。
Š 40 i/6: **ki~… --ta** 2 fattened rams (delivered) from**Apili<ya>**, for **In-nuri**	2 udu-niga, ki~ ***Á-pi$_5$-lí-<a>**--ta*, *mu~ **In-nu-rí**--šè*, *iti--ta ud-6 ba-ra-zal.* [*iti*] *-maš-dà-gu$_7$ mu-ús-sa é-Puzr$_4$-iš-^{d}Da-gan ba-dù.* (*PDT* 1 080 *P*125496)	*2 fattened rams* (*delivered*) *from***Apili<ya>**, for **In-nuri**, when the 6th day passed. [Month] of mašdà~gu$_7$, Year after that of the office of Puzriš-Dagan was built.	2只育肥公绵羊自**阿皮里【亚】**处（送人）为**尹努瑞**，于6日过去时。食瞪羚月，普兹瑞什达干司被建年之次年。
Š 40 i/20, 22: **zi-ga, butchered** 20th: 1 **butchered** duck was sent to the palace, 22nd: 1 duck, 5 doves **for "beer-pouring" of king**, were **withdrawn from Apiliya**	1 uz-tur-ba-úš, iti--ta **ud-20**-ba-ra-zal, **é-gal-la ba-an-ku$_4$**, 1 uz-tur, 5 tu-gur$_4$^{mušen}-tur, iti--ta **ud-22**-ba-ra-zal, **kaš-dé-a lugal**, zi-ga-***Á-pi$_5$-lí-a**. iti-maš-dà~gu$_7$*, *mu ús-sa é-Puzr$_4$-iš-^{d} Da-gan ba-dù.* (*AnOr* 01 002, P100993)	1**butchered** duck when the 20th day passed was **sent to the palace**, 1 duck, 5 doves when the 22nd day passed, **for "beer-pouring" of king**, were **withdrawn from Apiliya**. Month of mašda~gu$_7$, Year after that of the office of Puzriš-Dagan was built.	1只**宰杀鸭**于本月20日过去时**被送入宫殿**，1只鸭和5只野鸽于本月22日过去时，为**国王的倒啤酒宴会**，从**阿皮里亚支出了**。食瞪羚月，普兹瑞什达干司被建年之次年。
Š 40 i-ii: (**zi-ga**) 4 goats, 4 kids, 2 ewe, 3 rams, 2 lamb, 1 goat, for **monthly allowance of Belat-Suhnir, Belat-Darraban, Annunitum and Ulmašitum**	2 ud$_5$, 2 máš-nitá, 1 u$_8$, 2 udu-nitá, 1 sila$_4$, **iti-maš-dà~gu$_7$**; 2 ud$_5$, 1 máš-gal, 1 máš-nitá, 1 u$_8$, 1 udu-nitá, 1 máš-sila$_4$, 1 sila$_4$, **iti-ze$_x$-da~gu$_7$**, sá-dug$_4$~ ***^{d}Be-la-at-Suh -nir***, **^{d}Be-la-at-Dar-ra-ba-an**, **An-nu-ni-tum** *ù* **^{d}Ul-ma-ši-tum**, *mu ús-sa é-Puzr$_4$-iš-^{d} Da-gan ba-dù.* (*OIP* 115 057, *P*123498)	*2 she-goats*, *2 kids*, *1 ewe*, *2 rams*, *1 lamb*, *month of* **mašda~gu$_7$**; 2 she-goats, 1 kid, 1 he-goat, 1 ewe, 1 ram, 1 kid, 1 lamb, month of **zeda~gu$_7$**, for **monthly allowance of Belat-Suhnir**, **Belat-Darraban**, **Annunitum and Ulmašitum**, Year after that of the office of Puzriš-Dagan was built.	2母山羊、2公崽、1母绵羊、2公绵羊、1羔食**瞪羚月**；2母山羊、1公崽、1公山羊、1母绵羊、1公绵羊、1只公崽，1只羔**食豚月**，为**贝拉特苏赫尼尔、贝拉特达腊班、安努尼吞和乌勒马席吞月供**，普兹瑞什达干司被建年之次年。

续表

时间和摘要	文献内容	英文翻译	中文翻译
Š 40 ii/19： **mu-túm，ì-dab$_5$** 1+ fattened rams，1+ kid，from**Igi-anna-ke-zu**，when 19th day passed，3 grass rams，1 he-goat，1 lamb from **the wife of Apili**，5 fat-tailed sheep，1 ram from **Puzur-Ištar**，were deliveries for Šulgi-simti，**Apiliya took**	1+x udu-niga，1+ x máš，**Igi-an-na-ke$_4$-zu**，iti--ta ud-19 ba-ra-zal，3 udu-ú，1 máš-gal，1 sila$_4$，**dam-*Á-pi$_5$-lí***，5 *gukkal*，1 *udu-ú*，***Puzur$_4$-^{d}Iš$_8$-tár***，*mu-túm-*^{d}***Šul-gi-sí-im-ti***，***Á-pi$_5$-lí-a*** ì-dab$_5$. **iti-ze$_x$-da～gu$_7$**， mu ús-sa é-Puzr$_4$-iš-^{d}Da-gan ba-dù. （SACT 1 057，P128812）	1+ fattened rams，1+ kid，from**Igi-anna-ke-zu**，when 19th day passed，3 grass rams，1 he-goat，1 lamb from **the wife of Apili**，5 fat-tailed sheep，1 grass ram from **Puzur-Ištar**，were deliveries for Šulgi-simti，**Apiliya took over**.Month of zeda～gu$_7$， Year after that of the office of Puzriš-Dagan was built.	1+育肥公绵羊、1+只公崽，来自**伊吉安那凯朱**于19日过去时，3只食草公绵羊、1只公山羊、1只羊羔自**阿皮里之妻**，5只肥尾羊、1只食草公绵羊来自**普朱尔伊什塔尔**，为舒勒吉新提的送入项，**阿皮里亚接管**。食豚月，普兹瑞什达干司被建年之次年。
Š 40 ii/22： **zi-ga，butchered** 1**butchered** thicket piglet，the **weaver woman received**，when the 22nd day passed，**withdrawn from Apiliya**	1šáh^{zah}-tur-giš-gi ba-úš，**gemé-úš -bar-e-ne** šu～ba-ti-eš，iti--ta ud-22-ba-ra-zal，zi-ga ***Á-pi$_5$-lí-a***. *iti-ze$_x$-da～gu$_7$，mu ús-sa é-Puzur$_4$-iš-^{d}Da-gan ba-dù.* （*CST*050，*P*107562）	1**butchered** thicket piglet，the **weaver woman received**，when the 22nd day passed，**withdrawn from Apiliya**.Month of zeda～gu7，Year after that of the office of Puzuriš-Dagan was built.	1只宰杀的苇塘猪崽，**编织女工接收了**，于本月22日过去时，**从阿皮里亚支出**了。食豚月，普兹瑞什达干司被建年之次年。
Š 40 ii： **mu-túm，ì-dab$_5$** 1 female kid from **E-u-e**，deliveries for Šulgi-simti，**Apiliya took over**	1^{f}ašgar **É-u$_6$-e**，mu-túm-^{d} ***Šul-gi-sí-im-ti***，***Á-pi$_5$-lí-a*** *ì-dab$_5$，iti-ze$_x$-da～gu$_7$，mu ús-sa é-Puzr$_4$-iš-^{d} Da-gan ba-dù.* （*OIP* 115043，*P*123421）	1 *female kid from* **E-u-e**，deliveries for Šulgi-simti，**Apiliya took over**.Month of zeda～gu$_7$， Year after that of the office of Puzriš-Dagan was built.	1只雌山羊崽来自**埃乌埃**，为舒勒吉新提的送入项，**阿皮里亚接管了**。食豚月，普兹瑞什达干司被建年之次年。
Š 40 iii/1： **zi-ga** 1 ram of after ox-class for**food of An**，2 fat rams，2 rams for **Šeršerrum**，**Belat-S.and Belat-D.**，1 fat ram for **Urmasitum**，1 fattened bull，3 fattened rams for **the festival of Annunitum entered**，were **withdrawn from Apiliya，in Ur，via Beli-bani**	1 udugud-e-ús，**níĝ-gu$_7$-An-na**，2 udu-niga，2 udu-ú，***še-er-še-er -ru-um***，^{d}***Be-la-at-Suh-nir*** *ù* ^{d}***Be -la-at-Dar-ra-ba-an***，1 *udu-niga*，^{d} ***Ul-ma-si-tum***，1 *gud-niga*，3 *udu-niga*，**ezem-diĝir-ku$_4$-ku$_4$**，***An-nu-ni-tum***，*iti--ta ud-1-ba-ra-zal*，*zi-ga* ***Á-pi$_5$-lí-a***，*šà* **Uri$_5$**-ma^{ki}，*ĝìr* ***Be-lí-ba-ni***. *iti-u$_5$-bí-gu$_7$，mu ús-sa é-Puzr$_4$-iš-^{d} Da-gan ba-dù.* （*AnOr* 07 063，*P*101358）	1 *ram of after ox-class for***the food of An**，2 fattened rams，2 grass rams for **Šeršerrum**，**Belat-Suhnir and Belat-Darraban**，1 fattened ram for **Urmasitum**，1 fattened bull，3 fattened rams for **the festival of Annunitum entered**，when the 1st day passed，were **withdrawn from Apiliya**，**in Ur**，**via Beli-bani**. Month of ubi-gu$_7$，Year after that of the office of Puzriš-Dagan was built.	1牛后级公绵羊为**安神的食物**，2肥公绵羊和2食草公绵羊为**贝拉特苏赫尼尔和贝拉特达腊班的塞尔塞闰节**，1育肥公绵羊为**乌尔马席香**，1只育肥公牛和3只育肥公绵羊为**安努尼香的进入节**，于1日过去时，**从阿皮里亚支出**了，**于乌尔**，**经由贝里巴尼**。食乌比鸟月，普兹瑞什达干司被建年之次年。
Š 40 iii/8： **zi-ga** 1 duck，5 doves for**the food of my queen**，were **withdrawn from Apiliya**	1 uz-tur，5 tu-gur$_4$^{mušen}，**níĝ-gu$_7$- nin-ĝá**--šè，iti--ta ud-8 ba-ra-zal，zi-ga-***Á-pi$_5$-lí-a***. *iti-u$_5$-bí-gu$_7$，mu ús-sa é-Puzur$_4$-iš-^{d}Da-gan ba-dù.*（*TLB* 3 014，P134155）	1 *duck*，5 *doves for***the food of my queen**，when the 8th day passed，were **withdrawn from Apiliya**. Month of ubi-gu$_7$，Year after that of office of Puzriš-Dagan was built.	1只鸭和5只野鸽为**我的王后的食物**于8日过去时，**从阿皮里亚支出**了。食乌比鸟月，普兹瑞什达干司被建年之次年。

续表

时间和摘要	文献内容	英文翻译	中文翻译
Š 40 iii/2, 8, 15, 18, 27: **zi-ga, butchered** 2nd: 1 **butchered duck sent to the palace**, 8th: **1 butchered duck sent to the palace**, 15th: 1 ducklet, 5 doves **for "beer-pouring" of E-a-niša** (**lukur wife of Šul-gi**), 18th: 1 **butchered** ducklet **sent to the palace**, 27th: 1 ducklet, 3 doves on the day they were captured, for the **food of my queen**, were **withdrawn from Apiliya**	[1 uz-tur~ba-úš], **é-gal-la ba-an-ku$_4$**, iti--ta **ud-2** ba-ra-zal, 1 uz-tur-ba-úš, **é-gal-la** ba-an-ku$_4$, iti--ta **ud-8** ba-ra-zal, 1 amar-sag~ uz-tur, 5 tu-gur$_4$^{mušen}, kaš-dé-a, ***É-a-ni-ša***, *iti--ta* **ud-15** ba-ra-zal, 1 amar-sag~ uz-tur-ba-úš, **é-gal-la** ba-an-ku$_4$, iti--ta **ud-18** ba-ra-zal, 1 amar-sag~ uz-tur, 3 tu-gur$_4$^{mušen}, ud-1-kam, ud-dag$_5$-ba **níĝ-gu$_7$-nin-ĝá**--šè, iti--ta **ud-27** ba-ra-zal, zi-ga-***Á-pi$_5$-lí*** *a*. *iti-u$_5$-bí-gu$_7$*, *mu ús-sa é-Puzr$_4$-iš-^{d}Da-gan ba-dù*. (*OIP* 115 058, P123355)	1**butchered duck sent to the palace**, when **2nd** day passed, **1 butchered duck sent to palace**, when **8th** day passed, 1 ducklet, 5 doves **for "beer-pouring" of E-a-niša** (**lukur wife of Šul-gi**), when **15th** day passed, 1 **butchered** ducklet **sent to palace** when **18th** day passed, 1 ducklet, 3 doves on the day they were captured, for the **food of my queen**, when **27th** day passed, were **withdrawn from Apiliya**. Month of ubi-gu$_7$, Year after that of the office of Puzriš-Dagan was built.	1只**宰杀鸭被送入宫殿**于2日过去时，1只**宰杀鸭被送入宫殿**于8日过去时，1只幼鸭和5只野鸽**为埃阿尼沙（舒勒吉的神妻）的倒啤酒宴会**于15日过去时，1只**宰杀鸭被送入宫殿**于18日过去时，1只幼鸡和3只野鸽在它们被捕的当天，**为我的王后的食物**，于27日过去时，以上为**阿皮里亚支出**。食乌比鸟月，普兹瑞什达干司被建年之次年。
Š 40 iv/8, 13, 14, 20: **zi-ga, butchered** 8th: 1 pigeon, 13th: 1 white duck, 14th: 1 dove, **butchered ones were sent to the palace**; 14th: 1 duck was for the **food of my queen**, 20th: 1 **butchered** duck was **sent to the palace**, were**withdrawn from Apiliya**	1 ir$_7$^{mušen}, iti--ta **ud-8** ba-ra-zal, 1 uz-bar$_6$-bar$_6$, iti--ta **ud-13** ba-ra-zal, 1 tu-gur$_4$^{mušen}, iti--ta **ud-14** ba-ra-zal, ba-ug$_7$, **é-gal-la** ba-an-ku$_4$; 1 uz-tur, **níĝ-gu$_7$-nin-ĝá**--šè, iti--ta **ud-14** ba-ra-zal, 1 uz-tur-ba-úš, **é-gal-la** ba-an-ku$_4$, iti--ta**ud-20** ba-ra-zal, zi-ga-***Á-pi$_5$-lí-a***.*iti-ki-siki-^{d}Nin-a-zu*, *mu ús-sa é-Puzr$_4$-iš-^{d}Da-gan ba-dù*. (*OIP* 115059, *P*123448)	1 *pigeon when***8th** day passed, 1 white duck when **13th** day passed, 1 dove when **14th** day passed, **butchered ones were sent to the palace**; 1 duck was for the **food of my queen** when 14th day passed, 1 **butchered** duck was **sent to the palace**, when **20th** day passed, were **withdrawn from Apiliya**. Month of ki-siki-Ninazu, Year after that of the office of Puzriš-Dagan was built.	1只家鸽于**8**日过去时，1只白鸭于13日过去时，1只野鸽于14日过去时，**这些宰杀牲被送入宫殿**；1只鸭为**我的王后的食物**于14日过去时，1只**宰杀鸭被送入宫殿**， 于20日过去时， 以上为**阿皮里亚支出**。神宁阿朱羊毛作坊月， 普兹瑞什达干司被建年之次年。
Š 40 iv/7, 21: **mu-túm, ì-dab$_5$** 7th: 1+x dove from **Šara-kam, the son of Inim-Šara**, 21st: 4 ducklet from **Watrat** (**dowager**) **as overseer**, these were brought into, **Apiliya took over**	[1+x] tu-gur$_4$$^{mušen d}$Šará-kam dumu-Inim-^{d}Šará, iti--ta**ud-7** ba-ra-zal, 4 amar-sag~uz-tur ***Wa-at-ra-at*** *ugula*, *iti--ta***ud-21** ba-ra-zal, mu-túm, ***Á-pi$_5$-lí-a*** *ì-dab$_5$*. *iti-ki-siki-* [^{d}*N*] *in-a-zu*, *mu ús-sa é-Puzr$_4$-iš-^{d}Da-gan ba-dù*. (*PDT* 2 0993, *P*126339)	1+*x dove from***Šara-kam, the son of Inim-Šara**, when 7thday passed, 4 ducklet from **Watrat** (**dowager**) **the overseer**, when 21st day passed, these were brought into, **Apiliya took over**. Month of ki-siki-Ninazu, Year after that of the office of Puzriš-Dagan was built.	1+x只鸽来自**伊尼姆沙腊之子沙腊卡姆**，于7日过去时，4只幼鸭来自**监工瓦特腊特太后**，于21日过去时，送入**阿皮里亚接管**了。神宁阿朱羊毛作坊月，普兹瑞什达干司被建年之次年。

续表

时间和摘要	文献内容	英文翻译	中文翻译
Š 40 v: **mu-túm，ì-dab$_5$** 1 lamb from**Eue**，6 grass rams from **Rubatum**，the wife of Nunica，were deliveries for Šulgi-simti，**Apiliya took over**	1 sila$_4$，**É-u$_6$-e**，6 udu-ú，***Ru-ba-tum*** *dam-**Nu-ni-da***，*mu-túm-*^{d}***Šul-gi-sí-im-ti***， ***Á-pi$_5$-lí-a*** *ì-dab$_5$. iti-ezem-*^{d}*Nin-a-zu，mu ús-sa é-Puzr$_4$-iš-*^{d}*Da-gan ba-dù.* （*OIP* 115045，*P*123685）	1 *lamb from***Eue**，6 grass rams from **Rubatum**，the wife of Nunida，were deliveries for Šulgi-simti，**Apiliya took over**. Month of ezem-Ninazu，Year after that of the office of Puzriš-Dagan was built.	1只羊羔来自**埃乌埃**，6只食草公绵羊来自**如巴吞**，努尼达之妻，以上为舒勒吉新提的送入项，**阿皮里亚接管了**。神宁阿朱庆典月，普兹瑞什达干司被建之年次年。
Š 40 v/9: **mu-túm，ì-dab$_5$** 1 fattened bull，9 grass rams，1 kid from**the wife of Bani-ilum**，when the 9th day passed，were deliveries for Šulgi-simti，**Apiliya took ove**	1 gud-niga，9 udu-ú，1 máš，dam-***Ba-ni-ilum***，*iti--ta ud-10-lá-1-kam，mu-túm-*^{d} ***Šul-gi-sí-im-ti***，***Á-pi$_5$-lí-a*** *ì-dab$_5$. iti-ezem-*^{d}*Nin-a-zu，mu ús-sa é-Puzur-iš-*^{d} *Da-gan ba-dù.*（*Ontario* 1 011，*P*124424）	1 *fattened bull*，9 *grass rams*，1 *kid from***the wife of Bani-ilum**，when the 9th day passed，were deliveries for Šulgi-simti，**Apiliya took over**. Month of ezem-Ninazu，Year after that of the office of Puzriš-Dagan was built.	1只育肥公牛、9只育肥公绵羊和1只公崽来自**巴尼伊隆的妻子**，于9日过去时，为舒勒吉新提的送入项，**阿皮里亚接管了**。神宁阿朱庆典月，普兹瑞什达干司被建年次年。
Š 40 v/9: **zi-ga** 3 fattened rams for **the wife of Etel-pu-Dagan**，2 fattened rams for the **wife of Bani-ilum**，were **withdrawn from Apiliya**	3 udu-niga，mu ~ **dam-*E-te-el*! *-pù-*^{d} *Da-gan*--*šè*，2 *udu-niga，mu~* **dam-*Ba-ni-lum*--*šè***，*iti--ta ud-9 ba-ra-zal，zi-ga-**Á-pi$_5$-lí-a**. iti-ezem-*^{d}*Nin-a-zu，mu ús-sa é Puzur$_4$-iš-*^{d}*Da-gan ba-dù.* （*Torino* 1 182，*P*132026）	3 *fattened rams for t***he wife of Etel-pu-Dagan**，2 fattened rams for the **wife of Bani-ilum**，when 9th day passed，were **withdrawn from Apiliya**. Month of ezem-Ninazu，Year after that of the office of Puzriš-Dagan was built.	3只育肥公绵羊为埃**台勒普达干（舒勒吉子）之妻**，2只育肥公绵羊为**巴尼隆妻**，于第9天过去时，从**阿皮里亚支出了**。神宁阿朱庆典月，普兹瑞什达干司被建之年次年。
Š 40 v/19，20: **zi-ga，butchered** 19th：1 **butchered duck** and 1 **butchered dove were sent to the palace**，20th：1 duck（was delivered）from **Isinše**，**for Ušaga**，1 duck for the **food of my queen**，**withdrawn from Apilliya**	1 uz-tur ba-ug$_7$，1 tu-gur$_4$^{mušen} ba-ug$_7$，é-gal-la ba-an-ku$_4$，iti--ta **ud-19** ba-ra-zal，1 uz-tur **Ì-si-in^{ki}-šè** mu-**Ù-šag$_5$-a**--šè，1 uz-tur **níĝ-gu$_7$-nin-ĝá**--šè，iti--ta **ud-20** ba-ra-zal，zi-ga ***Á-pil-lí-a***. *iti-ezem-*^{d} *Nin-z-zu，mu-ús-sa é-PUZUR$_3$ ŠA-iš-*^{d}*Da-gan ba-dù.* （*AAICAB* 1，2 *Ashm.*1935-561）	1**butchered duck** and 1 **butchered dove were sent to the palace**，when the 19th day passed，1 duck from **Isinše**，**for Ušaga**，1 duck for the **food of my queen**，when the 20th day passed，**withdrawn from Apilliya**. Month of ezem-Ninazu，Year after that of office of Puzriš-Dagan was built.	1只**宰杀鸭**和1只**宰杀野鸽被送入宫殿**，于19日过去时，1只鸭从**伊辛塞处（送入）为乌萨旮**，1只鸭为**我的王后的食物**。于20日过去时，从**阿皮里亚支出了**。神宁阿朱庆典月，普兹瑞什达干司被建之年次年。
Š 40 v/24: **mu-túm，ì-dab$_5$** 2 pigeons from**Ninlil-tumimti**，when 24th day passed，were deliveries for Šulgi-simti，**Apiliya took over**	2 ir$_7$^{mušen}，^{d} ***Nin-líl-tum-im-ti***，*iti--ta ud-24 ba-ra-zal，mu-túm ~* ^{d}***Šul-gi-sí-im-ti***，***Á-pi$_5$-lí-a*** *ì-dab$_5$. iti-ezem-*^{d} *Nin-a-zu，mu ús-sa é-Puzr$_4$-iš-*^{d}*Da-gan ba-dù.* （*OIP* 115044，*P*123649）	2 *pigeons from***Ninlil-tumimti**，when 24th day passed，were deliveries for Šulgi-simti，**Apiliya took over**. Month of ezem-Ninazu，Year after that of the office of Puzriš-Dagan was built.	2只家鸽自**宁里勒吞伊媚提**，于24日过去时，为舒勒吉新提的送入项，**阿皮里亚接管了**。神宁阿朱庆典月，普兹瑞什达干司被建之年次年。

续表

时间和摘要	文献内容	英文翻译	中文翻译
Š 40 v/29： **mu-túm，ì-dab$_5$** 1 pigeon from**E-u-še**，2 pigeons from **Beli-bani**，when the 29th day passed，were deliveries for Šulgi-simti，**Apiliya took over**	1 ir$_7^{mušen}$，**É-u$_6$-šè**，2 ir$_7^{mušen}$，***Be-lí-ba-ni***，*iti--ta ud-30-lá-1 ba-ra-zal*，*mu-túm-*^{d}***Šul-gi-sí-im-ti***，***Á-pi$_5$-lí-a ì-dab$_5$***.*iti-ezem-*^{d}*Nin-a-zu*，*mu ús-saé-Puzr$_4$-iš-*^{d}*Da-gan ba-dù*. （*RT* 37 129 *ml* 2，*P*128395）	1 *pigeon from***E-u-še**，2 pigeons from **Beli-bani**，when the 29th day passed，were deliveries for Šulgi-simti，**Apiliya took over**. Month of ezem-Ninazu，Year after that of the office of Puzriš-Dagan was built.	1 只家鸽来自**埃乌塞**，2 只家鸽来自**贝里巴尼**，于 29 日过去时，为舒勒吉新提的送入项，**阿皮里亚接管**了。神宁阿朱庆典月，普兹瑞什达干司被建年之次年。
Š 40 vi： **mu-túm，ì-dab$_5$** 1 lamb，1 female lamb from**Ninlil-tum-imti**，were deliveries for Šulgi-simti，**Apiliya took over**	1 sila$_4$-nitá，1 kir$_{11}$，^{d}***Nin-líl-tum-im-ti***，*mu-túm-*^{d}***Šul-gi-sí-im-tum****-ma*，***Á-pi$_5$-lí-a*** *ì-dab$_5$*. *iti-á-ki-ti*，*mu ús-sa é-Puzr$_4$-iš-*^{d}*Da-gan ba-dù*. （*Torino* 1 035，*P*133846）	1 *lamb*，1 *female lamb from***Ninlil-tum-imti**，were deliveries for Šulgi-simti，**Apiliya took over**. Month of akiti， Year after that of the office of Puzriš-Dagan was built.	1 只雄羊羔和 1 只雌羔来自**宁里勒吞伊姆提**，为舒勒吉新提的送入项，**阿皮里亚接管**了。阿基提月，普兹瑞什达干司被建年之次年。
Š 40 vi/1，5： **mu-túm，ì-dab$_5$** 14 ducks of the**arrear repaid by Ipi-Sin，for Han-ini**，9 pigeons，2 doves from **Ninlil-hemti**，**were deliveries for Šulgi-simtum，Apiliya took over**	14 uz-tur，lá-ì su-ga **I-pi$_5$-^{d} Suen** mu～ Ha-ni-ni--šè，iti--ta ud-1 ba-ra-zal，9 ir$_7^{mušen}$，2 tu-gur$_4^{mušen}$，^{d}***Nin-líl-hé-em-ti***，*iti--ta ud-5 ba -ra-zal*，*mu-túm～* ^{d}***Šul-gi-sí-im-tum****-ma*，***Á-pi$_5$-lí-a*** *ì-dab$_5$*.*iti-á -ki-ti*，*mu ús-sa é-Puzr$_4$-iš-*^{d}*Da-gan ba-dù*.（*BIN* 3 363，*P*106169）	14 *ducks of the***arrear repaid by Ipi-Sin，for Hani-ni**，when the 1st day passed，9 pigeons，2 doves from **Ninlil-hemti**，when the 5th day passed，**were deliveries for Šulgi-simtum，Apiliya took over**. Month of akiti，Year after that of office of Puzriš-Dagan was built.	14 只鸭的**欠款由伊皮辛交付**了，为**哈尼尼**，于 1 日过去时，9 只家鸽和 2 只野鸽来自**宁里勒希姆提**，于 5 日过去时，**为舒勒吉新吞的送入**，**阿皮里亚接管**了。阿基提月，普兹瑞什达干司被建年之次年。
Š 40 vi/13： **zi-ga，butchered** 1 duck，5 doves for **supplies of Nin-kal-la**，1 **butchered dove sent to the palace**，were **withdrawn from Apiliya**	1 uz-tur，5 tu-gur$_4^{mušen}$，igi-kár～ **Nin$_9$-kal-la**，1 tu-gur$_4^{mušen}$-ba-úš，é-gal-la ba-an-ku$_4$，iti--ta **ud-13** ba-ra-zal，zi-ga-***Á-pi$_5$-lí_a***.*iti-á-ki-ti*，*mu ús-sa é-Puzr$_4$-iš-*^{d}*Da-gan ba-dù*. （*OIP* 115060，*P*123682）	1 *duck*，5 *doves for* **supplies of Nin-kal-la**，1 **butchered dove sent to the palace**，when 13th day passed，were **withdrawn from Apiliya**. Month of akiti，Year after that of the office of Puzriš-Dagan was built.	1 只鸭子和 5 只野鸽为**宁卡拉（舒勒吉神妻）的供奉**，1 只**宰杀的野鸽被送入宫殿**，于 13 日过去时，以上从**阿皮里亚支出**了。阿基提月，普兹瑞什达干司被建年之次年。

续表

时间和摘要	文献内容	英文翻译	中文翻译
Š 40 vii/5, 6, 7: **zi-ga** 5th: 8 ewes for **offering of disappearing place**, 2 fat rams for **sacrifice of temple of Belat-Suhnir and Belat-Darraban**; 6th: [1+ fat ram] for **temple of Nin-sun**, 1 fat ram and 1 ram for **temple of Adad-tug**, 1 fat ram for **temple of Allatum**, 2 ewes for **giranum of Annunitum and Ulmasitum**, **Ipiq-Erra as deputy**; 7th: 1 lamb, 1 fat bull, 4 fat rams, 1 lamb, 1 ram **when the god entered**, [1+] fattened bull for **food of fish and greenary**, **in the palace**, 1 ewe for **the goddess when she went into her temple**, **for "pouring-beer" festival of Annunitum**, **withdrawn from Apiliya**	2 u_8, **níĝ~ ki-zàh--šè**, 2 udu-niga, **siskúr--šè**, é-*[d]Be-la-at-Suh-nir* ù *[d]Be-la-at-Dar-ra-ba-an*, *iti--ta* **ud-5**ba-ra-zal; [1+ udu-niga] **é-[d]Nin-sún**, 1 udu-niga, 1 udu-ú, **é-[d]Iškur-túg**, 1 udu-niga, **é-*[d]Al-la-tum***, 2 u_8 ***gi-ra-núm An-nu-ni-tum*** ù ***[d]Ul-ma-si-tum***, ***I-pi$_5$-iq-Èr-ra*** *maškim*, *iti--ta* **ud-6**ba-ra-zal; 1 kir_{11}~$šag_4$-húl-la, 1 gud-niga, 4 udu-niga, 1 kir_{11}, 1 udu-ú, **diĝir-ku_4-ku_4-da-ni**, [1+] gud-niga, **níĝ- [ku_6] -nisig-ga--šè**, šà~ **é- [gal] -la**, 1 u_8, **diĝir é-a-ni-šè** ĝen-a-ni, kaš-dé-a ***An-nu-ni-tum***, *iti--ta* **ud-7**ba-ra-zal, zi-ga***Á-pi$_5$-lí-* [*a*]**. *iti-ezem-[d]Šul-gi*, *mu ús-sa é-Puzr$_4$-iš-[d]Da-gan ba-dù.* (*TRU* 273, *P*135037)	8 *ewes for***offering of disappearing place**, 2 fattened rams for **sacrifice of temple of Belat-Suhnir and Belat-Darraban**, when the 5thday passed; [1+ fattened ram] for **temple of Nin-sun**, 1 fattened ram and 1 grass ram for **temple of Adad-tug**, 1 fattened ram for **temple of Allatum**, 2 ewes for **giranum festival of Annunitum and Ulmasitum**, **Ipiq-Erra as royal deputy**, when the 6thday passed; 1 happy female lamb, 1 fattened bull, 4 fattened rams, 1 female lamb, 1 grass ram **when the god entered**, [1+] fattened bull for **food of fish and greenary**, **in the palace**, 1 ewe for **the goddess when she went into her temple**, **for "pouring-beer" festival of Annunitum**, when 7th day passed, were **withdrawn from Apiliya**. Month of ezem-Šulgi, Year after that of office of Puzriš-Dagan was built.	8只母绵羊为**消失处供奉**，2只育肥公绵羊为**贝拉特苏赫尼尔和贝拉特达腊班庙祭祀**， 于**5**日过去时； 【1+只育肥公绵羊】为**宁荪庙**，1只育肥公绵羊和1只食草公绵羊为**阿达德图格庙**，1只育肥公绵羊为**阿拉杏庙**，只2母绵羊为**安努尼吞和乌勒马席吞的吉腊努姆仪式**，**伊皮克埃腊督办**， 于**6**日过去时； 1只高兴雌羔、1只育肥公牛、4只育肥公绵羊、1雌羔、1只食草公绵羊为**神进入节**，【1+】头育肥公牛为**鱼食和蔬菜**，**于宫殿**，1只母绵羊当神走向她的神庙时，为**安努尼吞的倒啤酒宴会**， 于**7**日过去时， **从阿皮里亚支出**了。神舒勒吉庆典月，普兹瑞什达干司被建之年次年。
Š 40 vii: **zi-ga**, **butchered** 1 fat ram, 6 ewes, 3 rams, 1 female kid, **butchered ones were sent to the palace**, **in Ur**, **withdrawn from Apiliya**	1 udu-niga, 6 u_8, 3 udu-nitá, 1 [f]ašgar, ba-úš-úš, **é-gal-la** ba-an-ku_4, šà~ Uri_5[ki]-ma, zi-ga ***Á-pi$_5$-lí-a***. *iti-ezem-[d]Šul-gi*, *mu ús-sa é-Puzr$_4$-iš-[d]Da-gan ba-dù.* (*BIN* 5 073, *P*106507)	1 *fattened ram*, 6 *ewes*, 3 *rams*, 1 *female kid*, **butchered ones were sent to palace**, **in Ur**, **withdrawn from Apiliya**. Month of ezem-Šulgi, Year after that of the office of Puzriš-Dagan was built.	1肥公绵羊、6母绵羊、3公绵羊，1雌山羊崽，这些**宰杀牲送入为宫殿**，**于乌尔**，**从阿皮里亚支出**。神舒勒吉庆典月，普兹瑞什达干司被建之年次年。
Š 40 vii/26, 28, 30: **zi-ga**, **butchered** 26th: [1+x] **butchered pigeons**, 28th: 1 **butchered dove**, were **sent to the palace**, 30th: 1 pigeon, 1 dove, for **the provisions of U-šaga**, were **withdrawn from Apiliya**	[1+] ir_7[mušen]-ba-úš, *iti--ta* ud-26 ba-ra-zal, 1 $tu-gur_5$[mušen]-ba-úš, iti--ta ud-28 ba-ra-zal, **é-gal-la ba-an-ku_4**, 1 ir_7[mušen], 1 $tu-gur_5$[mušen], **igi-kár Ù-$šag_5$-a--šè**, iti--ta ud-30 ba-ra-zal, zi-ga- ***Á-pi$_5$-lí-a***. *iti-ezem-[d]Šul-gi*, *mu ús-sa é-Puzr$_4$-iš-[d]Da-gan ba-dù.* (*Rochester* 011, *P*128116)	[1 + *x*] **butchered pigeons** when the **26th**day passed, 1 **butchered dove** when the **28th**day passed, were **sent to the palace**, 1 pigeon, 1 dove, for **the provisions of U-šaga** when the **30th** day passed, were **withdrawn from Apiliya**. Month of ezem-Šulgi, Year after that of office of Puzriš-Dagan was built.	【1+x】**宰杀的家鸽**，于26日过去时，1只**宰杀的野鸽**，于28日过去时，**被送入宫殿**，1只家鸽和1只野鸽为**乌沙合供奉**，于30日过去时，**从阿皮里亚支出**了。神舒勒吉庆典月，普兹瑞什达干司被建之年次年。

续表

时间和摘要	文献内容	英文翻译	中文翻译
Š 40 viii/4, 5: **zi-ga** 4th: 1 [fattened] ram for ^{d}**Xsitum**, 1 fattened ram for **giranum festival of Inanna**, 5th: 1 fattened bull, 4 fattened rams and 1 kid for **temple of Ninlil**, 1 fat bull, 2 fat rams and 1 kid for **Alla-gula**, 1 fat ram for **Nin-tiug**, 1 fattened ram for **statue of king**, 1 ewe for the **lord of strength**, 1 ram for **Damgal-nunna**, 1 ewe for **Nintu**, 1 ewe for **Queen of Tummal**, **withdr.fr.Apiliya**	1 udu- [niga], x ^{d}*X-si$_4$$^{?}$-tum*, 1 *udu-niga**gi-ra-núm-***^{d}**Inanna**, iti--ta **ud-4**ba-ra-zal, 1 gud-niga, 4 udu-niga, 1 máš, **é-**^{d}**Nin-líl**, 1 gud-niga, 2 udu-niga, 1 máš, ^{d}***Al-la-gu-la***, 1 *udu-niga* ^{d}**Nin-ti-ug$_5$-ga**, 1 udu-niga, **alan-lugal**, 1 u$_8$ **en-á-nun**, 1 udu-ú ^{d}**Dam-gal-nun-na**, 1 u$_8$ ^{d}**Nin-tu**, 1 u$_8$-ú ^{d}**Nin-Tum-ma-al-la**, iti--ta**ud-5** ba-ra-zal, zi-ga***Á-pi$_5$-lí-a***. *iti-šu-eš-ša, mu ús-sa é-Puzur$_4$-iš-^{d} Da-gan ba-dù.* (*B.W.Ath.*6 45 06, *P*104742)	1 [*fattened*] *ram for* ^{d}**Xsitum**, 1 fattened ram for **giranum festival of Inanna**, when **4th** day passed, 1 fattened bull, 4 fattened rams and 1 kid for **temple of Ninlil**, 1 fattened bull, 2 fattened rams and 1 kid for **Alla-gula**, 1 fattened ram for **Nin-tiug**, 1 fattened ram for **statue of king**, 1 ewe for the **lord of strength**, 1 grass ram for **Damgal-nunna**, 1 ewe for **Nintu**, 1 grass ewe for **Queen of Tummal**, when **5th** day passed, were **withdrawn from Apiliya**.Month of šu-ešša, Year after that of office of Puzriš-Dagan was built.	1【育肥】公绵羊为X，1育肥公绵羊为**伊南那的吉腊努姆仪式**，于**4**日过去时，1育肥公牛、4育肥公绵羊和1公崽为**宁里勒庙**，1育肥公牛、2育肥公绵羊和1公崽为**阿拉古拉**，1育肥公绵羊为**宁提乌格**，1育肥公绵羊为**王像**，1母绵羊为**力量之主**，1食草公绵羊为**达姆旮勒农那**，1母绵羊为**宁图**，1食草母绵羊为**宁图马勒**，于**5**日过去时，**阿皮里亚支出**。三只手月， 普兹瑞什达干司被建年次年。
Š 40 viii/29, 30: **mu-túm, ì-dab$_5$** 29th: 3 ducks from **the bride of Inim-Šara**, 30th: 2 + ducks fr. **Ninlil-tumimti**, these were brought in, **Apiliya took over**	3 uz-tur, **é-gi$_4$-a-Inim-**^{d}**Šará**, iti--ta **ud-29**ba-ra-zal, 2 + uz-tur ^{d}**Nin-líl-tum-im-ti**, iti--ta ud-30 ba-ra-zal, mu-túm, ***Á-pi$_5$-lí-a*** *ì-dab$_5$. iti-šu-eš-ša, mu ús-sa é-Puzr$_4$-iš-^{d}Da-gan ba-dù.* (*CST*051, *P*107563)	3 *ducks from t***he bride of Inim-Šara**, when **29th** day passed, 2 + ducks from **Ninlil-tumimti**, when**30th**day passed, these were brought in, **Apiliya took over**.Month of šu-ešša, Year after that of office of Puzriš-Dagan was built.	3只鸭子自**伊尼姆沙腊的新娘**，于**29**日过去时，2+只鸭子来自**宁里勒吞伊姆提**，于**30**日过去时，**贡入品被阿皮里亚接管**了。三只手月，普兹瑞什达干司被建年次年。
Š 40iv-viii: (**zi-ga**) 40 ewes**for monthly allowance of Belat-Suhnir, Belat-Darraban, Annunitum and Ulmašitum** (each month 8 ewes, total 5 months)	8 u$_8$, iti-ki-siki-^{d}Nin-a-zu, 8 u$_8$, iti-ezem-^{d}Nin-a-zu, 8 u$_8$, iti-á-ki-ti, 8 u$_8$, iti-ezem-^{d}Šul-gi, 8 u$_8$, iti-šu-eš-ša, **sá-dug$_4$** ^{d} ***Be-la-at-Suh-nir***, ^{d} ***Be-la-at-Dar-ra-ba-an***, ***An-nu-ni-tum ù*** ^{d}***Ul-ma-ší-tum***. *mu ús-sa é-Puzur$_4$-iš-^{d}Da-gan ba-dù.* (*MVN* 03 185, *P*113745)	8 *ewes for month of ki-siki-Ninazu*, 8 *ewes for month of ezem-Ninazu*, 8 *ewes for month of akiti*, 8 *ewes for month of ezem-Šulgi*, 8 *ewes for month of šu-ešša*, *for* **monthly allowance of Belat-Suhnir, Belat-Darraban, Annunitum and Ulmašitum**.Year after that of the office of Puzriš-Dagan was built.	8只母绵羊为**宁阿朱羊毛作坊月**，8只母绵羊为**宁阿朱庆典月**，8只母绵羊为**阿基提月**，8只母绵羊为**舒勒吉庆典月**，8只母绵羊为三只手月，以上为**贝拉特苏赫尼尔、贝拉特达腊班、安努尼吞和乌勒马席吞的月供**。普兹瑞什达干司被建年次年。

续表

时间和摘要	文献内容	英文翻译	中文翻译
Š 40 ix/5: **zi-ga** 1 grass ram for **" cultic-table -room"**, 2 fattened lamb for the **food of king**, 2 fattened rams for **lament of Nanna**, 1 fattened ram for **sacrifice of Allatum**, 1 grass ram for **Ipiq-Erra**, 1 grass ram for **Šulgi-ili**, were withdrawn from **Apiliya**	1 udu-ú, **zà-gú-lá**--šè, 2 sila$_4$-niga, **níĝ-gu$_7$-lugal**--šè, 2 udu-niga, **ér su$_3$-a-^{d}Nanna**, 1 udu-niga, **siskúr-*^{d}Al-la-tum***, *iti--ta ud-5 ba-ra-zal*, 1 *udu-ú*, ***I-pi$_5$-iq-Èr-ra***, 1 *udu-ú*, ***^{d}Šul -gi-ì-lí***, *zi-ga-**Á-pi$_5$-lí-a**.iti-ezem-mah*, *mu ús-sa é-Puzr$_4$-iš-^{d}Da-gan ba-dù.* (*MVN* 03 178, *P*113738)	1 *grass ram for* **" cultic-table -room"**, 2 fattened lamb for the **food of king**, 2 fattened rams for **lament of Nanna**, 1 fattened ram for **sacrifice of Allatum**, when the 5th day passed, 1 grass ram for **Ipiq-Erra**, 1 grass ram for **Šulgi-ili**, were withdrawn from **Apiliya**. Month of ezem-mah, Year after that of the office of Puzriš-Dagan was built.	1食草公绵羊为**贡桌库**，2育肥羊羔为**国王的食物**，2育肥公绵羊为**南那神的哀悼祭**，1育肥公绵羊为**阿拉吞的祭祀**，于5日过去时，1食草公绵羊为**伊皮克埃腊**，1食草公绵羊为**舒勒吉伊里**，从**阿皮里亚支出了**。大庆典月，普兹瑞什达干司被建年次年。
Š 40 ix/10, 19: **mu-túm, ì-dab$_5$** 10th: 1 duck from the **bird-catcher**, 19th: 1 duck, 1 white duck from **Te ṣin-mama**, 1 white duck from **Sin-nada**, were deliveries for Šulgi-simti, **Apiliya took over**	1 uz-tur, **mušen-dù-ne**, iti--ta **ud-10**ba-ra-zal, 1 uz-tur, 1 uz-babbár, ***Te- ṣ i-in-Ma-ma***, 1 *uz-babbár*, ^{d} **Suen-na-da**, iti--ta **ud-20**lá-1 ba-ra-zal, mu-túm- ***^{d}Šul-gi-sí-im-ti***, ***Á-pi$_5$-lí-a*** *ì-dab$_5$. iti-ezem-mah*, *mu ús-sa é-Puzr$_4$-iš-^{d}Da-gan ba-dù.* (*BIN* 3 486, P106293)	1 *duck from the***bird-catcher** when the **10th**day passed, 1 duck, 1 white duck from **Te ṣin-mama**, 1 white duck from **Sin-nada**, when **19th**day passed, were deliveries for Šulgi-simti, **Apiliya took over**. Month of ezem-mah, Year after that of office of Puzriš-Dagan was built.	1只鸭来自**捕鸟人**，于**10**日过去时，1只鸭和1只白鸭来自**台岑妈妈**，1只白鸭来自**辛那达**，于**19**日过去时　为舒勒吉新提的送入项，**阿皮里亚接管**了。大庆典月，普兹瑞什达干司被建年之次年。
Š 40 ix/12: **zi-ga, butchered** 1 duck and 2 pigeons, **butchered ones were sent to palace, withdrawn from Apiliya**	1 uz-tur, 2 ir$_7$^{mušen} **ba-úš é-gal-la ba-ku$_4$**, iti--ta ud-12 ba-ra-zal, zi-ga ***Á-pi$_5$-lí-a.*** *iti-ezem-mah*, *mu ús-sa é-Puzur$_4$-iš-^{d}Da-gan ba-dù.* (*Van Kampen* 326, *P*200575)	1 *duck and* 2 *pigeons*, **butchered ones were sent to palace**, when 12th day passed, **withdrawn from Apiliya**. Month of ezem-mah, Year after that of office of Puzriš-Dagan was built.	1只鸭和2只家鸽，这些**宰杀牲被送入宫殿**，于12日过去时，从**阿皮里亚支出**了。大庆典月，普兹瑞什达干司被建年之次年。
Š 40 ix/16: **zi-ga** 1 fattened ram for**the sacrifice of Nin-Gubalaga, withdrawn from Apiliya**	1 udu- [niga], **siskúr-^{d}Nin-Gubalaga**, zi-ga-***Á-pi$_5$-lí-a***, *iti--ta ud*-16 *ba-ra-zal.* *iti-ezem-mah*, *mu ús-sa é-Puzr$_4$-iš-^{d}Da-gan ba-* [*dù*]. (*Torino* 1 183, *P*132071)	1 *fat ram for* **the sacrifice of Nin-Gubalaga, withdrawn from Apiliya**, when 16th day passed. Month of ezem-mah, Year after that of office of Puzriš-Dagan was built.	1只育肥公绵羊为**宁古巴拉旮的祭祀**，从**阿皮里亚支出了**， 于16日过去时。大庆典月，普兹瑞什达干司被建年次年。
Š 40 ix/19, 20: **zi-ga, butchered** 19th: 2 ducks, 5 doves, 20th: 2 ducks, 1 white bird, 10 doves, **butchered dead were sent to the palace, withdrawn from Apiliya**	2 uz-tur, 5 tu-gur$_4$^{mušen} iti--ta **ud-19** ba-ra-zal, 2 uz-tur, 1 uz-babbar, 10 tu-gur$_4$^{mušen}, iti--ta **ud-20** ba-ra-zal, **ba-ug$_7$-ug$_7$ é-gal-la ba-an-ku$_4$**, zi-ga ***Á-pi$_5$-lí-a.*** *iti-ezem-mah*, *mu ús-sa Puzur$_4$-iš-^{d} Da-gan ba-dù.* (*Nisaba* 08 381, *P*321032)	2 *ducks*, 5 *doves*, *when the* 19th *day passed*, 2 *ducks*, 1 *white bird*, 10 *doves*, *when* 20th *day passed*, **butchered ones were sent to the palace, withdrawn from Apiliya.** Month of ezem-mah, Year after that of the office of Puzriš-Dagan was built.	2只鸭和5只野鸽，于19日过去时，2只鸭、1只白鸟和10只野鸽，于20日过去时，以上**宰杀牲被送入宫殿**，**从阿皮里亚支出了**。大庆典月，普兹瑞什达干司被建年次年。

续表

时间和摘要	文献内容	英文翻译	中文翻译
Š 40 ix/22: **mu-túm, ì-dab$_5$** 1 fattened ram, 1 he-goat from**Nir-idagal**, when the 22nd day passed, were deliveries for Šulgi-simtum, **Apiliya took over**	1 udu-niga, 1 máš-gal, ***Nir-ì-da-ĝál***, *iti--ta ud-22 ba-ra-zal*, *mu-túm-*[d]***Šul-gi-sí-im-tum***, ***Á-pi$_5$-lí-a*** *ì-dab$_5$. iti-ezem-mah*, *mu ús-sa é-Puzr$_4$-iš-*[d]*Da-gan ba-dù.* (*RT* 37 129 *mr* 3, *P*128396)	1 *fattened ram*, 1 *he-goat from***Nir-idagal**, when the 22nd day passed, were deliveries for Šulgi-simtum, **Apiliya took over**. Month of ezem-mah, Year after that of the office of Puzriš-Dagan was built.	1只育肥公绵羊和1只公山羊来自**尼尔伊达旮勒**，于22日过去时，为舒勒吉新吞的送入项，**阿皮里亚接管**了。大庆典月，普兹瑞什达干司被建年次年。
Š 40 ix/30: **zi-ga** 2 fat rams, 1 ram, for **sacrifice of beginning of New Moon**, **in Uruk**, **via Mašum**, 1 fat ram for **giranum of Inanna**, 1 fattened ram, 1 goat for **sacrifice of Belat-Suhnir and Belat-Darraban**, 1 fat ram for **sacrifice of Nanna**, 1 fat kid for **sacrifice of Nin-sun**, 1 lamb for **disappearing place**, **in palace**, **withdr.fr.Apiliya**	2 udu-niga, 1 udu-ú, **siskúr sag-ud-sakar** šà ~ **Unug**[ki]-ga, gìr*Ma-šum*; 1 *udu-niga*, ***gi-ra-núm-***[d]**Inanna**, 1 udu-niga, 1 máš-gal, **siskúr-**[d] ***Be-la-at-Suh-nir*** *ù* [d] ***Be-la-at-Dar-ra-ba-an***, 1 *udu-niga*, **siskúr-**[d]**Nanna**, 1[f]ašgar-niga, **siskúr-**[d]**Nin-sún**, 1kir$_{11}$, **niĝ ~ ki-zàh** šà ~ **é-gal-la**, iti--ta ud-30 ba-ra-zal, zi-ga ***Á-pi$_5$-lí-a***. *iti-ezem-mah*, *mu ús-sa é-Puzr$_4$-iš-*[d]*Da-gan ba-dù.* (*AnOr* 07 065, *P*101360)	2 *fattened rams*, 1 *grass ram*, *for***sacrifice of beginning of the New Moon**, **in Uruk**, **via Mašum**, 1 fattened ram for **giranum festival of Inanna**, 1 fattened ram, 1 he-goat for **sacrifice of Belat-Suhnir and Belat-Darraban**, 1 fattened ram for **sacrifice of Nanna**, 1 fattened female kid for **sacrifice of Nin-sun**, 1 female lamb for **offering of disappearing place**, **in palace**, when 30th day passed, were **withdrawn from Apiliya**. Month of ezem-mah, Year after that of office of Puzriš-Dagan was built.	2只育肥公绵羊和1只食草公绵羊为**新月初祭**，于**乌鲁克**，**经由马顺**，1只育肥公绵羊为**伊南那的吉腊努姆仪式**，1只育肥公绵羊和1只公山羊为**贝拉特苏赫尼尔和贝拉特达腊班的祭祀**，1只育肥公绵羊为**南那的祭祀**，1只育肥雌山羊崽为**宁顺的祭祀**，1只雌羔为**消失处**，于**宫殿**，于第30天过去时，从**阿皮里亚支出**了。大庆典月，普兹瑞什达干司被建年次年。
Š 40 x/18: **zi-ga** 1 fat ram, 1 ram for the **temple of Nin-sun**, 1 fatteded ram, 1 grass ram for **the temple of Adad**, 1 fattened ram for **Puzur-Ištar**, 1 ram, 1 kid for **Geme-igi-sasaga** (**son of Šul-gi**), were **withdrawn from Apiliya**	1 udu-niga, 1 udu-ú, **é-**[d]**Nin-sún**, 1 udu-niga, 1 udu-ú, **é-**[d]**Iškur**, 1 udu-niga, ***Puzur$_4$-Iš$_8$-tár***, 1 *udu*, 1 *máš*, **Géme-igi-sa$_6$-sa$_6$-ga**, iti--ta ud-18 ba-ra-zal, zi-ga-***Á-pi$_5$-lí*** ***a***. *iti-ezem-An-na*, *mu ús-sa é-Puzr$_4$-iš-*[d]*Da-gan ba-dù.* (*OIP* 115061, *P*123568)	1 *fattened ram*, 1 *grass ram for the***temple of Nin-sun**, 1 fatteded ram, 1 grass ram for **the temple of Adad**, 1 fattened ram for **Puzur-Ištar**, 1 ram, 1 kid for **Geme-igi-sasaga** (**son of Šul-gi**), when 18th day passed, were **withdrawn from Apiliya**. Month of ezem-Anna, Year after that of office of Puzriš-Dagan was built.	1肥公绵羊和1食草公绵羊为**宁孙神庙**，1肥公绵羊和1食草公绵羊为**阿达德神庙**，1育肥公绵羊为**普朱尔伊什塔尔**，1公绵羊和1公崽为**吉美伊吉萨萨旮（舒勒吉之子）**于18日过去时，从**阿皮里亚支出**了。天神庆典月，普兹瑞什达干司被建年次年。

续表

时间和摘要	文献内容	英文翻译	中文翻译
Š 40 x/28: **zi-ga, butchered** 1 fattened ram, 2 he-goats for**sacrifice of New Moon in Uruk**, via **Erra-bani**, the cook, 1 fattened ram for **giranum festival of Inanna**, 1 fattened ram, 1 ewe for **sacrifice of Belat-S. and Belat-D.**, 1 fat ram for **sacrifice of Nanna**, 1 lamb for **"disappearing place"**, **in palace**, 1 kid for **Nin-sun**, 1 **butchered** ram, 1**butchered** ewe, **sent to palace**, **withdr.fr.Apiliya**	1 udu-niga, 2 máš-gal, **siskúr sag-ud-sakar** šà ~ **Un-ug^{ki}**-ga, gìr ***Èr-ra-ba-ni*** *muhaldim*, 1 *udu-niga* ***gi-ra-núm-^{d}Inan-na***, 1 udu-niga, 1 u_8, **siskúr-^{d}** ***Be-la-at-Suh-nir*** ù ***^{d}Be-la-at-Dar-ra-ba-an***, 1 *udu-niga*, **siskúr-^{d}Nanna**, 1 $sila_4$, **níĝ~ki-záh** šà **é-gal-la**, 1 máš, **siskúr-^{d}Nin-sún**, 1 udu-ú~ba-úš, a-rá 1-kam, 1 u_8~ba-úš, a-rá-2-kam, **é-gal-la ba-an-ku$_4$**, iti--ta ud-28 ba-ra-zal, zi-ga ***Á-pi$_5$-lí-a***. *iti-ezem-An-na*, *mu ús-sa é-Puzr$_4$-iš-^{d} Da-gan ba-dù*. (*AnOr* 07 066, *P*101361)	1 *fattened ram*, 2 *he-goats for***sacrifice of New Moon in Uruk**, via **Erra-bani**, the cook, 1 fattened ram for **giranum festival of Inanna**, 1 fattened ram, 1 ewe for **sacrifice of Belat-Suhnir and Belat-Darraban**, 1 fattened ram for **sacrifice of Nanna**, 1 lamb for **sacrifice of "disappearing place"**, **in the palace**, 1 kid for **sacrifice of Ninsun**, 1 **butchered** grass ram on 1st time, 1 **butchered** ewe on 2nd time, were **sent to palace**, when 28th day passed, **withdrawn from Apiliya**. Month of ezem-Anna, Year after that of the office of Puzriš-Dagan was built.	1只育肥公绵羊、2只公山羊为**新月祭于乌鲁克**，经由**厨师埃腊巴尼**，1只育肥公绵羊为**伊南那得吉腊努姆仪式**，1只育肥公绵羊和1只母绵羊为**贝拉特苏赫尼尔和贝拉特达腊班祭祀**，1只育肥公绵羊为**南那祭**，1只羊羔为**消失处供奉**，于**宫殿**，1只公崽为**宁荪祭**，1只**宰杀的**食草公绵羊第1次，1只**宰杀的**母绵羊第2次，**被送入宫殿**，于28日过去时，从**阿皮里亚支出**了。天神庆典月，普兹瑞什达干司被建年次年。
Š 40 xi/6, 8: **zi-ga, butchered** **6th**: 1 duck, 2 birds, 1 pigeon, **8th**: 1 duck, 1 pigeon, **butchered ones were sent to the palace, withdrawn from Apiliya**	1 uz-tur, 2 ir$_3$-mul^{mušen}, 1 ir$_7$^{mušen}, iti--ta **ud-6**ba-ra-zal, 1 uz-tur, 1 ir$_7$^{mušen}, iti--ta **ud-8**ba-ra-zal, ba-úš-úš, é-gal-la ba-an-ku$_4$, zi-ga ***Á-pi$_5$-lí-a***. <*iti-ezem-Me-ki-ĝál*> *mu ús-sa é-Puzr$_4$-iš-^{d}Da-gan ba-dù*. (*AfO* 40-41, 52, 1, *P*100296)	1 *duck*, 2 *birds*, 1 *pigeon*, *when the* **6th**day passed, 1 duck, 1 pigeon, when the **8th**day passed, **butchered ones were sent to the palace, withdrawn from Apiliya**. <Month of ezem-Mekiĝal>, Year after that of the office of Puzriš-Dagan was built.	1只鸭、2只鸟和1只家鸽于6日过去时，1只鸭和1只家鸽，于8日过去时，**这些宰杀牲被送入宫殿**， 以上从**阿皮里亚支出**了。<神美基旮勒庆典月>，普兹瑞什达干司被建年之次年。

续表

时间和摘要	文献内容	英文翻译	中文翻译
Š 40 xi/18: **zi-ga** 1 fattened ram, 2 lambs for**Ninlil**, 1 fattened ram, 2 lambs for **Enlil**, 1 ewe for **Nin-gagia**, 1 grass ram for **Alla-gula of dusk**; 1 fattened ram, 1 lamb for **Ninlil**, 1 kid for **Enlil**, 1 fattened ram for **Inanna**, 1 fattened ram for **Nin-urta**, 1 fattened ram for**Nusku of dawn**, **for the sacrifice of mourning in Nippur**, **via my queen**, **withdrawn from Apiliya**	1 udu-niga, 2 sila$_4$, ^{d}**Nin-líl**, 1 udu-niga, 2 sila$_4$, ^{d}**En-líl**, 1 u$_8$, ^{d}**Nin-ĝá-gi$_4$-a**, 1 udu-ú, ^{d}***Al-la-gu-la***, **á-ud-te-na-kam**; 1 udu-niga, 1 sila$_4$, ^{d}**Nin-líl**, 1 máš, ^{d}**En-líl**, 1 udu-niga ^{d}**Inanna**, 1 udu-niga ^{d}**Nin-urta**, 1 udu-niga ^{d}**Nusku**, **á-gú-zig-ga**, ér-siskúr--ra šà~ **Ni-bru^{ki}**, gìr **nin-ĝá**, iti--ta ud-18 ba-ra-zal, zi-ga-***Á-pi$_5$-lí-a***. *iti-ezem-Me-ki-ĝál*, *mu ús-sa é-Puzr$_4$-iš-^{d}Da-gan ba-dù.* (*SumRecDreh.*05, *P*130502)	1 *fattened ram*, 2 *lambs for***Ninlil**, 1 fattened ram, 2 lambs for**Enlil**, 1 ewe for **Nin-gagia**, 1 grass ram for**Alla-gula of dusk**; 1 fattened ram, 1 lamb for**Ninlil**, 1 kid for**Enlil**, 1 fattened ram for **Inanna**, 1 fattened ram for **Nin-urta**, 1 fattened ram for**Nusku of dawn**, **for the sacrifice of mourning in Nippur**, **via my queen**, when the 18th day passed, were **withdrawn from Apiliya**. Month of ezem-Mekiĝal, Year after that of the office of Puzriš-Dagan was built.	1育肥公绵羊和2羊羔为**宁里勒**，1育肥公绵羊和2羊羔为**恩里勒**，1母绵羊为**宁旮吉亚**，1食草公绵羊为**阿拉古拉**，为**黄昏祭**；1育肥公绵羊和1羊羔为**宁里勒**，1公崽为恩里勒，1育肥公绵羊为**伊南那**，1育肥公绵羊为**宁乌尔塔**，1育肥公绵羊为**努斯库**，**为晨祭**，**为于尼普尔德哀悼祭**，**经由我的王后**，于18日过去时，从阿皮里亚支出了。神美基旮勒庆典月，普兹瑞什达干司被建年次年。
Š 40 xi/25, 30: **zi-ga** 25th: 1 grass bull, 3 fattened rams for **the heaven boat**, 1 fattened ram for the **"night staying" shrine**, 1 grass ram for **Nanaya**, in **Uruk**, via **Ipiq-Erra**, 30th: 1fat goat for the **giranum festival of Inanna**, 1 fat ram, 1 fat goat for the **sacrifice of Belat-Suhnir and Belat-Darraban**, 1 fat ram for **Nanna**, 1 fat ram, 1 kid, for **sacrifice of Adad**, 1 kid for **Nin-sun**, 1 lamb for **disappearing place**, in the **palace**, **withdrawn from Apiliya**	1 gud-ú, 3 udu-niga, **má-an-na--šè**, 1 udu-niga, **ès-gi$_6$-zal**, 1 udu-ú, ^{d} **Na-na-a**, šà ~ **Unug^{ki}**-ga, gìr-***I-pi$_5$-iq-Èr-ra***, iti--ta**ud-25** ba-ra-zal; 1 máš-gal-niga, ***gi-ra-núm***-^{d}**Inanna**, 1 udu-niga, 1 máš-gal-niga, **siskúr-^{d}*Be-la-at-Suh-nir*** *ù* ^{d}***Be-la-at-Dar-ra-ba-an***, 1 *udu-niga*, ^{d}**Nanna**, 1 udu-niga, a-rú-1-kam; 1 máš, a-rú-2-kam, **siskúr-^{d}Iškur**, 1 ^{f}ašgar ^{d}**Nin-sún**, 1 kir$_{11}$, **níĝ~ ki-zàh**, šà~ **é-gal-la**, iti--ta **ud-30** ba-ra-zal, zi-ga-***Á-pi$_5$-lí_a***. *iti-ezem-Me-ki-ĝál*, *mu ús-sa é-Puzr$_4$-iš-^{d}Da-gan ba-dù.* (*OIP* 115062, *P*123428)	1 *grass bull*, 3 *fattened rams for* **the heaven boat**, 1 fattened ram for the **"night staying" shrine**, 1 grass ram for **Nanaya**, in **Uruk**, via **Ipiq-Erra**, when **25th** day passed, 1fattened he-goat for the **giranum festival of Inanna**, 1 fattened ram, 1 fattened he-goat for the **sacrifice of Belat-Suhnir and Belat-Darraban**, 1 fattened ram for **Nanna**, 1 fattened ram 1st time, 1 kid 2nd time, for the **sacrifice of Adad**, 1 female kid for **Nin-sun**, 1 female lamb for **offering of disappearing place**, in the **palace**, when **30th** day passed, were **withdrawn from Apiliya**. Month of ezem-Mekiĝal, Year after that of office of Puzriš-Dagan was built.	1食草公牛和3育肥公绵羊为**"天船"**，1育肥公绵羊为**黑夜圣殿**，1食草公绵羊为**那那亚**，于**乌鲁克**，**经由伊皮克埃腊**，于**25**日过去时；1育肥公山羊为**伊南那的吉腊努姆仪式**，1育肥公绵羊和1育肥公山羊为**贝拉特苏赫尼尔和贝拉特达腊班的祭祀**，1育肥公绵羊为**南那**，1育肥公绵羊第1次；1公羊崽第2次为**阿达德的祭祀**，1只雌崽为**宁苏**，1雌羔为**消失处供奉**，**在宫殿中**，于**30**日过去时，从**阿皮里亚支出了**。神美基旮勒庆典月，普兹瑞什达干司被建年次年。

续表

时间和摘要	文献内容	英文翻译	中文翻译
Š 40 xi： **mu-túm，ì-dab$_5$** 1 lamb from **Eue，the governor**，were delivery for Šulgi-simti，**Apiliya took over**	1 sila$_4$ É-u$_6$-e ensí，mu-túm ***^{d}Šul-gi-sí-im-ti*，*Á-pi$_5$-lí-a*** *ì-dab$_5$*. *iti-ezem-Me-ki-ĝál*，*mu ús-sa é-Puzur$_4$-iš-^{d}Da-gan ba-dù*. （*Nisaba* 08 169，*P*320588）	1 *lamb from* **Eue，the governor**，were delivery for Šulgi-simti，**Apiliya took over**. Month of ezem-Mekigal，Year after that of office of Puzriš-Dagan was built.	1只羊羔来自**埃乌埃总督**，为舒勒吉新提的送入项，**阿皮里亚接管了**。神美基旮勒庆典月，普兹瑞什达干司被建年次年。
Š 40 xii/25： **zi-ga，butchered** 1 fat ram for **giranum festival of Inanna**，1 ram，1 ewe and 1 lamb，**butchered ones for Imi-Sin**，were **withdrawn from Apiliya**	1 udu-niga，***gi-ra-núm-^{d}*Inanna**--šè，iti--ta **ud-25**-kam ba-ra-zal， 1 udu-ú，1 u$_8$，1 sila$_4$，ba-úš，***I-mi-^{d}Suen*--šè**，*zi-ga-**Á-pi$_5$-lí*-a**. iti-še-kin-kud*，*mu ús-sa é-Puzr$_4$-iš-^{d} Da-gan ba-dù*. （*Torino* 1 184，*P*132048）	1 *fattened ram for***giranum festival of Inanna**，when 25th day passed，1 grass ram，1 ewe and 1 lamb，**butchered ones for Imi-Sin，withdrawn from Apiliya**. Month of še-kin-kud，Year after that of the office of Puzriš-Dagan was built.	1肥公绵羊为**伊南那的吉腊努姆仪式**，于25日过去时，1食草公绵羊、1母绵羊和1羔，以上**宰杀牲为伊米辛**，**从阿皮里亚支出了**。大麦收割月，普兹瑞什达干司被建年次年。
Š 40ix-xii： （**zi-ga**） 9 rams，7 ewes，5 kids，1 lamb for**monthly allowance of Belat-Suhnir，Belat-Darraban，Annunitum and Ulmašitum**（total：4 months）	4 udu，2 u$_8$，**iti-ezem-mah**， 1 udu，3 u$_8$，**iti-ezem-An-na**， 2 udu，1 u$_8$，2 máš，1 sila$_4$，**iti-ezem-Me-ki-ĝál**， 2 udu，1 u$_8$，3 máš，**iti-še-kin-kud**，sá-dug$_4$ ***^{d}Be-la-at-Suh-nir*，*^{d} Be-la-at-Dar-ra-ba-an*，*An-nu-ni-tum* ù *^{d} Ul$^?$-ma-ši-tum***. *mu ús-sa é-Puzur$_4$-iš-^{d}Da-gan ba-dù*. （*BIN* 3 485，*P*106292）	4 *rams and* 2 *ewes for***month of ezem-mah**，1 ram and 3 ewes for **month of ezem-Anna**，2 rams，1 ewe，2 kids and 1 lamb for **month of Mekiĝal**，2 rams，1 ewe and 3 kids for **month of še-kin-kud**，for **monthly allowance of Belat-Suhnir，Belat-Darraban，Annunitum and Ulmašitum**. Year after that of the office of Puzriš-Dagan was built.	4公绵羊和2母绵羊为**大庆典月**，1公绵羊和3母绵羊为**安神庆典月**，2公绵羊、1母绵羊、2只公崽和1只羔为**神美基旮勒庆典月**，2公绵羊、1母绵羊和3公崽为**大麦收割月**，**以上为贝拉特苏赫尼尔贝拉特达腊班、安努尼吞和乌勒马席吞的月供**。普兹瑞什达干司被建年次年。
Š 41 i/4： **zi-ga** 1 fattened ram for **the sacrifice of Alla-tum**，when 4th day passed，**withdrawn from Apiliya**	1 udu-niga，**siskúr-*^{d} Al-la-tum***，*iti--ta* **ud-4** ba-ra-zal，zi-ga-***Á-pi$_5$-lí*-a**. *iti-maš-dà～gu$_7$*，*mu ús-sa é-Puzr$_4$-iš-^{d} Da-gan ba-dù mu-ús-sa-bi*. （*OIP* 115063，*P*123481）	1 *fattened ram for t***he sacrifice of Alla-tum**，when 4th day passed，**withdrawn from Apiliya**. Month of mašda-gu$_7$，Year after that of the office of Puzriš-Dagan was built；after that year.	1只育肥公绵羊为**阿拉吞的祭祀**，于4日过去时，**从阿皮里亚处被支出了**。食瞪羚月，普兹瑞什达干司被建年之次年：之次年。
Š 41 i/8，11，18： **zi-ga，butchered** 8th：1 duck for the **food of my queen**， 11th：1 **butchered dove sent to the palace**，18th：1 **butchered swallow sent to the palace，withdrawn from Apiliya**	1 uz-tur，**níĝ-gu$_7$-nin-ĝá**--šè，<u>iti--ta</u> **<u>ud-8</u>**<u>ba-ra-zal</u>，1 <u>tu-gur$_8$^{mušen}</u>**-ba-úš，é-gal-la ba-an-ku$_4$**，iti--ta **<u>ud-11</u>**<u>ba-ra-zal</u>，1 u$_5$-sim^{mušen} **ba-úš，é-gal-la ba-an-ku$_4$**，<u>ti--ta</u>**<u>ud-18</u>**<u>ba-ra-zal</u>，zi-ga ***Á-pi$_5$-lí-a***. *iti-maš-dà-gu$_7$*，*mu ús-sa é-Puzr$_4$-iš-^{d}Da-gan ba-dù mu ús-sa-bi*.（*PDT* 2 0970，*P*126318）	1 *duck for the***food of my queen**，<u>when</u> **8th**<u>day passed</u>，1 **butchered dove sent to palace**，<u>when</u>**<u>11th</u>** <u>day passed</u>，1 **butchered swallow sent to palace**，<u>when</u> **18th**<u>day passed</u>，were **withdrawn from Apiliya**. Month of mašda-gu$_7$，Year after that of the office of Puzriš-Dagan was built；after that year.	1只鸭子为**我的王后的食物**，于**8**<u>日过去时</u>，1只**宰杀野鸽被送入宫殿**于**<u>11</u>**<u>日过去时</u>，1只宰杀的**"舵燕鸦"被送入宫殿**于**<u>18</u>**<u>日过去时</u>，以上**从阿皮里亚支出了**。食瞪羚月，普兹瑞什达干司被建年之次年：之次年。

续表

时间和摘要	文献内容	英文翻译	中文翻译
Š 41 i/15: (zi-ga) 1 **butchered** lamb, 1 **butchered** kid for, were **sent to the palace**, 2 fattened rams and 1 grass [ram] for **sacrifice of Full Moon, in Uruk, via Ipiq-Erra**, 1 fattened ram for **giranum of Inanna**, 1 fattened ram and 1 grass ram for **sacrifice of Belat-Suhnir and Belat-Darraban**, 1 lamb for **sacrifice of Adad**	1 sila$_4$~ ba-úš a-rá-1-kam, 1 máš~ ba-úš a-rá-2-kam, **é-gal-la** ba-an-ku$_4$, 2 udu-niga, 1 [ram] -ú **siskúr é-ud-15** šà~ **Unug^{ki}-ga**, **gìr *I-pi$_5$-iq-Èr-ra***, 1 *udu-niga* **gi-ra-núm-^{d}*Inanna***, 1 udu-niga, 1 udu-ú **siskúr *^{d}Be-la-at-Suh-nir ù ^{d}Be-la-at-Dar-ra-ba-an***, 1 *sila$_4$* **siskúr ^{d}Iškur**, iti--ta ud-15 ba-ra-zal.iti-máš-kù-gu$_7$, mu ús-sa é-Puzur$_4$-iš-^{d}Da-gan ba-dù mu ús-sa-bi. (Ontario 1 016, P124429)	1**butchered** lamb for 1st time, 1 **butchered** kid for 2nd time, were **sent to the palace**, 2 fattened rams and 1 grass [ram] for **sacrifice of Full Moon, in Uruk, via Ipiq-Erra**, 1 fattened ram for **giranum of Inanna**, 1 fattened ram and 1 grass ram for **sacrifice of Belat-Suhnir and Belat-Darraban**, 1 lamb for **sacrifice of Adad**, when the 15th day passed, Month of mašku~gu$_7$, Year after that of the office of Puzriš-Dagan was built: after that year.	1只**宰杀羔**第1次，1只**宰杀的公山羊崽**第2次，**被送入宫殿**，2只育肥公绵羊和1只食草【公绵羊】**为满月牺牲，于乌鲁克，经由伊皮克埃腊**，1只肥公绵羊为**伊南那的吉腊努姆仪式**，1只育肥公绵羊和1只食草公绵羊为**贝拉特苏赫尼尔和贝拉特达腊班的牺牲**，1只羔为**阿达德**，于15日过去时。食瞪羚月，普兹瑞什达干司被建年之次年：次年。
Š 41 i/30: **zi-ga** 3 rams, 3 bulls for **sacrifice of New Moon**, in **Uruk**, **via Apiliya**, 1 fat ram for **giranum of Inanna**, 1 fat ram, 1 ram for **sacrifice of Belat-Suhnir and Belat-Darraban**, 1 fat ram for **sacrifice of Nanna**, 1 lamb for **"disappearing place" of New Moon in palace**, 1 kid for **Nin-sun**, **withdrawn from Apiliya**	3 udu-ú, 3 gud-ú, **siskúr sag ud-sakar** šà~ **Unug^{ki}**-ga, gìr ***Á-pi$_5$-lí-a***, 1 *udu-niga*, ***gi-ra-núm***-^{d}**Inanna**, 1 udu-niga, 1 udu-ú, **siskúr**-*^{d}**Be-la-at-Suh-nir*** *ù* ***^{d}Be-la-at-Dar-ra-ba-an***, 1 *udu-niga*, **siskúr-^{d}Nanna**, 1 sila$_4$, **níĝ~ ki-zàh**, **ud-sakar**, šà~ **é-gal-la**, 1 máš **siskúr-^{d}Nin-sún**--ka, iti--ta ud-30 ba-ra-zal, zi-ga ***Á-pi$_5$-lí-a***.*iti-maš-dà-gu$_7$*, *mu ús-sa é-Puzr$_4$-iš-^{d}Da-gan ba-dù mu-ús-sa-bi.* (*TRU* 274, P135038)	3 *grass rams*, 3 *grass bulls for***sacrifice of New Moon**, in **Uruk**, **via Apiliya**, 1 fattened ram for **giranum festival of Inanna**, 1 fattened ram, 1 grass ram for **sacrifice of Belat-Suhnir and Belat-Darraban**, 1 fattened ram for **sacrifice of Nanna**, 1 lamb for offering of **"disappearing place" of New Moon in palace**, 1 kid for sacrifice of **Nin-sun**, when 30th day passed, were **withdrawn from Apiliya**.Month of mašda-gu$_7$, Year after that of office of Puzriš-Dagan was built: after that year.	3只食草公绵羊和3只食草公牛为**新月祭于乌鲁克**，**经由阿皮里亚**，1只育肥公绵羊为**伊南那得吉腊努姆仪式**，1只肥公绵羊和1只食草公绵羊为**贝拉特苏赫尼尔和贝拉特达腊班的祭祀**，1只育肥公绵羊为**南那祭**，1只羊羔为**新月的消失处供奉**，于**宫殿**，1只公崽为**宁荪祭**，于30日过去时，**从阿皮里亚支出了**。食瞪羚月，普兹瑞什达干司被建年之次年：之次年。
Š 41/30: **zi-ga** 3 rams, 1 fat goat, for **elunum festival of temple of Belat-Suhnir and Belat-Darraban**, 1 bull, 3 fat rams, 1 ram for **ezem-Anna of temple of Annunitum and Ulmašitum**, in **Ur**, **via Ipiq-Erra** (withdrawn) from Apiliya	3 udu-ú, 1 máš-gal-niga, ***è-lu-núm*** *é-^{d}* ***Be-la-at-Suh$_6$-nir*** *ù* ***^{d}Be-la-at-Dar-ra-ba-an***, 1 *gud-ú*, 3 *udu-niga*, 1 *udu-ú*, *ezem-An-na*! (*tur*) *é-***An-nu-ni**! **-tum** *ù* ***^{d}Ul-ma-ši-tum***, šà~ **Uri$_5$^{ki}**-ma, gìr ***I-pi$_5$-iq-Èr-ra***, *iti--ta* ***Á-pi$_5$-lí-a***.*mu ús-sa é-Puzr$_4$-iš-^{d}Da-gan ba-dù.* (*SET* 044, *P*129454)	3 *grass rams*, 1 *fattened he-goat*, *for***elunum festival of temple of Belat-Suhnir and Belat-Darraban**, 1 grass bull, 3 fattened rams, 1 grass ram for**ezem-Anna of temple of Annunitum and Ulmašitum**, in **Ur**, **via Ipiq-Erra**, (withdrawn) from Apiliya. Year after that of the office of Puzriš-Dagan was built.	3只食草公绵羊和1只育肥公山羊为**贝拉特苏赫尼尔和贝拉特达腊班庙的埃鲁努姆节**，1只食草公牛、3只育肥公绵羊和1只食草公绵羊为**安努尼吞和乌勒马席吞庙的安神庆典**，于**乌尔**，**经由伊皮克埃腊**，从**阿皮里亚**处（支出），普兹瑞什达干司被建年之次年。

续表

时间和摘要	文献内容	英文翻译	中文翻译
Š 41 i： **zi-ga** 1 [grass] ram for**offering of "disappearing place" of Adad**，**Mašum as royal deputy**，**1 butchered lamb sent to the palace**，4 rams for **Mamaya**，1 ram for the **sacrifice of Allatum**，in **Ur**，**via Apiliya**，were **withdrawn from Apiliya**	1 udu-［ú］**níĝ~ki-zàh-^{d}Iškur**，*Ma-šum maškim*， 1 *sila$_4$-ba-úš*，**é-gal-la ba-an-ku$_4$**， 4 udu-ú，*Ma-ma-a*， 1 *udu-ú*，**siskúr-^{d}*Al-la-tum***， šà~ **Urim$_5$^{ki}**-ma， gìr-***Á-pi$_5$-lí-a***， zi-ga***Á-pi$_5$-lí-a***. *iti-maš-dà-gu$_7$，mu ús-sa é-Puzr$_4$-iš-^{d}Da-gan ba-dù mu-ús-sa-bi.*（*CST* 52，*P*107564）	1 [*grass*] *ram for***offering of "disappearing place" of Adad**，**Mašum as royal deputy**，**1 butchered lamb sent to the palace**，4 grass rams for **Mamaya**，1 grass ram for the **sacrifice of Allatum**，in **Ur**，**via Apiliya**，were **withdrawn from Apiliya**.Month of mašda-gu$_7$，Year after that of the office of Puzriš-Dagan was built：after that year.	1只【食草】公绵羊为**阿达德消失处供奉**，**马顺督办**， **1只宰杀羊羔被送入宫殿**，4只食草公绵羊为**妈妈亚**，1只食草公绵羊为**阿拉吞的祭祀**，于**乌尔**，**经由阿皮里亚**，以上从**阿皮里亚支出了**。 食瞪羚月，普兹瑞什达干司被建年之次年：次年。
[Š 41] i： **mu-túm，ì-dab$_5$** 1 duck，10 he-goats，1 lamb，from**the sister of Ṣ iluš-Dagan**，were deliveries for Šulgi-simtum，**Apiliya took over**	[...]，1 uz-tur，10 máš-gal，1 sila$_4$，　**nin$_9$-*Ṣ i-lu-uš-^{d}Da-gan***， *mu-túm-^{d}* ***Šul-gi-sí-im-tum****-ma*，***Á-pi$_5$-lí-a*** *ì-dab$_5$*. *iti-maš-dà~gu$_7$*，[*mu ús-sa é-Puzur$_4$-iš-^{d}Da-gan ba-dù mu ús-sa-bi*]. （*TRU* 076，*P*134840）	[...]，1 *duck*，10 *he-goats*，1 *lamb*，*from* **the sister of Ṣ iluš-Dagan**，were deliveries for Šulgi-simtum，**Apiliya took over**.Month of mašda~gu$_7$，[Year after that of the office of Puzriš-Dagan was built：after that year].	[...]，1只鸭、10只公山羊和1只羊羔来自**采鲁什达干之妹**，为舒勒吉新吞的送入项，**阿皮里亚接管了**。食瞪羚月， 【普兹瑞什达干司被建年之次年：次年】。
Š 41 ii/4： **zi-ga** 1 fat ram，1 fat goat，1 ram for **"pouring beer" festival of the daughter of Aba-Enlilgin**，1 fattened ram for **sacrifice of Allatum**，1 fattened ram for **Alla-gula**，2 fattened rams，1 lamb for **Ninlil**，1 fattened ram，1 kid for **Enlil**，1 grass ram for **Ningagia**，for **sacrifice of Moon of 7th**，in **Nippur**，**via my queen**，**withdrawn from Apiliya**	1 udu-niga，1 máš-gal-niga， 1 udu-ú，**kaš-dé-a dumu-munus-A-ba-^{d}En-líl-gin$_7$**， 1 udu-niga，**siskúr-*^{d}Al-la-tum***， 1 *udu-niga-**^{d}Al-la-gu-la***， 2 *udu-niga*，1 *sila$_4$*，**^{d}Nin-líl**， 1 udu-niga，1 máš，**^{d}En-líl**， 1 udu-ú，**^{d}Nin-ĝá-gi$_4$-a**，**siskúr é-ud-7** šà~ **Nibru^{ki}**， gìr **nin-ĝá**，iti-ta ud-4 ba-ra-zal，zi-ga ***Á-pi$_5$-lí-a***. *iti-ze$_x$-da-gu$_7$*， *mu ús-sa é-Puzr$_4$-iš-^{d}Da-gan ba-dù，mu ús-sa-bi.* （*AnOr* 07 068，*P*101363）	1 *fattened ram*，1 *fattened he-goat*，1 *grass ram for* **"pouring beer" festival of the daughter of Aba-Enlilgin**，1 fattened ram for **sacrifice of Allatum**，1 fattened ram for **Alla-gula**，2 fattened rams，1 lamb for **Ninlil**，1 fattened ram，1 kid for **Enlil**，1 grass ram for **Ningagia**，for **sacrifice of Moon of 7th**，in **Nippur**，**via my queen**，when the 4th day passed，**withdrawn from Apiliya**. Month of zeda-gu$_7$，Year after that of the office of Puzriš-Dagan was built：after that year.	1只育肥公绵羊、1只育肥公山羊和1只食草公绵羊为**阿巴恩里勒艮女倒啤酒宴会**，1只育肥公绵羊为**阿拉吞祭**，1只育肥公绵羊为**阿拉古拉**，1只育肥公绵羊和1只羊羔为**宁里勒**，1只育肥公绵羊和1只公崽为**恩里勒**，1只食草公绵羊为**宁旮吉阿**，**为初七上玄月于尼普尔**，**经由我的王后**，于4日过去时，从**阿皮里亚支出**。食豚月普兹瑞什达干司被建年之次年：之次年。

续表

时间和摘要	文献内容	英文翻译	中文翻译
Š 41 ii/[5]: **zi-ga, butchered** 1**butchered dove**[**was sent to palace**, [1+ fattened ram] for **Moon of 7th**, in **Nippur**, **withdrawn from Apiliya**	1ir$_7$^{mušen}-**ba-úš**, [**é-gal ba-an-ku$_4$**, iti-ta ud-5-ba]-ra-zal, [1+ udu-niga], rev. **é-ud-7** šà~ **Nibru^{ki}**, zi-ga-***Á-pi$_5$-lí*** *a. iti-ze$_x$-da-gu$_7$,* *mu ús-sa é-Puzr$_4$-iš-^{d}Da-gan ba-dù, mu ús sa-bi.* (*DoCu EPHE* 293, *P*109250)	1 **butchered dove**[**was sent to palace**, when 5th day passed, [1+ fattened ram] for **Moon of 7th**, in **Nippur**, **withdrawn from Apiliya**. Month of zeda ~gu$_7$, Year after that of the office of Puzriš-Dagan was built: after that year.	1只宰杀的家鸽【**被送入宫殿**】，于5日过去时，【1+公绵羊】**为初七上玄月祭**，**于尼普尔**，**从阿皮里亚支出了**。食豚月，普兹瑞什达干司被建年之次年：之次年。
Š 41 ii/20: **zi-ga, butchered** 2 fat rams for **Annunitum**, 1 goat for **Ulmašitum**, 2 goats for **Belat-Suhnir and Belat-Darraban**, **for elunum festival in Ur**, **via Mašum**, 1**butchered lamb was sent to palace**, were **withdrawn from Apiliya**	2 udu-niga ***An-nu-ni-tum***, 1 *máš-gal* ***^{d}Ul-ma-ši-tum***, 2 *máš-gal* ***^{d}Be-la-at-Suh-nir*** *ù* ***^{d}Be-la-at-Dar-ra-ba-an***, ***è-lu-núm*** *šà~* **Uri$_5$^{ki}**-ma, gìr***Ma-šum***, *iti-ta ud-20 ba-ra-zal*, 1 *sila$_4$* **ba-úš é-gal ba-an-ku$_4$**, zi-ga ***Á-pi$_5$-lí-a***. *iti-ze$_x$-da-gu$_7$, mu ús-sa é-Puzr$_4$-iš-^{d}Da-gan ba-dù,* *mu ús sa-bi.* (*AnOr* 07 067, *P*101362)	2 *fattened rams for* **Annunitum**, 1 he-goat for **Ulmašitum**, 2 he-goats for **Belat-Suhnir and Belat-Darraban**, **for elunum festival in Ur**, **via Mašum**, when 20th day passed, 1 **butchered lamb was sent to palace**, were **withdrawn from Apiliya**. Month of zeda~gu$_7$, Year after that of the office of Puzriš-Dagan was built: after that year.	2只育肥公绵羊为**安努尼吞**，1只公山羊为**乌勒马席吞**，2只公山羊为**贝拉特苏赫尼尔和贝拉特达腊班**，**为埃鲁努姆节**，**于乌尔**，**经由马顺**，于20日过去时，1只**宰杀的羊羔被送入宫殿**，以上从**阿皮里亚支出了**。食豚月，普兹瑞什达干司被建年之次年：之次年。
Š 41 ii/22: **mu-túm, ì-dab$_5$** 3 ducklet from**Išdum-kin**, were **deliveries for Šulgi-simti**, **Apiliya took over**	3 amar-sag~uz-tur, ***Išdum-ki-in***, *iti--ta ud-22 ba-ra-zal*, *mu-túm-*^{d}**Šul-gi-sim-ti**, ***Á-pi$_5$-lí-a***, *ì-dab$_5$. iti-ze$_x$-da-gu$_7$, mu ús-sa é-Puzr$_4$-iš-^{d}Da-gan ba-dù, mu ús sa-bi.* (*Torino* 1 036, *P*131968)	3 *ducklet from***Išdum-kin**, when 22nd day passed, were **deliveries for Šulgi-simti**, **Apiliya took over**. Month of zeda-gu$_7$, Year after that of the office of Puzriš-Dagan was built: after that year.	3只幼鸭来自**伊什杜姆金**，于22日过去时，**为舒勒吉新提的送入项**，**阿皮里亚接管了**。食豚月，普兹瑞什达干司被建年之次年：之次年。
Š 41 ii: **zi-ga, butchered** 12 **butchered** rams, 1 **butchered** lamb for fuller, in **Ur**, **the overseer**: **Qudašum**, **withdrawn from Apiliya**	12 udu-ú, 1 sila$_4$, ba-úš-úš, azlag, šà~ **Urim$_5$^{ki}**-ma--ka--šè, ugula ***Qú-da-šum***, *zi-ga-****Á-pi$_5$-lí*** *a. iti-šeš-da-gu$_7$, mu ús-sa é-Puzr$_4$-iš-^{d}Da-gan ba-dù, mu ús-sa-bi.* (*OIP* 115 064, *P*123496).	12 **butchered** grass rams, 1 **butchered** lamb for fuller, in **Ur**, **overseer**: **Qudašum**, **withdrawn from Apiliya**. Month of zeda~gu$_7$, Year after that of office of Puzriš-Dagan was built: after that year.	12只**宰杀的**食草公绵羊和1只**宰杀的**羊羔为**乌尔的漂洗工**，**苦达顺监管**，以上从**阿皮里亚支出了**。食豚月，普兹瑞什达干司被建年之次年：之次年。
Š 41 i-ii: (**zi-ga**) [...] 4 rams, 2 [...]; 6 sheep formonthly **allowance of Belat-Suhner and Belat-Darraban, Annunitum and Ulma**[**šitum**]	[...], 4 udu-níta, 2 [...], iti-maš-kù-g[u$_7$], 2 sila$_4$, 3 máš, 1 ^{f}ašgar, iti-ze$_x$-da-gu$_7$, **sá-dug$_4$**-***^{d}Be-la-at-Suh-ne-er*** *ù* ***^{d}Be-la-at-Dar-ra-ba-an***, ***An-nu-ni-t*** [***um***] *ù* ***^{d}Ul-ma-***[***ši-tum***]. *mu ús-sa é-*[*Puzur$_4$*] *-iš-^{d}Da-*[*gan ba-dù*] *mu ús-s*[*a-bi*]. (*Grégaire*, *AAICAB* 1, 4, *Bod.S*430)	[...], 4 *rams*, 2 [...], *month of mašku~gu$_7$*, 2 *lambs*, 3 *kids and* 1 *female kid month of zeda~gu$_7$*, *for the* **monthly allowance of Belat-Suhner and Belat-Darraban, Annunitum and Ulma**[**šitum**]. Year after that of the office of [Puzriš]-Da[gan was built]: aft[er] that year.	【……】，4只公绵羊和2【……】，食瞪羚月，2只羔、3只公崽和1只雌崽食豚月，为**贝拉特苏赫耐尔和贝拉特达腊班**，**安努尼吞和乌勒马【席吞】的月供**。【普兹瑞什】达【干司被建】年之【次】年：之次年。

续表

时间和摘要	文献内容	英文翻译	中文翻译
Š 41 iii: **ì-dab$_5$, butchered** 1 **butchered** kid on the 1st time, 1 **butchered** female lamb on the 2nd time, were **sent to the palace**, these deliveries **Apiliya took over**	1 máš**ba-úš**, a-rá-1-kam; 1 kir$_{11}$ ba-úš, a-rá-2-kam-aš, **é-gal-la ba-ku$_4$**, zi-ga, ***Á-pi$_5$-lí-a*** *ì-dab$_5$.iti-u$_5$-bí-gu$_7$, muús-sa é-Puzur$_4$-iš-^{d}Da-gan ba-dù mu ús-sa-bi.* (Princeton 1 008, P126697)	1 **butchered** kid on the 1st time, 1 **butchered** female lamb on the 2nd time, were **sent to the palace**, these were withdrawn, **Apiliya took over**. Month of ubi-gu$_7$, Year after that of office of Puzriš-Dagan was built: after that year.	1只**宰杀的公崽**第1次；1只**宰杀的雌羔**第2次，**被送入宫殿**，以上支出， **阿皮里亚接管**了。 食乌比鸟月， 普兹瑞什达干司被建年之次年：之次年。
Š 41 iii/1, 4: **zi-ga, butchered** 1st: 1 **butchered kid sent to palace**, 1 fat ram for **elunum festival**, as the gifts, 4th: 1 fattened ram for **sacrifice of Allatum**, were **withdrawn from Apiliya**	1 máš-ba-úš, **é-gal-la ba-an-ku$_4$**, 1 udu-niga, ***è-lu-núm*** **sag-rig$_7$-ke$_4$-ne**, iti--ta-**ud-1**-ba-ra-zal, 1 udu-niga, **siskúr-** ***^{d}Al-la-tum***, *iti--ta* **ud-4**ba-ra-zal, zi-ga-***Á-pi$_5$-lí*** ***a.*** *iti-u$_5$-bí-gu$_7$, mu ús-sa é-Puzr$_4$-iš-^{d} Da-gan ba-dù mu ús-sa-bi.* (*JCS* 52, 127, *P*145892)	1**butchered kid sent to palace**, 1 fattened ram for **elunum festival**, as the gifts, when **1st**day passed, 1 fattened ram for **sacrifice of Allatum**, when **4th** day passed, were **withdrawn from Apiliya**. Month of ubi-gu$_7$, Year after that of the office of Puzriš-Dagan was built: after that year.	1**宰杀的公崽被送入宫殿**，1肥公绵羊为**埃鲁努姆节作为礼品**，于**1日**过去时，1育肥公绵羊为**阿拉吞祭祀**，于**4日**过去时，从**阿皮里亚支出了**。 食乌比鸟月， 普兹瑞什达干司被建年之次年：之次年。
Š 41 iv/2, 5: **zi-ga, butchered** 2nd: 1 **butchered ducklet** was **sent to the palace**, 5th: 1 ducklet, 5 doves for **the Month of 7th**, **in Nippur**, **via my queen**, were **withdrawn from Apiliya**	1 amar-sag ~ uz-tur-ba-úš, iti--ta **ud-2**ba-ra-zal, **é-gal-la ba-an-ku$_4$**, 1 amar-sag ~ uz-tur, 5 tu-gur$_4$^{mušen}, **é-ud-7 šà ~ Nibru^{ki}**, gìr-**nin-ĝá**, iti--ta **ud-5**ba-ra-zal, zi-ga-***Á-pi$_5$-lí a.*** *iti-ki-siki-^{d} Nin-a-zu, mu ús-sa é-Puzr$_4$-iš-^{d} Da-gan ba-dù, mu ús-sa-bi.* (*SACT* 1 133, *P*128888)	1 **butchered ducklet** when**2nd**day passed **sent to the palace**, 1 ducklet, 5 doves for **the Month of 7th**, **in Nippur**, **via my queen**, when**5th**day passed, were **withdrawn from Apiliya**. Month of ki-siki-Ninazu, Year after that of the office of Puzriš-Dagan was built: after that year.	1只**宰杀的幼鸭**，于2日过去时**被送入宫殿**，1只幼鸭和5只野鸽为**神庙的初七上玄月祭**，于**尼普尔**，**经由我的王后**，于5日过去时，从**阿皮里亚支出了**。神宁阿朱羊毛作坊月，普兹瑞什达干司被建年之次年：之次年。
Š 41 iv: (**zi-ga**) 2 rams, 2 lamb, 2 kids for the**monthly allowance of Belat-Suhnir**, **Belat-Darraban**, **Annunitum and Ulmašitum**	2 udu-nitá, 2 sila$_4$, 2 máš, **sá-dug$_4$**-***^{d}Be-la-at-Suh-nir***, **^{d}Be-la-at -Dar-ra-ba-an**, **An-nu-ni-tum**, *ù* **^{d}Ul-ma-ši-tum**.*iti-ki-siki-^{d}Nin-a-zu, mu ús-sa é-Puzr$_4$-iš-^{d}Da-gan ba-dù, mu ús-sa-bi.* (*Aegyptus* 19 235 03, *P*100225)	2 *rams*, 2 *lamb*, 2 *kids for the***monthly allowance of Belat-Suhnir**, **Belat-Darraban**, **Annunitum and Ulmašitum**.Month of ki-siki-Ninazu, Year after that of the office of Puzriš-Dagan was built: after that year.	2只公绵羊、2只羊羔和2只公崽为**贝拉特苏赫尼尔**、**贝拉特达腊班**、**安努尼吞和乌勒马席吞的月供**。神宁阿朱羊毛作坊月，普兹瑞什达干司被建年之次年：之次年。
Š 41 v/8: **zi-ga, butchered** 2**butchered grass rams were sent to palace**, 1 fattened ram for **the wife of Nuida**, were **withdrawn from Apiliya**	2 udu-ú ~ ba-úš, **é-gal-la ba-an-ku$_4$**, 1 udu-niga, **dam-*Nu-ì-da--šè***, *iti--ta ud-8 ba-ra-zal, zi-ga* ***Á-pi$_5$-lí-a.*** *iti-ezem-^{d} Nin-a-zu, mu ús-sa é-Puzr$_4$-iš-^{d} Da-gan ba-dù, mu ús-sa-bi.* (*Ontario* 1 017, *P*124430)	2**butchered grass rams were sent to palace**, 1 fattened ram for **wife of Nuida**, when 8th day passed, were **withdrawn from Apiliya**. Month of ezem-Ninazu, Year after that of office of Puzriš-Dagan was built: after that year.	2只宰杀的**食草公绵羊被送入宫殿**，1只育肥公绵羊为**努伊达之妻**，于8日过去时，从**阿皮里亚支出了**。神宁阿朱庆典月，普兹瑞什达干司被建年之次年：之次年。

续表

时间和摘要	文献内容	英文翻译	中文翻译
Š 41 v: **zi-ga** 2 grass rams, 1 he-goat, 1 kid, 6 ewes for **Abum**, **in Ur**, **via Apiliya**, were **withdrawn from Apiliya**	2 udu-ú, 1 máš-gal, 1 máš, 6 u$_8$, ***A-bu-um*** *šà*~ **Urim^{ki}**-ma--ka--šè, gìr ***Á-pi$_5$-lí-a***, *zi-ga-* ***Á-pi$_5$-lí-a***. *iti-ezem-^{d}Nin-a-zu*, *mu ús-sa é-Puzr$_4$-iš-^{d}Da-gan ba-dù*, *mu ús-sa-bi*. (*Torino* 1 185, *P*131991)	2 *grass rams*, 1 *he-goat*, 1 *kid*, 6 *ewes for* **Abum**, **in Ur**, **via Apiliya**, were **withdrawn from Apiliya**. Month of ezem-Ninazu, Year after that of the office of Puzriš-Dagan was built: after that year.	2食草公羊、1公山羊、1公崽和6母羊为**阿布姆于乌尔**，**经由阿皮里亚**，**从阿皮里亚支出**。神宁阿朱庆典月，普兹瑞什达干司被建年之次年：之次年。
Š 41 vi/8, 10: **mu-túm, ì-dab$_5$** 12 doves from**Simat-Ištar**, 2 ducks from **Watrat**, the overseer, [1+] pigeon from **Mašmašliya**, were deliveries for **Šulgi-simti**, **Apiliya took over**	12 tu-gur$_4$^{mušen} ***Simat-^{d}Iš$_8$-tár***, *iti--ta* **ud-8** ba-ra-zal, 2 uz-tur ***Wa-at-ra-at*** *ugula*! [1+] *ir$_7$^{mušen}* ***Maš-maš-lí-a*** *iti--ta* **ud-10** ba-[ra]-zal, mu-túm ~ [^{d}] ***Šul-gi-*** [***sí***] ***-im-*** [***ti***], ***Á-*** [***pi$_5$***] ***-lí-*** [***a***] *ì-dab$_5$*. *iti-á-ki-ti mu ús-saé-Puzur$_4$-iš-^{d}Da-gan ba-dù-a mu ús-sa-bi*. (*BCT* 2 246, *P*105486)	12 *doves from***Simat-Ištar**, when **8th** day passed, 2 ducks from **Watrat**, the overseer, [1+] pigeon from **Mašmašliya**, when **10th** day passed, were deliveries for **Šulgi-simti**, **Apiliya took over**. Month of akiti, Year after that of the office of Puzriš-Dagan was built: after that year.	12只野鸽来自**席马特伊什塔尔**，于**8**日过去时，2只鸭来自**瓦特腊特监工**，【1+】家鸽来自**马什马什里亚**，于**10**日过去时，为**舒勒吉新提的送入项**，**阿皮里亚接管**了。阿基提月，普兹瑞什达干司被建年之次年：之次年。
Š 41 vi: **zi-ga** 2 fattened rams for**Annunitum**, 1 grass ram for **Ulmašitum**, when (their) erubatum festival, **in Ur**, **via the man of Urub**, **the envoy**	2 udu-niga, ***An-nu-ni-tum***, 1 *udu-ú*, ***^{d}Ul-ma-ši-tum*** *ud* ~ ***è-ru-ba-tum-ka*** **šà ~ Urim$_5$^{ki}-ma**, **gìr lú-Urub** (**URUxKÁR**) **^{ki} sukkal**. iti-á-ki-ti, mu ús-sa é-Puzur$_4$-iš-^{d} Da-gan ba-dù-a mu ús-sa-bi. (AnOr 07 167, P101462)	2 fattened rams for**Annunitum**, 1 grass ram for **Ulmašitum**, when (their) erubatum festival, **in Ur**, **via the envoy**, **the man of Urub**. Month of akiti, Year after that of the office of Puzriš-Dagan was built: after that year.	2育肥公绵羊为**安努尼吞**，1只食草公绵羊为**乌勒马席吞**，于她们的埃如巴吞节时，**于乌尔**，**经由国使乌如卜城之人**。阿基提月，普兹瑞什达干司被建年之次年：之次年。
Š 41 vii/2: **zi-ga** 1 fattened ram for **the gate (of ká) of bedroom of high priestess**, 1 fattened ram for **Nanaya**, 2 fattened rams, 1 lamb, for the **gate (of ká) of shrine**, **via my queen**, **withdrawn from Apiliya**	1 udu-niga, **ka~ĝe$_6$-pàr**, 1 udu-niga, ***^{d}Na-na-a***, 2 *udu-niga*, 1 *sila$_4$*, **ka~èš**, gìr**nin-ĝá**, iti--ta ud-2 ba-ra-zal, zi-ga-***Á-pi$_5$-lí-a***. *iti-ezem-^{d}Šul-gi*, *mu ús-sa é-Puzr$_4$-iš-^{d}Da-gan ba-dù*, *mu ús-sa-bi*. (*AnOr* 07 069, *P*101364)	1 *fattened ram for* **gate (of ká) of bedroom of high priestess**, 1 fattened ram for **Nanaya**, 2 fattened rams, 1 lamb, for **gate (of ká) of shrine**, **via my queen**, when 2nd day passed, **withdrawn from Apiliya**. Month of ezem-Šulgi, Year after that of office of Puzriš-Dagan was built: after that year.	1只育肥公绵羊为**修道院之门**，1只育肥公绵羊为**那那亚**，2只育肥公绵羊和1只羊羔为**圣地之门**，**经由我的王后**，于2日过去时，从**阿皮里亚支出**了。神舒勒吉庆典月，普兹瑞什达干司被建年之次年：之次年。

续表

时间和摘要	文献内容	英文翻译	中文翻译
Š 41 vii/26: **zi-ga** [1+] fat [rams] and [1+] fat [lambs] for [**the boat**] **of** [**An**], [1+] fat rams for **temple of Nanaya**, 1 ram for "**night staying" shrine**, in **Uruk**, via x-ni, 1 fat ram for **giranum festival of Inanna** on 1st time; 3 fattened rams, 3 fattened lambs for **the boat of An**, 1 ram for **Libur-simti**, 1 he-goat for **Ištar-ummi**, 1 grass ram for **giranum fesitival of Inanna** on 2nd time, were **withdrawn from Apiliya**, **in the storehouse**	[1+ udu] -niga, [1+ sila$_4$] -niga, [**má-an**] -**na**--šè, [1+x] udu-niga, **é-^{d}Na-na-a**, 1 udu-ú, **èš-ge$_6$-zal**, šà ~ **Unug^{ki}**-ga, gìr [x] -x-ni-[x], 1 udu-niga, ***gi-ra-núm*-^{d}Inanna**, a-rá-1-kam; 3 udu-niga, 3 sila$_4$-niga, **má-an-na**--šè, 1 udu, ***Li-bur-sí-im-ti***, 1 *máš-gal*, ***Iš$_8$-tár-um-mi***, 1 *udu-ú*, ***gi-ra-núm*-^{d}Inanna** [a] -rá 2-kam, [iti--ta] ud-26 ba-ra-zal, [zi-ga] ***-Á-pi$_5$-lí-a***, [*šà* ~ **é**] **-sag-da-** [**na**]. [iti-ezem-^{d}] Šul-gi, mu ús-sa é-Puzur$_4$-iš-^{d}Da-gan ba-dù mu ús-sa-bi. (TRU 275, P135039)	[1+] fattened [rams] and [1+] fattened [lambs] for [**the boat**] **of** [**An**], [1+] fattened rams for **temple of Nanaya**, 1 grass ram for "**night staying" shrine**, in **Uruk**, via x-ni, 1 fattened ram for **giranum festival of Inanna** on 1st time; 3 fattened rams, 3 fattened lambs for **the boat of An**, 1 ram for **Libur-simti**, 1 he-goat for **Ištar-ummi**, 1 grass ram for **giranum fesitival of Inanna** on 2nd time, when the 26th day passed, were **withdrawn from Apiliya**, **in the storehouse.** Month of ezem-Šulgi, Year after that of office of Puzriš-Dagan was built: after that year.	**[1+] 育肥【公绵羊】和【1+】育肥【羊羔】为【安神之船】**，**【1+】只育肥公绵羊为那那亚庙**，1只食草公绵羊为**黑夜圣殿**，于**乌鲁克**，**经由x-尼**，1只育肥公绵羊为**伊南那的吉腊努姆仪式第1次**；3只育肥公绵羊和3只育肥羊羔为**安神之船**，1只公绵羊为**里布尔新提**，1只公山羊为**伊什塔尔乌米**，1只食草公绵羊为**伊南那的吉腊努姆仪式第2次**，于26日过去时，**从阿皮里阿支出**，**于仓库中**。 神舒勒吉庆典月， 普兹瑞什达干司被建年次年：之次年。
Š 41 vii: (**zi-ga**) 6 sheep for **monthly allowance of Belat-Suhnir and Belat-Darraban**, **Annunitum and Ulmašitum**	2 udu-nitá, 2 u$_8$, 2 máš, sá-dug$_4$ ***^{d}Be-la-at-Suh-nir*** *ù* ***^{d}Be-la-at -Dar-ra-ba-an***, ***An-nu-ni-tum*** *ù* ***^{d}Ul-ma-ši-tum***. *iti-ezem-^{d}Šul-gi*, *mu ús-sa é-P* [*u*] *zur$_4$-iš-^{d}Da-gan ba-dù mu ús-sa-bi.* (*AnOr* 07 091, P101386)	2 *rams*, 2 *ewes and* 2 *kids for* **monthly allowance of Belat-Suhnir and Belat-Darraban**, **Annunitum and Ulmašitum**. Month of ezem-Šulgi, Year after that of office of Puzriš-Dagan was built: after that year.	2只公绵羊、2只母绵羊和2只公山羊崽为**贝拉特苏赫尼尔和贝拉特达腊班**，**安努尼吞和乌勒马席吞的月供**。神舒勒吉庆典月，普兹瑞什达干司被建年之次年：之次年。
Š 41 viii/17: **mu-túm**, **ì-dab$_5$** 9 fledglings from**Bagum**, the bird-catcher, when the 17th day passed, were **deliveries for Šulgi-simti**, **Apiliya took over**	9 mušen-tur, ***Ba-gu-um*** *mušen-dù*, *iti--ta ud-17-ba-ra-zal*, *mu-túm-* ***^{d}Šul-gi-si-im-ti***, ***Á-pi$_5$-lí-a*** *ì-dab$_5$*. *iti-šu-eš-ša*, *mu ús-sa é-Puzur$_4$-iš-^{d}Da-gan ba-dù mu ús-sa-bi.* (*SAT* 2 0294, P143494)	9 *fledglings frombird-catcher* **Bagum**, when 17th day passed, were **deliveries for Šulgi-simti**, **Apiliya took over.** Month of šu-eššá, Year after that of office of Puzriš-Dagan was built: after that year.	9只雏鸟来自**捕鸟人巴穌**于17日过去时， **为舒勒吉新提的送入项**，**阿皮里亚接管**了。 三只手月， 普兹瑞什达干司被建年之次年：次年。
Š 41 viii/23: **mu-túm**, **ì-dab$_5$** 3 ducks from**the sister of Ṣiluš-Dagan the bird-catcher**, were **deliveries for Šulgi-simtum**, **Apiliya took over**	3 uz-tur, **nin$_9$-*Ṣi-lu-uš-^{d}Da-gan*** *ba-dù*, *iti--ta ud-23 ba-ra-zal*, *mu-túm-* ***^{d}Šul-gi-sí-im-tum*--šè**, ***Á-pi$_5$-lí-a*** *ì-dab$_5$*. *iti-šu-eš-ša*, *mu ús-sa é-Puzur$_4$-iš-^{d} Da-gan ba-dù mu ús-sa-bi.* (*YOS* 18 005, P142399)	3 *ducks from***the sister of Ṣiluš-Dagan** (**ba-dù**), when 23rd day passed, were **deliveries for Šulgi-simtum**, **Apiliya took over**. Month of šu-ešša, Year after that of the office of Puzriš-Dagan was built: after that year.	3只鸭来自**采鲁什达干之妹**，于23日过去时， **为舒勒吉新吞的送入项**，**阿皮里亚接管**了。 三只手月， 普兹瑞什达干司被建年之次年：之次年。

续表

时间和摘要	文献内容	英文翻译	中文翻译
Š 41 viii/26, 30: **zi-ga** 26th: 1 pigeon, 5 doves when were took, for **the food of my queen**, 30th: 1 pigeon, 5 doves for **provisions of Ur-niĝar**, were**withdrawn from Apiliya**	1ir$_7$^{mušen}, 5 tu-gur$_4$^{mušen}, ud-dab$_5$-ba gu$_7$ **nin-ĝá**--šè, iti--ta **ud-26** ba-ra-zal, 1 ir$_7$^{mušen}, 5 tu-gur$_4$^{mušen}, **igi-kár-Ur-ni$_9$-ĝar**, iti--ta **ud-30** ba-ra-zal, zi-ga-***Á-pi$_5$-lí-a***. *iti-šu-eš$_5$-ša*, *mu ús-sa é-Puzur$_4$-iš-^{d}Da-gan ba-dù mu ús-sa-bi.* (*NYPL* 162, *P*122700)	1 *pigeon*, 5 *doves when were took*, *for***the food of my queen**, when the **26th** day passed, 1 pigeon, 5 doves for **provisions of Ur-niĝar**, when the **30th** day passed, were **withdrawn from Apiliya**. Month of šu-ešša, Year after that of the office of Puzriš-Dagan was built: after that year.	1只家鸽和5只野鸽于被抓住时为**我的王后的食物**于26日过去时，1只家鸽和5只野鸽为乌尔尼旮尔的月供，于本月30日过去时，从**阿皮里亚支出了**。三只手月，普兹瑞什达干司被建年之次年：之次年。
Š 41 ix: **ì-dab$_5$** 4 lambs and 2［ewes］, **Apiliya** took over, in **Ur**	4 sila$_4$ 2［u$_8$］, ***Á-pi$_5$-lí-a*** *ì-dab$_5$*, *šà*~ **Urim^{ki}**-ma. iti-ezem-mah, mu ús-sa é-Puzur$_4$-iš-^{d}Da-gan ba-dù mu ús-sa-bi.（PDT 1 330, 125746）	4 lambs and 2［ewes］, **Apiliya took over**, in **Ur**. Month of ezem-mah, Year after that of office of Puzriš-Dagan was built: after that year.	4羔和2**【**母绵羊**】**，**阿皮里亚接管**了，于**乌尔**。大庆典月，普兹瑞什达干司被建年之次年：之次年。
Š 41 ix/3: **zi-ga** 1 fattened ram for**sacrifice of Adad**, **withdrawn from Apiliya**	1 udu-niga, **siskúr-^{d} Iškur**, iti--ta ud-3 ba-ra-zal, zi-ga-***Á-pi$_5$-lí-a***. *iti-ezem-mah*, *mu ús-sa é-Puzr$_4$-iš-^{d}Da-gan ba-dù*, *mu ús-sa-bi.* (*DoCu EPHE* 313, *P*109269)	1 *fattened ram for***sacrifice of Adad**, when 3rd day passed, **withdrawn from Apiliya**. Month of ezem-mah, Year after that of the office of Puzriš-Dagan was built: after that year.	1只育肥公绵羊为**阿达德的祭祀**，于3日过去时，从**阿皮里亚支出**了。大庆典月，普兹瑞什达干司被建年之次年：之次年。
Š 41 ix/6, 10: **zi-ga**, **butchered** 6th: 2 **butchered** ducks, 1 **butchered** pigeon, **were sent to palace**, 10th: 2 pigeons, 15 ducks, for **lament of Nanna**, **withdrawn from Apiliya**	2 uz-tur~ba-úš, 1 ir$_7$^{mušen}~ba-úš, iti--ta **ud-6**ba-ra-zal, **é-gal-la ba-an-ku$_4$**, 2 ir$_7$^{mušen}, 15 tu-gur$_4$^{mušen}, **ér-sud-^{d} Nanna**--áš, iti--ta**ud-10**ba-ra-zal, zi-ga-***Á-pi$_5$-lí-a***. *iti-ezem-mah*, *mu ús-sa é-Puzr$_4$-iš-^{d} Da-gan ba-dù*, *mu ús-sa-bi.*（*AnOr* 07 064, *P*101359）	2**butchered** ducks, 1 **butchered** pigeon, when **6th** day passed, **were sent to palace**, 2 pigeons, 15 ducks, for **lament of Nanna**, when**10th**day passed, **withdrawn from Apiliya**. Month of ezem-mah, Year after that of the office of Puzriš-Dagan was built: after that year.	2只**宰杀鸭**和1只**宰杀家鸽**，于**6日**过去时，**被送入宫殿**，2只家鸽和15只鸭为**南那神的哀悼**，于**10日**过去时，从**阿皮里亚支出**了。大庆典月，普兹瑞什达干司被建年之次年：之次年。
Š 41 ix/10, 14: **mu-túm**, **ì-dab$_5$** 10th:［1+x］ducks from **daughter of Aganum**, **the musician**, 14th: 2 ducks from **strainer**, were deliveries for Šulgi-simti, **Apiliya took over**	［1+x］uz-tur, **dumu-munus-*A-ga-núm* nar**, iti--ta **ud-10** ba-ra-zal, 2 uz-tur, **in-nu-ri**, iti--ta **ud-14** ba-［ra-zal］, mu-［túm］-***^{d}Šul-*［*gi*］*-sí-im-ti***, ***Á-pi$_5$-lí-a***! *ì-dab$_5$*. *iti-ezem-mah*, *mu ús-sa é-Puzr$_4$-iš-^{d}Da-gan ba-dù*, *mu ús-sa-bi.* (*MVN* 03 179, *P*113739)	［1+x］*ducks from***daughter of Aganum**, **the musician**, when **10th** day passed, 2 ducks from **strainer**, when the **14th** day passed, were deliveries for Šulgi-simti, **Apiliya took over**. Month of ezem-mah, Year after that of the office of Puzriš-Dagan was built: after that year.	**【**1+x**】**只鸭来自**乐师阿旮农之女**，于本月10日过去时，2只鸭来自**捕猎网**，于本月第14日过去时， **为舒勒吉新提的送入项**， **阿皮里亚接管**了。 大庆典月， 普兹瑞什达干司被建年之次年：之次年。

续表

时间和摘要	文献内容	英文翻译	中文翻译
Š 41 ix/28: **zi-ga** 1 fattened ram for**gamamue festival, in palace**, 1 fattened ram for **giranum festival of Inanna**, were **withdrawn from Apiliya**	1 udu-niga, **ezem-ga-ma-am-mu-è**!, šà ~ **é-gal**, 1 udu-niga, ***gi-ra-núm-*^{d}Inanna**, iti--ta ud-30-lá!-2! ba-ra-zal, zi-ga-***Á-pi$_5$-lí-a***. *iti-ezem-mah*, *mu ús-sa é-Puzr$_4$-iš-^{d}Da-gan ba-dù*, *mu ús-sa-bi*. (*SET* 043, *P*129453)	1 *fattened ram for***gamamue festival, in palace**, 1 fattened ram for **giranum festival of Inanna**, when 28th day passed, were **withdrawn from Apiliya**. Month of ezem-mah, Year after that of the office of Puzriš-Dagan was built: after that year.	1 育肥公绵羊为 **gamamue 节于宫殿**，1 只育肥公绵羊**为伊南那的吉腊努姆仪式**，于 28 日过去时，**从阿皮里亚支出了**。 大庆典月， 普兹瑞什达干司被建年之次年：之次年。
Š 41 ix: **zi-ga, butchered** 2**butchered** lambs, 1 **butchered** ram, were sent to the palace, **were withdrawn from Apiliya**	2 sila$_4$~ ba-úš, 1 udu~ ba-úš, **é-gal-la** ba-an-ku$_4$, zi-ga-***Á-pi$_5$-lí-a***. *iti-ezem-mah*, *mu ús-sa é-Puzr$_4$-iš-^{d}Da-gan ba-dù*, *mu ús-sa-bi*. (*Princeton* 1 098)	2**butchered** lambs, 1 **butchered** ram, were sent to the palace, **were withdrawn from Apiliya**. Month of ezem-mah, Year after that of the office of Puzriš-Dagan was built: after that year.	2 只宰杀的羊羔和 1 只宰杀的公绵羊被送入宫殿（加工），**阿皮里亚支出了**。大庆典月， 普兹瑞什达干司被建年之次年：之次年。
Š 41 x: **zi-ga, butchered** 2 grass bulls, 26 ewes, 8 rams, 2 male lambs, 1 she-goat, 1 he-goat, 1 kid, which were**butchered**, **for the weaver slave women to eat**, were **withdrawn from Apiliya**	2 gud-ú, 26 u$_8$, 8 udu-nitá, 2 sila$_4$-nitá, 1 ud$_5$, 1 máš-gal, 1 máš, ug$_7$-ug$_7$-ga-àm, **géme-uš-bar-e-ne** ba-an-gu$_7$-éš, zi-ga-***Á-pi$_5$-lí-a***, *iti-ezem-an-na*, *mu ús-sa é-Puzr$_4$-iš-^{d}Da-gan ba-dù*, *mu ús-sa-bi*. (*OIP* 115066, *P*123343)	2 *grass bulls*, 26 *ewes*, 8 *rams*, 2 *male lambs*, 1 *she-goat*, 1 *he-goat*, 1 *kid*, *which were***butchered**, **for the weaver slave women to eat**, were **withdrawn from Apiliya**. Month of ezem-Anna, Year after that of the office of Puzriš-Dagan was built: after that year.	2 只食草公牛、26 只母绵羊、8 只公绵羊、2 只公羔、1 只母山羊、1 只公山羊和 1 只公崽，以上**宰杀牲为编织女工吃**，**从阿皮里亚支出了**。天神庆典月，普兹瑞什达干司被建年之次年：之次年。
Š 41 x: (**zi-ga**) 2 kids, 1 ewe, 1 lamb, 2 lambs for**allowance of Belat-Suhnir, Belat-Darraban, Annunitum and Ulmaštum**	2 máš, 1 u$_8$, 1 kir$_{11}$, 2 sila$_4$, **sá-dug$_4$**~ ***^{d}Be-la-at-Suh-nir***, **^{d}Be-la-at-Dar-ra-ba-an**, ***An-nu-ni-tum*** *ù* **^{d}Ul-ma-ši-tum**. *iti-ezem-an-na*, *mu ús-sa é-Puzr$_4$-iš-^{d}Da-gan ba-dù*, *mu ús-sa-bi*. (*OIP* 115 067, *P*123549)	2 *kids*, 1 *ewe*, 1 *female lamb*, 2 *lambs for***monthly allowance of Belat-Suhnir, Belat-Darraban, Annunitum and Ulmaštum**. Month of ezem-Anna, Year after that of the office of Puzriš-Dagan was built: after that year.	2 只公崽、1 只母绵羊、1 只雌羔和 2 只公羔为**贝拉特苏赫尼尔、贝拉特达腊班、安努尼吞和乌勒马什吞的月供**。天神庆典月，普兹瑞什达干司被建年之次年：之次年。

续表

时间和摘要	文献内容	英文翻译	中文翻译
Š 41 x/11 **zi-ga** 1 fattened bull, 4 fattened rams, 2 lambs, 1 fattened female kid, 1 lamb, for**food of fish**, 1 he-goat for **gagu offering of Meslam-taea** on the 1st time; 1 fattened bull, 2 fattened rams, 1 fattened he-goat, 2 fattened female kids for **the food of fish and greenery**, 1 ram, 1 he-goat for **the offering of "disappearing place"**; 1 fattened ram, 1 grass ram for **"beer-pouring" of Belat-S.and Belat-D.**, withdr.fr.Apiliya	1 gud-niga, 4 udu-niga, 2 sila$_4$, 1 ^{f}ašgar-niga, 1 sila$_4$, **níĝ-ku$_6$~** nisig (SAR) -ga--šè, 1 máš-gal, ga-gu$_7$ **^{d}Mes-lam-ta-è-a**, ud-1-kam; 1 gud-niga, 2 udu-niga, 1 máš-gal-niga, 2 ^{f}ašgar-niga, **níĝ-ku$_6$-nisig-ga**--šè, 1 udu, 1 máš, níĝ~ ki-zàh--šè, ud-2-kam; 1 udu-niga, 1 udu-ú, ud-3-kam; kaš-dé-a ***^{d}Be-la-at-Suh-nir*** *ù* **^{d}Be-la-at-Dar-ra-ba-an**, *iti--ta ud-11 ba-ra-zal*, *zi-ga-**Á-pi$_5$-lí-a**.iti-ezem-má-An-na*, *mu ús-sa é-Puzur$_4$-iš-^{d}Da-gan ba-dù, mu ús-sa-bi.* (*OIP* 115065, *P*123309)	1 *fattened bull*, 4 *fattened rams*, 2 *lambs*, 1 *fattened female kid*, 1 *lamb*, *for***food of fish**, 1 he-goat for **gagu offering of Meslam-taea** on the 1st time; 1 fattened bull, 2 fattened rams, 1 fattened he-goat, 2 fattened female kids for **the food of fish and greenery**, 1 ram, 1 he-goat for **the offering of "disappearing place"** on the 2nd time; 1 fattened ram, 1 grass ram on the 3rd time for **"beer-pouring" of Belat-Suhnir and Belat-Darraban**, when 11th day passed, were **withdrawn from Apiliya**. Month of ezem-ma-Anna, Year after that of office of Puzuriš-Dagan was built: after that year.	1头育肥公牛、4只育肥公绵羊、2只羊羔、1只育肥雌山羊崽和1只公山羊为**"鱼食"**，1只公山羊崽为**美斯兰塔埃阿的gagu供奉第1次**；1头育肥公牛、2只育肥公绵羊、1只育肥公山羊、2只育肥雌崽为**"鱼食和蔬菜"**，1只公绵羊、1只公山羊为**消失处供奉第2次**；1只育肥公绵羊、1只食草公绵羊**第3次**为**贝拉特苏赫尼尔和贝拉特达腊班的倒啤酒宴会**，于第11天过去时，从**阿皮里亚支出**了。天神安之船庆典月，普兹瑞什达干司被建年之次年。
Š 41 xi/26: **mu-túm, ì-dab$_5$** 1 fattened bull and 10 grass rams**deliveried by Kallamu**, the son of Inim-Šara, **Apilatum took over**	1 gud-niga, 10 udu-ú, **Kal-la-mu dumu-*Inim-^{d}Šará***, *mu-túm*, ***Á-pi$_5$-la-tum*** *ì-dab$_5$.iti-ezem-Me-ki-gál*, *<iti>-ta-ud-26 ba-ra-zal*, *mu ús-sa é-Puzr$_4$-iš-^{d}Da-gan ba-dù*, *mu ús-sa-bi.* (*Torino* 1 052, *P*131847)	1 *fattened bull and* 10 *grass rams***deliveried by Kallamu**, the son of Inim-Šara, **Apilatum took over.** Month of ezem-Mekigal, when 26th day passed, Year after that of the office of Puzriš-Dagan was built: after that year.	1只育肥公牛和10只食草公绵羊被**伊尼姆沙腊子卡拉穆送入**，**阿皮拉吞接管**了。神美基旮勒庆典月，于26日过去时，普兹瑞什达干司被建年之次年：次年。
Š 41 xii/1: **ì-dab$_5$** 4 thicket female piglets, 1 thicket male piglet, **these were new born**, **Apilatum took over** took	4 šáh^{zah}-tur-munus-giš-gi, 1 šah^{zah}-tur-nitá-giš-gi, ù-tu-da-àm, ***Á-* [*pi$_5$*] *-la-tum*** *ì-dab$_5$*, *iti--ta ud-1 ba-ra-zal.iti-še-kin-kud*, *mu ús-sa é-Puzr$_4$-iš-^{d}Da-gan ba-dù mu ús-sa-bi.* (*Torino* 1 073, *P*133859)	4 *thicket female piglets*, 1 *thicket male piglet*, **these were new born**, **Apilatum took over**, when 1st day passed. Month of še-kin-kud, Year after that of the office of Puzriš-Dagan was built: after that year.	4只苇塘雌豚和1只苇塘雄豚，以上为**新生**，**阿皮拉吞接管**了，于1日过去时。大麦收割月，普兹瑞什达干司被建年之次年：之次年。
Š 41 xii/2: **mu-túm, ì-dab$_5$** 2 ducks from**Ur-Ištaran**, these were deliveries, **Apilatum took over**	2 uz-tur**Ur-^{d}Ištaran**, iti--ta ud-2 ba-ra-zal, mu-túm, ***Á-pi$_5$-la-tum*** *ì-dab$_5$.iti-še-kin-kud*, *mu ús-sa é-Puzur$_4$-iš-^{d}Da-gan ba-dù-a mu ús-sa-bi.* (*Hirose* 016, *P*109487)	2 *ducks from***Ur-Ištaran**, when 2nd day passed, these were deliveries, **Apilatum took over.** Month of še-kin-kud, Year after that of the office of Puzriš-Dagan was built: after that year.	2只鸭来自**乌尔伊什塔蓝**，于2日过去时，以上送入，**阿皮拉吞接管**了。大麦收割月，普兹瑞什达干司被建年之次年：之次年。

续表

时间和摘要	文献内容	英文翻译	中文翻译
Š 41 xii/5： **zi-ga，butchered** 1 thicket sow was new born and 1 duck for**food of my queen**，2 thicket sows was new born and 1 dove，**butchered ones were sent to palace**，**withdrawn from Apilatum**	1šáh-zé-da-munus-giš-gi ù-tu-da，1 uz-tur **níĝ-gu$_7$-nin-ĝá**--šè，2 šáh-zé-da-munus-giš-gi ù-tu-da，1 tu-gur$_4$^{mušen} ri-ri-ga-àm **é-gal-la ba-an-ku$_4$**，iti--ta ud-5 ba-ra-zal，zi-ga ***Á-pi$_5$-la-tum***. *iti-še-kin-kud，mu ús-sa é-Puzur$_4$-iš-^{d}Da-gan ba-dù mu ús-sa-bi.* （*SET* 045，*P*129455）	1 *thicket sow was new born and* 1 *duck for***food of my queen**，2 thicket sows was new born and 1 dove，**butchered ones were sent to palace**，when 5th day passed，were **withdrawn from Apilatum**. Month of še-kin-kud，Year after that of the office of Puzriš-Dagan was built：after that year.	1只新生苇塘母猪和1只鸭为**我的王后的食物**，2只新生苇塘母猪和1只鸽，这些**宰杀牲被送入宫殿**，于5日过去时，从**阿皮拉吞支出了**。 大麦收割月， 普兹瑞什达干司被建年之次年：之次年。
Š 41 xii/［8］，9： **mu-túm，ì-dab$_5$** 8th：2 fat rams and 1 kid from **Nabium**，**the son of king**， 9th：4 fat rams and 1 lamb from［…］，**the son of king**， these were deliveries，**Apilatum took over**	2 udu-niga，1 máš ***Na-bí-um*** **dumu-lugal**， iti--ta **ud-［8］**ba-ra-zal， 4 udu-niga，1 sila$_4$［…］**dumu-lugal**，［iti--ta］**ud-9**ba-ra-zal， mu-túm，***Á -pi$_5$-la-tum*** *ì-dab$_5$. iti-še-kin-kud，mu ús-sa é-Puzur$_4$-iš-^{d} Da-gan ba-dù mu ús-sa-bi.*（*SET* 005，*P*129415）	2 *fattened rams and* 1 *kid from***Nabium**，**the son of king**，when［8th］day passed，4 fattened rams and 1 lamb from［…］，**the son of king**，when 9thday passed，these were deliveries，**Apilatum took over**. Month of še-kin-kud，Year after that of the office of Puzriš-Dagan was built：after that year.	2只育肥公绵羊和1只公崽来自**王子那比乌姆**，于【8】日过去时，4只育肥公绵羊和1只羔来自**国王之子【X】**，于9日过去时，以上送入，**阿皮拉吞接管了**。大麦收割月，普兹瑞什达干司被建年之次年：之次年。
Š 41 xii/15： **zi-ga，butchered** 1 lean domestic piglet and 1 lean thicket piglet were**dead**，1 thicket piglet for the **food of my queen**，were **withdrawn from Apilatum**	1 šáh^{zah}-tur-nitá-šà-uru-sig，1 šáh^{zah}-tur-giš-gi-munus-sig，ri-ri-ga-［àm］，1 šáh-ne-tur -nitá-giš-［gi］，**níĝ-gu$_7$-nin-ĝá**，zi-ga ***Á-pi$_5$-la-tum***，*iti--ta ud-15 ba-ra-zal.*［*iti*］*-še-kin-kud*，［*mu*］*ús-sa <é>-Puzur$_4$-iš-$^{[d]}$da-gan ba-dù mu ús-sa-bi.*（*Hirose* 017，*P*109488）	1 *lean domestic piglet and* 1 *lean thicket piglet were***dead**，1 thicket piglet for the **food of my queen**，were **withdrawn from Apilatum**，when 15th day passed. Month of še-kin-kud，Year after that of the office of Puzriš-Dagan was built：after that year.	1只瘦的驯养的雄豚和1只瘦的苇塘雌豚为**病死**，1只苇塘猪崽为**我的王后的食物**，从**阿皮拉吞支出了**，于15日过去时。 大麦收割月， 普兹瑞什达干司被建年之次年：之次年。
Š 41 xii/24，26，27，28，29： **zi-ga，butchered** 24th：1 thicket piglet， 26th：1 thicket piglet and 5 doves when were took，for **the food of my queen**， 27th 28th：1 pigeon and 1 dove，29th：1 thicket female piglet，**butchered ones were sent to palace**，**withdrawn from Apilatum**	1šáh^{zah}-tur-nitá-giš-gi，iti--ta **ud-24**ba-ra-zal，1 šáh^{zah}-tur-nitá-giš-gi，5 tu-gur$_4$^{mušen}，ud-dab$_5$-ba--šè，iti--ta **26**ba-ra-zal，**níĝ-gu$_7$-nin-ĝá**--šè，1 ir$_7$^{mušen}，1 tu-gur$_4$^{mušen}，iti--ta **ud-27**ba-ra-zal，a-rá-1-kam；iti--ta **ud-28**ba-ra-zal，a-rá-2-kam；1 šáh^{zah}-tur-munus-giš-gi，iti--ta **ud-29**ba-ra-zal，ri-ri-ga-àm **é-gal-la ba-an-ku$_4$**，zi-ga ***Á-pi$_5$-la-tum***. *iti-še-kin-kud-<min>，mu［ús-sa é-Puzur$_4$-iš-^{d} da-gan ba-dù mu ús-sa-bi.*（*SET* 046，*P*129456）	1 *thicket piglet*when **24th**day passed，1 thicket piglet and 5 doves when were took，when **26th**day passed，for **the food of my queen**，1 pigeon and 1 dove when **27th**day passed for 1st time，when **28th**day passed，for 2nd time，1 thicket female piglet when**29th**day passed，**butchered ones were sent to palace**，**withdrawn from Apilatum**. Month of še-kin-kud，Year after that of office of Puzriš-Dagan was built：after that year.	1只苇塘雄豚，于**24日**过去时，1只苇塘雄豚和5只野鸽于被抓住时， 于**26日**过去时， 为**我的王后的食物**，1只家鸽和1只野鸽于**27日**过去时第1次，于**28日**过去时第2次，1只苇塘雌豚于**29日**过去时，以上**宰杀牲被送入宫殿**，从**阿皮拉吞支出了**。大麦收割月，【普兹瑞什达干司被建年之次年：之次年】

续表

时间和摘要	文献内容	英文翻译	中文翻译
Š 41 xii: (**zi-ga**) 6 flocks for**allowance of Belat-Suhnir, Belat-Darraban, Annunitum and Ulmaštum**	2 u$_8$, 2 sila$_4$-nitá, 1 máš-nitá, 1 ^{f}ašgar, **sá-dug$_4$ ~ ^{d}*Be-la-at-suh-ni-ir*, ^{d} Be-la-at-dar-ra-ba-an, *An-nu-ni-tum* ù ^{d}Ul-ma-ši-tum**. *iti-še-kin-kud, mu ús-sa é-Puzr$_4$-iš-^{d}Da-gan ba-dù mu ús-sa-bi.* (*OIP* 115068, *P*123248)	*2 ewes, 2 he-lamb, 1 kid and 1 female kid, for-* **monthly allowance of Belat-Suhnir, Belat-Darraban, Annunitum and Ulmaštum**. Month of še-kin-kud, Year after that of the office of Puzriš-Dagan was built: after that year.	2只母绵羊、2只公羔、1只公崽和1只雌崽为**贝拉特苏赫尼尔、贝拉特达腊班、安努尼吞和乌勒马什吞的月供**。大麦收割月，普兹瑞什达干司被建年之次年：之次年。
Š 41 xii: **zi-ga** 1 thicket boar for the fattened boar, sent out for the sheep-shed, **withdrawn from Apilatum**	1 šáh-nitá-giš-gi, šáh-niga--šè, **gá-udu--šè** è-a, zi-ga ***Á-pi$_5$-la-tum***. *iti-še-kin-kud, mu ús-sa é-Puzur$_4$-iš-^{d} Da-gan ba-dù-a mu ús-sa-bi.* (*South Dakota* 01, P130302)	*1 thicket boar for the fattened boar, sent out for the sheep-shed*, **withdrawn from Apilatum**. Month of še-kin-kud, Year after that of the office of Puzriš-Dagan was built: after that year.	1头苇塘公猪为育肥公猪，为羊圈送走了，从**阿皮拉吞支出了**。 大麦收割月， 普兹瑞什达干司被建年之次年：之次年。
Š 41 xii: **zi-ga, butchered** 1 ram of after-ox-class and 1 lamb, **butchered** ones **were sent to the palace, withdrawn from Apillati**	1 udu-gud-e-ús-sa, 1 sila$_4$, ri-ri-ga-àm, **é-gal-la ba-an-ku$_4$**, zi-ga ***Á-pil-la-ti***. *iti-še-kin-kud, mu ús-sa é-Pu-zur$_4$-iš-^{d}Da-gan ba-dù-a mu ús-sa-bi.* (Gregire, AAICAB I-2, Ashm.1971-277).	1 ram of after-ox-class and 1 lamb, **butchered** ones **were sent to the palace, withdrawn from Apillati**.Month of še-kin-kud, Year after that of the office of Puzriš-Dagan was built: after that year.	1只牛后级公绵羊和1只羔为**宰杀牲被送入宫殿**，从**阿皮拉提支出了**。 大麦收割月， 普兹瑞什达干司被建年之次年：之次年。
Š 41 xii/25: **zi-ga** 1 fattened female kid for **the food of queen**, when 25th day passed, **withdrawn from Apilatum**	1^{f} ašgar-niga, **níĝ-gu$_7$-nin-ĝá**--šè, iti--ta ud-25-ba-ta-zal, zi-ga-***Á-pi$_5$-la-tum***. *iti-še-kin-kud-min, mu ús-sa é-Puzr$_4$-iš-^{d}Da-gan ba-dù mu ús-sa-bi.* (*Torino* 1 186, P131886)	*1 fattened female kid for* **the food of queen**, when 25th day passed, **withdrawn from Apilatum.Additional** month of še-kin-kud, Year after that of office of Puzriš-Dagan was built: after that year.	1只育肥雌山羊崽为**王后的食物**，于25日过去时，从**阿皮拉吞支出了**。闰加大麦收割月，普兹瑞什达干司被建年之次年：之次年。
Š 42 i/22: **mu-túm, ì-dab$_5$** 1 lamb fr. **en-priest of Inanna, in Uruk**, 1 kid fr. **Talim-Enlil**, 5 fat rams and 3 lambs fr.**Išdum-kin**, were deliveries for Šulgi-simtum, **Apilatum took over**	1 sila$_4$ **en-^{d}Inanna Unug^{ki}**-ga, 1 máš **Tá-lim-^{d}En-líl**, 5 udu-niga, 3 sila$_4$ ***Išdum-ki-in***, *iti--ta ud-22 ba-ra-zal, mu-túm ~* ***^{d}Šul-gi-sí-im-tum-ma***, ***Á-pi$_5$-la-tum*** *ì-dab$_5$. iti-maš-dà ~ gu$_7$, mu Ša-aš-ru^{ki} ba-hul.* (*SET* 006, P129416)	*1 lamb from* **en-priest of Inanna, in Uruk**, 1 kid from **Talim-Enlil**, 5 fattened rams and 3 lambs from **Išdum-kin**, when 22nd day passed, were deliveries for Šulgi-simtum, **Apilatum took over**. Month of mašda ~ gu$_7$, Year of Šašrum was destroyed.	1只羔来自**伊南那的祭司**，于**乌鲁克**，1只公崽来自**塔林恩里勒**，5只育肥公绵羊和3只羔来自**伊什杜金**，于22日过去时，为**舒勒吉新吞的送入项**，**阿皮拉吞接管了**。食瞪羚月，沙什润被毁之年。
Š 42 i/26: **mu-túm, ì-dab$_5$** 3 ducklets from **the palace**, were deliveries for Šulgi-simtum, **Apilatum took**	3 amar-sag ~ uz-tur, é-gal--ta, iti--ta ud-26-ba-ta-zal, mu-túm-***^{d}Šul-gi-sí-im-tum***, ***Á-pi$_5$-la-tum*** *ì-dab$_5$. iti-maš-dà-gu$_7$, mu Ša-aš-ru^{ki} ba-hul.* (*Torino* 1 037, P133847)	*3 ducklets from* **the palace**, when 26th day passed, were deliveries for Šulgi-simtum, **Apilatum took over**.Month of mašda-gu$_7$, Year of Šašrum was destroyed.	3只幼鸭来自**宫殿**，于26日过去时，为**舒勒吉新吞的送入项**，**阿皮拉吞接管了**。食瞪羚月，沙什润被毁之年。

续表

时间和摘要	文献内容	英文翻译	中文翻译
Š 42 i/26: **mu-túm, ì-dab$_5$** 2 fattened rams and 1 lamb from**Imid-ilum major-domo, deliveries for Šulgi-simtum, Apilatum took over**	2 udu-niga, 1 sila$_4$, ***I-mi-id-ilum*** šabra, iti--ta ud-26 ba-ra-zal, mu-túm-^{d} ***Šul-gi-sí-im-tum***, ***Á-pi$_5$-la-tum*** *ì-dab$_5$.iti-maš-dà-gu$_7$, mu Ša-aš-ru^{ki}ba-hul.* (*OIP* 115 069, P123665)	2 *fattened rams and* 1 *lamb from***Imid-ilum majordomo**, when 26th day passed, **deliveries for Šulgi-simtum, Apilatum took over**.Month of mašda-gu$_7$, Year of Šašrum was destroyed.	2 只育肥公绵羊和 1 只羊羔来自**庙总管伊米德伊隆**，于 26 日过去时，为**舒勒吉新吞的送入项，阿皮拉吞接管了**。食瞪羚月，沙什润被毁年。
Š 42 ii: **mu-túm, ì-dab$_5$** 1 lamb from**son of Bumiza, deliveries for Šulgi-simtum, Apilatum took over**	1 sila$_4$, **dumu-*Bù-mi-za***, *mu-túm-^{d}* ***Šul-gi-sí-im-tum***, ***Á-pi$_5$-la-tum*** *ì-dab$_5$.iti-šeš-da-gu$_7$, mu Ša-aš-ru^{ki}ba-hul.* (*OIP* 115070, P123595)	1 *lamb from the* **son of Bumiza, deliveries for Šulgi-simtum, Apilatum took over**.Month of zeda-gu$_7$, Year of Šašrum was destroyed.	1 只羊羔来自**布米扎之子，为舒勒吉新吞的送入项，阿皮拉吞接管了**。 食豚月， 沙什润被毁之年。
Š 42 ii/21, 22, 23, 24: **mu-túm, ì-dab$_5$** 21st: 2 pigeons were brought from **the palace**, 22nd: 1 [...], 4 [...], [...], 23rd: 13 pigeons of **arrears repaid by Ibi-Sin**, 24th: 3 pigeons from **Barbarliya**, were deliveries for Šulgi-simtum, **Apilatum took over**	2 ir$_7$^{mušen} **é-gal-** [**ta**] è-a, iti-- [ta **ud-21**ba] -ta-zal, 1 [...], 4 [...], [...] iti--ta **ud-22**ba-ta-zal, 13 ir$_7$^{mušen}, lá-ì su-ga **I-bí-^{d}Suen**, iti--ta **ud-23**ba-ta-zal, 3 ir$_7$^{mušen} ***Bar-bar-lí-a***, *iti--ta* **ud-24**ba-ta-zal, mu-túm ~ ***^{d}Šul-gi-sí-im-<im>-tum***, [***Á***] ***-pi$_5$-la-tum*** *ì-dab$_5$.iti-ze$_x$-da~gu$_7$, mu Ša-aš-šú-ru-um^{ki} ba-hul.* (*SET* 007, P129417)	2 *pigeons were brought from***the palace**, when[**21st**] day passed, 1 [...], 4 [...], [...], when **22nd** day passed, 13 pigeons of **arrears repaid by Ibi-Sin**, when**23rd**day passed, 3 pigeons from **Barbarliya**, when**24th**day passed, were deliveries for Šulgi-simtum, **Apilatum took over**.Month of zeda ~gu$_7$, Year of Šaššurum was destroyed.	2 只家鸽从**宫殿**带来，于 **21** 日过去时，1【……】，4【……】，【……】，于 **22** 日过去时，13 只家鸽来自**伊比辛交付的欠款**，于 **23** 日过去时，3 只家鸽来自**巴尔巴尔里亚**，于 **24** 日过去时，为**舒勒吉新吞的送入项，阿皮拉吞接管了**。食豚月，沙什润被毁之年。
Š 42 ii/30: **zi-ga** 1 fat ram for **giranum of Inanna**, 1 kid for **Nin-sun**, 1 lamb for **disappearing palce in the palace**, 1 fat ram and 1 goat for **Belat-S.and Belat-D.**, 1 fat ram for **Nanna**, 1 fat ram and 1 kid for **sacrifice in Uruk**, **via Mašum**, **for New Moon**, were withdr.	1 udu-niga, ***gi-ra-núm-*^{d}Inanna**, 1 máš **^{d}Nin-sún**, 1 sila$_4$ **níĝ-ki-zàh**, **šà~ é-gal**, 1 udu-niga, 1 máš-gal, ***^{d}Be-la-at-Suh-nir ù ^{d}Be-la-at-Dar-ra-ba-an***, 1 *udu-niga* **^{d}Nanna**, 1 udu-niga, 1 máš **siskúr šà~ Un-ug^{ki}**, gìr ***Ma-šum***, **siskúr ud-sakar**, iti--ta ud-30 ba-ta-zal, zi-ga. iti-ze$_x$-da-gu$_7$, mu Ša-aš-ru^{ki} ba-hul. (CST 467, P107982)	1 fattened ram for **giranum festival of Inanna**, 1 kid for **Nin-sun**, 1 lamb for **disappearing palce in the palace**, 1 fattened ram and 1 he-goat for **Belat-Suhnir and Belat-Darraban**, 1 fattened ram for **Nanna**, 1 fattened ram and 1 kid for **the sacrifice in Uruk**, **via Mašum**, **for the sacrifice of New Moon**, when 30th day passed, were withdrawn. Month ofzeda ~ gu$_7$, Year of Šaššurum was destroyed.	1 只育肥公绵羊为**伊南那的吉腊努姆仪式**，1 只公崽为宁苏，1 只羔为**宫殿的消失处**，1 只育肥公绵羊和 1 只公山羊为**贝拉特苏赫尼尔和贝拉特达腊班**，1 只育肥公绵羊为**南那**，1 只育肥公绵羊和 1 只公崽为**乌鲁克的祭祀**，**经由马顺**，以上为**新月祭**，于 30 日过去时， 支出了。食豚月， 沙什润被毁之年。

续表

时间和摘要	文献内容	英文翻译	中文翻译
Š 42 iii/［?］: **zi-ga, butchered** ［1+x**butchered** rams were **sent to**］ **the palace**, **withdrawn from Aplilatum**	［1+x udu ba-úš］ **é-gal-la b**［**a-an-ku$_4$**, iti--ta ud-x ba-ra-zal］, zi-ga-***Á-pi$_5$-l***［***a-tum***］. *iti-u$_5$-bí^{mušen}-gu$_7$*, *mu Ša-aš-ru-um^{ki}ba-hu*［*l*］.（*PDT* 2 1009, *P*126354）	［1+*x***butchered** rams were **sent to**］ **the palace**, ［when x day passed］, were **withdrawn from Apilatum**.Month of ubi-gu$_7$, Year of Šašrum was destroyed.	【1+x只宰杀的公绵羊被送入】宫殿，【于x日过去时】，从阿皮拉吞支出了。食乌比鸟月，沙什润被毁之年。
Š 42 iii/13, 14: **zi-ga** 13th: 1 fat ram for **festival of Inanna**, 1 fattened ram and 1 he-goat for **giranum festival of Belat-S. and Belat-D.**, 14th: 2 fattened rams and 1 he-goat, for **the sacrifice in Uruk**, via**Apiliya**, 1 fattened ram for **Allagula**, 2 fattened rams and 1 lamb for **Ninlil**, 2 fattened rams and 1 lamb for **Enlil**, 1 ram and 3［he-goats］of **kin-gi$_4$-a for acrifice in Nippur**, **for the Full Moon**, **withdr.fr.Apilatum**	1 udu-niga, ***gi-ra-núm-^{d}Inanna***, 1 udu-niga, 1 máš-gal, ***gi-ra-núm-*** ***^{d}Be-la-at-Suh-nir***, ù ***^{d}Be-la-at-Dar-ra-ba-an***, *iti--ta***ud-13**-ba-ta-zal, 2 udu-niga, 1 máš-gal, siskúr šà~ **Unug^{ki}**-ga, gìr-***Á-pi$_5$-lí-a***, 1 *udu-niga*, ***^{d}Al-la-gu-la***, 2 *udu-niga*, 1 *sila$_4$*, **^{d}Nin-líl**, 2［udu-niga］, 1 sila$_4$ ^{d}En-líl, 1 udu, 3［máš-gal］~ kin-gi$_4$-a, siskúr šà~ Nibru^{ki}, é-ud-15［…］, iti--ta **ud-14**ba-ta-zal, zi-ga-***Á-pi$_5$-la-tum***. *iti-u$_5$-bí-gu$_7$*, *mu a-aš-ru-um^{ki}ba-hul*. （*OrSP* 18 *pl*.06 21, *P*124865）	1 *fattened ram for* **giranum festival of Inanna**, 1 fattened ram and 1 he-goat for **giranum festival of Belat-Suhnir and Belat-Darraban**, when **13th**day passed, 2 fattened rams and 1 he-goat, for **the sacrifice in Uruk**, via**Apiliya**, 1 fattened ram for **Allagula**, 2 fattened rams and 1 lamb for **Ninlil**, 2 fattened rams and 1 lamb for **Enlil**, 1 ram and 3［he-goats］of **kin-gi$_4$-a for the sacrifice in Nippur**, **for the Full Moon**, when **14th**day passed, were **withdrawn from Apilatum**.Month of ubi-gu$_7$, Year of Šašrum was destroyed.	1育肥公绵羊为**伊南那的吉腊努姆仪式**，1育肥公绵羊和1公山羊为**贝拉特苏赫尼尔和贝拉特达腊班的吉腊努姆仪式**，于**13**日过去时；2育肥公绵羊和1公山羊为**于乌鲁克**的祭祀，**经由阿皮里亚**，1育肥公绵羊为**阿拉古拉**，2育肥公绵羊和1羊羔为**宁里勒**，2育肥公绵羊和1羊羔为**恩里勒**，1公绵羊和3 kin-gi$_4$-a公山羊为于**尼普尔的祭祀**，为**满月祭**，于**14**日过去时，从**阿皮拉吞支出了**。食乌比鸟月，沙什润被毁年。
Š 42 iv/1, 3: **zi-ga, butchered** 1st: 1 pigeon, for the 1st time; 3rd: 1 pigeon for the 2nd time, these were **butchered**, **sent to palace**, **withdr.fr.Apilatum**	1ir$_7$^{mušen}, iti--ta **ud-1**ba-ra-zal, a-rá 1-kam; 1 ir$_7$^{mušen}, iti--ta **ud-3**ba-ta-zal, a-rá-2-kam, ri-ri-ga-àm, **é-gal-la ba-an-ku$_4$**, zi-ga-***Á-pi$_5$-la-tum***. *iti-ki-siki-^{d}Nin-a-zu*, *mu Ša-aš-ru-um^{ki}ba-hul*. （*Torino* 1 187, *P*133900）	1 *pigeon*, *when the 1stday passed for the 1st time*; 1 *pigeon when the 3rdday passed for 2nd time*, *these were* **butchered**, **sent to palace**, **withdrawn from Apilatum**.Month of ki-siki-Ninazu, Year of Šašrum was destroyed.	1只家鸽于1日过去时，第一次；1只家鸽3日过去时，第二次，这些**宰杀牲被送入宫殿**，从**阿皮拉吞支出**了。神宁阿朱羊毛作坊月，沙什润被毁年。
Š 42 iv/3: **zi-ga, butchered** 1**butchered ram** of after-ox-class **sent to palace**, **withdrawn from Apilatum**	1 udu~gud-e-ús-sa, ba-úš, **é-gal-la ba-an-ku$_4$**, iti--ta ud-3 ba-ra-zal, zi-ga <***Á-pi$_5$-la-tum***>. *iti-ki-siki-^{d}Nin-a-zu*, *mu Ša-aš-ru^{ki}ba-hul*.（*OIP* 115 078, *P*123466）	1**butchered ram** of after-ox-class **sent to palace**, when the 3rd day passed, **withdrawn from Apilatum**.Month of ki-siki-Ninazu, Year of Šašrum was destroyed.	1只**宰杀的育肥牛后级公绵羊被送入宫殿**，于3日过去时，从**阿皮拉吞支出**了。神宁阿朱羊毛作坊月，沙什润被毁年。

续表

时间和摘要	文献内容	英文翻译	中文翻译
Š 42 v/21: **zi-ga** 1 duck and 5 doves for **the food of my queen**, were **withdrawn from Apilatum**, **in Ur**	1 uz-tur, 5 tu-gur$_5$^{mušen}, **níĝ-gu$_7$-nin-ĝá**--šè, iti--ta ud-21 ba-ta-zal, zi-ga ***Á-pi$_5$-la-tum***, *šà* ~ **Urim^{ki}**-ma. iti-ezem-^{d}Nin-a-zu, mu Ša-aš-ru^{ki} ba-hul. (Princeton 2 131, P201129)	1 duck and 5 doves for **the food of my queen**, when the 21st day passed, were **withdrawn from Apilatum**, **in Ur**. Month of ezem-Ninazu, Year of Šašrum was destroyed.	1只鸭和5只野鸽为**我的王后的食物**，于21日过去时，从**阿皮拉吞支出了**，**于乌尔**。 神宁阿朱庆典月， 沙什润被毁年。
Š 42 v/23: **mu-túm**, **ì-dab$_5$** 1 fattened ram, 1 ram of after-ox-class and 1 lamb from**Galaya**, **deliveries for Šulgi-simtum**, **Apilatum took over**	1 udu-niga, 1 udu-gud-e-ús-sa, 1 sila$_4$, ***Ga-la-a***, *iti--ta ud-23 ba-ta-zal*, *mu-túm*~ ***^{d}Šul-gi-sí-im-tum**-ma*, ***Á-pi$_5$-la-tum*** *ì-dab$_5$. iti-ezem-^{d}Nin-a-zu*, *mu Ša-aš-ru^{ki} ba-hul.* (*CST* 469, P107984)	1 *fattened ram*, 1 *ram of after-ox-class and* 1 *lamb from* **Galaya**, when 23rd day passed, were **deliveries for Šulgi-simtum**, **Apilatum took over**. Month of ezem-Ninazu, Year of Šašrum was destroyed.	1只育肥公绵羊、1只牛后级公绵羊和1只羔来自**旮拉亚**，于23日过去时， **为舒勒吉新吞的送入项**，**阿皮拉吞接管了**。 神宁阿朱庆典月， 沙什润被毁年。
Š 42 v/24: **zi-ga** 1 grass bull, 1 fattened bull and 1 fattened kid for**the house of Simat-Ištar**, **the son of king**, **withdrawn from Ur**	1 gud-ú, 1 gud-niga, 1 máš-gal-niga, ***é-Simat-Iš$_4$-tár*** *dumu Lugal--šè*, *iti--ta ud-24 ba-ta-zal*, *zi-ga šà* ~ **Urim$_5$^{ki}**-ma. iti-ezem-^{d}Nin-a-zu, mu Ša-aš-ru^{ki} ba-hul. (CST 470, P107985)	1 grass bull, 1 fattened bull and 1 fattened kid for**the house of Simat-Ištar**, **son of king**, when 24th day passed, **were withdrawn from Ur**. Month of ezem-Ninazu, Year of Šašrum was destroyed.	1头食草公牛、1头育肥公牛和1只育肥公山羊崽**为王子席马特伊什塔尔之房**，于24日过去时，从**乌尔支出了**。神宁阿朱庆典月，沙什润被毁年。
Š 42 v/28: **mu-túm**, **ì-dab$_5$** 3 pigeons from**Simat-Ištar**, **deliveries for Šulgi-simtum**, **Apilatum took over**, in Ur	3 ir$_7$^{mušen}, ***Simat-Iš$_4$-tár***, *iti--ta ud-28 ba-ta-zal*, *mu-túm-^{d}* ***Šul-gi-sí-im-tum***, ***Á-pi$_5$-la-tum*** *ì-dab$_5$*, *šà* ~ **Urim$_5$^{ki}**-ma. iti-ezem-^{d}Nin-a-zu, mu Ša-aš-ru^{ki} ba-hul. (Torino 1 039, P132068)	3 pigeons from**Simat-Ištar**, when the 28th day passed, **were deliveries for Šulgi-simtum**, **Apilatum took over**, in **Ur**. Month of ezem-Ninazu, Year of Šašrum was destroyed.	3只家鸽来自**席马特伊什塔尔**，于28日过去时，**为舒勒吉新吞的送入项**，**阿皮拉吞接管了**，于乌尔。神宁阿朱庆典月，沙什润被毁年。
Š 42 vi: **mu-túm**, **ì-dab$_5$** 4 rams and 1 kid fr. **Šukubum**, **for Šulgi-simtum**, **Apilatum took**, in **Tummal**	4 udu, 1 máš, ***Šu-ku-bu-um***, *mu-túm-* ***^{d}Šul-gi-sí-im-tum***, ***Á-pi$_5$-la-tum*** *ì-dab$_5$*, *šà* ~ **Tum-ma-al^{ki}**. iti-á-ki-ti, mu Ša-aš-ru-u^{ki}ba-hul. (PDT 2 983, P126330)	4 rams and 1 kid from **Šukubum**, **deliveries for Šulgi-simtum**, **Apilatum took over**, in **Tummal**. Month of akiti, Year of Šašrum was destroyed.	4只公绵羊和1只公崽来自**舒库布姆**，**为舒勒吉新吞的送入项**，**阿皮拉吞接管了**，**于图马勒**。阿基提月，沙什润被毁年。
Š 42 vi/8: **mu-túm**, **ì-dab$_5$** 1+ pigeons from**Watrat**, **the overseer**, were deliveries for **Šulgi-simtum**, **Apilatum took over**, in **Tummal**	1+ ir$_7$^{mušen} [***Wa-at***] ***-ra-at*** *ugula*, *iti--ta ud-8 ba-ta-zal*, *mu-túm*~ ***^{d}Šul-gi-sí-im-tum***, ***Á-pi$_5$-la-tum*** *ì-dab$_5$*, *šà*~ *Tum-ma-al^{ki}.iti-á-ki-ti*, *mu Ša-aš-ru^{ki} ba-hul.* (*SA* 045 (*Pl.*003), P128587)	1+ *pigeons from***Watrat**, **the overseer**, when 8th day passed, were deliveries for **Šulgi-simtum**, **Apilatum took over**, in **Tummal**. Month of akiti, Year of Šašrum was destroyed.	1+只家鸽来自**瓦特腊特监工**，于8日过去时，**为舒勒吉新吞的送入项**，**阿皮拉吞接管了**，**于图马勒**。阿基提月，沙什润被毁之年。

续表

时间和摘要	文献内容	英文翻译	中文翻译
Š 42 vi/24: **zi-ga** 1 **LAGAB** thicket piglet, 2 ducks, 3 pigeons, 14 doves, for **the boat of An**, were **withdrawn from Apilatum**	1šáh^{zah}-tur-nitá-giš-gi-**LAGAB**, 2 uz-tur, 3 ir$_7$^{mušen}, 14 tu-gur$_4$^{mušen}, **má$^!$-an-na**--šè, iti--ta ud-24 ba-ta-zal, zi-ga ***Á-pi$_5$-la-tum***. *iti-á-ki-ti*, *mu Ša-aš-ru^{ki}ba-hul.* (*ArOr* 25 562 23, *P*101878)	1 **LAGAB** thicket piglet, 2 ducks, 3 pigeons, 14 doves, for **the boat of An**, when 24th day passed, were **withdrawn from Apilatum**. Month of akiti, Year of Šašrum was destroyed.	1 只 **LAGAB** 苇塘雄豚、2 只鸭、3 只家鸽和 14 只野鸽为**安神之船**，于 24 日过去时，从**阿皮拉吞支出**了。阿基提月，沙什润被毁年。
Š 42 vii/5-9: **zi-ga** 5th: 1 fat ram for **Allatum**, 6th: 1 grass bull, 5 fat rams, 1 fat ewe, 1 fat goat for **kitchen**, 2 fat rams, 1 lamb, for **sacrifice**, 7th: 1 fattened ram in **sheepfold**, 1 lamb for **Ninsun**, 1 kid brought to **room**, 1 fat ram, 1 lamb, for **sacrifice**, 8th: 1 fattened ram, 1 ewe of the after-ox-class, 1 lamb, for the **offering of disappearing place**, 9th: 2 fattened rams for the **sacrifice**, 1 fattened lamb for the **food of king**, **sent to the sheepfold**, **these were withdrawn**	1 udu-niga, ^{d}***Al-la-tum***, *iti--ta* **ud-5**-ba-ta-zal, 1 gud-ú, 5 udu-niga, 1 u$_8$-niga, 1 ud$_5$-niga, **é-muhaldim**--šè, 2 udu-niga, 1 sila$_4$, **siskúr**--šè, ud-1-kam; iti--ta**ud-6**-ba-ta-zal, 1 udu-niga, **šà ~ gá-udu--ka**, 1 sila$_4$, ^{d} **Nin-sún**, 1 máš, zag túm-dè, 1 udu-niga, 1 sila$_4$, **siskúr**--šè, ud-2-kam; iti--ta**ud-7**-ba-ta-zal, 1 udu-niga, 1 u$_8$~ gud-e-ús-sa, 1 sila$_4$, **níĝ~ ki-zàh**--šè, ud-3-kam; iti--ta**ud-8**-ba-ta-zal, 2 udu-niga, **siskúr**--šè, 1 sila$_4$-niga, **níĝ-gu$_7$-lugal**--šè, ud-4-kam, iti--ta ud-9-ba-ta-zal, **gá-udu**--šè, **è-a**, zi-ga.iti-ezem-^{d}Šul-gi, mu Ša-aš-ru^{ki}ba-hul. (OIP 115079, P123240)	1 fattened ram for **Allatum**, when the5thday passed, 1 grass bull, 5 fattened rams, 1 fattened ewe, 1 fatteded she-goat for **kitchen**, 2 fattened rams, 1 lamb, for **the sacrifice** on once, when the 6thday passed, 1 fattened ram in **the sheepfold**, 1 lamb for **Ninsun**, 1 kid brought to the **room**, 1 fattened ram, 1 lamb, for **the sacrifice** on twice, when the 7thday passed, 1 fattened ram, 1 ewe of the after-ox-class, 1 lamb, for the **offering of disappearing place**, on 3rd time, when the 8thday passed, 2 fattened rams for the **sacrifice**, 1 fattened lamb for the **food of king**, on 4th time, when the 9thday passed, **sent to the sheepfold**, **these were withdrawn**. Month of ezem-Šulgi, Year of Šašrum was destroyed.	1 只育肥公绵羊为**阿拉吞**于第 5 天过去时，1 头食草公牛、5 只育肥公绵羊、1 头育肥公牛和 1 只育肥母山羊为**厨房**，2 只育肥公绵羊和 1 只羊羔为**祭祀**第一次，于第 6 天过去时，1 只育肥公绵羊为**羊圈**，1 只羊羔为**宁孙**，1 只公崽为**厢房**，1 只育肥公绵羊和 1 只羊羔为**祭祀**第 2 次，于第 7 天过去时，1 只育肥公绵羊、1 头牛后级母牛和 1 只羊羔为**消失处供奉**第 3 次，于第 8 天过去时，2 只育肥公绵羊为**祭祀**，1 只育肥羊羔为**国王的食物**第 4 次，于第 9 天过去时，被送入羊圈，以上支出了。 神舒勒吉庆典月， 沙什润被毁年。
Š 42 vii/15: **mu-túm, ì-dab$_5$** 4 fat rams and 1 lamb fr. **wife of Ur-Sin**, the governor of URxU, 2 rams fr. **Lusagga**, 1 lamb fr. **Ninlil-Tumimti**, 2 lambs fr. [...], were deliveries for Šulgi-simtum, **Apilatum took over**	4 udu-niga, 1 sila$_4$, **dam-Ur-^{d}Sîn** ensí ÚRxÚ^{ki}, iti--ta ud-15 ba-ta-zal, 2 udu **Lú-sag$_9$-ga**, 1 sila$_4$ ^{d} **Nin-líl-Tum-im-ti$_9$**, 2 sila$_4$ [...] ensí, mu-túm ~ ^{d}***Šul-gi-sí-im-tum***, ***Á-pi$_5$-la-túm*** *ì-dab$_5$*. *iti-ezem-^{d} Šul-gi*, *mu Ša-aš-ru^{ki} ba-hul.* (*Ontario* 1 012, *P*124425)	*4 fattened rams and* 1 *lamb from the***wife of Ur-Sin**, the governor of URxU, when the 15th day passed, 2 rams from **Lusagga**, 1 lamb from **Ninlil-Tumimti**, 2 lambs from [...], the governor, were deliveries for Šulgi-simtum, **Apilatum took over**. Month of ezem-Šulgi, Year of Šašrum was destroyed.	4 只育肥公绵羊和 1 只羔自 **UrxU 总督乌尔辛之妻**，于 15 日过去时，2 只公绵羊来自**卢萨旮**，1 只羔自**宁里勒吞伊姆提**，2 只羔自【……】总督，为**舒勒吉新吞的送入项**，**阿皮拉吞接管**了。神舒勒吉庆典月，沙什润被毁年。

续表

时间和摘要	文献内容	英文翻译	中文翻译
Š 42 vii/24： **mu-túm，ì-dab$_5$** 2 duck fr. **Šarrum-ili offical**，were **deliveries for Šulgi-simtum，Apilatum took over**	2 uz-tur，***Šar-ru-um-ìlí*** *sukkal*，*iti--ta ud-24-ba-ta-zal*，*mu-túm-*^{d} ***Šul-gi-sí-im-tum***，***Á-pi$_5$-la-tum*** *ì-dab$_5$*. *iti-ezem-*^{d}*Šul-gi*，*mu Ša-aš-ru*^{ki}*ba-hul*. （*Torino* 1 038，*P*133848）	2 *duck from***Šarrum-ili**，**the envoy**，when 24th day passed，were **deliveries for Šulgi-simtum**，**Apilatum took over**. Month of ezem-Šulgi，Year of Šašrum was destroyed.	2只鸭子来自**国使沙闰伊里**，于24日过去时，以上为**舒勒吉新吞的送入项**，**阿皮拉吞接管**了。神舒勒吉庆典月，沙什润被毁年。
Š 42 viii/5： **mu-túm，ì-dab$_5$** 8 ducks from**Bagum**，the **bird-catcher**，were deliveries **for Šulgi-simtum**，**Apilatum took over**	8 uz-tur ***Ba-gu-um*** *mušen-dù*！，*iti--ta ud-5 ba-ta-zal*，*mu-túm～*^{d}***Šul-gi-sí-im-tum***， ***Á-pi$_5$-la-tum*** *ì-dab$_5$*. *iti-šu-eš$_5$-ša*，*mu Ša-aš-ru*^{ki} *ba-hul*. （*MVN* 13 275，*P*117047）	8 *ducks from***Bagum**，the **bird-catcher**，when 5th day passed，were deliveries **for Šulgi-simtum**，**Apilatum took over**. Month of šu-ešša，Year of Šašrum was destroyed.	8只鸭来自**捕鸟人巴衮**，于5日过去时， **为舒勒吉新吞的送入项**， **阿皮拉吞接管**了。 三只手月， 沙什润被毁年。
Š 42 viii/20： （**zi-ga**） 1 fattened bull，2+ fattened rams for**Annunitum**，1 he-goat for **Nin-tin-u**［**gga**］，for **the nabrium festival of Annunitum in Ur**，**via Šulgi-ili**	1 gud-niga，2+ udu-niga，***An-nu-ni-tum***，1 *máš-gal*，^{d}**Nin-tin-u**［**g$_5$-ga**］，iti--ta-ud-20 ba-ra-zal，ezem ***na-ab-rí-um-An-nu-ni-tum*** *šà～* **Urim$_5$**^{ki}-ma，gìr^d***Šul-gi-ì-lí***，*zi-ga-**Á-pi$_5$-la-tum***. *iti-šu-eš$_5$-ša*，*mu Ša-aš-ru*^{ki} *ba-hul*. （*PDT* 2 0973，*P*126321）	1 *fattened bull*，2+ *fattened rams for***Annunitum**，1 he-goat for **Nin-tin-u**［**gga**］，when the 20th day passed，for **the nabrium festival of Annunitum in Ur**，**via Šulgi-ili**，were withdrawn from Apilatum. Month of šu-ešša，Year of Šašrum was destroyed.	1头育肥公牛和2+只育肥公绵羊为**安努尼吞**，1只公山羊为**宁廷【乌音】**，于20日过去时，为**安努尼吞于乌尔的那卜润节**，**经由舒勒吉伊里**，从阿皮拉吞支出了。三只手月，沙什润被毁年。
Š 42 viii/22： **mu-túm，ì-dab$_5$** 1 duck fr.**wife of Šarrum-ili**，the animal manager，this was delivery，**Apilatum took**	1 uz-tur **dam-*Šar-ru-um-ì-lí*** *šùš*，*iti--ta ud-22 ba-ra-zal*，*mu-túm*，***Á-pi$_5$-la-tum*** *ì-dab$_5$*. *iti-šu-eš$_5$-ša*，*mu Ša-aš-ru*^{ki} *ba-hul*. （*Princeton* 1 059，*P*126748）	1 *duck from***wife of Šarrum-ili** animal manager，when 22nd day passed，this delivery，**Apilatum took over**.Month of šu-ešša，Year of Šašrum was destroyed.	1只鸭来自**沙闰伊里牲畜长**，于22日过去时，这个送入，**阿皮拉吞接管**了。三只手月， 沙什润被毁年。
Š 42 viii/26，28： **zi-ga，butchered** 1**butchered** duck **sent to the palace**，1 female piglet for **the food of my queen**，were**withdrawn from Apilatum**	1 uz-tur，ba-úš，**é-gal-la ba-an-ku$_4$**，iti--ta **ud-26** ba-ra-zal，1 šáh-izi-tur-munus-giš-gi，**níĝ-gu$_7$-nin-ĝá**--šè，iti--ta **ud-28**-ba-ta-zal，zi-ga-***Á-pi$_5$-la-tum***. *iti-šu-eš-ša*，*mu Ša-aš-ru*^{ki}*ba-hul*. （*Torino* 1 188，*P*133901）	1**butchered** duck **sent to the palace**，when the **26th** day passed，1 female piglet for **the food of my queen**，when the **28th** day passed，were **withdrawn from Apilatum**.Month of šu-ešša，Year of Šašrum was destroyed.	1只宰杀的鸭**被送入宫殿**，于**26**日过去时，1只雌豚**为我的王后的食物**， 于**28**日过去时，以上从**阿皮拉吞支出**了。 三只手月， 沙什润被毁年。

续表

时间和摘要	文献内容	英文翻译	中文翻译
Š 42 viii/28, 30: **zi-ga, butchered** 28th: 1 **butchered** fat ram **sent to palace**, 1 fat ram for **Gamagamue festival**, 30th: 1 fat ram for **giranum of Inanna**, 1 fattened ram, 1 ewe for **giranum festival of Belat-Suhnir and Belat-Darraban**, 1 fattened ram for **the sacrifice of Nanna**, 1 lamb for **the center of the palace**, 1 lamb for **offering of "disappearing place"**, 1 kid for **Nin-sun**, 1 fat ram, 1 fat he-goat for **Uruk**, 2 **butchered** kids sent to palace, **withdrawn fr. Apilatum**	1 udu-gukkal-niga, ba-úš, **é-gal-la ba-an-ku$_4$**, 1 udu-niga, ezem-**ga-ma-ga-mu-è**--šè, iti--ta ud-28ba-ta-zal, 1 udu-niga, ***gi-ra-núm***-^{d}**Inanna**, 1 udu-niga, 1 u$_8$, *gi-ra-núm*-^{d}***Be-la-at-Suh-nir*** *ù* ^{d}**Be-la-at-Dar-ra-ba-an**, 1 *udu-niga*, *siskúr*-^{d}**Nanna**, 1 sila$_4$, šà~ **é-gal**, 1 sila$_4$, **níĝ~ ki-zàh**--šè, 1 máš, ^{d} **Nin-sún**, 1 udu-niga, 1 máš-gal-niga, šà ~ **Unug^{ki}**-ga--ka--šè, iti--ta **ud-30**-ba-ta-zal, 2 máš, ba-úš, **é-gal-la ba-an-ku$_4$**, zi-ga-***Á-pi$_5$-la-tum***. *iti-šu-eš-ša*, *mu Ša-aš-ru^{ki}ba-hul*. (*OIP* 115080, *P123252*)	1**butchered** fattened fat-tailed ram **sent to the palace**, 1 fattened ram for **Gamagamue festival**, when 28th day passed, 1 fattened ram for **giranum festival of Inanna**, 1 fattened ram, 1 ewe for **giranum festival of Belat-Suhnir and Belat-Darraban**, 1 fattened ram for **the sacrifice of Nanna**, 1 lamb for **the center of the palace**, 1 lamb for **offering of "disappearing place"**, 1 kid for **Nin-sun**, 1 fattened ram, 1 fattened he-goat for **the center of Uruk**, when 30th day passed, 2 **butchered** kids sent to the palace, **were withdrawn from Apilatum**. Month of šu-ešša, Year of Šašrum was destroyed.	1只宰杀的**育肥肥尾公绵羊被送入宫殿**，1只育肥公绵羊为 **Gamagamue 节**，于28日过去时，1只育肥公绵羊为**伊南那的 giranum 节**，1只育肥公绵羊和1只母牛为**贝拉特苏赫尼尔和贝拉特达腊班的 giranum 节**，1只育肥公绵羊为**南那的祭祀**，1只羊羔为**宫殿中心**，1只羊羔为**消失处供奉**，1只公崽为**宁孙**，1只育肥公绵羊和1只**育肥公山羊为乌鲁克中心**，于30日过去时，2只**宰杀的公崽被送入宫殿**，以上从**阿皮拉吞支出**了。三只手月，沙什润被毁年。
Š 42 viii: **mu-túm, ì-dab$_5$** 1 ram and 1 breast lamb fr. **Siyaya, for Šulgi-simtum, Apilatum took over**	1 udu-ú, 1 sila$_4$-gaba, ***Si-a-a***, *mu-túm*-^{d} ***Šul-gi-sím-tum***, ***Á-pi$_5$-la-tum*** *ì-dab$_5$*. *iti-šu-eš$_5$-ša*, *mu Ša-aš-ru^{ki} ba-hul*. (*Torino* 1040, *P133849*)	1 *grass ram and* 1 *breast lamb from* **Siyaya, were deliveries for Šulgi-simtum, Apilatum took over**. Month of šu-ešša, Year of Šašrum was destroyed.	1只食草公绵羊和1只胸羊羔来自**席亚亚**，以上为**舒勒吉新吞的送入项，阿皮拉吞接管**了。三只手月，沙什润被毁年。
Š 42 viii: **mu-túm, ì-dab$_5$** 2 rams and 1 kid fr. **Kurub-rra, for Šulgi-simtum, Apilatum over**	2 udu, 1 máš, ***Ku-ru-ub-Èr-ra***, *mu-túm*-^{d} ***Šul-gi-sím-tum***, ***Á-pi$_5$-la-tum*** *ì-dab$_5$*. *iti-šu-eš$_5$-ša*, *mu-Ša-aš-ru^{ki} ba-hul*. (*Torino* 1041, *P100271*)	2 *rams and* 1 *kid from* **Kurub-Erra**, were **deliveries for Šulgi-simtum, Apilatum took over**. Month of šu-ešša, Year of Šašrum was destroyed.	2只公绵羊和1只公崽来自**库如卜埃腊**，以上为**舒勒吉新吞的送入项，阿皮拉吞接管**了。三只手月，沙什润被毁年。
Š 42 viii: **zi-ga, butchered** 1**butchered ewe was sent to palace, withdr. fr. Apilatum**	1 u$_8$ ba-úš **é-gal-la ba-an-ku$_4$**, zi-ga ***Á-pi$_5$-la-tum***. *iti-šu-eš-ša*, *mu Ša-aš-ru^{ki} ba-hul*. (*Hirose* 018, *P109489*)	1**butchered ewe was sent to palace, withdrawn from Apilatum**. Month of šu-ešša, Year of Šašrum was destroyed.	1只**宰杀的母绵羊被送入宫殿，从阿皮拉吞支出**了。三只手月，沙什润被毁年。

续表

时间和摘要	文献内容	英文翻译	中文翻译
Š 42 x/13, 14: **zi-ga, butchered** 13th: 2 fattened rams for **the "pouring-beer" sacrifice of king**, 14th: 1 fat ram for **food of king, in the palace**, 1 fattened ram for **sacrifice of Inanna**, 1 fat ram and 1 ewe for **Belat-Suhnir**, 2 lambs for **offering of "disappearing place" of temple of Belat-Suhnir, via Ur-Dumuzida**, 1 fat ram, 1 fat goat and 1 ewe for **sacrifice Full Moon, in Uruk**, 4 rams, **butchered ones were sent to palace**, were**withdr.fr.Apilatum**	2 udu-niga**kaš-dé-a-lugal**, ud ~ Uru-sag-rig$_7$^{ki}--ta mu-túm--ra, iti--ta **ud-13**ba-ra-zal, 1 udu-niga**níĝ-gu$_7$-lugal**--šè šà ~ **é-gal-ka** , 1 udu-niga **siskúr-^{d} Inanna**, 1 udu-niga, 1 u$_8$, **siskúr-*^{d}Be-la-at-Suh-nir***, 2 *sila$_4$* **níĝ~ ki-zàh~ é-*^{d}Be-la-at-Suh-nir***, *gìr*-**Ur-^{d}Dumu-zi-da**, 1 udu-niga, 1 máš-gal-niga, 1 u$_8$, **siskúr šà~ Unug^{ki}-ga é-ud-15**, iti--ta **ud-14**ba-ta-zal, 4 udu-ú ri-ri-ga-àm **é-gal-la ba-an-ku$_4$**, zi-ga***Á-pi$_5$-la-tum***. *iti-ezem-An-na*, *mu Ša-aš-ru^{ki} ba-hul.* (*TRU* 284, *P*135048)	2 *fattened rams for***the "pouring-beer" sacrifice of king**, when from **Uru-sagrig** were deliveried, when **13th**day passed, 1 fattened ram for **food of king, in the palace**, 1 fattened ram for **sacrifice of Inanna**, 1 fattened ram and 1 ewe for **sacrifice of Belat-Suhnir**, 2 lambs for **offering of "disappearing place" of temple of Belat-Suhnir, via Ur-Dumuzida**, 1 fattened ram, 1 fattened he-goat and 1 ewe for **sacrifice Full Moon, in Uruk**, when**14th**day passed, 4 grass rams, **butchered ones were sent to palace**, were **withdrawn from Apilatum**.Month of ezem-Anna, Year of Šašrum was destroyed.	2育肥公绵羊为**国王的倒啤酒宴会**，当从乌鲁萨格瑞格送入时，于**13日**过去时，1育肥公绵羊为**国王的食物**，于**宫殿**，1育肥公绵羊为**伊南那的牺牲**，1育肥公绵羊和1母绵羊为**贝拉特苏赫尼尔的牺牲**，2羔为**贝拉特苏赫尼尔庙的消失处供奉**，**经由乌尔杜穆兹达**，1只育肥公绵羊、1只育肥公山羊和1只母绵羊为**满月牺牲**，**于乌鲁克**，于**14日**过去时，4只食草公绵羊，这些**宰杀牲被送入宫殿**，以上从**阿皮拉吞支出了**。天神庆典月，沙什润被毁年。
Š 42 x/23, 24: **mu-túm, ì-dab$_5$** 23rd: 1 duck from **Ayama**, 24th: 3 ducks from **Apili**, were **deliveries for Šulgi-simtum, Apilatum took over**	1 uz-tur, ***A-[a]-ma***, *iti--ta* **ud-23**ba-ra-zal, 3 uz-tur, ***Á-pi$_5$-lí***, *iti--ta* **ud-24**ba-ra-zal, mu-túm~ ***^{d}Šul-gi-sí-im-tum***, ***Á-pi$_5$-la-tum*** *ì-dab$_5$*. *iti-ezem-an-na*, *mu-Ša-aš-ru^{ki}ba-hul.* (*OIP* 115 071, *P*123318)	1 *duck from* **Ayama**, when the **23rd**day passed, 3 ducks from **Apili**, when the **24th**day passed, were **deliveries for Šulgi-simtum, Apilatum took over**. Month of ezem-Anna, Year of Šašrum was destroyed.	1只鸭来自**阿亚马**，于23日过去时， 3只鸭来自**阿皮里**，于24日过去时， 为**舒勒吉新吞的送入项，阿皮拉吞接管**了。天神安庆典月，沙什润被毁年。
Š 42 xi/29: **zi-ga** 1 thicket piglet for**food of my queen**, was **withdrawn from Apilatum**	1šáh-NE-tur-giš-gi, **níĝ-gu$_7$-nin-ĝá**--šè, iti--ta ud-29 ba-ra-zal, zi-ga ***Á-pi$_5$-la-tum***. *iti-ezem-Me-ki-ĝál*, [*mu Ša-aš-ru*]^{ki} *ba-hul.* (*OIP* 115 081, *P*123653)	1 *thicket piglet for***food of my queen**, when 29th day passed, was **withdrawn from Apilatum**. Month of ezem-Mekiĝ-al, Year of Šašrum was destroyed.	1只苇塘猪崽为**我的王后的食物**，于29日过去时，从**阿皮拉吞支出了**。神美基旮勒庆典月，沙什润被毁年。
Š 42 xi: **zi-ga** 6 sheep for **allowance of Belat-Suhnir, Belat-Darraban, Annunitum and Ulmasitum**	3 ud$_5$, 1 u$_8$, 1 máš-nitá, 1 sila$_4$-nitá, sá-dug$_4$-***^{d}Be-la-at-suh-ne-er***, ***^{d}Be-la-at-Dar-ra-ba-an***, ***An-nu-ni-tum*** ù **^{d}Ul-ma-si-tum**. *iti-ezem-Me-ki-ĝál*, *mu Ša-aš-ru^{ki} ba-hul-a.* (*SACT* 1180, *P*128935)	3 *she-goats*, 1 *ewe*, 1 *kid*, 1 *male lamb*, *for* **the monthly allowance of Belat-Suhner, Belat-Darra-ban, Annunitum and Ulmasitum**. Month of ezem-Mekiĝal, Year of Šašrum was destroyed.	3只母山羊、1只母绵羊、1只公崽和1只公羔，为**贝拉特苏赫耐尔、贝拉特达腊班、安努尼吞和乌勒马西吞的月供**。神美基旮勒庆典月，沙什润被毁年。

续表

时间和摘要	文献内容	英文翻译	中文翻译
Š 42 xi: **zi-ga, butchered** 1 female kid and 1 kid were**butchered, sent to the palace, withdr.fr.Apillatum**	1^{f}ašgar, 1 máš, ri-ri-ga-àm, é-gal-［la］ba-an-ku$_{4}$!, zi-ga ***Á-pil-la-tum***. *iti-ezem-Me-ki-ĝál. mu Ša-aš-ru^{ki} ba-hul.* (*MVN* 20, 188, *P*143121)	1 *female kid and* 1 *kid were***butchered, sent to the palace, withdrawn from Apillatum**. Month of ezem-Mekiĝal, Year of Šašrum was destroyed.	1只雌山羊崽和1只公山羊崽为**宰杀牲被送入宫殿**，从**阿皮拉吞支出**了。神美基旮勒庆典月，沙什润被毁年。
Š 42 xi/23: **zi-ga** 1 breast thicket female piglet, 2 thicket pigletsfor **Simat-Ištar**, were **withdrawn from Apilatum**	1 šáh^{zah}-tur-munus-giš-gi gaba, 1 šáh^{zah}-tur-munus-giš-gi, 1 šáh^{zah}-tur-nitá-giš-gi, **Simat-^{d} Iš$_{8}$-tár**--*šè*, *iti-ta ud-23 ba-ra-zal*, *zi-ga* ***Á-pi$_{5}$-la-tum***. *iti-ezem-Me-ki-ĝál*, *mu Ša-aš-ruki ba-hul.* (*BIN* 3 358, P106164)	1 *breast thicket female piglet*, 1 *thicket female piglet*, 1 *thicket piglet for* **Simat-Ištar**, when 23rd day passed, were **withdrawn from Apilatum**. Month of ezem-Meki-ĝal, Year of Šašrum was destroyed.	1头胸苇塘雌豚、1头苇塘雌豚和1头苇塘雄豚为**席马特伊什塔尔**，于23日过去时，从**阿皮拉吞支出**了。神美基旮勒庆典月，沙什润被毁年。
Š 42 xii: **mu-túm, ì-dab$_{5}$** 2 rams and 1 kid fr.**Garaya**, 1 lamb from **Te ṣin-Mama**, these were deliveries, **Apilatum took over**	2 udu-ú, 1 máš ***Ga-ra-a***, 1 *sila$_{4}$* ***Te-ṣí-in-Ma-ma***, *mu-túm*, ***Á-pi$_{5}$-la-tum*** *ì-dab$_{5}$.iti-še-kin-kud*, *mu Ša-aš-ru-um^{ki} ba-hul.* (*Hirose* 019, P109490)	2 *grass rams and* 1 *kid from***Garaya**, 1 lamb from **Te ṣ in-Mama**, these were deliveries, **Apilatum took over**.Month of še-kin-kud, Year of Šašrum was destroyed.	2只食草公绵羊和1只公崽来自**旮腊亚**，1只羔来自**台岑妈妈**， 以上送入，**阿皮拉吞接管**了。大麦收割月， 沙什润被毁年。
Š 42 xii/27, 30: **zi-ga** 2 fat rams for **provisions of Siyatum**, 1 fat ram for **giranum of Inanna**, 2 fat rams for **Belat-Suhnir and Belat-Darraban, were withdrawn from Apilatum**	2 udu-niga **igi-kár** ***Si-a-tum***, *iti--ta* **ud-27** ba-ra-zal, 1 udu-niga ***gi-ra-núm-^{d}Inanna***, 2 udu-niga ***^{d}Be-la-at-***［***Suh***］***-nir*** *ù* ***^{d}Be-la-at-Dar-ra-ba-an***, *iti--ta* **ud-30** ba-ra-zal, zi-ga ***Á-pi$_{5}$-la-tum***.*iti-še-kin-kud*, *mu Ša-aš-ru^{ki} ba-hul.* (*SA* 001 (*Pl*.033), *P*128616)	2 *fattened rams for* **provisions of Siyatum**, when **27th** day passed, 1 fattened ram for **giranum festival of Inanna**, 2 fattened rams for **Belat-Suhnir and Belat-Darraban**, when **30th** day passed, **were withdrawn from Apilatum**.Month of še-kin-kud, Year of Šašrum was destroyed.	2只育肥公绵羊为**席亚吞的供奉**，于**27日**过去时，1只育肥公绵羊为**伊南那的吉腊努姆仪式**，2只育肥公绵羊为**贝拉特苏赫尼尔和贝拉特达腊班**，于**30日**过去时，从**阿皮拉吞支出**了。大麦收割月，沙什润被毁年。
Š 43 i/15, 19, 22: **zi-ga, butchered** 15th: 1 piglet and 1 duck, 19th: 1 piglet, 1 duck and 5 doves, for **the king**, copy of the tablet, in Lamka. 22nd: 4 ducks and 1 swallow, **butchered dead were sent to the palace, withdrawn from Apillatum**	1šáh-zah-tur, 1 uz-tur, iti--ta **ud-15** ba-ra-zal, 1 šáh-zah-tur, 1 uz-tur, 5 tu-gur$_{4}$^{mušen}, iti--ta **ud-19** ba-ra-zal, **lugal**--ra gaba-ri-a, **šà~ Lam-ka**, 4 uz-tur, 1 u$_{5}$-sim^{mušen} **ri-ri-ga-àm**, é-gal-la ba-an-ku$_{4}$, iti--ta **ud-22** ba-ra-zal, zi-ga ***Á-pil-la-tum***. *iti-maš-kù-gu$_{7}$*, *mu ús-sa Ša-aš-ru^{ki} ba-hul.* (*AnOr* 07 088, P101383)	1 *piglet and* 1 *duck*,*when the* 15th*day passed*, 1 *piglet*, 1 *duck and* 5 *doves*, *when the* 19th*day passed*, *for* **the king**, copy of the tablet, in Lamka.4 ducks and 1 swallow, **butchered** ones **were sent to the palace**, when the 22ndday passed, **withdrawn from Apillatum**.Month of mašku ~ gu$_{7}$, Year after that of Šašrum was destroyed.	1只豚和1只鸭于15日过去时，1只豚、1只鸭和5只野鸽于19日过去时， **为国王**，泥板复件，于兰卡，4只鸭和1只燕，**为宰杀牲被送入宫殿**， 于22日过去时， 以上从**阿皮拉吞支出**了。食瞪羚月， 沙什润被毁年次年。

续表

时间和摘要	文献内容	英文翻译	中文翻译
Š 43 i/24, 26, 29: **zi-ga, butchered** 24th: 1 **butchered** ram was **sent to palace**, 26th: 2 fattened rams on 1st time, 29th: 1 fattened ram on 2nd time, for **the king**, copy of the tablet, in **Egaba**, 1 fattened ram for **sacrifice of Inanna**, 2 fattened rams for **Belat-Suhnir and Belat-Darraban**, 29th: 2 fattened rams, 1 ewe, for sacrifice in **Uruk of the beginning of New Moon, withdrawn from Apilatum**	1 udu-gud-e-ús-sa ~ ba-úš, **é-gal-la ba-an-ku$_4$**, iti--ta **ud-24**ba-ra-zal, 2 udu-niga a-rá-1-kam; iti--ta **ud-26**ba-ra-zal, 1 udu-niga a-rá-2-kam; **lugal**--ra gaba-ri-a šà ~ **É-ga-ba^{ki}**, 1 udu-niga, siskúr-^{d}**Inanna**, 2 udu-niga^{d}***Be-la-at-Suh-nir*** ù ^{d}**Be-la-at-Dar-ra-ba-an**, *iti--ta***ud-29**ba-ra-zal, 2 udu-niga, 1 u$_8$, **siskúr** šà ~ **Unug^{ki}**-ga **sag-ud-sakar**, iti--ta **ud-29**ba-ra-zal, zi-ga***Á-pi$_5$-la-tum***. *iti-maš-dà ~ gu$_7$*, *mu ús-sa Ša-aš-ru^{ki} ba-hul*. (*OIP* 115082, *P*123620)	1 **butchered** ram of after-ox-class was **sent to palace**, when 24thday passed, 2 fattened rams on 1st time, when 26thday passed, 1 fattened ram on 2nd time, for **the king**, copy of the tablet, in **Egaba**, 1 fattened ram for **sacrifice of Inanna**, 2 fattened rams for **Belat-Suhnir and Belat-Darraban**, when 29thday passed, 2 fattened rams, 1 ewe, for sacrifice in **Uruk of the beginning of New Moon**, when 29thday passed, were **withdrawn from Apilatum**. Month of mašda ~ gu$_7$, Year after that of Šašrum was destroyed.	1只**宰杀的**牛后级公绵羊被**送入宫殿**于本月**24**日过去时，2只育肥公绵羊第1次；于本月**26**日过去时，1只育肥公绵羊第2次为**国王**；泥板复件，于埃旮巴，1只育肥公绵羊为**伊南那祭**，2只育肥公绵羊为**贝拉特苏赫尼尔和贝拉特达腊班**，于本月**29**日过去时，2只育肥公绵羊和1只母绵羊为**于乌鲁克新月初祭**，于本月**29**日过去时，从**阿皮拉吞支出了**。食瞪羚月，沙什润被毁年次年。
Š 43 ii/1, 4, 9: **mu-túm, ì-dab$_5$** 1st: 2 pigeons from **Allamu**, the wood keeper, 4th: 4 ducklet from **Ninlil-tumimti**, 9th: 1 duck, 1 white duck, 2 pigeons, 10 doves from **Nir-idagal**, were deliveries for **Šulgi-simtum, Apilatum took over**	2 ir$_7$^{mušen}, ***Al-la-mu*** *santana*, *iti--ta***ud-1**ba-ra-zal, 4 amar-sag~ uz-tur ^{d}**Nin-líl-tum-im-ti**, iti--ta **ud-4**ba-ra-zal, 1 uz-tur, 1 uz-babbár, 2 ir$_7$^{mušen}, 10 tu-gur$_4$^{mušen}, ***Nir-ì-da-ĝál***, *iti--ta* **ud-9**ba-ra-zal, mu-túm-^{d}***Šul-gi-sí-im-tum***, ***Á-pi$_5$-la-tum*** *ì-dab$_5$*. *iti-ze$_x$-da ~ gu$_7$*, *mu en-^{d}Nanna máš-e ì-pà*. (*OIP* 115 072, *P*123495)	2 *pigeons from* **Allamu**, the wood keeper, when**1st** day passed, 4 ducklet from**Ninlil-tumimti**, when **4th**day passed, 1 duck, 1 white duck, 2 pigeons, 10 doves from**Nir-idagal**, when**9th**day passed, were deliveries for **Šulgi-simtum, Apilatum took over**. Month of zeda ~ gu$_7$, Year of en-priestess of Nanna was choosen by omen.	2只家鸽自**树林看守阿拉穆**，于**1**日过去时， 4只幼鸡自**宁里勒吞伊姆提**，于**4**日过去时， 1只鸭、1只白鸭、2只家鸽和10只野鸽自**尼尔伊达旮勒**，于**9**日过去时，为**舒勒吉新吞的送入项**，**阿皮拉吞接管了**。食豚月，南那的女祭司被占卜选中之年。

续表

时间和摘要	文献内容	英文翻译	中文翻译
Š 43 ii/11, 13, 16, 17: **zi-ga, butchered** 11th: 1 white bird and 1 dove on 1st time; 13th: 4 doves and 1 thicket piglet on 2nd time, 1 duck and 3 doves on 3rd time, **butchered ones were sent to the palace**, 16th: 1 thicket piglet and 1 ducklet on 1st time, 17th: 1 thicket piglet and 1 ducklet on 2nd time, for **the king**, copy of the tablet, in Kisurra, **withtdrawn from Apillatum**	1 uz-babbár, 1 tu-gur$_4$^{mušen} a-rá-1 -kam, iti--ta **ud-11-**ba-ra-zal; 4 tu-gur$_4$^{mušen}, 1 šáh-zah-tur-nitá-giš-gi, a-rá-2-kam, iti--ta **ud-13**-ba-ra-zal; 1 uz-tur, 3 tu-gur$_4$^{mušen}, a-rá-3-kam, iti--ta **ud-16**-ba-ra-zal, ri-ri-ga-ùm, é-gal-la ba-an-ku$_4$, 1 šáh-zah-tur-nitá-giš-gi, 1 amar-saĝ-uz-tur a-rá-1-kam, iti--ta **ud-16**-ba-ra-zal, 1 šáh-zah-tur-nitá-giš-gi, 1 amar-saĝ-uz-tur a-rá-2-kam, iti--ta **ud-17**-ba-ra-zal, lugal--ra gaba-ri-a, **šà~ Ki-sur-ra**^{ki}--ka, zi-ga ***Á-pil-la-tum***. *iti-ze$_x$-da-gu$_7$, mu en-^{d}Nanna maš-e ì-pàd.* (*AnOr* 07 070, *P*101365)	*1 white bird and 1 dove on 1st time, when the 11th day passed; 4 doves and 1 thicket piglet on 2nd time, when the 13thday passed; 1 duck and 3 doves on 3rd time, when 16thday passed*, **butchered ones were sent to the palace**, 1 thicket piglet and 1 ducklet on 1st time, when 16thday passed, 1 thicket piglet and 1 ducklet on 2nd time, when 17thday passed, for **the king**, copy of the tablet, in Kisurra, **withtdrawn from Apillatum**. Month of zeda~ gu$_7$, Year of en-priestess of Nanna was choosen by omen.	1只白鸟和1只野鸽第1次，于11日过去时；4只野鸽和1只苇塘雄豚第2次，于13日过去时；1只鸭和3只野鸽第3次，于16日过去时，以上宰杀**牲被送入宫殿**， 1只苇塘雄豚和1只幼鸭第1次，于16日过去时，1只苇塘雄豚和1只幼鸭第2次，于17日过去时，为**国王**，泥板复件，于**基苏腊**，从**阿皮拉吞支出**了。食豚月， 南那的女祭司被占卜选中之年。
Š 43 ii/21: **zi-ga** 1 fattened bull and 5 fattened rams for **"pouring-beer" festival of Tadin-Ištar**, were **withdrawn from Apilatu**	1 gud-niga, 5 udu-niga, kaš-dé-a ***Tá-din***$^!$***-Iš$_4$-tár***, *iti-ud-21 ba-ra-zal*, *zi-ga* ***Á-pi$_5$-la-tum***. *iti-ze$_x$-da~gu$_7$, mu en-^{d}Nanna maš-e ì-pàd.* (*Princeton* 2 354, *P*201353)	*1 fattened bull and 5 fattened rams for* **"pouring-beer" festival of Tadin-Ištar**, when 21st day passed, were **withdrawn from Apilatum**. Month of zeda~ gu$_7$, Year of en-priestess of Nanna was choosen by omen.	1头育肥公牛和5只育肥公绵羊为**塔丁伊什塔尔的倒啤酒宴会**，于21日过去时，从**阿皮拉吞支出**了。食豚月， 南那的女祭司被占卜选中之年。
Š 43 ii/20, 21, 22: **zi-ga, butchered** 20th: 1 **butchered** white duck **was sent to palace**, 21st: 1 thicket female piglet, 1 ducklet, 1 pigeon and 10 doves for **"pouring-beer" festival of Tadin-Ištar**, 22nd: 4 birds for the **food of my queen**, 1 **butchered** pigeon **was sent to palace**, were **withdrawn from Apilatum**	1 uz-babbár ba-úš **é-gal-la ba-an-ku$_4$**, iti--ta **ud-20**ba-ra-zal, 1šáh-NE-tur-munus-giš-gi, 1 amar-sag-uz-tur, 1 ir$_7$^{mušen}, 10 tu-gur$_4$^{mušen}, **kaš-dé-a-*Ta-din***$^!$***-Iš$_4$-tár***, *iti--ta* **ud-21**ba-ra-zal, 4 tu^{mušen} **níĝ-gu$_7$-nin-ĝá--šè**, 1 ir$_7$^{mušen} ba-úš **é-gal-la ba-an-ku$_4$**, iti--ta **ud-22**ba-ra-zal, zi-ga***Á-pi$_5$-la-tum***. *iti-ze$_x$-da ~ gu$_7$, mu en-^{d} Nanna maš-e ì-pàd.* (*NYPL* 079, *P*122615)	1**butchered** white duck **was sent to palace**, when the **20th**day passed, 1 thicket female piglet, 1 ducklet, 1 pigeon and 10 doves for **"pouring-beer" festival of Tadin-Ištar**, when the**21st**day passed, 4 birds for the **food of my queen**, 1 **butchered** pigeon **was sent to palace**, when the **22nd**day passed, were **withdrawn from Apilatum**. Month of zeda~ gu$_7$, Year of en-priestess of Nanna was choosen by omen.	1只**宰杀的白鸭被送入宫殿**，于**20**日过去时，1只苇塘雌豚、1只幼鸭、1只家鸽和10只野鸽为**塔丁伊什塔尔的倒啤酒宴会**，于**21**日过去时， 4只鸟为**我的王后的食物**，1只**宰杀的家鸽被送入宫殿**，于**22**日过去时， 从**阿皮拉吞支出**了。 食豚月， 南那的女祭司被占卜选中之年。

续表

时间和摘要	文献内容	英文翻译	中文翻译
Š 43 ii/30: **mu-túm, ì-dab$_5$** 1 ram and 1 kid from**Tabba-ili, the shepherd**, 3 fattened rams from **Watrat, the overseer**, 1 lamb and 1 kid fr.**Simat-Ištar**, were deliveries for **Šulgi-simtum, Apilatum took over**	1 udu, 1 máš ***Tab-ba-ì-lí*** *sipa*, 3 *udu-niga* ***Wa-at-ra-at*** *ugula*, *iti--ta ud-30 ba-ra-zal*, 1 *sila$_4$*, 1 *^{f}ašgar* ***Simat-Iš$_4$-tár***, *mu-túm~* ***^{d}Šul-gi-sí-im-tum****-ma*, ***Á-pi$_5$-la-tum*** *ì-dab$_5$*. *iti-ze$_x$-da~gu$_7$, mu en-^{d}Nanna maš-e ì-pàd.* (*OLP* 08 07 02, *P*124340)	1 *ram and* 1 *kid from***Tabba-ili, the shepherd**, 3 fattened rams from **Watrat, the overseer**, when 30th day passed, 1 lamb and 1 female kid from **Simat-Ištar**, were deliveries for **Šulgi-simtum, Apilatum took over**. Month of zeda~gu$_7$, Year of en-priestess of Nanna was choosen by omen.	1只公绵羊和1只公崽来自**牧羊人塔巴伊里**，3只育肥公绵羊来自**瓦特腊特监工**，于30日过去时，1只羔和1只雌崽来自**席马特伊什塔尔**，为**舒勒吉新吞的送入项，阿皮拉吞接管了**。食豚月，南那的女祭司被占卜选中之年。
Š 43 iii/25, 26, 29, 30: **zi-ga, butchered** 25th: 1 **butchered ducklet sent to palace**, 26th: 1 duck and 5 doves when were took for **food of my queen**, 29th: 1 ducklet, 1 dove, 30th: 1 duck **butchered ones were sent to the palace, withdrawn from Apilatum**	1 amar-sag-uz-tur~ba-úš, **é-gal-la ba-an-ku$_4$**, iti--ta **ud-25**ba-ra-zal, 1 uz-tur, 5 tu-gur$_4$^{mušen}, ud-dab$_5$-ba **níĝ-gu$_7$-nin-ĝá**--šè, iti--ta **ud-26**ba-ra-zal, 1 amar-sag-uz-tur, 1 tu-gur$_4$^{mušen}, iti--ta **ud-29** ba-ra-zal, a-rá-1-kam; 1 uz-tur, iti--ta **ud-30**ba-ra-zal, a-rá-2-kam, ba-úš, **é-gal-la ba-an-ku$_4$**, zi-ga***Á-pi$_5$-la-tum***. *iti-u$_5$-bí-gu$_7$,* *mu en-^{d}Nanna máš-e ì-pà.* (*OIP* 115083, *P*123478)	1**butchered ducklet sent to palace**when the **25th**day passed, 1 duck and 5 doves when were took for **food of my queen**, when the **26th**day passed, 1 ducklet, 1 dove when the **29th**day passed on 1st time, 1 duck when the **30th**day passed on 2nd time, **butchered ones were sent to the palace, withdrawn from Apilatum**.Month of ubi-gu$_7$, Year of the en-priestess of Nanna was chosen by omen.	1只**宰杀的幼鸭被送入宫殿**，于**25**日过去时， 1只鸭和5只野鸽于被抓住时为**我的王后的食物**，于**26**日过去时， 1只幼鸭和1只野鸽，于**29**日过去时第1次， 1只鸭于**30**日过去时第2次，**以上宰杀牲被送入宫殿**，**从阿皮拉吞支出了**。食乌比鸟月， 南那的女祭司被占卜选中之年。
Š 43 v: **zi-ga, butchered** [...], 4 kids, [x], 2 she-goats, **butchered ones were sent to palace, withdrawn from Apilatum**, in **Ur**	[...] 4 máš [x], 2 ud$_5$ ri-ri-ga **é-gal-la ba-an-ku$_4$**, zi-ga ***Á-pi$_5$-la-tum***, [*šà*] ~ **Urim^{ki}**-ma. [iti] -ezem-^{d}Nin-a-zu, [mu] en-^{d}Nanna [máš] -e ì-pàd. (MVN 13 820, P117593)	[...], 4 kids, [x], 2 she-goats, **butchered ones were sent to palace, withdrawn from Apilatum**, in **Ur**. Month of ezem-Ninazu, Year of the en-priestess of Nanna was chosen by omen.	【……】、4只公崽、【x】和2只母绵羊，**这些宰杀牲被送入宫殿，从阿皮拉吞支出了，于乌尔**。 神宁阿朱庆典月， 南那的女祭司被占卜选中之年。
Š 43 vii: **zi-ga** 1 ewe for palace, for**Beli-simti**, 1 lamb for **Uaba, withdrawn from Apilatum**	1 u$_8$, šà~ **é-gal-la**--šè, mu~ ***Be-lí-sí-im -ti***, 1 sila$_4$ mu~ ***U$_5$-a-ba***--šè, zi-ga ***Á-pi$_5$-la-tum***. *iti-ezem-^{d}Šul-gi, mu en-^{d}Nanna máš-e ì-pà.* (*OIP* 115 084, P123391)	1 *ewe for palace, for***Beli-simti**, 1 lamb for **Uaba**, were **withdrawn from Apilatum**. Month of ezem-Šulgi, Year of en-priestess of Nanna was chosen by omen.	1只母绵羊**为宫殿，为贝里新提**，1只羊羔**为乌阿巴**，**从阿皮拉吞支出了**。神舒勒吉庆典月，南那女祭司被占卜选中之年。
Š 43 viii: **mu-túm, ì-dab$_5$** [...] [forŠulgi] -sim [ti], [**Apilatum took over**],	[...] [mu-túm-***^{d}Šul-gi***] ***-sí-im-*** [***ti***], [***Á-pi$_5$-la-tum*** *ì-dab$_5$*], iti-šu-eš-ša, mu en-^{d}Nanna [máš-e ì-pà]. (OIP 115073, P123663)	[...] [deliveries forŠulgi] -sim [ti], [**Apilatum took over**], [Month] of [šu] -ešša, Year of en-priestess of Nanna was chosen by omen.	【……为舒勒吉】新【提】送入项，【阿皮拉吞接管了】，三只【手月】，南那女祭司被占卜选中年。

续表

时间和摘要	文献内容	英文翻译	中文翻译
Š 43 ix/17, 19, 20, 22: **mu-túm, ì-dab$_5$** 17th: 3 ducks, 19th: 2 ducks from **wife of Šarakam**, 20th: 2 ducks from **sister of Ṣiluš-Dagan**, 22nd: 2 ducks from **Zerara** were deliveries **for Šulgi-simtum, Apilatum took over**	3 uz-tur, iti--ta **ud-17**ba-ra-zal, 2 uz-tur, iti--ta **ud-19**ba-ra-zal, **dam-^{d}Šará-kam**, 2 uz-tur, **nin$_9$-*Ṣ i-lu-uš-^{d} Da-gan***, *iti--ta* **ud-20**ba-ra-zal, 2 uz-tur, **dam-Zé-ra-ra**, iti--ta **ud-22**ba-ra-zal, mu-túm-^{d} ***Šul-gi-sí-im-tum***, ***Á-pi$_5$-la-tum*** *ì-dab$_5$*. *iti-ezem-mah*, *mu en-^{d}Nanna máš-e ì-pà.* (*OIP* 115074, *P*123254)	3 *duckswhen the* **17th**day passed, 2 duckswhen the **19th**day passed, from **wife of Šarakam**, 2 ducks from **sister of Ṣ iluš-Dagan** (gov. of Simurrum) when**20th**day passed, 2 ducks from **Zerara** when **22nd**day passed, were deliveries **for Šulgi-simtum, Apilatum took over**. Month of ezem-mah, Year of en-priestess of Nanna was chosen by omen.	3 只鸭于 **17** 日过去时， 2 只鸭于 **19** 日过去时，自**沙腊坎的妻子**， 2 只鸭自**采鲁什达干的妹妹**，于 **20** 日过去时， 2 只鸭自**载腊腊**于 **22** 日过去时，为**舒勒吉新吞的送入项，阿皮拉吞接管**了。大庆典月，南那的女祭司被占卜选中之年。
Š 43 ix: **zi-ga** 6 sheep formonthly allowance of Belat-Suhnir, Belat-Darraban, Annuni-tum, Ulmašitum, withdrawn from **Akalla**	4 udu-nitá, 1 máš-niga, 1 ud$_5$, sá-dug$_4$-^{d} ***Be-la-at-Suh-nir***, **^{d}Be-la-at-Dar-ra-ba-an**, **An-nu-ni-tum** *ù* ^{d} **Ul-ma-ši-tum**, *zi-ga* ***A-kal-la***. *iti-ezem-mah*, *mu en-^{d} Nanna máš-e ì-pà.* (*OIP* 115 131, *P*123533)	4 *rams*, 1 *fattened he-goat*, 1 *goat for***monthly allowance of Belat-Suhnir, Belat-Darraban, Annunitum and Ulmašitum, withdrawn from Akalla**.Month of ezem-mah, Year of en-priestess of Nanna was chosen by omen.	4 只公绵羊、1 只育肥公山羊和 1 只山羊为**贝拉特苏赫尼尔、贝拉特达腊班、安努尼吞和乌勒马席吞月供，从阿拉拉支出**了。大庆典月，南那的女祭司被占卜选中年。
Š 43 x/4, 5: **zi-ga** 4th: 1 fattened ram for **Allatum**, 5th: 2 fattened rams and 1 lamb for **Ninlil**, 1 fattened ram and 1 kid for **Enlil**, 1 fattened ram for **Allagula**, 1 ram for **Ninĝagia**, for **sacrifice of 7th day of Moon**, **in Nippur**, were **withdr. from Apillatum**	1 udu-niga ^{d}***Al-la-tum***, *iti--ta ud-4-ba-ra-zal*; 2 *udu-niga*, 1 *sila$_4$*, **^{d}Nin-líl**, 1 udu-niga, 1 máš **^{d}En-líl**, 1 udu-niga^{d}***Al-la-gu-la***, 1 *udu* **^{d}Nin-ĝá-gi$_4$-a**, iti--ta **ud-5**-ba-ra-zal, **siskúr é-ud-7** šà~ **Nibru^{ki}**, zi-ga ***Á-pil-la-tum***.*iti-ezem-An-na*, *mu en-^{d}Nanna máš-e ì-pà.* (*AnOr* 07 071, *P*101366)	1 *fattened ram for***Allatum**, when 4thday passed; 2 fattened rams and 1 lamb for **Ninlil**, 1 fattened ram and 1 kid for **Enlil**, 1 fattened ram for **Allagula**, 1 ram for **Ninĝagia**, when the 5thday passed, for **sacrifice of the 7th day of Moon**, **in Nippur**, were **withdrawn from Apillatum**. Monthof ezem-Anna, Year of en-priestess of Nanna was chosen by omen.	1 肥公绵羊为**阿拉吞**于 4 日过去时；2 肥公绵羊和 1 只羔为**宁里勒**，1 只育肥公绵羊和 1 只公崽为**恩里勒**，1 只育肥公绵羊为**阿拉古拉**，1 只公绵羊为**宁旮吉阿**，于 5 日过去时，**为初七上弦月牺牲**，于**尼普尔**，从**阿皮拉吞支出**了。天神安庆典月，南那的女祭司被占卜选中年。

续表

时间和摘要	文献内容	英文翻译	中文翻译
Š 43 xi/30: **mu-túm, ì-dab$_5$** 1 ram and 1 lamb from**Idin-Erra**, 3 rams and 1 goat from **Zabar-dab**, 2 kids from **Puzur-Ištar**, 1 bull, 7 rams, 1 she-goat, 1 kid and 1 lamb from the **woman**, 1 grass ram and 1 female kid from **Aršiah**, 1 kid from **Imid-Sin**, 1 lamb from **Madati**, 2 kids from **Te ṣ in-Mama**, 1 lamb from **Šu-Ištar**, the son of king, 2 fattened rams, 1 he-goat and 1 kid from **Ṣ iluš-Dagan**, these were deliveries, **in the journey**, **Apilatum took over**	1 udu-ú, 1 sila$_4$, ***I-din-Èr-ra***, 3 *udu-ú*, 1 *ud$_5$*, **Zabar-dab$_5$**, 2 ^{f}ašgar ***Puzur$_4$-Iš$_4$-tár***, 1 *gud-ú*, 7 *udu-ú*, 1 *ud$_5$*, 1 *máš*, 1 *sila$_4$*, **ama-šu-gi$_4$**, 1 udu-ú, 1 ^{f}ašgar **Ar-ši-ah**, 1 máš ***I-mi-^{d}Suen***, 1 *sila$_4$* ***Ma-da-ti***, 2 *máš* ***Te-ṣí-in-Ma-ma***, 1 *sila$_4$* **Šu-Iš$_4$-tár** dumu-lugal, 2 udu-niga, 1 máš-gal, 1 máš ***Ṣi-lu-uš-^{d}Da-gan***, *iti--ta ud-30 ba-ra-zal*, *mu-túm*, *šà~* **kaskal-la *Á-pi$_5$-la-tum*** *ì-dab$_5$. iti-ezem-Me-ki-ĝál*, *mu en-^{d}Nanna máš-e ì-pàd.* (*RO* 11 96 01, *P*128094)	1 *grass ram and* 1 *lamb from***Idin-Erra**, 3 grass rams and 1 she-goat from **Zabar-dab**, 2 female kids from **Puzur-Ištar**, 1 grass bull, 7 grass rams, 1 she-goat, 1 kid and 1 lamb from the **woman**, 1 grass ram and 1 female kid from **Aršiah**, 1 kid from **Imid-Sin**, 1 lamb from **Madati**, 2 kids from **Te ṣ in-Mama**, 1 lamb from **Šu-Ištar**, the son of king, 2 fattened rams, 1 he-goat and 1 kid from **Ṣiluš-Dagan**, when 30th day passed, these were deliveries, **in the journey**, **Apilatum took over**. Month of ezem-Mekiĝal, Year of en-priestess of Nanna was chosen by omen.	1食草公绵羊和1羔自**伊丁埃腊**，3食草公绵羊和1母绵羊自**执青铜官**，2雌崽自**普朱尔伊什塔尔**，1食草公牛、7食草公绵羊、1母绵羊、1公崽和1羔自**妇女**，1食草公绵羊和1雌崽自**阿尔西阿赫**，1公崽自**伊米辛**，1羔来自**马达提**，2公崽自**台岑妈妈**，1羔自**王子舒伊什塔尔**，2育肥公绵羊、1公山羊和1公崽自**采鲁什达干**，于30日过去时，以上送入，**于旅途中**，**阿皮拉吞接管了**。神美基奋勒庆典月，南那的女祭司被占卜选中之年。
Š 43 xii: **íb-su-su** 1 bull, 48sheep, **the arrears that Beli-ṭab the fattener repaid** Beli-ṭab is the fattener of Šulgi-simtum.	1 gud, 48 udu-máš-hi-a, Si-ì-tum lá-ì, ***Be-lí-ṭàb*** *gurušda*, *íb-su-su. iti-še-kin-kud*, *mu en-^{d}Nanna máš-e ì-pàd.* (*Env.*) *lá-ì1 gud*, *lá-ì48 udu má* [*š-hi*] *-a*, **kišib *Be-lí-ṭ àb*guruš** [**da**], iti-še-kin-kud, mu en-^{d}Nanna máš-e ì-pàd. (Seal:) ***Be-lí-ṭ àb****gurušda*, ***^{d}Šul-gi-sí-im-tum****-ma.* (*AnOr* 07 144, *P*101439)	1 *bull*, 48*sheep*, **the arrears that Beli-ṭab the fattener repaid**. Month of še-kin-kud, Year of en-priestess of Nanna was chosen by omen. (Env.) the arrears of 1 bullandthe arrears of 48 sheep, **the receipt of Beli-ṭ ab, the fattener**. Month of še-kin-kud, Year of en-priestess of Nanna was chosen by omen. (Seal:) Beli-ṭ ab is the fattener of Šulgi-simtum.	1头公牛、48只羊为**育肥师贝里沓卜补交的欠账**。大麦收割月，南那的女祭司被占卜选中之年。 （文件：）1头公牛的欠账和48只羊的欠账，**为育肥师贝里沓卜的收据**。大麦月，南那的女祭司被占卜选中之年。 （印章：）贝里沓卜是舒勒吉新吞的育肥师。
Š 43 xii/8: **mu-túm, ì-dab$_5$** 1 duck fr. **wife of Šara-kam**, was **delivery for Šulgi-simtum**, **Apilatum took over**	1 uz-tur**dam-^{d} Šará-kam**, iti--ta ud-8 ba-ra-zal, mu-túm-***^{d} Šul-gi-sí-im-tum***, ***Á-pi$_5$-la-tum*** *ì-dab$_5$. iti-še-kin-kud*, *mu en-^{d}Nanna máš-e ì-pàd.* (*Hirose* 022, *P*109493)	1 *duck from***the wife of Šara-kam**, when 8th day passed, was **delivery for Šulgi-simtum**, **Apilatum took over**.Month of še-kin-kud, Year of en-priestess of Nanna was chosen by omen.	1只幼鸭来自**沙腊刊之妻**，于8日过去时，**为舒勒吉新吞的送入项**，**阿皮拉吞接管了**。大麦收割月，南那的女祭司被占卜选中之年。

续表

时间和摘要	文献内容	英文翻译	中文翻译
Š 44 i/27, 28, 29, 30: **mu-túm, ì-dab$_5$** 27th: 7 doves from **the wife of Ṣiluš-Dagan**, 28th: 32 doves for **Dagan from the food of Dagan**, 29th: 9 doves from **Inim-kugga**, 30th: 4 doves from **Dayati**, were deliveries for Šulgi-simtum, **Apilatum took over**	7 tu-gur$_4$^{mušen} **nin-*Ṣi-lu-uš-^{d}Da-gan***, *iti--ta ud-27 ba-ra-zal*, 32 *tu-gur$_4$^{mušen} ^{d}Da-gan gu$_7$ ^{d}Da-gan*, *iti--ta ud-28 ba-ra-zal*, 9 *tu-gur$_4$^{mušen}* **Inim-kug-ga**, iti--ta ud-29ba-ra-zal, 4 tu-gur$_4$^{mušen} ***Da-a-ti***, *iti--ta ud-30 ba-ra-zal*, *mu-túm* ***^{d}Šul-gi-sí-im-tum***, ***Á-pi$_5$-la-tum*** *ì-dab$_5$*. *iti-maš-dà ~ gu$_7$*, *mu Si-mu-ru-um^{ki} Lu-lu-bu^{ki} a-rá 9-kam-aš ba-hul.* (*MVN* 03 200, *P113760*)	*7 doves from* **the wife of Ṣiluš-Dagan**, when 27th day passed, 32 doves for **Dagan from the food of Dagan**, when 28thday passed, 9 doves from **Inim-kugga**, when 29thday passed, 4 doves from **Dayati**, when 30thday passed, were deliveries for Šulgi-simtum, **Apilatum took over**.Month of mašda ~ gu$_7$, Year of Simurrum and Lulubum were destroyed for the ninth time.	7只野鸽来自**采鲁什达干之妻**，于**27**日过去时，32只野鸽来自**达干的食物为达干**，于**28**日过去时，9只野鸽来自**伊尼姆库旮**，于**29**日过去时，4只野鸽来自**达亚提**，于**30**日过去时，为**舒勒吉新吞的送入**，**阿皮拉吞接管**了。食瞪羚月，席穆润和鲁鲁布第九次被毁之年。
Š 44 ii: **mu-túm, ì-dab$_5$** 1 kid from**Watrat**, was **delivery for Šulgi-simtum**, **Apilatum took over**	1 máš ***Wa-at-ra-at***, mu-túm-***^{d}Šul-gi-sí-im-tum***, ***Á-pi$_5$-la-tum*** *ì-dab$_5$*. *iti-ze$_x$-da ~ gu$_7$*, *mu Si-mu-ru-um^{ki} ù Lu-lu-bu^{ki} a-rá 9-kam-ma-aš ba-hul.* (*MVN* 03 201, *P113761*)	1 *kid from***Watrat**, was**delivery for Šulgi-simtum**, **Apilatum took over**. Month of zeda ~ gu$_7$, Year of Simurrum and Lulubum were destroyed for the ninth time.	1只公崽来自**瓦特腊特**，为**舒勒吉新吞的送入项**，**阿皮拉吞接管**了。 食豚月， 席穆润和鲁鲁布第九次被毁之年。
Š 44 ii: **mu-túm, ì-dab$_5$** 5 pigeons from**wife of Ur-ni**, 5 pigeons and 14 doves from X-ki, were **deliveries for Šulgi-simtum**, **Apilatum took over**	5 ir$_7$^{mušen} **dam-Ur-ni$_9$**, 5 ir$_7$^{mušen}, 14 tu-gur$_4$^{mušen}, [x] -x-x-ki [mu-túm] [***^{d}Šul-gi***] ***-sí-im-tum***, ***Á-pi$_5$-la-tum*** *ì-dab$_5$*. *iti-ze$_x$-da ~ gu$_7$*, *mu Si-mu-ru-um^{ki} ù Lu-lu-bu^{ki} a-rá 9-kam-ma-aš ba-hul.* (*YOS* 18 006, *P142400*)	5 *pigeons from***wife of Ur-ni**, 5 pigeons and 14 doves from X-ki, were **deliveries for Šulgi-simtum**, **Apilatum took over**.Month of zeda ~ gu$_7$, Year of Simurrum and Lulubum were destroyed for the ninth time.	5只家鸽来自**乌尔尼之妻**，5只家鸽和14只野鸽来自**X-基**，为**舒勒吉新吞的送入项**，**阿皮拉吞接管**了。食豚月，席穆润和鲁鲁布第九次被毁之年。
Š 44 ii/15: **mu-túm, ì-dab$_5$** 4 ducklets, 2 pigeons, from**Simat-Ištar**, were deliveries for **Šulgi-simtum**, **Apilatum took over**	4 amar-sag-uz-tur, 2 ir$_7$^{mušen}, ***Simat-Iš$_8$-tár***, *iti--ta ud-15 ba-ra-zal*, *mu-túm ~* ***^{d}Šul-gi-sí-im-tum***, ***Á-pi$_5$-la-tum*** *ì-dab$_5$*. *iti-ze$_x$-da-gu$_7$*, *mu Si-mu-ru-um^{ki} Lu-lu-bu-um^{ki} a-rá-9-kam-aš ba-hul.* (*OIP* 115075, *P123473*)	4 *ducklets*, 2 *pigeons*, *from***Simat-Ištar**, when 15th day passed, were deliveries for **Šulgi-simtum**, **Apilatum took over**. Month of zeda ~ gu$_7$, Year of Simurrum and Lulubum were destroyed for the ninth time.	4只幼鸭和2只家鸽自**席马特伊什塔尔**，于第15天过去时，为**舒勒吉新吞的送入项**，**阿皮拉吞接管**了。 食豚月，席穆润和鲁鲁布第九次被毁之年。

续表

时间和摘要	文献内容	英文翻译	中文翻译
Š 44 ii/15: **mu-túm, ì-dab$_5$** 1 lamb from **Imid-Ilum majordomo**, 1 grass bull and 10 grass rams from **Urnigar**, 2 fattened rams and 1 lamb from **Gallaya**, when the 15th day passed, were deliveries **for Šulgi-simtum, Apillatum took over**	1 sila$_4$ ***I-mi-id-ilum*** *šabra*, 1 *gud-ú*, 10 *udu-ú* **Ur-ni$_9$-<gar>**, 2 udu-niga, 1 sila$_4$ ***Gal-la-a***, *iti--ta ud-15-ba-ra-zal*, *mu-túm~* ***^{d}Šul-gi-sí-im-tum***, ***Á-pil-la-tum*** *ì-dab$_5$*. *iti-ze$_x$-da-gu$_7$*, *mu Si-mu-ru-um^{ki}*, *Lu-lu-bu-um^{ki} a-rá-9-kam-aš ba-hul.* (*AnOr* 07 007, *P*101302)	1 *lamb from* **Imid-Ilum majordomo**, 1 grass bull and 10 grass rams from **Urnigar**, 2 fattened rams and 1 lamb from **Gallaya**, when the 15th day passed, were deliveries **for Šulgi-simtum, Apillatum took over**. Month of zeda ~ gu$_7$, Year of Simurrum and Lulubum were destroyed for ninth time.	1只羔来自**伊米德伊隆庙总管**，1头食草公牛和10只食草公绵羊来自**乌尔尼旮尔**，2只育肥公绵羊和1只羔来自**旮拉亚**，于15日过去时， **为舒勒吉新吞送入项，** **阿皮拉吞接管了**。 食豚月，席穆润和鲁鲁布第九次被毁年。
Š 44 iii/7, 11: **mu-túm, ì-dab$_5$** 120 pigeons from **the gardeners**, 77 tu-birds from **the wife of Šarrum-ili**, 120 pigeons from **Ur-daga**, were **deliveries for Šulgi-simtum, Apilatum took over**	120 ir$_7$^{mušen}, ki ~ **nu-^{giš} kiri$_6$-ke$_4$-ne**--ta, 77 tu-mušen, **dam-*Šar-ru-um-ì-lí***, *iti--ta* **ud-7** ba-ra-zal, 120 ir$_7$^{mušen} **Ur-da-ga**, iti--ta **ud-11** ba-ra-zal, mu-túm-***^{d} Šul-gi-sí-im-tum***, ***Á-pi$_5$-la-tum*** *ì-dab$_5$*. *iti-u$_5$-bí-gu$_7$*, *mu Si-mu-ru-um^{ki}Lu-lu-bu^{ki}a-rá-9-kam-aš ba-hul.* (*Torino* 1 042, *P*133850)	120 *pigeons from* **the gardeners**, 77 tu-birds from **the wife of Šarrum-ili** when the **7th** day passed, 120 pigeons from **Ur-daga** when the **11th** day passed, were **deliveries for Šulgi-simtum, Apilatum took over**. Month of ubi ~ gu$_7$, Year of Simurrum and Lulubum were destroyed for the ninth time.	120只家鸽自**园丁们**和77只tu鸟来自**沙润伊里**，于本月7日过去时，120只家鸽自**乌尔达旮**于本月11日过去时， **为舒勒吉新吞的送入项，阿皮拉吞接管了**。 食乌比鸟月， 席穆润和鲁鲁布第九次被毁之年。
Š 44 iii/20, 28: **mu-túm, ì-dab$_5$** 5 pigeons from**the production norm of gardeners**, 5 pigeons from **Šu-Ištar**, the son of king, 1 pigeon and 8 doves from **wife of Urni**, were deliveries for **Šulgi-simtum, Apilatum took over**	5 ir$_7$^{mušen} á-giš-gar-ra nu-^{giš}kiri$_6$-ke$_4$-ne, 5 ir$_7$^{mušen} **Šu-Iš$_4$-tár** dumu-lugal, iti--ta ud-20 ba-ra-zal, 1 ir$_7$^{mušen}, 8 tu-gur$_8$^{mušen} **dam-Ur-ni$_9$**, iti-ta ud-28 ba-ra-zal, mu-túm ***^{d}Šul-gi-sí-im-tum***, ***Á-pi$_5$-la-tum*** *ì-dab$_5$*. *iti-u$_5$-bí ~ gu$_7$*, *mu Si-mu-ru-um^{ki}Lu-lu-bu^{ki}a-rá-9-kam-aš ba-hul.* (*RA* 19 192 07, *P*127737)	5 *pigeons from***the production norm of gardeners**, 5 pigeons from **Šu-Ištar**, the son of king, when 20th day passed, 1 pigeon and 8 doves from **wife of Urni**, when 28th day passed, were deliveries for **Šulgi-simtum, Apilatum took over**.Month of ubi~ gu$_7$, Year of Simurrum and Lulubum were destroyed for the ninth time.	5只家鸽来自**园丁们的生产产量**，5只家鸽来自**王子舒伊什塔尔**，于**20日**过去时，1只家鸽和8只野鸽来自**乌尔尼之妻**，于**28日**过去时，为**舒勒吉新吞的送入项，阿皮拉吞接管了**。食乌比鸟月，席穆润和鲁鲁布第九次被毁之年。

续表

时间和摘要	文献内容	英文翻译	中文翻译
Š 44 iii/27: **zi-ga** 2 fattened rams for**Ninlil with the vessel of drinking**, **via the priest of Nanše-kiaĝ**, the cupbearer, 5 fattened rams for **Lugal-kugzu**, **the cupbearer with the vessel of drinking**, **via Atu**, **the cupbearer**, **Nanše-ulgal as the royal deputy**, **withdrawn from Ahima**	2 udu-niga^{d}**Nin-líl**, an-za-am--da kur$_9$-ra--šè, gìr **En-^{d}Nanše-** [**ki-áĝ**] sagi, 5 udu-niga ^{d}**Lugal-kug-zu** sagi, an-za-am--da kur$_9$-ra--[šè], gìr ***A-tu!*** *sa* [*gi*], ^{d}**Nanše-ul$_4$-gal** [maškim], iti ud-27 ba- [zal], zi-ga-***A-hi-ma***, *iti-u$_5$-bí-gu$_7$*, *mu Si-mu-ru-um* [^{ki}] *ù* [*Lu*] *-lu-bu^{ki}a-rá 9-kam-aš ba-hul.* (*MVN* 2 333, *P*113632)	2 *fattened rams for***Ninlil with the vessel of drinking**, **via En-^{d}Nanše-kiaĝ**, the cupbearer, 5 fattened rams for **Lugal-kugzu**, **the cupbearer with the vessel of drinking**, **via Atu**, **the cupbearer**, **Nanše-ulgal as the royal deputy**, when 27th day passed, were **withdrawn from Ahima**. Month of ubi-gu$_7$, Year of Simurrum and Lulubum were destroyed for the ninth time.	2只育肥公绵羊为**宁里勒和饮酒器**， **经由恩南筛基阿格司酒**， 5只育肥公绵羊为**司酒卢旮勒库朱和饮酒器**， **经由司酒阿图**，**南筛乌勒旮勒督办**， 于27日过去时，以上从**阿希马支出**了。食乌比鸟月，席穆润和鲁鲁布第九次被毁之年。
Š 44 iv/15, 17, 19: **mu-túm, ì-dab$_5$** 15th: 1 pigeon, 4 doves from **Watarat**, 17th: 5 pigeons, from **the production norm of gardeners**, 19 doves from **Imid-ilum**, 19th: 4 pigeons from **the production norm of gardeners**, were **deliveries for Šulgi-simtum**, **Apilatum took over**	1 ir$_7$^{mušen}, 4 tu-gur$_4$^{mušen}, ***Wa-ta-ra-at***, *iti--ta ud-15 ba-ra-zal*, 5 *ir$_7$^{mušen}*, *á-giš-gar-ra nu-kiri$_6$-ke$_4$-ne*, 19 *tu-gur$_4$^{mušen}*, ***I-mi-id-ilum***, *iti--ta ud-17 ba-ra-zal*, 4 *ir$_7$^{mušen} á-giš-gar-ra nu-kiri$_6$-ke$_4$-ne*, *iti--ta ud-19 ba-ra-zal*, *mu-túm~* ^{d}***Šul-gi-sí-im-tum***, ***Á-pi$_5$-la-tum*** *ì-dab$_5$*. *iti-ki-siki-^{d}Nin-a-zu*, *mu Si-mu-ru-um^{ki}Lu-lu-bu^{ki}a-rá-9-kam-aš ba-hul.* (*OIP* 115076, *P*123231)	1 *pigeon*, 4 *doves from***Watarat** when the 15thday passed, 5 pigeons, from **the production norm of gardeners**, 19 doves from **Imid-ilum** when the 17th day passed, 4 pigeons from **the production norm of gardeners** when the 19thday passed, were **deliveries for Šulgi-simtum**, **Apilatum took over**. Month of ki-siki-Ninazu, Year of Simurrum and Lulubum were destroyed for the ninth time.	1只家鸽和4只野鸽自**瓦塔腊特**，于**15**日过去时，5只家鸽自**园丁们的生产定限**， 19只野鸽自**伊米德伊隆**于**17**日过去时， 4只家鸽自**园丁们的生产定限**，于**19**日过去时， 为**舒勒吉新吞的送入项**，**阿皮拉吞接管**了。 神宁阿朱羊毛作坊月， 席穆润和鲁鲁布第九次被毁之年。
Š 44 v/9: **mu-túm, ì-dab$_5$** 2 fattened female kids from**Puzur-Ištar**, the **general**, 2 grass rams and 1 kid from **the mother of Šu-Idim**, 2 grass rams and 1 kid from **Kudati**, 1 kid from **Watrat**, **were deliveries for Šulgi-simtum**, **Apilatum took over**	2^{f}ašgar-niga ***Puzur$_4$-Iš$_4$-tár*** *šakkan$_6$*, *iti--ta ud-9 ba-ra-zal*, 2 *udu-ú*, 1 *máš* **ama Šu-^{d}Idim**, 2 udu-ú, 1 máš ***Ku-da-ti***, 1 *máš* ***Wa-at-ra-at***, mu-túm~ ^{d}***Šul-gi-sí-im-tum***, ***Á-pi$_5$-la-tum*** *ì-dab$_5$*. *iti-ezem-^{d} Nin-a-zu*, *mu Si-mu-ru-um^{ki} ù Lu-lu-bu^{ki}a-rá 9-kam-aš ba-hul.* (*StOr* 09-1 22 (*pl.*6), *P*130407)	2 *fattened female kids from***Puzur-Ištar**, the **general**, when 9th day passed, 2 grass rams and 1 kid from **the mother of Šu-Idim**, 2 grass rams and 1 kid from **Kudati**, 1 kid from **Watrat**, **were deliveries for Šulgi-simtum**, **Apilatum took over**. Month of ezem-Ninazu, Year of Simurrum and Lulubum were destroyed for the ninth time.	2只育肥雌崽来自**普朱尔伊什塔尔将军**，于9日过去时，2只食草公绵羊和1只公崽来自**舒伊迪姆之母**，2只食草公绵羊和1只公崽来自**库达提**，1只公崽来自**瓦特腊特**，为**舒勒吉新吞的送入项**，**阿皮拉吞接管**了。神宁阿朱庆典月，席穆润和鲁鲁布第九次被毁年。

续表

时间和摘要	文献内容	英文翻译	中文翻译
Š 44 vi/15: **mu-túm，ì-dab$_5$** 1 ewe and 1 female kid were brought from **palace**，1 lamb was new born from **the house of fattener**，29 doves from **Bagum**，the bird-catcher，**were deliveries for Šulgi-simtum，Apilatum took over**	1 u$_8$，1 ^{f}ašgar，**é-gal**$^!$--ta$^!$ è-a，1 sila$_4$ ù-tu-da，**<é-gurušda>**， 29 tu-gur$_4$^{mušen} ***Ba-gu-um*** *mušen-dù*， *iti--ta ud-15 ba-ra-zal*，*mu-túm*~ ***^{d}Šul-gi-sí-im-tum***，***Á-pi$_5$-la-tum*** *ì-dab$_5$*. *iti-á-ki-ti*，*mu Si-mu-ru-um^{ki} Lu-lu-bu^{ki}a-rá 9-kam-aš ba-hul.* （*RT* 37 129 *mi.*4，*P*128394）	1 *ewe and* 1 *female kid were brought from* **palace**，1 lamb was new born from **the house of fattener**，29 doves from **Bagum**，the bird-catcher，when 15th day passed，**were deliveries for Šulgi-simtum，Apilatum took over**.Month of akiti，Year of Simurrum and Lulubum were destroyed for the ninth time.	1只母绵羊和1只雌崽从**宫殿带来**，1只新生羔来**自育肥房**， 29只野鸽来自**捕鸟人巴衮**， 于15日过去时， **为舒勒吉新吞的送入项，阿皮拉吞接管**了。阿基提月，席穆润和鲁鲁布第九次被毁之年。
Š 44 vi/22: **mu-túm，ì-dab$_5$** 2 fat rams fr.**the king**，these were deliveries，**Apilatum took**	2 udu-niga，ki~ **lugal**--ta，iti--ta ud-22 ba-ra-zal，mu-túm，***Á-pi$_5$-la-tum*** *ì-dab$_5$*. *iti-á-ki-ti*，*mu Si-mu-ru-um^{ki} a-rá-9-kam ba-hul.* （*Torino* 1 053，*P*132018）	2 *fattened rams from***the king**，when 22nd day passed，these were deliveries，**Apilatum took over**.Month of akiti，Year of Simurum was destroyed for 9th time.	2只育肥公绵羊来自**国王**于本月22日过去时，以上为送入，**阿皮拉吞接管**了。阿基提月，席穆润第九次被毁之年。
Š 44 vi/25: **mu-túm，ì-dab$_5$** 3 grass rams and 1 kid from **Ṣiluš-Dagan**，were **deliveries for Šulgi-simtum，Apilatum took over**	3 udu-ú，1 máš ***Ṣi-lu-uš-^{d}Da-gan***，*iti--ta ud-25 ba-ra-zal*，*mu-túm*~ ***^{d}Šul-gi-sí-im-tum***，***Á-pi$_5$-la-tum*** *ì-dab$_5$*. *iti-á-ki-ti*，*mu Si-mu-ru-um^{ki} Lu-lu-bu^{ki} a-rá 9-kam-aš ba-hul.* （*MVN* 15 324，*P*118589）	3 *grass rams and* 1 *kid from* **Ṣ iluš-Dagan**，when 25th day passed，were **deliveries for Šulgi-simtum，Apilatum took over**.Month of akiti，Year of Simurrum and Lulubum were destroyed for the ninth time.	3只食草公绵羊和1只公崽来自**采鲁什达干**， 于25日过去时， **为舒勒吉新吞的送入项，阿皮拉吞接管**了。 阿基提月，席穆润和鲁鲁布第九次被毁之年。
Š 44 vi: **mu-túm，ì-dab$_5$** 1 lamb fr. **Nam-zitarra**，was delivery for **Šulgi-simtum，Apilatum took over**	1 sila$_4$ **Nam-zi-tar-ra**，mu-túm~ ***^{d}Šul-gi-sí-im-tum***，***Á-pi$_5$-la-tum*** *ì-dab$_5$*. *iti-á-ki-ti*，*mu Si-mu-ru-um^{ki} Lu-lu-bu^{ki}a-rá 9-kam-aš ba-hul.*（*SAT* 2 0364，*P*143564）	1 *lamb from***Nam-zitarra**，was delivery for **Šulgi-simtum，Api-latum took over**. Month of akiti，Year of Simurrum and Lulubum were destroyed for the 9th time.	1只羔来自**那姆兹塔腊**，**为舒勒吉新吞的送入项，阿皮拉吞接管**了。阿基提月，席穆润和鲁鲁布第九次被毁之年。
Š 44 vii: **mu-túm，ì-dab$_5$** 4 [...]，1 [...]，1/3...，1 lamb from**Šu-Eštar**，the son of king，were deliveries for **Šulgi-simtum，Apilatum took over**	4 [...]，1 [...]，1/3 gu x] [x]，1 sila$_4$，Šu-Eš$_4$-tár dumu lugal，mu-túm~ ***^{d}Šul-gi-sí-im-tum***，***Á-pi$_5$-la-tum*** *ì-dab$_5$*.*iti-ezem-^{d}Šul-gi*，*mu Si-mu-ru-um^{ki} Lu-lu-bu^{ki} a-rá-9-kam-aš ba-hul.* （*ASJ* 09 318 12，*P*102376）	4 [...]，1 [...]，1/3...，1 *lamb from***Šu-Eštar**，the son of king，were deliveries for **Šulgi-simtum，Apilatum took over**.Month of ezem-Šulgi，-Year of Simurum and Lulubum were destroyed for 9th time.	4【……】、1【……】，1/3……，1只羔来自**王子舒埃什塔尔**，**为舒勒吉新吞的送入项，阿皮拉吞接管**了。舒勒吉庆典月，席穆润和鲁鲁布第九次被毁年。

续表

时间和摘要	文献内容	英文翻译	中文翻译
Š 44 vii/3, 6: **mu-túm, ì-dab$_5$** 1 lamb from**Ši-Ištar**, 1 fattened lamb from **Watrat**, the overseer, 7 fattened rams and 3 ram of after-ox-class from **the man of Urub**, the **envoy**, 5 lambs from X, 1 female lamb and 1 female kid were brought from **palace**, **these were deliveries**, **Apilatum took over**	1 sila$_4$ ***Ši-Iš$_4$-tár***, 1 *sila$_4$-niga* ***Wa-at-ra-at*** *ugula*, *iti--ta* **ud-3** ba-ra-zal, 7 udu-niga, 3 udu-gud-e-ús-sa, lú-Urub (URUxKÁR)^{ki} sukkal, iti--ta **ud-6** ba-[ra-zal], 5 sila$_4$ x-[x], 1 kir$_{11}$, 1 ^{f}aš [gar] é-gal--ta è-[a], mu-túm, ***Á-pi$_5$-la-tum*** *ì-dab$_5$*. *iti-ezem-^{d}Šul-gi*, *mu Si-mu-ru-um^{ki} Lu-lu-bu^{ki} a-rá-9-kam-aš ba-hul.* (*Hirose* 029, *P*109500)	1 *lamb from***Ši-Ištar**, 1 fattened lamb from **Watrat**, the overseer, when the **3rd** day passed, 7 fattened rams and 3 ram of after-ox-class from **the man of Urub**, the **envoy**, when **6th** day passed, 5 lambs from X, 1 female lamb and 1 female kid were brought from **palace**, **these were deliveries**, **Apilatum took over**. Month of ezem-Šulgi, Year of Simurum and Lulubum were destroyed for 9th time.	1只羔来自**席伊什塔尔**，1只育肥羔来自**监工瓦特腊特**，于**3日**过去时，7只育肥公绵羊和3只牛后级公绵羊来自**国使乌如卜城的人**，于**6日**过去时，5只羔来自X，1只雌羔和1只雌崽从**宫殿带来**，以上送入，**阿皮拉吞接管**了。舒勒吉庆典月，席穆润和鲁鲁布第九次被毁年。
Š 44 vii/17-20: **mu-túm, ì-dab$_5$** 3 fattened rams, 2 grass rams from**wife of Nuida**, 6 grass rams, 1 kid from **Nuida**, 2 fattened rams from the place of **king**, 2 fattened rams, 2 grass rams, 1 he-goat from **Ur-Nisaba**, the governer of Nippur, 3 fattened rams, 2 he-goats from **Watrat**, the overseer, 2 female kids from **Puzur-Ištar**, were deliveries for **Šulgi-simti**, **Apilatum took over**, in **Tummal**	3 udu-niga, 2 udu-ú **dam-*Nu-i-da***, 6 *udu-ú*, 1 *máš*, ***Nu-i-da***, *iti--ta ud-17 ba-ra-zal*, 2 *gud-niga ki*--**lugal**--ta, iti--ta ud-18 ba-ra-zal, 2 udu-niga, 2 udu-ú, 1 máš, **Ur-^{d}Nisaba énsi-Nibru^{ki}**, iti--ta ud-19 ba-ra-zal, 3 udu-niga, 2 máš, ***Wa-at-ra-at*** *ugula*, *iti--ta ud-20 ba-ra-zal*, 2 ^{f}*ašgar* ***Puzur$_4$-^{d}Iš$_8$-tár***, *mu-túm-^{d}**Šul-gi-sí-im-ti***, ***Á-pi$_5$-la-tum*** *ì-dab$_5$*, *šà ~ Tum-ma-al. iti-ezem-^{d}Šul-gi*, *mu Si-mu-ru-um^{ki} ù Lu-lu-bu^{ki} a-rá-9-kam-aš ba-hul.* (*OrSP* 18 *pl.*02 06, P124852)	3 *fattened rams*, 2 *grass rams from***wife of Nuida**, 6 grass rams, 1 kid from **Nuida**, when **17th** day passed, 2 fattened rams from the place of **king**, when **18th** day passed, 2 fattened rams, 2 grass rams, 1 he-goat from**Ur-Nisaba**, the governer of Nippur, when **19th** day passed, 3 fattened rams, 2 he-goats from**Watrat**, the overseer, when **20th** day passed, 2 female kids from **Puzur-Ištar**, were deliveries for **Šulgi-simti**, **Apilatum took over**, in **Tummal**. Month of ezem-Šulgi, Year of Simurum and Lulubum were destroyed for the 9th time.	3育肥公绵羊和2食草公绵羊自**努伊达之妻**，6食草公绵羊和1公崽自**努伊达**于**17日**过去时，2只育肥公绵羊自**国王**于**18日**过去时，2只育肥公绵羊、2只食草公绵羊和1只公山羊自**尼普尔总督乌尔尼萨巴**于**19日**过去时，3只育肥公绵羊和2只公山羊自**监工瓦特腊特**于**20日**过去时，2只雌山羊崽自**普朱尔伊什塔尔**，为**舒勒吉新提的送入项**，**阿皮拉吞接管了**，**于图马勒**。舒勒吉庆典月，席穆润和鲁鲁布第九次被毁年。
Š 44 ix: **mu-túm, ì-dab$_5$** 3 grass rams, 1 he-goat and 1 lamb from **Iti-Erra**, 1+ grass rams, 1 lamb and 1 kid from **Imid-ilum**, were deliveries for **Šulgi-simti**, **Apilatum took over**, in **Ur**	3 udu-ú, 1 máš-gal, 1 sila$_4$, ***I-ti-Èr-ra***, 1+ *udu-ú*, 1 *sila$_4$*, 1 *máš* ***I-mi-id-ilum***, *mu-túm ~* ***^{d}Šul-gi-sí-im-tum***, ***Á-pi$_5$-la-tum*** *ì-dab$_5$*, *šà ~ Urim^{ki}-ma. iti-ezem-mah*, *mu Si-mu-ru-um^{ki}Lu-lu-bu^{ki}a-rá 9-kam-aš ba-hul.* (*RT* 37 130 *ab.*6, *P*128397)	3 *grass rams*, 1 *he-goat and* 1 *lamb from* **Iti-Erra**, 1+ grass rams, 1 lamb and 1 kid from **Imid-ilum**, were deliveries for **Šulgi-simti**, **Apilatum took over**, in **Ur**.Month of ezem-mah, Year of Simurum and Lulubum were destroyed for the 9th time.	3只食草公绵羊、1只公山羊和1只羔自**伊提埃腊**，1+只食草公绵羊、1只羔和1只公崽自**伊米德伊隆**，**为舒勒吉新提的送入项**，**阿皮拉吞接管**了，于乌尔。大庆典月，席穆润和鲁鲁布第九次被毁年。
Š 44 ix/6: **mu-túm, ì-dab$_5$** 1 duck from**Simat-Ištar**, when the 6th day passed, **deliveries for Šulgi-simtum**, **Apilatum took over**, in **Ur**	1 uz-tur, ***Simat-Iš$_8$-tár***, *iti--ta ud-6 ba-ra-zal*, *mu-túm ~* ***^{d}Šul-gi-sí -im-tum***, ***Á-pi$_5$-la-tum*** *ì-dab$_5$*, *šà ~* **Urim^{ki}**-ma.iti-ezem-mah, mu Si-mu-ru-um^{ki}Lu-lu-bu^{ki}a-rá 9-kam-aš ba-hul. (Torino 1 043, P133851)	1 duck from**Simat-Ištar**, when the 6th day passed, **deliveries for Šulgi-simtum**, **Apilatum took over**, in **Ur**. Month of ezem-mah, Year of Simurum and Lulubum were destroyed for the 9th time.	1只鸭自**席马特伊什塔尔**于本月6日过去时，为**舒勒吉新吞的送入项**，**阿皮拉吞接管**了，于乌尔。大庆典月， 席穆润和鲁鲁布第九次被毁年。

续表

时间和摘要	文献内容	英文翻译	中文翻译
Š 44 x/13，14： **mu-túm，ì-dab$_5$** 13th：1 duck from **Šibat-ekur**，14th：1 duck from […]，were deliveries for **Šulgi-simtum**，**Apilatum took over**	1 uz-tur ***Ši-ba-at-é-kur***，iti--ta ud-13 ba-ra-zal，1 uz-tur […]，ud-［14］-kam，mu-túm～ ***^{d}Šul-gi-sí -im-tum***，***Á-pi$_5$-la-tum*** *ì-dab$_5$. iti-ezem-An-na，mu Si-mu-ru-um^{ki} Lu-lu-bu^{ki}a-rá 9-kam-aš ba-hul.* （*TRU* 077，*P134841*）	1 *duck from***Šibat-ekur**，when 13thday passed，1 duck from […]，on the ［14th］ day，were deliveries for **Šulgi-simtum**，**Apilatum took over**. Month of ezem-Anna，Year of Simurum and Lulubum were destroyed for the 9th time.	1 鸭自**席巴特埃库尔**，于 13 日过去时，1 只鸭自**【……】**，于【14】日，**为舒勒吉新吞的送入项，阿皮拉吞接管**了。天神庆典月，席穆润和鲁鲁布第九次被毁年。
Š 44 xi： **mu-túm，ì-dab$_5$** 1 female kid from **Imid-ilum**，2 rams and 1 kid from **Beli-bani**，were deliveries for **Šulgi-simtum**，**Apil-atum took over**	1 ^{f}ašgar ***I-mi-id-ilum***，2 *udu*，1 *máš* ***Be-lí-ba-ni***，*mu-túm*～ ***^{d}Šul-gi-sí-im-tum***，***Á-pi$_5$-la-tum*** *ì-dab$_5$. iti-ezem-Me-ki-ĝál，mu Si-mu-ru-um^{ki} Lu-lu-bu^{ki} a-rá 9-kam-aš ba-hul.* （*UCP* 9-2-2 070，*P136074*）	1 *female kid from* **Imid-ilum**，2 rams and 1 kid from **Beli-bani**，were deliveries for **Šulgi-simtum**，**Apil-atum took over**. Month of ezem-Mekiĝal，Year of Simurum and Lulubum were destroyed for the 9th time.	1 只雌崽来自**伊米德伊隆**，2 只公绵羊和 1 只公崽来自**贝里巴尼**，**为舒勒吉新吞的送入项，阿皮拉吞接管**了。神美基旮勒庆典月，席穆润和鲁鲁布第九次被毁年。
Š 44 xi = Š 45' vi'： **zi-ga** 1 fattened ram for**the shrine**，1 fattened ram for **gate of bedroom of high priestess**，1 ram of after-ox-class for **Nanaya**，were withdrawn in **Uruk**，from the place of Kalam-henagi，**via Šuhamati**，for the **festival of Full Moon**	1 udu-niga，**èš--šè**， 1 udu-niga **ká～ gi$_6$-par$_4$-ra**，1 udu-gud-e-ús-sa **^{d}Na-na-a**，zi-ga šà～ **Unug^{ki}**-ga，ki～ **Kalam-hé-na-gi**--ta，gìr **Šu-ha-ma-ti**，èš-èš **é-ud-15**. iti-ezem-Me-ki-ĝál，mu Ur-bí-lum^{ki}，Lu-lu-bu^{ki}，Si-mu-ru-um^{ki} ù Kará-har^{ki} aš-šè sag-bi šu-tibir bí-ra. （Rochester 013，P128118）	1 fattened ram for**the shrine**，1 fattened ram for **gate of bedroom of high priestess**，1 ram of after-ox-class for **Nanaya**，were withdrawn in **Uruk**，from the place of Kalam-henagi，**via Šuhamati**，for the **festival of Full Moon**. Month of ezem-Mekiĝal，Year of divine Šulgi king smashed with fist the heads of Urbilum，Lulubu，Simurrum and Karahar togeth-er.	1 只育肥公绵羊为**圣殿**，1 只育肥公绵羊为**祭司寝宫之门**，1 只牛后级公绵羊为**那那亚**，于**乌鲁克**，**卡兰希那吉**处支出了，**经由舒哈马提**，为**满月庆典**。神美基旮勒庆典月，神舒勒吉王以重拳一举击碎乌尔比隆、鲁鲁布、席穆润和卡腊哈尔之头颅年。
Š 44 xi/2： **mu-túm，ì-dab$_5$** 5 duck from**the wife of Šarrum-ili**，when 2nd day passed，were deliveries for **Šulgi-simtum**，**Apilatum took over**	5 uz-tur **dam-*Šar-ru-um-ì-lí***，*iti--ta ud-2 ba-ra-zal*，*mu-túm*～ ***^{d}Šul-gi-sí-im-tum***，***Á-pi$_5$-la-tum*** *ì-dab$_5$. iti-ezem-Me-ki-ĝál，mu Si-mu-ru-um^{ki} Lu-lu-bu^{ki} a-rá 9-kam-aš ba-hul.* （*BIN* 3 007，*P105814*）	5 *duck from***the wife of Šarrum-ili**，when 2nd day passed，were deliveries for **Šulgi-simtum**，**Apilatum took over**. Month of ezem-Mekiĝal，Year of Simurum and Lulubum were destroyed for the 9th time.	5 只鸭来自**沙润伊里之妻**，于 2 日过去时，**为舒勒吉新吞的送入项，阿皮拉吞接管**了。 神美基旮勒庆典月， 席穆润和鲁鲁布第九次被毁年。
Š 44 xi/21： **mu-túm，ì-dab$_5$** 2 grass rams and 1 kid from**Šimat-ekur**，2 fattened rams and 1 lamb from **the wife of Šara-kam**，deliv-eries for **Šulgi-simtum**，**Apilatum took over**	2 udu-ú，1 máš ***Ši-ma-at-é-kur***，2 udu-niga，1 sila$_4$，**dam-^{d}Šará-kam**，iti--ta ud-21 ba-ra-zal， mu-túm～ ***^{d}Šul-gi-sí-im-tum***，***Á-pi$_5$-la-tum*** *ì-dab$_5$. iti-ezem-Me-ki-ĝál，* *mu Si-mu-ru-um^{ki}Lu-lu-bu^{ki} a-rá 9-kam-aš ba-hul.* （*Orient* 16 041 6，*P124635*）	2 *grass rams and* 1 *kid from***Šimat-ekur**，2 fattened rams and 1 lamb from **the wife of Šara-kam**，when 21st day passed，were deliveries for **Šulgi-simtum**，**Api-latum took over**. Month of ezem-Mekiĝal，Year of Simurum and Lulubum were destroyed for the 9th time.	2 只食草公绵羊和 1 只公崽自**席马特埃库尔**，2 只育肥公绵羊和 1 只羔自**沙腊刊之妻**，于 21 日过去时，**为舒勒吉新吞的送入项，阿皮拉吞接管**了。 神美基旮勒庆典月， 席穆润和鲁鲁布第九次被毁年。

续表

时间和摘要	文献内容	英文翻译	中文翻译
Š 44 xii/4: **mu-túm, ì-dab$_5$** 4 pigeons from**Watrat, the overseer**, were deliveries **for Šulgi-simtum, Apilatum took over**	4 ir$_7$^{mušen}, ***Wa-at-ra-at*** *ugula, iti--ta ud-4 ba-ra-zal, mu-túm~* ***^{d}Šul-gi-sí-im-tum***, ***Á-pi$_5$-la-tum*** *ì-dab$_5$. iti-še-kin-kud, mu Si-mu-ru-um^{ki} Lu-lu-bu^{ki} a-rá-9-kam-aš ba-hul.* (*OIP* 115077, *P*123474)	4 *pigeons from***overseer Watrat**, when 4th day passed, were deliveries **for Šulgi-simtum, Api-latum took over**. Month of še-kin-kud, Year of Simurum and Lulu-bum were destroyed for 9th time.	4只家鸽自**瓦特腊特监工**于本月4日过去时，为**舒勒吉新吞的送入项，阿皮拉吞接管**了。大麦收割月，席穆润和鲁鲁布第九次被毁年。
Š 44 xii/7: **zi-ga** 1 he-goat of after-ox-class for**Meslam-taea**, via **Nin-hamati**, was withdrawn from **Kalam-henagi**	1 máš-gal-gud-e-ús-sa, ^{d} **Mes-lam-ta-è-a**, gìr **Nin-ha-ma-ti**, iti--ta ud-7-ba-ra-zal, zi-ga, **Kalam-hé-na-gi**. iti-še-kin-kud, mu Si-mu-ru-um^{ki} Lu-lu-bu^{ki}, a-rá-9-kam-aš ba-hul. (BPOA 6 1224, P292423)	1 he-goat of after-ox-class for**Meslam-taea**, via **Nin-hamati**, when the 7th day passed, was with-drawn from **Kalam-henagi**. Month of še-kin-kud, Year of Simurum and Lulu-bum were destroyed for 9th time.	1只牛后级公山羊为**美斯兰塔埃阿**，经由**宁哈马提**，于7日过去时，从**卡兰希那吉**处支出了。天麦收割月， 席穆润和鲁鲁布第九次被毁年。
Š 44 xii/15: **mu-túm, ì-dab$_5$** 2 white she-goat from**Inim-kugga**, were **deliveries for Šulgi-simtum, Apilatum took over**	2 ud$_5$-babbar **Inim-kug-ga**, mu-túm ~ ***^{d}Šul-gi-sí-im-tum***, ***Á-pi$_5$-la-tum*** *ì-dab$_5$, iti--ta ud-15 ba-ra-zal. iti-še-kin-kud, mu Si-mu-ru-um^{ki} Lu-lu-bu^{ki} a-rá-9-kam-aš ba-hul.* (*SACT* 1 058, *P*128813)	2 *white she-goat from***Inim-kugga**, were **deliveries for Šulgi-simtum, Apilatum took over**, when the 15th day passed. Month of še-kin-kud, Year of Simurum and Lulubum were destroyed for the 9th time.	2只白母山羊来自**伊尼姆库奋**， 为**舒勒吉新吞的送入项，阿皮拉吞接管**了，于15日过去时。 大麦收割月，席穆润和鲁鲁布第九次被毁年。
Š 43 x-Š 44 xii: **pisan dub-ba** The basket of tablets: **the account balance of Apilatum**, the **fattener**	pisan dub-ba, níg-kas$_7$ ak, ***Á-pi$_5$-la-tum*** **gurušda**$^!$, iti-ezem-an-na ud-17 zal-la, mu en-^{d}Nanna maš-e ì-pàd, iti-še- [kin-kud...] mu Si-mu- [ru-um^{ki}] Lu-lu-bu [^{ki} a-rá 9-kam] ba-hul.iti-bi 14 ud-17 (ASJ 04 065 05, P102137)	The basket of tablets: **the account balance of fattener Apilatum**, month of ezem-Anna, on the 17th day, year of en-priestess of Nanna was chosen by omen, month of še-kin-kud, year of Simurum and Lulubum were destroyed for the 9th time. 14 months and 17 days	档案箱：**育肥师阿皮拉吞的账目平衡**，天神庆典月，17日，南那的女祭司被占卜选中之年，大麦收割月，席穆润和鲁鲁布第九次被毁年。（总计）14个月，17天。
Š 44 xii: **mu-túm, ì-dab$_5$** 25 rams and 5 goats fr.**Ninlil-hemti**, 1 lamb fr. **wife of Zarara**, 1 kid fr. **Ur-niĝar**, animal manager, were **deliveries for Šulgi-simtum, Apilatum took over**	25 udu-ú, 5 máš-gal, **^{d}Nin-líl-hé-em-ti**, 1 sila$_4$ ***dam-Za-ra-ra***, 1 *máš* **Ur-ni$_9$-ĝar** šùš, mu-túm~ ***^{d}Šul-gi-sí-im-tum***, ***Á-pi$_5$-la-tum*** *ì-dab$_5$. iti-še-kin-kud, mu Si-mu-ru-um^{ki} Lu-lu-bu^{ki} a-rá-9-kam-aš ba-hul.* (*SET* 008, P129418)	25 *grass rams and* 5 *he-goats from***Ninlil-hemti**, 1 lamb from **the wife of Zarara**, 1 kid from **Ur-niĝar**, animal manager, were **deliveries for Šulgi-simtum, Apilatum took over**. Month of še-kin-kud, Year of Simurum and Lulubum were destroyed for the 9th time.	25只食草公绵羊和5只公山羊来自**宁里勒希姆提**，1只羔来自**扎腊腊之妻**，1只公崽来自**乌尔尼旮尔牲畜长**，为**舒勒吉新吞的送入项，阿皮拉吞接管**了。大麦收割月，席穆润和鲁鲁布第九次被毁年。

续表

时间和摘要	文献内容	英文翻译	中文翻译
Š 45 i: **mu-túm, ì-dab$_5$** 2 rams from **Ṣiluš-Dagan**, 2 lambs from **Te ṣin-Mama**, 1 male goat was new born from **the house of fattner**, 1 ram, 1 he-goat from **Puzur-Ištar**, 1 lamb from **Ur-niĝar**, 1 lamb from **Ninlil-tumimti**, **Apilatum took**	2 udu ***Ṣi-lu-uš-^{d}Da-gan***, 2 *sila$_4$* ***Te-ṣi-in-^{d}Ma-ma***, 1 *máš-gub-nita, ù-tu-da é-gurušda*, 1 *udu*, 1 *máš*, ***Puzur$_4$-Iš$_8$-tár***, 1 *sila$_4$* **Ur-ni$_9$-ĝar**, 1 sila$_4$ **Ninlil-*tum-im-ti***, *mu-túm*, ***Á-pi$_5$-la-tum*** *ì-dab$_5$.iti-maš-dà~gu$_7$, mu a-rá-3-kam-aš Kará-har^{ki} ba-hul.* (*BIN* 3 335, *P*106141)	2 *rams from* **Ṣiluš-Dagan**, 2 lambs from **Te ṣin-Mama**, 1 male goat was new born from **the house of fattner**, 1 ram, 1 he-goat from **Puzur-Ištar**, 1 lamb from **Ur-niĝar**, 1 lamb from **Ninlil-tumimti**, these were deliveries, Apilatum took over. Month of mašda~gu$_7$, Year of Kara-har was destroyed for the 3rd time.	2只公绵羊自**采鲁什达干**，2只羊羔自**台岑妈妈**，1只新生公山羊自**育肥房**，1只公绵羊和1只公山羊自**普朱尔伊什塔尔**，1只羊羔自**乌尔尼奋尔**，1只羊羔自**宁里勒吞伊姆提**，以上送入**阿皮拉吞接管**了。食瞪羚月，卡腊哈尔被第3次毁灭年。
Š 45 i/7, 10: **mu-túm, ì-dab$_5$** 1 lamb and 1 kid from**Puzur-Ištar**, 1 ducklet from **Simat-Ištar**, 1 kid from **the man of Magan**, 1 fattened bull from **Ikunum**, 10 grass rams from **Etealpu-Dagan**, 1 lamb from **Ninlil-tumimti**, were deliveries for Šulgi-simtum, **Apilatum took over**	1 sila$_4$, 1 máš ***Puzur$_4$-Iš$_4$-tár***, 1 *amar-sag-uz-tur* ***Simat-Iš$_4$-tár***, *iti--ta* **ud-7** ba-ra-zal, 1 máš **Lú-Má-gan^{ki}**, 1 gud-niga ***I-ku-núm***, *iti--ta* **ud-10** ba-ra-zal, 10 udu-ú ***E-te-al-pù-^{d}*Da-gan**, 1 sila$_4$ **^{d}Nin-líl-tum-im-ti**, mu-túm~ ***^{d}Šul-gi-sí-im-tum***, ***Á-pi$_5$-la-tum*** *ì-dab$_5$.* *iti-maš-dà~gu$_7$, mu ús-sa Si-mu-ru-um^{ki} Lu-lu-bu^{ki} a-rá-9-kam-aš ba-hul.* (*Babyl.*8 *Pupil* 17, *P*104826)	1 *lamb and* 1 *kid from***Puzur-Ištar**, 1 ducklet from **Simat-Ištar**, when 7th day passed, 1 kid from **the man of Magan**, 1 fattened bull from **Ikunum**, when 10th day passed, 10 grass rams from**Etealpu-Dagan**, 1 lamb from **Ninlil-tumimti**, were deliveries for Šulgi-simtum, **Apilatum took over**. Month of mašda~gu$_7$, Year after that of Simurum and Lulubu were destroyed for the 9th time.	1只羔和1只公崽自**普朱尔伊什塔尔**，1只幼鸭自**席马特伊什塔尔**，于**7**日过去时，1只公崽自**马干国的人**，1头育肥公牛自**伊库农**，于**10**日过去时，10只食草公绵羊来自**埃台阿勒普达干**，1只羔来自**宁里勒吞伊姆提**，为**舒勒吉新吞的送入项**，**阿皮拉吞接管**了。食瞪羚月，席穆润和鲁鲁布第九次被毁灭年次年。
Š 45 i/20, 23, 27: **mu-túm, ì-dab$_5$** 2 ducklet, 3 doves from**Ninlil-tumimti**, 40 doves from **Bagum**, **the bird-catcher**, when **23rd** day passed, 1 fattened ram from **Puzur-Ištar**, 1 lamb from **Imid-ilum**, were deliveries for **Šulgi-simtum**, **Apilatum took over**	2 amar-sag-uz-tur, 3 tu-gur$_4$^{mušen}, **^{d} Nin-líl-*tum-im-ti***, *iti--ta ud-20 ba-ra-zal*, 40 *tu-gur$_4$^{mušen}*, ***Ba-gu-um*** *mušen-dù*, *iti--ta ud-23 ba-ra-zal*, 1 *gud-niga* [***Puzur$_4$***] ***-Iš$_8$-tár***, *iti--ta ud-27 ba-ra-zal*, 1 *sila$_4$*, ***I-mi-id-ilum***, *mu-túm~* ***^{d}Šul-gi-sí-im-tum***, ***Á-pi$_5$-la-tum*** *ì-dab$_5$.iti-maš-dà~gu$_7$, mu ús-sa Simurrum^{ki} Lulubu^{ki} a-rá-9-kam-aš ba-hul.* (*Durand RA* 73, *no* 1)	2 *ducklet*, 3 *doves from***Ninlil-tumimti**, when **20th** day passed, 40 doves from **Bagum**, **the bird-catcher**, when **23rd** day passed, 1 fattened ram from **Puzur-Ištar**, when **27th** day passed, 1 lamb from **Imid-ilum**, were deliveries for **Šulgi-simtum**, **Apilatum took over**. Month of mašda~gu$_7$, Year after that of Simurum and Lulubu were destroyed for the 9th time.	2只幼鸭和3只野鸽自**宁里勒吞伊姆提**于本月**20**日过去时，40只野鸽自**捕鸟人巴鲧**于本月**23**日过去时，1只育肥公绵羊自**普朱尔伊什塔尔**于本月**27**日过去时，1只羊羔自**伊米德伊隆**，以上为**舒勒吉新吞的送入项**，**阿皮拉吞接管**了。食瞪羚月，席穆润和鲁鲁布第九次被毁灭年之次年。

续表

时间和摘要	文献内容	英文翻译	中文翻译
Š 45 i/22: **zi-ga** 2 fattened rams for **Belat-Suhnir**, 2 fattened rams for **Belat-Dara-ban**, 1 fattened bull, 3 fattened rams and 1 lamb for **Inanna**, 1 ram of after-ox-class for **Dayada**, 1 ram of after-ox-class for **Nin-šubur**, [⋯], [⋯], 1 ram for **Nin-x**, for **festival of gud-si -su**, **in Nippur**, withdr. fr. **Kalam-henagi**, **via my queen**	2 udu-niga ^{d}***Be-la-at-Suh-nir***, 2 *udu-niga*, ^{d} ***Be-la-at-Da-ra-ba-an***, 1 *gud-niga* 3 *udu-niga*, 1 *sila*$_4$ ^{d}**Inanna**, 1 udu-gud- [e] -ús-sa^{d}***Da-a-da***!, 1 *udu-ú gud-e-<ús>-sa* ^{d}**Nin-šubur**, [...], [...], 1 udu gud-e-ús-sa ^{d}**Nin-[...]**, iti-ta ud-22 ba-ra-zal, **ezem gud-si-su šà ~ Ni [bru^{ki}]**, zi-ga ki ~ **Kalam-hé-na-gi**, **gìr nin-ĝá**.iti maš-dà-gu$_7$, muús-sa Si-mu-ru-um^{ki}, Lu-lu-bu^{ki} a-rá-9-kam-aš ba-hul. (BPOA 6 0076, P 390714)	2 fattened rams for **Belat-Suhnir**, 2 fattened rams for **Belat-Dara-ban**, 1 fattened bull, 3 fattened rams and 1 lamb for **Inanna**, 1 ram of after-ox-class for **Dayada**, 1 grass ram of after-ox-class for **Nin-šubur**, [⋯], [⋯], 1 ram of after-ox-class for **Nin-x**, when 22nd day passed, for **festival of gud-si -su**, **in Nippur**, were withdrawn from **Kalam-henagi**, **via my queen**.Month of mašda ~ gu$_7$, Year after that of Simurum and Lulubu were destroyed for the 9th time.	2育肥公绵羊为**贝拉特苏赫尼尔**，2育肥公绵羊为**贝拉特达腊班**，1育肥公牛、3育肥公绵羊和1羔为**伊南那**，1牛后级公绵羊为**达亚达**，1食草牛后级公绵羊为**宁舒布尔**，【……】，1牛后级公绵羊为宁-x，于22日过去时，为**gud-si-su节**，**于尼普尔**，从**卡兰希那吉支出**，**经由我的王后**。食瞪羚月，席穆润和鲁鲁布第九次被毁灭年之次年。
Š 45 ii: **zi-ga** 1 ram for**Ninlil**, 1 ram of after-ox-class for **Enlil**, **via Aya-Nanna-arkalla**, were withdrawn from **Kalam-henagi**, for the festival of Full Moon	1 udu-gud-e-ús-sa ^{d}**Nin-líl**, 1 udu-gud- [e] -ús-sa ^{d} **En-líl**, gìr **A-a-**^{d}**Nanna-ar-kal-la**, zi-ga ki ~ **Kalam-hé-na-gi**--ta, èš-èš é-ud-15. iti-ze$_x$-da ~ gu$_7$, mu ús-sa Si-mu-ru-um^{ki} Lu-lu-bu a-rá 9-kam-aš ba-hul. (PDT 1 370, P125786)	1 ram of after-ox-class for**Ninlil**, 1 ram of after-ox-class for **Enlil**, **via Aya-Nanna-arkalla**, were withdrawn from **Kalam-henagi**, for **the festival of Full Moon**.Month of zeda ~ gu$_7$, Year after that of Simurum and Lulubu were destroyed for the ninth time.	1只牛后级公绵羊为**宁里勒**，1只牛后级公绵羊为**恩里勒**，**经由阿亚南那阿尔卡拉**，从**卡兰希那吉**处支出了，**为满月庆典**。食豚月，席穆润和鲁鲁布第九次被毁年之次年。
Š 45 iii/6: **mu-túm**, (**ì-dab$_5$**) 2 [rams], 4 he-goats, 2 ducks and 1 [lamb], **Watrat as the overseer**, 1 fattened ram from **the monthly allowance**, 1 kid, [...] from Šiba-[...], deliveries for **Šulgi-simtum**, **via Lugal-eden [na]**	2 [udu], 4 máš-gal, 2 uz-tur, 1 [sila$_4$], ***Wa-at-ra-at* ugula**, 1 udu-niga, sá!-dug$_4$!, 1 máš, [...], ***Ši-ba-*** **[...]**, *iti--ta ud-6-ba-ra-zal*, *mu-túm* ~ ^{d}***Šul-gi-sí-im-tum***, *gìr* **Lugal-eden- [na--ka]**.iti-u$_5$-bí-gu$_7$, mu ús-sa [Si-mu-ru-um^{ki} Lu-lu-bu^{ki}a-rá 9-kam-aš ba-hul]. (Ontario 1 013, P124426)	2 [rams], 4 he-goats, 2 ducks and 1 [lamb], **Watrat as the overseer**, 1 fattened ram from **the monthly allowance**, 1 kid, [...] from Šiba-[...], when the 6th day passed, were deliveries for **Šulgi-simtum**, **via Lugal-eden [na]**.Month of ubi ~ gu$_7$, Year after that [of Simurum and Lulubu were destroyed for 9th time].	2只【公绵羊】、4只公山羊、2只鸭和1【羔】，**瓦特腊特监工**，1只育肥公绵羊自**月供**，1只公崽、【……】来自**席巴-【x】**，于6日过去时，为**舒勒吉新吞德送入项**，**经由卢旮勒埃邓那**。食乌比鸟月，席穆润和鲁鲁布第九次被毁灭年之次年。

续表

时间和摘要	文献内容	英文翻译	中文翻译
Š 45 iii/2, 3, 5, 6: **zi-ga, butchered** 2nd: 1 thicket female piglet and 2 doves, 3rd: 1 duck and 1 pigeon, **butchered ones were sent to the palace**, 5th: 1 fattened ram for sacrifice of **Allatum**, 1 ram of after-ox-class for **the sacrifice of Ordeal Divine River**, 6th: 1 dove, **butchered ones were sent to palace, withdrawn from x- [x x x] tum**	1šáh-zah-tur-munus-giš-gi, 2 tu-gur$_4$^{mušen}, iti--ta ud-2-ba-ra-zal, 1 uz-tur, 1 ir$_7$^{mušen}, iti--ta ud-3-ba-ra-zal, ba-úš é-gal-la ba-an-ku$_4$, 1 udu-niga, **siskúr-^{d} *Al-la-tum***, 1 *udu-gud-e ús-sa*, **siskúr-^{d} *I$_7$-lú-ru-gú-*** [*ka*], *iti--ta ud-5$^?$-ba-* [*ra-zal*], 1 *tu-gur$_4$*$^{[mušen]}$, *iti--ta ud-6-* [*ba-ra-zal*], *ba-úš é-gal-* [*la ba-an-ku$_4$*], *zi-ga x* [*-x-x-x*] *-tum.* *iti-u$_5$-bí-gu$_7$*, *mu ús-sa Si-* [*mu-ru*] *-um^{ki} Lu-lu-bu-um^{ki} a-rá-9-kam-aš ba-hul.* (*BIN* 3 366, P106172)	1 *thicket female piglet and 2 doves*, *when the 2ndday passed*, 1 *duck and* 1 *pigeon when the 3rdday passed*, **butchered ones were sent to the palace**, 1 fattened ram for sacrifice of **Allatum**, 1 ram of after-ox-class for **the sacrifice of Ordeal Divine River**, when the 5thday passed, 1 dove when the 6thday passed, **butchered ones were sent to palace**, **withdrawn from x- [x x x] tum**. Month of ubi～gu$_7$, Year after that of Si [muru] m and Lulubu were destroyed for the 9th time.	1 只苇塘雌豚和 2 只野鸽于 2 日过去时，1 只鸭和 1 只家鸽，于 3 日过去时，以上**宰杀牲被送入宫殿**， 1 只育肥公绵羊为**阿拉吞的牺牲**， 1 只牛后级公绵羊为**神判河神的牺牲**，于 5 日过去时，1 只野鸽，于 6 日过去时，以上**宰杀牲被送入宫殿**，从 **x-［x x x］吞支出了**。食乌比鸟月，席【穆润】和鲁鲁布第九次被毁灭年之次年。
Š 45 iii/23: **mu-túm, ì-dab$_5$** 9 LAGAB-bird from**the man of Urub**, were deliveries for **Šulgi-simtum**, **Apilatum took over**	9 LAGAB^{mušen}, lú-Urub (URUxKÁR)^{ki}, iti--ta ud-23 ba-ra-zal, mu-túm～ ***^{d}Šul-gi -si-im-tum***, ***Á-pi$_5$-la-tum*** *ì-dab$_5$.iti-u$_5$-bí-gu$_7$*, *mu ús-sa Si-mu -ru-um^{ki} Lu-lu-bu^{ki} a-rá 9-kam-aš ba-hul.* (*RT* 37 129 *be.*5, P128393)	9 *LAGAB-bird from***the man of Urub**, when 23rd day passed, were deliveries for **Šulgi-simtum**, **Apilatum took over**. Month of ubi～gu$_7$, Year after that of Simurum and Lulubu were destroyed for the 9th time.	9 只 LAGAB 鸟来自**乌如卜城之人**，于 23 日过去时，为**舒勒吉新吞的送入项**，**阿皮拉吞接管了**。食乌比鸟月， 席穆润和鲁鲁布第九次被毁灭年之次年。
Š 45 v/12, 13, 14: **zi-ga** 12th: 1 fat ram for **Nanna**, 1 fat ram for **Ningal**, 13th: 1 lamb and 1 kid, **butchered ones were sent to palace**, 1 fat ram for **giranum of Inanna**, 14th: 1 fat bull, 3 fat rams, 1 lamb for **Inanna**, 1 ram for **Nin-nigar**, 1 ram for **Dada**, 1 ram for **Ordeal Divine River**, 1 grass ram for **Nin-šubur**, 1 lamb for **night food, in the palace**, 1 fattened ram for **center of palace**, 1 ram of after-ox-class for **Enlil**, 1 ram of after-ox-class for **Ninlil**, were **withdrawn from place of Kalam-henagi**	1 udu-niga^d **Nanna**, 1 udu-niga **^{d}Nin-gal**, iti-**ud-12**ba-zal, 1 sila$_4$, 1 máš ba-úš, **é-gal-la** ba-an-ku$_4$, 1 udu-niga ***gi-ra-núm-*^{d}Inanna**, iti-**ud-13**ba-zal, 1 gud-niga, 3 udu-niga, 1 sila$_4$**^{d}Inanna**, 1 udu-gud-e ús-sa **^{d}Nin-ni$_9$-gar**, 1 udu-gud-e-ús-sa **^{d}Da-da**, 1 udu-gud-e-ús-sa **^{d}I$_7$-lú-ru-gú**, 1 udu-ú **^{d}Nin-šubur**, 1 sila$_4$ níĝ-ĝi$_6$ šà～ **é-gal**, 1 udu-niga šà **é-gal-la**, 1 udu-gud-e-ús-sa **^{d}En-líl**, 1 udu-gud-e-ús-sa **^{d}Nin-líl**, iti-**ud-14**ba-zal, zi-ga ki～ **Kalam-hé-na-gi**.iti-ezem-^{d}Nin-a-zu, mu ús-sa Si-mu-ru^{ki} ù Lu-lu-bu^{ki} a-rá 9-kam-aš ba-hul. ed: 1 gud, 17 udu (PDT 1 645, P126061)	1 fattened ram for **Nanna**, 1 fattened ram for **Ningal**, when **12th**day passed, 1 lamb and 1 kid, **butchered ones were sent to palace**, 1 fattened ram for **giranum festival of Inanna**, when **13th**day passed, 1 fattened bull, 3 fattened rams, 1 lamb for **Inanna**, 1 ram of after-ox-class for **Nin-nigar**, 1 ram of after-ox-class for **Dada**, 1 ram of after-ox-class for **Ordeal Divine River**, 1 grass ram for **Nin-šubur**, 1 lamb for **night food, in the palace**, 1 fattened ram for **center of palace**, 1 ram of after-ox-class for **Enlil**, 1 ram of after-ox-class for **Ninlil**, when**14th**day passed, were **withdrawn from place of Kalam-henagi**. Month of Ninazu, Year after that of Simuru and Lulubu were destroyed for 9th time.	1 育肥公绵羊为**南那**，1 育肥公绵羊为**宁旮勒**，于 **12 日**过去时，1 羔和 1 公崽，这些**宰杀牲被送入宫殿**，1 育肥公绵羊为**伊南那的吉腊努姆仪式**，于 **13 日**过去时，1 头育肥公牛、3 育肥公绵羊和 1 羔为**伊南那**，1 牛后级公绵羊为**宁尼旮尔**，1 牛后级公绵羊为**达达**，1 牛后级公绵羊为**神判河神**，1 食草公绵羊为**宁舒布尔**，1 羔为**夜食于宫殿**，1 育肥公绵羊为**内殿**，1 牛后级公绵羊为**恩里勒**，1 牛后级公绵羊为**宁里勒**， 于 **14 日**过去时， 从**卡兰希那吉支出了**。神宁阿朱庆典月， 席穆如和鲁鲁布第九次被毁年次年。

续表

时间和摘要	文献内容	英文翻译	中文翻译
Š 45 v/22: **mu-túm, ì-dab$_5$** 4 rams and 1 kid from **Šarrum-ili, the governer**, 1 lamb fr.**Enlil-isa**, 2 fat rams and 1 fattened lamb from **Ikulum**, 2 pigeons from the **wife of Halaya**, deliveries for Šulgi-simtum, **Apilatum took over**	4 udu-ú, 1 máš, ***Šar-ru-um-ì-lí*** *ensí*, 1 *sila$_4$* ^{d}**En-líl-ì-sa$_6$**, 2 udu-niga, 1 sila$_4$-niga, ***I-ku-lum***, 2 *ir$_7$^{mušen}* **dam-*Ha-la-a***, *iti--ta ud-22 ba-ra-zal*, *mu-túm* ~ ^{d}***Šul-gi-sí-im-tum***, ***Á-pi$_5$-la-tum*** *ì-dab$_5$*. *iti-ezem-^{d}Nin-a-zu*, *mu ús-sa Si-mu-ru-um^{ki} Lu-lu-bu^{ki} a-rá 9-kam-aš ba-hul*. (*PDT* 1 475, P125891)	*4 grass rams and 1 kid from***Šarrum-ili, the governer**, 1 lamb from **Enlil-isa**, 2 fattened rams and 1 fattened lamb from **Ikulum**, 2 pigeons from the **wife of Halaya**, when 22nd day passed, were deliveries for Šulgi-simtum, **Apilatum took over**. Month of ezem-Ninazu, Year after that of Simurum and Lulubu were destroyed for the 9th time.	4只食草公绵羊和1只公崽自**沙润伊里总督**，1只羔自**恩里勒伊萨**，2只育肥公绵羊和1只育肥羔来自**伊库隆**，2只家鸽来自**哈拉亚之妻**，于22日过去时，为**舒勒吉新吞的送入项，阿皮拉吞接管**了。神宁阿朱庆典月， 席穆润和鲁鲁布第九次被毁灭年次年。
Š 45 vi: **mu-túm, ì-dab$_5$** 4 grass rams, 1 kid from**Inimkugga**, were deliveries for **Šulgi-simti, Apilatum took over**	4 udu-ú, 1 máš, **Inim-kug-ga**, mu-túm ~ ^{d}***Šul-gi-sí-im-ti***, ***Á-pi$_5$-la-tum*** *ì-dab$_5$*. *iti-á-ki-ti*, *mu ús-sa mu Si-mu-ru-um^{ki}ù Lu-lu-bu^{ki}a-rá-9-kam-<ma>-aš ba-hul*. (*PDT* 2 982, P126329)	4 *grass rams*, 1 *kid from***Inimkugga**, were deliveries for **Šulgi-simti, Apilatum took over**. Month of akiti, Year after that of Simurum and Lulubu were destroyed for the 9th time.	4只食草公绵羊和1只公崽自**伊尼姆库旮**，为**舒勒吉新提的送入项，阿皮拉吞接管**了。阿基提月，席穆润和鲁鲁布第九次被毁灭年之次年。
Š45 vi/15: **mu-túm, ì-dab$_5$** 1 ewe and 1 kid were brought from **the palace**, 1 lamb was new born from the **house of fattener**, 29 doves from Bagum, the bird-catcher, deliveries for **Šulgi-simtum, Apilatum took over**	1 u$_8$, 1 ^{f}ašgar, é-gal--ta è-a, 1 sila$_4$ ù-tu-da é-gurušda, 29 tu-gur$_4$^{mušen} ***Ba-gu-um*** *mušen-dù*, *iti--ta ud-15 ba-ra-zal*, *mu-túm* ~ ^{d}***Šul-gi-sí-im-tum***, ***Á-*** [***pi$_5$***] ***-la-tum*** [*ì*] *-dab$_5$*. *iti-* [*á*] *-ki-ti*, *mu ús-sa Si-mu-ru-um^{ki} ù Lu-lu-bu^{ki} a-rá-9-kam-aš ba-hul*. (*NABU* 1997: 099, P142631)	1 *ewe and* 1 *female kid were brought from***the palace**, 1 lamb was new born from the **house of fattener**, 29 doves from Bagum, the bird-catcher, when 15th day passed, were deliveries for **Šulgi-simtum, Apilatum took over**.Month of akiti, Year after that of Simurum and Lulubu were destroyed for the 9th time.	1只母绵羊和1只雌崽从**宫殿带来**， 1只新生羔来自**育肥房**，29只野鸽来自**捕鸟人巴衮**，于15日过去时， 为**舒勒吉新吞的送入项，阿皮拉吞接管**了。 阿基提月， 席穆润和鲁鲁布第九次被毁灭年之次年。
Š 45 vii/12, 13: **zi-ga, butchered** 12th: 1 dove for **the food of my queen** on the 3rd time, 9 doves, 1 pigeon, were **butchered sent to the palace**, 13th: 1 ram of after-ox-class for **giranum festival of Inanna**, were **withdrawn from Ur-Lugal-edinka**	1 tu-gur$_4$^{mušen}, **níĝ-gu$_7$-nin-ĝá**--šè, a-rá-3-kam, 9 tu-gur$_4$^{mušen}, 1 ir$_7$^{mušen}, ba-úš, **é-gal-la ba-an-ku$_4$**, iti--ta ud-12 ba-ra-zal, 1 udu-gud-e-ús-sa, ***gi-ra-núm*-Inanna**, iti--ta ud-13 ba-ra-zal, zi-ga-**Ur-^{d}Lugal-eden-ka**.iti-ezem-^{d}Šul-gi, mu ús-sa Si-mu-ru-um^{ki}Lu-lu-bu^{ki}a-rá-9-kam-aš ba-hul. (OIP 115 094, P123461)	1 dove for **the food of my queen** on the 3rd time, 9 doves, 1 pigeon, were **butchered sent to the palace**, when **12th**day passed, 1 ram of after-ox-class for **giranum festival of Inanna**, when the **13th**day passed, were **withdrawn from Ur-Lugal-edinka**. Month of ezem-Šulgi, Year after that of Simurum and Lulubu were destroyed for the 9th time.	1只野鸽为**我的王后的食物**第3次，9只野鸽和1只家鸽，**以上宰杀牲被送入宫殿**，于**12**日过去时，1只牛后级公绵羊为**伊南那的吉腊努姆仪式**，于**13**日过去时，**从乌尔卢旮勒埃丁卡支出了**。舒勒吉庆典月，席穆润和鲁鲁布第九次被毁灭年之次年。

续表

时间和摘要	文献内容	英文翻译	中文翻译
Š 45 vii /10，15: **zi-ga，butchered** 10th：1 ram for **sacrifice of Inanna**， 15th：1 ram for **giranum festival of Inanna** on 2nd time，2 fattened rams for **sacrifice of Full Moon in Uruk，via Ipiq-Erra**；1 ram for **offering of "disappearing place" of Adad**，1 fat ram and 1 ewe for **sacrifice of Belat-Suhnir and Belat-Darraban**，4 doves［**for the food of my queen?**］，1 ram and 1 breast lamb，**butchered ones were sent to palace**，in **Tummal**，withdrawn from **Ur-Lugal-edinka**	1 udu-gud-e-ús-sa，**siskúr-^{d} Inanna**，iti--ta**ud-10**ba-ra-zal，1 udu-gud-e-ús-sa，***gi-ra-núm*-^{d} Inanna**，a-rá 2-kam，2 udu-gud-e-ús-sa-niga，**siskúr é-ud-15** šà~ **Un-ug^{ki}**，gìr ***I-pi$_5$-iq-Èr-ra***；1 *udu-ú*，**níg-ki-záh-^{d}Iškur**，1 udu-niga，1 u_8，**siskúr-^{d}*Be-la-at-Suh-nir*** *ù* **^{d}*Be-la-at-Dar-ra-ba-an***，4 *tu-gur$_4$^{mušen}*，（*edge*）［**níĝ-gu$_7$-nin-ĝá**--šè?］，iti--ta **ud-15**ba-ra-zal，1 udu-ú，1 sila$_4$-gaba，ba-úš，**é-gal-la** ba-an-ku$_4$，šà~ Tum-ma-al^{ki}，zi-ga **Ur-^{d}Lugal-edin-<ka>**. iti-ezem-^{d}Šul-gi，mu ús-sa Si-mu-ru-um^{ki}Lu-lu-bu^{ki}a-rá-9-kam-aš ba-hul. （AnOr 07 072，P101367）	1 ram of after-ox-class，for **sacrifice of Inanna**，when **10th**day passed，1 ram of after-ox-class for **giranum festival of Inanna** on 2nd time，2 fattened rams of after-ox-class for **sacrifice of Full Moon in Uruk，via Ipiq-Erra**；1 grass ram for **offering of "disappearing place" of Adad**，1 fattened ram and 1 ewe for **sacrifice of Belat-Suhnir and Belat-Darraban**，4 doves［**for the food of my queen?**］，when **15th**day passed，1 grass ram and 1 breast lamb，**butchered ones were sent to palace**，in **Tummal**，were withdrawn from **Ur-Lugal-edinka**. Month of ezem-Šulgi，Year after that of Simurum and Lulubu were destroyed for the 9th time.	1只牛后级公绵羊为**伊南那祭**，于**10**日过去时，1只牛后级公绵羊为**伊南那的吉腊努姆仪式**第2次，2只牛后级育肥公绵羊为**满月祭于乌鲁克**，**经由伊皮克埃腊**；1只食草公绵羊为**阿达德的消失处供奉**，1只育肥公绵羊和1只母绵羊为**贝拉特苏赫尼尔和贝拉特达腊班消失处供奉**，4只野鸽【**为我的王后的食物**】，于**15**日过去时，1只食草公绵羊和1只胸（捧）公羔，以上**宰杀牲被送入宫殿于图马勒**，从**乌尔卢旮勒埃丁卡**支出了。舒勒吉庆典月，席穆润和鲁鲁布第九次被毁灭年之次年。
Š 45 vii/18: **zi-ga，butchered** 1 fattened ram，2 grass rams，1 he-goat，1 breast lamb，1 duck，7 doves，**butchered ones were sent to palace**，1 thicket female piglet for the **food of my queen**，were **withdrawn from Ur-Lugal-edinka**	1 udu-niga，2 udu-ú，1 máš-gal，1 sila$_4$-gaba，1 uz-tur，7 tu-gur$_4$^{mušen}，ba-úš **é-gal-la ba-an-ku$_4$**，1 šáh^{zah}-tur-munus-giš-gi，**níĝ-gu$_7$-nin-ĝá**--šè，iti--ta **ud-18** ba-ra-zal，zi-ga **Ur-Lugal-edin-ka**. iti-ezem-^{d}Šul-gi-mìn-kam，mu-ús-sa Si-mu-ru-um^{ki}Lu-lu-bu^{ki}a-rá-9-kam-aš ba-hul. （OIP 115 096，P123623）	1 fattened ram，2 grass rams，1 he-goat，1 breast lamb，1 duck，7 doves，**butchered ones were sent to palace**，1 thicket female piglet for the **food of my queen**，when 18th day passed，were **withdrawn from Ur-Lugal-edinka**. Month of second ezem-Šulgi-min-kam，Year after that of Simurum and Lulubu were destroyed for the 9th time.	1只肥公绵羊、2只食草公绵羊、1只公山羊、1只胸（捧）公羔、1只鸭和7只野鸽，以上**宰杀牲被送入宫殿**，1只苇塘雌豚为**我的王后的食物**，于18日过去时，从**乌尔卢旮勒埃丁卡支出了**。第二个舒勒吉庆典月，席穆润和鲁鲁布第九次被毁灭年之次年。
Š 45 vii/25: **zi-ga** 1 female kid for giranum festival of Inanna，**in the palace**，were **withdrawn from Ur-Lugal-edinka**	1^{f}ašgar ***gi-ra-núm*-Inanna**，šà~ **é-gal-la**，iti--ta ud-25 ba-ra-zal，zi-ga **Ur-^{d} Lugal-eden-ka**. iti-ezem-^{d}Šul-gi，mu ús-sa Si-mu-ru-um^{ki}Lu-lu-bu^{ki}a-rá-9-kam ba-hul. （OIP 115 095，P123424）	1 female kid for giranum festival of Inanna，**in the palace**，when the 25th day passed，were **withdrawn from Ur-Lugal-edinka**. Month of ezem-Šulgi，Year after that of Simurum and Lulubu were destroyed for the 9th time.	1只雌山羊崽为**伊南那得吉腊努姆仪式**，于**宫殿**，于25日过去时，**从乌尔卢旮勒埃丁卡支出了**。舒勒吉庆典月，席穆润和鲁鲁布第九次被毁灭年之次年。
Š 45 viii: **mu-túm，ì-dab$_5$** 1 female**kunga** onager was deliveries for **the king**，from Nasag，**Šulgi-ili took over**	1 anše-kungá-munus，mu-túm-**lugal**，ki~ ***Na-sag$_9$*--*ta***，***^{d}Šul-gi-ì-lí*** *ì-dab$_5$. iti-šu-eš$_5$-ša，mu Ur-bí-lum^{ki} ba-hul.* （*Torino* 1 092，*P*124597）	1 *female***kunga** onager was deliveries for **the king**，from Nasag，**Šulgi-ili took over**. Month of šu-ešša，Year of Urbilum was destroyed.	1头**kunga**母驴送入为国王，从那萨处，**舒勒吉伊里接管了**。 三只手月， 乌尔比隆被毁之年。

续表

时间和摘要	文献内容	英文翻译	中文翻译
Š 45 viii: **mu-túm, ì-dab$_5$** 1 cow, 1 grass cow, 10 rams, 10 goats, from the wife of **Šulgi-ili, the general**, were **deliveries for Šulgi-simtum, Ur-Lugal-edinka took**	láb, 1 áb-ú, 10 udu-ú, 10 máš-gal, **dam-^{d}*Šul-gi-ì-lí*** *šagina*, *mu-túm* ~ ***^{d}Šul-gi-sí-im-tum***, **Ur-^{d} Lugal-edin-ka** ì-dab$_5$. iti-šu-eš-ša, mu Ur-bí-lum^{ki}ba-hul. (RT 37 130 mi.7, P128399)	1 cow, 1 grass cow, 10 grass rams, 10 he-goats, from the wife of**Šulgi-ili, the general**, were **deliveries for Šulgi-simtum, Ur-Lugal-edinka took over**. Month of šu-ešša, Year of Urbilum was destroyed.	1只母牛、1只食草母牛、10只食草公绵羊和10只公山羊，自**将军舒勒吉伊里妻**，为**舒勒吉新吞的送入项，乌尔卢旮勒埃丁卡接管**了。三只手月，乌尔比隆被毁年。
Š 45 viii /10, 12, 15, 17, 18, 19: **zi-ga, butchered** 10th: 1 grass bull, 2 he-goats, 1 lamb, 2 ducks, 12th: 1 duck, **butchered ones were sent to the palace**, 15th: 1 fattened ram for **giranum festival of Inanna**, 1 ram of after-ox-class for **Adad**, 2 fattened rams for **Belat-Suhnir and Belat-Darraban**, 2 rams of after-ox-class, 1 grass ram for **sacrifice of the Full Moon in Uruk**, **via Ipiq-Erra**, 15th: 2 rams of after-ox-class for **anointing priest of Belat-S.and Belat-D.**, 17th: 1 female kid for **giranum festival of Inanna**, 1 female kid for **giranum festival of Inanna**, **via my queen**, 18th: 3 ducks, 19th: 2 ducks, 1 dove, **butchered ones were sent to palace**, **withdrawn from Ur-Lugal-edinka**	1 gud-ú, 2 máš-gal, 1 sila$_4$, 2 uz-tur, iti--ta ud-10 ba-ra-zal, 1 uz-tur, iti--ta ud-12 ba-ra-zal, ri-ri-ga é-gal-la ba-an-ku$_4$, 1 udu-niga, ***gi-ra-núm-*^{d}Inanna**, 1 udu-gud-e-ús-sa, **^{d}Iškur**, 2 udu-niga ***^{d}Be-la-at-Suh$_6$-nir*** *ù* ***^{d}Be-la-at-Dar-ra-ba-an***, 2 *udu-gud-e-ús-sa*, 1 *udu-ú*, **siskúr-é-ud-15** šà ~ **Unug^{ki}**, iti--ta ud-15 ba-ra-zal, gìr***I-pi$_5$-iq-Èr-ra***, 2 *udu-gud-e-ús-sa*, **gudug-*^{d}Be-la-at-Suh$_6$-nir*** (*rev.*) *ù* ***^{d}Be-la-at-Dar-ra-ba-an***, *iti--ta ud-15 ba-ra-zal*, 1^f *ašgar-niga* ***gi-ra-núm-*^{d} Inanna**, iti--ta ud-17 ba-ra-zal, a-rá 1-kam, 1 ^{f}ašgar ***gi-ra-núm-*^{d} Inanna** a-rá 2-kam, gìr **nin-ĝá**, 3 uz-tur, iti--ta ud-18 ba-ra-zal, 2 uz-tur, 1 tu-gur$_4$^{mušen}, iti--ta ud-19ba-ra-zal, ba-úš, **é-gal-la** ba-an-ku$_4$, zi-ga **Ur-^{d} Lugal-edin-ka**. iti-šu-eš$_5$-ša, mu Ur-bí-lum^{ki}ba-hul. (MVN 13 715, P117488)	1 grass bull, 2 he-goats, 1 lamb, 2 ducks, when **10th**day passed, 1 duck, when **12th**day passed, **butchered ones were sent to the palace**, 1 fattened ram for **giranum festival of Inanna**, 1 ram of after-ox-class for **Adad**, 2 fattened rams for **Belat-Suhnir and Belat-Darraban**, 2 rams of after-ox-class, 1 grass ram for **sacrifice of the Full Moon in Uruk**, when**15th**day passed, **via Ipiq-Erra**, 2 rams of after-ox-class for **anointing priest of Belat-Suhnir and Belat-Darraban**, when**15th** day passed, 1 female kid for **giranum festival of Inanna**, when **17th**day passed on 1st time, 1 female kid for **giranum festival of Inanna** on 2nd time, **via my queen**, 3 ducks, when **18th**day passed, 2 ducks, 1 dove, when **19th**day passed, **butchered ones were sent to palace**, were **withdrawn from Ur-Lugal-edinka**. Month of šu-ešša, Year of Urbilum was destroyed.	1食草公牛、2公山羊、1羊羔和2鸭，于**10日**过去时，1鸭，于**12日**过去时，以上**宰杀牲被送入宫殿**，1只育肥公绵羊为**伊南那吉腊努姆仪式**，1只牛后级公绵羊为**阿达德**，2只育肥公绵羊为**贝拉特苏赫尼尔和贝拉特达腊班**，2只牛后级公绵羊和1只食草公绵羊为**满月祭于乌鲁克**，于15日过去时，**经由伊皮克埃腊**，2只牛后级公绵羊为**贝拉特苏赫尼尔和贝拉特达腊班的涂油祭司**，于**15日**过去时，1只雌崽为**伊南那吉腊努姆仪式**，于**17日**过去时第1次，1只雌羊崽为**伊南那吉腊努姆仪式**第2次，**经由我的王后**，3只鸭，于**18日**过去时，2只鸭和1只野鸽，于**19日**过去，以上**宰杀牲被送入宫殿**，从**乌尔卢旮勒埃丁卡支出**。三只手月，乌尔比隆被毁之年。
Š 45 viii/25: **zi-ga** 1 bull, 3 fat rams for **Annunitum**, 1 ram for **Ulmasitum**, in the offering, 1 ram, 1 lamb, for **offering of disappearing place of Belat-S. and Belat-D.**, in **Ur**, **via Ipiq-Erra**, were **withdrawn from Ur-Lugal-edinka**	1 gud-ú, 3 udu-niga ***An-nu-ni-tum***, 1 *udu-ú*, ***^{d} Ul-ma-si-tum***, *ud na-ab-rí-um-ka*, 1 *udu-ú*, 1 *sila$_4$*, *níĝ-ki-zàh-****^{d}Be-la-at-Suh$_6$-nir*** *ù* ***^{d}Be-la-at-Dar-ra-ba-an***, *iti--ta ud-25 ba-ra-zal*, *šà~* **Urim$_5$^{ki}**-ma, gìr ***I-pi$_5$-iq-ìr-ra***, *zi-ga* **Ur-^{d} Lugal-edin-ka**. iti-šu-eš$_5$-ša, mu Ur-bí-lum^{ki} ba-hul. (PDT 1 162, P125579)	1 grass bull, 3 fattened rams for**Annunitum**, 1 grass ram for **Ulmasitum**, in the offering, 1 grass ram, 1 lamb, for **offering of disappearing place of Belat-Suhnir and Belat-Darraban**, when the 25th day passed, in **Ur**, **via Ipiq-Erra**, were **withdrawn from Ur-Lugal-edinka**. Month of šu-ešša, Year of Urbilum was destroyed.	1食草公牛和3育肥公绵羊为**安努尼吞**，1只食草公绵羊为**乌勒马席吞于供奉时**，1只食草公绵羊和1只羊羔为**贝拉特苏赫尼尔和贝拉特达腊班消失处祭**，于本月25日过去时于**乌尔**，**经由伊皮克埃腊**，从**乌尔卢旮勒埃丁卡支出**了。三只手月，乌尔比隆被毁之年。

续表

时间和摘要	文献内容	英文翻译	中文翻译
Š 45 viii/27: **mu-túm, ì-dab$_5$** 2 ducks, 2 birds, from**Watrat**, the overseer, **these were deliveries, Ur-Lugal-edinka took**	2 uz-tur, 2 u$_5$-sim^{mušen}, ***Wa-at-ra-at*** *ugula*, *iti--ta ud-27 ba-ra-zal*, *mu-túm*, **Ur-^{d} Lugal-edin-ka** ì-dab$_5$. iti-šu-eš$_5$-ša, mu Ur-bí-lum^{ki} ba-hul. (MVN 04 105, P114057)	2 ducks, 2 birds, from**Watrat**, the overseer, when the 27th day passed, **these were deliveries, Ur-Lugal-edinka took over**.Month of šu-ešša, Year of Urbilum was destroyed.	2只鸭和1只鸟自**监工瓦特腊特**，于本月27日过去时，以上送入**乌尔卢旮勒埃丁卡接管**了。 三只手月， 乌尔比隆被毁年。
Š 45 ix/13: **zi-ga** 1 ram with emblem, 1 ram for **Abzu**, 1 ram for **Alamuš**, 1 ram for **Ningal**, 1 ram for **Nin-eigara**, 1 kid for **Irhanša**, 1 kid for **Nimin-raba**, 1 kid for **Šulgi**, 1 fat bull, 4 fat rams, 1 lamb for **Dubla-mah**, 1 goat for **Alla-gagia**, 1 fat [ram] for **allowance**, 1 [ram], 1 lamb for **Nin-sun**, 1 [ram] for **allowance**, 1 [ram], 1+ he-goat for **Iškur**, **via my queen**; 2 lamb for **nenegar festival of Belat-Suhnir and Belat-Darraban**, **via Mašum**, were**withdrawn from Ur-Lugal-edinka**, in **Ur**	1 udu-ú-šu-nir, 1 udu-gud-e-ús-sa, **Abzu**--šè, 1 udu **^{d}Alamuš**, 1 udu**^{d}Nin-gal**, 1 udu **^{d}Nin-é-ì-gará**, 1 máš **^{d}Ìr-ha-an-ša**, 1 máš **^{d}Nimin-ra-ba**, 1 máš**^{d}Šul-gi** dumu-An-na, 1 gud-niga, 4 udu-niga, 1 sila$_4$, **Dub-lá-mah**--šè, 1 máš**^{d}Al-la~ gá-gi$_4$-a**, dag **níĝ-gu$_7$-^{d}Nanna**, 1 [udu] -niga, sá-dug$_4$, 1 [udu], 1 sila$_4$, **^{d}Nin-sún**, 1 [udu], sá-dug$_4$, 1 [udu], [1+] máš, **^{d}Iškur**, gìr **nin-ĝá**, 2 kir$_{11}$-ú, **ne-ne- [gar]** -***^{d}Be-la-at-Suh$_6$-nir*** [ù] ***^{d}Be-la-at-Dar-ra-ba-an***, *gìr* ***Ma-šum***, *iti--ta ud-13 ba-zal*, *zi-ga* **Ur-^{d}Lugal-edin-ka**, šà~ Uri$_5$^{ki}-ma.iti-ezem-mah, mu Ur-bí-lum^{ki}ba-hul. (AnOr 07 073, P101368)	1 grass ram with emblem, 1 ram of after-ox-class for**Abzu**, 1 ram for **Alamuš**, 1 ram for **Ningal**, 1 ram for **Nin-eigara**, 1 kid for **Irhanša**, 1 kid for **Nimin-raba**, 1 kid for **Šulgi**, the son of An, 1 fattened bull, 4 fattened rams, 1 lamb for **Dubla-mah**, 1 he-goat for **Alla-gagia**, on the side of the offering of Nanna, 1 fattened [ram] for **monthly allowance**, 1 [ram], 1 lamb for **Nin-sun**, 1 [ram] for **monthly allowance**, 1 [ram], 1+ he-goat for **Iškur**, **via my queen**; 2 grass female lamb for **nenegar festival (of Nippur v) of Belat-Suhnir and Belat-Darraban, via Mašum**, when 13th day passed, were **withdrawn from Ur-Lugal-edinka**, in **Ur**.Month of ezem-mah, Year of Urbilum was destroyed.	1食草标记公绵羊，1牛后级公绵羊为**阿卜朱**，1公绵羊为**阿拉穆什**，1公绵羊为**宁旮勒**，1公绵羊为**宁埃伊旮腊**，1公崽为**伊尔汉沙**，1公崽为**尼敏腊巴**，1公崽为安之子**舒勒吉**，1育肥公牛、4育肥公绵羊和1羔为**大门楼**，1公山羊为**女官院的阿拉女神**，**为南那食物**，1育肥公绵羊为**供奉**，1公绵羊和1羔为**宁苏**，1公绵羊为**供奉**，1公绵羊和1+公山羊为**伊什塔尔**，经**由我的王后**，2食草雌羔为**贝拉特苏赫尼尔和贝拉特达腊班 nenegar 节**，**经由马顺**，于13日过去时，从**乌尔卢旮勒埃丁卡支出了**，**于乌尔**。大庆典月，乌尔比隆被毁年。
Š 45 ix/29: **mu-túm, ì-dab$_5$** 7ducks from **Simat-Ištar**, 1 lamb from **Lugal-turše**, 10 ducks, the **arrears repaid by Apilatum**, were deliveries for **Šulgi-simtum**, **Ur-Lugal-edinka took over**	5 uz-tur, a-rá 1-kam, 2 uz-tur a-rá 2-kam, (Me) ***Simat-Iš$_4$-tár***, 1 *sila$_4$*, **Lugal-tur-šè**, 10 uz-tur, lá-ì su-ga, ***Á-pi$_5$-la-tum***, *iti--ta ud-29 ba-ra-zal*, *mu-túm* ~ ***^{d}Šul-gi-sí-im-tum***, **Ur-^{d}Lugal-edin-ka** ì-dab$_5$. iti-ezem-mah, mu Ur-bí-lum^{ki}ba-hul. (RA 49 86 04, P127829)	5 ducks on 1st time, 2 ducks on 2nd time, from **Simat-Ištar**, 1 lamb from **Lugal-turše**, 10 ducks, the **arrears repaid by Apilatum**, when 29th day passed, were deliveries for **Šulgi-simtum**, **Ur-Lugal-edinka took over**.Month of ezem-mah, Year of Urbilum was destroyed.	5只鸭第1次，2只鸭第2次，来自**席马特伊什塔尔**（**舒勒吉女**），1只羊羔自**卢旮勒图尔塞**，10只鸭自**阿皮拉吞补交的欠款**，于29日过去时，为**舒勒吉新吞的送入项**，**乌尔卢旮勒埃丁卡接管**了。大庆典月，乌尔比隆被毁年。
Š 45 ix /30: **zi-ga** 2+x thicket piglets, the food of today for **the food of my queen**, were **withdrawn from Ur-Lugal-edinka**	2 [+x šáh]^{zah}-tur-giš-gi, níg ud-ba **níĝ-gu$_7$-nin-ĝá**--šè, iti--ta ud-30 ba-ra-zal, zi-ga **Ur-^{d}Lugal-edin-ka**.iti-ezem-mah, mu Ur-bí-lum^{ki}ba-hul. (AnOr 07 074, P101369)	2+x thicket piglets, the food of today for **the food of my queen**, when the 30th day passed, were **withdrawn from Ur-Lugal-edinka**.Month of ezem-mah, Year of Urbilum was destroyed.	2+x只苇塘猪崽，当天的食物为**我的王后的食物**，于30日过去时，从**乌尔卢旮勒埃丁卡支出了**。大庆典月，乌尔比隆被毁年。

续表

时间和摘要	文献内容	英文翻译	中文翻译
Š 45 x/10，12，15： **zi-ga，butchered** 10th：1 fat ram，1 fat lamb，1 thicket piglet，1 duck，1 pigeon and 6 doves for **the food of king**， 12th：2 ducks and 1 pigeon，**butchered ones were sent to palace**， 15th：1 fat ram for **giranum of Inanna**，1 fat ram for **allowance of sacrifice of Adad**，1 fat ram for **allowance of Nin-hursagga**，2 fat rams，and 1 lamb for **Ninlil**，1 ram and 1 lamb for **Enlil**，1 ram for **Nin-gagia**，1 lamb for sacrifice of **Adad**，1 thicket piglet for **food of my queen**， 1**butchered dove** **was sent to palace**， **withdr.fr.Ur-Lugal-edinka**	1 udu-niga，1 sila$_4$-niga，1 šáh-tur-munus-giš-gi，1 uz-tur，1 ir$_7$^{mušen}，6 tu-gur$_4$^{mušen} **níĝ-gu$_7$-lugal**--šè，iti--ta ud-10 ba-ra-zal， 2 uz-tur，1 ir$_7$^{mušen} ba-úš **é-gal-la** ba-an-ku$_4$，iti--ta ud-12 ba-ra-zal，1 udu-niga，sá-dug$_4$ ***gi-ra-núm-*^{d}Inan-a**，1 udu-niga sá-dug$_4$ **siskúr-^{d}Iškur**，1 udu-niga sá-dug$_4$ **^{d}Nin-hur-sag-gá**，2 udu-niga，1 sila$_4$-gaba **^{d}Nin-líl**，1 udu-gud-e-ús-sa，1 sila$_4$，**^{d}En-líl**，1 udu-ú **^{d}Nin-gá-gi$_4$-a**，1 sila$_4$**siskúr-^{d}Iškur**，a-rá 2-kam，1 šáh-tur-munus-giš-gi，**níĝ-gu$_7$-nin-ĝá**--šè，1 tu-gur$_4$^{mušen} ba-úš **é-gal-la** ba-an-ku$_4$，iti--ta ud-15 ba-ra-zal，zi-ga **Ur-^{d}Lugal-eden-ka**.iti-ezem-An-na，mu Ur-bí-lum^{ki} ba-hul. （Nisaba 08 374，P321025）	1 fattened ram，1 fattened lamb，1 thicket female piglet，1 duck，1 pigeon and 6 doves for **the food of king**，when 10^{th}day passed，2 ducks and 1 pigeon，**butchered ones were sent to palace**，when 12^{th}day passed，1 fattened ram for **monthly allowance of giranum festival of Inanna**，1 fattened ram for **allowance of sacrifice of Adad**，1 fattened ram for **monthly allowance of Nin-hursagga**，2 fattened rams，and 1 breast lamb for **Ninlil**，1 ram of after-ox-class and 1 lamb for **Enlil**，1 grass ram for **Nin-gagia**，1 lamb for sacrifice of **Adad**，on the 2nd time，1 thicket female piglet for **food of my queen**，1 **butchered dove was sent to palace**，when 15^{th}day passed，were **withdrawn from Ur-Lugal -edinka**. Month of ezem-Anna，Year of Urbilum was destroyed.	1育肥公绵羊、1育肥羔、1苇塘雌豚、1鸭、1家鸽和6野鸽为**国王的食物**，于**10**日过去时， 2鸭和1家鸽，这些**宰杀牲被送入宫殿**， 于**12**日过去时， 1育肥公绵羊为**伊南那的吉腊努姆仪式的月供**，1育肥公绵羊为**阿达德牺牲的月供**，1育肥公绵羊为**宁胡尔萨旮的月供**，2育肥公绵羊和1胸羔为**宁里勒**，1牛后级公绵羊和1羔为**恩里勒**，1食草公绵羊为**宁旮吉阿**，1羔为**阿达德的牺牲**，第2次，1苇塘雌豚为**我的王后的食物**，1**宰杀野鸽被送入宫殿**，于**15**日过去时，**从乌尔卢旮勒埃丁卡支出**了。 安神庆典月，乌尔比隆被毁年。
Š 45 x/30： **zi-ga，butchered** [1+] rams，1 lamb，[1+] ducks，[1+] pigeonsand 1 thicket piglet，**butchered ones were sent to the palace**	[1+] udu，1 sila$_4$，[1+] uz-tur^{mušen}，[1+] ir$_7$^{mušen}，1 šáh-zah-tur-giš-gi，ba-ug$_7$ **é-gal-la ba-an-ku$_4$**，iti--ta **ud-30** ba-ra-zal，zi-ga. iti-ezem-An-na，mu Ur-bí-lum^{ki} ba-hul.（Nakahara，ST 8）	[1+] rams，1 lamb，[1+] ducks，[1+] pigeonsand 1 thicket piglet，**butchered ones were sent to the palace**，when the 30th day passed，withdrawn. Month of ezem-Anna，Year of Urbilum was destroyed.	1+只公绵羊、1只羔、1+鸭、1+只家鸽和1只苇塘吞为**宰杀牲被送入宫殿**，于30日过去时，支出了。安神庆典月，乌尔比隆被毁年。
Š 45 xi： **mu-túm，ì-dab$_5$** 2 lamb from**Me-Ištar**，were delivery for **Šulgi-simtum，Ur-Lugal-edinka took**	2 sila$_4$，***Simat-Iš$_4$-tár***，*mu-túm* ~ ***^{d}Šul-gi-sí-im-tum***，**Ur-^{d}Lugal-edin-［ka］** ì-dab$_5$.iti-ezem-Me-ki-ĝál.mu Ur-bí-lum^{ki}ba-hul.（OIP 115 085，P123243）	2 lamb from**Me-Ištar**，were delivery for **Šulgi-simtum，Ur-Lugal-edinka took over**. Month of ezem-Mekiĝal，Year of Urbilum was destroyed.	2只羊羔自**席马特伊什塔尔**，为**舒勒吉新吞的送入项**，**乌尔卢旮勒埃丁卡接管**了。神美基旮勒庆典月，乌尔比隆被毁年。
Š 45 xi： **mu-túm，ì-dab$_5$** 1 grass ram，1 lamb from **wife of Apili**，were deliveries for **Šulgi-simtum，Ur-Lugal-edinka took**	1 udu-ú，1 sila$_4$，**dam-*Á-pi$_5$-lí***，*mu-túm*-***^{d}Šul-gi-sí-im-tum***，**Ur-^{d} Lugal-edin-ka** ì-dab$_5$. iti-ezem-Me-ki-ĝál. mu Ur-bí-lum^{ki}ba-hul. （SACT 1 059，P128814）	1 grass ram，1 lamb from **wife of Apili**，were deliveries for **Šulgi-simtum，Ur-Lugal-edinka took over**. Month of ezem-Mekiĝal，Year of Urbilum was destroyed.	1只食草公绵羊和1只羊羔自**阿皮里之妻**，为**舒勒吉新吞的送入项**，**乌尔卢旮勒埃丁卡接管**了。神美基旮勒庆典月，乌尔比隆被毁年。

续表

时间和摘要	文献内容	英文翻译	中文翻译
Š 45 xi/4: **zi-ga, butchered** 1 bull, 1 ram, 1 duck, 1 pigeon, **butchered ones were sent to palace, withdrawn from Ur-Lugal-edinka**	1 gud-ú, 1 udu-ú, 1 uz-tur, 1 ir$_7$ [mušen], ba-úš **é-gal-la** ba-an-ku$_4$, iti--ta ud-4 ba-ra-zal, zi-ga **Ur-Lugal-edinka-ka**.iti-ezem-Me-ki-ĝál, mu Ur-bí-lum[ki] ba-hul. (OIP 115097, P123459)	1 grass bull, 1 grass ram, 1 duck, 1 pigeon, **butchered ones were sent to palace**, when 4th day passed, **withdrawn from Ur-Lugal-edinka**. Month of ezem-Mekiĝal, Year of Urbilum was destroyed.	1食草公牛、1食草公绵羊、1鸭和1家鸽，以上宰杀**牲被送入宫殿**，于4日过去时，**从乌尔卢旮勒埃丁卡支出**。神美基旮勒庆典月，乌尔比隆被毁年。
Š 45 xi/11, 12, 13, 14: **zi-ga, butchered** 11th: 1 **butchered** fattened ewe and 1 lamb was **sent to palace**, Dak-makešše as deputy, 1 kid for **Nin-hursag**, **via Aya-Nanna-arkalla**, 12th: 1 grass montain ram for **giranum festival of Inanna**, **via Aya-Nanna-arkalla**, 1 fattened ram, [1 lamb] for **Ninlil**, 1 fattened ram, 1 lamb for **Enlil**, via my queen, 1 **butchered** fattened ram was **sent to palace**, 13th: 2 grass rams for **Nin-tinug**, 2 ram for **Nin-šubur-e-egir**, **via Aya-Nanna-arkalla**, 1 lamb for **Nin-tinug**, 1 kid for **Šumah**, 1 fattened ram, 1 lamb for **Nin-šubur-e-egir**, 1 fattened bull, 3 fattened rams, 1 lamb for **Nin-tinug**, 2 grass rams for **Nin-nigar**, the early crop of **Nin-tinug**, **via my queen**, 14th: 1 lamb was **sent to palace**, **E-nigil-Nanna** as **deputy**, **withdrawn from Kalam-henagi**	1 u$_8$-niga ba-úš, 1 sila$_4$, **é-gal-la** ba-an-ku$_4$, **Da-ak-ma-kéš-šè** maškim, 1 máš **^{d}Nin-hur-sag** gìr**A-a-[^{d}Nanna]-ar-[kal]-la**, iti--ta ud-[11 ba]-ra-zal, 1 udu hur-s[ag]-ú, ***gi-ra-*[*núm*]-^{d} Inanna**, gìr **A-a-[^{d}Nanna]-ar-[kal]-la**, 1 udu-niga, [1 sila$_4$] **^{d}Nin-líl**, 1 udu-niga, 1 sila$_4$**^{d}En-líl**, gìr **nin-ĝá**, 1 udu-niga ba-úš **é-gal-la** ba-an-ku$_4$, iti--ta **ud-12** ba-ra-zal, 2 udu-ú **^{d}Nin-tin-ug$_5$-ga**, 2 udu-ú**^{d}Nin-šubur-é-egir**, gìr ***A-a-^{d}Nanna-ar-kal-la***, 1 *sila$_4$* **^{d}Nin-tin-ug$_5$-ga**, 1 máš **^{d}Šu-mah**, 1 udu-niga, 1 sila$_4$**^{d}Nin-šubur-é-egir**, 1 gud-niga, 3 udu-niga, 1 sila$_4$ **^{d} Nin-tin-ug$_5$-ga**, 2 udu-ú **^{d}Nin-ni-ĝar**, ú-saĝ **^{d}Nin-tin-ug$_5$-ga**, gìr **nin-ĝá**, iti--ta **ud-13** ba-ra-zal, 1 sila$_4$ **é-gal-la** ba-an-ku$_4$, **É-níĝ-íl-Nanna**maškim (PA.DU), iti--ta **ud-14** ba-ra-zal, zi-ga ki ~ **Kalam-hé-na-gi**--ta. iti-ezem-Me-ki-ĝál, mu Ur-bí-lum[ki] Lu-lu-bu[ki] Si-mu-ru-um[ki] ù Kará-har[ki]aš--šè sag-[du]-bi šu-búr-[a] bí-ra-[a]. (CDLJ 2007: 1 09, P361760)	1**butchered** fattened ewe and 1 lamb was **sent to palace**, Dak-makešše as royal deputy, 1 kid for **Nin-hursag**, **via Aya-Nanna-arkalla**, when [11[th]] day passed, 1 grass montain ram for **giranum festival of Inanna**, **via Aya-Nanna-arkalla**, 1 fattened ram, [1 lamb] for **Ninlil**, 1 fattened ram, 1 lamb for **Enlil**, via my queen, 1 **butchered** fattened ram was **sent to palace**, when 12th day passed, 2 grass rams for **Nin-tinug**, 2 grass ram for **Nin-šubur-e-egir**, **via Aya-Nanna-arkalla**, 1 lamb for **Nin-tinug**, 1 kid for **Šumah**, 1 fattened ram, 1 lamb for **Nin-šubur-e-egir**, 1 fattened bull, 3 fattened rams, 1 lamb for **Nin-tinug**, 2 grass rams for **Nin-nigar**, the early crop of **Nin-tinug**, **via my queen**, when 13th day passed, 1 lamb was**sent to palace**, **E-nigil-Nanna as royal deputy**, when 14th day passed, were **withdrawn from Kalam-henagi**.Month of Mekiĝal, Year of the divine Šulgi king smashed with fist the heads of Urbilum, Lulubu, Simurum and Karahar together.	1宰杀育肥母绵羊和1羔**被送入宫殿**，**达克马凯塞督办**；1公崽为**宁胡尔萨格**，**经由阿亚南那阿尔卡拉**，于【11】日过去时，1食草高山公绵羊**为伊南那的吉腊努姆仪式**，**经由阿亚南那阿尔卡拉**，1育肥公绵羊和【1羔】**为宁里勒**，1育肥公绵羊和1羔为**恩里勒**，**经由我的王后**，1宰杀的**肥公绵羊被送入宫殿**，于**12**日过去时，2食草公绵羊为**宁廷乌格**，2食草公绵羊为**宁舒布尔埃吉尔**，**经由阿亚南那阿尔卡拉**，1羔为**宁廷乌格**，1公崽为**舒马赫**，1育肥公绵羊和1羔为**宁舒布尔埃吉尔**，1育肥公牛、3育肥公绵羊和1羔为**宁廷乌格**，2食草公绵羊为**宁尼旮尔**，宁廷乌格的早稻，**经由我的王后**，于**13**日过去时，1羔被**送入宫殿**，**埃尼格伊勒南那督办**，于**14**日过去时，**从卡兰希那吉支出了**。美基旮勒庆典月，神舒勒吉王以重拳一举击碎乌尔比隆、鲁鲁布、席穆润和卡腊哈尔之头颅之年。

续表

时间和摘要	文献内容	英文翻译	中文翻译
Š 45 xi/17: **zi-ga** 1 fat kid for **food of king**, 1 fat bull, 3 fat rams, 1 lamb for **Nanaya**, 1 fat ram for **Šulgi** in midnight, 1 kid for **sacrifice of ^{d}Bil-ga-mes**, 2 fat rams, 1 lamb for **Nanaya**, 1 ram of after-ox-class for **Šulgi** in midnight, 1 female kid for **sacrifice of Gibil**, 1 lamb for **food of night**, on 2nd time, 2 fattened rams, 1 lamb for **"pouring beer" festival of Nanaya**, in palace, on 3rd time, **via my queen**, were **withdrawn from Kalam-henagi**	1^{f}ašgar-niga **níĝ-gu$_7$-lugal**--šè, 1 gud-niga, 3 udu-niga, 1 sila$_4$ **^{d}Na-na-a**, 1 udu-niga **^{d}Šul-gi**, á-gi$_6$-ba-a, 1^{f}ašgar **siskúr-^{d}Gibil**, ud-1-kam, 2 udu-niga, 1 sila$_4$ **^{d}Na-na-a**, 1 udu-gud-e-ús-sa **^{d}Šul-gi**, á-gi$_6$-ba-a, 1 ^{f}ašgar **siskúr-^{d}Gibil**, 1 sila$_4$ **níĝ-gi$_6$**--šè, ud-2-kam, 2 udu-niga, 1 sila$_4$ **kaš-dé-a-^{d}Na-na-a**, šà~ **é-gal** ud-3-kam, ĝìr **nin-ĝá**, zi-ga ki~ **Kalam-hé-na-gi**--ta, iti--ta ud-17 ba-ra-zal. iti-ezem-Me-ki-ĝál, mu Ur-bí-lum^{ki}ba-hul. (PDT 1 582, P125998)	1 fattened female kid for**food of king**, 1 fattened bull, 3 fattened rams, 1 lamb for **Nanaya**, 1 fattened ram for **Šulgi** in midnight, 1 female kid for **sacrifice of ^{d}Bil-ga-mes**, on 1st time, 2 fattened rams, 1 lamb for **Nanaya**, 1 ram of after-ox-class for **Šulgi** in midnight, 1 female kid for **sacrifice of Gibil**, 1 lamb for **food of night**, on 2nd time, 2 fattened rams, 1 lamb for **"pouring beer" festival of Nanaya**, in palace, on 3rd time, **via my queen**, were **withdrawn from Kalam-henagi**, when 17th day passed. Month of Mekiĝal, Year of Urbilum was destroyed.	1育肥雌崽为**国王的食物**，1育肥公牛、3育肥公绵羊和1羔为**那那亚**， 1育肥公绵羊为**舒勒吉**，于**午夜**，1雌崽为**吉比勒旮美斯的牺牲**，第1次， 2育肥公绵羊和1羔为**那那亚**，1牛后级公绵羊为**舒勒吉**，于**午夜**， 1雌崽为**吉比勒牺牲**，1羔为**黑夜的食物**第2次， 2育肥公绵羊和1羔为**那那亚的啤酒节**，于宫殿，第3次，**经由我的王后**， 从**卡兰希那吉处支出了**，于17日过去时。神美基旮勒庆典月， 乌尔比隆被毁年。
Š 45 xi/20: **zi-ga**, **butchered** 1 fattened ram for**allowance**, 1 goat, 1 fattened mature thicket she-piglet for **the provisions of Éa-nuhši**, via **Beli-bani**, 1 ram, 1 piglet, **butchered ones were sent to palace**, 1 thicket piglet for **food of my queen**, **withdrawn from Ur-Lugal-edinka**	1 udu-niga, **sá-dug$_4$**, 1 máš-gal-gud-e-ús-sa, 1 šáh-tur-munus-geš-gi-gur$_4$-niga, **igi-kár É-a-nu-úh-ši**--šè, ĝìr ***Be-lí-ba-ni***, 1 *udu*, 1 *šáh-tur-nitá*, *ba-úš* **é-gal-la** ba-an-ku$_4$, 1 šáh-tur-munus -geš-gi, **níĝ-gu$_7$-nin-ĝá**--šè, iti--ta ud-20 ba-ra-zal, zi-ga **Ur-^{d} Lugal-edin-ka**. iti-ezem-Me-ki-ĝál, mu Ur-bí-lum^{ki} ba-hul. (CST 484, P107999)	1 fattened ram for**monthly allowance**, 1 he-goat of after-ox -class, 1 fattened mature thicket she-piglet for **the provisions of Éa-nuhši**, via **Beli-bani**, 1 ram, 1 piglet, **butchered ones were sent to palace**, 1 thicket she-piglet for **the food of my queen**, when the 20th day passed, were **withdrawn from Ur-Lugal-edinka**. Month of ezem-Mekiĝal, Year of Urbilum was destroyed.	1只育肥公绵羊为**月供**，1只牛后级公山羊和1只育肥苇塘成熟雌豚为**埃阿努赫西的供给**，**经由贝里巴尼**，1只公绵羊和1只雄豚，这些**宰杀牲被送入宫殿**，1只苇塘雌豚为**我的王后的食物**，于20日过去时，从**乌尔卢旮勒埃丁卡支出了**。神美基旮勒庆典月，乌尔比隆被毁年。
Š 45 xi/24: **zi-ga**, **butchered** 1 ewe, 1 duck, **butchered** ones **were sent to palace**, **withdrawn from Ur-Lugal-edinka**	1 u$_8$, 1 uz-tur, **ba-úš é-gal-la ba-an-ku$_4$**, iti--ta ud-24 ba-ra-zal, zi-ga **Ur-Lugal-edinka-ka**. iti-ezem-Me-ki-ĝál, mu Ur-bí-lum^{ki} ba-hul. (OIP 115 098, P123453)	1 ewe, 1 duck, **butchered** ones **were sent to palace**, when the 24th day passed, **withdrawn from Ur-Lugal-edinka**. Month of ezem-Mekiĝal, Year of Urbilum was destroyed.	1只母绵羊和1只鸭，以上**宰杀牲被送入宫殿**于24日过去时，从**乌尔卢旮勒埃丁卡支出了**。 神美基旮勒庆典月， 乌尔比隆被毁年。

续表

时间和摘要	文献内容	英文翻译	中文翻译
Š 45 xii/**16**，**x**： **zi-ga**，**butchered** 1 fattened ram for **allowance of giranum festival of Inanna**，1 ram，1 duck，**butchered ones were sent to palace**，1 fattened ram of after-ox-class for **Nanna**，1 fat ram for **Adad**，1 ram for **allowance of**［^{d}**Inanna**］，［1+ **dead** bull］**sent to palace**，**withdrawn from Ur-Lugal-edinka**	1 udu-niga，**sá-dug$_4$** ***gi-ra-núm*-Inanna**，1 udu，1 uz-tur，ba-úš **é-gal-la** ba-an-ku$_4$，iti--ta **ud-16** ba-ra-zal， ［1］udu-niga-gud-e-ús-sa，［^{d}］**Nanna**，［1］udu-niga-gud-e-ús-sa，**Iškur**， ［1 udu］sá-dug$_4$［^{d}Inanna］， ［lines missing］，（rev.） ［1+gud］ba-úš **é-gal-la** ba-an］-ku$_4$，iti--ta **ud-x**ba］-ra-zal， zi-ga**Ur-Lugal-edinka-ka**.iti-še-kin-kud， mu Ur-bí-lum^{ki} ba-hul. （OIP 115 100，P123609）	1 fattened ram for **monthly allowance of giranum festival of Inanna**，1 ram，1 duck，**butchered ones were sent to palace**，when**16th**day passed，1 fattened ram of after-ox-class for **Nanna**，1 fattened ram of after-ox-class for **Adad**，1 ram for **monthly allowance of**［^{d}**Inanna**］，［1+ **dead** bull］**sent to palace**，when**xth**day passed，were **withdrawn from Ur-Lugal-edinka**.Month of še-kin-kud，Year of Urbilum was destroyed.	1育肥公绵羊为**伊南那得吉腊努姆仪式之月供**，1公绵羊和1鸭，**以上宰杀牲被送入宫殿**，于**16**日过去时，1只育肥牛后级公绵羊为**南那**，1只育肥牛后级公绵羊为**阿达德**，1只公绵羊为【**伊南那**】**的月供**，【1+】头【公牛】**被送入宫殿**，于**x**日过去时，从**乌尔卢旮勒埃丁卡支出**了。 大麦收割月， 乌尔比隆被毁年。
Š 45 xii/20-22： **zi-ga** 20th：1 fat ram for **allowance**，1 lamb for **Inanna**，1 kid for **Nin-urta**，1 kid for **Nusku**， 21st：1 fat ram，1 lamb for **Enlil**，1［fat ram for **allowance of Ninlil**］， 22nd：1 lamb for **Enlil**，1 fattened ram for **monthly allowance of Ninlil**，1 ram for **Nin-hursagga**，for sacrifice in **Nippur**，**via my queen**，**withdrawn from Ur-Lugal-edinka**	1 udu-niga**sá-dug$_4$**， 1 sila$_4$ ^{d}**Inanna**， 1 máš^{d}**Nin-urta**， 1 máš^{d} **Nusku**，iti--ta **ud-20** ba-ra-zal，1 udu-niga，1 sila$_4$，^{d}**En-líl**，1［udu-niga，sá-dug$_4$ ^{d}**Nin-líl**］， （rev.）iti-［ta**ud-21**ba-ra-zal］， 1 sila$_4$ **Enlil**，1 udu-niga sá-dug$_4$ **Nin-lil**，1 udu ^{d}**Nin-hur-sag-gá**，iti--ta ud-22 ba-ra-zal，ér-siskúr šà ~ **Ni-bru^{ki}**，gìr **nin-ĝá**，zi-ga **Ur-^{d}Lugal-edin-ka**.iti-še-kin-kud，mu Ur-bí-lum^{ki}ba-hul. （OIP 115099，P123551）	1 fattened ram for**monthly allowance**，1 lamb for **Inanna**，1 kid for **Nin-urta**，1 kid for **Nusku**，when **20th**day passed，1 fattened ram，1 lamb for **Enlil**，1［fattened ram for **monthly allowance of Ninlil**］，when［**21st**day passed］，1 lamb for **Enlil**，1 fattened ram for **monthly allowance of Ninlil**，1 ram for **Nin-hursagga**，when **22nd**day passed，for sacrifice in **Nippur**，**via my queen**，**withdrawn from Ur-Lugal-edinka**.Month of še-kin-kud，Year of Urbilum was destroyed.	1育肥公绵羊为**月供**，1羔为**伊南那**，1公崽为**宁乌尔塔**，1公崽为**努斯库**，于**20**日过去时，1育肥公绵羊和1羊羔为**恩里勒**，【育肥公绵羊为**宁里勒**，于**21**日过去时，1只羊羔为**恩里勒**，1【育肥公绵羊】为**宁里勒月供**，1只公绵羊为**宁胡尔萨旮**，于**22**日过去时，**尼普尔城中的哀悼祭祀**，**经由我的王后**，**从乌尔卢旮勒埃丁卡支出**了。大麦收割月，乌尔比隆被毁年。
Š 46 i/8，15： **mu-túm**，**ì-dab$_5$** 1 duck，5 doves from**Šalim-x**，20 doves，from the **son of Ṣiluš-Dagan**，3 pigeons from **Lu-kiri-zal**，8 doves from **the wife of Šarakam**，2 thicket boars from **Simat-Ištar**，were deliveries for **Šulgi-simtum**，**Ur-Lugal-edinka took over**	1 uz-［tur］，5 tu-［gur$_4$^{mušen}］，***Ša-lim-x-***［...］，20 tu-gur$_4$［^{mušen}］，**dumu** ***Ṣi-lu*$^{!}$*-<uš>-Da-gan***，*iti--ta* **ud-8** ba-ra-zal，3 ir$_7$^{mušen} **Lú-kirì -zal**，8 tu-gur$_4$^{mušen}，**dam-^{d}Šará -kam**，2 šáh^{zah}-tur-nitá-geš-gi，**Simat-Iš$_4$-tár**，*iti--ta* **ud-15** ba-ra-zal，mu-túm-^{d}***Šul-gi-sí -im-tum***，**Ur-^{d}Lugal-edin-ka** ì-［dab$_5$］.iti-maš-dà$^{!}$-［gu$_7$］，mu ús-sa Ur$^{?}$-［bí］-lum^{ki} ba-［hul］. （JCS 29 117 1，P112087）	1 duck，5 doves from**Šalim-x**，20 doves，from the **son of Ṣiluš-Dagan**，when the **8th** day， 3 pigeons from**Lu-kiri-zal**， 8 doves from**the wife of Šarakam**，2 thicket boars from **Simat-Ištar**，when the **15th** day passed，were deliveries for **Šulgi-simtum**，**Ur-Lugal-edinka took over**.Month of mašda ~ gu$_7$，Year after that of Urbilum was destroyed.	1只鸭和5只野鸽来自**沙林**，20只野鸽来自**采鲁什达干之子**，于**8**日过去时，3只家鸽来自**鲁基瑞扎勒**，8只野鸽来自**沙腊坎之妻**，2只苇塘公猪来自**席马特伊什塔尔**，于**15**日过去时，**为舒勒吉新吞的送入项**，**乌尔卢旮勒埃丁卡接管**了。食瞪羚月，乌尔比隆被毁年之次年。

续表

时间和摘要	文献内容	英文翻译	中文翻译
Š 46 i/18: **zi-ga, butchered** 1 fattened ram, 1 ewe fo**r the sacrifice in the palace, for Belat-Suhnir and Belat-Darraban**, 1 duck for the **sacrifice for bird house**, 1 **butchered duck was sent to the palace**, were **withdrawn from Ur-Lugal-edinka**	1 udu-niga**sá-dug$_4$**, 1 u$_8$ siskúr šà ~ é-gal, ^{d} ***Be-la-at-Suh-nir*** *ù* ^{d}***Be-la-at-Dar-ra-ba-an***, 1 uz-tur siskúr **é-mušen**, 1 uz-tur ba-úš **é-gal-la** <ba>-an-ku$_4$, iti--ta ud-18 ba-ra-zal, zi-ga-**Ur-^{d}Lugal-eden-ka**.iti-maš-dà ~ gu$_7$, mu ús-sa Ur-bí-lum^{ki} ba-hul. (OIP 115 101, P123679)	1 fattened ram, 1 ewe for **the sacrifice in the palace, for Belat-Suhnir and Belat-Darraban**, 1 duck for the **sacrifice for bird house**, 1 **butchered duck was sent to the palace**, when 18th day passed, were **withdrawn from Ur-Lugal-edinka**. Month of mašda ~ gu$_7$, Year after that of Urbilum was destroyed.	1只育肥公绵羊和1只母绵羊为**于宫殿的祭祀，为贝拉特苏赫尼尔和贝拉特达腊班**，1只鸭为**家禽房的祭祀**，1只**宰杀鸭被送入宫殿**， 于18日过去时， **从乌尔卢旮勒埃丁卡支出了**。食瞪羚月， 乌尔比隆被毁年之次年。
Š 46 ii/1 =45'（ús-sa）ix': **mu-túm, ì-dab$_5$** 1 lamb, 1 thicket male piglet, [x] from**the man of Urub**, 1 lamb from [**the man of...**], [1+] dove from **X-Dagandan**, [1] lamb was brought from **the palace**, 1 lamb from **Imid-ilum**, were **deliveries for Šulgi-simti**, **Ur-Lugal-edinka-ka took**	1 sila$_4$, 1 šáh^{zah}-tur-nitá-giš-< gi >, [x] **lú-Urub** (**URUxKÁR**)^{ki}, [1] sila$_4$ [lú-X]^{ki}, [1+ tu]-gur$_4$^{mušen}, [**X-^{d}**] ***Da-gan-dan***, [1] *sila$_4$* [*é-g*] *al-la--ta è-a*, [1] *sila$_4$* ***I-mid-ilum***, *iti--ta ud-1 ba-ra-zal*, *mu-túm-* ^{d}***Šul-gi-sí-im-ti***, **Ur-^{d} Lugal-eden-ka** ì-dab$_5$. iti-ze$_x$-da ~ gu$_7$, mu ús-sa Ur-bí-lum^{ki} ba-hul. (OIP 115086, P123485)	1 lamb, 1 thicket male piglet, [x] from**the man of Urub**, 1 lamb from [**the man of...**], [1+] dove from **X-Dagandan**, [1] lamb was brought from **the palace**, 1 lamb from **Imid-ilum**, when 1st day passed, were **deliveries for Šulgi-simti**, **Ur-Lugal-edinka-ka took over**. Month of zeda ~ gu$_7$, Year after that of Urbilum was destroyed.	1只羔和1只苇塘雄豚，【x】来自**乌如卜城的人**，1只羔来自【……**的人**】，【1+】只野鸽来自**X-达干丹**，【1】只羔从**宫殿带来**，1只羔来自**伊米德伊隆**，于1日过去时，**为舒勒吉新提的送入项**，**乌尔卢旮勒埃邓卡接管**了。食豚月，乌尔比隆被毁年之次年。
Š 46 ii=45'（ús-sa）ix' /4, 6: **zi-ga, butchered** 4th: 1 kid for **Nin-egal**, 1 lamb for **Inanna**, 1 lamb for **Nin-sun**, 1 fattened lamb for **Inanna** on 2nd time, 1 fattened he-goat, 1 **butchered** grass ram **sent to palace**, 1 ducklet for **food of my queen**, 6th: 1 fattened ram for **offering of Allatum**, 1 ram for **Ordeal Divine River**, were **withdrawn from Ur-Lugal-edinka-ka**	1^f ašgar-gud-e-ús-sa ^{d}**Nin-é-gal**, 1 sila$_4$ ^{d} **Inanna**, 1 sila$_4$ ^{d} **Nin-sún**, 1 sila$_4$-niga ^{d}**Inanna** a-rá-2-kam, 1 máš-gal-niga, 1 udu-ú **ba-úš é-gal-la** ba-an-ku$_4$, 1 amar-sag-uz-tur níĝ-gu$_7$-**nin-ĝá**--šè, iti--ta-**ud-4**ba-ra-zal, 1 udu-niga sá-dug$_4$-^{d} ***Al-la-tum***, 1 *udu* ^{d}**I$_7$-lú-ru-gú**, iti--ta **ud-6**ba-ra-zal, zi-ga-**Ur-^{d} Lugal-edin-< ka >**. iti-ze$_x$-da ~ gu$_7$, mu ús-sa Ur-bí-lum^{ki} ba-hul. (OIP 115 102, P123404)	1 female kid of after-ox-class for**Nin-egal**, 1 lamb for **Inanna**, 1 lamb for **Nin-sun**, 1 fattened lamb for **Inanna** on 2nd time, 1 fattened he-goat, 1 **butchered** grass ram **sent to palace**, 1 ducklet for **food of my queen**, when 4thday passed, 1 fattened ram for **offering of Allatum**, 1 ram for **Ordeal Divine River**, when 6thday passed, were **withdrawn from Ur-Lugal-edinka-ka**. Month of zeda ~ gu$_7$, Year after that of Urbilum was destroyed.	1只牛后级雌崽为**宁埃旮勒**，1只羔为**伊南那**， 1只羔为**宁苏**，1只育肥羔为**伊南那第2次**， 1只育肥公山羊，1只**宰杀的食草公绵羊被送入宫殿**，1只幼鸭为**王后的食物**，于**4日**过去时， 1只育肥公绵羊为**阿拉吞的供奉**，1只公绵羊为**神判河神**，于**6日**过去时，**从乌尔卢旮勒埃丁卡支出了**。食豚月， 乌尔比隆被毁年之次年。
Š 46 iii =45'（ús-sa）x': **mu-túm, ì-dab$_5$** 81 sows, 108 mature boars, 15mother sows, 15 pigs, which were brought fr. **Naqabtum fold**, fr. **Kalam-he-nagi**, **Buqušum took over**	81 sáh-gur$_4$-mí, 108 sáh-gur$_4$-nitá, 15 sáh-ama-gan, 15 sáh-nitá, ***Na-qab-tum***--*ta è-a*, *ki* **Kalam-hé-na-gi**--ta ***Bu-qú-šum*** *ì-dab$_5$.iti-u$_5$-bí-gu$_7$*, *mu ús-sa Ur-bí-lum^{ki} ba-hul.* (*OIP* 115 132, *P123569*)	81 *mature sows*, 108 *mature boars*, 15*mother sows*, 15 *pigs*, *which were brought from* **Naqabtum fold**, from **the place of Kalam-he-nagi**, **Buqušum took over**.Month of ubi ~ gu$_7$, Year after that of Urbilum was destroyed.	81成熟只母猪、108成熟只公猪、15只母猪和15只公猪，**从王家兽苑卡兰希那吉**处带来了，**布苦顺接管**了。食乌比乌月，乌尔比隆被毁年之次年。

续表

时间和摘要	文献内容	英文翻译	中文翻译
Š 46 iii=45'（ús-sa）x' /3： **mu-túm，ì-dab$_5$** 6 pigeons from**Etelpu-Dagan**，the fattener，5 grass rams from **Babatum，wife of Nunida**，were deliveries for **Šulgi-simtum，Ur-Lugal-edinka-ka took**	6 ir$_7$^{mušen}［*E-te-el*］*-pù-^{d}Da-gan gurušda*!，5 *udu-ú* ***Ba-ba-tum* dam-*Nu-ni-d*** ［*a*］，［*iti*］*--ta-ud-3*［*ba-ra-zal*］，［*m*］*u-tú*［*m～*］***^{d}Šul-gi*］*-s*［*í-im-tum*］**，*Ur-*^{d} **Lugal-eden-ka** ì-dab$_5$.iti-u$_5$-bí-gu$_7$，［mu］-ús-sa Ur-bí-［lum$^{k]i}$ ba-hul. （PDT 2 1035，P126375）	6 pigeons from**Etelpu-Dagan**，the fattener，5 grass rams from **Babatum，wife of Nunida**，when the 3rd day passed，were deliveries for **Šulgi-simtum，Ur-Lugal-edinka-ka took over**.Month of ubi～gu$_7$，Year after that of Urbilum was destroyed.	6只家鸽来自**埃台勒普达干育肥师**，5只食草公绵羊来自**努尼达之妻巴巴吞**，于本月3日过去时，**为舒勒吉新吞的送入项，乌尔卢旮勒埃邓卡接管**了。食乌比鸟月，乌尔比隆被毁年之次年。
Š 46 iii=45'（ús-sa）x' /6： **zi-ga，butchered** 1 lamb，1 pigeon and 2 doves，**butchered** ones **were sent to palace，withdrawn from Ur-Lugal-edenka**	1 sila$_4$，1 ir$_7$^{mušen}，2 tu-gur$_4$^{mušen}，ba-ug$_7$ **é-gal-la ba-an-ku$_4$**，iti--ta ud-6 ba-ra-zal，zi-ga **Ur-^{d} Lugal-eden-ka**.iti-u$_5$-bí～gu$_7$，mu ús-sa Ur-bí-lum^{ki} ba-hul. （AAICAB 1，2，Ashm.1935-554）	1 lamb，1 pigeon and 2 doves，**butchered** ones **sent to palace**，when 6th day passed，**withdrawn from Ur-Lugal-edenka**. Month of ubi～gu$_7$，Year after that of Urbilum was destroyed.	1只羔、1只家鸽和2只野鸽**为宰杀牲被送入宫殿**，于6日过去时，**从乌尔卢旮勒埃邓卡支出了**。食乌比鸟月，乌尔比隆被毁年之次年。
Š 46 iii=45'（ús-sa）xi' /26-29： **zi-ga，butchered** 26th：1 thicket piglet and 5 doves for **the food of my queen**，when they were catched in the New Moon，27th：1 thicket male piglet for **the food of my queen**，4 ducks and 1 pigeon were **butchered**，sent to palace，28th：1 **butchered** ram was **sent to palace**， 29th：1 fattened ram for **giranum festival of**［…］，1 fattened ram for **sacrifice of Inanna，in the palace**，1 fat ram for **allowance**，1 ram and 1 kid for **sacrifice of New Moon，in Uruk**，2 ewes，1 he-goat and 5 lambs for **Abum，in Ur**，**via Ur-Dumuzida**，2 rams and 2 goats for **sister of Ṣiluš-Dagan**，**withdrawn from Ur-Lugal-edenka**	1šáh-zah-tur-munus-giš-gi，5 tu-gur$_4$^{mušen}，**níĝ-gu$_7$-nin-ĝá**--šè，ud-dab$_5$-ba，**ud-sakar**，iti--ta ud-26 ba-ra-zal， 1šáh-zah-tur-níta-giš-gi，**níĝ-gu$_7$-nin-ĝá**--šè，4 uz-tur，1 ir$_7$^{mušen}，ba-ug$_7$，**é-gal-la ba-an-ku$_4$**，iti--ta ud-27 ba-ra-zal， 1 udu-gud-e-ús-sa，ba-ug$_7$ **é-gal-la ba-an-ku$_4$**，iti--ta ud-28 ba-ra-zal， 1 udu-niga，***gi-ra-núm-^{d}***［…］，1 udu-niga **sískur-^{d} Inanna**，šà～é-gal-la，1 udu-niga，**sá-dug$_4$**，1 udu-niga-e-ús-sa，1 máš **siskur-ud-sakar**，**šà～Unug^{ki}-ga**，2 u$_8$，1 máš-gal，5 sila$_4$，***A-bu-um*--šè**，**šà～Urim$_5$^{ki}-ma**，［iti］--ta ud-30-lá-1 ba-ra-zal， gìr **Ur-^{d}Dumu-zi-da**， 2 udu，2 máš-gal，**nin$_9$-*Ṣi-lu-uš-^{d}Da-gan*--šè**， *zi-ga***Ur-^{d}Lugal-eden-ka**.iti-u$_5$-bí～gu$_7$，mu ús-sa Ur-bí-lum^{ki} ba-hul. （AAICAB 1，4 Trampitsch 81）	1 thicket female piglet and 5 doves for **the food of my queen**，when they were catched in the New Moon，when the **26th**day passed；1 thicket male piglet for **the food of my queen**，4 ducks and 1 pigeon were **butchered**，sent to palace，when the **27th**day passed；1 **butchered** ram of after-ox-class was **sent to palace**，when the **28th**day passed；1 fattened ram for **giranum festival of**［…］，1 fattened ram for **sacrifice of Inanna，in the palace**，1 fattened ram for **monthly allowance**，1 ram of after-ox-class and 1 kid for **sacrifice of New Moon，in Uruk**，2 ewes，1 he-goat and 5 lambs for **Abum，in Ur**，when the 29thday passed，**via Ur-Dumuzida**，2 rams and 2 he-goats for **the sister of Ṣiluš-Dagan**，were **withdrawn from Ur-Lugal-edenka**. Month of ubi～gu$_7$，Year after that of Urbilum was destroyed.	1苇塘雌豚和5野鸽为**我的王后的食物**，当它们在新月初被抓住，于26日过去时；1苇塘雄豚为**我的王后的食物**，4鸭和1家鸽为宰杀牲被送入宫殿， 于27日过去时；1**宰杀的牛后级公绵羊被送入宫殿**，于28日过去时， 1只育肥公绵羊为【……】**的吉腊努姆仪式**，1育肥公绵羊为**宫殿中的伊南那牺牲**，1育肥公绵羊为**月供**，1牛后级公绵羊和1公崽为**新月牺牲，于乌鲁克**，2只母绵羊、1只公山羊和5只羔为**阿布姆，于乌尔**，于29日过去时，**经由乌尔杜穆兹达**，2只公绵羊和2只公山羊为**采鲁什达干之妹**，以上**从乌尔卢旮勒埃邓卡支出了**。 食乌比鸟月， 乌尔比隆被毁年之次年。

续表

时间和摘要	文献内容	英文翻译	中文翻译
Š 46 iv=45'（ús-sa）xi' /24： **mu-túm，ì-dab$_5$** 1 lamb fr. **Ninlil-hemti**，1 lamb new born at **the house of fattener**，3 pigeons，1 lamb fr. **Ninlil-hemti**，deliveries for **Šulgi-simtum**，**Ur-Lugal-edinka took over**	1 sila$_4$ ^{d}**Nin-líl-hé-em-ti**，1 sila$_4$ ù-tu-da **é-gurušda**，3 ir$_7$^{mušen} a-rá 1-kam，1 sila$_4$ a-rá 2-kam，^{d}**Nin-líl-hé-em-ti**，iti--ta ud-24 ba-ra-zal，mu-túm ~ ***^{d}Šul-gi-sí-im-tum***，**Ur-^{d}Lugal-edin-ka** ì-dab$_5$. iti-ki-siki-^{d}Nin -a-zu，mu ús-sa Ur-bí-lum^{ki} ba-hul.（MVN 13 664，P117437）	1 lamb from**Ninlil-hemti**，1 lamb new born at **the house of fattener**，3 pigeons on 1st time，1 lamb on 2nd time，from **Ninlil-hemti**，when 24th day passed，were deliveries for **Šulgi-simtum**，**Ur-Lugal-edinka took over**. Month of ki-siki-Ninazu，Year after that of Urbilum was destroyed.	1只羔来自**宁里勒希姆提**，1只新生羔来自育肥房，3只家鸽第1次，1只羔第2次，来自**宁里勒希姆提**，于24日过去时，**为舒勒吉新吞的送入项**，**乌尔卢旮勒埃丁卡接管了**。神宁阿朱羊毛作坊月，乌尔比隆被毁年之次年。
Š 46 v=45'（ús-sa）xii' /20： **zi-ga**，**butchered** 1 lamb for **"disappearing place" of Nanaya**，3 **butchered doves were sent to palace**，1 kid for **the gate of bedroom of high priestess**，2 doves for **food of my queen**，**withdr. fr. Ur-Lugal-edinka**，in **Uruk**	1 sila$_4$ **níĝ~ ki-zàh-^{d}Na-na-a**， 3 tu-gur$_4$^{mušen} ba-úš **é-gal-la ba-an-ku$_4$**， 1 máš**ká~ĝi$_6$-par$_4$-ra**， 2 tu-gur$_4$^{mušen} **níĝ-gu$_7$-nin-ĝá**--šè，iti--ta ud-20 ba-ra-zal，zi-ga-**Ur-^{d} Lugal-edin-ka**，šà ~ **Unug^{ki}**-ga. iti-ezem-^{d}Nin-a-zu，mu ús-sa Ur-bí-lum^{ki} ba-hul. （OIP 115 103，P123592）	1 lamb for**sacrifice of "disappearing place" of Nanaya**，3 **butchered doves were sent to palace**，1 kid for **the gate of bedroom of high priestess**，2 doves for **food of my queen**，when 20th day passed，were **withdrawn from Ur-Lugal-edinka**，in **Uruk**. Month of ezem-Ninazu，Year after that of Urbilum was destroyed.	1只羔为**那那亚的消失处供奉**，3只**宰杀的野鸽被送入宫殿**，1只公崽为**女观院之门**，2只野鸽为**我的王后的食物**， 于20日过去时，**从乌尔卢旮勒埃丁卡支出了**， 于**乌鲁克**。 神宁阿朱庆典月，乌尔比隆被毁年之次年。
Š 45'（ús-sa）xii' =46 v/21： **zi-ga** 1 kid for Adad，**via Šulgi-ili**， 2 kids for**Belat-Suhnir and Belat-Darraban**， **via Nur-Sin**， 2 fat rams，1 ram，1 goat，1 lamb，1 kid for **Belat-Suhnir and Belat-Darraban**，1 kid for **Ordeal Divine River**，**via my queen**，were**withdrawn from Ur-Lugal-edinka**，in **Ur**	1 máš^{d}**Iškur**，gìr ***^{d}Šul-gi-ì-lí***，2 *máš* ***^{d}Be-la-at-Suh-nir*** *ù* ***^{d}Be-la-at-Dar-ra-ba-an***，gìr **Nu-úr-^{d}Suen**，2 udu-niga，1 udu-ú，1 máš-gal，1 sila$_4$，1 máš ***^{d}Be-la-at-Suh-nir*** *ù* ***^{d}Be-la-at-Dar-ra-ba-an***，1 *máš* **^{d}I$_7$-lú-ru-gú** gìr **nin-ĝá**，iti--ta ud-21 ba-ta-zal，zi-ga **Ur-^{d} Lugal-edin-ka**，šà~ **Urim^{ki}**-ma. iti-ezem-^{d}Nin-a-zu，mu ús-sa Ur-bí-lum^{ki}ba-hul. （JCS 35 183 1，P112145）	1 kid for Adad，**via Šulgi-ili**，2 kids for **Belat-Suhnir and Belat-Darraban**，**via Nur-Sin**，2 fattened rams，1 grass ram，1 he-goat，1 lamb，1 kid for **Belat-Suhnir and Belat-Darraban**，1 kid for **Ordeal Divine River**，**via my queen**，when 21st day passed，were **withdrawn from Ur-Lugal-edinka**，in **Ur**. Month of ezem-Ninazu，Year after that of Urbilum was destroyed.	1公崽为**阿达德**，**经由舒勒吉伊里**，2公崽为**贝拉特苏赫尼尔和贝拉特达腊班**，**经由努尔辛**，2育肥公绵羊、1食草公绵羊、1公山羊、1羔和1公崽为**贝拉特苏赫尼尔和贝拉特达腊班**，1公崽为**神判河神**，**经由我的王后**，于21日过去时，**从乌尔卢旮勒埃丁卡支出**，于**乌尔**。神宁阿朱庆典月，乌尔比隆被毁年之次年。
Š 46 v=45'（ús-sa）xii'： **mu-túm，ì-dab$_5$** 2 la［mbs］fr. **Ninlil-Tumimti**，were **delivery for Šulgi-simti**，**Apilliya took over**	2 si［la$_4$］^{d}**Nin-líl-Tu［m］-im-ti**，mu-túm~ ***^{d}Šul-gi-sí-im-ti***，***Á-pil-lí-a*** *ì-dab$_5$. iti-ezem-^{d}N［in -a-zu］*，*mu-ús-［sa Ur］-b［í-lum^{ki} ba-hul］*.（*Torino* 44）	2 *la［mbs］from***Ninlil-Tumimti**，were **delivery for Šulgi-simti**，**Apilliya took over**. Month of ezem-N［inazu］，Year af［ter］that of Urb［ilum was destroyed］.	2只羔来自**宁里勒吞伊姆提**，**为舒勒吉新提的送入项**，**阿皮拉提接管了**。神宁阿朱庆典月，乌尔比隆被毁年之次年。

续表

时间和摘要	文献内容	英文翻译	中文翻译
Š 46 vi=46'（ús-sa）i' /22: **zi-ga，butchered** 1 dove for **food of my queen**，1 duck，3 pigeons，2 doves，**butchered ones were sent to the palace**，**withdrawn from Ur-Lugal-edinka**	1 tu-gur$_4^{mušen}$，**níĝ-gu$_7$-nin-ĝá**--šè，1 uz-tur，3 ir$_7^{mušen}$，2 tu-gur$_4^{mušen}$，ba-úš **é-gal-la ba-an-ku$_4$**，iti--ta ud-22 ba-ra-zal，zi-ga-**Ur-^{d}Lugal-edin-ka**.iti-á-ki-ti，mu ús-sa Ur-bí-lum^{ki}ba-hul.（TRU 280，P135044）	1 dove for **the food of my queen**，1 duck，3 pigeons，2 doves，**butchered ones were sent to the palace**，when the 22nd day passed，were **withdrawn from Ur-Lugal-edinka**. Month of akiti，Year after that of Urbilum was destroyed.	1只野鸽为**我的王后的食物**，1只鸭、3只家鸽和2只野鸽，**这些宰杀牲被送入宫殿**，于22日过去时，**从乌尔卢旮勒埃丁卡支出了**。阿基提月，乌尔比隆被毁年次年。
Š 46 vi=46'（ús-sa）i' /25: **zi-ga，butchered** [1] fattened bull，3 fattened rams for**the boat of An**，1 grass ram for **"night staying" shrine**，1 kid for **Nanaya**，in **Uruk**，**via Nur-Sin**，**withdr. fr. Ur-Lugal-edinka**	[1] gud-niga，3 udu-niga，**má-An-na**--šè，1 udu-ú，èš-gi$_6$~zal--šè，1 máš，**^{d}Na-na-a**--šè，iti--ta ud-25 ba-ra-zal，šà~**Unug^{ki}**-ga，ĝìr **Nu-úr-^{d}Suen**，zi-ga-**Ur-^{d}Lugal-edin-ka**.iti-á-ki-ti，mu ús-sa Ur-bí-lum^{ki} ba-hul.（Torino 1 189，P133902）	[1] fattened bull，3 fattened rams for**the boat of An**，1 grass ram for **"night staying" shrine**，1 kid for **Nanaya**，when 25th day passed，in **Uruk**，**via Nur-Sin**，were **withdrawn from Ur-Lugal-edinka**. Month of akiti，Year after that of Urbilum was destroyed.	1育肥公牛和3育肥公绵羊为**安神之船**，1只食草公绵羊为"**黑夜圣殿**"，1公崽为**那那亚**，于25日过去时，**于乌鲁克**，**经由努尔辛**，**从乌尔卢旮勒埃丁卡**支出了。阿基提月，乌尔比隆被毁年次年。
Š 46 vi=46'（ús-sa）i'： **lá-ì su-ga** 1 ram，arrear repaid by Apilatum，Ur-Lugal-edinka took	1 udu-ú，lá-ì su-ga，***Á-pi$_5$-la-tum***，**Ur-^{d}Lugal-edin-ka** ì-dab$_5$. iti-á-ki-ti，mu ús-sa Ur-bí-lum^{ki}ba-hul.（BIN 3 310，P106116）	1 grass ram，**the arrear repaid by Apilatum**，**Ur-Lugal-edinka took over**. Month of akiti，Year after that of Urbilum was destroyed.	**阿皮拉吞补交的1食草公绵羊的欠款，乌尔卢旮勒埃丁卡接管**。阿基提月，乌尔比隆被毁年次年。
Š 46 vii=46' ii'： **mu-túm，ì-dab$_5$** 118 sheep and 2 big he-goats，delivered from**king**，from **Naram-ili**，**Šulgi-simti** took over	118 udu，2 máš-gal，mu-túm-lugal，ki~***Na-ra-am-ì-lí--ta***，***^{d}Šul-gi-sí-im -ti*** *ì-dab$_5$.iti-ezem-^{d}Šul-gi*，*mu Ki-maš^{ki} ù Hu-ur$_5$-ti^{ki} ba-hul.*（*Torino* 1 023，*P*131922）	118 *sheep and* 2 *big he-goats*，*delivered from***king**，from **Naram-ili**，**Šulgi-simti** took over. Month of Ezem-Šulgi. Year of Kimaš and Hurti were destroyed.	118绵羊和2公山羊，**王送牲**，**从那冉伊里处**，**舒勒吉希姆提接管了**。神舒勒吉庆典，基马什和胡尔提被毁灭之年。
Š 46 vi=46'（ús-sa）i'： **zi-ga** 1 ewe and 1 kid for **temple of Belat-Suhnir**，1 fattened ram for **sacrifice of Nanna**，2 fattened rams，1 duck，2 pigeons，5 doves and 1 thicket male piglet for **the king**，**in Karzida**，2 lambs for the **disappearing place of [Belat-Su] hnir and [Belat] -Dar [raban]**	1 u$_8$，1 máš **é-*^{d}Be-la-at-Suh-nir***，*má-^{d}Nanna á-ki-ti ĝen-a-ni*，1 *udu-niga* **sískur-^{d}Nanna** ud-á-ki-ti，2 udu-niga，1 uz-tur，2 ir$_7^{mušen}$，5 tu-gur$_4^{mušen}$，1 šáh-zah-tur-níta-giš-gi ki-**lugal**--šè，Kar-zi-da^{ki}--šè，2 sila$_4$，níĝ-ki-zàh ***^{d}[Be-la-at-Su] h-nir*** *ù* [***^{d}Be-la-at***] ***-Dar-[ra-ba-an]***，[…]，*iti-á-ki-ti*，*mu ús-sa Ur-bí-lum^{ki} ba-hul.*（*NYPL* 048，*P*122584）	1 *ewe and* 1 *kid for* **the temple of Belat-Suhnir**，when she went in the boat of Nanna in the month of akiti，1 fattened ram for **the sacrifice of Nanna**，in the month of akiti，2 fattened rams，1 duck，2 pigeons，5 doves and 1 thicket male piglet for **the king**，**in Karzida**，2 lambs for the **disappearing place of [Belat-Su] hnir and [Belat] -Dar [raban]**，[…]，Month of akiti，Year after that of Urbilum was destroyed.	1只母绵羊和1只公崽为**贝拉特苏赫尼尔庙**，当**她于阿基提月走进南那神的船时**，1只育肥公绵羊为**南那的牺牲**，于阿基提月，2只育肥公绵羊、1只鸭、2只家鸽、5只野鸽和1只苇塘雄豚为**国王**，于卡尔兹达，2只羔为**贝拉特苏赫尼尔和贝拉特达腊班的消失处**，【……】。阿基提月，乌尔比隆被毁年次年。

续表

时间和摘要	文献内容	英文翻译	中文翻译
Š 46 viii = 46' iii'： **zi-ga** 1 fattened ram for **allowance of anointing priest of Belat-Suhnir**，3［fat rams for **Belat-D.**］，**withdrawn from Ur-Lugal-edenka**	1 udu-niga sá-dug$_4$ **gudug-^{d}*Be-la-at-Suh-nir***，3［*udu-niga*，**^{d}Be-la-at-Dar-ra-ban**］，*zi-ga*［*ki*～ **Ur-lugal**］**-eden-ka**.iti-šu-eš-ša，mu Ki-maš^{ki} ù Hu-ur$_5$-ti^{ki} ba-hul. （YOS 18 007，P142401）	1 fattened ram for **monthly allowance of the anointing priest of Belat-Suhnir**，3［fattenen rams for **Belat-Darraban**］，**withdrawn from Ur-Lugal-edenka**.Month of šu-ešša，Year of Kimaš and Hurti were destroyed.	1 只育肥公绵羊为**贝拉特苏赫尼尔的祭司的月供**，3【只育肥公绵羊为**贝拉特达腊班**】，**从乌尔卢旮勒埃丁卡支出**了。三只手月，基马什和胡尔提被毁之年。
Š 46 viii =46' iii' /5，6： **zi-ga**，**butchered** 5th：1 fat ram for **Allatum**，1 goat for **Ordeal Divine River**，2 ducks，20 doves，1 domestic female piglet for **the food of my queen**， 6th：1 she-goat，1 kid，7 ducks，5 pigeons，25 doves，**butchered ones were sent to palace**，**withdrawn from Ur-Lugal-edinka**	1 udu-niga～gud-［e］-ús-sa，^{d}***Al-la-tum***，1 *máš-gal*，^{d} **I$_7$-lú-ru-gú**，2 uz-tur，20 tu-gur$_4$^{mušen}，1 šáh-izi-tur-munus-uru，**níg-gu$_7$-nin-ĝá**--šè，iti--ta ud-5 ba-ra-zal，1 ud$_5$，1 máš，7 uz-tur，5 ir$_7$^{mušen}，25 tu-gur$_4$^{mušen}，ba-úš **é-gal-la** ba-an-ku$_4$，iti--ta ud-6 ba-ra-zal，zi-ga **Ur-^{d}Lugal-edin**. iti-šu-eš-ša，mu Ki-maš^{ki} ù Hu-ur-ti^{ki} ba-hul. （TLB 3 013，P134154）	1 fattened ram of after-ox-class for**Allatum**，1 he-goat for **Ordeal Divine River**，2 ducks，20 doves，1 domestic female piglet for **the food of my queen**，when 5thday passed，1 she-goat，1 kid，7 ducks，5 pigeons，25 doves，**butchered ones were sent to palace**，when 6thday passed，were **withdrawn from Ur-Lugal-edinka**. Month of šu-ešša，Year of Kimaš and Hurti were destroyed.	1 只肥牛后级公绵羊为**阿拉吞**，1 只公山羊为**神判河神**，2 只鸭、20 只野鸽和 1 只驯养的雌豚为**我的王后的食物**，于 5 日过去时，1 只母山羊、1 只公崽、7 只鸭、5 只家鸽和 25 只野鸽，以上**宰杀牲被送入宫殿**，于 6 日过去时，**从乌尔卢旮勒埃丁卡支出**了。三只手月，基马什和胡尔提被毁之年。
Š 46 viii： **zi-ga** 1 bull and 2 fat rams for **allowance**，1 ram and 1 goat for **the nabrium festival of Annunitum**，**in Ur**，**via Ur-Dumuzida**	1 gud-ú，2 udu-niga sá-dug$_4$，1 udu-ú，1 máš-gal，**ezem-*na-ab-rí* *-um* *An-nu-ni-tum***，*šà* ～ *Urim$_5$^{ki}-ma*，*gìr* **Ur-^{d}Dumu-zi-da**，iti--ta ud-20 ba-ra-zal.iti-šu-eš-ša，mu Ki-maš^{ki} ba-hul. （Sigrist，NSTROM 2，204，5-R06	1 grass bull and 2 fattened rams for**monthly allowance**，1 grass ram and 1 he-goat for **the nabrium festival of Annunitum**，**in Ur**，**via Ur-Dumuzida**，when the 20th day passed.Month of šu-ešša，Year of Kimaš was destroyed.	1 头食草公牛和 2 只肥公绵羊为**月供**，1 只食草公绵羊和 1 只公山羊为**安努尼吞那卜润节**，**于乌尔**，**经由乌尔杜穆兹达**，于 20 日过去时。三只手月，基马什被毁年。
Š 46 viii =46' iii' /［x］+2： **zi-ga** 1 fattened lamb，1 thicket piglet，1 duck for**the provisions of Ninlil-hemti**，**withdrawn from Ur-Lugal-edinka**	1 sila$_4$-niga，1 šáh-izi-tur-nitá-giš-gi，1 uz-tur，**igi-kár-^{d}Nin-líl-hé-em-ti**，iti--ta［ud-x］+2，［ba］-ra-zal，zi-ga **Ur-^{d} Lugal-edin-ka**. iti-šu-eš$_5$-ša，mu Ki-maš^{ki} ù Hu-［ur$_5$-ti］^{ki} ba-hul.（MVN 13 679，P117452）	1 fattened lamb，1 thicket piglet，1 duck for**the provisions of Ninlil-hemti**，when［x］+2 day passed，were **withdrawn from Ur-Lugal-edinka**. Month of šu-ešša，Year of Kimaš and Hurti were destroyed.	1 只育肥羔、1 头苇塘猪崽和 1 只鸭为**宁里勒希姆提的供应**，于【x】+2 天过去时，**从乌尔卢旮勒埃丁卡支出**了。 三只手月，基马什和胡尔提被毁之年。

续表

时间和摘要	文献内容	英文翻译	中文翻译
Š 46 viii =46' iii'： lá-ì arrear of 1 piglet，19 ducks，22 pigeons 4 doves，Ur-Lugal-edinka repaid	lá-ì 1 šáh^{zah}-tur-nitá-giš-gi，lá-ì 19 uz-tur，lá-ì 22 ir$_{7}^{mušen}$，lá-ì 4 tu-gur$_{4}^{mušen}$，Ur-^{d} Lugal-eden-ka gurušda，su-su-dam. iti-šu-eš$_{5}$-ša，mu Ki-maš^{ki} ù Hu-ur$_{5}$-ti^{ki} ba-hul. （seal）：^{d}Šul-gi-sí-im-ti，lukur ki-ág lugal，Ur-^{d}Lugal-eden-ka，dub-sar dumu Ku$_{5}$-da-［x］［árad-zu］. （PDT 1 530，P125946）	the arrear of 1 thicket piglet，the arrear of 19 ducks，the arrear of 22 pigeons，the arrear of 4 doves，Ur-Lugal-edinka fattener repaid. Month of šu-ešša，Year of Kimaš and Hurti were destroyed. （seal）：Šulgi-simti，the loved lukur of the king，Ur-Lugal-edinkala，the scribe，son of Kuda-x，was your servent.	1头苇塘猪崽、19只鸭、22只家鸽和4只野鸽，乌尔卢旮勒埃邓卡育肥师补交了。三只手月，基马什和胡尔提被毁之年。 （印章）：舒勒吉新提，国王喜爱的 lukur 神妻，库达-X之子乌尔卢旮勒埃邓卡书吏是你的仆人。
Š 46 viii=46' iii'： mu-túm，ì-dab$_{5}$ 5 rams from Rubatum，49 rams，1 lamb from Ṣiluš-Dagan，20 rams from［…］，son of Rapipil，were deliveries for Šulgi-simti，Ur-Lugal-edinka took	5 udu-ú*Ru-ba-tum*，49 *udu-ú* 1 *sila$_{4}$* *Ṣi-lu-uš-^{d}Da-gan*，20 *udu-ú*　［…］-*dumu* *Ra-pi$_{5}$-pil*，*mu-túm-^{d}Šul-gi-sí-im-ti*，Ur-^{d}Lugal-eden-ka ì-dab$_{5}$. iti-šu-eš$_{5}$-ša，mu Ki-maš^{ki} ù Hu-ur$_{5}$-ti^{ki} ba-hul. （PDT 2 1013，P126355）	5 grass rams fromRubatum，49 grass rams，1 lamb from Ṣiluš-Dagan，20 grass rams from［…］，son of Rapipil，were deliveries for Šulgi-simti，Ur-Lugal-edinka took over. Month of šu-ešša，Year of Kimaš and Hurti were destroyed.	5只食草公绵羊来自如巴吞，49只食草公绵羊和1只羊羔自采鲁什达干，20食草公绵来自X，腊皮皮勒之子，为舒勒吉新提送入，乌尔卢旮勒埃邓卡接管了。三只手月，基马什和胡尔提被毁年。
Š 46 viii=46' iii' /18： zi-ga，butchered 2 butchered ducks were sent to the palace，withdrawn from Ur-Lugal-edinka	2 uz-tur ba-úšé-gal-la ba-an-ku$_{4}$，iti--ta ud-18 ba-ra-zal，zi-ga-Ur-^{d} Lugal-edin-ka. iti-šu-eš-ša，mu Ki-maš^{ki} ba-hul. （OIP 115 104，P123447）	2 butchered ducks were sent to the palace，when 18th day passed，withdrawn from Ur-Lugal-edinka. Month of šu-ešša，Year of Kimaš was destroyed.	2只宰杀鸭被送入宫殿，于本月18日过去时，从乌尔卢旮勒埃丁卡支出了。 三只手月，基马什被毁灭之年。
Š 46 viii=46' iii' /27： zi-ga，butchered 1 fattened ram forsacrifice of Inanna，in palace，1 fat ram and 1 fat goat for sister of Ṣiluš-Dagan，1 kid for Nin-sun，2 rams and 5 kids，butchered ones sent to the palace，were withdrawn from Ur-Lugal-edinka	1 udu-niga sá-dug$_{4}$ siskúr-^{d}Inanna šà~ é-gal， 1 udu-niga，1 máš-gal-niga， mu~ nin$_{9}$-*Ṣi-lu-uš-^{d}Da-gan*--šè， 1 *máš*，^{d}Nin-sún， 2 udu-ú，5 máš，ba-úš é-gal-la ba-an-ku$_{4}$. iti--ta ud-27 ba-ra-zal，zi-ga Ur-^{d} Lugal-edin-ka. iti-šu-eš$_{5}$-ša，mu Ki-maš^{ki} ba-hul. （AnOr 07 075，P101370）	1 fattened ram formonthly allowance of the sacrifice of Inanna，in the palace，1 fattened ram and 1 fattened he-goat for the sister of Ṣiluš-Dagan，1 kid for Nin-sun，2 grass rams and 5 kids，butchered ones sent to the palace，when the 27th day passed，were withdrawn from Ur-Lugal-edinka. Month of šu-ešša，Year of Kimaš was destroyed.	1只育肥公绵羊为伊南那牺牲的月供，于宫殿，1只育肥公绵羊和1只育肥公山羊为采鲁什达干之妹，1只公崽为宁荪，2只食草公绵羊和5只公崽，这些宰杀牲被送入宫殿， 于27日过去时， 从乌尔卢旮勒埃丁卡支出了。三只手月，基马什被毁灭之年。

续表

时间和摘要	文献内容	英文翻译	中文翻译
Š 46 viii = 46' iii' /30: **zi-ga, butchered** 1 piglet, 1 duck, 5 doves, for**food of my queen**, 2 thicket female piglets, 1 duck, 13 doves, **butchered ones were sent to palace, withdrawn from Ur-Lugal-edinka**	1 šáh^{zah}-tur-munus-geš-gi, 1 uz-tur, 5 tu-gur$_4^{mušen}$, **níĝ-gu$_7$-nin-ĝá**--šè, 2 šáh-izi-tur-munus-geš-gi, 1 uz-tur, 13 tu-gur$_4^{mušen}$, ba-úš **é-gal-la ba-an-ku$_4$**, iti--ta ud-30 ba-ra-zal, zi-ga-**Ur-^{d} Lugal-edin - [ka]**. iti-šu-eš$_5$-ša, mu Ki-maš^{ki} ba-hul. (TRU 281, P135045)	1 thicket female piglet, 1 duck, 5 doves, for**the food of my queen**, 2 thicket female piglets, 1 duck, 13 doves, **butchered ones were sent to palace**, when 30th day passed, **withdrawn from Ur-Lugal-edinka**.Month of šu-ešša, Year of Kimaš was destroyed.	1只苇塘雌豚、1只鸭和5只野鸽为**我的王后的食物**，2只苇塘雌豚、1只鸭和13只野鸽，**以上宰杀牲被送入宫殿**，于30日过去时，**从乌尔卢旮勒埃丁卡支出了**。三只手月，基马什被毁灭之年。
Š 44 vi-Š 46 viii = 46' iii': **lá-ì** 8 bulls, 49 kids, 55 ducks, 41 pigeons, 278 doves, were capital fr. it, total 58 sheep, total 45 ducks, total 225 doves, these were withdrawn, the arrear of 1 bull, the arrears of 41 pigeons, the arrears of 53 doves, **account was made by Apilatum**	8 gud, 49 máš, 55 uz-tur, 41 ir$_7^{mušen}$, 278 tu-gur$_4^{mušen}$, sag-níĝ -gur$_{11}$-ra-kam, šà-bi-ta, 7 gud, 16 [máš], 19 x, 23 [x], {45 [x] }, 45 uz-tur, [225 tu-gur$_4^{mušen}$], šu-nigín 7 [gud], šu-nigín 58 [udu] - máš-hi -a, šu-nigín 45 uz-tur, šu-nigín 225 tu-gur$_4^{mušen}$, **[zi-ga] -àm**, lá-ì 1 gud, lá-ì 41 ir$_7^{mušen}$, lá-ì 53 tu-gur$_4^{mušen}$ **níg-kas$_7$ ak *Á-pi$_5$-la-tum* gurušda**. iti-á-ki-ti, mu Si-mu-ru-um ù Lu-lu-bu^{ki} a-rá 9-kam-aš ba-hul--**ta**, iti-šu-eš$_5$-ša, mu Ki-maš^{ki} ù Hu-ur$_5$-ti^{ki} ba-hul--**šè**. (MVN 13 649, P117422) (see below)	8 bulls, 49 kids, 55 ducks, 41 pigeons and 278 doves, were the capital from it, 7 bulls, 16 [kids], 19 x, 23 x, 45 x, 45 ducks, 225 doves, total 7 bulls, total 58 sheep, total 45 ducks, total 225 doves, these were withdrawn, the arrear of 1 bull, the arrears of 41 pigeons, the arrears of 53 doves, **the account was made by Apilatum**. **From** the month of akiti of Year of Simurum and Lulubum were destroyed for the 9th time **to** the month of šu-ešša of the Year of Kimaš and Hurti were destroyed.	8头公牛、49只公崽、55只鸭、41只家鸽和278只野鸽，这些为可用资产，7头公牛、16只【公崽】，19 X，23 X，45 X，45只鸭，225只野鸽，总计7头公牛，总计58只羊，总计45只鸭，总计225只野鸽，以上为支出，1头牛的欠款，41只家鸽的欠款，53只野鸽的欠款，**阿皮拉吞账目平衡**。从席穆润和鲁鲁布第九次被毁之年的阿基提月到基马什和胡尔提被毁之年的三只手月。
Š 46 viii = 46' iii': **lá-ì** the arrear of 1 bull, the arrears of 41 pigeons, **the arrears of 53 doves, imposed on Apilatum fattener from the receipt, it is abstracted**	lá-ì 1 gud, lá-ì 41 ir$_7^{mušen}$, [lá] -ì 53 tu-gur$_4^{mušen}$, ***Á-pi$_5$-la-tum*** **gurušda, in-da-gál, kišib-ta tur-ra**. iti-šu-eš-ša, mu Ki-maš^{ki} ù Hu-ur$_5$-ti^{ki} ba-hul. (CST 129, P107641) (see above)	(sum of the above text) the arrear of 1 bull, the arrears of 41 pigeons, **the arrears of 53 doves, imposed on Apilatum fattener from the receipt, it is abstracted**.Month of šu-ešša, Year of Kimaš and Hurti were destroyed.	(上一文件的片断，阿皮拉吞的欠账) **1头牛的欠款、41只家鸽的欠款和53只野鸽的欠款，育肥师阿皮拉吞从收据中摘要出**。三只手月，基马什和胡尔提被毁之年。

续表

时间和摘要	文献内容	英文翻译	中文翻译
Š 46 ix =46' iv' /6: **zi-ga** 1 ram for **An**, 2 rams for **"disappearing place"**, 2 bulls, 2 fat rams, 2 fat rams, 2 kids for **nabrium festival**, **Belat-Suhnir and Belat-Darraban**, 1 fattened ram, 1 lamb for **Allatum**, 1 grass ram, 1 kid for **Išhara and Belat-Nagu**, 1 lamb for **Annunitum**, 1 kid for **Nanaya**, **withdrawn from Ur-Lugal-edinka**, in **Ur**	1 udu-ú **An**, 2 udu-ú **níĝ-ki-zàh**--šè, 2 gud-ú, 2 udu-niga, 2 udu-niga-gud-e-ús-sa, 2 máš, ***na-ab-ri-um***--šè, ^{d}***Be-la-at-Suh-nir*** *ù* ^{d}***Be-la-at-Dar-ra-ba-an***, 1 *udu-niga*, 1 *sila*$_{4}$ ^{d}***Al-la-tum***, 1 *udu-ú*, 1 *máš* ^{d}***Iš-ha-ra*** *ù* ^{d}***Be-la-at-Na-gú***, 1 *sila*$_{4}$ ***An-nu-ni-tum***, 1 *máš* ^{d}***Na-na-a***, *iti--ta ud-6 ba-ra-zal*, *zi-ga*-**Ur-^{d}Lugal-edin-** [**ka**], šà~ **Urim**$^{[ki]}$-ma.iti-ezem-mah, mu Ki-maš^{ki} ba-hul. (TRU 282, P135046)	1 grass ram for **An**, 2 grass rams for **the offering of "disappearing place"**, 2 grass bulls, 2 fattened rams, 2 fattened rams of after-ox-class, 2 kids for **nabrium festival**, **Belat-Suhnir and Belat-Darraban**, 1 fattened ram, 1 lamb for **Allatum**, 1 grass ram, 1 kid for **Išhara and Belat-Nagu**, 1 lamb for **Annunitum**, 1 kid for **Nanaya**, when the 6th day passed, **were withdrawn from Ur-Lugal-edinka**, in **Ur**. Month of ezem-mah, Year of Kimaš was destroyed.	1食草公绵羊为**安**，2食草公绵羊为**消失处供奉**，2头食草公牛、2育肥公绵羊、2牛后级育肥公绵羊和2公崽为**贝拉特苏赫尼尔和贝拉特达腊班的nabrium节日**，1育肥公绵羊和1羔为**阿拉吞**，1食草公绵羊和1公崽为**伊什哈腊和贝拉特那古**，1羔为**安努尼吞**，1公崽为**那那亚**，于6日过去时，**从乌尔卢旮勒埃丁卡支出了**，于**乌尔**。大庆典月，基马什被毁灭之年。
Š 46 ix =46' iv' /6: **mu-túm, ì-dab$_{5}$** 2 fat goats from **Nir-idagal**, 3 fat rams, 4 rams, 3 kids from **Simat-Ištar**, 1 ram from **Šibat-ekur**, 2 fattened rams, 1 female kid from **Imid-Šabra**, were deliveries for **Šulgi-simti**, **Ur-Lugal-edinka took**	2 máš-gal-niga***Nir-í-da-ĝál***, 3 *udu-niga*, 4 *udu-ú*, 3 *máš* ***Simat-^{d}Iš$_{8}$-tár***, 1 *udu* ***Ši-ba-at-é-kur***, 2 udu-niga, 1 ^{f}ašgar-niga ***I-mi-id-^{d}Šabra***, *iti--ta ud-6 ba-ra-zal*, *mu-túm*-^{d}***Šul-gi-sí-im-ti***, **Ur-^{d}Lugal-edin-<ka>** ì-dab$_{5}$.iti-ezem-mah, mu Ki-maš^{ki} ba-hul. (DoCu EPHE 302, P109258)	2 fattened he-goats from**Nir-idagal**, 3 fattened rams, 4 grass rams, 3 kids from **Simat-Ištar**, 1 ram from **Šibat-ekur**, 2 fattened rams, 1 female kid from **Imid-Šabra**, when the 6th day passed, were deliveries for **Šulgi-simti**, **Ur-Lugal-edinka took over**. Month of ezem-mah, Year of Kimaš was destroyed.	2育肥公山羊自**尼尔伊达旮勒**，3育肥公绵羊、4食草公绵羊和3公崽自**席马特伊什塔尔**，1公绵羊自**席巴特埃库尔**，2育肥公绵羊和1雌崽自**伊米德沙卜腊**，于6日过去时，**为舒勒吉新提的送入，乌尔卢旮勒埃丁卡接管了**。大庆典月，基马什被毁之年。
Š 46 ix=46' iv' /27: **zi-ga** 1 duck for**the food of my queen**, were **withdrawn from Ur-Lugal-edinka**	1 uz-tur, **níĝ-gu$_{7}$-nin-ĝá**--šè, iti--ta ud-27 ba-ra-zal, zi-ga-**Ur-^{d} Lugal-edin-ka**. iti-ezem-mah, mu Ki-maš^{ki} ba-hul. (Torino 1 190, P133903)	1 duck for**the food of my queen**, when the 27th day passed, were **withdrawn from Ur-Lugal-edinka**. Month of ezem-mah, Year of Kimaš was destroyed.	1只鸭为**我的王后的食物**，于27日过去时，**从乌尔卢旮勒埃丁卡支出了**。大庆典月，基马什被毁之年。
Š 46' v' = x: **mu-túm, ì-dab$_{5}$** 1 lamb from**Simat-Ištar**, 1 kid from **Apili**, 1 lamb from **Kurub-Erra**, were deliveries **for Šulgi-simtum, Ur-Lugal-edinka took**	1 sila$_{4}$, **Simat-Iš$_{8}$-tár**, 1 *máš* ***Á-pi$_{5}$-lí***, 1 *sila*$_{4}$ ***Ku-ru-ub-Èr-ra***, *mu-túm*-^{d}***Šul-gi-sí-im-tum***, **Ur-^{d}Lugal-edin-na** ì-dab$_{5}$.iti-ezem-An-na, mu Ki-maš^{ki}ba-hul. (Aegyptus 29 108 37, P100270)	1 lamb from**Simat-Ištar**, 1 kid from **Apili**, 1 lamb from **Kurub-Erra**, were deliveries**for Šulgi-simtum, Ur-Lugal-edinka took over**. Month of ezem-Anna, Year of Kimaš was destroyed.	1只羔来自**席马特伊什塔尔**，1只公崽来自**阿皮里**，1只羔来自**库如卜埃腊**，**为舒勒吉新吞的送入项，乌尔卢旮勒埃丁卡接管了**。天神安庆典月，基马什被毁之年。
Š 46 x =46' v': **mu-túm, ì-dab$_{5}$** 16 thicket female piglets, 14 thicket male piglets of 5 mother sows, **new born in the house of fattener**, **the deliveries for Šulgi-simti, Ur-Lugal-edinka took**	16 šáh-tur-munus-giš-gi, 14 šáh-tur-nitá-giš-gi, šáh-ama-gan-bi 5-àm, ù-tu-da é-gurušda, mu-túm-^{d} ***Šul-gi-sí-im-ti***, **Ur-^{d}Lugal-edin-na** ì-dab$_{5}$.iti-ezem-An-na, mu Ki-maš^{ki} ù Hu-ur$_{5}$-ti^{ki}ba-hul. (OIP 115 087, P123508)	16 thicket female piglets, 14 thicket male piglets of 5 mother sows, **new born in the house of fattener**, **the deliveries for Šulgi-simti, Ur-Lugal-edinka took over**. Month of ezem-Anna, Year of Kimaš and Hurti were destroyed.	16只苇塘雌豚、14只苇塘雄豚，它们的母猪的数量为5只，**新生于育肥房，为舒勒吉新提的送入项，乌尔卢旮勒埃丁卡接管了**。天神安庆典月，基马什和胡尔提被毁灭之年。

续表

时间和摘要	文献内容	英文翻译	中文翻译
Š 46’ v’ = x: **mu-túm，ì-dab$_5$** 1 fat domestic boar，1 fat mature domestic boar from **Ur-Lugal-edinka**，5 domestic piglets，5 piglets for monthly allowance of regimont，**were deliveries for Šulgi-simti，Ur-Lugal-edinka took**	1 šáh-nita-uru-niga，1 šáh-nita-uru -gur$_4$-niga，**Ur-^{d}Lu-gal-edin-ka**，5 šáh^{zah}-tur-nitá-uru，5 šáh^{zah}-tur-nitá，sá-dug$_4$ **ku$_5$-ta**，mu-túm-^{d}***Šul-gi-sí-im-ti***，**Ur-^{d} Lugal-edin-ka** ì-dab$_5$. iti-ezem-An-na，mu Ki-maš^{ki} ù Hu-ur$_5$-ti^{ki} ba-hul. (AnOr 07 009，P101304)	1 fattened domestic boar，1 fattened mature domestic boar from**Ur-Lugal-edinka**，5 domestic piglets，5 piglets for monthly allowance of regimont，**were deliveries for Šulgi-simti，Ur-Lugal-edinka took over**.Month of ezem-Anna，Year of Kimaš and Hurti were destroyed.	1只育肥驯养的公猪、1只育肥成年的驯养的公猪来自**乌尔卢旮勒埃丁卡**，5只驯养的猪崽和5只猪崽为**军团的月供**，**为舒勒吉新提的送入项**，乌尔卢旮勒接管了。天神安庆典月，基马什和胡尔提被毁灭之年。
Š 46 x=46’ v’: **zi-ga，butchered** 1 bull，40 rams，19 kids，14 female kids，**butchered ones were sent to the palace，withdr.fr.Ur-Lugal-edinka**	1 gud，40 udu，20-lá-［1］máš，14 ^{f}ašgar，ug$_7$-ug$_7$-ga-àm，**é-gal-la** ba-an-ku$_4$，zi-ga-**Ur-^{d} Lugal-edin-ka**. iti-ezem-An-na，mu Ki-maš^{ki} ba-hul.（CST 139，P107651）	1 bull，40 rams，19 kids，14 female kids，**butchered ones were sent to the palace，withdrawn from Ur-Lugal-edinka**.Month of ezem-Anna，Year of Kimaš and Hurti were destroyed.	1公牛、40公绵羊、19公崽和14只雌崽，这些**死牲被送入宫殿，从乌尔卢旮勒埃丁卡支出了**。天神安庆典月，基马什和胡尔提被毁灭之年。
Š 46 x=46’ v’ /7: **zi-ga** 1 fat ram for **allowance of Nanna**，1 fat bull，2 fat rams for **allowance of the shrine**，1 fat ram for **allowance**，［x］［...］，［2 lines missing］the 7th day［**of Moon，in Uruk**］，**via my queen**，1 female kid for sacrifice of **Inanna，in the palace，withdrawn from Ur-Lugal-edinka**	1 udu-niga**sá-dug$_4$-^{d}Nanna**，1 gud-niga，2 udu-niga **sá-dug$_4$-èš**--šè，1 udu-niga **sá-**［**dug$_4$**］~［x］［...］，［2 lines missing］é-［ud-7 šà ~ Unug/Nibur］^{ki}，gìr **nin-ĝá**，1 ^{f}ašgar-niga **siskúr-^{d}Inanna** šà ~ é-gal，iti--ta ud-7 ba-ra-zal，zi-ga-**Ur-^{d}Lugal-edin**-ka.iti-ezem-An-na，mu Ki-maš^{ki} ba-hul. (OIP 115 105，P123571)	1 fattened ram for **monthly allowance of Nanna**，1 fattened bull，2 fattened rams for **monthly allowance of the shrine**，1 fattened ram for **monthly allowance**，［x］［...］，［2 lines missing］the 7th day of［Moon **in Uruk**］，**via my queen**，1 female kid for sacrifice of **Inanna，in the palace**，when 7th day passed，**were withdrawn from Ur-Lugal-edinka**.Month of ezem-Anna，Year of Kimaš was destroyed.	1只育肥公绵羊为**南那的月供（7天）**，1头育肥公牛和2只育肥公绵羊为**圣殿月供**，1只育肥公绵羊为**月供**，［x］［...］，为【**初七上弦月，于乌鲁克**】，**经由我的王后**，1只雌崽为**伊南那金星的牺牲**，**于宫殿**，于7日过去时，**从乌尔卢旮勒埃丁卡支出了**。天神安庆典月，基马什被毁灭之年。
Š 46 x=46’ v’ /20: **zi-ga，butchered** 1 grass ram for**sacrifice of Adad**，1 fattened lamb in the palace，1 fattened bull，3 grass rams，3 kids，1 kid，**butchered ones were sent to the palace**，were **withdrawn from Ur-Lugal-edinka**	1 udu-ú **siskúr-^{d} Iškur**，1 sila$_4$-niga，šà **é-gal**--šè，1 gud-niga，3 udu-ú，3 ^{f}ašgar，1 máš，**ba-úš é-gal-la** ba-an-ku$_4$，iti--ta ud-20 ba-ra-zal，zi-ga-**Ur-^{d} Lugal-edin-na**. iti-ezem-An-na，mu Ki-maš^{ki} ù Hu-ur-ti^{ki} ba-hul. (SAT 2 0491，P143691)	1 grass ram for**sacrifice of Adad**，1 fattened lamb，in the **palace**，1 fattened bull，3 grass rams，3 female kids，1 kid，**butchered ones were sent to palace**，when 20th day passed，**withdrawn from Ur-Lugal-edinka**. Month of ezem-Anna，Year of Kimaš and Hurti were destroyed.	1只食草公绵羊为**阿达德的牺牲**，1只育肥羔，于**宫殿**，1头育肥公牛、3只食草公绵羊、3只雌崽和1只公崽，**这些宰杀牲被送入宫殿**，于本月20日过去时，**从乌尔卢旮勒埃丁卡支出了**。天神安庆典月，基马什被毁灭之年。

续表

时间和摘要	文献内容	英文翻译	中文翻译
Š 46 x=46' v' /28: **zi-ga, butchered** 1 thicket female piglet, 2 ducks, when they were seized for **the food of my queen**, 2 **butchered ducks were sent to the palace**, **withdr. fr. Ur-Lugal-edinka**	1šáh-tur-munus-giš-gi, 2 uz-tur, ud-dab$_5$-ba **níĝ-gu$_7$-nin-ĝá**--šè, 2 uz-tur ba-úš **é-gal-la** ba-an-ku$_4$, iti--ta ud-28 ba-ra-zal, zi-ga-**Ur-^{d} Lugal-edin-ka**. iti-ezem-An-na, mu Ki-maš^{ki} ba-hul. (OIP 115 106, P123565)	1 thicket female piglet, 2 ducks, when they were seized for **the food of my queen**, 2 **butchered ducks were sent to the palace**, when the 28th day passed, were **withdrawn from Ur-Lugal-edinka**. Month of ezem-Anna, Year of Kimaš was destroyed.	1只苇塘雌豚和2只鸭被抓住时为**我的王后的食物**， 2只**宰杀鸭被送入宫殿**， 于28日过去时，从**乌尔卢旮勒埃丁卡支出了**。天神安庆典月， 基马什被毁灭之年。
Š 46 x=46' v' /28: **mu-túm, ì-dab$_5$** 5 ducks from **Ṣiluš-Dagan**, 8 ducks from **Agešgar bird-catcher**, from **the place of Ur-Šulpa-e**, 1 duck from **Ka-kugga**, deliveries for Šulgi-simti, **Ur-Lugal-edinka took**	5 uz-tur **Ṣ i-lu-uš-^{d} Da-gan**, 8 *uz-tur* **Á-geš-gar-ra** mušen-dù, ki ~ **Ur-^{d} Šul-pa-è**, 1 uz-tur **Ka-kug-ga**, iti--ta ud-28 ba-ra-zal, mu-túm-^{d} ***Šul-gi-sí-im-ti***, **Ur-^{d} Lugal-edin-ka** ì-dab$_5$. iti-ezem-An-na, mu Ki-maš^{ki} ba-hul. (PDT 1 056, P125472)	5 ducks from **Ṣiluš-Dagan**, 8 ducks from**Agešgar bird-catcher**, from **the place of Ur-Šulpa-e**, 1 duck from **Ka-kugga**, when the 28th day passed, were deliveries for Šulgi-simti, **Ur-Lugal-edinka took over**. Month of ezem-Anna, Year of Kimaš was destroyed.	5只鸭来自**采鲁什达干**，8只鸭来自**阿吉什旮尔捕鸟人**，来自**乌尔舒勒帕埃处**，1只鸭来自**卡库旮**，于28日过去时，**为舒勒吉新提的送入项**，**乌尔卢旮勒埃丁卡接管了**。 天神安庆典月， 基马什被毁灭年。
Š 46 x=46' v' /30: **zi-ga, butchered** 1 fattened ram for**allowance**, 2 rams for **sacrifice of New Moon**, in **Uruk**; 2 kids for **Belat-S. and Belat-D.**, **in Ur**, **via Ur-Dumuzida**; 11 kids for **Nin-Sun**, 1 fat lamb [...], 1 fat ram for **sacrifice of Inanna**, **in palace**; 1 lamb for **offering of "disappearing place"**, **in (her) palace**; 1 fattened female kid, 1 fattened ram for **Belat-Suhnir and Belat-Darraban**, 3 rams, 1 he-goat, 2 female kids, **butchered ones sent to the palace**, **withdrawn from Ur-Lugal-edinka**	1 udu-niga sá-dug$_4$, 2 udu **siskúr ud-sakar šà ~ Unug^{ki}-ga**; 2 máš^{d}***Be-la-at-Suh$_6$-nir*** ù ^{d}***Be-la-at-Dar-ra-ba-an***, **šà~ Urim^{ki}**-ma, gìr**Ur-^{d}Dumu-zi-da**; 11 máš^{d}**Nin-sún**, 1 sila$_4$-niga-gud-e-ús-sa [...], 1 udu-niga siskúr-^{d}**Inanna** šà~ **é-gal**; 1 sila$_4$ níg-ki-zàh šà~ **é-gal**; 1^{f}ašgar-niga, 1 udu-niga, ^{d}***Be-la-at-Suh$_6$-nir*** ù ^{d}***Be-la-at-Dar-ra-ba-an***, 3 *udu*, 1 *máš-gal*, 2^{f}*ašgar*, *ba-úš* **é-gal-la** ba-an-ku$_4$, iti--ta ud-30 ba-ra-zal, zi-ga-**Ur-^{d}Lu-gal-edin-na**. iti-ezem-An-na, mu Ki-maš^{ki} ù Hu-ur$_5$-ti^{ki} ba-hul. (PDT 1 414, P125830)	1 fattened ram for**monthly allowance**, 2 rams for **sacrifice of New Moon**, in **Uruk**; 2 kids for **Belat-Suhnir and Belat-Darraban**, **in Ur**, **via Ur-Dumuzida**; 11 kids for **Nin-Sun**, 1 fattened lamb of after-ox-class [...], 1 fattened ram for **sacrifice of Inanna**, **in palace**; 1 lamb for **offering of "disappearing place"**, **in (her) palace**; 1 fattened female kid, 1 fattened ram for **Belat-Suhnir and Belat-Darraban**, 3 rams, 1 he-goat, 2 female kids, **butchered ones**, **were sent to the palace**, when the 30th day of passed, **were withdrawn from Ur-Lugal-edinka**. Month of ezem-Anna, Year of Kimaš and Hurti were destroyed.	1只育肥公绵羊为**月供**，2只公绵羊为**新月牺牲**，于**乌鲁克**； 2只公崽为**贝拉特苏赫尼尔和贝拉特达腊班**，于**乌尔**，**经由乌尔杜穆孜达**，11只公崽为**宁苏**，1只育肥牛后级羔【……】，1只育肥公绵羊为**伊南那的牺牲于宫殿**；1只羔为**消失处供奉于宫殿**；1只育肥雌崽和1育肥公绵羊为**贝拉特苏赫尼尔和贝拉特达腊班**，3只公绵羊、1只公山羊和2只雌崽，**这些宰杀牲被送入宫殿**，于30日过去时，从**乌尔卢旮勒埃丁卡支出了**。 安神庆典月， 基马什和胡尔提被毁年。

续表

时间和摘要	文献内容	英文翻译	中文翻译
Š 46 xi=46' vi': **mu-túm, ì-dab$_5$** 1 lamb from**Zak-ili**, were **deliveries for Šulgi-simti, Ur-Lugal-edinka took over**	1 sila$_4$ ***Za-ak-ì-lí***, *mu-túm-*^{d}***Šul-gi-sí-im-ti***, **Ur-**^{d}**Lugal-edin-ka** ì-dab$_5$. iti-ezem-Me-ki-ĝál, mu Ki-maš^{ki} ba-hul. (MVN 13 675, P117448)	1 lamb from**Zak-ili**, was **deliveries for Šulgi-simti, Ur-Lugal-edinka took over**. Month of ezem-Mekiĝal, Year of Kimaš was destroyed.	1只羔来自**扎克伊里**，为**舒勒吉新提的送入项**，**乌尔卢旮勒埃丁卡接管**了。神美基旮勒庆典月，基马什被毁之年。
Š 46 xi=46' vi' /7: **zi-ga, butchered** 1 fat ram for**allowance of Enlil**, 1 fat ram for **Ninlil**, 1 fat ram of after-ox-class for **Nin-hursag**, for **the sacrifice of the 7th day of Month**, in **Nippur**, 1 fattened ram of after-ox-class for **Allatum**, 1 grass ram for **Ordeal Divine River**, 1 lamb for **Nanna**, 1 **butchered kid was sent to the palace**, **withdrawn fr.Šu (Ur) -Lugal-edinka**	1 udu-niga **sá-dug$_4$**-^{d} **En-líl**, 1 udu-niga ^{d}**Nin-líl**, 1 udu-niga-gud-e-ús-sa ^{d}**Nin-hur-sag-gá**, **siskúr-é-ud-7** šà ~ **Nibru**^{ki}, 1 udu-niga-gud-e-ús-sa ^{d}***Al-la-tum***, 1 *udu-ú* ^{d}**I$_7$-lú-ru-gú**, 1 sila$_4$-^{d}**Nanna**. 1 ^{f}ašgar ba-úš **é-gal-la ba-an-ku$_4$**, iti-ta ud-7 ba-ra-zal, zi-ga-**Šu (= Ur) -**^{d}**Lugal-edin-ka**. iti-ezem-Me-ki-ĝál, mu Ki-maš^{ki} ba-hul. (Babyl 7 pl 19 04, P104778)	1 fattened ram for**monthly allowance of Enlil**, 1 fattened ram for **Ninlil**, 1 fattened ram of after-ox-class for **Nin-hursag**, for **the sacrifice of the 7th day of Month**, in **Nippur**, 1 fattened ram of after-ox-class for **Allatum**, 1 grass ram for **Ordeal Divine River**, 1 lamb for **Nanna**, 1 **butchered female kid was sent to the palace**, when 7th day passed, were **withdrawn from Šu (Ur) -Lugal-edinka**. Month of ezem-Mekiĝal, Year of Kimaš was destroyed.	1只育肥公绵羊为**恩里勒的月供**，1只育肥公绵羊为**宁里勒**，1只牛后级育肥公绵羊为**宁胡尔萨格**，**为初七上弦月牺牲**， 于**尼普尔**，1只牛后级育肥公绵羊为**阿拉吞**，1只食草公绵羊为**神判河神**，1只羔为**南那**，1只**宰杀的雌崽被送入宫殿**，于7日过去时，从**舒卢旮勒埃丁支出了**。 神美基旮勒庆典月， 基马什被毁之年。
Š 46 xi =46' vi' /8, 9: **zi-ga, butchered** 8th: 1 fat ram for **allowance**, 1 lamb for **Inanna**, 1 ram and 1 kid for **Nin-urta**, 1 kid for **Nusku**, 9th: 1 fattened ram and 1 lamb for **Enlil**, 1 fattened ram for **monthly allowance**, 1 kid for **Ninlil**, **for the lament sacrifice**, **in Nippur**, **via my queen**, 1 grass ram, 5 female kids and 1 lamb, **butchered ones were sent to palace**, x x, withdrawn **from Ur-Lugal-ed [en]**	1 udu-niga sá-dug$_4$, 1 sila$_4$ ^{d}**Inanna**, 1 udu-ú, 1 máš ^{d}**Nin-urta**, 1 máš ^{d}**Nusku**, iti--ta ud-8-ba-ra-zal, 1 udu-niga, 1 sila$_4$, ^{d}**En-líl**, 1 udu-niga**sá-dug$_4$**, 1 máš ^{d}**Nin-líl** iti--ta ud-9-ba-ra-zal, **ér-siskúr** šà~ Nibru^{ki} gìr **nin-ĝá**, 1 udu-ú, 5 ^{f}[aš] -gar, 1 sila$_4$, ba-úš é-gal- [la?], x x zi-ga **Ur-**^{d}**Lugal-ed [en]**.iti-ezem-Me-ki-ĝál, mu Ki-maš^{ki} ba-hul. (AnOr 07 076, P101371)	1 fattened ram for**monthly allowance**, 1 lamb for **Inanna**, 1 grass ram and 1 kid for **Nin-urta**, 1 kid for **Nusku**, when the 8thday passed, 1 fattened ram and 1 lamb for **Enlil**, 1 fattened ram for **monthly allowance**, 1 kid for **Ninlil**, when the 9thday passed, **for the lament sacrifice**, **in Nippur**, **via my queen**, 1 grass ram, 5 female kids and 1 lamb, **butchered dead were sent to the palace**, x x, withdrawn **from Ur-Lugal-ed [en]**.Month of ezem-Mekiĝal, Year of Kimaš was destroyed.	1只育肥公绵羊为**月供**，1只羔为**伊南那**， 1只食草公绵羊和1只公崽为**宁乌尔塔**，1只公崽为**努斯库**，于**8日**过去时，1只育肥公绵羊和1只羔为**恩里勒**，1只育肥公绵羊为**月供**，1只公崽为**宁里勒**，于**9日**过去时，**为于尼普尔的哀悼牺牲**，**经由我的王后**，1只食草公绵羊、5只雌崽和1只羔为**宰杀牲被送入宫殿**，xx，神美基旮勒庆典月， 基马什被毁之年。

续表

时间和摘要	文献内容	英文翻译	中文翻译
Š 46 xi =46' vi' /15: **zi-ga，butchered** 1 fat ram for **allowance**，1 ram for **Belat-Suhnir and Belat-Darraban**，1 ram for **sacrifice of Adad**，1 fattened ram，1 lamb for **Ninlil**，1 fattened ram for **monthly allowance**，1 kid for **Enlil**，in **Nippur**，**via my queen**，2 grass rams，1 he-goat，1 female kid **fell down of ill sent to the palace**，**withdrawn from Ur-Lugal-edinka**	1 udu-niga **sá-dug$_4$**，1 udu-ú ^{d}***Be-la-at-Suh-nir*** *ù* ^{d}***Be-la-at-Dar-ra-ba-an***， 1 *udu-ú* **siskúr-^{d}Iškur**， 1 udu-niga，1 sila$_4$ ^{d}**Nin-líl**， 1 udu-niga **sá-dug$_4$**， 1 máš ^{d}**En-líl**，šà~ **Nibru^{ki}** gìr**nin-ĝá**， 2 udu-ú，1 máš-gal，1 ^{f}ašgar ri-ri-ga-àm **é-gal-la** ba-an-ku$_4$，iti--ta ud-15 ba-ra-zal，zi-ga- **Ur-^{d}Lugal-edin-<ka>**. iti-ezem-Me-ki-ĝál，mu Ki-maš^{ki} ba-hul.（AnOr 07 077，P101372）	1 fattened ram for**monthly allowance**，1 grass ram for **Belat-Suhnir and Belat-Darraban**，1 grass ram for **sacrifice of Adad**，1 fattened ram，1 lamb for **Ninlil**，1 fattened ram for **monthly allowance**，1 kid for **Enlil**，in **Nippur**，**via my queen**，2 grass rams，1 he-goat，1 female kid **fell down of ill sent to the palace**，when the 15th day passed，were **withdrawn from Ur-Lugal-edinka**. Month of ezem-Mekiĝal，Year of Kimaš was destroyed.	1育肥公绵羊为**月供**，1食草公绵羊为**贝拉特苏赫尼尔和贝拉特达腊班**，1食草公绵羊为**阿达德的牺牲**，1育肥公绵羊和1羔为**宁里勒**，1育肥公绵羊为**月供**，1公崽为**恩里勒**，于**尼普尔**，**经由我的王后**，2食草公绵羊、1公山羊和1雌崽**病死被送入宫殿**，于15日过去时，**从乌尔卢旮勒埃丁卡支出了**。美基旮勒庆典月，基马什被毁年。
Š 46 xi =46' vi' /29: **zi-ga，butchered** 1 fat ram of after-ox-class，1 ewe，3 kids，**fell down of ill were sent to palace**，**withdrawn from Ur-Lugal-edinka**	1 udu-niga-gud-e-ús-sa，1 u$_8$，3 máš，**ri-ri-ga-àm**，**é-gal-la** ba-an-ku$_4$，iti--ta ud-29 ba-ra-zal，zi-ga-**Ur-^{d}Lu-gal-edin-ka**.iti-ezem-Me-ki-ĝál，mu Ki-maš^{ki} ba-hul. （RA 49 87 06，P127831）	1 fattened ram of after-ox-class，1 ewe，3 kids，**fell down of ill were sent to palace**，when the 29th day passed，**withdrawn from Ur-Lugal-edinka**. Month of ezem-Mekiĝal，Year of Kimaš was destroyed.	1只牛后级育肥公绵羊、1只母绵羊和3只公崽，**病死被送入宫殿**，于29日过去时，**从乌尔卢旮勒埃丁卡支出了**。 美基旮勒庆典月， 基马什被毁年。
Š 46 xi=46' vi': **mu-túm，ì-dab$_5$** 2 lambs new born infattened house，these were delivery，**Ur-Lugal-edinka took**	2 sila$_4$ ù-tu-da é-gurušda，mu-túm，**Ur-^{d}Lugal-edin-na** ì-dab$_5$.iti-ezem-Me-ki-ĝál， mu Ki-maš^{ki} ba-hul. （OIP 115088，P123483）	2 lambs new born in thefattened house，these were delivery，**Ur-Lugal-edinka took over**. Month of ezem-Mekiĝal，Year of Kimaš was destroyed.	2只新生羔于**育肥房**，**送入项**，**乌尔卢旮勒埃丁卡接管了**。 美基旮勒庆典月，基马什被毁年。
Š 46 xi=46' vi' /20: **zi-ga** 4 fat goats，1 goat，for **the provisions of son of Ṣiluš-Dagan**，**via Apiliya**，**were withdrawn from Ur-Lugal-edin-ka**	4 máš-gal-niga，1 máš-gal，**igi-kár dumu-*Ṣ i-lu-uš-^{d}Da-gan***，*iti--ta ud-20 ba-ra-zal*，*gìr* ***Á-pi$_5$-lí-a***，*zi-ga-* **Ur-^{d} Lugal-edin-ka**. iti-ezem-Me-ki-ĝál，mu Ki-maš^{ki} ù Hu-ur$_5$-ti^{ki}ba-hul. （NYPL 168，P122706）	4 fattened he-goats，1 he-goat，for**the provisions of son of Ṣiluš-Dagan**，when 20th day passed，**via Apiliya**，**were withdrawn from Ur-Lugal-edin-ka**. Month of ezem-Mekiĝal，Year of Kimaš and Hurti were destroyed.	4只育肥公山羊和1只公山羊为**采鲁什达干之子的供奉**，于本月20日过去时，**经由阿皮里亚**，**从乌尔卢旮勒埃丁卡支出了**。神美基旮勒庆典月，基马什和胡尔提被毁年。
Š 46 xi=46' vi' /29: **zi-ga，butchered** 1 fattened ram of after-ox-class，1 ewe，3 kids，**fell down of ill were sent to palace**，**withdrawn from Ur-Lugal-edinka**	1 udu-niga-gud-e-ús-sa，1 u$_8$，3 máš，**ri-ri-ga-àm**，**é-gal-la** ba-an-ku$_4$，iti--ta ud-29 ba-ra-zal，zi-ga-**Ur-^{d}Lu-gal-edin-ka**.iti-ezem-Me-ki-ĝál，mu Ki-maš^{ki} ba-hul. （RA 49 87 06，P127831）	1 fattened ram of after-ox-class，1 ewe，3 kids，**fell down of ill were sent to palace**，when the 29th day passed，**withdrawn from Ur-Lugal-edinka**. Month of ezem-Mekiĝal，Year of Kimaš was destroyed.	1只牛后级育肥公绵羊、1只母绵羊和3只公崽，**病死被送入宫殿**，于29日过去时，**从乌尔卢旮勒埃丁卡支出了**。 美基旮勒庆典月， 基马什被毁年。

续表

时间和摘要	文献内容	英文翻译	中文翻译
Š 46 xi=46' vi': **ì-dab$_5$** 4 lambs which were new born, **Šulgi-ili took over**	4 sila$_4$ ù-tu-[da], ***^{d}Šul-gi-ì-lí*** *ì-dab$_5$*. *iti-ezem-Me-ki-ĝál*, *mu Ki-maš^{ki} ba-hul.* (*OIP* 115 492, *P*123297)	*4 lambs which were new born*, **Šulgi-ili took over**. Month of *ezem-Mekiĝal*, Year of Kimaš was destroyed.	**4只新生羔，舒勒吉伊里接管**了。神美基旮勒庆典月，基马什被毁之年。
Š 46 xii=46' vii': **zi-ga, butchered** 53 rams, 28 kids, **butchered ones sent to palace**, **withdr.from Ur-Lugal-edinka**	53 udu, 28 máš **ri-ri-ga-àm é-gal-la** ba-an-ku$_4$, zi-ga **Ur-^{d}Lugal-edin-ka**.iti-še-kin-kud, mu Ki-maš^{ki} ba-hul. (AnOr 07 078, P101373)	53 rams, 28 kids, **butchered ones were sent to the palace**, were **withdrawn from Ur-Lugal-edinka**.Month of še-kin-kud, Year of Kimaš was destroyed.	53只公绵羊和28只公崽，以上**宰杀牲被送入为宫殿**，**从乌尔卢旮勒埃丁卡支出了**。大麦收割月，基马什被毁之年。
Š 46 xii=46' vii': **mu-túm, ì-dab$_5$** 1 lamb fr.**Išdum-kin**, 1 lamb fr.**Amur-Utu**, 1 kid fr.**Imid-ilum**, 1 lamb fr.**Puzur-Ištar**, **for Šulgi-simti**, **Ur-Lugal-edinka took**	1 sila$_4$ ***Išdum-gi-in***, 1 *sila$_4$* ***A-mur-^{d}Utu***, 1 *máš* ***I-mi-id-ilum***, 1 *sila$_4$* ***Puzur$_4$-Iš$_4$-tár***, *mu-túm-*^{d}***Šul-gi-sí-im-ti***, **Ur-^{d} Lugal-edin-ka** ì-dab$_5$. iti-še-kin-kud, mu Ki-maš^{ki} ba-hul.(AnOr 07 011, P101306)	1 lamb from**Išdum-kin**, 1 lamb from **Amur-Utu**, 1 kid from **Imid-ilum**, 1 lamb from **Puzur-Ištar**, were deliveries **for Šulgi-simti**, **Ur-Lugal-edinka took over**.Month of še-kin-kud, Year of Kimaš was destroyed.	1羔自**伊什杜姆金**，1羔自**阿穆尔乌图**，1公崽自**伊米德伊隆**，1羔自**普朱尔伊什塔尔**，以上为**舒勒吉新提的送入项**，**乌尔卢旮勒埃丁卡接管**了。大麦收割月，基马什被毁之年。
Š 46 xii=46' vii' /13, 14: **zi-ga, butchered** 2 domestic piglets, 3 ducks, 1 pigeon, 4 ducks, 2 pigeons, **butchered ones were sent to the palace**, **were withdrawn from Ur-Lugal-edinka**	2 šáh^{zah}-tur-nita-uru, 3 uz-tur, 1 ir$_7$^{mušen}, iti--ta **ud-13** ba-ra-zal, 4 uz-tur, 2 ir$_7$^{mušen}, iti--ta **ud-14** ba-ra-zal, ba-úš **é-gal-la** ba-an-ku$_4$, zi-ga-**Ur-^{d} Lugal-edin-**ka.iti-še-kin-kud, muKi-maš^{ki} ba-hul.(AnOr 07 080, P101375)	2 domestic piglets, 3 ducks, 1 pigeon, when**13th** day passed, 4 ducks, 2 pigeons, when **14th** day passed, **butchered ones were sent to palace**, **were withdrawn from Ur-Lugal-edinka**.Month of še-kin-kud, Year of Kimaš was destroyed.	2只驯养的猪崽、3只鸭和1只家鸽于**13日**过去时，4只鸭和2只家鸽于**14日**过去时，以上**宰杀牲被送入宫殿**，**从乌尔卢旮勒埃丁卡支出了**。 大麦收割月， 基马什被毁之年。
Š 46 xii=46' vii' /15, 18, 22: **mu-túm, ì-dab$_5$** 15th: 3 fat thicket boars fr.**Šarrum-ili**, **the secretary**, **in Nippur**, 18th: 3 ducks, 3 pigeons, from **Simat-Ištar**, **in Puzriš-Dagan**, 22nd: 20 ducks from **Ištar-alšu**, 1 duck from **Urmes**, **Ur-Lugal-edinka took**	3šáh^{zah}-nitá-tur-giš-gi-niga ***Šar-ru-um-ì-lí*** sukkal, iti--ta **ud-15**ba-ra-zal, šà~ **Nibru^{ki}**, 3 uz-tur, 3 ir$_7$^{mušen} ***Si-mat-^{d} Iš$_8$-tár***, *iti--ta* **ud-18**ba-ra-zal, šà ~ **Puzr$_4$-iš-^{d} Da-gan**, 20 uz-tur ***^{d}Iš$_8$-tár-al-šu***, 1 *uz-tur* **Ur-mes**, iti--ta **ud-22**ba-ra-zal, mu-túm, **Ur-^{d} Lugal-edin-<ka>** ì-dab$_5$. iti-še-kin-kud, mu Ki-maš^{ki} ba-hul.(OIP 115 89, P123670)	3 fattened thicket boars from**Šarrum-ili**, **the envoy**, when **15th**day passed, **in Nippur**, 3 ducks, 3 pigeons, from **Simat-Ištar**, when **18th**day passed, **in Puzriš-Dagan**, 20 ducks from **Ištar-alšu**, 1 duck from **Urmes**, when **22nd**day passed, these were deliveries, **Ur-Lugal-edinka took over**.Month of še-kin-kud, Year of Kimaš was destroyed.	3肥苇塘公猪来自**沙润伊里国使**，于15日过去时，于**尼普尔**，3鸭和3家鸽来自**席马特伊什塔尔**，于18过去时，于**普兹瑞什达干**，20鸭自**伊什塔尔阿勒舒（王子）**，1只鸭来自**乌尔美斯**，于22日过去时，以上送入，**乌尔卢旮勒埃丁卡接管**了。大麦收割月，基马什被毁之年。

续表

时间和摘要	文献内容	英文翻译	中文翻译
Š 46 xii=46' vii' /22: **mu-túm, ì-dab$_5$** [3+] lambs, 10 fat rams, 1 fattened bull, 9 rams, 1 he-goat, 1 gazelle, from **Ištar-alšu**, 2 lambs on 1st time, 10 grass rams on 2nd time, 3 fattened rams, 1 lamb on 3rd time, 2 lambs on 4th time, from **Ur-mes**, the scribe, [1+] grass bull, 6+ grass rams, 3 he-goats, 1 lamb from **Bu-Dagan**, 1 kid from **Amur-Utu**, 2 lambs from **Imid-Ilum**, the administrator, when 22nd day passed, total 1 + bulls, total 30+ rams and kids, were **deliveries for Šulgi-simti**, **Ur-Lugal-edinka took**	[1+] sila$_4$ [a] -rá-1-kam, 2 sila$_4$ a-rá-2-kam, 10 udu-niga a-rá-3-kam, 1 gud-niga, 9 udu-ú, 1 máš-gal, 1 maš-dà a-rá-4-kam, ***^{d}Iš$_8$-tár-al-šu* dumu-lugal**, 2 sila$_4$ a-rá-1-kam, 10 udu-ú a-rá-2-kam, 3 udu-niga, 1 sila$_4$ a-rá-3-kam, 2 sila$_4$ a-rá-4-kam, **Ur-mes** dub-sar, [1+] gud-ú, 6+ udu-ú, 3 máš-gal, 1 sila$_4$ x x il? ***Bù-^{d}Da-gan***, 1 *máš* ***A-mur-^{d} Šamaš***, 2 *sila$_4$* ***I-mi-id-Ilum*** *šabra*, *iti--ta ud-22 ba-ra-zal*, *šu-nigín* [...] 1+ *gud*, *šu-nigín* [...] 30+ [*udu*] *-máš-hi-a*, [*mu-túm-^{d} Šul*] ***-gi-sí-im-ti***, [**Ur-^{d}Lugal-edin**] **-ka** ì-dab$_5$, šà~ [...] -du^{ki}. iti- [še-kin] -kud, [muKi-maš]^{ki} ù Hu-ur$_5$-ti^{ki} ba-hul. (MVN 13 794, P117567)	[1+] lamb on 1st time, 2 lambs on 2nd time, 10 fattened rams on 3rd time, 1 fattened bull, 9 grass rams, 1 he-goat, 1 gazelle on 4th time, from **Ištar-alšu**, the son of king, 2 lambs on 1st time, 10 grass rams on 2nd time, 3 fattened rams, 1 lamb on 3rd time, 2 lambs on 4th time, from **Ur-mes**, the scribe, [1+] grass bull, 6+ grass rams, 3 he-goats, 1 lamb from **Bu-Dagan**, 1 kid from **Amur-Utu**, 2 lambs from **Imid-Ilum**, the majordomo, when 22nd day passed, total 1+ bulls, total 30+ rams and kids, were **deliveries for Šulgi-simti**, **Ur-Lugal-edinka took over**, in [...] du.Month of še-kin-kud, Year of Kimaš and Hurti were destroyed.	【1+】羔第1次，2羔第2次，10育肥公绵羊第3次，1头育肥公牛、9食草公绵羊、1公山羊和1瞪羚第4次，**自王子伊什塔尔阿勒舒**，2羔第1次，10食草公绵羊第2次，3育肥公绵羊和1羔第3次，2羔第4次，**自乌尔美斯书吏**，【1+】头食草公牛、6+食草公绵羊、3公山羊和1羔来自**布达干**，1公崽来自**阿穆尔乌图**，2羔自**伊米德伊隆庙总管**，于第22日过去时，总计1+公牛，总计30+公绵羊和公崽，**为舒勒吉新提的送入项，乌尔卢旮勒埃丁卡接管了**，于【……】杜。大麦收割月，基马什和胡尔提被毁年。
Š 46 xii=46' vii' /28: **zi-ga, butchered** 1 ram for**allowance of giranum festival of Inanna**, 1 **butchered helm swallow was sent to palace**, **withdr.fr.Ur-Lugal-edin-ka**	1 udu**sá-dug$_4$ *gi-ra-núm*-^{d}Inanna**, 1 u$_5$-sim^{mušen} ba-úš **é-gal-la ba-an-ku$_4$**, iti--ta ud-28 ba-ra-zal, zi-ga-**Ur-^{d}Lugal-edin**-ka.iti-še-kin-kud, mu ús-sa Ur-bí-lum^{ki} ba-hul. (PDT 1 061, P125477)	1 ram for**monthly allowance of giranum festival of Inanna**, 1 **butchered helm swallow was sent to palace**, when 28th day passed, **withdrawn from Ur-Lugal-edin-ka**.Month of še-kin-kud, Year after that of Urbilum was destroyed.	1只公绵羊为**伊南那的吉腊努姆仪式的月供**，1只**宰杀的舵燕被送入宫殿**， 于本月28日过去时， **从乌尔卢旮勒埃丁卡支出了**。大麦收割月， 乌尔比隆被毁年之次年。
Š 46 xii=46' vii' /30: **zi-ga** 1 lamb for **Inanna**, 1 lamb for **Ninlil**, 1 lamb for **Enlil**, 1 lamb for **Inanna**, 1 lamb for **Ninlil**, 1 fat ram for **sacrifice of Inanna**, in **Nippur**, 1 ewe, 1 female kid for **sacrifice of New Moon**, in **Uruk**, 4 female kids for **temple of Belat-Suhnir and Belat-Darraban**, **in Ur**, **via Ipiq-Erra**, **withdrawn from Ur-Lugal-edinka**	1 sila$_4$**^{d}Inanna**, 1 sila$_4$**^{d}Nin-líl**, 1 sila$_4$**^{d}En-líl**, a-rá-1-kam, 1 sila$_4$**^{d}Inanna**, 1 sila$_4$**^{d}Nin-líl**, a-rá-2-kam, 1 udu-niga siskúr-**^{d}Inanna**, a-rá-3-kam, šà~ **Nibru^{ki}**, 1 u$_8$, 1^{f}ašgar, **siskúr~ ud-sakar**, šà~ **Unug^{ki}**-ga, 4^{f} ašgar, **é-*^{d}Be-la-at-Suh-nir*** *ù* ***^{d}Be-la-at-Dar-ra-ba-an--šè***, *šà~* **Urim^{ki}**-ma, gìr ***I-pi-iq-Èr-ra***, *iti--ta ud-30 ba-ra-zal*, *zi-ga*-**Ur-^{d}Lugal-edin**-ka. iti-še-kin-kud, mu Ki-maš^{ki} ba-hul. (SumRecDreh.10, P130507)	1 lamb for **Inanna**, 1 lamb for **Ninlil**, 1 lamb for **Enlil**, on 1st time, 1 lamb for **Inanna**, 1 lamb for **Ninlil**, on 2nd time, 1 fattened ram for **sacrifice of Inanna**, on 3rd time, in **Nippur**, 1 ewe, 1 female kid for **sacrifice of New Moon**, in **Uruk**, 4 female kids for **temple of Belat-Suhnir and Belat-Darraban**, **in Ur**, **via Ipiq-Erra**, when the 30th day passed, were **withdrawn from Ur-Lugal-edinka**. Month of še-kin-kud, Year of Kimaš was destroyed.	1羔为**伊南那**，1羔为**宁里勒**，1羔为**恩里勒**——第1次，1羔为**伊南那**，1羔为**宁里勒**——第2次，1育肥公绵羊为**伊南那的牺牲**——第3次，于**尼普尔**，1母绵羊和1雌崽为**新月牺牲**，于**乌鲁克**，4雌崽为**贝拉特苏赫尼尔和贝拉特达腊班**，**于乌尔**，**经由伊皮克埃腊**，于第30日过去时，**从乌尔卢旮勒埃丁卡支出了**。大麦收割月，基马什被毁年。

续表

时间和摘要	文献内容	英文翻译	中文翻译
Š 47 i =46' viii' /1，2： **zi-ga** 1st：1 lamb for **gate of shrine**，1 fattened ram for **monthly allowance**，1 lamb for **gate of bedroom of high priestess**，1 lamb for **Nanaya**，1 lamb for **gate of bedroom of high priestess**， 2nd：1 fattened ram for **monthly allowance**，1 lamb for **gate of bedroom of high priestess**，**withdrawn from Ur-Lugal-edinka**，in **Uruk**	1 $sila_4$ **ká~èš**， 1 udu-niga **$sá-dug_4$**， 1 $sila_4$ **ká~$\hat{g}e_6$-par_4**-ra， 1 $sila_4$ **^{d}Na-na-a**，a-rú-1-kam， 1 $sila_4$ **ká~$\hat{g}e_6$-par_4**-ra a-rú-2-kam， iti--ta **ud-1**ba-ra-zal， 1 udu-niga **$sá-dug_4$**， 1 $sila_4$ **ká~$\hat{g}e_6$-par_4**--ra a-rú-3-kam， iti--ta **ud-2** ba-ra-zal，zi-ga-**Ur-^{d} Lugal-edin-ka**，šà ~ **Unug^{ki}**-ga.iti-maš-dà~gu_7，mu ús-sa Ki-maš^{ki} ba-hul. （BJRL 64 111 66，P106860）	1 lamb for **gate of shrine**，1 fattened ram for **monthly allowance**，1 lamb for **gate of bedroom of high priestess**，1 lamb for **Nanaya**，on 1st time，1 lamb for **gate of bedroom of high priestess**，on 2nd time，when 1stday passed，1 fattened ram for **monthly allowance**，1 lamb for **gate of bedroom of high priestess**，on 3rd time，when 2ndday passed，**withdrawn from Ur-Lugal-edinka**，in **Uruk**. Month of mašda ~ gu_7，Year after that of Kimaš was destroyed.	1 只羔为**圣殿门**， 1 只育肥公绵羊为**月供**， 1 只羔为**祭司寝宫**， 1 只羔为**那那亚**——第 1 次，1 只羔为**祭司寝宫**——第 2 次， 于第 1 日过去时， 1 只育肥公绵羊为**月供**， 1 只羔为**祭司寝宫**——第 3 次， 于第 2 日过去时， **从乌尔卢旮勒埃丁卡支出了**，于**乌鲁克**。 食瞪羚月，基马什被毁年之次年。
Š 47 i =46' viii' /7： **zi-ga** 1 lamb for **monthly allowance of dusk**，1 fat ram for **monthly allowance of dawn**，**of gate of bedroom of high priestess**，1 kid for **Ordeal Divine River**，**withdr.from Ur-Lugal-edinka**	1 $sila_4$，**á~ud-te-na**， 1 udu-niga**$sá-dug_4$**，**á~gú-zi-ga**，**ká~$\hat{g}i_6$-pàr**， 1 máš**^{d}I_7-lú-ru-gú**， iti--ta ud-7 ba-zal，zi-ga-**Ur-^{d}Lugal-edin**-ka.iti-maš-dà~gu_7，mu ús-sa Ki-maš^{ki} ù Hu-ur_5-ti^{ki} ba-hul. （Torino 1 191，P132056）	1 lamb for **monthly allowance of dusk**，1 fattened ram for **monthly allowance of dawn**，**of the gate of bedroom of high priestess**，1 kid for **Ordeal Divine River**，when 7th day passed，were **withdrawn from Ur-Lugal-edinka**. Month of mašda ~gu_7，Year after that of Kimaš was destroyed	1 只羔为**黄昏祭月供**， 1 只育肥公绵羊为**祭司寝宫的晨祭月供**， 1 只公崽为**神判河神**， 于本月 7 日过去时 ，**从乌尔卢旮勒埃丁卡支出了**。 食瞪羚月， 基马什被毁年之次年。
Š 47 i =46' viii' /8： **zi-ga** 1 lamb for**dusk**，1 fattened ram for **dawn**，for **the gate of bedroom of high priestess**，**were withdrawn from Ur-Lugal-edinka**	1 $sila_4$ á~ud-te-na，1 udu-niga á~gú-zi-ga，**ká~$\hat{g}e_6$-pàr**-ra，iti--ta ud-8 ba-ra-zal，zi-ga-**Ur-^{d}Lugal-edin**-ka. iti-maš-dà~gu_7，mu ús-sa Ki-maš^{ki} ba-hul.（edge）2 （Orient 16 042 11，P124637）	1 lamb for**dusk**，1 fattened ram for **dawn**，for **the gate of bedroom of high priestess**，when the 8th passed，**were withdrawn from Ur-Lugal-edinka**. Month of mašda~gu_7，Year after that of Kimaš was destroyed.sum：2	1 只羔为**黄昏祭**，1 只育肥公绵羊为**晨祭**，为**祭司寝宫**，于 8 日过去时， **从乌尔卢旮勒埃丁卡支出了**。食瞪羚月， 基马什被毁年之次年。总计：2
Š 47 i =46' viii' /11： **mu-túm，ì-dab_5** 1 duck，2 pigeons from **Nir-idagal**，**were deliveries for Šulgi-simti**，**Ur-Lugal-edinka took**	1 uz-tur，2 ir_7^{mušen}，***Nir-ì-da-ĝál***，*iti--ta ud*-11 *ba-ra-zal*，*mu-túm-^{d}* ***Šul-gi-sí-im-ti***，**Ur-^{d} Lugal-edin-ka** ì-dab_5.iti-maš-dà~gu_7，mu ús-sa Ki-maš^{ki} ba-hul.（TRU 078，P134842）	1 duck，2 pigeons from **Nir-idagal**，when 11th day passed，**were deliveries for Šulgi-simti**，**Ur-Lugal-edinka took over**. Month of mašda ~ gu_7，Year after that of Kimaš was destroyed.Š	1 只鸭和 2 只家鸽来自**尼尔伊达旮勒**，于 11 日过去时，为**舒勒吉新提的送入项**，**乌尔卢旮勒埃丁卡接管了**。食瞪羚月，基马什被毁年之次年。

续表

时间和摘要	文献内容	英文翻译	中文翻译
Š 47 i =46’ viii’ /13: **zi-ga** 1 fat ram, 1 kid for shrine, 1 fat ram for gate of bedroom of high priestess, 1 fat for Nanaya, withdrawn from**Ur-Lugal-edinka**	1 udu-niga, 1 máš, **ká ~ èš**, 1 udu-niga, **ká ~ ĝe$_6$-par$_4$-ra**, 1 udu-niga-gud-e-ús-sa **^{d}Na-na-a**, iti--ta ud-13 ba-ra-zal, zi-ga-**Ur-^{d}Lugal-edin-ka**.iti-maš-dù ~ gu$_7$, mu ús-saKi-maš^{ki} ù Hu-ur-ti^{ki} ba-hul. (CST 159, P107671)	1 fattened ram, 1 kid for**gate of shrine**, 1 fattened ram for **gate of bedroom of high priestess**, 1 fattened ram of after-ox-class for **Nanaya**, when the 13th day passed, were **withdrawn from Ur-Lugal-edinka**.Month of mašda ~ gu$_7$, Year after that of Kimaš and Hurti were destroyed.	1只育肥公绵羊和1只公崽为**圣殿门**，1只育肥公绵羊为**祭司寝宫**，1只育肥牛后级公绵羊为**那那亚**，于13日过去时，从**乌尔卢旮勒埃邓卡支出**了。食瞪羚月， 基马什和胡尔提被毁年之次年。
Š 47 i =46’ viii’ /19: **zi-ga, butchered** 2 doves for **the food of my queen**, 2 **butchered** doves were **sent to the palace**, were **withdrawn from Ur-Lugal-edinka**, in **Uruk**	2 tu-gur$_4$^{mušen} **níĝ-gu$_7$-nin-ĝá**--šè, 2 tu-gur$_4$^{mušen} ba-úš **é-gal-la** ba-an-ku$_4$, iti--ta ud-19 ba-ra-zal, zi-ga-**Ur-^{d} Lugal-edin**-ka, šà ~ **Unug^{ki}**-ga. iti-maš-dù ~ gu$_7$, mu ús-sa Ki-maš^{ki} ba-hul. (OIP 115 107, P123477)	2 doves for **the food of my queen**, 2 **butchered** doves were **sent to the palace**, when the 19th day passed, were **withdrawn from Ur-Lugal-edinka**, in **Uruk**. Month of mašda ~ gu$_7$, Year after that of Kimaš was destroyed.	2只野鸽为**我的王后的食物**，2只**宰杀的野鸽被送入宫殿**，于19日过去时，从**乌尔卢旮勒埃丁卡支出了**，**于乌鲁克**。 食瞪羚月， 基马什被毁年之次年。
Š 47 i =46’ viii’ /20: **mu-túm, ì-dab$_5$** 13 doves from **Ṣiluš-Dagan**, were **deliveries for Šulgi-simti, Ur-Lugal-edinka took over**	13 tu-gur$_4$^{mušen}, **Ṣi-lu-uš-^{d}Da-gan**, *iti--ta ud-20 ba-ra-zal*, *mu-túm-^{d}* ***Šul-gi-sí-im-ti***, **Ur-^{d} Lugal-edin-ka** ì-dab$_5$.iti-maš-dù ~ gu$_7$, mu ús-sa Ki-maš^{ki} ba-hul. (SA 041, P128593)	13 doves from **Ṣiluš-Dagan**, when the 20th day passed, were **deliveries for Šulgi-simti, Ur-Lugal-edinka took over**.Month of mašda ~ gu$_7$, Year after that of Kimaš was destroyed.	13只野鸽来自**采鲁什达干**，于20日过去时，为**舒勒吉新提的送入项，乌尔卢旮勒埃丁卡接管**了。食瞪羚月，基马什被毁年之次年。
Š 47 i =46’ viii’ /23: **mu-túm, ì-dab$_5$** 2 ducklets from**Šu-Ištar**,, **were deliveries for Šulgi-simti, Ur-Lugal-edinka took over**	2 amar-sag-uz-tur***Šu-^{d} Iš$_8$-tár***, *iti--ta ud-23 ba-ra-zal*, *mu-túm-****^{d}Šul-gi-sí-im-ti***, **Ur-^{d}Lugal-eden-ka** ì-dab$_5$.iti-maš-dù ~ gu$_7$, mu ús-sa Ki-maš^{ki} ba-hul. (PDT 2 1022, P126364)	2 ducklets from**Šu-Ištar**, when the 23rd day passed, **were deliveries for Šulgi-simti, Ur-Lugal-edinka took over**.Month of mašda ~ gu$_7$, Year after that of Kimaš was destroyed.	2只幼鸭来自**舒伊什塔尔**，于23日过去时，为**舒勒吉新提的送入项，乌尔卢旮勒埃邓接管**了。 食瞪羚月，基马什被毁年之次年。
Š 47 i =46’ viii’ /28: **zi-ga** 1 fattened lamb, 1 female kid and 1 female lamb for**the gate of bedroom of high priestess**, 1 kid for **the harp**, 1 kid for **Šurupak**, **withdrawn from Ur-Lugal-edinka**, in **Uruk**	1 sila$_4$-niga, 1 ^{f}ašgar {x gud DU}, 1 kir$_{11}$$^?$ ká ~ ĝe$_6$-par$_4$-ra, 1 máš, balag, 1 máš Šurupak^{ki} (SUxKURx-Lu), iti--ta ud-28 ba-ra-zal, zi-ga-**Ur-^{d} Lugal-edin**-ka šà ~ **Unug^{ki}**.iti-maš-dù ~ gu$_7$, mu ús-sa Ki-maš^{ki} ba-hul. (Princeton 1 099, P126788)	1 fattened lamb, 1 female kid and 1 female lamb for**the gate of bedroom of high priestess**, 1 kid for **the harp**, 1 kid for **Šurupak**, when 28th day passed, were **withdrawn from Ur-Lugal-edinka**, in **Uruk**. Month of mašda ~ gu$_7$, Year after that of Kimaš was destroyed.	1只育肥羔、1只雌崽和1只雌羔为**祭司寝宫**，1只公崽为**竖琴**，1只公崽为**舒如帕克**， 于本月28日过去时， 从**乌尔卢旮勒埃丁卡支出了**，**于乌鲁克**。 食瞪羚月， 基马什被毁年之次年。

续表

时间和摘要	文献内容	英文翻译	中文翻译
Š 47 i =46’ viii’ /29: **mu-túm, ì-dab$_5$** 2 fattened rams, 1 lamb from**Ur-Ištaran**, deliveries **for Šulgi-simti, Ur-Lugal-edinka took**	2 udu-niga, 1 sila$_4$, **Ur-^{d}Ištaran**, iti--ta ud-29 ba-ra-zal, mu-túm-^{d} ***Šul-gi-sí-im-ti***, **Ur-^{d} Lugal-edin-ka** ì-dab$_5$. iti-maš-dà ~ gu$_7$, mu ús-sa Ki-maš^{ki} ba-hul. (SACT 1 060, P128815)	2 fattened rams, 1 lamb from**Ur-Ištaran**, when 29th day passed, were deliveries **for Šulgi-simti, Ur-Lugal-edinka took over**.Month of mašda ~ gu$_7$, Year after that of Kimaš was destroyed.	2 育肥公绵羊和 1 羔来自**乌尔伊什塔蓝**，于 29 日过去时，**为舒勒吉新提的送入项，乌尔卢旮勒埃丁卡接管了**。食瞪羚月，基马什被毁年次年。
Š 47 i =46’ viii’ /30: **zi-ga** 1 kid for **sacrifice**, 1 kid for **“disappearing place”, for gate of bedroom of high priestess**, 1 kid for **“disappearing place” of Nanaya, at dusk**, 1 fat ram, 1 kid for **gate of shrine**, 1 fat ram for **gate of bedroom of high priestess**, 1 goat for **Nanaya, at drawn, withdr. fr. < Ur-Lugal-edinka>**, in **Uruk**	1 máš siskúr--šè, 1 máš **níĝ-ki-zàh**--šè, **ká~ĝi$_6$-pàr**-ra, 1 máš**níĝ-ki-zàh ^{d}Na-na-a**, á~ud-ten-na, 1 udu-niga, 1 máš, **ká~èš**, 1 udu-niga**ká~ĝi$_6$-pàr-ra**, 1 máš-gal^{d} **Na-na-a**, á ~ gú-zi-ga, iti--ta ud-30 ba-ra-zal, zi-ga **<Ur-^{d}Lugal-edin-ka>** šà~ **Unug^{ki}**. iti-maš-dà~gu$_7$, mu ús-sa Ki-maš^{ki} ba-hul. (DoCu EPHE 289, P109246)	1 kid for **sacrifice**, 1 kid for **offering of “disappearing place”, for the gate of bedroom of high priestess**, 1 kid for **offering of “disappearing place” of Nanaya, at dusk**, 1 fattened ram, 1 kid for **gate of shrine**, 1 fattened ram for **gate of bedroom of high priestess**, 1 he-goat for **Nanaya, at drawn**, when 30th passed, were **withdrawn from < Ur-Lugal-edinka >**, in **Uruk.** Month of mašda~gu$_7$, Year after that of Kimaš was destroyed.	1 只公山羊崽为**牺牲**， 1 只公山羊崽为**祭司寝宫的消失处牺牲**， 1 只公山羊崽为**那那亚消失处牺牲，于黄昏时**， 1 只育肥公绵羊和 1 只公山羊崽为**圣殿门**， 1 只育肥公绵羊为**祭司寝宫**，1 只公山羊为**那那亚，于晨时**，于 30 日过去时，以上从**<乌尔卢旮勒埃丁卡>支出，于乌鲁克**。 食瞪羚月， 基马什被毁年次年。
Š 47 i =46’ viii’: **mu-túm, ì-dab$_5$** 2 lambs from**overseer Watrat, deliveries for Šulgi-simti, Ur-Lugal-edinka took**	2 sila$_4$ ***Wa-at-ra-at*** *ugula*, *mu-túm-^{d}* ***Šul-gi-sí-im-ti*, Ur-^{d}Lugal-edin-ka** ì-dab$_5$. iti-maš-dà ~ gu$_7$, mu ús-sa Ki-maš^{ki} ba-hul. (AnOr 07 016, P101311)	2 lambs from**overseer Watrat**, were **deliveries for Šulgi-simti, Ur-Lugal-edinka took over**.Month of mašda~gu$_7$, Year after that of Kimaš was destroyed.	2 只羔来自**瓦特腊特监工，为舒勒吉新提的送入项，乌尔卢旮勒埃丁卡接管了**。食瞪羚月，基马什被毁年次年。
Š 47 i =46’ viii’: **mu-túm, ì-dab$_5$** 1 lamb from **Kurub-Erra**, 1 lamb from **Imi-Sin**, were **deliveries for Šulgi-simti, Ur-Lugal-edinka took**	1 sila$_4$ ***Ku-ru-ub-Èr-ra***, 1 *sila$_4$* **I-mi-^{d}Suen**, *mu-túm-^{d}* ***Šul-gi-sí-im-ti*, Ur-^{d}Lugal -edin-ka** ì-dab$_5$.iti-maš-dà~gu$_7$, mu ús-sa Ki-maš^{ki} ba-hul. (PDT 1 113, P125529)	1 lamb from **Kurub-Erra**, 1 lamb from **Imi-Sin**, were **deliveries for Šulgi-simti, Ur-Lugal-edinka took over**.Month of mašda~gu$_7$, Year after that of Kimaš was destroyed.	1 只羔来自**库如卜埃腊**，1 只羔来自**伊米辛，为舒勒吉新提的送入项，乌尔卢旮勒埃丁卡接管了**。食瞪羚月，基马什被毁年次年。
Š 47 i =46’ viii’: **mu-túm, ì-dab$_5$** 2 grass rams, 1 he-goat from**Tabba-ili**, the shepherd, 7 kids from [...] -Utu, were **deliveries for Šulgi-simti, Ur-Lugal-edinka took**	2 udu-ú 1 máš-gal***Tab-ba-ì-lí*** *sipa*, 7 *máš* [..] -^{d}*Utu*, *mu-túm-^{d}**Šul-gi-sí-im-tum***, **Ur-^{d}Lugal-edin-ka** ì-dab$_5$. iti-maš-dà~gu$_7$, mu ús-sa Ki-maš^{ki} ba-hul. (TCS 335, P132120)	2 grass rams, 1 he-goat from**Tabba-ili**, the shepherd, 7 kids from [...] -Utu, were **deliveries for Šulgi-simti, Ur-Lugal-edinka took over**.Month of mašda~gu$_7$, Year after that of Kimaš was destroyed.	2 只食草公绵羊和 1 只公山羊来自**塔巴伊里牧羊人**，7 只公崽来自 **X-乌图，为舒勒吉新提的送入项，乌尔卢旮勒埃丁卡接管了**。食瞪羚月，基马什被毁年次年。

续表

时间和摘要	文献内容	英文翻译	中文翻译
Š 47 i =46' viii': **zi-ga** 1 lamb for **gate of bedroom of high priestess, withdr.fr.Ur-Lugal-edinka**, in **Uruk**	1 sila$_4$ **ká ~ ĝe$_6$-par$_4$-ra**, zi-ga-**Ur-^{d}Lugal-edin-ka**, šà ~ **Unug^{ki}**-ga. iti-maš-dù ~ gu$_7$, mu ús-sa Ki-maš^{ki} ba-hul. (CST 157, P107669)	1 lamb for **the gate of bedroom of high priestess, withdrawn from Ur-Lugal-edinka**, in **Uruk**. Month of mašda ~ gu$_7$, Year after that of Kimaš was destroyed.	1只羔为**祭司寝宫**，从**乌尔卢旮勒埃丁卡支出了**，于**乌鲁克**。食瞪羚月，基马什被毁年次年。
Š 47 ii = 46' ix': **mu-túm, ì-dab$_5$** 1 kid from **Imid-ilum, the majordomo**, was **delivery for Šulgi-simti, Ur-Lugal-edinka took over**	1 máš, ***I-mi-id-ilum*** *šabra*, *mu-túm-**Šul-gi-sí-im-ti***, **Ur-^{d}Lugal-edin-ka** ì-dab$_5$.iti-ze$_x$-da ~ gu$_7$, mu ús-sa Ki-maš^{ki} ba-hul. (Torino 1 046, P132008)	1 kid from **the majordomo Imid-ilum**, was **delivery for Šulgi-simti, Ur-Lugal-edinka took over**. Month of zeda ~ gu$_7$, Year after that of Kimaš was destroyed.	1公崽来自**伊米德伊隆庙总管**，为**舒勒吉新提的送入项**，**乌尔卢旮勒埃丁卡接管**。食豚月，基马什被毁年次年。
Š 47 ii = 46' ix': **mu-túm, ì-dab$_5$** 1 lamb from**Šarrum-ili, the secretary, delivery for Šulgi-simti, Ur-Lugal-edinka took**	1 sila$_4$ ***Šar-ru-um-ì-lí*** *sukkal*, *mu-túm ~ **^{d}Šul-gi-sí-im-ti***, **Ur-^{d}Lugal-edin-ka** ì-dab$_5$.iti-ze$_x$-da ~ gu$_7$, mu ús-sa Ki-maš^{ki} ba-hul. (OIP 115 091, P123275)	1 lamb from**Šarrum-ili, the envoy**, was **delivery for Šulgi-simti, Ur-Lugal-edinka took over**. Month of zeda ~ gu$_7$, Year after that of Kimaš was destroyed.	1只羔来自**沙润伊里国使**，**为舒勒吉新提的送入项**，**乌尔卢旮勒埃丁卡接管了**。食豚月，基马什被毁年次年。
Š 47 ii = 46' ix' /2: **mu-túm, ì-dab$_5$** 1 bull, 5 rams from **Kara**, 1 fat bull, 7 rams, 3 goats from **Šara-kam**, 1 lamb from **priest of Inanna**, 2 fat rams, 1 kid from **Nir-idagal**, 1 kid from **Ṣiluš-Dagan**, **deliveries for Šulgi-simti, Ur-Lugal-edinka took over**	1 gud-ú, 5 udu-ú **Ka-ra**, 1 gud-niga, 7 udu-ú, 3 máš-gal **^{d}Šará-kam**, 1 sila$_4$ **en-^{d} Inanna**, 2 udu-niga, 1 máš, ***Nir-ì-da-ĝál***, 1 *máš **Ṣ i-lu-uš-^{d} Da-gan***, *iti--ta ud-2 ba-ra-zal*, *mu-túm-**^{d}Šul-gi-sí-im-ti***, **Ur-^{d}Lugal-edin-<ka>** ì-dab$_5$. iti-ze$_x$-da ~ gu$_7$, mu ús-sa Ki-maš^{ki} ba-hul. (OIP 115090, P123420)	1 grass bull, 5 grass rams from**Kara**, 1 fattened bull, 7 grass rams, 3 he-goats from **Šara-kam**, 1 lamb from **the priest of Inanna**, 2 fattened rams, 1 kid from **Nir-idagal**, 1 kid from **Ṣ iluš-Dagan**, when 2nd day passed, **were deliveries for Šulgi-simti, Ur-Lugal-edinka took over**. Month of zeda ~ gu$_7$, Year after that of Kimaš was destroyed.	1食草公牛和5食草公绵羊自**卡腊**，1育肥公牛、7育肥公绵羊和3公山羊自**沙腊刊**，1羔自**伊南那的祭司**，2育肥公绵羊和1公崽自**尼尔伊达旮勒**，1公崽自**采鲁什达干**，于本月2日过去时，**为舒勒吉新提的送入项，乌尔卢旮勒埃丁卡接管了**。食豚月，基马什被毁年次年。
Š 47 ii = 46' ix' /14: **zi-ga** 1 fattened ram for**monthly allowance of the gate of bedroom of high priestess, withdrawn from Ur-Lugal-edinka**, in **Uruk**	1 udu-niga **sá-dug$_4$ ká ~ ĝe$_6$-pàr**--ra, iti--ta ud-14 ba-ra-zal, zi-ga **Ur-^{d}Lugal-edin-ka**, šà ~ **Unug^{ki}**.iti-ze$_x$-da ~ gu$_7$, mu ús-sa Ki-maš^{ki} ba-hul. (AnOr 07 082, P101377)	1 fattened ram for**monthly allowance of the gate of bedroom of high priestess**, when 14th of month passed, **withdrawn from Ur-Lugal-edinka**, in **Uruk**. Month of zeda ~ gu$_7$, Year after that of Kimaš was destroyed.	1只育肥公绵羊为**祭司寝宫的月供**， 于本月14日过去时， 从**乌尔卢旮勒埃丁卡支出了**，于**乌鲁克**。 食豚月， 基马什被毁年次年。

续表

时间和摘要	文献内容	英文翻译	中文翻译
Š 47 ii = 46' ix' /16: **zi-ga, butchered** 2 bulls, 2 fattened rams of after-ox-class, 2 fattened lambs, 9 grass rams, 1 female kid, 9 he-goats and 1 gazelle, **fell down of ill, were sent to the palace**, were **withdrawn from Ur-Lugal-edinka**	2 gud, 2 udu-niga-gud-e-［ús-sa］, 2 sila$_4$-niga, 9 udu-ú, 1 ^{f}ašgar, 9 máš-gal, 1 maš-dà, **ri-ri-ga-àm, é-gal-la** ba-an-［ku$_4$］, iti--ta ud-16-kam, zi-ga **Ur-^{d}Lugal-edin-ka**. iti-ze$_x$-da ~ gu$_7$, mu ús-sa Ki-maš^{ki} ba-hul. （CST 165, P107677）	2 bulls, 2 fattened rams of after-ox-class, 2 fattened lambs, 9 grass rams, 1 female kid, 9 he-goats and 1 gazelle, **fell down of ill, were sent to the palace**, when 16th day passed, were **withdrawn from Ur-Lugal-edinka**. Month of zeda ~ gu$_7$, Year after that of Kimaš was destroyed.	2头公牛、2只牛后级育肥公绵羊、2只育肥羔、9只食草公绵羊、1只雌崽、9只公山羊和1头瞪羚， **病死被送入宫殿**， 于本月16日过去时， **从乌尔卢旮勒埃丁卡支出**了。食豚月，基马什被毁年次年。
Š 47 ii = 46' ix' /26: **mu-túm, ì-dab$_5$** 2 pigeons from**Ši-Lammasi**, these **were deliveries, Ur-Lugal-edinka took over**	2ir$_7$^{mušen} ***Ši-La-ma-sí***, *iti--ta ud-26 ba-ra-zal*, *mu-túm*, **Ur-^{d}Lugal-edin-ka** ì-dab$_5$.iti-ze$_x$-da ~ gu$_7$, mu ús-sa Ki-maš^{ki} ba-hul. （MVN 13 677, P117450）	2 pigeons from**Ši-Lammasi**, when the 26th day passed, these **were deliveries, Ur-Lugal-edinka took over**.Month of zeda ~ gu$_7$, Year after that of Kimaš was destroyed.	2只家鸽来自**席拉马斯**，于26日过去时， 以上**送入项**， **乌尔卢旮勒埃丁卡接管**了。食豚月， 基马什被毁年次年。
Š 47 ii = 46'ix' /26: **mu-túm, ì-dab$_5$** 1 fattened ram for **monthly allowance of Nin-tiug, withdrawn from Ur-Lugal-edinka**	1 udu-niga**sá-dug$_4$ ^{d}Nin-ti-ug$_5$-ga**, iti--ta ud-26 ba-ra-zal, zi-ga-**Ur-^{d}Lugal-eden-ka**.iti-ze$_x$-da ~ gu$_7$, mu ús-sa Ki-maš^{ki} ba-hul. （PDT 20988, P126334）	1 fattened ram for **monthly allowance of Nin-tiug**, when the 26th day passed, **withdrawn from Ur-Lugal-edinka**.Month of zeda ~ gu$_7$, Year after that of Kimaš was destroyed.	1只育肥公绵羊为**宁提乌格神的月供**， 于26日过去时， **从乌尔卢旮勒埃邓支出**了。食豚月， 基马什被毁年次年。
Š 47 iii = 46' x': **mu-túm, ì-dab$_5$** 2 rams, 1 lamb fr. **Kurub-Erra, deliveries for Šulgi-simti, Ur-Lugal-edinka took**	2 udu-ú, 1 sila$_4$ ***Ku-ru-ub-Èr-ra***, *mu-túm-^{d}* ***Šul-gi-sí-im-ti***, **Ur-^{d}Lugal-eden-ka** ì-dab$_5$. iti-ze$_x$-da ~ gu$_7$, mu ús-sa Ki-maš^{ki} ba-hul.（PDT 2 1003, P126348）	2 grass rams, 1 lamb from**Kurub-Erra**, were **deliveries for Šulgi-simti, Ur-Lugal-edinka took over**.Month of zeda ~ gu$_7$, Year after that of Kimaš was destroyed.	2只食草公绵羊和1只羔来自**库如卜埃腊**，为**舒勒吉新提的送入项，乌尔卢旮勒埃邓接管**了。食豚月，基马什被毁年次年。
Š 47 iii = 46' x' /7: **zi-ga** 1+ fat ram for **allowance**, 1 lamb for **gate of shrine**, 1 fattened ram for **monthly allowance of gate of bedroom of high priestess**, 1 lamb for **Nanaya, withdrawn from Ur-Lugal-edin-ka**, in **Uruk**	1+ udu-niga **sá-dug$_4$**, 1 sila$_4$ **ka ~ èš**, 1 udu-niga **sá-dug$_4$ ka ~ ĝe$_6$-par$_4$-ra**, 1 sila$_4$ **^{d}Na-na-a**, iti--ta ud-7 ba-ra-zal, zi-ga-**Ur-^{d}Lugal-edin-ka**, šà ~ **Unug^{ki}**.iti-u$_5$-bí ~ gu$_7$, mu ús-sa Ki-maš^{ki} ba-hul. （CST 167, P107679）	1+ fattened ram for**monthly allowance**, 1 lamb for **gate of shrine**, 1 fattened ram for **monthly allowance of gate of bedroom of high priestess**, 1 lamb for **Nanaya**, when 7th day passed, were **withdrawn from Ur-Lugal-edin-ka**, in **Uruk**. Month of ubi ~ gu$_7$, Year after that of Kimaš was destroyed.	1+只育肥公绵羊为**月供**，1只羔为**圣殿门**， 1只育肥公绵羊为**祭司寝宫的月供**， 1只羔为**那那亚**， 于7日过去时， **从乌尔卢旮勒埃丁卡支出**了，于**乌鲁克**。 食乌比乌月， 基马什被毁年次年。

续表

时间和摘要	文献内容	英文翻译	中文翻译
Š 47 iii = 46' x' /15: **zi-ga, butchered** 1 thicket female piglet, 1 thicket male piglet, 1 ducklet,…1 duck, 4 thicket male piglets, 4 ducks, 11 doves, **butchered ones were sent to the palace, withdr.from Ur-Lugal-eden**	1šáh-zah-tur-munus-giš-gi, 1 šáh-zah-tur-nitá-giš-gi, 1 amar-sag̃~ uz-tur,…1 uz-tur, 4 šáh-zah-tur-nitá-giš-gi, 4 uz-tur, 11 tu-gur$_4$^{mušen} ri-ri-ga-àm é-gal-la ba-an-ku$_4$, iti--ta ud-15-ba-ra-zal, zi-ga **Ur-^{d} Lugal-eden.** iti-u$_5$-bí-gu$_7$, mu ús-sa Ki-maš^{ki} ba-hul. (AnOr 07 081, P101376)	1 thicket female piglet, 1 thicket male piglet, 1 ducklet,…1 duck, 4 thicket male piglets, 4 ducks, 11 doves, **butchered ones were sent to the palace**, when the 15th day passed, **withdrawn from Ur-Lugal-eden.** Month of ubi~gu$_7$, Year after that of Kimaš was destroyed.	1只苇塘雌豚、1只苇塘雄豚、1只幼鸭……1只鸭、4只苇塘雄豚、4只鸭、11只野鸽为**宰杀牲被送入宫殿**，于15日过去时，**从乌尔卢旮勒埃邓支出了**。食乌比鸟月，基马什被毁年次年。
Š 47 iii = 46' x' /16: **zi-ga** 1 fat ram for **allowance of sacrifice of Nin-hursag**, 4 grass rams, 4 lamb for **the father in the center of Ur**, **via Beli-bani**, **withdrawn from Ur-Lugal-edinka**	1 udu-niga**sá-dug$_4$**, **siskúr -^{d} Nin-hur-sag-gá**, iti--ta ud-16 ba-ra-zal, 4 udu-ú, 4 sila$_4$, ***a-bu-um*** *šà ~ Urim^{ki}-ma--ka--šè*, *gìr* ***Be-lí-ba-ni***, *zi-ga*-**Ur-^{d} Lugal-e-den-ka**.iti-u$_5$-bí~gu$_7$, mu ús-sa Ki-maš^{ki} ba-hul. (Torino 1 192, P133904)	1 fattened ram for**monthly allowance of sacrifice of Nin-hursag**, when 16th day passed, 4 grass rams, 4 lamb for **the father in the center of Ur**, **via Beli-bani**, **withdrawn from Ur-Lugal-edinka.** Month of ubi~gu$_7$, Year after that of Kimaš was destroyed.	1只育肥公绵羊为**宁胡尔萨格牺牲的月供**，于16日过去时，4只食草公绵羊和4只羔为**于乌尔中心的父亲**，**经由贝里巴尼**，**从乌尔卢旮勒埃邓支出了**。食乌比鸟月，基马什被毁年次年。
Š 47 iii = 46' x' /21: **mu-túm, ì-dab$_5$** 4 ducklets from **Apil-kin**, **were deliveries for Šulgi-simti**, **Ur-Lugal-edinka took over**	4 amar-sag-uz-tur***A-pil-ki-in***, *iti--ta ud-21 ba-ra-zal*, *mu-túm-^{d}***Šul-gi-sí-im-ti**, **Ur-^{d} Lugal-edin-ka** ì-dab$_5$. iti-u$_5$-bí~gu$_7$, mu ús-sa Ki-maš^{ki} ba-hul. (OIP 115 092, P123684)	4 ducklets from **Apil-kin**, when 21st day passed, **were deliveries for Šulgi-simti**, **Ur-Lugal-edinka took over.** Month of ubi~gu$_7$, Year after that of Kimaš was destroyed.	4只幼鸭来自**阿皮勒金**，于21日过去时，**为舒勒吉新提的送入项**，**乌尔卢旮勒接管了**。食乌比鸟月，基马什被毁年次年。
Š 47 iv = 46' xi': **mu-túm, ì-dab$_5$** 1 ram, 1 lamb from **Išdum-kin**, 1 she-goat from **Te ṣin-mama**, [1+] lamb from **Šu-Eštar**, were deliveries for **Šulgi-simti**, **Šulgi-ili took**	1 udu-ú, 1 kir$_{11}$, ***Išdum-ki-in***, 1 *ud$_5$*, ***Te- ṣ i-in-ma-ma***, [1+] *sila$_4$ Šu-Eš$_4$-tár*, *mu-túm-^{d}***Šul-gi-sí-im-ti**, ***^{d} Šul-gi-ì-lí*** *ì-dab$_5$.iti-ki-siki-^{d}Nin-a-zu*, *mu ús-sa Ki-maš^{ki} ba-hul.* (*Torino* 1 024, *P*131931)	1 *grass ram*, 1 *female lamb from***Išdum-kin**, 1 she-goat from **Te ṣ in-mama**, [1+] lamb from **Šu-Eštar**, were deliveries for **Šulgi-simti**, **Šulgi-ili took over.** Month of ki-siki-Ninazu, Year after that of Kimaš was destroyed.	1食草公绵羊和1雌羔自**伊什杜姆金**，1母山羊自**台岑妈妈**，**【1+】**只羔自**舒埃什塔尔**，**为舒勒吉新提送入**，**舒勒吉伊里接管了**。宁阿朱羊毛作坊月，基马什被毁年次年。
Š 47 iv = 46' xi' /3: **mu-túm, ì-dab$_5$** 1 fat ram from **allowance**, 1 fattened ram, 2 grass rams, 1 kid from **Šibat-ekur**, **deliveries for Šulgi-simti**, **Ur-Lugal-edinka took over**	1 udu-niga **sá-dug$_4$**, 1 udu-niga-gud-e-ús-sa, 2 udu-ú, 1 máš ***Ši-ba-at-é-kur***, iti--ta ud-3 ba-ra-zal, mu-túm-***^{d} Šul-gi-sí-im-ti***, **Ur-^{d} Lugal-edin-ka** ì-dab$_5$. iti-ki-siki-^{d} Nin-a-zu, mu ús-sa Ki-maš^{ki} ba-hul. (PDT 1 157, P125574)	1 fattened ram from **monthly allowance**, 1 fattened ram of after-ox-class, 2 grass rams, 1 kid from **Šibat-ekur**, when 3rd day passed, were **deliveries for Šulgi-simti**, **Ur-Lugal-edinka took over.** Month of ki-siki-Ninazu, Year after that of Kimaš was destroyed.	1育肥公绵羊来自**月供**，1牛后级育肥公绵羊、2食草公绵羊和1公崽来自**席巴特埃库尔**，于3日过去时，**为舒勒吉新提的送入项**，**乌尔卢旮勒埃丁卡接管了**。神宁阿朱羊毛作坊月，基马什被毁年次年。

续表

时间和摘要	文献内容	英文翻译	中文翻译
Š 47 iv=46' xi' /7: **zi-ga, butchered** 1 duck, 5 doves for **food of my queen**, 1 **butchered duck was sent to the palace**, were **withdrawn from Ur-Lugal-edinka**	1 uz-tur, 5 tu-gur$_4$^{mušen}, **níĝ-gu$_7$-nin-ĝá**--šè, 1 uz-tur, ba-úš **é-gal-la** ba-an-ku$_4$, iti--ta ud-7 ba-ra-zal, zi-ga-**Ur-^{d}lugal-edin-ka**.iti-ki-siki-^{d}Nin-a-zu, mu ús-sa Ki-maš^{ki} ba-hul. (Torino 1 404, P133987)	1 duck, 5 doves for **the food of my queen**, 1 **butchered duck was sent to the palace**, when 7th day passed, were **withdrawn from Ur-Lugal-edinka**. Month of ki-siki-Ninazu, Year after that of Kimaš was destroyed.	1只鸭和5只野鸽为**我的王后的食物**，1只**宰杀鸭被送入宫殿**，于7日过去时，**从乌尔卢旮勒埃丁卡支出了**。神宁阿朱羊毛作坊月，基马什被毁年次年。
Š 47 iv=46' xi' /10: **zi-ga** 1 ducklet and 5 doves for**the food of my queen**, were **withdrawn from Ur-Lugal-edenna**	1 amar-saĝ-uz! -tur, 5 tu-gur$_4$^{mušen}, **níĝ-gu$_7$-nin-ĝá**--šè, iti--ta ud-10 ba-ra-zal, zi-ga **Ur-lugal-eden-na**. iti-ki-siki-^{d}Nin-a-zu, mu ús-sa Ki-maš^{ki} ba-hul. (SAT 2 0541, P143741)	1 ducklet and 5 doves for**the food of my queen**, when the 10th day passed, were **withdrawn from Ur-Lugal-edenna**. Month of ki-siki-Ninazu, Year after that of Kimaš was destroyed.	1只幼鸭和5只野鸽为**我的王后的食物**，于10日过去时，**从乌尔卢旮勒埃邓那支出了**。神宁阿朱羊毛作坊月，基马什被毁年次年。
Š 47 iv=46' xi' /14: **zi-ga, butchered** 1 fat ram for**allowance of food of my queen**, 1 fat ram for **monthly allowance of giranum festival of Inanna**, 1 fattened ram for **monthly allowance**, 1 fattened he-goat for **Belat-Suhnir and Belat-Darraban**, 1 lamb for **sacrifice of Full Moon, via Arad-zuni**, 1 **butchered** fattened ram **was sent to the palace, withdrawn from Ur-Lugal-edinka**	1 udu-niga sá-dug$_4$ **níĝ-gu$_7$-nin-ĝá**--šè, 1 udu-niga **sá-dug$_4$** ***gi-ra-núm***-**^{d}Inanna**, 1 udu-niga **sá-dug$_4$**, 1 máš-gal-niga ***^{d}Be-la-at-Suh-nir*** *ù* ***^{d}Be-la-at-Dar-ra-ba-an***, [2 *lines missing*] 1 *sila$_4$* **siskúr-ud-15-kam**, gìr**Arád-zu-ni**, 1 udu-niga-gud-e-ús-sa, ba-úš **é-gal-la** ba-an-ku$_4$, iti--ta ud-14 ba-ra-zal, zi-ga-**Ur-^{d} Lugal-edin-ka**.iti-ki-siki-^{d}Nin-a-zu, mu ús-sa Ki-maš^{ki} ba-hul. (CST 170, P107682)	1 fattened ram for**monthly allowance of food of my queen**, 1 fattened ram for **monthly allowance of giranum festival of Inanna**, 1 fattened ram for **monthly allowance**, 1 fattened he-goat for **Belat-Suhnir and Belat-Darraban**, [2 lines missing], 1 lamb for **sacrifice of Full Moon, via Arad-zuni**, 1 **butchered** fattened ram of after-ox-class **was sent to the palace**, when 14th day passed, **withdrawn from Ur-Lugal-edinka**. Month of ki-siki-Ninazu, Year after that of Kimaš was destroyed.	1育肥公绵羊为**我的王后的食物的月供**， 1育肥公绵羊为**伊南那的吉腊努姆仪式的月供**， 1育肥公绵羊为**月供**， 1只育肥公山羊为**贝拉特苏赫尼尔和贝拉特达腊班**，【两行缺失】， 1只羔为**满月牺牲**， **经由阿腊德朱尼**， 1只**宰杀的育肥牛后级公绵羊被送入宫殿**，于14日过去时，**从乌尔卢旮勒埃丁卡支出了**。神宁阿朱羊毛作坊月，基马什被毁年次年。
Š 47 iv=46' xi' /18: **zi-ga** 1 fattened ram and 1 fattened lamb were**sent to the center of palace**, were **withdrawn from Ur-Lugal-edinka**	1 udu-niga, 1 sila$_4$-niga, **šà ~ é-gal**--šè, ba-an-ku$_4$, iti--ta ud-18 ba-ra-zal, zi-ga-**Ur-^{d} Lugal-edin-ka**. iti-ki-siki-^{d}Nin-a-zu, mu ús-sa Ki-maš^{ki} ba-hul. (OIP 115 108, P123323)	1 fattened ram and 1 fattened lamb were**sent to the center of palace**, when 18th day passed, **withdrawn from Ur-Lugal-edinka**. Month of ki-siki-Ninazu, Year after that of Kimaš was destroyed.	1只育肥公绵羊和1只育肥羔**被送入宫殿中心**，于18日过去时，**从乌尔卢旮勒埃丁卡支出了**。神宁阿朱羊毛作坊月，基马什被毁年次年。
Š 47 iv=46' xi' /28: **zi-ga, butchered** 5 butchered ducks were **sent to palace, withdrawn from Ur-Lugal-edinka**	5 uz-tur ba-úš **é-gal-la** ba-an-ku$_4$, iti--ta ud-28 ba-ra-zal, zi-ga-**Ur-^{d} Lugal-edin-< ka >**. iti-ki-siki-^{d} Nin-a-zu, mu ús-sa Ki-maš^{ki} ba-hul. (CST 173, P107685)	5**butchered ducks were sent to palace**, when 28th day passed, **withdrawn from Ur-Lugal-edin-ka**. Month of ki-siki-Ninazu, Year after that of Kimaš was destroyed.	5只**宰杀鸭被送入宫殿**，于28日过去时，**从乌尔卢旮勒埃丁卡支出了**。神宁阿朱羊毛作坊月，基马什被毁年次年。

续表

时间和摘要	文献内容	英文翻译	中文翻译
Š 47 iv=46’ xi’ /30: **zi-ga** 1 thicket female piglet, 1 thicket male piglet, for**the food of my queen**, 1 thicket male piglet for **the provision of Simat-Ištar**, were **withdrawn from Šulgi-ili**	1 šáh^{zah}-tur-munus-giš-gi, 1 šáh^{zah}-tur-nita-giš-gi, **níĝ-gu$_7$-nin-ĝá**--šè, 1 šáh^{zah}-tur-nita-giš-gi, **igi-kár-*Simat-Ištar***, *iti--ta ud-30 ba-ra-zal*, *zi-ga-^{d}* ***Šul-gi-ìlí***. *iti-ki-siki-^{d}Nin-a-zu*, *mu ús-sa Ki-maš^{ki} ba-hul.* (*OIP* 115 116, *P*123270)	1 *thicket female piglet*, 1 *thicket male piglet*, *for***the food of my queen**, 1 thicket male piglet for **the provision of Simat-Ištar**, when 30th day passed, were **withdrawn from Šulgi-ili**. Month of ki-siki-Ninazu, Year after that of Kimaš was destroyed.	1头苇塘雌豚和1头苇塘雄豚为**我的王后的食物**，1头苇塘雄豚为**席马特伊什塔尔的供奉**，于30日过去时，从**舒勒吉伊里支出**了。神宁阿朱羊毛作坊月，基马什被毁年次年。
Š 47 v=46’ xii’: **mu-túm, ì-dab$_5$** 1 female kid from**Puzur-Ištar**, **deliveries for Šulgi-simtum**, **Šulgi-ili took**	1^f ašgar ***Puzur$_4$-Iš$_4$-tár***, *mu-túm-^{d}* ***Šul-gi-sí-im-tum***, *^{d}* ***Šul-gi-ì-lí*** *ì-dab$_5$*. *iti-ezem-^{d}Nin-a-zu*, *mu ús-sa Ki-maš^{ki} ba-hul.* (*AnOr* 07 014, *P*101309)	1 *female kid from***Puzur-Ištar**, were **deliveries for Šulgi-simtum**, **Šulgi-ili took over**. Month of ezem-Ninazu, Year after that of Kimaš was destroyed.	1雌崽来自**普朱尔伊什塔尔**，**为舒勒吉新吞的送入**，**舒勒吉伊里接管**了。神宁阿朱庆典月，基马什被毁年次年。
Š 47 v=46’ xii’: **zi-ga** 2 rams for **Belat-S. and Belat-D.**, 1 kid for **Iškur**, in **Ur**, **via Beli-bani**, 1 kid for the **gate of bedroom of high priestess**, in **Uruk**, <u>**via Mašum**</u>, **withdr.fr.Šulgi-ili**	2 udu-ú, ***^{d}Be-la-at-Suh-nir*** *ù* ***^{d}Be-la-at-Dar-ra-ba-an***, 1 *máš* **^{d}Iškur**, šà~ **Urim^{ki}**-ma, gìr ***Be-lí-ba-ni***, 1 *máš ka-ge$_6$-par$_4$-ra*, *šà ~* **Unug^{ki}**-ga, <u>gìr *Ma-šum*</u>, *zi-ga-^{d}* ***Šul-gi-ì-lí***. *iti-ezem-^{d}Nin -a-zu*, *mu ús-sa Ki-maš^{ki} ba-hul.* (*SAT* 2 0557, *P*143757)	2 *grass rams for***Belat-Suhnir and Belat-Darraban**, 1 kid for **Iškur**, in **Ur**, **via Beli-bani**, 1 kid for the **gate of bedroom of high priestess**, in **Uruk**, <u>**via Mašum**</u>, were **withdrawn from Šulgi-ili**. Month of ezem-Ninazu, Year after that of Kimaš was destroyed.	2食草公绵羊为**贝拉特苏赫尼尔和贝拉特达腊班**，1公崽为**阿达德**，**于乌尔**，**经由贝里巴尼**，1公崽为**祭司寝宫**，**于乌鲁克**，<u>**经由马顺**</u>，从**舒勒吉伊里支出**了。神宁阿朱庆典月，基马什被毁年次年。
Š 47 v=46’ xii’ /14: **zi-ga**, **butchered** 1 thicket male piglet and 2 doves for **the food of my queen**, 1 **butchered duck sent to the palace**, **withdrawn from Šulgi-ili**	1 šáh^{zah}-tur-nita-giš-gi, 2 tu-gur$_4$^{mušen}, **níg-gu$_7$-nin-ĝá**--šè, 1 uz-tur ba-úš **é-gal-la** ba-an-ku$_4$. iti--ta ud-14 ba-ra-zal, zi-ga-***^{d}Šul-gi-ì-lí***. *iti-ezem-^{d}Nin-a-zu*, *mu ús-sa Ki-maš^{ki} ba-hul.* (*Ontario* 2 278, *P*209796)	1 *thicket male piglet and* 2 *doves for* **the food of my queen**, 1 **butchered duck sent to the palace**, when 14th day passed, were **withdrawn from Šulgi-ili**. Month of ezem-Ninazu, Year after that of Kimaš was destroyed.	1只苇塘雄豚和2只野鸽为**我的王后的食物**，1只**宰杀鸭被送入宫殿**，于14日过去时，从**舒勒吉伊里支出**了。神宁阿朱庆典月，基马什被毁之年。
Š 47 v=46’ xii’ /20: **zi-ga**, **butchered** 1 fattened thicket sow for**the food of the king**, 1 thicket piglet, 1 duck for **the provisions of Te ṣin-Mama**, 1 domestic sow for **provision of the wife of Šarrum-ili**, 1 **butchered duck was sent to palace**, **withdrawn from Šulgi-ili**	1 šáh-munus-giš-gi-nigín-niga, **níĝ-gu$_7$-lugal**--šè, 1 šáh-tur-munus-giš-gi, 1 uz-tur **igi-kár-*Te- ṣi-in-Ma-ma***, 1 *šáh-tur-munus-uru* **igi-** [**kár-da**] **m-*Šar-ru-um-ì-lí***, 1 *uz-tur ba-úš* **é-gal-la** ba-na-ku$_4$, iti--ta ud-20 ba-ra-zal, zi-ga-*^{d}* ***Šul-gi-ì-lí***. *iti-ezem-Nin-a-zu*, *mu ús-sa Ki-maš^{ki} ba-hul.* (*OIP* 115 117, *P*123660)	1 *fattened thicket sow for***the food of the king**, 1 thicket piglet, 1 duck for **the provisions of Te ṣin-Mama**, 1 domestic sow for **provision of the wife of Šarrum-ili**, 1 **butchered duck was sent to the palace**, when 20th day passed, were **withdrawn from Šulgi-ili**. Month of ezem-Ninazu, Year after that of Kimaš was destroyed.	1只育肥苇塘公猪为**我的国王的食物**，1只苇塘猪崽和1只鸭为**台岑妈妈的供奉**，1只驯养的公猪为**沙润伊里之妻的供奉**，1只**宰杀鸭被送入宫殿**，于20日过去时，从**舒勒吉伊里支出**了。神宁阿朱庆典月，基马什被毁年次年。

续表

时间和摘要	文献内容	英文翻译	中文翻译
Š 47 v=46' xii' /30: **zi-ga, butchered** 20**butchered doves were sent to palace, withdrawn from Šulgi-ili**	20 tu-gur$_4$^{mušen} ba-úš **é-gal-la** ba-na-ku$_4$, iti--ta ud-30 ba-ra-zal, zi-ga-^{d}***Šul-gi-ì-lí***.*iti-ezem-Nin -a-zu, mu ús-sa Ki-maš^{ki} ba-hul.* (*OIP* 115 118, *P*123717)	20**butchered doves were sent to palace**, when 30th day passed, **withdrawn from Šulgi-ili**. Month of ezem-Ninazu, Year after that of Kimaš was destroyed.	20只**宰杀野鸽被送入宫殿**，于30日过去时，从**舒勒吉伊里支出**了。 神宁阿朱庆典月，基马什被毁年次年。
Š 47 v=46' xii' /30: **zi-ga** 1 fat ram for **allowance**, 1 fat ram, 1 lamb for **sacrifice of New Moon**, in **Uruk**, **via Ipi-Sin**, 1 fattened ram for **giranum festival of Inanna**, 1 fat ram for **allowance**, [1+] fat kid for **sacrifice of Inanna**, **in palace**, [1 fattened ram] for **offering of disappearing place**, **in palace**, [1 fattened ram] for **sacrifice of Nin-sun**, [1+] fattened [ram] for **monthly allowance of sacrifice of Nanna**, x+2 fattened rams for **monthly allowance**, [1+] he-goat for **sacrifice of Belat-Suhnir and Belat-Darraban**, **withdrawn fromŠulgi-ili**	1 udu-niga **sá-dug$_4$**, 1 udu-niga-gud-e-ús-sa, 1 sila$_4$ **siskúr-ud-sakar** šà ~ **Unug^{ki}**, **gìr *I-pi$_5$-^{d}Suen***, 1 *udu-niga* **sá-dug$_4$ *gi-ra-núm*-^{d}Inanna**, 1 udu-niga **sá-dug$_4$**, [1+] ^{f}ašgar-niga **siskúr-^{d}Inanna** šà~ **é-gal**, [1 udu-niga] **níĝ-ki-zàh** šà~ **é-gal**, [1 udu-niga] **siskúr-^{d}Nin-sún**, [1 udu] -niga **sá-dug$_4$ siskúr-^{d}Nanna**, [x] +2 udu-niga **sá-dug$_4$**, [1+] máš-gal, **siskúr-^{d} *Be-la-at-Suh-nir*** ù ^{d}***Be-la-at-Dar-ra-ba-an***, *iti--ta ud-30 ba-ra-zal*, *zi-ga-* ^{d}***Šul-gi-ì-lí***.*iti-ezem-^{d}Nin-a-zu*, *mu ús-saKi-maš^{ki}ù Hu-ur$_5$-ti^{ki}ba-hul.* (*OrAnt* 11 273 2, *P*124605)	1 *fattened ram for***monthly allowance**, 1 fattened ram of after-ox-class, 1 lamb for **sacrifice of New Moon**, in **Uruk**, **via Ipi-Sin**, 1 fattened ram for **monthly allowance of giranum festival of Inanna**, 1 fattened ram for **monthly allowance**, [1+] fattened female kid for **sacrifice of Inanna**, **in palace**, [1 fattened ram] for **offering of disappearing place**, **in palace**, [1 fattened ram] for **sacrifice of Nin-sun**, [1+] fattened [ram] for **monthly allowance of sacrifice of Nanna**, x+2 fattened rams for **monthly allowance**, [1+] he-goat for **sacrifice of Belat-Suhnir and Belat-Darraban**, when 30th day passed, were **withdrawn from Šulgi-ili**. Month of ezem-Ninazu, Year after that of Kimaš and Hurti were destroyed.	1只育肥公绵羊为**月供**，1只牛后级育肥公绵羊和1只羔为**新月牺牲**， 于乌鲁克，**经由伊皮辛**， 1只育肥公绵羊为**伊南那的吉腊努姆仪式的月供**， 1只育肥公绵羊为**月供**，【1+】只育肥雌崽为**伊南那的牺牲，于宫殿**， 【1只育肥公绵羊】为**消失处供奉，于宫殿**， 【1只育肥公绵羊】为**宁荪的牺牲**， 【1+】只育肥【公绵羊】**为南那的牺牲的月供**，2+只育肥公绵羊**为月供**， 【1+】只公山羊为**贝拉特苏赫尼尔和贝拉特达腊班**，于30日过去时， 从**舒勒吉伊里支出**了。 神宁阿朱庆典月， 基马什被毁年次年。
(Š 47?) ii-v: **ì-dab$_5$** **its workdays were 3680 women slave for 1 day, for 4 months, the clay tablet of barley ration, Šulgi-ili took over**	26 gemé sag-dub, 7 gemé á $^{2}/_{3}$, itize$_x$- [da] ~gu$_7$--ta, iti-ezem- [^{d}] Nin-a-zu--šè, á-bi 3680 gemé ud-1--šè, iti-4-kam, im še-ba--ta, ^{d}***Šul-gi-ì-lí*** *ì-dab$_5$*. (*SET* 267, *P*129677)	26 *women slave of full ration laborers*, 7 *laborers with 2/3 workday's ration*, *from month of zeda~gu$_7$ to month of ezem- Ninazu*, **its workdays were 3680 women slave for 1 day**, **for 4 months**, **the clay tablet of barley ration**, **Šulgi-ili took over**.	26个全额劳工的女奴， 7个2/3工作日份额的劳工， 从食豚月到神宁阿朱月，**3680个女奴工作一天一共4个月**， **此大麦份额的泥板**， **舒勒吉伊里接管**了。
Š47 vi=47' i' /7: **zi-ga, butchered** 2 doves for the **food of my queen**, 7 **butchered doves were sent to the palace**, **withdrawn from Šulgi-ili**	2 tu-gur$_4$^{mušen} **níĝ-gu$_7$-nin-ĝá**--šè, 7 tu-gur$_4$^{mušen} ba-úš **é-gal-la** ba-na-ku$_4$, iti--ta ud-7 ba-ra-zal, zi-ga-^{d}***Šul-gi-ì-lí***.*iti-á-ki-ti*, *mu ús-sa Ki-maš^{ki} ba-hul.* (*OIP* 115 119, *P*123657)	2 *doves for***the food of my queen**, 7 **butchered doves were sent to the palace**, when 7th day passed, **withdrawn from Šulgi-ili**. Month of Akiti, Year after that of Kimaš was destroyed.	2只野鸽为**我的王后的食物**，7只**宰杀野鸽被送入宫殿**，于7日过去时，从**舒勒吉伊里支出**了。阿基提月，基马什被毁年之次年。

续表

时间和摘要	文献内容	英文翻译	中文翻译
Š47 vi=47' i' /10: **zi-ga** 2 doves for **food of my queen**, were **withdrawn from Šulgi-ili**	2 tu-gur$_4$^{mušen} **níĝ-gu$_7$-nin-ĝá**--šè, iti--ta ud-10 ba-ra-zal, zi-ga- ***^{d}Šul-gi-ì-lí***. *iti-á-ki-ti*, *mu ús-sa Ki-maš^{ki} ù Hu-ur$_5$-ti^{ki}ba-hul.* (*OIP* 115 120, *P*123497)	2 *doves for* **food of my queen**, when 10th day passed, were **withdrawn from Šulgi-ili**. Month of Akiti, Year after that of Kimaš and Hurti were destroyed.	2 只野鸽为**我的王后的食物**，于 10 日过去时，从**舒勒吉伊里支出了**。阿基提月，基马什和胡尔提被毁年之次年。
Š47 vi=47' i' /15: **zi-ga** 2 ducks for**food of my queen**, were **withdrawn from Šulgi-ili**	2 uz-tur **níĝ-gu$_7$-nin-ĝá**--šè, iti--ta ud-15 ba-ra-zal, zi-ga-***^{d}Šul-gi-ìlí***.*iti-á-ki-ti*, *mu ús-sa Ki-maš^{ki} ù Hu-ur$_5$-ti^{ki} ba-hul.* (*OIP* 115 121, *P*123566)	2 *ducks for***food of my queen**, when 15th day passed, were **withdrawn from Šulgi-ili**. Month of Akiti, Year after that of Kimaš and Hurti were destroyed.	2 只鸭为**我的王后的食物**，于 15 日过去时，从**舒勒吉伊里支出了**。阿基提月，基马什和胡尔提被毁年之次年。
Š47 vi=47' i' /16: **zi-ga** 1 fattened ram for**monthly allowance of Adad**, 2 grass rams for **Belat-Suhnir and Belat-Darraban**, **were withdrawn from Šulgi-ili**	1 udu-niga **sá-dug$_4$^{d}Iškur**, 2 udu-ú ***^{d}Be-la-at-Suh-nir** ù **^{d}Be-la-at-Dar-ra-ba-an***, *iti--ta ud-16 ba-ra-zal*, *zi-ga-**^{d}Šul-gi-ì-lí**.iti-á-ki-ti*, *mu ús-sa Ki-maš^{ki} ù Hu-ur$_5$-ti^{ki} ba-hul.* (*Princeton* 2 126, *P*201124)	1 *fattened ram for***monthly allowance of Adad**, 2 grass rams for **Belat-Suhnir and Belat-Darraban**, when 16th day passed, **were withdrawn from Šulgi-ili**.Month of Akiti, Year after that of Kimaš and Hurti were destroyed.	1 只育肥公绵羊为**阿达德的月供**，2 只食草公绵羊为**贝拉特苏赫尼尔和贝拉特达腊班**，于 16 日过去时，从**舒勒吉伊里支出了**。阿基提月，基马什和胡尔提被毁年次年。
Š47 vi=47' i' /19, 21: **zi-ga** 19th: 1 fat ram for **allowance of Nanna**, 2 fat rams, 2 fat rams of after-ox-class, 2 kids for **Belat-Suhnir and Belat-Darraban**, 1 kid for **Ordeal Divine River**, 21st: 2 rams for **giranum of Annunitum and Ulmašitum**, 1 kid for **Raduria**, 1 fat bull, 4 fat rams, for **allowance**, 1 lamb for **Dawn**, 1 fat kid for **the vegetable food**, 1 kid for **god went to his temple**, 1 grass ram for the "**pouring beer**" **festival of Ulmašitum and Annunitum**, **in palace**, **withdrawn from Šulgi-ili**, **in Ur**	1 udu-niga **sá-dug$_4$-^{d}Nanna**, 2 udu-niga, 2 udu-niga-gud-e-ús-sa, 2 máš ***^{d}Be-la-at-Suh-nir** ù **^{d}Be-la-at-Dar-ra-ba-an***, 1 *máš***^{d}I$_7$-lú-ru-gú**, iti--ta **ud-19**ba-ra-zal, 2 udu-ú ***gi-ra-núm*** ***An-nu-ni-tum** ù **Ul-ma-ši-tum***, 1 *máš***^{d}Ra-du$_8$-ri-a**, 1 gud-niga, 2 udu-niga, 2 udu-niga sá-dug$_4$, 1 sila$_4$ **á ~ gú-zi-ga**, 1 ^{f}ašgar-niga **níĝ-gu$_7$-nisig** (**SAR**) - **ga**--šè, 1 mášdiĝir é--a-ni--šè ĝen-né, 1 udu-ú ***^{d}Ul-ma-ši-tum** káš-dé-a **An-nu-ni-tum***, **šà ~ é-gal-la**, iti--ta ud-**21**ba-ra-zal, zi-ga-***^{d}Šul-gi-ì-lí***, *šà* ~ **Urim^{ki}**-ma. iti-á-ki-ti, mu ús-sa Ki-maš^{ki} ù Hu-ur$_5$-ti^{ki} ba-hul. (AnOr 07 083, P101378)	1 fattened ram for**monthly allowance of Nanna**, 2 fattened rams, 2 fattened rams of after-ox -class, 2 kids for **Belat-Suhnir and Belat-Darraban**, 1 kid for **Ordeal Divine River**, when **19th**day passed, 2 grass rams for **giranum festival of Annunitum and Ulmašitum**, 1 kid for **Raduria**, 1 fattened bull, 2 fattened rams, 2 fattened rams for **monthly allowance**, 1 lamb for **Dawn**, 1 fattened female kid for **the vegetable food**, 1 kid for **the god went to his temple**, 1 grass ram for the "**pouring beer**" **festival of Ulmašitum and Annunitum**, **in palace**, when **21st**day passed, were **withdrawn from Šulgi-ili**, **in Ur**. Month of akiti, Year after that of Kimaš and Hurti were destroyed.	1 育肥公绵羊为**南那的月供**，2 育肥公绵羊、2 牛后级育肥公绵羊、2 公崽为**贝拉特苏赫尼尔和贝拉特达腊班**，1 公崽为**神判河神**，于 19 日过去时，2 食草公绵羊为**安努尼吞和乌勒马席吞的吉腊努姆仪式**，1 公崽为**腊杜瑞阿**，1 育肥公牛、2 育肥公绵羊、2 育肥公绵羊为**月供**，1 羔为**黄昏**，1 育肥雌崽为**蔬菜食物**，1 只公崽为**神走向他的庙宇**，1 只食草公绵羊为**乌勒马席吞和安努尼吞的啤酒节**，**于宫殿**，于 21 日过去时，从**舒勒吉伊里支出了**，**于乌尔**。阿基提月，基马什和胡尔提被毁年次年。

续表

时间和摘要	文献内容	英文翻译	中文翻译
Š47 vi=47' i' /22: **zi-ga** 2 rams for **Belat-Suhnir and Belat-Darraban, via Mašum**, 1 fat ram, 1 fat lamb, 1 fat kid for **the gaba-ri-a offering of king**, when he left Karzida, **withdrawn from Šulgi-ili**, in **Ur**..	2 udu-ú ***ᵈBe-la-at-Suh-nir*** *ù* ***ᵈBe-la-at-Dar-ra-ba-an***, *gìr* ***Ma-šum***, 1 *udu-niga*, 1 *sila₄-niga*, 1 *ᶠašgar-niga*, **lugal**--ra gaba ~ ri <-a>, Kar-zi-da^ki^--ta ĝen-na, iti--ta ud-22 ba-ra-zal, zi-ga-***ᵈŠul-gi-ì-lí***, *šà* **Urim^ki^**-ma. iti-á-ki-ti, mu ús-sa Ki-maš^ki^ ba-hul. (AnOr 07 084, P101379)	2 grass rams for**Belat-Suhnir and Belat-Darraban, via Mašum**, 1 fattened ram, 1 fattened lamb, 1 fattened female kid for **the gaba-ri-a offering of king**, when he left Karzida, when 22nd day passed, **withdrawn from Šulgi-ili**, in **Ur**. Month of akiti, Year after that of Kimaš was destroyed.	2食草公绵羊为**贝拉特苏赫尼尔和贝拉特达腊班，经由马顺**，1育肥公绵羊、1育肥羔和1育肥雌崽**为国王的供奉**，当他离开卡尔兹达时，于本月22日过去时，从**舒勒吉伊里支出了**，于**乌尔**。阿基提月，基马什被毁年次年。
Š47 vi=47' i': **mu-túm, ì-dab₅** 1 kid fr. **Zaklili**, was **delivery for Šulgi-simti, Šulgi-ili took**	1 máš***Za-ak-ì-lí*** *mu-túm-* ***ᵈŠul-gi-sí-im-ti***, ***ᵈŠul-gi-ì-lí*** *ì-dab₅.iti-á-ki-ti*, *mu ús-sa Ki-maš^ki^ ba-hul.* (*OIP* 115 109, *P*123541)	1 *kid from* **Zak-ili**, was **delivery for Šulgi-simti, Šulgi-ili took over**.Month of akiti, Year after that of Kimaš was destroyed.	1公崽自**扎克伊里**，为**舒勒吉新提的送入项，舒勒吉伊里接管**。阿基提月，基马什被毁年之次年。
Š 47vii=47' ii': **mu-túm** 2níglám clothes, its weight is 3 mana, 1 guzza clothes, its weight is 5 mana, 7 guzza clothes, its weight is 28 $^{1}/_{3}$ mana, 1 weaved clothes, its weight is 8 $^{2}/_{3}$ mana, **weighted clothes were deliveries, from the place ofŠulgi-ili**	2^túg^níg-lám 3-kam-ús, ki-lá-bi 3 ma-na, 1 ^túg^guz-za-3-kam-ús, ki-lá-bi 5 ma-na, 7 ^túg^guz-za-4-kam-ús, ki-lá-bi 281/3 ma-na, 1 túg-uš-bar, ki-lá-bi 8 2/3 ma-na, **túg ki-lá tag-ga,** **mu-túm,** ki ~ ***ᵈŠul-gi-ì-lí***--*ta.iti-ezem-ᵈŠul-gi*, *mu ús-saKi-maš^ki^ ba-hul.* (*AnOr* 07 152, *P*101447)	2*níglám clothes of 3rd class, the weight of which is 3 mana, 1 guzza clothes of 3rd class, the weight of which is 5 mana, 7 guzza clothes of 4th class, the weight of which is 28 $^{1}/_{3}$ mana, 1 weaved clothes, the weight of which is 8 $^{2}/_{3}$ mana*, **weighted clothes were deliveries, from the place of Šulgi-ili**.Month of ezem-Šulgi, Year after that of Kimaš was destroyed.	2件三级的布料，其重量为3斤，1件三级的guzza布料，其重量为5斤， 7件四级的guzza布料，其重量为$28^{1}/_{3}$斤， 1件编织布料，其重量为$8^{2}/_{3}$斤， **已经称重的布料为送入，自舒勒吉伊里处**。 舒勒吉庆典月，基马什被毁年之次年。
Š 47 vii=47' ii': **mu-túm, ì-dab₅** 1 kid from**Šu-Ištar**, 1 kid from **Garaya**, were **deliveries for Šulgi-simti, Šulgi-ili took**	1 máš***Šu-Iš₄-tár***, 1 *máš* ***Ga-ra-a***, *mu-túm-****ᵈŠul-gi-sí-im-ti***,***ᵈŠul -gi-ì-lí*** *ì-dab₅.iti-ezem-ᵈŠul-gi*, *mu ús-sa Ki-maš^ki^ ba-hul.* (*Princeton* 1 036, *P*126725)	1 *kid from***Šu-Ištar**, 1 kid from **Garaya**, were **deliveries for Šulgi-simti, Šulgi-ili took over**.Month of ezem-Šulgi, Year after that of Kimaš was destroyed.	1公崽自**舒伊什塔尔**，1公崽自**旮腊亚**，为**舒勒吉新提的送入项，舒勒吉伊里接管了**。舒勒吉庆典月，基马什被毁年之次年。
Š 47 vii=47' ii': **mu-túm, ì-dab₅** 3 rams and 1 kid fr.**Šukubum**, were deliveries **for Šulgi-simti, Šulgi-ili took**	3 udu-ú, 1 máš ***Šu-ku-bu-um*** *mu-túm ~* ***ᵈŠul-gi-sí-im-[ti]***, ***ᵈ*** ***[Šul-gi-ì-lí]*** *ì-dab₅. iti-ezem-ᵈŠul-gi*, *mu ús-sa Ki-maš^ki^ ba-hul.* (*Princeton* 1 041, *P*126730)	3 *grass rams and* 1 *kid from***Šukubum**, were deliveries **for Šulgi-simti, Šulgi-ili took over**. Month of ezem-Šulgi, Year after that of Kimaš was destroyed.	3食草公绵羊和1只公崽来自**舒库布姆**，为**舒勒吉新提的送入项，舒勒吉伊里接管**。舒勒吉庆典月，基马什被毁年之次年。

续表

时间和摘要	文献内容	英文翻译	中文翻译
Š 47 vii=47' ii' /15: **zi-ga, falling down** 1 lamb for **gate of shrine**, 1 kid for **gate of bedroom of high priestess, via my queen**, 2 fat rams for **allowance**, 1 kid for **sacrifice of Full Moon, in Uruk, via Nur-Sin**, 13 fat rams, 14 grass rams and 4 female kids, **falling down ones were sent to the palace, withdrawn from Šulgi-ili**	1 sila$_4$ **Ká~èš**, 1 máš **Ká~gi$_6$-par$_4$-ra**, gìr**nin-ĝá**, 2 udu-niga **sá-dug$_4$**, 1 máš**siskúr-é-ud-15**, šà~ **Unug^{ki}**-ga, gìr*Nu-úr-^{d}Sîn*, 13 *udu-niga-gud-e-ús-sa*, 14 *udu-ú* 4^{f}*ašgar*, **ri-ri-ga-àm, é-gal-la ba-an-ku$_4$**, iti--ta ud-15 ba-ra-zal, zi-ga-^{d} ***Šul-gi-ì-lí***. *iti-ezem-^{d} Šul-gi, mu ús-sa Ki-maš^{ki} ba-hul.* (*OIP* 115 122, *P*123658)	1 *lamb for***the gate of shrine**, 1 kid for the **gate of bedroom of high priestess, via my queen**, 2 fattened rams for **monthly allowance**, 1 kid for **sacrifice of Full Moon, in Uruk, via Nur-Sin**, 13 fattened rams of after-ox-class, 14 grass rams and 4 female kids, **falling down ones were sent to the palace**, when 15th day passed, were **withdrawn from Šulgi-ili**. Month of ezem-Šulgi, Year after that of Kimaš was destroyed.	1只羔为**圣殿门**, 1只公崽为**祭司寝宫**, **经由我的王后**, 2只育肥公绵羊为**月供**, 1只公崽为**满月牺牲**, **于乌鲁克**, **经由努尔辛**,13只牛后级育肥公绵羊、14只食草公绵羊和4只雌崽,为**病死被送入宫殿**,于15日过去时,从**舒勒吉伊里支出**了。舒勒吉庆典月,基马什被毁年之次年。
Š 47 vii=47' ii' /22: **mu-túm, ì-dab$_5$** 1 duck, 4 doves from**the sisiter of Ṣiluš-Dagan**, were **deliveries for Šulgi-simti, Šulgi-ili took over**	1 uz-tur, 4 tu-gur$_4$^{mušen} **nin$_9$-*Ṣi-lu-uš-^{d}Da-gan***, *iti--ta ud-22 ba-ra-zal, mu-túm-^{d}* ***Šul-gi-sí-im-ti***, ^{d} ***Šul-gi-ì-lí*** ì-dab$_5$.iti-ezem-^{d}Šul-gi, mu ús-sa Ki-maš^{ki} ba-hul. (OIP 115 110, P123542)	1 duck, 4 doves from**the sisiter of Ṣiluš-Dagan**, when 22nd day passed, were **deliveries for Šulgi-simti, Šulgi-ili took over**. Month of ezem-Šulgi, Year after that of Kimaš was destroyed.	1只鸭和4只野鸽**自采鲁什达干的妹妹**,于本月22日过去时,**为舒勒吉新提的送入项,舒勒吉伊里接管了**。舒勒吉庆典月,基马什被毁年之次年。
Š 47 vii=47' ii' /22: **zi-ga, butchered** 10 ducks, 2 birds, for**the food of my queen**, 5 **butchered ducks were sent to the palace, withdrawn from Šulgi-ili**	10 tu-gur$_4$^{mušen}, 2 tu^{mušen} **níĝ-gu$_7$-nin-ĝá**--šè, 5 tu-gur$_4$^{mušen} **ba-úš é-gal-la ba-an-ku$_4$**, iti--ta ud-22 ba-ra-zal, zi-ga-^{d} ***Šul-gi-ì-lí***. *iti-ezem-^{d} Šul-gi, mu ús-sa Ki-maš^{ki} ba-hul.* (*OIP* 115 123, *P*123681)	10 *ducks*, 2 *birds*, *for***the food of my queen**, 5 **butchered ducks were sent to the palace**, when 22nd day passed, were **withdrawn from Šulgi-ili**. Month of ezem-Šulgi, Year after that of Kimaš was destroyed.	10只鸭和2只鸟**为我的王后的食物**, 5只**宰杀鸭被送入宫殿**, 于22日过去时, **从舒勒吉伊里支出**了。舒勒吉庆典月,基马什被毁年之次年。
Š 47 vii=47' ii' /24, 25, 26, 27, 28: **zi-ga** 8 doves for (**allowance of**) **dawn**, 1 thicket sow, 1 duck, 2 pigeons, 7 doves for (**allowance of**) **dusk**, 1 pigeon, 9 doves, 1 pigeon, 9 doves, 1 pigeon, 9 doves, 1 thicket sow, 1 duck, 1 dove, were **withdrawn from Šulgi-ili**	8 tu-gur$_4$^{mušen} **á~gú-zi-ga**, 1 sáh-tur-munus-giš-gi, 1 uz-tur, 2 ir$_7$^{mušen}, 7 tu-gur$_4$^{mušen} **á~ud-ten-na**, iti--ta ud-24 ba-ra-zal, 1 ir$_7$^{mušen}, 9 tu-gur$_4$^{mušen}, iti--ta ud-25 ba-ra-zal, 1 ir$_7$^{mušen}, 9 tu-gur$_4$^{mušen}, iti--ta ud-26 ba-ra-zal, 1 ir$_7$^{mušen}, 9 tu-gur$_4$^{mušen}, iti--ta ud-27 ba-ra-zal, 1 sáh-tur-munus-giš-gi, 1 uz-tur, 1 tu-gur$_4$^{mušen}, iti--ta [ud-28 ba-ra-zal], [zi-ga-^{d}***Šul-gi-ì-lí***]. *iti-ezem-^{d} Šul-gi, mu ús-sa Ki-maš^{ki} ba-hul.* (*OIP* 115 124, *P*123494)	8 *doves for* (**allowance of**) **dawn**, 1 thicket sow, 1 duck, 2 pigeons, 7 doves for (**allowance of**) **dusk**, when 24th day passed, 1 pigeon, 9 doves, when 25th day passed, 1 pigeon, 9 doves, when 26th day passed, 1 pigeon, 9 doves, when 27th day passed, 1 thicket sow, 1 duck, 1 dove, [when 28th day passed], were **withdrawn from Šulgi-ili**. Month of ezem-Šulgi, Year after that of Kimaš was destroyed.	8只野鸽为**晨时(月供)**,1只苇塘母猪、1只鸭、2只家鸽和7只野鸽为**黄昏时(月供)**,于24日过去时,1只家鸽和9只野鸽,于25日过去时,1只家鸽和9只野鸽,于26日过去时,1家鸽和9只野鸽,于27日过去时,1苇塘母猪、1鸭和1野鸽,于【28日过去时】,从【**舒勒吉伊里**】**支出**。舒勒吉庆典月,基马什被毁年之次年。

续表

时间和摘要	文献内容	英文翻译	中文翻译
Š 47 vii=47' ii': **zi-ga, butchered** 2 kids, **butchered ones were sent to the palace, were withdrawn from Šulgi-ili**	1 ^{f}ašgar, 1 máš, **ba-úš é-gal-la ba-an-ku$_4$**, zi-ga-***^{d}Šul-gi-ì-lí***.*iti-ezem-^{d}Šul-gi*, *mu ús-sa Ki-maš^{ki} ba-hul.* (*OIP* 115 125, *P123675*)	1 *female kid*, 1 *kid*, **butchered ones were sent to the palace, were withdrawn from Šulgi-ili**. Month of ezem-Šulgi, Year after that of Kimaš was destroyed.	1只雌崽和1只公崽**为宰杀牲被送入宫殿**，从**舒勒吉伊里支出**了。舒勒吉庆典月，基马什被毁年之次年。
Š 47vii=47' ii': **mu-túm, ì-dab$_5$** [1+] lamb from **Šu-Ištar**, 1 kid from **Madati**, were **deliveries for Šulgi-simti, Šulgi-ili took over**	[1+] sila$_4$, ***Šu-^{d}Iš$_8$-tár***, 1 *máš*, **Ma-da-ti**, mu-túm-***^{d}Šul-gi-sí-im-ti***, ***^{d}Šul-gi-ì-lí***, *ì-dab$_5$*. *iti-ezem-^{d}Šul-gi*, *mu ús-sa Ki-maš^{ki} ba-hul.* (*Torino* 1 047, *P133853*)	[1+] *lamb from* **Šu-Ištar**, 1 kid from**Madati**, were**deliveries for Šulgi-simti, Šulgi-ili took over**. Month of ezem-Šulgi, Year after that of Kimaš was destroyed.	【1+】只羔来自**舒伊什塔尔**，1只公崽来自**马达提**，**为舒勒吉新提的送入项，舒勒吉伊里接管了**。 舒勒吉庆典月， 基马什被毁年之次年。
Š47 viii=47' iii' /8: **zi-ga, butchered** 1 thicket sow, 1 duck, 1 pigeon, 20 doves, for the**food of my queen**, 1 thicket boar, 2 ducks, 21 doves, **butchered** ones were **sent to palace, withdrawn from Šulgi-ili**	1 sáh-tur-munus-giš-gi, 1 uz-tur, 1 ir$_7$^{mušen}, 20 tu-gur$_4$^{mušen}, **níĝ-gu$_7$-nin-ĝá**--šè, 1 sáh-tur-giš-gi, 2 uz-tur, 21 tu-gur$_4$^{mušen} **ba-úš é-gal-la ba-an-ku$_4$**, iti--ta ud-8 ba-ra-zal, zi-ga-***^{d}Šul-gi-ì-lí***. *iti-šu-eš-ša*, *mu ús-sa Ki-maš^{ki} ba-hul.* (*OIP* 115 126, *P123715*)	1 *thicket sow*, 1 *duck*, 1 *pigeon*, 20 *doves*, *for the*-**food of my queen**, 1 thicket boar, 2 ducks, 21 doves, **butchered** ones were **sent to palace**, when 8th day passed, were **withdrawn from Šulgi-ili**. Month of šu-ešša, Year after that of Kimaš was destroyed.	1苇塘母猪、1鸭、1只家鸽和20只野鸽，**为我的王后的食物**，1只苇塘公猪、2只鸭和21只野鸽，**为宰杀牲被送入宫殿**，于本月8日过去时，从**舒勒吉伊里支出**了。三只手月，基马什被毁年之次年。
Š 47 ix=47' iv': **zi-ga, butchered** 1 ewe, 1 ram, 1 kid, **butchered ones were sent to palace, withdr.from Šulgi-ili**	1 u$_8$, 1 udu-ú, 1 ^{f}ašgar, **ba-úš é-gal-la ba-an-ku$_4$**, zi-ga-***^{d}Šul-gi-ì-lí***.*iti-ezem-mah*, *mu ús-sa Ki-maš^{ki} ba-hul.* (*AnOr* 07 085, *P101380*)	1 *ewe*, 1 *grass ram*, 1 *female kid*, **butchered ones were sent to palace, withdrawn from Šulgi-ili**. Month of ezem-mah, Year after that of Kimaš was destroyed.	1只母绵羊、1只食草公绵羊、1只雌山羊崽——**宰杀牲被送入宫殿，从舒勒吉伊里支出**了。大庆典月，基马什被毁之年。
Š 47 ix=47' iv' /2: **mu-túm, ì-dab$_5$** 2 ducks from **Ka-kugga**, were **deliveries for Šulgi-simti, Šulgi-ili took over**	2 uz-tur Ka-kug-ga, iti--ta ud-2 ba-ra-zal, mu-túm-***^{d}Šul-gi-sí-im-ti***, ***^{d}Šul-gi-ì-lí*** *ì-dab$_5$*.*iti-ezem-mah*, *mu ús-sa Ki-maš^{ki} ba-hul.* (*SACT* 1 061, *P128816*)	2 *ducks from* **Ka-kugga**, when 2nd day passed, were **deliveries for Šulgi-simti, Šulgi-ili took over**.Month of ezem-mah, Year after that of Kimaš was destroyed.	2只鸭来自**卡库旮**，于本月2日过去时，**为舒勒吉新提的送入项，舒勒吉伊里接管**了。大庆典月，基马什被毁之年。
Š 47 ix=47' iv' /2: **mu-túm, ì-dab$_5$** 1 kid fr.**Ama-barú**, 2 fat rams for **monthly allowance fr.man of Urub**, 2 rams, 1 lamb fr.**Kurub-Erra**, were **deliveries for Šulgi-simti, Šulgi-ili took**	1 mášAma-barú, 2 udu-niga **sá-dug$_4$** Lú-Urub^{ki} (URUxKÁR), 2 udu-ú, 1 sila$_4$, ***Ku-ru-úb-Èr-ra***, *iti--ta ud-2 ba-ra-zal*, *mu-túm-**^{d}Šul-gi-sí-im-ti***, ***^{d}Šul-gi-ì-lí*** *ì-dab$_5$*.*iti-ezem-mah*, *mu ús-saKi-maš^{ki} ba-hul.* (*AnOr* 07 015, *P101310*)	1 *kid from***Ama-barú**, 2 fattened rams for **monthly allowance from man of Urub**, 2 grass rams, 1 lamb from **Kurub-Erra**, when 2nd day passed, were **deliveries for Šulgi-simti, Šulgi-ili took over**.Month of ezem-mah, Year after that of Kimaš was destroyed.	1只公崽**自王座之母**，2只育肥公绵羊自**乌如卜城的人的月供**，2只食草公绵羊和1只羔来自**库如卜埃腊**，于2日过去时，**为舒勒吉新提的送入项，舒勒吉伊里接管**了。大庆典月，基马什被毁之年。

续表

时间和摘要	文献内容	英文翻译	中文翻译
Š 47 ix=47' iv' /9, 10: **zi-ga** 9th: 1 ram of after-ox-class for **Inanna**, 1 grass he-goat for **Meslam-ta-ea**, 1 kid for **Nanaya**, 10th: 1 grass ram for **Inanna of Uruk**, 1 grass he-goat for **Inanna of Nippur**, **via Aya-Nanna-arkalla**, were **withdrawn from Kalam-henagi**	1 udu-gud-e-ús-sa ^{d}**Inanna**, 1 máš-gal-ú ^{d}**Mes-lam-ta-è-a**, 1 máš ^{d}**Na-na-a**, iti--ta **ud-9**ba-ra-zal, 1 udu-ú ^{d}**Inanna Unug**^{ki}-ga, 1 máš-gal-ú ^{d}**Inanna Ni-bru**^{ki}, iti--ta **ud-10**ba-ra-zal, gìr ***A-a-***^{d}***Nanna-ar-kal-la***, *zi-ga ki* ~ **Kalam-hé-na-gi**--ta. iti-ezem-mah, mu ús-sa Ki-maš^{ki} [Hu] -ur$_5$-ti^{ki} ba-hul. (BIN 3 337, P106143)	1 ram of after-ox-class for**Inanna**, 1 grass he-goat for **Meslam-ta-ea**, 1 kid for **Nanaya**, when 9th day passed, 1 grass ram for **Inanna of Uruk**, 1 grass he-goat for **Inanna of Nippur**, when **10th** day passed, **via Aya-Nanna-arkalla**, were**withdrawn from Kalam-henagi**. Month of ezem-mah, Year after that of Kimaš and Hurti were destroyed.	1只牛后级公绵羊为**伊南那**，1只食草公山羊为**美斯兰塔埃阿**，1只公崽为**那那亚**，于**9日**过去时，1只食草公绵羊为**乌鲁克的伊南那**，1只食草公山羊为**尼普尔的伊南那**，于**10日**过去时，**经由阿亚南那阿尔卡拉**，**从卡兰希那吉处支出**了。大庆典月，基马什和胡尔提被毁年之次年。
Š 47 ix=47' iv' /11: **mu-túm, ì-dab$_5$** 3 ducks from the **wife of Šarrum-ili captain**, when 11th day passed, were **deliveries for Šulgi-simti, Šulgi-ili took**	3 uz-tur, dam- ***Šar-ru-um-ì-lí*** *nu-bandà*, *iti--ta ud*-11 *ba-ra-zal*, *mu-túm-* ^{d}***Šul-gi-sí-im-ti***, ^{d}***Šul-gi-ì-lí*** ì-dab$_5$. iti-ezem-mah, mu ús-sa Ki-maš^{ki} ba-hul. (OIP 115 111, P123683)	3 ducks from the **wife of Šarrum-ili captain**, when 11th day passed, were **deliveries for Šulgi-simti, Šulgi-ili took over**. Month of ezem-mah, Year after that of Kimaš was destroyed.	3只鸭来自**沙如姆伊里军尉之妻**，于本月11日过去时，为**舒勒吉新提的送入项**，**舒勒吉伊里接管**了。大庆典月， 基马什被毁之年。
Š 47 ix=47' iv' /13: **mu-túm, ì-dab$_5$** 2 kids from**Simat-Ištar**, 2 fat rams and 1 fat goat from **Ikunum**, 1 kid from **Šarrum-ili**, 1 grass ram and 1 kid from **Nir-idagal**, 1 lamb from **en-priest of Inanna**, 1 lamb from **Adda-tur**, were **deliveries for Šulgi-simti, Šulgi-ili took over**	2 máš ***Simat-Iš$_8$-tár***, 2 *udu-niga-gud-e ~ ús-sa*, 1 *máš-gal-niga-gud-e-ús-sa*, ***I-ku-nu-um***, 1 *máš* ***Šar-ru-um-ì-lí***, 1 *udu-ú*, 1 *máš* ***Nir-ì-da-ĝál***, 1 *sila$_4$* **en-**^{d}**Inanna**, 1 sila$_4$ **Ad-da-tur**, iti--ta ud-13 ba-ra-zal, mu-túm ~ ^{d}***Šul-gi-sí-im-ti***, ^{d}***Šul-gi-ì-lí*** *ì-dab$_5$*. *iti-ezem-mah*, *mu ús-sa Ki-maš^{ki}* [*ba-hul*]. (*Orient* 16 044 16, *P*124644)	2 *kids from***Simat-Ištar**, 2 fattened rams of after-ox-class and 1 fattened he-goat of after-ox-class from **Ikunum**, 1 kid from **Šarrum-ili**, 1 grass ram and 1 kid from **Nir-idagal**, 1 lamb from **en-priest of Inanna**, 1 lamb from **Adda-tur**, when 13th day passed, were **deliveries for Šulgi-simti, Šulgi-ili took over**. Month of ezem-mah, Year after that of Kimaš was destroyed.	2只公崽自**席马特伊什塔尔**，2只牛后级育肥公绵羊和1只牛后级育肥公山羊自**伊库农**，1只公崽来自**沙润伊里**，1只食草公绵羊和1只公崽自**尼尔伊达旮勒**，1只羔自**伊南那的祭司**，1只羔自**阿达图尔**，于13日过去时，为**舒勒吉新提的送入项**，**舒勒吉伊里接管**了。大庆典月，基马什被毁之年。
Š 47 ix=47' iv' /15: **mu-túm, ì-dab$_5$** 1 fattened bull, 3 fattened rams, 5 grass rams, 1 fattened he-goat, 1 fattened female kid, from**Nir-idagal**, **deliveries for Šulgi-simti, Šulgi-ili took over**	1 gud-niga, 3 udu-niga, 5 udu-ú, 1 máš-gal-niga, 1 ^{f} ašgar-niga, ***Nir-ì-da-ĝál***, *iti--ta ud*-15 *ba-ra-zal*, *mu-túm-*^{d}***Šul-gi-sí-im-ti***, ^{d}***Šul-gi-ì-lí*** *ì-dab$_5$*. *iti-ezem-mah*, *mu ús-sa Ki-maš^{ki} ba-hul*. (*BIN* 3 021, *P*105828)	1 *fattened bull*, 3 *fattened rams*, 5 *grass rams*, 1 *fattened he-goat*, 1 *fattened female kid*, *from***Nir-idagal**, when 15th day passed, were **deliveries for Šulgi-simti, Šulgi-ili took over**. Month of ezem-mah, Year after that of Kimaš was destroyed.	1头育肥公牛、3只育肥公绵羊、5只食草公绵羊、1只育肥公山羊和1只育肥雌崽来自**尼尔伊达旮勒**，于15日过去时，为**舒勒吉新提的送入项**，**舒勒吉伊里接管**了。大庆典月，基马什被毁之年。

续表

时间和摘要	文献内容	英文翻译	中文翻译
Š 47 ix=47' iv' /18: **mu-túm，ì-dab$_5$** 2 ducks from**the wife of Kara**，were deliveries **for Šulgi-simti，Šulgi-ili took**	2 uz-tur，**dam-Ka-ra**，iti--ta ud-18 ba-ra-zal，mu-túm-^{d}***Šul-gi-síim-ti***，^{d}***Šul-gi-ì-lí*** *ì-dab$_5$*. *iti-ezem-mah*， *mu ús-saKi-maš^{ki} ba-hul.* （*Torino* 1 048，*P*133854）	2 *ducks from***the wife of Kara**，when 18th day passed，were deliveries **for Šulgi-simti，Šulgi-ili took over**.Month of ezem-mah，Year after that of Kimaš was destroyed.	2只鸭来自**卡腊之妻**，于本月18日过去时，为**舒勒吉新提的送入项**， **舒勒吉伊里接管**了。 大庆典月， 基马什被毁之年。
Š 47 ix=47' iv' /20: **zi-ga** 1 fattened ram and 1 kid for**Belat-Suhnir and Belat-Darraban，withdrawn from Šulgi-ili**	1 udu-niga，1 máš，^{d}***Be-la-at-Suh$_6$-nir*** *ù* ^{d}***Be-la-at-Dar-ra-ba-an***，*iti--ta ud-20 ba-ra-zal*，*zi-ga-* ^{d}***Šul-gi-ì-lí***. *iti-ezem-mah*，*mu ús-sa Ki-maš^{ki} ba-hul.*（*Torino* 1 193，*P*131971）	1 *fattened ram and* 1 *kid for***Belat-Suhnir and Belat-Darraban**，when 20th day passed，were **withdrawn from Šulgi-ili**. Month of ezem-mah，Year after that of Kimaš was destroyed.	1只育肥公绵羊和1只公崽为**贝拉特苏赫尼尔和贝拉特达腊班**，于本月20日过去时，**从舒勒吉伊里支出了**。大庆典月，基马什被毁之年。
Š 47 ix=47' iv' /20: **mu-túm，ì-dab$_5$** 2 fattened rams，1 fattened kid from**Apil［ati］**，1 fattened ram from **Šukubum**，were **deliveries for Šulgi-simti，Šulgi-ili took over**	2 udu-［niga］，1 máš-gal-niga，***A-pi$_5$-***［***la***?］-［***ti***?］（*erasure*：*ib-ni*），1 *udu-niga*，***Šu-ku$_8$-bu-um***，*iti-ta ud-20 ba-ra-zal*，*mu-túm-*^{d}**Šul-gi-sí-im-ti**，［^{d}***Šul***］***-gi-ì-lí***［*ì*］*-dab$_5$*.［*iti*］*-ezem-mah*，［*mu ús*］*-sa Ki-maš^{ki}*［*ba-hul*］. （*OIP* 115 112，*P*123576）	2 *fattened rams*，1 *fattened kid from***Apil［ati］**，1 fattened ram from **Šukubum**，when 20th day passed，were **deliveries for Šulgi-simti，Šulgi-ili took over**. Month of ezem-mah， Year after that of Kimaš was destroyed.	2只育肥公绵羊和1只育肥公山羊崽来自**阿皮【拉提】**，1只育肥公绵羊来自**舒库布姆**，于第20天过去时，为**舒勒吉新提的送入项，舒勒吉伊里接管**了。大庆典月，基马什被毁年之次年。
Š 47 ix=47' iv' /20: **zi-ga，butchered** 2 fat lambs and 1 fat kid for **food of king**，1 ram for **Nin-sun**，2 fat rams for **disappearing place，in the sheep-shed**，1 fattened ram for **monthly allowance**，2 grass rams in the palace，for **sacrifice of Inanna，my queen brought for the sheep-shced**，1 grass bull，3 rams and 1 lamb，**butchered** ones **were sent to the palace，with-drawn**	2 sila$_4$-niga，1 ^{f}ašgar-niga，**níĝ-gu$_7$-lugal**--šè， 1 udu-ú，^{d}**Nin-sún**， 2 udu-niga **sá-dug$_4$**，**níĝ-ki-zàh**--šè šà~ gá-udu-ka， 1 udu-niga**sá-dug$_4$**，2 udu-ú šà~ é-gal-la， **sískur-^{d}Inanna**，nin-mu gá-udu--šè è-a， 1 gud-ú，3 udu-ú，1 sila$_4$，ba-ug$_7$ **é-gal-la ba-an-ku$_4$**， iti--ta ud-20 ba-ra-zal，zi-ga.iti-ezem-mah， mu ús-sa Ki-maš^{ki}ba-hul. （DC 1，299）	2 fattened lambs and 1 fattened female kid for **the food of king**，1 grass ram for **Nin-sun**，2 fattened rams for **monthly allowance of disappearing place，in the sheep-shed**，1 fattened ram for **monthly allowance**，2 grass rams in the palace，for **sacrifice of Inanna，my queen brought for the sheep-shced**，1 grass bull，3 grass rams and 1 lamb，**butchered** ones **were sent to the palace**，when 20th day passed，**withdrawn**. Month of ezem-mah，Year after that of Kimaš was destroyed.	2只育肥羔和1只育肥雌崽为**国王的食物**， 1只食草公绵羊为**宁荪**， 2只育肥公绵羊为**消失处的月供，于羊圈**， 1只育肥公绵羊为**月供**， 2只食草公绵羊，于宫殿，**为伊南那的牺牲**， 我的王后送入到羊圈， 1头食草公牛、3只食草公绵羊和1只羔为**宰杀牲被送入宫殿**， 于20日过去时，支出了。大庆典月，基马什被毁年之次年。
Š 47 ix=47' iv' /23: **mu-túm，ì-dab$_5$** 10 ducks from**the wife of Apili**，were **deliveries for Šulgi-simti，Šulgi-ili took**	10 uz-tur **dam-*Á-pi$_5$-lí***，*iti--ta ud-23 ba-ra-zal*，*mu-túm-*^{d}***Šul-gi-sí-im-tum***，^{d}***Šul-gi-ì-lí*** *ì-dab$_5$.iti-ezem-mah*， *mu ús-sa Ki-maš^{ki} ba-hul.* （*CST* 184，*P*107696）	10 *ducks from***the wife of Apili**，when 23rd day passed，were **deliveries for Šulgi-simti，Šulgi-ili took over**. Month of ezem-mah，Year after that of Kimaš was destroyed.	10只鸭来自**阿皮里之妻**，于23日过去时，为**舒勒吉新提的送入项**， **舒勒吉伊里接管**了。 大庆典月， 基马什被毁年之次年。

续表

时间和摘要	文献内容	英文翻译	中文翻译
Š 47 ix=47' iv': **zi-ga** 2 rams for **Belat-Suhnir and Belat-Darraban**, 1 ram for **Adad**, in **Ur**, **via Mašum**, **withdrawn from Šulgi-ili**	2 udu-ú^{d}***Be-la-at-Suh-nir*** *ù* ^{d}**Be-la-at-Dar-ra-ba-an**, 1 *udu-ú* ^{d}**Iškur**, šà~ **Urim^{ki}**-ma, gìr ***Ma-šum***, *zi-ga-*^{d}***Šul-gi-ì-lí***. *iti-ezem-mah*, *mu ús-sa Ki-maš^{ki} ba-hul.* (*OIP* 115 127, *P*123583)	2 *grass rams for* **Belat-Suhnir and Belat-Darraban**, 1 grass ram for **Adad**, in **Ur**, **via Mašum**, were **withdrawn from Šulgi-ili**. Month of ezem-mah, Year after that of Kimaš was destroyed.	2食草公绵羊为**贝拉特苏赫尼尔和贝拉特达腊班**，1食草公绵羊为**阿达德**，于**乌尔**，**经由马顺**，**舒勒吉伊里支出**。大庆典月，基马什被毁年之次年。
Š 47 ix=47' iv': **mu-túm, ì-dab$_5$** 2 grass bulls, 16 grass rams, 4 he-goats from**Šulgi-ili, the general**, 1 lamb from **Zak-ili**, were **deliveries for Šulgi-simti, Šulgi-ili took**	2 gud-ú, 16 udu-ú, 4 máš-gal, ***Šul-gi-ì-lí*** *šagina*, 1 *sila$_4$*, ***Za-ak-ì-lí***, *mu-túm-*^{d}***Šul-gi-sí-im-ti***, ^{d}***Šul-gi-ì-lí*** *ì-dab$_5$*. *iti-ezem-mah*, *mu ús-sa Ki-maš^{ki} ba-hul.* (*OIP* 115 113, *P*123654)	2 *grass bulls*, 16 *grass rams*, 4 *he-goats from***Šulgi-ili, the general**, 1 lamb from **Zak-ili**, were **deliveries for Šulgi-simti, Šulgi-ili took over**. Month of ezem-mah, Year after that of Kimaš was destroyed.	2头食草公牛、16只食草公绵羊和4只公山羊来自**舒勒吉伊里将军**，1只羔自**扎克伊里**，为**舒勒吉新提的送入项**，**舒勒吉伊里接管了**。大庆典月，基马什被毁年次年。
Š 47 x=47' v' mu-túm, ì-dab$_5$ 2 lambs from **Ninlil-tumimti**, were deliveries for **Šulgi-simti, Šulgi-ili took**	2 sila$_4$ ^{d}**Nin-lil-*tum-im-ti***, *mu-túm-*^{d} ***Šul-gi-sí-im-ti***, ^{d} ***Šul-gi-ì-lí*** *ì-dab$_5$*. *iti-ezem-An-na*, *mu ús-sa Ki-maš^{ki} ba-hul.* (*OIP* 115 114, P123362)	2 *lambs from* **Ninlil-tumimti**, were deliveries for **Šulgi-simti**, **Šulgi-ili took over**. Month of ezem-Anna, Year after that of Kimaš was destroyed.	2只羔自**宁里勒吞伊姆提**，为**舒勒吉新提的送入项**，**舒勒吉伊里接管了**。天神安庆典月，基马什被毁年之次年。
Š 47 x=47' v' /15: **zi-ga** 1 fat ram for **monthly allowance of gate (for ká?) of shrine**, 1 fat ram for **monthly allowance of the gate (for ká?) of bedroom of high priestess**, 1 grass ram for **Nanaya**, were **withdrawn from Šulgi-ili**, in **Uruk**	1 udu-niga**sá-dug$_4$**, **ka~èš**, 1 udu-niga**sá-dug$_4$**, **ka~ĝi$_6$-pàr-ra**, 1 udu-ú^{d}**Na-na-a**, iti--ta ud-15 ba-ra-zal, zi-ga- ^{d}***Šul-gi-ì-lí***, *šà*~ **Unug^{ki}**-ga. iti-ezem-An-na, mu ús-saKi-maš^{ki} ba-hul. (Aegyptus 29 109 40, P100273)	1 fattened ram for**monthly allowance of gate (for ká?) of shrine**, 1 fattened ram for **monthly allowance of the gate (for ká?) of bedroom of high priestess**, 1 grass ram for **Nanaya**, when 15th day passed, were **withdrawn from Šulgi-ili**, in **Uruk**. Month of ezem-Anna, Year after that of Kimaš was destroyed.	1只育肥公绵羊为**圣殿门的月供**， 1只育肥公绵羊为**祭司寝宫的月供**， 1只食草公绵羊为**那那亚**，于本月15日过去时，从**舒勒吉伊里支出了**， **于乌鲁克**。 天神安庆典月，基马什被毁年之次年。

续表

时间和摘要	文献内容	英文翻译	中文翻译
Š 47 x=47’ v’ /19: **zi-ga** 1 fat goat for (**allowance of**) **the gate** (**for ká?**) **of bedroom of high priestess**, 1 fat ram for **allowance of Adad**, 2 grass rams for **offering of "disappearing place" of Belat-Suhnir and Belat-Darraban**, in **Ur**, **withdrawn from Šulgi-ili**	1 máš-gal-niga**ka~ĝi$_6$-par$_4$-ra**, 1 udu-niga sá-dug$_4$ **^{d}Iškur**, iti--ta ud-19 ba-ra-zal, 2 udu-ú**niĝ-ki-zàh** *^{d}Be-la-at-Suh-nir* ù **^{d}Be-la-at-Dar-ra-ba-an**, *šà*~ **Urim^{ki}**-ma, zi-ga-*^{d}Šul-gi-ì-lí*. *iti-ezem-An-na*, *mu ús-saKi-maš^{ki}ba-hul.* (*MVN*02 165, *P*113464)	1 *fattened he-goat for* (**allowance of**) **the gate** (**for ká?**) **of bedroom of high priestess**, 1 fattened ram for **monthly allowance of Adad**, when 19th day passed, 2 grass rams for **offering of "disappearing place" of Belat-Suhnir and Belat-Darraban**, in **Ur**, **withdrawn from Šulgi-ili**. Month of ezem-Anna, Year after that of Kimaš was destroyed.	1只育肥公山羊为**祭司寝宫（月供）**， 1只育肥公绵羊为**阿达德的月供**， 于19日过去时，2只食草公绵羊为**贝拉特苏赫尼尔和贝拉特达腊班的消失处供奉**， 于**乌尔**，从**舒勒吉伊里支出**了。天神安庆典月， 基马什被毁年之次年。
Š 47 x=47’ v’ /28: **mu-túm**, **ì-dab$_5$** 6 ducks from **Bagum**, the **bird-catcher**, **were deliveries for Šulgi-simti**, **Šulgi-ili took over**	6 uz-tur***Ba-gu-um*** *mušen-dù*, *iti--ta ud-28 ba-ra-zal*, *mu-túm-^{d}* [***Šul-gi***] ***-sí-im-ti***, ***^{d}Šul-gi-ì-lí*** *ì-dab$_5$*. *iti-ezem-An-na*, *mu ús-sa Ki-maš^{ki} ba-hul.* (*PDT* 1 139, *P*125556)	6 *ducks from* **Bagum**, the **bird-catcher**, when 28th day passed, **were deliveries for Šulgi-simti**, **Šulgi-ili took over**. Month of ezem-Anna, Year after that of Kimaš was destroyed.	6只鸭来自**捕鸟人巴鲧**，于本月28日过去时，为**舒勒吉新提的送入项**，**舒勒吉伊里接管**了。天神安庆典月，基马什被毁年之次年。
Š 47 x=47’ v’ /30: **zi-ga**, **butchered** 2 ducks, 1 domestic sow, **butchered ones were sent to the palace**, were **withdrawn from Šulgi-ili**	2 uz-tur, 1 šáh-izi-tur-munus-uru, **ba-úš é-gal-la ba-an-ku$_4$**, iti--ta ud-30 ba-ra-zal, zi-ga- ***^{d}Šul-gi-ì-lí***. *iti-ezem-An-na*, *mu ús-sa Ki-maš^{ki} ba-hul.* (*Babyl.*7 78 14, *P*104772)	2 *ducks*, 1 *domestic sow*, **butchered ones were sent to the palace**, when 30th day passed, were **withdrawn from Šulgi-ili**. Month of ezem-Anna, Year after that of Kimaš was destroyed.	2只鸭和1只驯养的母猪，这些**死牲被送入宫殿**，于30日过去时，从**舒勒吉伊里支出**了。 天神安庆典月， 基马什被毁年之次年。
Š 47 x=47’ v’: **zi-ga** [1+] fat ram for (**gate of**) **the shrine**, 1 fat ram for **gate of bedroom of high priestess**, 1 ram for **Nanaya**, **via Ahuwaqar**, were withdrawn, in **Uruk**, **from Kalam-henagi**, for shrine, **in the New Moon**	[1+] udu-niga <ká->**èš**--šè, 1 udu-niga **ká~ĝi$_6$-pàr-ra**, 1 udu-gud-e-ús-sa **^{d}Na-na-a**, gìr ***A-hu-wa-qar***, *zi-ga šà*~ **Unug^{ki}**-ga, ki~ **Kalam-hé-na-gi**--ta, **èš**--šè **ud-sakar**. iti-ezem-An-na, [mu] ús-sa Ki-maš^{ki} ù [Hu-ur$_5$-ti]^{ki} ba-hul. (PDT 2 1272, P126599)	[1+] fattened ram for (**the gate of**) **the shrine**, 1 fattened ram for **the gate of bedroom of high priestess**, 1 ram of after-ox-class for **Nanaya**, **via Ahuwaqar**, were withdrawn, in **Uruk**, **from Kalam-henagi**, for the shrine, **in the New Moon**. Month of ezem-Anna, Year after that of Kimaš and Hurti were destroyed.	[1+] 只育肥公绵羊为**圣殿（门）**，1只育肥共勉为**祭司寝宫**，1只牛后级公绵羊为**那那亚**，**经由阿胡瓦喀尔**，这些支出了，于**乌鲁克**，**从卡兰希那吉处**，**为圣殿**，**于新月时**。天神安庆典月， 基马什和胡尔提被毁年之次年。
Š 47 xi=47’ vi’ /5: **mu-túm**, **ì-dab$_5$** 2 ducks from **Lugal-me-lam**, **the secretary**, were **deliveries for Šulgi-simti**, **Šulgi-ili took over**	2 uz-tur, **Lugal-me-lám sukkal**, iti--ta ud-5 ba-ra-zal, mu-túm-***^{d}Šul-gi-*** [***sí-im-ti***], ***^{d}Šul-gi-ì-lí*** *ì-dab$_5$*. *iti-ezem-Me-ki-ĝál*, *mu ús-sa Ki-maš^{ki}ba-hul.* (*OIP* 115 115, *P*123530)	2 *ducks from* **Lugal-me-lam**, **the envoy**, when 5th day passed, were **deliveries for Šulgi-simti**, **Šulgi-ili took over**. Month of ezem-Mekiĝal, Year after that of Kimaš was destroyed.	2只鸭来自**卢旮勒美兰国使**，于5日过去时，为**舒勒吉新提的送入项**，**舒勒吉伊里接管**了。神美基旮勒庆典月， 基马什被毁年之次年。

续表

时间和摘要	文献内容	英文翻译	中文翻译
Š 47 xi=47’ vi’ /5，10： **zi-ga，butchered** 1 fattened bull and 3 grass rams，1 fattened bull and 1 grass ram，**butchered ones**，were **withdrawn from Kalam-henagi，sent to palace**	1 gud-niga，3 udu-ú，iti--ta ud-5 ba-ra-zal，1 gud-niga，1 gud-ú，**ba-úš** iti--ta ud-10 ba-ra-zal， zi-ga ki～ **Kalam-hé-na-gi**--ta，**é-gal-la ba-an-ku$_4$**. iti-ezem-Me-ki-ĝál，mu ús-sa Ki-maš^{ki} ba-hul. （AUCT 1 881，P103726）	1 fattened bull and 3 grass rams，when**5th** day passed，1 fattened bull and 1 grass ram，**butchered ones**，when **10th** day passed，were **withdrawn from Kalam-henagi，sent to palace**. Month of Mekiĝal，Year after that of Kimaš was destroyed.	1头育肥公牛和3只食草公绵羊于**5日**过去时，1头育肥公牛和1只食草公绵羊，以上为**宰杀牲**，于**10日**过去时，从**卡兰希那吉处支出**了，被送入宫殿。神美基旮勒庆典月，基马什被毁年之次年。
Š 47 xi=47’ vi’ /7： **zi-ga，butchered** 3 ducks and 1 pigeon，**butchered ones were sent to the palace，withdrawn from Šulgi-ili**	3 uz-tur，1 ir$_7$^{mušen} **ba-úš é-gal-la ba-an-ku$_4$**，iti--ta ud-7 ba-ra-zal，zi-ga **^{d}Šul-gi-ì-lí**. *iti-ezem-Me-ki-ĝál*，*mu ús-sa Ki-maš^{ki} ba-hul.* （*AnOr* 07 086，*P*101381）	3 *ducks and* 1 *pigeon*，**butchered ones were sent to the palace**，when 7th day passed，**withdrawn from Šulgi-ili**. Month of ezem-Mekiĝal，Year after that of Kimaš was destroyed.	3只鸭和1只家鸽，这些**宰杀牲被送入宫殿**，于7日过去时，从**舒勒吉伊里支出**了。神美基旮勒庆典月，基马什被毁年之次年。
Š 47 xi=47’ vi’ /7： **zi-ga** ［1+］ram for **Adad**，［1+］ram for **Gula，in the palace**，1 lamb for **disappearing place of Nanaya**，1 fat ram for **allowance**，1 lamb for **gate（for ká）of bedroom of high priestess**，1 fat ram，1 lamb for **Nanaya**，1 fattened bull，2 fattened rams，1 lamb for **gate of shrine of e-zar-zar**，in **Uruk**，**via my queen**，**withdrawn from Šulgi-ili**	［1+］udu-ú［^{d}］**Iškur**， ［1+］udu-ú［^{d}］**Gú-lá** šà～ é-gal--šè，1 sila$_4$ níĝ-ki-záh-**^{d}Na-na-a**， 1 udu-niga **sá-dug$_4$**， 1 sila$_4$ **ka～ĝe$_6$-pàr**， 1 udu-niga-gud-e ús-sa，1 sila$_4$ **^{d}Na-na-a** a-rá 2-kam-aš， 1 gud-niga，2 udu-niga，1 sila$_4$，**ka～èš**，e-ZAR-ZAR šà～ **Unug^{ki}**-ga， iti--ta ud-7 ba-ra-zal， gìr **nin-ĝá**， zi-ga-**^{d}Šul-gi-ì-lí**. *iti-ezem-Me-ki-ĝál*，*mu ús-sa Ki-maš^{ki} ba-hul.* （*AnOr* 07 087，*P*101382）	［1+］*grass ram for***Adad**，［1+］grass ram for **Gula，in the palace**，1 lamb for **offering of disappearing place of Nanaya**，1 fattened ram for **monthly allowance**，1 lamb for **gate（for ká）of bedroom of high priestess**，1 fattened ram of after-ox-class，1 lamb for **Nanaya** on 2nd time，1 fattened bull，2 fattened rams，1 lamb for **gate of shrine of e-zar-zar**，in **Uruk**，when 7th day passed，**via my queen，withdrawn from Šulgi-ili**. Month of ezem-Mekiĝal，Year after that of Kimaš was destroyed.	【1+】只食草公绵羊为**阿达德**，【1+】只食草公绵羊为**古拉，于宫殿**，1只羔为**那那亚消失处的供奉**，1只育肥公绵羊为**月供**，1只羔为**祭司寝宫**，1只牛后级育肥公绵羊和1羔为**那那亚**第2次，1只育肥公牛、2只育肥公绵羊和1只羔为**e-zar-zar的圣殿门**，于**乌鲁克**， 于7日过去时， **经由我的王后**，从**舒勒吉伊里支出**。 神美基旮勒庆典月， 基马什被毁年之次年。
Š 47 xi=47’ vi’ /19： **zi-ga，butchered** 1 thicket sow to the center of palace，7 ducklets and 1 dove，**dead of ill，were sent to the palace，withdrawn from Šulgi-ili**	1 šáh-izi-tur-munus-geš-gi，šà～ **é-gal**--šè，7 uz-tur，1 tu-gur$_4$^{mušen} ri-ri-ga-àm **é-gal-la ba-an-ku$_4$**，iti--ta ud-19 ba-ra-zal，zi-ga-**^{d} Šul-gi-ì-lí**. *iti-ezem-Me-ki-ĝál*，*mu ús-sa Ki-maš^{ki} ba-hul.* （*SET* 053，*P*129463）	1 *thicket sow to the center of palace*，7 *ducklets and* 1 *dove*，**dead of ill，were sent to the palace**，when 19th day passed，were **withdrawn from Šulgi-ili**. Month of ezem-Mekiĝal，Year after that of Kimaš was destroyed.	1只苇塘母猪到**内殿**，7只幼鸭和1只野鸽——**病死牲被送入宫殿**，于本月19日过去时，从**舒勒吉伊里支出**了。神美基旮勒庆典月，基马什被毁年之次年。

续表

时间和摘要	文献内容	英文翻译	中文翻译
Š 47 xi=47' vi' /25: **zi-ga** 1 ram of after-ox-class for **giranum festival of Inanna**, 1 fattened bull and 3 fattened rams for **Inanna**, 1 fattened ram for **Nanaya**, 1 ram was **sent to the palace for Igi-kur**, 2 grass rams for **the rent of hiring 2 boats, for the boat of An, in Uruk, from Kalam-henagi, via Ahu-wagar**	1 udu-gud-e-ús-sa ***gi-ra-núm-*****^{d}Inanna**, 1 gud-niga, 3 udu-niga**^{d}Inanna**, 1 udu-niga, ***^{d}Na-na-a***, 1 *udu-gud-e-ús-sa*, **é-gal ^{d}Igi-kur**, 2 udu-ú á-má-2-a ba-huĝ, zi-ga**má-An-na**, **šà ~ Unug^{ki}**-ga, ki ~ **Kalam-hé-na-gi**--ta, **gìr *A-hu-wa-gar***.*iti-ezem-Me-ki-ĝál*, *ud-25*, *mu ús-sa Ki-maš^{ki}* ù [*Hu-mur*] *-ti^{ki} ba-hul.* (*SumRecDreh.*12, P130509)	1 *ram of after-ox-class for* **giranum festival of Inanna**, 1 fattened bull and 3 fattened rams for**Inanna**, 1 fattened ram for **Nanaya**, 1 ram of after-ox-class was **sent to the palace for Igi-kur**, 2 grass rams for **the rent of hiring 2 boats, for the boat of An, in Uruk, from Kalam-henagi, via Ahu-wagar**. Month of ezem-Mekiĝal, on 25th day, Year after that of Kimaš was destroyed	1只牛后级公绵羊为**伊南那的吉腊努姆仪式**，1头育肥公牛和3只育肥公绵羊为**伊南那**，1只育肥公绵羊为**那那亚**，1只牛后级公绵羊为**伊吉库尔神被送入宫殿**，2只食草公绵羊为**租2条船的费用，为安神之船，于乌鲁克，自卡兰希那吉，经由阿胡瓦甘尔**。神美基旮勒庆典月，于25日，基马什被毁年之次年。
Š 47 xi=47' vi': **kišib** the arrear of 115 minas wool, the arrear of workdays are 3247 women slave for one days, the**receipt of Šulgi-ili**	lá-ì 1 gú 55 ma-na siki ~ gin, lá-ì 3247 ú gemé ud-1--šè, kišib ***^{d}Šul-gi-ì-lí***.*iti-ezem-Me-ki-ĝál*, *mu ús-saKi-maš^{ki} ba-hul.* (*AnOr* 07 145, *P*101440)	*the arrear of* 115 *minas wool, the arrear of workdays are* 3247 *women slave for one days*, *the***receipt of Šulgi-ili**.Month of ezem-Mekiĝal, Year after that of Kimaš was destroyed.	115斤羊毛的欠款，3247个女奴工作一天的欠款，**舒勒吉伊里的收据**。 神美基旮勒庆典月， 基马什被毁年之次年。
Š 48 i=47' viii' /10: **zi-ga** 1 kid for **Tigris**, 1 fattened ram for **Ninlil**, 1 fattened ram and 1 fattened lamb for **food of king**, **were withdrawn**, **in the field of meadow**, **from Kalam-henagi**	1 máš **^{d}I$_{7}$-idigna**, 1 udu-niga**^{d}Nin-líl**, 1 udu-niga, 1 sila$_{4}$-niga **níĝ-gu$_{7}$-lugal**--šè, zi-ga šà ~ a-šà a-gará, ki ~ **Kalam-hé-na-gi**, iti--ta ud-10 ba-ra-zal.iti maš-dà ~ gu$_{7}$, mu ús-sa Ki-maš^{ki} ù Hur-ti^{ki} ba-hul, mu ús-sa-a-bi. (Rochester 022, P128127)	1 kid for **Tigris**, 1 fattened ram for **Ninlil**, 1 fattened ram and 1 fattened lamb for **food of king**, **were withdrawn**, **in the field of meadow**, **from Kalam-henagi**, when 10th day passed. Month of mašda ~ gu$_{7}$, Year after that of Kimaš and Hurti were destroyed, after that.	1公崽为**底格里西斯河神**，1育肥公绵羊为**宁里勒**，1育肥公绵羊和1育肥羔为**国王的食物**，于牧场的田地中，从**卡兰希那吉处支出了**，于10日过去时。食瞪羚月，基马什和胡尔提被毁年之次年：之次年。
Š 48 ii=47' ix' /10: **zi-ga**, **butchered** 1 ram of after-ox-class for**Nanaya** and 1 sucking lamb for **the food of king**, **via Šumama**, 1 **butchered** lamb, were withdrawn from the place of **Kalam-he-nagi**	1 udu-gud-e-ús-sa **^{d}Na-na-a**, 1 sila$_{4}$-ga níĝ-gu$_{7}$-**lugal**--šè, gìr **Šu-ma-ma**, 1 sila$_{4}$-ga ba-úšzi-ga ki ~ **Kalam-hé-na-gi**, iti--ta ud-10 ba-ra-zal.iti-ze$_{x}$-da ~ gu$_{7}$, mu ús-sa Ki-maš^{ki} ba-hul mu ús-sa-a-bi. (PDT 1 339, P125755)	1 ram of after-ox-class for**Nanaya** and 1 sucking lamb for **the food of king**, **via Šumama**, 1 **butchered** lamb, were withdrawn from the place of **Kalam-he-nagi**, when 10th day passed. Month of zeda ~ gu$_{7}$, Year after that of Kimaš was destroyed: after that.	1只牛后级公绵羊为**那那亚**，1只吃奶羔为**国王的食物**，**经由舒马马**， 1只**宰杀羔**， 从**卡兰希那吉处支出了**，于10日过去时。食豚月，基马什被毁年之次年：之次年。

续表

时间和摘要	文献内容	英文翻译	中文翻译
Š 48 ii=47' ix'： **šu~ ba-ti** 10 bán of oil and 140 minas of gypsum，for the clothes，from **the man of URUxKÁR，Apilatum received**	0.0.1 ì-giš，2 gú 20 ma-na im-babbár，mu~ túg šù-ha-šè，ki lú-Urub（URUxKÁR）^{ki}--ta，***Á-pi$_5$-la-tum*** *šu~ ba-ti. iti-ze$_x$-da~gu$_7$，mu ús-sa Ki-maš^{ki} ba-hul，mu ús-sa-bi.* （*OIP* 115 480，*P*123668）	10 *bán of oil and* 140 *minas of gypsum*，*for the clothes*，*from* **the man of URUxKÁR，Apilatum received**. Month of zeda~gu$_7$， Year after that of Kimaš was destroyed：after that.	10 斗油和 140 斤石膏为布料， **来自乌如卜城的人，阿皮拉吞接收了**。 食豚月， 基马什被毁年之次年：之次年。
Š 48 ix=48' iv'： **mu-túm，ì-dab$_5$** 40rams delivered from **king**，from **Naram-ili，Šulgi-simtum took over**	40 udu，mu-túm-lugal，ki~***Na-ra-am-ì-lí***--*ta*，***^{d}Šul-gi-sí-im-tum*** *ì-dab$_5$. iti-ezem-mah，mu Ha-ar-ši^{ki} Ki-maš^{ki} ù Hu-ur$_5$-ti^{ki} ba-hul.* （*OIP* 115，13，*P*123249）	40*rams delivered from* **king**，from **Naram-ili，Šulgi-simtum took over**. Month of Ezem-mah. Year of Harši，Hurti and Kimaš were destroyed.	40 只绵羊为**王送牲**，从**那冉伊里**处，**舒勒吉新吞（王后）接管**了。大庆典月，哈尔西、基马什和胡尔提被毁之年。
Š 48 x=48' v'： **mu-túm，ì-dab$_5$** 70 sheep，10 he-goats for king，fr. Naram-ili，**Šulgi-ili** took，**seal of Šulgi-simtum**	70 udu，10 máš-gal，mu-túm-lugal，ki~ ***Na-ra-am-ì-lí***--*ta*， **^{d}Šul-gi-ì-lí** *rá-gaba ì-dab$_5$*， *kišib* ***^{d}Šul-gi-sí-im-tum***. *iti-ezem-An-na，mu Ha-ar-ši^{ki} ù Ki-maš^{ki} ba-hul.* （*Princeton* 1037，*P*126726）	70 *sheep*，10 *he-goats were* **deliveries of king**，from the place of **Naram-ili，Šulgi-ili，the knight took over，the seal of Šulgi-simtum**. Month of ezem-Anna，Year that of Harši and Kimaš was destroyed.	70 只公绵羊和 10 只公山羊为**国王的送入**， 从**那冉伊里**处， **骑使舒勒吉伊里接管**了，**舒勒吉新提的印章**。天神安庆典月，哈尔希和基马什被毁之年。
Š 48 x =48' v'： **mu-túm，ì-dab$_5$** 70 rams and 10 he-goats were deliveries for **the king**，from the place of **Naram-ili，Ninhamati，the knight took over，the seal of Ninkalla**	70 udu，10 máš-gal，mu-túm~ **lugal**，ki~ ***Na-*［*ra*］*-am-ì-lí*--*ta***，**Nin-ha-ma-ti** rá-gaba ì-dab$_5$， kišib**Nin-kal-la**. iti-ezem-An-na，mu Ha-ar-ši^{ki} ù Ki-maš^{ki}ba-hul. （OIP 115 014，P123546）	70 rams and 10 he-goats were deliveries for **the king**，from the place of **Naram-ili，Ninhamati，the knight took over，the seal of Ninkalla**. Month of ezem-Anna，Year of Harši and Kimaš were destroyed.	70 只公绵羊和 10 只公山羊为**国王的送入项**， 从**那冉伊里**处， **宁哈马提骑使接管**了， **宁卡拉的印章**。 天神安庆典月，哈尔希和基马什被毁之年。

续表

时间和摘要	文献内容	英文翻译	中文翻译
Š? v/7: **mu-túm, ì-dab$_5$** 1 better fattened female kid for**Inanna**, **Enlil-zišagal as royal deputy**, **on the dawn**; 2 better fattened rams and 1 lamb for **Nanna**, **for the sacrifice in palace**, when the king entered, 1 fattened ram of 4-class for Nin-x, were deliveries for **Šulgi-simti**, **Enlil-zišagalas royal deputy**, **on the dusk**, from **the palce of Ahuwer were withdrawn**, **via Šulgi-almah scribe**	1^f asgar-niga [sig$_5$-ús], ^{d} **Inanna**, ^{d} **En-líl-zi-šà-gál** maškim, **á-gi$_6$-ba-a**; 2 udu-niga-sig$_5$-ús, 1 sila$_4$, ^{d}**Nanna**, **siskúr šà~ é-gal**, lugal ku$_4$-ra, 1 udu-niga-4-kam-ús, ^{d} Nin- [...], [mu-túm ^{d}**Šul-gi**] **-sí-im-ti**, ^{d}*En-líl-zi-šà-gál maškim*, **á-u$_4$-te-na**, iti-ud-7 ba-zal, ki~ ***A-hu-We-er--ta***, *ba-zi*, gìr ^{d}**Šul-gi-al-mah**dub-sar.iti-ezem-^{d}Nin-a-zu, mu ús-sa [^{d}Šul-gi], lugal-e [...], edge.5 udu. Seal: ^{d}Šul-gi-al-mah, dub-sar, dumu [...]. (Rochester 007, P128112)	1 better fattened female kid for**Inanna**, **Enlil-zišagal as royal deputy**, **on the dawn**; 2 better fattened rams and 1 lamb for **Nanna**, **for the sacrifice in palace**, when the king entered, 1 fattened ram of 4-class for Nin-x, were deliveries for **Šulgi-simti**, **Enlil-zišagalas royal deputy**, **on the dusk**, when the 7th day passed, from **the palce of Ahuwer were withdrawn**, **via Šulgi-almah scribe**. Month of ezem-Ninazu, Year after that of Šulgi, the king, (sum:) 5 rams. (seal:) Šulgi-almah scribe was the son of…	1只次优等育肥雌崽为**伊南那**，**恩里勒兹沙旮勒督办**，为晨祭；2只次优等育肥公绵羊和1只羔为**南那**，以上为于宫殿的祭祀，当国王进入时，1只四等育肥公绵羊为宁-X，**为舒勒吉新提的送入项**，**恩里勒兹沙旮勒督办**，为黄昏祭，于7日过去式，自**阿胡维尔处支出**，**经由舒勒吉阿勒马赫书吏**。神宁阿朱庆典月，舒勒吉国王……之年，(共:) 5只羊。 (印章:) 舒勒吉阿勒马和书吏是X之子。
Š ? **zi-ga** [1+] fat ram, via [...], 1 fat ram, [x], **via Mašum**, 2 rams of after-ox-class, for **temple of Belat-Suhnir and Belat-Darban**, 1 ram of after-ox-class for **sacrifice of Inanna by the wall**, 1 ram for **temple of Belat-Daraban**, **for allowance of** [...], 1 bull for **Šukubum**	[1+] udu- [niga], gìr [...], 1 udu-niga, [x] [...], gìr ***Ma* - [*šum*...]**, 2 *udu ~ gud-e-* [*ús-sa...*], *é-*^{d}***Be-la-at-Suh-* [*nir*]** *ù* ^{d}***Be-la-at-* [*Dar-ba*] *-an***, 1 *udu ~ gud-e-ús siskúr-*^{d}*Inanna-da-bàd*, 1 *udu ~ gud-e-ús é-*^{d}***Be-la-at-Da-ra-* [*ban*]**, *sá-dug$_4$-* [...], 1 *gud* ***Šu-* [*ku$_8$*] *-* [*bu*] *-* [*um*]**, 1 *sila$_4$* [*níĝ-x*] - [...], *šà é-* [*gal*] [...] (*OIP* 115 134, *P*123608)	[1+] *fattened ram*, *via* [...], 1 *fattened ram*, [*x*], **via Mašum**, 2 rams of after-ox-class, for **temple of Belat-Suhnir and Belat-Darban**, 1 ram of after-ox-class for **sacrifice of Inanna by the wall**, 1 ram of after-ox-class for **temple of Belat-Daraban**, **for monthly allowance of** [...], 1 bull for **Šukubum**, 1 lamb for the food of x, in palace, [...]	【1+】只育肥公绵羊，**经由X**，1只育肥公绵羊，**经由马顺**，2只牛后级公绵羊为**贝拉特苏赫尼尔和贝拉特达腊班之庙**，1只牛后级公绵羊为**伊南那的牺牲于城墙**，1只牛后级公绵羊为**贝拉特达腊班之庙**，**为【……】月供**，1头公牛为**舒库布姆**，1只羔为X食物，**于宫殿**
Š ? vi/10: **zi-ga** 2 fat rams for **Belat-Suhnir and Belat-Darraban**, 1 fat ram for **Nanna**, 1 fat ram for **Inanna**, were **withdrawn from Apiliya**	2 udu-niga^d***Be-la-at-Suh-nir*** *ù* ^{d}***Be-la-at-Dar-ra-ba-an***, 1 *udu-niga* ^{d}**Nanna**, 1 udu-niga ^{d}**Inanna**, iti--ta ud-10 ba-zal, zi-ga [***Á-pi$_5$***] ***-lí-a***. [*iti-á-ki*] *-ti*, [*mu...*^{d}] *Šul-gi* [...]. (*MVN* 15 306, *P*106170)	2 *fattened rams for***Belat-Suhnir and Belat-Darraban**, 1 fattened ram for **Nanna**, 1 fattened ram for **Inanna**, when 10th day passed, were **withdrawn from Apiliya**.Month of akiti, Year of ……	2只育肥公绵羊为**贝拉特苏赫尼尔和贝拉特达腊班**，1只育肥公绵羊为**南那**，1只育肥公绵羊为**伊南那**，于10日过去时，从**阿皮里亚支出了**。阿基提月，……年
Š?: **zi-ga**, **butchered** 1 fat ram for cloister, 1**butchered** fat ewe sent to palace	…1 udu-niga sá-dug$_4$, é-gi$_6$-par$_4$-r [a], 1 u$_8$-niga ba-úš é-gal-la ba-an-ku$_4$,… (OIP 115 135, P123652)	…1 fattened ram for monthly allowance of the cloister, 1**butchered** fattened ewe was sent to the palace,…	……1只育肥公绵羊为女观院的月供，1只宰杀的育肥母绵羊被送入宫殿……

续表

时间和摘要	文献内容	英文翻译	中文翻译
Š ? ix/23: **zi-ga** [1+] fat goat for **Ulmašitum**, **via Nin-hamati**, 1 fat goat for **Inanna**, 1 fat goat for **Nin-šubur**, **via Dakma-kešše**, **withdr.fr.Kalam-henagi**	[1+] máš- [gal-niga] ***dUl-ma-ši-tum*** *gìr* **Nin-ha-ma-ti**, 1 máš-gal-niga **dInanna**, 1 máš-gal-niga, **d Nin-šubur**, gìr**Da-ak-ma-kéš-šè**, zi-ga ki ~ **Kalam-hé-na-gi**--ta, iti--ta ud-23 ba-ra-zal.iti-ezem-mah, [mu...] (TRU 286, P135050)	[1+] fattened he-goat for**Ulmašitum**, **via Nin-hamati**, 1 fattened he-goat for **Inanna**, 1 fattened he-goat for **Nin-šubur**, **via Dakma-kešše**, **were withdrawn from Kalam-henagi**, when 23rd day passed.Month of ezem-mah, [Year of]	【1+】只育肥公山羊为**乌勒马席吞**，**经由宁哈马提**，1只育肥公山羊为**伊南那**，1只育肥公山羊为**宁舒布尔**，**经由达克马凯塞**，**从卡兰希那吉处支出了**，于23日过去时。大庆典月，【……年】。
Š? xii/14, 16: **zi-ga** 14th: [1+] fat ram and 1 ewe for **sacrifice of the Full Moon**, **in giš-zu-di-ga**, 16th: 3 fat rams for **place of Kin-kin-da**, **with-drawn from Apilatum**	[1+] udu-niga, 1 u_8, **siskúr** šà~ **giš-zu-di-ga** é-ud-15, iti--ta **ud-14**ba-ra-zal; 3 udu-niga, ki **Kin-kin-da lugal x gaba-ri**, iti--ta **ud-16** ba-ra-zal, zi-ga ***Á-pi5-la-tum***. [*iti*] *-še-kin-kud.* (*Babyl.*8 *HG* 07, *P*104804)	[1+] *fattened ram and* 1 *ewe for***sacrifice of the Full Moon**, **in giš-zu-di-ga**, when 14thday passed; 3 fattened rams for **the place of Kin-kin-da**, the king copied (the tablet), when the 16th day passed, were **withdrawn from Apilatum**. Month of še-kin-kud.	【1+】育肥公绵羊和1只母绵羊为**满月牺牲**，于**giš-zu-di-ga**，于14日过去时；3只育肥公绵羊为**Kin-kin-da**，**国王复制了**（泥板），于16日过去时，**从阿皮拉吞支出了**。大麦收割月。
Š 46 x: ki~...--*ta* 55*minas of worse wool from* **the place of Šulgi-ili**, **were sent to the palace**	55 ma-na siki-mug ki ~ ***dŠul-gi-ì-lí***--*ta*, *é-gal-la ba-an-ku4.iti-ezem-An-na*, *mu Ki-maški ù Hu-ur5-tiki ba-hul.* (*TCS* 350, *P*132135)	55*minas of worse wool from* **the place of Šulgi-ili**, **were sent to the palace**.Month of ezem-Anna, Year of Kimaš and Hurti were destroyed.	55斤次羊毛来自**舒勒吉伊里处**，**被送入宫殿**。 天神安庆典月， 基马什和胡尔提被毁灭之年。
Š 46 x: **mu-túm** 1guzza textile of 4th class, weight of which is 4 pounds, textile which is weighted, **the delivery**, **from Šulgi-ili**	1túgguz-za-4-kam-ús, ki-lá-bi 4 ma-na, **túg ki-lá tag-ga**, **mu-túm**, ki~ ***dŠul-gi-ì-lí***--*ta.iti-ezem-an-na*, *mu Ki-maški ba-hul.* (*OIP* 115 470, *P*123256)	1*guzza textile of 4th class*, *the weight of which is* 4 *pounds*, *textile which is weighted*, **the delivery**, **from the palce of Šulgi-ili**. Month of ezem-Anna, Year of Kimaš was destroyed.	1件4等级的guzza衣料，其重量是4斤， **这件被称了的衣料**， **为送入**，**从舒勒吉伊里**处。天神庆典月， 基马什被毁之年。
Š 46 ix: **mu-túm** 2niĝlam textile of 4th class, 7 guzza textile of 4th class, the prepared textiles, **were delivery**, **from Šulgi-ili**	2túgníĝ-lám-4-kam-ús, 7túgguz-za-4-kam-ús, túg sa ~ gi4-a, mu-túm, ki ~ ***dŠul-gi-ì-lí***--*ta. iti-ezem-mah*, *mu Ki-maški ba-hul.* (*NYPL* 104, *P*122640)	2*niĝlam textile of 4th class*, 7 *guzza textile of 4th class*, *the prepared textiles*, **were delivery**, **from Šulgi-ili**. Month of ezem-mah, Year of Kimaš was destroyed.	2件4等级的niĝlam的衣料和7件4等级的guzza衣料，完成的衣料，**为送入项**，**从舒勒吉伊里**处。大庆典月， 基马什被毁之年。

档案二　阿比新提王太后的档案重建

时间和摘要	文献内容	英文翻译	中文翻译
AS 1 xi/2: **ba-zi** ［1］fat［bull］, 4 sheep for **Enlil**, 1 fat bull, 4 sheep for **Ninlil**, 2 for **Šulgi**, 61 was betrothal gift for **Šelebutum**, 22 sheep for **Abi-simti**, 6 flocks for **Raši**, 2 rams and 2 kids for **x-na**, 1 ram, 1 kid for **Ti-x-ti**, fr. deliveries of Zikur-ili, 31 eliminated flocks to **kitchen**, **Arad-mu** as deputy, fr.**Abba-saga withdr.**	［1 gud］-niga, 2 udu, 2 máš, ^{d}**En-líl**, 1 gud-niga, 2 udu, 2 máš, ^{d} **Nin-líl**, 1 udu, 1 máš, ^{giš} **gu-za** ^{d}**Šul-gi**--ra, 50 udu, 11 máš, níĝ-mí-ús-sa ***Tu-pu-tu-pu***, *ki* ~ ***Še-le-bu-tum--ma--šè***, 2 *gud*, 10 *udu*, 10 *máš*, ***A-bí-sí-im-ti***, 1 *gud*, 5 *udu*［…］*x*, ***Ra-ši*** *lú Zi-da-nu-um*^{ki}, 2 *udu*, 2 *máš*, **x**］-［**x-na** lú *Ši-ma-nu-um*^{ki}, 1 udu, 1 máš, ***Ti-***［***x***］***-ti*** *lú Ha-ar-ši*^{ki}, *šà* ~ *mu-*［*túm*］***Zi-kur-ì-lí***, 8 *udu*, 10 *máš*, 13 *ud*$_5$, *šu-gíd é-muhaldim--šè*, **Arád-mu** maškim, ud-2-kam, ki ~ **Ab-ba-sa$_6$-ga**--ta, ba-zi. iti-ezem-Me-ki-ĝál, mu ^{d}Amar-^{d} Suen lugal, (left) 158. (AUCT 1 110, P102956)	［1］fattened［bull］, 2 rams and 2 kids for **Enlil**, 1 fattened bull, 2 rams and 2 kids for **Ninlil**, 1 ram and 1 kid for the **throne of Šulgi**, 50 rams and 11 kids was the **betrothal gift of Tuputupu** (bridegroom), for the place of Šelebutum (bride), 2 bulls, 10 rams and 10 kids for **Abi-simti**, 1 bull and 5 rams for **Raši**, the man of Zidanum, 2 rams and 2 kids for **x-na**, the man of Šimanum, 1 ram and 1 kid for **Ti-x-ti**, the man of Harši, from the deliveries of Zikur-ili, 8 rams, 10 kids and 13 she-goats were eliminated to the **kitchen**, **Arad-mu** as royal deputy, on the 2nd day, from the place of **Abba-saga**, were withdrawn. Month of ezem-Mekiĝal, Year of the divine Amar-Sin became king, (sum:) 158	【1】肥【公牛】, 2公绵羊和2公崽为**恩里勒**, 1肥公牛、2公绵羊和2公崽为**宁里勒**, 1公绵羊和1公崽为**舒勒吉的王座**, 50公绵羊和11公崽是图普图普（新郎）的聘礼, 为塞莱布吞公主（新娘）, 2公牛、10公绵羊和10公崽为**阿比新提**, 1公牛和5公绵羊为兹达农城人腊席, 2公绵羊和2公崽为席马农城人X-那, 1公绵羊和1公崽为哈尔席城人提-x-提, 自兹库尔伊里德送入项中, 8公绵羊、10公崽和13母山羊为淘汰级到**厨房**, **阿腊德穆督办**, 2日, 从**阿巴萨旮**处被支出。美基旮勒庆典月, 阿马尔辛成为王之年。(总计:) 158

续表

时间和摘要	文献内容	英文翻译	中文翻译
AS 2 i/1: **ba-zi** 2 for**Annunitum**, 1 for **Nanaya**, via **Abi-simti**, 2 for **Annunitum**, 2 for **Nanaya**, sent by king for cultic meal in palace, **N.** as deputy, 5 fat sheep for **Dada**, by **A.**, **A.**as deputy, 1 for **Enlil**, 1 for **Ninlil**, 1 for **Nanna**, by **Š.**, **Z.**as deputy, 2 to kitchen, fr. **Abba-saga**, **withdr.**	2 sila$_4$ ***An-nu-ni-tum***, 1 *sila$_4$* ^{d}***Na-na-a***, *gìr* ***A-bí-sí-im-ti***, 2 *sila$_4$* ***An-nu-ni-tum***, 2 *sila$_4$* ^{d}***Na-a-a***, *lugal ku$_4$-ra*, *gišbun$_x$ šà ~ é-gal*, ^{d} **Nanše-ul $_4$(ád) -galmaškim**, 4 udu-niga, 1 sila$_4$-niga, **Da-da** gala, mu-túm **Arád-mu**, **Arád-mu maškim**, 1 amar-maš-dà ^{d}**En-líl**, 1 amar-maš-dà ^{d}**Nin-líl**, 1 amar-maš-dà ^{d}**Nanna**, mu-túm **Šeš-kal-la**, **zabar-dab$_5$maškim**, 1 udu, 1 maš šu-gíd, é-muhaldim, ud-1-kam, ki~ **Ab-ba-sa$_6$-ga**--ta, ba-zi. iti-maš-dà ~ gu$_7$, mu ús-sa ^{d}Amar-^{d}Suen lugal, 18. (SAT 2 0693, P143893)	2 lambs for**Annunitum**, 1 lamb for **Nanaya**, via **Abi-simti**, 2 lambs for **Annunitum**, 2 lambs for Nanaya, sent by the king for cultic meal in palace, **Nanše-ulgal**as royal deputy, 4 fattened rams and 1 fattened lamb for **Dada**, the singer, delivered by **Arad-mu**, **Arad-mu**as royal deputy, 1 kid of gazelle for **Enlil**, 1 kid of gazelle for **Ninlil**, 1 kid of gazelle for **Nanna**, delivered by **Šeš-kalla**, **zabar-dab**as royal deputy, 1 ram and 1 kid were eliminated to kitchen, on 1st day, from **Abba-saga**, were withdrawn. Month of mašda~ gu$_7$, Year after that of Amar-Sin became king, (sum:) 18	1 羔为**安努尼吞**，1 羔为**那那亚**，经由**阿比新提**；2 羔为**安努尼吞**，2 羔为**那那亚**，由国王送入为于宫殿的圣餐，**南塞乌勒旮勒督办**，4 育肥公绵羊和 1 育肥羔为歌手达达，阿腊德穆送入，**阿腊德穆督办**，1 幼瞪羚为**恩里勒**，1 幼瞪羚为**宁里勒**，1 幼瞪羚为**南那**，塞什卡腊送入，**执青铜官督办**，1 公绵羊和 1 公崽为淘汰级到厨房，于 1 日，自**阿巴萨旮**处，被支出了。食瞪羚月，神阿马尔辛成为王之年之次年，(总计:) 18
AS 2 v (1-30): **ba-zi** 30 fat rams for**Abi-simti** of 1 month, **Nuhi-ilum** envoy as deputy, fr. Šulgi-ayamu, were **withdr**.	30 udu-niga, sá-dug$_4$ ***A-bí-sí-im-ti***, *iti-1-kam*, ***Nu-hi-ilum****sukkal maškim*, *ki~* ^{d}***Šul-gi-a-a-mu***--*ta*, *ba-zi. iti-ezem-^{d} Nin-a-zu*, *mu ^{d}Amar-^{d}Suen lugal-e Ur-bí-lum^{ki}mu-hul*, (*left*) 30. (*SumRecDreh.*15, *P*130512)	30 *fattened rams for the monthly allowance of***Abi-simti** of 1 month, **Nuhi-ilum**, theenvoy as royal deputy, from the place of **Šulgi-ayamu**, were withdrawn. Month of ezem-Ninazu, Year of the divine Amar-Sin the king destroyed Urbilum. (sum:) 30	30 只育肥公绵羊为**阿比新提**一个月的月供，**努希伊隆国使督办**，自**舒勒吉阿亚穆**处，被支出了。神宁阿朱庆典月，神阿马尔辛王毁灭乌尔比隆之年。(总计:) 30
AS 2 xii/10: **ba-zi** 1 fat <bull> for**runners**, 3 fat sheep for **Abi-simti**, 3 fat rams for **Geme-eanna**, 1 fat ram for **Raši**, via **Lugal-kagina**, **Arad-mu**as deputy, fr. palce of **Lu-diĝirra**, were **withdrawn**	1<gud>-niga, mu~ **kaš$_4$-ke$_4$-ne**--šè, 2 udu-niga, 1 gukkan-niga, mu ~ ***A-bí-sí-im-ti***--*šè*, 3 *udu-niga*, *mu* **Gemé-é-an-na**[é] -gi$_4$-a **Arád-mu** sukkal-mah--šè, [é] **-muhaldim**--šè, 1 udu-niga, ***Ra-ši*** *lú-Zi-da-nu-um^{ki}*, *gìr***Lugal-ka-gi-na**sukkal, **Arád-mu** maškim, iti-ud-10 ba-zal, ki ~ **Lú-diĝir-ra**--ta ba-zi. iti-še-kin-kud, mu ^{d}Amar-^{d}Suen lugal-e Ur-bí-lum^{ki} mu-hul, (left) 8. (OIP 121 009, P123740)	1 fattened <bull> for the**messengers**, 2 fattened rams and 1 fattened big-tailed sheep for **Abi-simti**, 3 fattened rams for **Geme-eanna** daughter-in-law of Arad-mu, the ambassor, 1 fattened ram for **Raši**, the man of Zidanum, via **Lugal-kagina**secretary, **Arad-mu**as royal deputy, when the 10th day passed, from the palce of **Lu-diĝirra**, were withdrawn. Month of še-kin-kud, Year of the divine Amar-Sin the king destroyed Urbilum, (sum:) 8	1 头育肥公牛为**信使**，2 只育肥公绵羊和 1 只育肥肥尾绵羊为**阿比新提**，3 只育肥公绵羊为**阿腊德穆**国务卿的儿媳吉美埃安那，1 只育肥公绵羊为腊西——孜达农城之人，**经由卢旮勒卡吉那使官**，**阿腊德穆**督办，于 10 日过去时，从**卢迪弥腊**处，被支出了。大麦收割月，神阿马尔辛王毁灭乌尔比隆之年。(总计:) 8

续表

时间和摘要	文献内容	英文翻译	中文翻译
AS 3 i/1: **ba-zi** 1 for**Enlil** by Šulgi-ili, Papanšen as deputy; 1 for **Abi-simti**, by Puzur-Ištar, Linisin as deputy, fr. Abba-saga, **withdr.**	1 $sila_4$ ^{d}**En-líl**, mu-túm ^{d}***Šul-gi-ì-lí***, ***Pá-pá-an-še-en*** **(zabar-dab$_5$) maškim**; 1 amar-maš-dà, ***A-bí-sí-im-ti***, *mu-túm* **Puzur$_4$-Iš$_8$-tár**, ***Li-ni-si-in****maškim*, *ud-1-kam*, *ki*~ **Ab-ba-sa$_6$-ga**--ta ba-zi.iti-maš-dà~gu_7, mu ús-sa [Ur-bí-lum^{ki}] ba!-hul, (left) 2. (AUCT 2 152, P103970)	1 lamb for**Enlil**, was delivered by Šulgi-ili, Papanšen as royal deputy; 1 kid of gazelle for **Abi-simti**, was delivered by Puzur-Ištar, Linisin as royal deputy, on the 1st day, from the place of Abba-saga, were withdrawn. Month of mašda~gu_7, Year after that of [Urbilum] was destroyed, (sum:) 2	1只羔为**恩里勒**，舒勒吉伊里送人，**帕盘鑫督办**； 1只瞪羚幼崽为**阿比新提**，普朱尔伊什塔尔送入，**里尼辛督办**，于1日，从**阿巴萨旮处**， 被支出了。 食瞪羚月， 【乌尔比隆】被毁年之次年，（总计：）2
AS 3 ii (1-30): **ba-zi** 30 fat rams for**Abi-simti**, **Nuhi-ilum** as deputy, fr. **Lu-diĝirra**, **withdr.**	30 udu-niga, sá-dug_4 ***A-bí-sí-im-ti***, ***Nu-hi-ilum****sukkal maškim*, *iti-1-kam*, *ki*~ **Lú-diĝir-ra**--ta, ba-zi.iti-ze$_x$-da~gu_7, mu ^{d}Gu-za ^{d}En-líl-lá ba-dím, (left) 30. (OIP 121 011, P123742)	30 fattened rams for the monthly allowance of**Abi-simti**, **Nuhi-ilum**envoy as royal deputy, for 1 month, from **Lu-diĝirra**, were withdrawn. Month of zeda~gu_7, Year of the throne of Enlil was made. (sum:) 30	30只肥公绵羊为**阿比新提**的月供，**努希伊隆国使督办**，为一个月，自**卢迪弥腊**处，被支出了。食豚月，神恩里勒的王座被造之年。（总计：）30
AS 3 ix: **lá-ì** 132 goats among for**king**, 10 goat for **Abi-simti**, were arrear of **Ṣiluš-Dagan**, 8 rams and 120 goats were arrear of **Šuruš-kin**, 2 flocks stayed in sheep-house	132 máš, šà mu-túm-**lugal**, 10 máš, šà mu-túm ***A-bí-sí-im-ti***, *lá-ì* ***Ṣi-lu-uš-^{d}Da-gan***, 8 *udu*, 120 *máš-gal*, *lá-ì* ***Šu-ru-uš-ki-in***, 1 *máš*, *a-rá-1-kam*, 1 $sila_4$ *a-rá-2-kam*, *é-udu-ka gub-ba. iti-ezem-mah*, *mu* ^{d}*Gu-za ba-dím.* (*Seal*): *Lú-sa$_6$-ga*, *dub-sar*, *dumu Gu-za-ni.* (*SAT* 2 0759, *P*143959)	132 *goats among the deliveries for***king**, 10 goats among the deliveries for **Abi-simti**, were the arrear of **Ṣiluš-Dagan** (gov. of Simurrum), 8 rams and 120 he-goats were the arrear of **Šuruš-kin** (general of É-bal/A. HA), 1 kid for 1st time, 1 lamb for 2nd time stayed in the sheep-house. Month of ezem-mah, Year of the throne (of Enlil) was made. (Seal): Lu-saga scribe was the son of your thorne.	132只山羊为**国王**的送入，10只山羊为**阿比新提**的送入，以上为**采鲁什达干的欠款**，8只公绵羊和120只公山羊为**舒如什金的欠款**，1只公崽第1次，1只羔第2次留在羊圈中。大庆典月，（神恩里勒的）王座被造之年。 （印章）：卢萨旮书吏是你的王座之子。

续表

时间和摘要	文献内容	英文翻译	中文翻译
AS 3 xi^2/25: **ba-zi** 1 lamb for Enlil, delivered byŠu-x, 1 for Ninlil, **N.** as deputy, 2 fat goats by **Ṣiluš-Dagan.**, 34 flocks by **Ir.**, 1 goat and 4 kids by **Ig.**, 1 by **governor of Marda**, these for **Abi-simti**, **Arad-mu** as deputy, fr. **Abba-saga**, were **withdr**.	1 sila$_4$ ^{d} [**En-líl**], mu-túm **Šu-** [**...**], 1 sila$_4$ ^{d} [**Nin-líl**], ^{d}**Nanše-ul$_4$-gal maškim**, 2 máš-gal-*Ši$_x$-maški*-niga, mu-túm ***Ṣ i-lu-uš-^{d}* [*Da*] *-gan***, 3 *gud*, 25 *udu*, 1 *sila$_4$*, 5 *máš-gal*, *mu-túm* ***I-ri-bu-um***, 1 *ud$_5$*, 4 *máš-ga*, *mu-túm* ***I-gi$_4$-ru-um***, 1 *sila$_4$ mu-túm ensí Már-da^{ki}*, ***A-bí-sí-im-ti***, **Arád-mu** maškim, ud-25-kam, ki ~ **Ab-ba-sa$_6$-ga**--ta ba-zi.iti-**diri**-ezem-Me-ki-ĝál, mu^{d}Gu-za ^{d}En- [líl-lá] ba-dím, (left) 44. (AUCT 2 099, P103917)	1 lamb for [Enlil], delivered byŠu-x, 1 lamb for [Ninlil], **Nanše-ulgal** as rayal deputy, 2 fattened *Šimaški* he-goats delivered by **Ṣiluš-Dagan**, 3 bulls, 25 rams, 1 lamb and 5 he-goats, delivered by **Iribum**, 1 she-goat and 4 suckling kids delivered by **Igirum**, 1 lamb delivered by the **governor of Marda**, these for **Abi-simti**, **Arad-mu** as royal deputy, on the 25th day, from **Abba-saga**, were withdrawn. Additional Month of Mekiĝal, Year of the throne of En [lil] was made, (sum:) 44	1只羔为【恩里勒】，舒-X送入，1只羔为【宁里勒】，**南塞乌勒旮勒督办**，2育肥 西马什基公山羊，采鲁什达干送入，3公牛、25公绵羊、1羔和5公山羊，伊瑞布送入，1母山羊和4吃奶崽，伊吉润送入，1羔，马尔达的总督送入，以上为**阿比新提**，**阿腊德穆**督办于25日，自阿巴萨旮处被支出了。增加的神美基旮勒庆典月（闰月），神恩【里勒】的王座被造之年。（总计：）44
AS 3 xi^2/26: **ba-zi** 5 flocks for**Abi-simti**, by Naram-E., Eštar-i., Šulgi-i., Ku-N. **Arad-mu** as deputy, 1 fat kid to **kitchen of state**, by **N.**, **Ur-Baba** as deputy, fr. **Abba-saga withdr.**	1^{f}ašgar mu-túm ***Na-ra-am-É-a***, 2 *sila$_4$ mu-túm x* ***Eš$_4$-tár-il-šu***, 1 *sila$_4$ mu-túm* ***^{d}Šul-gi-ì-lí***, 1 *sila$_4$ mu-túm* **Kù-^{d} Nin-gal**, ***A-bí-sí-im-ti***, **Arád-mu maškim**, 1 ^{f}ašgar-niga é-uz-ga, mu-túm ***Nir-ì-da-ĝál***, **Ur-^{d}Ba-ba$_6$** maškim, ud-26-kam, ki ~ **Ab-ba-sa$_6$-ga**--ta, ba-zi. iti-**diri**-ezem-Me-ki-ĝál ~ ús-sa, mu ^{d}Gu-za šà húl-la ^{d}En-líl-lá ba-dím, (left) 6. (TAD 55, P131097)	1 female kid delivered by**Naram-Ea**, 2 lambs delivered by **Eštar-ilšu**, 1 lamb delivered by **Šulgi-ili**, 1 lamb delivered by **Ku-Ningal**, these for **Abi-simti**, **Arad-mu**as royal deputy, 1 fattened female kid to the **kitchen of state**, delivered by **Nir-idagal**, **Ur-Baba** as royal deputy, on the 26th day, from the place of **Abba-saga**, were withdrawn. Additional Month of Mekiĝal, Year of the throne of Enlil was made, (sum:) 6	1雌崽，**那冉埃阿**送入，2羔，**埃什塔尔伊里舒**送入，1只羔，**舒勒吉伊里**送入，1只羔，**库宁旮勒**送入，以上为阿比新提，**阿腊德穆督办**，1只育肥雌崽到御膳房，尼尔伊达旮勒送入，**乌尔巴巴督办**，于26日，自**阿巴萨旮**处，被支出。在神美基旮勒庆典月之后的闰月，神恩里勒的王座被造之年。（总计：）6

续表

时间和摘要	文献内容	英文翻译	中文翻译
AS 4 ii/2, 11: **ba-zi, butchered** 1 gezelle to**kitchen of State**, **Aya-kalla as deputy**, 2 **butchered** to **storeroom**, by Adatum, 1 to **kitchen of State**, **Ur-Baba as deputy**, 2 gezelles to **storeroom**, by Šulgi-naga, [3], 1 lamb delivered by **Ahu-[ma]**, 1 by **man of X**, for **Abi-simti**, **N.**as deputy, …, fr.**Abba-saga**, were **withdr.**	1 amar-maš-dù é-uz-ga, ***A-a-kal-la*maškim**, 2 amar-maš-dù ba-úš, é-kišib-ba--šè, mu-túm ***A-da-tum***, 3, *ud-2-kam*, 1 *maš-dà é-uz-ga*, **Ur-^{d}Ba-ba$_6$ maškim**, 2 maš-dà é-kišib-ba--šè, mu-túm **^{d}Šul-gi-na-da**, [2]+1, [ud-x-kam], […], ud-[x-kam], 1 sila$_4$ mu-túm ***A-hu-*[*ma*]** *ensí* [*Pu-úš^{ki}*], 1 *sila$_4$ mu-túm* **lú-[…] -x**, ***A-bí-sí-im-*[*ti*]**, ***Nu-úr-^{d}Adad*rá-[gaba] maškim**, 2, ud-11-[kam], 2 sila$_4$ ^{d}Nin-[…], mu-túm […], x-x-[…], […], […], […], šu-nigin […], šu-nigin […], šu-nigin 1 […], šu-nigin 14 […], šu-nigin 5 […], šu-nigin 56 […], ki ~ **Ab-ba-sa$_6$-ga**--ta ba-zi. iti-ze$_x$-da~ gu$_7$, muús-sa ^{d}Gu-za ^{d}En-líl-lá ba-dím. (PDT 2 1293, P126617)	1 young gezelle to the**kitchen of State**, **Aya-kalla as royal deputy**, 2 **butchered** young gezelles to the **storeroom**, delivered by Adatum, 3, on the 2nd day, 1 gezelle to the **kitchen of State**, **Ur-Baba as royal deputy**, 2 gezelles to the **storeroom**, delivered by Šulgi-naga, [3], on the x day, […], on the [x] day, 1 lamb delivered by **Ahu-[ma]**, governor of [Pus], 1 lamb delivered by **man of X**, these for **Abi-simti**, **Nur-Adad knight as royal deputy**, (sum:) 2, on 11th day, 2 lambs for Nin-[…], delivered by […], […], total […], total […], total 1 […], total 14 […], total 5 […], total 56 […], from **Abba-saga**, were withdrawn.Month of zeda~ gu$_7$, Year after that of the divine throne of Enlil was installed.	1 幼瞪羚到**御膳房**，**阿亚卡拉督办**；2 **宰杀的**幼瞪羚到**库房**，阿达吞送人，（计）3，于2日，1 瞪羚到**御膳房**，**乌尔巴巴督办**；2 瞪羚到**库房**，舒勒吉那旮送人，（计）3，于x天，【……】，于【x】天，1只羔由【普斯】的总督阿胡【马】送人，1只羔由X城之人送人，以上为**阿比新提**，**努尔阿达德骑使督办**，（总计:）2羊，于11日，2羔为宁-【……】，【……】送人，……，总计1【……】，14【……】，5【……】，56【……】， 自阿巴萨旮处，被支出。食豚月，恩里勒的圣王座被造之年。
AS 4 iii/2: **šu ùr-dam** 10 cattle fr. anoiting priest of Zimudar for **Abi-simti overseer: Šu-ili**, via **Erra-bani**, erased fr.account of king	8 gud, 2 áb, gú-un ~ gudá ~ èš-didli Zi-mu-dar^{ki}, ugula ***Šu-ì-lí***, ***A-bí-sí-im-ti*** *ba-na-sum*, *gìr* **Èr-ra-ba-ni** gurušda, mu-túm **lugal**--ta, šu ùr-dam, ud-2-kam.iti-u$_5$-bí~ gu$_7$, mu En-mah-gal-an-na en^{d}Nanna ba-hun. (ZA 68 37 NCBT 1628, P142569)	8 bulls and 2 cows from the anoiting priest of shrine of Zimudar, the overseer: Šu-ili, **Abi-simti** was given, via Erra-bani fattener, from delivery account of the king erased, on the 2nd day. Month of ubi~ gu$_7$, Year of En-mahgal-anna, en-priest of Nanna was installed.	8 公牛和2 母牛，**自孜穆达尔城圣殿的涂油祭司**，**监工为舒伊里**，阿比新提被给予，**经由埃腊巴尼育肥师**，从国王的送入账目删除了于2日。 食乌比鸟月， 神南那的女祭司恩马赫旮勒安那被任命之年。

续表

时间和摘要	文献内容	英文翻译	中文翻译
AS 4 vii/27: **ba-zi** ［1］ to kitchen by Lugal-magurre, **Ur-baba as deputy**, 1 fat ram by Ṣiluš-Dagan, 2 fat by Abuni, ［x x］ by Adaya, ［x］ by governor of Urum, ［x］ by Aba-Enlilgen, ［x x］ by Ur-Sin, **these for ［Abi］-simti**, **Ri ṣ-ilum knight as deputy**, fr. Abba-saga withdr.	［1 udu］ **é-uz-ga**, mu-túm **Lugal-má-gur$_8$-re**, **Ur-^{d}Ba-ba$_6$ maškim**, 1 udu-lú-ulù-um-niga mu-túm ***Ṣ i-lu-uš-^{d} Da-gan***, 1 *u$_8$-niga*, 1^{f} *ašgar-niga mu-túm* **A-bu-ni**, ［x x］ mu-túm ***Á-da-a***, ［…*mu*］*-túm ensí Urúm^{ki}* (*ÚRxÚ*), ［*x x mu-túm*］ **A-ba-^{d}En-líl-gen$_7$**, ［x x］ mu-túm **Ur-^{d}Suen** ［*A-bí*］ ***-sí-im-ti***, ［*x x*］ **Me-^{d} Ištaran**, mu-túm **Šu-kab-tá**, ***Ri-i ṣ-ilum****rá-gaba maškim*, *ud-27-kam*, *ki* ~ **Ab-ba-sa$_6$-ga**-ta ba-zi. ［iti-ezem］-^{d} Šul-gi, ［mu］ En-mah-gal-an-na en ^{d}Nanna ba-hun, (ed.) 9. (BIN 3 081, P105887)	［1 ram］ to the kitchen of state, delivered by Lugal-magurre, **Ur-baba as royal deputy**, 1 fattened lulum ram was delivered by Ṣiluš-Dagan, 1 fattened ewe and 1 fattened female kid were delivered by Abuni, ［x x］ delivered by Adaya, ［x］ was delivered by the governor of Urum, ［x was delivered］ by Aba-Enlilgen, ［x x］ delivered by Ur-Sin, **these for ［Abi］-simti**, ［x x］ Me-^{d}Ištaran, delivered by Šu-kubta, **Ri ṣ-ilum knight as royal deputy**, on 27th day, withdrawn from Abba-saga. ［Month of ezem］-Šulgi, ［Year］ of En-mahgal-anna, en-priest of Nanna was installed, (sum:) 9	【1公绵羊】到**御膳房**，卢旮勒马古雷送人，**乌尔巴巴督办**，1肥鲁鲁姆公绵羊采鲁什达干送人，1肥母绵羊和1肥雌崽阿布尼送人，【x】阿达亚送人，【x】乌如姆城的总督送人，【x】阿巴恩里艮【送人】，【x】由乌尔辛送人，以上为**【阿比】新提**，【x】美伊什塔阑，由舒库卜塔送人，**瑞施伊隆骑使督办**，于27日，自**阿巴萨旮**支出。舒勒吉庆典月，神南那的女祭司恩马赫旮勒安那被任命之年。（总计：）9只羊
AS 4 ix/8: **ba-zi**, **butchered** 2 sheep for**Šulgi**, Š. as deputy; 22 for **Bizua**, U. **as deputy**; Mešinunu delivered, 1 to **kitchen**, by Ṣ eluš-Dagan, **Ur-Baba as deputy**; 17 **butchered** gezelles to storeroom, fr. **Abba-saga**	1 udu, 1 m［áš-gal］, **gu-za ^{d}Šul-［gi］**-ra, **Šà-ta-kù-zu rá-gaba maškim**; 2 gud, 18 udu, 2 máš-gal, ***Bí-zu-a*** *nin$_9$-nin*, ***Ú-ta1-mi-šar-ra-am*** **rá-gaba maškim**; šà ~ mu-túm Me-ši-nu-nu Ú.SU, 1 sila$_4$ é-uz-ga, mu-túm ***Ṣe-lu-uš-^{d}Da-gan***, **Ur-^{d}Ba-ba$_6$ maškim**; 17 maš-dà, ba-ug$_7$ é-kišib-ba-šè, šà mu-túm ***Ì-làl-lum***, *ud-8-kam*, *ki* ~ **Ab-ba-sa$_6$-ga**-ta, ba-zi. iti-ezem-mah, mu En-［mah-gal-an-na］en ^{d}［Nanna ba-hun］, (ed.) 42. (OIP 121 164, P123894)	1 ram and 1 he-goat for the**throne of Šulgi**, **Šatakuzu knight as royal deputy**; 2 bulls, 18 rams and 2 he-goats for **Bizua**, the sister of Queen, **Utalmi-šarram knight as royal deputy**; among deliveries Mešinunu LÚ.SU delivered, 1 lamb to **the kitchen of state**, delivered by Ṣeluš-Dagan, **Ur-Baba as royal deputy**; 17 **butchered** gezelles to the storeroom, delivered by Ilallum, on the 8th day, from **Abba-saga** withdrawn. Month of ezem-mah, ［Year］ of En-mahgal-anna, en-priest of Nanna was installed, (sum:) 42.	1只公绵羊和1只公山羊为**舒勒吉王座**，**沙塔库朱骑使督办**；2头公牛、18公绵羊和2只公山羊为**王后的姊妹比朱阿**，**乌塔勒米沙阑骑使督办**；美席努努送人，1只羔到**厨房**，采鲁什达干送人，**乌尔巴巴督办**；17**宰杀的瞪羚由伊拉隆送入仓库**，于8日，自**阿巴萨旮**支出。大庆典月，神南那的女祭司恩马赫旮勒安那被任命之年，（总计：）42只牲。

续表

时间和摘要	文献内容	英文翻译	中文翻译
AS 4 ix/26: **ba-zi** 9 lambs and 2 fat flocks**for Abisimti**, **delivered** by Ur-Engal-dudu, Adatum, Hun-Šulgi, Ur-sasaga, Šulgi-Lamma-mu, priest of Šara, Adaya, Abuni and Itib-šinat, **Ri ṣ-ilum as deputy**, 2 lambs to **kitchen of state**, **Ur-Baba**as deputy, fr. **Abba-saga**, were **withdr**.	1 sila$_4$ mu-túm **Ur-^{d}En-gal-du-du**, 1 sila$_4$ mu-túm ***A-da-tum***, 1 *sila$_4$ mu-túm* ***Hu-un-^{d}Šul-gi***, 1 *sila$_4$ mu-túm* **Ur-sa$_6$-sa$_6$-ga**, 1 sila$_4$ mu-túm **^{d}Šul-gi-^{d}Lamma-mu** šùš, 1 sila$_4$ mu-túm **lú-mah ^{d}Šará**, 1 sila$_4$ mu-túm ***Á-da-a***, 1 *u$_8$-niga*, 1 *^{f}ašgar-niga*, 1 *sila$_4$*, *mu-túm* ***A-bu-ni***, 1 *sila$_4$ mu-túm* ***I-ti-ib-ši-na-at***: ***A-bí-sí-im-ti***, ***Ri-i*** **ṣ-ilumrá-gabamaškim**, 1 sila$_4$ mu-túm ***Za-zi***, 1 *sila$_4$ mu-túm* **Lú-kù-zu**, **é-uz-ga**, **Ur-^{d}Ba-ba$_6$maškim**, ud-26-kam, ki~ **Ab-ba-sa$_6$-ga**--ta ba-zi. iti-ezem-mah, mu En-mah-gal-an-na en ^{d}Nanna ba-hun, (left) 13. (Princeton 1 081, P126770)	1 lamb was delivered by**Ur-Engal-dudu**, 1 lamb delivered by **Adatum**, 1 lamb delivered by **Hun-Šulgi**, 1 lamb delivered by **Ur-sasaga**, 1 lamb delivered by **Šulgi-Lammamu** animal manager, 1 lamb delivered by the **priest of Šara**, 1 lamb delivered by **Adaya**, 1 fattened ewe, 1 fattened female kid and 1 lamb delivered by **Abuni**, 1 lamb delivered by **Itib-šinat**, these for **Abi-simti**, **Ri ṣ-ilum knight as deputy**, 1 lamb delivered by **Zazi**, 1 lamb delivered by **Lukuzu**, these to the **kitchen of state**, **Ur-Baba**as royal deputy, on the 26th day, from the lace of **Abba-saga**, were withdrawn. Month of ezem-mah, Year of En-mahgal-anna, en-priest of Nanna was installed, (sum:) 13	1只羔乌尔恩旮勒杜杜送入，1只羔阿达吞送入，1只羔混舒勒吉送入，1只羔乌尔萨萨旮送入，1只羔舒勒吉兰马穆**牲畜长**送入，1只羔沙腊神的祭司送入，1只羔阿达亚送入，1只育肥母绵羊、1只育肥雌崽和1只羔阿布尼送入，1只羔伊提卜席那特送入，**以上为阿比新提**，**瑞施伊隆骑使督办**；1只羔扎孜送入，1只羔卢库朱送入，**以上到御膳房**，**乌尔巴巴督办**，于26日，自**阿巴萨旮**处，被支出。大庆典月，神南那的女祭司恩马赫旮勒安那被任命之年。（总计：）13只羊
AS 4 x/26: **ba-zi** 1 best fat ram for the dark moon was sent to palace, for**Abi-simti**, via **Šulgi-ayamu**, fr. **Šulgi-ayamu**	1 udu-niga-sig$_5$, ud-nú-a-ka é-gal ba-an-[ku$_4$], ***A-bí-sí-im-ti***, *gìr* ***^{d}Šul-gi-a-a-mu***, *iti-ud-26 ba-zal*, *ki~ ^{d}* ***Šul-gi-a-a-mu****--ta.iti-ezem-An-na*, *mu En-mah-gal-an-na en^{d}Nanna ba-hun*, (*left*) 1 *udu*. (*OIP* 121 048, *P*123778)	1 *best fattened ram for the dark moon was sent to the palace for***Abi-simti**, via **Šulgi-ayamu**, when the 26th day passed, from the place of **Šulgi-ayamu**.Month of ezem-Anna, Year of En-mahgal-anna, en-priest of Nanna was installed, (sum:) 1	1优等肥公绵羊为晦月被送入宫殿，为**阿比新提**，**经由舒勒吉阿亚穆**，于26日过去时，自**舒勒吉阿亚穆**处（被支出）。安神庆典月，神南那的女祭司恩马赫旮勒安那被任命之年。（计：）1

续表

时间和摘要	文献内容	英文翻译	中文翻译
AS 4 xi/1： **ba-zi** 29 [fat] rams for daily**offering**, 1 fat for **Full Moon**, 1 for **New Moon**, extra for **Šulgi**, 30 fat rams for **Abi-simti**, **Nuhi-ilum** as deputy, fr. **Šulgi-ayamu**, were **withdr.**	29 udu- [niga], **šu-a-gi-** [**na** ud] -29-kam, 1 udu-niga [**é-ud**] **-15**, 1 udu-niga**é-** [**ud**] **-sakar**, níĝ-diri, sá-dug$_4$ ^{d}**Šul-gi**, 30 udu-niga, sá-dug$_4$ ***A-bí-sí-im-ti***, *ud-1-kam*, ***Nu-hi-ilum*****sukkal maškim**, ki ~ ^{d}***Šul-gi-a-a-mu--ta*** *ba-zi. iti-ezem-Me-ki-ĝál, mu en* ^{d}*Nanna ba-* [*hun*], (*left*) 61. (*Torino* 1 259, *P*133933)	29 [*fattened*] *rams for daily***offering** of 29 days, 1 fattened ram for **Full Moon**, 1 fattened ram for **New Moon**, above extra for monthly allowance of **Šulgi**, 30 fattened rams for monthly allowance of **Abi-simti**, on the 1st day, **Nuhi-ilum**, the-envoy as royal deputy, from the palce of **Šulgi-ayamu**, were withdrawn. Month of ezem-Mekiĝal, Year of the en-priest of Nanna was installed, (sum:) 61	29只【肥】公绵羊为29天的日供应，1只育肥公绵羊为**满月**，1只育肥公绵羊为**新月**，以上剩余的为**舒勒吉的月供**，30只育肥公绵羊为**阿比新提的月供**，于1日，**努希伊隆**国使督办，自**舒勒吉阿亚穆**处，被支出。美基旮勒庆典月，神南那的祭司被任命之年。（总计：）61
AS5 i： **ba-zi** 15 fat flocks and 20 rams for **Abi-simti**, **T.as deputy**; 4 fat flocks and 7 rams fr. **Libanu-a.**, for Libanug-šabaš, 2 rams for **Šulgi-abi**, 1 for **Hun-Šulgi**, 4 fat flocks and 10 for **Naplanum**, **U. as deputy**; 1 fat bull and 10 rams for **Habruša**, **T.as deputy**, 2 fat bulls and 20, …, fr. **Abba-saga** withdr.	5 gud-niga, 10 udu-niga, 20 udu, ***A-bí-sí-im-ti***, ***Tu-ra-am-***^{d}***Da-gan*****maškim**, 1 gud-niga, 3 udu-niga, 7 udu, **Li-ba-nu-aš-gu-bi** lú-kin-gi-a Li-ba-nu-ug-ša-ba-aš ensí Mar-ha-ši^{ki}, 2 udu ^{d}***Šul-gi-a-bí***, 1 *udu* ***Hu-un-***^{d} ***Šul-gi***, 2 *gud-niga*, 2 *udu-niga-3-kam-ús*, 10 *sila$_4$*, ***Na-ap-la-*** [***núm***] *mar-tu*, **Ur-šar-ru-gen$_7$ maškim**; 1 gud-niga, 10 udu, **Ha-ab-ru-ša**, ***Tah-ša-tal*****maškim**, 2 gud-niga, 20 udu, mu-túm […], Ur-^{d} […], 2 […], 3 […], ki na-[…], ú-la- […], šà ~ mu- [er$_{10}$--ra--ta], ud- [x-kam], ki~ **Ab-** [**ba-sa$_6$-ga--ta**], ba-[zi].iti-maš- [dà-gu$_7$], mu En- [Unu$_6$] -gal ^{d}Inanna [ba-hun]. (PDT 2, p.20, P134700)	5 fattened bull, 10 fattend rams and 20 rams for **Abi-simti**, **Turam-Daganas royal deputy;** 1 fattened bull, 3 fattened rams and 7 rams from**Libanu-ašgubi messenger**, for the governor of Marhaši Libanug-šabaš, 2 rams for **Šulgi-abi**, 1 ram for **Hun-Šulgi**, 2 fattened ram, 2 3rd class of fattened rams and 10 lambs for **Naplanum**, the Amorite, **Uršarrugen as royal deputy**; 1 fattened bull and 10 rams for **Habruša**, **Tahšatal as royal deputy**, 2 fattened bulls and 20 rams, …, from the deliveries, on the [x] day, from the place of **Abba-saga** were withdrawn.Month of mašda ~ gu$_7$, Year of En-unugal- (an-na), en-priest of Inanna was installed.	5肥公牛、10肥公绵羊和20公绵羊为**阿比新提**，**图冉达干督办**，1育肥公牛、3肥公绵羊和7公绵羊自**里巴努阿什古比信使**，为马尔哈席的总督里巴努格沙巴什，2公绵羊为**舒勒吉阿比**，1公绵羊为**混舒勒吉**，2肥公绵羊、2三等肥公绵羊和10羔为阿摩利人**那坡拉农**，**乌尔沙如艮督办**；1育肥公牛和10公绵羊为**哈卜如沙**，**塔赫沙塔勒督办**，2肥公牛和20公绵羊，……自送入项，于x天，自**阿巴萨旮**处被支出。食瞪羚月，女神伊南那的祭司恩乌努旮勒被任命之年。

续表

时间和摘要	文献内容	英文翻译	中文翻译
AS 5 i/25: **ba-zi** 1 lamb and 1 gazelle for**Abi-simti**, by Ur-dam, Lugal-k. as deputy, fr. **Abba-saga**, were **withdr.**	1 $sila_4$, 1 amar-maš-dà, ***A-bí-sí-im-ti***, *mu-túm* **Ur-dam** ud-da-tuš, **Lugal-kù-zumaškim**, ud-25-kam, ki ~ **Ab-ba-sa_6-ga**--ta, ba-zi. iti-maš-dà ~ gu_7, mu En-unu_6-gal-^{d}Inanna ba-hun, (left) 2. (BAOM 6 141 179, P109650)	1 lamb and 1 kid of gazelle for**Abi-simti**, delivered by Ur-dam, the jester, Lugal-kuzu as royal deputy, on the 25th day, from the place of **Abba-saga**, were withdrawn. Month of mašda ~ gu_7, Year of En-unu-gal- (an-na), en-priest of Inanna, was installed, (sum:) 2.	1 只羔和 1 只幼瞪羚为**阿比新提**，**乌尔达姆弄臣**送人，**卢旮勒库朱督办**，于 25 日，自**阿巴萨旮**处，被支出。食瞪羚月，女神伊南那的祭司恩乌努旮勒被任命之年。（总计：）2
AS 5 i/26: **ba-zi** 11 fat flocks and 6 lambs/ kids for**Abi-simti**, when she goes to Du and served her in the ship, **delivered** by Abuni, Nir-idagal, Ilallum, Beli-arik, Masasa, Ibi-Istaran, Šu-Mama, Ur-Engal-dudu, Šulgi-ili and Ur-mes, **Nur-Adad**knight as royal deputy, rom place of **Abba-saga**, were withdrawn	1 u_8-niga, 1 ^{f}ašgar-niga, mu-túm ***A-bu-ni***, 2 *máš-gal a-$dara_4$-niga*, *mu-túm* ***Nir-ì-da-ĝál***, 2 *máš-gal a-$dara_4$-niga*, *mu-túm* ***Ì-làl-lum***, 2 *udu-niga mu-túm* ***Be-lí-a-rí-ik***, 1 $sila_4$ mu-túm **Má-sa_6-sa_6**, 1 amar-maš-dà mu-túm ***I-bí-^{d}Ištaran***, 1 *$sila_4$ mu-túm* **Šu-Ma-ma** ensí, 3 udu-niga, 1 $sila_4$ mu-túm **Ur-^{d} En-gal-du-du**, 1 $sila_4$ mu-túm ***^{d}Šul-gi-ì-lí***, 1 *$sila_4$ mu-túm* **Ur-mes** ensí (of Uru-sag-rig_7), ***A-bí-sí-im-ti*** *DU^{ki}--šè du-ni má ba-na-a-gub*, **Nu-úr-^{d}Adad** *rá-gaba* ⌊*maškim*⌋, *ud-26-kam*, *ki* ~ **Ab-ba-sa_6-ga**--ta ba-zi. iti-maš-dà ~ gu_7, mu En-unu_6-gal ^{d}Inanna ba-hun, (left) 17. (MVN 13 849, P117621)	1 fattened ewe and 1 fattened female kid were delivered by**Abuni**, 2 fattened wild he-goats delivered by **Nir-idagal**, 2 fattened wild he-goats delivered by **Ilallum**, 2 fattened rams delivered by **Beli-arik**, 1 lamb delivered by **Masasa**, 1 kid of gazelle delivered by **Ibi-Istaran**, 1 lamb delivered by **Šu-Mama** governor (of Kazalla), 3 fattened rams and 1 lamb delivered by **Ur-Engal-dudu**, 1 lamb delivered by **Šulgi-ili**, 1 lamb delivered by **Ur-mes** governor, these for **Abi-simti**, when she goes to DU and served for her in the ship, **Nur-Adad**knight as royal deputy, on the 26th day, from place of **Abba-saga**, were withdrawn. Month of mašda ~ gu_7, Year of En-unu-gal- (an-na), en-priest of Inanna, was installed, (sum:) 17	1 只育肥母绵羊和 1 只育肥雌崽阿布尼送人，2 只育肥野生公山羊尼尔伊达旮勒送人，2 只育肥野生公山羊伊拉隆送人，2 只育肥公绵羊贝里阿瑞克送人，1 只羔马萨萨送人，1 只幼瞪羚伊比伊什塔蓝送人，1 只羔舒马马**总督**送人，3 只育肥公绵羊和 1 只羔乌尔恩旮勒杜杜送人，1 只羔舒勒吉伊里送人，1 只羔乌尔美斯总督送人，**以上为阿比新提**，当她前往 DU 城时，为在船上的她，**努尔阿达德骑使督办**，于 26 日，自**阿巴萨旮**处，被支出。食瞪羚月，女神伊南那的祭司恩乌努旮勒被任命之年。（总计：）17

续表

时间和摘要	文献内容	英文翻译	中文翻译
AS 5 ii: **ba-zi** 7 basin, 1 kundu vessel, 16 cups, 4šušala vessels, 1 gigid instrument and 1 šendili kundu vessel for **Abi-simti**, X as deputy, 2 rings of silver, in palace, fr.**Lu-diĝirra withdr.**	1 šu-ša-gar^{zabar}, 1 kun-dù^{zabar}, 16 gal^{zabar}, 6 za-hum^{zabar}, 4 šu-ša-lá^{zabar}, 1 gi-gíd^{zabar}, 1 šen-dilí kun-dù^{zabar}, ***A-bí-sí-im-ti***, *ud* ~ è-lu-núm-^{d} *Inanna* ***Ha-bu-rí-tum-ma***, *in-ak-a*, *in-ba*, *x maškim*, 2 *har kù-babbar*, 10 *gín-ta*, *šà* ~ *é-gal-šè*, ***Li-ni-si-in****maškim*, *ki* ~ **Lú-diĝir-ra**--ta, ba-zi, šà ~ **Puzur$_4$-iš-^{d} Da-gan**. iti-ze$_x$-kù ~ gu$_7$, mu en Unug^{ki}-ga ba-hun, (left) 32. (MVN 20, 031, P142964)	1 basin, 1 kundu vessel, 16 cups, 6 zahum basins, 4šušala vessels, 1 gigid instrument and 1 šendili kundu vessel for **Abi-simti**, in the elunum festival of Inanna-Haburitum, present to her, **X as royal deputy**, 2 rings of silver, each 10 shekels, **in the palace**, **Lisin as royal deputy**, from the place of Lu-diĝirra, were withdrawn, in **Puzuriš-Dagan**. Month of ze-ku ~ gu$_7$, Year of en-priest of Uruk was installed, (sum:) 32.	1个盆、1个 kundu 容器、16个杯子、6个 zahum 盆、4个 šušala 容器、1个 gigid 工具和1个 šendili kundu 容器为**阿比新提**，于伊南那哈布瑞吞的埃鲁农节时赠予了，**X 督办**，2环银子，每环10锱于宫殿，**里尼辛督办**，自卢迪弥腊处被支出，于**普兹瑞什达干**。食豚月，乌鲁克的女祭司被任命之年。(总计:) 32
AS 5 viii/16: **ba-zi** 16 fat flocks, 16 x x and 1 kid for**Abi-simti**, **Ri ṣ-ilum**as deputy; 1 fat kid to kitchen of state, **Aya-kalla**asdeputy, fr. **Aba-saga** were **withdr**.	8 udu-niga, 4 máš-gal-niga, 2 ^{f}aš [gar] -niga, 16 x x, 1 máš, ***A-bí-sí-*** [***im***] ***-ti***, ***Ri-i ṣ-ilum***rá-gaba **maškim**; 1^{f} ašgar-niga **é-uz-** [**ga**], ***A-a-kal-la****maškim*, *šà* ~ *mu-er$_{10}$--ra--ta*, *ud*-16-*kam*, *ki* ~ **Ab-ba-sa$_6$-ga**--ta, ba-zi.iti-šu-eš$_5$-ša, mu En-unu$_6$-gal ^{d}Inanna Unug-ga [ba] -hun. (left) 32 (Orient 16 046 28, P124655)	8 fattened rams, 4 fattened he-goats, 2 fattened female kids, 16 x x and 1 kid for**Abi-simti**, **Ri ṣ-ilum**knight as royal deputy; 1 fattened female kid to the kitchen of state, **Aya-kalla**as royal deputy, from the deliveries, on 16th day, from **Aba-saga** were withdrawn. Month of šu-ešša, Year of En-unu-gal- (an-na), en-priest of Inanna, was installed. (sum:) 32	8只育肥公绵羊、4只育肥公山羊、2只育肥雌崽、16 x x 和1只公崽为**阿比新提**，**瑞施伊隆骑使督办**；1只育肥雌崽到御膳房，**阿亚卡拉督办**，**从送入项中**，于16日，自**阿巴萨旮**处，被支出了。三只手月，女神伊南那的祭司恩乌努旮勒被任命之年。（总计:) 32
AS 5 ix/11: **ba-zi** 130 flocks for**Abi-simti**, 60 for **Me-Ištaran**, **Beli-ili** as **deputy**; 2 for **throne of Šulgi**, **Utu-du as deputy**; 11 for **Dada**, 5 for **Šu-Dagan**, 20 for **Ṣ i-Iškur**, 20 bulls for **Ama-naya**, 10 for **Ilallum**, **Arad-mu** as deputy, fr.**Abba-saga withdr**.	10 gud, 120 udu-bar-gál, ***A-bí-sí-im-ti***, 60 *udu-bar-gál* **Me-^{d} Ištaran**, ***Be-lí-ì-lí*****maškim**; 1 udu 1 máš-gal, **gu-za-^{d} Šul-gi**, ^{d} **Utu-du$_{10}$ maškim**; 1 gud, 10 udu, **Da-da gala**, 5 udu**Šu-^{d} Da-gan**, 10 udu, 10 máš-gal, ***Ṣ i-li-^{d} Iškur***, 20 *gud* **Ama-na-a** nu-bandà, 10 udu***Ì-làl-lum***, **Arád-mu maškim**, šà ~ mu-er$_{10}$--ra--ta, ud-11-kam, ki ~ **Ab-ba-sa$_6$-ga**--ta ba-zi.iti-ezem-mah, mu en ^{d}Inanna ba-hun, 31 gud, 227 udu. (OIP 121 271, P124001)	10 bulls and 120 rams with fleece for**Abi-simti**, 60 rams with fleece for **Me-Ištaran**, **Beli-ili as royal deputy**; 1 ram and 1 goat for **throne of Šulgi**, **Utu-du as royal deputy**; 1 bull and 10 rams for**Dada**, the singer, 5 rams for **Šu-Dagan**, 10 rams and 10 goats for **Ṣi-Iškur**, 20 bulls for **Ama-naya** soldier, 10 rams for **Ilallum**, **Arad-mu as royal deputy**, from the deliveries, on the 11th day, from the place of **Abba-saga** were withdrawn. Month of ezem-mah, Year of the en-priest of Inanna was installed. (sum): 31 bulls, 227 rams	10公牛和120带毛公绵羊为**阿比新提**，60带毛公绵羊为**美伊什塔蓝**，**贝里伊里督办**；1公绵羊和1公山羊为**舒勒吉的王座**，**乌图杜督办**；1公牛和10公羊为歌手**达达**，5公羊为**舒达干**，10公绵羊和10公山羊为**采伊什库尔**，20公牛为士兵**阿马那亚**，10公绵羊为**伊拉隆**，**阿腊德穆督办**，自送入项中，于11日，从**阿巴萨旮**处被支出了。大庆典月，女神伊南那的祭司被任命之年。计：31头公牛，227羊。

续表

时间和摘要	文献内容	英文翻译	中文翻译
AS 5 ix/23: **ba-zi** 1 lamb for**Enlil**, 1 for **Ninlil**, **<u>Ilum-D.</u>as <u>deputy</u>**, 1 for **Abi-simti**, by priest of Š., **Nur-Adad** as deputy, fr. [**Abba-saga**] **withdr.**	1 sila$_4$ ^{d}**En-líl**, 1 sila$_4$ ^{d}**Nin-líl**, mu-túm ***Ṣe-lu-uš-^{d}Da-gan***, ***<u>Ilum-Dan</u>**<u>sukkal</u>* **<u>maškim</u>**, 1 máš ***A-bí-sí-im-ti***, *mu-túm* **lú-mah-^{d} Šará**, ***<u>Nu-úr-^{d}Adad</u>**<u>rá-gabamaškim</u>*, *ud-23-kam*, *ki* ~ [**Ab-ba-sa$_6$**] **-ga**--ta [ba] -zi. iti-ezem-mah, mu en ^{d}Inanna ba-huĝ, 3. (OIP 121 283, P124013)	1 lamb for**Enlil**, 1 lamb for **Ninlil**, were delivered by **Ṣeluš-Dagan**, **<u>Ilum-dan</u>**, <u>theenvoy as royal deputy</u>, 1 kid for **Abi-simti**, delivered by the lú-mah priest of Šara, **<u>Nur-Adad</u>** <u>knight as royal deputy</u>, on the 23rd day, from [**Abba-saga**] were withdrawn. Month of ezem-mah, Year of the en-priest of Inanna was installed.	1只公羔为**恩里勒**，1只公羔为**宁里勒**，由采鲁什达干送人，**<u>伊隆丹国使督办</u>**，1只公崽为**阿比新提**，由沙腊神的祭司送入，**<u>努尔阿达德骑使督办</u>**，于23日，自**阿巴萨旮**处被支出。大庆典月，女神伊南那的祭司被任命之年。
AS 5 xi/1-29: **ba-zi** 29 fat flocks for**offering** of 29 days; 1 fat ram for **Full Moon**, 1 fat ram for **New Moon**, 30 fat flocks for allowance of **Abi-simti**, <u>via**Nuhi-ilum**</u>, fr. **Šulgi-ayamu**, were **withdr.**	10 udu-niga, 12 u$_8$-niga, 7 ud$_5$-niga, **šu-a-gi-na ud-29-kam**; 1 udu-niga **é-ud-15**, 1 udu-niga**é-ud-sakar**, (erasure: 2? x-niga), 12 udu-niga, 8 u$_8$-niga, 10 ud$_5$-niga, sá-dug$_4$~ ***A-bí-sí-im-ti***, *iti-1-kam*, *<u>gìr</u>* ***<u>Nu-hi-ilum</u>**<u>rá-gaba</u>*, *ki* ~ ***^{d}Šul-gi-a-a-mu***--*ta ba-zi.iti-ezem-Me-ki-ĝál*, *mu en^{d}Inanna ba-hun*, 61 *udu.* (*Nisaba* 08 373, *P*321024)	10 *fattened rams*, 12 *fattened ewes and* 7 *fattened she-goats for the* **daily offering** of 29 days; 1 fattened ram for **Full Moon**, 1 fattened ram for **New Moon**, 12 fattened rams, 8 fattened ewes and 10 fattened she-goats for the monthly allowance of **Abi-simti**, for 1 month, <u>via**Nuhi-ilum**knight</u>, from place of **Šulgi-ayamu**, were withdrawn. Month of Mekiĝal, Year of the en-priest of Inanna was installed. (sum): 61 rams.	10只肥公绵羊、12只肥母绵羊和7只肥母山羊为**29天的日供**；1只肥公绵羊为**满月**，1只肥公绵羊为**新月**，12肥公绵羊、8肥母绵羊和10肥母山羊为**阿比新提的一个月的月供**，**<u>经由努希伊隆骑使</u>**，自**舒勒吉阿亚穆**处被支出。神美基旮勒庆典月，女神伊南那的祭司被任命之年。总计：61只公绵羊
AS 6 ii/16: **ba-zi** 1 fat ram fr. Zubuš for **Iabrat**, **<u>via Ur-Haya</u>**, **in Nippru**, 13 fat flocks for **messengers**, 5 ewes for **soldiers**, to kitchen, 2 rams for **Abi-simti**, to palace, via Šul., 1 fat ram fr. Libanš. for **Libanu.**, via **<u>Šu-Šulgi</u>**, 1 fat ram fr. Dannali. for **Hu.**, via **<u>Lalamu</u>**, **<u>Arad-mu</u>**as <u>deputy</u>, fr. **Ahu-Wer** were **withdr.**	1 udu-niga***Zu-bu-uš*** *lú-kin-gi$_4$-a* ***Ià-ab-ra-at*** *LÚ.SU^{ki}*, *<u>gìr</u>* **<u>Ur-^{d}Ha-ià</u>**<u>sukkal</u>, šà ~ Nibru^{ki}, 2 udu-niga uzu-ud--šè, 1 gud-niga, 10 udu-niga, mu~ **kaš$_4$-e-ne**--šè, 5 u$_8$ šu-gíd mu~ **agà-ús-ne**--šè, é muhaldim--šè, 2 udu***A-bí-sí-im-ti***, *šà é-gal--šè*, *<u>gìr</u>* **<u>^{d}Šul-gi-uru-mu</u>**, 1 udu-niga***Li-ba-an-aš-gu-bi*** *lú-kin-gi$_4$-a* ***Li-ba-nu-ug-ša-ba-aš*** *ensí Mar-ha-ši^{ki}*, *<u>gìr</u>* **<u>Šu-^{d}Šul-gi</u>** <u>sukkal</u>, 1 udu-niga ***Dan-na-li*** *lú-kin-gi$_4$-a* ***Hu-li-bar*** *lú Du$_8$-du$_8$-<lí>^{ki}*, *gìr* ***La-la-mu*** *sukkal*, **<u>Arád-mu</u>** <u>maškim</u>, iti-ud-16 ba-zal, ki~ ***A-hu-We-er***--*ta ba-zi.iti-ze$_x$-da~ gu$_7$*, *mu Ša-aš-ru^{ki} ba-hul*, 1 *gud*, 22 *udu.* (*Ontario* 1 048, *P*124461)	1 *fattened ram from Zubuš messenger* **for Iabrat** of LÚ.SU, **<u>via Ur-Haya</u>**, <u>the ambassor</u>, **in Nippur**, 2 fattened rams as boiled meat, 1 fattened bull and 10 fattened rams for the **messengers**, 5 eliminated ewes for the **soldiers**, to the kitchen, 2 rams for **Abi-simti**, to the palace, **<u>via Šulgi-urumu</u>**, 1 fattened ram from Liban-ašgubi messenger for **Libanug-šabaš**, the governor of Marhaši, **<u>via Šu-Šulgienvoy</u>**, 1 fattened ram from Dannali messenger for **Hulibar**, the man of Duduli, <u>via **Lalamu**secretary</u>, **<u>Arad-mu</u>**<u>as royal deputy</u>, when the 16th day passed, from the place of **Ahu-Wer** were withdrawn. Month of zeda ~ gu$_7$, Year of Šašru was destroyed, (sum): 1 bull and 22 rams.	1肥公绵羊由朱布什信使给LÚ.SU的亚卜腊特，**<u>经由乌尔哈亚国务卿</u>**，**于尼普尔**，2肥公绵羊为水煮肉，1肥公牛和10肥公绵羊为**信使**，5淘汰级母绵羊为**士兵们**，到厨房，2公绵羊为**阿比新提**，到宫殿，**<u>经由舒勒吉乌如穆</u>**，1肥公绵羊由里班什古比信使给**马尔哈希德总督里巴努格沙巴什**，**<u>经由舒舒勒吉国使</u>**，1肥公绵羊由丹那里信使给杜杜里城的人胡里巴尔，**<u>经由拉拉穆使官</u>**，**<u>阿腊德穆督办</u>**，于16日过去时，自**阿胡维尔**处被支出。食豚月，沙什如被毁之年。总计：1公牛和22只公绵羊

续表

时间和摘要	文献内容	英文翻译	中文翻译
AS 6 ii/3, 5, 11, 17, 20, 23, 25, 26: **ba-zi, butchered** 1 lamb to**kitchen**, by Utami-š., **Hababatum as deputy**; 1 for **Enlil**, 1 for **Ninlil**, by Watarum, **Šarrum-ili as deputy**; 1 lamb to **kitchen**, by Arad-mu, **Hababatum as deputy**; 4 flocks for **Ilallum**, 2 for **Dada**, 2 for Ur-N., **Arad-mu as deputy**; 1 for **Enlil**, 1 for **Ninlil**, **P.as deputy**; 1 gezelle by Šulgi-a., 2 by H., these to **kitchen**, **H.as deputy**; 1 gezelle to **kitchen H. as deputy**, 1 **butchered** gezelle to storeroom; 1 for **Enlil**, 1 for **Ninlil**, **P.as deputy**; 1 ewe for **priest of Inanna of Uruk**, **Nur-I. as deputy**, 1 **butchered** gezelle to **storeroom**; 7 fat, 8 for **Abi-simti**, **N. as deputy**; fr. **Abba-saga** withdr.	1 sila$_4$ é-uz-ga, mu-túm ***Ú-tá-mi-šar-ra-am***, ***H*** ［***a-b***］ ***a-ba-tum*****muhaldim maškim**, 1, ud-3-kam, 1 sila$_4$ ^{d}**En-líl**, 1 sila$_4$ ^{d}**Nin-líl**, mu-túm ***Wa-tá-ru-u*** ［***m***］ *sanga*, ***Šar-ru-um-ì-lí*****sagi maškim**, 2, ud-5-kam, 1 sila$_4$ **é-uz-ga**, mu-túm Arád-mu, ***Ha-ba-ba-tum*** **muhaldim maškim**, 1, ud-11-kam, 1 gud, 3 udu-a-lum, ***Ì-làl-lum***, 2 *udu* **Da-da gala**, 2 udu Ur-^{d}Nin-gubalag nar, **Arád-mu maškim**, 1 sila$_4$ ^{d}**En-líl**, 1 sila$_4$ ^{d} **Nin-líl**, ***Pá-pá-an-še-en*****maškim**, šà mu-er$_{10}$--ra--ta, 10, ud-17-kam, 1 amar-maš-dà mu-túm ^{d}***Šul-gi-a-bi***, 1 *sila$_4$*, 1 *máš*, *mu-túm* **Ha-ab-ru-ša!**, é-uz-ga, ***Ha-ba-ba-tum*****muhaldim maškim**, 3, ud-20-kam, 1 mar-maš-dà é-uz-ga, ***Ha-ba-ba-tum*** **muhaldim maškim**, 1 maš-dà ba-úš, **é-kišib-ba**--šè, 2, ud-21-kam, 1 sila$_4$ ^{d} **En-líl**, 1 sila$_4$ ^{d}**Nin-líl**, ***Pá-pá-an-še-en*****maškim**, šà mu-er$_{10}$--ra--ta, 2, ud-23-kam, 1 u$_8$ **en-^{d} Inanna** Unug^{ki}, ***Nu-úr-^{d}Adad*****rá-gaba maškim**, 2 maš-dà, ba-úš **é-kišib-ba**--šè, šà ~ mu-er$_{10}$--ra--ta 3, ud-25-kam, 6 udu-niga, 1 máš-gal-niga, 7 sila$_4$, 1 máš, ***A-bí-sí-im-ti***, **Nam-ha-ni sukkal maškim**, 15, ud-26-kam, šu-nígin 9 sila$_4$, …, ki ~ **Ab-ba-sa$_6$-ga**--ta, ba-zi.iti-ze$_x$-da ~ gu$_7$, mu ^{d}Amar-^{d}Suen lugal-e Ša-aš-ru^{ki} mu-hul. （Nisaba 08 026, P108672）	1 lamb to the**kitchen of State**, delivered by Uta-mi-šarram, **Hababatum cook as royal deputy**, 1, on the 3rd day, 1 lamb for **Enlil**, 1 lamb for **Ninlil**, delivered by Watarum, the bishop, **Šarrum-ili cup-bearer as royal deputy**, 2, on the 5th day, 1 lamb to **kitchen of State**, delivered by Arad-mu, **Hababatum cook as royal deputy**, 1, on 11th day, 1 bull and 3 aslum rams for **Ilallum**, 2 rams for **Dada**, the singer, 2 rams for Ur-Nin-gubalag, the musician, **Arad-mu as royal deputy**; 1 lamb for**Enlil**, 1 lamb for **Ninlil**, **Papanšen as royal deputy**, from the deliveries, 10, on the 17th day, 1 young gezelle delivered by Šulgi-abi, 1 lamb and 1 kid delivered by Habruša, these to **kitchen of State**, **Hababatun cook as royal deputy**, 3, on 20th day, 1 young gezelle to **kitchen of State**, **Hababatun cook as royal deputy**, 1 **butchered** gezelle to the storeroom, 2, on 21st day, 1 lamb for **Enlil**, 1 lamb for **Ninlil**, **Papanšen as royal deputy**, from the deliveries, , on the 23rd day, 1 ewe for **the priest of Inanna of Uruk**, **Nur-Adad knight as royal deputy**, 1 **butchered** gezelle to the **storeroom**, from the deliveries, 3, on 25th day, 6 fattened rams, 1 fattened goat, 7 lambs and 1 kid for**Abi-simti**, **Nam-hali envoy as royal deputy**, 15, on the 26th day, total: 9 lambs, …, from the place of **Abba-saga** were withdrawn.Month of zeda ~ gu$_7$, Year of Amar-Sin king destroyed Šašru.	1羔到御膳房，乌塔米沙冉送人，**哈巴巴吞厨师督办**，（计）：1，于3日；1羔为恩里勒，1羔为宁里勒，**瓦塔润祭司送入**，**沙润伊里司酒督办**，（总计：）2，于5日；1羔到御膳房，阿腊德穆送入，**哈巴巴吞厨师督办**，（计：）1，于11日；1公牛和3 aslum绵羊为伊拉隆，2公绵羊为歌手达达，2公绵羊为乐师乌尔宁古巴拉格，**阿腊德穆督办**；1羔为恩里勒，1羔为宁里勒，**帕盘鑫督办**，自送入项中，（总计：）10，于17日；1幼瞪羚舒勒吉阿比送入，1羔和1公崽哈卜如沙送入，以上为御膳房，**哈巴巴吞厨师督办**，（计）3，于20日；1幼瞪羚到御膳房，**哈巴巴吞厨师督办**，1**宰杀**瞪羚到仓库，（计）2，于21日；1羔为恩里勒，1羔为宁里勒，**帕盘鑫督办**，自送入项中，（计）2，于23日；1母绵羊为乌鲁克的伊南那神的祭司，**努尔阿达德骑使督办**，1宰杀的瞪羚到仓库，自送人项中，（计）3，于25日；6只育肥公绵羊、1只育肥公山羊、7只羔和1只公崽为**阿比新提**，**那姆哈里国使督办**，（计）15，于26日，总计：9羔……自**阿巴萨旮**处被支出。食豚月，阿马尔辛国王摧毁沙什如年。

续表

时间和摘要	文献内容	英文翻译	中文翻译
AS 6 iii: **ba-zi, butchered** 16 shekels silver fr.**Nuhi-ilum**, for **Abi-simti**, **Ri ṣ-ilum**as deputy, 16 and 1 fr.**daughter of Lugal-a.**, **Šitelani** as deputy, 1 bronze for **Ahansibu**, <Mašum> as deputy, fr.**Lu-diĝirra** withdr., in Puzuriš-Dagan	2 har kù-babbar, 8 gín-ta, ***Nu-hi-ilum*** *sukkal* ***A-bí-sí-im-ti***, ***Ri-i*** ***ṣ-ilum****maškim*, 2 *har kù-babbar*, 8 *gín-ta*, 1 *dalla kù-babbar*, *dumu-munus* **Lugal-an-na-ab-du** dam ***Šar-ru-um-ì-lí*** *nu-bandà lú Šušin*[ki]*-ka*, ***Ši$_x$-te-lá-ni****maškim*, *ud ~ ba-nú-ša-a*, 1 *gal zabar*, ***A-ha-an-si-bu*** [giš]*pana* (*ban*), *in-ba*, <***Ma-šum***>*maškim*, *ki* ~ **Lú-diĝir-ra**--ta, ba-zi, šà ~ Puzur$_4$-iš-[d]Da-gan. iti-u$_5$-bí[mušen] ~ gu$_7$, mu Ša-aš-ru[ki] ba-hul, (left) 6. (JCS 10 31 11, P111905)	2 rings of sliver, (weighted) 8 shekels each from**Nuhi-ilum envoy**[!] (for knight), for **Abi-simti**, **Ri ṣ-ilum as royal deputy**, 2 rings of silver, 8 shekels each, 1 dalla ring of silver from the **daughter of Lugal-annb-du**, for the wife of Šarrum-ili captain of the ruler of Susa, **Šitelani as roya deputy**, when the dark moon, 1 cup bronze presented to **Ahansibu** bowman, <Mašum> as royal deputy, from **Lu-diĝirra** were withdrawn, in Puzuriš-Dagan. Month of ubi ~ gu$_7$, Year of Šašru was destroyed. (sum:) 6.	2 环银，每环重 8 舍克勒，自努希伊隆国使处，**为阿比新提**，**瑞施伊隆督办**，2 环银，每环重 8 舍克勒，1dalla 环银自卢旮勒安那卜杜的女儿， 为苏萨的统治者沙润伊里军尉的妻子，**西台拉尼督办**，于晦月时，1 杯青铜赠予阿哈斯布弓射手， **<马顺>督办**， 自**卢迪弥腊**处被支出，于**普兹瑞什达干**。 食乌比鸟月， 沙什如被毁之年。
AS 6 iii/25: **ba-zi** 1 fat kid when dark moon to palace for**Abi-simti**, via **Ahuwer**, 5 flocks to **kitchen**, **Arad-mu** as deputy, fr. Ahuwer **withdr.**	1[f] ašgar-niga-sig$_5$, ud-nú-a-ka é-gal-la ba-an-ku$_4$, ***A-bí-sí-im-ti***, *gìr* ***A-hu-We-er***, 3 *sila$_4$*, 2 *ud$_5$*, *šu-gíd é-muhaldim*, *mu ~* **agà-ús-e-ne**--šè, **Arád-mu**maškim, iti-ud-25 ba-zal, ki ~ ***A-hu-We-er***--*ta*, *ba-zi. iti-u$_5$-bí-gu$_7$*, *mu Ša-aš-ru*[ki]*ba-hul*, 6 *udu*. (*NYPL* 133, *P122669*)	1 *best fattened female kid when the dark moon was sent to the palace for***Abi-simti**, **via Ahuwer**, 3 lambs and 2 she-goats to the **kitchen** for the soldiers, **Arad-mu as royal deputy**, when the 25th day passed, from the place of Ahuwer, were withdrawn. Month of ubi ~ gu$_7$, Year of Šašru was destroyed, (sum): 6 rams.	1 只优等育肥雌崽于晦月时被送入宫殿，为**阿比新提**，**经由阿胡维尔**，3 只羔和 2 只母山羊**到厨房**，为士兵，**阿腊德穆督办**，于 25 日过去时，自**阿胡维尔**处，被支出。食乌比鸟月，沙什如被毁之年。总计：6 只公绵羊。

续表

时间和摘要	文献内容	英文翻译	中文翻译
AS 6 iv/26: **ba-zi** 3 fat rams for**sacrifice of Malkum**, **Ur-Baba** as deputy, 1 fat goat sent to palace for **Abi-simti**, **via Ahu-Wer**, 1 fat goat fr. Liban-a., for Libanug-š., **via Lu-Damu envoy**, 1 fat goat for Ili-Dagan, **via Nabi-Sîn**, 1 fat goat for Šu-I., **via Šiteli**, **Arad-mu as deputy**, fr. **Ahu-Wer**, were withdrawn	3 udu-niga, **siskúr** ^{d}***Ma-al-kum-ma***, **Ur-**^{d}**Ba-ba$_6$ muhaldim maškim**, 1 máš-gal-niga-sig$_5$, ud nú-a-ka é-gal-la ba-an-ku$_4$, ***A-bí-sí-im-ti***, *gìr* ***A-hu-We-er***, 1 *máš-gal-niga*, **Li-ba-an-aš-gu-bi** lú-kin-gi$_4$-a Li-ba-nu-ug-ša-ba-aš ensí Mar-ha-ši^{ki}, **gìrLú-**^{d}**Da-mu sukkal**, 1 máš-gal-niga***Ì-lí-***^{d}***Da-gan*** *lú Eb-la*^{ki}, **gìr*****Na-bí-***^{d}***Suen*****sukkal**, 1 máš-gal-niga, **Šu-**^{d}**Iš-ha-ra** lú Ma-rí^{ki}, **gìr*****Ši$_x$-te-li*****sukkal**, **Arád-mumaškim**, iti-ud-26-ba-zal, ki ~ ***A-hu-We-er*****-**-*ta*, *ba-zi. iti-ki-siki-*^{d}*Nin-a-zu*, *mu Ša-aš-ru*^{ki}*ba-hul*, 7 *udu.* (*MVN* 11 146, *P*116159)	3 *fattened rams for the***sacrifice of Malkum**, **Ur-Baba cook as royal deputy**, 1 best fattened he-goat when dark moon was sent to palace for**Abi-simti**, **via Ahu-Wer**, 1 fattened he-goat from Liban-ašgubi messenger for Libanug-šabaš, the governor of Marhaši, **via Lu-Damu envoy**, 1 fattened he-goat for Ili-Dagan, the man of Ebla, **via Nabi-Sîn envoy**, 1 fattened he-goat forŠu-Išhara, the man of Mari, **via Šiteli envoy**, **Arad-mu as royal deputy**, when the 26th day passed, from the place of**Ahu-Wer**, were withdrawn. Month of ki-siki-Ninazu, Year of Šašru was destroyed, (sum): 7 rams.	3只育肥公绵羊为**马勒昆神的祭祀**，**乌尔巴巴厨师**督办，1只优等育肥公山羊于晦月时被送入宫殿为**阿比新提**，**经由阿胡维尔**， 1育肥公山羊自里班阿什古比信使为马尔哈席德总督里巴努格沙巴什， **经由卢达穆国使**， 1育肥公山羊为伊里达干，埃卜拉城之人， **经由那比辛国使**， 1育肥公山羊为舒伊什哈腊，马瑞城之人， **经由席台里国使，阿腊德穆督办**，于26日过去时，自**阿胡维尔**处，被支出。神宁阿朱羊毛作坊月，沙什如被毁之年。总计：7只公绵羊
AS 6 v/26: **ba-zi** 1 wild kid sent to palace for**Abi-simti**, fr. **Lu-diĝirra withdr.**	1^{f} ašgar-a-dara$_4$$^{?}$, ud-nú-a-ka, é-gal-la ba-an-ku$_4$, ***A-bí-sí-im-ti***, *ki* ~ **Lú-diĝir-ra**--ta, ba-zi, iti-ud-26, ba-zal. iti-ezem-^{d} Nin -a-zu, mu Ša-aš-ru^{ki} ba-hul, 1. (Torino 1 249, P131883)	1 wild female kid when dark moon was sent to palace for **Abi-simti**, from place of **Lu-diĝirra**, was withdrawn, when 26th day passed. Month of ezem-Ninazu, Year of Šašru was destroyed, (sum): 1	1只野生雌崽于晦月时被送入宫殿，为**阿比新提**，自**卢迪弥腊**处被支出，于26日过去时。神宁阿朱庆典月，沙什如被毁之年。总计：1

续表

时间和摘要	文献内容	英文翻译	中文翻译
AS 6 ix/13: **ba-zi** 183 flocks for**Abi-simti**, by **people of URUxA**, **Arad-mu**as deputy, fr. **Abba-saga withdr.**	3 gud, 70 udu, 110 máš-gal, ***A-bí-sí-im-ti***, *mu-túm* **erín-URUxA**^{ki}, **Arád-mu**maškim, ud-13-kam, ki~ **Ab-ba-sa$_{6}$-ga**--ta, ba-zi. iti-ezem-mah, mu Ša-aš-ru^{ki} ba-hul, 3 gud, 180 udu. (SAT 2 0914, P144114)	3 bulls, 70 rams and 110 he-goat for**Abi-simti**, were delivered by people of URUxA, **Arad-mu**as royal deputy, on the 13th day, from Abba-saga were withdrawn. Month of ezem-mah, Year of Šašru was destroyed, (sum): 3 bulls and 180 sheep.	3 头公牛、70 只公绵羊和 110 只公山羊为**阿比新提**, URUxA 的人送入, **阿腊德穆督办**, 于 13 日, 自**阿巴萨旮**处被支出。大庆典月, 沙什如被毁之年。总计: 3 头公牛和 180 只羊
AS 6 ix: **šu~ ba-ti** 180 gur of barley for village of**Abi-simti**, fr. **Lugal-hegal**, **Lu-Nin-šubur received**	180.0.0 še gur, sá-dug$_{4}$ še-ba--šè, é-duru$_{5}$ **<A >$^{?}$-*bí-sí-im-ti*--*šè***, *ki*~ **Lugal-hé-gál**--ta, **Lú-^{d}Nin-šubur** (Šu-Nin-šubur ra-gaba) šu~ ba-ti. iti-ezem-mah, mu Ša-aš-ru^{ki}ba-hul. (PDT 2 1174, P126509)	180 gur of barley, the barley for the monthly allowance and barley rations of the irrigation village of**Abi-simti**, from place of Lugal-hegal, **Lu-Nin-šubur** (šabra of An) received. Month of ezem-mah, Year of Šašrum was destroyed.	180 钟大麦为**阿比新提**灌溉村庄的**月供和大麦口粮**, 自**卢旮勒希旮勒**处, **卢宁舒布尔**接收了。大庆典月, 沙什润被毁之年。
AS 6 x/25: **ba-zi** 6 fat flocks, 14 flocks and 1 gazelle for **Abi-simti**, **Šu-N.as deputy**, 1 fat ram for **Lu.**, **Arad-mu as deputy**, fr. **Abba-saga**, were **withdr.**	5 udu-niga, 1 máš-gal-niga, 2 udu, 12 sila$_{4}$, 1 maš-dà, ***A-bí-sí-im-ti***, **Šu-^{d}Nin-šubur rá-gaba maškim**, 1 udu-niga **Lugal-má-gur$_{8}$-re**, **Arád-mu maškim**, šà mu-túm ud-nú-a-< ka >, ud-25-kam, ki~ **Ab-ba-sa$_{6}$-ga**--ta ba-zi. iti-ezem-An-na, mu Ša-aš-ru^{ki} ba-hul.22 (TRU 315, P135079)	5 fattened rams, 1 fattened he-goat, 2 rams, 12 lambs and 1 gazelle for **Abi-simti**, **Šu-Nin-šubur knight as royal deputy**, 1 fattened ram for **Lugal-magurre**, **Arad-mu as royal deputy**, from deliveries for Dark Moon on the 25th day, from the place of **Abba-saga**, were withdrawn. Month of ezem-Anna, Year of Šašru was destroyed, (sum): 22	5 育肥公绵羊、1 只育肥公山羊、2 只公绵羊、12 只羔和 1 只瞪羚为**阿比新提**, **舒宁舒布尔骑使督办**, 1 只育肥公绵羊为**卢旮勒马古瑞**, **阿腊德穆督办**, 自送入项为晦月, 于 25 日, 自**阿巴萨旮**处被支出。安神庆典月, 沙什如被毁之年。总计: 22

续表

时间和摘要	文献内容	英文翻译	中文翻译
AS 6 xi/1, 3, 4, 5, 7, 11, 13, 15, 20, 21, 24, 25, 27: **ba-zi** 1st: 1 for Enlil, 1 for Ninlil, 1 for Iškur, **Maštur as deputy**; 3rd: 25 flocks for Ilallum, **Arad-mu as deputy**, 1 to kitchen, **Ur-Baba as deputy**, 10 for Ribagada, **Beli-ili as deputy**; 4th: 5 for Dada, by I., **Ula-i.as deputy**; 5th: 1 to kitchen, **Ur-B. as deputy**, 1 fat for Ilallum, **Šu-Š.as deputy**; 7th: 2 for Dada, **Arad-mu as deputy**, 2 for Me-Ištaran, **Nanna-k. as deputy**; 11th: 3 fat, 13 for Me-Ištaran, **N.as deputy**, 1 for Nusku, [1 for Ninurta], [⋯], **Aya- [k.as deputy]**, 1 by x-mu, 1 by [Wa] t., 1 by Bur-M., 1 by I., these to kitchen of State, **Aya-k. as deputy**; 13th: 6 gezelles to kitchen, **Šulgi-u. as deputy**, 10 for Ur-N., **Arad-mu as deputy**; 15th: 1 to kitchen, **Ur-B. as deputy**; 20th: 1 for Enlil, 1 for Ninlil, **Maštur as deputy**; 21st: 1 for Dada, **Arad-mu as deputy**; 24th: 2 by **Nir-i.**, to kitchen, **Ur-Baba as deputy**, 4 fat and 9 lambs for **Abi-simti**, **Šu-Nin-šubur as deputy**; 1 for Enlil, **Maštur as deputy**, 25th: 1, 27th: 1 kid for Ur-Nin-gubalag, **Ilallum as deputy**, ⋯, fr.**Abba-saga** withdr.	[1] sila$_4$ ^{d}En-líl, [1] sila$_4$ ^{d}Nin-líl, [1] sila$_4$ ^{d}Iškur, **Maš-tur sagi maškim**, [š] à~ mu-er$_{10}$--ra--ta, 3, ud-1-kam; 20 udu, 1 udu-a-lum, 4 gukkal, ***Ì-làl-lum***, **Arád-mu maškim**, 1 sila$_4$ é-uz-ga, **Ur-^{d}Ba-ba$_6$maškim**,...., ***Be-lí-ì-lí*** **maškim**, šà~ mu-er$_{10}$--ra--ta, 36, ud-3-kam; 5 udu **Da-da** gala, mu-túm ***I-gi$_4$-ha-lum***, ***Ú-la-i-* [*ni-iš*maškim]**, 5, ud-4-kam; 1 sila$_4$ é-uz-ga, **Ur-^{d}Ba-ba$_6$ maškim**, 1 gukkal-niga, *Ì-làl-lum*, **Šu-^{d}Šul-gi**rá-gaba maškim, 2, ud-5-kam; 1 máš-gal, 1 ^{f}ašgar, **Da-da** gala, **Arád-mu maškim**, 1 ud$_5$, 1 máš-gùn-a, Me-^{d}Ištaran, **^{d}Nanna-kam sukkal maškim**, šà ~ mu-er$_{10}$--ra--ta, 4, ud-7-kam; 3 udu-niga, 12 sila$_4$, 1 máš, **Me-^{d}Ištaran**, **Nin-ha-ma-ti rá-gaba maškim**, 1 sila$_4$ **^{d}Nusku**, [1 sila$_4$ ^{d}Nin-urta], [...], ***A-a-* [*kal-la*maškim?]**, 1 sila$_4$ m [u-túm x] -mu, 1 sila$_4$ mu-t [úm ***Wa***] ***-tá-ru-um***, 1 *sila$_4$ mu-túm* **Bur-Ma-ma**, 1 sila$_4$ mu-túm ***Ik-šu-dum***, *é-uz-ga*, ***A-a-kal-la*maškim**, šà~ mu-er$_{10}$--ra--ta, 22, ud-11-kam; 6 maš-dà šu-gíd, é-muhaldim, **^{d}Šul-gi-uru-mumaškim**, 10 udu **Ur-^{d} Nin-gubalag** nar, **Arád-mu**maškim, 16, ud-13-kam; 1 sila$_4$ é-uz-ga, **Ur-^{d}Ba-ba$_6$maškim**, 1, ud-15-kam; 1 sila$_4$ ^{d}En-líl, 1 sila$_4$ ^{d}Nin-líl, **Maš-tur sagi maškim**, šà ~ mu-er$_{10}$--ra--ta, 2, ud-20-kam; 1 sila$_4$ **Da-da** gala, **Arád-mu maškim**, šà~ mu-er$_{10}$--ra--ta, 1, ud-21-kam; 1 ud$_5$-máš-nu-a, 1 sila$_4$, mu-túm ***Nir-ì-da-ĝál***, *é-uz-ga*, **Ur-^{d}Ba-ba$_6$maškim**, 1 udu-gi$_6$-niga, 1 gukkal-niga, 2 máš-gal-niga, 9 sila$_4$, ***A-bí-sí-im-ti***, **Šu-^{d} Nin-šuburrá-gaba maškim**, 15, ud-24-kam; 1 sila$_4$ ^{d}En-líl, mu-túm ***I-din-^{d}Suen***, **Maš-tur**sagi maškim, 1, ud-25-kam; 1 máš**Ur-^{d}Nin-gubalag** nar, ***Ì-làl-lum*** *maškim*, 1, *ud-27-kam*; *šu-nígin* 16 *sila$_4$*, …, *ki*~**Ab-ba-sa$_6$-ga**--ta ba-zi.iti-ezem-Me-ki-ĝál, mu Ša-aš-ru^{ki} ba-hul. (Nisaba 08 036, P108661)	1 lamb for Enlil, 1 lamb for Ninlil, 1 lamb for Iškur, **Maštur cup-bearer as royal deputy**, from the deliveries, (sum) 3, on the 1st day; 20 rams, 1 aslum ram and 4 fat-tailed sheep for Ilallum, **Arad-mu as royal deputy**, 1 lamb to kitchen of State, **Ur-Baba as royal deputy**, 10 he-goats for Ribagada knight, for ? **eli-ili as royal deputy**, from the deliveries, (sum) 36, on the 3rd day; rams for Dada, the singer, delivered by Igihalum, **Ula-inišas royal deputy**, 5, on the 4th day; lamb to kitchen of State, **Ur-Baba as royal deputy**, 1 fattened fat-tailed sheep for Ilallum, **Šu-Šulgi knight as royal deputy**, (sum) 2, on the 5th day; he-goat and 1 female kid for Dada, the singer, **Arad-mu as royal deputy**, 1 she-goat and 1 spot kid for Me-Ištaran, **Nanna-kam envoy as royal deputy**, from the deliveries, (sum) 4, on 7th day; 3 fattened ram, 12 lambs and 1 kid for Me-Ištaran, **Ninhamati knight as royal deputy**, 1 lamb for Nusku, [1 lamb for Ninurta], [⋯], **Aya- [kalla as royal deputy]**, 1 lamb was delivered by x-mu, 1 lamb delivered by [Wa] tarum, 1 lamb delivered by Bur-Mama, 1 lamb delivered by Ikšudum, these to kitchen of State, **Aya-kalla as royal deputy**, from deliveries, (sum) 22, on 11th day; 6 eliminated gezelles to kitchen, **Šulgi-urumu as royal deputy**, 10 rams for Ur-Nin-gubalag, the musician, **Arad-mu as royal deputy**, (sum) 16, on 13th day; 1 lamb to the kitchen of State, **Ur-Baba as royal deputy**, (sum) 1, on the 15th day; 1 lamb for Enlil, 1 lamb for Ninlil, **Maštur cup-bearer as royal deputy**, from deliveries, (sum) 2, on 20th; 1 lamb for Dada, the singer, **Arad-mu as royal deputy**, from deliveries, (sum) 1, on 21st; 1 she-goat without kid and 1 lamb were delivered by **Nir-idagal**, to the kitchen of state, **Ur-Baba as royal deputy**, 1 fattened black ram, 1 fattened big-tailed sheep, 2 fattened he-goats and 9 lambs for **Abi-simti**, **Šu-Nin-šubur knight as royal deputy**, (sum) 15, on the 24th day; 1 lamb for Enlil, delivered by Idin-Sîn, **Maštur cup-bearer as royal deputy**, (sum) 1, on the 25th day; 1 kid for Ur-Nin-gubalag, the musician, **Ilallum as royal deputy**, (sum) 1, on the 27th day; total: 16 lambs, ⋯, from **Abba-saga** were withdrawn. Month of ezem-Mekiĝal, Year of Šašru was destroyed.	1羔为恩里勒，1羔为宁里勒，1羔为伊什库尔，**马什图尔司酒督办**，自送入项中，(总) 3，于1日； 20公绵羊、1 aslum公绵羊和4肥尾绵羊为伊拉隆，**阿腊德穆督办**，1羔到御膳房，**乌尔巴巴督办**，10公山羊为瑞巴旮达骑使……**贝里伊里督办**，自送入项中，(总) 36，于3日；5公绵羊为歌手达达，伊吉哈隆送入，**乌拉伊尼什督办**，(总) 5，于4日；1羔到御膳房，**乌尔巴巴督办**，1育肥肥尾绵羊为伊拉隆，**舒舒勒吉骑使督办**，(总) 2，于5日；1公山羊和1雌崽为歌手达达，**阿腊德穆督办**，1母山羊和1斑点公山羊崽为美伊什塔蓝，**南那刊国使督办**，自送入项，(总) 4，于7日；3育肥公绵羊、12羔和1公崽为美伊什塔蓝，**宁哈姆提骑使督办**，1羔为努斯库，【1羔为宁乌尔塔】，【……】，**阿亚【卡拉督办】**，1羔X-穆送入，1羔【瓦】塔润送入，1羔布尔马马送入，1羔伊克舒杜姆送入，以上到御膳房，**阿亚卡拉督办**，自送入项中，(总) 22，于11日；6淘汰级瞪羚到厨房，**舒勒吉乌如穆督办**，10公绵羊为乐师乌尔宁古巴拉格，**阿腊德穆督办**，(总) 16，于13日；1羔到御膳房，**乌尔巴巴督办**，(总) 1，于15日；1羔为恩里勒，1羔为宁里勒，**马什图尔司酒督办**，自送入项，(总) 2，20日；1羔为歌手达达，**阿腊德穆督办**，自送入项，1，21日；1只无崽母山羊和1只羔尼尔伊达旮勒送入，到御膳房，**乌尔巴巴督办**，1只育肥黑公绵羊、1只育肥的肥尾绵羊、2只育肥公山羊和9只羔为**阿比新提**，**舒宁舒布尔骑使督办**，(总) 15，于24日；1羔为恩里勒，伊丁辛送入，**马什图尔司酒督办**，(总) 1，于25日；1公崽为乐师乌尔宁古巴拉格，**伊拉隆督办**，(总) 1，27日；总计：16只羔……自**阿巴萨旮**处被支出。神美基旮勒庆典月，沙什如被毁之年。

续表

时间和摘要	文献内容	英文翻译	中文翻译
AS 6 xii/25： **ba-zi** 1 lamb for dark moon was sent to palace for **Abi-simti**, fr。**Lu-diĝirra withdr.**	1 sila$_4$-ga ~ *Ši$_x$-maški*, ud ~ nú-a-ka, é-gal-la ba-an-ku$_4$, ***A-bí-sí-im-ti***, *iti-ud-25 ba-zal*, [*ki*] ~ **Lú-diĝir-ra**--ta, [ba] -zi. iti-še-kin-kud, mu Ša-aš-ru^{ki} ba-hul. (Prima dell' alfabeto no.17, P112529)	1*Šimaški* sucking lamb for the dark moon day (27-29) was sent to the palace for **Abi-simti**, when the 25th day passed, from the palce of **Lu-diĝirra**, was withdrawn. Month of še-kin-kud, Year of Šašrum was destroyed.	1只西马什基吃奶羔为晦月被送入宫殿，为**阿比新提**，于25日过去时，自**卢迪弥腊**处被支出了。大麦收割月， 沙什润被毁之年。
AS 7 iii/26： **ba-zi** 1 fat kid for dark moon sent to palace for **Abi-simti**, <u>**via Ahu-Wer**</u>, fr. **Ahu-Wer** with-dr.	1^{f}ašgar-a-dara$_4$-niga-sig$_5$, **ud nú-a-ka é gal-la ba-an-ku$_4$**, ***A-bí-sí-im-ti***, <u>*gìr*</u> <u>***A-hu-We-er***</u>, *iti-ud-26 ba-zal*, *ki* ~ ***A-hu-We -er***-*-ta*, *ba-zi*. *iti-u$_5$-bí~gu$_7$*, *mu Hu-úh-nu-ri^{ki} ba-hul*, 1. (*OIP* 121 027, *P*123757)	1 *best fattened wild female kid for the dark moon was sent to palace for***Abi-simti**, <u>**via Ahu-Wer**</u>, when the 26th day passed, from the place of **Ahu-Wer** was withdrawn. Month of ubi ~ gu$_7$, Year of Huhnuri was destroyed. (sum)：1	1只优等育肥野生雌崽为晦月被送入宫殿，为**阿比新提**，<u>**经由阿胡维尔**</u>，于26日过去时，自**阿胡维尔**处被支出。食乌比乌月，胡赫努瑞被毁之年。总计：1
AS 7 v/26： **ba-zi** 1 sow, 10 fat flocks, 10 lamb and 1 gazelle, these for **Abi-simti**, for the níĝ-dab$_5$ offering of Dark Moon, fr. **Abba-saga** were **withdrawn**	1 šeg$_9$-bar munus, 5 udu-niga, 1 sila$_4$-niga, 2 u$_8$-a-lum-niga, 2 máš-gal-niga, 10 sila$_4$, 1 maš-dà-munus, ***A-bí-sí-im-ti***, *níĝ-dab$_5$-ud-nú-a*, *ud-26-kam*, *ki*~ **Ab-ba-sa$_6$-ga**--ta, ba-zi. iti-ezem-^{d}Nin-a-zu, mu Hu-úh-nu-ri^{ki} ba-hul, 22. (Ontario 1 075, P124488, see Nisaba next) 1 šeg$_9$-bar munus, 5 udu-niga, 1 sila$_4$-niga, 2 u$_8$-a-lum-niga, 2 máš-gal-niga, 10 sila$_4$, 1 maš-dà-munus, ***A-bí-sí-im-ti***, *níĝ-dab$_5$-ud-nú-a*, *ud-26-kam*, *ki* ~ **Ab-ba-sa$_6$-ga**--ta, ba-zi. iti-ezem-^{d} Nin-a-zu, mu Hu-úh-nu-ri^{ki} ba-hul, 22. (Ontario 1 075, P124488, see Nisaba next)	1 wild sow, 5 fattened rams, 1 fattened lamb, 2 fattened aslum ewe, 2 fattened he-goats, 10 lamb and 1 female gazelle, these for **Abi-simti**, for the níĝ-dab$_5$ offering of Dark Moon, on the 26th day, from the place of **Abba-saga** were withdrawn. Month of ezem-Ninazu, Year of Huh-nuri was destroyed. (sum)：22	1头 *sapparu* 野母猪、5只肥公绵羊、1只肥羔、2只育肥 aslum 母绵羊、2只育肥公山羊、10只羔和1只雌瞪羚，以上为**阿比新提**，为晦月的 níĝ-dab$_5$ 供奉，于26日，自**阿巴萨旮**处被支出。神宁阿朱庆典月，胡赫努瑞被毁之年。总计：22

续表

时间和摘要	文献内容	英文翻译	中文翻译
AS 7 v/2, 6-8, 11, 13, 14 18, 21-24, 26, 29, 30: ba-zi 2nd: 10 for Lugal-m., Ur-Baba as deputy, 6 for Dada, 4 for Ur-N., Turam-D.as deputy; 6th: 1 for Enlil, delivered by H., Enlil-zišagal as deputy; 7th: 5 for bride of Nanipatal of Urbilum, via Šulgi-hasis, 300 for wife of Lu-Nanna, Arad-mu as deputy; 8th: [2] for Lugal-m., Ula-inišas deputy; 11th: 3 wild pigs, 1 donkey, 8 fat flocks, 8 flocks for Me-Ištaran, Ninhamati asdeputy, 1 sow for village, Arad-mu as deputy; 13th: 1 fat for cultic table, for the delivery of níg-dab$_{5}$ offering of Amar-Sîn, Atu as deputy, 14th: 2 fat flocks to kitchen of State, by Ṣ iluš-Dagan, Ur-Baba as deputy; 18th: 2 fat for Ilallum, by governor of Kiš, Dayati as deputy; 21st: 1 goat to kitchen of State, by Katar, Ur-Baba as deputy; 22nd: 5 for Ilallum, 5 for Lugal-m., U.as deputy; 23rd: 1 to the, fr. temple of Nintin-ugga, by Me-Eštar, Enlil-z.as deputy; 24th: 5 flocks Arad-mu as deputy, 6 sheep for Šu-Sîn, Utami-š.as deputy; 26th: 1 sow, 10 fat flocks, 10 lambs and 1 gazelle for Abi-simti; 29th: 1 for Enlil, 1 for Ninlil, Enlil-z.as deputy, 1 lamb to kitchen of State, Ur-Baba as deputy, 5 fat ram, 5 rams for Me-Ištaran, 1 ram for Lugal-m.1 ram for Dada, 1 sheep for Enlil-z., Utami-š. as deputy, 1 for Šu-Mama, Dayati as deputy; 10 for Lugal-m., Lini-šin as royal deputy, from the deliveries, 10, on the 30th day, total: 1 wild sow, ···, fr. Abba-saga withdr.	10 udu**Lugal-má-gur$_{8}$-re**, Ur-^{d}Ba-ba$_{6}$maškim, 6 udu **Da-da** gala, 3 udu, 1 sila$_{4}$, Ur-^{d}Nin-gubalag nar, *Tu-ra-am-^{d}Da-gan**maškim*, *šà ~ mu-er$_{10}$-ra-ta*, 20, *ud-2-kam*; 1 *sila$_{4}$* ^{d}En-líl, mu-túm *Ha-ab-ru-še-er*, ^{d}En-líl-zi-šà-gál maškim, 1, ud-6-kam; 5 udu, é-gi$_{4}$-a *Na-ni-pá-tal*, Ur-bí-lum^{ki}-šè, gìr ^{d}*Šul-gi-ha-sí-is*, 276 *udu*, 24 *máš-gal*, [d] am Lú-^{d}Nanna, [dumu U] r-nigar, [Arád-mu?] maškim, [300], [ud-7] -kam; [1 udu-a] -lum, [1 gu] kkal, [Lugal-má-gur$_{8}$?] -re, *Ú-la-ì-ni-iš**maškim*, *šà ~ mu-er$_{10}$-ra-ta*, 2, *ud-8-kam*; 2 *šeg$_{9}$-bar-níta*, 1 *šeg$_{9}$-bar-munus*, 1 *anše-eden-na-níta-mu-1*, 5 *udu-niga*, 1 *udu-a-lum-niga*, 1 *máš-gal-niga*, 1 *^{f}ašgar-niga*, 2 *gukkal*, 5 *sila$_{4}$*, 1 *^{f}ašgar*, Me-^{d}Ištaran, níg-dab$_{5}$ é-ud-15, Nin-ha-ma-tirá-gaba maškim, 1 šeg$_{9}$-bar-munus é-duru$_{5}$ DU./DU šà ~ é-^{d}En-líl-lá, Arád-mu maškim, šà ~ mu-er$_{10}$-ra-ta, 21, ud-11-kam; 1 udu-niga**zà-gú-lá**-šè, mu-túm níg-dab$_{5}$, ^{d}Amar-^{d}Suen, é-^{d}En-líl-lá-ta, A-tusagimaškim, 1, ud-13-kam, 1 udu *Šimaškí*^{ki}-niga, 1 ud$_{5}$-*Šimaškí*^{ki}-niga, é-uz-ga, mu-túm *Ṣ i-lu-uš-^{d}Da-gan*, Ur-^{d}Ba-ba$_{6}$ maškim, 2, ud-14-kam; 2 udu-niga *Ì-làl-lum*, *mu-túm ensí Kiš^{ki}*, *Da-a-a-ti**dub-sar maškim*, 2, *ud-18-kam*; 1 *ud$_{5}$-máš-nu-a*, é-uz-ga, mu-túm Ka-tar nu-^{giš}kiri$_{6}$, Ur-^{d}Ba-ba$_{6}$maškim, 1, ud-21-kam; 5 udu-a-lum, *Ì-làl-lum*, 5 *udu-a-lum*, Lugal-má-gur$_{8}$-re, *Ú-tá-mi-šar-ra-am**maškim*, *šà ~ mu-er$_{10}$-ra-ta*, 10, *ud-22-kam*; 1 *sila$_{4}$-GAM*, é duru$_{5}$ DU. DU šà ~ é ^{d}Nin-tin-ug$_{5}$-ga, mu-túm Me-Eš$_{4}$-tár, ^{d}En-líl-zi-šà-gál maškim, 1, ud-23-kam; 3 gukkal-giš-dù, 2 udu-a-lum-giš-dù, Arád-mu <maškim>, 6 gukkal-giš-dù, Šu-^{d} Suen, *Ú-tá-mi-šar-ra-am**maškim*, *šà ~ mu-er$_{10}$-ra-ta*, 11, *ud-24-kam*; 1 *šeg$_{9}$-bar-munus*, 5 *udu-niga*, 1 *sila$_{4}$-niga*, 2 *u$_{8}$-a-lum-niga*, 2 *máš-gal-niga*, 10 *sila$_{4}$*, 1 *maš-dà-munus*, *A-bi-sí-im-ti*, níĝ-dab$_{5}$ud-nú-a, 22, ud-26-kam; 1 sila$_{4}$ ^{d}En-líl, 1 sila$_{4}$ ^{d}Nin-líl, ^{d}En-líl-zi-šà-gál maškim, 1 sila$_{4}$ gukkal, é-uz-ga, Ur-^{d}Ba-ba$_{6}$ muhaldim maškim, 5 gukkal, 3 udu-a-lum, 2 udu-a-lum-giš-dù, Me-^{d}Ištaran, 1 udu-a-lum-giš-dù, Lugal-má-gur$_{8}$-re, 1 udu-a-lum-giš-dù, Da-da gala, 1 gukkal-giš-dù, ^{d}En-líl-zi-šà-gál, *Ú-tá-mi-šar-ra-am**maškim*, 1 *máš* Šu-Ma-ma ud-da-tuš, *Da-a-a-ti**dub-sar maškim*, *šà ~ mu-er$_{10}$-ra-ta*, 17, *ud-29-kam*; 10 *udu* Lugal-má-gur$_{8}$-re, *Li-ni-ši-in**maškim*, *mu-er$_{10}$-ra-ta*, 10, *ud-30-kam*, *šu-nígin* 1 *šeg$_{9}$-bar-munus*, ···, *ki~* Ab-ba-sa$_{6}$-ga-ta ba-zi. iti-ezem-^{d}Nin-a-zu, mu ^{d}Amar-^{d}Suen lugal-e, Bí-tum-ra-bí-um^{ki}Ì-ab-ru^{ki} ma-da ma-da-bi ù Hu-úh-nu-ri^{ki}mu-hul. (Nisaba 08 070, P108671, see above)	10 rams for Lugal-magurre, Ur-Baba as royal deputy, 6 rams for Dada, the singer, 3 rams and 1 lamb for Ur-Nin-gubalag, the musician, Turam-Dagan as royal deputy, from the deliveries, (sum) 20, on the 2nd day; 1 lamb for Enlil, delivered by Habrušer, Enlil-zišagal as royal deputy, (sum) 1, on the 6th day; 5 ram for the bride of Nanipatal of Urbilum, viaŠulgi-hasis, 276 rams and 24 he-goats for the wife of Lu-Nanna, son of Ur-nigar, Arad-mu as royal deputy, [300], on the 7th day; [1] aslum ram and [1] fat-tailed sheep for Lugal-magurre, Ula-inišas royal deputy, from the deliveries, (sum) 2, on the 8th day; 2wild boars, 1 wild sow, 1 donkey of 1 year-old, 5 fattened rams, 1 fattened aslum ram, 1 fattened he-goat, 1 fattened female kid, 2 fat-tailed sheep, 5 lambs and 1 female kid for Me-Ištaran, for the níg-dab$_{5}$ offering of Full Moon, Ninhamati knight asroyal deputy, 1 wild sow for the village, from the temple of Enlil, Arad-mu as royal deputy, from the deliveries, (sum) 21, on 11th day; 1 fattened ram for the cultic table, for the delivery of níg-dab$_{5}$ offering of Amar-Sîn, from the temple of Enlil, Atu cup-bearer as royal deputy, (sum) 1, on 13th day, 1 fattened *Šimaškí* ram, 1 fattened *Šimaškí* she-goat to the kitchen of State, delivered by *Ṣ iluš-Da-gan*, Ur-Baba asroyal deputy, (sum) 2, on the 14th day; 2 fattened rams for Ilallum, delivered by governor of Kiš, Dayati scribe as royal deputy, (sum) 2, on the 18th day; 1 she-goat without kid to the kitchen of State, delivered by Katar gardener, Ur-Baba as royal deputy, (sum) 1, on 21st day; 5 aslum ram for Ilallum, 5 aslum rams for Lugal-magurre, Utamišarram as royal deputy, from the deliveries, (sum) 10, on the 22nd day; 1 lamb to the village, from the temple of Nintin-ugga, delivered by Me-Eštar, Enlil-zišagal as royal deputy, (sum) 1, on the 23rd day; 3 fat-tailed sex mature sheep and 2 sex mature aslum ram, Arad-mu as royal deputy, 6 fat-tailed sex mature sheep for Šu-Sîn, Utami-šarram as royal deputy, from the deliveries, (sum) 11, on the 24th day; 1 wild sow, 5 fattened rams, 1 fattened lamb, 2 fattened aslum ewe, 2 fattened he-goats, 10 lambs and 1 female gazelle, these for Abi-simti, for the níĝ-dab$_{5}$ offering of Dark Moon, (sum) 22, on the 26th day; 1 lamb for Enlil, 1 lamb for Ninlil, Enlil-zišagal as royal deputy, 1 fat-taild lamb to the kitchen of State, Ur-Baba cook as royal deputy, 5 fat tailed-sheep, 3 aslum rams and 2 sex mature aslum rams for Me-Ištaran, 1 sex mature aslum ram for Lugal-magurre, 1 sex mature aslum ram for Dada, the singer, 1 sex mature fat-tailed sheep for Enlil-zišagal, Utami-šarram as royal deputy, 1 kid for Šu-Mama, the jester, Dayati scribe as royal deputy, from the deliveries, (sum) 17, on the 29th day; 10 rams for Lugal-magurre, Lini-šin as royal deputy, from the deliveries, (sum) 10, on the 30th day, total: 1 wild sow, ···, from the place of Abba-saga were withdrawn. Month of ezem-Ninazu, Year of Amar Sin king destroyed Bitum-rabum, Iabru and Huhnuri.	10公绵羊为卢旮勒马古瑞，乌尔巴巴督办，6公绵羊为歌手达达，3公绵羊和1羔为乌尔宁古巴拉格乐师，图冉达干督办，自送入项中，(总) 20，于2日；1羔为恩里勒，哈卜如筛尔送入，恩里勒兹沙旮勒督办，(总) 1，于6日；5公绵羊为乌尔比隆城的那尼帕塔勒的新娘，经由舒勒吉哈席斯，276公绵羊和24公山羊为乌尔尼旮尔之子：卢南那的妻子，阿腊德姆督办，【300】，于7日；【1】aslum公绵羊和【1】肥尾绵羊为卢旮勒马古瑞，乌拉伊尼什督办，自送入项中，(总) 2，于8日；2野公猪，1野母猪、1头1岁驴、5育肥公绵羊、1育肥aslum公绵羊、1育肥公山羊、1育肥雌崽、2肥尾羊、5羔和1雌崽为美伊什塔蓝，为满月的níg-dab$_{5}$供奉，宁哈马提骑使督办，1野公猪为村庄，自恩里勒庙中，阿腊德穆督办，自送入项中，(总) 21，于11日；1育肥公绵羊为圣桌，为阿马尔辛的níg-dab$_{5}$供奉，自恩里勒庙中，阿图司酒督办，(总) 1，于13日，1育肥西马什基公绵羊和1育肥西马什基母山羊到御膳房，采鲁什达干送入，乌尔巴巴督办，(总) 2，于14日；2育肥公绵羊为伊拉隆，基什的总督送入，达亚提书吏督办，(总) 2，于18日；1无崽母山羊到御膳房，卡塔尔园丁送入，乌尔巴巴督办，(总) 1，于21日；5 aslum公绵羊为伊拉隆，5 aslum公绵羊为卢旮勒马古瑞，乌塔米沙蓝督办，自送入项中，(总) 10，于22日；1羔到村庄，自宁廷乌旮庙，美埃什塔尔送入，恩里勒兹沙旮勒督办，(总) 1，于23日；3肥尾性成熟羊和2性成熟aslum公绵羊，阿腊德穆督办，6肥尾性成熟羊为舒辛，乌塔米沙蓝督办，自送入项中，(总) 11，于24日；1头*sapparu*野母猪、5只肥公绵羊、1只肥羔、2只育肥aslum母绵羊、2只育肥公山羊、10只羔和1只雌瞪羚，以上为阿比新提，为晦月的níĝ-dab$_{5}$供奉，(总) 22，于26日；1羔为恩里勒，1羔为宁里勒，恩里勒兹沙旮勒督办，1肥尾羔到御膳房，乌尔巴巴厨师督办，5肥尾羊、3 aslum公绵羊和2性成熟aslum公绵羊为美伊什塔蓝，1性成熟aslum公绵羊为卢旮勒马古瑞，1性成熟aslum公绵羊为歌手达达，1性成熟肥尾羊为恩里勒兹沙旮勒，乌塔米沙蓝督办，1崽为舒马马弄臣，达亚提书吏督办，自送入项中，(总) 17，于29日；10公绵羊为卢旮勒马古瑞，里尼审督办，自送入项中，(总) 10，于30日，总计：1野生公猪……自阿巴萨旮处被支出。神宁阿朱庆典月，王阿马尔辛摧毁比吞腊布、亚卜如何胡赫努瑞之年。

续表

时间和摘要	文献内容	英文翻译	中文翻译
AS 8: **ba-zi** 1 ram from Lugal-magur, 1 ram from Lugal-kuzu, the mouth of canal of Abi-simti, Habtum-lipdu as royal deputy, were withdrawn from X.	1 udu**Lugal-má-gur$_8$-re**, 1 udu **Lugal-kù-zu**, ud~ gán udu erím-ak, **ka i$_7$** ***A-bí-sí-im-ti*** *ì-ib-*[...], ***Ha-ba-tum-li-ip-du*** *maškim*, [*ki~ X ba-zi*], [*iti-x*] *-da-gu$_7$*, *mu En-nun-e-^{d}Amar-^{d}Suen-ra-ki-áĝ en Eridu^{ki} ba-hun*, 2 *udu*. (*Seal*): **Ad-da-kal-la**, dub-sar, dumu Níĝ-erím-ga-sug-ga. (SAT 2 1112, P144312)	1 ram from Lugal-magurre, 1 ram from Lugal-kuzu, when the ram eat the field, the mouth of canal of Abi-simti?, Habtum-lipdu as royal deputy, [were withdrawn from X], Month of x-da~gu$_7$, Year of En-nune-kiag-Amar-Sin, the en-priest of Eridu was installed, (sum:) 2 rams. (seal:) Adda-kalla scribe was the son of Nig-erim-gasugga.	1公绵羊自卢旮勒马古瑞、1只公绵羊自卢旮勒库朱，当羊啃田地时，**阿比新提的河渠之口?**，**哈卜吞里坡杜督办**，【自X处被支出】。食X月，埃瑞都的女祭司恩嫩埃基阿格阿马尔辛被任命之年，（总计:）2只羊。 （印章:）阿达卡拉书吏是尼格埃壬旮苏旮之子。
AS 8 i/18: (**ba-zi**) […] for Abi-simti, **via Šu-mama**, 1 fat ram for Adda-gina, 1 for Marhuni, via […], [1+] fr. Dabuduk for Iabrat, **via Lalamu**, 1 ram for Gadabi, **via Dua envoy**, **in Nippur**, 5+ fat rams from **Naplanum** (were withdrawn)	[...], ***A-bi-sí-im-*** [***ti***], **gìr Šu-ma-ma**, 1 udu-niga **Ad-da-gi-na**, ensí Ha-ar-ši^{ki}, 1 udu-niga ***Ma-ar-hu-ni***, *lú-*[*Mar*] *-ha-ši^{ki}*, **gìr** **[...]**, [1+] udu-niga ***Da-bu-d*** [***u-uk***], *lú-kin-gi$_4$-a* ***Ià-ab-ra-at*** *LÚ. SU^{ki}*, **gìr*La-la-mu***sukkal, 1 *udu* **Ga-da-bi** lú Ne-gi-ne-hu-um^{ki}, gìr **Dù-a** sukkal, šà~ Nibru^{ki}, 5+ udu-niga ki ***Na-ap-la-núm***, [...]. [*iti-maš*] *-dà-gu$_7$*, [*mu*] *en Eridu^{ki}ba-hun*. (*Seal*:) **Bu-lu-** [...], dub- [sar] arád^{d}Nin- [...]. (MVN 13 636, P117409)	[⋯] for Abi-simti, **via Šu-mama**, 1 fattened ram for Adda-gina, the governor of Harši, 1 fattened ram for Marhuni, the man of [Mar] haši, **via [⋯]**, [1+] fattened ram from Dabuduk messenger for Iabrat of LÚ.SU^{ki}, **via Lalamu, theenvoy**, 1 ram for Gadabi, the man of Negine-um, **via Dua envoy**, **in Nippur**, 5+ fattened rams from the place of **Naplanum** (were withdrawn). [Month of maš] da~ gu$_7$, [Year] of en-priest of Eridu was installed. (seal:) Bulu- [⋯] scribe was the servant of Nin- [⋯].	【……】为**阿比新提**，**经由舒马马**，1肥公羊为哈尔席总督阿达吉那，1肥公绵羊为马尔胡尼，马尔哈席城之人，**经由【X】**，【1+】肥公羊自达布杜克信使为LÚ.SU^{ki}城的亚卜腊特，**经由拉拉姆国使**，1公绵羊为耐吉耐混城之人旮达比，**经由杜阿国使**，于**尼普尔**，5+肥公绵羊自**那坡拉农**处。食【瞪羚羊】月，埃瑞都的女祭司被任命年。（印文:）布鲁【X】书吏是宁-【X】的仆人。
AS 8 ii/26: **ba-zi** 1 lamb for **Abi-simti**, via **Šu-Mama**, **Ilum-Dan** as deputy, fr.**Šu-Mama** was **withdr.**	1 sila$_4$-ga, ***A-bí-sí-im-ti***, *mu-túm ud~nú-a-ka-ni ki-ba ba-na-a-gar*, **gìr Šu-Ma-ma**, ***Ilum-Dan****sukkal***maškim**, iti-ud-26 ba-zal, ki~ **Šu-Ma-ma**-ta, ba-zi. iti-ze$_x$-da ~ gu$_7$, mu en Eridu^{ki} ba-hun.left: 1 udu (BIN 3 165, P105971)	1 suckling lamb for **Abi-simti**, for her deliveries of Dark Moon offered on site, **via Šu-Mama**, **Ilum-Dan, theenvoy as royal deputy**, when 26th day passed, from Šu-Mama was withdrawn. Month of zeda~ gu$_7$, Year of en-priest of Eridu was installed. (sum): 1 ram	1只吃奶羔为**阿比新提**，为她的晦月的贡入项奉献在现场，**经由舒马马**，**伊隆丹国使督办**，于26日过去时，自**舒马马**处被支出。食豚月，埃瑞都的女祭司被任命之年。（总计）：1只绵羊

续表

时间和摘要	文献内容	英文翻译	中文翻译
AS 8 ii/26: **ba-zi** 1 lamb for**Abi-simti**, **via Ur-Baba cook**, 20 eliminated flocks to kitchen for soldiers, **Arad-mu as deputy**, fr.**Duga** were withdr.	1 sila$_4$ ***A-bí-sí-im-ti***, *mu-túm ud-nú-a-ka-na ki-ba ba-na-a-gar*, **gìr Ur-^{d}Ba-ba$_6$ muhaldim**, 5 udu, 9 u$_8$, 2 máš-gal, 4 ud$_5$, šu-gíd é mu-haldim, mu ~ **gàr-du**-e-ne--šè, **Arád-mu maškim**, ud-26-kam, ki ~ Du$_{11}$-ga--ta, ba-zi. iti-ze$_x$-da ~ gu$_7$, mu en Eridu^{ki} ba-hun, left: 21. (BIN 3 403, P106210)	1 lamb for**Abi-simti**, for her deliveries of Dark Moon offered on site, **via Ur-Baba cook**, 5 rams, 9 ewes, 2 he-goats and 4 she-goats were eliminated to the kitchen for the soldiers, **Arad-mu as royal deputy**, on the 26th day, from **Duga** were withdrawn. Month of zeda ~ gu$_7$, Year of en-priest of Eridu was installed. (sum): 21	1羔为阿比新提，为她的晦月的贡入项奉献在现场，**经由乌尔巴巴厨师**，5只公绵羊、9只母绵羊、2只公山羊和4只母山羊为淘汰级**到厨房为士兵们**，**阿腊德穆督办**，于26日，自**杜旮**处被支出。食豚月，埃瑞都的女祭司被任命之年。（总计）：21
AS 8 iv/26: **ba-zi** … **Ur-mes** musician, via **Šulgi-litiš**, **Ilum-Dan** as deputy, 2 lambs for **Abi-simti**, via **Ur-Baba**, 20 eliminated sheep to kitchen for **soldiers**, from **Dugga** were **withdrawn**	[1…] x-tu mu […] -ba Ur-mes nar, ud~ ba-ug$_7$-a, gìr ***^{d}Šul-gi-li-ti-iš*** *sukkal*, ***Ilum-Dan-*** **sukkal maškim**, 2 sila$_4$ ***A-bí-sí-im-ti***, *mu-túm ud-nú-a-ka-na ki-ba ba-na-a-gá-ar*, gìr **Ur-^{d}Ba-ba$_6$ muhaldim**, 2 udu, 18 u$_8$, [šu] -gíd é muhaldim, mu~ **gàr-du**-e-ne--šè, ud-26-kam, ki **Du$_{11}$-ga**--ta ba-zi. [iti] -ki-siki-^{d}Nin-a-zu, mu en Eridu^{ki}ba-hun, 23. (PDT 2 1145, P126480)	… **Ur-mes musician**, on the day she was dead, **via Šulgi-litišenvoy**, **Ilum-Dan envoy as royal deputy**, 2 lambs for **Abi-simti**, for her deliveries of Dark Moon offered on site, **via Ur-Baba cook**, 2 rams and 18 ewes were eliminated to the kitchen for the **soldiers**, on the 26th day, from **Dugga** were withdrawn. Month of ki-siki-Ninazu, Year of the en-priest of Eridu was installed, (sum): 23	……，乌尔美斯乐师，当她死时，**经由舒勒吉里提什国使**，**伊隆丹国使督办**，2只羔为**阿比新提**，为她的晦月的贡入项奉献在现场，**经由乌尔巴巴厨师**，2公绵羊和18只母绵羊为淘汰级**到厨房**，**为士兵们**，于26日，自**杜旮**被支出。神宁阿朱羊毛作坊月，埃瑞都的女祭司被任命之年。（总计）：23
AS 8 v/25: **ba-zi** 1 lamb for**Abi-simti** when Dark Moon, via **Ur-Baba**, fr. **Dugga** was withdrawn	1 sila$_4$, ***A-bí-sí-im-ti***, *mu-túm ud-nú-a-ka-na ki-ba ba-na-a-gá-ar*, gìr **Ur-^{d}Ba-ba$_6$**, ud-25-kam, ki ~ Du$_{11}$-ga--ta, ba-zi. iti-ezem-^{d} Nin-a-zu, mu en Eridu^{ki}ba-hun, left: 1. (ASJ 07 123 19, P102197)	1 lamb for**Abi-simti**, for her deliveries of Dark Moon offered on site, via **Ur-Baba**, on the 25th day, from **Dugga** was withdrawn.Month of ezem-Ninazu, Year of the en-priest of Eridu was installed, (sum): 1	1只羔为**阿比新提**，为她的晦月的贡入项奉献在现场，**经由乌尔巴巴**，于25日，自**杜旮**被支出。神宁阿朱庆典月，埃瑞都的女祭司被任命之年。（总计）：1

续表

时间和摘要	文献内容	英文翻译	中文翻译
AS 8 vi/27: **ba-zi** 1 lamb for**Abi-simti**, **via Aya-kalla cook**, 10 flocks were eliminated to kitchen for soldiers, in **Ur**, fr. **Dugga** were withdr.	1 sila$_4$, ***A-bí-sí-im-ti***, *mu-túm ud~ nú-a-ka-na ki-ba ba-na-a-gá-ar*, *gìr**A-a-kal-la**muhaldim*, *2 udu, 5 u$_8$, 3 máš, šu-gíd é-muhaldim, mu* ~ **gàr-du**-e-ne--šè, šà ~ **Urim$_5$^{ki}**-ma, ud-27-kam, ki~ **Du$_{11}$-ga**--ta, ba-zi.iti-á-ki-ti, mu en Eridu^{ki} ba-hun, left: 11. (CTNMC 05, P108736) (CTNMC 05, P108736)	1 lamb for**Abi-simti**, for her deliveries of Dark Moon offered on site, **via Aya-kalla cook**, 2 rams, 5 ewes, 3 kids, were eliminated to the kitchen for the soldiers, in **Ur**, on the 27th day, from **Dugga** were withdrawn. Month of akiti, Year of the en-priest of Eridu was installed, (sum): 11.	1只羔为**阿比新提**，为她的晦月的贡入项奉献在现场，**经由阿亚卡拉厨师**，2只公绵羊、5只母绵羊和3只公崽为淘汰级**到厨房**，**为士兵们**，于**乌尔**，于27日，自杜旮被支出。阿基提月，埃瑞都的女祭司被任命之年。(总计)：11
AS 8 vi/27: **ba-zi** 1 lamb to kitchen of state, **Aya-kalla** cook as deputy; 13 fat flocks and 9 flocks for **Abi-simti**, for the níĝ-dab$_5$ offering of Dark Moon among the deliveries, from the place of **Abba-saga** were **withdrawn.**	1 sila$_4$ **é-uz-ga**, ***A-a-kal-la****muhaldim* **maškim**, 5 udu-niga-3-kam-ús, 2 udu-a-lum-niga, 1 u$_8$-a-lum-niga-3-kam-ús, 1 sila$_4$-niga, 1 kir$_{11}$-niga, 1 máš-gal-Ši$_x$-maš^{ki}-niga-sig$_5$, 1 máš-gal-a-dara$_4$-niga, 1 ^{f}ašgar-niga, 6 sila$_4$, 1 ^{f}ašgar, 2 ^{f}ašgar-Má-gan, ***A-bí-sí-im-ti***, *níĝ-dab$_5$ ud-nú-a-a-ka-ni, šà mu-er$_{10}$--ra--ta, ud-27-kam, ki ~* **Ab-ba-sa$_6$-ga**--ta, ba-zi. iti-á-ki-ti, mu En-nun-e-^{d}Amar-^{d}Suen-ra-ki-áĝ en Eridu^{ki} ba-hun, 23 udu. (SAT 2 1089, P144289)	1 lamb to the kitchen of state, **Aya-kalla** cook as royal deputy, 5 fattened rams of 3rd class, 2 fattened aslum rams, 1 fattened aslum ewe of 3rd class, 1 fattened lamb, 1 fattened female lamb, 1 best fattened *Šimaški* he-goat, 1 fattened wild he-goat, 1 fattened female kid, 6 lambs, 1 female kid and 2 Magan femlae kids, these for **Abi-simti**, for the níĝ-dab$_5$ offering of her Dark Moon among the deliveries, on the 27th day, from **Abba-saga** were withdrawn. Month of akiti, Year of En-nune-kiaĝ-Amar -Sin, the en-priest of Eridu was installed, (sum:) 23 rams	1只羔到**御膳房**，**阿亚卡拉厨师督办**，5只三等肥公绵羊、2只肥aslum公绵羊、1只三等肥aslum母绵羊、1只肥羔、1只肥雌羔、1只优等西马什基公山羊、1只育肥野生公山羊、1育肥雌崽、6羔、1只雌崽和2马干雌崽，以上为**阿比新提**，为送入项中她的晦月的níĝ-dab$_5$供奉，于27日，自**阿巴萨旮**处被支出。阿基提月，埃瑞都的女祭司恩嫩埃基阿格阿马尔辛被任命之年，(总计) 23羊
AS 8 vii/26: **ba-zi** 7 fat flocks and 11 flocks for**Abi-simti**, for the níĝ-dab$_5$ offering of Dark Moon among the deliveries, fr. **Abba-saga** were withdrawn	1 udu-niga, 2 udu-a-lum-niga, 1 máš-gal-niga, 3 ^{f}ašgar-niga, 4 udu-a-lum, 1 gukkal, 6 sila$_4$, ***A-bí-sí-im-ti***, *níĝ-dab$_5$ ud-nú-a-ka-ni*, *šà mu-er$_{10}$--ra--ta, ud-26-kam, ki~* **Ab-ba-sa$_6$-ga**--ta, ba-zi. iti-ezem-^{d}Šul-gi, mu en Eridu^{ki} ba-hun, (left) 18. (UDT 129, P136263)	1 fattened ram, 2 fattened aslum rams, 1 fattened he-goat, 3 fattened female kids, 4 aslum ram, 1 big-tailed sheep and 6 lambs for**Abi-simti**, for the níĝ-dab$_5$ offering of her Dark Moon among the deliveries, on the 26th day, from the place of **Abba-saga** were withdrawn. Month of ezem-Šulgi, Year of en-priest of Eridu was installed, (sum:) 18.	1肥公绵羊、2育肥aslum公绵羊、1只育肥公山羊、3育肥雌崽、4只aslum公绵羊、1只肥尾绵羊和6只羔为**阿比新提**，为送入项中她的晦月的níĝ-dab$_5$供奉，于26日，自**阿巴萨旮**处被支出。舒勒吉庆典月，埃瑞都的女祭司被任命之年，(总计:) 18

续表

时间和摘要	文献内容	英文翻译	中文翻译
AS 8 vii/27: **ba-zi** 1 fat bull for**Nin-tin-ugga**, via **Abi-simti**, 1 fat for meat, 10 rams in **Nippur**, 10 for soldiers, via Šulgi-urumu, Ilum-Dan envoy as deputy, fr. **Igi-Enlilše** withdr.	1 gud-niga ^{d}Nin-tin-ug$_5$-ga, gìr ***A-bí-sí-im-ti***, 1 *gud-niga ba-kúš*, *mu-du-lum--šè*, 10 *udu šà~Nibru*^{ki}, 10 *udu*? *šu-gíd é-muhaldim*, *mu* **gàr-du-ne**--šè, **gìr** ^{d}**Šul-gi-uru-mu**, ***Ilum-Dan****sukkal maškim*, *iti-ud-27 ba-zal*, *ki~* **Igi-**^{d}**En-líl-šè**--ta, ba-zi.iti-ezem-^{d}Šul-gi, mu en Eridu^{ki} ba-hun, (left) 2 gud, 20 udu. (NYPL 2448, P122782)	1 fattened bull for**Nin-tin-ugga**, **via Abi-simti**, 1 mad fattened bull for the preserved meat, 10 rams in **Nippur**, 10 eliminated rams to the **kitchen**, for the soldiers, **via Šulgi-urumu**, **Ilum-Dan envoy as royal deputy**, when the 27th day passed, from the place of **Igi-Enlilše** were withdrawn. Month of ezem-Šulgi, Year of en-priest of Eridu was installed, (sum:) 2 bulls and 20 rams.	1肥公牛为宁廷乌旮，**经由阿比新提**，1头疯肥公牛为肉干，10公绵羊于**尼普尔**，10淘汰级公绵羊**到厨房，为士兵们**，**经由舒勒吉乌如穆，伊隆丹国使督办**，于27日过去时，自**伊吉恩里勒筛**被支出了。舒勒吉庆典月，埃瑞都的女祭司被任命之年，（总计:）1头牛和20只羊
AS 8 viii/18: **mu-túm, ì-dab$_5$** 1 fat bull, 376 fat flocks and 58 rams from**Ilallum**, these were deliveries for **Abi-simti**, from the place of **Ur-Igalim fattener**, these deliveries **Abba-saga** took over	1 gud-niga, 37 udu-niga-3-kam-ús, 30 udu-a-lum-niga-3-kam-ús, 248 udu-niga, 16 udu-niga-gud-e-ús-sa, 45 máš-gal-niga, 58 udu, ***Ì-làl-lum***, *mu-túm* ***A-bí-sí-im-ti***, *ki~* **Ur-**^{d} **Ig-alim gurušda**--ta, ud-18-kam, mu-túm **Ab-ba-sa$_6$-ga** ì-dab$_5$. iti-šu-eš$_5$-ša, mu en Eridu^{ki} ba-hun, 1 gud, 434 udu. (Nik.2 488, P122171)	1 fattened bull, 37 fattened rams of 3rd class, 30 fattened aslum rams of 3rd class, 248 fattened rams, 16 fattened rams of after-ox-class, 45 fattened he-goats and 58 rams from **Ilallum** (general), these were deliveries for **Abi-simti**, from the place of **Ur-Igalim fattener** (of queen), on the 18th day, these deliveries **Abba-saga** took over. Month of šu-ešša, Year of the en-priest of Eridu was installed, (sum): 1 bull and 434 rams.	1肥公牛、37肥三等公绵羊、30肥三等 aslum 公绵羊、248肥公绵羊、16肥牛后级公绵羊、45肥公山羊和58公绵羊自伊拉隆（将军），以上为**阿比新提的送入项**，自**乌尔伊格阿林（王后）育肥师**处，于18日，以上送入**阿巴萨旮**接管了。三只手月，埃瑞都的女祭司被任命之年。（总计）：1公牛和434公绵羊
AS 8 ix (1-30): **ba-zi** 30 fat flocks for**Abi-simti**, for 1 month, from **Zubaga** were **withdr.**	21 udu-niga, 9 máš-gal-niga, **sá-dug$_4$** ***A-bí-sí-im-ti***, *iti-1-kam*, *ki~* ***Zu-ba-ga***--*ta*, *ba-zi.iti-ezem-mah*, *mu en Eridu*^{ki} *ba-hun*, 30 *udu*. (*OIP* 121 556, *P*124286)	21 *fattened rams and* 9 *fattened he-goats for monthly allowance of***Abi-simti**, for 1 month, from the place of **Zubaga** were withdrawn. Month of ezem-mah, Year of en-priest of Eridu was installed, (sum:) 30 rams	21只育肥公绵羊和9只育肥公山羊为**阿比新提一个月的月供**，自**朱巴旮**处被支出。大庆典月，埃瑞都的女祭司被任命之年。（总计:）30只羊

续表

时间和摘要	文献内容	英文翻译	中文翻译
AS 8 ix/9: **mu-túm, ì-dab$_5$** 40 fat flocks and 90 flocks for **banquet**, **via Enlil-zišagal**, deliveries for **Abi-simti**, fr. **Ur-Igalim fattener of queen**, **Abba-saga** took over	10 gud-niga, 16 udu-niga, 4 udu-niga-gud-e-ús-sa, 10 máš-gal-niga, 70 udu, 20 máš-gal, kaš-dé-a, gìr **^{d}En-líl-zi-šà-gál**, mu-túm ***A-bí-sí-im-ti***, *ki*~ **Ur-^{d}Ig-alim gurušda nin--ta**, ud-9-kam, mu-túm **Ab-ba-sa$_6$-ga** ì-dab$_5$.iti-ezem-mah, mu en Eridu^{ki} ba-hun, (left) 130 (SumRecDreh. 19, P130516)	10 fattened bulls, 16 fattened rams, 4 fattened rams of after-ox-class, 10 fattened he-goats, 70 rams and 20 he-goats for the **banquet**, **via Enlil-zišagal**, were deliveries for **Abi-simti**, from the place of **Ur-Igalim fattener of queen**, on the 9th day, these deliveries **Abba-saga** took over. Month of ezem-mah, Year of en-priest of Eridu was install, (sum:) 130	10肥公牛、16只肥公绵羊、4只牛后级肥公绵羊、10只肥公山羊、70只公绵羊和20只公山羊为宴会，**经由恩里勒孜沙旮勒**，以上送入为**阿比新提**，自**乌尔伊格阿林王后育肥师**处，于9日，以上送入阿巴萨旮接管了。大庆典月，埃瑞都的女祭司被任命之年。（总计：）130
AS 8 ix/18: **mu-túm, ì-dab$_5$** 106 flocks and 10 fat bulls for **Abi-simti**, fr. **people of URUxA** and **Iram-Dagan**, **o-verseer: Šulgi-zimu**, fr. **Ur-Igalim Abba-saga took**	3 gud, 1 udu, 2 máš-gal, erín URUxA^{ki}, ugula ***^{d}Šul-gi-zi-mu***, 10 *gud-niga*, 69 *udu*, 1 *sila$_4$*, 30 *máš-gal*, ***I-* [*ra-am*] *-^{d}Da-gan***, *mu-túm* ***A-bí-sí-im-ti***, *ki*~ **Ur-^{d}Ig-alim gurušda nin**--ta, ud-18-kam, mu-túm **Ab-ba-sa$_6$-ga** ì-dab$_5$.iti-ezem-mah, mu en Eridu^{ki} ba-hun, (left) 293. (TRU 126, P134890)	3 bulls, 1 ram and 2 he-goats from**people of URUxA**, **the overseer: Šulgi-zimu**, 10 fattened bulls, 69 rams, 1 lamb and 30 he-goats from **Iram-Dagan**, were deliveries for **Abi-simti**, from the place of **Ur-Igalim**, the fattener of queen, on the 18th day, these deliveries **Abba-saga** took over. Month of ezem-mah, Year of en-priest of Eridu was install, (sum:) 293.	3公牛、1公绵羊和2公山羊自乌如阿城之人，**监工：舒勒吉孜穆**，10肥公牛、69公绵羊、1只羔和30只公山羊自伊冉达干，为**阿比新提**的送人，从**乌尔伊格阿林王后育肥师**处，于18日，以上送入**阿巴萨旮**接管了。大庆典月，埃瑞都的女祭司被任命之年。293
AS 8 ix/26: **ba-zi** 1 fat ram for**Mušgula**, **Enlil-zišagal** as deputy, 2 flocks to **kitchen of state**, **Ur-Baba** as deputy, 4 fat flocks, 52 flocks and 70 *Šimaški* kids, these for **Abi-simti**, from **Abba-saga** were withdrawn, via**Dayati**	1 udu-nigaMuš$^?$-gú-lá--šè, **^{d}En-líl-zi-šà-gál maškim**, 1 udu, 1 sila$_4$, **é-uz-ga**, **Ur-^{d}Ba-ba$_6$ muhaldim maškim**, 2 gud-niga, 1 gud, 2 udu-niga, 19 udu, 4 gukkal, 1 udu-a-lum, 14 sila$_4$, 1 kir$_{11}$-gukkal, 10 máš-gal, 2 máš, 70 ^{f}ašgar Ši$_x$-maški, ***A-bí-sí-im-ti***, **níĝ-dab$_5$ ud-nú-a**, ud-26-kam, ki~ **Ab-ba-sa$_6$-ga**--ta, ba-zi, gìr ***Da-a-a-ti****dub-sar*, *iti-ezem-mah*, *mu en Eridu^{ki} ba-hun*, (*left*) 130 *la*2 1. (*UDT* 095, *P*136229)	1 *fattened ram for***Mušgula**, **Enlil-zišagal as royal deputy**, 1 ram and 1 lamb to the **kitchen of state**, **Ur-Baba cook as royal deputy**, 2 fattened bulls, 1 bull, 2 fattened rams, 19 rams, 4 big-tailed sheep, 1 aslum ram, 14 lambs, 1 big-tailed female lamb, 10 he-goats, 2 kids and 70 female Šimaški *kids*, *these for* **Abi-simti**, for the níĝ-dab$_5$ offering of dark moon, on the 26th day, from **Abba-saga** were withdrawn, **via Dayati scribe**. Month of ezem-mah, Year of the en-priest of Eridu was installed, (sum:) 129	1肥公绵羊为**穆什古拉**，**恩里勒兹沙旮勒督办**，1公绵羊和1羔到**御膳房**，**乌尔巴巴厨师督办**，2肥公牛、1公牛、2肥公绵羊、19公绵羊、4肥尾绵羊、1aslum公绵羊、14羔、1肥尾雌羔、10公山羊、2公崽和70西马什基雌崽，为**阿比新提**，为晦月的níĝ-dab$_5$供奉，于26日，自**阿巴萨旮**处被支出，**经由达亚提书吏**。大庆典月，埃瑞都女祭司被任命之年，129

续表

时间和摘要	文献内容	英文翻译	中文翻译
AS 9 ii/26: **ba-zi** 3 [⋯], 2 [⋯], 1 fat ram for **table**, **Atu**as deputy, 2 rams for **Amar-Sin**, 5 fat flocks, 5 flocks and 1 kid, for safe-greeting, 1 fat ram for **Naplu-num**, via **Ur-baba**, 1 kid for dark moon sent to palace for **Abi-simti**, in Ur, **via Zubaga**, ⋯, fr. **Zubaga** withdr., via **Adda-kalla**	3 [...], 2 [...], 1 udu-niga zà-gú-lá šà é [...], ***A-tu****sagi maškim*, 2 *udu* gišgu-za dAm-ar-dSuen, 1 gud-niga, 2 udu, 3 máš-gal a-rá-1-kam, 4 udu-niga, 1 fašgar a-rá 2-kam, mu ~ **GÌR-ke₄-ne**--šè, 1 udu-niga mu ***Na-ap-la-núm*** *Mar-tu--šè*, *é muhaldim--šè*, *gìr* **Ur-dBa-ba₆** muhaldim, 1 fašgar ud-nú-a-ka šà ~ é-gal-la ba-an-ku₄, ***A-bí-sí-im-ti***, *Urim₅ki-ma--šè*, *gìr* ***Zu-ba-ga***, ⋯, *iti-ud-26 ba-zal*, *ki* ~ **Zu-ba-ga**--ta ba-zi, gìr ***Ad-da-kal-la****dub-sar*. *iti-ze$_x$-da-gu$_7$*, *mu en^d Nanna kar-zi-da ba-hun*, 1 *gud*, 28 *udu*. (*SET* 066, *P*129476)	3 [⋯], 2 [⋯], 1 *fattened ram for the* **cultic table** in the palace, **Atu cup-bearer as royal deputy**, 2 rams for the **throne of Amar-Sin**, 1 fattened bull, 2 rams and 3 he-goats for 1st time, 4 fattened rams and 1 female kid for 2nd time, for the safe-greeting, 1 fattened ram for **Naplunum**, the Amorite, to the kitchen, **via Ur-baba cook**, 1 female kid for dark moon was sent to palace for **Abi-simti**, in Ur, **via Zubaga**, ⋯, when the 26th day passed, from the place of **Zubaga** were withdrawn, **via Adda-kalla scribe**. Month of zeda ~ gu₇, Year of en-priest of Nanna of Karzida was installed, (sum:) 1 bull and 28 rams.	3【x】、2【x】和1肥公绵羊为宫殿的圣桌，**阿图司酒督办**，2公绵羊为**阿马尔辛的王座**，1肥公牛、2公绵羊和3公山羊第1次，4肥公绵羊和1雌崽第2次，为问安礼，1肥公绵羊为**阿摩利人那坡拉农**，**到厨房**，**经由乌尔巴巴厨师**，1雌崽为晦月被送入宫殿，为**阿比新提**，于乌尔，**经由朱巴旮**……于26日过去时，自**朱巴旮**处被支出，**经由阿达卡拉书吏**。食豚月，卡尔兹达的南那神的祭司被任命之年，（总计）1牛和28羊
AS 9 ii/26: **ba-zi** 2 fat ram for Naplanum, via **Lugal-kagina**, 21 fat flocks, 7 rams, 27 lambs, 5 goats, 3 kids of gazelle, for **Abi-simti**, via **Ulališ**. **Arad-mu**among deputy of deliveries, fr. **Abba-saga** withdr., via **Nur-Sin**	2 udu-niga***Na-ap-la-num*** *Mar-tu*, *gìr* **Lugal-KA-gi-na**sukkal, 8 udu-niga, 9 udu-a-lum-niga, 1 máš-gal-niga-sig₅-ús, 3 máš-gal-niga, 7 udu, 27 sila₄, 5 máš-gal, 3 amar-maš-dà nitá, ***A-bí-sí-im-ti***, *níĝ-dab₅ ud-nú-a-ka-ni*, *gìr**Ú-la-lí-iš**rá-gaba*, **Arád-mu**maškim, šà mu-túm-ra-ta, ud-26-kam, ki ~ **Ab-ba-sa₆-ga**--ta, ba-zi, gìr ***Nu-úr-dSuen****dub-sar*. *iti-ze$_x$-da-gu$_7$*, *mu en dNanna Kar-zi-da ba-hun*, 65. (*PDT* 1 579, *P*125995)	2 *fattened ram for Naplanum*, *theAmorite*, **via Lugal-kagina envoy**, 8 fattened rams, 9 fattened aslum rams, 1 better fattened he-goat, 3 fattened he-goats, 7 rams, 27 lambs, 5 he-goats, 3 kids of gazelle, these for **Abi-simti**, for the níĝ-dab₅ offering of her dark moon, via Ulališ knight, **Arad-mu among the royal deputy of deliveries**, on the 26th day, from **Abba-saga** were withdrawn, **via Nur-Sin scribe**. Month of zeda ~ gu₇, Year of en-priest of Nanna of Karzida was installed, (sum:) 65.	2肥公绵羊为**阿摩利人那坡拉农**，**经由卢旮勒卡吉那国使**，8肥公绵羊、9肥aslum公绵羊、1较好肥公山羊、3肥公山羊、7公绵羊、27羔、5公山羊和3瞪羚公崽，以上为**阿比新提**，为她晦月的níĝ-dab₅供奉，**经由乌拉里什骑使**，**阿腊德穆于贡品督办中**，于26日，自**阿巴萨旮**处被支出，**经由努尔辛书吏**。食豚月，卡尔兹达的南那什的祭司被任命之年，（总计：）65

续表

时间和摘要	文献内容	英文翻译	中文翻译
AS 9 iii: **ba-zi** 16 shekels silver, fr. **Šatakuzu** for **Abi-simti**, fr. Uruk brought, 16 for palace, **La-ilišas [deputy]**, fr. **Puzur-rra** were withdrawn, in **Uru-sag-rig**	2 har kù-babbar, 8 gín-ta, **Šà-ta-kù-zu** sukkal, mu silim-ma ***A-bí-sí-im-ti***, *Unug*[ki]*--ta mu-de$_6$-a--šè*, *2 har kù-babbar*, *8 gín-ta*, *šà é-gal--šè*, ***La-ì-lí-iš*** *[maškim]*, *ki~* ***Puzur$_4$-Èr-ra****--ta*, *ba-zi*, *šà~ Uru-sag-rig$_7$*[ki]. *iti-u$_5$-bí*[mušen]*~gu$_7$*, *mu en*[d]*Nanna ba-hun* (*left*) 4. (*JCS* 10 30 10, *P*111904)	2 *rings of silver*, 8 *shekels each*, *from* **Šatakuzu** envoy for the sate-greeting of **Abi-simti**, from Uruk were brought (to Ur), 2 rings of silver, 8 shekels each, for the palace, **La-ilišas [royal deputy]**, from **Puzur-Erra** were withdrawn, in **Uru-sag-rig**. Month of ubi~gu$_7$, Year of en-priest of Nanna of Karzida was installed, (sum:) 4.	2环银子，每环8舍克勒，自沙塔库朱国使为**阿比新提的问安礼**，他（使者）从乌鲁克送入（到乌尔），2环银子，每环8舍克勒，为宫殿，**拉伊里什【督办】**，自**普朱尔埃腊**处被支出，于**乌如萨格瑞格**。食乌比鸟月，卡尔兹达的南那什的祭司被任命之年，（总计）4。
AS 9 iii/15: **ba-zi** 3 fat rams as boiled meat, 4 fat rams, king sent (them) to **Inanna**, 3 fat rams for the gate of high priestess, 2 fat rams for Nanaya, **via Abi-simti**, fr. **Nalu** withdr., in **Uruk**, **via Lu-Nin-šubur**	3 udu-niga, uzu-a-bala, 2 udu-niga-3-kam-ús, 2 udu-niga, lugal ku$_4$-ra, [d] **Inanna**, **siskúr-gu-la**, 3 udu-niga **ká~ gi$_6$-pàr**, 2 udu-niga [d]Na-na-a, gìr ***A-bí-sí-im-ti***, *iti-ud*-15 *ba-zal*, *ki~* **Na-lu$_5$**--ta ba-zi, šà~ Unug[ki]-ga, **[gìr] Lú-dNin-šubur dub-sar**. iti-u$_5$-bí-gu$_7$, mu en [d]Nanna Kar-zi-da ba-hun, (left) 10 udu. (NYPL 357, P122895)	3 fattened rams as boiled meat, 2 fattened rams of 3rd class, 2 fattened rams, king sent (them), of/to **Inanna**, as great sacrifice, 3 fattened rams for **the gate of the chamber of high priestess**, 2 fattened rams for Nanaya, **via Abi-simti**, when the 15th day passed, from **Nalu** were withdrawn, in **Uruk**, **via Lu-Nin-šubur scribe**. Month of ubi~gu$_7$, Year of en-priest of Nanna of Karzida was installed, (sum:) 10 rams.	3肥公绵羊为水煮肉，2肥三等公绵羊、2肥公绵羊，王送入为/到**伊南那**，以上是**大祭祀**，3肥公绵羊为**最高女祭司寝宫门**，2肥公绵羊为**那那亚**，**经由阿比新提**，于15日过去时，从**那鲁**处被支出，于**乌鲁克**，**经由卢宁舒布尔书吏**。食乌比鸟月，卡尔兹达的南那什的祭司被任命之年，（总计：）10只羊
AS 9 iv/25: **ba-zi** 6 fat flocks, 14 sheep **for níg-dab$_5$ of her dark moon**, **Nin-lil-amamu** as deputy, [1+] fat ram, **Ula-inišas** deputy, 1 gezelle for Nin-Nin-gublag, [X] as deputy, fr. deliveres, fr. **Abba-saga** with-drawn, via **Nanna-maba scribe**	1 udu-niga-sig$_5$-ús, 2 udu-niga-3-kam-ús, 1 gukkal-niga, 1 máš-gal-niga, 1 [f]ašgar-niga, 4 udu, 10 sila$_4$, **níg-[dab$_5$] ud-nú-a-ka-ni**, [d] **Nin-líl-ama-mu rá-gaba** maškim, [x] udu-niga-3-kam-ús, [x] -x en-na, ***Ú-la-ì-ni-iš*** **rá-gaba** maškim, 1 amar-maš-dà **Ur-**[d] **Nin-gublag nar**, [...] rá-gaba maškim, šà~ [mu-er$_{10}$-ra] --ta, ud-25[?]-kam, ki **Ab-ba-sag$_6$-ga**--ta ba-zi, gìr [d]**Nanna-ma-ba dub-sar**. iti-ki-siki-[d]Nin-a-zu, mu en [d]Nanna Kar-zi-da[ki] ba-hun, (ed.) 20 udu, 1 maš-dà. (DoCu EPHE 259, P109227)	1 better fattened ram, 2 fattened ram of 3rd class, 1 fattened big-tailed sheep, 1 fattened kid, 1 fattened female kid, 4 rams and 10 lambs **for the níg-dab$_5$ offering of her dark moon**, **Ninlil-amamu knight** as royal deputy, [1+] fattened ram of 3rd class, x en-na, **Ula-inišk-night** as royal deputy, 1 young gezelle for **Nin-Nin-gublag** musician, [X] as royal deputy, from the deliveres, on the 25th day, from **Abba-saga** were withdrawn, **via Nanna-maba scribe**. Month of ki-siki-Ninazu, Year of en-priest of Nanna of Karzida was installed, (sum:) 20 rams and 1 gezelle.	1次等肥公绵羊、2三等肥公绵羊、1肥肥尾绵羊、1肥公崽、1肥雌崽、4公绵羊和10羔为**她的晦月的níg-dab$_5$供奉**，**宁里勒阿马穆骑使督办**，【1+】三等肥公绵羊，x en-na，**乌拉伊尼什骑使督办**，1幼瞪羚为宁宁古卜拉格乐师，【x】督办，自送入项，于25日，**自阿巴萨旮处被支出**，**经由南那马巴书吏**。神宁阿朱羊毛作坊月，卡尔兹达的南那什的祭司被任命之年，（总计：）20只公绵羊和1只瞪羚。

续表

时间和摘要	文献内容	英文翻译	中文翻译
AS 9 v/26: **ba-zi** 1 ram to**kitchen of state**, **Arad-mu**as deputy, 9 fat flocks, 15 lambs and 2 kids, for **Abi-simti**, for the requisition of her dark moon among the deliveries, from **Abba-saga** were withdr., via **Nur-Sin** scribe.	1 udué-uz-ga, **Arád-dNanna muhaldim maškim**, 1 udu-niga, 2 udu-bar-gál-niga, 1 gukkal-niga, 3 udu-a-lum-niga, 1 udu-*Lú-ulù-um*-niga, 1 máš-gal *Ši$_x$-maški*-niga-3-kam-ús, 15 sila$_4$, 2 máš, ***A-bí-sí-im-ti***, *níĝ-dab$_5$ ud-nú-a*, *šà mu-er$_{10}$--ra--ta*, *ud-26-kam*, *ki*~ **Ab-ba-sa$_6$-ga**--ta, ba-zi, gìr ***Nu-úr-^{d}Suen****dub-sar*. *iti-ezem-^{d}Nin-a-zu*, *mu en^{d}Nanna kar-zi-da ba-hun*, (*left*) 27. (*PDT* 2, *p*.19, *P*134715)	1 *ram to the* **kitchen of state**, **Arad-mu cook as royal deputy**, 1 fattened ram, 2 fattened rams with fleece, 1 fattened big-tailed sheep, 3 fattened alum rams, 1 fattened Lulum ram, 1 fattened Ši$_x$-maški he-goat of 3rd class, 15 lambs and 2 kids, these for **Abi-simti**, for the níĝ-dab$_5$ offering of dark moon among the deliveries, on the 26th day, from the place of **Abba-saga** were withdrawn, via **Nur-Sin** scribe. Month of ezem-Ninazu, Year of en-priest of Nanna of Karzida was installed, (sum:) 27 rams.	1 公绵羊到**御膳房**，**阿腊德穆厨师督办**，1 肥公绵羊、2 带毛肥公绵羊、1 肥肥尾绵羊、3 肥 aslum 公绵羊、1 肥鲁鲁姆公绵羊、1 肥三等西马什基公山羊，15 羔和 2 公崽，以上为**阿比新提**，以上为阿比新提，为贡入项中晦月的 níĝ-dab$_5$供奉，于 26 日，自**阿巴萨旮**处被支出，**经由努尔辛书吏**。神宁阿朱庆典月，卡尔兹达的南那什的祭司被任命之年，（总计:）27 羊。
AS 9 ix (1-30): **ba-zi** 30 fat rams for**Abi-simti** for 1 month, via **Erra-bani**, fr.**Zuzuga withdr.**	30 udu-niga, sá-dug$_4$ ***A-bí-si-im-ti***, *iti-1-kam*, gìr ***Èr-ra-ba-ni***, *ki*~ ***Zu-ba -ga***--*ta*, *ba-zi*. *iti-ezem-mah*, *mu en ^{d}Nanna Kar-zi-da ba-hun*, (*left*) 30 *udu*. (*JCS* 52 10 35, *P*145829)	30 *fattened rams for the monthly allowance of***Abi-simti** for 1 month, **via Erra-bani**, from the place of **Zuzuga** were withdrawn. Month of ezem-mah, Year of en-priest of Nanna of Karzida was installed, (sum:) 30 rams.	30 只育肥公绵羊为**阿比新提一个月的月供**，**经由埃腊巴尼**，自**朱巴旮**处被支出。大庆典月，卡尔兹达的南那什的祭司被任命之年，（总计:）30 只羊。
AS 9 xi/18: **ba-zi** 3 fat rams for bride of Ur-Iškur, Šu-N. as deputy, 1 fat for Haburitum, 1 fat for Dagan, 1 fat for Išhara, for **Abi-simti**, **Atu** as deputy, fr. **Zubaga** withdr., via **Addakalla**	3 udu-niga, **igi-kár é-gi$_4$-a Ur-^{d}Iškur** ensí Ha-ma-zí^{ki}, **Šu-^{d}Nin-šubur**rá-gaba **maškim**, 1 udu-niga ***^{d}Ha-bu-rí-tum***, 1 *udu-niga* **^{d}Da-gan**, 1 udu-niga ***^{d}Iš-ha-ra***, *mu* ~ ***A-bí-sí-im-ti***--*šè*, **A-tu***sagi maškim*, *iti-ud*-18 *ba-zal*, *ki*~ ***Zu-ba-ga***--*ta*, *ba-zi*, gìr ***Ad-da-kal-la****dub-sar*. *iti-ezem-Me-ki-ĝál*, *mu en^{d}Nanna kar-zi-da ba-hun*, (*left*) 6 *udu*. (*Ontario* 1 160, *P*124573)	3 *fattened rams for provisions of bride of Ur-Iškur*, *the governor of Hamazi*, **Šu-Nin-šubur knight as royal deputy**, 1 fattened ram for Haburitum, 1 fattened ram for Dagan, 1 fattened ram for Išhara, these for **Abi-simti**, **Atu cup-bearer as royal deputy**, when 18th day passed, from **Zubaga** were withdrawn, **via Addakalla scribe**. Month of Mekiĝal, Year of en-priest of Nanna of Karzida was installed, (sum:) 6 rams.	3 肥公绵羊为**哈马兹的总督乌尔伊什库尔的新娘的供应**，**舒宁舒布尔骑使督办**，1 只肥公绵羊为**哈布瑞吞神**，1 肥公绵羊为**达干**，1 肥公绵羊为**伊什哈腊**，为**阿比新提**，**阿图司酒督办**，于 18 日过去时，自**朱巴旮**处被支出，**经由阿达卡拉书吏**。神美基旮勒庆典月，卡尔兹达的南那什的祭司被任命之年，（总计:）6。

续表

时间和摘要	文献内容	英文翻译	中文翻译
ŠS 1 ii/10: **ba-zi** 4 fat rams, 4 lambs and 1 gazelle for **Abi-simti**, **Beli-ili**as deputy, fr. **Inta-ea** withdr., via **Nanna-maba**	4 udu-niga, 4 sila$_4$, 1 amar-maš-dà-nitá, ***A-bí-sí-im-*** [***ti***], ***Be-lí-ì-lí***[*maškim*], *šà mu-er*$_{10}$*--ra--* [*ta*], *ud*-10- [*kam*], *ki* ~ ***In-ta-*** [***è***] ***-a****--ta ba-* [*zi*], **gìr dNanna-** [**ma**] **-ba dub-sar**. iti-ze$_x$-da ~ gu$_7$, mu ^{d}Šu-^{d} Suen lugal, (left) 9. (BCT 1 094, P105196)	4 fattened rams, 4 lambs and 1 kid of gazelle for **Abi-simti**, **Beli-ili as among the royal deputy**, from the deliveries, on the 10th day, from the place of **Inta-ea** were withdrawn, **via Nanna-maba scribe**. Month of zeda ~ gu$_7$, Year of the divine Šu-Sin became king, (sum:) 9.	4只育肥公绵羊、4只羔和1只公瞪羚崽为**阿比新提**，**贝里伊里督办**，**自贡入项中**，于10日，自**尹塔埃阿**处被支出，**经由南那马巴书吏**。食豚月，神舒辛成为王之年，（总计:）9
ŠS 1 ii/24: **ba-zi** 6 fat flocks, 5 lambs and 1 kid of gazelle for**Abi-simti**, from the place of **Inta-ea were** withdrawn, via Nanna-maba scribe	3 udu-niga, 2 udu-a-lum-niga, 1 ^{f}ašgar-niga, 5 sila$_4$, 1 amar-maš-dà-nitá, ***A-bí-sí-im-ti***, *níĝ-dab*$_5$ *ud-nú-a-ka-ni*, *šà mu-er*$_{10}$*--ra--ta*, *ud-24-kam*, *ki* ~ ***In-ta-è-a****--ta*, *ba-zi*, *gìr dNanna-ma-ba dub-sar*.*iti-ze*$_x$*-da-gu*$_7$, [*mu*^{d}] *Šu-*^{d}*Suen lugal*.12 (*PDT* 1 470, *P*125886)	3 *fattened rams*, 2 *fattened aslum rams*, 1 *fattened female kid*, 5 *lambs and* 1 *kid of gazelle for***Abi-simti**, for the níĝ-dab$_5$ offering of her dark moon among the deliveries, on the 24th day, from **Inta-ea** were withdrawn, via Nanna-maba scribe.Month of zeda ~ gu$_7$, Year of the divine Šu-Sin became king, (sum:) 12.	3肥公羊、2肥aslum公绵羊、1肥雌崽、5羔和1**瞪羚公崽为阿比新提**，以上为**阿比新提**，为贡入项中的她的晦月的níĝ-dab$_5$供奉，于24日，自尹塔阿处被支出，经由**南那马巴书吏**。食豚月，食豚月，神舒辛成为王之年，（总计:）12
ŠS 1 iv/29: **ba-zi** 2 rams for Dumu-zi, 2 rams for Inanna, 1 ram for Išar, 1 ram for Mišar, 1 she-goat for Nin-šubur, in Pa-tibira, via **Abi-simti**, from Duga withd., via **Nur-Adad**	2 udu^d **Dumu-zi**, 2 udu ^{d}**Inanna**, 1 udu ^{d}**I-šar**, 1 udu ^{d}**Mi-šar**, 1 ud$_5$ ^{d} **Nin-šubur**, šà ~ Bàd-tibira^{ki}, gìr ***A-bí-sí-im-ti***, *ud*-29- [*kam*,] *ki* ~ **Du$_{11}$-ga**--ta, ba-zi, gìr ***Nu-úr-***^{d}***Adad****dub-sar*. *iti-ki-siki-*^{d} *Nin-a-zu*, *mu* ^{d}*Šu-*^{d} *Suen lugal*, (*left*) 7 *udu*. (*seal*:) Nu-úr-^{d}Adad, *dumu Šu-*^{d}*Adad*, *šùš lugal*. (*BIN* 3 215, *P*106021)	2 *rams for Dumu-zi*, 2 *rams for Inanna*, 1 *ram for Išar*, 1 *ram for Mišar*, 1 *she-goat for Nin-šubur*, *in Bad-tibira*, **via Abi-simti**, on the 29th day, from Dugga were withdrawn, **via Nur-Adad scribe.** Month of ki-siki-Ninazu, Year of the divine Šu-Sin became king, (sum:) 7 rams. (seal:) Nur-Adad, the son ofŠu-Adad was the animal managerof king.	2公羊为**杜穆兹**，2羊为**伊南那**，1公羊为**伊沙尔**，1公羊为**米沙尔**，1公山羊为**宁舒布尔**，于巴德**提比拉**，**经由阿比新提**，于29日，自**杜旮**处被支出，**经由努尔阿达德书吏**。神宁阿朱羊毛作坊月，神舒辛成为王之年。（总计:）7羊。（印章）舒阿达德之子努尔阿达德是国王的牲畜长。

续表

时间和摘要	文献内容	英文翻译	中文翻译
ŠS 1 v: **šu~ ba-ti** 10 [leather…], 5 leathers of dead bulls, these for **Abi-simti**, for AS 8-A S 9, for leather workshop, from **Šunamugi**, **Ur-mes received**	8 [kuš...], 2 kuš [...], 3 kuš áb- [úš], 2 kuš gud-úš, kuš gud-ri-ri-ga, ***A-bí-sí-im-ti***, *un-ga$_{6}$* (*tl*) *unù*, *mu en-Eridu^{ki} ba-hun*, *ù mu en ^{d}Nanna Kar-zi-da ba-hun*, *kuš gíd giš-kin-ti--šè*, *ki ~* ***Šu-na-mu-gi$_{4}$***--*ta*, **Ur-mes** dub-sar, šu~ ba-ti. iti-ezem-^{d}Nin-a- [zu], mu ^{d}Šu-^{d}Suen [lugal]. (MVN 15 198, P118478)	8 [leather…], 2 leather […], 3 leathers of dead cow, 2 leathers of dead bull, these were dead bulls for **Abi-simti** servant, for year of en-priest of Eridu was installed and year of en-priest of Nanna of Karzida was installed, the leather dragged to the craft workshop, from **Šunamugi**, **Ur-mes** scribe received. Month of ezem-Ninazu, Šu-Sin became king.	8 张 x 皮、2 张 x 皮、3 张死母牛皮，2 张死公牛皮，以上死牛皮为**阿比新提家仆**，为埃瑞都的女祭司被任命之年和卡尔兹达德南那神的女祭司被任命之年的制皮作坊，自**舒那穆吉**处，**乌尔美斯书吏**接收了。神宁阿朱庆典月，神舒辛成为王之年。
ŠS 1 viii/5: **ba-zi** 21, 35, 64 kids, 20 x-[…], for **Abi-simti**, 4 + […], 4 bulls and 1 cow **butchered** for **soldiers**, **Arad-mu**as deputy, fr.**Duga** withdr., ia **Nur-Adad**	21? […], 35 […], 64 máš […], 20 x-[…], ***A-bí-sí-im-ti***, *ud~ lugal-ra-* […] *-na-* […], 4 + […] *x*, *šu-* [*gíd*], 4 *gud*, 1 [*áb*], *ba-* [*ug$_{7}$*], *é-muhaldim*, *mu~* **agà-ús-e-ne**--šè, **Arád-mu**maškim, ud-5-kam, ki ~ **Du$_{11}$-ga**--ta ba-zi, gìr ***Nu-úr-^{d}Adad****dub-sar*. *iti-šu-eš$_{5}$-ša*, *mu^{d} Šu-^{d} Suen lugal*, 5 *gud*, 150 *udu*. (*PDT* 2 1036, *P*126376	21 […], 35 […], 64 *kids* […], 20 *x*-[…], *for* **Abi-simti**, when the king […], 4+ eliminated […], 4 bulls and 1 cow, these were **butchered** for the **soldiers**, **Arad-mu as royal deputy**, on the 5th day, from the place of **Duga** were withdrawn, **via Nur-Adad scribe**. Month ofšu-ešša, Year of the divine Šu-Sin became king, (sum:) 5 bulls and 150 rams.	21 x、35 x、64 只公崽、20 x，以上为**阿比新提**，于国王【……】，4+为淘汰级，4 头公牛和 1 头母牛，**以上宰杀牲为士兵们**，**阿腊德穆督办**，于 5 日，自**杜旮**处被支出，**经由努尔阿达德书吏**。三只手月，神舒辛成为王之年，（总计：）5 头牛和 150 只羊。
ŠS 1 xii/12: **ba-zi** 2 fat for**Allatum**, via **Abi-simti**, **Dada** as deputy, 3 fat for Šu- [x], **Arad-mu** as deputy, 2 rams […], 3 fat for ?, **Lugal-magurre**as deputy, for bride, from **Zubaga** withdrawn, via **Išdum-kin**	2 udu-niga, ***^{d}Al-*** [***la***] ***-tum***, *siskúr šà ~ é-gal*, *gìr* ***A-bí-sí-im-ti***, ***Da-da*** **sagi maškim**, 3 udu-niga, igi-kár *Šu-* [x-x-x]^{ki} **Arád-**[**mumaškim**], 2 udu […], 3 udu-niga, siskúr giš-nú gub-ba, **Lugal-má-gur$_{8}$-remaškim**, mu ~ é-gi$_{4}$-a ***Šar-ru-um-ba-ni***--*šè*, *iti-ud-*12 *ba-zal*, *ki ~* ***Zu-ba-ga***--*ta ba-zi*, *gìr* ***Išdum-ki-in***dub-sar.iti-še-kin-kud, mu^{d}Šu-^{d}Suen lugal, (left) 10 udu. (Trouvaille 16, P134689)	2 fattened rams for**Allatum**, for the sacrifice in palace, via **Abi-simti**, **Dada cup-bearer as royal deputy**, 3 fattened rams for provisions of Šu- [x], **Arad-mu as royal deputy**, 2 rams […], 3 fattened rams for sacrifice of bed-setting, **Lugal-magurre as royal deputy**, for bride of Šarrum-bani, when 12th day passed, from **Zubaga** were withdrawn, **via Išdum-kin scribe**. Month of še-kin-kud, Year of the divine Šu-Sin became king, (sum:) 10 rams.	2 育肥公绵羊为**阿拉吞**，为于宫殿的祭祀，**经由阿比新提**，**达达司酒督办**，3 育肥公绵羊为**舒-X** 的供应，**阿腊德穆督办**，2 只公绵羊【……】，3 只育肥公绵羊为**放床处**，**卢旮勒马古瑞督办**，为沙润巴尼的新娘，于 12 日过去时，自**朱巴旮**处被支出，**经由伊什杜金书吏**。大麦收割月，神舒辛成为王之年，（总计：）10 只羊。

续表

时间和摘要	文献内容	英文翻译	中文翻译
ŠS 2: **ì-dab$_5$** 1 fat bull,? in Nippur, **via Nanna-k.**, 1 fat, **via Lugal-a.**, 15 fat ram, **via Ku-N.**, fr. **Ahu-Wer**, **Ṣ iluš-D.** took, **via Urušgidda**	1 gud-niga, ud~ ***A-bí-sí-im-ti*** *^{d}Ištaran in-da-a*, *šà* ~ **Nibru^{ki}** gìr^d**Nanna-kù-zu**, 1 gud-niga, gìr **Lugal-amar-kù**dumu Na-sa$_6$, 15 udu-niga, gìr**Kù-^{d}Nanna**, ki ~ ***A-hu-We-er--ta***, ***Ṣ i-lu-uš-^{d}Da-gan*** *ì-dab$_5$*, *gìr* **Ur-uš-gíd-da**, mu má darà ^{d}En-ki ba-ab-du$_8$. (TAD 28, P131070)	1 fattened bull, when Abi-simtiin-da-a Ištaram, in Nippur, **via Nanna-kuzu**, 1 fattened bull, **via Lugal-amarku**, the son of Nasa, 15 fattened ram, **via Ku-Nanna**, from the place of**Ahu-Wer**, **Ṣiluš-Dagan** took over, **via Urušgidda**, Year of the boat of wild buck of Apsu of Enki was caulked.	1头育肥公牛，于阿比新提 in-da-a 伊什塔兰，于**尼普尔**，**经由南那库朱**，1头育肥公牛**经由那萨之子卢旮勒阿马尔库**，15肥公绵羊，**经由库南那**，自**阿胡维尔**处，**采鲁什达干接管**，**经由乌如什吉达**，恩基的阿坡朱的野山羊船被密封年。
ŠS 2 iii/27: **ba-zi** 3 fat rams, 8 lambs, 3 gazelles, these for**Abi-simti**, for requisition of her dark moon among deliveries, from the place of **Inta-ea** were withdrawn, **via Nanna-maba scribe**	2 udu-niga-4-kam-ús, 1 udu-a-lum-niga-4-kam-ús, 8 sila$_4$, 2 amar-maš-dà-nitá, 1 amar-maš-dà-munus, ***A-bí-sí-im-ti***, *níĝ-dab$_5$ ud-nú-a-ka-ni*, *šà mu-er$_{10}$--ra--ta*, *ud-27-kam*, *ki~* **In-ta-è-a**--ta ba-zi, **gìrdNanna-ma-ba dub-sar**. iti-u$_5$-bí ~ gu$_7$, mu má darà-abzu ^{d}En-ki-ka ba-ab] - [du$_8$], 14. (seal:) ^{d}Nanna- [ma-ba], dub-[sar], [dumu Û-na-ap-še-en$_6$]. (JEOL 34, 28, 2, P142645)	2 fattened rams of 4th class, 1 fattened aslum ram of 4th class, 8 lambs, 2 kids of gazelle and 1 female kid of gazelle, these for **Abi-simti**, for the níĝ-dab$_5$ offering of her dark moon among the deliveries, on the 27th day, from the place of **Inta-ea** withdrawn, **via Nanna-maba scribe.** Month of ubi ~ gu$_7$, Year of the boat of wild buck of Apsu of Enki was caulked, (sum:) 14. (seal:) Nanna-maba scribe was the son of Unapšen.	2只肥四等公绵羊、1只育肥四等 aslum 公绵羊、8只羔、2只瞪羚公崽和1只瞪羚雌崽，以上为**阿比新提**，为贡入项中她的晦月的 níĝ-dab$_5$供奉，于27日，自**尹塔埃阿**处被支出，**经由南那马巴书吏**。食乌比鸟月，恩基的阿坡朱的野山羊船被密封之年，（总计：）14。（印文：）南那马巴书吏是乌那坡鑫之子。
ŠS 2 ix/23: **ba-zi** 2 fat bulls to**kitchen**, for messengers, **Nanna-kam envoy as royal deputy**, 39 fat flocks and 40 flocks for **Abi-simti**, in Nippur, ⋯, from the place of **Ahu-Wer** were withdrawn, **via Ur-Lugal-banda and Ur-Bilgames**	2 gud-niga é-muhaldim, mu ~ **kaš$_4$-e-ne**--šè, **dNanna-kam sukkal maškim**, 3 gud-niga-3-kam-ús, 2 gud-niga, 20 udu-niga-4-kam-ús, 10 máš-gal-niga, 30 udu a-rá-1-kam, 4 gud-niga, 10 áb a-rá-2-kam, ***A-bi-sí-im-ti*** *ud ~ ^{d}Ištaran in-da-a*, *šà* ~ **Nibru^{ki}** ⋯ iti-ud-23-ba-zal, ki~ ***A-hu-We-er--ta***, *ba-zi*, **gìr Ur-dLu-gal-bàn-da dub-sar ùUr-dBìl-ga-mes ša-ra-ab-du.** iti-ezem-mah, mu má darà-abzu ^{d}En-ki-ka ba-ab-du$_8$, (left) 21 gud, 65 udu. (BIN 3 559, P106366)	2 fattened bulls to the**kitchen**, for the messengers, **Nanna-kam envoy as royal deputy**, 3 fattened bull of 3rd class, 2 fattened bulls, 20 fattened rams of 4th class, 10 fattened he-goats, 30 rams for 1st time, 4 fattened bulls and 10 cows for the 2nd time, these for **Abi-simti** in-da-a Ištaran, in Nippur, ⋯, when the 23rd day passed, from the place of **Ahu-Wer** were withdrawn, **via Ur-Lugal-banda scribe and Ur-Bilgames administrator**. Month of ezem-mah, Year of the boat of wild buck of Apsu of Enki was caulked, (sum:) 21 bulls and 65 rams.	2头肥公牛到厨房，为**信使们**，**南那刊国使督办**，3头三等肥公牛、2头肥公牛、20四等肥公绵羊、10肥公山羊、30公绵羊第1次，4头肥公牛和10头母牛第2次，以上为**阿比新提** in-da-a 伊什塔兰，于**尼普尔**，……，于23日过去时，自**阿胡维尔**处被支出，**经由乌尔卢旮勒班达书吏和乌尔比尔旮美斯行政官**。大庆典月，恩基的阿坡朱的野山羊船被密封之年，（总计：）21头公牛和65只羊

续表

时间和摘要	文献内容	英文翻译	中文翻译
ŠS **2 x: ba-zi** 29 fat rams for daily offering of 29 days, 1 fat ram for **Full Moon**, 1 fat ram for **New Moon**, above extra for **Šulgi**, 29 fat for offering of 29 days, 1 fat for **Full Moon**, 1 fat for **New Moon**, extra for **Amar-Sin**, [1+] fat for **Abi-simti**, 9+ fat for **Haršitum**, [1+] fat x for **Kubatum**, [1+] fat for **Abba-bašti**, 2+ fat for **Una-bari**, 3 rams for **Binahu**, 6 fat for **Ṣ ilili**, 17 fat for allowance of 17 days, fr. **Min-niš** for **offering**, fr. **Ahu-Wer** withdr., <u>via Ur-ušgidda and Qurad-ili</u>	29 udu-niga, **šu-a-gi-na** ud-29-kam, 1 udu-niga **é-ud-15**, 1 udu-niga**é-ud-sakar**, níĝ-diri **sá-dug$_4$ ^{d}Šul-gi**, 29 udu-niga, **šu-a-gi-na** ud-29-kam, 1 udu-niga **é-ud-15**, [1] udu-niga **é-ud-sakar**, [níĝ] -diri **sá-dug$_4$ ^{d}Amar-^{d}Suen**, [6? +] udu-niga, [**sá**] **-dug$_4$** ***A-bí-sí-im-ti***, 9 *udu-niga*, [**sá**] **-dug$_4$** ***Ha-ar-ši-tum***, [1+] *udu-niga* [1+] *udu-niga-gud-e-ús-sa*, [**sá-dug$_4$**] rá-gaba, rev. [1 udu-niga], [...] -na-tum? [1+ udu] -niga-gud-e-ús-sa, [**sá-dug$_4$**] ***Ku-ba-tum***, [1+] *udu-niga-gud-e-ús-sa*, [**sá**] **-dug$_4$ A-ab-ba-ba-aš-ti** (**Tiamat-bašti**), 2+ udu-niga **sá-dug$_4$** ***Ú-na-ba-ri***, 3 *udu* **siskúr é-*Bi-na-hu***, 6 *udu-niga-gud-e-ús-sa*, **sá-dug$_4$** ***Ṣ í-li-li***, 17 *udu-niga* **sá-dug$_4$** ud-17-kam, *Min-ni-iš* lú *Ri-mu-uš^{ki}*, **sá-dug$_4$ šu-a-gi-na** iti-1-kam, ki~ ***A-hu-We-er***-*-ta ba-zi*, <u>*gìr Ur-uš-gíd-da dub-sarùQú-ra-ad-ì-líšár-ra-ab-du x.*</u> *iti-ezem-An-na*, *mu má ^{d}En-ki ba-ab-du$_8$*. (*left*) *x* [*udu*] (*BIN* 3 558, *P*106365)	29 *fattened rams for***daily offering of 29 days**, 1 fattened ram for **Full Moon**, 1 fattened ram for **New Moon**, additional ones for monthly allowance of **Šulgi**, 29 fattened ram for daily offering **of 29 days**, 1 fattened ram for **Full Moon**, 1 fattened ram for **New Moon**, additional ones for monthly allowance of **Amar-Sin**, [1+] fattened ram for monthly allowance of **Abi-simti**, 9 + fattened ram for monthly allowance of **Haršitum**, [1+] fattened ram and [1+] fattened ram of after-ox-class, [⋯] knight, [⋯], [⋯] nutum, [1+] fattened [ram] of after-ox-class, [x x] x **Kubatum**, [1+] fattened ram of after-ox-class for monthly allowance of **Abba-bašti** (**lukur of ŠS**), 2+ fattened rams for monthly allowance of **Unabari**, 3 rams for sacrifice of temple of **Binahu**, 6 fattened rams of after-ox-class for monthly allowance of **Ṣilili**, 17 fattened rams for monthly allowance of 17 days, from **Min-niš**, man of Rimuš for d**aily offering** of 1 month, from **Ahu-Wer** were withdrawn, <u>via Ur-ušgidda scribe and Qurad-ili administrator</u>. Month of ezem-Anna, Year of boat of Enki was caulked, (sum:) x rams	29 只育肥公绵羊为 29 天的**日供**，1 育肥公绵羊为**满月**，1 育肥公绵羊为**新月**，增加的供应为**舒勒吉的月供**，29 只育肥公绵羊为 29 天的**日供**，1 育肥公绵羊为**满月**，1 育肥公绵羊为**新月**，增加的供应为**阿马尔辛的月供**，【1+】育肥公绵羊为**阿比新提的月供**，9+育肥公绵羊为**哈尔西吞的月供**，【1+】育肥公绵羊和【1+】牛后级育肥公绵羊……骑使，【……】，【1+】牛后级育肥【公绵羊】为**库巴吞**，【1+】牛后级育肥公绵羊为**阿巴巴什提的月供**，2+育肥公绵羊为**乌那巴瑞的月供**，3 公绵羊为**比那胡庙的祭祀**，6 牛后级育肥公绵羊为**采里里的月供**， 17 育肥公绵羊为 17 天的月供，自瑞穆什城的人敏尼什处为 1 个月的日供，自**阿胡维尔**处被支出，<u>经由**乌尔乌什吉达书吏和苦腊德伊里行政官**</u>。安神庆典月，恩基的船被封之年。 （总计：）x 只羊

续表

时间和摘要	文献内容	英文翻译	中文翻译
ŠS 2 x/2, 4, 5, 9, 11, 14, 16, 19, 24, 25: **ba-zi** 6 bulls for the**gate of Inanna** [⋯], for sacrifice of Lugal-ezem, x, via Abi-simti, 3 bulls **to kitchen**, 2 bulls **to kitchen** for, ⋯, sum 28 bulls, 1 3-year bull, 1 2-year bull, 18 cows, fr. **Enlilla** withdr.	6 gud ká-^{d} Inanna [...], siskúr Lugal-ezem-è-[x x], gìr ***A-bí-sí-im-ti***, **ud-2**-kam; 3 gud šu-gíd **é-muhaldim ud-4**-kam; 1 gud, 1 gud-mu-2 šu-gíd **é muhaldim**, **ud-5**-kam;..., šu-nigín 28 gud, šu-nigín 1 gud-mu-3, šu-nigín 1 gud-mu-2, šu-nigín 18 áb, ki~ **^{d}En-líl-lá**--ta ba-zi.iti-ezem-An-na, mu má darà abzu ^{d}En-ki-ka ba-ab-du$_{8}$, (left) 48 gud. (MVN 10 142, P115912)	6 bulls for the **gate of Inanna** [⋯], for the sacrifice of king festival, x, via Abi-simti, on the 2nd day, 3 eliminated bulls **to the kitchen** on the 4th day, 1 bull, 1 eliminated 2-year bull **to the kitchen** on the 5th day, ⋯, sum 28 bulls, sum 1 3-year bull, sum 1 2-year bull, sum 18 cows, from the place of**Enlilla** were withdrawn. Month of ezem-Anna, Year of Enki caulked the boat of wild buck of Apsu, (sum:) 48 bulls.	6头公牛为**伊南那门【……】**，为国王节日的祭祀，x，经由**阿比新提**，于2日，3头淘汰级公牛到厨房于4日，1头公牛和1淘汰级2岁公牛到厨房于5日…… 总计28公牛，总计1头3岁公牛，总计1头2岁公牛，总计18母牛，自**恩里拉**处被支出。安神庆典月，恩基密封阿坡朱的野山羊船之年，（总计：）48头牛。
ŠS 2 xi/24: **ba-zi** 1 fat ram and 1 ram fr. **Bab-duša**, for Iabrat of LÚ. SU, [1+] fat ram fr. **Šilatir**, for Dayazite, **via Bazaza envoy**, [1+] fat ram for**Kirb-ulme**, **via Šukubum**, 1 fat ram for **Aridubuk**, **via Laqipum**, 1 fat ram for **Š.**, **via Lalamu**, **Arad-mu as deputy**, 1 lamb for **Abi-simti**, **K. as deputy**, fr. **Ahu-Wer** withdr., **via Ur-L.and Ahanišu**	1 udu-niga, 1 udu, ***Ba-ab-du-ša*** *lú-kin-gi$_{4}$-a* [***Ià***] ***-ab-ra-at*** *LÚ.SU^{ki}*, [1+] *udu-niga* ***Ši-la-ti-ir*** *lú-kin-gi$_{4}$-a* **Da-a-zi**$^{!}$ **-te** lú An-ša-an^{ki}, gìr ***Ba-za-za*** **sukkal**, [1+] udu-niga ***Ki-rí-ib-ul-me*** *lú Si-mu-ru-um^{ki}*, gìr ***Šu-ku-bu-um*****sukkal**, 1 udu-niga***A-ri-du-bu-uk*** *lú Ša-aš-ru^{ki}*, gìr ***La-qí-pu-um*****sukkal**, 1 udu-niga, ***Še-et-pá-tal*** *lú Gi-gi-ib-ni^{ki}*, gìr ***La-la-mu****sukkal*, **Arád-mumaškim**, 1 sila$_{4}$-ga ***A-bí-sí-im-ti***, ***Ku-ub-za-gi-mu*** **maškim**, iti-ud-24 ba-zal, ki~ ***A-hu-We-er***--*ta ba-zi*, gìr **Ur-^{d}Lugal-bàn-da**ù**A-ha-ni-šu**šár-ra-ab-du. iti-ezem-Me-ki-ĝál, mu má ^{d}En-ki ba-ab-du$_{8}$. (Babyl.8 Pupil 30, P104839)	1 fattened ram and 1 ram from**Bab-duša** messenger, for Iabrat of LÚ.SU, [1+] fattened ram from **Šilatir** messenger, for Dayazite, the man of Anšan, **via Bazaza envoy**, [1+] fattened ram for **Kirb-ulme**, the man of Simurum, **via Šukubum envoy**, 1 fattened ram for **Aridubuk**, the man of Šašru, **via Laqipum envoy**, 1 fattened ram for **Šetpatal**, the man of Gigibni, **via Lalamu envoy**, **Arad-mu**as royal deputy, 1 suckling lamb for**Abi-simti**, **Kubzagimu as royal deputy**, when the 24th day passed, from the place of**Ahu-Wer**, were withdrawn, **via Ur-Lugal-banda and Ahanišu administrator**. Month of ezem-Mekiĝal, Year of the boat of wild buck of Apsu was caulked.	1肥公绵羊和1公绵羊自**巴卜杜沙信使**，为LÚ.SU城的亚卜腊特，**【1+】**肥公绵羊自**西提尔信拉使**，为安山城之人达亚孜台，**经由巴扎扎国使**，**【1+】**肥公绵羊为**席穆润城之人基尔卜乌勒美**，**经由舒库布姆国使**，1肥公绵羊为沙什如城之人阿瑞杜布克，**经由拉齐普姆国使**，1肥公绵羊为吉吉卜尼城之人塞特帕塔勒，**经由拉拉穆国使**，**阿腊德穆督办**，1吃奶羔为**阿比新提**，**库卜扎吉穆督办**，于24日过去时，自**阿胡维尔**处被支出，**经由乌尔卢旮勒班达和阿哈尼舒行政官**。神美基旮勒庆典月，阿坡朱的野山羊船被密封之年。

续表

时间和摘要	文献内容	英文翻译	中文翻译
ŠS 3 iii: **ba-zi** [1 fat bull] for [**Enlil**], [1] fat for **Ninlil**, king sent, 1 fat for **Inanna**, **via Abi-simti**, in **Nippur**, 1 fat for **Abu-ṭab**, 1 fat for **E.**, **via Naram-Iškur**, **Arad-mu** as deputy, fr. **Ahu-Wer**, withdr., **via Ur-Lugal-banda, Lu-Nanna**	[1 gud-niga], [^{d}**En-líl**], [1] gud-niga, ^{d}**Nin-líl**, **siskúr-gu-la**, lugal ku_4-ra, 1 gud-niga ^{d}**Inanna**, gìr ***A-bí-sí-im-* [*ti*]**, *šà* ~ *Ni-bru*^{ki}, 1 *udu-niga*, ***A-bu-ṭàb*** *lú Ma-rí*^{ki}, 1 *udu-niga* ***E-zu-un-^{d}Da-gan*** *lú Eb-la*^{ki}, gìr***Na-ra-am-^{d}A-dad*sukkal**, **Arád-mumaškim**, iti-ud-6-ba-zal, ki ~ ***A-hu-We-er*** *--ta*, *ba-zi*, *gìr* **Ur-^{d}Lugal-bànd- [da] dub-sarùLú-^{d}Nannašár-ra-ab-du**.iti-u_5-bí ~ gu_7, muśs-sa má darà [abzu ba-du_8], 3 gud, 2 udu. (Ebla 1975-1985 287 B, P200528)	[1 fattened bull] for [**Enlil**], [1] fattened bull for **Ninlil**, these for the great sacrifice, the king sent, 1 fattened bull for **Inanna**, **via Abi-simti**, in **Nippur**, 1 fattened ram for **Abu-ṭab**, the man of Mari, 1 fattened ram for **Ezun-Dagan**, the man of Ebla, **via Naram-Iškur envoy**, **Arad-mu as royal deputy**, when the 6th day passed, from **Ahu-Wer**, were withdrawn, **via Ur-Lugal-banda scribe and Lu-Nanna administrator**. Month of ubi ~ gu_7, Year after that of boat of wild buck of Apsu was caulked, (sum:) 3 bulls and 3 rams.	【1肥公牛】为【**恩里勒**】，【1】肥公牛为**宁里勒**，为大祭祀，国王送入，1肥公牛为**伊南那**，**经由阿比新提**，于**尼普尔**，1肥公绵羊为马瑞城之人阿布塔卜，1肥公绵羊为埃卜拉城人埃樽，**经由那冉伊什库尔国使**，**阿腊德穆督办**，于6日过去时，自**阿胡维尔**处被支出，**经由乌尔卢旮勒班达书吏和卢南那行政官**。食乌比乌月，阿坡朱的野山羊船被密封年之次年，3头牛和3只羊。
ŠS 3 iv: **ba-zi** 1 better fattened bullfor **Annu-nitum**, **via Abi-simti, the queen, Sin-abi cup-bear as royal deputy**, x, from the [place] of **Ma- [šum]**, was withdrawn, in Ur	1 gud-niga-sig_5- (hi erased?) -ús, ***An-nu-ni-tum***, *gìr* ***A-bí-sí-< im >-ti*nin-a**, **^{d}Suen-a-bísagi maškim**, x UD? - [...], [ki?] ***Ma***$^{?}$-[***šu-um***] *--ta*, *ba-zi šà* **Urim$_5$^{ki}**-ma.iti-ki- [si-ki-^{d}Nin -a-zu], mu [ús-sa má darà] -abzu [ba-ab] -du_8. (Seal:) Šu-^{d}Suen, lugal-kal-ga, lugal Urim$_5$^{ki}-ma, lugal an-ub-da limmú-ba-ke_4, ^{d}Suen-a-bí, sagi, arád-da-ni--ir, in-na-ba. (Studies Pettinato 160, 167 09, 171, P332417)	1 better fattened bull for**Annunitum**, **via Abi-simti, the queen (dowager), Sin-abi cup-bear as royal deputy**, x, from the [place] of**Ma- [šum]**, was withdrawn, in **Ur**. Month of ki- [siki-Ninazu], Year [after that of the boat of wild buck] of Apsu was caulked. (seal:) Šu-Sin, the strong king, king of Ur, king of four-quarter present to Sin-abi cup-bear, his servant (this seal).	1头次优育肥公牛为**安努尼吞**，**经由阿比新提王后（皇太后）**，**辛阿比司酒督办**，x，自马【**顺处**】，被支出，于**乌尔**。【神宁阿朱羊毛作坊月】，【阿坡朱的野山羊船】被密封之年之【次年】。 （印章：）舒辛，强大之王，乌尔之王，四方之王赠予了他的仆人辛阿比司酒（该印章）。

续表

时间和摘要	文献内容	英文翻译	中文翻译
ŠS 3 vi/7: **ba-zi** [3] fat flocks for**Enlil**, 3 fat flocks for **Ninlil**, via **Abi-simti**, **Enlil-zišagal**as deputy, **butchered** fat ram to storeroom, from **Kur-bilak** were withdr., via**Nur-Sin**scribe	[1] udu-niga-3-kam-ús, [1] udu-niga-4-kam-ús, [1] máš-gal-niga-4-kam-ús, ^{d} **En-líl**, 1 udu-niga-3-kam-ús, 2 udu-niga-4-kam-ús, ^{d}**Nin-líl**, gìr ***A-bí-sí-im-ti***, ^{d}**En-líl-zi-šà-gálmaškim**, 1 udu-niga-gud-e-ús-sa, ba-úš, **é-kišib-ba--šè**, iti-ud-7$^{!}$ba-zal, ki~ ***Kur-bi-la-ak***--*ta ba-zi*, *gìr* ***Nu***$^{!}$***-úr***$^{!}$***-***^{d} ***Suen*** *dub-sar. iti-á-ki-ti*, *mu Si-ma-núm*^{ki} *ba-hul*, *7 udu.* (*seal*:) [*Kur-bi*] *-la-ak*$^{(?)}$ (*PDT* 2 1219, *P*126549)	[1] *fattened ram of* 3rd *class*, [1] *fattened ram of* 4th *class and* [1] *fattened he-goat of* 4th *class for* **Enlil**, 1 fattened ram of 3rd class and 2 fattened rams of 4th class for **Ninlil**, **via Abi-simti**, **Enlil-zišagal as royal deputy**, 1 **butchered** fattened ram of after-ox-class to the storeroom, when the 7th day passed, from the place of **Kur-bilak** were withdrawn, **via Nur-Sin scribe.** Month of akiti, Year of Simanum was destroyed, (sum:) 7 rams.	【1】育肥三等公绵羊、【1】育肥四等公绵羊和【1】育肥四等公山羊为**恩里勒**，1育肥三等公绵羊和2育肥四等公绵羊为**宁里勒**，**经由阿比新提**，**恩里勒孜沙旮勒督办**，1宰杀牛后级育肥公绵羊到**仓库**，于7日过去时，**自库尔比拉可**处被支出，**经由努尔辛书吏**。阿基提月，席马农被毁之年，（总计：）7只羊。
ŠS 3 xii/10: **ba-zi** 2 fat rams and 2 lambs for**Dagan**, 2 fat rams and 2 lambs for **Išhara**, 1 fat ram and 1 lamb for **Inanna**, for scrifice in palace, **via Abi-simti**, **Nanna-igidu cup-bearer**, from **Ibni-Sin** were withdrawn	1 udu-niga-3-kam-ús, 1 udu-niga, 2 sila$_4$ ^{d} **Dagan**, 1 udu-niga-4-kam-ús, 1 udu-niga, 2 sila$_4$, ^{d}***Iš-ha-ra***, 1 *udu-niga-4-kam-ús*, 1 *sila*$_4$, ^{d} **Inanna**, siskúr é-gal, gìr ***A-bí-sí-im-ti***, ^{d} **Nanna-igi-dusagi**, iti-ud-10 ba-zal, ki~ ***Ib-ni-***^{d} ***Suen***--*ta ba-zi. iti-še-kin-kud*, *mu Si-ma-núm*^{ki}*ba-hul.* (*seal*:) ^{d}*Amar-*^{d}*Suen*, *lugal-kal-ga*, *lugal Urim*$_5$^{ki}*-ma*, *lugal an-ub-da limmú-ba*, *Ur-*^{d}*Šul-pa-èdub-sar*, *dumu Ur-*^{d}*Ha-ià*, *arád-zu.* (*PDT* 1 269, *P*125685)	1 *fattened ram of* 3rd *class*, 1 *fattened ram and* 2 *lambs for* **Dagan**, 1 fattened ram of 4th class, 1 fattened ram and 2 lambs for **Išhara**, 1 fattened ram of 4th class and 1 lamb for **Inanna**, for the scrifice in palace, **via Abi-simti and Nanna-igidu cup-bearer**, when the 10th day passed, from **Ibni-Sin** were withdrawn. Month of še-kin-kud, Year of Simanum was destroyed. (seal:) Amar-Sin, the strong king, king of Ur, king of four-quarter, Ur-Šulpae scribe, son of Ur-haya was your servant.	1肥三等公绵羊、1育肥公绵羊和2羔为**达干**，1育肥四等公绵羊、1育肥公绵羊和2羔为**伊什哈腊**，1育肥四等公绵羊和1羔为**伊南那**，以上为宫殿的祭祀，**经由阿比新提和南那伊吉杜司酒**，于10日过去时，自伊比尼辛处被支出。大麦收割月，席马农被毁之年。（印章）阿马尔辛，强大之王、乌尔王、四方之王，乌尔哈亚之子乌尔舒勒帕埃书吏是你的仆人。
ŠS 4 iii: **ba-zi** 1 knife, **Elala** presented to **Abi-simti**, fr. **Lu-diĝirra** withdr., in **Nippur**	1 gír gi-ka, zabar kù-sig$_{17}$ gar-ra, mu-túm ***E-la-la*** *tibira*, ***A-bí-sí-im-ti***, *in-ba*, *ki*~ **Lú-diĝir-ra**--ta, ba-zi, šà~ **Nibru^{ki}**. iti-ze$_x$-da~gu$_7$, mu ús-sa ^{d}Šu-^{d}Suen [lugal-e] Si-ma-núm^{ki} mu-hul. (SET 296, P129705)	1 knife with bronze and gold, delivered by**Elala**, **coppersmith**, presented to **Abi-simti**, from the place of **Lu-diĝirra** withdrawn, in **Nippur**. Month of zeda~gu$_7$, Year after that of Šu-Sin, king of Ur destroyed Simanum.	1把青铜和金刀，埃拉拉铜匠送人，赠予**阿比新提**，自**卢迪弥腊**处被支出，于**尼普尔**。食豚月，乌尔之王舒辛毁灭席马农之年之次年。

续表

时间和摘要	文献内容	英文翻译	中文翻译
ŠS 4 iii/4: **ba-zi** [1+] fat [ram] **Nin-Isina** of Umma, in palace, **A [tu] cup-bearer as deputy**, **in Nippur**, [2+] fat for **Dagan**, [2+] fat for **Išhara**, 1 fat for **Inanna**, 1 fat for **Nin-nigar**, 1 fat [⋯] for **sacrifice in orchard**, 2 rams and 1 lamb for **Haburitum**, via **Abi-simti**, **Sin-abušu as deputy**, fr. **Ur-Nanna**, withdr., via **Ur-Tummal**	[1 + udu] -niga-4- [kam] -ús, ^{d} **Nin-Isín-na** Umma$^{[ki]}$ šà ~ é-gal, **A- [tu]** sagi maškim, [šà] ~ Nibru^{ki}, [1+ udu] -niga-4-kam-ús, [1+] udu-niga, [… ^{d}] **Da-gan**, [1+] udu-niga-4-kam-ús, [1+] udu-niga, ^{d}**Iš-ha-ra**, 1 udu-niga ^{d}**Inanna**, 1 udu-niga ^{d}**Nin-nigar**$_{x}$, 1 udu-niga […], **siskúr šà** ~ ^{giš}**kiri**$_{6}$, 1 udu-niga-4-kam-ús, 1 udu-niga, 1 sila$_{4}$-ga, ^{d} ***Ha-bu-ri-tum***, gìr ***Á-bí-sí-im-ti***, ^{d}**Suen-a-bu-šusagi maškim**, iti-ud-4 ba-zal, ki ~ **Ur-**^{d} **Nanna**--ta, ba-zi, gìr **Ur-Tum-ma-al**šár-ra-ab-du. [iti] -ze$_{x}$-da ~ gu$_{7}$, [mu ús] -sa ^{d}Šu-^{d}Suen [lugal-e] Si-ma-núm^{ki} mu-hul. (MVN 05 125, P114345)	[1+] fattened [ram] of 4th class for **Nin-Isina** of Umma, in palace, A [tu] cup-bearer as royal deputy, **in Nippur**, [1+] fattened [ram] of 4th class and [1+] fattened ram for **Dagan**, [1+] fattened ram of 4th class and [1+] fattened ram for **Išhara**, 1 fattened ram for **Inanna**, 1 fattened ram for **Nin-nigar**, 1 fattened ram [⋯] for **sacrifice in the orchard**, 1 fattened ram of 4th class, 1 fattened ram and 1 suckling lamb for **Haburitum**, via Abi-simti, Sin-abušu cup-bear as royal deputy, when the 4th day passed, from **Ur-Nanna**, were withdrawn, via**Ur-Tummal**administrator. [Month] of zeda~gu$_{7}$, [Year aft] er that of Šu-Sin, king of Ur destroyed Simanum.	【1+】肥四等【公绵羊】为温马的**宁伊辛那**女神，于宫殿，阿【图】司酒督办，于尼普尔，【1+】肥四等【公绵羊】和【1+】肥公绵羊为**达干**，【1+】肥四等【公绵羊】和【1+】肥公绵羊为**伊什哈腊**，1肥公绵羊为**伊南那**，1肥公绵羊为**宁尼旮尔**，1肥公绵羊为果园的祭祀，1肥四等公绵羊、1肥公绵羊和1吃奶羔为**哈布瑞吞**神，经由阿比新提，辛阿布书司酒督办，于4日过去时，自**乌尔南那**处被支出，经由**乌尔吞马勒行政官**。食豚【月】，乌尔之王舒辛毁灭席马农之年之【次年】。
ŠS 4 v/6: **ba-zi** 5 fat rams to **kitchen**, for provisions of Apilaša, **Abi-simti** sent, **Arad-mu as deputy**, fr. **Ur-Nanna** withdr., via **Ur-Tummal**	5 udu-niga**é-muhaldim**, igi-kár ***é-Á-pi***$_{5}$***-la-ša--šè***, ***A-bí-sí-im-ti***, *šu* ~ *bí-in-ús*, **Arád-mu maškim**, iti-ud-6 ba-zal, ki~ **Ur-**^{d}**Nanna**--ta, ba-zi, gìr **Ur-Tum-ma-al** šár-ra-ab-du. iti-ki-kisi-^{d} Nin-a-zu, mu ús-sa ^{d}Šu-^{d} Suen lugal Urim$_{5}$^{ki}-ma--ke$_{4}$ Si-ma-núm^{ki} mu-hul. (SA 005 (Pl.042), P128623)	5 fattened rams to **the kitchen**, for the provisions of the house of Apilaša (general of Kazallu), **Abi-simti** sent, **Arad-mu as royal deputy**, when the 16th day passed, from the place of **Ur-Nanna**, were withdrawn, via **Ur-Tummal** administrator. Month of ki-siki-Ninazu, Year after that of Šu-Sin, king of Ur destroyed Simanum.	5只育肥公绵羊到**厨房**，为阿皮拉沙（卡扎鲁的将军）房的供奉，**阿比新提送入**，**阿腊德穆督办**，于16日过去时，自**乌尔南那**处被支出，**经由乌尔吞马勒行政官**。神宁阿朱羊毛作坊月，乌尔之王舒辛毁灭席马农之年之次年。

续表

时间和摘要	文献内容	英文翻译	中文翻译
ŠS 4 ix/14, 25: **ki~...-ta** 8 bulls and 1 cow, for **Abi-simti**, 8 bulls and 1 cow, were deliveries for **Kubatum**, 18, deliveries, 4 bulls, 4, Beli-ili took, 2 bulls, 2, Zabar-dab took, 2 bulls, 2, Ahuwer took, 4 bulls and 1 cow, 5, Ibni-Sîn took, 4 bulls and 1 cow, 5, Ur-Nanna took, fr. **Inta-ea** withdr.	8 gud-ú, 1 áb-ú, mu-túm ***A-bí-sí-im-ti***, 8 *gud-ú*, 1 *áb-ú*, *mu-túm* ***Ku-ba-tum***, 18, *mu-túm ud-14-kam*, *šà-bi-ta*, 4 *gud-ú*, 4, ***Be-lí-i-lí*** *ì-*[*dab$_5$*], 2 *gud-ú*, 2, *zabar-dab$_5$ ì-dab$_5$*, 2 *gud-ú*, 2, ***A-hu-We-e****r ì-dab$_5$*, 4 *gud-ú*, 1 *áb-ú*, 5, ***Ib-ni-^{d}Suen*** *ì-dab$_5$*, 4 *gud-ú*, 1 *áb-ú*, 5, **Ur-^{d}Nanna** ì-dab$_5$, šà~ ki-bi gi$_4$-a ud-25-kam, ki~ **In-ta-è-a-ta**. iti-ezem-^{d}Šu-^{d}Suen, mu bàd Mar-tu *Mu-ri-iq Ti-id-ni-im* ba-dù. (AUCT 1 032, P102878)	8 grass bulls and 1 grass cow, were deliveries for **Abi-simti**, 8 grass bulls and 1 grass cow, were deliveries for **Kubatum**, 18, from the deliveries, on the 14th day, 4 grass bulls, 4, Beli-ili took over, 2 grass bulls, 2, Zabar-dab took over, 2 grass bulls, 2, Ahuwer took over, 4 grass bulls and 1 grass cow, 5, Ibni-Sîn took over, 4 grass bulls and 1 grass cow, 5, Ur-Nanna took over, these return to its place, on the 25th day, from**Inta-ea** were withdrawn. Month of ezem-Šu-Sin, Year of the divineŠu-Sin, king of Ur, built the Amorite Wall.	8食草公牛和1食草母牛，为**阿比新提**的送入项，8食草公牛和1食草母牛，为**库巴吞**的送入，18，自送入项中，于14日，4食草公牛，4，贝里伊里接管，2食草公牛，2，执青铜官接管，2食草公牛，2，阿胡维尔接管，4食草公牛和1食草母牛，5，伊卜尼辛接管，4食草公牛和1食草母牛，5，乌尔南那接管，以上返还到该地，于25日，自**尹塔埃阿**处。舒辛庆典月，乌尔王神舒辛建了名为穆瑞可提宁德阿摩利城墙之年。
ŠS 4 xii/27: **ba-zi** 4 fat flocks for**Kur-bilake**, stay in that place, 9 fat flocks, 3 grass rams, 7 lambs and 1 big-tailed lamb, these for **Abi-simti**, for the requisitions of her dark moon among the deliveries, from **Inta-ea**, were withdrawn, <u>**via Nanna-maba scribe**</u>	1 gukkal-niga-sig$_5$, 2 udu-niga-3-kam-ús, 1 udu-a-lum-niga-3-kam-ús, udu-bi **Kur-bi-la-ak-e**, ki-ba bí-in-gá-ar, 3 udu-niga-3-kam-ús, 1 udu *Ši$_x$-maški*-niga-3-kam-ús, 1 udu-a-lum-niga-3-kam-ús, 2 udu-niga-4-kam-ús, 2 udu-a-lum-niga-4-kam-ús, 3 udu-a-lum-ú, 7 sila$_4$, 1 sila$_4$ gukkal, ***A-bí-sí-im-ti***, **níĝ-dab$_5$ ud-nú-a-ka-ni**, šà mu-túm-ra-ta, ud-27-kam, ki~ **In-ta-è-a--ta** ba-zi, gìr <u>**^{d}Nanna-ma-ba**dub-sar</u>. iti-ezem-Me-ki-ĝál, mu ^{d}Šu-^{d} Suen lugal Urim$_5$^{ki}-ma--ke$_4$ bàd mar-tu *Mu-ri-iq Ti-id-ni-im* mu-dù, (left) 24 udu. (BCT 1 100, P105202)	1 best fattened big-tailed sheep, 2 fattened rams of 3rd class, 1 fattened aslum ram of 3rd class, these rams for **Kur-bilak**, placed in the place, 3 fattened rams of 3rd class, 1 fattened *Ši$_x$ maški* ram of 3rd class, 1 fattened aslum ram of 3rd class, 2 fattened rams of 4th class, 2 fattened aslum rams of 4th class, 3 grass aslum rams, 7 lambs and 1 big-tailed lamb, these for **Abi-simti**, for her níĝ-dab$_5$ offering of her dark moon among the deliveries, on the 27th day, from **Inta-ea**, were withdrawn, <u>**via Nanna-maba scribe**</u>. Month of ezem-Mekiĝal, Year of the divineŠu-Sin, king of Ur, built the Amorite Wall, (sum:) 24 rams.	1优等肥肥尾绵羊、2肥三等公绵羊、1肥三等aslum公绵羊、以上公绵羊为**库尔比拉可**，放于那个地方，3肥三等公绵羊、1肥三等西马什基公绵羊、1肥aslum三等公绵羊、2肥四等公绵羊、2肥aslum四等公绵羊、3食草aslum公绵羊、7羔和1肥为羔，以上为**阿比新提**，为贡入项中她的晦月的níĝ-dab$_5$供奉，于27日，自**尹塔埃阿**，被支出，<u>**经由南那马巴书吏**</u>。神美基吞勒庆典月，<u>乌尔王神舒辛建了名为穆瑞可提宁德阿摩利城墙之年</u>，24只羊。

续表

时间和摘要	文献内容	英文翻译	中文翻译
ŠS 6 xi/14: **ba-zi** 3 fat flocks for**scrifice of Inanna**, in palace, **Nanna-igidu** cup-bearer as deputy in midnight, 10 fat flocks for Izin-Dagan, 3 fat rams for Kurbilak, 10 fat flocks for Abu-Du, 5 fat rams for Ibiq-reu, 5 fat rams for Iuša, via Urluh envoy, Arad-mu as royal deputy, 10 fat flocks for **Abi-simti**, **Turam-Dagan** as deputy on dusk, [fr. **Aba-Enlil-gin**, withdrawn, in **Nippur**, via Lu-Nin-šubur scribe	[1+] máš-niga-3-kam-ús, 1 udu-niga-4-kam-ús, 1 ^{f}ašgar-niga-4-kam-ús, **siskúr-^{d}Inanna** šà ~ é-gal, **<u>dNanna-igi-du sagi maškim</u>**, **á-gi$_6$-ba-a**, 5 udu-niga-gud-e-ús-sa, 5 máš-gal-niga-gud-e -ús-sa, ***I-zi-in-^{d}Da-gan***, 3 udu-niga-gud-e-ús-sa, ***Kur-bi-la-ak***, *lú Eb-la^{ki}-me-éš*, 5 *udu-niga-gud-e-ús-sa*, 5 *máš-gal -niga-gud-e-ús-sa*, **A-bu-DU$_{10}$** lú Ma-rí^{ki}, 5 udu-niga-gud-e-ús-sa, ***I-bi-iq-re-e-ú*** *mar-tu* ***Ì-a-ma-ti-um***, **uru-ne-ne-šè du-ni**, **má-a ba-ne-gub**, 3 udu-niga-gud-e-ús-sa, 2 máš-gal-niga-gud-e-ús-sa, ***Ì-ù-ša*** *dumu Me-gu$_4$-* [*x*] *LÚ.SU*, gìr **Ur-luh** sukkal, **<u>Arád-mu maškim</u>**, 2 udu-niga-sig$_5$-ús, 8 udu-niga-3-kam-ús, ***A-bí-sí-im-ti***, ***<u>Tu-ra-am-^{d}Da-gan</u>*****<u>maškim</u>**, **á-ud**! **-te-na**, ud-14-kam, [ki~ **A**] **-ba-^{d}En-líl-gin$_7$**--ta, [ba] -zi, [šà] ~ Nibru^{ki}, <u>gìr</u> **<u>Lú-^{d}Nin-šubur</u>** <u>dub-sar</u>. iti-**ezem-^{d}Šu-^{d}Suen**, mu ^{d}Šu-^{d}Suen lugal Urim$_5$^{ki}-ma--ke$_4$ na-rú-a mah, ^{d}En-líl [^{d}] Nin-líl-ra [mu] -ne-dù (Amorites 21 (pl. 10), P100986)	[1+] fattened kid of 3rd class, 1 fattened ram of 4th class, 1 fattened female kid of 4th class, for **scrifice of Inanna**, in palace, **<u>Nanna-igidu cup-bearer as royal deputy in midnight</u>**, 5 fattened rams of after-ox-class and 5 fattened he-goats of after-ox-class for Izin-Dagan, 3 fattened rams of after-ox-class for Kurbilak, the man of Ebla, 5 fattened rams of after-ox-class and 5 fattened he-goats of after-ox-class for Abu-du, the man of Mari, 5 fattened rams of after-ox-class for Ibiq-reu, the Amorite, when Iyamatium went to the cities and placed in the boat, 3 fattened rams of after-ox-class and 2 fattened he-goats of after-ox-class for the son of Megu- [x], Iuša, via Urluh envoy, Arad-mu as royal deputy, 2 better fattened rams, 8 fattened rams of 3rd class, these for **Abi-simti**, **<u>Turam-Dagan as royal deputy ondusk</u>**, on the 14th day, [from the place of **Aba-Enlil-gin**, were withdrawn, in **Nippur**, **<u>via Lu-Nin-šubur scribe</u>**. Month of ezem-Šu-Sin, Year of the divine Šu-Sin, king of Ur, built a magnificent stele for Enlil and Ninlil.	【1+】育肥三等公崽、1只育肥四等公绵羊和1只育肥四等雌崽为**伊南那于宫殿的祭祀**，**<u>南那伊吉杜司酒督办于午夜</u>**，5育肥牛后级公绵羊和5育肥牛后级公山羊为**伊珍达干**，3育肥牛后级公绵羊为**库尔比拉可**，埃卜拉城之人，5育肥牛后级公绵羊和5育肥牛后级公山羊为**阿布杜**，马瑞城之人，5育肥牛后级公绵羊为**阿摩利人伊比可瑞乌**，当伊亚马提温走向城市时，放于船上，3育肥牛后级公绵羊和2育肥牛后级公山羊为美古-【x】之子：**伊乌沙**，**<u>经由乌尔卢赫国使，阿腊德穆督办</u>**，2只较好育肥公绵羊和8只育肥三等公绵羊为**阿比新提**，**<u>图冉达干督办</u>**，于黄昏时，于14日，【自】**阿巴恩里勒艮处**，被支出，于**尼普尔**，**<u>经由卢宁舒布尔书吏</u>**。舒辛庆典月，乌尔王舒辛为神恩里勒和宁里勒建造丰碑之年。

续表

时间和摘要	文献内容	英文翻译	中文翻译
ŠS 7 v/1: **ba-zi** 1 x, 1+ [x] ram and 1 lamb for**Abi-simti**, on the 1st day, from **Inta-ea** were withdrawn, **via Nanna-maba**scribe	1 x- [x], 1+ [x] udu [x], 1 sila$_4$, ***A-bí-sí-im***!- [***ti***], *ud-1-kam*, *ki*~ **In-ta-è-a**--ta, ba-zi, gìr d**Nanna-ma**!**-ba**dub-sar. iti-ki-siki-d Nin-a-zu, mu dŠu-d Suen lugal Urim$_5$ki-ma-- [ke$_4$] ma-da Za-ab-ša- [li]ki mu- [hul], (left) 6 udu. (UCP 9-2-2 085, P136089)	1 x, 1+ [x] ram and 1 lamb for**Abi-simti**, on the 1st day, from the place of **Inta-ea** were withdrawn, **via Nanna-maba**scribe. Month of ki-siki-Ninazu, Year of the divineŠu-Sin, king of Ur, destroyed the land of Zabšali, (sum:) 6 rams.	1x, 1+【x】公绵羊和1羔为**阿比新提**，于1日，自**尹塔埃**阿处被支出，**经由南那马巴书吏**。神宁阿朱羊毛作坊月， 乌尔王神舒辛毁灭扎卜沙里国之年， （总计：）6只羊。
ŠS 7 vi/8: **ba-zi** 1 kid of gazelle for**Abi-simti**, **Šu-S.** knight as deputy, 4 flocks for **U-amar-bašu**, **Nanna-kam envoy as deputy**, fr. **Ur-kununna** withdr., **via Lušalim**	1 amar-maš-dà-nita, ***A-bí-sí-im-ti***, d***Šu***-d***Suen-na-ra-am***-d***En-líl*** **rá-gaba maškim**, 2 udu-ú, 2 máš-gal-ú, **Ù-amar-ba-šu** nar, d**Nanna-ka-msukkal maškim**, ud-8-kam, ki ~ **Ur-kù-un-na**--ta, ba-zi, gìr***Awīl-ša-lim***dub-sar. *iti-ezem*-d *Nin-a-zu*, *mu* d*Šu*-d *Suen lugal Urim$_5$*ki-*ma--ke$_4$ ma-da Za-ab-ša-li*ki *mu-hul*, (*left*) 4 *udu*, 1 *maš-dà*. (*BIN* 3 342, *P*106148)	1 *kid of gazelle for***Abi-simti**, **Šu-Sin-naram-Enlil, knight as royal deputy**, 2 grass rams and 2 grass he-goats for **U-amar-bašu musician**, **Nanna-kam envoy as royal deputy**, on the 8th day, from **Ur-kununna** were withdrawn, **via Lušalim scribe**.Month of ezem-Ninazu, Year of the divine Šu-Sin, king of Ur, destroyed the land of Zabšali, (sum:) 4 rams and 1 gazelle.	1只瞪羚公崽为**阿比新提**，**舒辛那冉恩里勒骑使督办**，2只食草公绵羊和2只食草公山羊为**乌阿马尔巴舒乐师**，**南那刊国使督办**，于8日，自**乌尔库依那**处被支出，**经由卢沙林书吏**。神宁阿朱庆典月，乌尔王神舒辛毁灭扎卜沙里国之年，（总计：）4只羊和1只瞪羚。
ŠS 7 vi/14: **ba-zi** 5 fat flocks for**Nusku, Atu cup-bearer as royal deputy**, 1 fattened ram of 4th class, 1 fattened ram for **Ama-razu**, **via Abi-simti**, **Sin-abušu cup-bearer as deputy**, 1 lamb for Angle of king, **Kaspuša cup-bearer as deputy**, from **Šuli-ili** withdrawn	2 udu-niga-4-kam-ús, 3 udu-niga, uzu-a-bala, d **Nusku**, ***A-tu*****sagi maškim**, 1 udu-niga-4-kam-ús, 1 udu-niga, d **Ama-ra-zu**, gìr ***A-bí-sí-im-ti***, d***Suen-a-bu-šu*****sagi maškim**, 1 sila$_4$ d Lamma-lugal, šà gištukul zabar-dab$_5$, ***Kàs-pu-ša***sagi, **á-gi$_6$-ba-a**maškim, ud-14-kam, ki ~ d ***Šul-gi-ì-lí***--*ta ba-zi. iti-ezem*-d *Nin-a-zu*, *mu* d *Šu*-d *Suen lugal Urim$_5$*ki*-ma--ke$_4$ ma-da Za-ab-ša-li*ki*mu-hul*, 8. (*AUCT* 3 099, *P*103324) (*seal:*) d*Šu*-d*Suen*, *lugal-kalag-ga*, *lugal Urim$_5$*ki*-ma*, *lugal an-ub-da limmú-ba*, *Ur*-d *Šul-pa-è*, *dub-sar*, *dumu Ur*-d *Ha-iàarád-zu*. (*AUCT* 1 479, *P*103324)	2 *fattened rams of 4th class and 3 fattened ram as boiled meat*, *these for* **Nusku**, **Atu cup-bearer as royal deputy**, 1 fattened ram of 4th class, 1 fattened ram for **Ama-razu**, **via Abi-simti**, Sin-abušu cup-bearer as royal deputy, 1 lamb for the Angel of king on bronze weapon, **Kaspuša, cup-bearer of dark as royal deputy**, on the 14th day, from the place of **Šuli-ili** were withdrawn.Month of ezem-Ninazu, Year of the divine Šu-Sin, king of Ur, destroyed the land of Zabšali. (seal:) Šu-Sin, the strong king, king of Ur, king of four-quarter, Ur-Šul-pae scribe, son of Ur-Haya was your servant.	2育肥四等公绵羊和3育肥公绵羊为水煮肉，以上为**努斯库**，**阿图司酒督办**，1肥四等公绵羊和1肥公绵羊为**阿马腊朱**，**经由阿比新提**，**辛阿布舒司酒督办**，1羔为**国王的保护神于青铜武器之上**，**卡斯普沙傍晚司酒督办**，于14日，自**舒勒吉伊里**处被支出。神宁阿朱庆典月，乌尔王神舒辛毁灭扎卜沙里国之年。 （印章：）（印章：）舒辛，强大之王、乌尔之王、四方之王，乌尔哈亚之子乌尔舒勒帕埃书吏是你的仆人。

续表

时间和摘要	文献内容	英文翻译	中文翻译
ŠS 7 vii/4: **ba-zi** 1 fattened ram for**Nin-kununna**, **via Abi-simti**, **Sin-abušu as royal deputy**, n the 4th day, from **Aba-Enlilgin** was withdrawn, in **Ur**	1 udu-niga, ^{d}**Nin-kù-nun-na**, gìr ***A-bí-sí-im-ti***, ^{d}***Suen-a-bu-šu*** **maškim**, ud-4-kam, ki ~ **A-ba-^{d}En-líl-gin$_7$**--ta ba-zi, šà ~ **Urim$_5$^{ki}**-ma. iti-á-ki-ti, mu ^{d}Šu-^{d}Suen lugal Urim$_5$^{ki}-ma--ke$_4$ ma-da Za-ab-ša-li^{ki} mu-hul. (seal:) ^{d}Šu-^{d}Suen, lugal-kal-ga, lugal Urim$_5$^{ki}-ma, lugal an-ub-da limmú-ba, ^{d}Suen-a-[bu-šu], sagi, arád-da-ni--ir, in-na-ba. (PDT 1 610, P126026)	1 fattened ram for**Nin-kununna**, **via Abi-simti**, **Sin-abušu as royal deputy**, on the 4th day, from **Aba-Enlilgin** was withdrawn, in **Ur**. Month of akiti, Year of the divine Šu-Sin, king of Ur, destroyed the land of Zabšali. (seal:) Šu-Sin, the strong king, king of Ur, king of four-quarter presented to Sin-a [bušu] cup-bearer, his servant (this seal).	1只育肥公绵羊为**宁库依那**，**经由阿比新提**，**辛阿布舒督办**，于4日，自**阿巴恩里勒艮**处被支出，于乌尔。阿基提月，乌尔王神舒辛毁灭扎卜沙里国之年。 （印章：）舒辛，强大之王、乌尔之王、四方之王赠予了辛阿【布舒】司酒，他的仆人（该印章）。
ŠS 7 vii/14: **ba-zi** 1 kid of gazelle for **Abi-simti**, **Ninlil-amamu as royal deputy**, fr. **Inta-ea** withdr., via **Nanna-maba**	1 amar-maš-dà-nitá, ***A-bí-sí-im-ti***, ^{d}**Nin-líl-ama-mu**maškim, ud-14-kam, ki ~ **In-ta-è-a**--ta, ba-zi, gìr ^{d}**Nanna-ma-ba** dub-sar. iti-á-ki-ti, mu ^{d}Šu-^{d}Suen lugal Urim$_5$^{ki}-ma-ke$_4$ ma-da Za-ab-ša-li^{ki} mu-hul, 1 maš-dà. (Nisaba 08 076, P200513)	1 kid of gazelle for **Abi-simti**, **Ninlil-amamu as royal deputy**, on the 14th day, from the place of **Inta-ea**, was withdrawn, via **Nanna-mabascribe**. Month of akiti, Year of the divine Šu-Sin, king of Ur, destroyed the land of Zabšali, (sum:) 1 gazelle.	1只瞪羚公崽为**阿比新提**，**宁里勒阿马穆督办**，于14日，自**尹塔埃阿**处被支出，**经由南那马巴书吏**。阿基提月，乌尔王神舒辛毁灭扎卜沙里国之年，（总计：）1只瞪羚。
ŠS 7 vii/18: **ba-zi** 1 lamb for**Dagan**, 1 fattened ram for **Haburitum**, via **Abi-simti**, **Sin-abušu** cup-bearer as royal deputy, fr. **Puzur-Enlil** were withdrawn	1 sila$_4$, ^{d}**Da-gan**, 1 udu-niga ^{d}***Ha-bu-rí-tum***, gìr ***A-bí-sí-im-ti***, ^{d}***Suen-a-bu-šu*** **sagi maškim**, ud-18-kam, ki ~ **Puzur$_4$-^{d}En-líl**--ta, ba-zi. iti-á-ki-ti, mu ^{d}Šu-^{d} Suen lugal Urim$_5$^{ki}-ma--ke$_4$ ma-da Za-ab-ša-li^{ki} mu-hul. (seal:) ^{d}Šu-^{d}Suenlugal-kal-gal, lugal Urim$_5$^{ki}-ma, lugal an-ub-da limmú-ba, [...], arád-da-ni--[ir] in-na-[ba]. (CST 440, P107955)	1 lamb for**Dagan**, 1 fattened ram for **Haburitum**, via **Abi-simti**, **Sin-abušu** cup-bearer as royal deputy, on the 18th day, from the place of **Puzur-Enlil** were withdrawn. Month of akiti, Year of the divine Šu-Sin, king of Ur, destroyed the land of Zabšali. (seal:) Šu-Sin, the strong king, king of Ur, king of four-quarter presented to x, his servant (this seal).	1只羔为**达干**，1只育肥公绵羊为**哈布瑞吞神**，**经由阿比新提**，**辛阿布舒司酒督办**，于18日，自**普朱尔恩里勒**处被支出。阿基提月，乌尔王神舒辛毁灭扎卜沙里国之年。 印章：舒辛，强大之王、乌尔之王、四方之王赠予了X，他的仆人（该印章）。

续表

时间和摘要	文献内容	英文翻译	中文翻译
ŠS 7 ix/9: **ba-zi** 5 fat rams for**Haršitum**, **Abi-simti as royal deputy**, 5 fat rams for **Eštar-tukulti**, 1 fat ram for **Gablulu**, **Arad-mu as deputy**, for ? fr. **Puzur-Enlil** withdr., via **Erréšum**administrator	5 udu-niga-gud-e-ús-sa, ***Ha-ar-ši-tum***, ***A-bí-sí-im-ti*maškim**, 5 udu-niga-gud-e-ús-sa, **Eš$_4$-tár-tu-kúl-ti** um-me-da Gemé-^{d}En-líl-lá dumu lugal, 1 udu-niga ***Ga-ab-lu-lu*** *lú Zi-da-ah*$^!$*-re*^{ki}, **Arád-mu** maškim, á-gi$_6$-ba-a, ud-9-kam, ki~ **Puzur$_4$-^{d}En-líl**-ta, ba-zi, gìr ***Èr-re-šum****šár-ra-ab-du*. *iti-ezem-*^{d} *Šu-*^{d} *Suen*, *mu* ^{d}*Šu-*^{d} *Suen lugal Urim*$_5$^{ki}*-ma--ke*$_4$ *ma-da Za-ab-ša-li*^{ki} *mu-hul*, (*left*) [1] 1 *udu*. (*ASJ* 03 092 2, *P*102021)	5 *fattened rams of after-ox-class for***Haršitum**, **Abi-simti as royal deputy**, 5 fattened rams of after-ox-class for **Eštar-tukulti**, the wet-nurse of Geme-Enlilla, the son of king, 1 fattened ram for **Gablulu**, the man of Zidahre, **Arad-mu as royal deputy**, for (the sacrifice of) dawn, on the 9th day, from the place of **Puzur-Enlil** were withdrawn, **via Errešum administrator**. Month of ezem-Šu-Sin, Year of the divineŠu-Sin, king of Ur, destroyed the land of Zabšali, (sum:) 11 rams.	5只牛后级育肥公绵羊为**哈尔西吞**，**阿比新提督办**，5只牛后级育肥公绵羊为**埃什塔尔图库勒提**——国王之子吉美恩里拉的奶妈，1只育肥公绵羊为孜达赫瑞城之人旮卜鲁鲁，**阿腊德穆督办**，为"黎明"祭，于9日，自**普朱尔恩里勒**处被支出，**经由埃瑞顺行政官**。舒辛庆典月，乌尔王神舒辛毁灭扎卜沙里国之年，（总计：）11只公绵羊。
ŠS 7 x/6: **ba-zi** 16 rams for**Abi-simti**, 10 for **Kubatum**, for chamber, **Lukuzu as deputy**, in **Ur**, fr. **Ur-kununna** withdr., **via Lušalim scribe**	16 udu-ú, ***A-bí-sí-im-ti***, 10 *udu-ú*, ***Ku-ba-tum***, *igi-kár ki-pàr--šè*, **Lú-kù-zu maškim**, šà~ Urim$_5$^{ki}-ma, ud-6-kam, ki~ **Ur-kù-nun-na**--ta ba-zi, **gìr Lú-ša-lim dub-sar**. iti-ezem-mah, mu ^{d}Šu-^{d}Suen lugal Urim$_5$^{ki}-ma--ke$_4$ ma-da Za-ab-ša-li^{ki} mu-hul, 20 udu. (PDT 1 431, P125847)	16 grass rams for**Abi-simti**, 10 grass rams for **Kubatum**, for the provisions of place of chamber, **Lukuzu as royal deputy**, in **Ur**, on the 6th day, from the place of **Ur-kununna** were withdrawn, via Lušalim scribe. Month of ezem-mah, Year of the divine Šu-Sin, king of Ur, destroyed the land of Zabšali, (sum:) 20 rams.	16食草公绵羊为**阿比新提**，10食草公绵羊为**库巴吞**，为寝宫的供奉，**卢库朱督办**，于**乌尔**，于6日，自**乌尔库依那**处被支出，**经由卢沙林书吏**。大庆典月，乌尔王神舒辛毁灭扎卜沙里国之年，（总计：）20只羊。
ŠS 8 ii/26: **ba-zi** 7 fat flocks, 12 lambs and 1 kid of gazelle for**Abi-simti**, for the requisitions of her dark moon, via**Ninlil-amamu**knight, from **Inta-ea** withdrawn, **via Nanna-maba scribe**	1 udu-niga, 3 gukkal-niga, 3 udu-a-lum-niga, 12 sila$_4$, 1 amar-maš-dà-nitá, ***A-bí-sí-im-ti***, **níĝ-dab$_5$ ud nú-a-ka-ni**, **gìr ^{d}Nin-líl-ama-mu rá-gaba**, ud-26-kam, ki~ **In-ta-è-a**--ta, ba-i, **gìr ^{d}Nanna-ma-ba dub-sar**. ba-zi, gìr ^{d}Nanna-ma-ba dub-sar. iti-maš-dà~ gu$_7$, [mu ^{d}] Šu-^{d}Suen [lugal] Urim$_5$^{ki}-ma--ke$_4$, [má] -gur$_8$ mah ^{d}En-líl ^{d}Nin-líl-ra mu-ne-dím, (left) [19 udu], 1 maš-dà. (YOS 18 020, P142414)	1 fattened ram, 3 fattened big-tailed sheep, 3 fattened aslum rams, 12 lambs and 1 kid of gazelle for**Abi-simti**, for the níĝ-dab$_5$ of her dark moon, via**Ninlil-amamu**knight, on the 26th day, from the place of **Inta-ea** were withdrawn, **via Nanna-maba scribe**. Month of mašda~gu$_7$, Year of the divine Šu-Sin, king of Ur, made a magnificent boat for Enlil and Ninlil, (sum:) [19 rams] and 1 gazelle.	1只育肥公绵羊、3只育肥肥尾绵羊、3只育肥 aslum 公绵羊、12只羔和1只瞪羚公崽为**阿比新提**，为她的晦月的 níĝ-dab$_5$供奉，经由**宁里勒阿马穆骑使**，于26日，自**尹塔埃阿**处被支出，**经由南那马巴书吏**。食瞪羚月，乌尔王神舒辛为神恩里勒和神宁里勒建造了巨船之年，（总计：）【19只羊】和1只瞪羚。

续表

时间和摘要	文献内容	英文翻译	中文翻译
ŠS 9 iii/25: **ba-zi, butchered** 1 fat ram for**Nin-tinugga**, 5 for **Sin-abušu**, 12 fat flocks for **Girsu**, 3 fat for **Abi-simti**, were withdr., 1 **butchered** fat ram fr. temple in sacrifice, **via Nur-Eštar**	1 udu-niga^{d} **Nin-tin-ug$_5$-ga**, **níĝ-dab$_5$ a-tu$_5$-a lugal**, 5 udu-niga ^{d}***Suen-a-bu-šu***, 12 *udu-máš-niga-hi-a*, *Gír-su^{ki}--šè*, 3 *udu-niga* ***A-bí-sí-im-ti***, *mu-túm ud-nú-a-ka-ni*, *zi-ga-àm*, 1 *udu-niga-4-kam-ús ba-ús*, *é siskúr-ra--ta*, **gìr*Nu-úr-Eš$_4$-tár***, *é--ta è-a*, *sila--ta ku$_4$-ra*, *ud-25-kam. iti-ze$_x$-da ~ gu$_7$*, *mu é-^{d}Šará ba-dù.* (*AUCT* 2 170, *P*103988)	1 *fattened ram for***Nin-tinugga**, for the níĝ-dab$_5$ lustration rite of king, 5 fattened rams for **Sin-abušu**, 12 fattened sheep for **Girsu**, 3 fattened rams for **Abi-simti**, these deliveries for her Dark Moon were withdrawn, 1 **butchered** fattened ram of 4th class from the temple in sacrifice, **via Nur-Eštar**, from the temple brought to the street, on the 25th day. Month of zeda ~ gu$_7$, the temple of Šara was built.	1 肥公绵羊为**宁廷乌旮**，为国王的洁净仪式的 níĝ-dab$_5$ 供奉，5 肥公绵羊为**辛阿布舒**，12 肥羊为**吉尔苏**，3 只育肥公绵羊为**阿比新提**，以上为她的晦月祭支出，1 宰杀的育肥四等公绵羊自祭祀中的神庙，**经由努尔埃什塔尔**，自神庙带到街道，于 25 日。食豚月，沙腊的神庙被建之年。
ŠS 9 v/3: **ba-zi** 5 fat rams for**Enlil**, 1 fat fr. Aba-Enlilgen for symbol of Enlil, in temple of Enlil, 5 fat rams for **Ninlil**, **Atu cup-bearer as deputy**, 3 fat rams for **Sîn**, 1 fat ram, …, 1 fat ram for x, 1 fat ram for **Dam-galnunna**, in palace, when king entered into Nippur, 1 fat ram for **Nin-tinug [ga]**, 1 fat for **Nin-egal**, 2 fat rams for **Nanna**, via**Abi-simti**, **Sin-abušu**cup-bearer as royal deputy, in **Puzuriš-Dagan**, 4 fat rams to kitchen, for generals, from **Puzur-Enlil** were withdrawn	2 udu-niga, 3 udu-niga-gud-e-ús-sa ^{d}**En-líl**, 1 udu-niga-gud-e-ús-sa, ^{d} **Gu-za** ^{d}**En-líl-lá**, 1 udu-niga-gud-e-ús-sa, ^{d} A-ba-^{d} En-líl-gen$_7$ šu-nir ^{d}**En-líl**, šà ~ é-^{d}En-líl-lá, 2 udu-niga, 3 udu-niga-gud-e-ús-sa, ^{d} **Nin-líl**, udu-gi$_6$-kam, **A-tu sagi maškim**, 1 udu-niga-sig$_5$-ús, 2 udu-niga 2-kam-ús, ^{d}**Suen**, 1 udu-niga [...], ^{d}Nin- [...], 1 [...], ^{d} [...], 1 [...], ^{d}Nin- [...], siskúr ki ~ [^{d}] EN. [...], 1 udu-niga x x, 1 udu-niga ^{d}**Dam-gal-nun-na**, šà ~ é-gal lugal ku$_4$-ra, šà ~ Nibru^{ki}, 1 udu-niga ^{d}**Nin-tin-ug$_5$-[ga]**, 1 udu-niga gud-e-ús-sa ^{d}**Nin-é-gal**, 1 udu-niga-sig$_5$-ús, 1 udu-niga-2-kam-ús, ^{d} **Nanna**, gìr ***A-bí-sí-im-ti***, ^{d}***Suen-a-bu-šu* sagi maškim**, šà ~ ***Puzur$_4$-iš-^{d} Da-gan^{ki}***, 4 *udu-niga-gud-e-ús-sa*, *é muhaldim mu ~ šakkan$_6$-ne--šè*, ^{d} **Nanna-kam sukkal maškim**, á-gi$_6$-ba-a ud-3-kam, ki ~ **Puzur$_4$-^{d} En-líl**--ta ba-zi. iti-ki-siki-^{d}Nin-a-zu, mu^{d}Šu-^{d}Suen lugal Urim$_5$^{ki}-ma--ke$_4$ é ^{d}Šará Umma^{ki}-ka mu-dù, (left) 28. (MVN 13 098, P116870)	2 fattened rams and 3 fattened rams of after-ox-class for**Enlil**, 1 fattened ram of afer-ox-class for the **throne of Enlil**, 1 fattened ram of after-ox-class from Aba-Enlilgen, for the symbol of Enlil, in the temple of Enlil, 2 fattened rams and 3 fattened rams of afer-ox-class for **Ninlil**, these were black rams, **Atu cup-bearer as royal deputy**, 1 better fattened ram and 2 fattened rams of 2nd class for **Sîn**, 1 fattened ram, [···] for Nin-[···], 1 [x] for [X], 1 [x] for [X], for the sacrifice, 1 fattened ram for x, 1 fattened ram for **Dam-galnunna**, in palace, when the king entered into Nippur, 1 fattened ram for **Nin-tinug [ga]**, 1 fattened ram of after-ox-class for **Nin-egal**, 1 better fattened ram and 1 fattened ram of 2nd class for **Nanna**, **via Abi-simti**, **Sin-abušu cup-bearer as royal deputy**, in **Puzuriš-Dagan**, 4 fattened rams of after-ox-class to the kitchen, for the generals, **Nanna-kam envoy as royal deputy**, for (the sacrifice of) dawn, on the 3rd day, from the place of **Puzur-Enlil** were withdrawn. Month of ki-siki-Ninazu, Year of the divine Šu-Sin, king of Ur, built the temple of Šara of Umma, (sum:) 28.	2 只育肥公绵羊和 3 只牛后级育肥公绵羊为**恩里勒**，1 牛后级育肥公绵羊为**恩里勒的王座**，1 牛后育肥公绵羊自阿巴恩里勒艮为恩里勒的标志，于**恩里勒庙**，2 育肥公绵羊和 3 牛后级育肥公绵羊为**宁里勒**，以上为黑羊，**阿图司酒督办**，1 次优育肥公绵羊和 2 二等育肥公绵羊为**辛神**，1 育肥公绵羊为【……】……1 育肥公绵羊为 X，1 育肥公绵羊为**旦旮勒侬那**，于宫殿，当国王进入尼普尔时，1 育肥公绵羊为**宁廷乌【旮】**，1 牛后级育肥公绵羊为**宁埃旮勒**，1 次优育肥公绵羊和 1 二等育肥公绵羊为**南那**，**经由阿比新提**，**辛阿布舒司酒督办**，于普兹瑞什达干，4 只牛后级育肥公绵羊到厨房，为将军们，**南那刊国使督办**，为"黎明"（祭），于 3 日，自**普朱尔恩里勒**处被支出。神宁阿朱羊毛作坊月，乌尔王神舒辛建成温马的沙腊神庙之年，（总计：）28。

续表

时间和摘要	文献内容	英文翻译	中文翻译
ŠS 9 vi/15: **ba-zi** 1 fat bull for**Dagan**, 1 fat for **Išhara**, via **Abi-simti, Sin-abuni (as deputy)**, in Puzuriš-Dagan, fr. **Puzur-[Enlil]** withdrwan	1 gud-niga ^{d}**Da-gan**, 1 gud-niga ^{d}**Iš-ha-ra**, gìr ***A-bí-si-im-ti***, ^{d}*Suen-a-bu-ni sagi(maškim)*, šà **Puzur$_4$-iš-^{d} Da-gan**, á-gi$_6$-ba-a, ud-15-kam, ki ~ **Puzur$_4$-^{d} [En-líl]** ba-zi. iti-ezem-^{d} Nin-a-zu, mu^{d}Šu-^{d}Suen lugal Urim^{ki}-ma--ke$_4$ é ^{d}Šará Um-ma^{ki}-ka mu-dù, (ed.) 2 gud. (SAT 3 1871, P145071)	1 fattened bull for**Dagan**, 1 fattened bull for **Išhara**, via **Abi-simti, Sin-abuni cup-bearer (as royal deputy)**, in **Puzuriš-Dagan**, in dark, on the 15th day, from **Puzur-[Enlil]** were withdrawn. Month of ezem-Ninazu, Year of the divineŠu-Sin, king of Ur, built the temple of Šara of Umma, (sum:) 2 bulls.	1 头育肥公牛为**达干**，1 头育肥公牛为**伊什哈腊**，**经由阿比新提，辛阿布尼司酒**（督办），于**普兹瑞什达干**，在傍晚时，于 15 日，**自普朱尔恩里勒**支出了。神宁阿朱庆典月，乌尔王神舒辛建成温马的沙腊神庙之年，（总计）2 头公牛。
ŠS 9 x: **ba-zi** 20 rams for **temple of Enlil**, 17 rams for **temple of Ninlil**, these for **sacrifice of throne**, 56 flocks were eliminated to kitchen, **Arad-mu as deputy, in Nippur**, 103 flocks for **temple of Inanna** for **sacrifice of throne**, 10 rams were eliminated to kitchen, **Lugal-magurre as deputy**, 15 rams for **Inanna**, **via Abi-simti, Sin-abušu as deputy**, …, fr. **Ur-kununna** withdr., via **Nur-Sin**	20 udu-ú-alan-didli, **šà ~ é-^{d} En-líl-lá**, 17 udu-ú-alan-didli, **šà ~ é-^{d} Nin-líl-lá**, uzu-a-bal, siskúr-gu-la, lugal ku$_4$-ra, 1 áb-ú, 20 udu-ú, 17 u$_8$-ú, 18 máš-gal-ú, šu-gíd é-mu-haldim, lugal Urim$_5$^{ki}--šè du-ni má-a ba-a-gar, **Arád-mu maškim**, šà ~ Nibru^{ki}, 1 gud, 92 udu, ud-1-kam, 10 udu-ú-alan-didli, **šà ~ é-^{d} Inanna**, uzu-a-bal, **siskúr-gu-la**, lugal ku$_4$-ra, šà ~ Unug^{ki}-ga, 10 udu-ú, šu-gíd é-mu-haldim, mu ~ **lú šuku-ra-ke$_4$-ne**--šè, **Lugal-má-gur$_8$-re maškim**, šà ~ Unug^{ki}-ga, 10 udu, ud-28-kam, 5 udu-ú ^{d}Inanna, gìr ***A-bí-sí-im-ti***, ^{d}***Suen-a-bu-šu****sagi maškim*, …, …, *ki* ~ **Ur-kù-nun-na**--ta, ba-zi, gìr ***Nu-úr-^{d} Suen*** *dub-sar.iti-ezem-mah*, *mu ^{d}Šu-^{d}Suen lugal Urim$_5$^{ki}-ma--ke$_4$*, *é ^{d}Šará Umma^{ki}-ka*, *mu-dù*. (*AnOr* 07 108, *P*101403)	20 *various grass rams for* **the temple of Enlil**, 17 various grass rams for **the temple of Ninlil**, these were boiled meat for **sacrifice of throne**, when the king entered, 1 grass cow, 20 grass rams, 17 grass ewes and 18 grass goats were eliminated to the kitchen, when the king went to Ur, placed in the boat, **Arad-mu as royal deputy, in Nippur**, 1 bull, 92 rams on the 1st day, 10 various grass rams for the **temple of Inanna**, these were boiled meat, for **sacrifice of throne**, when the king entered into Uruk, 10 grass rams were eliminated to the kitchen, for the man's food allocation, **Lugal-magurre as royal deputy**, 10 rams on the 28th day, 5 grass rams for **Inanna**, **via Abi-simti, Sin-abušu cup-bearer as royal deputy**, total: 7 grass bulls, …, from the place of **Ur-kununn**a were withdrawn, **via Nur-Sin scribe**. Month of ezem-mah, Year of the divine Šu-Sin, king of Ur, built the temple of Šara of Umma.	20 各种食草公绵羊为**恩里勒庙**，17 各种食草公绵羊为**宁里勒庙**，以上水煮肉为**王座的祭祀**，于国王进入时，1 食草母牛、20 食草公绵羊、17 食草母绵羊和 18 食草公山羊为淘汰级到厨房，当国王走向乌尔时，放于船上，**阿腊德穆督办，于尼普尔**，1 公牛、92 公绵羊第 1 日，10 各种食草公绵羊为**伊南那庙**，以上为水煮肉，为**王座的祭祀**，于国王进入乌鲁克时，10 食草公绵羊为淘汰级到厨房，为人的食物份额，**卢旮勒马古瑞督办**，10 公绵羊于 28 日，5 食草公绵羊为**伊南那**，**经由阿比新提，辛阿布舒司酒督办**，计：7 食草公牛……自**乌尔库依那**处被支出，**经由努尔辛书吏**。大庆典月，乌尔王神舒辛建成温马的沙腊神庙之年。

续表

时间和摘要	文献内容	英文翻译	中文翻译
ŠS 9 xii/17: **ba-zi** 3 fat rams for**Allatum**, 3 fat rams to EN. DÍM. GIG, these for libation place of **Abi-simti**, **via Nanna-kam**, in **Ur**, fr. **Šulgi-ili** withdr., **via Lu-Nanna**	3 udu-niga-4-kam-ús, **níĝ-dab$_5$ *^{d} Al-la-tum***, 3 *udu-niga-4-kam-ús*, *EN. DÍM. GIG^{ki}-šè*, **ki-a-nag *A-bí-sí-im-ti***, **gìr dNanna-kam šu-i**, šà Urim$_5$^{ki}-ma, ud-17-kam, ki ~^{d} ***Šul-gi-ì-lí--ta*** *ba-zi*, **gìr Lú-dNanna šár-ra-ab-du**. iti-ezem-^{d}Me-ki-ĝál, mu^{d}Šu-^{d}Suen lugal Urim$_5$^{ki}-ma--ke$_4$ é ^{d}Šará Um-ma^{ki}-ka mu-dù, (left) 6 udu. (ASJ 03 092 3, P102022)	3 fattened rams of 4th class for the níĝ-dab$_5$ offering of **Allatum**, 3 fattened rams of 4th class to EN. DÍM. GIG, these for the libation place of **Abi-simti**, **via Nanna-kam barber**, in **Ur**, on the 17th day, from the place of **Šulgi-ili** were withdrawn, **via Lu-Nanna administrator**. Month of ezem-Mekiĝal, Year of the divine Šu-Sin, king of Ur, built the temple of Šara of Umma, (sum:) 6 rams.	3只育肥四等公绵羊为**阿拉吞的níĝ-dab$_5$供奉**，3只育肥四等公绵羊到EN. DÍM. GIG，以上为**阿比新提的"饮水地"**，**经由南那刊理发师**，于乌尔，于17日，自**舒勒吉伊里**处被支出，**经由卢南那行政官**。神美基旮勒庆典月，乌尔王神舒辛建成温马的沙腊神庙之年，（总计：）6羊
? vi/13: **ba-zi** …, 1 lamb for **Nanna**, via **Abi-simti**, 1 fat ram for **Nin-sun**, **Enlil-zišagal** as deputy, …, fr. **Inim-Nanna** withdr., via Erre-šum	…, 1 sila$_4$-ga **^{d}Nanna ki siskúr**--ra, gìr ***A-bí-sí-im-ti***, 1 *udu-niga* **^{d}Nin-sún**, **^{d} En-líl-zi-šà-gál maškim**, …, iti-ud-13 ba-zal, **Inim-^{d} Nanna**--ta ba-zi, [gìr] ***Èr-re-šum****šár-* [*ra-ab-du*]. [*iti-ki-siki*]?-^{d} [*Nin-a-zu*]? [*mu*…], 26 *udu*. (*ASJ* 04 140 01, *P*102164)	…, 1 *suckling lamb for* **Nanna** in the place of sacrifice, via **Abi-simti**, 1 fattened ram for **Nin-sun**, **Enlil-zišagal** as royal deputy, …, when the 13th day passed, from **Inim-Nanna** were withdrawn, via Erre-šum administrator. [Month of ki-siki-Ninazu], [Year of…], (sum:) 26 rams.	……1只吃奶羔为**祭祀地的那南**，**经由阿比新提**，1育肥公绵羊为**宁荪**，**恩里勒孜沙旮勒督办**……，于13日过去时，自**伊尼姆南那**被支出，经由**埃瑞顺**行政官。【神宁阿朱庆典月】，【……年】，（总计：）26只羊。
? **ba-zi** 1 fat ram for x, **via Sin-abušu** cup-bearer, 1 fat ram for **Abi-simti**, …	…, 1 udu-niga, x x, gìr ***^{d}Suen-a-bu-šu*sagi**, 1 udu-niga-sig$_5$, ***A-bí-sí-im-ti***, …, (*AR RIM* 01 23 *H* 36*c*, *P*101758)	…, 1 *fattened ram for x*, **via Sin-abušu cup-bearer**, 1 best fattened ram for **Abi-simti**, …, from the place of x were withdrawn, via …, (sum:) 55.	……，1肥公羊为x，**经由辛阿布舒司酒**，1优等肥公羊为**阿比新提**，……自x处被支出，经由……（总计：）55.

续表

时间和摘要	文献内容	英文翻译	中文翻译
? xi/16: **ba-zi** 4 + kids of gazelle for**Abi-simti**, 5 for **Kubatum**, **Amur-ilum as deputy**, 32 flocks for soldiers, **Arad-mu as deputy**, fr. **Ur-kunnuna**, via **Nur-Sin**	[3?] amar-maš-dà-nitá, 3 + amar-maš-dà-munus, ***A-bí-sí-im-ti***, 3 *amar-maš-dà-nitá*, 2 *amar-maš-dà-munus*, ***Ku-ba-tum***, ***A-mur-ilum*rá-gaba maškim**, 26 udu-ú, 6 máš-gal-ú, é-muhaldim, mu **agà-ús-e-ne--šè**, **Arád-mu maškim**, iti-16-kam, ki ~ **Ur-kù-nun-na--ta**, [gìr] **Nu-úr-d [Suen]**. [iti] -ezem-An-[na], [mu] d[...] (left) 22 + udu, 18 maš-dà. (AUCT 1 399, P103244)	[1+] kid of gazelle and 3+ female kids of gazelle for**Abi-simti**, 3 kids of gazelle and 2 female kids of gazelle for **Kubatum**, **Amur-ilum knight as royal deputy**, 26 grass rams and 6 grass he-goats to the kitchen, for the soldiers, **Arad-mu as royal deputy**, on the 16th day, from the place of **Ur-kunnuna**, via **Nur-Sin**. [Month] of ezem-An [na], [Year] of […], (sum:) 22+ ramsand 18 gazelles.	【1+】瞪羚公崽和3+瞪羚雌崽为**阿比新提**，3只瞪羚公崽和2只瞪羚雌崽为**库巴吞**，**阿穆尔伊隆骑使督办**，26只食草公绵羊和6只食草公山羊到**厨房**，**为士兵们**，**阿腊德穆督办**，于16日，自**乌尔库依那**处（被支出），经由**努尔辛**。安神庆典【月】，【……年】，（总计:）22+只公绵羊和18只瞪羚羊。
?: **ba-zi** …, 2 fat rams and 1 lamb for Nanna, in orchard, **Sin-abušu cup-bearer as royal deputy**, when **Abi-simti**, ? [1 +] fat big-tailed ram for Iškur, [1 +] ram for Enki, withdr. fr.X	…, 2 udu-niga-sig5-ús, 1 sila4 **dNanna** šàgiš ki-ri6, [d] ***Suen-a-bu-šu*sagi maškim**, [ud?] [*A*] ***-bí-sí-im-ti* túg-šu-gur-ra ì-in-íl-lá-a**, [1 +] udu-gukkal-dù-niga **dIškur**, [1+] udu **dEn-ki** [ki~ ba-zi]. (seal:) dŠu-dSuen, lugal-kal-ga, lugal Urim5ki-ma, lugal an-ub-da limmú-ba, Ur-dŠul-pa-è, dub-sar, dumu Ur-dHa-ià, [arád-zu]. (Ripon 1, P145557)	…, 2 better fattened rams and 1 lamb for Nanna, in the orchard, **Sin-abušu, cup-bearer as royal deputy**, [when] Abi-simti wears turban, [1+] fattened big-tailed ram for Iškur, [1+] ram for Enki, [were withdrwn from X]. (seal:) Šu-Sin, the strong king, king of Ur, king of four-quarter, Ur-Šulpae scribe, son of Ur-Haya was your servant.	……2只较好育肥公绵羊和1只羔为**南那**，于**椰枣园**中，**辛阿布舒司酒督办**，于阿比新提戴上头巾时，【1+】育肥肥尾公绵羊为**伊什库尔**，【1+】公绵羊为**恩基**，【从X处被支出】。 （印章:）舒辛，强大之王、乌尔王、四方之王，乌尔哈亚之子乌尔舒勒帕埃书吏是你的仆人。

续表

时间和摘要	文献内容	英文翻译	中文翻译
? /29: **ba-zi** […], [3+] fat flocks for **Nanna**, 2 fat rams for **Big Tower**, 1 fat for **Ningal**, 2 fat and 2 breast lambs for **Nin-sun**, 2+ fat for **Nin-gublaga**, [2+] fat, [1+] lamb, […], 2 fat flocks for **Nanna**, 2 fat for **Abzu**, 3 fat flocks, in the courtyard, for **Nanna**, 1 fat ram for **Big Tower**, 1 fat for **Ningal**, 1 fat for **Nungal**, 2 fat for **Nin-kunnunna**, 1 fat for throne of **Ur-Namma**, 2 fat, 3 breast flocks for **Gula**, 1 fattened ram of after-ox-class for **Allatum**, 1 fattened he-goat of 4th class, these for New Moon, via **Abi-simti**, **Nur-Utu** as deputy, 24 flocks, in Ur, fr.**Puzur-Enlil** withdr.	[…], [1 gud] -niga-3- [kam-ús], [1] udu-niga-sig$_5$-ús, [x] GIŠ ^{d}**Nanna**, [1] udu-niga-sig$_5$-ús, 1 udu-niga, **Dub-lá-mah**, 1 udu-niga-gud-e-ús-sa, ^{d}**Nin-gal**, 1 udu-niga, 1 udu-niga-gud-e-ús-sa, 2 sila$_4$-gaba ^{d}**Nin-sún**, 1 + udu-niga-3-kam-ús, 1+ udu-niga-gud-e-ús-sa, ^{d}**Nin-gublaga**, [1+] udu-niga-3-kam-ús, [1+] udu-niga, [1+] sila$_4$, […] ud-23-kam, 1 udu-niga-sig$_5$-ús, [1+] máš-gal-niga-sig$_5$-ús, níg-dab$_5$ šáh-zé-da ^{d}**Nanna**, 1 udu-a-lum-niga-sig$_5$-ús, 1 udu-a-lum-niga-sig$_5$-ús!, **Abzu**--šè, 1 gud-niga-3-kam-ús, 1 udu-niga-sig$_5$-ús, 1 u$_8$-niga-sig$_5$-ús, šà ~ kisal!-lá, ^{d}**Nanna**, 1 udu-niga, **Dub-lá-mah**, 1 gukkal-niga-sig$_5$-ús, ^{d}**Nin-gal**, 1 udu-niga-gud-e-ús-sa, ^{d} **Nun-gal**, 1 máš-gal-niga, 1 udu-niga-gud-e-ús-sa, ^{d} **Nin-kù-nun-na**, 1 máš-gal-niga, ki^{giš}**gu-za Ur-**^{d}**Namma**, 1 udu-niga-3-kam-ús, 1 udu-niga-gud-e-ús-sa, 2 sila$_4$-gaba, 1 máš-gaba, ^{d}**Gu-la**, 1 udu-niga-gud-e-ús-sa, ^{d}***Al-la-tum***, 1 *máš-gal-niga-4-kam-ús*, […] *-x-tum*, […] [*èš*] *-èš* **é-ud-sakar--šè**, gìr ***A-bí-sí-im-ti***, ***Nu-úr-***^{d}***Šamaš*****rá-gaba maškim**, 1 gud, 23 udu, ud-29-kam, šà **Urim$_5$**^{ki}-ma, ki ~ **Puzur$_4$-**^{d} **En-líl**--*ta*, *ba-*[*zi*] […] (*MVN* 13 550, *P*117323)	[…], [1] *fattened* [*bull of* 3rd *class*], [1] *better fattened ram*, [1+] *for* **Nanna**, [1] better fattened ram and 1 fattened ram for **Big Tower**, 1 better fattened ram for**Ningal**, 1 fattened ram, 1 better fattened ram and 2 breast male lambs for **Ninsun**, 1+ better fattened ram and 1+ better fattened ram for**Nin-gublaga**, [1+] fattened ram of 3rd class, [1+] fattened ram, [1+] lamb, […], on the 23rd day, 1 better fattened ram and [1+] better fattened he-goat for pig-níg-dab$_5$ offering of **Nanna**, 1 better fattened aslum ram, 1 better fattened aslum ram for **Abzu**, 1 fattened bull of 3rd class, 1 better fattened ram and 1 better fattened ewe, in the courtyard, for **Nanna**, 1 fattened ram for **Big Tower**, 1 better fattened fat-tailed sheep for **Ningal**, 1 fattened ram of after-ox-class for **Nungal**, 1 fattened he-goat and 1 fattenen ram of after-ox-class for **Nin-kunnunna**, 1 fattened he-goat for the place of throne of**Ur-Namma**, 1 fattened ram of 3rd class, 1 fattened ram of after-ox-class, 2 breast male lambs and 1 breast male kid for **Gula**, 1 fattened ram of after-ox-class for**Allatum**, 1 fattened he-goat of 4th class, these for New Moon,…, via**Abi-simti**, **Nur-Utu** knight as royal deputy, 1 bull and 23 rams on the 29th day, in **Ur**, from the place of **Puzur-Enlil** were withdrawn, …	【……】,【1】育肥【三等】公牛、【1】次优育肥公绵羊、【1+】为**南那**,【1】次优育肥公绵羊和1育肥公绵羊为**大门楼**, 1次优育肥公绵羊为**宁旮勒**, 1育肥公绵羊、1次优育肥公绵羊和2胸前雄羔为**宁苏**, 1+次优育肥公绵羊和1+次优育肥公绵羊为**宁古卜拉旮**,【1+】育肥三等公绵羊,【1+】育肥公绵羊、【1+】羔,【……】,于23日, 1次优育肥公绵羊和【1+】次优育肥公山羊为**南那的 níg-dab$_5$ 猪供奉**, 1次优育肥 aslum 公绵羊和1次优育肥 aslum 公绵羊为**阿卜朱**, 1育肥三等公牛、1次优育肥公绵羊和1次优育肥母绵羊,于庭院中,为**南那**, 1育肥公绵羊为**大门楼**, 1次优育肥肥尾绵羊为**宁旮勒**, 1育肥牛后级公绵羊为**侬旮勒**, 1育肥公山羊和1育肥牛后级公绵羊为**宁库侬那**, 1育肥公山羊为**乌尔那马的王座地**, 1育肥三等公绵羊、1育肥牛后级公绵羊、2胸前雄羔和1胸前雄崽为**古拉**, 1育肥牛后级公绵羊为**阿拉吞**, 1育肥四等公山羊,以上为新月,……,经由**阿比新提**,**努尔乌图**骑使督办, 1头公牛和23只公绵羊于29日,于乌尔,自**普朱尔恩里勒**被支出……

档案三　阿什尼乌的档案重建

时间和摘要	文献内容	英文翻译	中文翻译
Š 40 iv/1-30: **ugula: Aš-ni -ulù** **464** flocks for 1.5, 1, 1/2, 1, 1/2, 1, its barley **1332** bán for fodder of fattened rams for 30 days, **Ayakalla** fattener took over; **168** flocks for 1.5, 1, its barley **639** bán for fodder of fattened rams for 30 days, **Nalu** fattener took over; **80** pigs for 1.5, 1, 1.5, 1, 1/3, 1/3, its barley **218** bán for the fodder of thicket pigs on 30th day, **Šusamu** took over; its barley **120** bán for fodder of birds on 30th day, **Buzuya** took over; total its barley **2309** bán for fodder of fattened rams, pigs and birds, for 1 month in **Tummal**, **Ašni-ulu** as supervisor	104 udu-niga-sig$_5$- {NI}, 1.5 silà--ta, 158 udu-niga, 1 silà --ta, 136 udu, 1/2 silà--ta, 38 sila$_4$-niga, 1 silà--ta, 8 máš-gal, 1/2 silà--ta, 20 ud$_5$, 1 silà --ta, še-bi 44.2.0 gur, šà-gal~ udu-niga, ud-30-kam, **A-a-kal-la** gurušda ì-dab$_5$; 90 udu -niga, 1.5 silà--ta, 78 udu-niga, 1 silà--ta, še-bi 21.1.3 gur, šà-gal~udu-niga, ud-30-kam, **Na-lu$_5$** gurušda, ì-dab$_5$; 1 šah-giš-gi-nitá-gal, 1.5 silà, 10 šah-nitá-sa-gi$_4$-a, 1 silà--ta, 23 šah-ama-gan, 1.5 silà--ta, 17 šah-munus -gur$_4$, 1 silà--ta, 14 šah-zé-da -nitá, 1/3 silà--ta, 15 šah-zé-da-munus, 1/3 silà--ta, še-bi 7.1.2 gur, šà-gal~šah-giš - gi -kam, ud 30-kam, ***Šu-sa$_6$-mu*** *ì-dab$_5$*; 4.0.0 *še gur*, *šà-gal~ mušen -tur-tur*, *ud-30-kam*, ***Bù-zu-a*** *ì-dab$_5$*; *šu-nigín* 194 *udu-niga*, 1.5 *silà--ta*, *šu-nigín* 236 *udu-niga*, 1 *silà--ta*, *šu-nigín* 136 *udu*, 1/2 *silà --ta*, *šu-nigín* 38 *sila$_4$-niga*, 1 *silà--ta*, *šu-nigín* 8 *máš-gal*, 1/2 *silà--ta*, *šu-nigín* 20 *ud$_5$*, 1 *silà--ta*, *šu-nigín* 1 *šah-giš-gi-nitá-gal*, 1.5 *silà*, *šu-nigín* 10 *šah-nitá-sa-gi$_4$-a*, 1 *silà--ta*, *šu-nigín* 23 *šah-ama-gan*, 1.5 *silà--ta*, *šu-nigín* 17 *šah-munus-gur$_4$*, 1 *silà--ta*, *šu-nigín* 14 *šah-zé-da-nitá*, 1/3 *silà--ta*, *šu-nigín* 15 *šah-zé-da-munus*, 1/3 *silà--ta*, *šu-nigín* 4.0.0 *še gur*, *šà-gal~ mušen-tur-tur*; *šu-nigín še-bi* 76.4.5 *gur*, *šà-gal~udu-niga*, *šah ù mušen-na*; *iti-1-kam*, *šà* **Tum-ma-al**^{ki}, ugula**Aš-ni-ulù**. iti-ki-siki-^{d}Nin-a-zu, mu ús-sa é Puzur$_4$-iš-^{d}Da-gan ba-dù. (PDT 2, 1049, P126389)	104 fine fattened rams, 1.5 litres each, 158 fattened rams, 1 litre each, 136 rams, 1/2 litres each, 38 fattened lambs, 1 litre each, 8 kids, 1/2 litres each, 20 she-goats, 1 litre each: its barley **1332** bán for the fodder of fattened rams for 30 days, **Ayakalla fattener** took over; 90 fattened rams, 1.5 litres each, 78 fattened rams, 1 litre each: its barley**639** bán for the fodder of fattened rams for 30 days, **Nalu fattener** took over; 1 thicket boar, 1.5 litres, 10 ready boars, 1 litre each, 23 mother sows, 1.5 litres each, 17 thick gilts, 1 litre each, 14 he-piglets, 1/3 litre each, 15 she-piglets, 1/3 litre each: its barley**218** bán for the fodder of thicket pigs on 30th day, **Šusamu** took over; its barley 120 bán for the fodder of birds for 30th day, **Buzuya** took over; total 194 fattened rams, 1.5 litre each, total 236 fattened rams, 1 litre each, total 136 rams, 1/2 litre each, total 38 fattened lambs, 1 litre each, total 8 kids, 1/2 litre each, total 20 she-goats, 1 litre each, total 1 thicket boar, 1.5 litre, total 10 ready boars, 1 litre each, total 23 mother sows, 1.5 litre each, total 17 thick gilts, 1 litre each, total 14 he-piglets, 1/3 litre each, total 15 she-piglets, 1/3 litre each, total 120 bán of barley for fodder of birds; **total its barley 2309 bán for fodder of fattened rams, pigs and birds, for 1 month, in Tummal,** **Ašni-ulu as supervisor**. Month of ki-siki-Ninazu, Year after that of the office of Puzriš-Dagan was built.	104优等育肥公绵羊，每只1.5升，158肥公绵羊，每只1升，136公绵羊，每只1/2升，38肥羊羔，每只1升，8公山羊，每只1/2升，20母山羊，每只1升：其大麦共1332斗为肥公绵羊（和其他）30天的饲料，**阿亚卡拉育肥师接管**了；90肥公绵羊，每只1.5升，78肥公绵羊，每只1升：其大麦共639斗为育肥公绵羊30天的饲料，**那鲁育肥师接管**了；1苇塘公猪，每头1.5升，10成年公猪，每头1升，23母猪，每头1.5升，17成年母猪，每头1升，14公猪豚，每头1/3升，15母猪豚，每头1/3升，其大麦共218斗为苇塘猪30天的饲料，**舒萨穆接管**了；其大麦120斗为鸟30天的饲料，**布朱亚接管**了；总计194肥公绵羊，每只1.5升，总计236肥公绵羊，每只1升，总计136公绵羊，每只1/2升，总计38肥羊羔，每只1升，总计8雄山羊崽，每只1/2升，总计20雌山羊，每只1升，总计1苇塘公猪，每头1.5升，总计10成年公猪，每头1升，总计23母猪，每头1.5升，总计17成年母猪，每头1升，总计14公猪豚，每头1/3升，总计15母猪豚，每头1/3升，总计120升大麦为鸟的饲料。总计其大麦共2309斗为肥公绵羊、猪和鸟的1个月饲料于**图马勒**，**阿什尼乌鲁监管**。宁阿朱羊毛作坊月，普兹瑞什达干司被建年之次年。

续表

时间和摘要	文献内容	英文翻译	中文翻译
Š 40 v: **ugula Aš-ni-u$_{18}$**. 509+x flocks for 1.5, 1, 1/2, 1, 2/3, 1, 1.5, 1, 1, 1, its barley**1725.5** bán for fodder of fattened rams, for 30 days, **Akalla** fattener took over; 22+x flocks for 1.5, 1, 1/2, [⋯] its barley **801** bán for fodder of fattened rams, for 30 days, **Nalu** fattener took over; 80 pigs for 1.5, 1, 1, 1.5, 1, 1/2, 4 piglets, the barleys of which were not took over.its barley **222** bán for the fodder of the thicket boars, for 30 days, **Šusamu** took over; **120** bán of barley for the fodder of birds, **Buzuya** took over; total **2871.5** bán of barley for fodder of pigs and birds, in **Tummal**, **Ašniu** as supervisor	111 udu-niga-sig$_{5}$- {NI}, 1.5 silà-ta, 196 udu-niga, 1 silà -ta, 90 udu, 1/2 silà-ta, 33 sila$_{4}$-niga, 1 silà-ta, 61 sila$_{4}$-niga, 2/3 silà-<1>-ta, [x] u$_{8}$, [1 silà-ta, x] sila$_{4}$- nitá, **ga-bi**, [10] máš-gal, 1.5 silà-ta, [6] máš-gal, 1 silà -ta, [2] ^{f}ašgar, 1 silà-ta, [x] ud$_{5}$, 1 silà-ta, [še] -bi 57.2.3 5 silà gur, [šà] -gal~udu-niga, [ud] -30-kam, [A] **-kal-la gurušda**, ì-dab$_{5}$; x+20 udu- niga, 1.5 silà-ta, x+1 udu, 1 silà-ta, [x udu, 1/2] silà-ta, [...] -ta, še-bi 26.3. 3 gur šà-gal~udu-niga, ud-30-kam, **Na-lu$_{5}$ gurušda**, ì-dab$_{5}$; 1 šáh-giš-gi-nitá-gal, 1.5 silà, 10 šáh-nitá-sa-gi$_{4}$-a, 1 silà -ta, 3 šáh-nitá-giš, 1 silà-ta, 23 šáh-ama-gan, 1.5 silà-ta, 13 šáh-munus-gur$_{4}$, 1 silà -ta, 26 šáh-mú, 1/2 silà-ta, 4 šáh-zé-da, še nu-dab$_{5}$, še-bi 7.2.3 gur šà-gal~šáh-giš-gi- kam, ud-30-kam, ***Šu-sa$_{6}$-mu*** *ì-dab$_{5}$*; 4.0.0 *še gur šà-gal~ mušen-tur-tur*, ***Bù-zu-a*** *ì-dab$_{5}$*; *šu-nigín*111 *udu-* *niga-sig$_{5}$- {NI}*, 1.5 *silà-ta*, *šu-nigín* [196 *udu-niga*, 1 *silà-ta*], *šu-nigín* 4 *sila$_{4}$*, 1/2 [*silà-ta*], *šu-nigín* 33 *sila$_{4}$*- *niga*, 1 *silà-ta*, *šu-nigín* 61 *sila$_{4}$-niga*, 2/3 *silà-ta*, *šu-* *nigín* 10 *máš-gal*, 1.5 *silà-ta*, *šu-nigín* 6 *máš-gal*, 1 *silà-ta*, *šu-nigín* 2 ^{f}*ašgar*, 1 *silà-ta*, *šu-nigín* 20 *ud$_{5}$*, 1 *silà-ta*, *šu-nigín* 24 *šáh*, 1.5 *silà-ta*, *šu-nigín* 26 *šáh*, 1 *silà-ta*, *šu-nigín* 26 *šáh*, 1/2 *silà-ta*, *šu-nigín* 4 *šáh-zé-da še nu-dab$_{5}$*, *šu-nigín* 4.0.0 *še gur*, *šà-gal~mušen-tur-tur*, *šu-nigín še-bi* 95.3.3 5 *silà gur*, *šà-gal~udu-niga*, *šáh ù mušen-na*, *šà~* **Tum-ma-al^{ki}**, [ugula] **Aš-ni-u$_{18}$**.iti-ezem-^{d}Nin-a-zu, muš-sa é-Puzur$_{4}$-iš-^{d}Da-gan ba-dù. (MVN 15 064, P118344)	111 fine fattened rams, 1.5 litres each, 196 fattened rams, 1 litre each, 90 rams, 1/2 litres each, 33 fattened lamb, 1 litre each, 61 fattened lamb, 2/3 litre each, 1+x ewes, 1 litre each, 1+x lambs, **ga-bi?** 10 kids, 1.5 litre each, 6 kids, 1 litre each, 2 female kids, 1 litre each, 1+x she-goats, 1 litre each, its barley 1725.5 bán for the fodder of fattened rams, for 30 days, **Akalla fattener took over**; x+20 fattened rams, 1.5 litres each, x+1 rams, 1 litre each, 1+x rams, 1/2 litres each, [⋯] its barley 801 bán for the fodder of fattened rams, for 30 days, **Nalu fattener took over**; 1 thicket boar, 1.5 litre each, 10 ready boars, 1 litre each, 3 sex mature boars, 1 litre each, 23 mother sows, 1.5 litres each, 13 growing-up pigs, 1 litre each, 26 young boars, 1/2 litre each, **4 piglets**, **the barleys of which were not took over**. its barley 222 bán for the fodder of pigs, for 30 days, **Šusamu took over**; 120 bán of barley for the fodder of birds, **Buzuya took over**; total all of 111 fine fattened rams, 1.5 litre each, total 196 fattened rams, 1 litre each, total 4 lambs, 1/2 litre each, total 33 fattened lambs, 1 litre each, total 61 fattened lambs, 2/3 litre each, total 10 kids, 1.5litre each, total 6 kids, 1 litre each, total 2 female kids, 1 litre each, total 20 she-goats, 1 litre each, total 24 pigs, 1.5 litre each, total 26 pigs, 1 litre each, total 26 pigs, 1/2 litre each, **total 4 piglets**, **the barley of which were not took over**, total 120 bán barley for fodder of birds, total its barley 2871.5 bán for fodder of pigs and birds, **in Tummal**, **Ašniu as supervisor**. Month of ezem-Ninazu, Year after that of the office of Puzriš-Dagan was built.	111优等肥公绵羊，每只1.5升，196肥公绵羊，每只1升，90只公绵羊，每只1/2升，33肥羊羔，每只1升，61肥羊羔，每只2/3升，1+x母绵羊，每只1升，**1+x羊羔**？10山羊崽，每只1.5升，6山羊崽，每只1升，2雌山羊崽，每只1升，1+x母山羊，每只1升，其大麦共1725.5斗为肥公绵羊30天的饲料，**阿卡拉育肥师接管**；x+20肥公绵羊，每只1.5升，x+1只公绵羊，每只1升，1+x公绵羊，每只1/2升，【⋯⋯】其大麦共801斗大麦为育肥公绵羊30天的饲料，**那鲁育肥师接管**；1苇塘公猪，每只1.5升，10成年公猪，每头1升，3性成熟公猪，每头1升，23生育母猪，每头1.5升，13成长猪，每头1升，26年轻猪，每头1/2升，4猪崽的大麦没有**接管**，其大麦共222斗为苇塘猪30天的饲料，**舒萨穆接管**；120斗大麦为鸟的饲料，**布朱亚接管**了；总计111优等肥公绵羊，每只1.5升，总计196肥公绵羊，每只1升，总计4羔，每只1/2升，总计33肥羔，每只1升，总计61肥羔，每只2/3升，总计10山羊崽，每只1.5升，总计6山羊崽，每只1升，总计2母山羊崽，每只1升，总计20母山羊，每只1升，总计24猪，每头1 1/2升，总计26猪，每头1升，总计26猪，每头1/2升，总计4猪崽的大麦没有**接管**，总计120斗大麦为鸟的饲料，总计其大麦共2871.5斗为猪和鸟的饲料于**图马勒**，**阿什尼乌监管**。宁阿朱庆典月，普兹瑞什达干司被建年之次年。
Š 40 vii/5-7: **šu~ ba-ti**, **butchered** 5th: 1 **butchered** fat lamb, 6th: 1 ram, 7th: 1+x kids, **butchered** ones, in **Tummal**, from **Ašniu**, **Bamu** reveived	1 sila$_{4}$-niga~ba-úš, ud-5-kam, 1 udu, ud-6-kam, [1+x] [máš-gal], [ud] - [7] -kam, ba-úš, šà~ **Tum-ma-<al>**, ki **Aš-ni-** [**u$_{18}$**] -ta, **Ba-mu** [*šu*] ~ *ba-ti. iti-ezem-^{d}Šul-gi*, *mu ús-sa é-Puzur$_{4}$-iš-^{d}Da-gan ba-dù*. (*OIP* 115 138, *P*123255)	1**butchered** fattened lamb, on 5th day, 1 ram, on 6th day, 1+x kids on 7th day, ones **butchered**, **in Tummal**, **from the place of Ašniu**, **Bamu (son of AS) reveived**.Month of ezem-Šulgi, Year after that of the office of Puzriš-Dagan was built.	1宰杀肥羔于5日，1公绵羊于6日和1+x羊羔于7日，以上宰杀牲于**图马勒**，从**阿什尼乌**处，**巴穆（阿马尔辛之子）接收了**。神舒勒吉庆典月，普兹瑞什达干司被建年之次年。

续表

时间和摘要	文献内容	英文翻译	中文翻译
Š 41 i: **mu-túm, ì-dab$_5$** 1 gazelle delivery of the king, from the place of**Naram-ili**, **Ašniu** took over	1 maš-dà, mu-túm-lugal, ki ***Na-ra-am-ì-lí*--*ta***, **Aš-ni-u$_{19}$**, ì-dab$_5$. iti-maš-dà ~ gu$_7$, mu ús-sa é-Puzur$_4$-iš-^{d}Da-gan ba-dù-a mu ús-sa-bi. (BIN 3 365, P106171)	1 gazelle delivery of the king, from the place of Naram-ili, Ašniu took over. Month of mašda ~ gu7, Year after that of the office of Puzriš-Dagan was built; after that year.	1只瞪羚羊为国王的送入，从**那冉伊里处**，**阿什尼乌接管了**（于图马勒）。食瞪羚月，普兹瑞什达干司被建年之次年：之次年。
Š 41 i-iv: **šu~ ba-ti** 9716 bán of barley for fodder of flocks, pig and bird, 2496 bán for **allowance of woman who dwelled in city of An**, 48 bán of barley, 48 bán of emmer for **cultic table which in palace of city of An**, 1216 bán of barley for **slaves and children**, total 13477 bán of barley, total 48 bán of emmer, from of **Kitušlu**, **Ašniu** received	323.4.2 še [gur] ~lugal šà-gal-udu-máš-hi-a, šáh ù mušen, 83.1.0 gur, sá-dug$_4$ ~ kaš-ninda-munus uru-An-na--ka ~ tuš-a-ne, 1.3.0 še gur, 1.3.0 zíz gur, (^{giš}banšur) zà-gú-lá, é-gal uru-An-na, 40.2.4 gur še-ba gemé-dumu; šu-nigín 449.1.0 še gur, šu-nigín 1.3.0 zíz gur, ki **Ki-tuš$^!$-lú**--ta, **Aš-ni-u$_{18}$** šu ~ ba-ti, kišib **Aš-ni-u$_{18}$**, ki **Ki-tuš$^!$-lú**--ka, mu-gál-la, gaba-ri-bi. **iti-maš-dà ~ gu$_7$**--ta, **iti-ki-siki-^{d} Nin-a-zu**, iti-bi, iti 4-am$_3$, mu ús-sa é-Puzur$_4$-iš-^{d}Da-gan ba-dù, mu ús-sa-a-bi. (Princeton 1 123, P126812)	9716 royal bán of barley for the fodder of sheep and goats, pigs and birds, 2496 bán for **the monthly allowance of beer and bread of woman who dwelled in the city of An**, 48 bán of barley, 48 bán of emmer for **cultic table which in palace of the city of An**, 1216 bán of barley for **slaves and children**, total 13477 bán of barley, total 48 bán of emmer, **from the place of Kituš-lu, Ašniu received**, the receipt of Ašniu was put in the place of Kitušlu. This is its copy, from Month of mašda ~ gu$_7$ to month of ki-siki-Ninazu, its month are 4 months, Year after that of the office of Puzriš-Dagan was built; after that year.	9716王斗大麦为羊群、猪和鸟的饲料，2496斗为**住在天神安之城的女人的啤酒和面包月供**，48斗大麦和48斗红小麦为**天神安之城的宫殿的圣桌**，1216斗大麦为**女奴和孩子们**，总计13476斗大麦，总计48斗红小麦， **从基图什鲁处**， **阿什尼乌收到了**。 **阿什尼乌**的收据被置于基图什鲁处， 这是复制品， 从食瞪羚月到神宁阿朱羊毛作坊月，共4个月，普兹瑞什达干司被建年之次年：之次年。
Š 41 vii: **mu-túm, ì-dab$_5$** 73 fat rams, 4 fat lambs, 6 fat kids, 1 kid, 264 rams, 83 kids, **delivery of the king, from Naram-ili, Ašniu took**	73 udu-niga, 4 sila$_4$-niga, 6 máš-gal-niga, 1 ^{f}ašgar-niga, 264 udu, 83 máš-gal, **mu-túm-lugal**, ki ***Na-ra-am-i-lí*--*ta***, **Aš-ni-u$_{18}$** ì-dab$_5$. iti-ezem-^{d} Šul-gi, mu ús-sa é-Puzur$_4$-iš-^{d}Da-gan ba-dù-a, mu-ús-sa-bi. (Torino 1 020, P133843)	73 fattened rams, 4 fattened lambs, 6 fattened kids, 1 female kid, 264 rams, 83 kids, **were delivery of the king, from the place of Naram-ili, Ašniu took over**. Month of ezem-Šulgi, Year after that of the office of Puzriš-Dagan was built; after that year.	73只育肥公绵羊、4只育肥羊羔、6只育肥山羊崽，1只雌山羊崽，264只公绵羊，83只羊羔，**为国王的送入项**，从**那冉伊里处**，**阿什尼乌接管了**。神舒勒吉庆典月，普兹瑞什达干司被建年之次年：之次年。
Š 41 vii: **šu~ ba-ti** 58 ready birds from the place of**Ašniu**, **Ur-Ig-alim** received	58 gú gi-ru-uš, ki **Aš-ni-u$_{18}$**--ta, **Ur-^{d}Ig-alim** šu ~ ba -ti. iti-ezem-^{d}Šul-gi, mu ús-sa é-Puzur$_4$-iš-^{d}Da-gan [ba-dù], mu ús-sa- [bi]. (seal) Ur-^{d}Ig-alim dub-sar dumu Na-ba-sá. (ASJ 19 201 03, P102694)	58 piles of gi-ru-uš reed from the place of Ašniu, Ur-Ig-alim received. Month of ezem-Šulgi, Year after that of the office of Puzriš-Dagan was built; after that year. (**seal**): Ur-Ig-alim scribe, the son of Nabasa.	58堆giruš芦苇来自**阿什尼乌处**，**乌尔伊格阿林接收了**。神舒勒吉庆典月，普兹瑞什达干司被建年之次年：之次年。（印章）那巴萨之子——乌尔伊格阿林书吏。

续表

时间和摘要	文献内容	英文翻译	中文翻译
Š 41 vii/4: **šu~ ba-ti** 1 ready bird, from the place of**Ašniu**, **Ur-Ig-alim** received	1 gú gi-ru-uš, ki **Aš-ni-u$_{19}$**--ta, **Ur-^{d}Ig-alim** šu~ ba-ti.iti-ezem-^{d}Šul-gi--ta ud-4 ba-ra-zal, mu ús-sa é-Puzur$_{4}$-^{d}Da-gan ba-dù-a, mu ús-sa-bi. (seal) Ur-^{d}Ig-alim dub-sar dumu Na-ba-sá. (PDT 1 257, P125673)	1 pile of gi-ru-uš reed, **from the place of Ašniu, Ur-Ig-alim received**.from the month of ezem-Šulgi, when the 4th day passed, Year after that of the office of Puzriš-Dagan was built; after that year.Ur-Ig-alim scribe, the son of Nabasa.	1堆 giruš 芦苇来自**阿什尼乌处**，**乌尔伊格阿林接收**了。从舒勒吉庆典月的第4天过去时，普兹瑞什达干司被建年之次年：之次年。（印章）那巴萨之子——乌尔伊格阿林书吏。
Š 41 vii/30: ki**Aš-ni-u$_{18}$**, 1**butchered** lamb, in **Tummal**, from the place of **Ašniu**	1 sila$_{4}$-nitá~ba-úš, ud-30-kam, šà~ **Tum-ma-al^{ki}**, ki **Aš-ni-u$_{18}$**.iti-ezem-^{d}Šul-gi, mu ús-sa é-Puzur$_{4}$-iš-^{d}Da-gan ba-dù, mu ús-sa-bi. (Torino 1 405, P133988)	1**butchered** lamb on the 30th day, in Tummal, from the place of Ašniu. Month of ezem-Šulgi, Year after that of the office of Puzriš-Dagan was built; after that year.	1只宰杀的雄羊羔在第30天，于**图马勒**，于**阿什尼乌处**（支出），神舒勒吉庆典月，普兹瑞什达干司被建年之次年：之次年。
Š 41 ix: **šu~ ba-ti** 1145 bán of barley for the fodder of rams, from **Ašniu**, **Ur-Nintu** received	38.0.5 še gur, šà- [gal] -udu--šè, ki **Aš-ni-u$_{18}$**--ta, **Ur-^{d}Nin-tu** šu~ ba-ti.iti ezem-mah, mu ús-sa é-Puzur$_{4}$-iš-^{d}Da-gan ba-dù mu ús-sa-bi. (ASJ 07 124 22, P102200)	1145 bán of barley for the fodder of rams, **from the place of Ašniu, Ur-Nintu received**. Month of ezem-mah, Year after that of the office of Puzriš-Dagan was built; after that year.	1145斗大麦为公绵羊的饲料，来自**阿什尼乌处**，**乌尔宁图接收了**。大庆典月，普兹瑞什达干司被建年之次年：之次年。
Š 41 x: **šu~ ba-ti** 1560royal bán of barley for fodder of rams, from the place of **Ašniu**, **Ayakalla** received	52. [0.0 še gur, lugal] šà-gal~ udu- [-šè], ki **Aš-ni-u$_{18}$**-- [ta], **A-a-kal-la** *šu~ ba-ti.iti-ezem-An-na, mu ús-sa é-Puzur$_{4}$-iš-^{d}Da-* [*gan*] *mu ús-sa-bi.* (*AUCT* 1 733, *P103578*)	1560*royal bán of barley for* **fodder of rams, from the place of Ašniu, Ayakalla received**.Month of ezem-Anna, Year after that of the office of Puzriš-Dagan was built; after that year. (Umma scribe)	1560王斗大麦为公绵羊的饲料，来自**阿什尼乌处**，**阿亚卡拉接收了**。 天神庆典月， 普兹瑞什达干司被建年之次年：之次年。
Š 42: **šu~ ba-ti** 427 bundles fr. Tummal, **Ašniu**, **Lugal-šala** received, via Ur-x.	5.34.0 **sa-gi**, 1.31.20 sa gi-bíl, Tum-ma-al--ta, ki **Aš-ni-u$_{18}$**--ta, **Lugal-šà-lá** šu~ba-ti, gìr Ur- [...], iti [...], mu Ša-aš-ru-um^{ki} ba-hul. (SAT 2 0999, P144199)	334 ready bundles, 93 ready bundles, from**Tummal, from the place of Ašniu, Lugal-šala received, via Ur-x**.Month of [···], Year of Šašrum was destroyed.	334堆芦苇捆，93堆芦苇捆来自**图马勒**，**阿什尼乌处**，**鲁旮勒沙拉接收了**，经由乌尔-X，【?】月，沙什润被毁之年。
Š 42 vi: **zi-ga** 1+x [fat] rams for···**Ninlil**, withdr.fr.**Ašniu** in **Tummal**	[1+x] udu- [niga], [x] KA [x] **Nin-líl-lá**, [iti] -1-kam, [z] i-ga [šà] ~ Tum-ma-al^{ki}, [ki] **Aš-ni-u$_{18}$**. [iti] - [á] -ki-ti, [...] [Ša-aš] -ru^{ki} [ba] - [hul]. (OIP 115 140, P123636)	1+x [fattened] rams for··· **mouth of Ninlil**, for 1 month, **withdrawn from Ašniu, in Tummal**. Month of akiti, Year of Šašrum was destroyed.	1+x只【育肥】公绵羊为……**宁里勒之口**，为1个月，从**图马勒**，**阿什尼乌处**支出了。阿基提月，沙什润被毁之年。

续表

时间和摘要	文献内容	英文翻译	中文翻译
Š 42 vi/12: **zi-ga** 2 fat rams for**allowance of** […], 6 fat rams, 2 rams for **king**, 2 fat rams, 1 ram for **allowance of ki-a-naĝ of Ur-Nammu**, 1 fat ram for **monthly allowance of Nun-gal**, withdr.fr.**Tummal**, **Ašniu**	2 udu-niga, sá- [dug$_4$…], 6 udu-niga, 2 udu, **sá-dug$_4$~ lugal**, 2 udu-niga, 1 udu, **sá-dug$_4$~ki-a-naĝ Ur-^{d}Namma**--ka, 1 udu-niga, **sá-dug$_4$~ ^{d}Nun-gal**, iti--ta ud-12, ba-ra-zal, zi-ga šà~ **Tum-ma-al^{ki}**, ki**Aš-ni-u$_{18}$**.iti-á-ki-ti, mu Ša-aš-ru^{ki} ba-hul. (OIP 115 139, P123638)	2 fattened rams for**the monthly allowance of** […], 6 fattened rams and 2 rams for **the monthly allowance of king**, 2 fattened rams and 1 ram for **the monthly allowance of ki-a-naĝ of Ur-Nammu**, 1 fattened ram for **the mounthly allowance of Nungal**, when 12th day passed, were **withdrawn from Tummal**, **the place of Ašniu**. Month of akiti, Year of Šašrum was destroyed.	2只育肥公绵羊为【……】月供， 6只育肥公绵羊和2只公绵羊为**国王的月供**， 2只育肥公绵羊和1只公绵羊**乌尔那穆"饮水地"的月供**，1只育肥公绵羊为**农舍勒神**的月供， 于本月第12天过去时，从**图马勒**，**阿什尼乌**处支出了。阿基提月，沙什润被毁之年。
Š 42 vi/1: **zi-ga** 30 fat rams for allowance of Ninlil 1st day, withdr. fr. **Tummal**, **Ašniu**	30 udu-niga, sá-dug$_4$~ ^{d}Nin-líl-lá, ud-1-kam, zi-ga šà**Tum-ma-al^{ki}**, ki**Aš-ni-u$_{18}$**.iti-á-ki-ti, mu Ša-aš-ru^{ki} ba-hul. (Torino 1 196, P133905)	30 fattened rams for **the monthly allowance of Ninlil**, on the 1st day, were **withdrawn from Tummal**, **the place of Ašniu**. Month of akiti, Year of Šašrum was destroyed.	30只育肥公绵羊为**宁里勒的月供**，于本月第1天，从**图马勒**， **阿什尼乌**处支出了。 阿基提月， 沙什润被毁之年。
Š 42 viii/22: **zi-ga** 3 fat rams, 1 lamb for Enlil, 2 fat rams, 1 lamb for Nin-lil, **Nanše-adgal** as deputy, withdrawn from **Tummal**, place of **Ašniu**	3 udu-niga, 1 sila$_4$, ^{d}En-líl, 2 udu-niga, 1 sila$_4$, ^{d}Nin-líl, siskúr-gi$_6$-kam, **^{d}Nanše-ul$_4$-gal** maškim, zi-ga šà~ **Tum-ma-al^{ki}**, ki **Aš-ni-u$_{19}$**--ta, iti--ta ud-22 ba-ra-zal.iti-šu-eš-ša, mu Ša-aš-ru^{ki} ba-hul. (AUCT 1 686, P103531)	3 fattened rams, 1 lamb for **Enlil**, 2 fattened rams, 1 lamb for **Ninlil**, these for **night sacrifice**, **Nanše-ulgal as royal deputy**, were **withdrawn from Tummal**, **the place of Ašniu**, when the 22nd day passed. Month of šu-ešša, Year of Šašrum was destroyed.	3育肥公绵羊和1只羊羔为恩里勒，2只育肥公绵羊和1只羊羔为宁里勒，这些为"夜祭"，南筛乌勒台勒督办，以上从**图马勒**，**阿什尼乌**处支出了，于本月第22天过去时。三只手月，沙什润被毁之年。
Š 43 ii/17, 22: **šu~ba-ti**, **butchered** 17th: 1 ram, 22nd: 1 **butchered** ram, in **Tummal**, fr.Ašniu, Beliyarik received	1 udu, ud-17-kam, 1 udu~ ba-úš, ud-22-kam, šà~ **Tum-ma-al^{ki}**, ki **Aš-ni-u$_{18}$--ta**, ***Be-lí-a-rí-ik*** *šu~ba-ti. iti-ze$_x$* (*šeš*) *-da~gu$_7$*, *mu En-ubur-zi-an-na ^{d}Nanna maš-e ì-pàd.* (*Torino* 1 268, *P*131918)	1 *ram on* 17th *day*, 1 **butchered** ram on 22nd day, **in Tummal**, **from the place of Ašniu**, **Beliyarik received**. Month of zeda~gu$_7$, Year of En-ubur-zianna was chosen as en-priestess of Nanna by omen.	1只公绵羊于第17天，1只宰杀的公绵羊于第22天，于**图马勒**，来自**阿什尼乌**，**贝里阿瑞克接收了**。食豚月，南那的女祭司被占卜选中之年。
Š 43 ii/25-28: **šu~ba-ti**, **butchered** 1 ram on 25th, 1 ram, 1 ewe on 26th, 1 fat lamb on 27th, 1 ewe on 28th, **butchered** ones, in **Tummal**, fr.**Ašniu**, **Beliyarik** received	1 udu ud-25-kam, 1 udu, 1 u$_8$, ud-26-kam, 1 sila$_4$-nitá, ud-27-kam, 1 u$_8$, ud-30-lá-2-kam, ba-úš, šà~ **Tum-ma-al^{ki}**, ki **Aš-ni-u$_{19}$**--ta, ***Be-lí-a-rí-ik*** *šu~ba-ti. iti-ze$_x$* (*šeš*) *-da~gu$_7$*, *mu En-ubur-zi-an-na ^{d}Nanna maš-e ì-pàd.* (*MVN* 13 861, P117633)	1 *ram on the* 25th *day*, 1 *ram*, 1 *ewe on the* 26th *day*, 1 *fattened lamb on* 27th *day*, 1 *ewe on* 28th *day*, **butchered** ones, **in Tummal**, **from the place of Ašniu**, **Beliyarik received**. Month of zeda~gu$_7$, Year of En-ubur-zianna was chosen as en-priestess of Nanna by omen.	1公绵羊于第25天，1公绵羊和1母绵羊于本月第26天，1育肥羊羔于第27天，1母绵羊于第28天，以上宰杀牲于**图马勒**，自**阿什尼乌**处，**贝里阿瑞克接收了**。食豚月，南那的女祭司被占卜选中之年。

续表

时间和摘要	文献内容	英文翻译	中文翻译
Š 43 ii/30: **šu~ba-ti, butchered** 1**butchered** ram, in Tummal, from of Ašniu, Beliyarik received	1 udu~ba-úš, ud-30-kam, šà~ **Tum-ma-al^{ki}**, ki **Aš-ni-u$_{18}$**-ta, ***Be-lí-a-rí-ik*** *šu~ba-ti.iti-ze$_x$* (*šeš*) *-da~gu$_7$*, *mu En-ubur-zi-an-na en-^{d}Nanna maš-e ì-pàd.* (*RT* 37 136 *l*, *P*128407)	1**butchered** ram on the 30th day, **in Tummal, from the place of Ašniu, Beliyarik received**.Month of zeda~gu$_7$, Year of En-ubur-zianna was chosen as en-priestess of Nanna by omen.	1只宰杀的公绵羊于本月第30天，**于图马勒，来自阿什尼乌处，贝里阿瑞克接收了**。食豚月，南那的女祭司被占卜选中之年。
Š 43 iii/8: **šu~ba-ti, butchered** 1**butchered** ram on the 8th day, in Tummal, from the place of Ašniu, Beliyarik received	1 udu~ba-úš, ud-8-kam, šà~ **Tum-ma-al**, ki **Aš-ni-u$_{18}$**-ta, ***Be-lí-a-ri-ik***, *šu~ba-ti.iti-u$_5$-bí-gu$_7$*, *mu En-ubur-zi -an-na en-^{d} Nanna maš-e ì-pad$_3$.* (*RA* 09 040 *SA* 01, *P*127322)	1**butchered** ram on the 8th day, **in Tummal, from the place of Ašniu, Beliyarik received**.Month of ubi~gu$_7$, Year of En-ubur-zianna was chosen as en-priestess of Nanna by omen.	1只宰杀的公绵羊于本月第8天，**于图马勒**，来自**阿什尼乌处，贝里阿瑞克接收了**。食乌比鸟月，南那的女祭司被占卜选中之年。
Š 43 iii/10, 13, 14: **šu~ba-ti, butchered** 10th: 1 ram [⋯], 13th: 2 rams, 14th: 1 ram, **butchered** ones in **Tummal**, fr. **Ašniu**, **Beliyarik** received	1 udu [...], ud-10-kam, 2 udu, ud-13-kam, 1 udu, ud-14-kam, ba-úš, šà~ Tum-ma-al^{ki}, ki **Aš-ni-u$_{19}$**-ta, Be-lí-a-ri-ik šu~ba-ti.iti-u$_5$-bí~gu$_7$, mu En-ubur-zi-an-na en-^{d}Nanna maš-e ì-pàd. (AnOr 01 005, P100996)	1 ram [⋯], on the 10th day, 2 rams on the 13th day, 1 ram on the 14th day, **butchered** ones **in Tummal, from the place of Ašniu, Beliyarik received**. Month of ubi~gu$_7$, Year of En-ubur-zianna was chosen as en-priestess of Nanna by omen.	1公绵羊【……】于第10天，2公绵羊于第13天，1公绵羊于第14天，以上宰杀牲，**于图马勒**，**自阿什尼乌处，贝里阿瑞克接收**。食乌比鸟月，南那的女祭司被占卜选中之年。
Š 43 iv/1, 2: **šu~ba-ti, butchered** 1st: 1 ram on theday, 2nd: 1 **butchered** ram, in Tummal, fr.Ašniu, Beliyarik received	1 udu, ud-1-kam, 1 udu~ ba-úš, ud-2-kam, šà~ **Tum-ma-al^{ki}**, ki **Aš-ni-u$_{18}$**-ta, ***Be-lí-a-rí-ik*** *šu~ba-ti.iti-ki-siki-^{d}Nin-a-zu*, *mu en-^{d}Nanna maš-e ì-pàd.* (*Sumer* 24, 72 08, *P*134033)	1 *ram on the 1st day*, 1 **butchered** ram on the 2nd day, **in Tummal, from the place of Ašniu, Beliyarik received**.Month of ki-siki-Ninazu, Year of was chosen as en-priestess of Nanna by omen.	1只公绵羊于第1天，1只宰杀的公绵羊于第2天，**于图马勒，自阿什尼乌处，贝里阿瑞克接收了**。神宁阿朱羊毛作坊月，南那的女祭司被占卜选中之年。
Š 43 v/9, 10: **šu~ba-ti, butchered** 9th: 1 ram, 10th: 1 **butchered** ram, in Tummal, fr. Ašniu, Beliyarik received	1 udu, ud-9-kam, 1 udu~ ba-úš, ud-10-kam, šà~ **Tum-ma-al^{ki}**, ki **Aš-ni-u$_{18}$**-ta, ***Be-lí-a-rí-ik*** *šu~ba-ti.iti-ezem-^{d}Nin-a-zu*, *mu en-^{d}Nanna máš-e ì-pàd.* (*Nisaba* 08 190, *P*320609)	1 *ram on the 9th day*, 1 **butchered** ram on the 10th day, **in Tummal, from the place of Ašniu, Beliyarik received**.Month of ezem-Ninazu, Year of was chosen as en-priestess of Nanna by omen.	1只公绵羊于第9天，1只宰杀的公绵羊于第10天，**于图马勒，自阿什尼乌处，贝里阿瑞克接收了**。神宁阿朱庆典月，南那的女祭司被占卜选中之年。
Š 43 v/26, 28: **šu~ba-ti, butchered** 26th: 1 gazelle, 28th: 2 **butchered** rams, in **Tummal**, from the place of **Ašniu**	1 maš-dà, ud-26-kam, 2 udu~ba-úš, ud-28-kam, šà~ **Tum-ma-al**, ki **Aš-ni-u$_{19}$**.iti-ezem-^{d}Nin-a-zu, mu en-^{d}Nanna maš-e ì-pàd. (BIN 3 005, P105812)	1 gazelle on the 26th day, 2 **butchered** rams on 28th day, **in Tummal, from the place of Ašniu**.Month of ezem-Ninazu, Year of was chosen as en-priestess of Nanna by omen.	1只瞪羚羊于本月第26天，2只宰杀的公绵羊于本月第28天，**于图马勒，自阿什尼乌处**。神宁阿朱庆典月，南那的女祭司被占卜选中之年。

续表

时间和摘要	文献内容	英文翻译	中文翻译
Š 43 vi/4： **zi-ga** 2 fat rams for Inanna，in palace，**Erranada as deputy**，1 lamb as boiled meat to kitchen of state，Ur-Šulgi as deputy，withdr.fr.**Tummal**，**Ašniu**	2 udu-niga，siskúr~ ^{d}Inanna，šà é-gal，***Èr-ra-na-da*** *maškim*，1 *sila$_4$-nitá*，［...］*uzu a-b*［*ala*］，*é-uz-*［*ga*］，**Ur-dŠul-gi［maškim］**，iti--ta ud-4-ba-ra-za［1］，zi-ga šà **Tum-ma-al**，ki **Aš-ni-u$_{19}$**（URU）.iti-á-ki-ti，mu en-^{d}Nanna maš-e ì-pàd. （JCS 52 07 02，P145796）	2 fattened rams for the**sacrifice of Inanna in the palace**，**Erranada as royal deputy**，1 lamb as boiled meat for **é-uz-ga**，**Ur-Šulgi as［royal deputy］**，when the 4th day passed，withdrawn from **Tummal**，**the place of Ašniu**. Month of akiti，Year of was chosen as en-priestess of Nanna by omen.	2只育肥公绵羊为**宫中的伊南那的牺牲**，**埃腊那达督办**，1只公羊羔为水煮肉，**为御膳房**，**乌尔舒勒吉［督办］**，于本月第4天过去时，从**图马勒**，**阿什尼乌**处支出了。阿基提月，南那的女祭司被占卜选中之年。
Š 43 vi/5： **zi-ga** 5 fat rams for place of Sîn，1 fat ram for Inanna，**Erranada as deputy**，1 ewe to kitchen of state，**Ur-Šulgi as deputy**，withdr.fr.**Tummal**，place of **Ašniu**	2 udu-niga-sig$_5$-úš，3 udu-niga，ki ^{d}Suen，1 udu-niga，siskúr-^{d}Inanna，šà é-gal，***Èr-ra-na-da*** *maškim*，1 *u$_8$-sila$_4$-nú-a é-uz-ga*，**Ur-^{d}Šul-gi** maškim!，iti--ta ud-5 ba-ra-zal，zi-ga šà **Tum-ma-al**，ki **Aš-ni-u$_{18}$**.iti-á-ki-ti，mu en-^{d}Nanna maš-e ì-pàd. （MVN 15 051，P118331）	2better fattened rams，3 fattened rams，for **the place of Sîn**，1 fattened ram for **the sacrifice of Inanna in the palace**，**Erranada as deputy**，1 ewe without lamb for **é-uz-ga**，**Ur-Šulgi as royal deputy**，when the 5th day passed，withdrawn from **Tummal**，**the place of Ašniu**.Month of akiti，Year of was chosen as en-priestess of Nanna by omen.	2只次优育肥公绵羊和3只育肥公绵羊为辛之地，1只育肥公绵羊为宫中的伊南那的牺牲，**埃腊那达督办**，1只小母羊为御膳房，**乌尔舒勒吉督办**，于本月第5天过去时，从**图马勒**，**阿什尼乌**处支出了。阿基提月，南那的女祭司被占卜选中之年。
Š 43 vi/24： **šu~ba-ti**，**butchered** 1 fat kid，1 ram，**butchered** ones on，in **Tummal**，fr. **Ašniu**，**Beli-arik** received	1 máš-gal-niga，1 udu，ba-úš，ud-24-kam，šà~ Tum-ma-al，ki **Aš-ni-u$_{18}$**--ta，***Be-lí-a-ri-ik*** *šu~ba-ti.iti-á-ki-ti，mu en-^{d}Nanna maš-e ì-pàd.* （*RA* 09 040 *SA* 02，P127323）	1 *fattened kid*，1 *ram*，**butchered** ones on the 24th day，**in Tummal**，**from the place of Ašniu**，**Beli-arik received**.Month of akiti，Year of was chosen as en-priestess of Nanna by omen.	1肥山羊崽和1公绵羊为宰杀牲于第24天，在图马勒，来自**阿什尼乌**处，**贝里阿瑞克接收**了。阿基提月，南那的女祭司被占卜选中之年。
Š 43 vi： **šu~ba-ti** 60 bán of barley for king，return into this place，fr. **Ursagga**，**Ašniu** received	2.0.0 še gur，lugal，še ki-ba，si-gi$_4$，ki **Ur-sag$_9$-ga**，sipa-gud--ta，**Aš-ni-u$_{18}$**šu~ba-ti. iti á-ki-ti， mu en-^{d}Nanna máš-e ì-pàd. （AUCT 1 746，P103591）	60royal bán of barley，return into this place（Tummal?），from **Ursagga**，**the oxpherd**，**Ašniu received**.Month of akiti，Year of was chosen as en-priestess of Nanna by omen.	60王斗大麦，返还到原地（**图马勒**），从**乌尔萨旮牛牧**处，**阿什尼乌**接收了。阿基提月， 南那的女祭司被占卜选中之年。
Š 43 vi： **šu~ba-ti** 2 pounds of silver from **Šeškalla**，from the place of **Ašniu**，**Lu-diĝir**-ra received，in **Tummal**	2 ma-na kug-babbar，**Šeš-kal-la**，šu-ku$_6$-^{d}En-líl-lá，［ki］**Aš-ni-u$_{18}$**--ta，［**Lú**］-**diĝir-ra**［šu］ba-ti，［šà］Tum-ma-al^{ki}.iti á-ki-ti，mu en ^{d}Nanna maš-e ì-pàd.（AUCT 1 910，P103755）	2 pounds of silver from**Šeškalla**，the fisherman of Enlil，from the **place of Ašniu**，**Lu-diĝir-ra received**，**in Tummal**. Month of akiti，Year of was chosen as en-priestess of Nanna by omen.	2斤银来自塞什卡拉，恩里勒的渔夫， 自**阿什尼乌**处（支出），**卢迪弥腊接收**了，于**图马勒**。阿基提月，南那的女祭司被占卜选中之年。
Š 43 vii-x/15： **pisan~ dub-ba** pisan ~ dub-ba，níg-šid，ak-ka-lú-a，**Aš-ni-u$_{18}$**，［iti］-ezem ^{d}Šul-gi--ta，［iti］-ezem-An-na，ud-15-ba-［zal］--šè，iti［3］ud-15-kam	pisan~ dub-ba，níg-šid，ak-ka-lú-a，**Aš-ni-u$_{18}$**，［iti］-ezem ^{d}Šul-gi--ta，［iti］-ezem-An-na，ud-15-ba-［zal］--šè，iti［3］ud-15-kam.mu en-^{d}Nanna maš-e ì-pàd.**dub-sag-níg-gur$_{11}$--ra --ka-ni ù dub ba-úš-bi ì-sá ì-gál.**（OIP 115 141，P123368）	The basket of tablets：the account of remainder，Ašniu，from **month of ezem-Šulgi** to **month of ezem-Anna** and 15th day passed，for 3 months and 15 days.Year of was chosen as en-priestess of Nanna by omen.He compared and put his first property and the dead tablet.	档案箱：剩余的账目，**阿什尼乌**，从舒勒吉庆典月到天神庆典月的第15天，为3个月15天。南那的女祭司被占卜选中之年。他（**阿什尼乌**）比较并建立了他的财富和死的泥板。

续表

时间和摘要	文献内容	英文翻译	中文翻译
Š 44 i/12: **mu-túm** 2 lambs, 1 gazelle fr. **governor of Nippur**, 1 lamb fr. **Girni-ida** captain, 2 kids of gazelle fr. **Larabum**, 5 kids of gazelle fr. **Halliya**, 5 kids of gazelle fr. **Ašniu**, 1 lamb fr. **governor of Marda**,	2 sila$_4$, 1 amar-maš-dà, ensí-Nibru^{ki}, 1 sila$_4$, ***Gìr-ni-ì-sa$_6$***, *nu-bandà*, 2 *amar-maš-dà*, ***La-ra-bu-um*** *nu-bandà*, 5 *amar-maš-dà*, ***Hal-lí-a***, 5 *amar-maš-dà*, **Aš-ni-u$_{18}$**, 1 sila$_4$, ensí-Már-da^{ki} mu-túm. iti-maš-dà~gu$_7$, mu Si-mu-ru-um^{ki} Lu-lu-bu^{ki} a-rá 10 lá 1-kam-ma-aš ba-hul-a ud-12-kam. (SACT 1 001, P128758)	2 lambs, 1 kid of gazelle from the governor of Nippur, 1 lamb from Girni-ida captain, 2 kids of gazelle from Larabum captain, 5 kids of gazelle from Halliya, 5 kids of gazelle from Ašniu, 1 lamb from the governor of Marda, these were delivered. Month of mašda~gu$_7$, Year of Simurrum and Lulubum were destroyed for the ninth time, on the 12th day.	2只羊羔和1只瞪羚崽来自尼普尔的总督，1只羊羔来自吉尔尼伊萨军尉，2只瞪羚崽来自拉腊布姆军尉，5只瞪羚崽来自哈里亚，5只瞪羚崽来自**阿什尼乌**，1只羊羔来自马尔达的总督， 这些为送入。 食瞪羚月，席穆润和鲁鲁布第九次被毁之年，于第12天。
v/7: **šu~ba-ti, butchered** 1**butchered** ewe, in **Tummal**, fr. **Ašniu**	1 u$_8$~ba-úš, šà~ **Tum-ma-al^{ki}**, ki Aš-ni-u$_{18}$, ud-7-kam, iti-ezem-^{d}Nin-a-zu (Hirose 005, P109476)	1**butchered** ewe, in Tummal, from Ašniu, on the 7th day, Month of ezem-Ninazu.	1只宰杀的母绵羊于**图马勒**，来自**阿什尼乌**处，于本月第7天， 神宁阿朱庆典月。

档案四　贝里阿瑞克的档案重建

一　早期死牲官员贝里阿瑞克的档案重建

时间和摘要	文献内容	英文翻译	中文翻译
Š 42 xi： **šu~ba-ti，butchered** 401 corpses of bulls and sheep delivered from **Naram-ili**，**Beli-arik** cup-bearer and **Ur-niĝar** received	78 ad_6 gud，11 ad_6 amar-ga，312 ad_6 udu-máš-hi-a，ad_6 gud-udu ba-úš，ki~ ***Na -ra-am-ì-lí***--*ta*，*mu-túm*，***Be-lí-a-rí-ik*** *ù* **Ur-ni$_9$-ĝar**，šu~ ba-ab-ti.iti-ezem-Me-ki-ĝál，mu Ša-aš-ru^{ki} ba-hul. （BIN 3，611，P106418）	78 corpses of bulls，11corpses of sucking calves and 312 corpses of sheep and goats，corpses of **butchered** oxen and flocks，**from Naram-ili**，these deliveries **Beli-arik and Ur-niĝar received**.Month of ezem-Mekiĝal，Year of Šašru was destroyed.	78 头牛尸和 11 头吃奶牛犊尸和 312 只羊尸是宰杀的牛羊，从**那冉伊里**处送来了，这些送入项， **贝里阿瑞克（祭酒）和乌尔尼旮尔**收到了。 美基旮勒庆典月， 沙什如被毁之年。
Š 42 xi： **šu~ba-ti，butchered** 94 oxen，1063 flocks = 1157 corpses fr. Naram -ili delivered，**Beli-arik** and **Ur-niĝar** received.	42 ad_6 gud，39 ad_6 amar，13 ad_6 amar-ga，1063 ad_6 udu-máš-hi-a，ki~ ***Na-ra -am-ì-lí***--*ta*，*mu-túm*，***Be-lí -a-rí -ik*** *ù* **Ur-ni$_9$-ĝar**，šu ~ ba-an-ti，iti-ezem-me-ki！（igi）-ĝál，mu Ša-aš-ru^{ki} ba-hul. （TIM 6，27，P134032）	42corpses of bulls，39 corpses of calves，13 corpses of suckling calves and 1063 corpses of sheep and goats，**from Naram-ili，delivered，Beli-arik and Ur-niĝar received**.Month of ezem-Meki-ĝal，Year of Šašru was destroyed.	42 头公牛尸、39 头牛犊尸，13 头吃奶牛犊尸和 1063 只羊尸， 从**那冉伊里**处送来了， **贝里阿瑞克和乌尔宁旮尔**收到了。 神美基旮勒庆典月， 沙什如被毁之年。

续表

时间和摘要	文献内容	英文翻译	中文翻译
Š 42 xii: **šu～ba-ti, butchered** 215 corpses of oxen, 1401 corpses of flocks = 1616, from **Naram-ili** delivered, **Beli-arik cup-bearer** and **Ur-niĝar cook** received	159 ad$_6$ gud, 25 ad$_6$ amar, 31 ad$_6$ amar-ga, 1385 ad$_6$ udu-máš-hi-a, 16 ad$_6$ máš-sila$_4$ $^{hi-a}$, ki～ ***Na-ra-am-ì-lí***--*ta*, *mu-túm*, ***Be-lí-a-ri-ik*** ù **Ur-ni$_9$-ĝar**--ke$_4$ šu～ ba-an-ti-éš, iti-še-kin-kud, mu Ša-aš-ru^{ki} ba-hul. (**Seal 1**) ^{d}Šul-gi, nita-kalag-ga, lugal Urim$_5$ ^{ki}-ma, Ur-ni$_9$-ĝar, dumu Ti-ru, muhal-dim arád-zu. (**Seal 2**) ^{d}Šul-gi, nita kalag-ga, lugal Urim$_5$ ^{ki}-ma, lugal an-ub-da limmú-ba, *Be-lí-a-ri-ik*, sagi, arád-zu. (NYPL 278, P122816)	159 corpses of bulls, 25 corpses of calves, 31 corpses of suckling calves, 1385 corpses of sheep and goats, 16 corpses of kids and lambs, **from Naram-ili, delivered, Beli-arik and Ur-niĝar received**. Month of še-kin-kud, Year of Šašru was destroyed. (**Seal 1**) Šulgi, the strong man, the king of Ur, Ur-niĝar, son of Tiru, cook, was yourservant. (**Seal 2**) Šulgi, the strong man, the king of Ur, the king of four quarters, Beli-arik, the cupbearer, was yourservant.	159 头牛尸、25 头犊尸和 31 头吃奶犊尸，1385 只羊尸和 16 只羔和山羊崽尸从**那冉伊里**处送来了，**贝里阿瑞克和乌尔尼旮尔**收到了。大麦收割月，沙什如被毁灭年。 (印章 1：) 舒勒吉强大之人，乌尔之王，提如之子——**乌尔尼旮尔厨师**是你的仆人。 (印章 2：) 舒勒吉强大之人，乌尔之王，四方之王，**司酒贝里阿瑞克**是你的仆人。
Š 42 xii: **šu～ba-ti, butchered** 10**butchered** bulls to store-room, **Beli-arik** received, fr. **Enlilla**	10 gud～ ba-úš, é-kišib -ba--šè, ***Be-lí-a-rí-ik*** *šu～ ba-ti*, *zi-ga* ^{d}**En-líl-lá**. iti-še-kin-kud, mu Ša-aš-ru^{ki} ba-hul. (NYPL 256, P122794)	10**butchered** bulls to the storehouse, **Beli-arik received**, were**withdrawn from Enlilla**. Month of še-kin-kud, Year of Šašrum was destroyed.	10 只宰杀的公牛为仓库， **贝里阿瑞克收到了**， 从**恩里拉**支出了。 大麦收割月， 沙什润被毁之年。
Š 43 ii/17, 22: **šu～ba-ti, butchered** 1 ram on 17th, 1 **butchered** ram on 22nd, in **Tummal**, from **Ašniu**, **Beli-arik** received	1 udu, **ud-17**-kam, 1 udu～ ba-úš **ud-22**-kam, šà～ Tum-ma-al^{ki}, ki～ Aš-ni-u$_{18}$--ta, ***Be-lí-a-rí-ik*** *šu～ ba-ti.iti-ze$_x$-da～gu$_7$*, *mu En-ubur -zi-an-na ^{d}Nanna maš-e ì-pàd.* (*Torino* 1 268, *P*131918)	1 *ram on the 17th day*, 1 **butchered** ram on the 22nd day, **in Tummal, from the place of Ašniu, Beli-arik received**. Month of zeda～gu$_7$, Year of En-ubur-zianna was chosen as en-priestess of Nann by omen.	1 只公绵羊本月第 17 天，1 只**宰杀的公绵羊**于本月第 22 天，于**图马勒**， 自**阿什尼乌**处，**贝里阿瑞克**接收了。食豚月， 南那的女祭祀被占卜选中之年。

续表

时间和摘要	文献内容	英文翻译	中文翻译
Š 43 ii/25-28: **šu～ba-ti, butchered** 1 ram on 25th, 1 ram, 1 ewe on 26th, 1 fat lamb on 27th, 1 ewe on 28th, **butchered** ones in **Tummal**, fr.**Ašniu**, **Beli-arik** received	1 udu ud-25-kam, 1 udu, 1 u$_8$, ud-26-kam, 1 sila$_4$-nitá, ud-27-kam, 1 u$_8$, ud-28-kam, ba-úš, šà～ **Tum-ma -al^{ki}**, ki **Aš-ni-u$_{19}$**--ta, ***Be-lí -a-rí-ik*** *šu～ ba-ti. iti-ze$_x$-da～gu$_7$, mu En-ubur-zi-an-na ^{d}Nanna maš-e ì-pàd.* (*MVN* 13 861, *P*117633)	1 *ram on the* 25th *day*, 1 *ram*, 1 *ewe on the* 26th *day*, 1 *fattened lamb on* 27th *day*, 1 *ewe on* 28th *day*, **butchered** ones, **in Tummal, from the place of Ašniu, Beli-arik received**. Month of zeda～gu$_7$, Year of En-ubur-zianna was chosen as en-priestess of Nanna by o-men.	1只公绵羊于本月第25天，1只公绵羊和1只母绵羊于本月第26天，1只育肥羊羔于第27天，1只母绵羊于第28天，为**宰杀牲**，于**图马勒**，来**自阿什尼乌**处，**贝里阿瑞克接收了**。食豚月，南那的女祭司被占卜选中之年。
Š 43 ii/30: **šu～ba-ti, butchered** 1**butchered** ram, in **Tummal**, from place of **Ašniu**, **Beli-arik** re-ceived	1 udu～ ba-úš, ud-30-kam, šà～ **Tum-ma-al^{ki}**, ki **Aš-ni -u$_{18}$**--ta, ***Be-lí-a-rí-ik*** *šu～ ba-ti. iti-ze$_x$-da～gu$_7$, mu En-ubur-zi-an-na en-^{d} Nan-na* maš-e ì-pàd. (RT 37 136 1, P128407)	1**butchered** ram on the 30th day, **in Tummal, from place of Ašniu, Beli-arik received**. Month of zeda～gu$_7$, Year of En-ubur-zianna was chosen as en-priestess of Nanna by omen.	1只**宰杀的公绵羊**于本月第30天，于**图马勒**，来**自阿什尼乌处**，**贝里阿瑞克**接收了。 食豚月，南那的女祭司被占卜选中之年。
Š 43 iii/8: **šu～ba-ti, butchered** 1**butchered** ram, in **Tummal**, from the place of **Ašniu**, **Beli-arik** received	1 udu～ ba-úš, ud-8-kam, šà～ **Tum-ma-al**, ki **Aš-ni -u$_{18}$**--ta, ***Be-lí-a-ri-ik***, *šu～ ba-ti. iti-u$_5$-bí-gu$_7$, mu En-ubur-zi-an-na en-^{d} Nanna maš-e ì-pad$_3$.* (*RA* 09 040 *SA* 01, *P*127322)	1**butchered** ram on the 8th day, in Tummal, **from the place of Ašniu, Beli-arik received**. Month of ubi～gu$_7$, Year of En-ubur-zianna was chosen as en-priestess of Nanna by omen.	1只宰杀的公绵羊于本月第8天，于**图马勒**，来自**阿什尼乌处**，**贝里阿瑞克**接收了。食乌比乌月，南那的女祭司被占卜选中之年。
Š 43 iii/10, 13, 14: **šu～ba-ti, butchered** 1 ram, on 10th, 2 rams on 13th, 1 ram on 14th, **butchered** ones in **Tummal**, fr. **Ašniu**, **Beli-arik** received	1 udu [...], ud-10-kam, 2 udu, ud-13-kam, 1 udu, ud -14-kam, ba-úš, šà～ Tum -ma-al^{ki}, ki **Aš-ni-u$_{19}$**--ta, ***Be-lí-a-ri-ik*** *šu～ ba-ti. iti-u$_5$-bí～gu$_7$, mu En-ubur-zi-an-na en-^{d}Nanna maš-e ì-pàd.* (*AnOr* 01 005, *P*100996)	1 *ram* [⋯], *on the* 10th *day*, 2 *rams on the* 13th *day*, 1 *ram on the* 14th *day*, **butchered** ones in Tummal, **from the place of Ašniu, Beli-arik received**. Month of ubi～gu$_7$, Year of En-ubur-zi-anna was chosen as en-priestess of Nanna by omen.	1只公绵羊【……】于第10天，2只公绵羊于本月第13天，1只公绵羊于本月第14天，以上宰杀牲，于**图马勒**，自**阿什尼乌处**，**贝里阿瑞克**接收了。食乌比乌月，南那的女祭司被占卜选中之年。

续表

时间和摘要	文献内容	英文翻译	中文翻译
Š 43 iv/1，2： **šu~ba-ti，butchered** 1 ram on 1st，1 **butchered** ram on 2nd，in Tummal，fr. place of **Ašniu**，**Beli-arik** received	1 udu，ud-1-kam，1 udu~ ba-úš，ud-2-kam，šà~ **Tum-ma-al**^{ki}，ki **Aš-ni-u$_{18}$** --ta，***Be-lí-a-rí-ik*** *šu~ ba-ti. iti-ki-siki-^{d} Nin-a-zu，mu en-^{d} Nanna maš-e ì-pàd.* （*Sumer* 24，72 08，*P*134033）	1 *ram on the 1st day*，1 **butchered** ram on the 2nd day，**in Tummal，from the place of Ašniu，Beli-arik received**. Month of ki-siki-Ninazu，Year of en-priestess of Nanna was chosen by omen.	1只公绵羊于本月第1天，1只宰杀的公绵羊于本月第2天，于**图马勒**，自**阿什尼乌**处，**贝里阿瑞克**接收了。神宁阿朱羊毛作坊月，南那的女祭司被占卜选中之年。
Š 43 v/9，10： **šu~ba-ti，butchered** 1 ram on 9th，1 **butchered** ram on 10th，in **Tummal**，from **Ašniu**，**Beli-arik** received	1 udu，ud-9-kam，1 udu ~ ba-úš，ud-10-kam，šà ~ **Tum-ma-al**^{ki}，ki **Aš-ni-u$_{18}$** --ta，***Be-lí-a-rí-ik*** *šu~ ba-ti. iti-ezem-^{d} Nin-a-zu，mu en-^{d} Nanna máš-e ì-pàd.*（*Nisaba* 08 190，*P*320609）	1 *ram on the 9th day*，1 **butchered** ram on the 10th day，**in Tummal，from the place of Ašniu，Beli-arik received.** Month of ezem-Ninazu，Year of en-priestess of Nanna was chosen by omen.	1只公绵羊于本月第9天，1只宰杀的公绵羊于本月第10天，于**图马勒**，自**阿什尼乌处**，**贝里阿瑞克**接收了。神宁阿朱庆典月，南那的女祭司被占卜选中之年。
Š 43 v/12： **mu-túm** 1 gazelle for palace，fr. Ku-u，1 fat lamb for Utu，fr. governor of N. 1 kid for Enlil，fr. brother of Dada，1 lamb for N.，fr. Ur-n.，1 lamb for palace，fr. Ur-Enlil，Zabardab as deputy，2 **butchered** for storeroom，70 flocks for soldiers，**Beli-arik** as deputy	1 maš-dà，**šà~ é-gal**--šè，mu-túm Ku-ù， 1 sila$_{4}$-niga $^{\mathbf{d}}$**Utu**，mu-túm ensí-Nibru^{ki}， 1 ^{f}ašgar-niga $^{\mathbf{d}}$**En-líl**， mu-túm šeš-Da-da sanga， 1 sila$_{4}$ $^{\mathbf{d}}$ **Nin-gá-gi$_{4}$ -a**，mu-túm Ur-ni$_{9}$-gar ka-guru$_{7}$，1 sila$_{4}$ **é-gal-mah**， mu-túm Ur-^{d}En-líl -lá，Zabar-dab$_{5}$ maškim， 1 udu，1 u$_{8}$，ba-úš，é-kišib-ba --šè，3 udu，26 u$_{8}$，6 máš，35 ud$_{5}$，**é-muhaldim mu agà-ús-e-ne**--šè， *Be-lí-a-rí-ik*maškim，ud-12-kam，zi-ga. ［iti-ezem］-^{d} Nin-a-zu，mu en-^{d} Nanna maš-e ì-pàd. （OIP 115 222，P123370）	1 gazelle for the palace，delivered by Ku-u，1 fattened lamb for Utu，delivered by the governor of Nippur，1 female kid for Enlil，delivered by the brother of Dada，the official，1 lamb for Nin-gagia，delivered by Urnigar，the granary supervisor，1 lamb for the great palace，delivered by Ur-Enlil，**Zabar-dab as royal deputy**，1 ram，1 ewe，**butchered** ones for the storehouse，3 rams，26 ewes，6 he-goats，35 goats to the kitchen for the soldiers，**Beli-arik as royal deputy**，on the 12th day，these were withdrawn. Month of ezem-Ninazu，Year of en-priestess of Nanna was chosen by omen.	1只瞪羚为**宫殿** 库乌送入， 1只育肥羔为**乌图**，尼普尔的总督送入， 1只雌山羊崽为**恩里勒**，官员达达之兄送入， 1只羊羔为**宁旮吉阿**，仓库监管乌尔尼旮尔送入，1只羊羔为**大宫殿**，乌尔恩里勒送入， **执青铜官督办**， 1只公绵羊、1只母绵羊，以上宰杀牲为仓库，3只公绵羊、26只母绵羊、6只公山羊和35只山羊到厨房为士兵们， **贝里阿瑞克督办**， 以上为支出。神宁阿朱庆典月，南那的女祭司被占卜选中之年。

续表

时间和摘要	文献内容	英文翻译	中文翻译
Š 43 v: **šu~ba-ti, butchered** 1 cow, 6 sheep, **butchered** ones fr. **Nasa**, **Beli-arik**, **Urnigar** received	1áb ~ mu-1, 4 u_8, 1 udu, 1 ud_5, ba-úš ki **Na-sa$_6$**, ***Be-lí-a-rí-ik*** *ù* **Ur-ni$_9$-gar** šu ~ ba-ti. iti-ezem-^{d} Nin -a-zu, mu en ^{d}Nanna maš-e ì-pàd. (OIP 115 296, P123629)	1 cow of one-year old, 4 ewes, 1 ram, 1 goat, **butchered** ones **from Nasa, Beli-arik and Urnigar received**. Month of ezem-Ninazu, Year of en-priestess of Nanna was chosen by omen.	1头1岁母牛、4只母绵羊、1只公绵羊和1只山羊，为宰杀牲时从**那萨处，贝里阿瑞克和乌尔尼旮尔接收了**。神宁阿朱庆典月，南那女祭司被占卜选中年。
Š 43 vi/24: **šu~ba-ti, butchered** 1 fat goat, 1 ram, **butchered** ones, in **Tummal**, from **Ašniu**, **Beli-arik** received	1 máš-gal-niga, 1 udu, ba-úš, ud-24-kam, šà ~ Tum-ma-al, ki **Aš-ni-u$_{18}$** --ta, ***Be-lí-a-ri-ik*** *šu ~ ba-ti. iti-á-ki-ti, mu en-^{d} Nanna maš-e ì-pàd.* (*RA* 09 040 *SA* 02, *P*127323)	1 *fattened goat and* 1 *ram*, **butchered** ones on the 24th day, in Tummal, **from the place of Ašniu, Beli-arik received**. Month of akiti, Year of was chosen as en-priestess of Nanna by omen.	1只育肥山羊和1只公绵羊为宰杀牲于本月第24天，在**图马勒**，来**自阿什尼乌**处，**贝里阿瑞克**接收了。阿基提月，南那的女祭司被占卜选中之年。

二 苏萨的总督贝里阿瑞克的档案重建

时间和摘要	文献内容	英文翻译	中文翻译
Š 43 v/12: …, 2 butchered sheep **to storeroom**, 70 flocks to **kitchen for soldiers**, **Beli-arik as deputy**, were withdrawn	…, 1 udu, 1 u_8, ba-úš, é-kišib-ba--šè, 3 udu, 26 u_8, 6 máš, 35 ud_5, é-muhaldim mu ~ agà-ús-e-ne--šè, ***Be-lí-a-rí-ik*** *maškim*, *ud-12-kam*, *zi-ga*…, (*OIP* 115 222, *P*123370)	…, 1 *ram and* 1 *ewe were butchered* **to the storeroom**, 3 rams, 26 ewes, 6 kids and 35 goats to **the kitchen for soldiers**, **Beli-arik as royal deputy**, on 12th day, were withdrawn, …	……1公绵羊和1母绵羊为**宰杀牲到仓库**，3公绵羊、26母绵羊、6公山羊崽和35公山羊到**厨房为士兵们**，**贝里阿瑞克督办**，于12日，为支出……
Š 44vi: 1 ewe fr.**Beli-arik**, were deliveries	…, 1 u_8 hur-sag, ***Be-lí-a-rí-ik***, …, *mu-túm*, … (*OIP* 115 174, *P*123359)	…, 1 *mountain ewe from* **Beli-arik**, … these were deliveries, …	……1高山母绵羊自**贝里阿瑞克**，……以上为送入……
Š 46x: 1 ewe fr.**Beli-arik**, were deliveries	…, 1 u_8 hur-sag, ***Be-lí-a-rí-ik*** … *mu-túm*, …, (*Torino* 1 015, *P*132003)	…, 1 *mountain ewe from* **Beli-arik**, … these were deliveries, , …	……1高山母绵羊自**贝里阿瑞克**，……以上为送入……

续表

时间和摘要	文献内容	英文翻译	中文翻译
Š 46v/21： 1 lamb，1 kid and 1 ram fr. **Beli-arik，** were deliveries	…，1 sila$_4$-giš-dù，1 ^{f}áš-gàr 1 udu，***Be-lí-a-rí-ik*，**…，*mu-túm*，… （*Nik*.2 465，*P*122148）	…，1 *breeding lamb*，1 *female kid and* 1 *ram from* **Beli-arik**，… these were deliveries，…	……1 种羔、1 雌山羊崽和 1 公绵羊来自**贝里阿瑞克**…以上为送入……
Š 47ix/13： …，［1+ rams］，6 goats and 1 kid for **E.**，**Beli-arik delivered**，… **Nasa** withdr.	…，［1+ udu］，6 máš-gal，1 ^{f}áš-gàr，［Èš］-ta-ab-è šidim，mu-túm ***Be-lí-a-rí-ik*** …*ki~ Na-sa$_6$--ta ba-zi*，… （*MVN* 02 309，*P*113608）	…，［1+ *rams*］，6 *he-goats and* 1 *female kid for* **Eštabe**，the builder，**Beli-arik delivered**，… from the place of **Nasa** withdrawn，…	……【1+公绵羊】、6 公山羊和 1 雌山羊崽为**瓦工埃什塔贝**，**贝里阿瑞克送入**……**从那萨**处支出……
Š 48 xi/16： …，1 lamb for **Nanna**，**Beli-arik** delivered，…，**Nasa** withdr.	…1 sila$_4$ ^{d}Nanna［…］，mu-túm ***Be-lí-a-rí-ik*** …，*ki~ Na-sa$_6$--ta ba-zi*，… （*MVN* 20，078，*P*143011）	…，1 *lamb for* **Nanna**，［…］，**Beli-arik** delivered，…，from the place of **Nasa** withdrawn，…	……1 羔为**南那神**，【……】**贝里阿瑞克送入**……**从那萨**处支出……
AS 1 iii/11： …，1 lamb，1 kid and 11 bulls fr. **Beli-arik**， Nasa took	… 1 sila$_4$，1 máš，11 gud，***Be-lí-a-rí-ik***，*mu-túm Na-sa$_6$ ì-dab$_5$*… （*PDT* 1 422，*P*125838）	…，1 *lamb*，1 *kid and* 11 *bulls from* **Beli-arik**，these deliveries Nasa took over…	……1 羔、1 崽和 11 牛来自**贝里阿瑞克**，以上送入**那萨**接管了……
AS 2 xi： …，6 rams，4 goats and 1 kid fr. **Beli-arik**，… for **king**，**Abba-saga** took	…6 udu，4 máš-gal，1 máš，***Be-lí-a-rí-ik***…，*mu-túm lugal*，*Ab-ba-sa$_6$-ga ì-dab$_5$*，… （*Studies Levine* 115-119，*P*292620）	…，6 *rams*，4 *he-goats and* 1 *kid from* **Beli-arik**，… these deliveries for the **king**，**Abba-saga** took over，…	……6 公绵羊、4 公山羊和 1 公崽来自**贝里阿瑞克**……**为国王送入**，**阿巴萨旮接管**了……
AS 4 ix/19： … fr. **Beli-arik**，**Abba-saga** with-drawn	…šà~ mu-túm ***Be-lí-a-rí-ik***，*ud-19-kam*，*ki~* **Ab-ba-sa$_6$-ga**--ta，ba-zi，…（JCS 58 56，P136231）	… from the deliveries of **Beli-arik**，on the 19th day，from the place of **Abba-saga** withdrawn…	……来自**贝里阿瑞克的送入项**，于 19 日，**自阿巴萨旮**处支出了……

续表

时间和摘要	文献内容	英文翻译	中文翻译
AS 4 ix/21: 2 bulls, 1 cow, 30 flocks fr. **Beli-arik**, …, fr. **Abba-saga**, **Šulgi-ayamu** took	2 gud, 1 áb, 20 udu, 10 máš-gal, kaš-dé-a ***Be-lí-a-rí-ik***…, *ki*~ **Ab-ba-sa$_6$-ga**--ta, ^{d}Šul-gi-a-a-mu ì-dab$_5$…, kaš-dé-a***Be-lí-a-rí-ik***…, *ki*~ **Ab-ba-sa$_6$-ga**--ta, ^{d}Šul-gi-a-a-mu ì-dab$_5$…, (PDT 1 190, P125607)	2 bulls, 1 cow, 20 rams and 10 he-goats from the pouring-beer festival of**Beli-arik**…, from the place of **Abba-saga**, **Šulgi-ayamu** took over, …	2公牛、1母牛、20公绵羊和10公山羊自贝里阿瑞克的倒啤酒宴会……自阿巴萨旮处，舒勒吉阿亚穆接管了……
AS 4 ix/21: 2 bulls, 1 cow, 20 rams and 10 goats fr. **Beli-arik**, fr. **Abba-saga**, **Ahu-Wer** took	2 gud, 1 áb, 20 udu, 10 máš-gal, kaš-dé-a ***Be-lí-a-rí-ik***, …, *ki*~ **Ab-ba-sa$_6$-ga**--ta, ***A-hu-We-er*** *ì-dab$_5$*…, (*AUCT* 1 603, *P*103448)	2 *bulls*, 1 *cow*, 20 *rams and* 10 *he-goats from the***pouring-beer festival of Beli-arik**, …, from the place of **Abba-saga**, **Ahu-Wer** took over, …	2公牛、1母牛、20公绵羊和10公山羊自贝里阿瑞克的倒啤酒宴会，……自阿巴萨旮处，阿胡维尔接管了……
AS 4 x: …2 fat rams fr. **Beli-arik**, …, were withdr.fr.king	…2 udu-niga mu-túm***Be-lí-a-rí-ik*** …, *zi-ga lugal*, … (*MVN* 11 182, *P*116195)	…2 *fattened rams from the deliveries of* **Beli-arik**, …, were withdrawn from the king, …	……2育肥公绵羊来自贝里阿瑞克的送入项……自国王支出……
AS 4x/27: 1 lamb for **Me-I.**, from **Beli-arik**, **Arad-mu as deputy**, fr. Abba-saga withdrawn	1 sila$_4$ **Me-^{d} Istaran**, mu-túm ***Be-lí-a-rí-ik***, **Arád-mu** maškim, ud-27-kam, ki~ **Ab-ba-sa$_6$-ga--ta** ba-zi, … (AUCT 1 585, P103430)	1 lamb for **Me-Istaran**, from the deliveries of **Beli-arik**, **Arad-mu as royal deputy**, on the 27th day, from the place of Abba-saga withdrawn, …	1羔为美伊斯塔兰，来自贝里阿瑞克的送入项，阿腊德穆督办，于27日，自阿巴萨旮处支出……
AS 4 xii/13: … fr. **Beli-arik**, …, **Abba-saga** took	… [...***Be***] ***-lí-a-rí-i*** [***k***…, **Ab-ba-sa$_6$-ga** ì-dab$_5$, … (Nisaba 08 037, P127615)	… from [**Be**] **li-ari** [**k**], …, **Abba-saga** took over, …	……来自【贝】里阿瑞【克】……阿巴萨旮接管了……
AS 5 i/10: …, 1 lamb fr. **Beli-arik** …, **Abba-saga** took	…1 sila$_4$ ***Be-lí-a-rí-ik***…, *mu-túm* **Ab-ba-sa$_6$-ga** ì-dab$_5$, … (MVN 13 662, P117435)	…, 1 lamb from **Beli-arik**…, these deliveries, **Abba-saga** took over, …	……1羔来自贝里阿瑞克……以上送入阿巴萨旮接管了……
AS 5 i/26: …, 2 fat rams from **Beli-arik**…, from **Abba-saga** withdrawn	…2 udu-niga mu-túm***Be-lí-a-rí-ik*** …, *ki*~ **Ab-ba-sa$_6$-ga**--ta ba-zi, … (MVN 13 849, P117621)	…, 2 fattened rams from the deliveries of **Beli-arik** …, from the place of **Abba-saga** withdrawn, …	……2育肥公绵羊来自贝里阿瑞克的送入项……自阿巴萨旮处支出……

续表

时间和摘要	文献内容	英文翻译	中文翻译
AS 5 iii/26： 2 fat rams and 1 lamb fr. **Beli-arik** …，**Abba-saga** took	…2 udu-niga，1 $sila_4$，***Be-lí-a-rí-ik***…，*mu-túm* **Ab-ba-sa$_6$-ga** ì-dab_5，… （OIP 121 083，P123813）	…，2 fattened rams and 1 lamb from **Beli-arik** …，these deliveries，**Abba-saga** took over，…	……2 肥公绵羊和 1 羔自**贝里阿瑞克**……以上送入**阿巴萨旮接管**了……
AS 5 iv/24： …，3 fat rams，1 fat goat，2 rams and 1 lamb fr. **Beli-arik**，…**Abba-saga**took over，…	…2 udu-niga，1 udu-a-lum-niga，1 máš-gal-niga，2 gukkal-giš-dù，1 $sila_4$，***Be-lí-a-rí-ik***，…，*mu-túm* **Ab-ba-sa$_6$-ga** ì-dab_5，… （PDT 1 167，P125584）	…，2 fattened ram，1 fattened aslum ram，1 fattened he-goat，2 breeding fat-tailed ram and 1 lamb from **Beli-arik**，… these deliveries，**Abba-saga** took over，…	……2 育肥公绵羊、1 育肥 aslum 公绵羊、1 育肥公山羊、2 种肥尾公绵羊和 1 羔来自**贝里阿瑞克**……以上送入**阿巴萨旮接管**了……
AS 5 iv/26： …，［1］ram and 1 lamb fr. **Beli-arik**，… **Abba-saga** took	…［1］udu hur-sag，1 $sila_4$，***Be-lí-a-rí-ik***，…*mu-túm* **Ab-ba-sa$_6$-ga** ì-dab_5，… （OIP 121 086，P123816）	…，［1］mountain ram and 1 lamb from **Beli-arik**，… these deliveries，**Abba-saga** took over，…	……【1】高山公绵羊和 1 羔来自**贝里阿瑞克**……以上送入**阿巴萨旮接管**了……
AS 5 viii/22： 41goats fr. **Beli-arik**，…**Abba-saga**took	14$dara_4$-níta，27 $dara_4$-munus ***Be-lí-a-rí-ik***，…，*mu-túm* **Ab-ba-sa$_6$-ga** ì-dab_5，… （OIP 121 096，P123826）	14 mountain he-goats and 27 mountain she-goats from**Beli-arik**，…these deliveries，**Abba-saga** took over，…	14 高山公山羊和 27 高山母山羊来自**贝里阿瑞克**……以上送入**阿巴萨旮接管**了……
AS 5 viii/23： 7 goats fr. **Beli-arik**，… these deliveries，**Abba-saga** took	4 máš-gal-gùn-a，3 $dara_4$ nita，***Be-lí-a-rí-ik***…，*mu-túm* **Ab-ba-sa$_6$-ga** ì-dab_5，… （NYPL 272，P122810）	4 spot he-goats and 3 wild he-goats from**Beli-arik**，… these deliveries，**Abba-saga** took over，…	4 斑点公山羊和 3 野公山羊来自**贝里阿瑞克**……以上送入**阿巴萨旮接管**了……
AS 5 x/9： 1 lamb fr. **Beli-arik**，… **Abba-saga** took	…，1 $sila_4$ ***Be-lí-a-rí-ik***，…，*mu-túm* **Ab-ba-sa$_6$-ga** ì-dab_5，… （JCS 17 008 2，P131594）	…，1 lamb from **Beli-arik**，… these deliveries，**Abba-saga** took over，…	……1 羔来自**贝里阿瑞克**……以上送入**阿巴萨旮接管**了……
AS 6 iii/9： 3600 flocks for fatten-ed room，in-Susa，…，**Beli-arik** took	3586 udu，14 máš-gal，é-udu-niga，šà ～ Šušin[ki]，… ***Be-lí-a-rí-ik*** *ì-dab$_5$*… （*Nik.*2 479，*P*122162）	3586 *rams and* 14 *he-goats for the fattened room*，*inSusa*，…，**Beli-arik** took over…	3586 公绵羊和 14 公山羊为育肥房，于苏萨……**贝里阿瑞克接管**了……

续表

时间和摘要	文献内容	英文翻译	中文翻译
AS 6 iv: 150 goats for fattened room, fr. **Abba-saga**, **Beli-arik** took	150 máš-gal, é-udu-niga--šè, ki~ **Ab-ba-sa$_6$-ga**--ta, ***Be-lí-a-rí-ik***, *ì-dab$_5$* …（*AAICAB* 1/3, *Bod.A* 081, *P*131058）	150 *he-goats for the fattened room*, *from***Abba-saga**, **Beli-arik** took over, …	150公山羊为育肥房，来自**阿巴萨旮**，**贝里阿瑞克接管**了……
AS 6 xi/2: 1 lamb fr. **Beli-arik**, …, **Inta-ea** took	1 sila$_4$***Be-lí-a-rí-ik***, …, **In-ta-è-a** ì-dab$_5$…（OrSP 47-49 098, P124987）	1 lamb from **Beli-arik**, …, **Inta-ea** took over, …	1羔来自**贝里阿瑞克**……，**尹塔埃阿接管**了……
AS 7 vi: 29 eliminated flocks, were rams of**Beli-arik**, fr. **Inta-ea**, **Šu-mama** took	27 udu, 2 máš-gal, šu-gíd udu ***Be-lí-a-rí-ik***, *ki*~ **In-ta-è-a**--ta, **Šu-ma-ma** ì-dab$_5$…（OrSP 47-49 106, P124995）	27 rams and 2 he-goats, eliminated, were rams of**Beli-arik**, from the place of **Inta-ea**, **Šu-mama** took over, …	27公绵羊和2公山羊，淘汰级，为**贝里阿瑞克**的羊，自**尹塔埃阿**处，**舒马马接管**了……
AS 8: 8 workers for 3 days, for weir ofvillage of **Beli-arik**	8 guruš ud-3--šè, kun-zi-da, é-duru$_5$, ***Be-lí-a-rí-ik***--*šè*, …（*Rochester* 178, *P*128283）	8 *workers for 3 days*, *for the weir of village of***Beli-arik**, …	8个工人工作三天为**贝里阿瑞克的庄园的大坝**……
AS 9 x/7: … 3 fat rams and 1 lamb fr. **Beli-arik**, …, **Inta-ea** took over	…3 udu-niga, 1 sila$_4$, ***Be-lí-a-rí-ik***…, *mu-túm*, **In-ta-è-a** ì-dab$_5$, …（BIN 3 546, P106353）	… 3 fattened rams and 1 lamb from **Beli-arik**, …, these deliveries, **Inta-ea** took over, …	……3肥公绵羊和1羔来自**贝里阿瑞克**……以上送入，**尹塔埃阿接管**……
AS 9? xi/16: 1 fat ram to kitchen, for **Beli-arik's wife**, …, from place of Zubaga withdrawn	1 udu-niga gud-e-ús-sa, **é-muhaldim**, igi-kár mu ~ **dam-*Be-lí-a-rí-ik*--*šè***, … *ki* ~ **Zu-ba-ga**--ta ba-zi, …（Hirose 297, P109768）	1 fattened ram of after-ox-class to the kitchen, for **the provisions of Beli-arik's wife**, …, from the place of Zubaga withdrawn, …	1牛后级育肥公绵羊到厨房，为**贝里阿瑞克的妻子**……自**朱巴旮**处支出了……
ŠS 1 vi/1: … 2 fat rams and 1 lamb fr. **Beli-arik**, …, **Inta-ea took**	… 2 udu-niga, 1 sila4, ***Be-lí-a-rí-ik*** … *mu-túm*, **In-ta-è-a** ì-dab$_5$, …（BPOA 7 2650, P303414）	… 2 fattened rams and 1 lamb from **Beli-arik**, …, these deliveries, **Inta-ea took over**, …	……2肥公绵羊和1羔自**贝里阿瑞克**……以上送入，**尹塔埃阿接管**了……

续表

时间和摘要	文献内容	英文翻译	中文翻译
ŠS 1 xii： 24 rams for**pouring-beer of Beli-arik**，…，	… 24 udu kaš-dé-a***Be-lí-a-rí-ik*** …， *zi-ga-àm*，… （*TLB* 3 095，*P*134236）	…，24 *rams for* **pouring-beer festival of Beli-arik**，…，these were withdrawn，…	……24 公绵羊为**贝里阿瑞克的倒啤酒宴会**……以上为支出……
ŠS 4 iv/5： 12 fat rams and 1 lamb from**Beli-arik**，…，for **the king**，**Inta-ea** took over	4 udu-a-lum-niga -3-kam-ús，8 udu-niga-4-kam-ús，1 $sila_4$，***Be-lí-a-rí-ik***，…，*mu-túm* **lugal**，**In-ta-è-a** ì-dab_5，… （Akkadica 21 48，P100328）	4 fattened aslum rams of 3rd class，8 fattened rams of 4th class and 1 lamb from **Beli-arik**，…，were deliveries for **the king**，**Inta-ea** took over，…	4 三等育肥 aslum 公绵羊、8 四等育肥公绵羊和 1 羔来自**贝里阿瑞克**……**为国王的送入**，**尹塔埃埃接管**了……
ŠS 4 viii： …，for **the prince Beli-arik**，when he went to Nippur	…，dumu lugal ***Be-lí-a-rí-ik***，*Nibru*ki*--šè ĝen-na*，*gìr* **NI.URU-dŠul-gi**…． （MVN 16 0933，P118981）	…，for **the prince Beli-arik**，when he went to Nippur，via NI.URU-Šulgi，…	……**为贝里阿瑞克王子**，当他走向尼普尔时，经由 NI. URU 舒勒吉……
ŠS 5 xi/16： 120 rams for**Beli-arik**，…，withdr. fr. **king**，fr. **pouring-beer of Inta-ea**	… 120 udu-ú***Be-lí-a-rí-ik***，…，*zi-ga* **lugal**，ki **kaš-dé-a In-ta-è-a--ta**，… （SET 091，P129501）	… 120 grass rams for **Beli-arik**，…，were withdrawn from **the king**，from **the place of the pouring-beer festival of Inta-ea**，…	……120 食草公绵羊为**贝里阿瑞克**……**从国王支出**，**自尹塔埃阿的倒啤酒宴会**……
ŠS 5 xi/18： 3 goats and 2 kids fr. **Beli-arik**，…，**Inta-ea** put on that place	…1 ud_5-ú 2 máš-gal BI，2 fáš-gàr-ga BI，***Be-lí-a-rí-ik***…，*ki-bi* gi_4*-a In-ta-è-a*，… （*BPOA* 7 2824，*P*303606）	… 1 *grass she-goat*，2 *he-goats and* 2 *female kids from* **Beli-arik**，…，**Inta-ea** put on that place，…	1 食草母山羊、2 公山羊和 2 雌崽来自**贝里阿瑞克**……**尹塔埃阿放于那处**……
ŠS 6 xi/29： 7 fat bulls，1 fat donkey，1 fat goat，30 fat rams，60 rams and 25 goats fr. **pouring-beer festival of Beli-arik**，…，**Inta-ea took** over	7 gud-niga， 1 anše-niga， 1 $šeg_9$-bar-niga， 30 udu-niga，60 udu-ú，25 máš-gal-ú，kaš-dé-a，***Be-lí-a-rí-ik***…，*mu-túm*， *In-ta-è-a ì-dab*$_5$，… （*PDT* 1 564，*P*125980）	7 *fattened bulls*，1 *fattened donkey*，1 *fattened mountain goat*，30 *fattened rams*，60 *grass rams and* 25 *grass he-goats from the***pouring-beer festival of Beli-arik**，…，these deliveries，**Inta-ea took** over，…	7 育肥公牛、1 育肥驴、1 育肥高山公山羊、30 育肥公绵羊、60 食草公绵羊和 25 食草公山羊来自**贝里阿瑞克的倒啤酒宴会**……以上送入，**尹塔埃阿接管了**……
ŠS 7 xii/25： 2 fat rams and 1 lamb fr. **Beli-a.**，**Inta-ea took over**	2 udu-niga-sig_5-ús，1 $sila_4$，***Be-lí-a-rí-ik***…，*mu-túm* **lugal**，**In-ta-è-a** ì-dab_5，… （TRU 181，P134945）	2 better fattened rams and 1 lamb from**Beli-arik**，…，were **deliveries for the king**，**Inta-ea took over**，…	2 次优育肥公绵羊和 1 羔来自**贝里阿瑞克**……以上**为国王的送入**，**尹塔埃阿接管**了……

续表

时间和摘要	文献内容	英文翻译	中文翻译
ŠS 8 xii: 45 bán beer and 45 bán bread for **Beli-arik**	…1.2.3 kaš gur, 1.2.3 ninda gur, ***Be-lí-a-rí-ik*** *ensí*, *Šušin*^{ki}…, (*TÉL* 046, *P*133553)	45 *bán beer and* 45 *bán bread for* **Beli-arik**, the governor of Susa, …	45 升啤酒和 45 升面包为**苏萨的总督贝里阿瑞克**……
ŠS 9 xi: 1 bull fr.bulls delivery of**Beli-arik**, 1 cowvia **Ur-ba**, fr. **Puzur-Enlil**, **Ur-kununa took**	1 gud-ú, šà~ gud ***Be-lí-a-rí-ik***, 1 *áb-ú*, *gìr* **Ur-ba**, ki ~ Puzur$_4$-^{d} En-líl--ta, Ur-kù-nun-na ì-dab$_5$ … (BIN 3 588, P106395)	1 grass bull from the bulls delivery of**Beli-arik**, 1 grass cow via **Ur-ba**, were from **Puzur-Enlil**, **Ur-kununa took over**, …	1 食草公牛来自**贝里阿瑞克**的牛送牲，1 食草母牛**经由乌尔巴**，来自**普朱尔恩里勒处，乌尔库农那接管**了……
?: 2 goats, 1+ fat rams and 1+lamb from**Beli-arik**	…2 dara$_4$-nitá, ***Be-lí-a-rí-ik***, …, *ugula* ***Be-lí-a-rí-ik***, …, … [*x*] *udu-niga*, [*x*] *sila*$_4$, [***Be***] ***-lí-a-rí-ik***, … (*PDT* 2 0959, *P*126313)	…, 2 *wild he-goats from* **Beli-arik**, …, the overseer: Beli-arik, …, [1+] fattened rams and 1+ lambs from **Beli-arik**, …	……2 只野公山羊自**贝里阿瑞克**……监工：**贝里阿瑞克**……1+育肥公绵羊和 1+羔来自**贝里阿瑞克**……
?: 2 fat rams and 1 lamb from**Beli-arik**	…2 udu-a-lum-niga, 1 sila$_4$, ***Be-lí-a-rí-ik***…, (*AAICAB* 1/1, *Ashm.*1911-241, *P*142752)	…, 2 *fattened aslum rams and* 1 *lamb from* **Beli-arik**, …	……2 育肥 aslum 公绵羊和 1 羔来自**贝里阿瑞克**……
?: 4 fat rams and 1 lamb fr. **Beli-a.**, **Abba-saga** took	…4 udu-niga, 1 sila$_4$ ***Be-lí-a-rí-ik***…, *mu-túm*, **Ab-ba-sa$_6$-ga** [ì] -dab$_5$, … (PDT 2 0915, P126273)	… 4 fattened rams and 1 lamb from **Beli-arik**, …, these deliveries, **Abba-saga** took over, …	……4 肥公绵羊和 1 羔自**贝里阿瑞克**……以上送入，**阿巴萨旮接管**了……
?: 45 rams fr. deliveries of**Beli-arik**, …, 120 from **Beli-a.**	…45 udu, šà~ udu-niga ***Be-lí-a-rí-ik***…, 120 *udu*, *ki~* ***Be-lí-a-rí-ik*** …… (*AUCT* 1 973, *P*103818)	…, 45 *rams from the fattened rams deliveries of* **Beli-arik**, …, 120 rams from the place of **Beli-arik**, …	……45 公绵羊来自**贝里阿瑞克**的育肥公绵羊送入……120 公绵羊来自**贝里阿瑞克处**……
?: 40 fat bulls, 5 fat rams, 628 fat rams, 41 fat goats and 1 lamb from**Beli-arik**	… 40 gud-niga, 5 udu-niga-4-kam-ús, 628 udu-niga-gud-e-ús-sa, 41 máš-gal-niga gud-e ús-sa, 1 sila$_4$, ***Be-lí-a-rí-ik*** *ensí Šušin*^{ki}, … (*SACT* 1 189, *P*128944)	…40 *fattened bulls*, 5 *fattened rams of* 4th *class*, 628 *fattened rams of after-ox-class*, 41 *fattened he-goats of after-ox-class and* 1 *lamb from* **Beli-arik**, the governor of Susa, …	……40 育肥公牛、5 四等育肥公绵羊、628 育肥牛后级公绵羊、41 育肥牛后级公山羊和 1 羔来自苏萨的总督**贝里阿瑞克**……

续表

时间和摘要	文献内容	英文翻译	中文翻译
?: 45 bán beer and 45 bán coarse barley flour for **Beli-arik**	1.2.3 kaš-gen gur, 1.2.3 dabin gur, ***Be-lí-a-rí-ik*** *ensí Šušin*[ki], *Šušin*[ki]*--ta ĝen-ni*… (*ITT* 5 06779, *P*111489)	45 *bán beer and* 45 *bán coarse barley flour for* **Beli-arik**, the governor of Susa, When he left from Susa, …	45升普通啤酒和45升粗麦面粉为**苏萨的总督贝里阿瑞克**，当他离开苏萨时……
?: 12 bán beer, 16 bán bread and 1 bán oil for **Beli-arik**	…0.2.0 kaš 0.2.4 ninda, 1 silà ì-giš, ***Be-lí-a***[!]***-rí-iq*** *ensí Šušin*[ki]… (*ITT* 3 05241, *P*111149)	…, 12 *bán beer*, 16 *bán bread and* 1 *bán sesame oil for* **Beli-arik**, the governor of Susa, …	……12升啤酒、16升面包和1升芝麻油为**苏萨的总督贝里阿瑞克**……
? i: 45 bán beer and 45 bán bread for **Beli-arik**	1.2.3 kaš-gen gur, 1.2.3 ninda gur, ***Be-lí-a-rí-ik*** *ensí Šušin*[ki], *Šušin*[ki]*--šè ĝen-ni*, …. (*RT* 22 153 3, *P*128388)	45 *bán beer and* 45 *bán bread for* **Beli-arik**, the governor of Susa, When he went to Susa, …	45升普通啤酒和45升面包为**苏萨的总督贝里阿瑞克**，当他走向苏萨时……
(Š ? x/2: ［1+ fat bull］ fr.**Beli-arik**, ［1+x］ grass ［ram］ fr.troops of Balue, **overseer**: **Beli-arik**, 1 fat bull, 10 grass sheep fr.Šunikib, man of Pil)	［1+ gud-niga?］ ***Be-lí-a -rí-ik***, ［1+ *udu*］ *-ú*, *érin Ba-lu-e*[ki], *ud-* ［1[?]］ *-kam*, ［*iti-ezem*］ *-an-na*, *ugula* ***Be-lí-a-rí-ik***, 1 *gud-niga*, 5 *udu-ú*, 5 *máš-gal-ú*, **Šu-ni -ki-ib** lú-Pi-il[ki], ud-2-kam.iti-ezem-an-na, ［ugula］ ***Ṣi-lu-uš-***[d]***Da-gan***. (*AUCT* 1 004, *P*102850)	［1+ *fattened bull*］ *from Beli-arik*, ［1 +］ *grass* ［*ram*］ *from the troops of Balue*, *on the* ［$1^{st?}$］ *day*, *month of ezem-Anna*, **the overseer**: **Beli-arik**, 1 fattened bull, 5 grass rams, 5 grass goats, from Šunikib, the man of Pil, on the 2nd day. Month of ezem-Anna, the overseer: Ṣiluš-Dagan.	【1+肥公牛】自**贝里阿瑞克**，【1+】食草【公绵羊】从**巴鲁埃军队**，第【1[?]】天，天神安庆典月，**监工**：**贝里阿瑞克**，1育肥公牛、5食草公绵羊和5只食草公山羊自皮勒城之人，于本月2日。天神安庆典月，监工：采鲁什达干（席穆润的总督）。

参考文献

亚述学和乌尔第三王朝时期文献出版物英文缩写

缩写	作者（编者），书名，出版地，日期
CDLI	国际亚述学研究网站（《楔形文字数字图书馆工程》加利福尼亚大学洛杉矶分校 http：//www.cdli.ucla.edu/index_ html）
BDTNS	《新苏美尔原文数据库》马德里，高等科学研究院语言研究所 http：//bdts.filol.csic.es/
A	Tablets in the Collections of the Oriental Institute，Univ.of Chicago.
A l'ombre deBabel	E.Gubel（ed.），in de Schaduw Van Babel.de Kunst Van Het Oude Nabije Oosten in Belgische Verzamelingen/A L' Ombre de Babel.L' Art du Proche-Orient Ancien Dans Les Collections Belges，Leuven 1995.
AAA	Annals of Archaeology and Anthropology，issued by the Institute of Archaeology，Liverpool.
AAS	J.P.Grégoire，*Archives Administratives Sumériennes*，Paris 1970.
ABAA	E. Weidner，*Alter und Bedeutung der Babylonischen Astronomie und Astrallehre*，*Nebst Studien Uber Fixsternhimmel und Kalender*，Leipzig 1914.
ABAW N.F	Abhandlungen der Bayerischen Akademie der Wissenschaften. Philosophisch-Historische Abteilung，München.
ABTR	W.R.Arnold，*Ancient-Babylonian Temple Records in the Columbia University Library*，New-York，1896.
ActOrHun Or	Acta Orientalia Academiae Scientiarum Hungaricae.
ActSocHun Or	Acta Societatis Hungaricae Orientalis.
Aegyptus	Rivista（Italiana）Di Egittologia E Di Papirologia.Milano.
Aevum	Rassegna Di Scienze Storiche，Linguistiche E Filologiche，Milano.
AfO	Archiv für Orientforschung，Wien.
AION	Annali Istituto Universitario Orientale，Nápoles.
AIPHOS	Annuaire deI' Institut de Philologie et d'Histoire Orientales et Slaves，Universite Libre de Belgique，Bruxelles.
AJ	The Antiquaries Journal，being the Journal of the Society of Antiquaries of London（Jsal）.

续表

缩写	作者（编者），书名，出版地，日期
AJSL	American Journal of Semitic Languages and Literatures, Chicago.
Akkadica	Périodique Bimestriel dela Fondation Assyriogique Gorges Dossin, Musées Royaux d'Art et d'Histoire, Bruxelles.
Al Rafidan	Journal of Western Asiatic Studies, Kokushikan University, Japan.
Aleppo	M. Touzalin, *L' Administration Palatiale À L' Époque de la Troisième Dynastie d'Ur: Textes Inédits du Musée d'Alep*, Thèse de Doctorat de Troisième Cycle Soutenue À L' Université de Tours 1982.
Amherst	Th.G.Pinches, *The Amherst Tablets I*, London 1908.
Ammann-Festgabe	Ammann-Festgabe I. Teil, Innsbrucker Beiträge Zur Kulturwissenschaft I. Band, Innsbruck, 1953.
Amorites	G.Buccellati, *The Amorites of the Ur III Period*, Nápoles 1966.
Anadolu Arastirmalari	Anadolu Arastirmalari / Jahrbuch Für Kleinasiatische Forschung.
AnBiblica/AnBi	Analecta Biblica, Rome.
AncMesArt	E.Porada, *Ancient Mesopotamian Art and Selected Texts: the Pierpont Library*, New York, 1976.
ANESJ	K. Ishida (ed.), *Ancient Near Eastern Seals in Japan [in Japanese]*, Tokyo 1991.
Annuaire EPHE 1978-79	Annuaire de L' École Pratique des Hautes Études, Ive Section - Sciences Historiques et Philologiques, Paris.
AnOr	Analecta Orientalia, Rome.
AnOr 7.	M.N.Schneider, *Die Drehem und Djoha-Urkunden der Strassburger Universitäts und Landesbibliothek*, Analects Orientalia, Roma, 1931.
AnSt	Anatolian Studies, London.
AOAT	Alter Orient und Altes Testament, Neukirchen-Vluyn / Münster, 1979.
AoF	Altorientalische Forschungen, Leipzig.
AoN	Altorientalische Notizen, Höchberg.
AOS	American Oriental Series, New Haven.
AR RIM	Annual Review of the Royal Inscriptions of Mesopotamia Project, Toronto.
Archaic Bookkeeping	H.J.Nissen - P. Damerow - R. K. Englund, *Archaic Bookkeeping. Writing and Techniques of Economic Administration in the Ancient Near East*, Chicago 1993 (1990).
ArOr	Archiv Orientální, Praga.
Art of the Eastern World	G.Fehérvári et Al., *Art of the Eastern World*, London 1996
AS	Assyriological Studies, University of Chicago.
ASJ	Acta Sumerologica, Hiroshima, Japan 1979.
Atiqot	Atiqot, Jerusalem.Journal of the Israel Department of Antiquities, Jerusalem.

续表

缩写	作者（编者），书名，出版地，日期
AUCT	M.Sigrist, *Neo-Sumerian Account Texts in the Horn Archaeological Museum*, *Andrews University Cuneiform Texts* 1-3, Berrien Sprigs Michigan 1984-1988.
Auktionshaus Nagel 19921017	Anonymous, Auktionshaus F. Nagel. 1 Sonderauktion Aussereuropäische und Antike Kunst, Versteigerung: 17.Oktober 1992, Nr.594.
AuOr	Aula Orientalis, Sabadell (Barcelona).
AuOr Suppl.	Aula Orientalis - Supplementa, Barcelona.
AUWE	Ausgrabungen in Uruk-Warka Endberichte, Mainz Am Rhein.
B.Rhode Island	Bulletin of the Museum ofArt, Rhode Island School of Design.
B.W.Ath.	BulletinWadsworth Atheneum.
BAAL	Bulletin d'Archéologie et d'Architecture Libanaises, Beirut.
BabClayTab.	R.J.Gillings, et Al., *Babylonian Clay Tablets*, *Technology*, May 1965, pp. 6-10.
Babel und Bibel	Babel und Bibel. Annual of Ancient Near Eastern, Old Testament, and Semitic Studies, Winona Lake.
Babyl.	Babyloniaca.Études de Philologie Assyro-Babylonienne, Paris.
Babylonisches Schriftum	E.Unger, Babylonisches Schriftum, Leipzig, 1921.
Bala, Diss.	T.M.Sharlach, Bala: *Economic Exchange Between Center and Provinces in the Ur III State*, Ph.D.Diss.Harvard University 1999.
BaM	Baghdader Mitteilungen (Deutsches Archaologisches Institut Abteilung Baghdad), Berlin, Mainz.
BAOM	Bulletin of the Ancient Orient Museum, Japan.
BbJ	Von Babylon Bis Jerusalem.Die Welt der Altorientalischen Königsstädte, Bd.1 (Eds.W.Seipel - A.Wieczorek), und 2 (Eds.F.Blocher - J.G.Westenholz), Mailand 1999.
BBVO	Berliner Beiträge Zum Vorderen Orient, Berlin.
BCT 1	P.J.Watson, *Catalogue of Cuneiform Tablets in Birmingham City Museum I*: Neo-Sumerian Texts from Drehem, Warminster, 1986. =Watson Birmingham.
BCT2	P.J.Watson with Horowitz, Catalogue of Cuneiform Tablets in Birmingham City Museum 2: Neo-Sumerian Texts from Umma and other Sites, Warminster 1993.
BE	The Babylonian Expedition of the University of Pennsylvania.Philadelphia.
Berens	Th.G.Pinches, *The Babylonian Tablets of the Berens Collection*, Asiatic Society Monographs16, London 1915.
BGDLWU	Bulletin of the Graduate Division of Literature of Waseda University, Tokyo.
BiMes	Bibliotheca Mesopotamica. Primary Sources and Interpretive Analyses for the Study of Mesopotamian Civilization and Its Influences from the Late Prehistoric to the End of the Cuneiform Tradition, Malibu.

续表

缩写	作者（编者），书名，出版地，日期
BIN	Babylonian Inscriptions in the Collection of B.J.Nies, New Haven Yale University Press, 1917.
BIN 3	C.E.Keiser, with S-T.Kang, *Neo-Sumerian Account Texts from Drehem*, Babylonian Inscriptions in the Collection of J.B.Nies 3, New Haven 1971.
BiOr	Bibliotheca Orientalis, Leiden.
BJRL	Bulletin of the John Rylands University Library, Manchester.
BM	Museum Siglum of the British Museum, Manchester, 1903.
BMC Roma	Bolletino Dei Musei Communali Di Rome.
BMHBA	Bulletin du Musée Hongrois des Beaux-Arts.
BPOA	Biblioteca Del Próximo Oriente Antiguo, Madrid.
BRM	*Babylonian Records in the Library of J.Pierpont Morgan*, New Haven, 1923.
Brown Collection	Cuneiform Tablets from the University of Victoria - Brown Collection, Victoria Bc, Canada, Http: //Gateway1.Uvic.Ca/Spcoll.
BSA	Bulletin on Sumerian Agriclture, Cambridge UK.
Bull.Buffalo SNS	Bulletin of the Buffalo Society of Natural Sciences.
Bulletin Okayama	Revue de Recherche du Musée d'orient de Okayama.
BW Essays Gordon	G.Rendsburg - R.Adler - M.Arfa - N.H.Winter (Eds.), *The Bible World, Essays in Honor of Cyrus H.Gordon*, New York 1980.
Care of the Elderly	M.Stol - S.P.Vleeming (Eds.), *The Care of the Elderly in the Ancient Near East*, Leiden - Boston - Köln 1998.
Cat RSM	S.Dalley, *A Catalogue of the Akkadian Cuneiform Tablets in the Collection of the Royal Scottish Museum, Edinburgh*, With Copies of the Texts, Edinburgh, 1979.
CBCT-PUL	E.Chiera, *Catalogue of the Babylonian Cuneiform Tablets in the Princeton University Library*, Princeton 1921.
CBCY	Catalogue of the Babylonian Collections at Yale, Bethesda.
CBT	Catalogue of the Babylonian Tablets in the British Museum, London.
CBTLCU	I.Mendelsohn, *Catalogue of the Babylonian Tablets in the Library of Columbia University*, New York, 1943.
CCh	Virolleaud, C., *Comptabilite Chaldeenne*, 1903.
CCL I	L.Delaporte, *Catalogue des Cylindres Orientaux*, *Cachets et Pierres Gravées du Musée du Louvre* I, *Fouilles et Missions*, Paris 1920.
CCL II	L.Delaporte, *Catalogue des Cylindres Orientaux*, *Cachets et Pierres Gravées du Musée du Louvre II*, *Acquisitions*, Paris 1923.
CDLB	Cuneiform Digital Library Bulletin, http: //cdli.ucla.edu/pubs/cdlb.html.
CDLI	Cuneiform Digital Library Initiative, http: //cdli.ucla.edu.
CDLJ	Cuneiform Digital Library Journal, http: //cdli.ucla.edu/pubs/cdlj.html.

续表

缩写	作者（编者），书名，出版地，日期
CDLN	Cuneiform Digital Library Notes, http: //cdli.ucla.edu/pubs/cdln.html.
CHANE	Culture and History of the Ancient Near East, Leiden - Boston - Köln.
Charles Ede	Cuneiform Texts Offered by Charles Ede Ltd. (Antiquarian), London, http: //www.charlesede.com.
CHEU	G.Contenau, *Contribution À L'histoire Économique d'umma*, Paris 1915.
Christie's	Cuneiform Texts offered by Christie's (Auction House), London.
CM	Cuneiform Monographs, Leiden.
Coll.de Clerq	L. de Clercq, *Collection de Clercq. Catalogue Méthodique et Raisonné: Antiquités Assyriennes, Cylindres Orientauz, Cachets, Briques, Bronzes, Bas-Reliefs, etc*, Paris 1888.
Comptabilité	C.Virolleaud, *Comptabilité Chaldéenne* (Époque de la Dynastie Dite Seconde d'our), Poitiers, 1903.
Cooks and Kitchens	L.B.Allred, *Cooks and Kitchens: Centralilzed Food Production in Late Third Millennium Mesopotamia*, Ph.D.Diss.Johns Hopkins University 2006.
Creating Economic Order	M.Hudson - C.Wunsch (Eds.), *Creating Economic Order. Record-Keeping, Standardization, and the Development of Accounting in the Ancient Near East*, Bethesda 2004.
CRRAI	Compte Rendu Rencontre Assyriologique Internationale.
CSA	Cahiers dela Société Asiatique, Paris.
CST = Fish Rylands	T.Fish, Catalogue of Sumerian Tablets in the John Rylands Library, Manchester 1932.
CT	Cuneiform Texts from Babylonian Tablets in the British Museum, London.
CT St Louis	R.D.Freedman, The Cuneiform Tablets in St.Louis, Ph.D..Diss.New York Columbia University 1975.
CTMMA	*Cuneiform Texts in the Metropolitan Museum of Art*, New York.
CTNMC	Th. Jacobsen, *Cuneiform Texts in the National Museum, Copenhagen*, Leiden 1939.
CuCa	M. E. Cohen, The*Cultic Calendars of the Ancient Near East*, Bethesda Md 1993.
Cuneiform	C.B.F.Walker, *Cuneiform*, *Reading the Past* 1, London 1987.
CUSAS	Cornell University Studies in Assyriology and Sumerology, New York.
CUT CUA	M.Johnston, *Catholic University Cuneiform Texts*, 1969.
Cylinder Seals	H.Frankfort, *Cylinder Seals.A Documentary Essay on the Art and Religion of the Ancient Near East*.London 1939.
DAA	de Anatolia Antiqua, Paris.
DAS	B.Lafont, *Documents Administatifs Sumériens Provenant du Site de Tello et Conservés au Musée du Louvre*, Paris 1985.

续表

缩写	作者（编者），书名，出版地，日期
Dec.Chaldée =DC	Sarzec，E De，*Decouvertes en Chaldee*，Ouvrage Accompagné de Planches，Publié Par Les Soins de Léon Heuzey，Avec Le Concours de Arthur Amiaud et F.Thureau-Dangin Pour la Partie Épigraphique. **Premier Volume**：Texte，**Second Volume**：Partie Épigraphique et Planches，Paris 1884-1912.
DCS	Charpin，D. & Durand，J-M.，*Documents Cuneiformes de Stras-Bourg Conserves a la Bibliotheque Nationale et Universitaire*，1981.
DDU	Schmeider，N.，*Die Drehem-und Djoha-Urkunden der Stabburger Universitats-und Landesbibliothek in Autotraphie und Mit Systematischen Woterverzeichmissen Herausgegehen*，1931.
Debt and Economic Renewal	M.Hudson - M.Van de Mieroop（eds.），*Debt and Economic Renewal* in the Ancient Near East. A Colloquium Held at Columbia University（November 1988），Vol.III，Bethesda 2002.
DoCu EPHE	J.-M.Durand，*Documents Cunéiformes de la Ive Section de L'école Pratique des Hautes Études*，Tome I：Catalogue et Copies Cunéiformes，Genève - Paris 1982.
DoCu Strasbourg	D.Charpin - J.M.Durand，Documents Cunéiformes de Strasbourg Conservés Àla Bibliothèque Nationale et Universitaire，Études Assyriologiques 4，Paris 1981.
Dynastie Chald.	C.-G.Janneau，Une Dynastie Chaldéenne：Le Rois d'Ur，Paris，1911.
EAMES=AOS 32	Oppenheim，L.，*Catalogue of the Cuneiform Tablets of the Wilberforce Eames Babylonian Collection in the New York Public Library.Tablets of the Time of the Third Dynasty of Ur*，1948.
Ebay	Cuneiform Texts offered Through Ebay Inc.，San Jose，Http：//Www. Ebay.Com.
EBH	H.Radau，*Early Babylonian History* Down to the End of the Fourth Dynasty to Which is Appended An Account of " The E.A.Hoffman Collection" of Babylonian Tablets in the General Theological Seminary，New York. New York，1900.
Ebla 1975-1985	L.Cagni Ed.，Ebla 1975 - 1985，Napoli 1987.
ECH	R.Menegazzi（Ed.），*An Endangered Cultural Heritage*：Iraqi Antiquities Recovered In Jordan，Monografie Di Mesopotamia Vii，Firenze 2005.
Economy and Settlement	N.Miller（ed.），*Economy and Settlement in the Near East.Analyses of Ancient Sites and Materials*，Philadelphia 1990.
ELO Gallery	Cuneiform Texts offered by E.L.Owen（Antiquarian），Lake Hopatcong，Http：//Www.Edgarlowen.Com.
ELS	P.Attinger，*Eléments de Linguistique Sumérienne.la Construction de* Du_{11}*/E/Di "Dire"*，Göttingen 1993.
ENES	B.Buchanan，*Early Near Eastern Seals in the Yale Babylonian Collection*，New Haven 1981.
Epigraphie 1	Limet，H.，*Textes Sumetiens de la IIIE Dynastie d'Ur*，1976.
FAOS	Freiburger Altorientalische Studien，Wiesbaden.Stuttgart.

续表

缩写	作者（编者），书名，出版地，日期
Farmer's Instructions	M.Civil, The*Farmer's Instructions.A Sumerian Agricultural Manual*, Aula Orientalis - Supplementa 5, Sabadell 1994.
Finkelstein J. J. Menorial Volume	*Essays on the Ancient Near East*, 1977.
Foods AME	Anonymous, "Sumerian Economical Document", *Foods in the Ancient* [Sic] *Middle East*, Special Lectures on the Fifteenth Anniversary of the Middle Eastern Culture Center in Japan, 1994.
Frühe Schrift	H.J.Nissen - P.Damerow - R.K.Englund, *Frühe Schrift und Techniken der Wirtschaftsverwaltung Im Alten Vorderen Orient*, Berlin 1990.
FS.Ammann	Immsbrucker Beitrage Zur Kulturwissenschaft, 1953.
FS.A.Deimel	ANOR 12, 1935.
Fs.N.Egami	Estschrift N.Egami, Tokyo, 1984.
Fs.C.H.Gordon 1973	AOAT 22, 1973.
Fs.C.H.Gordon 1979	AOAT 203, 1979.
Fs.T.B.Jones	Owen, D.I., Wasilewska, E.2006 Owner Church of Jesus Christ of Latter Day Saints - Museum of Church History and Art Salt Lake City, *Ut Usa So Live the Works of Man*, *Seventieth Anniversary Volume Honoring Edgar Lee Hewett*, 1939.
Fs.H.V.Hilprecht	Hilprecht Anniversary Volume, 1909.
Fs.P.Koschaker	Symbolae Koschaker, Sd II, 1939.
Fs.G.R.Luciani	Studi Sull' Oriente Ela Bibbia, Genova, 1967.
Fs.L.Matous	Fs.L.Matous, 1978<1980>.
Fs.J.Pirenne	Melanges J.Pirenne, Aiphos 20, 1968-72
Fs.K.Oberhuber	Im Bannkreis des Alten Orients, Innsbrucker Beitrage Zurkulturwissenschaft24, 1986.
Fs.V.V.Struve	Assiriologija I Egyptologija, Sbornik Statej Akademikyv.V.Struve, 1964.
FT	H.de Genouillac, Fouilles de Tello, Paris 1934-1936.
FTUPM	H.P.Martin - F.Pomponio - G.Visicato - A.Westenholz., The*Fara Tablets in the University of Pennsylvania Museum of Archaeology and Anthropology*, Bethesda 2001.
Genava	Genava.Bulletin du Musée d'Art et d'Histoire de Genève.
Geschlechtsreife	E. W. Müller (ed.), *Geschlechtsreife und Legitimation Zur Zeugung*, Freiburg 1985.
Gratz AJS	Gratz Annual of Jewish Studies.
HAV	Hilprecht Anniversary Volume, Leipxig, 1909.
Hermitage 3	N.Koslova, Ur III- Texte der St.Petersburger Ermitage, Iii, Unpubl.Ms.Oppenheim.

续表

缩写	作者（编者），书名，出版地，日期
Hirose	T.Gomi - Y.Y K.Hirose, *Neo-Sumerian Account Texts of the Hirose Collection*, Potomac, Maryland 1990.
HLC	G.A.Barton, Harverford Library Collection of Cuneiform Texts Or Documents from the Temple Archives of Telloh, Vols.1-3, Philadelphia 1905-1914.
HMU	C.J.Gadd, *History and Monuments of Ur*, London 1929.
HSS	Harvard Semitic Series, Cambridge.
HUCA	Hebrew Union College Annual, Cincinnati.
HWYR	R.J.Gelinas, *History of the World for Young Readers*, 1965.
IAMY	Istanbul Arkeoloji Müzelerei Yilligi.
ICAANE	International Congress on the Archaeology of the Ancient Near East.
IMGULA 5	M.Hilgert, *Akkadisch in der Ur III-Zeit*, *Imgula* 5, Münster 2002.
Inanna Temple	R.L.Zettler, The*Ur III Inanna Temple at Nippur*, Ph. D. Diss. University of Chicago 1984.
IOS	Israel Oriental Studies.
IRAIMK	Izvestija Rossijskoj Akademii Istorii Material' Noj Kul' Tury.
Iraq	Iraq.British School of Archaeology in Iraq, London, 1934.
Isin	D.O.Edzard - S.C.Wilcke, "Vorläufiger Bericht Über Die Inschriftfunde Frühjahr 1973, Frühjahr 1974, Herbst1974", B. Hrouda, Isin - Isan Bahriyat.I, München 1977, pp.83–91.
ITT	Inventaire des Tablettes de Tello Conservées Au Musée Impérial Ottoman, Paris.
JA	Journal Asiatique, Paris.
JAC	Journal of Ancient Civilizations, Changchun.
JANES	Journal of the Ancient Near Eastern Society of Columbia University, New York.
JAOS	Journal of the American Oriental Society, Boston.
JCS	Journal of Cuneiform Studies, New Haven, Yale University Press, Boston, 1947.
JCS 57	T.Sharlach, *Diplomacy and Rituals of Politics at Ur III Court*, Jcs 57, 2005, Pp 27-29, No.1-11 (3-7 = Drehem, 1-2, 8, 11 = Umma, 9 = Messen., U, 10 = Drehem?) P. Michalowski/P. Daneshmand, An Ur III Tablet from Iran, p.31.
JEOL	Jaarbericht Van Het Vooraziatisch-Egyptisch Genootschap " Ex Oriente Lux", Leiden.1933 Ff.
JESHO	Journal of the Economic and Social History of the Orient, Leiden, 1933.
JMEOS	Journal of theManchester Egyptian and Oriental Society, Manchester.
JNES	Journal of Near Eastern Studies, Chicago.

续表

缩写	作者（编者），书名，出版地，日期
Journal Asiatique	Journal Asiatique.Paris.
JRAS	Journal of the Royal Asiatic Society ofGreat Britain and Ireland, London.
JSOR	Journal of the Society of Oriental Research, Chicago - Toronto.
JOAS	Journal of Otsuka Archaeological Socity, Otsuka, Japan.
JSS	Journal of Semitic Studies, Manchester.
Jubileum LB	F. M. Th. de Liagre Böhl, Jubileumstentoonstelling 1898-1938, Amsterdam, 1938.
Kaskal	Kaskal.Rivista Di Storia, Ambienti E Culture Del Vicino Oriente Antico, Padova.
KAV	Kramer Anniversary Volume, AOAT 25, 1976.
Kennelmen	P.Mander, An Archive of Kennelmen and Other Workers in Ur III Lagash, Supplemento N.80 Agli Annali - Vol.54, 1994, Fasc.3, Napoli 1994.
KHMS	Cuneiform Texts from the Kunsthistorisches Museum, Vienna.
KM	Cuneiform Texts from the Kelsey Museum of Archaeology, Ann Arbor Mi.
Kricheldorf	H.H.Kricheldorf, Auktionskatalog, Stuttgart 1957.
Kultische Kalender	W.Sallaberger, der*Kultische Kalender der Ur III - Zeit. I-II*, Berlin - New York 1993.
Kykladen und Alter O-rient	E.Rehm, Kykladen und Alter Orient.Bestandskatalog des Badischen Landes-museums Karlsruhe, Karlsruhe 1997.
Kyoto = ST	Y.Nakahara, The Sumerian Tablets in the Imperial University of Kyoto, Kyoto 1928.
L' ufficio e il docu-mento	C.Mora - P.Piacentini (Eds.), L´ufficio E Il Documento.I Luoghi, I Modi, Gli Strumenti Dell´amministrazione in Egitto E Nel Vicino Oriente Antico, Quaderni Di Acme 83, Milan 2006.
L' uomo	G. Pettinato, *L' Uomo Cominciò A Scrivere. Iscrizioni Cuneiformi Della Collezione Michail*, Milan 1997.
Ladders to Heaven	O.W.Muscarella (ed.), *Ladders to Heaven.Art Treasures from Lands of the Bi-ble*, Toronto 1981.
Lamas Bolaño	Lamas Bolaño.Arte, Inversi6n Y Collecionismo, Barcelona.
Landless and Hungry	B.Haring - R.de Maaijer (Eds.), Landless and Hungry? Access to Land in Early and Traditional Societies.Proceedings of A Seminar Held in Leiden, 20 and 21 June, 1996, Cnws Publications 67, Leiden 1998.
LB	Cuneiform Tablets from the F.M.Th.de Liagre Böhl Collection, Leiden.
Ledgers	D.Snell, Ledgers and Prices.*Early Mesopotamian Merchant Accounts*, *Yale Near Easter Researches* 8, New Haven - London 1982.
Letters	P.Michalowski, *Letters from Early Mesopotamia*, *Sbl Writings from the Ancient World* 3, Winona Lake 1993.

续表

缩写	作者（编者），书名，出版地，日期
Ley más antigua	M. Molina, la Ley Más Antigua. Textos Legales Sumerios, Madrid - Barcelona 2000.
Liber Annuus	Liber Annuus.Studium Biblicum Francescanum, Jerusalem.
Library of Congress	M.Sigrist, Cuneiform Tablets from the Library of Congress, Washington Dc, Http: //Hdl.Loc.Gov/Loc.Amed.
Life in the ANE	D.C.Snell, Life in the Ancient Near East, New Haven - London 1997.
London antiquities	W.G.Lambert, London Antiquities, Unpubl.Ms.
Looting of the Iraq Museum	A.M. H. Schuster - M. Polk (Eds.), The Looting of the Iraq Museum, Baghdad.the Lost Legacy of Ancient Mesopotamia, New York 2005.
MAD	Materials for the Assyrian Dictionary, Chicago.
MAOG	Mitteilungen der Altorientalischen Gesellschaft, Berlin, Leipzig.
MARI	Mari.Annales de Recherches Interdisciplinaires, Paris.
MC	Mesopotamian Civilizations, Winona Lake.
MCS	Manchester Cuneiform Studies, Manchester.
MDAI/MDAIK= DAI	Mitteilungen des Deutschen Archäologischen Instituts, Abt. Kairo, Mainz, 1956--. (Nesbit. =Nesbit Drehem. =Sumrecdreh.W.Nesbit, *Sumerian Records from Drehem* = Columbia University Oriental Studies 8, New York 1914, Reprint New York 1966.)
MDOG	Mitteilungen der Deutschen Orientgesellschaft Zu Berlin.
MDP	Mémoires dela Délégation En Perse, Paris.
Mél.Steve	L.de Meyer - H.Gasche - F.Vallat (Eds.), Fragmenta Historiae Aelamicae. Mélanges offerts À M.-J.Steve, Paris 1986.
Mem.Cagni	S.Graziani (ed.), Studi Sul Vicino Oriente Antico Dedicati Alla Memoria Di Luigi Cagni, Istituto Orientali Di Napoli Dsa, Series Minor Lxi, 4 Vols., Napoli 2000.
Mem.Finkelstein	M.de J.Ellis (ed.), Essays on the Ancient Near East in Memory of Jacob Joel Finkelstein, Memoirs of the Connecticut Academy of Arts and Sciences 19, Hamden Conn.1977.
Mesopotamia	Mesopotamia.Rivista Di Archeologia A Cura Del Centro Ricerche Archeologiche E Scavi Di Torino Per Il Medio Oriente E d'Asia, Turín.
Mesopotamia 8	B.Alster (ed.), Death in Mesopotamia, Xxvie Rencontre Assyriologique Internationale - Mesopotamia Csa 8, Copenhagen 1980.
Messaggeri, Diss.	P.Notizia, Testi Di Messaggeri Di Ur III, Tesi Di Dottorato, Unpubl.Ms.
Messenger Texts, Diss.	R.C.Mcneil, *The "Messenger Texts" of the Third Ur Dynasty*, Ph.D.Diss.University of Pennsylvania 1970.
Métal	H.Limet, *Le Travail du Métal Au Pays de Sumer Au Temps de la III Dynastie d'ur*, Paris 1960.
MFM	Medelhavsmuseet.Focus on the Mediterranean, Stockholm.

续表

缩写	作者（编者），书名，出版地，日期
MHAQ	Mount Holyoke Alumnae Quarterly，Sounth Hadley，Massach-Usetts.
Minuscule Monuments of Art	A.Glock，Minuscule Monuments of Ancient Art，Catalogue of Near Eastern Stamp and Cylinder Seals Collected by Virginia E.Bailey，The New Jersey Museum of Archaeology 1988.
MJ	The Museum Journal，University Museum，University ofpennsylvania.
MLVS	Bohl，F.M.T.de Liagre，Mededeelingen Uit de Leidsche Verzameling Van Spijkerschrift-Inscripties，Amsterdam，1933-1936.
MMA Guide	V.E.Crawford，et Al.，The Metropolitan Museum of Art.Guide to the Collections.Ancient Near Eastern Art，New York 1966.
MonOT	I.M.Price et Alii，The Monuments and the Old Testament，2 Edition，1958.
Mt Holyoke A.Q.	Mount Holyoke Alumnae Quarterly.South Burlington，Vermont.
MTBM	M.Sigrist，Messenger Texts from the British Museum，Ann Arbor 1990.
Museo Barracco	M. G. Biga et Al.，Museo Barracco. Arte Del Vicino Oriente Antico，Rome 1996.
Museon	Le Muséon.Revue d'Etudes Orientales，Leuven.
Museum Journal	Museum Journal，Philadelphia.
MVAG	Mitteilungen der Vorderasiatisch（-Ägyptisch）En Gesellschaft，Leipzig.
MVN	G. Pettinato-H. Waetzoldt，*Materiali Per Il Vocabolario Neosumerico*，Roma，1974.
MVN 15	D Owen，Neo-Sumerian Texts from American Collections，Materiali Per Il Vocabulario Neosumerico 15，Roma 1991.
Mycenaean	A.Uchitel，Mycenaean and Near Eastern Economic Archives，Ph.D.Diss.London University 1985（Thesis N° Dx188419）.
NABU	Nouvelles Assyriologiques Brèves et Utilitaires，Paris.
Naissance de l' écriture	B.andré-Leickman - A.Ziegler，Naissance de L' Écriture：Cunéiformes et Hiéroglyphes，Paris 1982.
Nasha，Diss.	S.B.Nelson，*Nasha：A Study of Administrative Texts of the Third Dynasty of Ur*，Ph.D.Diss.University of Minnesota 1972.
NATN	D.I.Owen，Neo-Sumerian Archival Texts Primarily from Nippur in the University Museum，The Oriental Institute and the Iraq Museum，Winona Lake 1982.
Nebraska	N. W. Forde，*Nebraska Cuneiform Texts of the Sumerian Ur Dynasty*，Lawrence，1967.
Newark Public Library	Neo-Sumerian Cuneiform Tablets from the Newark Public Library，Newark Nj.
NFT	G.Cros，*Nouvelles Fouilles de Tello*，Publiées Avec Le Concours de Léon Heuzey，Fçois Thureau-Dangin，Paris，1910.
Nik	Nikol´skij，Drevnosti Vostocnyja.

续表

缩写	作者（编者），书名，出版地，日期
Nik 1	Dokumenty Sobraniia N.P.Likhacheva, Part Iii/2, St.Petersburg 1908, Edit. G.Selz, FAOS 15/1 (Nik 1).
Nik 2 = DV5	M.V.Nikolskij, Dokumenty Chozjajstevnnoj Otcetnosti Drevnej Epochi Chaldei Iz Sobranija N.P.Lichaceva, Cast´ II: Èpocha DinastiiAgade I Època Dinastii Ura, Drevnosti Vostocnyja 5, Moscú 1915.Collations by M.Powell, Acta Sum 3, 125ff.
Nisaba	Nisaba.Studi Assiriologici Messinesi, Messina.
Nisaba 8	J. Politi and L. Verderame, *The Drehem Texts in the Brutush Museum* (DTBM), Nisaba-8, Messina 2005.
NRVN 1	M.Çig - H.Kizilyay, Neusumerische Rechts- und Verwaltungsurkunden Aus Nippur I = Yeni Sumer Cagina Ait Nippur Hukukî Ve Idarî Belgeleri I, Ankara 1965.
NATN = NSATN	Owen, D.I., *Neo-Sumerian Archival Texts Prinarily from Nippur in the University Museum, the Oriental Institute and the Iraq Museum*, 1982.
NSGU	A. Falkenstein, Die Neusumerischen Gerichtsurkunden 1-3, München 1956-1957.
NYPL	H.Sauren, Les Tablettes Cunéiformes de L´époque d'ur des Collections dela New York Public Library, Publications de L´institut Orientaliste de Louvain 19, Lovaina 1978.
OA	Oriens Antiquus, Roma.
OBO	Orbis Biblicus et Orientalis, Göttingen.
OBTR	R.J. Lau, Old Babylonian Temple Records, Columbia University Oriental Series 3, Obtr, New York, 1906.
OECT	Oxford Editions of Cuneiform Texts, Oxford.
OIC	Oriental Institute Communications, Chicago.
OIP	Oriental Institute Publications, Chicago.
ÖL	Österreichische Lehrerzeitung, Wien.
OLP	Orientalia Lovaniensia Periodica.
OLZ	Orientalistische Literaturzeitung, Berlin.
OMRO	Oudheidkundige Mededelingen Nit Het Rijksmuseum Van Oudheden Te Leiden, Leiden.
Ontario1 = TROM = NSTROM	Sigrist, M.*Neo-Sumerian Account Texts from the Royal Ontario Museum I. the Administration at Drehem*, Bethesda 1995.
Ontario 2	M.Sigrist, *Neo-Sumerian Texts from the Royal Ontario Museum II, Administrative Texts Mainly from Umma*, Bethesda 2004.
Oppenheim Nachlass	M. Civil, *Cuneiform Texts from Oppenheim's Unpublished Manuscripts*, Unpubl.Ms.
OrAnt	Oriens Antiquus, Rome, 1962.
Orient	Orient.Report of the Society of Near Eastern Studies in Japan, Tokyo.

续表

缩写	作者（编者），书名，出版地，日期
OrNS = Or.	Orientalia Nova Series, Rome.
OrSP	Orientalia Series Prior, Rome.
Patesis	C.E.Keiser, *Patesis of the Ur Dynasty*, *Yale Oriental Series*, *Researches* 4: 2, New Haven 1919.
PBS	The Museum of the University of Pennsylvania: Publications of the Babylonian Section, Philadelphia.
PDT	Die Puxris-Dagan-Texte.
PDT 1	M.Çig, H.Kizilyay and H.Salonen, *Die Puzriš-Dagan-Texte der Istanbuler Archäologischen Museen Teil I*: *Nr.* 1-725, Aasf. B. T. 92, 1954/1956. Helsinki 1954.
PDT 2 = FAOS 16	F.Yildiz - T.Gomi, *Die Puzriš-Dagan-Texte der Istanbuler Archäologischen Museen II*: *Nr.*726-1379, Freiburger Altorientalische Studien 16, Stuttgart 1988.
PIOL = PIOL 19	H.Sauren, *Les Tablettes Cuneiformes de l' Epoque d'Ur des Collections de la New York Public Library*, Publications de I ' Institut Orientaliste de Louvain, 1978.
Pisan-dub-ba Texts, Diss.	R.C.Nelson, *Pisan-dub-ba Texts from the Sumerian Ur III Dynasty*, Ph.D. Diss.University of Minnesota 1976.
PPAC	Periodic Publications on Ancient Civilizations, Changchun.
PRAK	Premières Recherches Archéologiques À Kich, Paris, 1925.
Priests and Officials	K.Watanabe (ed.), *Priests and officials in the Ancient Near East.Papers of the Second Colloquium on the Ancient Near East* - the City and Its Life, Held at the Middle Eastern Culture Center in Japan (Mitaka, Tokyo. March 22-24, 1996), Heidelberg 1999.
Prima dell´ alfabeto	M. Fales, *Prima Dell ´ alfabeto. la Storia Della Scrittura Attraverso Testi Cuneiformi Inediti*, Venezia 1989.
Princeton 1	M.Sigrist, *Tablettes du Princeton Theological Seminary.Époque d'ur III*, Philadelphia 1990.
Princeton 2	M.Sigrist, *Tablets from the Princeton Theological Seminary. Ur III Period. Part* 2, Occasional Publications of the Samuel Noah Kramer Fund 18, Philadelphia 2008.
PSBA	Proceedings of the Society of Biblical Archaeology, London.
QqTabCun.	E.Dantinne, *Quelques Tablettes Sumériennes d´Ur*, *Hüy*, Belgique, 1900.
RA	Revued´Assyriologie et d´Archéologie Orientale, Paris, 1886–.
RAH	Cuneiform Tablets in the Real Academia dela Historia (Madrid).
RAI	Renconter Assyriologique Internationale.
RAI 4	Cahiers dela Societe Asiatique 13, Paris, 1954.
RAI 20	Publications de I' Institut Historique et Archeologique Neerlandais de Stamoulxxxvii, 1975.
RB	Revue Biblique, Paris.

续表

缩写	作者（编者），书名，出版地，日期
RCU	P. Michalowski, *The Royal Correspondence of Ur*, Ph. D. Diss. Yale University, 1976.
RIAA = Recueil	Speleers, L., *Recueil des Inscriptions de l' Asie Antérieure des Musées Royaux du Cinquantenaire A Bruxelles*, 1925.
Rend Ac.Linc	Reale Accademia Nazionale Dei Lincei, Rendiconti Della Classe Di Scienze Morali, Storiche E Filologiche, Rome.
RevSem	Revue Sémitique d'Épigraphie et d'Histoire Ancienne.Paris.
RIM	The Royal Inscriptions of Mesopotamia, Toronto - Buffalo - London.
RJM	F.Joannès (ed.), *Rendre la Justice En Mésopotamie. Archives Judiciaires du Proche-Orient Ancien (IIIe-Ier Millénaires Avant J.-C.)*, Saint Denis 2000.
RlA	Reallexikon der Assyriologie, Berlin - Leipzig 1932-, Vol.1 (1932); Vol.2 (1938); Vol.3 (1957-71); Vol.4 (1972-75); Vol.5 (1976-80); Vol.6 (1980-83); Vol.7 (1987-90); Vol.8 (1993-97); Vol.9 1/2 (1998).
RO	Rocznik Orientalistyczny, Varsovia.
Rochester = DTCR	M.Sigrist, *Documents from Tablet Collections in Rochester, New York*, CDL Bethesda, Maryland 1991.
Rocznik MNW	Rocznik Muzeum Narodowego W Warszawie, Warszawa.
Rocznik Toruniu	Rocznik Muzeum W Toruniu.
RSen	Revue Semitique d' Epigraphie et d'Histoire Ancienne (S), Paris.
RSO	Rivista Degli Studi Orientali, Rome.
RT	Recueil de Travaux Relatifs Àla Philologie et À L´archéologie Égyptienne et Assyriennes, Paris.
RTC	F.Thureau-Dangin, Recueil de Tablettes Chaldéennes, Paris 1903.
SA	Ch.F.Jean, *Šumer et Akkad.Contribution à L' Histoire de la Civilisation Dans la Basse-Mésopotamie*, Paris 1923.
SACT	S.T.Kang, *Sumerian and Akkadian Cuneiform Texts in the Collection of the World Heritage Museum of the University of Illinois*, Urbana - Chicago - London, 1972.
Sadberk Museum	V.Donbaz, *Sadberk Hanim Muzesi´nde Bulunan Civiyazili Belgeler - Cuneiform Tablets in the Sadberk Museum*, Istanbul 1999.
SAKF	Oberhuber, K, *Sumerische und Akkadische Keilschriftdenkmäler des Archäologischen Museums Zu Florenz*, Innsbruck 1958–1960.
SAKI	F. Thureau-Dangin, *Die Sumerischen und Akkadischen Königsinschriften*, *Vorderasiatische Bibliothek I/1*, Leipzig 1907.
Sale Documents = FAOS 17	P. Steinkeller, *Sale Documents of the Ur-III Period*, Freiburger Altorientalische Studien 17, Stuttgart 1989.
Salesianum	Periodicum Internationale Trimestro Editum A Professoribus Pontificiae Studiorum Universitatis Salesiane, Rome.
Salmanticensis	Salmanticensis, Salamanca.

续表

缩写	作者（编者），书名，出版地，日期
SAOC	Studies in Ancient Oriental Civilizations, Chicago.
SAT 1-3	M.Sigrist, *Sumerian Archival Texts*, SAT 1 = *Texts from the British Museum*. (CDL Press 1993). (= Texts from the British Museum, TBM); SAT 2 = *Texts from the Yale Babylonian Collection*, *Part I*.CDL Press 2000, = TYBC I, 1-1176; SAT 3 = *Texts from the Yale Babylonian Collection*, *Part II*. CDL Press 2000, = TYBC II, 1177-2223.
SaU	C.Fischer, *Seal Impressions from Ur*, Unpubl.Ms.
Schätze	R.-T. Speler, *Schätze Aus Den Sammlungen und Kabinetten*. 300 Jahre Universität Halle, 1694-1994, Karlsruhe 1994.
Schreiberwesen	H.Waetzoldt, *Das Schreiberwesen in Mesopotamien Nach Texten Aus Neusumerischer Zeit*, *Unveröff.Habilitationsschrift*, Heidelberg 1973.
Security for Debt	R.Westbrook - R.Jasnow (Eds.), *Security for Debt in Ancient Near Eastern Law*, *Culture and History of the Ancient Near East* 9, Leiden 2001.
SD	Studia et Documenta Ad Jura Orentis Antiqui Pertinentia.
Sefarad	Sefarad.Revista de Estudios Hebraicos, Sefardíes Y de Oriente Próximo, Madrid.
SEL	Studi Epigrafici E Linguistici Sul Vicino Oriente Antico, Verona.
SET	T.B.Jones - J.W.Snyder, *Sumerian Economic Texts from the Third Ur Dynasty*, Minneapolis 1961.
Shemshara Archives 2	J. Eidem, *The Shemshara Archives* 2. *the Administrative Texts*, Copenhagen 1992.
SLA	The Sumerian Lexicon Project. Sla, Http://www-oi. uchicago. edu/oi/proj/sum/sla/sumer.html, 1998.
SmithCS 38	C. Gordon, *Smith College Tablets*; 110 *Cuneiform Texts Selected from the College Collection*, *Northampton* (Massachusetts), Smith College Studies in History 38, 1952.
Smithsonian	Cuneiform Tablets from the Smithsonian Institution, Washington Dc.
SMS	Monographic Journals of the Ancient Near East.Syro – Mesopotamian Studies, Malibu.
SNAT	T.Gomi - S.Sato, *Selected Neo-Sumerian Administrative Texts from the British Museum*, Chuo-Gakuin University 1990.
South Dakota	N.W.Forde, *Neo-Sumerian Texts from South Dakota University*, *Luther and Union Colleges*, Lawrence, Kansas 1987.
SRU	D.O.Edzard, *Sumerische Rechtsurkunden des III.Jahrtausends Aus der Zeit Vor der III.Dynastie Von Ur*, München 1968.
STA	E. Chiera, *Selected Temple Accounts from Telloh*, *Yokha and Drehem. Cuneiform Tablets in the Library of Princeton University*, Philadelphia 1922.
StBibFran.	Studium Biblicum Franciscanum Museum, Jerusalem.
STD	Margolis, E., *Sumerian Temple Documents*, 1915.
StOr	Studia Orientalia, Helsinki.

续表

缩写	作者（编者），书名，出版地，日期
Stovall Museum	A.J.Heisserer（ed.）, *The Collection of the Stovall Museum of Science and History*, *The University of Oklahoma.Classical Antiquities*, Norman 1986.
StrKT	C. Frank, *Straßburger Keilschrifttexte in Sumerischer und Babylonischer Sprache*, Straßburg, 1928.
STU	C.L.Bedale, *Sumerian Tablets from Umma in the John Rylands Library - Manchester*, Manchester 1915.
Studi Levi della Vida	Studi Orientalistici in Onore Di Giorgio Levi Della Vida, Pubblicazioni Dell´istituto Per L´oriente, Rome 1956.
Studi Scerrato	M.V.Fontana - B.Genito（Eds.）, *Studi in Onore Di Umberto Scerrato Per Il Suo Settantacinquesimo Compleanno I*, Napoli 2003.
Studi Tamburello	F.Mazzei - P.Carioti（Eds.）, *Studi in Onore Di A.Tamburello*, Napoli（in Press）.
Studies Astour	G. Young - M. Chavalas - R. Averbeck（Eds.）, *Crossing Boundaries and Linking Horizons*: *Studies in Honor of Michael C.Astour on His 80th Birthday*, Bethesda 1997.
Studies Dietrich	O.Loretz - K.A.Metzler - H.Schaudig（Eds.）, *Ex Mesopotamia et Syria Lux. Festschrift Für Manfried Dietrich Zu Seinem* 65. Geburstag, AOAT 281, Münster 2002.
Studies Gordon	H.A.Hoffner（ed.）, *Orient and Occident*: *Essays Presented to Cyrus H.Gordon on the Occasion of His Sixty-Fifth Birthday*, Alter Orient und Altes Testament 22, Kevelaer 1973.
Studies Graefe	A.I. Blöbaum - J. Kahl - S. D. Schweitzer, Ägypten - Münster. *Kulturwissenschaftliche Studien Zu Ägypten*, *Dem Vorderen Orient und Verwandten Gebieten*. Donum Natalilcium Viro Doctissimo Erharto Graefe Sexagenario Ab Amicis Collegis Discipulis Ex Aedibus Schlaunstrasse 2/ Rosenstrasse 9 Oblatum, Wiesbaden 2003.
Studies Greenfield	Z.Zevit - S.Gitin - M.Sokoloff（Eds.）, *Solving Riddles and Untying Knots.Biblical*, *Epigraphic and Semitic Studies in Honor of Jonas C.Greenfield*, Winona Lake 1995.
Studies Haas	T.Richter - D.Prechel - J.Klinger（Eds.）, *Kulturgeschichten.Altorientalische Studien Für Volkert Haas Zum* 65.Geburstag, Saarbrücken 2001.
Studies Hallo	M.E.Cohen - D.C.Snell - D.B.Weisberg（Eds.）, *The Tablet and the Scroll. Near Eastern Studies in Honour of W.W.Hallo*, Bethesda 1993.
Studies Hewett	D.D.Brand - F.E.Harvey（Eds.）, *So Live the Works of Men*: *Seventieth Anniversary Volume Honoring Edgar Lee Hewett*, Albuquerque 1939.
Studies Hilprecht	*Hilprecht Anniversary Volume*: *Studies in Assyriology and Archaeology Dedicated to Hermann V.Hilprecht Upon the Twenty-Fifth Anniversary of His Doctorate and His Fiftieth Birthday*（July 28）by His Colleagues, Friends and Admirers, Leipzig-London-Paris-Chicago, 1909.
Studies in Neo-Sumerian, Diss.	M.Cooper, *Studies in Neo-Sumerian Administrative Procedures*, Ph.D.Diss.University of Minnesota 1980.
Studies Jones	M.A.Powell - R.H.Sack（Eds.）, *Studies in Honor of Tom B.Jones*, Alter Orient und Altes Testament 203, Kevelaer - Neukirchen Vluyn 1979.

续表

缩写	作者（编者），书名，出版地，日期
Studies Klein	Y.Sefati et Al., *An Experienced Scribe Who Neglects Nothing*. Ancient Near Eastern Studies in Honor of Jacob Klein, Bethesda Md 2005.
Studies Koschaker SDJD 2	J.Friedrich - J.G.Lautner - J.Miles (Eds.), *Symbolae Ad Iura Orientis Antiqui Pertinentes Paulo Koschaker Dedicatae*, Leiden 1939.
Studies Kraus	G.Van Driel et Al. (Eds.), *Zikir Šumim: Assyriological Studies Presented to F.R.Kraus on the Occasion of His Seventieth Birthday*, Leiden 1982.
Studies Leichty	A.K.Guinan, et Al. (Eds.), *If A Man Builds A Joyful House: Assyriological Studies in Honor of Erle Verdun Leichty*, Cuneiform Monographs 31, Leiden 2006.
Studies Limet	Ö.Tunca - D.Deheselle (Eds.), Tablettes et Images Aux Pays de Sumer et d'Akkad. Mélanges offerts À Monsieur H. Limet, A. P. H. A. Mémoires 1, Liège 1996.
Studies Lipinski	K.Van Lerberghe - A.Schoors (Eds.), Inmigration and Emigration Within the Ancient Near East. Festschrift E.Lipinski, Orientalia Lovaniensia Analecta 65, Leuven 1995.
Studies Matous	B.Hruška - G.Komoróczy (Eds.), *Festschrift Lubor Matouš*, Budapest 1978.
Studies Moran	T.Abusch - J. Huehnergard - P. Steinkeller (Eds.), *Lingering Over Words. Studies in Ancient Near Eastern Literature in Honor of William J. Moran*, Atlanta 1990.
Studies Oberhuber	W. Meid - H. Trenkwalder, *Im Bannkreis des Alten Orients: Studien Zur Sprach- und Kulturgeschichte des Alten Orients und Seine Ausstrahlungsraumes*, Innsbruck 1986.
Studies Pettinato	H.Waetzoldt (ed.), Von Sumer Nach Ebla und Zurück. *Festscrift Giovanni Pettinato Zum 27. September 1999 Gewidmet Von Freunden, Kollegen und Schülern*, Heidelberger Studien Zum Alten Orient 9, Heidelberg 2004.
Studies Renger = AOAT 267	B.Böck - E.Cancik-Kirschbaum - T.Richter, *Munuscula Mesopotamica. Festschrift Für Johannes Renger*, Alter Orient und Altes Testament 267, Münster 1999.
Studies Rinaldi	*Studi Sull' Oriente Ela Bibbia offerti Al P. Giovanni Rinaldi Nel* 60 *Compleanno Da Allievi, Colleghi, Amici*, Genoa 1967.
Studies Röllig = AOAT 247	B.Pongratz-Leisten - H.Kühne - P.Xella (Eds.), *Ana Šadî Labnâni Lû Allik. Beiträge Zu Altorientalischen und Mittelmeerischen Kulturen. Festschrift Für Wolfgang Röllig*, Alter Orient und Altest Testament 247, Neukirchen-Vluyn 1997.
Studies Sigrist	P.Michalowski (ed.), *On the Third Dynasty of Ur. Studies in Honor of Marcel Sigrist*, Journal of Cuneiform Studies Supplements 1, Boston 2008 (in Press).
Studies Sjöberg = OPKF 11	H.Behrens - D.Loding - M.T.Roth (Eds.), *Dumu-E$_2$-Dub-Ba-A. Studies in Honor of Ake W.Sjöberg*, Occasional Publications of the Samuel Noah Kramer Fund 11, Philadelphia 1989.
Studies Struve	Assiriologija I Egyptologija Sbornik Statej Akademiky, Struve V. V., Leningrad 1964.

续表

缩写	作者（编者），书名，出版地，日期
Studies Szarzynska	J.Braun - K.Lyczkowska - M.Popko - P.Steinkeller（Eds.），*Written on Clay and Stone.Ancient Near Eastern Studies Presented to Krystyna Szarzynska on the Occasion of Her 80th Birthday*，Warsaw 1998.
Studies Tadmor	M.Cogan - I.Eph' Al（Eds.），Ah，Assyria.*Studies in Assyrian History and Ancient Near Eastern Historiography Presented to Hayim Tadmor = Scripta Hierosolymitana* 33，Jerusalem 1991.
Studies Veenhof	W.H.Van Soldt（ed.），*Veenhof Anniversary Volume.Studies Presented to Klaas R.Veenhof on the Occasion of His Sixty-Fifth Birthday*，Istanbul 2001.
Studies Volterra	*Studi in Onore Di Edoardo Volterra*，Milan 1971.
Subartu	Subartu，Turnhout.
Sumer	A Journal of Archaeology and History in Iraq，Baghdad（Since 1973），Was Arab World.（Baghdad 1945 Ff.）
SumRecDreh. = Nesbit Drehem. = Nesbit.	W.N.Nesbit，*Sumerian Records from Drehem* = Columbia University Oriental Studies 8，New York 1914.Reprint New York 1966.
SumTemDocs.	E.Margolis，*Sumerian Temple Documents*，New York 1915.
SVS	Studi Per Il Vocabolario Sumerico，Rome.
Syracuse	M.Sigrist，*Textes Économiques Néo-Sumeriens de L´université de Syracuse*，Paris 1983.
Syria	Syria，Revue d'Art Oriental et d'Archéologie，Paris.
TA	Tel Aviv，Jounal of the Tel Aviv University Institute of Archaeology.
TAD	S.H.Langdon，*Tablets from the Archives of Drehem*，*With A Complete Account of the Origin of the Sumerian Calendar*，*Translation*，*Commentary and 23 Plates*，*Tad*，Paris，1911.
TCCBI 2	F.Pomponio - M.Stol - A.Westenholz（Eds.），*Le Tavolette Cuneiformi Delle Collezioni Della Banca d'Italia. Ii. Tavolette Cuneiformi Di Varia Provenienza Delle Collezioni Della Banca d'Italia*，Rome 2006.
TCL	Musee Di Louvre，Departement des Antiquites Orientales，Textes Cuneiforms，Paris.
TCND =TCNSD	A.Archi and F.Pomponio，*Testi Cuneiformi Neo-Sumerici Da Drehem*，*N. 0001-0412*，*Catalogo Del Museo Egizio Di Torino*，*Ser.Ii*，7，Torino 1990.
TCS	G.Boson，*Tavolette Cuneiformi Sumere Degli Archivi Di Drehem E Di Djoha*，*Dell´ultima Dinastia Di Ur*，Milan 1936.
TCS#	Texts from Cuneiform Sources.（New York 1966 Ff.）
TCS 1	E.Sollberger，*The Business and Administrative Correspondence under the Kings of Ur*，*Texts from Cuneiform Sources* 1，Locust Valley N.Y.1966.
TCTI/TCT	Tablettes Cunéiformes de Tello Au Musée d'Istanbul.
TÉL	M.Lambert，*Tablettes Économiques de Lagash*（*Époque de la Iiie Dynastie d'ur*）*Copiées En* 1900 *Au Musée Impérial Ottoman Par Charles Virolleaud*，Cahiers de la Société Asiatique 19，Paris，1968.

续表

缩写	作者（编者），书名，出版地，日期
Tel-Aviv	Tel-Aviv.Journal of the Sonia Nd Marco Nadler Institute of Archaeology. Tel-Aviv.
TENUS/ TÉNS = Syracuse	Sigrist, M., *Textes Economiques Sumeriens de I ' Universite de Syracuse*, 1983.
Ternbach Collection	R.Merhav, *A Glimpse Into the Past*: *the Joseph Ternbach Collection*, Jerusalem, 1981.
Texts and Impressions	A.Hattori, *Texts and Impressions*: *A Holistic Approach to Ur III Cuneiform Tablets from the University of Pennsylvania Expeditions to Nippur*, Ph.D.Diss. University of Pennsylvania 2002.
TIM	Texts in theIraq Museum, Baghdad, 1964.
TJAMC FM	E.Szlechter, *Tablettes Juridiques et Administratives de la Iiie Dynastie d'ur et de la Ier Dynastie de Babylone*, *Conservées Au Musée de L'université de Manchester et À Cambridge*, *Au Musée Fitzwilliam*, *À L'institut d'études Orientales et À L' institut d'egyptologie*, Paris 1963.
TLB	Tabulae Cuneiformes A F. M. Th. de Liagre Böhl Collectae, Leidae Conservatae, Leiden.1954 ff.
TMH NF	Texte und Materialien der Frau Professor Hilprecht-Sammlung Vorderasiatischer Altertümer Im Eigentum der Friedrich-Schiller-Universität Jena, Neue Folge, Berlin.
Torino 1	A.Archi - F.Pomponio, *Testi Cuneiformi Neo-Sumerici Da Drehem*, *N.*0001-0412, *Catalogo Del Museo Egizio Di Torino VII*, Milan 1990.
Torino 2	A.Archi - F.Pomponio - G.Bergamini, *Testi Cuneiformi Neo-Sumerici Da Umma. N N.* 0413-0723, *Catalogo del Museo Egizio Di Torino VIII*, Turín 1995.
TPTS	Sigrist, M., *Tablettes du Princeton Theological Seminary*, *Epoque d'Ur III*, 1990.
Trouvaille/TrD	H.de Genouillac, la *Trouvaille de Dréhem*, Paris 1911.
TRU	L.Legrain, *Le Temps des Rois d'Ur*, Bibliothèque de L' École des Hautes Études 199, Paris 1912.
TSDU	Lemét, H., *Textes Sumeriens de la IIIe Dynastie d'Ur*, Musées Royaux d'Art et d'Histoire, Parc du Cinquantenaire, 1973.
TUT	G.Reisner, *Tempelurkunden Aus Telloh*, Berlin 1901.
UCP	University of California Publications in Semitic Philology, Los Angeles.
UCP 9/2	*Sumerian Temple Records of the Late Ur Dynasty*, University of Californian Publications in Semitic Philology 9/2, 1-2, Berkeley 1928.
UCU	M.Widell, *The Administrative and Economic Ur III Texts from the City of Ur*, Piscataway 2003.
UDT	J.B.Nies, *Ur Dynasty Tablets.Texts Chiefly from Tello and Drehem Written During the Reigns of Dungi*, *Bur-Sin*, *Gimil-Sin and Ibi-Sin*, Leipzig = Ab 25, 1920.
UE	Ur Excavations, Oxford.

续表

缩写	作者（编者），书名，出版地，日期
UET	Ur Excavations Texts, Pennsylvania - London.
UF	Ugarit-Forschungen, Neukirchen-Vluyn.
Umma	G.Contenau, *Umma Sous la Dynastie d'ur*, Paris 1916.
UNL	G.Pettinato, *Untersuchungen Zur Neusumerischen Landwirtschaft I. Die Felder* 1-2, Nápoles 1967.
UNT	H. Waetzoldt, *Untersuchungen Zur Neusumerischen Textilindustrie*, Rome 1972.
UTI 3	F.Yildiz - T.Gomi, *Die Umma-Texte Aus Den Archäologischen Museen Zu Istanbul. Band III* (*Nr.*1601-2300), Bethesda Md 1993.
UVB	Vorlaufiger Bericht Uber Die Von der Notgemeinschaft der Deutschen Wissenschaft in Uruk-Warka 7, Berlin.
VAMZ	Vjesnik Arheoloskog Muzeja U Zagrebu.
VDI	Vestnik Drevnej Istorii (= Journal of Ancient History), Moskva.
VO	Vicino Oriente, Rome.
Walla Walla College	M.Vincent, *The Transcription*, *Translation and Analysis of the Small Walla Walla College Cuneiform Collection*, Unpubl.Ms.
Warka	J.N.Strassmaier, *Die Altbabylonischen Verträge Aus " Warka"*, 5. *Kongress*, *Zweiter Theil*, *Erste Hälfte P.*315-364 *und* 144 *Tafeln*, 1882.
WMAH	H.Sauren, *Wirtschaftsurkunden Aus der Zeit der III. Dynastie Von Ur Im Besitz des Musée d'art et d'histoire in Genf. I*: Umschrift und Übersetzung, Indizes, Naples 1969.
WO	Die Welt des Orients, Göttingen, 1947.
WroteClay	E.Chiera, *They Wrote on Clay*, Chicago, 1938, P.88 = Les Tablettes Babyloniennes, Paris, 1939.
WZKM	Wiener Zeitschrift Für Die Kunde des Morgenlandes, Wien.
YBC	Tablet Siglum, Yale Babylonian Collection, New Haven.
YNER	Yale Near Easterm Researches.
YOS	Yale Oriental Series, Babylonian Texts, New Haven.
YOS 18	D.Snell and C, H.Lager, *Economic Texts from Sumer*, *Yale Oriental Series*, *Babylonian Texts*, New Haven, 1991.
ZA	Zeitschrift Für Assyriologie und Vorderasiatische Archäologie, Berlin.
ZapKlass.	Zapiski Klassiceskago Otdeleniya Imperatorskago Russkago Archeologiceskago Obåcestva.
Zinbun	Memoirs of the Research Institute for Humanistic Studies, Kyoto University.
ZVO	Zapiski Vostocnago Otdelenija Russkago Archeologiceskago Obsccestva. St. Petersburg.

中文文献

［1］刘文鹏主编：《古代西亚北非文明》，中国社会科学出版社 1999 年版。

［2］张文安：《中国与两河流域神话比较研究》，中国社会科学出版社 2009 年版。

［3］拱玉书：《日出东方——苏美尔文明探秘》，云南人民出版社 2001 年版。

［4］吴于廑、齐世荣、朱寰：《世界史——古代史（上卷）》，高等教育出版社 1994 年版。

［5］朱寰主编：《世界上古中世纪史》，北京大学出版社 1990 年版。

［6］吴宇虹等：《古代两河流域楔形文字经典举要》，黑龙江人民出版社 2006 年版。

［7］刘家和、廖学盛主编：《世界古代文明史研究导论》，高等教育出版社 2001 年版。

［8］王俊娜、吴宇虹：《乌尔第三王朝贡牲中心出土舒勒吉新提王后贡牲机构苏美尔语档案文献研究》，《古代文明》2010 年第 2 期。

［9］王俊娜、吴宇虹：《阿比新提王太后和舒勒吉新提身份同一研究》，《东北师大学报》2011 年第 2 期。

［10］李学彦、吴宇虹：《奴隶劳动在两河流域家庭农业中的重要作用——以两件分家泥板文书为例》，《古代文明》2011 年第 1 期。

［11］李学彦、吴宇虹：《从一件大礼品单看乌尔第三王朝国王和王后的豪华生活》，《历史教学》2011 年第 8 期。

［12］王光胜：《乌尔第三王朝贡牲中心家畜官员卢迪弥尔腊第二的档案重建》，硕士学位论文，东北师范大学古典文明史研究所，2010 年。

［13］王颖杰：《乌尔第三王朝贡牲中心羊牲育肥官员那鲁的档案重建》，博士学位论文，东北师范大学古典文明史研究所，2009 年。

［14］付世强：《乌尔第三王朝厨房死牲官员舒勒吉乌如穆的档案重建》，硕士学位论文，东北师范大学古典文明史研究所，2009 年。

［15］齐霄：《乌尔第三王朝贡牲中心羊圈管理官员乌尔库依那的档案重建》，硕士学位论文，东北师范大学古典文明史研究所，2008 年。

［16］杨勇：《乌尔第三王朝贡牲中心羊牲管理官员阿胡尼的档案重

建》，硕士学位论文，东北师范大学古典文明史研究所，2007 年。

［17］杨柳凌：《乌尔第三王朝厨房死牲官员乌尔尼旮尔的档案重建》，硕士学位论文，东北师范大学古典文明史研究所，2006 年。

［18］谢胜杰：《乌尔第三王朝贡牲中心牛圈管理官员恩里拉的档案重建》，硕士学位论文，东北师范大学古典文明史研究所，2006 年。

［19］齐兵：《乌尔第三王朝贡牲中心运送官员那冉伊里的档案重建》，硕士学位论文，东北师范大学古典文明史研究所，2005 年。

英文文献

[1] Wu Yuhong. High Ranking Scribes and Intellectual Governors during the Akkadian and Ur III Periods [J], JAC, 1995.

[2] Wu Yuhong. The Ewes without Lambs and Lambs Cooked in É-uz-ga, "The Private House of Kings", in the Drehem Archives [J], JAC, 1996.

[3] Wu Yuhong. How did They Change from Mašda Years to Akiti Years from Šulgi 45 to Šulgi48 in Puzriš-Dagan [J], JAC, 2000.

[4] Wu Yuhong. Calendar Synchronization and Intercalary Months in Umma, Puzriš-Dagan, Nippur, Lagash and Ur during the Ur III Period [J], JAC, 2002.

[5] Wu Yuhong. Differentiating Šulgi 43 and Amar-Suen 4 in Cuneiform Digital Library Notes = CDLN = 2010: 001, http://cdli.ucla.edu/pubs/cdln/http://cdli.ucla.edu/pubs/cdln/ (105).

[6] Wu Yuhong, The Anonymous Nasa and Nasa of the Animal Center during Šulgi 44-48 and the Wild Camel (gú-gur$_5$), Hunchbacked Ox (gur$_8$-gur$_8$), ubi, habum and the Confusion of the Deer (lulim) with Donkey (anše) or šeg$_9$, [J], JAC, 2010.

[7] Wu Yuhong. *Naram-ili*, Šu-Kabta and *Nawir-ilum* in the Archives of Ĝaršana, Puzriš-Dagan and Umma [J]. JAC, 2008.

[8] Tohru Gomi. The Calendars of Ur and Puzriš-Dagān in the Early Ur-III Period [J]. Jounal of ACTA Sumerological, 1979, 1.

[9] Tohru Gomi. Bringing (mu-túm) livestock and the Puzurish-Dagan organization in the Ur III dynasty [J]. Jounal of ACTA Sumerological, 1989, 11.

[10] Tohru Gomi. Shulgi-simti and her Libation Place (ki-a-nag) [J]. O-

rient, 1976, 12.

[11] Diane W, Samuel N K. Inanna——Queen of Heaven and Earth [M].New York: Harper & Row, Publishers, Inc, 1983.

[12] Bottéro J.Religion in Ancient Mesopotamia [M], Chicago: The University of Chicago Press, 2001.

[13] Setsuko O. On the Function of the Maškim [J], Jounal of ACTA Sumerological, 1983, 5.

[14] P.Steinkeller.More on the Ur III Royal Wives [J].ASJ, 1981, 3.

[15] Tom B.Jones and John W.Snyder.Sumerian Economic Texts from the Third Ur Dynasty [M], University of Minnesota Press, 1961.

[16] Frauke Weiershäuser.Die königlichen Frauen der III.Dynastie von Ur [M], Göttingen: Universitätsverlag Göttingen, 2008.

[17] Jacob L. Dahl. The Ruling Family of Ur III Umma: A Prosopographical Analysis of an Elite Family in Southern Iraq 4000 Years Ago [M], Leiden: Nederlands Instituut voor het Nabije Oosten, 2007.

[18] D.Frayne.The Royal Inscription of Mesopotamia [M], Toronto: University of Toronto Press, 1993.

[19] David I. Owen. On the Patronymy of Šu-Suen [J], N. A. B. U. Nouvelles Assyriologiques Brevs et Utilitaires, 2001.

[20] Yitschak Sefati. Love Songs in Sumerian Literature [M], Ramat Gan: Bar-Ilan University Press, 1998.

[21] Kazuko Watanabe. Priests and Officials in the Ancient Near East [M], Heidelberg: Universitätsverlag C.Winter, 1996.

[22] Samuel Noah Kramer. The Sumerians, their history, culture, and character [M], Chicago & London: The University of Chicago Press, 1963.

[23] Harriet Crawford. Sumer and the Sumerians [M], London: Cambrige University Press, 1991.

[24] Marcel Sigrist.Drehem [M], Bethesda, MD: CDL Press, 1992.

[25] Marc Van De Mieroop. The Ancient Mesopotamian City [M], Oxford University Press, 1997.

[26] McGuire Gibson and Robert D.Biggs.Seals and Sealing in the Ancient

Near East [M], Malibu: Undena Publications, 1977.

[27] Mark E.Cohen. The Cultic Calendars of the Ancient Near East [M], Bethesda, Maryland: CDL Press, 1993.

[28] P.Steinkeller.More on the Ur III Royal Wives [J].ASJ, 1981, 3.

附录一　年名表

年序	原文	英文和中文
24	mu Karú-har[ki] ba-hul（RlA 2 137 43）	Year of Karahar was destroyed. 卡腊哈尔被毁之年。
（25-ús-sa）	i-iii，mu ús-sa Karú-har[ki] ba-hul	Year after that of Karahar was destroyed. 卡腊哈尔被毁年之次年。
25	mu Si-mu-ru-um[ki] ba-hul（RlA 2 137 44）	Year of Simurrum was destroyed. 席穆润被毁之年。
Š 26	mu a-rá-2-kam-aš Si-mu-ru-um[ki] ba-hul.（TRU 1） mu-**ús-sa** Si-mu-ru-um[ki] ba-hul（OIP 115，1）	Year of Simurrum was destroyed for the second time.席穆润第二次被毁之年。Year after that of Simurrum was destroyed 席穆润被毁年之次年。
（Š 27 **ús-sa**）	mu-**ús-sa** Si-mu-ru-um[ki] ba-hul.	Year after that of Simurrum was destroyed. 席穆润被毁之年之次年。
Š 27	mu Ha-ar-ši[ki] ba-hul.（PDT 1 209）	Year of Harši was destroyed. 哈尔西被毁之年。
Š 28 （-29 ús-sa）	mu En-nam-šita$_4$-^{d} Šul-gi-ra-ke$_4$-gub-ba ba-huĝ.（YBC 859= SAT 2，6） mu En-nam-šita$_4$-^{d} Šul-gi-ra-ke$_4$-ba-gub ~ **en-** $^{\mathbf{d}}$**En-ki~ Eridug**[ki]-ga dumu-^{d}Šul-gi ~ nita-kalag-ga ~ lugal-Urím[ki]-ma ~ lugal-an-ub-da-limmú-ba-ka ba-a-huĝ（BM 26209）. **mu en-Eridu**[ki] **ba-huĝ**.（PDT 1，516）	Year of En-namšita-Šulgirake-guba（of Eridu）was installed.恩楠西塔舒勒吉腊凯古巴（女祭司）被任命之年。Year the Ennamšita-Šulgirake-guba，priestess of Enki of Eridug，daughter of Šulgi，the strong man，the king of Ur and the king of the four quarters，was installed.恩楠西塔舒勒吉腊凯古巴——埃瑞杜的恩基女祭司和强健者、乌尔王和四方之王舒勒吉之女被任命之年。Year of the en priestess（of Enki）of Eridu was installed.埃瑞都的（恩基神的）女祭司被任命之年。

续表

年序	原文	英文和中文
Š 29 **ús-sa** **正式**	mu**ús-sa** En-nam-šita-^{d} Šul-gi-ra-ke$_4$-gub-ba ba-huĝ-ĝá. (Iraq 22 pl.19) mu ús-sa En-nam-šita$_4$-^{d}Šul-gi-ra-ke$_4$- ba-gub-ba--šè šùd-saĝ en- ^{d}En-ki ~ **Eridug**^{ki}-ga dumu-^{d} Šul-gi ~ nita-kalag-ga ~ lugal-Urím^{ki}-ma ~ lugal-an-ub-da-limmú-ba-ke$_4$ ba-a-hun (YBC 859); mu**ús-sa** **en-Eridu**^{ki} **ba-huĝ** (TCL 2 5537, i-xii)	Year after that of En-namšita-Šulgirake$_4$-guba (en-priestess) was installed. 恩楠西塔舒勒吉腊凯古巴（女祭司）被任命年之次年。 Year after that of the Ennamšita-Šulgirake-guba-sudsaĝ, priestess of Enki of Eridug, daughter of Šulgi, the strong man, the king of Ur and the king of the four quarters, was installed. 恩楠西塔舒勒吉腊凯古巴苏德桑——埃瑞杜的恩基女祭司和强健之人乌尔王四方之王舒勒吉之女被任命之年之次年。
Š 30	mu dumu-munus-lugal énsi-An-ša-an^{ki}--ke$_4$ ba-an-tuku (BIN 3 407)	Year of the daughter of king was married by the governor of Anšan. 王之女被安山的总督娶走之年。
Š 31 i-xiii	mu a-rá-2 (mìn) -kam-aš Kára-har^{ki} ba-hul. (OIP 115, 2 = A 5149, i-xiii PDT 374) **see Š 24**	Year of Karahar was destroyed for the second time.24-31 卡腊哈尔第二次被毁灭之年。(第一次是 24 年)
Š 32 (-33ús-sa)	mu 3-kam. (Princeton 2 046). **see Š 25-26** mu a-rá-3-kam Si-mu-ru-um^{ki} ba-hul. mu a-rá-3-kam-aš Si-mu-ru-um^{ki} ba-hul. (PDT 1, 373, TCL 2 5538 i-xii)	Year of Simurrum was destroyed for the third time.25-26-32 席穆润第三次被毁灭之年。 (第一和第二次是 25 年和 26 年)
Š 33 **ús-sa** **正式**	mu**ús-sa** a-rá-3-kam-aš Si-mu-ru-um^{ki} ba-hul. mu**ús-sa** a-rá-3-kam Si-mu-ru-um^{ki} ba-hul. (TPTS 93)	Year of Simurrum was destroyed for the third time.32-33 席穆润第三次被毁之年次年。
Š 34	mu An-ša-an^{ki} ba-hul. (34-35 ús-sa)	Year of Anšan was destroyed. 安山被毁之年。
Š 35 **正式**	mu ús-sa An-ša-an^{ki} ba-hul (RlA 2 137 54)	Year after that of Anšan was destroyed 安山国被毁之年之次年。
(Š 36 **ús-sa**)	mu ús-sa An-ša-an^{ki} ba-hul, mu ús-sa-bi	Year after that of Anšan was destroyed: after that. 安山国被毁之次年：之次年。
Š 36	mu^{d} Nanna Ga-eš^{ki} é-ba-a ba-ku$_4$ (BM 18746)	Year of Nanna of Gaeš was brought into his temple 旮埃什的神南那被送入他的庙宇之年。
Š 36	mu^{d} Nanna Kar-zi-da^{ki} **a-rá-2-kam-ma-aš** é-a-na ba-an-ku$_4$. (formula used in Drehem) mu^{d} Nanna Kar-zi-da^{ki} a-rá-2-kam-ma--**šè** é-a-na ba-an-ku$_4$ (formula used in Nippur) mu^{d} Nanna-Kar-zi-da a-rá-2-kam é-a-na ba-kur$_9$/ku$_4$.	Year of Nanna of Karzida was for the second time brought into his temple. 卡尔孜达的神南那第二次被送入他的庙宇之年。 (第一次是 15 年)

续表

年序	原文	英文和中文
Š 36	mu ^{d}Nanna Kar-zi-da^{ki} é-a-na ba-an-ku$_4$	Year of Nanna of Karzida was brought into his temple. (formula used in Lagaš) 卡尔孜达的神南那被送入他的庙宇之年。
Š 36 Ur	mu^{d} Nanna Kar-zi-da^{ki} é-**nun**-na--šè / agrun-na--šè (ba-an-ku$_4$) (in Ur)	Year of Nanna of Karzida (was brought into the temple), Enunna. 卡尔孜达的神南那（被送入）他的庙宇之年。
(Š 37 **ús-sa**)	mu ús-sa^{d}Nanna Kar-zi-da^{ki} a-rá-2-kam é-a-na ba-an-ku$_4$	Year after that of Nanna of Karzida was for the second time brought into his temple. 卡尔孜达的神南那被送入他的庙宇之次年。
Š 37	mu^{d} Nanna ù ^{d}Šul-gi lugal-e bàd ma-da mu-dù (YBC 476) mu bàd ma-da ba-dù	Year of Nanna and Šulgi king built the wall of the land. 神南那和国王舒勒吉建立国家的城墙之年。 Year of the wall of the land was built 国家的城墙建被立之年。
Š 38 ús-sa 正式	mu ús-sa bàd ma-da ba-dù (RlA 2 137 57)	Year after that of wall of the land was built. 国家城墙被建立年之次年。
Š 39**ús-sa**	mu ús-sa bàd ma-da ba-dù, **mu ús-sa-bi** (RlA 2 137 59)	Year after that of the wall of the land was built. 国家城墙被建立年之次年：**之次年**。
Š 39	mu^{d} Šul-gi ~ lugal-Urim^{ki}-ma--ke$_4$ lugal-an- ub-da-4-ba--ke$_4$ É-Puzur$_4$-iš-^{d} Dagan^{ki} é-^{d} Šul-gi-ra mu-dù (BM 23420, 28018) **mu É-Puzur$_4$-iš-^{d}Da-gan ba-dù**. (PIOL 19, 280 = Eames S8)	Year of Šulgi, king of Ur and king of the four quarters, built the Office of Puzriš-Dagan, the house of Šulgi. 乌尔之王和四方之王神舒勒吉建立普兹瑞什达干司即神舒勒吉的官府之年。 Year of the Office of Puzriš-Dagan was built. 普兹瑞什达干司被建之年。
Š 40 ús-sa 正式	mu ús-sa É-Puzur$_4$-iš-^{d} Da-gan^{ki} ba-dù-a (JSOR 14, 49 61)	Year after that of the Office of Puzriš-Dagan was built. 普兹瑞什达干司被建年之次年。
Š 41 ús-sa-bi 正式	mu ús-sa É-Puzur$_4$-iš-^{d} Da-gan^{ki} ba-dù-a mu ús-sa-a-bi (RlA 2 137 60)	Year after that of the Office of Puzriš-Dagan was built; after that year 普兹瑞什达干司被建年之次年：之次年。
Š 42	mu^{d} Šul-gi lugal-e Ša-aš-ru-um^{ki} mu-hul (RlA 2 137 61) mu Ša-aš-ru-um^{ki} ba-hul	Year of the divine Šulgi king destroyed Šašrum 神舒勒吉王毁灭沙什润之年。 Year of Šašrum was destroyed. 沙什润被毁之年。
Š 43	mu En-ubur-zi-an-na en-^{d} Nanna maš/máš--e ì-pàd (见 AS 4 ba-huĝ)	Year of En-ubur-zianna was chosen as en-priestess of Nanna by omen 南那的女祭司被占卜选中之年 RlA 2 137 62。

续表

年序	原文	英文和中文
Š 44	mu Si-mu-ru-um[ki] ù Lu-lu-bu-um[ki]/Lu-lu-bím[ki] a-rá-9-kam-aš ba-hul（RlA 2 142 63） mu Si-mu-ru-um[ki] a-rá-9-kam-aš ba-hul（OIP 115，372）	Year Simurrum and Lulubum were destroyed for the ninth time. 席穆润和鲁鲁布第九次被毁之年。 Year of Simurum was destroyed for the 9th time.席穆润第九次被毁之年。
Š44’ **ús -sa** viii’-xii’（45 i-v）	mu Si-mu-ru-um[ki] ù Lu-lu-bu-um[ki] a-rá-9-kam-aš ba-hul，mu-ús-sa-bi.（TRU 279）. mu ús-sa Si-mu-ru-um[ki] ù Lu-lu-bu-um[ki] a-rá-9-kam-aš ba-hul（SACT 1，72）	Year of Simurum and Lulubu were destroyed for the 9th time：after that.席穆润和鲁鲁布第九次被毁灭年：之次年。 Year after that of Simurum and Lulubu were destroyed for the 9th time.席穆润和鲁鲁布第九次被毁年之次年。
Š44’ viii’-xii’ iti-**mìn**	iti-zex（ses）-da-gu$_7$-**mìn**-kam，mu Si-mu-ru-um[ki]<ù> Lu-lu-bu[ki] a-rá-9-kam-aš ba-hul.（OIP 115，303）	Month of the second zeda-gu$_7$，Year of Simurum and Lulubu were destroyed for 9th time.第二个食豚月，席穆润和鲁鲁布第九次被毁灭之年。
Š45’ ús- sa-bi，i’	mu ús-sa Lu-lu-bum a-rá-9-kam ba-hul，mu~ ús-sa-bi（YBC 14406）	Year after that of Lulubum was destroyed for the 9th time：after that.鲁鲁布第九次被毁年之次年：之次年。
Š 45’ i’ -v’	mu[d] Šul-gi lugal-e Ur-bí-lum[ki] Lu-lu-bu[ki] Si-mu-ru-um[ki] ù Kará-har[ki] aš--šè saĝ-du-bi šu-tibir-a bí-in-ra-a.（MVN-10，224）	Year of the divine Šulgi king smashed with fist the heads of Urbilum，Lullubu，Simurrum and Karahar together.神舒勒吉王以重拳一举击碎乌尔比隆、鲁鲁布、席穆润和卡腊哈尔之头颅之年。
Š 45’ i’ -xii’	mu Ur-bí-lum[ki] ba-hul（Hirose 39）	Year of Urbilum was destroyed 乌尔比隆被毁之年。
Š46’ ús- sa i’ - ii’	mu ús-sa Ur-bí-lum[ki] ba-hul（OIP 115，400）	Year after that of Urbilum was destroyed 乌尔比隆被毁之年之次年。
Š46’	mu Ki-maš[ki] ù Hu-ur$_5$-ti[ki] ba-hul（CST 116） mu Ki-maš[ki] ba-hul（AUCT 1，666）	Year of Kimaš and Hurti were destroyed. 基马什和胡尔提被毁之年。 Year of Kimaš was destroyed. 基马什被毁之年。
Š47’ ús-sa 正式	mu ús-sa Kimaš[ki] ù Hu-ur$_5$-ti[ki] ba-hul（Hirose 74） mu ús-sa Ki-maš[ki] ba-hul（BM 117410）	Year after that of Kimaš and Hurti were destroyed 基马什和胡尔提被毁之年之次年。 Year after that of Kimaš was destroyed. 基马什被毁之年之次年。
Š48’ ús-sa i’ -ii’	mu ús-sa Ki-maš[ki] ba-hul：mu ~ ús-sa-bi（AUCT 1，688）	Year after that of Kimaš was destroyed：after that 基马什被毁之年之次年：之次年。

续表

年序	原文	英文和中文
Š48' i' -vii'（仅7个月）	mu Ha-ar-ši^{ki} Hu-ur$_5$-ti^{ki} Ki-maš^{ki} ù ma-da-bi ud-1-a ba-hul（AUCT 1，8 74） mu Ha-ar-ši^{ki} Ki-maš^{ki} ù Hu-ur$_5$-ti^{ki} ba-hul（AUCT 1，499） mu Ha-ar-ši^{ki} ù Ki-maš^{ki} ba-hul（TCND 294） mu Ha-ar-ši^{ki} ba-hul（MVN 2，320）	Year of Harši，Hurti，Kimaš and their territories were destroyed in one day. 哈尔西、胡尔提、基马什及它们领土同一天被毁之年。 Year of Harši，Kimaš and Hurti were dstroyed. 哈尔西、基马什和胡尔提被毁之年。 Year of Harši and Kimaš were destroyed 哈尔西和基马什被毁之年。 Year of Harši was destroyed 哈尔西被毁之年。
Š48'	mu Ki-maš^{ki} a-rá 2-kam ba-hul	Year Kimaš was destroyed for the second time 基马什第二次被毁灭之年。
Š48'	mu 2-kam Ha-ar-ši^{ki} ba-hul	Year for the second time Harši was destroyed 哈尔西第二次被毁之年。（第一次27年）
AS 1 ús-sa	mu ús-sa Ha-ar-ši^{ki} ù Ki-maš^{ki} ba-hul（AnOr 13 24 1a）（新历取消，恢复旧历）	Year after that of Harši and Kimaš were destroyed 哈尔西和基马什被毁之年之次年。
AS 1	mu^{d} Amar-^{d} Enzu lugal-àm（AnOr 13 24 1b） mu^{d} Amar-^{d}Sin lugal.（MVN13，122）	Year of the divine Amar-Sin became king. 神阿马尔辛成为王之年。
AS 2 ús-sa	mu ús-sa^{d} Amar-^{d}Enzu lugal（UDT 62）	Year after that of the divine Amar-Sin became king. 神阿马尔辛成为王之年之次年。
AS 2	mu^{d} Amar-^{d} Enzu lugal-e Ur-bí-lum^{ki} mu-hul（AnOr 13 24 2b）	Year of the divine Amar-Sin the king destroyed Urbilum. 神阿马尔辛王毁灭乌尔比隆之年。
AS 2/Š45'	mu Ur-bí-lum^{ki} ba-hul（CST 130）	Year of Urbilum was destroyed 乌尔比隆被毁之年。
AS 3 ús-sa	mu ús-sa^{d} Amar-^{d} Enzu lugal-e Ur-bí-lum^{ki} mu-hul（AnOr 13 24 3a）	Year after that of the divine Amar-Sin king destroyed Urbilum. 神阿马尔辛王毁灭乌尔比隆之年之次年。
AS 3	mu^{d} Amar-^{d} Sîn lugal-e ^{d}Gu-za-mah-^{d} En-líl-lá in-dím.（AnOr 13 24 3b） mu^{d} Amar-^{d}Sîn lugal-e ^{geš}gu-za ^{d}En-líl in-dím.（Aleppo 7） mu^{geš} gu-za-^{d} En-líl-lá ba-dím（Hirose 137） mu^{d}gu-za- ^{d}En-líl-lá ba-dím.（Nisaba 8，243）	Year of the divine Amar-Sin king made joyfully a magnificent throne for Enlil. 神阿马尔辛王制造了神恩利勒的宏伟圣座之年。 Year of the divine Amar-Sin king made a magnificent throne for Enlil. 神阿马尔辛王制造了神恩利勒的王座之年。 Year of the throne of Enlil was made. 神恩利勒的王座被造之年。 Year of the divine throne of Enlil was made. 神恩利勒的圣王座被造之年。

续表

年序	原文	英文和中文
AS 4	mu en^{d}Nanna ba-huĝ. (OrSP 47, 49 120, P125009) mu En-mah-gal-an-na en^{d} Nanna ba-huĝ. (AUCT 1, 408, P103253)	Year of the en-priest of Nanna was installed.神南那的女祭司被任命之年。 Year of En-mahgal-anna, en-priestess of Nanna, was installed.神南那的女祭司恩马赫旮勒安那被任命之年。
AS 5**ús-sa**	mu ús-sa En-mah-gal-an-na en^{d}Nanna ba-huĝ.(BIN 3 538, P106345)	Year after that of the en-priest of divine Nanna was installed.神南那的女祭司恩马赫旮勒安那被任命之年之次年。
AS 5	mu en-^{d}Inanna ba-huĝ.(AUCT 3, 381, P 104592) mu en-Unug^{ki}-ga ba-huĝ. mu En-unu$_{6}$-gal-(an-na) ^{d}Inanna ba-huĝ. (TRU 183 = ASJ 07, 175, P134947)	Year of the en-priest of Inanna was installed.女神伊南那的祭司被任命之年。 Year of the en-priest of Uruk was installed.乌鲁克的祭司被任命之年。 Year of En-unu-gal-(an-na), en-priest of Inanna, was installed.女神伊南那的祭司恩乌努旮勒被任命之年。
AS 6	mu Ša-aš-ru^{ki} ba-hul. (YBC 1378 = SAT 2, 0997, P144197)	Year of Šašru was destroyed. 沙什如被毁之年。
AS 7	mu Hu-úh-nu-ri^{ki} ba-hul. (AUCT 3, 377, P104588)	Year of Huhnuri was destroyed. 胡赫努瑞被毁灭之年。
AS 8	mu En～nun-e-ki～ág～^{d}Amar-^{d}Sin—<ra> en-Eridu^{ki} ba-huĝ. mu En～nun-e～^{d}Amar-^{d}Sîn-ra～ki～ág en-Eridu^{ki} ba-huĝ.(left) 5 gud 52 udu (P125964 PDT 1: 0548) mu en-Eridu^{ki} ba-huĝ. (MVN 2, 331 = OLP 04, 35 27, P113630)	Year of En-nune-kiag-Amar-Sin, the en-priestess of Eridu was installed.埃瑞都的女祭司（名为）"神王爱阿马尔辛"女祭司被任命之年。 Year of En-nune-Amar-Sinra-kiag, the priestess of Eridu was installed. Year of the en-priestess of Eridu was installed.埃瑞都的女祭司被任命之年。
AS 9	1) mu en-^{d}Nanna～Kar-zi-da ba-huĝ. (CTMMA 1, 30, P108714) 2)	Year of the en-priest of Nanna of Karzida was installed. 卡尔孜达的神南那的女祭司被任命之年。
ŠS 1	mu^{d}Šu-^{d}Sîn lugal.(Princeton 2 447, P 201446)	Year of the divine Šu-Sin became king 神舒辛成为王之年。
ŠS 2	mu má-darà-Absu ba-ab-du$_{8}$. (AUCT 3, 001, P104235)	Year of the boat of wild buck of Apsu was caulked.阿坡朱的野山羊船被密封之年。
ŠS 3	mu Si-ma-núm^{ki} ba-hul. (MVN 15, 294, P118559)	Year of Simanum was destroyed. 席马农被毁之年。
ŠS 4 ús-sa	mu ús-sa Si-ma-núm^{ki} ba-hul. (SAT 3, 1440, P144640)	Year after that of Simanum was destroyed. 席马农被毁之年之次年。
ŠS 4	mu^{d} Šu-^{d} Sîn～lugal-Urim$_{5}$^{ki}-ma-ke$_{4}$ bàd Mar-tu *Mu-ri-iq Ti-id-ni-im* mu-dù.(CST 427, P107942)	Year of the divine Šu-Sin, king of Ur, built the Amorite Wall (called) "*Murīq-Tidnim*".乌尔王神舒辛建了名为穆瑞可提德恁的阿摩利城墙之年。

续表

年序	原文	英文和中文
ŠS 5- 全年 **ús-sa**	mu ús-sa^{d} Šu-^{d} Sîn lugal Urim$_5$^{ki}-ma-ke$_4$ bàd Mar-tu *Mu-ri-iq Ti-id-ni-im* mu-dù. （BCT 1，029，P105131）	Year after that of the divine Šu-Sin, king of Ur, built the Amorite Wall (called) "*Murīq-Tidnim*".乌尔王神舒辛建了名为穆瑞可提德尼姆的阿摩利城墙之年之次年。
ŠS 6	mu^{d} Šu-^{d} Sîn ~ lugal Urim$_5$^{ki}-ma-ke$_4$, [na] -rú-a-mah ^{d}En-líl ~ [^{d}Nin] -líl--ra mu-ne-dù. （MVN 13，485，P117258）	Year of the divine Šu-Sin, king of Ur, built a magnificent stele for Enlil and Ninlil. 乌尔王神舒辛为神恩利勒和神宁利勒建造丰碑之年。
ŠS 7	mu^{d} Šu-^{d} Sîn ~ lugal-Urim$_5$^{ki}-ma-ke$_4$ ma-da-Za-ab-ša-li^{ki} mu-hul.（TRU 254 = ASJ 7，179，P135018）	Year of the divine Šu-Sin, king of Ur, destroyed the land of Zabšali. 乌尔王神舒辛毁灭扎卜沙里国之年。
ŠS 8	mu^{d}Šu-^{d}Sîn ~ lugal-Urim$_5$^{ki}-ma-ke$_4$, má-gur$_8$-mah ^{d}En-líl ~ ^{d}Nin-líl--ra mu-ne-dím. （BIN 3，328，P106134）	Year of the divine Šu-Sin, king of Ur, made a magnificent boat for Enlil and Ninlil. 乌尔王神舒辛为神恩利勒和神宁利勒建造了巨船之年。
ŠS 9	mu^{d} Šu-^{d} Sîn ~ lugal Urim$_5$^{ki}-ma-ke$_4$ É-^{d} Šará- Umma^{ki}-ka mu-dù.（AUCT 3，096，P104326）	Year of the divine Šu-Sin, king of Ur, built the temple of Šara of Umma.乌尔王神舒辛建成温马的沙腊神庙之年。
IS 1	mu^{d} I-bí-^{d} Sîn lugal.（AUCT 3，027，P104260）	Year of divine Ibbi-Sin (became) king. 神伊比辛成为国王之年。
IS 2	mu en-^{d}Inanna-Unug^{ki}-ga máš-e ì-pàd,（YOS 4，60，P142124）	Year of the en-priest of Inanna of Uruk was chosen by omens 乌鲁克的女神伊南那的祭司被占卜选中之年。

附录二　月名表

i：iti-maš-dà~gu$_7$	Month of mašda-gu$_7$	食瞪羚月
ii：iti-ze$_x$（ses）-da~gu$_7$	Month of zeda~gu$_7$	食豚月
iii：iti-u$_5$-bí$^{(\text{mušen})}$~gu$_7$	Month of ubi-gu$_7$	食乌比鸟月
iv：iti-ki-siki-^{d}Nin-a-zu	Month of ki-siki-Ninazu	神宁阿朱羊毛作坊月
v：iti-ezem-^{d}Nin-a-zu	Month of ezem-Ninazu	神宁阿朱庆典月
vi：iti-á-ki~ti	Month of akiti	阿基提月
vii：iti-ezem-^{d}Šul-gi	Month of ezem-Šulgi	神舒勒吉庆典月
viii：iti-šu-eš-ša （舒辛 3 年以前使用）	Month of šu-eššа	三只手月
viii：iti-ezem-^{d}Šu-Sîn （舒辛 3 年开始使用）	Month of ezem-Šu-Sin	神舒辛庆典月
ix：iti-ezem-mah	Month of ezem-mah	大庆典月
x：iti-ezem-An-na	Month of ezem-Ana	天神庆典月
xi：iti-ezem-$^{(d)}$Me-ki-ĝál	Month of ezem-Mekiĝal	神美基旮勒庆典月
xii：iti-še-kin-kud	Month of še-kin-kud	大麦收割月
xiii：iti-diri-še-kin~kud	Additional Month of še-kin-kud	闰加大麦收割月

附录三　舒勒吉新提王后贡牲机构官员职衔表

名字	官衔	时间	文献出处
It-ra-ak-ì-lí	lú Ma-rí^{ki}	Š 34 v	AnOr 07 147
nin$_9$-*A-da-làl*	ugula-uš-bar	Š 35 vii	Royal Ontario Museum 1，10
A-da-na-ah	mušen-dù	Š 38 vi	AnOr 01 001
Ad$_6$-mu	na-gada	Š 39 v	AnOr 07 003
Al-la-mu	santana	Š 43 ii/1，4，9	OIP 115 07
Ar-ši-ah	ensí Babilim^{ki}	Š 43 xi/30	RO 11 96 01
Á-geš-gar-ra	mušen-dù	Š 46 x	PDT 1 056
A-mur-^{d}*Utu*	lú-kaš$_4$	Š 46 xii	AnOr 07 011
dumu-munus-A-ba-^{d} En-líl-gin$_7$	rá-gaba	Š 36 i	BIN 3 347
dumu-munus-*A-ga-núm*	nar	Š 41 ix/10，14	MVN 03 179
Ba-a-la-a	nu-bandà	Š 36 v	Orient 16 040 3
Be-lí-ba-ni	sanga-Inanna	Š 40 v/29	RT 37 129 ml 2
Ba-gu-um	mušen-dù	Š 42 viii/5	MVN 13 275
Da-a-ti	kuš$_7$	Š 44 i/27-30	MVN 03 200
E-te-［*el*］*-pù-*^{d} *Da-*［*gan*］	dumu-lugal	Š 29 xi	OIP 115016
É-a-ba-ni	ensí Eréš^{ki}	Š 32 ix	YOS 4 079
^{d}En-líl-ì-sa$_6$	šabra	Š 45 v/22	PDT 1 475
En-ni-a	nar-mí	Š 39 iii	OIP 115037
É-u$_6$-e	ensí	Š 40 ii	OIP 115043
Gìr-ni-ì-sa$_6$	šbara-Gu-la	Š 32 v	Torino 1 001

续表

名字	官衔	时间	文献出处
Ga-la-a	rú-gaba lugal	Š 42 v/23	CST 469
Hu-ba-a	šagina	Š 33 v	CST042
dam-*Ha-la-a*	ugula-60-da	Š 45 v/22	PDT 1 475
é-gi_4-a-Inim-^{d}Šarú	dub-sar	Š 40viii/29, 30	CST051
Ilum-ba-ni	šabra/ensí Kiš^{ki}	Š 33 iv	MVN 03 136
Igi-an-na-ke_4-zu	šabra-^{d}Nanna	Š 34 v	AnOr 07 147
I-ṭì-ib-ši-na-at	ugula, erén-I-$šur_6$^{ki}	Š 34 vi	MVN 13 415
I-mi-^{d}Sîn	sukkal	Š 36 viii	OIP 115024
I-mi-id-ilim,	na-gada	Š 38 viii	AnOr 7042
I-zu-a-ri-ik	énsi	Š 39 viii	CST049
Išdum-kí-in dumu Ur-niĝar	lú-*Mar-ha-ši*^{ki}	Š 40 i	AUCT 1 089
I-mi-id-ilum	šabra	Š 42 i/26	OIP 115 069
I-din-Èr-ra	^{lú}azlág	Š 43 xi/30	RO 11 96 01
^{d}*$Iš_8$-tár-al-šu*	dumu-lugal	Š 46 xii	MVN 13 794
Ku-li-mu	šabra	Š 31 iv	OIP 115017
Ku-li	šabra	Š 32 v	DoCu Strasbourg 53
Ka-lu-um	ensí	Š 33 iv	MVN 03 136
Lugal-ha-ma-ti	dub-sar	Š 31 i	NYPL 163
La-ra-bu-um	na-gada	Š 38 viii	AnOr 7042
Lugal-ezem	šùš/ lú ensí Šuruppag^{ki}	Š 39 v	AnOr 07 003
Lú-sag_9-ga	šabra^{d}Nin-urta	Š 42 vii/15	Ontario 1 012
Lugal-tur-šè	sukkal	Š 45 ix/29	RA 49 86 04
Lú-kirì-zal	na-gada	Š 46 i/8, 15	JCS 29 117 1
Lugal-me-lám	sukkal/ensí Nibru^{ki}	Š 47 xi	OIP 115 115
Nin-ù-ma	uš-bar	Š 31 vi	BIN 3 360
Nir-ì-da-gál	šakkana ÚR×A.HA^{ki}	Š 36 ix	AnOr 07 002
Nin-kal-la	lukur	Š 36 ix	AnOr 07 002
Ni-da-ga	na-gada	Š 39 v	AnOr 07 003
dam- Nu-ni-da	šabra	Š 39 xi/25	OIP 115 042
Na-bí-um	dumu- lugal	Š 41 xii/ [8], 9	SET 005

续表

名字	官衔	时间	文献出处
Nam-zi-tar-ra	ensí Gú-du$_8$-a^{ki}	Š 44 vi	SAT 2 0364
Puzur$_4$-^{d}Utu	šakkan$_6$	Š 35 viii:	MVN 03 143
Puzur-Iš$_8$-tár	šakkana Mari^{ki}	Š 38 vi	OIP 115036
Si-a-a	na-gada	Š 42 viii	Torino 1 040
Simat-É-*a*	lukur	Š 29 xi	OIP 115016
Simat-^{d}*Iš*$_8$*-tár*	*Simat-Iš*$_4$*-tár* dumu Lugal	Š 42 v/24	CST 470
dam-Šu-^{d}Kabta	šakkana, a-zu	Š 36 viii	OIP 115024
dam-Šu-^{d}Šamaš	sipa <udu>-gú-gur$_5$	Š 38 viii	AnOr 7042
Šar-ru-um-ì-lí	sukkal/ ensí Unug^{ki} (Š 45 v)	Š 42 vii/24	Torino 1 038
Šu-Iš$_4$-tár	dumu-lugal	Š 43 xi/30	RO 11 96 01
dam-^{d}*Šul-gi-ì-lí*	šagina	Š 45 viii	RT 37130 mi.7
^{d}Šará-kam	ensí Gír-su^{ki}, dumu In-im-^{d}Šará	Š 47 ii	OIP 115090
Ši-la-ma-sí	ugula	Š 47 ii	MVN 13 677
nin$_9$*-Ṣi-lu-uš-*^{d}*Da-gan*	ensí Si-mu-ru-um^{ki}	Š 44 i/27-30	MVN 03 200
Te-ṣi-en$_6$*-Ma-* [*ma*]	daughter of AS	Š 29 xi	OIP 115016
Ṫa-ba-Da-ra-ah	lú Si-mu-ru-um^{ki}	Š 34 ii	OIP 115021
Tab-ba-ì-lí	sipa	Š 43 ii/30	OLP 08 07 02
Ur-ni$_9$-gar	dumu-lugal/ ensí Šuruppag^{ki}	Š 33 v	CST042
Ur-^{d}Za-ba$_4$-ba$_4$	nu-bandà	Š 33 iv	MVN 03 136,
Ur-^{d}Šul-pa-è	sukkal-mah Lagaš^{ki}	Š 36 ix	AnOr 07 002
Ur-^{d}Kug-nun-na	^{lú}azlág	Š 38 v	SACT 1 055
^{d}Utu-ellati	šagina	Š 38 viii	Torino 1 030
Ur-^{d}Nin-mug	agà-ús	Š 39 iii	OIP 115037
Ur-mes	na-gada	Š 39 v	AnOr 07 003
Ur-^{d}Šul-gi-ra	šakkana	Š 39 viii/25	CST048
Ur-^{d}Ištaran	son of AS	Š 41 xii/2	Hirose 016
dam-Ur-^{d}Sîn	ensí ÚRxÚ^{ki}	Š 42 vii/15	Ontario 1 012
Ur-da-ga	engar	Š 44 iii/7, 11	Torino 1 042

续表

名字	官衔	时间	文献出处
dam-Ur-ni_9	šabra-^{d}Nin-a-mu-túm	Š 44 iii/20，28	RA 19 192 07
Ur-^{d}Nisaba	énsi-$Nibru^{ki}$	Š 44 vii/17-20	OrSP 18 pl.02 06
Ur-mes	dub-sar	Š 46 xii	MVN 13 794
Za-la-a	ugula	Š 32 iv	MVN 2 308
Za-ak-ì-lí	šabra	Š 40 i	AUCT 1 089
Wa-at-ra-at	ugula，dowager	Š 38ix	BIN 3 001

附录四　地图

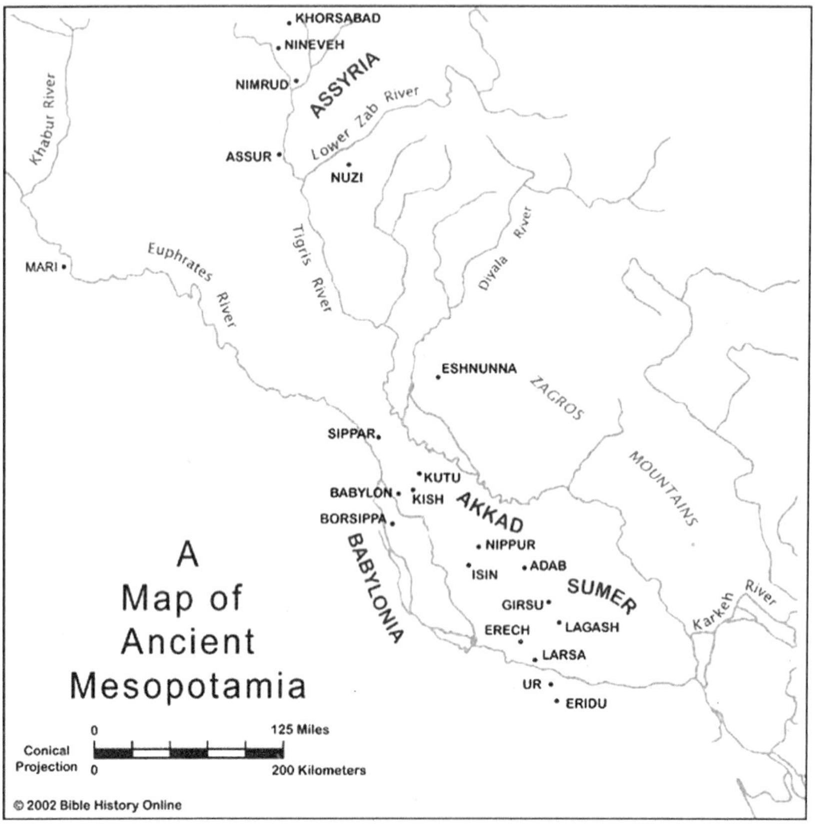

KHORSABAD
NINEVEH
NIMRUD
ASSYRIA
Lower Zab River
ASSUR
NUZI
Khabur River
MARI
Euphrates River
Tigris River
Diyala River
ESHNUNNA
ZAGROS
MOUNTAINS
SIPPAR
KUTU
BABYLON
KISH
AKKAD
BORSIPPA
BABYLONIA
NIPPUR
ISIN
ADAB
SUMER
GIRSU
LAGASH
ERECH
LARSA
UR
ERIDU
Karkeh River
A Map of Ancient Mesopotamia
0
125 Miles
0
200 Kilometers
Conical Projection
© 2002 Bible History Online

附录五　度量衡

重量单位

苏美尔语	英文名称	现代重量	中文译名
še	grain	约 0.05 克	**“黍”**（粒，秦汉 1 豆 = 16 黍）
gín = 180 še（波斯：米底锱 = 2/3 锱，Daric = 1 锱，10 锱 = *karša*，6 *karša* = 1 斤	shekel	约 8.3 克	**锱**（古 1 斤 = 16 两 = 64 锱；1 两 = 4 锱；现代 1 斤 = 500 克，1/64 斤 = 7.8 克。秦 1 锱 = 36 豆 = 576 黍）
ma-na = 60 gín	mina	约 500 克	（秦汉斤 = 250 克，北朝 = 520-600，隋 = 700，唐 = 670 克，宋元 = 630 克，明清 = 590 克）
gú = gú-un = 60 ma-na	talent	约 30 公斤	**钧**或 60 斤

容量单位

苏美尔语和进位	英文名	现代容积	中译名
1 silà	quart	约 1 公升	**升**（秦汉晋梁陈 = 0.2 公升，北齐 = 0.3 公升，北魏 = 0.4 公升。隋唐宋 = 0.6 公升，**元明清** = 0.96-1 公升）
1bán = 10 silà（古苏美尔拉旮什 1 bán = 6 silà）		约 10 公升	**斗**（中国斗 = 10 升，**隋唐宋** 1 斗 = 6 公升， **元明清 1** 斗 = 10 公升）
1nigida，ba-rí-ga = 6 bán = 60 silà（古苏美尔和新晚巴比伦 = 6 bán = 36 silà）		约 60 公升	**斛**（战国齐 1 区 = 4 豆/斗，**隋唐宋斛** = 10 斗 = **60** 公升。宋代将一斛（或称一石）改为 5 斗（30 公升），十斗（二斛）为一石，元明清 1 斛 = 5 斗 = 50 公升）
$guru_7$“堆、仓”用于古苏美尔，在 Fara/苏如帕克 = 2400 gur 钟，其他城 = 3600 钟	heap	300 公升×3600 = 1080000 公升	**仓**

附录六　东北师范大学古典所中西文专有名词对译字表

	Ø	a 阿’ a **ia、ea 亚**	e 希腊’ η or ∈/ε	i/**y** 伊 = 希腊 **ι;**	u 乌希腊 **u =Yυ ου 土耳其 u，ü**	**O 欧** (希腊 **o，Ωω**)	am 按	an 安	em / im 寅	en 恩	iņ 尹	um 温	un 文	**on 翁 oe 奥伊**	ao 奥 au/aw (英 ou)	ai/ ae/**ay** 艾	iu/ü/ ew/eu/ ev 尤	**ei 诶;**
b	b 卜	ba 巴	be 贝	bi 比	bu 布	bo 波	bam 板	ban 班	bem/ im 奔	ben 本	bin 宾	bum 布姆	bun 贲	**bon 崩**	bao/ au 保	bai/ ae/ **ay** 白	biu/ü/ ew/eu/ ev 比尤	bei 倍
土耳其 ç	汉语 q	洽	切	**çi 齐**	ç**ü** 屈	**俅**	Ç = 英 ch											
d/ dh	d 德	da 达	de 戴	**di 迪** (狄)	du 杜	**do 多**	dam 旦	dan 丹	dem 邓	den 登	din 丁	dum 杜姆	dun 顿	**don 东**	dao/ au/ aw 道	dai/ ae/代	diu/ü/ ew/eu/ ev 丢	dei 带
dj 埃及	**dj 捷**	**dja’ 加**	**dje 杰**	**dji 季**	**dju 居**					**djen 晋**						**/ay**		

续表

	Ø	a 阿，a **ia**、**ea** 亚	e 希腊，η or ∈/ε	i/**y** 伊 = 希腊 **ι**；	u 乌希腊 **u = Yυ ου 土耳其 u，ü**	**O 欧（希腊 o，Ωω）**	am 按	an 安	em / im 寅	en 恩	in 尹	um 温	un 文	**on 翁 oe 奥伊**	ao 奥 au/aw（英 ou）	ai/ ae/**ay** 艾	iu/ü/ ew/eu/ ev 尤	**ei 诶；**
f = **ph/φ**	弗	fa 发	fe 费	**fi 菲**	fu 夫	fo 缶	fam 凡	fan 梵	fem 奋	芬 fen	fin 纷	fum 份	fun 冯	fon/丰	fao/ au/ aw 佛	fai/ ae/法	fiu/ü/ ew/eu/ ev 霏	fei 腓
g/ gh	格	ga 旮	**ge** 吉/ 埃及盖	**gi** 吉	gu 古	go 勾、戈	gam 甘	gan 干	gem 根	根 gen	gin 艮	gum 鲧	gun 衮	gon/宫	gao/ au/ aw 皋	gai/ ae/垓	giu/ü/ ew/eu/ ev 苟	gei 给
h = 埃及 h/ **kh** = 希腊 **'a/ e/u/ o/i**	h 赫希腊''	h a/ kha 哈 **'a**	h e/ khe，埃及赫希 **'e**	**h i/** khi **希，'i**	hu/khu 胡，**'u**	**ho/** kho **霍，'o**	**ham/** kham **汉**	han/ khan 韩	hem/ im/ khem/ im 恒	hen/ khen 痕	h in/ kh 欣	h um/ kh 珲	h un/ kh 混	**h on/** kh 弘	hao/au /aw 昊	hai/kh ae/ **ay** 亥	hiu/ü/ ew/eu/ ev 修	h/khei 黑
埃及 h	*h* 荷	ha' 亥	he 荷	hi 喜	hu 忽	ho 霍	ha '合											
k = c	k 克	卡 ka	ke 凯	**ki** 基	**ku** 库 kü	**ko** 廓	kam 坎	**k**an 刊	**k**em 垦	ken 肯	kin **恳**	kum 坤	kun 昆	**k**on/孔	kao/ au/ aw 考	kai/ ae/开	kiu/ü/ ew/eu/ ev 咎	**k**ei 凯
l	l 勒	la 拉	le 莱	**li** 里	lu 鲁 lü =ly 吕	**lo** 罗	lam 兰	lan 阑	lem/ im 林	len/ lon 伦	lin 临	lum 隆	lun 仑	**lon 伦龙**	lao/au /aw 劳	lai/ ae/徕	liu/ü/ ew/eu/ ev 流	lei 耒
m	姆	ma 马	me 美	m**i** 米	mu 穆 mü	m**o** 摩	mam 蛮	man 曼	mem/ im 闽（孟）	men 门 /（蒙）	min 敏	mum 萌	mun 蒙	mon/ men 蒙	mao/ au/ aw 卯	mai/ ae/ **ay** 麦	miu/ü/ ew/eu/ ev 缪	mei 梅

续表

	Ø	a 阿’a ia、ea 亚	e 希腊’η or ∈/ε	i/y 伊 = 希腊 ι;	u 乌希腊 u =Yυ ου 土耳其 u, ü	O 欧（希腊 o, Ωω）	am 按	an 安	em / im 寅	en 恩	in 尹	um 温	un 文	on 翁 oe 奥伊	ao 奥 au/aw（英 ou）	ai/ ae/ay 艾	iu/ü/ ew/eu/ ev 尤	ei 诶;
n	‘n 恩	na 那	ne 奈	ni 尼	nu 努	no 诺	nam 楠	nan 南	nem/ im 恁	nen 嫩	nin 宁	num 农	nun 侬	non 浓	nao/au /aw 瑙	nai/ ae/乃	niu/ü/ ew/eu/ ev 纽	nei 内
p	p 坡	pa 帕	pe 派	pi 皮	pu 普	po 坡	pam 盘	pan 潘	pem/ im 喷	pen 盆	pin 品	pum 彭	pun 篷	pon/朋	pao/au /aw 咆	pai/ ae/徘	piu/ü/ ew/eu/ ev 皮尤	pei 裴
q = k = ch 希腊 χ/ ch	q 可	qa 喀	qe 科	qi 科	qu 苦	qo 寇	qam 堪	qan 侃	qem/ im 亘	qen 肯	qin 肯	qum 崑	qun 琨	qon/崆	qao/au /aw 栲	qai/ ae/ ay 恺	qiu/ü/ ew/eu/ ev 邱	qei 科
r = rh	r 尔	ra 腊	re 瑞	ri 瑞	ru 如	ro 若	ram 冉	ran 蓝	rem/ im 荏	ren 任	rin 壬	rum 润	run 闰	r on/荣	rao/au /aw 荛	rai/ ae/睐	riu/ü/ ew/eu/ ev 琉	rei 睿
埃及 r =l	r 尔	ra ‘拉	re ‘拉	ri 瑞	ru 如	ro 若												
s	s 斯	sa 萨	se 塞 埃及斯	si 席 埃及西	su 苏 sy = sü 叙	so 索	sam 叁	san 散	sem/ im 新	sen 森	sin 辛	sum 孙	sun 荪	son/松	sao/au /aw 梢	sai/ ae/赛	siu/ü/ ew/eu/ ev 休	sei 塞
ṣ	ṣ施	ṣa 嚓	ṣe 采	ṣi 采	ṣu 簇	0	ṣam 璨	an 参	ṣ em/ im 琛	ṣen 辰	ṣin 岑	ṣ um 淳	ṣun 春	ṣ on/琮	ṣao/au /aw 超	ṣ ai/ ae/材	0	0

续表

	Ø	a 阿' a **ia、ea 亚**	e 希腊' η or ∈/ε	i/**y** 伊 = 希腊 **ι;**	u 乌希腊 **u = Yυ ου 土耳其 u, ü**	**O 欧**（希腊 **o, Ωω**）	am 按	an 安	em / im 寅	en 恩	in 尹	um 温	un 文	**on 翁 oe 奥伊**	ao 奥 au/aw （英 ou）	ai/ ae/**ay** 艾	iu/ü/ ew/eu/ ev 尤	**ei 诶;**
š = **sh** = 土耳其 ş	ş 什	ša 沙	**še 筛**	ši 西	šu 舒	**šo 朔**	šam 闪	šan 珊 shan	šem/ im 莘	šen 鑫	š/ shin 审	šum 顺	shun 舜	**šon/宋**	šao/au /aw 绍	šai/ ae/晒	šiu/ü/ ew/eu/ ev 秀	šei 垂
t	t 特	ta 塔	**te 泰**	**ti 提**	tu 图	**to 托**	tam 覃	tan 坦	tem/ im 汀	ten 藤	tin 廷	tum 吞	tun 屯	ton/**同**	tao/au /aw 陶	tai/ ae// **ay** 台	tiu/ü/ ew/eu/ ev 提尤	tei 推
ṭ /**th/ tj/θ**	ṭ 忒埃及王特	ṭ a 沓	ṭ e 忒	**ṭ i** 梯	ṭ u 突	**ṭ o** 脱	ṭ / tham 檀	ṭ an 坛	ṭ em/ im 登	ṭ en 鼎	ṭ in 定	um 盾	thun 敦	thon/ 仝	ṭ ao/ au /aw 套	ṭ ai/ ae// **ay** 岱	ṭ iu/ ü/ew/ eu/ev 梯尤	ṭ ei 忒
y/**j/i**	伊	ya/ ia 亚	ye 耶	伊 **yi**	yu 于 yü	**yo 约**	yam 延	yan 严	yem/ im 彦	yen 寅	yin 尹	yum 雍郧	yun 芸	yon/雍	yao/au / aw 尧	0	yiu/ü/ ew/eu/ ev 于	yei 耶
w/v	乌	wa 瓦	we 维	**wi** 维	wu 乌	**wo** 沃	wam 皖	an 万	wem/ im 宛	wen 文	win 汶	wum 温	wun 蕹	won/**翁**	wao/au /aw 窝	wai/ ae/ **ay** 外	wiu/ü/ ew/eu/ ev 维尤	wei 威
z	兹	za 扎	ze 载	**zi** 孜	zu 朱	**zo** 佐	zam 瓒	zan 昝	zem/ im 金	zen 箴	zin 珍	zum 樽	zun 尊	zon/宗	皂 zao/ au/aw	zai/ ae/甾	ziu/ü/ ew/eu/ ev 邹	zei 宰

苏美尔语特殊音节对译字表

	a 阿	e 埃 é/ = “房”	i 伊	u 乌	（鼻音）iĝ/aĝ/uĝ
鼻音 ĝ	玛 **ĝa** = gá “我的”，ĝál 玛勒 “存在”；ĝanun “仓、房” **ĝar** 玛尔 “制定、设立	梅 **ĝe**：**ĝeš** 梅什 “木”，ĝéš = 60、ĝèš 男，**ĝen** 扪 “走”	弥：**ĝi** = ĝi$_6$ “黑” **ĝi**dru “权杖” ĝir 鱼 **ĝír** “石刀”、**ĝìr** “足”	牟 **ĝu** = gu$_{10}$ = mu “我的” **ĝu**ruš “男子 壮丁”	
dr h k/l	**hé** 海 = “让” **dru/dù/rú** 篤 “建筑”	**lú** 卢 = “人”，**lugal** 卢旮勒 = “王”	**kiĝ** 精 “工作”，**áĝ** 昂 ki ~ áĝ “爱” **huĝ = hun** 弘 “雇用” **naĝ** 囊 “饮”，**saĝ = 桑** “头”		

后　记

求学东师，一晃六年。

六年学习和生活的点点滴滴，如今回忆起来依然清晰如昨。恩师吴宇虹教授骑车风雨无阻来上课的画面、兢兢业业伏在案后给弟子们授业解惑的画面、率领我们这些业余选手在排球场上顽强拼搏的画面、在KTV高歌《敖包相会》的画面……帧帧在目。恩师严谨的治学态度、敏锐的学术思维、活泼的教学方式以及乐观的生活心态使我终身受益，尤其是恩师在亚述学领域的精深造诣与认真求实的治学精神将永远激励我前行。在此，向恩师吴宇虹教授表示崇高的敬意和深深的谢意。师恩如海，铭记于心。

毕业至今，又是六年。

六年的时间，沧海桑田。从刚毕业时的稚嫩青涩到现在的稳重成熟，从初入职场时的忐忑不安到现如今的淡定坦然，从原先的茫然躁动到此时的坚定安宁，历经坎坷，终又回到这个梦想开始的地方、这个熟悉热爱的领域。在此，向鼓励我重回本专业并督促我进步的车效梅老师致以真诚的谢意。知遇之恩，衔环以报。

人生十二年，瞬时一轮回。

从跟随恩师入门亚述学，到研究成果出版在即，整整十二年。我将以此为点，砥砺前行！

感谢日本学者尾崎亨（Ozaki Tohru）博士对本书稿原始文献的修改和补充。

感谢东北师范大学世界古典文明史研究所的张强老师、郭丹彤老师、李晓东老师在我求学期间给予我学习和生活中的诸多支持和帮助，感谢周秀文老师为我查找和借阅资料提供便利，感谢刘燕老师为我提供生活上的帮助。

感谢师兄李海峰、袁指挥、刘军、阴元涛，师姐王颖杰、李学彦，同学徐昊、刘虹博、马晓玲、师学良，师弟张宝利、刘昌玉、蒋家瑜、尹成浩，师妹陈艳丽、张静、张丽媛在学习上的热情帮助。感谢寝室姐妹黄馨、燕青、张冬梅在生活上的快乐分享。

感谢山西师范大学历史与旅游文化学院的仝建平老师、王志超老师、徐跃勤老师、徐继承老师、谢立忱老师、王霏老师、阎海燕老师在生活上和工作中给予我的帮助和支持。

还要特别感谢中国社会科学出版社的任明老师以及为本书的出版做出努力的所有工作人员。

最后，要把感谢送给我的家人和朋友。感谢父母的大爱无私、谆谆教诲和殷殷关怀。感谢挚友的信任和扶持。